The Cumulated Indexes
to the
Public Papers of the Presidents
of the
United States

U.S. " President.,
_"_
t= Public papers.

LYNDON B. JOHNSON
1963–1969

kto press

A U. S. Division of Kraus-Thomson Organization Ltd.
Millwood, New York
1978

ISBN 0-527-20751-9

First Printing
Printed in the United States of America

PREFACE

In his Foreword to the 1965 volume of the *Public Papers of the Presidents*, Lyndon B. Johnson writes, "The public statements of a president occupy a unique place in history. Every president speaks, of necessity, to his own time . . . Yet the words and deeds of any president, serving as spokesman and Chief Executive for his own contemporaries, also reach to future generations . . . and become landmarks for posterity." *The Cumulated Indexes to the Public Papers of the Presidents* provide, for the first time in one volume, full access to the papers of each presidential administration issued in this government series.

The *Public Papers* offer a remarkable view of the American presidents and of American history. The character of a president, the individuals with whom a president interacts, the historical events that are shaped by a president and that, in turn shape his presidency, are all to be found within the pages of the *Public Papers*.

A resolution passed by the United States Congress on July 17, 1894, provided that a compilation of "all the annual, special, and veto messages, proclamations, and inaugural addresses" of all the presidents from 1789 to 1894 be printed. The publication was to be prepared by James D. Richardson, a representative from Tennessee, under the direction of the Joint Committee on Printing, of which Richardson was a member. The official set was issued in two series of ten volumes each. A joint resolution of May 2, 1896, provided for the distribution of the set to members of Congress, with the remainder to be delivered to the compiler, James Richardson. An act passed about a year later provided that the plates for *A Compilation of the Messages and Papers of the Presidents* be delivered to Richardson "without cost to him." Representative Richardson then made arrangements for the commercial publication of the set. Several other compilations of presidential papers were commercially published in the first half of the nineteenth century; these usually contained only selected documents.

The Richardson edition of the *Messages and Papers*, however, was the only set authorized by Congress and published by the government until

1957, when the official publication of the public messages and statements of the presidents, the *Public Papers of the Presidents of the United States*, was initiated based on a recommendation made by the National Historical Publications Commission (now the National Historical Publications and Records Commission). The Commission suggested that public presidential papers be compiled on a yearly basis and issued in a uniform, systematic publication similar to the *United States Supreme Court Reports* and the *Congressional Record*. An official series thus began in which presidential writings and statements of a public nature could be made promptly available. These presidential volumes are compiled by the Office of the Federal Register of the General Services Administration's National Archives and Record Service.

As might be expected, the "public papers" vary greatly in importance and content; some contain important policy statements while others are routine messages. They include, in chronological order, texts of such documents as the president's messages to Congress, public addresses, transcripts of news conferences and speeches, public letters, messages to heads of state, remarks to informal groups, etc. Executive orders, proclamations, and similar documents that are required by law to be published in the *Federal Register* and *Code of Federal Regulations* are not reprinted, but are listed by number and subject in an appendix in each volume.

The *Public Papers of the Presidents* are kept in print, and are available from the Superintendent of Documents, United States Government Printing Office. The *Papers* of each year are published in single volumes, with each volume containing an index for that calendar year. *The Cumulated Indexes to the Public Papers of the Presidents* combines and integrates the separate indexes for a president's administration into one alphabetical listing.

References to all of the volumes of a president's public papers can thus be found by consulting this one-volume cumulated index. *See* and *see also* references have been added and minor editorial changes have been made in the process of cumulating the separate indexes.

References in *The Cumulated Indexes to the Public Papers of the Presidents* are to item numbers. Individual volumes are identified in the *Index* by year, as are the actual volumes of the *Papers*. The year identifying the volume in which a paper is located appears in boldface type. When page references are used, they are clearly noted in the entry.

Other volumes in the set of *The Cumulated Indexes to the Public Papers of the Presidents* include Richard M. Nixon, 1969–1974; John F. Kennedy, 1961–1963; Dwight D. Eisenhower, 1953–1961; and Harry S. Truman, 1945–1953. Forthcoming volumes will index the papers of Herbert C. Hoover and Gerald R. Ford, as well as those of future presidents when their administrations are completed.

KTO PRESS

LYNDON B. JOHNSON
1963–1969

A-7 bomber, **1965**: 26
A7A bomber, **1963-64**: 382
A-11 aircraft, **1965**: 219
A-11 jet interceptor, world speed record, **1963–64**: 201 [2], 256 [3]
A. W. Chesterton Co., **1963-64**: 350n.
Abe, Mr. and Mrs. Kazuhisa, **1966**: 532
Abel, I. W., **1965**: 454 [1, 3], 466, 483; **1966**: 184n.; **1967**: 326; **1968-69**: 106n.
Abele, Repr. Homer E., **1963-64**: 323
Abell, Mrs. Bess, **1966**: 351; **1968-69**: 570, 648
Abernathy, Rev. Ralph D., **1968-69**: 223 [9]
Abernethy, Byron R., **1968-69**: 626n.
Abilene, Kans., **1968-69**: 537
"Ability Counts" awards, **1963-64**: 302
ABM.
See Antiballistic missiles.
"Abraham Lincoln: The Prairie Years and the War Years," Carl Sandburg, **1963-64**: 796n.
Abraham Lincoln-Benito Juárez scholarships, **1967**: 451; **1968-69**: 66
Abraham Lincoln Scholarships, **1968-69**: 66
Abram, Morris B., **1965**: 548, 613; **1967**: 87n.
Abrams, Gen. Creighton W., Jr., **1967**: 166, 554 [1], 567; **1968-69**: 189, 191 [5, 6]
 Commander, United States Military Assistance Command, Vietnam, **1968-69**: 472, 557 [7], 572, 630
Absentee voting, **1968-69**: 314
Abu Simbel, American Committee to Preserve **1967**: 198
Academy of Sciences, National, **1966**: 461; **1967**: 101; **1968-69**: 107
Accident prevention, **1963-64**: 234; **1965**: 73, 287n., 460, 488
 See also Safety.
 Industrial, **1963-64**: 421
 Traffic, **1963-64**: 234, 565
Accident victims, rescue, **1968-69**: 111
Acheson, David C., **1966**: 204

Acheson, Dean, **1963-64**: 244, 349n., 358, 511, 560 [4], 563 [5], 568, 591, 608, 688 [8], 696, 796; **1966**: 134, 235, 236 [5], 247 [8]
Ackerman, Bishop Richard H., **1968-69**: 499
Ackermann, William C., **1963-64**: 231n.
Ackley, Gardner (Chairman, Council of Economic Advisers), **1963-64**: 486 [2], 550; **1965**: 22 [2], 46 [14], 54, 62, 319 [3], 326n., 347 [4], 418, 506, 617, 641, 663; **1966**: 8 [15], 33, 44, 158 [4], 201, 236 [13], 247 [1], 333, 373ftn. (p. 805), 379, 492 [1], 494 [1], 630 [2, 5, 8], 631, 635 [1, 2, 8, 16, 18], 636; **1968-69**: 1 [17], 2, 46n., 76
 See also Council of Economic Advisers, Chairman (Gardner Ackley).
Acreage allotments, **1965**: 47, 168; **1966**: 62, 203, 281; **1968-69**: 39 (p. 100)
Acton, John Emerich Edward Dalberg, Lord, **1966**: 97
Acts approved.
 See Legislation, remarks or statements upon approval.
Adair, Repr. E. Ross, **1965**: 163, 188
Adams, Abigail, **1965**: 536, 551, 613; **1966**: 271; **1968-69**: 648
Adams, Repr. Brock, **1966**: 23
Adams, Charles S., **1968-69**: 499
Adams, Eugenia, **1963-64**: 323
Adams, Eva (Director, Bureau of the Mint), **1965**: 297
Adams, Henry, **1965**: 369; **1968-69**: 66, 172
 "The Education of Henry Adams," **1967**: 344
Adams, John, **1963-64**: 536, 590, 662n.; **1965**: 77, 88, 334; **1966**: 101, 120, 189, 609; **1967**: 124, 485 [3]; **1968-69**: 291n., 576, 648
Adams, John G., **1965**: 117 [3]
Adams, John Quincy, **1966**: 300
Adams, Roger, **1965**: 56n.

Adams, Samuel, **1963-64:** 362
Adams, Tom, **1963-64:** 709, 712, 713
Addabbo, Repr. Joseph P., **1967:** 391
Addams, Jane, **1967:** 39; **1968-69:** 87
Addiss, Stephen, **1965:** 159
Addonizio, Hugh J., **1965:** 434; **1966:** 504
Addresses to the Nation
  Bombing halt of North Vietnam, **1968-69:** 572
  Detroit civil disorders, **1967:** 322
  Kennedy, Sen. Robert F., shooting of, **1968-69:** 293
  King, Rev. Martin Luther, Jr., death, **1968-69:** 180
  North Korean situation, **1968-69:** 35
  Reelection, decision not to seek, **1968-69:** 170
  Vietnam, steps to limit the war, **1968-69:** 170
Addresses or remarks on commemorative or special occasions
  Agudas Achim Synagogue, dedication, **1963-64:** 77
  Airline strike settlement, **1966:** 360
  Alfred E. Smith Memorial Foundation, dinner, **1963-64:** 662; **1968-69:** 540
  Alliance for Progress
    3d anniversary, **1963-64:** 220
    4th anniversary, **1965:** 429
    5th anniversary, **1966:** 386
    6th anniversary, **1967:** 357
  Amalgamated Clothing Workers, 50th anniversary, **1963-64:** 334
  "America Days" in Turku, Finland, **1965:** 491
  American Heritage Foundation, "register and vote" ceremony, **1963-64:** 508
  Amistad Dam, Mexico, inspection tour, **1966:** 639
  AMVETS Headquarters, dedication, **1966:** 345
  Apollo 7 astronauts, return, **1968-69:** 552
  Armed Forces Radio and Television Service, 25th anniversary, **1966:** 648
  Austin Oaks Housing Project, Austin, Texas, **1968-69:** 625
  Ball, George W., farewell ceremony, **1966:** 502
  Baylor University commencement, **1965:** 286
  Boy Scouts of America, 55th anniversary, **1965:** 55
  Brookings Institution, 50th anniversary, **1966:** 493
  Brooks, Repr. Jack, dinner honoring, **1968-69:** 109
  Brown University, 200th anniversary, **1963-64:** 601
  Budget Message (1970) signing, **1968-69:** 677
  C-5A cargo plane rollout ceremony, **1968-69:** 110
  Cancer Control Month, opening of, **1965:** 154
  Cancer Crusade, opening of, **1966:** 156
  Cape Kennedy trip with Chancellor Erhard, **1966:** 485

Addresses or remarks – *continued*
  Capitol Page School, commencement, **1965:** 316; **1966:** 270; **1967:** 262; **1968-69:** 301
  Carl Vinson Hearing Room, Rayburn House Office Building, dedication, **1965:** 157
  Catholic University of America, commencement, **1965:** 302
  Central Texas College, dedication, **1967:** 532
  Chamizal boundary completion, **1968-69:** 623
  Chamizal boundary settlement, **1967:** 453
  Chamizal Zone agreement, U.S.-Mexico, ceremony marking, **1963-64:** 596
  Christmas message, **1967:** 573
  Civic meeting, Anchorage, Alaska, **1966:** 568
  Civil disorders, **1967:** 326
  Clark, Ambassador Edward, introduction, **1968-69:** 206
  Cleveland, Ohio, Parade of Progress, dedication, **1963-64:** 543
  Coast Guard Academy, commencement, **1963-64:** 382
  Columbia State Community College, dedication, **1967:** 117
  Columbus Day, **1965:** 563
  Columbus Day dinner, **1966:** 513
  Commerce, Department of, change in leadership, **1963-64:** 806
  Communication satellite service, opening of commercial, **1965:** 333
  Communications cable, U.S.-Venezuela, inauguration, **1966:** 366
  Congress
    Dinners for Democratic Members, **1963-64:** 228; **1965:** 329, 330
    Reception for Members, **1965:** 183
    Reception for new Democrats in, **1963-64:** 799
    Salute to Members of, **1963-64:** 527; **1965:** 559
  Congressional dinners, **1966:** 221, 520; **1967:** 216
  Congressional leadership reception, **1968-69:** 655
  Connally, Gov. John B., birthday dinner, **1968-69:** 97
  Consular convention, United States-Soviet, proclaiming of, **1968-69:** 309
  Cost reduction awards, **1968-69:** 174
  Crossland Vocational Center, Camp Springs, Md., dedication, **1967:** 193
  Czestochowa, Shrine of Our Lady of, dedication, **1966:** 528
  Dallastown, Pa., 100th anniversary, **1966:** 428
  Dante, 700th anniversary of birth, **1965:** 367
  Daughters of the American Revolution, 73d continental congress, **1963-64:** 275
  D-day, 20th anniversary, **1963-64:** 384

Addresses or remarks – *continued*
  Defense Department cost reduction cere-
    mony, **1966**: 324; **1967**: 324
  Democratic-Farmer-Labor Party Convention,
    1963-64: 433
  Democratic Party Conference, **1967**: 514
  Democratic Party dinners, **1963-64**: 199, 287,
    338, 372, 373, 413, 415, 431, 434;
    1966: 228, 312; **1967**: 150, 251, 270,
    421; **1968-69**: 210
    Cook County, Ill., **1965**: 299
  Denver, University of, honorary degree, **1966**:
    414
  Dirksen, Sen. Everett McK., dinner honoring,
    1967: 502
  District of Columbia reception, **1968-69**: 698
  Dollars for Democrats Drive, **1966**: 403
  Economic Report, signing, **1968-69**: 683
  Education, Office of, centennial, **1967**: 82
  Eisenhower, General and Mrs. Dwight D.,
    wedding anniversary, **1966**: 300
  Election victory, radio and TV remarks, **1963-
    64**: 765
  Ellenville (N.Y.) Community Hospital dedica-
    tion, **1966**: 395
  Employment Act of 1946, 20th anniversary,
    1966: 83
  Encyclopaedia Britannica, 200th anniversary,
    1967: 540
  Eufaula Dam, dedication, **1963-64**: 597
  EXPO '67, U.S. Pavilion model unveiling, **1966**:
    644
  EXPO '67 visit, **1967**: 237
  Farewell dinner, New York City, **1968-69**: 672
  Federal Building, San Francisco, Calif., dedica-
    tion, **1963-64**: 411
  Federal Home Loan Bank System, 35th anni-
    versary, **1967**: 420
  Federal Science Exhibit, opening of, **1965**: 170
  First official remarks following oath of office,
    1963-64: 1
  Fishtrap Dam, Ky., dedication, **1968-69**: 565
  Flathead Tunnel, Mont., opening, **1968-69**:
    330
  Florida Atlantic University, dedication, **1963-
    64**: 709
  Florida cross-state barge canal, ground breaking,
    1963-64: 198
  Foreign policy conference, business executives,
    1967: 519
  Foreign Service Institute's Vietnam Training
    Center, **1968-69**: 149
  Foreign Service seminar graduation, **1966**: 261
  Friendly Sons of St. Patrick dinner, New York
    City, **1963-64**: 224
  Gallaudet College centennial banquet, **1963-64**:
    389

Addresses or remarks – *continued*
  Gary Job Corps Center, San Marcos, Tex., dedi-
    cation, **1965**: 179
  Gemini 5 mission, completion of, **1965**: 462
  Gemini space program conclusion, **1966**: 625
  George C. Marshall Research Library, dedica-
    tion, **1963-64**: 359
  Georgetown University, 175th anniversary,
    1963-64: 788
  GI bill of rights, 20th anniversary, **1963-64**:
    419
  Glassboro State College, commencement, **1968-
    69**: 288
  Gonzalez, Repr. Henry B., reception honoring,
    1965: 621
  Graduate Research Center of the Southwest,
    dedication, **1963-64**: 738
  Hall of Heroes dedication, Pentagon, **1968-69**:
    246
  Harry S. Truman Center for the Advancement
    of Peace, establishment, **1966**: 22
  Hayden, Sen. Carl, reception for, **1968-69**: 228
  Holy Cross, College of the, commencement,
    1963-64: 396
  Hopkins, William J., ceremony honoring, **1966**:
    330
  Housing and Urban Development, Department
    of, dedication of building, **1968-69**: 470
  Housing and Urban Development, Department
    of, 1st anniversary, **1966**: 604
  Howard University anniversary, **1967**: 81
  Howard University, commencement, **1965**: 301
  Human Rights Year, 1968, meeting of Com-
    mission for Observance of, **1968-69**:
    611
  Illinois State Federation of Labor, convention,
    1963-64: 637
  Inaugural, **1965**: 27
  Inauguration of George Washington, 175th
    anniversary, **1963-64**: 303
  Independence Day, **1968-69**: 359
  India, grain shipment to, **1966**: 311
  Indiana and Kentucky State Democratic
    leaders, breakfast, **1963-64**: 643
  Indiana statehood, 150th anniversary, **1966**:
    346
  Indianapolis businessmen's luncheon, **1966**:
    347
  International Ladies Garment Workers Union
    Health Center, New York City, 50th
    anniversary, **1963-64**: 387
  Iran, 25th anniversary of Shah's reign, **1965**:
    517
  J. Percy Priest Project, dedication, **1968-69**:
    345
  Jackson, Andrew, 200th anniversary of birth,
    1967: 115

Addresses or remarks — *continued*
  John F. Kennedy, memorial services for,
    1963-64: 64; **1965:** 623
  John F. Kennedy bust, unveiling, **1963-64:** 773
  John F. Kennedy Center for the Performing
    Arts, ground breaking, **1963-64:** 784
  John F. Kennedy Educational, Civic and Cul-
    tural Center, Mitchel Field, N.Y., dedica-
    tion, **1963-64:** 337
  John F. Kennedy Square, Texarkana, dedica-
    tion, **1963-64:** 599
  Johnson City High School, commencement,
    1963-64: 374
  Joseph H. Hirschhorn Museum and Sculpture
    Garden, ground breaking, **1968-69:** 660
  Kenya, independence, **1963-64:** 34
  Land banks, 50th anniversary, **1967:** 156
  Law and order postage stamp, issuance, **1968-
    69:** 257
  Lincoln, Abraham, birthday commemoration,
    1965: 64; **1967:** 49; **1968-69:** 70
  Lincoln, Abraham, statue dedication, **1966:**
    175
  Magna Carta anniversary ceremony, **1965:** 376
  Malta, independence, **1963-64:** 585
  McCormack, Repr. John W., dinner honoring,
    1967: 206
  McNamara, Secretary Robert S., farewell cere-
    mony, **1968-69:** 101
  Meany, George, dinner honoring, **1967:** 484
  Medical assistance, inauguration of Federal-
    State program, **1966:** 157
  Medicare, medical leaders' meeting, **1966:** 271
  Memorial Day service, **1966:** 246
  Methodism, American, bicentennial, **1966:** 189
  Michoud Assembly Facility (NASA), inspec-
    tion, **1967:** 533
  Military installations tour, **1968-69:** 81
  Miller, Tom, bust unveiling, **1967:** 210
  Minimum wage increase, effective date, **1967:**
    30
  Monetary reserve asset creation, **1967:** 371
  Mora, Dr. José, luncheon honoring, **1968-69:**
    239
  Morgantown, W. Va., Airport, dedication,
    1963-64: 586
  Museum of History and Technology, Washing-
    ton, D.C., dedication, **1963-64:** 141
  National Cathedral School for Girls, com-
    mencement, **1965:** 289
  National Christmas Tree lighting, **1963-64:**
    810; **1965:** 653; **1966:** 646; **1967:** 544;
    1968-69: 629
  National Collection of Fine Arts, dedication,
    1968-69: 225
  National Geographic Society building, dedica-
    tion, **1963-64:** 117

Addresses or remarks — *continued*
  National Heart Institute, 20th anniversary,
    1968-69: 589
  National Institutes of Health tour, **1967:** 319
  National War College and Industrial College of
    the Armed Forces, convocation, **1963-
    64:** 533
  Navajo people, centennial banquet, **1968-69:**
    28
  Navy League luncheon, **1966:** 397
  New York World's Fair, opening of, **1963-64:**
    282
  North Atlantic Treaty
    15th anniversary, **1963-64:** 244
    17th anniversary, **1966:** 163
  Northwest-Southwest power transmission inter-
    tie, breakfast saluting, **1963-64:** 578
  Nuclear nonproliferation treaty, signing, **1968-
    69:** 349
  Nuclear reactor, 25th anniversary, **1967:** 515
  Nuclear test ban treaty, first anniversary, **1963-
    64:** 486 [1], 653
  Oceanographer, commissioning, **1966:** 326
  Odlum, Floyd B., dinner honoring, **1968-69:**
    262
  Older Americans, ceremony inaugurating pro-
    gram of community service projects,
    1968-69: 75
  Olympic games (1964), luncheon for U.S.
    medal winners, **1963-64:** 782
  Opportunities Industrialization Center, Phila-
    delphia, **1967:** 291
  Organization of African Unity, 3d anniversary,
    1966: 243
  Organization of American States, ratification
    of the Protocol of Amendments to
    Charter, **1968-69:** 205
  Peace Corps
    4th anniversary, **1963-64:** 759
    5th anniversary, **1966:** 93
  Plasterers' and Cement Masons' International
    Association of the United States and
    Canada, Operative, 100th anniversary,
    1963-64: 547
  Polish millenium, **1966:** 200
  Port of Houston, 50th anniversary, **1963-64:**
    766
  Prayer breakfast, presidential, **1963-64:** 172;
    1965: 45; **1966:** 78; **1967:** 32;
    1968-69: 43
  Presidential appointees dinner, **1965:** 213
  Presidential Scholars, reception, **1967:** 266
  President's Club dinner, **1967:** 281
  President's portrait, unveiling of, **1965:** 285
  Pryor, Okla., industrial site, ground breaking,
    1966: 416
  Pulaski, Casimir, anniversary of death, **1965:**
    562

Addresses or remarks – *continued*
  Reception for President Johnson given by
      Negro Presidential appointees, **1968-69**:
      631
  Red Cross campaign, opening of, **1966**: 92
  Red Cross Month, opening of, **1963-64**: 202
  Ribicoff, Sen. Abraham, unveiling of portrait
      of, **1965**: 94
  Roosevelt, Franklin D., 82d anniversary of
      birth, **1963-64**: 165
  Roosevelt, Theodore, 46th anniversary of
      death, **1965**: 3
  Rusk, Secretary of State, and Mrs. Rusk, fare-
      well reception for, **1968-69**: 681
  St. Louis University, tree-planting ceremony,
      1963-64: 188
  Salute to U.S.-Canadian partnership in progress,
      1963-64: 577
  Salutes to the President, **1963-64**: 363, 642
  Sam Rayburn Dam, dedication of, **1965**: 236
  Samuel I. Newhouse Communications Center,
      dedication, **1963-64**: 499
  San Antonio, Texas, 250th anniversary, **1966**:
      160
  San Francisco Bay area rapid transit test track,
      ground breaking, **1963-64**: 410
  Sandburg, Carl, memorial service, **1967**: 387
  Sanders, Dr. William, luncheon honoring, **1968-
      69**: 239
  Savings bond campaign opening, **1963-64**: 306
  Senate reception, **1968-69**: 690
  Senate visit, **1968-69**: 258
  Shah of Iran, 25th anniversary of reign, **1965**:
      517
  Sibelius, Jean, centennial of birth, **1965**: 1
  Smithson, James, bicentennial celebration,
      1965: 519
  Social Security Act, 30th anniversary, **1965**:
      425
  Southwest Texas State College, summer com-
      mencement, **1968-69**: 459
  Space program members, dinner honoring,
      1968-69: 616
  Space treaty
      Entry into force, **1967**: 425
      Signing, **1967**: 18
  S.S. *Louise Lykes*, keel-laying ceremony, **1963-
      64**: 110
  Staggers, Repr. Harley O., dinner honoring,
      1968-69: 567
  Stamp unveilings, **1966**: 358, 500
  Stevenson, Adlai E., commemorative stamp
      unveiling, **1965**: 504
  Summersville Dam, W. Va., dedication, **1966**:
      427
  Swarthmore College, centennial celebration,
      1963-64: 391

Addresses or remarks – *continued*
  Swearing-in ceremonies, **1963-64**: 144, 146,
      200, 203, 207, 273, 360, 437, 442,
      445, 469, 550, 613, 677, 771; **1965**: 25,
      66, 78, 98, 155, 177, 209, 290, 339,
      341, 345, 371, 383, 421, 433, 443, 468,
      478, 595, 596
      See also main heading, Swearing-in ceremo-
      nies.
  Tchaikovsky International Music Competition
      winners, reception, **1966**: 440
  Texas Christian University, commencement,
      1968-69: 282
  Theodore Roosevelt Memorial, dedication,
      1967: 450
  Thomas More College, dedication, **1968-69**:
      499
  Tree-planting ceremony at the White House,
      1963-64: 673
  Trowbridge, Alexander B., reception honoring,
      1968-69: 139
  200 millionth American, birth, **1967**: 498
  UCLA, 96th charter day observance, **1963-64**:
      192
  United Community Campaigns, **1967**: 402
  United Nations
      19th anniversary, **1963-64**: 698
      20th anniversary, **1965**: 331
  United Nations General Assembly, endorse-
      ment of the nuclear nonproliferation
      treaty, **1968-69**: 308
  United States Marshals, 175th anniversary of
      service, **1963-64**: 523
  United States Pavilion at World's Fair, dedica-
      tion, **1963-64**: 283
  University of California, Irvine Campus, dedi-
      cation, **1963-64**: 414
  University of Kentucky, 100th anniversary,
      1965: 80
  University of Texas, commencement, **1963-64**:
      375
  U.S.S. *Casimir Pulaski*, commissioning, **1963-
      64**: 515
  U.S.S. *John F. Kennedy,* christening, **1967**:
      241
  U.S.S. *Pargo,* keel-laying ceremony, **1963-64**:
      383
  U.S.S. *Sam Rayburn*
      Commissioning, **1963-64**: 786
      Launching, **1963-64**: 59
  U.S.S. *Vallejo,* keel-laying ceremony, **1963-64**:
      449
  Veterans Day tour of military installations,
      1967: 485
  Vice President, Speaker of the House, and Chief
      Justice, dinner honoring, **1965**: 42;
      1967: 7; **1968-69**: 32

Addresses or remarks — *continued*
  Vice President's return from Europe, **1967**: 169
  Vietnam conflict veterans, pilot program for training as teachers, **1968–69**: 419
  Vinson, Repr. Carl, 85th birthday, **1968–69**: 592
  Warsaw Uprising, 20th anniversary, **1963–64**: 491
  Westmoreland, Gen. William C., luncheon honoring, **1967**: 195
  White House personnel, farewell to, **1968–69**: 588, 595, 602
  Women, recent appointees, reception for, **1963–64**: 257
  Woodrow Wilson School for Public and International Affairs, dedication, **1966**: 216
  Wright, Repr. James C., reception, **1968–69**: 281
  Year of the Bible, ceremony marking, **1966**: 19
  Young Democrats fundraising dinner, **1963–64**: 372
  Zambia, independence, **1963–64**: 721
  Zanzibar, independence celebration, **1963–64**: 32
Addresses or remarks during election campaign. *See* Election campaign, addresses, remarks.
Addresses or remarks to foreign or international groups.
  See also Visits to foreign countries.
  Alliance for Progress, Ambassadors of participating countries, **1963–64**: 340
  Ambassadors, foreign, **1968–69**: 357
  American Field Service students, **1963–64**: 465; **1965**: 372
  Argentine senators, **1963–64**: 269
  Atomic Energy, International Conference on the Peaceful Uses of, **1963–64**: 545
  Austrian good will delegation, **1966**: 272
  Benito Juárez Scholars, **1967**: 451; **1968–69**: 66
  Development Assistance Committee, **1966**: 343
  Diplomatic Corps, **1963–64**: 42; **1965**: 63
  Electrical Workers, International Union of, **1963–64**: 590
  Exchange teachers, **1966**: 406
  Foreign editors, **1968–69**: 177
  Foreign students in D.C. colleges, **1963–64**: 313
  Inter-American Committee on the Alliance for Progress, **1963–64**: 726
  International Bank for Reconstruction and Development, **1968–69**: 500
  International Executive Service Corps, **1963–64**: 402
  International Labor Press Association, **1963–64**: 297; **1966**: 237
  International Ladies Garment Workers Union, **1963–64**: 387, 388; **1968–69**: 270
  International Monetary Fund, **1968–69**: 500

Addresses or remarks — *continued*
  International rural development conference delegates, **1963–64**: 482
  Italian artists, **1965**: 82
  Italian journalists, **1963–64**: 149
  Japanese Cabinet ministers, **1967**: 381
  Japanese Governors, **1967**: 234
  Korean National Assembly, **1966**: 565
  Latin American Ambassadors, **1967**: 151
  Lyndon B. Johnson Australian Science Scholars, **1967**: 1
  Machinists Union, International, **1963–64**: 571
  Mexican-American Conference, **1967**: 452
  Mexico-United States Interparliamentary Conference, **1968–69**: 199
  NATO nations, parliamentarians, **1963–64**: 582
  Organization of American States, foreign ministers, **1967**: 395
  Pan American Congress of Architects, **1965**: 315
  United Nations General Assembly, **1963–64**: 51
  Urban Development Seminar, **1965**: 511
  World Bank, **1968–69**: 500
  World Press Institute, **1965**: 378
Addresses or remarks to national groups
  Advertising Council, **1963–64**: 314
  AFL–CIO
    Building and Construction Trades Department, **1963–64**: 235; **1965**: 223; **1967**: 261; **1968–69**: 154
    Committee on Political Education, **1968–69**: 164
    Delegates, **1965**: 644
    Executive council, **1963–64**: 22
    General board of, **1963–64**: 548
    National convention, **1967**: 534
    National headquarters, **1968–69**: 670
    Rally, **1966**: 431
  African Methodist Episcopal Church, Bishops' Council, **1966**: 484
  Agricultural Stabilization and Conservation Service, committeemen and director, **1967**: 228
  All American Council, Democratic National Committee, **1968–69**: 568
  American Alumni Council, **1965**: 124; **1966**: 325
  American Association of School Administrators, **1965**: 250
  American Bar Association, **1963–64**: 511; **1968–69**: 263
  American Committee on Italian Migration, **1968–69**: 352
  American Field Service Students, **1966**: 339
  American Institute of Architects, **1965**: 315
  American Legion, **1968–69**: 472

Addresses or remarks – *continued*
  American Legion National Convention, **1966:** 420

  American Physical Society, **1967:** 192

  American Society of Newspaper Editors, **1963–64:** 270

  Association of American Editorial Cartoonists, **1965:** 246; **1968–69:** 260

  B'nai B'rith, **1968–69:** 474

  Boy Scout Jamboree, **1963–64:** 473

  Boy Scouts of America, **1965:** 55; **1966:** 57; **1967:** 41

  Boys Nation, **1967:** 323

  Business Council, **1967:** 524; **1968–69:** 241, 612

    Telephone remarks to members, **1965:** 632

  Business Group for Latin America, **1963–64:** 169

  Campaign Conference for Democratic Women, **1963–64:** 305

  Chamber of Commerce of the United States, **1963–64:** 295

  Citizens Advisory Committee for Recreation and Natural Beauty, **1968–69:** 167

  Communications Workers of America, **1963–64:** 406

  Conference of State Commissions on the Status of Women, **1966:** 299

  Conference of State Committees on Criminal Administration, **1966:** 526

  Conference on Women in the War on Poverty, **1967:** 211

  Construction industry representatives, **1965:** 41

  Consumer Assembly '67, **1967:** 465

  Consumer organizations, representatives, **1967:** 393

  Cooperative League of the U.S.A., **1963–64:** 352

  Cooperative organizations, conference, **1967:** 415

  Council of International Programs for Youth Leaders and Social Workers, **1967:** 365

  Daughters of the American Revolution, **1963–64:** 275

  Democratic Governors, **1967:** 296

  Democratic National Committee, **1963–64:** 542

    Advisory Committee on Youth Activities, **1968–69:** 17

  Educational leaders, **1967:** 490; **1968–69:** 644

    Foreign policy conference, **1968–69:** 327

  Farm leaders, **1967:** 63

  Farm Policy and Rural Life Conference, **1968–69:** 155

  Federal Home Loan Bank System officials, **1967:** 420

Addresses or remarks – *continued*
  Foreign Policy Conference for Educators, **1967:** 272

  Fraternal organizations, representatives, **1967:** 397

  Future Farmers of America, **1968–69:** 390

  Girls Nation, **1967:** 332

  Governors' conference, **1967:** 123-125; **1968–69:** 100, 102, 406

  Incorporators, National Housing Partnership, **1968–69:** 506

  Insurance executives, **1967:** 380

  Internal Revenue commissioners, **1966:** 96

  International Association of Chiefs of Police, **1967:** 382

  International Conference on Water for Peace, **1967:** 230

  International Conference on the World Crisis in Education, **1967:** 423

  International Federation of Commercial, Clerical, and Technical Employees, **1967:** 442

  International Labor Press Association, **1963–64:** 297; **1966:** 237

  Italian-American Professional and Businessmen's Association, **1966:** 513

  Jewish Labor Committee dinner, **1967:** 484

  Lawyers Conference on Crime Control, **1967:** 221

  League of Women Voters, **1963–64:** 289

  Marshals, national conference, **1966:** 487

  Mayors of Nation's larger cities, **1966:** 525

  Milk Producers, Inc., convention, **1968–69:** 462

  National Alliance of Businessmen, **1968–69:** 37, 141

  National Association of Broadcasters, **1968–69:** 172

  National Association of Counties, **1963–64:** 509

  National Association of Home Builders, **1965:** 243

  National Association of Postmasters, **1968–69:** 498

  National Bar Association, convention, **1968–69:** 429

  National Committee for International Development, **1965:** 7

  National Conference of Christians and Jews, **1968–69:** 78

  National Conference on Crime Control, **1967:** 146

  National Conference of Editorial Writers, **1966:** 503

  National Conference on Foreign Policy, editors and broadcasters, **1963–64:** 280

[References are to items except as otherwise indicated]

Addresses or remarks – *continued*
  National Congress of American Indians, **1963–64**: 120
  National Council on Aging, **1968–69**: 117
  National Council on the Arts, **1968–69**: 601
  National Council on Crime and Delinquency, **1967**: 276
  National Council of Senior Citizens, **1966**: 253
  National Education Association, **1965**: 340
  National Farmers Union, **1968–69**: 142
    Telephone remarks, **1963–64**: 225
  National Grange, convention, **1967**: 496
  National Industrial Conference Board, **1965**: 76
  National League of Cities, **1966**: 155
  National Legislative Conference, **1967**: 409
  National Legislative Leaders Conference, **1966**: 273
  National Medical Association, **1968–69**: 442
  National Recreation and Park Association, **1966**: 518
  National Rural Electric Cooperative Association, **1965**: 308, 357; **1968–69**: 96
    Student contest winners, **1968–69**: 305
    Youth Conference, **1967**: 267
  National Urban League's Community Action Assembly, **1963–64**: 800
  National Water Commission, **1968–69**: 600
  National Youth Conference on National Beauty and Conservation, **1966**: 295
  New England Governors' conference, **1967**: 222
  Newspaper Farm Editors Association, **1963–64**: 344
  Nongovernmental national organizations, leaders, **1968–69**: 143
  101st Airborne Division, **1966**: 348
  Physical Fitness Leadership Award winners, **1967**: 160
  Presidential Scholars, **1966**: 257; **1968–69**: 300
  President's Committee on Consumer Interests, **1967**: 430
  President's Committee on Mental Retardation, **1967**: 373
  Radio Free Europe, business supporters of, **1963–64**: 785
  Railroad labor dispute board, **1967**: 386
  Selective Service State directors, **1967**: 205
  Senate Youth Program, **1968–69**: 33
  Senate Youth Program participants, **1965**: 48; **1966**: 35
  Southern Baptist Christian Citizenship Seminar, **1968–69**: 156
  Southern Baptists, seminar, **1963–64**: 238
  State commerce directors, **1967**: 148
  State Employment Service Directors, **1968–69**: 86

Addresses or remarks – *continued*
  Tennessee State Legislature, Vietnam policy, **1967**: 116
  United Automobile Workers of America, **1963–64**: 233; **1966**: 235
  United States Attorneys, **1968–69**: 209
  United States Jaycees, **1967**: 23, 286
  United Steelworkers of America, **1963–64**: 290, 589
  Urban Institute, Board of Trustees, **1968–69**: 215
  Veterans Administration directors and managers, **1967**: 161
  Veterans of Foreign Wars, **1968–69**: 132, 452
  Veterans organizations
    Leaders, **1967**: 493
    Representatives, **1963–64**: 611
  Vocational Industrial Clubs, representatives, **1968–69**: 238
  White House Conference "To Fulfill These Rights," **1966**: 248
  White House Correspondents Association, **1968–69**: 242
  White House Fellows, **1967**: 201; **1968–69**: 227
  White House summer interns, **1966**: 388
  Women's National Press Club, **1963–64**: 208
  YMCA Youth Governors Conference, **1965**: 335; **1966**: 306; **1968–69**: 332
  Young Democrats, **1968–69**: 165
Addresses or remarks at presentation ceremonies. *See also* Awards and citations.
  AAA lifesaving awards, School Safety Patrol, **1963–64**: 317; **1965**: 232
  American Football Coaches Association award, **1966**: 7
  Anti-Defamation League Award, acceptance, **1965**: 44
  Army battle flag, acceptance, **1963–64**: 119
  Beautification award, **1966**: 353
  Beautification program leadership certificate, acceptance, **1965**: 315
  Big Brother of the Year Award, **1966**: 213
    Acceptance, **1963–64**: 239
  Boy Scouts of America "Report to the Nation," **1966**: 57; **1967**: 41
  Bronze Star, **1967**: 475
  Canada, gift from U.S., **1967**: 238
  Certificates of Merit, **1963–64**: 467; **1967**: 324
  Charles B. Stillman Award, acceptance, **1965**: 539
  Collier Trophy, Clarence L. Johnson, **1963–64**: 593
  Commemorative book, education legislation, **1968–69**: 644
  Commission to Lt. Col. John H. Glenn, Jr., **1963-64**: 725

Addresses or remarks – *continued*
Cost reduction awards, Department of Defense, **1965**: 387; **1968–69**: 516
Disciples of Christ Historical Society citation, acceptance, **1963–64**: 279
Distinguished Federal Civilian Service Awards. *See* Distinguished Federal Civilian Service, President's Award for.
Distinguished Service Medal, **1967**: 235, 308, 567; **1968–69**: 34, 353, 384, 669
  Clifton, Maj. Gen. Chester V., **1965**: 399
  Felt, Adm. Harry D., **1963–64**: 454
  Gerhart, Gen. John K., **1965**: 158
  Harkins, Gen. Paul D., **1963–64**: 425
  LeMay, Gen. Curtis E., **1965**: 37
  McKee, Gen. William F., **1963–64**: 487
  Power, Gen. Thomas S., **1963–64**: 783
  Shoup, Gen. David M., **1963–64**: 127
  Smith, Adm. Harold Page, **1965**: 228
"E" flag awards, **1963–64**: 350; **1966**: 144; **1967**: 231
8th Armored Division Association peace award, **1966**: 377
Eleanor Roosevelt commemorative stamps, acceptance, **1963–64**: 35
Eleanor Roosevelt Golden Candlestick award, Judge Anna M. Kross, **1963–64**: 208
Employer of the Year Award, **1967**: 388; **1968–69**: 548
Enrico Fermi Award, **1968–69**: 608
  Oppenheimer, J. Robert, **1963–64**: 19
  Rickover, Vice Adm. Hyman G., **1965**: 17
Equal opportunity awards, **1968–69**: 596
Fannie and John Hertz Foundation Award, **1966**: 194
Federal Aviation Agency award, Mrs. Russell (Jerrie) Mock, **1963–64**: 310
Federal Woman's Award, **1965**: 91; **1966**: 89; **1967**: 93; **1968–69**: 138
Government Employees Incentive Awards, **1963–64**: 790
Harmon International Aviation Trophies, **1963–64**: 569; **1967**: 431; **1968–69**: 610
Hearst Foundation Journalism Award, **1963–64**: 339
  Hall, Hal David, **1965**: 260
  Powers, Charles, **1965**: 260
  University of Florida, **1965**: 260
Heart-of-the-Year Award, **1966**: 49
Heart-of-the-Year Award, Vice Adm. Hyman G. Rickover, **1963–64**: 164
Hirshhorn, Joseph H., art collection, **1966**: 226
Holland Society's Award for Distinguished Achievement, **1968–69**: 661
Honorary degree, **1967**: 448
Honorary membership in National Forensic League, acceptance, **1963–64**: 343

Addresses or remarks – *continued*
Interama Cultural and Trade Center, acceptance of book on, **1963–64**: 710
International Narcotics Enforcement Officers Association award, **1968–69**: 217
International Platform Association, annual award, acceptance, **1968**: 397
Johnson, Andrew, papers, **1967**: 538
Joseph P. Kennedy, Jr., Foundation awards, **1963–64**: 174
Lasker, Albert, special award, **1966**: 166
Legion of Merit, **1967**: 475
"Magna Carta" book, acceptance of copy, **1965**: 376
Medal of Honor, **1963–64**: 793; **1966**: 87, 183, 288, 456, 641; **1967**: 9, 102, 166, 202, 361, 407, 446, 494, 567; **1968–69**: 48, 129, 221, 246, 487, 594, 617, 688
  See also under Awards and Citations.
Minuteman Award, **1968–69**: 12
NASA awards, **1965**: 134; **1968–69**: 574, 662
NASA Exceptional Service Award
  Mathews, Charles W., **1965**: 318
  McDivitt, Lt. Col. (Maj.) James A., **1965**: 318
  White, Lt. Col. (Maj.) Edward H., 2d, **1965**: 318
National Civil Service League's Career Service Awards, **1965**: 263
National Education Award of 1966, **1966**: 77
National Freedom Award, **1966**: 86
National Medal of Science, **1963–64**: 98; **1965**: 56; **1966**: 61; **1967**: 37; **1968–69**: 71, 695
National Security Medal, **1966**: 387
Parents' Magazine award, acceptance, **1965**: 614
Pledge to law and authority, **1968–69**: 163
Postal Service's Honor Award, **1968–69**: 630
Presidential Citation, Stephen Gallatti, Sr., posthumously, **1963–64**: 465
Presidential limousine, acceptance, **1968–69**: 549
Presidential Medal of Freedom, **1963–64**: 27, 157, 568; **1968–69**: 99, 616, 691
Presidential Scholars award, **1963–64**: 397; **1965**: 306
Presidential Unit Citation, **1966**: 20; **1967**: 106, 384; **1968–69**: 267, 541, 675
President's Committee on Employment of the Handicapped Distinguished Service Award, Walter Mason, **1963–64**: 235
President's Committee on Employment of the Handicapped 1964 award, **1963–64**: 389
Rhode Island, University of, honorary degree, **1966**: 396

Addresses or remarks – *continued*
  Robert H. Goddard Trophy, **1966:** 134
  Roosevelt, Eleanor, President's acceptance of
      bust of, **1965:** 210
  Roosevelt, Franklin D., portrait, **1967:** 28
  Safety Awards, President's, **1963–64:** 351
  Salute to Eisenhower Week, proclamation,
      1968–69: 488
  Salvation Army award, acceptance, **1965:** 643
  Savings bond program award, **1968–69:** 537
  Savings bond purchases awards, **1967:** 315
  Scholastic achievement awards to blind students,
      1966: 220; **1968–69:** 230
  Silver Star, Sgt. Harry A. Walling, posthumously,
      1963–64: 535
  Small Businessman of the Year award
      Berkley W. Bedell, **1963–64:** 362
      Dominic Donatello, **1965:** 270
  Social security check to 20-millionth benefi-
      ciary recipient, **1965:** 231
  Stevenson, Adlai E., bust, **1968–69:** 53
  Swords Into Plowshares award, **1968–69:** 310
  Teacher of the Year Award
      Dayton, Mona M., **1966:** 165
      Graf, David E., **1968–69:** 219
      Klinck, Richard E., **1965:** 171
      Tenney, Roger, **1967:** 182
      Trout, Lawana, **1963–64:** 309
  10th International Games for the Deaf cere-
      monial pass, acceptance of, **1963–64:**
      808
  Thanksgiving Day turkey, acceptance, **1963–64:**
      772
  Treasury Exceptional Service Award, Rufus W.
      Youngblood, **1963–64:** 21
  Tuss McLaughry Award, **1966:** 7
  U.S. Veterans Advisory Commission awards,
      1968–69: 599
  Veritas Medal of Providence College, Speaker
      of the House of Representatives John W.
      McCormack, **1965:** 237
  Vietnam Civilian Service Awards, **1967:** 352
  William Randolph Hearst Foundation, jour-
      nalism awards
    See Hearst Foundation Journalism Award,
      above.
  Young American Medals, **1963–64:** 315; **1965:**
      336; **1966:** 289; **1967:** 275; **1968–69:**
      236
Adenauer, Konrad, **1967:** 191n., 347n., 351, 554
      [5]
  Death, **1967:** 181
Adler, Richard, **1963–64:** 363, 373
Administrative budget, **1966:** 26 (pp. 49, 50, 52
      55), 635 [6, 17]; **1967:** 13 (pp. 41, 43,
      45, 46, 59), 358 [12]; **1968–69:** 39 (p.
      84)

Administrative Conference of the United States,
      Chairman (Jerre S. Williams), **1968–69:**
      31
Adminstrative Conference of the United States,
      Council, **1968–69:** 31n., 208
Administrative Office of the United States Courts,
      1967: 35
Admissions taxes, **1965:** 255
Adult Basic Education, National Advisory Com-
      mittee on, **1968–69:** 484
Adult education, **1963–64:** 213, 327, 658; **1965:**
      75; **1966:** 111, 189; **1967:** 77, 277;
      1968–69: 6, 54, 154, 262, 484, 538, 648
Adult illiteracy, **1963–64:** 213
Adult Indian Vocational Training Act, amend-
      ment, **1965:** 204
Adulyadej, King Bhumibol (Thailand), **1966:**
      554n., 555n., 557n., 558n.; **1967:** 289,
      290, 293
Advertising Council, **1963–64:** 314, 403, 508
Advertising practices, deception in, **1963–64:**
      173
Advisory Board on National Parks, Historic Sites,
      Buildings and Monuments, **1965:** 538n.
Advisory Board on the Presidential Election Cam-
      paign Fund, **1967:** 236
Advisory Commission on Food and Fiber, Nation-
      al, **1965:** 597
Advisory Commission on Intergovernmental Re-
      lations, **1966:** 606, 607 [1]; **1968–69:**
      598
Advisory Commission on Narcotic and Drug
      Abuse, President's, **1963–64:** 159, 179,
      458; **1965:** 102
Advisory Committee on Foreign Assistance Pro-
      grams, General, **1965:** 136
Advisory Committee on International Monetary
      Arrangements, **1965:** 365; **1968–69:**
      218
Advisory Committee on Labor-Management
      Policy, President's, **1963–64:** 126, 213;
      1965: 428
Advisory Committee on Older Americans, **1965:**
      642
Advisory Committee on Private Enterprise in
      Foreign Aid, **1963–64:** 227; **1965:** 18,
      450; **1966:** 41
Advisory Committee on Supersonic Transport,
      President's, **1965:** 339
Advisory Committee on Youth Activities, Demo-
      cratic National Committee, **1968–69:** 17
Advisory Council on Health Insurance for the
      Disabled, **1968–69:** 346n.
Advisory Council on Insured Loans to Students,
      1966: 3
Advisory Council on International Monetary and
      Financial Problems, National, **1965:** 110,
      282

Advisory Council of the Small Business Administration, National, **1965**: 270n.
Advisory Council on the Status of Women, Citizens', **1965**: 392n.
Advisory Panel on Personnel Interchange, **1968–69**: 490, 498
AEC.
See Atomic Energy Commission.
Aeronautics, International Federation of, **1965**: 219
Aeronautics Association, National, **1963–64**: 593
Aeronautics and Space Act of 1958, **1968–69**: 616
Aeronautics and space activities report, **1963–64**: 155; **1966**: 40; **1967**: 24; **1968–69**: 41
Aeronautics and Space Administration, National, **1967**: 76, 315; **1968–69**: 39 (pp. 92, 100, 111), 107, 467 [3], 507, 533, 574, 610, 616, 646 [12], 662, 678 (pp. 1281, 1304)
Aeronautics and Space Council, National, **1968–69**: 41n.
Aerospace and Agricultural Implement Workers of America, International Union of United Automobile, **1966**: 535
Aerospace Workers, International Association of Machinists and, **1966**: 256n., 322, 360, 535
AFDC (Aid to Families with Dependent Children), **1967**: 16 (p. 83), 39
Afghanistan, **1967**: 143–145, 449, 452
  King Mohammed Zahir, **1967**: 143–145
  Peace Corps projects, **1966**: 126
  Prime Minister Mohammad Hashim Maiwandwal, **1967**: 143–145
  Queen Homaira, **1967**: 143–145
  U.N. Ambassador Abdul Rahman Pazhwak, **1967**: 143
AFL-CIO (American Federation of Labor-Congress of Industrial Organizations)
See main heading American Federation of Labor-Congress of Industrial Organizations.
Africa, **1963–64**: 272, 280, 297 [1], 544, 721, 780 [2, 16], 788; **1965**: 142, 144, 272, 295 [10, 14], 378; **1966**: 6 (p. 9), 243, 489, 610 [8], 654 [3]; **1967**: 51n., 52, 100, 356, 426, 488, 495 [5]; **1968–69**: 137, 140, 157, 159, 204, 508
See also specific countries.
African-American labor center, **1965**: 450
Assistance, **1963–64**: 45, 227, 617; **1965**: 7, 18, 136; **1966**: 45, 243; **1968–69**: 63, 524
Chiefs of State, **1965**: 141n.
  Meeting, **1963–64**: 460
Communist aggression, **1963–64**: 702; **1965**: 18; **1966**: 346

Africa – *continued*
  Conference of independent states, **1968–69**: 159
  Eastern states, **1963–64**: 170 [1]
  Economic and social development, **1965**: 450; **1966**: 41, 243, 261; **1967**: 44, 272, 403, 442, 444; **1968–69**: 110, 157, 159n., 181, 365, 394, 482, 508
  Health problems, **1965**: 262
  Health programs for, **1963–64**: 396
  Independence movement, **1963–64**: 32, 34
  New nations, **1963–64**: 32, 34; **1965**: 2, 141, 142n.
  Peace Corps projects in, **1965**: 83
  Regional cooperation, **1968–69**: 14 (p. 26), 140n., 365, 508, 511
  U.N. Economic Commission, **1963–64**: 191
  U.S. policy, **1967**: 3 (p. 9), 44; **1968–69**: 249, 255
  U.S. relations with, **1965**: 141, 142n.; **1966**: 273, 414
African Development Bank, **1966**: 41, 243, 654 [3]; **1967**: 16 (p. 80), 44, 100; **1968–69**: 63, 365, 500, 508
African and Malagasy States, Union of, **1965**: 144
African Methodist Episcopal Church, **1966**: 484
African Unity, Organization of, **1963–64**: 191, 460; **1965**: 571; **1966**: 243; **1967**: 51n., 52; **1968–69**: 140n., 157, 181, 433, 482, 508, 511n.
Afro-Americans, **1967**: 426
Age Discrimination in Employment Act of 1967, **1967**: 548
Agena launch vehicle, **1966**: 625
Agence France-Presse, **1968–69**: 169 [17]
Agency for International Development, **1966**: 11, 18, 26 (p. 58), 41, 45, 62, 153–154, 308n., 368, 406, 549ftn. (p. 1261), 629, 630 [4]; **1967**: 33, 44, 149, 357n., 489, 568; **1968–69**: 39 (p. 99), 47 (p. 138), 63, 79 [6], 149n., 181, 438, 679
See also International Development, Agency for.
  Iran, **1967**: 509
  Memorandum, **1968–69**: 11
  Partners of the Alliance program, **1968–69**: 63
  Vietnam programs, **1967**: 73, 116, 235
Agency for International Development, Administrator.
See also International Development, Agency for, Administrator.
  David E. Bell, **1966**: 247 [1, 15], 261
  William S. Gaud, **1966**: 368, 407; **1967**: 352; **1968–69**: 11, 63, 631, 691
Aggrey, Dr. James, **1966**: 243
Aging, Administration on, **1966**: 431
Aging, National Council on, **1968–69**: 75n., 117

Aging, President's Council on, **1963–64**: 178, 415; **1965**: 72

Agitators in racial disturbances, **1966**: 338 [8]

Agnew, Gov. Spiro T., **1967**: 286; **1968–69**: 184
  Vice-President elect, **1968–69**: 598, 599, 604, 696 [20]
  Vice-Presidential candidacy, **1968–69**: 529, 540, 567

Agnew, Mrs. Spiro T., **1968–69**: 598

Agreement for Facilitating the International Circulation of Visual and Auditory Materials of an Educational, Scientific, and Cultural Character (Beirut Agreement), **1966**: 45, 519

Agreement on the Importation of Educational, Scientific, and Cultural Materials, **1965**: 292, 604

Agreement on the Importation of Educational, Scientific, and Cultural Materials (Florence Agreement), **1966**: 45, 519, 601

Agreement on Tariffs and Trade, General.
  See General Agreement on Tariffs and Trade.

Agreement of Tax Incentives, Central American, **1968–69**: 366

Agreements, international.
  See International agreements.

Agricultural Act of 1964, **1963–64**: 54 [9], 242 [12], 255, 344, 631, 650, 669, 719; **1965**: 47

Agricultural Advisory Commission, National, **1963–64**: 484; **1965**: 47

Agricultural advisory corps, Vietnam, **1966**: 331

Agricultural commodities, **1963–64**: 124 (p. 162), 132 (p. 187), 598, 701, 757; **1965**: 35 (p. 111), 47, 319 [8], 377, 597
  Consumption, **1963–64**: 757
  Emergency reserves, **1965**: 47
  Exports, **1963–64**: 71 [8, 13], 475 [2], 484, 592, 634, 636, 757; **1965**: 18, 47, 139, 149, 168, 192, 307, 377, 597, 661
  Imports, **1963–64**: 757
  Marketing programs, **1963–64**: 255, 455 [7], 631, 634, 641, 757; **1965**: 46 [1], 47, 139, 149, 168, 192, 307, 377, 597
  Prices, **1963–64**: 255, 267; **1965**: 46 [1], 47, 168, 377

Agricultural Extension Service, **1963–64**: 414; **1965**: 513

Agricultural Food Fund, **1967**: 33

Agricultural Implement Workers of America, International Union of United Automobile, Aerospace and, **1966**: 535

Agricultural resources development, **1963–64**: 132 (p. 176)

Agricultural Service, Foreign, **1966**: 308n.

Agricultural Stabilization and Conservation Service, **1966**: 225; **1967**: 228; **1968–69**: 303

Agricultural surpluses, **1963–64**: 132 (p. 187), 255; **1965**: 47, 377
  See also Agriculture and agricultural programs.
  Distribution, **1965**: 18, 139, 149
  Distribution in Appalachian area, **1963–64**: 300
  Reduction, **1963–64**: 246 [12]; **1965**: 597
  Sale to United Arab Republic, **1965**: 46 [2], 661

Agricultural Trade Development and Assistance Act of 1954, **1963–64**: 132 (p. 187), 641; **1965**: 661; **1966**: 308
  Extension, **1968–69**: 417, 696 [14]

Agriculture, College of (University of the Philippines), **1966**: 550

Agriculture, Department of, **1963–64**: 132 (p. 181), 173, 179, 255, 482n., 567, 690n., 792n.; **1965**: 18, 47, 54, 85, 90, 127, 149, 168, 197, 224, 249n., 287n., 418, 492, 503, 512n., 514, 560, 569, 618; **1966**: 26 (pp. 54, 59), 62, 69, 140, 245n., 308n., 312, 334 [2], 374, 595, 630 [4]; **1967**: 13 (pp. 46, 50, 59), 405; **1968–69**: 39 (p. 101), 155n., 247n., 388, 389, 534, 678 (p. 1289)
  Appropriations, **1967**: 417 [1]; **1968–69**: 678 (p. 1281)
  Cost reduction program, **1966**: 164; **1968–69**: 174, 678 (p. 1304)
  Federal Extension Service, **1968–69**: 91
  Food stamp program, **1968–69**: 39 (p. 105)
  Inspection services, **1963–64**: 132 (p. 187)
  News conference remarks, **1963–64**: 211 [28], 218 [16], 619 [1]
  Purchases of beef, **1963–64**: 344
  School lunch program, **1966**: 340
  Spending cutbacks, **1967**: 6 [8]

Agriculture, House Committee on, **1968–69**: 85, 94

Agriculture, Secretary of (Orville L. Freeman), **1963–64**: 23, 67, 178n., 217, 242 (p. 428), 255, 320, 321, 322, 323, 325, 326, 327, 328, 341, 344, 358, 432, 433, 434, 489, 711, 758; **1965**: 2, 32 (p. 91), 46 [1], 47, 54, 112, 168, 277, 492, 555, 569, 597, 632; **1966**: 28, 52 [1, 2], 54, 56, 62, 69n., 86, 95, 106n., 141 [10], 153–154, 164, 188 [4], 203, 214, 245n., 281, 312, 331n., 343, 424n., 477 [5], 508, 516 [1], 595, 607 [1, 8]; **1967**: 13 (p. 50), 29, 33, 57, 63, 114, 138n., 144, 199, 228, 258, 294, 358 [9], 375 [20], 405, 415, 418, 541; **1968–69**: 39 (p. 100), 85, 91, 94, 113, 122, 136, 142, 155, 168, 364, 388, 417, 451, 505, 510, 534
  Letters, **1965**: 85, 197; **1966**: 340, 376
  Memorandums, **1966**: 425, 606; **1967**: 186, 259; **1968–69**: 389

Agriculture, Secretary of – *continued*
News conference remarks on, **1963–64:** 71 [8, 11] and ftn. (p. 89), 54 [9], 170 [4], 256 [14], 266 [21], 316 [3, 4]
Reports, **1965:** 249n., 358n., 545
Agriculture, Senate Committee on, **1968–69:** 85, 94
Agriculture Adjustment Act of 1938, **1968–69:** 94
Agriculture and agricultural programs, **1963–64:** 132 (p. 176), 434; **1965:** 32 (p. 91), 35 (p. 116), 46 [1], 168; **1966:** 414; **1967:** 16 (p. 79), 63, 442, 496, 508, 525; **1968–69:** 39 (p. 100), 96, 142, 155, 174, 695
See also Farm economy; Farm programs; Farmers; Food.
Acreage allotments, **1965:** 47, 168; **1966:** 62, 203; **1968–69:** 39 (p. 100)
Commission to examine policies on, proposed, **1965:** 46 [1]
Commodity exchanges, **1968–69:** 85, 94
Credit, **1967:** 156, 415; **1968–69:** 94, 450
Economy, **1966:** 6 (p. 5), 34 (pp. 96, 103), 62, 203, 240, 312
Exports, **1966:** 62, 272, 308n., 312, 355, 461; **1967:** 63, 228; **1968–69:** 29, 39 (p. 100), 94, 176, 247, 406, 417, 684 (p. 1319)
Farm and rural life conference, **1968–69:** 155
Federal aid, **1966:** 26 (p. 59), 188 [6]; **1968–69:** 425 [2], 439
Foreign aid, **1968–69:** 63, 679, 684 (p. 1321)
Foreign assistance, **1966:** 6 (p. 8), 26 (p. 58), 34 (p. 105), 153–154, 177, 272, 343; **1967:** 33, 44, 63, 264 [19]
Imports, **1968–69:** 439
Income, farm, **1966:** 6 (p. 5), 34 (p. 96), 189, 228, 334 [4], 346–347, 355, 403, 412, 415, 428, 436–437, 451, 479, 654 [3]; **1967:** 3 (p. 7), 13 (p. 50), 16 (p. 73), 63, 156, 228, 270, 305, 329, 358 [9], 496, 525; **1968–69:** 14 (pp. 28, 29, 31), 39 (p. 100), 47 (p. 128), 91, 94, 142, 155, 247, 462, 534, 683, 684 (p. 1312)
Legislation, **1965:** 168, 319 [1]; **1966:** 403; **1967:** 44, 63; **1968–69:** 534
Loans, **1967:** 6 [8], 305; **1968–69:** 247
Message to Congress, **1965:** 47; **1968–69:** 94
Migrant workers, **1967:** 3 (p. 5), 97, 114, 199, 201; **1968–69:** 91, 536
National food bank, **1968–69:** 247
Prices, **1966:** 312, 346, 355, 428, 635 [18]; **1967:** 63, 156, 305, 329, 358 [9], 496; **1968–69:** 94, 142, 534
Production, **1963–64:** 124 (p. 162), 132 (p. 187), 570; **1965:** 47, 168, 377, 597; **1966:** 26 (p. 59), 62, 281, 355, 461, 550; **1967:** 156, 496, 525; **1968–69:** 63, 94, 406, 534, 679, 696 [14]

Agriculture – *continued*
Research, **1963–64:** 124 (p. 162); **1965:** 47, 54, 168; **1966:** 62, 441, 550; **1967:** 13 (p. 60)
Surpluses, **1966:** 52 [1], 62, 164, 281, 353, 355, 403, 436, 515, 608; **1967:** 13 (p. 50), 63, 228, 305, 449, 469; **1968–69:** 94, 247
See also Agricultural surpluses.
Technology research, **1968–69:** 176
Waste products, **1968–69:** 122
World, **1968–69:** 500
Agriculture Organization, Food and, **1966:** 94
Agriculture Organization of the United Nations, Food and, **1967:** 33
Agriculture and Related Agencies Appropriation Act of 1969, **1968–69:** 94n.
Agudas Achim Synagogue, Austin, Tex., dedication, **1963–64:** 77
Aguilar, Gilberto, **1968–69:** 370
Aguirre, Mr. and Mrs. Braulio Fernandez, **1966:** 639
Ahidjo, El Hadj Ahmadou (President of Cameroon), **1967:** 444
Ahmed, Ghulam, **1965:** 649
Ahmed, Mrs. Ghulam, **1965:** 649
AID.
See Agency for International Development; International Development, Agency for.
Aid to Families with Dependent Children (AFDC), **1967:** 16 (p. 83), 39
Aiken, Frank, **1963–64:** 366
Aiken, Sen. George D., **1963–64:** 136n., 546, 575, 577, 605; **1965:** 412 [2, 4], 415, 555; **1966:** 396–399, 403, 417 [5], 428, 455; **1967:** 204 [16], 405
Aikin, A. M., Jr., **1965:** 285
Ailes, Stephen.
See Army, Secretary of the (Stephen Ailes).
Ainsworth, Miller, **1963–64:** 763
Air Defense Command, North American, **1965:** 158
Air Force, Department of the, **1963–64:** 285 [16], 308, 351, 516 [3]; **1965:** 448 [1]; **1968–69:** 18 [2]
Procurement, **1963–64:** 703
Air Force, Secretary of the (Harold Brown), **1966:** 20; **1967:** 9, 106; **1968–69:** 48, 110, 556, 610, 669, 688
Air Force, Secretary of the (Eugene M. Zuckert), **1963–64:** 37, 256 [13], 285 [16], 409, 510, 612, 783; **1965:** 37n. 656
Air Force, United States, **1963–64:** 52, 199, 647, 665, 716; **1965:** 26, 158, 219, 223, 287; **1968–69:** 39 (p. 98), 81 [3], 144, 153 [5], 231, 251, 254, 266, 268, 269, 318, 337, 379, 478, 516, 543, 597, 603, 610, 627, 628, 696 [17]
Air Force Reserve, **1967:** 159
Air Force safety record, **1966:** 75

[References are to items except as otherwise indicated]

Air Museum, National, **1966**: 630 [4]

Air National Guard, **1967**: 159

Air pollution, **1963–64**: 50, 132 (p. 189), 179,
      357, 422, 562, 578, 599, 620, 650, 667,
      669, 732, 736, 747, 755, 760; **1966**: 6
      (p. 6), 26 (p. 62), 82, 353, 398, 403,
      485–486, 515, 545; **1967**: 3 (p. 5), 13
      (p. 53), 20, 149, 186, 216, 222, 295,
      329, 503, 534; **1968–69**: 14 (p. 28), 39
      (pp. 89, 103), 84, 87, 95, 122, 123,
      167, 345, 409, 420, 447, 470, 648, 653,
      678 (p. 1296), 684 (pp. 1311, 1321)

Air pollution control, **1965**: 2, 9, 15, 32 (p. 94),
      35 (p. 115), 54, 90, 94, 175, 277, 433,
      568, 602, 659

Air Quality Act of 1967, **1967**: 16 (p. 85), 20,
      186, 503; **1968–69**: 122, 409, 420

Air Quality Advisory Board, **1968–69**: 409

Air safety, **1963–64**: 391

Air traffic, **1967**: 149, 392

Air Transport Agreement, United States-Japan,
      1965: 15; **1966**: 64

Air Transport Association, International, **1968–
69**, 116

Air travelers, protection, **1963–64**: 173

Aircraft, **1966**: 98, 141 [5]; **1968–69**: 41, 169
      [18]
    See also Aircraft, military; Aviation.
    C-5A transport, **1966**: 26 (p. 56); **1967**: 13
      (p. 48); **1968–69**: 39 (p. 98), 109, 110,
      125
    Convention on offenses aboard, **1968–69**: 494
    FB-111 bomber, **1966**: 26 (p. 56); **1968–69**:
      39 (p. 98), 169 [10, 18]
    J-58 aircraft engine, **1963–64**: 201 [2]
    Mach 2.3, proposed, **1963–64**: 310
    Military, **1968–69**: 39 (p. 98)
    Noise, **1968–69**: 122
    Noise reduction, **1966**: 98; **1967**: 139, 328
      [15]
    Procurement, **1963–64**: 216; **1965**: 261n.
    Procurement, Federal, **1966**: 159; **1967**: 13
      (p. 48)
    Supersonic civil transport, **1963–64**: 132 (p.
      188), 201 [2], 242 [9], 294 [6], 355,
      789; **1965**: 32 (p. 89), 319 [19], 339;
      1966: 6 (pp. 6, 7), 26 (pp. 56, 61), 98,
      654 [12]; **1967**: 13 (pp. 48, 52), 31n.,
      197; **1968–69**: 39 (p. 102)
    X-15, **1968–69**: 610
    XB-70 supersonic, **1967**: 431n.

Aircraft, military, **1963–64**: 132 (p. 184), 736
    See also Aviation.
    A-11, **1965**: 219
    A-11 jet interceptor, world speed record, **1963–
      64**: 201 [2], 256 [3]
    Airlift capacity, **1963–64**: 132 (p. 184), 199,
      382, 413, 467; **1965**: 26, 387

Aircraft, military — *continued*
    Bombers, **1963–64**: 266 [18], 382, 635; **1965**:
      26, 158, 284, 339
    See also Aircraft; Aviation.
    A7A, **1963–64**: 382
    COIN (counter-insurgency), **1963–64**: 516
      [3]
    F-111, **1963–64**: 382
    RB-66 reconnaissance, **1963–64**: 170 [1],
      182, 232 [2], 242 [18, 26], 246 [4]
    SR-71 reconnaissance, **1963–64**: 475 [1];
      1965: 26, 339
    C-5A cargo transport, proposed, **1965**: 26
    Sale to Israel, **1968–69**: 524n.
    XB-70A research, **1965**: 339
    YF-12A speed record, **1965**: 219

Aircraft Noise Panel, jet, **1966**: 98ftn. (p. 261)

Airlines, **1963–64**: 215; **1966**: 98
    See also Aircraft; Aviation.
    Accident compensation, **1966**: 98
    Labor dispute, **1966**: 256–257, 322, 338 [3],
      360, 373 [5, 7, 12], 399
    User charges, **1966**: 26 (pp. 53, 54), 34 (p.
      106), 403

Airports, **1966**: 98, 244
    Appalachian region, **1968–69**: 701
    Federal aid, **1963–64**: 215, 410, 453, 598
    Land use in vicinity, **1967**: 139, 328 [15]
    Safety, **1968–69**: 47 (p. 144)
    Urban, **1968–69**: 93

Airspace System, National, **1968–69**: 39 (p. 111)

Akamine, Drusilla C., **1967**: 275

Akers, Robert W., **1965**: 395 [1]

Akron, Ohio
    Campaign remarks, **1963–64**: 693
    Mayor Edward Erickson, **1963–64**: 693

Alabama, **1965**: 201
    Economic boycott, question of, **1965**: 156 [4]
    Federal courts in, **1965**: 106 [1], 117 [5]
    Gov. George C. Wallace, **1963–64**: 246 [7],
      256 [7, 19], 285 [1], 316 [14, 18, 21],
      455 [19], 475 [18]; **1965**: 106 [1],
      114, 117 [1, 5], 126n.; **1966**: 122 [1, 2]
    Murder of civil rights workers, **1965**: 107, 135
    National Guard, **1965**: 114, 117 [1, 5, 11]
    Poll tax, **1965**: 409
    Primary election, **1963–64**: 316 [14, 21]
    School desegregation, **1965**: 470
    Selma-to-Montgomery civil rights march, **1965**:
      104, 114, 117 [1, 5, 10], 126n., 135
    Troops in, question of, **1965**: 106 [5], 117 [1,
      5] and ftn. (p. 307), 161
    Voter rights and registration, **1965**: 46 [3, 13],
      106 [1, 7, 9]

Alamo, **1968–69**: 696 [1]

Alaska, **1965**: 189, 270, 435, 448 [10]; **1968–69**:
    341, 621

Alaska — *continued*
  Disaster relief, **1967**: 369
  Earthquake relief, **1963–64**: 241, 242 [1, 16],
      286, 294 [7], 308, 319, 368, 371, 615;
      1966: 74
  Fisheries, **1963–64**: 559
  Floods, **1968–69**: 98
  Gov. William A. Egan, **1963–64**: 241, 242 [16],
      615; **1966**: 244, 567–568; **1967**: 369
  Gov. Walter J. Hickel, **1967**: 555
  Land rights, **1968–69**: 113
  Rural electrification, **1968–69**: 629n.
  Statehood, **1966**: 244
  Visit to, question of, **1963–64**: 242 [16]
Alaska, Federal Field Committee for Develop-
    ment Planning in, **1963–64**: 615
Alaska, Federal Reconstruction and Develop-
    ment Planning Commission for, **1963–
    64**: 241n., 294 [7], 308, 319, 368, 615
Alaska, President's Review Committee for De-
    velopment Planning in, **1963–64**: 615n.
Alaska Omnibus Act, **1966**: 244
  Amendment, **1963–64**: 286, 371
  1964 Amendments to the, **1965**: 435
Alaska Purchase Centennial, 1967, **1966**: 147
Alaska Railroad, **1963–64**: 615
Albert, Repr. Carl, **1963–64**: 341n., 516 [20],
      540, 542, 587 [2], 597; **1965**: 133,
      179, 181, 183, 329, 330, 340, 394, 559;
      1966: 334 [1], 410, 413, 415–416, 505,
      524, 578 [1], 599 [6], 628 [11]; **1967**:
      216; **1968–69**: 212, 461n., 467 [1],
      655, 676 (p. 1270)
Albert D. Lasker Foundation, **1968–69**: 589n.
Alberto Masferrer Normal School, San Andrés,
    El Salvador, **1968–69**: 370
Albin, Spencer K., **1967**: 324n.
Albuquerque, N. Mex., campaign remarks, **1963–
    64**: 732
Alcohol
  Addiction, **1966**: 27, 95; **1967**: 15, 35, 71,
      285; **1968–69**: 59, 536, 561
  Crime and accident cause, **1968–69**: 57, 59
Alcoholic beverages, excise taxes, **1965**: 255
Alcoholic rehabilitation bill of 1968, **1968–69**:
    59
Alcoholism, Advisory Committee on, **1966**: 95
Alcott, Amos B., **1963–64**: 360
Alden, Mr. and Mrs. Vernon R., **1963–64**: 323
Aldrich, Daniel C., **1963–64**: 414
Aldrich, Dr. Robert A., **1967**: 373; **1968–69**:
    493
Aldrin, Lt. Col. Edwin E., Jr., **1966**: 618, 625;
    1967: 431
Alemán, Roberto, **1965**: 532
Alexander, Clifford L., Jr., **1965**: 448 [6]; **1966**:
    65 [1], 408n.; **1967**: 291, 333, 460 [1];
    1968–69: 17, 42, 429, 596, 631

Alexander, Jesse N., Jr., **1968–69**: 332
Alexander, Myrl E., **1966**: 463; **1967**: 317n.
Alexander, Shana, **1968–69**: 525n.
Alexander the Great, **1965**: 378
Alexandria, Va., campaign remarks, **1963–64**: 628
Alfred, James V., **1963–64**: 763; **1967**: 211
Alfred E. Smith Memorial Foundation, **1963–64**:
      662; **1968–69**: 540
Alger, Horatio, **1968–69**: 459
Algeria, **1967**: 245
"Alice in Wonderland," Lewis Carroll, **1967**: 431
Alien Property, Office of, **1965**: 309; **1966**: 303;
      1968–69: 514
Alien Property Custodian, Office of, **1965**: 309
Aliens in U.S., **1968–69**: 88, 498
Alioto, Joseph, **1968–69**: 333, 339 [3], 568
All American Council, Democratic National
      Committee, **1968–69**: 568
Allen, Rear Adm. Edward C., **1967**: 485 [8]
Allen, Rev. Frank, **1967**: 117
Allen, Fred, **1963–64**: 314
Allen, George V., **1966**: 519; **1968–69**: 149
Allen, Mr. and Mrs. Ivan, Jr., **1963–64**: 330
Allen, Wally, **1966**: 332n.
Alliance for Progress, **1963–64**: 45, 46, 66, 69,
      91 (p. 117), 123, 132 (p. 186), 192–193,
      194, 218 [34], 227, 245, 269, 272, 438,
      441, 443, 561, 590, 596, 607, 769;
      1965: 2, 7, 18, 32 (p. 90), 139, 149,
      272, 295 [15], 319 [16], 393, 484,
      558, 593, 624; **1966**: 6 (p. 8), 16,
      26 (p. 58), 41, 62, 175, 254, 261, 277
      [3], 320 [12], 341, 366, 469, 610 [8,
      10], 642 [2], 649; **1967**: 3 (p. 9), 10,
      13 (p. 49), 16 (p. 80), 44, 110, 152,
      171, 175–177, 272, 357, 394, 395, 436,
      451, 495 [5]; **1968–69**: 39 (p. 99), 63,
      147, 148n., 205, 206, 207, 239, 289,
      290, 359, 366, 375, 376, 500, 524, 665
  3d anniversary, **1963–64**: 220
  4th anniversary, **1965**: 429
  5th anniversary, **1966**: 125, 386
  Agricultural credit program, **1966**: 177
  Ambassadors of participating countries, **1963–
      64**: 316 [9], 340
  California-Chile project, **1963–64**: 227
  Campaign remarks, **1963–64**: 695, 702
  News conference remarks, **1963–64**: 71 [5, 16],
      150 [7], 285 [6, 13], 455 [16], 560
      [2]
  U.S. support of, **1963–64**: 9, 316 [9]; **1965**:
      18, 131, 429
Alliance for Progress, Inter-American Committee
      on the, **1963–64**: 211 [8], 220, 227,
      340, 475 [3], 726, 769; **1965**: 18, 136,
      393, 429; **1966**: 41, 125, 158 [2], 177,
      386n., 501 [1]; **1968–69**: 290

Allied capitals, visits of Henry Cabot Lodge, **1963–64**: 504 [9]

Allied Health Professions Personnel Training Act of 1966, **1966**: 490, 573; **1968–69**: 111, 447

Allied Motion Picture Theater Owners of Maryland, Inc., **1963–64**: 354

Allied States Association of Motion Picture Exhibitors, **1963–64**: 354

Allis-Chalmers Manufacturing Co., **1963–64**: 350n.

Allon, Yigal, **1968–69**: 474

Allott, Sen. Gordon, **1966**: 410, 413–414

Alphand, Hervé, **1963–64**: 188, 189

Alphand, Mme. Hervé, **1963–64**: 188, 189

Al-Salim al-Sabah, Shaikh Abdullah, **1965**: 629

Alsop, Joseph, **1967**: 518 [16]

Altamaha River Basin, Georgia, **1963–64**: 716

Aluminum, release from stockpile, **1965**: 632

Aluminum stockpiles, **1966**: 283n., 390, 572n.

Alumni Council, American, remarks to, **1965**: 124

Alvarez, Luis W., **1963–64**: 98

Alvim, General of the Army Hugo Panasco, **1965**: 286, 295 [1, 4], 299, 319 [4, 16], 342

Amalgamated Clothing Workers, 50th anniversary, **1963–64**: 334

Ambassadors, foreign, **1968–69**: 357

Ambassadors, U.S., appointments, **1963–64**: 242 [2]

Ambassadors, U.S., to Latin America, **1963–64**: 71 [9], 211 [8], 218 [34]

Ambassadors from American Republics, **1963–64**: 316 [9], 340, 455 [16]

"America Days" celebration in Turku, Finland, **1965**: 491

America Illustrated magazine, **1966**: 483

American Airlines, Inc., **1966**: 373 [12]

American Alumni Council, **1966**: 325
  Remarks to, **1965**: 124

American Association of School Administrators, **1965**: 250; **1966**: 77

American Automobile Association Lifesaving Medal, **1963–64**: 317; **1965**: 232

American Ballet Theatre, **1967**: 53

American Banker, The, **1967**: 420

American Bankers Association, **1963–64**: 455 [13]; **1966**: 265

American Bar Association, **1963–64**: 511; **1965**: 75; **1967**: 114; **1968–69**: 87, 263, 425 [1]
  Special Committee on Crime Prevention and Control, **1967**: 455

American Bible Society, **1966**: 19

American Broadcasting Co., **1967**: 554 [8]; **1968–69**: 648n.

American Cancer Society, **1966**: 156

American Chemical Society, **1965**: 88, 403

American Committee on Italian Migration, **1968–69**: 352

American Committee to Preserve Abu Simbel, **1967**: 198

American Editorial Cartoonists, Association of, **1965**: 246; **1968–69**: 260

American Education Placement Service, **1966**: 45

American Education Week, **1965**: 609

American Federation of Labor, **1963–64**: 430n

American Federation of Labor-Congress of Industrial Organizations, **1963–64**: 22, 111, 195, 221, 235, 255, 379 [7], 548, 745; **1965**: 223, 438, 641 [7], 644; **1966**: 88 [20], 125, 431, 535; **1967**: 30, 534; **1968–69**: 50, 154, 164, 165, 241, 670, 686
  Building and Construction Trades Department, **1968–69**: 154
  Committee on Political Education, **1968–69**: 50, 164, 165

American Federation of Teachers, **1965**: 539

American Field Service students, **1965**: 372; **1966**: 339
  Remarks to, **1963–64**: 465

American Film Institute, **1968–69**: 686
  Proposed, **1965**: 534

American Football Coaches Association, **1966**: 7

American G.I. Forum of the United States, **1966**: 236 [14]

American Heart Association, **1965**: 52

American Heart Association award, presentation, **1963–64**: 164

American Heritage Foundation, **1963–64**: 508, 560 [1]

American Hospital Association, **1966**: 271, 314, 490

American Independent Party, **1968–69**: 360n.

American Indians, National Congress of, **1963–64**: 120

American Institute of Architects, **1965**: 315

American Integration Fund, Central, **1967**: 44

American Legion, **1963–64**: 640; **1965**: 388 [5], 438; **1966**: 420, 421; **1967**: 323, 332n., 375 [19]; **1968–69**: 472

American Legion Distinguished Service Medal, **1968–69**: 472

American Medical Association, **1965**: 295 [3], 394; **1966**: 271, 395, 490; **1968–69**: 438

American Merchant Marine Institute, **1965**: 428

American-Mexican Chamizal Convention Act of 1964, **1963–64**: 58n.

American Motor Corp., **1963–64**: 745

American National Red Cross, **1966**: 92, 470; **1967**: 22, 287; **1968–69**: 55, 121

American Nurses Association, **1966**: 490

American Optometric Association, **1965**: 467

American Philosophical Society, **1968–69**: 695

American Physical Society, **1967**: 192

American Plywood Association, **1966**: 144n.
American Public Health Association, **1966**: 185n.
American Radio Association, **1965**: 428
American Republics, **1963-64**: 220, 232 [1]; **1965**: 2, 218, 221, 223, 286, 393; **1966**: 16, 125, 386
See also Inter-American Committee on the Alliance for progress; Latin America; Organization of American States; *specific countries.*
Ambassadors from, **1963-64**: 316 [9], 340, 455 [16]
U.S. Ambassadors to, **1963-64**: 71 [9], 211 [8], 218 [34]
American Revolution, **1963-64**: 321, 417; **1966**: 200; **1967**: 485 [3], 495 [11]; **1968-69**: 211n., 250n., 271n., 289
American Revolution, Daughters of the, **1963-64**: 275; **1966**: 478, 503
American Revolution Bicentennial Commission, **1966**: 120, 323
American River, **1965**: 477
American Samoa, **1966**: 537, 539; **1967**: 218, 559; **1968-69**: 370
Gov. Owen S. Aspinall, **1967**: 559
Gov. H. Rex Lee, **1966**: 266, 537
Visit, **1966**: 537
Watch imports to U.S., **1966**: 600
American Samoan Tropical Medical Center, **1966**: 537
American selling price system, **1968-69**: 274, 275 [2]
American Society of Newspaper Editors, **1963-64**: 266 [1], 270, 285ftn., (p. 524)
American States, Organization of.
See Organization of American States.
American Telephone and Telegraph Co., **1965**: 298
American Trade Centers, **1963-64**: 722
American Trial Lawyers Association, **1966**: 47
Ames, Ed, **1967**: 281
Amistad Dam, Mexico, **1963-64**: 193; **1966**: 630 [2, 10], 638-640; **1967**: 408 [5], 447; **1968-69**: 623n., 624n.
Ammann, Othmar H., **1965**: 56n.
AMMI.
See American Merchant Marine Institute.
Amster, Daniel, **1963-64**: 660
AMVER.
See Automated Merchant Vessel Report.
AMVETS Headquarters, dedication, **1966**: 345
Anaconda, Mont., unemployment, **1963-64**: 99
Anacostia Naval Air Station, Washington, D.C., **1966**: 452
Anchorage, Alaska, **1963-64**: 242 [1]; **1966**: 567, 568; **1967**: 369

Andean common market, proposed, **1968-69**: 365
Andean Development Corporation, **1968-69**: 205, 365
Andean Group, **1968-69**: 362, 665
Andelman, Dr. Samuel L., **1967**: 419n.
Anders, Lt. Col. William A., **1968-69**: 616, 637n., 647, 652, 662
Anders, Mrs. William A., **1968-69**: 645n.
Andersen, Hans Christian, **1963-64**: 394
Andersen, Martin, **1963-64**: 712
Andersen Air Force Base, Guam, **1967**: 134
Anderson, Sen. Clinton P., **1963-64**: 105, 273, 294 [7], 368, 461, 554, 608, 615, 732; **1965**: 122, 133, 134, 143, 329, 375, 394, 417; **1966**: 22, 134, 193, 221, 271; **1967**: 227, 258; **1968-69**: 160, 510, 624
Medical care bill.
See King-Anderson medical care bill.
Report on Alaska reconstruction, **1963-64**: 319
Water conversion act.
See Saline water conversion act of 1961.
Anderson, Mrs. Clinton P., **1963-64**: 273
Anderson, Mrs. Eugenie M., **1965**: 448 [4], 533; **1967**: 526
Anderson, Evelyn, **1963-64**: 204n.
Anderson, Marian, **1963-64**: 27; **1965**: 273; **1967**: 484
Anderson, Peyton T., Jr., **1963-64**: 716
Anderson, Robert B., **1963-64**: 245, 285 [6], 316 [11], 604, 612, 659, 747, 809; **1965**: 400, 532; **1967**: 85n.
Anderson, Robert J., **1968-69**: 388n.
Anderson, Judge Robert P., **1967**: 223 [2]
Anderson, Maj. Rudolf, **1966**: 246
Anderson, Stanley J., **1967**: 406, 466n.
Anderson, William, **1965**: 420
Anderson, William R., **1963-64**: 645, 701; **1966**: 348; **1968-69**: 345
Anderson, Repr. and Mrs. William R., **1967**: 117
Andolsek, L. J., **1963-64**: 434
Andover, Maine, **1965**: 68n.
Andre, Lt. Col. Daniel, **1965**: 219
Andreas, Dwayne, **1963-64**: 255
Andrews Air Force Base, Md., **1966**: 146n.; **1967**: 135
Remarks upon arrival, **1963-64**: 1
Angeles National Forest, Calif., **1967**: 418
Angelina River Basin, **1965**: 236
Angotti, Samuel J., **1968-69**: 567n.
Animal disease control, **1966**: 45
Animal research, humane treatment, **1966**: 395, 402
Ankrah, Lt. Gen. Joseph A. (Chairman, National Liberation Council, Republic of Ghana), **1967**: 426
Ankrah, Mrs. Joseph A., **1967**: 426

Ann Arbor, Mich., **1963-64**: 357n.

Annunzio, Repr. Frank, **1965**: 299; **1966**: 228; **1967**: 391

Antarctic exploration and research, international cooperation, **1965**: 220, 265

Antarctic Operation Deep Freeze, **1968-69**: 522n.

Antarctic Treaty, **1963-64**: 551; **1966**: 411; **1968-69**: 288

Antarctic Treaty (1959), **1967**: 18n.

Antarctica
   Nuclear weapons prohibition, **1967**: 59
   U.S. policy and international cooperation in, report, **1963-64**: 551

Anthony, Susan B., **1963-64**: 257, 298, 666

Antiballistic missiles, **1966**: 607 [16]; **1967**: 3 (p. 11), 13 (p. 48), 157, 167, 225 [17], 328 [25]; **1968-69**: 39 (p. 92), 557 [6], 676 (p. 1268)

Anti-Defamation League (B'nai B'rith), **1965**: 44

Anti-Defamation League Award (B'nai B'rith), acceptance, **1965**: 44

Antidumping Act (1921), **1968-69**: 559

Antidumping Code, International, **1968-69**: 559

Antipoverty programs, **1963-64**: 89, 91 (pp. 112, 114), 124 (p. 164), 132 (pp. 176, 182), 160, 179, 182, 183, 194, 199, 218 [17], 220, 228, 233, 235, 238, 239, 248, 268, 269, 270, 272, 275, 278, 280, 293, 295, 300, 311, 314, 340, 357, 388, 391, 394, 396, 398, 406, 415, 431, 433, 477, 496, 528, 550, 650, 669, 677, 728, 732, 747, 754, 757, 759, 770, 778, 798, 800, 801, 802, 811; **1965**: 2, 9, 24, 27, 32 (pp. 83, 85, 91, 94), 33, 35 (pp. 107, 113, 116), 75, 86, 90, 100, 154, 156 [2], 179, 193, 208 [5, 13], 210, 224, 286, 322, 323, 329, 489, 501; **1966**: 6 (pp. 3, 5), 34 (p. 100), 49, 140, 189, 237, 346, 353; 394, 396, 406, 431, 484, 504, 526, 545, 650 [11, 24]; **1967**: 3 (pp. 2-3), 13 (p. 54), 15, 16 (pp. 76, 82), 23, 87n., 97, 114, 211, 221, 222, 251, 267, 270, 276, 277, 286, 297 [10], 329, 347, 358 [8], 397, 413, 421, 484, 514, 517, 532, 534, 554 [15]; **1968-69**: 3, 4, 14 (p. 31), 39 (pp. 104, 105), 47 (p. 130), 50, 87, 94, 96, 100, 103, 111, 162, 165, 263, 327, 390, 429, 437, 459, 555, 557 [8], 565, 567-569, 672, 676 (pp. 1265, 1266), 678 (pp. 1273, 1286, 1290, 1296, 1300, 1301, 1303), 684 (pp. 1314, 1324), 696 [9]
   See also specific programs.
   Aid to education, **1963-64**: 124 (p. 164)
   Aid to health programs, **1963-64**: 124 (p. 164)

Antipoverty programs – *continued*
   Aid for unemployed workers, **1963-64**: 124 (p. 165), 219, 267, 288, 289; **1965**: 132
   Antipoverty act.
     See Economic Opportunity Act of 1964.
   Antipoverty bill, **1963-64**: 221, 246 [15], 266 [21], 267, 294 [2], 297, 305, 332 352, 386, 504ftn. (p. 939), 521 [13]
     See also Economic Opportunity Act of 1964.
   Appalachian area, **1963-64**: 124 (p. 165), 132 (p. 184), 211 [28], 219, 242 [19, 21], 246 [6], 256 [14], 285 [2], 292, 293, 294 [2, 18], 295, 316 [15], 320, 321, 322, 323, 324, 325, 326, 327, 328, 329, 330, 331, 332, 334, 336 [9, 10], 338, 342; **1965**: 80, 554; **1966**: 123; **1967**: 11, 114, 211, 514, 570; **1968-69**: 173
   Appropriations, **1963-64**: 218 [15]; **1966**: 26 (pp. 50, 55, 63), 492 [9]; **1967**: 13 (p. 54), 211, 286, 312 [6], 554 [6, 16]; **1968-69**: 87, 114
   Business participation in, **1963-64**: 297 [1], 314, 336 [20]
   California, **1963-64**: 580
   Campaign remarks, **1963-64**: 541, 548, 566, 589, 605, 606, 635, 648, 654, 661, 666, 680, 734, 736, 742, 746, 748, 751, 760
   Community action program, **1963-64**: 124 (p. 165), 132 (pp. 181, 184, 189, 194), 219, 289; **1965**: 9, 32 (p. 93), 75, 80, 90, 100, 132, 455
   Criticism of, **1965**: 208 [13]
   Defense Department support, **1965**: 288
   District of Columbia, **1965**: 70
   Employment for young persons, **1963-64**: 246 [20]
   Expansion of coverage, question of, **1963-64**: 294 [9]
   Extension act, **1966**: 594
   Farmers, **1963-64**: 219
   Government agency for, question of, **1963-64**: 218 [16]
   Indians, **1963-64**: 120; **1965**: 204; **1966**: 594
   Job Corps.
     See main heading, Job Corps.
   Labor organizations, participation in, **1963-64**: 297, 336 [20]
   Legal services, **1966**: 594
   Legislation, **1968-69**: 655
   Message to Congress, **1963-64**: 219; **1967**: 114
   Neighborhood centers, **1967**: 15, 114, 458, 467; **1968-69**: 19, 20, 39 (p. 110)
   Neighborhood Youth Corps.
     See main heading Neighborhood Youth Corps.
   New York, **1963-64**: 334

Antipoverty programs – *continued*
News conference remarks, **1963–64**: 54 [9],
170 [4, 19], 211 [28], 242 [19, 21],
246 [6, 15, 20], 256 [14], 266 [21],
285 [2], 294 [2, 9, 18], 316 [15],
336 [9, 10, 20], 516 [4, 12], 521 [13]
Nondiscrimination policy, **1963–64**: 256 [14]
North Carolina, **1963–64**: 103
Older persons serving, **1963–64**: 712
Peace Corpsmen, former, participation in,
1963–64: 347
Preschool program.
See Project Head Start (preschool program).
Private citizens participation, **1963–64**:
316 [28], 336 [20]
Private organizations participation, **1965**: 529
Private organizations role, **1966**: 223
Relation to foreign policy, **1963–64**: 280
Republican criticism, **1966**: 510
Role of women, **1963–64**: 289
Role of youth, **1963–64**: 323
Rural areas, **1963–64**: 54 [9], 132 (p. 184),
219, 225, 344, 434, 528; **1967**: 3 (p. 5)
Urban areas, **1963–64**: 132 (p. 184), 528;
1965: 90; **1967**: 312 [6], 328 [19]
VISTA.
See Volunteers in Service to America.
Volunteers, **1963–64**: 219, 289
Antiquities Act, **1968–69**: 707
Anti-Racketeering Act, **1968–69**: 59
Anti-Semitism, **1968–69**: 474
Antitank missile system, **1963–64**: 170 [3], 382
Antitrust laws, **1965**: 60
Antitrust legislation, **1968–69**: 534
Antonini, Luigi, **1968–69**: 270
Anzalduas Dam, **1967**: 408 [6]
ANZUS Council (Australia, New Zealand, U.S.),
1963–64: 426, 464
ANZUS treaty (Australia, New Zealand and
United States Treaty Council),
1968–69: 271n., 277, 522n., 525, 528
Apollo space program, **1963–64**: 211 [32];
1965: 318; **1967**: 24, 48, 533;
1968–69: 39 (pp. 92, 100), 41, 616
7 mission, **1968–69**: 533, 552
8 mission, **1968–69**: 637, 646 [1, 8, 12],
645, 647, 652, 660, 662, 672, 676
(p. 1264)
Spacecraft, **1966**: 26 (p. 59), 485, 625
Spacecraft fire, **1967**: 19n., 104 [18];
1968–69: 41
Apostle Islands National Lakeshore, Wis., **1966**:
82; **1967**: 20; **1968–69**: 39 (p. 101),
122
Apostolic Delegate (Msgr. Egidio Vagnozzi),
1966: 478
Appalachia, Federal Development Planning
Commission for, **1963–64**: 711;
1965: 117 [3]

Appalachian area, **1963–64**: 728; **1965**: 32 (pp.
83, 95); **1966**: 26 (p. 60), 122 [1, 2],
123, 403, 426; **1967**: 11
See also Area redevelopment; *specific States.*
Antipoverty program, **1963–64**: 124 (p. 165),
132 (p. 184), 211 [28], 219, 242 [19,
21], 246 [6], 256 [14], 285 [2], 292,
293, 294 [2, 18], 291, 316 [15], 320,
321, 322, 323, 324, 325, 326, 327, 328,
329, 330, 331, 332, 334, 336 [9, 10],
338, 342; **1965**: 80, 554
See also under main heading, Antipoverty
programs.
Economic development, **1963–64**: 91 (p. 114),
126, 132 (p. 184), 213, 300, 711
Education, **1963–64**: 321; **1965**: 103
Federal aid, **1963–64**: 314, 711; **1965**: 32
(p. 88), 35 (p. 115), 100, 103, 215, 245
Governors, **1963–64**: 285 [2], 293, 294 [2],
300, 711; **1965**: 103
Group representing, remarks to, **1965**: 554
Highways, **1963–64**: 300; **1965**: 245
Income, **1965**: 103
Legislation, **1965**: 99
Mining practices, **1965**: 54
President's visit to, **1963–64**: 280 [1]
Schools, **1963–64**: 325
Unemployment, **1963–64**: 213, 246 [6], 321,
325
Appalachian Commission, Federal-State, proposed
establishment, **1963–64**: 294 [2]
Appalachian development, **1967**: 11, 114, 211,
514, 576; **1968–69**: 173, 345, 564, 566,
567, 648, 701
Appalachian Governors, Council of, **1963–64**:
300
Appalachian Regional Commission, President's,
1963–64: 293n., 294 [2], 300; **1965**:
117 [3], 132, 245; **1966**: 111, 122 [2],
123; **1967**: 11; **1968–69**: 58, 173, 701
Appalachian Regional Development Act, **1968–69**:
173n., 345, 567
Appalachian Regional Development Act of 1965,
1965: 103, 117 [3], 173, 245, 418;
1966: 123; **1967**: 11, 300, 514
Appalachian Regional Development Act
Amendments of 1967, **1967**: 11n.,
114n.
Appalachian Trail, **1965**: 54; **1966**: 82;
1968–69: 510
Apparel industry, **1967**: 414
Appel, Dr. James Z., **1967**: 419n.
Appleseed, Johnny (John Chapman), **1968–69**:
227
Appliance safety, **1968–69**: 56
Applied Science, Korean Institute for Industrial
Technology and, **1965**: 257, 344, 407
Appointments and nominations
Air Quality Advisory Board, **1968–69**: 409

Appointments — *continued*
  Ambassadors
    Ambassador at Large, **1966**: 501 [1]; **1967**: 132 [11]
    Dominican Republic, **1966**: 277 [2]
    France, **1968–69**: 153 [1, 5, 10]
    Italy, **1968–69**: 1 [17]
    Soviet Union, **1966**: 501 [1]
    Switzerland, **1966**: 401 [18]
  Architectural Barriers to Rehabilitation of the Handicapped, National Commission on, Chairman and members, **1966**: 192
  Army
    Chief of Staff, **1968–69**: 79n. (p. 234), 283 [1]
    Vice Chief of Staff, **1968–69**: 283 [1]
  Atomic Energy Commission, members, **1966**: 277 [5], 320 [5]
  Budget, Bureau of the, Deputy Director, **1966**: 88 [6]
  Central Intelligence Agency, Director, **1966**: 277 [5, 14]
  Civil Aeronautics Board, Chairman, **1968–69**: 79 [2]
  Civil Aeronautics Board, member, **1966**: 516 [4]
  Codes, Zoning, Taxation and Development Standards, Commission on, Chairman, **1967**: 4
  Commerce, Secretary of, **1968–69**: 79 [1]
  Commission on the Federal Budget, **1967**: 85
  Commission on Income Maintenance Programs, members, **1968–69**: 3
  Comptroller General, **1966**: 65 [1], 88 [6]
  Consumer Advisory Council, Chairman and members, **1967**: 342
  Council of Economic Advisers, Chairman, **1968–69**: 76
  Courts
    Appeals, **1966**: 88 [1], 304 [4]
    District, **1966**: 304 [4]
  Defense, Secretary of, **1968–69**: 18 [1, 2]
  District of Columbia
    City Council, **1967**: 406
    Commissioner and Assistant Commissioner, **1967**: 377
  Economic Opportunity, National Advisory Council on, **1967**: 87n.
  Emergency Planning, Office of, Director, **1966**: 124 [6]
  Federal Communications Commission, Chairman and member, **1966**: 277 [5], 278
  Federal Deposit Insurance Corporation, Board of Directors, Director, **1966**: 88 [3]
  Federal Power Commission, Chairman and member, **1966**: 88 [8], 268

Appointments — *continued*
  Federal Reserve System, Board of Governors, member **1966**: 88 [2]
  Federal Trade Commission, Commissioner, **1967**: 518 [2]
  Food and Drugs, Commissioner of, **1966**: 580 [8]
  Health, Education, and Welfare, Department of, Assistant Secretary for Education, **1966**: 320 [5]
  Health, Education, and Welfare, Secretary of, **1968–69**: 79ftn. (p. 232), 153 [2, 5]
  Heart Institute, National, Director, **1966**: 580 [8]
  Housing and Urban Development, Department of
    Assistant Secretary for Demonstrations and Intergovernmental Relations, **1966**: 207n.
    Assistant Secretary for Metropolitan Planning and Development, **1966**: 12
    Assistant Secretary for Mortgage Credit, **1966**: 12
    Assistant Secretary for Renewal and Housing Assistance, **1966**: 207n.
    Deputy Under Secretary for Policy Analysis and Program Evaluation, **1966**: 12
    Secretary, **1966**: 8 [1], 12
    Under Secretary, **1966**: 8 [1], 12
  Indian Claims Commission, members, **1967**: 518 [3]
  Insured Loans to Students, Advisory Council on, members, **1966**: 3
  Interior, Department of the, Assistant Secretary—Water Pollution Control, **1966**: 320 [5]
  Internal Revenue Service, Chief Counsel, **1966**: 88 [5]
  International Bank for Reconstruction and Development, President, **1967**: 511
  Justice, Department of
    Assistant Attorney General
      Civil Rights Division, **1967**: 411 [1]
      Office of Legal Counsel, **1966**: 88 [5]
      Tax Division, **1966**: 88 [5]
    Assistant Attorney General for Administration, **1966**: 88 [5]
    Deputy Attorney General, **1967**: 269
    Solicitor General, **1967**: 411 [2, 8]
  Manpower development consultative committee, members, **1966**: 536
  Marine Corps Commandant, **1967**: 518 [1, 7]
  National Advisory Commission on Health Facilities, Chairman and members, **1967**: 419
  National Advisory Council on Education Professions Development, members, **1967**: 396

Appointments – *continued*
National Advisory Council on Supplementary
Centers and Services, **1968–69**: 52
National Council on the Humanities, **1968–69**:
61
National Housing Partnership, incorporators,
1968–69: 471
National Institutes of Health, Director, **1968–
69**: 396
Organization of American States, U.S. Repre-
sentative to Council, **1966**: 501 [1]
Pacific, Commander in Chief, **1968–69**:
191 [4]
Peace Corps, Director, **1966**: 12
Population and Family Planning, Committee
on, members, **1968–69**: 393
Post Office Department, Postmaster General,
1968–69: 191 [2]
President's Commission for the Observance of
Human Rights Year, 1968, **1968–69**: 42
President's Committee on Urban Housing,
Chairman and members, **1967**: 252
President's foreign visitor program, **1968–69**:
116
President's staff, **1968–69**: 191 [3]
Savings Bonds, Interdepartmental Committee
for, Chairman, **1966**: 137
Science mission to Australia, members,
1968–69: 513
Small Business Administration, Deputy
Administrator, **1966**: 613
State, Department of
Assistant Secretary for Inter-American
Affairs, **1966**: 13
Assistant Secretary for Public Affairs,
1966: 65 [1]
Counselor, **1966**: 320 [3]
Policy Planning Council, Chairman, **1966**:
277 [5]
Under Secretary for Political Affairs, **1966**:
474 [17]
Supreme Court
Associate justice, **1967**: 263; **1968–69**:
339 [2], 425 [11]
Chief Justice of the United States, **1968–69**:
339 [2], 425 [11], 467 [2, 5], 509,
527, 696 [6]
Transportation, Department of, Secretary,
1966: 580 [5, 14]
Treasury, Department of the, Assistant
Secretary (International Affairs),
1966: 277 [5]
Treasury, Secretary of, **1968–69**: 582n.
United Nations U.S. Representative,
1968–69: 213 [1], 496
Urban Transportation Administration, Director,
1966: 442

Appointments – *continued*
Vietnam
Commander of U.S. Forces, **1968–69**: 191 [5]
Deputy Commander of U.S. Forces, **1968–69**:
191 [6]
Water Pollution Control Administration,
Federal, Commissioner, **1966**: 88 [4]
White House staff
Counsel, **1966**: 88 [7]
Deputy Press Secretary, **1966**: 65 [2]
Deputy Special Counsel, **1966**: 65 [1]
Special Assistant for Consumer Affairs,
1967: 86
Special Assistants, **1966**: 141 [8], 158 [1, 2]
Special Counsel, **1966**: 65 [1]
Women, Citizens' Advisory Council on the
Status of, Chairman, **1966**: 299
Appropriations, House Committee on, **1967**:
195, 358 [12], 362; **1968–69**: 39 (p.
107), 223 [11], 226, 229, 339 [7, 9],
510
Appropriations, Senate Committee on, **1967**: 195;
1968–69: 39 (p. 107), 380
Approval of acts of Congress.
See Legislation, statements upon approval.
Aqaba, Gulf of, **1967**: 233, 270
Arab-Israeli conflict.
See Middle East; Middle East conflict.
Arab nations, **1965**: 295 [10, 14]; **1968–69**:
250n., 474, 524n., 676 (p. 1269)
U.S. relations with, **1963–64**: 258, 265
Arango, Daniel, **1966**: 16n.
Araujo Castro, João de (Foreign Minister of
Brazil), **1963–64**: 66
Arbuckle, Ernest, **1968–69**: 470, 471
Arbuckle, Ernest C., **1963–64**: 622
Arches National Monument, Utah, **1968–69**:
707n.
Archimedes, **1967**: 376
Architects, American Institute of, **1965**: 315
Architects, Eleventh Pan American Congress of,
1965: 315
Architectural barriers to the handicapped,
elimination, **1968–69**: 287, 440
Architectural Barriers to Rehabilitation of the
Handicapped, National Commission
on, **1966**: 192; **1968–69**: 287
"Architectural Standards for Federal Buildings,"
report, **1965**: 249n.
Arco, Idaho, **1966**: 411
Arctic Circle park area, Alaska, proposed,
1968–69: 707
Arctic exploration, **1968–69**: 124
Area Manpower Planning System, Cooperative,
1968–69: 24

Area redevelopment, **1963–64**: 598, 729; **1965**: 47, 132, 148, 454 [5]
  Appalachian area, **1963–64**: 91 (p. 114), 213, 300; **1965**: 100, 245
  Area redevelopment bill, **1965**: 329, 330
  Depressed areas, **1965**: 2, 132, 492
  Federal aid, **1963–64**: 124 (p. 165), 132 (p. 188), 213
  Message to Congress, **1965**: 132
  Rural areas, **1965**: 47, 90, 132
Area Redevelopment Act, **1963–64**: 22, 124 (p. 165), 213, 219, 290, 297, 642; **1965**: 32 (p. 92), 35 (p. 115), 47, 99, 100, 132
Area Redevelopment Administration, **1963–64**: 99, 323, 606; **1965**: 132, 148
Area Redevelopment Administrator (William L. Batt), **1963–64**: 67
Arends, Repr. Leslie C., **1963–64**: 96; **1966**: 240; **1968–69**: 655
Argentina, **1963–64**: 143ftn. (p. 219); **1965**: 220; **1968–69**: 205, 362
  Ambassador Norbert M. Barrenechea, **1965**: 473n.
  Argentine senators, remarks to, **1963–64**: 269
  Assistance, **1963–64**: 269
  President Arturo Illia, **1966**: 175
  Ships for, **1965**: 600
Argonne National Laboratory, **1966**: 411n.
Arias Espinosa, Ricardo, **1965**: 532
Aristotle, **1963–64**: 287, 357, 391; **1965**: 90
Arizona, **1963–64**: 590; **1965**: 119, 477; **1968–69**: 228, 259, 501
  Campaign remarks, **1963–64**: 649
  Dispute with California, **1963–64**: 294 [12], 733
  Glen Canyon Dam, **1963–64**: 256 [16]
  Gov. Paul Fannin, **1963–64**: 649
  Gov. Sam Goddard, **1966**: 494 [1, 2]
  Public land, **1968–69**: 563
  Visit to, question of, **1963–64**: 280 [3]
Arkansas, **1963–64**: 486 [7]; **1965**: 132, 223, 239, 363; **1967**: 270
  Campaign remarks, **1963–64**: 599
  Gov. Orval E. Faubus, **1963–64**: 599
Arkansas Red River Basin, pollution, **1966**: 82
Arkansas River, **1966**: 415, 416; **1968–69**: 511
Arkansas River navigation project, **1963–64**: 486 [7], 597, 598
Arlington, Texas, Mayor Thomas Vandergriff, **1967**: 4n.
Arlington National Cemetery, **1967**: 19n.
  Memorial Day Service, **1966**: 246
Armah, Kwesi, **1965**: 388ftn. (p. 799)
Armco Steel Corp., **1967**: 231n.
Armed Forces, Committee on Equal Opportunity in the, **1963–64**: 816
Armed Forces, Industrial College of the, **1963–64**: 533

Armed Forces, U.S., **1963–64**: 213, 379 [9], 409, 783; **1965**: 26, 84, 174, 280, 319 [12], 493, 572; **1966**: 246, 324, 388, 435; **1968–69**: 332, 341, 452
See also Military, U.S.; Military personnel.
  Alabama, **1965**: 106 [5], 117 [1, 5] and ftn. (p. 307), 161
  Antipoverty program participation, **1965**: 288
  Asia, South Asia, and Southeast Asia, **1965**: 261n., 573; **1966**: 144, 324; **1967**: 554 [1]; **1968–69**: 5, 144, 231, 251, 254, 266, 268, 269, 318, 337, 379, 452, 478, 597, 627, 628, 635, 648
  Baltimore, Md., **1968–69**: 184
  Casualties in, **1963–64**: 770
  Chicago, Ill., **1968–69**: 183
  Christmas message, **1966**: 647; **1967**: 549; **1968–69**: 642
  Comments on, **1966**: 350, 409, 420–421; **1967**: 361, 375 [1], 431, 441, 475, 485 [1–8], 493, 494, 495 [14], 546, 565–567, 573; **1968–69**: 81 [1, 2, 3], 99, 129, 142
  Congo, **1963–64**: 780 [2, 16]; **1965**: 319 [16]
  Conventional forces, **1963–64**: 91 (p. 116), 132 (p. 184), 703; **1965**: 32 (p. 90)
  Defense procurement and research appropriation authorization, **1963–64**: 230
  Detroit, Mich., **1967**: 321, 322, 328 [2], 331
  Dominican Republic, **1965**: 212, 216, 217, 221, 223, 227, 286, 289, 295 [1, 15, 16], 299, 319 [4, 16], 342; **1966**: 577 [15]
  Draft.
    See Selective Service System.
  Equal opportunity, **1963–64**: 816
  Europe, **1963–64**: 49, 132 (p. 184), 382; **1965**: 235, 300; **1966**: 445 [24], 486, 506; **1967**: 348; **1968–69**: 223 [14]
  Germany, **1963–64**: 76; **1967**: 204 [2, 3], 348, 519, 554 [5]
  Incentive awards, **1968–69**: 248
  Incentive cash award program, **1965**: 528
  Increase in strength, **1963–64**: 132 (p. 184), 382, 467, 611, 775; **1965**: 26, 347 [9], 353 [6], 387, 388 [1], 396
  Integration, **1968–69**: 611
  Korea, **1965**: 257; **1966**: 563, 570, 577 [8]; **1968–69**: 51 [15], 170
  Land-use program, **1965**: 54
  Losses since World War II, **1965**: 347 [1]
  Materiel support, **1966**: 496
  Messages to
    Christmas, **1965**: 654
    Memorial Day, **1968–69**: 279
    On death of President Kennedy, **1963–64**: 6
    Thanksgiving Day, **1963–64**: 779; **1965**: 626

Armed Forces, U.S. – *continued*
National Guard, **1966**: 124 [9]
See also National Guard.
Nuclear forces, **1963-64**: 132 (p. 184), 467;
1965: 300
Overseas, **1963-64**: 31, 227, 732, 816; **1965**:
319 [8]
Pacific area, **1966**: 37
Panama, **1965**: 532
Parachute jumping, incentive pay for hazardous
duty involving, **1965**: 633
Personnel.
See Military personnel.
President's service in, **1963-64**: 426, 493
Recruitment programs, **1963-64**: 619 [3]
Red Cross services, **1967**: 22; **1968-69**: 55
Reduction, **1963-64**: 271 [16]
Reserve forces, mobilization, **1963-64**: 382
Reserves, **1965**: 26, 353 [6, 9], 388 [1],
395 [5], 396; **1966**: 65 [14], 124 [9],
324, 521; **1967**: 309 [1]; **1968-69**:
170, 448
Schools, occupational training in, **1963-64**:
213
Special Forces, **1963-64**: 382; **1965**: 26, 387
Strength, **1968-69**: 14 (p. 27), 39 (p. 98),
678 (p. 1273)
Strength increase, **1966**: 26 (pp. 56-57), 65
[14], 67
Thailand, **1967**: 565, 573
Vietnam, **1963-64**: 26, 83, 211 [33], 223,
294 [5], 314, 379 [10], 793; **1965**:
47 [7, 11], 51, 206, 208 [20], 227,
229, 234, 261, 289, 295 [13], 319,
[17], 347 [1, 9], 353 [1, 12, 14, 21],
388 [1, 5, 11, 14], 395 [2], 396, 412
[4], 421, 439, 445, 448 [11, 12, 20],
561n., 573, 588, 632, 633
See also Vietnam; Vietnam, South.
Women, **1963-64**: 298; **1966**: 8 [16]
Armed Forces Institute, United States, **1967**: 199
Armed Forces Radio Network, **1968-69**: 642n.
Armed Forces Radio and Television Service,
1966: 648
Armed Services, House Committee on, **1967**:
195, 358 [10], 475; **1968-69**: 169 [18]
Armed Services, Senate Committee on, **1967**:
195, 204ftn. (p. 497), 358 [10];
1968-69: 18 [2], 51 [5, 11]
Armistice, 50th anniversary, **1968-69**: 583
Arms control and disarmament, **1963-64**: 140,
232 [8], 272, 382, 388, 394n., 395,
475 [7], 541, 562, 577, 607, 719, 764,
797, 820; **1965**: 15, 20, 196, 284, 331,
347 [2], 386, 493, 523, 537, 660;
1966: 6 (p. 8), 70, 320 [9], 411, 480,
483, 486, 497, 503; **1967**: 3 (p. 11),
38, 59, 64, 80 [2, 5, 7], 162, 167, 281,

Arms control and disarmament – *continued*
283, 328 [24], 340n., 491; **1968-69**:
14 (p. 26), 16, 27, 39 (p. 98), 69, 73,
288, 308, 310, 345, 349, 350, 378, 387,
392, 394, 425 [9], 467 [5, 8, 17], 474,
531, 557 [6], 567, 568, 590 [6], 654,
663, 667 [8, 17], 676 (p. 1268), 678
(p. 1292)
See also Weapons.
French proposal for conference on, **1965**:
208 [11]
Geneva conferences.
See Geneva conferences.
U.S. proposals for, **1963-64**: 122, 129, 130,
131
Arms Control and Disarmament Act, **1965**:
173, 284; **1966**: 480
Arms Control and Disarmament Act, amend-
ment, **1968-69**: 27n.
Arms Control and Disarmament Act of 1961,
1967: 59
Arms Control and Disarmament Agency, United
States, **1967**: 59; **1968-69**: 27, 69, 73n.
See also United States Arms Control and
Disarmament Agency.
Director (William C. Foster), **1968-69**: 27, 69
Arms race, **1963-64**: 693; **1965**: 15, 284, 331,
386; **1966**: 32
Armstrong, Neil, **1966**: 134, 135
Armstrong, Dr. W. T., **1968-69**: 442
Armstrong-Jones, Antony (Lord Snowdon),
1965: 616
Army, Department of the, **1965**: 26, 117 [3],
140; **1966**: 595; **1968-69**: 18 [2],
153 [16]
Transfer of land, **1963-64**: 422
Army, Secretary of the (Stephen Ailes), **1963-64**:
422, 510, 612, 711, 809; **1965**: 161,
319 [10], 418, 587
Army, Secretary of the (Stanley R. Resor),
1966: 288; **1967**: 102, 166, 331, 384,
407, 494, 558; **1968-69**: 58, 221, 353,
384, 487, 594, 669, 688
Army, Secretary of the (Cyrus R. Vance), **1963-
64**: 37, 119n, 127
Memorandum to, **1963-64**: 81n.
Army, United States, **1963-64**: 665; **1965**: 223,
274n., 288n., 293; **1966**: 282, 348, 353;
1968-69: 39 (p. 98), 81 [3], 153 [5],
221, 283 [6], 323, 353, 410, 456, 487,
491, 516, 544, 546, 594, 603, 609, 688
Battle flag, presentation to the President,
1963-64: 119
Chief of Staff, **1963-64**: 420 [3]
Chief of Staff (Gen. Harold K. Johnson),
1966: 348
Increase in strength, **1963-64**: 132 (p. 184),
199, 467, 611, 703, 716

Army, United States — *continued*
   Riot training, **1963-64**: 600
Army Command, Continental, **1967**: 326
Arnold, Thurman W., **1967**: 204 [13]
Arrest warrants, **1967**: 71
Arrow Lakes Dam, **1963-64**: 135
Art
   District of Columbia, **1968-69**: 660
   Student, **1968-69**: 64
Art, Metropolitan Museum of, **1967**: 198
Art, National Gallery of, **1966**: 227; **1968-69**:
   133
Arteriosclerosis, **1966**: 271
Arthritis, **1963-64**: 755; **1966**: 271; **1967**: 77;
   1968-69: 64, 262
Arthritis Foundation, **1968-69**: 262
Arthur, Chester A., **1965**: 98; **1968-69**: 667
Articles of Confederation, **1966**: 261
Artigas, José, **1967**: 171
Arts, **1965**: 405
   Exhibition of, **1965**: 328
   Federal aid, **1963-64**: 784; **1965**: 2, 105, 314,
     405, 534; **1966**: 587
   Growth in U.S., **1963-64**: 391; **1965**: 177, 314,
     405, 534
   Iranian exhibit in U.S., **1963-64**: 369, 385
   Presidential Board, proposed, **1963-64**: 266 [6]
Arts, National Council on the, **1963-64**: 524,
   784; **1965**: 177, 534; **1966**: 440; **1967**:
   53n.; **1968-69**: 64, 601, 686
Arts, National Endowment for the, **1966**: 440;
   1967: 53; **1968-69**: 54, 64, 686
Arts, White House Festival of the, **1965**: 314
Arts and the Humanities, Federal Council on
   the, **1966**: 327; **1967**: 274
Arts and the Humanities, National Foundation
   on the, **1965**: 2, 105, 314, 534; **1967**:
   77; **1968-69**: 54
Arts and humanities bill, **1965**: 329, 330, 340,
   405, 534
Artworks, international exchanges, **1966**: 519
ARVN (Army of the Republic of Vietnam).
   See Vietnam, South.
Asbestos stockpiles, **1966**: 218, 283n.
Asbury, Bishop Francis, **1966**: 189
Ascension Island, **1963-64**: 780 [2]
Asgeirsson, Asgeir (President of Iceland), **1967**:
   313
Asheville, N.C., **1968-69**: 648
Ashley, Repr. Thomas L., **1963-64**: 323, 642;
   1965: 190; **1966**: 155
Ashmore, Repr. Robert T., **1963-64**: 719; **1966**:
   335
Ashtray, acceptance of gift, **1965**: 11
Asia, South Asia, and Southeast Asia, **1963-64**:
   150 [15], 211 [27], 475 [3], 626n.,
   788; **1965**: 15, 22 [4], 117 [2], 179,

Asia — *continued*
   194, 203, 208 [2], 248, 272, 302, 331,
   347 [2], 353 [1, 8], 355n., 388 [1,
   10], 390, 448 [21], 463 [5], 524, 650;
   1966: 6 (p. 9), 246, 311, 328, 411, 415,
   484, 654 [3]; **1967**: 3 (p. 10), 248,
   249n., 281, 289, 297 [2], 433, 434,
   487, 491; **1968-69**: 44, 193n., 194,
   198, 223 [1], 233, 271, 277, 283 [4,
   5], 384, 398n., 474
See also specific countries.
Appropriations and expenditures, **1968-69**:
   39 (p. 88), 241, 678 (pp. 1273, 1274,
   1277, 1282)
Assistance, **1963-64**: 45, 186, 189, 227, 379 [1],
   420 [1], 500, 597, 617, 627, 662n., 675,
   686, 693, 797; **1965**: 7, 18, 26, 106
   [4], 130, 136, 172, 176 [1, 3], 179,
   199, 208 [17], 227, 229, 294, 295
   [3], 357, 628; **1966**: 11n., 18, 26
   (pp. 50, 54, 56, 58), 45, 133, 420;
   1967: 13 (pp. 46, 48), 44; **1968-69**:
   39 (pp. 91, 94), 63, 170, 524, 678 (pp.
   1273, 1274)
Black, Eugene R.
   Mission, **1966**: 88 [1]
   Visit to, **1968-69**: 467 [4]
Chinese Communist threat to, **1965**: 15, 172,
   229, 246
Communism in, **1966**: 325, 397
Communist aggression, **1963-64**: 170 [1, 5,
   10, 18], 182, 189, 201 [5, 17], 218
   [24], 272, 280 [8], 285 [12], 379
   [1], 420 [1], 474, 499, 662, 702;
   1965: 2, 18, 46 [11], 106 [6], 130,
   227, 246, 256n., 300, 388 [1]; **1966**:
   85, 461, 542, 549, 551-552, 560-561,
   565, 568; **1967**: 3 (p. 11), 127n., 212n.,
   246n., 347, 397, 401, 407, 409, 438n.,
   442, 446, 495 [14], 519; **1968-69**:
   109, 129, 142, 143, 186, 384, 452, 528
Conference proposal, **1967**: 312 [8], 328 [18],
   375 [14], 518 [19]
Conferences.
   See Honolulu Conference; Manila Conference.
Cultural presentations program, **1965**: 159
Dignitaries, U.S., visits to, **1966**: 56, 85-86,
   88 [16]
Economic and social development, **1965**: 295
   [3], 355n., 628, 637, 660; **1966**: 41,
   88 [1], 128, 133, 261, 277 [7], 304,
   329, 420, 437, 450, 459, 516 [1], 517,
   533, 540, 542, 549, 561, 565, 566a,
   568, 570; **1967**: 3 (p. 13), 44, 272,
   381, 401, 435, 442, 519; **1968-69**:
   39 (p. 99), 63, 109, 110, 170, 200,
   233, 271n., 277, 394

Asia – *continued*
  Health problems, U.S.-Japan cooperation,
    1965: 12, 15, 175, 214, 544
  International relations, **1966**: 533
  Military operations, appropriation, **1967**: 14
  Neutralization of Southeast Asia, question of,
    1963-64: 170 [14]
  New nations, **1965**: 2
  Nuclear weapons use in, question of, **1965**:
    208 [18]
  Peace prospects, **1968-69**: 557 [1], 572, 611,
    652
  Philippine assistance to, **1963-64**: 626, 627
  President's report of 1961, **1965**: 176 [3]
  Regional cooperation, **1968-69**: 14 (p. 26),
    237, 277
  Security, **1966**: 566, 566a; **1967**: 293, 435,
    486n., 495 [14], 534
  Smallpox eradication, international coopera-
    tion, **1965**: 262
  Trade with U.S., **1967**: 231
  Trip to.
    See Visits to foreign countries.
  United Nations operations, **1965**: 169, 172,
    176 [1, 3], 246
  U.S. military dependents, return home, **1963-
    64**: 475 [10]
  U.S. policy, **1963-64**: 420 [1], 607, 626n.;
    1965: 106 [4], 172, 199, 200, 203,
    229, 257, 321n.; **1966**: 26 (p. 48), 88
    [1], 216, 325, 338 [9], 418, 437, 443,
    450, 459, 482, 501 [17], 514, 533,
    542, 577 [16]; **1967**: 357, 434, 446,
    460 [9], 519; **1968-69**: 50, 81 [3],
    109, 170, 178, 200, 201, 221, 225,
    232n., 233, 237, 255, 273, 400, 452,
    462, 472, 522, 676 (p. 1269), 678
    (pp. 1273, 1274), 682, 683
  U.S. troops in, **1965**: 261n., 573; **1966**: 144,
    324; **1967**: 554 [1]; **1968-69**: 5, 144,
    231, 251, 254, 266, 268, 269, 318, 337,
    379, 452, 478, 597, 627, 628, 635, 648
  Vietnam assistance, **1966**: 312, 516 [13], 553
  Visit of Robert F. Kennedy, **1963-64**: 156,
    170 [1]
Asia and Far East, Economic Commission for,
    1966: 461, 557
Asia and the Far East, United Nations Economic
    Commission for, **1965**: 353ftn. (p. 736);
    1968-69: 237
Asian Development Bank, **1965**: 199, 246, 300,
    353ftn. (p. 736), 412 [2], 628, 637,
    660; **1966**: 14, 41, 88 [1, 16], 93, 128,
    304, 325, 328-329, 348, 420, 458-459,
    461, 516 [1], 517, 533, 542, 565-566;
    1967: 3 (p. 13), 16 (p. 80), 44, 73,
    100, 111, 112n., 212, 219, 401, 459,

Asian Development Bank – *continued*
    486, 491, 492; **1968-69**: 14 (p. 27),
    39 (p. 99), 47 (p. 138), 63, 275 [6],
    500, 525, 678 (p. 1282), 684 (p. 1321)
  U.S. contribution message, **1967**: 401
Asian Development Bank Act, **1965**: 628n.
Asian Development Bank Act of 1966, **1966**:
    93n., 133
Asian Highway, **1966**: 557
Asian and Pacific Council, **1966**: 542, 565-566;
    1967: 44, 111, 219; **1968-69**: 365, 525
Askin, Mr. and Mrs. Robin W., **1966**: 544, 545
ASPAC (Asian and Pacific Council), **1966**: 542,
    565-566
Aspinall, Gov. and Mrs. Owen S., **1967**: 559
Aspinall, Repr. Wayne N., **1963-64**: 554, 658;
    1965: 143, 375, 417, 521; **1966**: 119,
    410-411, 413-414; **1967**: 227; **1968-
    69**: 150, 386, 411, 457, 477, 501, 505,
    510
Water conversion act.
    See Saline water conversion act of 1961.
Aspiras, José D., **1966**: 548
Assassination of President John F. Kennedy,
    Commission to Report Upon the,
    1967: 80 [5]
Assateague Island National Seashore, Maryland-
    Virginia, **1965**: 54, 521; **1966**: 518;
    1968-69: 122, 411, 547, 601
Associated Press, **1963-64**: 272; **1966**: 492 [9];
    1968-69: 467 [10]
Association for the Advancement of Colored
    People, National, **1965**: 443
Association of American Editorial Cartoonists,
    1965: 246
Association of Chiefs of Police, International,
    1967: 382, 385
Association of Educational Broadcasters, Na-
    tional, **1967**: 474
Association of Home Builders, National, **1965**:
    243
Association of Manufacturers, National, **1965**:
    438
Association of School Administrators, American,
    1965: 250
Association of Southeast Asia, **1966**: 560;
    1968-69: 365
Association of State Aviation Officials, National,
    1963-64: 215
Association of State Colleges and Universities,
    1967: 490n.
Association of State Universities and Land-Grant
    Colleges, National, **1967**: 490n.
Aston, James W., **1968-69**: 3
Astor, Vincent, **1968-69**: 672n.
Astor Foundation, **1967**: 15
Astronauts, **1968-69**: 387, 507, 616
  Apollo 7, **1968-69**: 533, 552, 574

Astronauts – *continued*
 Apollo 8, **1968–69**: 616, 637, 645, 646 [1, 8,
   12], 647, 652, 660, 662, 672
 Rescue, U.N. agreement, **1967**: 557; **1968–69**:
   14 (p. 27), 41, 288, 309, 387, 662
 Soviet cosmonauts, **1968–69**: 161, 387
   Gagarin, Maj. Yuri, **1965**: 318
   Komarov, Col. Vladimir, **1967**: 190
   Leonov, Lt. Col. Aleksei, **1965**: 116
 United States, **1966**: 40
   See also Manned space flights; Space research
     and exploration.
   Aldrin, Lt. Col. Edwin E., Jr., **1966**: 618,
     625; **1967**: 431
   Armstrong, Neil, **1966**: 134, 135
   Borman, Lt. Col. Frank, **1965**: 636, 656
   Chaffee, Lt. Comdr. Roger B., **1967**: 19, 38
   Conrad, Lt. Comdr. (Comdr.) Charles, Jr.,
     1965: 462, 463 [2]; **1966**: 485
   Cooper, Lt. Col. (Maj.) L. Gordon, **1963–64**:
     569, 572; **1965**: 310, 462, 463 [2]
   Glenn, Lt. Col. John H., Jr., **1963–64**: 374,
     725, 733
   Gordon, Comdr. Richard F., Jr., **1966**: 485
   Grissom, Lt. Col. (Maj.) Virgil I., **1965**: 120,
     121, 134, 310; **1967**: 19, 38
   Lovell, Capt. (Comdr.) James A., Jr., **1965**:
     636, 656; **1966**: 618, 625; **1967**: 431
   McDivitt, Lt. Col. (Maj.) James A., **1965**:
     304, 306, 310, 318, 320
   Promotion and decoration policy, **1965**:
     463ftn. (p. 944)
   Schirra, Capt. Walter M., Jr., **1965**: 647, 656
   Scott, Lt. Col. David, **1966**: 134, 135
   Stafford, Maj. Thomas P., **1965**: 647, 656
   White, Lt. Col. (Maj.) Edward H., 2d, **1965**:
     304, 306, 310, 318, 320; **1967**: 19, 38
   Young, Lt. Comdr. John W., **1965**: 120, 121,
     134
Aswan High Dam, Egypt, **1967**: 198
Ataturk, Mustafa Kemal, **1963–64**: 416, 418;
     1967: 155, 158
Atchley, Dr. Dana W., **1965**: 163
Athenagoras I, Patriarch, **1963–64**: 147
Athens, Greece, **1966**: 497
Athens, Ohio, **1963–64**: 323
Athletic achievement, comments on, **1963–64**:
     106, 401
Atlanta, Ga., **1963–64**: 330
 Housing, **1967**: 531
 Mayor Ivan Allen, Jr., **1963–64**: 330
Atlantic Alliance, **1963–64**: 102n., 109, 582,
     608, 610, 685, 780 [1], 788, 797;
     1965: 200n., 203, 205, 300, 660;
     1966: 142n., 482n., 486, 503; **1967**:
     162, 272, 391n., 572; **1968–69**: 214

Atlantic City, N.J., **1963–64**: 233, 589; **1966**:
     77; **1968–69**: 270
 Democratic Committee dinner, **1963–64**: 338
 Democratic National Committee, remarks to,
     1963–64: 542
 Democratic National Convention, **1963–64**:
     218 [19], 256 [22], 539, 540
   Acceptance address, **1963–64**: 541
Atlantic community, **1963–64**: 49, 102n., 244,
     400, 608, 610, 696, 780 [1], 788;
     1965: 2, 256, 632; **1966**: 6 (p. 8), 142,
     359n., 486
Atlantic Missile Range, Station No. 1, redesigna-
     tion, **1963–64**: 13
Atlantic Ocean
 Canal to Gulf of Mexico, **1963–64**: 198
 Canal to Pacific Ocean, **1963–64**: 266 [5], 594
 U.S. Coastline, **1965**: 521
Atlantic-Pacific Interoceanic Canal Study
     Commission, **1965**: 400; **1966**: 384;
     1967: 336; **1968–69**: 466
Atlantic-Pacific sea level canal, proposed, **1965**:
     400
Atlantic partnership, **1963–64**: 49, 72, 76, 91
     (p. 117), 109, 186, 244, 272, 384, 394,
     612, 662n., 788; **1965**: 112, 235, 507,
     659, 660
Atlas booster rockets, **1966**: 625
Atlas missiles, **1965**: 26
Atmospheric sciences program, **1966**: 222
Atomic bombs, **1963–64**: 297 [2]
Atomic energy, **1963–64**: 132 (pp. 176, 191);
     1965: 196; **1966**: 412
 Control of, **1963–64**: 562, 577; **1965**: 196,
     319 [5]; **1966**: 411, 480
 Peaceful uses, **1963–64**: 29, 69, 396, 545,
     560 [6], 715, 718, 719; **1965**: 17, 32
     (p. 92), 196, 271, 319 [5], 325, 523,
     537; **1966**: 48n., 179, 361, 411, 427,
     480; **1967**: 64, 176, 442, 448, 491,
     515, 545
 Private industry, **1966**: 179
 Research, **1967**: 76
 Use for aircraft carriers, proposed, **1963–64**:
     170 [12]
 Water desalination, **1967**: 13 (p. 51), 227
 Weapons.
   See Nuclear weapons.
Atomic Energy, International Conference on the
     Peaceful Uses of, **1963–64**: 545; **1965**:
     537
Atomic Energy Act of 1946, **1966**: 361; **1968–
     69**: 378
Atomic Energy Act of 1954, **1963–64**: 439
 Amendment, **1965**: 446
Atomic Energy Agency, International, **1963–64**:
     29, 175, 545, 715; **1965**: 319 [5], 523,

Atomic Energy Agency, International — *continued*
537, 558; **1966**: 32, 48n., 177, 516 [3];
1967: 59, 64, 515; **1968–69**: 349, 378,
392
Atomic Energy Commission, **1963–64**: 276, 298,
437, 480; **1965**: 17, 32 (p. 92), 127,
143, 196, 274n., 319 [5], 325, 446,
493n., 514; **1966**: 26 (pp. 54, 60), 48,
225, 227 [5], 319, 320 [5], 361, 410;
1967: 13 (pp. 50, 51), 76, 329; **1968–
69**: 466, 608, 653n.
Appointments to, **1966**: 361
Appropriations, **1968–69**: 39 (p. 92), 467
[3], 678 (p. 1281)
Electron volt accelerators, **1967**: 515
News conference remarks, **1963–64**: 211 [28],
420 [2], 486 [2], 560 [6], 619 [1]
Report, **1963–64**: 715n.
Safety record, **1966**: 75
Spending cutbacks, **1967**: 6 [9], 98
Water desalination, **1966**: 26 (p. 60)
Atomic Energy Commission, Chairman (Glenn T.
Seaborg), **1963–64**: 19, 29, 276, 439,
538, 546n., 715; **1965**: 17, 88, 196,
319 [1, 5], 417, 418, 523; **1966**: 48,
179, 361, 410–411; **1967**: 227, 504,
515; **1968–69**: 310, 608, 695
Memorandum, **1963–64**: 62, 440; **1968–69**:
361
News conference remarks on, **1963–64**: 294
[10], 688 [1], 780 [22]
Atomic Energy Community, European
(Euratom), **1966**: 48n.
Atomic energy research, **1968–69**: 145
Atomic information, U.S.-NATO exchange of,
agreement, **1963–64**: 439, 440
Attlee, Clement, death, **1967**: 422
Attorney General (Ramsey Clark), **1967**: 20, 35,
55, 71, 79, 104 [15], 114, 146, 221,
223 [2], 236, 264 [8], 269, 275, 276,
310, 322, 335, 372, 443, 530; **1968–69**:
17, 26, 36, 42, 56, 57, 59, 60, 79 [6],
100, 153 [16], 169 [5], 209, 236, 257,
263, 292n., 298, 320, 325, 339 [3],
388, 425 [11], 471, 553, 557 [8], 570,
631
Memorandum, **1967**: 441; **1968–69**: 389
Swearing in, **1967**: 105
Attorney General (Nicholas deB. Katzenbach),
1965: 66, 102, 114, 135, 181, 250,
309n., 336, 346, 366, 382, 409, 422n.,
433, 437, 440, 443, 500, 509, 516, 526,
546, 608n., 613, 615; **1966**: 45, 51,
59, 82, 88 [5], 105, 116, 139, 196,
204–205, 216, 241, 247 [1, 10], 227
[24], 286, 289, 394, 401 [3], 417
[6], 453, 474 [14]

Attorney General — *continued*
See also Katzenbach, Nicholas deB.
Letter, **1966**: 463
News conference remarks on, **1965**: 106 [1, 9],
117 [5], 208 [15], 319 [12], 353
[16], 448 [9, 22]
Reports, **1965**: 409n., 437n., 546n.
Resignation, **1966**: 474 [17]
Attorney General (Robert F. Kennedy), **1963–
64**: 218 [10], 315, 401, 428n., 452,
489, 523
Letter, **1963–64**: 537
News conference remarks on, **1963–64**: 170 [4],
211 [15], 256 [14], 266 [21], 285 [11],
504 [13]
Report on organized crime and racketeering,
1963–64: 90
Resignation, **1963–64**: 556
Visit to London and Asia, **1963–64**: 156
Visit to Malaysia, **1963–64**: 150 [17]
Visit to Southeast Asia, **1963–64**: 170 [11
Attorney General, Acting (Ramsey Clark), **1966**:
474 [17], 487, 526, 602, 607 [1],
609, 611, 614, 635 [2, 3], 636–637,
650 [22]
See also Clark, Ramsey; Attorney General
(Ramsey Clark).
General Electric Co. labor dispute injunction,
1966: 535
Memorandum, **1966**: 606
Attorney General, Acting (Nicholas deB.
Katzenbach), **1963–64**: 641, 684,
688 [5], 780 [4, 13]
See also Attorney General (Nicholas deB.
Katzenbach); Katzenbach, Nicholas
deB.
Letters, **1963–64**: 614, 752
Attorney General, question of appointment,
1966: 474 [17], 477 [5], 516 [18],
635 [11], 650 [22]; **1967**: 70 [2]
Attorneys, United States, **1968–69**: 209
Assistant, **1968–69**: 14 (p. 30), 59, 209
Remarks to, **1963–64**: 452
Attorneys General, National Association of,
1968–69: 334
Atwood, Albert W., **1963–64**: 389n.
Atwood, J. Lee, **1968–69**: 616
Auburn, Norman P., **1963–64**: 693
Auburn Dam, California, **1965**: 477
Auburn-Folsom South project bill, approval,
1965: 477
Auchincloss, Mrs. Hugh D., **1963–64**: 784
Auchincloss, Repr. James C., **1963–64**: 422
Auditory Materials of an Educational, Scientific,
and Cultural Character, Agreement for
Facilitating the International Circula-
tion of Visual and (Beirut Agreement),
1966: 45, 519

Augusta, Ga., campaign remarks, **1963–64**: 718
Augusta, U.S.S., **1967**: 485 [5]
Austin, J. Paul, **1968–69**: 25, 92, 114, 115, 141, 227
Austin, Warren R., **1963–64**: 605; **1965**: 370
Austin, Tex., **1963–64**: 67n., 68n., 69n., 70n., 72, 77, 78n., 79n., 80n., 81n., 82n., 83n., 84n., 85n., 86n., 89n., 241n., 375, 376n., 547n., 616n., 653n., 763, 765, 814n., 815n., 816n., 817n., 820n.; **1965**: 1n., 23n., 116n., 142, 180n., 193n., 195n., 196n., 197n., 285n., 287n., 288n., 332n., 342n., 343n., 344n., 348n., 349n., 351n., 352n., 396n., 422n., 423n., 424n., 425n., 426n., 427n., 428n., 460n., 461n., 484n., 485n., 486n., 487n., 488n., 490n., 491n., 492n., 493n., 494n., 495n., 496n., 497n., 498n., 501n., 587n., 588n., 589n., 590n., 591n., 592n., 593n., 594n., 597n., 598n., 599n., 600n., 601n., 602n., 604n., 605n., 606n., 607n., 608n., 609n., 610n., 611n., 622n., 624n., 625n., 626n., 627n., 628n., 629n., 630n., 631n., 633n., 634n., 635n., 636n., 637n., 639n., 640n., 645n., 646n., 647n., 661n., 662n., 663n.; **1967**: 210, 270; **1968–69**: 646 [15]
  Community antenna system v.KTBC-TV monopoly, **1963–64**: 256 [15], 266 [14]
  Housing projects, **1968–69**: 435, 625
  Mayor Lester Palmer, **1963–64**: 72n., 763; **1967**: 210
  Releases, **1966**: 623–624, 627, 629, 631–634, 637, 640, 643n., 649, 651–652; **1968–69**: 88–92, 202, 284, 285, 313, 398n., 403–405, 432–441, 443–451, 457, 458, 460, 463, 626
  News conferences, **1966**: 630, 635, 642
  Remarks, **1968–69**: 97, 625
Austin Oaks Housing Project, Austin, Texas, **1968–69**: 625
Australia, **1963–64**: 475 [3]; **1965**: 68n., 220, 628; **1966**: 14, 133, 328, 516 [1], 542–543; **1967**: 551, 555; **1968–69**: 604
  Ambassador Keith Waller, **1967**: 1, 246; **1968–69**: 273
  Armed Forces, **1968–69**: 283 [4, 5]
  Assistance to Vietnam, **1963–64**: 426
  Foreign policy, **1968–69**: 528
  Governor-General Richard G. Casey, **1966**: 541; **1967**: 239, 561
  India food aid, **1967**: 33
  Lyndon B. Johnson science scholars, **1966**: 545–546; **1967**: 1; **1968–69**: 453

Australia – *continued*
  Menzies, Robert G., **1963–64**: 426
  Prime Minister John Gorton, **1968–69**: 223 [7], 271, 273, 275 [1, 2], 276, 277, 283 [1, 3–6], 290, 513n.
  Prime Minister Harold E. Holt, **1966**: 304–305, 328–329, 492 [4], 514, 541–547, 549, 630 [12]; **1967**: 246, 248, 267, 272, 328 [9], 409, 550, 551, 555, 561, 564, 565, 567, 573
  Prime Minister John McEwen, **1967**: 561, 562
  Prime Minister Robert G. Menzies, **1965**: 303; **1966**: 24
  Releases, **1967**: 560, 562–564
  Ships for, **1965**: 600
  U.S. Ambassador Edward Clark, **1966**: 305, 543–544; **1967**: 248, 551, 562
  U.S. relations with, **1965**: 303; **1966**: 304n.–305; **1967**: 555; **1968–69**: 277, 283 [3]
  U.S. science mission, **1968–69**: 513
  Vietnam assistance, **1966**: 53, 304, 516 [13], 520, 543, 546; **1967**: 83, 246, 555, 562, 567; **1968–69**: 271n., 273, 277, 283 [3, 4], 525
  Visit, **1966**: 541–547; **1967**: 561–564
Australia, New Zealand and United States Treaty Council (ANZUS), **1963–64**: 426, 464; **1968–69**: 271n., 277, 522n., 525, 528
Australian Broadcasting Co., **1967**: 551
Austria, **1966**: 272, 605
  Ambassador Ernst Lemberger, **1966**: 272
  Chancellor Josef Klaus, **1965**: 87; **1968–69**: 190, 193, 194
  President Franz Jonas, **1966**: 605; **1968–69**: 193
  President Adolf Schaerf, **1965**: 87
  Relations with U.S., **1968–69**: 190n., 194
  U.N. Ambassador Kurt Waldheim, **1966**: 272
  U.S. Ambassador James W. Riddleberger, **1966**: 272
Auto theft prevention bill of 1968, **1968–69**: 59
Automated Merchant Vessel Report, **1965**: 312
Automatic data processing
  Federal, **1966**: 26 (p. 66), 27, 296
  Government use of, **1965**: 93
Automatic data processing equipment, **1968–69**: 39 (p. 111)
Automatic merchandising, **1965**: 297
Automation, **1963–64**: 99, 126, 213, 233, 388, 406, 525, 589; **1965**: 428; **1966**: 34 (p. 97)
Automation, Commission on, proposed, **1963–64**: 91 (p. 114), 124 (p. 162)
Automation and Economic Progress, National Commission on Technology, **1963–64**: 214, 525; **1965**: 100, 258; **1966**: 111

Automobile, Aerospace and Agricultural Imple-
    ment Workers of America, International
    Union of United, **1966**: 535
Automobile industry, **1963–64**: 233, 455 [3],
    521 [10], 745; **1965**: 375; **1966**: 449
  Automotive products trade agreement, U.S.–
    Canada, **1965**: 21, 22 [9], 147, 574, 575
  Labor contracts, **1963–64**: 624
  Labor disputes, **1963–64**: 687, 733, 780 [3];
    1967: 375 [11]
  Sales, **1963–64**: 124 (p. 160), 246 [15], 271
    [3], 336 [1], 563 [6], 624, 780 [3];
    1965: 590; **1968–69**: 47 (p. 129)
  Unemployment, **1963–64**: 67, 288, 289, 295,
    297, 462 [3], 463, 486 [2]
Automobile Workers of America, United,
    1963–64: 67, 233, 336 [17], 563 [2],
    624, 687, 713, 733; **1966**: 235
Automobiles, **1966**: 98, 426; **1967**: 286
  Accidents.
    See Safety.
  Air pollution, **1967**: 20, 503
  Driver education, **1966**: 187
  Excise taxes on, **1965**: 255, 326
  Exhaust fumes, air pollution, **1965**: 54
  Federal procurement, **1967**: 6 [7]
  Imports, **1968–69**: 241
  Insurance, study, **1968–69**: 14 (p. 30), 56, 264
  Junkyards, **1966**: 398; **1967**: 295
  Junk
    Highway disfigurement, **1963–64**: 642, 669;
      1965: 54, 277, 279
  Prices, **1966**: 474 [3], 492 [5]; **1968–69**: 485,
    492
  Safety, **1968–69**: 56, 212, 244, 264, 270, 545,
    693
    See also Highways.
  Safety standards, **1966**: 98, 187, 252, 290–291,
    449, 474 [3]
  Tariffs, **1968–69**: 274
  Taxes, **1966**: 6 (p. 5), 8 [14], 17, 26 (pp. 49,
    52), 155; **1967**: 329; **1968–69**: 39 (p.
    88), 47 (p. 132), 678 (p. 1277), 684
    (p. 1322)
  Theft, **1968–69**: 59
Automotive products, exports, **1965**: 21, 22 [9],
    147, 574
Automotive Products Trade Act of 1965,
    1965: 574; **1967**: 137; **1968–69**: 256,
    274, 275 [2], 465
Automotive products trade agreement, U.S.-
    Canada, **1965**: 21, 22 [9], 147, 574, 575;
    1967: 137; **1968–69**: 256, 465
Avery, Col. Jacob M., **1968–69**: 210
Avery, Gov. William H., **1966**: 407n., 494 [1]
Aviation, **1963–64**: 132 (pp. 180, 181); **1965**: 26;
    1966: 98; **1967**: 139, 431; **1968–69**: 125
  See also Aircraft; Aircraft, military; Airlines.
  Airways congestion, **1966**: 187

Aviation – *continued*
  Civil air agreement with Soviet Union,
    1968–69: 14 (p. 26), 288, 387
  Civil aviation, **1963–64**: 215; **1965**: 32 (p. 88),
    255
  Excise taxes, **1965**: 32 (p. 88), 35 (p. 116), 255
  Expansion of network, **1968–69**: 39 (p. 102)
  Facilities, cost, **1967**: 13 (p. 44), 16 (p. 86)
  Paris Air Show, **1965**: 320
  Safety, **1966**: 98, 321; **1968–69**: 14 (p. 31),
    39 (p. 102), 41, 47 (p. 144), 693
  Taxes, **1966**: 26 (p. 54)
  Traffic control, **1967**: 392
  Transoceanic routes, **1966**: 64
  User charges, **1966**: 26 (pp. 53–54), 34
    (p. 106), 403
Aviation Administration, Federal, **1967**: 392;
    1968–69: 39 (p. 111), 93, 693
Aviation Agency, Federal, **1966**: 26 (p. 54);
    1967: 139n.
Aviation Committee, Women's, **1963–64**: 310
Aviation Officials, National Association of State,
    1963–64: 215
Aviation Trophies, Harmon International,
    presentation, **1963–64**: 569
Awards and citations
  See also Addresses or remarks at presentation
    ceremonies.
  AAA lifesaving awards, **1963–64**: 317
    School Safety Patrol, **1965**: 232
  "Ability Counts" awards, **1963–64**: 302
  American Football Coaches Association award,
    1966: 7
  American Legion Distinguished Service Medal,
    President Johnson, **1968–69**: 472
  Anti-Defamation League Award, acceptance,
    1965: 44
  Astronauts, policy for, **1965**: 463ftn. (p. 944)
  Beautification award, Jeffersonville, Ind.,
    1966: 353
  Beautification program leadership certificate,
    acceptance, **1965**: 315
  Big Brother of the Year Award, **1966**: 213
    Acceptance, **1963–64**: 239
  Bronze Star, Maj. Marie L. Rodgers, **1967**: 475
  Certificate of Commendation, **1963–64**: 163
  Certificates of Merit, **1963–64**: 467;
    1967: 324n.
  Charles B. Stillman Award, acceptance,
    1965: 539
  Charter Oak Leadership Medal, acceptance,
    1963–64: 604n.
  Civil Service League awards, **1966**: 198
  Collier Trophy, **1963–64**: 593
  Commission to Lt. Col. John H. Glenn, Jr.,
    1963–64: 725
  Conservation plaque, Secretary Udall, Mrs.
    Lyndon B. Johnson, Laurance S.
    Rockefeller, **1968–69**: 411

[References are to items except as otherwise indicated]

Awards and citations – *continued*
  Cost reduction awards
    Agriculture Department, **1968–69**: 174
    Department of Defense, **1965**: 387;
      1968–69: 516
  Denver, University of, honorary degree,
    1966: 414
  Disciples of Christ Historical Society citation,
    acceptance, **1963–64**: 279
  Distinguished Federal Civilian Service Awards
    See Distinguished Federal Civilian Service,
    President's Award for.
  Distinguished Flying Cross, Maj. William J.
    Knight, **1968–69**: 610
  Distinguished Service Award of the President's
    Committee on Employment of the
    Handicapped, **1963–64**: 235, 302n., 389
  Distinguished Service Medal, **1963–64**: 127,
    425, 487, 783
    Abrams, Gen. Creighton W., **1967**: 567
    Bringle, Vice Adm. William F., **1967**: 567
    Clifton, Maj. Gen. Chester V., **1965**: 399
    Cushman, Lt. Gen. Robert E., **1967**: 567
    Gerhart, Gen. John K., **1965**: 158
    Greene, Gen. Wallace M., Jr., **1968–69**: 34
    Humphreys, Maj. Gen. James W., Jr.,
      1967: 235
    Johnson, Gen. Harold K., **1968–69**: 353
    LeMay, Gen. Curtis E., **1965**: 37
    McDonald, Adm. David L., **1967**: 308
    Momyer, Lt. Gen. William W., **1967**: 567
    Palmer, Lt. Gen. Bruce, **1967**: 567
    Smith, Adm. Harold Page, **1965**: 228
    Veth, Rear Adm. Kenneth L., **1967**: 567
    Westmoreland, Gen. William C., **1967**: 567;
      1968–69: 384
    Wheeler, Gen. Earle G., **1968–69**: 669
  Distinguished Unit Citation
    1st Battalion (Airborne), 503d Infantry,
      173d Airborne Brigade (Separate), USA,
      1966: 282
    121st Aviation Company (Air Mobile Light),
      USA, **1966**: 107
  "E" Awards, **1966**: 144; **1967**: 231
  "E" flag awards, **1963–64**: 350
  Education, citation for contributions to,
    1967: 490n.
  8th Armored Division Association peace award,
    1966: 377
  Eleanor Roosevelt Golden Candlestick award,
    1963–64: 208
  Employer of the Year Award, **1967**: 388;
    1968–69: 548
  Enrico Fermi award, **1963–64**: 19
    Vice Adm. Hyman G. Rickover, **1965**: 17
    Dr. John A. Wheeler, **1968–69**: 608
  Equal opportunity awards, **1968–69**: 596
  Exceptional Service Award of the Treasury,

Awards and citations – *continued*
  Exceptional Service Award – *continued*
    1963–64: 21
  Fannie and John Hertz Foundation Award, Ali
    Javan and Theodore H. Maiman,
    1966: 194
  Federal Aviation Agency award, **1963–64**: 310
  Federal Home Loan Bank Presidents, citation,
    1967: 420n.
  Federal incentive awards program, **1965**: 540
  Federal Woman's Award, **1965**: 91; **1966**: 89;
    1967: 93; **1968–69**: 138
  Franklin D. Roosevelt Birthday Memorial
    Award, **1967**: 21
  Government Employees Incentive Awards,
    1963–64: 467n., 790
  Harmon International Aviation Trophies,
    1963–64: 569; **1967**: 431
    Maj. William J. Knight, **1968–69**: 610
  Head Start insignia, Mrs. Lyndon B. Johnson,
    1965: 323
  Hearst Foundation Journalism Awards, **1963–
    64**: 339
    Hall, Hal David, **1965**: 260
    Powers, Charles, **1965**: 260
    University of Florida, **1965**: 260
  Heart of the Year Award, **1963–64**: 164
    Repr. John E. Fogarty, **1966**: 49
  Holland Society, Award for Distinguished
    Achievement, President Johnson,
    1968–69: 661
  Honorary degree, President Johnson,
    1968–69: 282
  Honorary degrees, President Johnson and
    President Diaz Ordaz, **1967**: 448
  International Narcotics Enforcement Officers
    Association award, President Johnson,
    1968–69: 217
  International Platform Association, annual
    award, acceptance, **1965**: 397
  Labor Human Rights Award, George Meany,
    1967: 484n.
  Lasker, Albert, special award, **1966**: 166
  Legion of Merit, Col. Ethel A. Hoefly,
    1967: 475
  Medal of Freedom
    See also Presidential Medal of Freedom
    Bunker, Ellsworth, **1967**: 567
    Komer, Robert W., **1967**: 567
    Locke, Eugene M., **1967**: 567
  Medal of Honor, **1968–69**: 141, 690, 691
    Baker, Sgt. John F., Jr., **1968–69**: 221
    Connor, S. Sgt. Peter S., **1967**: 202
    Davis, Sgt. Sammy L., **1968–69**: 594
    Dethlefsen, Maj. Merlyn H., **1968–69**: 48
    Dix, S. Sgt. Drew D., **1968–69**: 688
    Dolby, Sgt. David C., **1967**: 407
    Donlon, Capt. Roger H. C., **1963–64**: 793
    Fernandez, Sp4c. Daniel, **1967**: 166
    Fisher, Maj. Bernard F., **1967**: 9

Awards and citations – *continued*
  Medal of Honor – *continued*
    Foley, Capt. Robert F., **1968–69**: 221
    Hagemeister, Sp5c. Charles C., **1968–69**: 246
    Hibbs, 2d Lt. Robert J., **1968–69**: 148
    Howard, Gunnery Sgt. Jimmie E., **1967**: 361
    Jackson, Lt. Col. Joe M., **1968–69**: 688
    Jennings, S. Sgt. Delbert O., **1968–69**: 487
    Joel, Sp6c. Lawrence, **1967**: 102
    Johnson, Sp5c. Dwight H., **1968–69**: 594
    Keller, Sgt. Leonard B., **1968–69**: 487
    Lassen, Lt. Clyde E., **1968–69**: 688
    Lee, Maj. Howard V., **1967**: 446
    Liteky, Chaplain (Capt.) Anglo J.,
      1968–69: 594
    McGintry, 2d Lt. John J., III, **1968–69**: 129
    McNerney, 1st Sgt. David H., **1968–69**: 487
    Modrzejewski, Maj. Robert J., **1968–69**: 129
    Morris, Staff Sgt. Charles B., **1967**: 494
    Olive, Pfc. Milton L., III, **1966**: 183
    O'Malley, Sgt. Robert E., **1966**: 641
    Pierce, S. Sgt. Larry S., **1966**: 87
    Pittman, Sgt. Richard A., **1968–69**: 246
    Pitts, Capt. Riley L., **1968–69**: 617
    Pless, Maj. Stephen W., **1968–69**: 688
    Shields, PO Marvin G., **1966**: 456
    Stumpf, S. Sgt. Kenneth E., **1968–69**: 487
    Taylor, Capt. James A., **1968–69**: 594
    Wetzel, Sp4c. Garry C., **1968–69**: 594
    Williams, Lt. Charles Q., **1966**: 288
    Williams, Boatswain's Mate I/C James E.,
      1968–69: 246
    Wright, Sp4c. Raymond R., **1968–69**: 487
    Young, Capt. Gerald O., **1968–69**: 246
  Military incentive, **1967**: 208; **1968–69**: 248
  Minuteman award, Tactical Air Command's
    12th Air Force, **1968–69**: 12
  NASA awards, **1965**: 134, 391n.
  NASA Distinguished Service Medal
    Anders, Lt. Col. William A., **1968–69**: 662
    Borman, Col. Frank, **1968–69**: 662
    Lovell, Capt. James A., **1968–69**: 662
    Webb, James E., **1968–69**: 574
  NASA Exceptional Service Medal
    Cunningham, R. Walter, **1968–69**: 574
    Eisele, Lt. Col. Donn F., **1968–69**: 574
    Mathews, Charles W., **1965**: 318
    McDivitt, Lt. Col. (Maj.) James A.,
      1965: 318
    Schirra, Capt. Walter M., Jr., **1968–69**: 574
    White, Lt. Col. (Maj.) Edward H., 2d,
      1965: 318
  National Civil Service League's Career Service
    Awards, presentation, **1965**: 263
  National Conference of Christians and Jews
    Brotherhood Award, President Johnson,
    1968–69: 78n.
  National Education Award of 1966, **1966**: 77

Awards and citations – *continued*
  National Freedom Award, **1966**: 86
  National Governors' Conference Special Award,
    President Johnson, **1968–69**: 406n.
  National Medal of Science, **1963–64**: 98;
    1966: 61, 652; **1967**: 37; **1968–69**: 71,
    695
    Presentation, **1965**: 56
    Recipients, **1965**: 646
  National Security Medal
    Fitz-Gerald, Desmond, **1967**: 383
    McCone, John A., **1965**: 209n.
    Raborn, Vice Adm. William F., Jr.,
      1966: 387
    Rowlett, Frank Byron, **1966**: 99
  Pan American Society Gold Medal Award,
    President Johnson, **1968–69**: 665
  Parents' Magazine award, acceptance,
    1965: 614
  Physical Fitness Leadership Awards, **1965**:
    222, 645; **1967**: 160
  Postal Service's Honor Award, President John-
    son, **1968–69**: 630
  Presidential Citation, **1963–64**: 465
  Presidential Medal of Freedom, **1963–64**: 27,
    157, 447, 568
    McNamara, Secretary Robert S., **1968–69**: 99
    Rusk, Secretary Dean, **1968–69**: 691
    Webb, James, E., **1968–69**: 616
  Presidential Scholars award, **1963–64**: 397
    Presentation, **1965**: 306
  Presidential Unit Citation recipients.
    See Presidential Unit Citations.
  Presidential Unit Citations, **1967**: 61, 106, 226,
    302, 334, 384, 424, 456, 457
    U.S. and Vietnamese troops in Vietnam,
      1965: 206, 588; **1966**: 20, 616–617,
      621
  President's Award for Distinguished Federal
    Civilian Service, **1963–64**: 417; **1965**:
    269, 296; **1966**: 25, 266; **1967**: 317;
    1968–69: 604
  President's Committee on Employment of the
    Handicapped Distinguished Service
    Award, **1963–64**: 235, 302n., 389
  President's Safety Awards, **1963–64**: 351;
    1965: 73, 287
  President's Trophy for the Handicapped Ameri-
    can of the Year, **1963–64**: 302n.
  Rhode Island, University of, honorary degree,
    1966: 396
  Robert H. Goddard Trophy, **1966**: 134
  Salvation Army award, acceptance, **1965**: 643
  Savings bond promotion award, President
    Johnson, **1968–69**: 537
  Savings bond purchases, **1967**: 315
  Scholastic achievement, blind students,
    1966: 220
    Baker, Larry Dale, **1968–69**: 230

[References are to items except as otherwise indicated]

Awards and citations — *continued*
  Scholastic achievement — *continued*
    DuBoff, Leonard David, **1968–69**: 230
    Peterson, Sherrill Rae, **1968–69**: 230
   Silver Star, **1963–64**: 535
    Pfc. Charles William Bosley, **1966**: 350
   Small Businessman of the Year award,
    1963–64: 362
    Dominic Donatello, **1965**: 270
   Swords Into Plowshares award, President
    Johnson, **1968–69**: 310
   Teacher of the Year award, **1963–64**: 362
    Dayton, Mrs. Mona, **1966**: 165
    Graf, David E., **1968–69**: 219
    Klinck, Richard E., **1965**: 171
    Tenney, Roger, **1967**: 182
    Trout, Mrs. Lawana, **1963–64**: 309
  Tuss McLaughry Award, **1966**: 7
  UAW Social Justice Award, **1966**: 235n.
  U.S. Veterans Advisory Commission awards,
    1968–69: 599
  Veritas Medal of Providence College, Speaker
    of the House of Representatives John
    W. McCormack, **1965**: 237
  Vietnam Civilian Service Awards, **1967**: 352
  World Leadership Award, President Johnson,
    1968–69: 459n.
  Young American Medals, **1963–64**: 315;
    1965: 336; **1966**: 289; **1967**: 275
    Capilia, Carmalita, **1968–69**: 236
    Donohue, Mary Lynne, **1968–69**: 236
    Glynn, William G., **1968–69**: 236
  Youth Opportunity Campaign, certificates for
    participating corporations, **1965**: 298n.
Ayers, Repr. William H., **1968–69**: 554n.
Ayub Khan, Mohammed, **1965**: 208, 529, 641
    [3], 648, 649, 650; **1966**: 247 [7],
    273, 514; **1967**: 569
Azalea Festival, Norfolk, Va., crowning of
    queen, **1965**: 205

B-17 bombers, **1965**: 158
B-47 and B-52 bombers, **1965**: 26
Babcock, Gov. Tim M., **1963–64**: 267, 575;
    1966: 491n., 492 [1]
Babcock, Mrs. Tim M., **1963–64**: 267
Babelthuap Island, **1967**: 133n.
Babiarz, John E., **1966**: 515
Bachelder, Toinette M., **1966**: 186
Backlash, white, **1966**: 401 [6], 580 [15, 20],
    599 [3]
Bacon, Donald W., **1966**: 240n.
Bacon, Edmund, **1965**: 277n.
Bacon, Francis, **1963–64**: 141

Badeau, John S., **1963–64**: 455 [6]
Baer, Walter S., **1968–69**: 513n.
Bagge, Carl E., **1965**: 117 [3]
Bail practices, **1967**: 13 (p. 56), 71, 221
Bail Reform Act of 1966, **1966**: 116, 286, 487,
    526, 611; **1967**: 13 (p. 56), 221;
    1968–69: 39 (p. 107)
Bailey, Charles W., 2d, **1967**: 70 [3], 104 [7];
    1968–69: 51 [9]
Bailey, Mrs. Charles W., **1967**: 342n.
Bailey, John M., **1966**: 403; **1967**: 216, 251,
    421, 514; **1968–69**: 210, 631
  See also Democratic National Committee,
    Chairman.
Bailey, Joseph Weldon, **1963–64**: 607, 645,
    652, 719
Bailey, Mrs. Oriole, **1963–64**: 150 [8]
Bailey, Robert D., **1966**: 426–427
Bailey, Stephen K., **1968–69**: 694
Bailey, Thomas D., **1963–64**: 709, 712, 713
Bainbridge, U.S.S., **1963–64**: 619 [5]
Baines, George Washington, Sr., **1963–64**: 238,
    631; **1965**: 286n.; **1968–69**: 156
Baird, Charles F., **1967**: 361
Baird, Maj. Robert, **1967**: 485 [6]
Baja California, Mexico, **1967**: 303
Baker, Mrs. Annette, **1963–64**: 709, 712, 713
Baker, Cathy May, **1963–64**: 284, 290
Baker, Cole, **1963–64**: 636
Baker, David L., **1967**: 4n.
Baker, George, **1967**: 168n.
Baker, John A., **1968–69**: 505
Baker, Sgt. John F., Jr., **1968–69**: 221
Baker, Larry Dale, **1968–69**: 230
Baker, Newton D., **1968–69**: 78
Baker, Robert C., **1967**: 27
Baker, Robert G., **1963–64**: 143 [4], 150 [9],
    201 [4], 218 [13], 455 [21], 563 [15],
    728; **1965**: 46 [10]
Bakersfield College Choir, remarks to, **1965**: 405
Bakke, Oscar, **1966**: 198n.
Balaguer, Joaquin (President of the Dominican
    Republic), **1966**: 277 [3, 25], 320 [6];
    1967: 436
Balance of payments, **1963–64**: 76, 91 (p. 117),
    124 (pp. 158, 160, 161, 166), 132 (p.
    190), 196, 227, 248, 295, 296, 299, 400,
    472, 477, 617, 714, 740, 753, 775, 787,
    797; **1965**: 2, 18, 32 (p. 84), 35 (pp.
    104, 105, 107, 109, 110, 111, 117), 47,
    76, 77, 110, 146, 192, 338, 365, 418,
    419, 450, 541, 570, 638, 660;
    1966: 34 (pp. 97–98), 41, 155, 359,
    444, 445 [6], 461, 486, 506, 596, 612;
    1967: 13 (pp. 49, 51), 16 (pp. 74, 75,
    80, 81, 88), 44, 103, 329, 401, 491,
    492, 519, 524, 545; **1968–69**: 1 [12], 2,

Balance of payments – *continued*
10, 39 (pp. 84, 86), 46, 47 (pp. 127,
130, 137, 138, 144), 63, 88, 94, 106,
112, 136, 218, 223 [14], 304, 350, 425
[1], 427, 449, 500, 528, 648, 678 (pp.
1275, 1276), 684 (pp. 1311, 1313,
1319), 696 [12]
Agricultural exports, impact, **1966**: 355
Cabinet Committee on, **1965**: 638; **1967**: 231
Deficit, **1965**: 60, 77, 338; **1966**: 6 (p. 5), 26
(p. 49), 33, 114–115, 144
Foreign assistance, impact, **1966**: 11
Memorandum, **1966**: 114
Message to Congress, **1965**: 60
News conference remarks, **1963–64**: 246 [12,
18], 266 [2], 379 [6], 475 [2];
1965: 22 [11], 46 [12], 319 [8, 19],
347 [2, 4]
Report, **1965**: 249n.
Statement, **1963–64**: 722
Steps to improve, **1968–69**: 1 [1, 8, 15], 11,
14 (p. 33), 15, 39 (pp. 99, 102), 47
(pp. 128, 133–35), 62, 83, 146, 170,
241, 274, 277, 377, 422
Statement on program, **1968–69**: 2
Surplus, **1968–69**: 676 (p. 1268)
United Kingdom, **1963–64**: 780 [3];
1966: 359n.
U.S. position, **1965**: 139, 149
Balboa, Praxedis, **1965**: 179n.
Balboa High School, Panama Canal Zone,
1963–64: 143ftn. (p. 219)
Baldanzi, George, **1963–64**: 590
Baldwin, John F., Jr., **1966**: 401 [11]
Baldwin, Robert H. B., **1965**: 319 [11, 13]
Balfour Declaration (1917), **1968–69**: 250n.
Balick, Sidney, **1966**: 515
Ball, Edgar L., **1963–64**: 761
Ball, George W., **1963–64**: 26, 27, 69, 150ftn.
(p. 229), 157, 182, 237n., 274, 417,
511, 568, 678, 680, 797; **1965**: 172n.,
295 [16], 296, 319 [14], 347 [2], 448
[15], 451, 535n., 557; **1966**: 236 [5],
247 [1, 8], 261, 266, 474 [17], 502,
566n.; **1967**: 113; **1968–69**: 221, 223
[1, 6], 691, 696 [14]
See also United Nations.
Appointment as United Nations Representa-
tive, **1968–69**: 213 [1]
News conference remarks on, **1963–64**: 71
[9], 201 [13], 246 [4], 455 [16],
780 [9]
Resignation as U.S. Representative to United
Nations, **1968–69**: 496
Ball, Mrs. George W., **1966**: 502n.;
1968–69: 335, 691
Ball, Robert M., **1966**: 253, 509
Ballard, Frederick A., **1965**: 366

Ballet Company, National, proposed,
1965: 534
Ballet Theatre, American, **1967**: 53
Ballif, Mrs. Angie E., **1967**: 419n.
Baltimore, Md., **1965**: 95
Campaign remarks, **1963–64**: 612, 703
Civil disorders, **1968–69**: 184
Mayor Theodore R. McKeldin, **1963–64**: 516
[16], 703; **1965**: 521; **1966**: 155, 189,
394n.; **1967**: 87n., 286
Baltimore Baseball Club, Inc. (Orioles),
1966: 509
Baltimore New Car Dealers Association,
1967: 286
Baltimore Sun, **1967**: 264 [12]
Banda, H. Kamuzu (President of Malawi),
1967: 256
Bandag, Inc., **1966**: 144n.
Bandstra, Repr. Bert, **1966**: 312
Bane, Frank, **1963–64**: 285 [7]; **1967**: 319
Bang Saen, Thailand, **1966**: 554
Bangkok, Thailand, **1966**: 554–555, 557;
1968–69: 232, 233, 237
Lord Mayor Cham Nan Yuvabul, **1966**: 554n.
Releases, **1966**: 559n., 560
Bank, African Development, **1967**: 16 (p. 80),
44, 100; **1968–69**: 63, 365, 500, 508
Bank, Asian Development, **1967**: 3 (p. 13), 16
(p. 80), 44, 73, 100, 111, 112n., 212,
219, 401, 459, 486, 491, 492;
1968–69: 14 (p. 27), 39 (p. 99), 47
(p. 138), 63, 275 [6], 500, 525, 678
(p. 1282), 684 (p. 1321)
Bank, Inter-American Development, **1966**: 26
(p. 58), 41, 125, 177, 386n.;
1967: 16 (p. 80), 44, 110, 176, 177n.,
394, 401; **1968–69**: 39 (p. 99), 63,
206, 239, 290, 366, 500, 665
Bank Board, Federal Home Loan, **1966**: 473,
530, 642, [3, 19]; **1967**: 3 (p. 8), 6
[11], 16 (p. 87), 88, 315n., 420;
1968–69: 72
Bank for Economic Integration, Central
American, **1968–69**: 363, 365, 366, 375
Bank for International Settlements,
1963–64: 472, 780 [3]
Bank Protection Act of 1968, **1968–69**: 59
Bank for Reconstruction and Development,
International, **1966**: 41, 94, 125, 152–
154, 565; **1967**: 13 (p. 49), 33, 44,
153, 401, 511, 554 [15]; **1968–69**: 39
(p. 99), 63, 99, 102, 290, 500
Bank regulations, **1963–64**: 226; **1965**: 60
Bank System, Federal Home Loan, **1967**: 420
Bank of the United States, Export-Import,
1968–69: 2, 39 (p. 96), 47 (p. 136),
136, 146, 377, 422

Bank of Washington, Export-Import, **1967**: 13
  (p. 49), 16 (p. 81), 176
Bankers, remarks to, **1965**: 77
Bankers Association, American, **1966**: 265
Bankhead-Jones Farm Tenant Act, amendment,
  1966: 595
Banking and Currency, House Committee on,
  1968-69: 319
Bankruptcy legislation, **1968-69**: 59
Banks and banking, **1966**: 34 (pp. 104, 108),
  141 [5], 582; **1967**: 16 (p. 86-87);
  1968-69: 141
  Balance of payments role, **1966**: 6 (p. 5), 26
    (p. 49)
  Comments on, **1963-64**: 144; **1965**: 156 [5]
  Cooperatives, **1968-69**: 94
  Credit, **1966**: 444, 473
  Deposits, **1966**: 34 (p. 108), 338 [14], 530;
    1967: 200, 393
  Federal land, **1967**: 156
  Foreign investments, **1968-69**: 47 (p. 135)
  Insurance on deposits, **1967**: 57
  Mutual savings, **1968-69**: 87
  Robberies, **1968-69**: 59
  Student loans, **1966**: 265
  Urban areas role, **1968-69**: 114, 115
Baptist Church, **1966**: 273
Baptists, **1968-69**: 156
Baptists, Southern, Christian Leadership Seminar,
  1963-64: 238
Bar Association, American, **1963-64**: 511;
  1965: 75; **1967**: 114, 455; **1968-69**:
  87, 263, 425 [1]
Barbados, **1968-69**: 476, 479
  Declaration of Rights, **1968-69**: 479
  Prime Minister Errol W. Barrows, **1968-69**: 476,
    479
  U.S. Ambassador Fredric R. Mann,
    1968-69: 476
Barbour, Al, **1963-64**: 562; **1966**: 431
Barbour County, West Va., **1968-69**: 567
Barclay, Rev. John, **1965**: 623n.
Barclay, Rev. and Mrs. John, **1967**: 210
Bardeen, Dr. John, **1965**: 646n.; **1966**: 61n.,
  637n.
Baring, Repr. Walter S., **1963-64**: 655
Barkan, Alexander E., **1966**: 431, 437
Barker, Horace A., **1968-69**: 695n.
Barkley, Alben W., **1963-64**: 277, 295, 644;
  1968-69: 174
Barley production, **1966**: 62
Barnard, Dr. Christiaan, **1968-69**: 108n.
Barnard College, **1963-64**: 150ftn. (p. 231)
Barnes, Ben, **1965**: 285; **1967**: 409
Barnes, Melvin W., **1963-64**: 266 [4]
Barnett, Peter, **1967**: 551
Barr, Joseph M., **1963-64**: 290, 728;
  1966: 350, 536

Barr, Joseph W., **1963-64**: 144; **1965**: 155n.,
  628, 637; **1967**: 6ftn. (p. 24), 252n.,
  338, 417 [1]
  See also Treasury, Secretary of the.
Barr, Mrs. Joseph W., **1963-64**: 144
Barrenechea, Norbert M., **1965**: 473n.
Barrett, Repr. William A., **1963-64**: 742;
  1965: 415; **1967**: 291
Barrientos Ortuño, Gen. René, **1966**: 338 [16];
  1968-69: 362
Barron, Gov. William W., **1963-64**: 217, 293,
  360, 586
Barrow, Errol W. (Prime Minister of the Bar-
  bados), **1968-69**: 476, 479
Barrow, Mrs. Errol W., **1968-69**: 476, 479
Bartlett, Gov. Dewey, **1968-69**: 46n.
Bartlett, Sen. E. L., **1966**: 567-569
  Death, **1968-69**: 621
Bartlett, Mrs. Margaret Patterson, **1963-64**: 61
Bartlett, Paul D., **1968-69**: 695n.
Bartley, Mrs. Samuel E., **1965**: 236
Barton, Clara, **1963-64**: 557
Barton, John J., **1966**: 346-347
Barton, Mrs. John J., **1966**: 346
Baruch, Bernard M., **1965**: 273, 327; **1967**: 59
  Atomic energy control plan (1946),
    1968-69: 378
Barwick, Sir Garfield E. J. and Lady, **1966**: 541-
  542
Baskin, Robert E., **1966**: 417 [15]
Bass, Ross, **1963-64**: 324, 325, 645, 701, 702;
  1966: 599 [1]
Bass, Mrs. Ross, **1963-64**: 324
Bataan, the Philippines, **1963-64**: 623; **1966**:
  551
Bates, Harry C., **1965**: 539
Bates, Lester, L., **1963-64**: 719
Bator, Francis M., **1967**: 371
Batt, William L., **1963-64**: 67, 294 [4]
Batten, William M., **1963-64**: 455 [7]
Battery Park, Burlington, Vt., **1966**: 398
Battin, Repr. James F., **1963-64**: 267
Battle, Lucius D., **1963-64**: 455 [6];
  1968-69: 169 [20]
Battle Creek, Mich., **1966**: 432-433
  Mayor Harry Wilklow, **1966**: 433
Baudouin, King, **1965**: 627
Baugh, Sam, **1963-64**: 136n.; **1968-69**: 282
Baumgartner, Leona, **1965**: 594n.
Bauxite stockpiles, **1966**: 173
Bay of Pigs, Cuba (attempted invasion),
  1968-69: 18 [2]
Bayh, Sen. Birch, **1963-64**: 67, 233, 288, 639,
  640, 729; **1965**: 88, 188, 242;
  1966: 346-347, 350, 353, 579;
  1967: 68
Bayh, Mrs. Birch, **1963-64**: 640; **1966**: 346,
  350, 353

Baylor University, **1965**: 286, 295 [4];
    1968-69: 156
Beach, Gen. Dwight E., **1968-69**: 283 [2]
Beadle, George W., **1965**: 424n., 594n.
Beagles, the President's, **1963-64**: 316 [19],
    334, 347
Beal, Lt. Col. Arthur, **1967**: 106n.
Beall, Sen. J. Glenn, **1963-64**: 320, 321
Beame, Abraham D., **1963-64**: 668
Beams, Jesse W., **1968-69**: 71n.
Bear River Wilderness, Utah, **1968-69**: 700
Beatrix, Princess (Netherlands), **1966**: 118
Beaumont, Tex., **1965**: 641 [1]; **1968-69**: 108,
    109
Beaurepaire, Mr. and Mrs. I. F., **1966**: 543
Beautification programs, **1965**: 2, 32 (p. 83),
    446, 448 [19], 529, 545; **1966**: 26
    (p. 50), 105, 119, 202, 263, 295, 346,
    353, 395, 500, 515; **1967**: 3 (pp. 2, 5),
    295; **1968-69**: 14 (p. 31), 96, 122,
    167, 311, 411, 458, 470, 567, 648
    Certificate for leadership in, acceptance, **1965**:
      315
    District of Columbia, **1965**: 545
    Federal aid, **1965**: 54, 545
    Highways and countryside, **1965**: 2, 30, 54,
      279, 545, 576; **1966**: 119, 202, 398,
      500; **1967**: 20, 295
    Industrial support, **1966**: 295
    Johnson, Mrs. Lyndon B., support, **1966**: 202,
      295, 500, 501 [18], 518
    Messages to Congress, **1965**: 53, 54
    Natural resources, **1965**: 53, 54, 277
    Post offices, **1966**: 353
    Postage stamp, "Plant for a More Beautiful
      America," **1966**: 500
    Public support, **1965**: 48
    Rapid transit facilities, **1966**: 84
    Report, **1965**: 277n.
    River basins, **1966**: 6 (p. 6)
    Rural areas, **1965**: 54; **1966**: 500
    Urban areas, **1965**: 54, 90; **1966**: 26 (p. 61),
      394, 500; **1967**: 295
    White House conference.
      See White House Conference on Natural
      Beauty.
    Youth activities, **1966**: 653; **1967**: 114
"Beauty for America—Proceedings of the White
    House Conference on Natural Beauty,"
    Laurence S. Rockefeller, **1965**: 418
    ftn. (p. 870)
Bechill, William D., **1965**: 642n.; **1968-69**: 117
Bechtel, S. B., Jr., **1967**: 252n.
Becker, Ralph E., letter, **1963-64**: 369
Beckman, Arnold, **1965**: 522n.
Beckman, Vincent, **1963-64**: 679
Beckman Instruments, Inc., **1967**: 231n.
Bedell, Berkeley W., **1963-64**: 362

Beebe, Leo C., **1968-69**: 25, 37, 92, 241, 498
Beech, Mrs. Olive Ann, **1963-64**: 741
Beef
    Exports, **1963-64**: 316 [6], 657
    Imports, **1963-64**: 211 [31], 516 [14], 732,
      657
    Sale of, **1963-64**: 316 [6], 344, 657
Behn, Gerald A., **1963-64**: 619 [11]
Beirne, Joseph A., **1963-64**: 406, 745; **1966**:
    208n.; **1967**: 500
Beirut Agreement (Agreement for Facilitating
    the International Circulation of Visual
    and Auditory Materials of an Educa-
    tional, Scientific, and Cultural Char-
    acter), **1966**: 45, 519
Belcher, Repr. Page, **1963-64**: 309; **1966**: 410,
    413, 415-416
Belen, Frederick C., **1963-64**: 207
Belgian Foreign Minister Pierre Harmel, **1966**:
    236 [5]
Belgium, **1965**: 68n.
    King Baudouin, **1965**: 627
    Operations in Congo, **1963-64**: 780 [2, 16]
    Queen Elisabeth, **1965**: 627
Belieu, Kenneth E., **1963-64**: 59; **1965**: 319
    [11, 13]
Bell, David, **1967**: 168n.
Bell, David E. (Administrator, Agency for Inter-
    national Development), **1963-64**: 48,
    69, 227, 402; **1965**: 7, 18, 60, 77, 136,
    407, 638, 649; **1966**: 52 [2], 141 [10,
    16], 247 [1, 15], 261, 368
Bell, Edward, **1968-69**: 429
Bell, Elliott V., **1963-64**: 285 [9], 299
Bell, Spurgeon, **1966**: 493
Belleau Wood, battle of, **1968-69**: 541
Bellet, Dr. Samuel, **1963-64**: 211 [6]
Belleville, Ill., campaign remarks, **1963-64**: 694
Bellmon, Gov. Henry, **1963-64**: 597, 598; **1966**:
    401 [7], 415-416, 417 [1], 491n., 492
    [1, 10]
Bellotti, Francis X., **1963-64**: 727
Beloe, Vice Adm. I. W. T., **1963-64**: 244
Belt Railway Company, Chicago, **1968-69**: 626
Bemis, Samuel Flagg, **1963-64**: 303
Bender, Raymond E., **1965**: 496n.
Benedict, Joseph T., **1967**: 420n.
Benediktsson, Bjarni, **1963-64**: 521ftn. (p. 978)
Benerito, Ruth Rogan, **1968-69**: 138n.
Benet, Stephen Vincent, **1965**: 314
Benito Juárez-Abraham Lincoln scholarships,
    1967: 451; **1968-69**: 66
Benito Juárez Scholars, **1968-69**: 66
Benjamin, Robert S., **1963-64**: 161n.; **1965**: 96,
    273
Bennett, Repr. Charles E., **1963-64**: 199, 713
Bennett, James William, **1966**: 289
Bennett, Robert L., **1968-69**: 259

Bennett, Mr. and Mrs. Robert L., **1966**: 193
Bennett, Tony, **1963–64**: 751
Bennett, W. Tapley, Jr., **1965**: 212n., 221, 223n., 227, 295 [1, 16], 319 [16], 342, 364n., 482; **1966**: 277 [2]
Bennett, Sen. Wallace F., **1966**: 188 [11]
Bennett, William A. C., **1963–64**: 575, 576
Benny, Jack, **1968–69**: 102n.
Benson, Ezra Taft, **1967**: 421; **1968–69**: 534
Bent, James E., **1963–64**: 71 [3]
Benton, William, **1963–64**: 211 [7], 379ftn. (p. 738); **1965**: 273; **1967**: 540
Berg, Sherwood O., **1965**: 597; **1967**: 525
Bergen, William B., **1966**: 625n.
Bergen, N. J., campaign remarks, **1963–64**: 660
Berger, Samuel D., **1963–64**: 796n.; **1967**: 113
Bergstrom Air Force Base, Texas, **1963–64**: 71 [6]; **1967**: 210; **1968–69**: 12n.
Berkeley, Marvin H., **1966**: 404n.; **1967**: 184
Berkeley County, West Va., **1968–69**: 567
Berkner, Lloyd V., **1963–64**: 738
Berlin, Irving, **1965**: 242
Berlin, **1963–64**: 72, 87, 349, 400, 703; **1965**: 37, 235, 600; **1966**: 482; **1968–69**: 142, 204, 313, 590 [3]
  Airlift, **1966**: 503
  Airlift (1948–49), **1968–69**: 154, 165
  Blockade, **1967**: 397, 409
  Communist aggression, **1968–69**: 339 [6]
  Defense, **1966**: 6 (p. 7)
  Mayor Willy Brandt, **1963–64**: 266 [8], 349
  New Year message to, **1963–64**: 87
  U.S. policy, **1968–69**: 474
  U.S. troops (1961), **1968–69**: 472
  Wall dividing city, **1963–64**: 349, 516 [18]; **1967**: 554 [4]; **1968–69**: 387
Bernhard, Berl I., **1965**: 548n.
Bernhardt, Sarah, **1967**: 388
Bernstein, Edward, **1965**: 365n.
Bernstein, Leonard, **1963–64**: 266 [4]
Berwind, Charles G., **1963–64**: 238n.
Beryl ore, **1968–69**: 47 (p. 144)
Betancourt, Rómulo, **1963–64**: 335; **1965**: 221, 429
Bethesda, Md., **1967**: 319
Bethesda (Md.) Naval Hospital, **1965**: 559n., 560n., 561n., 562n., 563n., 564n., 565n., 566n., 567n., 568n., 569n., 570n., 572; **1966**: 575, 610 [1]; **1968–69**: 632–640, 646
  Departure remarks, **1966**: 622
  Releases, **1966**: 619–620, 622
Bethlehem Steel Co., **1965**: 663; **1968–69**: 425 [1, 3, 5], 427
Bethune, Mrs. Mary McLeod, **1963–64**: 298
Better Business Bureau, National, **1968–69**: 56
Bhumibol Adulyadej, King (Thailand), **1968–69**: 232n., 233, 237

Bhutto, Zulfikar Ali (Foreign Secretary of Pakistan), **1965**: 649
Bible, Sen. Alan, **1963–64**: 575, 577, 652, 655; **1965**: 330, 486; **1966**: 522; **1967**: 399; **1968–69**: 510
Bible, gift, **1966**: 19
Bible, The Holy, **1967**: 356; **1968–69**: 117, 276
Bible, Year of the (1966), **1966**: 19
Bible Society, American, **1966**: 19
Bicentennial of American Independence, **1968–69**: 14 (p. 33)
Biddle, Mrs. Margaret Thompson, **1963–64**: 24
Biemiller, Andrew J., **1963–64**: 255; **1965**: 223; **1966**: 404n.; **1967**: 184; **1968–69**: 154
Big Bend National Park, Texas, **1966**: 202
Big Brother of the Year Award, **1966**: 213
  Acceptance, **1963–64**: 239
Big Brothers of America, **1965**: 438; **1966**: 213
Big Thicket, Texas, proposed wilderness area, **1968–69**: 702
Biggs, John, Jr., **1966**: 88 [11]
Bighorn Canyon National Recreation Area, Montana-Wyoming, **1965**: 54; **1966**: 82, 518, 522; **1967**: 20
Bihar, India, **1967**: 33
Bikle, Paul F., **1963–64**: 409
Bilingual education, **1968–69**: 4, 54, 68, 91, 437
Bill of Rights, **1965**: 27, 34, 48, 108, 397; **1966**: 96, 273, 299, 646; **1967**: 286
Bills approved.
  See Legislation, remarks or statements upon approval.
Bindzi, Benoit, **1967**: 444
Bing, Dr. Peter, **1967**: 500
Binger, Lawrence, **1966**: 404n.; **1967**: 184
Bingham, Barry, **1963–64**: 211 [6]; **1966**: 351
Bingham, Repr. Jonathan B., **1966**: 394–395, 510
Bingham, William S., **1967**: 532
Biomedical research, **1966**: 293; **1967**: 76, 77, 540
  Report, **1965**: 115
"Biomedical Science and Its Administration," report, **1965**: 115n.
Birch, Francis, **1968–69**: 71n.
Birch Islands Wilderness, Maine, **1968–69**: 168
Birch Society, **1963–64**: 462 [6], 656
Bird, Rear Adm. Horace V., **1967**: 126
Birendra, Crown Prince (Nepal), **1967**: 459n., 461n., 462
Birkenstock, James, **1966**: 637n.
Birmingham, Ala., **1963–64**: 642; **1965**: 135, 490
  Disarming of bombs in, **1965**: 161
  Mayor Albert Boutwell, **1965**: 161
Birth defects, **1967**: 214n.
Birthday, the President's, **1963–64**: 541n., 544n; **1965**: 458, 463 [1]; **1966**: 406, 417 [1, 2, 6, 10, 14]; **1968–69**: 460

Birthplace, the President's, **1965**: 2
Biscayne National Monument, Fla., establishment, **1968-69**: 547
Bismarck, Otto von, **1967**: 349
Bismuth stockpiles, **1966**: 218; **1967**: 506
Bista, Kirti Nidhi, **1967**: 462
Bitker, Bruno, **1968-69**: 42
Bittinger, Donald S., **1965**: 366
Bjergo, Allen Clifford, **1966**: 331n.
Bjerknes, Jacob Aall Bonnevie, **1966**: 652n.; **1967**: 37n.
Black, Eugene R., **1963-64**: 71 [9], 150 [7], 201 [2], 242 [9], 563 [5], 591; **1965**: 172, 176 [1, 3], 177, 199, 246, 294, 295 [3], 353 [1], 388 [2], 412 [2], 628, 637; **1966**: 14, 88 [1], 133, 493, 517, 577 [3, 6], 630 [14], 642 [1]; **1967**: 3 (p. 13), 44, 73, 401; **1968-69**: 237, 275 [6], 467 [4], 500
Black, Fred B., Jr., **1963-64**: 285 [16]
Black, Hugo, Jr., **1967**: 4n.
Black, Justice Hugo L., **1963-64**: 208; **1965**: 290, 383, 443; **1968-69**: 425 [11]
Black Madonna, **1966**: 200
Black power, **1966**: 338 [7]; **1967**: 328 [10]
Blackburn, William M., Jr., **1968-69**: 17
Blackie, William, **1965**: 4
Blackmon, Larry, **1966**: 338 [14]
Blackstone, Sir William, **1966**: 196
Blacutt Mendoza, Mario, **1968-69**: 66
Blaine, Wash., **1963-64**: 576
Blair, William McC., Jr., **1963-64**: 394, 626; **1966**: 550
Blair, Mrs. William McC., Jr., **1963-64**: 394
Blaisdell, Neal S., **1967**: 555
Blake, Rev. Eugene Carson, **1963-64**: 301
Blanch, Gertrude, **1963-64**: 204n.
Blanton, Repr. Ray, **1968-69**: 345
Blatnik, Repr. John A., **1963-64**: 433, 434; **1965**: 452
Blatt, Genevieve, **1963-64**: 289, 566, 661, 728, 742; **1965**: 422n.
Blaustein, Jacob, **1965**: 273
Blind, Inc., Recording for the, **1966**: 220n.; **1968-69**: 230n.
Blind persons, **1965**: 556; **1966**: 220, 277 [1], 327, 362; **1968-69**: 230, 446, 503, 548
Blind Youth and Adults, National Center for Deaf, **1967**: 77, 413
Blindness, **1967**: 77, 319, 413
Blindness, National Institute of Neurological Diseases and, **1968-69**: 446
Bliss, Ray, **1966**: 610 [13]
Blizzards, **1967**: 31n.; **1968-69**: 28
Blood donations, Government employees, **1965**: 525
Bloomington Dam, **1963-64**: 320
Bloomington, Ill., **1965**: 373n., 504n.

Blough, Roger M., **1963-64**: 246 [19], 290; **1965**: 76
Blue baby surgical procedure, **1966**: 49n.
Blue Bonnet Cooperative, **1965**: 230
Blumenthal, W. Michael, **1967**: 545
B'nai B'rith, **1966**: 273, 395
B'nai B'rith, Anti-Defamation League of, **1965**: 44
B'nai B'rith 125 anniversary, **1968-69**: 474
Board of Education, Washington, D.C., **1966**: 27
Boating safety, **1968-69**: 56
Boca Raton, Fla., campaign remarks, **1963-64**: 709
Bodine, Leo V., **1968-69**: 548
Boe, Gov. Nils A., **1966**: 494 [1, 2]
Boeing Aircraft Co., **1967**: 197, 388
Boeing Co., **1965**: 339
Boggs, Repr. Hale, **1963-64**: 14, 15, 542n., 646, 648; **1965**: 112, 124, 133, 183, 330, 361, 372n., 394, 568n.; **1966**: 221, 599 [6], 628 [11], 630 [5]; **1967**: 6 [17], 216, 533; **1968-69**: 233, 293, 655
Boggs, Mrs. Hale (Lindy), **1963-64**: 648; **1965**: 372
Boggs, Sen. J. Caleb, **1965**: 568n.; **1966**: 22; **1967**: 405
Boggs, Thomas Hale, Jr., **1963-64**: 648
Bogotá, Act of, **1963-64**: 45; **1965**: 429; **1966**: 62, 125, 175, 177, 386; **1967**: 110; **1968-69**: 205
Bohen, Frederick M., **1968-69**: 17
Bohlen, Charles E., **1963-64**: 211 [19], 218 [24]; **1966**: 134, 485n.
Bohr, Niels, **1963-64**: 394; **1968-69**: 608
Boise, Idaho
  Campaign remarks, **1963-64**: 659
  Mayor Eugene Shellworth, **1963-64**: 660n.
Boise, Tom, **1963-64**: 659
Boland, Repr. Edward P., **1963-64**: 727
Bolívar, Simón, **1963-64**: 340, 438n.; **1965**: 221, 286, 429; **1967**: 110, 176; **1968-69**: 205
Bolivia, **1967**: 453; **1968-69**: 205
  Ambassador Tomas Guillermo Elio, **1968-69**: 362n.
  Ambassador Julio Sanjines-Goytia, **1965**: 473n.
  Assistance, **1963-64**: 340
  Economic and social development, **1968-69**: 362
  Paz Estenssoro, Victor, **1963-64**: 52
  Peace Corps projects in, **1965**: 83
  Rene Barrientos Ortuno, **1966**: 338 [16]; **1968-69**: 362
  U.S. assistance, **1968-69**: 21
  U.S. officials held captive in, **1963-64**: 52, 60
Bolling, Mrs. Barbara, **1963-64**: 208
Bolling, Repr. Richard, **1963-64**: 189

Bolling Air Force Base, Washington, D.C., **1966**: 452

Bolte, Sir Henry E. and Lady, **1966**: 543

Bolton, Repr. Frances P., **1967**: 475

Bolton, Repr. Oliver P., **1963–64**: 323

Bombers.

See Aircraft, military.

Bombs.

See also Missiles; Nuclear weapons; Nuclear weapons tests; Weapons.

Atomic, **1963–64**: 297 [2]

Walleye, **1963–64**: 170 [3]

Bond, Charles, **1968–69**: 419

Bond, Gen. Charles R., Jr., **1968–69**: 12

Bonds, **1966**: 141 [3, 5], 382, 472; **1967**: 315, 460 [12]

See also Savings bonds.

Bonds, Interdepartmental Committee for Savings, **1966**: 137

Bonin Islands, **1965**: 15; **1967**: 491, 492

Return to Japanese administration, **1968–69**: 340

Bonn, West Germany, **1967**: 190n., 191, 347

Trilateral meeting, **1966**: 506

Bonnelly, Rafael F., **1966**: 277 [3]

Bonner, Repr. Herbert C., **1963–64**: 327, 328

Bonus army, **1963–64**: 250

Book, commemorative, gift to the President, **1968–69**: 644n.

Boone, Daniel, **1963–64**: 644

Booth, John Wilkes, **1967**: 49

Borah, William E., **1965**: 319 [14]; **1966**: 516 [9]

Borch, Fred, **1967**: 168n.

Border Development and Friendship, United States-Mexico Commission for, **1967**: 451; **1968–69**: 223 [2], 354, 623, 624n.

Borg, Andy, **1968–69**: 599n.

Bork, Bill, **1963–64**: 741

Bor-Komorowski, Gen. Tadeusz, **1963–64**: 491

Borman, Frank, **1965**: 636, 656; **1968–69**: 616n., 637n., 647, 652, 662

Borman, Mrs. Frank, **1968–69**: 645n.

Bosch, Juan, **1965**: 212n., 221, 227, 295 [16]; **1966**: 277 [3, 25]

Bosley, Pfc. Charles William, **1966**: 350

Boston, Everett D., **1966**: 289

Boston, Raymond, **1968–69**: 419

Boston, Mass., **1965**: 2

Campaign remarks, **1963–64**: 727

Mayor John F. Collins, **1963–64**: 727

Boston College alumni, **1967**: 206n.

Boston Red Sox, **1967**: 429

Boston Symphony Orchestra, **1968–69**: 102n.

Botulism, **1968–69**: 56

Boulder Canyon Project Act, **1965**: 586

Boundary and Water Commission, United States and Mexico, International, **1966**: 177,

Boundary and Water Commission – *continued* 467–468; **1967**: 47, 303, 408 [2, 8], 451, 454n.; **1968–69**: 623

Bourguiba, Habib (President of Tunisia), **1968–69**: 249, 250, 255

Boutin, Bernard L., **1963–64**: 171n., 411, 481n.; **1965**: 243, 415; **1966**: 231, 397, 613, 637; **1967**: 325n., 412; **1968–69**: 36

Boutin, Mrs. Bernard L., **1966**: 231

Boutwell, Albert, **1965**: 161

Bow, Repr. Frank T., **1965**: 190; **1967**: 85n.; **1968–69**: 677

Bowdler, Bill, **1968–69**: 362n.

Bowen, Mrs. Catherine Drinker, **1963–64**: 303

Bowen, Howard R., **1963–64**: 525n.

Bowers, Dr. Raymond, **1967**: 416n.

Bowes, Wayne, **1963–64**: 578n.

Bowie, Robert B., **1966**: 320 [3]

Bowles, Chester, **1965**: 273; **1967**: 33; **1968–69**: 1ftn. (p. 4)

Bowman, Barbara Ann, **1966**: 220

Boy Scouts of America, **1966**: 295n., 472

55th anniversary, **1965**: 55

Jamboree, Valley Forge, Pa., **1963–64**: 473

"Report to the Nation," **1966**: 57; **1967**: 41

Boyd, Alan S., **1965**: 208 [6], 290; **1966**: 580 [5], 607 [8]

See also Transportation, Secretary of.

Boyd, Mrs. Alan S., **1966**: 580 [5, 14]; **1967**: 5

Boyd, Forrest, **1966**: 338 [10]; **1967**: 278n.

Boyls, Fannie M., **1966**: 89

Boys, National Training School for, **1967**: 15

Boys' Clubs of America, **1966**: 295n.

Boys Nation, **1967**: 323

Bozeman, Judge Howard, **1963–64**: 325

Brademas, Repr. John, **1963–64**: 67, 211 [1], 288; **1965**: 188, 368, 369, 449

Bradford, R. D., **1968–69**: 106n.

Bradley, Michael J., **1963–64**: 742

Bradley, Gen. Omar N., **1963–64**: 244, 359, 384, 563 [5], 591, 688 [3], 696; **1965**: 399; **1966**: 141 [11], 165; **1968–69**: 353, 384

Bradley Field, Conn., **1967**: 222, 223

Brady, Nyle C., **1968–69**: 513n.

Brain, George B., **1966**: 77

Braman, J. D., **1963–64**: 577

Branch, Gen. Irving L., **1963–64**: 409

Brandeis, Louis D., **1965**: 44; **1967**: 3 (p. 6), 35, 105; **1968–69**: 270, 467 [2]

Branding iron, gift to the President, **1968–69**: 537n.

Brandt, Raymond P., **1966**: 65 [6]

Brandt, Willy, **1963–64**: 266 [8], 349; **1967**: 347, 348, 349, 351

Branigin, Roger D., **1963–64**: 639, 729; **1965**: 188; **1966**: 228, 346–348, 350, 353, 491n., 492 [1]

Branigin, Mrs. Roger D., **1966**: 346, 350
Branscomb, Lewis M., **1965**: 166n.; **1968-69**: 513n.
Brasco, Frank J., **1966**: 510; **1967**: 391
Bray, Repr. William G., **1965**: 188; **1966**: 350
Brazil, **1963-64**: 243, 688 [8], 726, 749; **1965**: 429, 600; **1966**: 11n., 41; **1967**: 17, 44; **1968-69**: 205
   AID programs, **1968-69**: 63, 679
   Ambassador Vasco Laitao da Cunha, **1966**: 455
   Araujo Castro, João de (Foreign Minister), **1963-64**: 66
   Assistance, **1963-64**: 340
   Castelo Branco, Humberto, **1963-64**: 561
   Constitutional government, **1963-64**: 246 [4], 256 [17]
   Debt payments, **1963-64**: 66
   Expropriation of foreign-owned properties, **1963-64**: 246 [3]
   Goulart, João, **1963-64**: 66
   Mazzilli, Ranieri, **1964-65**: 243, 256ftn. (p. 458)
   President-elect Arthur da Costa e Silva, **1967**: 17
   Support of United Nations, **1963-64**: 561
   U. S. Ambassador Lincoln Gordon, **1963-64**: 561n.; **1966**: 13
   U. S. relations with, **1963-64**: 246 [1], 560 [7], 561
Breakfast programs, school, **1966**: 508
Breathitt, Gov. Edward T., Jr., **1963-64**: 41, 217, 291, 292, 643, 644, 678, 729; **1965**: 80; **1966**: 122 [1], 228, 348
Breathitt, Mrs. Edward T., Jr., **1966**: 348
Breit, Gregory, **1968-69**: 71n.
Breitel, Judge Charles D., **1965**: 422n.
Brennan, Justice and Mrs. William J., Jr., **1968-69**: 148
Bress, David G., **1965**: 448 [7]
Bretton Woods, N. H.
   Agreements Act of 1945, **1965**: 110, 541
   Monetary Conference (1944), **1967**: 373; **1968-69**: 218, 317, 500, 582
Brevard Music Center, N. C., **1966**: 406n.
Brewster, Sen. Daniel B., **1963-64**: 316 [15], 320, 321, 612, 703; **1965**: 172; **1966**: 189, 499; **1967**: 193, 286
Brewster, Kingman, Jr., **1965**: 422n.; **1966**: 315n.
Brezhnev, Leonid, **1963-64**: 82; **1966**: 516 [7], 577 [6]
   Visit to U. S., question of, **1965**: 46 [4]
Bridge of the Americas, **1967**: 454
Bridge safety, **1967**: 558
Bridgeport, Conn., Troubadors Drum and Bugle Corps, **1966**: 178
Bridwell, Lowell K., **1967**: 6ftn. (p. 17)
Bright, Arthur, **1963-64**: 645, 701

Briley, Beverly, **1967**: 115n.; **1968-69**: 345
Brimmer, Andrew F., **1965**: 453; **1966**: 88 [2], 115, 136n., 248n.; **1967**: 81; **1968-69**: 631
Bringle, Vice Adm. William F., **1967**: 567
Brink, Frank, Jr., **1963-64**: 98n.
Brinkley, David, **1963-64**: 218
Brinkley, Repr. Jack, **1967**: 485 [1]
Brinkmeier, Robert E., **1963-64**: 747
Brisbane, Australia, **1966**: 546
British Columbia, **1963-64**: 134, 135
British Museum, **1967**: 423
British Overseas Airways Corporation, **1966**: 64
Broadcasters, National Association of, **1968-69**: 172
Broadcasters, National Association of Educational, **1967**: 474
Broadcasting, Corporation for Public, **1967**: 77, 474; **1968-69**: 370
Broadcasts.
   See Interviews of the President; Messages to the American people.
Broderick, Mrs. Faye, **1963-64**: 606
Brodie, Bernard B., **1968-69**: 695n.
Brodman, Estelle, **1966**: 424n.
Bronk, Detlev W., **1963-64**: 568; **1968-69**: 695n.
Brontë, Charlotte, **1965**: 616
Bronze Star, **1967**: 475
Brook, William, **1963-64**: 54ftn. (p. 68)
Brooke, Sen. Edward W., **1967**: 81, 326
Brooke Hospital, San Antonio, Texas, **1966**: 580 [2, 17]
Brookings Institution, **1963-64**: 622ftn. (p. 1206); **1966**: 493; **1968-69**: 38
Brooklyn, N. Y., **1966**: 511
   Campaign remarks, **1963-64**: 668
Brooks, Repr. Jack, **1963-64**: 481, 599, 760; **1965**: 236; **1966**: 296; **1968-69**: 108, 109, 267
Brooks, Mrs. Jack (Charlotte), **1965**: 236; **1968-69**: 109
Brooks, Mrs. Opal Way, **1966**: 165
Brosio, Manlio (Secretary General, North Atlantic Treaty Organization), **1963-64**: 587 [2], 608, 609, 610, 612; **1966**: 506; **1967**: 521
   Letters, **1963-64**: 495, 685
Brotherhood of Electrical Workers, International, **1965**: 298
Brotherhood of Locomotive Engineers, **1963-64**: 252, 284
Brotherhood of Railroad Trainmen, **1968-69**: 626
Brotherhood Week, **1966**: 81
   Memorandum, **1963-64**: 113
Brown, Repr. Clarence J., death of, **1965**: 441

Brown, D. Mahlon, **1963–64**: 652n.

Brown, Edgar A., **1963–64**: 719

Brown, Gov. Edmund G. (Pat), **1963–64**: 163n., 192, 194, 409, 410, 411, 413, 414, 415, 579, 580n., 767; **1965**: 291n., 331, 426, 453, 477; **1966**: 56, 236ftn. (p. 537), 338 [15]; **1968–69**: 3

See also California, Gov. Edmund G. (Pat) Brown.

Campaign remarks on, **1963–64**: 650, 651, 733, 734, 735, 736

News conference remarks on, **1963–64**: 294 [9, 12], 462 [6, 7], 521 [5]

Brown, Mrs. Edmund G., **1963–64**: 194, 579, 736, 767

Brown, Elizabeth Ann, **1967**: 93n.

Brown, F. Stewart, **1965**: 641 [1]; **1966**: 198n.

Brown, George, **1966**: 520, 607 [3], 654ftn. (p. 1458); **1967**: 278, 404

Brown, Mrs. George, **1963–64**: 211 [7]

Brown, Harold (Secretary of the Air Force), **1966**: 20; **1967**: 9, 106; **1968–69**: 48, 110, 556, 610, 669, 688

Brown, Hugh B., **1963–64**: 737

Brown, Hy, **1963–64**: 751

Brown, Judge John R., **1965**: 341

Brown, John Young, **1966**: 351

Brown, Kathleen, **1963–64**: 579

Brown, Marshall, **1963–64**: 648

Brown, Ray, **1965**: 594n.

Brown, Mrs. Virginia Mae, **1963–64**: 208, 360

Brown, Winthrop G., **1966**: 566; **1967**: 223 [8, 12]

Brown University, **1963–64**: 601; **1968–69**: 212

Brown v. Board of Education of Topeka, Kans., **1966**: 235ftn. (p. 528), 501 [13]; **1967**: 55; **1968–69**: 78

Brownell, Herbert, Jr., **1967**: 68

Browning, Gordon, **1963–64**: 645; **1968–69**: 345

Browning, Robert, **1968–69**: 65

Brownstein, Philip N., **1965**: 566; **1966**: 12; **1968–69**: 114

Bruce, David K. E., **1963–64**: 796; **1965**: 46 [6]; **1966**: 236 [5]

Bruce, Mrs. Mellon, **1967**: 470

Bruce, Preston, **1968–69**: 631

Bruff, John, **1966**: 431

Bruhn, William G. (Bill), **1963–64**: 737

Bruno, Louis, **1966**: 210n.

Brunt, A. William, **1966**: 411

Brussels NATO conference, **1966**: 273

Bryan, William Jennings, **1965**: 397

Bryant, Farris, **1963–64**: 12, 198, 199, 567, 571, 709, 710n., 712, 713, 719; **1966**: 121 [7], 124 [6], 145, 187, 228, 252, 273, 408n., 416, 509, 584, 606, 607 [1], 635 [2], 636n., 650 [15]; **1968–69**: 102, 483n., 539

Bryant, Farris – *continued*

See also Emergency Planning, Office of, Director.

Bryant, Mrs. Farris, **1966**: 145

Bryant, William Benson, **1967**: 81

Bryant, William S., **1966**: 427

Bryce, James, **1963–64**: 513

Bubel, Neil F., **1963–64**: 666

Buchanan, James, **1967**: 115

Buchanan School, D. C., **1968–69**: 648

Buck, Raymond E., **1968–69**: 281

Buckley, Repr. Charles A., **1963–64**: 39n.

Buckley, James P., **1963–64**: 746

Buckner, Walker G., **1965**: 643

Budapest Industrial Fair, **1966**: 272

Buddha, **1967**: 459

Budget, **1963–64**: 295, 299, 328, 338, 431, 598, 724, 775, 776, 787; **1965**: 2, 35 (p. 106), 362, 403; **1966**: 11, 240, 492 [1]; **1967**: 16 (p. 89), 225 [3, 14], 330, 375 [16]; **1968–69**: 170, 223 [11], 467 [3], 684 (p. 1317, 1318)

Administrative, **1966**: 26 (pp. 49, 50, 52, 55), 635 [6, 17]; **1967**: 13 (pp. 41, 43, 45, 46, 59), 358 [12]; **1968–69**: 39 (p. 84)

Appropriations, **1967**: 417, 495 [9]

Cash budget, **1967**: 13 (pp. 41, 45, 59)

Cutbacks, **1966**: 630 [2, 4, 18], 631; **1967**: 6 [2, 6, 7, 9, 12], 358 [12], 417 [10, 13], 460 [12], 556; **1968–69**: 14 (p. 32), 38, 39 (pp. 83, 86, 90, 92), 54, 142, 170, 226, 343, 654, 678 (pp. 1278, 1282)

Deficits, **1966**: 6 (p. 4), 26 (pp. 49–50), 320 [8], 477 [3], 654 [14]; **1967**: 6 [13], 13 (pp. 41, 43, 45, 56), 312 [4], 329, 330 [1], 343, 358 [12], 362, 374, 420, 495 [9], 503, 518 [9], 524; **1968–69**: 1 [14], 14 (p. 32), 39 (pp. 84, 85, 87, 96, 108), 47 (pp. 127, 131), 170, 241, 632, 677, 678 (pp. 1274, 1288), 684 (pp. 1313–1315)

District of Columbia, **1965**: 29, 40, 151; **1966**: 27, 586; **1967**: 15, 71; **1968–69**: 95, 689

Effect on economy, **1963–64**: 723

Expenditure account, **1968–69**: 39 (p. 84), 678 (p. 1274)

Fiscal 1955, **1963–64**: 780 [4]

Fiscal 1959, **1966**: 121 [10]

Fiscal 1963, **1966**: 477 [3]

Fiscal 1964, **1963–64**: 124 (p. 159), 132 (p. 176), 211 [28], 227, 271 [3, 7], 379 [3], 462 [2], 604, 619 [12], 640; **1965**: 326; **1966**: 121 [10], 181

Fiscal 1965, **1963–64**: 17, 37, 68, 91 (pp. 112, 113), 96, 120, 124 (p. 159), 139, 178, 179, 182, 216, 218 [15], 219, 222, 227, 229, 307, 316ftn. (p. 616), 327, 347,

Budget – *continued*
  Fiscal 1965 – *continued*
        348, 486 [7], 597, 603, 604, 606, 607,
        630, 631, 640, 643, 654, 655, 659, 661,
        679, 723, 749, 750, 775, 778; **1965**: 18,
        32 (pp. 84, 97), 208 [4], 227, 255, 326;
        1966: 11, 121 [10], 477 [3]
    Message to Congress, **1963-64**: 132
    News conference remarks, **1963-64**: 28 [5,
        10], 54 [6, 9], 71 [10, 11], 150 [3],
        211 [9, 28], 266 [2], 271 [3, 7], 294
        [2, 18], 336 [4], 379 [3], 455 [1],
        619 [1, 2, 12], 688 [6]
    Signing of, **1963-64**: 121
  Fiscal 1966, **1963-64**: 307, 780 [4, 21]; **1965**:
        5, 9, 10, 18, 22 [6], 35 (p. 108), 43, 47,
        54, 60, 75, 83, 90, 92, 100, 131, 143,
        225, 249, 255, 319 [6], 321, 381n.,
        512; **1966**: 124 [15], 158 [10], 181,
        185, 197, 235, 236 [8, 10], 238, 321,
        324, 337, 444, 477 [3], 654 [9]
    Message to Congress, **1965**: 32
  Fiscal 1967, **1963-64**: 170 [2]; **1965**: 249,
        506, 512; **1966**: 6 (p. 4), 17, 34 (p.
        101), 44, 83, 95, 100-101, 108, 112,
        116, 121 [10], 122 [2], 130, 140, 141
        [5], 155, 159, 181, 185, 193, 197, 199,
        234, 247 [4], 277 [18], 296, 321, 333,
        334 [1, 6, 10, 12], 371, 444, 445 [1],
        474 [8], 477 [3], 494 [1, 3, 9, 13],
        628 [1, 3], 654 [9]; **1967**: 3 (p. 8), 6
        [3], 23, 27, 120, 140, 211, 217
    Message to Congress, **1966**: 25-27
  Fiscal 1968, **1965**: 447; **1966**: 197, 370, 373
        [15], 441, 521, 578 [2, 3, 10], 603, 628
        [6, 8]; **1967**: 3 (p. 8), 13, 16 (p. 77),
        77, 85, 98, 114, 121, 163, 329, 410,
        411 [10], 417 [1], 518 [6, 9], 546;
        1968-69: 39 (p. 84), 632, 684 (p.
        1315)
    Message to Congress, **1967**: 13, 329
  Fiscal 1969, **1967**: 518 [4, 6], 546; **1968-69**:
        1 [14], 14 (p. 32), 38-40, 226, 252,
        275 [4], 283 [8], 320n., 344, 676
        (p. 1267), 678 (p. 1282)
    Message to Congress, **1968-69**: 39
  Fiscal 1970, **1968-69**: 654, 658, 659, 676 (pp.
        1266, 1267), 677, 678 (pp. 1279-1282)
    Message to Congress, **1968-69**: 678
    Signing, **1968-69**: 677
  Impact on national economy, **1968-69**: 241,
        678 (pp. 1274, 1276), 684 (pp. 1312,
        1313)
  National income, **1966**: 635 [6, 17]
  National income accounts, **1967**: 13 (pp. 41,
        45, 59), 16 (pp. 76, 77), 339 [1]; **1968-
        69**: 47 (p. 131)
  News conference, **1967**: 6

Budget – *continued*
    Reform, **1968-69**: 14 (p. 32), 39 (p. 108)
    Salary reform, provision for, **1968-69**: 694
    Surplus, **1968-69**: 632, 646 [3], 654, 676 (p.
        1267), 677, 678 (pp. 1273, 1274), 684
        (p. 1313)
  Budget, Bureau of the, **1963-64**: 121, 150 [3],
        534, 583; **1965**: 32 (p. 97), 46 [8], 49,
        93, 127, 138n., 244, 319 [3, 6], 321,
        362, 497, 508, 512, 618; **1966**: 27, 88
        [6], 113-114, 225, 296, 376n., 580
        [18], 607 [1]; **1967**: 223 [7], 225
        [22], 315n., 346; **1968-69**: 38, 39 (p.
        109), 100, 654
  Budget, Bureau of the, Director (Kermit Gordon),
        1963-64: 18, 69, 100, 121n., 240, 286,
        466, 588n., 659, 714, 775, 790; **1965**:
        32 (p. 98), 46 [8], 47, 49, 54, 66, 93,
        127, 129, 183, 264n.
    Memorandums to, **1963-64**: 62, 261
    News conference remarks on, **1963-64**: 336
        [4], 462 [2], 486 [4], 563 [10], 619
        [1, 12], 780 [4, 5, 24], 818 [4]
  Budget, Bureau of the, Director (Charles L.
        Schultze), **1965**: 249, 290, 297, 319
        [6, 8], 324, 332, 347 [8], 362, 404, 418,
        447, 506, 512, 560; **1966**: 18n., 25, 28,
        67, 82, 104, 108, 114, 129-131, 143,
        170, 181-182, 224, 234, 239, 244, 273,
        294, 296, 370, 374, 379n., 404n., 470,
        592, 603, 606, 620, 631, 650ftn. (p.
        1450); **1967**: 14n., 77, 85, 88, 92, 103,
        114, 121, 124, 157, 163, 184, 232, 294,
        295, 329, 330 [4], 343, 358 [12], 379,
        417 [1], 420, 458, 518 [9], 554 [13];
        1968-69: 1 [16], 2n., 15, 36
    Memorandum, **1966**: 425; **1967**: 89, 186
    News conference remarks on, **1966**: 121 [10],
        158 [4], 236 [8], 277 [18], 373 [15],
        417 [5], 477 [2], 492 [1, 10], 494
        [1, 13], 578 [1], 580 [7], 628 [1],
        630 [2], 635 [18]; **1967**: 6
  Budget, Bureau of the, Director (Charles J.
        Zwick), **1968-69**: 38, 54, 75, 89, 90,
        153 [16], 169 [1], 283 [10], 303,
        344, 391, 467 [3], 480n., 581, 587,
        590 [4], 677
  Budget, Commission on the Federal, **1967**: 85
  Budget and Accounting Procedures Act of 1950,
        1966: 239
  Budget Concepts, President's Commission on,
        1968-69: 39 (pp. 84, 96, 107, 108),
        678 (p. 1274)
  Budget Messages, **1967**: 13, 329
    Comments, **1967**: 121, 330
  Budgeting system
    Government-wide planning and, **1965**: 447, 448
        [3]

Budgeting system – *continued*
  Planning-Programming, **1966**: 129, 620; **1967**:
    121; **1968–69**: 39 (p. 108), 678 (pp.
    1303, 1304)
Buehler, Arthur W., **1963–64**: 586
Buenos Aires, Argentina, **1965**: 593; **1966**: 175;
    1968–69: 205n.
Buenos Aires, Inter-American conference, **1967**:
    70 [4]
Buffalo, N. Y., **1966**: 391n., 392
  Campaign remarks, **1963–64**: 667
  Mayor Chester Kowal, **1963–64**: 667
  Mayor Frank A. Sedita, **1966**: 392
Buford, Anthony, **1963–64**: 695
Bui Vien, **1967**: 130
Building codes, **1965**: 90
Building and Construction Trades Department,
    AFL-CIO, **1965**: 223; **1967**: 261; **1968–
    69**: 154
Building materials, exports, **1968–69**: 434
Buildings and Monuments, Advisory Board on
    National Parks, Historic Sites, **1965**:
    538n.
Bulgaria, **1968–69**: 204
Bullitt, John C., **1963–64**: 69
Bunche, Ralph J., **1963–64**: 27; **1965**: 273;
    1967: 81
Bundy, McGeorge, **1963–64**: 175, 504 [4], 513,
    539, 709, 747, 780 [5, 6], 818 [4];
    1965: 22 [1], 46 [7, 11], 172n., 221,
    260, 295 [4, 16], 319 [16, 21], 347
    [2, 6], 370n., 421 [2], 454 [2], 641
    [2]; **1966**: 52 [2], 56, 85, 88 [15,
    16], 158 [6], 404n.; **1967**: 184, 255,
    375 [17]; **1968–69**: 18 [2], 215
Bundy, William P., **1963–64**: 69, 201 [1, 18],
    272, 274; **1966**: 397, 566, 577 [3, 6],
    607 [12], 610 [8]; **1967**: 219, 352,
    562; **1968–69**: 188, 398n., 425 [4]
Bunker, Ellsworth, **1963–64**: 27, 54ftn. (p. 70),
    486 [3]; **1965**: 221, 227, 347 [3], 353
    [2], 364, 448 [18], 472, 473, 482, 632;
    1966: 277 [2, 4, 25], 501 [1], 516 [3],
    607 [1]; **1967**: 126–128, 130n., 131,
    134, 166, 352, 461, 490, 493, 503, 526,
    567; **1968–69**: 51 [1], 109, 185, 187–
    189, 197, 398n., 401
  News conference remarks, **1967**: 132 [1, 4, 7,
    13], 225 [2], 309 [1], 358 [2], 460
    [11], 495 [6, 13, 14]
Bunn, V. Rev. Edward B., **1963–64**: 788
Bunshaft, Gordon, **1968–69**: 660
Buntin, Mrs. Horatio B., **1967**: 115
Bunting, John, **1963–64**: 437n.
Bunting, Mrs. Mary Ingraham, **1963–64**: 242
    [3], 289, 298, 437; **1965**: 91; **1966**:
    208n., 277 [5]; **1967**: 500
Burch, Dean (Chairman, Republican National
    Committee), **1963–64**: 508

Burdick, Sen. Quentin N., **1968–69**: 457, 477
Burdon, George, **1963–64**: 590
Burial, veterans, **1968–69**: 40
Burke, Edmund, **1966**: 228, 420, 493
Burke, Repr. James A., **1963–64**: 727; **1968–69**:
    275 [4]
Burke, Walter F., **1966**: 625n.
Burkhardt, Robert J., **1966**: 504
Burkley, George G., **1963–64**: 619 [11]; **1965**:
    46 [9], 549; **1966**: 575, 580 [18], 599
    [4]; **1968–69**: 668
Burlingame, Anson, **1967**: 213
Burlington, Vt., **1966**: 398
  Campaign remarks, **1963–64**: 605
  Mayor Francis J. Cain, **1966**: 398
Burma, **1966**: 446, 450; **1967**: 409
  Chairman of the Revolutionary Council,
    General Ne Win, **1966**: 443, 446, 450,
    514
Burnham, Donald C., **1966**: 184n.; **1968–69**: 3,
    471n.
Burnham, Linden F. (Prime Minister of Guyana),
    1966: 341–342
Burns, Haydon, **1963–64**: 571, 712, 713; **1965**:
    248; **1966**: 494 [1]
Burns, Hugh M., **1963–64**: 415, 579
Burns, James MacGregor, **1963–64**: 303; **1968–
    69**: 262
Burns, Gov. John A., **1963–64**: 336 [6]; **1966**:
    121 [1], 326, 459n., 484, 532–533;
    1967: 555; **1968–69**: 197–199, 398n.
Burns, Mrs. John A., **1966**: 532–533
Burns, John J., **1967**: 251
Burr, Aaron, **1968–69**: 109
Burro Club, **1968–69**: 212
Burroughs, John, **1963–64**: 767; **1968–69**: 167
Burt, William E., **1966**: 436–437
Burton, Clarence G., hospital act.
  See Hospital Survey and Construction Amend-
    ments of 1949.
Burton, Harold H., **1963–64**: 693n.; **1966**: 395
Burton, Repr. Phillip, **1963–64**: 651
Burton, Robert, **1968–69**: 595
Bus fares, **1966**: 403
Busby, Horace, Jr., **1963–64**: 246 [13], 613n.;
    1965: 22 [1], 250, 319 [21, 22], 412;
    1967: 87n.; **1968–69**: 171
Busch, Col. August A., Jr., **1963–64**: 188, 189
Bush, John W. (Chairman, Interstate Commerce
    Commission), **1966**: 240, 322, 434, 436–
    437
Bush, Vannevar, **1963–64**: 98; **1965**: 250, 522
Business, National Federation of Independent,
    1965: 438
Business, U.S., **1963–64**: 124 (pp. 157, 160, 161),
    295, 299, 415, 555, 679, 708, 712, 722,
    724; **1965**: 2, 23, 25, 371; **1966**: 26
    (p. 49), 34 (pp. 97, 99, 102), 125, 155,
    158 [4, 9], 199, 347, 444; **1967**: 121,
    524, 554 [13]; **1968–69**: 241
  See also Corporations; Industry; Small business.

Business − *continued*
  Adverse effect of foreign imports, protection
      from, **1968-69**: 47 (p. 137)
  Antipoverty program participation, **1963-64**:
      297 [1], 314, 336 [20]
  Balance of payments responsibilities, **1965**: 338
  Civil rights responsibilities, **1963-64**: 139, 250,
      314, 342, 350
  Community development, **1966**: 30; **1967**: 114
  Cooperation.
      See Government cooperation with business,
          education, and labor.
  Cooperation with colleges, Government, etc.,
      1963-64: 124 (p. 163), 139, 295, 708,
      742, 787
      See also Government cooperation with business,
          education, and labor.
  Corporate.
      See Corporations.
  Cultural exchange participation, **1965**: 553
  Depreciation allowances, **1966**: 26 (p. 52), 596;
      1967: 329
  Economic responsibilities, **1963-64**: 266 [2],
      294 [23], 506; **1965**: 35 (pp. 106, 111);
      1966: 34 (pp. 104, 109), 115, 347, 399,
      431, 453, 477 [2]
  Employment responsibilities, **1963-64**: 448;
      1965: 153, 207, 268, 384, 438
  Equal employment opportunity agreements,
      1963-64: 40, 111, 139, 250, 342, 448
  Executives
      Foreign policy conference, **1967**: 519
      Overseas consultations, **1968-69**: 63
  Expansion, **1963-64**: 23, 605; **1968**: 35 (p.
      106)
  Exports, **1965**: 465
  Federal aid, **1968-69**: 39 (p. 102)
  Foreign aid participation, **1963-64**: 227, 402,
      617; **1965**: 18, 154
  Foreign investments, **1963-64**: 169, 296
  Foreign operations, balance-of-payments coop-
      eration, **1968-69**: 14 (p. 33), 684 (p.
      1319), 696 [15]
  Free enterprise system, **1966**: 98, 187, 396,
      403, 444, 451, 473, 483
  Indiana leaders, remarks to, **1966**: 347
  Insurance for inner city, **1968-69**: 278
  Inventories, **1967**: 16 (p. 78)
  Investments, **1963-64**: 124 (p. 160), 285 [9];
      1965: 60, 132, 149, 255, 319 [8]
      See also Investments.
  Job training.
      See Occupational training.
  Loans, **1966**: 26 (pp. 55, 63, 66), 141 [3, 5],
      155, 199, 445 [5]; **1967**: 427
  Meetings with leaders, **1966**: 158 [3]
  Minimum wage impact, **1966**: 479

Business − *continued*
  News conference remarks, **1963-64**: 211 [3],
      246 [12], 266 [2], 271 [15], 285 [9],
      294 [23], 336 [20], 379 [5], 619 [4]
  Reports to the Government, **1963-64**: 583
  Small, **1966**: 26 (p. 63), 30, 231, 582;
      1967: 427, 504; **1968-69**: 39 (p. 87),
      227
  Tax benefits, **1963-64**: 197, 227, 246 [12],
      379 [5]; **1965**: 326
  Tax increases, reactions, **1967**: 330 [7]
  Taxes, **1966**: 121 [3], 444, 445 [21], 596,
      631, 642 [6], 654 [6]
  Technical services to, **1966**: 26 (p. 60); **1967**:
      13 (pp. 51, 57)
  Vietnam conflict impact, **1966**: 34 (p. 97)
  Youth Opportunity Campaign participation,
      1965: 298
Business Advisers, Committee on, **1963-64**: 271
      [15]
Business Committee for Tax Reduction, **1963-64**:
      93, 299
Business Council, **1963-64**: 23, 250, 336ftn. (p.
      660), 787; **1965**: 632; **1966**: 158 [3];
      1967: 524; **1968-69**: 25, 241, 612
Business Group for Latin America, **1963-64**:
      169, 688 [8]
Business International roundtable, Moscow, **1965**:
      4
Business and Labor, Department of, proposed,
      1967: 3 (p. 4), 11, 13 (p. 57), 16 (p. 86),
      121, 148
Business Week magazine, **1965**: 463 [9]
Businessmen, National Alliance of, **1968-69**: 24,
      25, 37, 74, 92, 100, 105, 115, 141, 220,
      227, 328, 506, 678 (p. 1294), 684
      (p. 1324)
Businessmen, remarks to, **1963-64**: 506, 531,
      604, 630; **1965**: 4, 77
Butler, Lady, **1963-64**: 184, 187
Butler, Melissa Ann, **1963-64**: 631
Butler, Richard A., **1963-64**: 184, 186, 187n.
Butte, Mont., **1963-64**: 99
  Campaign remarks, **1963-64**: 656
Button import tariffs, **1966**: 601
Byrd, Sen. Harry Flood, **1963-64**: 148, 197, 295,
      358, 359, 643, 775; **1965**: 113, 133,
      176 [2], 251, 321; **1968-69**: 257
  Letter, **1963-64**: 92
  News conference remarks on, **1963-64**: 28 [9],
      54 [9], 143 [2], 150 [3], 271 [3], 294
      [4], 316 [4], 462 [2], 563 [10]
Byrd, Sen. Robert C., **1963-64**: 360, 586; **1965**:
      151; **1966**: 426-427; **1967**: 216, 405;
      1968-69: 566, 567
Byrne, Garrett, **1965**: 422n.
Byrne, Repr. James A., **1963-64**: 742; **1967**: 291,
      330 [1, 4], 495 [9], 518 [5]

Byrne, Joseph A., **1968-69**: 670
Byrnes, Repr. John W., **1963-64**: 619 [16]; **1965**:
    113; **1966**: 88 [22], 132, 157, 199;
    1968-69: 658
Byron, M. Sgt. Marvin M., **1965**: 161n.

C-5A cargo transport, proposed, **1965**: 26
C-5A transport aircraft, **1966**: 26 (p. 56); **1967**:
    13 (p. 48); **1968-69**: 39 (p. 98), 109,
    110, 125
Cabell, Repr. Earle, **1968-69**: 281
Cabinet, **1963-64**: 105, 201 [9], 218 [3, 4, 8],
    307, 513; **1965**: 25, 334, 355, 362, 468;
    1966: 72, 88 [23], 137, 379; **1967**:
    221, 315, 417 [10, 14], 460 [1], 500,
    518 [16], 556; **1968-69**: 1 [1], 32, 238,
    631, 670, 696 [14]
  Changes in, **1963-64**: 780 [13]
  Election campaign, **1968-69**: 223 [10]
  Memorandums to
    Budget preview and program planning for
      fiscal 1967, **1965**: 249
    Federal staff retirement systems, **1965**: 49
    June buying, **1965**: 267
    News conference remarks on, **1965**: 22 [12],
      319 [12], 347 [11], 353 [15, 22], 448
      [3]
  Remarks following meeting with, **1963-64**: 689
  Reports to the President, **1965**: 249n.
  Salary increase, **1963-64**: 297
  Statement to
    Cost reduction program, **1965**: 512
    Employee health services, Federal, **1965**:
      324
    Excise tax reductions, **1965**: 321
    Government-wide planning and budgeting
      system, **1965**: 447
    Manpower utilization and control, **1963-64**:
      38
    Project Head Start, **1965**: 323
    Science, strengthening academic capability
      for, **1965**: 514
  Tribute to John F. Kennedy, **1963-64**: 370
Cabinet Committee on Balance of Payments,
    1965: 638; **1967**: 231
Cabinet Committee on Export Expansion, **1963-
    64**: 248, 592
Cabinet Committee on Federal Staff Retirement
    Systems, **1966**: 108; **1967**: 25
  Proposed, **1965**: 49
Cabinet Committee on Price Stability, **1968-69**:
    46, 47 (p. 140), 76, 89, 90, 404, 425 [1,
    3], 469, 485, 492, 612n., 684 (p. 1317)
Cabinet Coordinating Committee on Economic
    Planning for the End of Vietnam Hos-
    tilities, **1968-69**: 684 (pp. 1318, 1319)

Cabot, John M. (U.S. Ambassador to Poland),
    1963-64: 420 [5]
Cabot, Theodore, **1966**: 320 [4]
Caglayangil, Ihsan Sabri, **1967**: 162
Cahill, Thomas J., **1965**: 422n.
Cain, Francis J., **1966**: 398
Cain, Dr. James C., **1965**: 549; **1966**: 141 [10],
    208n., 575; **1967**: 500
Cairo, Egypt, **1963-64**: 460
  Nonaligned nations conference, **1963-64**: 625
Caladino Farm Seeds, Inc., **1963-64**: 350n.
Caldwell, Arthur A., **1966**: 542
Caldwell, Harry B., **1963-64**: 54ftn. (p. 68), 255
Calhoun, John C., **1967**: 68, 115; **1968-69**: 109,
    551, 592
Califano, Joseph A., Jr., **1965**: 387, 395 [2];
    1966: 158 [1], 247 [1], 370, 373 [15],
    478, 492 [1], 524n., 635 [1, 18, 20];
    1967: 6 [17], 157, 343n., 379, 380n.,
    391; **1968-69**: 1 [1], 17, 25, 276, 425
    [3]
California, **1966**: 320 [14], 338 [15]; **1967**:
    418, 485 [2-4]; **1968-69**: 501
  Alliance for Progress participation, **1963-64**:
    227
  Antipoverty program, **1963-64**: 580
  Auburn-Folsom South project, **1965**: 477
  Campaign remarks, **1963-64**: 579, 650, 651,
    733, 734, 735, 736
  Candidates for public office, **1963-64**: 411, 413,
    650, 733, 734, 735, 736
  Defense contracts, **1963-64**: 409
  Democratic Party, **1967**: 281
  Dispute with Arizona, **1963-64**: 294 [12], 733
  Floods, **1965**: 74, 477
  Gov. Edmund G. (Pat) Brown, **1963-64**: 163n.,
    192, 194, 294 [9, 12], 409, 410, 411,
    413, 414, 415, 462 [6, 7], 521 [5], 579,
    580n., 650, 651, 733, 734, 735, 736,
    767; **1965**: 291n., 331, 426, 453, 477;
    1966: 56, 236ftn. (p. 537), 338 [15]
    See also Brown, Gov. Edmund G. (Pat).
  Gubernatorial election, **1966**: 577 [13], 599
    [3]
  Population, **1963-64**: 413
  Public lands, **1968-69**: 563
  Redwood forests, **1963-64**: 427
  Redwood preservation, **1968-69**: 14 (p. 31),
    122, 167
  Remarks, **1968-69**: 81 [2]
  Space program, **1963-64**: 409
  Water desalination, **1965**: 325; **1967**: 227
California, Metropolitan Water District of
    Southern, **1967**: 284
California Youth Authority, **1967**: 35
Calkins, Robert D., **1966**: 404n., 493; **1967**: 184
Callaghan, James, **1965**: 335
Callan, Repr. Clair A., **1966**: 311-312

Callegary, Claude, **1968–69**: 599
Calleja, Joseph, **1963–64**: 585
Calnek, Gary, **1963–64**: 315
Cam Lo, South Vietnam, **1967**: 446
Cam Ranh Bay, South Vietnam, **1966**: 552–553,
  570; **1967**: 14, 25, 134, 446, 568n., 573;
  1968–69: 79 [8]
  Visit, **1967**: 566, 567
Cambodia, **1966**: 401 [15]; **1967**: 480, 132 [3,
  4]
  Chief of State Prince Norodom Sihanouk,
    1968–69: 1 [9], 634
  Communist sanctuary, **1968–69**: 1 [9]
  Release of detained Americans, **1968–69**: 634
Cambodian Conference, **1965**: 319 [14]
Camden, N. J., Mayor Alfred R., Pierce, **1965**:
  434
Cameroon, **1967**: 444; **1968–69**: 433n.
  Foreign Minister Benoit Binozi, **1967**: 444
  President El Hadj Ahmadou Ahidjo, **1967**: 444
Camp, William B., **1967**: 85
Camp David, Md., **1965**: 162; **1967**: 272; **1968–
  69**: 187–189
Camp Fire Girls, **1966**: 295n.
Camp Nam Dong, **1963–64**: 793
Camp Pendleton, Calif., **1967**: 485 [3, 4], 493
Camp Smith, Honolulu, **1968–69**: 401
Camp Springs, Md., **1967**: 193
Camp Stanley, Korea, visit, **1966**: 563
Campaign addresses or remarks.
  See Election campaign, addresses or remarks.
Campaign Conference for Democratic Women,
  1963–64: 305
Campaign Costs, President's Commission on,
  1967: 236
Campaigns.
  See Elections.
Campbell, Very Rev. Gerard J., **1963–64**: 788;
  1965: 519
Campbell, Gov. Jack M., **1963–64**: 732; **1966**:
  413, 416, 491n., 492 [1]
Campbell, Joseph (Comptroller General of the
  United States), **1963–64**: 18, 261; **1965**:
  60
Campbell, Walter, **1965**: 529
Campbell, Judge William J., **1966**: 228
Campobello International Park and Park Com-
  mission, Roosevelt, New Brunswick,
  1963–64: 455 [14]; **1965**: 350; **1966**:
  448
Campobello Island, New Brunswick, Canada,
  1966: 400
  Conversion to International park, **1963–64**:
    136n., 137, 138, 140
CAMPS (Cooperative Area Manpower Planning
  System), **1968–69**: 24, 444
Campus unrest, **1968–69**: 499

Canada, **1965**: 68n., 194, 451; **1966**: 14, 133;
  1967: 16 (p. 80), 83, 401; **1968–69**:
  218
  Aid to developing nations, **1963–64**: 227;
    1965: 18
  Ambassador A. Edgar Ritchie, **1966**: 644n.;
    1967: 237
  Automobile industry, **1965**: 21, 147, 574
  Automotive products trade agreement with
    U.S., **1965**: 21, 22 [9], 147, 574, 575;
    1967: 137; **1968–69**: 256, 274, 275
    [2], 465
  Communist China, relations with, **1965**: 21n.,
    22 [19]
  Fisheries in North Pacific, **1963–64**: 559
  Foreign exchange reserves, **1965**: 60
  Foreign investments, **1968–69**: 290
  Foreign Secretary Paul J. J. Martin, **1967**: 237,
    238
  Governor-General Roland Michener, **1967**: 577
  Great Lakes shipping, **1963–64**: 140
  India, assistance to, **1966**: 153–154; **1967**: 33
  Martin, Paul, **1963–64**: 134, 135, 140; **1965**:
    21, 22 [1]
  Prime Minister Lester B. Pearson, **1966**: 269,
    400, 417 [5]; **1967**: 237, 239, 272,
    543
    See also Pearson, Lester B.
  Prime Minister Pierre Elliott Trudeau, **1968–69**:
    339 [11]
  U.S. agreements with
    Columbia River agreement, **1963–64**: 134,
      135, 140, 563 [3], 574, 576, 598, 599,
      656
    Roosevelt Campobello International Park
      agreement, **1963–64**: 136n., 137, 138,
      140
  U.S.-Canada Committee on Trade and Economic
    Affairs, **1963–64**: 140
  U.S.-Canada Joint Ministerial Committee on
    Defense, **1963–64**: 140
  U.S. cooperation with
    Columbia River development, **1965**: 186
    Electric energy resources development, **1965**:
      350
    Great Lakes pollution control, **1965**: 54
  U.S. relations with, **1963–64**: 80, 128, 136,
    138, 140, 574, 575, 576, 577; **1965**:
    60, 162, 352, 432; **1966**: 448, 644
  U.S. trade with, **1965**: 21, 22 [9], 147, 574,
    575, 638n.; **1967**: 137, 508
  Visit, **1963–64**: 575, 576; **1967**: 237–239
Canada-United States, Permanent Joint Board on
  Defense, **1965**: 432
Canadian Universal and International Exhibition
  (EXPO '67), **1966**: 644; **1967**: 239, 245;
  1968–69: 204
  Visit, **1967**: 237, 238

Canal Study Commission, Atlantic-Pacific Inter-
    oceanic, **1966**: 384; **1967**: 336; **1968–
    69**: 466
Canal Zone, **1968–69**: 466
    Dispute, U.S.-Panama, **1963–64**: 95, 104, 114,
        182, 189, 192, 218 [30], 220, 235, 245,
        544, 607, 643, 648, 652, 726, 749, 809
    Joint cooperation committee, **1963–64**: 104,
        245
    News conference remarks, **1963–64**: 143
        [1], 150 [2, 14], 201 [6], 232 [1, 3,
        9], 242 [11], 246 [4]
Canals, sea-level, proposed
    Atlantic-Pacific canal, **1963–64**: 266 [5], 594;
        1965: 400
    Central America, **1963–64**: 809
    Florida, **1963–64**: 198
    Panama, **1965**: 532
Canberra, Australia, **1966**: 541–542, **1967**: 560–
    564
Cancer, **1966**: 95, 156, 189, 271, 395, 403, 436,
    515; **1967**: 6 [15], 77, 319, 477; **1968–
    69**: 39 (p. 103), 111, 536, 695
    President's Commission on Heart Disease, Can-
        cer, and Stroke, **1963–64**: 179, 211 [6],
        268, 617, 798; **1965**: 5, 343
    Prevention, **1963–64**: 268, 391, 656, 667, 669,
        733, 755, 798; **1965**: 2, 5, 32 (p. 94),
        89, 154, 156 [3], 329, 330, 343, 401,
        406, 433, 551, 594
        Crusade Against Cancer postage stamp, issu-
            ance, **1965**: 154
Cancer, International Agency for Research on,
    1965: 343
Cancer Crusade (1966), **1966**: 156
Cancer Institute, National, **1966**: 156
Cancer Society, American, **1966**: 156
Candidacy for reelection, the President's (1964),
    1963–64: 218 [22]
    News conference remarks, **1963–64**: 54 [7],
        71 [15], 170 [9, 11], 201 [10], 242
        [14, 22], 256 [22], 271 [10], 336 [11,
        13], 420 [7, 10]
    Nomination, remarks accepting, **1963–64**: 541
Candidacy for reelection, the President's (1968),
    1966: 320 [20]; **1967**: 104 [13], 225
        [19], 411 [9], 495 [8], 518 [17], 554
        [9]; **1968–69**: 1 [7], 153 [13, 15],
        169 [11, 15]
    Decision not to seek
        Address to Nation, **1968–69**: 170
        Comments on, **1968–69**: 171, 172, 212, 223
            [5, 6], 242, 260, 262, 301, 452, 564,
            568, 572, 575, 655, 677, 690, 691
Candidates for President, **1968–69**: 153 [13, 14],
    171, 191 [12], 229, 360, 461n., 467 [7,
    14, 16], 486, 497, 529, 540, 557 [4, 8,
    10], 565–569, 575, 576, 578, 579

Candidates for President – *continued*
    Availability of information to, **1963–64**: 272,
        280 [6], 285 [1, 17], 294 [15], 462
        [9], 516 [11]
    Executive power, transfer plans, **1968–69**: 480
    News conference remarks on, **1963–64**: 179 [9],
        246 [4], 280 [6], 285 [1, 17], 294
        [15], 420 [7, 10], 462 [9], 516 [11]
    Secret Service protection, **1968–69**: 292n.
Candidates for public office
    California, **1963–64**: 411, 413, 650, 733, 734,
        735, 736
    Delaware, **1963–64**: 749, 750
    Florida, **1963–64**: 712
    Idaho, **1963–64**: 659
    Illinois, **1963–64**: 635, 636, 747, 748
    Indiana, **1963–64**: 639, 640, 729
    Kansas, **1963–64**: 741
    Kentucky, **1963–64**: 643, 644
    Maine, **1963–64**: 606
    Maryland, **1963–64**: 703
    Michigan, **1963–64**: 745
    Minnesota, **1963–64**: 435
    Missouri, **1963–64**: 695
    Montana, **1963–64**: 656
    Nevada, **1963–64**: 652, 655
    New Hampshire, **1963–64**: 607
    New Jersey, **1963–64**: 338, 660
    New Mexico, **1963–64**: 732
    New York, **1963–64**: 666, 667, 668, 669, 670,
        751
    North Carolina, **1963–64**: 631
    Ohio, **1963–64**: 642, 678, 679, 680, 693
    Pennsylvania, **1963–64**: 566, 661, 728, 742
    Tennessee, **1963–64**: 645, 701, 702
    Texas, **1963–64**: 544, 760, 761, 762
    Vermont, **1963–64**: 605
    Virginia, **1963–64**: 628
    Wisconsin, **1963–64**: 746
    Wyoming, **1963–64**: 657
Candidates for Vice President, **1963–64**: 170
    [11], 211 [12, 15, 17], 242 [20], 285
    [18, 20], 294 [17], 455 [10], 475
    [14], 486 [9, 16], 489, 516 [7], 521
    [12], 539, 540; **1968–69**: 486, 529,
    565, 567–569, 575, 576
Caniff, Milton, **1965**: 554n.
Cannon, Repr. Clarence, **1963–64**: 263n., 271
    [7], 455 [1]
Cannon, Sen. Howard W., **1963–64**: 256 [13],
    575, 577, 652, 655
Cannon, Joseph G., **1965**: 521; **1966**: 398; **1968–
    69**: 386
Cantinflas (Mario Moreno Reyes), **1965**: 621;
    1967: 449
Cantor, Eddie, **1963–64**: 163
Canyonlands National Park bill, **1963–64**: 554n.
Cao Van Vien, General, **1966**: 548

Cape Canaveral, Fla., **1963–64:** 12
Cape Kennedy, Fla., **1963–64:** 12, 162n., 572; **1965:** 120; **1966:** 485; **1968–69:** 611
Cape Lookout National Seashore, N.C., **1965:** 54; **1966:** 82, 119; **1967:** 20; **1968–69:** 122
Capilla, Carmalita, **1968–69:** 236
Capital, National Committee for a More Beautiful, **1966:** 500, 501 [18]
Capital, outflow from U.S., **1965:** 60
Capital gains taxes, **1963–64:** 132 (p. 179)
Capital Housing Authority, National, **1967:** 180; **1968–69:** 133
Capital improvement programs, District of Columbia, **1965:** 29, 40, 61, 151
Capital Market, Central Americans, **1968–69:** 366
Capital Planning Commission, National, **1966:** 27, 452; **1967:** 15, 71; **1968–69:** 133
Capital Regional Planning Council, National, **1966:** 302
Capital Transportation Agency, National, **1967:** 15, 154
Capitalism, comments on, **1963–64:** 530
Capitol Historical Society, **1968–69:** 655
Capitol Page School, commencement, **1965:** 316; **1966:** 270; **1967:** 262; **1968–69:** 301
Capitol Reef Monument, Utah, **1968–69:** 707n.
Capitol Visitor Center, **1968–69:** 128
Caplin, Mortimer M., **1963–64:** 182; **1965:** 150
Car Dealers Association, Baltimore New, **1967:** 286
Caracristi, Ann Z., **1965:** 91n.
Caraway, Mrs. Hattie Wyatt, **1965:** 223
Cardenas, Col. Robert L., **1967:** 485 [6]
Cardozo, Benjamin N., **1965:** 449
CARE
See Cooperative for American Remittances to Europe.
Career Advancement, President's Task Force on, **1966:** 404
Carey, Repr. Hugh L., **1963–64:** 668; **1965:** 305; **1966:** 510–511
Carey, James B., **1963–64:** 590, 622
Carey, Walter F., **1963–64:** 295
Cargo Preference Laws, **1963–64:** 617
Caribbean area, **1963–64:** 186
  Communism, defense against, **1963–64:** 37
Caribbean regional cooperation, **1968–69:** 476
Carlson, Sen. Frank, **1963–64:** 172; **1965:** 45, 413; **1966:** 78; **1967:** 32
Carlson, Dr. Paul, **1963–64:** 780ftn. (p. 1612)
Carlyle, Thomas, **1963–64:** 181, 343, 352; **1965:** 9; **1966:** 588
Carmichael, Leonard, **1963–64:** 141; **1965:** 88, 519
Carnegie, Andrew, **1963–64:** 181
Carnegie Commission, **1967:** 474
Carnegie Foundation, **1963–64:** 622; **1965:** 334

Caroline Islands, **1967:** 360
Carpco Research and Engineering, Inc., **1966:** 144n.
Carpenter, Mrs. Elizabeth S., **1963–64:** 560 [13]; **1965:** 392, 554; **1966:** 165; **1968–69:** 368, 648
Carpenter, Paul B., **1963–64:** 736
Carpenter, Capt. William S., Jr., **1966:** 273
Carper, Elsie, **1963–64:** 208
Carpet tariffs, **1967:** 428
Carr, Edward R., **1968–69:** 629
Carr, Robert S., **1963–64:** 712
Carr, Thomas W., **1966:** 210n.; **1967:** 201
Carr, Waggoner, **1963–64:** 763
Carr, William G., **1965:** 89, 340; **1966:** 77; **1968–69:** 644
Carrillo Flores, Antonio, **1963–64:** 58, 596, 767; **1966:** 175, 247 [15]; **1967:** 447, 449, 452, 454n.
Carrillo Flores, Mrs. Antonio, **1967:** 447, 449, 452
Carroll, Diahann, **1963–64:** 751
Carroll, John A., **1963–64:** 658; **1966:** 413
Carroll, Lewis, "Alice in Wonderland," **1967:** 431
Carson, Rachael, **1963–64:** 341
  "Silent Spring," **1965:** 568ftn. (p. 1067)
Carstens, Dr. Karl, **1966:** 506
Carter, Edward, **1963–64:** 414
Carter, Dr. H. E., **1965:** 646n.; **1966:** 61n., 652n.; **1967:** 37n.
Carter, John, **1963–64:** 211 [6]
Carter, Sir John, **1966:** 342
Carter, Launor, **1966:** 424n.
Cartmill, George E., Jr., **1967:** 419n.
Cartoonists, Association of American Editorial, **1965:** 246
Cartoons on the President, **1965:** 554
Carvel, Gov. Elbert N., **1963–64:** 338, 749, 750
Carver, John A., Jr., **1966:** 410–413
Cary, William L., **1963–64:** 530
  See also Securities and Exchange Commission, Chairman (William L. Cary).
Casals, Pablo, **1963–64:** 27; **1967:** 484
Case, Sen. Clifford P., **1963–64:** 422; **1965:** 117 [3], 368, 369
Case Institute of Technology, **1965:** 225
Casey, Repr. Bob, **1963–64:** 760, 761, 762; **1968–69:** 575
Casey, Lady, **1966:** 541
Casey, Richard G. (Governor-General of Australia), **1966:** 541; **1967:** 239, 561
Cash budget, **1967:** 13 (pp. 41, 45, 59)
Casimir Pulaski, U.S.S., **1963–64:** 515
Casper, Wyo., campaign remarks, **1963–64:** 657
Cass, Lewis, **1966:** 257
Cassatt, Mary, **1968–69:** 648
Cassidy, Gloria, **1967:** 275

Cassidy, Robert C., **1967**: 458n.
Cassidy, Lt. Gen. William F., **1965**: 418n., 434n.
Castelo Branco, Humberto, **1963-64**: 561
Castor oil, **1968-69**: 47 (p. 144)
Castro, Fidel, **1963-64**: 175, 177, 272, 295, 330,
     652; **1965**: 546n.; **1967**: 395
     Campaign remarks on, **1963-64**: 544, 607,
          612, 634, 635, 639, 642, 645, 736,
          750
     News conference remarks on, **1963-64**: 246
          [5], 316 [23], 455 [22]
Catavi-Siglo Viente, Bolivia, **1963-64**: 60n.
Cater, S. Douglass, Jr., **1963-64**: 513; **1965**: 22
     [1], 319 [21, 22], 340; **1966**: 106n.,
     298n., 519, 578 [10], 629; **1968-69**: 1
     [16], 696 [1]
Catholic Church, **1966**: 273
Catholic Inter-American Cooperation Program,
     1963-64: 123
Catholic Relief Services, National Catholic
     Welfare Conference, **1965**: 293, 431,
     450
Catholic University of America, **1965**: 302
Catholics, **1968-69**: 78
Catoctin, Md., Job Corps Center, **1965**: 106 [8]
Cattle.
     See Livestock.
Cattle industry, **1963-64**: 246 [18], 316 [6],
     516 [14], 732
Catto, Henry E., Jr., **1963-64**: 392
Catto, Mrs. Henry E., Jr. (Jessica), **1963-64**: 392
Catton, Bruce, **1963-64**: 211 [7]
Caulfield, Genevieve, **1963-64**: 27
Cavanagh, Edward F., Jr., **1963-64**: 224; **1966**:
     155
Cavanagh, Jerome P., **1963-64**: 356, 431, 562;
     1966: 155, 401 [4], 431, 536; **1967**:
     321, 322, 325, 328 [5, 14]; **1968-69**:
     452
Caves, Tommy, **1965**: 179
CBS radio network, **1968-69**: 569n.
CCC.
     See Commodity Credit Corporation.
Cedar Keys Wilderness, Fla., **1968-69**: 168
Cederberg, Repr. Elford A., **1965**: 242
Celebrezze, Anthony J., **1965**: 385, 433
     See also Health, Education, and Welfare,
          Secretary of (Anthony J. Celebrezze).
Celebrezze, Mrs. Anthony J., **1963-64**: 642;
     1965: 433
Celeste, Frank, **1963-64**: 642
Celestite stockpiles, **1966**: 283n.
Celler, Repr. Emanuel, **1963-64**: 387; **1965**: 394,
     546; **1966**: 286, 335; **1967**: 68, 251;
     1968-69: 57, 553
     Packaging bill.
          See Hart-Celler packaging bill.
Cement costs, **1966**: 445 [7]

Cement Masons' International Association of the
     United States and Canada, Operative
     Plasterers' and, **1963-64**: 547
Census, Bureau of the, **1965**: 497; **1967**: 270,
     460 [2], 463, 498; **1968-69**: 94, 423,
     429
Center for Advanced Study in the Health
     Sciences, Fogarty International, **1967**:
     217; **1968–69**: 408
Center for Advanced Study in the Visual Arts,
     1967: 470
Center for Deaf-Blind Youth and Adults,
     National, **1967**: 77, 413
Center for Educational Cooperation (HEW),
     1966: 406, 533, 627
Center for Environmental Health Sciences,
     National, proposed, **1965**: 54
Center for Population Studies and Human Re-
     production, **1968-69**: 111
CENTO.
     See Central Treaty Organization.
Central America, **1966**: 41, 384
     See also Latin America.
     Assistance, **1968-69**: 364
     Economic and social development, **1968-69**:
          366, 394
     Presidents, joint statement, **1968-69**: 366
     Sea-level canal, proposed, **1963-64**: 809
     Visit, **1968-69**: 363, 365-375
Central American Agreement on Tax Incentives,
     1968-69: 366
Central American Bank for Economic Integra-
     tion, **1965**: 393; **1968-69**: 363, 365,
     366, 375
Central American Common Market, **1963-64**:
     438, 443, 769; **1965**: 393, 429; **1966**:
     41, 177, 254, 263-264; **1967**: 44; **1968-**
     69: 205, 239, 289, 363, 365, 366, 375,
     376, 500, 665
Central American Institute of Industrial Research
     and Technology, **1968-69**: 366
Central American Institute for Public Adminis-
     tration, **1968-69**: 366
Central American Integration Fund, **1967**: 44
Central American Monetary Council, **1968-69**:
     365, 366
Central American States, Organization of, **1968-**
     69: 365-67
Central American University Council, **1968-69**:
     366
Central Arizona project, **1968-69**: 39 (p. 101),
     122
Central Intelligence Agency, **1963-64**: 272, 645,
     664; **1965**: 209; **1966**: 88 [23], 310,
     387; **1967**: 116, 104 [6], 147
     Director
          Richard Helms, **1966**: 277 [5, 14], 310;
               1967: 147, 255; **1968-69**: 585

Central Intelligence Agency — *continued*
  Director — *continued*
    John A. McCone, **1963-64**: 207, 664,
      780ftn. (p. 1616)
      Campaign remarks on, **1963-64**: 612, 667,
        678, 680, 702, 747
      News conference remarks on, **1963-64**: 71
        [7, 10], 242 [9], 462 [9], 563 [1],
        688 [1], 818 [4]
    William F. Raborn, **1965**: 209; **1966**: 277
      [5, 14]
Central Intelligence Agency Retirement Act of
  1964 for Certain Employees, approval,
  1963-64: 664
Central Park, New York City, sniper attack,
  1968-69: 356
Central Radio Propagation Laboratory (Depart-
  ment of Commerce), **1965**: 247; **1967**:
  31n.
Central Texas College, Killeen, Tex., **1967**: 532
Central Treaty Organization, **1963-64**: 416;
  1965: 319 [21]; **1967**: 109
Central Valley, California, **1965**: 477
Cereals Arrangement, International, **1967**: 33
Cerebral Palsy, **1968-69**: 111, 329
Cermak, Anton, **1968-69**: 298
Certificates, participation, **1967**: 13 (p. 44), 329,
  330 [1], 420; **1968-69**: 39 (pp. 96,
  108)
Certificates of Merit, presentation, **1963-64**:
  467
Cessna Aircraft Co., **1963-64**: 350n.
Chad, **1968-69**: 508
  President Francois Tombalbaye, **1968-69**:
    508, 511
Chafee, Gov. John H., **1963-64**: 601; **1966**: 396–
  397, 494 [1, 2]; **1967**: 222n., 223 [2,
  3]
Chaffee, Lt. Comdr. Roger B., **1967**: 19, 38;
  1968-69: 387
Chaldea, **1965**: 302
Chalk, Gordon W. W., **1966**: 547
Chamber of Commerce, United States Junior,
  1963-64: 403; **1965**: 222
Chamber of Commerce of the United States,
  1963-64: 211 [18], 295, 297 [1],
  402; **1965**: 438, 554; **1968-69**: 25,
  220
Chamberlain, Joshua, **1963-64**: 606; **1966**: 399
Chamberlain, Neville, **1965**: 88; **1968-69**: 142,
  148, 646 [14]
Chamberlin, Guy W., Jr., **1967**: 458n.
Chambers, Justice M., **1963-64**: 336 [7]
Chamizal boundary and highway, **1966**: 177,
  597
Chamizal boundary settlement, United States–
  Mexico, **1967**: 447, 451–454; **1968-69**:
  199, 623, 624

Chamizal Convention of 1910, **1967**: 453
Chamizal Convention of 1963, **1967**: 454
Chamizal Memorial Park, Texas, **1965**: 487;
  1966: 597
Chamizal Zone agreement, U.S.–Mexico, **1963–
  64**: 58, 193, 194, 316 [10], 587 [6],
  596, 598, 599; **1965**: 487
Champassak, Sisouk Na, **1967**: 439
Chancellor, John, **1965**: 189, 388 [3], 412 [3]
Chanceries.
  See Embassies, U.S.
Chanceries in District of Columbia, **1967**: 71
Chandler, A.B. (Happy), **1963-64**: 643, 644
Chandler, Mrs. Norman, **1963-64**: 208; **1967**:
  526
Chandler, Otis, **1965**: 422n.
Chandler, Dr. Robert, **1966**: 550
Chandler, Walter, **1963-64**: 701
Chandrasekhar, Subrahmanyan, **1966**: 652n.;
  1967: 37n.
Chaney, Connie Ray, **1963-64**: 317n.
Chaney, Earl D., **1963-64**: 321
Chaney, Mrs. Earl D., **1963-64**: 321
Chang, Key Young, **1965**: 257; **1966**: 562, 566
Chang, Mrs. Key Young, **1966**: 562
Chapman, John (Johnny Appleseed), **1968-69**:
  227
Chapman, Leonard F., Jr., **1967**: 518 [1,7];
  1968-69: 34, 129, 232, 267, 541
Chapman, Mrs. Leonard F., **1968-69**: 232
Chapman, Oscar L., **1965**: 210; **1966**: 232
Charisse, Cyd, **1963-64**: 199
Charles I, King (England), **1968-69**: 38
Charles II, King (England), **1963-64**: 390; **1968–
  69**: 38
Charles I (Spain), **1966**: 411
Charleston, W. Va., **1966**: 426, 427; **1967**: 514
  Mayor John A. Shanklin, **1966**: 426
Charter, U.N.
  See United Nations.
Charter Oak Leadership Medal, acceptance,
  1963-64: 604n.
Charter of San Salvador, **1968-69**: 366
Charusathiara, Gen. Prapas, **1963-64**: 476; **1966**:
  557n.
Chase, Francis S., **1963-64**: 116n., 457n.
Chase, Milton, **1963-64**: 480
Chase, Salmon P., **1968-69**: 612
Chatelain, Leon, Jr., **1966**: 192n.
Chattanooga, Tenn.
  Campaign remarks, **1963-64**: 702
  Mayor Ralph H. Kelley, **1963-64**: 702
Chattanooga Times, **1963-64**: 702
Chavez, Dennis, **1963-64**: 732
Cheeley, H. H., **1965**: 458
Chelf, Repr. Frank., **1963-64**: 643, 644, 678;
  1965: 336
Chemical pollutants, **1966**: 280n.

Chemical Society, American, **1965:** 88, 403
Chemical warfare in Vietnam, question of,
    1965: 208 [19]
Chemicals, tariffs, **1968–69:** 274
Chen Yi, **1966:** 445 [23]
Chena River, Alaska, **1967:** 369
Chermayeff, Ivan, **1968–69:** 698n.
Cherne, Leo, **1966:** 86n.
Cherry, Francis A., **1965:** 363
Cherry, Mrs. Francis A., **1965:** 363
Chesapeake Bay, **1967:** 101
Chesterfield, Lord, **1963–64:** 531
Chiang Kai-shek, **1963–64:** 274; **1965:** 388 [9];
    1967: 212n., 540
Chiang Kai-shek, Madame, **1966:** 516 [16];
    1967: 212n.
Chiari, Roberto F. (President of Panama), **1963–
    64:** 95, 201 [6], 232 [1], 245, 316
    [11], 607
Chicago, Ill., **1965:** 299; **1966:** 401 [6, 9], 338
    [7]; **1967:** 114
  Campaign remarks, **1963–64:** 748
  Civil disorders, Armed Forces use, **1968–69:**
    183
  Democratic convention, disorders sur-
    rounding, **1968–69:** 467 [11]
  Democratic fundraising dinner, **1963–64:** 287
  Democratic Party dinner, **1966:** 228
  Mayor Richard J. Daley, **1963–64:** 287, 455
    [10], 521 [5], 748; **1965:** 299, 415;
    1966: 183, 228; **1967:** 216, 223 [10],
    515; **1968–69:** 171, 172, 183, 210
  Remarks, **1968–69:** 172, 210
Chicago, University of, **1967:** 391
Chicago Tribune, **1968–69:** 79 [12], 212
Chief Joseph Dam, **1965:** 186
Chief Justice of the United States (Earl Warren),
    1963–64: 2, 14, 15, 27, 117, 141, 153,
    172, 426, 427, 733, 796; **1965:** 25, 42,
    46 [6], 516, 519; **1966:** 22, 86, 570;
    1967: 18, 52, 105, 146, 263, 278, 387,
    394, 395, 443, 450, 470; **1968–69:** 78,
    99, 104, 140, 180, 304, 335, 425 [11],
    510, 527, 542, 611, 660, 662, 694
  Dinner honoring, **1967:** 7; **1968–69:** 32
  Letter, **1963–64:** 595
  Resignation, letter of, **1968–69:** 339 [1]
Chief Justice of the United States, nomination,
    1968–69: 339 [2], 425 [11], 467 [2,
    5], 509, 527, 696 [6]
Chiefs of Police, International Association of,
    1966: 354; **1967:** 382, 385
Chiefs of Staff.
  See Joint Chiefs of Staff.
Child Health and Human Development, National
    Institute of, **1963–64:** 403; **1966:** 95;
    1968–69: 111

Child health improvement and protection bill of
    1968, **1968–69:** 111
Child Nutrition Act of 1966, **1966:** 77, 95,
    340n., 394, 508; **1967:** 405
Child Protection Act of 1966, **1966:** 140, 307,
    576; **1967:** 57, 200
Children.
  See also Youth.
  AFDC (Aid to Families with Dependent
    Children), **1967:** 16 (p. 83), 39
  Aid for, **1966:** 26 (p. 63), 27, 95, 108
  Aid for children of unemployed workers, **1963–
    64:** 133, 160; **1965:** 29
  Aid for children of veterans, **1965:** 542
  Bilingual, **1968–69:** 39 (p. 106), 91
  Birth defects, **1967:** 214n.
  Crippled, **1968–69:** 111, 503
  Day care programs, **1967:** 15; **1968–69:** 3, 39
    (p. 105), 47 (p. 142), 678 (p. 1294)
  Disadvantaged, **1966:** 30, 632; **1967:** 16 (p.
    82), 39, 53, 55, 77, 114, 292; **1968–69:**
    39 (pp. 104, 106), 47 (pp. 141, 142),
    54, 281, 329, 493, 678 (p. 1293)
  District of Columbia, **1966:** 27
  Education, **1965:** 527n., 592; **1966:** 26 (p. 64),
    95, 108, 210, 223, 238, 270, 273, 319,
    353, 392, 394, 533, 589, 632, 654 [3];
    1967: 3 (pp. 2, 5), 13 (p. 55), 15, 16
    (p. 85), 53, 55, 77, 110, 114, 183, 222,
    286, 292, 423, 452, 479, 532, 540;
    1968–69: 4, 39 (p. 106), 50, 52, 87,
    102, 111, 142, 154, 164, 270, 329, 442,
    444, 462, 493, 503, 536, 538, 564, 566,
    567, 568, 644, 676 (p. 1264), 678
    (p. 1286), 684 (p. 1324)
  Food assistance, **1968–69:** 678 (p. 1297)
  Foster grandparent programs, **1967:** 12, 114
  Handicapped, **1965:** 401, 592; **1966:** 95, 317,
    362; **1967:** 13 (pp. 55, 59), 39, 77,
    260, 517; **1968–69:** 4, 39 (p. 106), 54,
    111, 329, 503, 678 (p. 1293)
  Health and welfare, **1963–64:** 403, 490, 590,
    755; **1965:** 2, 5, 6, 29, 32 (p. 94), 70,
    149, 259, 401, 406, 453, 467, 501, 594;
    1966: 26 (p. 62), 27, 45, 95, 157, 271,
    317, 392, 395, 508, 569, 573, 576, 580
    [11], 589, 654 [3]; **1967:** 13 (p. 53),
    16 (pp. 75, 85), 39, 57, 63, 77, 86, 160,
    176, 200, 222, 251, 353, 405; **1968–
    69:** 3, 4, 14 (p. 29), 26, 39 (pp. 89,
    103, 104), 47 (p. 143), 111, 113, 262,
    270, 322, 406, 429, 442, 446, 567–569,
    596, 622, 676 (p. 1265), 678 (pp. 1295–
    1297), 684 (p. 1324)
  Labor, **1967:** 39
  Malnutrition, **1968–69:** 21, 63
  Medical care, **1967:** 13 (p. 60), 39, 114
  Mentally ill, **1967:** 285

Children – *continued*
 Mentally retarded, **1965**: 592; **1968–69**: 39 (p. 106), 54, 111, 493
 Message to Congress, **1967**: 39, 40
 Orphans, **1965**: 496
 Philippine, **1966**: 505
 Physical fitness, **1968–69**: 111
 Preschool program.
  See Project Head Start (preschool program).
 Presence at news conference, **1963–64**: 316 [1]
 Recreational facilities, **1966**: 105, 394; **1967**: 160, 203, 209
 School lunch and milk programs, **1966**: 26 (p. 63), 95, 340, 508, 520; **1967**: 15, 39, 63, 228, 353, 405
 "Share Your Summer" program, **1967**: 209
 Social security benefits, **1965**: 501; **1966**: 581; **1968–69**: 3
 Task force on, **1966**: 317
 Toys safety, **1966**: 576; **1967**: 200, 393, 465
 Welfare payments, **1968–69**: 322
Children, National Advisory Council on the Education of Disadvantaged, **1966**: 210, 238, 632; **1967**: 77, 183n.
Children, National Planning Conference on the Education of Disadvantaged, **1966**: 238
Children's Bureau, **1963–64**: 590; **1966**: 95; **1967**: 39, 114; **1968–69**: 329
Children's Fund, United Nations (UNICEF), **1963–64**: 227; **1965**: 149, 353; **1966**: 41
Children's Hospital, District of Columbia, **1967**: 15
Childs, Marquis, **1966**: 474 [17]
Childs, Steven, **1963–64**: 317n.
Chile, **1963–64**: 143ftn. (p. 219), 688 [8], 726, 749; **1965**: 220; **1966**: 11n., 41; **1967**: 44; **1968–69**: 205
 Assistance, **1963–64**: 227; **1968–69**: 63, 679
 Disaster assistance, **1965**: 431
 Election, **1963–64**: 560 [2]
 Frei Montalva, Eduardo, **1963–64**: 560 [2]; **1965**: 431; **1966**: 649
 Peace Corps movement in, **1965**: 83
China, Communist, **1963–64**: 272, 420 [5], 607, 619 [15], 627, 693, 703, 737, 780 [12]; **1965**: 208 [11], 388 [1, 5], 448 [21]; **1966**: 228, 311, 320 [18], 325, 346, 437; **1967**: 272, 409, 519, 554 [1]
 Aid to developing nations, **1965**: 18
 Aid to North Vietnam, **1965**: 26
 Canadian relations with, **1965**: 21n., 22 [19]
 Chen Yi, **1966**: 445 [23]
 Cultural revolution, **1967**: 219
 Economy, **1963–64**: 686
 First nuclear device, **1963–64**: 673, 675, 676, 678, 679, 686, 688 [1], 693, 735, 736, 737, 745, 780 [23], 797

China, Communist – *continued*
 Foreign policy, **1966**: 445 [23], 533; **1967**: 554 [14]
 Indian relations, **1966**: 152–153
 Japanese relations with, **1965**: 15
 Nuclear arsenal, **1967**: 491
 Nuclear capability, **1968–69**: 39 (p. 98)
 Nuclear explosions, **1966**: 560, 654 [4]
 Premier Chou En-lai, **1967**: 225 [8]
 Recognition by France, **1963–64**: 150 [11, 15], 170 [1], 218 [31, 32]
 Soviet relations with, **1963–64**: 182, 246 [11], 643, 686
 Soviet supplies, transportation in, **1966**: 642 [13]
 Threat to Asia, **1963–64**: 627; **1965**: 15, 172, 229, 246
 Threat to Vietnam, question of, **1963–64**: 201 [5]; **1965**: 208 [12]
 Trade restrictions, **1966**: 338 [12]
 U.N. membership, question of, **1963–64**: 170 [6], 218 [32]; **1965**: 46 [5]; **1966**: 141 [7], 338 [9]; **1967**: 219
 U.S. policy, **1966**: 141 [7], 417 [13], 445 [23]; **1968–69**: 14 (p. 26)
 U.S. relations with, **1963–64**: 504 [15], 662; **1967**: 3 (p. 13), 225 [18], 312 [15], 554 [14]
 Vietnam conflict role, **1966**: 311, 607 [3]; **1967**: 34 [2], 358 [7]
 View of Western Alliance, **1963–64**: 246 [14]
 Visit of Aleksei N. Kosygin, **1965**: 46 [7]
China, Republic of, **1963–64**: 122, 617; **1966**: 41, 368; **1967**: 44, 272
 Ambassador Chow Shu-kai, **1967**: 219
 Assistance, **1965**: 7; **1968–69**: 63
 Chiang Kai-shek, **1963–64**: 274; **1965**: 388 [9]; **1967**: 212n., 540
 Defense of, **1963–64**: 272
 Economic and social development, **1967**: 212, 213, 219
 Economy of, **1965**: 18
 Food aid, **1968–69**: 176
 Japanese relations with, **1965**: 15
 Mutual defense treaty, **1967**: 213, 219
 U.N. Ambassador Liu Chieh, **1967**: 219
 U.S. Ambassador Walter P. McConaughy, **1967**: 219
 U.S. relations with, **1965**: 15, 18
 U.S. scientific mission, **1967**: 416
 Vice President C. K. Yen, **1967**: 212, 213, 416n.
 Vietnam assistance, **1967**: 219
China Lake (California) Naval Ordnance Test Station, **1963–64**: 170 [3]
Cholera, **1966**: 45, 166, 395; **1968–69**: 286, 685
Chongkol, Lady Thanpuying, **1968–69**: 232, 233

[References are to items except as otherwise indicated]

Chou En-lai (Premier of Communist China),
   1967: 225 [8]
Chow Shu-kai, **1967**: 219
Christchurch, New Zealand, **1965**: 220
Christian, George E., **1966**: 419n., 514, 517,
   521, 578 [11], 580 [1, 6, 8], 591n.,
   599 [1], 605n., 607 [1, 2, 14], 610
   [1, 3], 635 [1, 14], 642 [15], 643n.,
   650 [1]; **1967**: 50n., 69n., 70 [4], 79,
   132 [1], 204, 254n., 255n., 263,
   264ftn. (p. 612), 269, 297 [9], 312 ftn.
   (p. 699), 318n., 325, 328 [1], 371n.,
   375ftn. (p. 821), 404, 411 [1, 3, 4],
   472n., 518 [2], 529; **1968–69**: 1 [14,
   16], 5, 7n., 18n., 25, 51 [6], 79 [1, 2,
   3, 9, 11], 161n., 171, 178n., 187, 188,
   191 [1], 242, 275 [1], 292n., 339 [15],
   398n., 401, 425 [4, 5], 427n., 460 [3],
   461n., 467 [5, 7, 11], 557 [1], 592,
   604, 629n., 634n., 654
Christian Citizenship Seminar, Southern Baptist,
   1968–69: 156
Christian Leadership, Inc., International,
   1967: 32n.; **1968–69**: 43n.
Christian Science Monitor, **1966**: 401 [11],
   599 [3]
Christians and Jews, National Conference of,
   1963–64: 113; **1968–69**: 78
Christianson, Edwin, **1963–64**: 255
Christmas, the President's, **1963–64**: 54 [16]
Christmas mail for servicemen in Asia,
   1965: 573
Christmas messages
   American people, **1967**: 573
   Americans in Vietnam, **1963–64**: 313
   Armed Forces, **1965**: 654; **1966**: 647;
      1967: 549; **1968–69**: 642
Christmas Tree, National Community,
   1963–64: 65, 810; **1965**: 653;
      1966: 646; **1967**: 544; **1968–69**: 629
Christopher, George, **1965**: 449
Christopher, Warren, **1967**: 269, 325, 335;
   1968–69: 209, 425 [11]
Chromite stockpiles, **1966**: 218
Chrysler Corp., **1963–64**: 563 [2], 587 [9], 745;
   1968–69: 485, 492
Chulalongkorn University (Thailand), **1966**: 557;
   1968–69: 232n.
Chung, Il Kwon, **1966**: 561–564, 566; **1967**: 111–
   113; **1968–69**: 79 [13]
Chung, Mrs. Il Kwon, **1966**: 561–562
Church, Sen. Frank, **1963–64**: 659; **1965**: 46 [7];
   1966: 410–411, 417 [5]; **1967**: 262;
   1968–69: 457, 477
Church, Mrs. Frank, **1963–64**: 659
Church World Service, **1965**: 293, 431, 450
Churches of Christ in the U.S.A., National Coun-
   cil of, **1965**: 438

Churchill, Sir Winston S., **1963–64**: 184, 199,
   263, 382, 764, 796n.; **1965**: 22 [3],
   301, 303, 504, 583; **1966**: 86, 88 [19],
   189, 228, 328n., 540, 568; **1967**: 134,
   246, 249, 407, 485 [5]; **1968–69**: 148,
   262, 281, 406, 420, 429, 442, 472, 479,
   565, 567, 596, 631, 672, 695, 696 [12]
   Death of, **1965**: 31
   Funeral, U.S. delegation to, **1965**: 46 [6]
   Letter, **1963–64**: 781
   Memorial Library, **1963–64**: 263
Churin, Aleksandr I., **1963–64**: 480n.
CIA.
   See Central Intelligence Agency.
CIAP.
   See Inter-American Committee on the Alliance
      for Progress.
Cicero, **1963–64**: 421; **1966**: 200
Cieplinski, Michel, **1963–64**: 588n.; **1967**: 397
Cigarroa, Dr. Leonides G., **1967**: 419n.
Cincinnati, Ohio, **1963–64**: 217; **1968–69**: 406
   Campaign remarks, **1963–64**: 678, 679
Citations.
   See Awards and citations.
Cities.
   See Urban areas.
Cities, demonstration.
   See Model cities program.
Cities, National League of, **1965**: 438; **1966**: 155,
   536
Citizens' Advisory Committee on Recreation and
   Natural Beauty, **1966**: 202, 653;
      1967: 295; **1968–69**: 122, 167
Citizens' Advisory Council on the Status of
   Women, **1965**: 392n.; **1966**: 299
Citizens' Commission, National, **1966**: 370
Citizens Committee for Tax Reduction and
   Revision, **1963–64**: 93
Citizens Crusade Against Poverty, **1965**: 75
Citizens for Humphrey-Muskie, **1968–69**: 569
Citizens for Johnson and Humphrey, **1967**: 421n.
City Managers Association, National, **1965**: 438
Ciudad Acuña, Mexico, **1966**: 639
Ciudad Juárez, Mexico, **1967**: 451, 454
Civic Affairs, Youth Councils on, **1965**: 508
Civil Aeronautics Act of 1938, **1968–69**: 125
Civil Aeronautics Board, **1965**: 117 [3], 567;
   1966: 98, 187, 322, 516 [4];
      1968–69: 116, 125
   Chairman (John H. Crooker, Jr.), **1968–69**: 125
   Chairman (Charles S. Murphy), **1966**: 64, 322;
      1968–69: 79 [2, 4]
Civil air agreement, United States-Soviet,
   1967: 80 [2]; **1968–69**: 14 (pp. 2, 6),
   288, 387
Civil Air Transport Agreement, United States-
   Japan, **1965**: 15
Civil aviation, **1963–64**: 215

Civil Aviation Organization, International,
  1968–69: 494
Civil defense, **1968–69**: 196
Civil Defense, Office of, **1965**: 418
Civil Defense, Office of (Army), **1965**: 174
Civil Defense Advisory Council, National,
  1968–69: 196
Civil disorders, **1963–64**: 472, 475 [15, 20],
    511, 560 [14], 541, 563 [9, 11, 13],
    665, 680; **1965**: 102; **1967**: 55, 225
    [1], 264 [8], 327, 328 [5, 19], 328
    [7], 382, 420, 481, 554 [6];
    1968–69: 14 (pp. 28, 31), 26, 59, 100,
    114, 126, 153 [16], 155, 178n., 180n.,
    195, 209, 561, 596, 611, 625
  Address to the Nation, **1967**: 326
  Anti-riot gas, use in, **1965**: 156 [12]
  Baltimore, Md., **1968–69**: 184
  Birmingham, Ala., **1965**: 161
  Chicago, Ill., **1968–69**: 183
  Detroit, Mich., **1967**: 321, 322, 325, 326, 328
    [2], 331, 466; **1968–69**: 51 [11], 86,
    114
  Disaster relief, **1967**: 325, 328 [20]
  District of Columbia, **1968–69**: 180n.
  Insurance in areas of, **1968–69**: 36, 87, 287
  Los Angeles, Calif., **1965**: 426, 436, 448 [17],
    452, 453, 454 [5], 463 [15]
  Memphis, Tenn., **1968–69**: 166
  New York City, **1963–64**: 468
  Newark, N.J., **1967**: 312 [6]; **1968–69**: 86, 114
  Plainfield, N.J., **1967**: 312 [6]
  Police action, **1968–69**: 213 [9]
  Prevention and control, **1967**: 575;
    1968–69: 59, 153 [16], 690
  Riot control training, **1967**: 326
  Statement, **1963–64**: 600
  Watts area, Los Angeles, Calif., **1968–69**: 114
Civil Disorders, National Advisory Commission
    on, **1967**: 326, 327, 328 [1, 10, 23];
    1968–69: 59, 114, 142, 153 [16], 191
    [9], 301
Civil rights, **1963–64**: 51, 91 (p. 112), 111, 124
    (pp. 165, 166), 139, 161, 182, 199, 238,
    267, 268, 269, 277, 279, 287, 289, 295,
    301, 302, 313, 323, 325, 330, 332, 334,
    337, 340, 342, 352, 357, 373, 391, 396,
    406, 412, 413, 415, 431, 433, 452, 472,
    473, 477, 488, 506, 511, 522, 560 [10,
    14], 628n., 650, 669, 677, 721, 787,
    800; **1965**: 27, 33, 64, 85, 102, 108,
    201, 301, 353 [3, 18, 19], 397, 409,
    436, 548, 613; **1966**: 6 (p. 6), 247 [11],
    263, 273, 346, 375, 396, 399, 408, 436,
    484, 501 [6], 545, 646, 650 [24];
    1967: 3 (pp. 2, 5), 81, 105, 115, 124,
    146, 216, 267, 333, 382, 421, 443, 452,
    463, 481, 484, 534, 554 [6];
    1968–69: 164, 209

Civil rights — *continued*
  See also Integration; Nondiscrimination;
    specific subjects.
  Agitators, professional, **1966**: 338 [8]
  Armed Forces, compliance, **1963–64**: 816
  Boy Scouts' compliance, **1965**: 55
  Business responsibilities, **1963–64**: 139, 250,
    314, 342, 350
  Campaign remarks, **1963–64**: 541, 562, 566,
    589, 637, 639, 648, 655, 667, 695, 719,
    728, 751
  Churches' role, **1963–64**: 301
  Civil rights bill.
    See Civil rights bills.
  Clergy, role of, **1966**: 484
  Demonstrations, **1963–64**: 218 [35], 242 [13],
    266 [9], 285 [11], 290, 336 [19], 486
    [15]; **1965**: 126n., 301, 397; **1966**: 277
    [10], 338 [7], 347, 396, 401 [6, 9], 484
    Selma, Ala., **1965**: 106 [1, 7], 107
    Selma-Montgomery march, **1965**: 104, 114,
      117 [1, 5, 10], 126n., 135
  Director of Conciliation, proposed,
    1963–64: 420 [11, 13]
  Disappearance of workers in Mississippi, in-
    vestigation, **1963–64**: 420 [12], 455
    [9], 504 [3, 8], 563 [9]
  Effect of Democratic primaries on,
    1963–64: 246 [7]
  Effect on elections, **1963–64**: 266 [23], 420
    [10], 796n.
  Employment.
    See Equal employment opportunity.
  Enforcement, **1966**: 6 (pp. 3, 5), 59
  Exercise of, violators, **1968–69**: 26, 82
  Federal compliance, **1963–64**: 446, 792, 800,
    812; **1965**: 50, 128, 197, 530
  Federal programs, **1966**: 59, 60n., 501 [13]
  Hawaii, **1963–64**: 534
  Housing, **1963–64**: 91 (p. 116); **1966**: 6 (pp. 3,
    5), 30, 196, 247 [10], 375, 474 [14],
    475
  Indians, **1968–69**: 113
  Jury selection, **1967**: 55
  Labor responsibilities, **1963–64**: 139, 221, 314,
    342, 350
  Legislation, **1965**: 412 [3]; **1966**: 26 (p. 64),
    196, 277 [24], 403, 474 [14], 475;
    1967: 55, 81, 114, 251, 258, 291, 484;
    1968–69: 14 (p. 31), 26, 82, 126, 158,
    164, 191 [1], 195, 212, 262, 406, 442,
    459, 596, 655, 676 (p. 1266)
    See also specific acts.
  Litigation, **1968–69**: 26
  March on Washington, **1968–69**: 51 [14]
  Medicare, compliance under, **1966**: 253, 271,
    395; **1967**: 298
  Message to Congress, **1965**: 107; **1966**: 196;
    1968–69: 26

Civil rights – *continued*
  Murder of civil rights workers, **1965**: 107, 135
  Negroes, **1967**: 81
  News conference remarks, **1963–64**: 242 [13],
      266 [9, 20], 285 [11], 336 [19], 420 [9,
      11, 12, 13], 455 [9], 462 [5], 475 [9,
      17], 486 [15], 504 [3, 8], 560 [10, 14],
      563 [9]
  President's view of, **1965**: 353 [19]
  Press, responsibilities of, **1963–64**: 496
  Public accommodations.
      See Public accommodations, equal access to.
  Racial and religious discrimination, **1966**: 30,
      34 (p. 100), 341
  Riots, **1963–64**: 600
  State enforcement, **1966**: 6 (p. 3)
  Voting rights.
      See Voting rights.
  White House conference "To Fulfill These
      Rights," **1965**: 183, 301, 453, 548, 613;
      1966: 51, 88 [10], 196, 247 [11], 248,
      407–408
Civil Rights, Commission on, **1965**: 85, 197,
      530n., 613, 615; **1967**: 55; **1968–69**: 26,
      42
Civil Rights Acts
  1957, **1963–64**: 800; **1965**: 108, 301, 436;
      1966: 59; **1967**: 55, 298; **1968–69**: 26
  1960, **1965**: 108, 301, 436; **1966**: 59, 196;
      1967: 55
  1963, **1963–64**: 800
  1964, **1963–64**: 446, 448, 452, 466, 478n.,
      486 [15], 522, 620, 642, 667, 669,
      680, 728, 744, 792; **1965**: 2, 46 [3, 13],
      50, 85, 100, 106 [1, 9], 108, 117 [10],
      201, 249n., 301, 340, 345, 436, 470;
      1966: 59, 60n., 250, 271, 475, 494ftn.
      (p. 1106); **1967**: 12, 55, 77, 216, 333,
      548; **1968–69**: 26, 87, 91, 111, 195,
      212, 347, 596, 611
  1965 (Voting Rights Act), **1968–69**: 26, 87,
      111, 195, 212, 332, 341, 596, 611, 631,
      676 (p. 1266), 696 [9]
  1968, **1968–69**: 82, 126, 131, 158, 182, 191
      [1, 13], 192, 195, 212, 380, 596, 611,
      676 (p. 1266), 678 (p. 1289)
Civil rights bills
  1964, **1963–64**: 11, 22, 158, 218 [35], 228,
      233, 238, 250, 270, 290, 292, 297, 301,
      314, 334, 342, 388, 397, 412, 413, 434
    Amendment to include women, question of,
      1963–64: 170 [16]
    Approval, **1963–64**: 446
    News conference remarks, **1963–64**: 28 [4],
      143 [2], 150 [4], 170 [13, 16], 201
      [16], 211 [16, 20], 218 [35], 242 [13,
      15], 246 [9], 256 [11], 266 [9, 20, 21],
      285 [11], 316 [13], 336 [10, 14], 379
      [8, 20], 420 [9–11], 462 [11], 475 [9]

Civil rights bills – *continued*
  1964 – *continued*
    Public accommodations section,
      1963–64: 201 [16]
    Senate debate on, **1963–64**: 211 [20], 218
      [35], 246 [9], 256 [11], 316 [13], 336
      [14], 379 [20]
  1966, **1966**: 373 [10], 375, 394, 436, 474
      [7, 14], 475
  1967, **1967**: 55, 56, 353, 358 [3]
Civil service, **1965**: 125; **1966**: 6 (p. 3), 487,
      499, 619
  See also Government employees.
Civil Service Act, **1966**: 499; **1968–69**: 667
Civil Service Commission, **1963–64**: 205, 302,
      345, 403, 688 [4], 812n.; **1965**: 49, 91,
      93, 233, 241, 244, 379, 530n., 591, 631;
      1966: 136, 239, 376n., 438, 499, 630
      [8]; **1967**: 95n., 121, 148, 265, 379,
      502; **1968–69**: 437, 498, 539, 548
  Annual report, **1963–64**: 168
  Reports to Congress, **1968–69**: 84, 667
Civil Service Commission, Chairman (John W.
      Macy, Jr.), **1963–64**: 178n., 302, 622,
      775, 777, 790; **1965**: 91, 117 [3], 126,
      140, 170, 183, 240, 241, 263, 324, 395
      [1], 403, 448 [9], 515, 591, 612;
      1966: 8 [1], 88 [12], 105, 108, 116,
      129, 136–137, 158 [1], 198, 208, 216,
      239, 241, 247 [2], 266, 276, 388, 404,
      438, 580 [5]; **1967**: 95, 121, 163, 184,
      232, 343, 379, 388, 546; **1968–69**: 15,
      40, 67, 227, 303, 480n., 498, 526, 539,
      570, 581, 604
  Letters, **1963–64**: 100, 151; **1965**: 264, 631;
      1968–69: 464
  Memorandum to, **1965**: 379
  Reports, **1965**: 249n., 409n., 540, 591
Civil Service League awards, **1966**: 198
Civil Service League's Career Service Awards,
      National, presentation, **1965**: 263
Civil Service System, **1968–69**: 40
Civil War, **1963–64**: 605; **1965**: 39, 64;
      1966: 248, 414, 558; **1967**: 49, 115,
      361, 487, 495 [11]; **1968–69**: 271n.,
      273n.
Civilian Conservation Corps, **1966**: 417 [2];
      1967: 258
Civilian Service Awards Board, Distinguished,
      1968–69: 604
Claims by or against the Government, **1966**: 335
Claims Fund, War, **1965**: 309
Clairmont Dueñas, Ramón de, **1965**: 472, 473
Clapp, Verner, **1966**: 424n.
Clarizio, Emanuele (Papal Nuncio to the Domini-
      can Republic), **1965**: 212n., 216, 223,
      295 [16]
Clark, Lt. Gen. Albert P., **1968–69**: 12

Clark, Edward, **1966**: 305, 543-544; **1967**: 248, 551, 562; **1968-69**: 206, 273, 357, 359

Clark, Mrs. Edward, **1968-69**: 273, 359

Clark, Repr. Frank M., **1963-64**: 728; **1966**: 428

Clark, George Rogers, **1966**: 350

Clark, Heather Lynn, **1966**: 289

Clark, James Beauchamp (Champ), **1967**: 495 [14]

Clark, Dr. James W., **1967**: 117

Clark, Sen. Joseph S., **1963-64**: 55, 289, 390, 566, 661, 728, 742; **1965**: 319 [14], 503; **1966**: 151; **1967**: 291

Clark, Gen. Mark W., **1967**: 104 [12]

Clark, Mary Ramsey, **1967**: 79

Clark, Dr. R. Lee, **1963-64**: 211 [6]

Clark, Ramsey, **1965**: 66, 117 [1], 126, 264n., 448 [17], 453, 486; **1966**: 231, 236 [13]
  See also Attorney General; Attorney General, Acting.

Clark, Mrs. Ramsey, **1967**: 105

Clark, Justice Tom C., **1965**: 45, 66, 443, 468, 478; **1966**: 474 [17]; **1967**: 79, 105, 263, 266, 466; **1968-69**: 42, 425 [11]

Clark, William G., **1963-64**: 635, 636, 637, 747; **1968-69**: 210

Clark Hill Reservoir, Georgia-South Carolina, **1963-64**: 718

Clarke, John H., **1968-69**: 270

Clarke, John L., **1963-64**: 660n.

Clarke, Lloyd E., **1968-69**: 229

Classification Act of 1949, **1963-64**: 711

Clay, Henry, **1963-64**: 644; **1965**: 80; **1968-69**: 592

Clay, Gen. Lucius D., Jr., **1963-64**: 349n., 462 [2]; **1966**: 482n.

Clayman, Jacob, **1967**: 465

Clean Air Act, **1963-64**: 179; **1965**: 54, 568; **1966**: 82; **1967**: 503; **1968-69**: 122
  Approval, **1963-64**: 50

Clean Water Restoration Act of 1966, **1966**: 91, 232, 394n., 518, 574; **1967**: 20; **1968-69**: 122

Clement, Frank G., **1963-64**: 324, 325, 645, 701, 702; **1966**: 122 [1, 2], 494 [1, 2], 599ftn. (p. 1358); **1968-69**: 345

Clement, Mrs. Frank G., **1963-64**: 324, 325

Clement, Howard W., **1966**: 637n.

Clements, Earle, **1963-64**: 643, 644

Clements, Raymond, **1968-69**: 419

Clendinen, James A., **1966**: 503

Clergy, civil rights role, **1966**: 484

Clergy, comments on, **1963-64**: 742; **1965**: 106 [1]

Clerical, and Technical Employees, International Federation of Commercial, **1967**: 442

Cleveland, Grover, **1966**: 430; **1968-69**: 576

Cleveland, Harlan, **1963-64**: 616n.; **1965**: 265, 507; **1967**: 167

Cleveland, Ohio, **1963-64**: 405, 406; **1966**: 338 [7]
  Campaign remarks, **1963-64**: 642
  Mayor Ralph S. Locher, **1963-64**: 405, 406, 543, 642
  Mayor Carl Stokes, **1968-69**: 141
  Parade of Progress, dedication, **1963-64**: 543

Clevenger, Repr. Raymond F., **1966**: 431

Cliburn, Van, **1963-64**: 75; **1966**: 440

Clifford, Clark M., **1966**: 320 [2]; **1967**: 328 [9, 12, 16, 18], 352; **1968-69**: 51 [5], 53, 99
  See also Defense, Secretary of.
  Appointment as Secretary of Defense, **1968-69**: 18 [1, 2]

Clifford, Mrs. Clark M., **1968-69**: 18 [2], 104, 616

Clifford B. Harmon Trust, **1967**: 431n.

Clifton, Maj. Gen. Chester V., **1963-64**: 773; **1965**: 399

Clifton, Mrs. Chester V., **1965**: 399

Clifton, N. J., **1963-64**: 338

Clinical Laboratories Improvement Act of 1967, **1967**: 57; **1968-69**: 14 (p. 29)

Clock import tariffs, **1966**: 600

Clothing taxes, **1965**: 255

Clothing Workers, Amalgamated, 50th anniversary, **1963-64**: 334

Clynes, Mr. and Mrs. George I., **1966**: 581

Coal industry, unemployment, **1963-64**: 292, 295, 297

Coal mines
  Disaster, West Va., **1968-69**: 607
  Health and safety bill, **1968-69**: 475, 607, 684 (p. 1323)
  Safety, **1966**: 151, 237

Coal and Steel Community, European, **1963-64**: 788; **1965**: 429

Coast and Geodetic Survey, **1963-64**: 308; **1965**: 247; **1966**: 326; **1967**: 31n.

Coast Guard, **1963-64**: 216; **1965**: 312; **1966**: 98, 158 [10], 159, 188 [6], 447, 630 [4]; **1967**: 72, 101, 240, 485 [8]; **1968-69**: 93, 248, 297, 693
  Cost reduction program, **1968-69**: 39 (p. 111)
  Cuban fishermen in U.S. waters, arrest of, **1963-64**: 175

Coast Guard Academy, **1963-64**: 382

Cobb, Dr. Montague, **1965**: 594n.

Cochran, Jacqueline (Mrs. Floyd B. Odlum), **1968-69**: 262, 616

Cochran, Lt. John F., **1966**: 645n.

Cocoa, **1965**: 429

Codes, Zoning, Taxation and Development Standards, Commission on, **1966**: 394; **1967**: 4, 16 (p. 84)

Codes, Zoning, Taxation and Development Standards, Temporary National Commission on, proposed, **1965**: 90

Cody, Archbishop John P., **1966**: 228; **1967**: 87n.
Coffee, **1967**: 10, 175; **1968–69**: 23, 207, 366
 Prices, **1965**: 272
Coffee Agreement, International, **1963–64**: 193,
  662, 728; **1965**: 272, 429; **1966**: 9, 125;
  1967: 10, 175, 176; **1968–69**: 23, 207,
  366, 559
Coffee Diversification and Development Fund,
  1967: 175
Coffey, A. Langley, **1968–69**: 626n.
Coffey, Matthew, **1968–69**: 17
Cogen, Charles, **1965**: 539
Coggeshall, Dr. Lowell T., **1965**: 594n.
Cogo, Rev. Joseph A., **1968–69**: 325
Cohen, Joe, **1963–64**: 77
Cohen, Manuel F., **1963–64**: 455 [8];
  1968–69: 418
 See also Securities and Exchange Commission,
   Chairman (Manuel F. Cohen).
Cohen, Paul J., **1968–69**: 71n.
Cohen, Rabbi Seymour J., **1966**: 228
Cohen, Sheldon S., **1963–64**: 818 [2]; **1965**: 150,
  478; **1966**: 96, 204
Cohen, Wilbur J., **1963–64**: 356; **1965**: 72, 208
  [6], 231, 394, 406, 410; **1966**: 157,
  253, 293n., 298, 509; **1967**: 413, 539;
  1968–69: 79ftn. (p. 232), 100, 153 [2,
  5]
 See also Health, Education, and Welfare, Secre-
   tary of.
COIN (counter-insurgency) aircraft,
  1963–64: 516 [3]
Coinage, Joint Commission on the, proposed,
  1965: 297
Coinage, U.S., **1965**: 297
 Coin shortage, **1965**: 252
 Minerals used in, **1965**: 297, 380
Coinage Act of 1965, **1965**: 329, 330
 Approval, **1965**: 380
Coinage Study, Treasury Staff Silver and,
  1965: 297
Coin-operated machines, **1965**: 297
Coke, Bishop Thomas, **1966**: 189
Colavito, Rocky, **1966**: 435
Cold war, **1963–64**: 396, 409
Cole, David L., **1966**: 535n.
Cole, Kenneth S., **1968–69**: 71n.
Cole, Phillip L., **1968–69**: 330
Cole, W. Sterling (Stub), **1965**: 157
Coleman, J. P., **1965**: 319 [22]
Coleman, William L., **1963–64**: 406, 642, 680
Coleman, William T., Jr., **1965**: 548, 613;
  1967: 291
Coles, John, **1963–64**: 688 [3]
Collective bargaining, **1963–64**: 124 (p. 157),
  218 [36], 233, 251, 270, 280 [11],
  284, 287, 290, 295, 297 [2], 589, 637,
  638, 639, 642, 643, 669, 670, 680,

Collective bargaining – *continued*
  719, 745, 746; **1965**: 41, 58, 208 [4],
  258, 463 [3, 12], 466, 483; **1966**: 34
  (p. 106), 347, 414; **1967**: 170, 174,
  188, 204 [5], 207, 310
 News conference remarks, **1963–64**: 232
  [10], 242 [8], 256 [1, 6], 266 [3, 12],
  455 [3], 780 [5]
 President's function in, **1963–64**: 266 [12]
College of the Holy Cross, **1963–64**: 396
College Students Registration Week,
  1963–64: 560 [1]
Colleges and universities, **1963–64**: 513, 658,
  754; **1965**: 401, 405, 457; **1966**: 3n.,
  27, 45, 111, 312; **1967**: 286, 413, 490,
  532, 540
 See also Education; Government cooperation
  with business, education and labor;
  Schools; Students; *specific schools.*
 AID-financed contracts, **1963–64**: 482
 Appalachian region, **1968–69**: 701
 Community colleges, **1963–64**: 47; **1965**: 111
 Community development participation,
  1965: 9, 54, 455
 Community services and continuing education,
  1968–69: 39 (p. 106), 54, 312
 Construction program, **1963–64**: 413
 Cooperation with business and Government,
  1963–64: 124 (p. 163), 231, 456
  See also Government cooperation with business,
   education, and labor.
 District of Columbia, **1963–64**: 116, 457n.;
  1965: 70, 111; **1966**: 586; **1968–69**: 95
 Enrollment, **1968–69**: 54, 538n., 684 (p. 1313)
 Extension service, **1963–64**: 414
 Federal aid, **1963–64**: 47, 132 (p. 182), 338,
  413, 414; **1965**: 2, 9, 100, 225, 368,
  369, 415, 455, 479, 514, 522, 539;
  1966: 95, 584; **1968–69**: 39 (p. 106),
  54, 567, 678 (p. 1293)
 Foreign assistance participation, **1965**: 18
 Graduate schools, **1968–69**: 54
 Graduates, income, **1968–69**: 26
 Grants, **1965**: 455
 Housing, **1965**: 90, 415, 585; **1966**: 26 (p. 63),
  182; **1967**: 179; **1968–69**: 678 (p.
  1281)
 Increase, **1963–64**: 601
 Indians, **1968–69**: 259n.
 Land-grant, **1965**: 9, 18
 Libraries, **1965**: 9, 455, 479
 Negro, fundraising, **1963–64**: 79
 Overseas assistance, **1968–69**: 63
 Participation in foreign assistance, **1963–64**: 617
 Pollution research, **1965**: 54
 Presidents of, meeting, **1963–64**: 485, 513
 Role in public affairs, **1963–64**: 709
 ROTC programs, **1963–64**: 665

Colleges and universities – *continued*
  Scholarships and fellowships, **1963–64**: 601;
      1965: 2, 6, 9, 100, 340, 368, 369, 374,
      479, 514, 603
  Science teaching, **1968–69**: 687
  Scientific research, **1965**: 32 (p. 95), 92, 115,
      196, 514
  Sea grant, **1967**: 101; **1968–69**: 122, 124
  State supported, **1963–64**: 482; **1965**: 18
  Student loan program, **1963–64**: 47, 53, 132
      (p. 189), 413, 676, 755; **1965**: 2, 5, 9,
      100, 455, 479, 539, 578, 603
  Students, **1968–69**: 39 (pp. 104, 106, 110),
      47 (p. 129), 50, 113, 230, 282, 459,
      672, 676 (p. 1264)
    Aid, **1967**: 114, 304, 338, 413, 423, 490;
      1968–69: 14 (p. 31), 47 (p. 143), 54,
      113, 678 (p. 1293)
    Summer intern program, **1963–64**: 428;
      1965: 403
  Water resources research, **1963–64**: 231
  Work-study programs, **1967**: 13 (p. 55), 77,
      304n., 378; **1968–69**: 39 (p. 106), 54
Colleges and Universities, Association of State,
      1967: 490n.
Collier Trophy, presentation, **1963–64**: 593
Collins, John F., **1963–64**: 727
Collins, LeRoy, **1963–64**: 446, 521 [2], 522,
      588n., 744; **1965**: 106 [1], 345, 448
      [17], 483; **1966**: 51, 185n.
Collins, Lester, **1963–64**: 635
Collins, Linton M., **1963–64**: 389, 613
Colombia, **1963–64**: 143ftn. (p. 219), 809;
      1967: 44, 336; **1968–69**: 63, 205, 364
  Ambassador Eduardo Uribe, **1965**: 473n.
  Assistance, **1963–64**: 227, 340; **1968–69**: 63,
      679
  Canal site survey, **1966**: 384
  Economic development, **1963–64**: 352
  Peace Corps, **1968–69**: 103
  Peace Corps projects in, **1965**: 83
  Sea-level canal survey, **1963–64**: 266 [5]
Colombo plan, **1963–64**: 471n.; **1966**: 542;
      1967: 459
Colonialism, **1963–64**: 244; **1966**: 6 (p. 9)
Colorado, **1966**: 95
  Campaign remarks, **1963–64**: 658
  Floods, **1965**: 319 [20]
  Gov. John A. Love, **1965**: 319 [20];
      1966: 413–414, 491n., 492 [1]
  Oil shale processing, **1967**: 358 [11]
Colorado River, **1966**: 427; **1967**: 408 [6];
      1968–69: 501, 510, 511
  Land ownership, **1966**: 615; **1968–69**: 563
  Salinity control, **1963–64**: 193; **1965**: 119;
      1966: 177; **1967**: 227
Colorado River Basin Project Act, **1968–69**: 122,
      345, 501, 511

Colored People, National Association for the
      Advancement of, **1965**: 443; **1968–69**:
      696 [12]
ColorTran Industries, Inc., **1966**: 144n.
Columbia, S.C.
  Campaign remarks, **1963–64**: 719
  Mayor Lester L. Bates, **1963–64**: 719
Columbia, Tenn., **1967**: 117
Columbia College, **1965**: 124
Columbia River, **1968–69**: 330n.
  Power projects, **1963–64**: 135, 563 [3], 574;
      1966: 269
Columbia River Treaty, U.S.-Canada,
      1963–64: 134, 135, 140, 563 [3], 574,
      576, 598, 599, 656; **1965**: 186;
      1966: 269; **1967**: 237
Columbia State Community College, Tenn.,
      1967: 117
Columbia University, **1965**: 347 [5]
Columbus, Christopher, **1963–64**: 651; **1965**: 88;
      1966: 478, 513; **1967**: 515, 533
Columbus, Ohio, Mayor M. E. Sensenbrenner,
      1966: 436
Columbus Day, **1963–64**: 651; **1965**: 563;
      1968–69: 342
  Dinner, **1966**: 513
  Proclamation, **1966**: 478
Combined Federal Campaign, **1967**: 288
Combs, Bert T., **1963–64**: 41, 174, 643, 644
Comfort, Texas, **1967**: 493
Commemorative occasions.
  See Addresses or remarks on commemorative
      or special occasions.
Commerce, **1963–64**: 132 (p. 187); **1965**: 32
      (p. 92), 148
  International, **1967**: 346
  Interstate, **1966**: 121 [3]
Commerce, Chamber of, **1968–69**: 25, 220
Commerce, Department of, **1963–64**: 124 (p.
      163), 711, 722, 805; **1965**: 25, 30, 35
      (p. 116), 46 [12], 62, 93, 127, 132,
      138n., 167, 247, 268, 345, 460, 465,
      487, 503, 512n., 513, 530n., 536, 618,
      641 [2]; **1966**: 26 (p. 60), 59, 60n., 98,
      110, 115, 140, 296, 445 [5], 592, 601,
      630 [4], 635 [18], 642 [6]; **1967**: 8,
      31, 103, 104 [1], 139n., 225 [9], 268,
      412, 428; **1968–69**: 2, 30 (p. 109), 80,
      127, 146, 204, 241n., 678 (p. 1302)
  Appropriations, **1967**: 417 [1]
  Economic Development Administration,
      1968–69: 153 [16]
  Hard-core unemployment, program,
      1968–69: 37
  Lard, embargo on, proposed, **1963–64**: 201 [14]
  Maritime Commission, proposed transfer to
      Department of Transportation,
      1968–69: 678 (p. 1302)

Commerce, Department of – *continued*
  Personnel changes, **1963–64**: 806
  Proposed merger with Department of Labor,
    1968–69: 670
  Reorganization, **1967**: 3 (p. 4), 11, 13 (p. 57),
    16 (p. 86), 121, 148
Commerce, Secretary of (Connor, John T.),
    1965: 25, 38, 54, 58, 60, 77, 79, 91,
    97, 112, 132, 207, 247, 250, 268, 297,
    298, 339, 345, 433, 438, 452, 460,
    466, 483, 513, 530n., 536, 575, 617,
    638; **1966**: 51, 88 [2], 105, 115, 139,
    143, 172, 184n., 187. 201, 202n., 237,
    275, 277 [8], 326, 373 [3–4, 17], 394,
    449, 496, 576, 592, 607 [1, 8], 635
    [2–3, 20], 636–637, 654 [11];
    1967: 6 [17, 18], 8, 31, 186
  See also main heading, Connor, John T.
  Letters, **1965**: 30, 153
  Memorandums, **1966**: 425, 606
  News conference remarks on, **1965**: 156 [1],
    176 [1], 319 [8], 347 [4]
  Reports, **1965**: 249n., 545
Commerce, Secretary of (Hodges, Luther H.),
    1963–64: 23n., 67, 178n., 203, 248,
    288, 350, 358, 522, 531, 537, 588n.,
    615, 631, 711, 806; **1965**: 4
  Letters, **1963–64**: 234, 705, 805
  Memorandum to, **1963–64**: 62
  News conference remarks, **1963–64**: 242 [9],
    285 [2], 294 [2], 316 [3]
Commerce, Secretary of (Smith, C. R.),
    1968–69: 79 [1], 106, 112, 113, 122,
    127, 136, 139, 141, 146, 173, 274, 422,
    425 [5], 587
  Memorandum, **1968–69**: 361
  Swearing in, **1968–69**: 115
Commerce, Secretary of (Trowbridge, Alexander
    B.), **1967**: 13 (p. 587), 70ftn. (p. 221),
    72, 74, 113, 199, 223 [2], 231, 295,
    420, 460 [1], 498, 499, 512, 539;
    1968–69: 1 [1], 2, 17, 24, 25, 36, 37,
    47 (p. 135), 56, 90, 94, 105, 112
  Memorandums, **1967**: 89, 412; **1968–69**: 89
  Reception honoring, **1968–69**: 139
  Resignation, **1968–69**: 79 [1, 3], 80
  Swearing in, **1967**: 268
Commerce Commission, Interstate, **1965**: 281
Commercial, Clerical, and Technical Employees,
    International Federation of, **1967**: 442
Commission for Appalachia, Federal Develop-
    ment Planning, **1965**: 117 [3]
Commission on Architectural Barriers to Re-
    habilitation of the Handicapped, Na-
    tional, **1966**: 192
Commission for Asia and the Far East, Economic,
    1965: 353ftn. (p. 736); **1966**: 461, 557

Commission on Civil Rights, **1965**: 85, 197, 530n.,
    613, 615; **1967**: 55; **1968–69**: 26, 42
Commission on Codes, Zoning, Taxation and
    Development Standards, **1966**: 394;
    1967: 4, 16 (p. 84)
Commission on Codes, Zoning, Taxation and
    Development Standards, Temporary
    National, **1965**: 90
Commission on the Coinage, Joint, proposed,
    1965: 297
Commission on Community Health Services,
    National, **1966**: 185
Commission on Crime in the District of Colum-
    bia, President's, **1965**: 70, 366, 381,
    526n.; **1966**: 116, 219, 354, 611, 656
Commission of the European Communities,
    1968–69: 62, 348
Commission on Executive, Legislative, and
    Judicial Salaries, **1968–69**: 676 (pp.
    1266, 1267), 678 (p. 1305), 694
Commission on the Federal Budget, **1967**: 85
Commission on Fine Arts, **1963–64**: 700
Commission on Food and Fiber, National Ad-
    visory, **1965**: 597
Commission on Food Marketing, National,
    1965: 567; **1966**: 294
Commission on Health Manpower, National
    Advisory, **1966**: 169, 208, 301, 490,
    536
Commission on Heart Disease, Cancer, and
    Stroke, President's, **1963–64**: 179, 211
    [6], 268, 617, 798; **1965**: 5, 343
Commission on Income Maintenance Programs,
    1968–69: 3, 47 (p. 143), 678 (p. 1298),
    684 (p. 1325)
Commission on Law Enforcement and Admini-
    stration of Justice, President's,
    1965: 102, 381, 382, 422, 437, 500,
    526; **1966**: 116, 491, 492 [1], 494 [1],
    526, 611, 630 [9]
Commission on Libraries, National Advisory,
    1966: 424
Commission on Marine Science, Engineering, and
    Resources, **1967**: 101
Commission on Money and Credit, **1966**: 182,
    199
Commission on Narcotic and Drug Abuse, Presi-
    dent's Advisory, **1963–64**: 159, 179;
    1965: 102
Commission on Organization of the Executive
    Branch of the Government (Hoover
    Commission), **1963–64**: 71 [12];
    1966: 190, 438, 523; **1967**: 99, 121;
    1968–69: 59, 60, 227
Commission on Pennsylvania Avenue, proposed,
    1965: 538
  See also President's Council on Pennsylvania
    Avenue.

Commission on Political Activity of Government Personnel, **1966**: 499

Commission on Postal Organization, **1967**: 168

Commission on Presidential Scholars, **1963–64**: 266 [4], 309; **1965**: 171; **1966**: 257

Commission on Product Safety, National, **1967**: 57, 342, 499

Commission on Reform of Criminal Laws in the District of Columbia, **1967**: 71

Commission on Reform of Federal Criminal Laws, National, **1966**: 598

Commission on Registration and Voting Participation, President's, **1963–64**: 57, 167

Commission to Report Upon the Assassination of President John F. Kennedy, **1963–64**: 14, 232 [5], 280 [10], 281, 462 [8], 780 [11]; **1966**: 577 [11]; **1967**: 80 [5]

  Appointment of, executive order, **1963–64**: 15

  Report, **1963–64**: 595, 619 [11, 17]

Commission on Rural Poverty, National Advisory, **1966**: 28

Commission on Selective Service, National Advisory, **1966**: 315n., 388, 536

Commission on Statehood for Puerto Rico, **1963–64**: 242 [5]

Commission on the Status of Women, Governor's, **1965**: 392

Commission on the Status of Women, President's, **1963–64**: 294 [21]; **1965**: 392

Commission on Technology, Automation, and Economic Progress, National, **1963–64**: 214, 525; **1965**: 100, 258; **1966**: 111, 258

Commission on Urban Problems, **1968–69**: 704

Commission on U.S. Food and Fiber Policy, proposed, **1965**: 47

Commission on White House Fellows, President's, **1963–64**: 622; **1965**: 334; **1968–69**: 227

Commissioners, U.S., **1968–69**: 542

Commissioner's Committee on Community Development, **1967**: 15n.

Commissions on Organization of the Executive Branch of the Government, **1965**: 441

Committee on the Alliance for Progress, Inter-American, **1963–64**: 220, 227, 475 [3]; **1965**: 18, 136, 393, 429; **1966**: 41, 125, 158 [2], 177, 386n., 501 [1]

Committee on Balance of Payments, Cabinet, **1965**: 638

Committee on Business Advisers, **1963–64**: 271 [15]

Committee on Consumer Interests, President's, **1963–64**: 173; **1965**: 567; **1966**: 140

Committee on Corporate Pension Funds and Other Private Retirement and Welfare Programs, Presidential, **1965**: 35 (p. 113)

Committee for Development Planning in Alaska Federal Field, **1963–64**: 615n.

  President's Review, **1963–64**: 615

Committee on Disarmament, 18-Nation, **1965**: 20, 353 [5, 11], 386, 430

Committee for Economic Development, **1963–64**: 775

Committee on the Economic Impact of Defense and Disarmament, **1963–64**: 62, 486ftn. (p. 908); **1965**: 493

Committee on Education, Interagency, **1965**: 100

Committee on Employment of the Handicapped, President's, **1963–64**: 302

  Distinguished Service Award, **1963–64**: 235, 302n.

  1964 award, **1963–64**: 389

Committee on Environmental Quality, **1968–69**: 577n.

Committee on Equal Employment Opportunity, President's, **1963–64**: 40, 111, 139, 205, 213, 221, 277, 342, 379 [7], 448; **1965**: 448 [6], 530n.; **1966**: 196

  Report, **1963–64**: 812n.

Committee on Equal Opportunity in the Armed Forces, **1963–64**: 816

Committee on Federal Credit Programs, **1966**: 182, 199

Committee on Federal Staff Retirement Systems, Cabinet, **1966**: 108

  Proposed, **1965**: 49

Committee on Food and Fiber, **1965**: 597

Committee on Foreign Assistance Programs, General Advisory, **1965**: 136

Committee for International Development, National, **1965**: 7

Committee on International Meteorological Programs, Interagency, **1966**: 143

Committee on International Monetary Arrangements, Advisory, **1965**: 365

Committee for Johnson and Humphrey, National Independent, **1963–64**: 555

Committee on Juvenile Delinquency and Youth Crime, President's, **1963–64**: 334, 537, 704n.; **1965**: 282, 381

Committee on Labor-Management Policy, President's Advisory, **1963–64**: 126, 213; **1965**: 428; **1966**: 111, 184, 201, 474 [20]

Committee on Libraries, President's, **1966**: 424

Committee on Manpower, President's, **1963–64**: 212, 213, 264; **1965**: 100; **1966**: 111

Committee on Mental Retardation, **1966**: 95

Committee for a More Beautiful Capital, National, **1966**: 500, 501 [18]

Committee on the National Medal of Science, President's, **1963–64**: 98n.; **1965**: 646n.; **1966**: 61n.; **1967**: 37n.

Committee on Nuclear Proliferation, **1965**: 28

Committee on Older Americans, Advisory, **1965**: 642

Committee on Political Education (COPE), **1968–69**: 50, 164, 165

Committee on Population and Family Planning, **1968–69**: 393, 659

Committee for the Preservation of the White House, **1963–64**: 211 [7, 35]

Committee on Private Enterprise in Foreign Aid, Advisory, **1963–64**: 227; **1965**: 18, 450; **1966**: 41

Committee on Public Higher Education in the District of Columbia, President's, **1963–64**: 116n., 457

  Report, **1965**: 111

Committee of the Red Cross, International, **1966**: 338 [1], 549

Committee on Reduction of Nonessential Federal Expenditures, **1963–64**: 316 [4]

Committee on Retirement Policy for Federal Personnel, **1965**: 49

Committee on Scientific Cooperation, United States-Japan, **1965**: 15

Committee on Supersonic Transport, President's Advisory, **1963–64**: 242 [9, 17], 294 [6]; **1965**: 339

Committee on Trade and Economic Affairs, Joint United States-Japan, **1965**: 15, 355

Committee on Trade on Economic Affairs, U.S.-Canada, **1963–64**: 140

Committee on Trade Negotiations, Public Advisory, **1963–64**: 278

Committee for Traffic Safety, President's, **1963–64**: 565; **1966**: 98

Committee on Utilization of Scientific and Engineering Manpower, **1963–64**: 271 ftn. (p. 488), 456n.

Committee on Veterans Facilities, Special, **1965**: 163

Committee on Water Resources Research, **1965**: 275, 418; **1966**: 138

Commodity Credit Corporation, **1963–64**: 132 (p. 187); **1965**: 47, 139, 149, 377; **1966**: 49, 62, 272, 281n., 355; **1967**: 13 (p. 46), 33, 138n., 305; **1968–69**: 94, 467 [3], 534, 678 (pp. 1281, 1282)

  Report, **1968–69**: 247

Commodity Exchange Act, amendments, **1968–69**: 14 (p. 29), 85

Commodity exchanges, **1968–69**: 94

Common markets.

  See Central American Common Market; European Economic Community.

Commonwealth Prime Ministers Conference (London), **1963–64**: 474; **1965**: 319 [14], 331

Communicable diseases, **1966**: 6 (p. 8), 41, 45–46, 166, 189, 461

Communications, **1966**: 145, 246, 337; **1967**: 474; **1968–69**: 39 (p. 102), 41

  See also Communications satellites.

  Excise taxes on, **1965**: 255

  Message to Congress, **1967**: 346

  Police, **1968–69**: 59

  Policy task force, **1967**: 346

  Standard Code for Information Interchange, **1968–69**: 127

  Task force, presidential, **1968–69**: 59

  Technological progress, **1963–64**: 517, 788; **1965**: 305, 378, 468

  U.S.-Germany, direct line, **1966**: 486

  U.S.-Japan, trans-Pacific telephone, **1963–64**: 408

  U.S.-Soviet ("Hotline") direct line, **1963–64**: 395, 413, 435, 504 [12], 607, 662n., 667, 686; **1965**: 20; **1967**: 59, 264 [16], 297 [3]

  U.S.-Venezuela submarine cable, **1966**: 366

  Worldwide, **1968–69**: 507

Communications Act of 1934, **1967**: 346

Communications Satellite Act of 1962, **1963–64**: 180; **1965**: 68, 69; **1966**: 103; **1967**: 122, 346; **1968–69**: 175

Communications Satellite Corporation (ComSat), **1963–64**: 180, 517, 587 [1]; **1965**: 68n., 69, 333, 353 [4], 468; **1966**: 103; **1967**: 122, 346; **1968–69**: 175, 506

Communications satellites, **1963–64**: 132 (p. 187), 180, 408n., 517; **1965**: 333, 334, 378; **1966**: 40, 103, 243; **1967**: 176, 346, 389, 423, 425, 474; **1968–69**: 14 (p. 27), 77, 175, 233, 288

  Global commercial system, international agreement, **1963–64**: 532; **1965**: 68, 69, 81

  Relay, **1963–64**: 779n.

  Syncom, **1963–64**: 180n., 632, 779n.

Communications System, National, **1968–69**: 127

Communications Workers of America, **1963–64**: 406

Communism, **1963–64**: 244, 462 [12]; **1965**: 289, 316; **1967**: 34 [7]; **1968–69**: 472, 531

  U.S. policy on, **1963–64**: 619 [18]

  Versus democracy, **1963–64**: 8, 91 (p. 116), 139, 227, 280, 413, 531, 562, 589, 598, 604, 607, 617, 631, 633, 638, 640, 643, 648, 650, 652, 655, 668, 669, 678, 686, 694, 695, 702, 703, 709, 726, 734, 735, 736, 737; **1965**: 2, 18, 221, 294, 295 [15], 340

Communist aggression, **1963-64**: 132 (p. 176),
227, 272, 413, 416, 424, 516 [19], 607,
627, 702; **1965**: 117 [3], 229, 330, 347
[1]; **1966**: 26 (p. 48), 345, 347;
1968-69: 565
Africa, **1963-64**: 702; **1965**: 18; **1966**: 346
Asia, South Asia, and Southeast Asia,
1963-64: 170 [1, 5, 10, 18], 182, 189,
201 [5, 17], 218 [24], 272, 280 [8], 285
[12], 379 [1], 420 [1], 474, 499, 662,
702; **1965**: 2, 18, 46 [11], 106 [6], 130,
227, 246, 256n., 300, 388 [1];
1966: 85, 397, 411, 461, 542, 549, 551-
552, 560, 565, 568; **1967**: 3 (p. 11),
127n., 212n., 246n., 347, 397, 401,
407, 409, 438n., 442, 446, 495 [14],
519; **1968-69**: 109, 129, 142, 143, 186,
384, 452, 528
Bolivia, **1967**: 453
Burma, **1967**: 409
Caribbean area, **1963-64**: 37
China, Republic of, **1967**: 219
Cuba, **1966**: 6 (p. 7)
Czechoslovakia, **1968-69**: 455, 462, 467ftn.
(p. 929), 472, 474, 676 (p. 1269)
Developing and new nations, **1965**: 18; **1966**:
420
Dominican Republic, **1965**: 216, 221, 227,
286, 295 [9, 16]
Europe, Eastern, **1968-69**: 467 [15], 472
Formosa Straits, **1966**: 6 (p. 7)
Germany, **1968-69**: 142, 154, 165, 339 [6]
Greece, **1966**: 6 (p. 7); **1967**: 397, 409;
1968-69: 142, 154, 165
India, **1965**: 227
Indonesia, **1967**: 409
Korea, **1966**: 6 (p. 7), 562, 565, 568;
1967: 111; **1968-69**: 35, 109, 142,
154, 165, 201, 472
Laos, **1963-64**: 201 [7], 294 [16], 400, 420
[1, 5], 500, 504 [4]; **1965**: 26;
1967: 80 [4], 83, 132 [3, 4], 409, 480,
554 [1]
Latin America, **1963-64**: 220, 272, 443, 702;
1965: 18, 295 [10]; **1967**: 395;
1968-69: 110
Malaysia (Malaya), **1963-64**: 471; **1966**: 568-
569
Philippines, **1966**: 568
Thailand, **1967**: 293, 409; **1968-69**: 237
Turkey (1947), **1966**: 6 (p. 7); **1967**: 397,
409
U.S. response, **1966**: 261, 311-312, 397, 400,
411, 416, 420, 434, 497, 542, 563;
1967: 126, 158, 397, 453, 491,
519
Venezuela, **1963-64**: 486 [3]; **1967**: 453

Communist aggression – *continued*
Vietnam, **1963-64**: 37, 83, 170 [1, 5, 10, 18],
201 [5, 17], 211 [33], 218 [24], 223,
272, 280 [8], 313, 316 [27], 348, 379
[1], 400, 475 [3], 497, 498, 499, 500,
504 [4], 507, 509, 511, 560 [3], 561,
563 [1], 591, 627, 662, 693, 793;
1965: 2, 26, 46 [11], 51, 117 [2], 130,
145, 152, 156 [11], 172, 194, 206, 208
[2, 14, 16], 227, 229, 234, 246, 254,
276, 295 [3], 300, 319 [17], 331, 353
[1, 12], 388 [1, 5, 16], 397, 412 [4],
421; **1966**: 6 (p. 7), 53, 55, 77, 86, 93-
94, 128, 188 [10], 236, [1, 9], 246,
273-274, 277 [7], 287, 304, 311, 329,
346, 377, 383, 411, 415-416, 420, 431,
437, 445 [25], 474 [10], 540, 549, 553,
565-566, 568, 570, 577 [15], 607 [3]
See also Vietnam, North; Vietnam, South.
Western Hemisphere, **1963-64**: 26, 316 [23],
635; **1965**: 18, 223, 286, 295 [4, 15];
1966: 175
Communist bloc, **1963-64**: 124 (p. 162), 686,
689, 702, 737, 746; **1965**: 299, 302;
1966: 6 (p. 9), 414
See also specific countries.
Civil war, spread of, **1963-64**: 192
Sino-Soviet rift, effect on U.S., **1963-64**: 246
[11], 643
Trade with, **1963-64**: 294 [20, 22], 641
U.S. relations with, **1963-64**: 696
View of U.S. morals, **1963-64**: 280 [5]
Community action programs, **1965**: 9, 32 (p.
93), 75, 80, 90, 100, 132, 455;
1966: 8 [3], 28, 111, 140, 189, 594
Community Assistance, Federal Task Force on,
proposed, **1965**: 493n.
Community Campaigns, United, **1966**: 476
Community Development, Commissioner's
Committee on, **1967**: 15n.
Community Development, Department of
Housing and, proposed, **1963-64**: 132
(p. 194), 152
Community development district bill, **1966**: 28n.
Community Development Service, Rural,
1966: 28, 111
Community Health Services, National Commis-
sion on, **1966**: 185
Community Health Services Extension Amend-
ments of 1965, **1965**: 406
Community mental health centers bill,
1965: 329, 330
Approval, **1965**: 401
Community programs and development,
1963-64: 124 (p. 163), 132 (p. 188),
189, 219, 289, 757; **1965**: 9, 90;
1966: 6 (p. 5), 26 (pp. 50, 55, 61, 63),
28-30, 518; **1967**: 13 (pp. 52, 54, 58),

Community development – *continued*
15n., 16 (p. 75), 39, 114, 199, 372;
1968–69: 28, 39 (pp. 103, 104), 75n.,
87, 94, 312, 315, 354, 471, 678 (pp.
1290, 1291, 1295), 684 (pp. 1321,
1322)
Colleges, participation, **1965**: 9, 54, 455
Federal aid, **1963–64**: 124 (p. 165), 132 (pp.
181, 184, 189, 194), 152, 219, 289;
1965: 32 (p. 93), 35 (pp. 106, 114,
115), 54, 90, 401, 493
Health centers, **1968–69**: 111, 536, 678 (p. 1295)
Health services, **1967**: 285, 353
Indian, **1968–69**: 113
Message to Congress, **1963–64**: 152;
1965: 90
Older persons, **1968–69**: 75
Private organizations participation, **1965**: 529
Task force, **1965**: 100, 493n.
Community Relations, National Citizens Commit-
tee for, **1963–64**: 522
Community Relations Service, **1963–64**: 446;
1965: 345, 530n.; **1966**: 51, 59–60,
196; **1967**: 13 (p. 57), 55; **1968–69**: 26,
39 (p. 109), 678 (p. 1301)
Comprehensive Health Planning and Public
Health Service Amendments of 1966,
1966: 490, 573; **1967**: 223 [6]
Compton, Arthur, **1967**: 391, 515
Comptroller General (Joseph Campbell),
1963–64: 18, 261; **1965**: 60
Comptroller General (Elmer B. Staats),
1966: 25, 65 [1], 88 [6], 113, 239, 612;
1967: 16 (p. 87), 236
Computers
Data systems, **1968–69**: 127
Education use, **1967**: 77; **1968–69**: 54, 145
Use and management, **1966**: 296
Computing Activities, Office of, **1968–69**: 145
ComSat.
See Communications Satellite Corporation.
Conant, James B., **1963–64**: 27
Concentrated employment program, **1968–69**: 24,
39 (p. 104), 40, 47 (p. 142), 94, 113,
220, 678 (p. 1294)
Conciliation Service, Federal Mediation and,
1963–64: 614n.; **1967**: 104 [15];
1968–69: 112
Concord, Calif., rapid transit system,
1963–64: 410
Con-Edison power system, **1965**: 608n.
Cone Mills, **1968–69**: 548
Confederation, Articles of, **1966**: 261
Conference on Civil Rights, **1965**: 183, 301, 453,
548, 613; **1966**: 51, 88 [10], 196, 247
[11], 248, 407–408
Conference on Crime Control, National,
1967: 146, 221

Conference on Cultural and Educational Inter-
change, Joint United States-Japan,
1965: 15
Conference on Development and Utilization of
Natural Resources, United States-Japan,
1967: 491
Conference of Editorial Writers, National,
1966: 501 [2], 503–504
Conference on Education, International,
1966: 627
Conference on Education, White House,
1965: 183, 291, 340, 374, 385
Conference on the Education of Disadvantaged
Children, National Planning, **1966**: 238
Conference on Educational Legislation, National,
1965: 89
Conference for Educators, Foreign Policy,
1967: 272
Conference on the 18-Nation Committee on Dis-
armament, **1965**: 430
Conference on Equal Employment Opportunity,
White House, **1965**: 384, 436
Conference of Federal Executive Board Chair-
men, National, **1965**: 264
Conference on Health, White House, **1965**: 183,
424, 594
Conference on International Cooperation, White
House, **1965**: 96, 630, 632; **1966**: 370;
1967: 157
Conference on International Rural Development,
1963–64: 482
Conference of Mayors, United States, **1965**: 438;
1966: 536; **1967**: 337
Conference on Medical Costs, National,
1967: 77
Conference on Natural Beauty, White House,
1965: 2, 30, 54, 183, 277, 446
Conference on Natural Beauty and Conservation,
National Youth, **1966**: 295
Conference on Occupational Safety, **1963–64**: 421
Conference of Returned Peace Corps Volunteers,
1965: 33
Conference of State Commissions on the Status
of Women, **1966**: 299
Conference of State Committees on Criminal
Administration, **1966**: 491, 492 [1],
526
Conference "To Fulfill These Rights," White
House, **1965**: 183, 301, 453, 548, 613;
1966: 51, 88 [10], 196, 247 [11], 248,
407–408
Conference on Trade and Development, United
Nations, **1967**: 100
Conference on Water for Peace, International,
1966: 427, 593; **1967**: 230
Conference on Women in the War on Poverty,
1967: 211
Conference on the World Crisis in Education,
International, **1967**: 423

Conference on World Peace Through Law,
   1965: 516
Confucius, **1967**: 434
Congo (Kinshasa), **1968–69**: 433n.
Congo, Republic of the (Leopoldville)
   Belgian troops in, **1963–64**: 780 [2, 16]
   Civil disorder in, **1963–64**: 780 [2, 10]
      Civilian rescue operations, **1963–64**: 780
         [2, 16]
      Rebel forces, **1963–64**: 780 [10]
   Tshombe, Moise, **1963–64**: 455 [12], 475 [8]
   United Nations operations, **1965**: 169
   U.S. relations with, **1963–64**: 780 [2]; **1967**:
      519
   U.S. troops in, **1963–64**: 780 [2, 16];
      1965: 319 [16]
Congress, **1965**: 115; **1966**: 8 [8], 445 [19]
   Adjournment, question of, **1963–64**: 516 [5]
   Antipoverty bill, House action on,
      1963–64: 505
   Appropriation bills, House action on,
      1963–64: 455 [1]
   Appropriations, **1966**: 141 [3], 188 [6], 444
      For foreign aid, **1963–64**: 218 [33]
   Area redevelopment bill, House action on,
      1965: 329, 330
   Civil rights bill, Senate debate on, **1963–64**: 211
      [20], 218 [35], 246 [9], 256 [11], 316
      [13], 336 [14], 379 [20]
   Coinage bill, Senate passage of, **1965**: 329, 330
   Comments on, **1963–64**: 536, 619 [6], 735;
         1965: 22 [14], 141, 143, 156 [9], 316,
         397, 406, 413, 417, 418, 433, 454 [5],
         463 [15], 522, 536, 559; **1966**: 65 [5],
         141 [12], 277 [19], 444, 510, 515, 599
         [1–2, 6]; **1967**: 6 [17], 34 [4], 225
         [12], 375 [8], 417 [4], 420, 460 [14];
         1968–69: 4, 26, 661, 690, 696 [12]
   Committees.
      See other part of title.
   Democratic dinners, **1965**: 329, 330
   Democratic Members, administrative assistants,
      1968–69: 212
   Dinners for Members, **1966**: 188 [12], 221;
      1967: 216
   District of Columbia home rule petition, signing
      by House Members, **1965**: 481
   District of Columbia representation, **1967**: 71;
      1968–69: 39 (p. 107)
   Education Act, Senate approval, **1963–64**: 36
   Education bills, action on, **1965**: 137, 178,
      455, 479
   Ethical standards, **1967**: 297 [8]
   Excise tax reduction bill, passage, **1965**: 321
   Excise taxes, House action on, **1963–64**: 407
   Executive branch relations, **1963–64**: 11, 81,
      777; **1965**: 440, 495, 502, 515;
      1966: 206, 216, 270, 292

Congress – *continued*
   Federal budget procedures, **1968–69**: 684
      (p. 1317)
   Federal Reserve Bank presidents, selection
      process, **1968–69**: 684 (p. 1318)
   Foreign Assistance Appropriation Act of 1965,
      passage by House, **1965**: 502
   Holidays spent in session, **1963–64**: 71 [14]
   Housing and urban development bill, House
      action on, **1965**: 319 [2], 337
   IDA bill, House action on, **1963–64**: 346
   Investigations
      Robert G. Baker, **1963–64**: 201 [4], 218
         [13], 455 [21], 563 [15]
      Extremist organizations, question of,
         1965: 135
      National security, **1965**: 106 [3]
   Juvenile delinquency bill, House action on,
      1965: 329, 330
   Leadership
      Breakfast, **1968–69**: 654
      Meetings, **1963–64**: 688 [1]; **1965**: 133, 221,
         227; **1966**: 628 [1]; **1968–69**: 658
      Reception for President, **1968–69**: 655
   Legislative record, **1963–64**: 53, 71 [16], 78, 91
      (p. 112), 143 [2], 150 [5], 170 [13],
      179, 201 [9], 228, 242 [22], 271 [7],
      307, 338, 342, 350, 434, 482, 488, 504
      [2], 514, 520, 521 [2], 527, 549, 554,
      578, 603, 605, 620, 640, 642, 643, 645,
      650, 652, 657, 658, 667, 669, 676, 678,
      695, 703, 728, 729, 756, 761; **1965**: 156
      [9], 173, 329, 330, 354, 362, 385, 489,
      525, 559, 579, 597, 603, 644; **1966**: 6
      (p. 3), 26 (pp. 63, 65), 77, 95, 141 [12],
      164, 166, 221, 232, 237, 247 [14], 270,
      307, 341, 353, 392, 403, 406, 417 [6],
      418, 436–437, 470, 487, 501 [6, 10],
      504, 509–512, 515, 516 [7], 518, 520,
      522, 524–525, 545, 569, 573, 576, 579,
      588, 604, 610 [6]; **1967**: 575n.
   Medicare bill, Senate passage of, **1963–64**: 552;
      1965: 348
   Members, pay and allowances, **1963–64**: 132
      (p. 194), 222, 267, 270, 271 [10];
      1968–69: 676 (p. 1267), 677, 694
   Members at a press conference, **1963–64**: 285
      [19]
   New Democratic Members, **1963–64**: 776, 799
   President's service in, **1963–64**: 22, 37, 51, 96,
      120, 124 (p. 155), 170 [9], 182, 215,
      242 [26], 250, 289, 295, 297, 330, 334,
      336 [14], 337, 342, 372, 388, 413, 486
      [11], 512, 550, 560 [10], 562, 578, 589,
      591, 597, 605, 608n., 617, 635, 637,
      642, 643, 645, 648, 652, 658, 676, 678,
      680, 694, 695, 702, 703, 712, 716, 718,
      728, 729, 733, 734, 736, 741, 742, 747,

Congress — *continued*
  President's service in — *continued*
    748, 749, 750, 762, 764, 799, 808;
    1965: 81, 183, 196, 248, 301, 310, 317,
    409, 415, 514; **1966**: 51, 52 [3], 88
    [17], 168, 353
  Reaction to closing of military installations,
    1963–64: 71 [11]
  Reception for Members of, **1965**: 183
  Receptions for the President, **1968–69**: 690,
    691
  Relationship with District of Columbia,
    1965: 39
  Remarks, to, **1968–69**: 258
  Reorganization plans, Presidential submittal,
    1968–69: 39 (p. 109)
  Salute to Members of, **1963–64**: 462 [11], 527;
    1965: 559
  Social Security Amendments of 1965, House
    approval, **1965**: 176 [2]
  Southeast Asia, Joint Resolution on, passage,
    1963–64: 503
  Special session, possibility, **1963–64**: 316 [13];
    1968–69: 590 [6]
  Tax legislation procedures, **1968–69**: 684 (p.
    1318)
  Term of office, **1966**: 6 (pp. 3–4, 7), 21
  Vietnam, appropriations for military require-
    ments in, **1965**: 261
  Vietnam conflict
    Involvement, **1966**: 52 [3], 65 [6], 88 [16–
      17], 474 [4]
    Views, **1967**: 132 [10], 358 [2, 10], 518
      [12]
  Voting rights bill
    House action on, **1965**: 349
    Senate passage of, **1965**: 278
Congress, letters to members of.
  See also Congress, messages to; Congress, re-
    ports to, messages transmitting.
  Adams, Repr. Brock, Vietnam conflict, **1966**:
    23
  Anderson, Sen. Clinton P., Alaska reconstruc-
    tion, **1963–64**: 319
  Bible, Sen. Alan, District of Columbia school
    board, **1967**: 399
  Buckley, Repr. Charles A., renaming of National
    Cultural Center, **1963–64**: 39
  Byrd, Sen. Harry Flood, reduction in tax with-
    holding rate, **1963–64**: 92
  Byrd, Sen. Robert C., education budget for the
    District of Columbia, **1965**: 151
  Dulski, Repr. Thaddeus J., mail service to Viet-
    nam, **1966**: 651
  Harris, Repr. Oren, transportation, **1963–64**:
    154
  Hart, Sen. Philip, civil rights bill, **1968–69**: 82
  Hartke, Sen. Vance, Vietnam conflict, **1966**:
    36

Congress, letters to members of — *continued*
  Hill, Sen. Lister, college student loans, **1967**:
    338n.
  Jackson, Sen. Henry M., bombing of North
    Vietnam, **1967**: 83
  Long, Sen. Russell B., tariff imports on repro-
    cessed wool fabrics and blends, **1968–
    69**: 671
  Magnuson, Sen. Warren G., transportation,
    1963–64: 154
  Mansfield, Sen. Mike
    Crime control and safe streets bill, **1968–69**:
      235
    Middle East conflict, **1967**: 257
    Railroad labor dispute, **1967**: 310
    Steel price increase, **1968–69**: 427
    Urban legislation, **1967**: 353
  McMillan, Repr. John L., District of Columbia
    Charter Act, **1965**: 486
  McNamara, Sen. Pat, renaming of National
    Cultural Center, **1963–64**: 39
  Mills, Repr. Wilbur D.
    Tariff imports on reprocessed wool fabrics
      and blends, **1968–69**: 671
    Tax bill, **1963–64**: 196
    Tax proposals, **1966**: 17
  Moss, Repr. John E., executive privilege, **1965**:
    160
  Patman, Repr. Wright, business investments,
    1966: 110
  Perkins, Repr. Carl D., college student loans,
    1967: 338n.
  President pro tempore of the Senate and
      Speaker of the House of Representa-
      tives
    Alaska Omnibus Act, proposed amendment,
      1963–64: 286
    Alaskan reconstruction legislation, **1963–64**:
      368
    Appalachian area, **1963–64**: 300
    Arms Control and Disarmament Agency,
      1965: 20
    Civil rights program, appropriations for,
      1963–64: 466
    Fair Labor Standards Act, amendments pro-
      posed, **1963–64**: 166
    Food industry, study proposed, **1963–64**:
      242 [10]
    Highway construction in the District of
      Columbia, **1965**: 19
    National Commission on Automation and
      Technological Progress, proposed, **1963–
      64**: 214
    National Council on the Arts, proposed
      establishment, **1963–64**: 524
    National Oceanographic Program, **1963–64**:
      229
    Pay bill, **1963–64**: 222
    Peace Corps appropriations, **1963–64**: 112

Congress, letters to members of – *continued*
  President pro tempore – *continued*
    Reduction in cost of operating the Government, **1963–64**: 240
    Technological revolution, **1963–64**: 214
    Water resources program, **1963–64**: 231
  President of the Senate and Speaker of the House of Representatives
    Alaska, earthquake recovery assistance to, **1965**: 435
    Alaskan disaster relief, **1966**: 74; **1967**: 369
    American Revolution Bicentennial Commission, **1966**: 120
    Antipoverty program, **1965**: 75
    Appalachian program, **1967**: 11
    Arms Control and Disarmament Agency, **1968–69**: 27
    Automatic data processing equipment, Government use of, **1965**: 93
    Automotive products trade agreement, U.S.-Canada, **1965**: 147
    Civil rights bill, **1968–69**: 131
    Coal mine health and safety bill, **1968–69**: 475
    Credit, substitution of private for public, **1966**: 182
    District of Columbia, **1965**: 40, 111, 402
      Government reorganization, **1967**: 337
      National Visitor Center, **1966**: 90
      Public safety, **1968–69**: 355
      School board, **1967**: 350
    Economic Opportunity, Office of, **1967**: 203
    Educational, Scientific and Cultural Materials, Agreement on the Importation of, **1965**: 292
    Election reform bill, **1966**: 241
    Exports, actions to increase American, **1968–69**: 146
    Fair housing bill, **1968–69**: 182
    Farm bill, **1965**: 168
    Federal Council for Science and Technology, **1966**: 222
    Federal Water Resources Research Program (1966), **1965**: 275
    Firearms control bill, **1967**: 385
    Flood control policy, **1966**: 374
    Foreign Affairs Personnel System, **1965**: 233
    Foreign Service, **1965**: 185
    Foreign visitors, entry, **1968–69**: 88
    Grand Coulee Dam, proposed power-plant, **1965**: 186
    Gun control legislation, **1968–69**: 296
    Highway beautification legislation, proposed, **1965**: 279
    Hirshhorn, Joseph H., Museum and Sculpture Garden, **1966**: 227
    Immigration bill, **1965**: 449

Congress, letters to members of – *continued*
  President of the Senate – *continued*
    Income tax surtax, **1968–69**: 226
    International Monetary Fund, increased fund quotas, proposed, **1965**: 110
    Medicare enrollment extension, **1966**: 161
    Military officers, taxes, **1966**: 389
    Military operations in Asia, appropriation, **1967**: 14
    Mining, strip and surface, **1967**: 300
    National Teacher Corps, **1966**: 67
    Oceanographic programs, 1966, **1965**: 92; **1966**: 229
    Office of Emergency Planning, name change, **1968–69**: 483
    Pacific Islands, Trust Territory of the, **1967**: 360
    Passamaquoddy-St. John River Basin development, **1965**: 350
    Patent system, **1967**: 65
    Peace Corps appropriations, **1965**: 83
    Pennsylvania Avenue National Historic Site, **1965**: 538
    Public Works and Economic Development Act, proposed, **1965**: 148
    Railroad labor dispute, **1967**: 194, 310
    Rapid transit system for Nation's capital, proposed, **1965**: 61
    Rent supplement program, **1966**: 67
    Reorganization Act of 1949, proposed amendment, **1965**: 43
    San Rafael Wilderness, Calif., **1967**: 29
    Selective Service System, **1966**: 67
    Southeast Asia, appropriations, **1966**: 18
    Southern Rhodesia, trade with, **1967**: 74
    Steel price increase, **1968–69**: 427
    Summer youth programs, **1967**: 203
    Tax bill, **1968–69**: 322
    Tax reform, **1968–69**: 651
    Teaching Professions Act of 1965, proposed, **1965**: 368
    Tennessee Valley Authority, **1966**: 233
    Transportation, high-speed systems, research and development, **1965**: 97
    United States-Mexico Commission for Border Development and Friendship, **1968–69**: 354
    U.S. chancery in Saigon, proposed construction, **1965**: 152
    Voting rights, bill to eliminate barriers to, **1965**: 109
    Washington Metropolitan Area Transit Authority, **1966**: 262
    Water desalinization, **1965**: 143
    Water resources
      Assessment of Nation's, **1968–69**: 593
      Research, **1966**: 138
    Wilderness preservation, **1967**: 418

Congress, letters to members of — *continued*
  President of the Senate - *continued*
    Wilderness Preservation System, National,
      1968–69: 168
    Saltonstall, Sen. Leverett, **1965**: 662
    Sparkman, Sen. John, Housing and Urban De-
      velopment Act of 1968, **1968–69**: 278
Congress, Library of, **1965**: 412 [1]; **1966**: 362;
  1967: 423
Congress, messages to.
  See also Congress, letters to Members of; Con-
    gress, reports to, messages transmitting.
  Agriculture, **1965**: 47
  Aircraft based offenses, convention, **1968–69**:
    494
  Area and regional economic development, **1965**:
    132
  Asian Development Bank, **1966**: 14; **1967**: 401
  Assistance to Vietnam, **1963–64**: 348
  Astronaut Assistance and Return Agreement,
    1968–69: 387
  Balance of payments, **1965**: 60
  Budget, **1963–64**: 132; **1965**: 32; **1966**: 26;
    1967: 13, 329
    Fiscal 1969, **1968–69**: 39
    Fiscal 1970, **1968–69**: 678
  Children and youth, **1967**: 39, 40
  Civil rights, **1965**: 107; **1966**: 196; **1968–69**:
    26
  Coffee Agreement, International, **1968–69**: 207
  Coinage system, **1965**: 297
  Communications policy, **1967**: 346
  Congressional term of office, **1966**: 21
  Conservation and beautification of natural re-
    sources, **1965**: 53, 54; **1968–69**: 122
  Constitutional amendments, **1966**: 21
  Consumer interests, **1963-64**: 173; **1966**: 140;
    1967: 57, 58; **1968–69**: 56
  Crime and law enforcement, **1966**: 116–117;
    1967: 35, 36
  Customs Cooperation Council, U.S. accession to
    Convention establishing, **1968–69**: 261
  Depreciation allowances, **1967**: 103
  District of Columbia, **1965**: 29, 30, 70; **1968–
    69**: 133
    Budget, **1963-64**: 133; **1966**: 27; **1967**: 15
    Fiscal year 1969, **1968–69**: 95
    Fiscal year 1970, **1968–69**: 689
  Economic Report, **1965**: 35; **1966**: 33–34;
    1967: 16; **1968–69**: 47, 684
  Economy, **1967**: 329
  Education, **1966**: 95; **1967**: 77, 78; **1968–69**:
    54
  Educational opportunity, **1965**: 9
  Election reform, **1967**: 236
  Electoral college system, **1966**: 21
  Employment, the right to earn a living, **1968–
    69**: 24
  Equal justice, **1967**: 55, 56

Congress, messages to — *continued*
  Farmers and rural America, **1968–69**: 94
  Federal employees, pay, **1966**: 108
  Federal military and civilian pay rates increase,
    1965: 244
  Fiscal policy, **1966**: 444
  Food for freedom program, **1966**: 62, 63
  Foreign aid, **1963–64**: 227; **1965**: 18; **1966**:
    41–42; **1967**: 44, 45; **1968–69**: 63
  Government, American, quality of, **1967**: 121
  Government employees pay, **1967**: 163
  Gun control legislation, **1968–69**: 334
  Health, national, **1963–64**: 179; **1965**: 5; **1966**:
    95; **1967**: 77; **1968–69**: 111
  Housing and community development, **1963–
    64**: 152
  Immigration, **1965**:13
  Income tax protocol, U.S.-Germany, **1965**: 535
  India food aid, **1966**: 153–154; **1967**: 33
  Indians, American, **1968–69**: 113
  Insurance, **1967**: 343
  International education and health, **1966**: 45–
    46
  International Grains Arrangement, **1968–69**: 29
  International monetary system, **1968–69**: 218
  Investment tax credit, **1967**: 103
  Kennedy, John F.
    Death of, **1963–64**: 11
    50-cent pieces, coinage, **1963–64**: 33
  Labor, **1965**: 258
  Latin American summit meeting, **1967**: 110
  Law enforcement and administration of justice,
    1965: 102
  Manpower Report of the President, **1963–64**:
    213; **1967**: 199
  Narcotics convention, **1967**: 94
  National security, **1965**: 26
  Nation's cities, **1965**: 90
  Natural heritage preservation, **1966**: 82
  Natural resources conservation, **1967**: 20
  North Vietnam attacks on U.S. vessels, **1963–
    64**: 500
  Nuclear nonproliferation treaty, **1968–69**: 378
  Older Americans, **1967**: 12
  Postal rates, **1967**: 163
  Poverty, **1963–64**: 219
  Presidential disability and related matters,
    1965: 34
  Railroad labor dispute, **1967**: 170, 207
  Refugees, protocol relating to the status of,
    1968–69: 428
  Reorganization plans, **1965**: 125, 247, 281,
    282, 283; **1966**: 59, 91, 190, 267, 302
    District of Columbia, **1967**: 247
      Recreation, **1968–69**: 134
    District of Columbia Redevelopment Land
      Agency, **1968–69**: 135
    Narcotics and drug abuse control, **1968–69**:
      60

Congress, messages to – *continued*
  Reorganization plans – *continued*
    Ships' mortgages, **1967**: 72
    Tariff Commission, U.S., **1967**: 99
    Urban mass transportation, **1968–69**: 93
  Rural America and farmers, **1968–69**: 94
  Rural areas, **1966**: 28–29
  Rural and urban poverty, **1967**: 114
  Salaries, Federal, **1968–69**: 694
  Selective service, **1967**: 92
  Servicemen and veterans, **1967**: 25, 26; **1968–69**: 40
  Southeast Asia, foreign aid for, **1965**: 294
  Space treaty, **1967**: 38
  State of the Union, **1963–64**: 91; **1965**: 2; **1966**: 6; **1967**: 3; **1968–69**: 14, 676
  Trade agreements, multinational, **1967**: 508
  Transit trade of land-locked states, convention on, **1968–69**: 383
  Transportation, **1966**: 98
  United Nations Charter, proposed amendments, **1965**: 169
  Urban areas, **1966**: 30–31
  Urban problems, **1968–69**: 87
  Urban and rural poverty, **1967**: 114
  Vietnam, appropriations for military requirements in, **1965**: 229
  Voting by 18-year-olds, **1968–69**: 341
  Voting rights, **1965**: 108
  World trade, **1968–69**: 274
  Youth Councils on Civic Affairs, veto of incorporation, **1965**: 508
Congress, reports to, list, Appendix C, **1967**: 1225; **1968–69**: 1401
Congress, reports to, messages transmitting.
  See also Congress, letters to Members of; Congress, messages to.
  Adult education, **1968–69**: 484
  Aeronautics and space, **1963–64**: 155; **1967**: 24; **1968–69**: 41
  Alaskan disaster relief, **1966**: 74
  Alien Property, Office of, **1965**: 309; **1966**: 303; **1968–69**: 514
  Antarctica, U.S. policy and international cooperation in, **1963–64**: 551
  Appalachian Regional Commission, **1968–69**: 173, 701,
  Architectural barriers to rehabilitation of the handicapped, **1968–69**: 287
  Armed Forces, incentive awards, **1968–69**: 248
  Arms Control and Disarmament Agency, **1966**: 70; **1968–69**: 69
  Atlantic-Pacific Interoceanic Canal Study Commission, **1965**: 400; **1966**: 384; **1967**: 336; **1968–69**: 466
  Atomic information, exchange with NATO and member nations, **1963–64**: 439
  Automatic data processing equipment, Government use of, **1965**: 93

Congress, reports to – *continued*
  Automotive products agreement with Canada, **1967**: 137; **1968–69**: 256, 465
  Civil Service Commission, **1968–69**: 84, 667
  Coffee Agreement, International, **1967**: 10; **1968–69**: 23
  Commodity Credit Corporation, **1965**: 377; **1966**: 355; **1967**: 305; **1968–69**: 247
  Communications Satellite Corporation, **1965**: 69; **1966**: 103; **1967**: 122; **1968–69**: 175
  Community work and training program, **1967**: 91
  Cooperative Medical Science Program, U.S.-Japan, **1968–69**: 286, 685
  Department of Labor, manpower resources, **1966**: 111–112
  Disaster relief assistance, Federal, **1968–69**: 98
  Economic opportunity, **1968–69**: 315
  Economic Opportunity, Office of, **1967**: 277
  Economic reports, **1963–64**: 124; **1968–69**: 47, 684
  Excise taxes and user charges, **1965**: 255
  Federal Council for Science and Technology, **1966**: 222
  Federal statutory salary systems, **1968–69**: 303
  Federal Water Resources Research Program (1966), **1965**: 275
  Flood disaster relief, **1966**: 381
  Food aid programs, **1967**: 469
  Food for freedom program, **1968–69**: 176
  Food for peace program, **1965**: 149; **1966**: 308
  Foreign assistance programs, **1963–64**: 617; **1966**: 11; **1968–69**: 21, 679
  Grand Coulee Dam, proposed powerplant, **1965**: 186
  Great Lakes Basin Commission, **1968–69**: 666
  Health research facilities construction program, **1968–69**: 468
  Highway Safety Act of 1966, administration, **1968–69**: 243
  Housing, national goals, **1968–69**: 699
  Housing and Home Finance Agency, **1965**: 585
  Housing and Urban Development, Department of, **1967**: 179; **1968–69**: 697
  Incentive awards, Armed Forces, **1968–69**: 248
  International Atomic Energy Agency, U.S. participation, **1965**: 537
  International Coffee Agreement, **1966**: 9
  International Educational and Cultural Exchange Program, **1965**: 36, 552; **1966**: 378; **1967**: 344
  International exhibitions, special, **1965**: 553; **1967**: 245; **1968–69**: 204
  Manpower programs, **1968–69**: 220, 706
  Manpower resources, **1965**: 100
  Marine resources and engineering, **1967**: 101; **1968–69**: 124, 692
  Medical programs, regional, **1967**: 477

Congress, reports to – *continued*
  Military incentive awards, **1967**: 208
  National Advisory Committee on Adult Basic
      Education, **1968–69**: 484
  National Advisory Council on Economic Oppor-
      tunity, **1968–69**: 315
  National Advisory Council on the Education of
      Disadvantaged Children, **1966**: 210
  National Advisory Council on Extension and
      Continuing Education, **1967**: 185; **1968–
      69**: 312
  National Aeronautics and Space Administration,
      1965: 584; **1967**: 220
  National Aeronautics and Space Council, **1966**:
      40
  National Capital Housing Authority, **1967**: 180;
      1968–69: 152
  National Capital Transportation Agency, **1966**:
      68; **1967**: 154
  National Endowment for the Arts, **1967**: 53;
      1968–69: 64, 686
  National Endowment for the Humanities, **1967**:
      54; **1968–69**: 45, 703
  National Science Foundation, **1965**: 71; **1966**:
      38, 79; **1967**: 165, 314; **1968–69**: 145,
      495, 687
  National Traffic and Motor Vehicle Safety Act
      of 1966, administration, **1968–69**: 244
  National Wilderness Preservation System, **1967**:
      96; **1968–69**: 311, 700
  New England River Basins Commission, **1968–
      69**: 666
  Pacific Northwest River Basins Commission,
      1968–69: 666
  Passamaquoddy-St. John River Basin develop-
      ment, **1965**: 350
  Peace Corps, **1966**: 126; **1967**: 90; **1968–69**:
      103, 656
  President's Appalachian Regional Commission,
      1963–64: 300
  President's Manpower Report, **1963–64**: 213
  Railroad Retirement Board, **1967**: 244; **1968–
      69**: 331
  Rapid transit system for the Nation's Capital,
      1965: 61
  Saint Lawrence Seaway Development Corpora-
      tion, **1967**: 398; **1968–69**: 252
  Souris-Red-Rainy River Basins Commission,
      1968–69: 666
  Surgeon General, **1967**: 260
  Surgeon General on health research facilities
      construction program, **1968–69**: 468
  Tariff schedules, textured yarns, **1966**: 43
  Trade agreements program, **1963–64**: 592;
      1965: 564; **1966**: 471; **1967**: 445;
      1968–69: 517
  Transportation, Secretary of, **1968–69**: 693

Congress, reports to – *continued*
  United Nations, U.S. participation, **1963–64**:
      529; **1966**: 94; **1967**: 100, 488; **1968–
      69**: 504
  United States Arms Control and Disarmament
      Agency, **1967**: 59
  United States-Japan Cooperative Medical
      Science program, **1968–69**: 286, 685
  Urban transportation, **1968–69**: 130, 306
  Water resources, assessment, **1968–69**: 593
  Weather modification, **1965**: 271; **1967**: 314;
      1968–69: 495
  Wilderness preservation system, **1966**: 69
Congress of Industrial Organizations.
  See American Federation of Labor–Congress
      of Industrial Organizations.
Congressional committee reports, **1963–64**: 307
Congressional Fellows, **1965**: 515
Congressional Medal of Honor.
  See Medal of Honor *under* Awards and
      Citations.
Congressional Record, **1967**: 332
Connally, Gov. John B., **1963–64**: 72n., 280 [10],
      281, 375, 596, 597, 598, 599, 738, 760,
      761, 763, 765, 767, 778; **1965**: 179,
      285, 291n.; **1966**: 121 [1], 277 [6],
      415–416, 417 [3], 520, 630 [2], 635
      [14], 638–639, 641, 650n.; **1967**: 408
      [1, 4, 8], 452; **1968–69**: 97, 171, 191
      [3], 260, 357, 359
Connally, Mrs. John B. (Nellie), **1963–64**: 596,
      763, 767; **1966**: 630 [2], 638–639;
      1968–69: 97, 359
Connally, Tom T., **1965**: 406n.
Connarn, John P., **1966**: 398
Connecticut, **1963–64**: 383; **1967**: 223 [2, 11],
      542
  Campaign remarks, **1963–64**: 603, 604
  Gov. John N. Dempsey, **1963–64**: 285 [7], 382,
      383, 603; **1967**: 222n., 223 [1, 2, 11]
  Remarks, **1967**: 222, 223
Connecticut River National Recreation Area,
      1966: 82
Connell, Ted C., **1968–69**: 599n.
Connell, William, **1966**: 85
Conner, Doyle E., **1963–64**: 709, 712, 713
Connett, Lt. Col. James A., **1966**: 246
Connor, Cecilia, **1967**: 202n.
Connor, Edward, **1966**: 536
Connor, Mrs. Harold E., **1967**: 202n.
Connor, John T., **1963–64**: 806; **1965**: 4; **1967**:
      268
  See also Commerce, Secretary of (John T. Con-
      nor).
Connor, Mrs. John T., **1965**: 25; **1966**: 326; **1967**: 8
Connor, S. Sgt. and Mrs. Peter S., **1967**: 202
Conrad, Charles, Jr., **1965**: 462, 463 [2]; **1966**:
      485

Conservation, National Youth Conference on
　　Natural Beauty and, **1966**: 295, 653
Conservation camps, **1963–64**: 267
Conservation Corps, Civilian, **1966**: 417 [2];
　　1967: 258
Conservation and development of natural re-
　　sources, **1963–64**: 132 (pp. 176, 187),
　　219, 267, 287, 391, 396, 427, 554, 578,
　　597, 599, 606, 644, 650, 654, 667, 669,
　　673, 713, 719, 729, 737, 760, 787; **1965**:
　　30, 32 (pp. 83, 91, 96), 35 (pp. 106,
　　115), 47, 48, 54, 132, 143, 148, 168,
　　471, 477, 521, 545, 576; **1966**: 26 (pp.
　　48, 59–60), 119, 232, 237, 295, 353,
　　393–394, 398, 415, 486, 509, 512, 518,
　　545, 579; **1967**: 13 (p. 51), 20, 96, 295,
　　495 [5], 532, 534, 553; **1968–69**: 14
　　(p. 122), 39 (p. 101), 50, 109, 167, 168,
　　212, 311, 330, 345, 386, 411, 510, 547,
　　593, 601, 612, 622, 644, 646 [13], 648,
　　666, 684 (p. 1321), 696 [16], 700, 702,
　　707
　　See also specific resources.
　　Appalachia, **1966**: 26 (p. 60), 123
　　Beautification programs, **1965**: 53, 54, 277
　　　See also Beautification programs.
　　Development areas, **1968–69**: 94
　　Indian lands, **1968–69**: 113
　　Legislation, **1963–64**: 620; **1966**: 515, 520,
　　　522, 524; **1968–69**: 345, 411, 565, 567,
　　　655
　　Message to Congress, **1966**: 82; **1967**: 20; **1968–
　　　69**: 122, 123
　　Presidential policy paper, **1963–64**: 756
　　Taxation policies on, **1965**: 54
　　TVA contributions, **1966**: 382
　　Urban open land, **1967**: 16 (p. 85)
　　Veterans use, **1968–69**: 419
　　Wilderness, **1967**: 29, 418
　　Youth activities, **1966**: 653; **1967**: 114
Conservation Fund, Land and Water, **1965**: 47,
　　54; **1966**: 398; **1967**: 13 (p. 51), 20,
　　553; **1968–69**: 39 (p. 101), 122, 386
Conservation Service, Agricultural Stabilization
　　and, **1966**: 225; **1967**: 228; **1968–69**:
　　303
Conservation Year proclamation, Youth for
　　Natural Beauty and, **1966**: 653
Consolidated Farmers Home Administration Act,
　　amendments, **1968–69**: 450
Consolidated Farmers Home Administration Act
　　of 1961, **1966**: 398, 403, 428
Constantine, King (Greece), **1963–64**: 209
　　Message, **1967**: 108
Constellation, U.S.S., **1968–69**: 81 [3], 102, 109
Constitution, U.S., **1963–64**: 81, 250, 270, 453,
　　462 [5], 511; **1965**: 27, 34, 48, 106
　　[1], 107, 108, 155, 169, 295 [7], 301,

Constitution, U.S. – *continued*
　　317, 329, 436, 440, 443, 448 [22], 481,
　　486, 515, 518, 587; **1966**: 6 (pp. 4, 7),
　　21, 96, 261–262, 299, 504; **1967**: 55,
　　65, 105, 328 [2], 331, 358 [2, 10], 375
　　[1], 376, 443, 455, 460 [11], 482, 554
　　[8]; **1968–69**: 14 (p. 25), 42, 50, 158,
　　214n., 219, 226, 320, 406, 472, 479,
　　499, 557 [4, 8], 611, 648, 676 (pp.
　　1266, 1270)
　　1st amendment, **1967**: 286, 352, 495 [13]
　　13th and 14th amendments, **1968–69**: 76
　　14th amendment, **1967**: 55
　　15th amendment, **1968–69**: 76, 341
　　　Enforcement of provisions, **1965**: 107, 108,
　　　409
　　19th amendment, **1968–69**: 332, 341
　　23rd amendment, **1968–69**: 332, 341
　　24th amendment, **1968–69**: 332, 341
　　　Adoption, **1963–64**: 145
　　　Certification, **1963–64**: 171
　　25th amendment, **1968–69**: 263
　　　Ratification ceremony, **1967**: 68
　　Bill of Rights, **1965**: 27, 34, 48, 108, 397
　　Federal employees, upholding of, **1965**: 128
　　Presidential succession, amendment proposed,
　　　1963–64: 211 [13, 29], 218 [9]; **1965**: 34
　　Voting, 18-year-olds, proposed amendment,
　　　1968–69: 332, 341
Constitutional Convention, **1965**: 45; **1966**: 21,
　　261; **1968–69**: 499
Construction, **1966**: 30, 155, 445 [7]; **1967**: 6
　　[9], 13 (pp. 44, 45), 16 (p. 75), 261
　　Cutbacks, **1968–69**: 39 (p. 92)
　　Education facilities, **1968–69**: 39 (p. 106), 678
　　　(p. 1293)
　　Electric power projects, **1968–69**: 39 (p. 91)
　　Employment, **1967**: 199; **1968–69**: 87
　　Government and federally financed, **1968–69**:
　　　39 (pp. 90, 92, 101), 587, 678 (pp.
　　　1281, 1293)
　　Health facilities, **1968–69**: 39 (p. 92)
　　Highways, **1966**: 630 [2, 4], 631; **1967**: 261;
　　　1968–69: 173, 223 [11], 458, 567
　　Hospitals and medical care facilities, **1966**: 26
　　　(p. 62), 95, 253, 394, 406, 515; **1967**:
　　　261, 353, 419; **1968–69**: 111, 536, 678
　　　(p. 1296)
　　Housing, **1966**: 141 [3], 445 [7], 451, 596,
　　　628 [1], 642 [3]; **1967**: 4, 16 (pp. 75,
　　　78, 85), 70 [6], 88, 103, 114, 180, 353,
　　　369, 411 [11], 417 [5, 6], 420, 430, 531,
　　　554 [6]; **1968–69**: 14 (pp. 28, 29, 31),
　　　26, 39 (p. 102), 47 (pp. 128, 129, 132,
　　　133, 141), 84, 87, 91, 154, 164, 229,
　　　319, 382, 406, 434, 445, 506, 568, 569,
　　　622, 625, 631, 676 (p. 1265), 678 (pp.
　　　1288, 1289), 684 (pp. 1321, 1322), 699

Construction – *continued*
 Libraries, **1967**: 507
 Loans, **1968–69**: 587
 Military, **1966**: 155; **1967**: 417 [14], 440, 460
  [5]
 Schools, **1967**: 532, 540
 Seasonal, **1968–69**: 587
 Ships, **1967**: 13 (p. 48), 410, 528; **1968–69**:
  39 (p. 98), 535
 Subway, **1967**: 20
 Technological research, **1968–69**: 684 (p. 1322)
 Vietnam contracts, **1966**: 642 [21]
 Waste disposal facilities, **1967**: 16 (p. 85)
 Water resources projects, **1968–69**: 39 (p. 101)
 Workers' wages, **1966**: 445 [7]
Construction industry, jurisdictional disputes
 agreement, **1965**: 41
Consular convention, United States-Soviet, **1967**:
 3 (p. 10), 34 [1], 80 [2], 104 [11],
 119, 157, 225 [17], 519; **1968–69**:
 14 (p. 26), 288, 309, 387
Consumer Advisory Council, **1963–64**: 43, 86,
 173; **1965**: 567; **1967**: 86, 342, 393,
 465
Consumer Affairs, Senate Subcommittee on,
 1968–69: 56
Consumer Affairs, Special Assistant to the
 President for, **1967**: 200; **1968–69**: 14
 (p. 30), 56, 154, 336
Consumer Assembly '67, remarks, **1967**: 465
Consumer Complaints Bureau, **1966**: 140
Consumer Credit Protection Act, **1968–69**: 14
 (p. 29), 49, 56, 105, 164, 280, 281
Consumer Finance, National Commission on,
 1968–69: 280
Consumer Interests, President's Committee on,
 1963–64: 86, 173; **1965**: 567; **1966**:
 140; **1967**: 86, 200, 393, 430, 465;
 1968–69: 56, 336
Consumer and Marketing Service, **1965**: 492;
 1966: 140, 245n.
Consumer Price Index, **1963–64**: 124 (p. 160),
 211 [3], 463, 619 [4]; **1965**: 35 (p.
 104); **1966**: 88 [22], 185, 336, 373
 [6], 401 [2], 403; **1967**: 417 [5], 430
Consumer Protection and Environmental Health
 Service, **1968–69**: 336
 See also Safety.
Consumers, **1963–64**: 233; **1965**: 2; **1966**: 26
 (p. 52), 34 (pp. 97, 101); **1967**: 16
 (p. 78), 393
 Counsel, **1968–69**: 14 (p. 30)
 Credit, **1963–64**: 173; **1966**: 6 (p. 6), 34 (p.
  108), 140, 394, 445 [8]; **1967**: 16
  (p. 86), 200; **1968–69**: 280
 Drugs, **1965**: 5, 102, 202, 361, 567
 Education programs, **1965**: 567
 Housewives' strike, **1966**: 158 [7]

Consumers – *continued*
 Income, **1966**: 26 (p. 49), 34 (p. 99)
 Message to Congress, **1963–64**: 173; **1966**: 140;
  1967: 57, 58; **1968–69**: 56
 Prices, **1966**: 494 [1]; **1967**: 3 (p. 7), 13 (p.
  40), 16 (pp. 78, 88), 430, 465; **1968–
  69**: 39 (p. 86)
 Protection of, **1963–64**: 43, 173, 179, 242
  [10], 391, 740, 787, 803; **1965**: 5, 35
  (p. 115), 47, 94, 272; **1966**: 4, 6 (p. 6),
  8 [5], 34 (p. 108), 140, 307, 524, 576;
  1967: 3 (p. 6), 57, 86, 200, 214, 342,
  430, 442, 465, 499, 503, 520, 534, 537;
  1968–69: 14 (p. 29), 39 (p. 101), 47 (p.
  143), 49, 56, 105, 142, 209, 212, 264,
  270, 280, 336, 338, 390, 441, 451, 545,
  565, 567, 655, 678 (p. 1296), 684 (pp.
  1321, 1322)
  Drugs, **1963–64**: 159, 458
  Pesticides, **1963–64**: 341
 Publications, **1963–64**: 173
 Regional conferences, proposed, **1963–64**: 173
 Spending, **1963–64**: 124 (pp. 157, 159, 160),
  173, 197, 233, 379 [5], 459, 506, 546,
  563 [6], 619 [4], 630, 724, 757, 771;
  1965: 23, 35 (pp. 104, 105, 106, 108),
  38, 100, 255, 297, 319 [3], 326, 567,
  632; **1966**: 34 (pp. 99, 101), 294, 347,
  399, 444; **1968–69**: 47 (p. 133), 684
  (p. 1315)
 Voluntary organizations, **1967**: 393
Conte, Repr. Silvio O., **1967**: 391
Continental Army Command, **1967**: 326
Continental Congress, **1965**: 481; **1968–69**: 246
Continental Grain Co., **1963–64**: 195n.
Continental Shelf, **1963–64**: 353; **1968–69**: 567
 Mapping, **1968–69**: 124
 Oil, **1968–69**: 411, 547, 567, 646 [13]
 Outer, **1968–69**: 39 (p. 101)
Contract auditing, Vietnam construction, **1966**:
 642 [21]
Contracts, Government, **1966**: 58, 199, 231n.,
 313, 336, 401 [3]; **1967**: 13 (p. 44),
 121, 410; **1968–69**: 26, 587, 678
 (p. 1280)
 AID-financed, **1963–64**: 482, 617
 Aircraft development, **1963–64**: 355n.
 Defense, **1963–64**: 18, 170 [2], 285 [16],
  409, 486 [2], 563 [6], 690n., 741;
  1965: 26, 211, 493
 Employees of contractors, **1965**: 582
 Equal employment opportunity under, **1963–
  64**: 792
 Scientific research, **1965**: 514
 Uranium, **1963–64**: 294 [10]
Control Commission, International, **1966**: 65ftn.
 (p. 177)
Convention Establishing Customs Cooperation
 Council, **1968–69**: 261

Convention for the High Seas Fisheries of the North Pacific Ocean, **1965**: 15

Convention on Narcotic Drugs, Single, **1967**: 35, 94

Convention on slavery, supplementary, **1968-69**: 42

"Conversation With the President" television program, **1967**: 554

Conway, Jack T., **1965**: 453

Conyers, John, Jr., **1963-64**: 745; **1966**: 431; **1967**: 358 [8]

Cook, Donald, **1965**: 157

Cook, Eliza, **1965**: 183

Cook, James, **1968-69**: 25

Cook, Capt. James, **1968-69**: 525

Cooke, Most Rev. Terrence J., **1968-69**: 293, 540

Cooley, Repr. Harold D., **1963-64**: 327, 328, 546, 631; **1965**: 555; **1966**: 164, 508, 599 [6]

Cooley, Harry H., **1966**: 398

Coolidge, Calvin, **1965**: 298; **1967**: 382; **1968-69**: 138, 330

Coombs, Charles, **1963-64**: 296

Cooney, Capt. James P., **1965**: 219

Co-Op Month, 1967, National, **1967**: 415

Cooper, Chester L., **1965**: 319 [21]

Cooper, Sen. John Sherman, **1963-64**: 14, 15, 150 [7], 291, 292; **1965**: 80; **1966**: 348, 351

Cooper, L. Gordon, **1963-64**: 569, 572, 598; **1965**: 310, 462, 463 [2]

Cooper, Prentice, **1963-64**: 645; **1968-69**: 345

Cooper, R. Conrad, **1965**: 454 [1, 3], 466, 483

Cooperative for American Remittances to Europe (CARE), **1965**: 293, 431, 450; **1967**: 33, 153

Cooperative Area Manpower Planning System (CAMP), **1968-69**: 24, 444

Cooperative Extension Service, **1966**: 331n.

Cooperative housing, **1965**: 511

Cooperative League of the U.S.A., **1963-64**: 352, 617

Cooperative organizations, conference, **1967**: 415

Cooperative Research Act, amendments proposed, **1965**: 9

Cooperatives, Banks for, **1968-69**: 94

COPE (Committee on Political Education), **1968-69**: 50, 164, 165

Copenhagen, Denmark, **1963-64**: 394; **1966**: 195

Copland, Aaron, **1963-64**: 568

Copper, **1966**: 445 [7]
　Release from national stockpile, **1965**: 599, 617, 632; **1966**: 139, 390, 635 [2, 7, 15, 20], 636
　Use in coinage system, **1965**: 297

Copper industry
　Labor dispute, **1967**: 375 [12]; **1968-69**: 106, 112, 141, 169 [21]
　Prices, **1968-69**: 169 [21]

Corbett, Repr. Robert J., **1965**: 413

Corcoran, Thomas G., **1963-64**: 601

Corcoran, William, **1966**: 227

Cordage fiber stockpiles, **1966**: 283n.

Cordova, Alaska, **1963-64**: 242 [1]

Corita, Sister Mary, **1967**: 396n.

Corman, Repr. James C., **1967**: 326

Cormier, Frank, **1963-64**: 211 [17]; **1966**: 247 [16], 338 [1], 474 [21]; **1967**: 34 [2]; **1968-69**: 242

Corn prices, **1968-69**: 94

Corn shipments to India, **1966**: 153

Cornelius Co., The, **1966**: 144n.

Cornell, Douglas, **1963-64**: 587 [9]; **1968-69**: 79 [15], 339 [15]

Cornell University, **1968-69**: 145

Corner, Frank H., **1968-69**: 525

Cornette, James P., **1967**: 490

Corporate Pension Funds and Other Private Retirement and Welfare Programs, Presidential Committee on, **1965**: 35 (p. 113)

Corporation for Public Broadcasting, **1967**: 77, 474; **1968-69**: 39 (p. 106), 54, 370

Corporations, **1966**: 6 (p. 5), 34 (p. 99), 141 [3]
　Dividends, **1963-64**: 285 [15]
　Income, **1963-64**: 731; **1967**: 13 (p. 42)
　Profits, **1963-64**: 23, 124 (pp. 156, 157, 161), 132 (p. 178), 266 [2], 285 [15], 294 [3, 23], 295, 297, 299, 311, 314, 316 [5], 327, 379 [5], 404, 405, 411, 472, 477n., 506, 531, 544, 555, 562, 589, 631, 635, 636, 645, 650, 652, 655, 657, 658, 659, 667, 689, 694, 695, 712, 713, 724, 731, 733, 735, 746, 749, 750; **1965**: 23, 35 (p. 104), 60, 76, 223, 250, 285, 298, 326, 406, 590, 632, 644; **1966**: 17, 34 (p. 96), 155, 199, 347, 444; **1967**: 3 (p. 7), 13 (p. 40), 16 (p. 73), 329; **1968-69**: 76, 109, 229, 612, 678 (p. 1276), 684 (p. 1312)
　Securities, **1965**: 60
　Taxes, **1963-64**: 124 (p. 159), 132 (pp. 179, 180), 139, 197, 218 [15], 724; **1965**: 23, 35 (p. 109), 226, 406, 505n.; **1966**: 6 (p. 5), 17, 26 (pp. 49, 52), 34 (p. 102), 124 [13], 155, 444, 445 [9]; **1967**: 6 [13], 13 (p. 41), 16 (p. 77), 329, 330 [1, 6, 7], 417 [1]; **1968-69**: 39 (pp. 85, 87), 47 (p. 132), 229, 678 (p. 1277)

Corps of Engineers, **1963-64**: 132 (p. 187), 198, 217, 308, 567, 718; **1965**: 32 (p. 92), 174, 400, 418, 560; **1966**: 98, 374, 427, 630 [4]; **1967**: 6 [5, 10, 13], 120, 240,

Corps of Engineers – continued
        408 [2, 4]; 1968–69: 39 (p. 101), 223
        [11], 252, 297
    Appropriations, 1968–69: 39 (p. 92), 467 [3]
Correctional institutions, 1966: 491; 1967: 71,
        146; 1968–69: 57, 59
    District of Columbia, 1968–69: 95
    Reform, 1968–69: 39 (p. 107), 320
    Youth, 1968–69: 59
Correctional Rehabilitation Study Act of 1965,
        1965: 509
Corrections, District of Columbia Department of,
        1967: 71
Corrections service, United States, proposed,
        1968–69: 59
Corregidor, the Philippines, 1963–64: 623; 1966:
        551
Correspondents Association, White House, 1968–
        69: 242
Corriere Della Sera, Milan, 1963–64: 149
Corrigan, Douglas G., 1968–69: 125
Corso, Frank M., Jr., 1966: 512
Corson, John J., 1968–69: 694
Cortez, Hernando, 1966: 411
Cosmetics, consumer protection, 1963–64: 173,
        179; 1965: 5; 1966: 6 (p. 6), 34 (p.
        108), 140
Cost of living, 1966: 158 [3], 201, 236 [8], 239,
        347, 373 [17], 401 [2], 413, 431, 444;
        1967: 16 (p. 79), 63, 170, 417 [5, 6];
        1968–69: 111, 684 (p. 1313)
Cost Reduction, President's Advisory Council on,
        1967: 121, 232; 1968–69: 678 (p. 1304)
"Cost Reduction Notes," pamphlet, 1966: 181
Cost reduction programs, Federal, 1965: 2, 7, 14,
        26, 32 (pp. 85, 90, 97, 98), 35 (p. 108),
        73, 76, 168, 184, 208 [4], 211, 249n.,
        264, 267, 274, 311, 319 [6], 324, 326,
        387, 395 [2], 497; 1966: 6 (p. 4), 25,
        26 (pp. 55, 66), 104, 114, 124 [16],
        141 [3], 155, 181, 197, 296, 313, 321,
        324, 334 [2–3, 8], 444, 492 [9–10],
        596; 1967: 13 (pp. 40, 41, 42, 44), 232,
        556; 1968–69: 39 (pp. 83, 86, 90, 98,
        111), 169 [21], 174, 229, 241, 275 [4],
        283 [8, 10], 322, 344, 458, 467 [3],
        678 (p. 1304), 684 (p. 1316)
    Agriculture Department, 1966: 164
    Defense, Department of, 1967: 13 (pp. 44, 48),
        121, 232, 324, 329, 410
    District of Columbia, 1967: 15
    Government-wide planning, 1965: 447, 448
        [3]; 1966: 129, 444, 445 [1], 477 [2],
        620; 1967: 121
    Incentive awards, 1965: 387, 540
    Low priority expenditures, 1966: 444, 445 [1,
        12, 17], 473, 492 [1], 494 [3]
    Memorandum, 1965: 360; 1966: 464, 620;
        1968–69: 403

Cost reduction programs – continued
    National Aeronautics and Space Administration
        (NASA), 1966: 58; 1967: 121
    News conference remarks, 1967: 6 [9], 411
        [10], 417 [1, 2, 3, 10, 12]
    Overseas expenditures, 1965: 60, 129
    Statements, 1965: 127, 211, 512; 1966: 464,
        603, 631
    Task force on, 1965: 362
    Veterans Administration, 1967: 161
Costa Rica, 1963–64: 809; 1967: 44, 336; 1968–
        69: 368
    Canal route mapping, 1966: 384
    Economic and social development, 1963–64:
        438n.; 1968–69: 289, 290, 291n.
    Education, 1968–69: 374, 375
    Floods, 1963–64: 438, 443
    Mount Irazu, volcanic eruption, 1963–64:
        438n., 443
    Orlich, Francisco J., 1963–64: 438, 441, 443,
        455 [16]
    President José Joaquín Trejos Fernandez,
        1968–69: 289, 290, 291, 366, 374, 421,
        430
    U.S. Ambassador Raymond Telles, 1963–64:
        54 [5]
    U.S. relations with, 1963–64: 438, 441
    Visit, 1968–69: 374
    Volcano disaster, 1968-69: 421, 430
Costa e Silva, Arthur da (President-elect of
        Brazil), 1967: 17
Costa e Silva, Madame, 1967: 17
Costello, Timothy W., 1963–64: 669
Costin, Thomas P., Jr., 1968–69: 498n.
Cotter, William R., 1965: 334n.
Cotton, Sen. Norris, 1967: 474
Cotton, 1963–64: 132 (p. 187), 225, 249; 1965:
        47; 1967: 223 [3], 375 [20], 508
    Consumption, 1963–64: 255
    Cotton bill, 1965: 319 [1]
    Cotton-wheat bill.
        See Agricultural Act of 1964.
    Extra-long staple, imports, 1968–69: 439
    Imports and exports, 1963–64: 193, 717
    Insect control, 1963–64: 758
    Marketing programs, 1965: 47
    Prices, 1963–64: 255, 641; 1968–69: 94, 439
    Production, 1963–64: 758; 1965: 168; 1968–
        69: 39 (p. 100), 94, 247
    Shipments to India, 1966: 153–154
    Textile industry, 1963–64: 602
Cotton Institute, International, 1966: 177
Cotulla, Mayor W. Paul, 1966: 589
Cotulla, Tex., 1963–64: 194; 1966: 589; 1968–
        69: 68, 595, 596, 624, 631
Coulter, Robert C., 1968-69: 388n.
Council on Aging, President's, 1963–64: 178,
        415; 1965: 72

Council of Appalachian Governors, **1963-64**: 300

Council on the Arts, National, **1965**: 177, 534; **1966**: 440; **1967**: 53n.; **1968-69**: 64

Council on the Arts and the Humanities, Federal, **1966**: 327; **1967**: 274

Council of Chief State School Officers, **1966**: 165; **1967**: 182n.; **1968-69**: 219n.

Council of Churches of Christ in the U.S.A., National, **1965**: 438

Council on Cost Reduction, President's Advisory, **1967**: 121, 232

Council on Crime and Delinquency, National, **1967**: 276

Council of Economic Advisers, **1963-64**: 40, 295, 472, 477, 506, 550, 771; **1965**: 35 (p. 111), 46 [12], 226, 319 [3], 321, 567, 589, 590n., 639, 663; **1966**: 34 (p. 103), 44, 83, 95, 108-110, 139, 228, 474 [3], 577ftn. (p. 1321), 592, 635 [5]; **1967**: 6 [17, 18], 16n., 17n., 70 [6], 103, 312 [4], 420, 554 [13]; **1968-69**: 76, 350, 654, 683, 684 (p. 1317)

News conference remarks on, **1963-64**: 271 [15], 294 [23], 379 [5], 455 [2], 563 [10]

Report, **1963-64**: 124 (pp. 161, 162)

Council of Economic Advisers, Chairman (Gardner Ackley), **1963-64**: 771, 818 [4]; **1965**: 22 [2], 46 [14], 54, 62, 319 [3], 326n., 347 [4], 418, 506, 617, 641, 663; **1966**: 8 [15], 33, 44, 158 [4], 201, 236 [13], 247 [1], 333, 373ftn. (p. 805), 379, 492 [1], 494 [1], 630 [2, 5, 8], 631, 635 [1-2, 8, 16, 18], 636; **1967**: 16 (p. 87), 20, 77, 88, 294, 330 [4, 8], 371, 375 [4], 460 [1, 6], 518 [19]; **1968-69**: 1 [17], 2, 46n., 76

Memorandums, **1967**: 89, 186

Council of Economic Advisers, Chairman (Walter W. Heller), **1963-64**: 296, 297, 314, 433, 434, 513, 531, 550, 714

Memorandum to, **1963-64**: 62

News conference remarks on, **1963-64**: 54 [9], 266 [2], 486 [4]

Council of Economic Advisers, Chairman (Arthur M. Okun), **1968-69**: 47 (p. 140), 76, 89, 90, 100n., 169 [21], 350, 467 [3], 612n., 677, 683

Memorandums, **1968-69**: 89, 469n.

Council of Economic Opportunity, National Advisory, **1963-64**: 802; **1967**: 87n., 114

Council on the Education of Disadvantaged Children, National Advisory, **1966**: 210, 238, 632; **1967**: 77

Council on Education Professions Development, National Advisory, **1967**: 396

Council on Equal Opportunity, President's, **1965**: 50, 530n.

Council on Extension and Continuing Education, National Advisory, **1967**: 185

Council on Foreign Relations, **1967**: 306n.

Council of Governments, Metropolitan Washington, **1966**: 302

Council on Human Relations, District of Columbia, **1967**: 15

Council for Human Rights, National Trade Union, **1967**: 484n.

Council on the Humanities, National, **1966**: 101; **1968-69**: 45, 61

Council on Insured Loans to Students, Advisory, **1966**: 3

Council on International Education, **1966**: 45

Council on International Monetary and Financial Problems, National Advisory, **1965**: 110, 282

Council of International Programs for Youth Leaders and Social Workers, **1967**: 365

Council of Jewish Women, National, **1965**: 438

Council on Latin America, **1966**: 125

Council on Marine Resources and Engineering Development, National, **1966**: 326; **1967**: 20, 101, 240

Council of Motion Pictures Organizations, Inc., **1963-64**: 354

Council on Pennsylvania Avenue, President's, **1963-64**: 379 [12], 700; **1965**: 538

Council on Physical Fitness, President's, **1963-64**: 188, 490; **1965**: 625, 645n.; **1967**: 160

Council on Recreation and Natural Beauty, President's, **1966**: 202, 653; **1967**: 295

Council for Science and Technology, Federal, **1965**: 92, 271, 275, 514; **1966**: 138, 222; **1967**: 478

Council for Scientific, Professional and Cultural Employees, AFL-CIO, **1968-69**: 686

Council of Senior Citizens, National, **1966**: 253

Council of the Small Business Administration, National Advisory, **1965**: 270n.

Council for Small Business Management Development, National, **1965**: 270n.

Council of the Southern Mountains, **1963-64**: 41

Council of State Governments, **1963-64**: 178n.

Council on the Status of Women, Citizens' Advisory, **1965**: 392n.

Councils on Civic Affairs, Youth, **1965**: 508

Counselors, District of Columbia, **1966**: 27

Counties, National Association of, **1963-64**: 509; **1966**: 536; **1968-69**: 416

Courts, **1966**: 6 (p. 3), 64, 116, 196, 335, 491, 526; **1967**: 35, 146, 382, 560

Appeals, **1967**: 55

Appointments.

See Appointments and nominations.

Criminal, **1965**: 70, 102, 381, 526

Courts — *continued*
  District of Columbia, **1967**: 15, 71, 350; **1968–
    69**: 95, 133, 542
  Federal, **1965**: 106 [1], 117 [5]; **1968–69**: 14
    (p. 30), 59
    Appeals, **1965**: 353 [3], 385
  Illinois nominations, question of, **1966**: 401
    [16]
  Juvenile, **1967**: 15, 39, 71
  Reform, **1968–69**: 39 (p. 107), 57, 59, 209,
    320, 355
Courts, Administrative Office of the United
    States, **1967**: 35
Couve de Murville, Maurice, **1965**: 78; **1966**:
    607 [2, 7]
Covington, Ky., **1968–69**: 499n.
Cow Palace, San Francisco, Calif., **1963–64**: 415
Cowles, Gardner, **1965**: 420
Cowles, John, **1963–64**: 563 [5], 591
Cox, Archibald, **1963–64**: 315; **1965**: 336n.,
    353 [3], 443
Cox, James M., **1963–64**: 680
Cox, Ohlen, **1965**: 459
Craig, Mrs. May, **1963–64**: 606; **1965**: 635
Craig, Walter E., **1963–64**: 511n.
Craig Air Force Base, Alabama, **1965**: 117 [5]
Craley, Repr. N. Neiman, Jr., **1966**: 428
Cramer, John F., **1963–64**: 514
Crane, Roy, **1965**: 554n.
Crangle, Joseph F., **1966**: 392
Crank, Marion, **1963–64**: 285 [7]
Craters of the Moon Wilderness, Idaho, **1968–69**:
    168
Cravalho, Elmer F., **1966**: 532
Crawford, Bryce L., **1968–69**: 71n., 695n.
Creative federalism, **1966**: 34 (p. 98), 416, 606,
    607 [1]; **1967**: 13 (p. 57), 296
Credit, **1963–64**: 132 (p. 187), 350, 775, 780
    [3]; **1965**: 35 (pp. 106, 112), 110, 639;
    1966: 141 [5], 419, 444, 445 [3, 5],
    477 [2], 596; **1967**: 415
  Availability, **1967**: 3 (p. 7), 13 (pp. 41, 43),
    16 (pp. 75, 81, 88), 312 [4], 329, 417
    [1, 5, 6], 420, 430; **1968–69**: 39 (p.
    87), 46, 47 (pp. 132, 133), 229, 326,
    684 (p. 1313)
  Banking policies, **1966**: 444, 473
  Consumer, **1963–64**: 173; **1966**: 6 (p. 6), 34
    (p. 108), 140, 445 [8]; **1967**: 16 (p.
    86), 200
  Expansion, **1963–64**: 708, 714; **1965**: 506
  Farm, **1965**: 377; **1967**: 156, 415; **1968–69**:
    94, 142, 450, 679
  Federal programs, **1963–64**: 787; **1965**: 60, 77;
    1966: 26 (pp. 55, 66), 34 (p. 102), 182,
    199, 451
  Federal Reserve policies, **1966**: 635 [13]

Credit — *continued*
  Housing, **1966**: 338 [14], 445 [7], 451, 473,
    642 [3, 19]; **1967**: 420; **1968–69**: 87,
    699
  Low-income families, **1967**: 415
  Rural development, **1968–69**: 94, 450
  State and local governments, **1968–69**: 39 (p.
    87)
  Truth in lending, **1967**: 16 (p. 86), 57, 342,
    393, 430, 460 [5], 465, 499, 503, 520,
    534, 539; **1968–69**: 49, 154, 164, 270,
    280, 281, 545
Credit, Commission on Money and, **1966**: 182,
    199
Credit Corporation, Commodity, **1967**: 13 (p.
    46), 33, 138n.; **1968–69**: 94, 247, 467
    [3], 534, 678 (pp. 1281, 1282)
Credit Programs, Committee on Federal, **1966**:
    182, 199
Credit Union National Association, **1963–64**:
    617
Credit unions, **1967**: 537
Creighton, Rt. Rev. William F., **1963–64**: 810n.;
    1965: 289
Crespi Morbio, Mario, **1963–64**: 149
Crew, Albert C., **1967**: 420n.
Crider, Otto, **1963–64**: 413
Crime, **1963–64**: 523; **1965**: 102, 361; **1966**:
    116–117, 388, 492 [1], 526; **1967**: 146,
    279ftn. (p. 673), 382, 427
  See also Law enforcement.
  Adult offenders, **1965**: 509
  Aircraft based, **1968–69**: 494
  Campaign remarks, **1963–64**: 630, 666, 668,
    680
  Commissions.
    See President's Commission on Crime in the
      District of Columbia; President's Com-
      mission on Law Enforcement and Ad-
      ministration of Justice.
  Control, **1965**: 102, 366
  Correctional institutions, **1966**: 491
  District of Columbia, **1963–64**: 704; **1965**: 29,
    70, 102, 366, 381; **1966**: 27, 219, 354,
    611, 656; **1967**: 15, 27, 71, 337, 466,
    575; **1968–69**: 133, 355, 689
  Evidence in trials, **1968–69**: 320
  Increase, **1965**: 90, 102, 422, 526; **1968–69**:
    14 (pp. 28, 30)
  Investigations, **1967**: 468; **1968–69**: 59, 678
    (p. 1292)
  Legislation, **1966**: 417 [6], 487, 526; **1967**:
    13 (p. 56), 146, 221, 276, 297 [7], 358
    [3], 382, 385, 455, 468, 575
  Material witnesses, **1966**: 611
  Message to Congress, **1966**: 116; **1967**: 35, 36;
    1968–69: 59

Crime – *continued*
  Organized, **1966**: 116, 204–205, 487; **1967**:
    35, 382, 468; **1968–69**: 39 (p. 107), 59,
    553, 561
  Prevention and control, **1965**: 2, 382, 500,
    509, 526; **1966**: 6 (p. 63), 26 (p. 64),
    116–117, 205, 487, 491, 492 [1], 526,
    633, 656; **1967**: 3 (p. 6), 13 (p. 56), 15,
    23, 35, 60, 105, 146, 216, 297 [7], 382,
    421, 468, 482, 530, 575; **1968–69**: 14
    (p. 30), 39 (pp. 89, 107), 50, 59, 60,
    100, 156, 164, 202, 209, 235, 257, 320,
    325, 355, 406, 424, 542, 553, 561, 676
    (p. 1266), 678 (pp. 1281, 1291)
  Federal programs, **1968–69**: 57, 59, 235
  Reports, **1963–64**: 90, 752
  Research, **1965**: 2, 102, 381, 422, 437, 500,
    509, 526; **1966**: 526; **1967**: 35, 382
  Statement to Governors, **1966**: 491
  Statistics, **1966**: 487, 491; **1967**: 35, 60, 71,
    146, 276, 530
  Urban areas, **1966**: 30; **1967**: 353, 455; **1968–
    69**: 59, 82, 87
  Weapons use, **1968–69**: 59, 257, 296, 302, 324,
    333, 334, 355, 356, 678 (p. 1292)
  Youth, **1963–64**: 537, 658; **1965**: 90, 102,
    509; **1966**: 491, 494 [1]; **1967**: 35,
    382; **1968–69**: 39 (p. 107), 57, 59, 329,
    424, 457 [8], 553, 678 (p. 1291)
Crime commission.
  See President's Commission on Law Enforce-
    ment and Administration of Justice.
Crime Control, Lawyers Conference on, **1967**:
    221
Crime Control, National Conference on, **1967**:
    146
Crime control and safe streets bill.
  See Omnibus Crime Control and Safe Streets
    Act of 1968.
Crime and Delinquency, National Council on,
    1967: 276
Crime in the District of Columbia, President's
    Commission on, **1965**: 70, 366, 381,
    526n.; **1966**: 116, 219, 354, 611, 656;
    1967: 15, 27, 71
Crime Information Center, National, **1968–69**:
    334
Criminal Administration, Conference of State
    Committees on, **1966**: 491, 492 [1],
    526
Criminal Justice, National Institute of Law
    Enforcement and, **1968–69**: 59, 320
Criminal Justice, Office of, **1965**: 102
Criminal Justice Assistance, Office of Law
    Enforcement and, **1967**: 35
Criminal law, **1966**: 116, 196, 611
Criminal Laws, National Commission on Reform
    of Federal, **1966**: 598; **1968–69**: 59

Criminal Laws in the District of Columbia, Com-
    mission on Reform of, **1967**: 71
Criminal Statistics, District of Columbia Bureau,
    1967: 71
Criminals, rehabilitation, **1966**: 611
Crimmins, John Hugh, **1966**: 277 [2]
Crippled children, **1968–69**: 111, 503
Crippled children's programs, **1967**: 39
Criswell, John B., **1967**: 421
Crockett, David, **1963–64**: 645, 702
Crockett, William J., **1963–64**: 26, 242 [7]
Crofut, William E., II, **1965**: 159
Cromley, Allan W., **1968–69**: 696ftn. (p. 1350)
Cromwell, Oliver, **1965**: 94
Croneis, Carey, **1968–69**: 107
Cronkite, Walter, **1963–64**: 527; **1968–69**: 460
    [1]
Crook, W. H., **1965**: 603
Crook, William, **1968–69**: 273n.
Crooker, John H., Jr., **1968–69**: 79 [2], 125
Crooker, Mrs. John H., Jr., **1968–69**: 125
Crooker, John H., Sr., **1968–69**: 125
Croplands
  Adjustment program, **1965**: 47, 597
  Decline in need for, **1963–64**: 132 (p. 187);
    1965: 168
Crosby, Edwin L., **1966**: 185n., 314
Cross, Maj. Carl S., death of, **1966**: 259
Cross, James U., **1965**: 399n.; **1967**: 536; **1968–
    69**: 345
Crossland Vocational Center, Camp Springs, Md.,
    1967: 193
Crotty, Peter J., **1963–64**: 667
Crouch, W. T., **1968–69**: 462
Crowe, David E., **1966**: 289
Crown, Henry, **1965**: 273
Cruikshank, Dr. Nelson H., **1965**: 594n.
Crumm, Maj. Gen. William J., **1967**: 134
Cuba, **1963–64**: 48, 399n., 475 [13], 688 [8],
    703; **1966**: 6 (p. 8), 346, 602, 608;
    1967: 409; **1968–69**: 110
  Bay of Pigs, **1965**: 347 [5]; **1968–69**: 18 [2]
  Castro, Fidel.
    See main heading, Castro, Fidel.
  Claims of U.S. nationals against, **1963–64**: 684
  Communism in, **1963–64**: 562, 607, 612, 631,
    640, 643, 650, 652, 655, 678, 726
  Cuban fishermen, arrest in U.S. waters, **1963–
    64**: 175, 182
  Defectors to U.S., **1963–64**: 232 [6]
  Economic isolation, **1963–64**: 150ftn. (p. 231),
    272, 294 [22], 316 [23], 635
  Guantanamo Naval Base.
    See main heading, Guantanamo Naval Base,
    Cuba.
  Guevara, Ernesto, **1963–64**: 246 [5]
  Missile crisis (1962), **1963–64**: 91 (p. 116),
    638, 686; **1967**: 554 [4]; **1968–69**:
    27, 291, 387, 472

Cuba — *continued*
  Missile crisis — *continued*
    Campaign remarks, **1963–64**: 612, 642, 643,
      645, 646, 648, 650, 652, 656, 657, 659,
      666, 667, 669, 678, 694, 702, 727, 728,
      733, 734, 736, 741, 745, 746, 747, 749,
      750, 762
  Refugees from, **1965**: 546, 601, 618
  Soviet bombers, missiles, and weapons in,
    1963–64: 285 [22]
  Soviet technicians and supplies for, **1963–64**:
    285 [22]
  Soviet troops in, withdrawal, **1963–64**: 256
    [20]
  Subversive activities in Latin America, **1963–64**:
    186, 486 [3]
  Trade with U.K., **1963–64**: 150 [13]
  U.S. aerial reconnaissance, **1963–64**: 280 [9],
    285 [22], 316 [17], 379 [15]
  U.S. policy on, **1963–64**: 316 [23]
  U.S. relations with, **1963–64**: 242 [11], 246
    [5], 455 [22]
Cullen, Joseph M., **1963–64**: 411
Culp, Dr. Ormond, **1965**: 549n.
Cultural Affairs, Bureau of Educational and,
  1966: 378n.
Cultural Center, National, renaming, **1963–64**: 39
Cultural Council, Inter-American, **1966**: 16;
  1968–69: 66, 77
Cultural and Educational Interchange, Joint
  United States-Japan Conference on,
  1965: 15
Cultural exchanges, **1963–64**: 280, 369, 385;
  1965: 36, 292, 552, 553; **1966**: 16,
  378, 483; **1967**: 53, 80 [2], 272, 344
Cultural life in U.S., **1963–64**: 784; **1965**: 314,
  534
Cultural Materials, Agreement on the Importation
  of Educational, Scientific, and (Florence
  Agreement), **1965**: 202, 604; **1966**: 45,
  519, 601
Cultural Organization, United Nations Educa-
  tional, Scientific, and, **1963–64**: 480;
  1967: 198n.
Cultural and Trade Center, Interama, Miami,
  Fla., **1963–64**: 710
Culver, Repr. John C., **1966**: 312
Cumberland, Md., **1963–64**: 320, 321
  Mayor Earl D. Chaney, **1963–64**: 321
Cumberland Gap, Md., **1965**: 103
Cummings, James H., **1967**: 116
Cummings, Walter J., Jr., **1966**: 320 [4]
Cunha, Vasco Laitao da, **1966**: 455
Cunningham, R. Walter, **1967**: 533; **1968–69**:
  533n., 552, 574
Currency
  Automatic merchandising use of, **1965**: 297
  Control of, **1965**: 156 [5]

Currency — *continued*
  Foreign, **1965**: 110, 149
  John F. Kennedy 50-cent pieces, **1963–64**: 33;
    1965: 297
  Minerals used in, **1965**: 297, 380
  Silver dollar coinage, **1965**: 252, 297
Currigan, Thomas G., **1966**: 413–414
Curry, Bryce, **1967**: 420n.
Curry, Nathaniel T., **1967**: 275
Curry, Neil J., **1965**: 329, 330
Curtin, William J., **1966**: 360
Curtis, Kenneth M., **1963–64**: 606; **1967**: 222n.,
  223 [3, 6], 225 [21]
Curtis, Thomas B., **1963–64**: 189, 619 [16],
  642; **1966**: 199
Cushing, Richard Cardinal, **1963–64**: 2
Cushman, Lt. Gen. Robert E., Jr., **1967**: 567;
  1968–69: 34, 185n.
Cusick, Leo J., **1966**: 442
Custer, Gen. George A., **1968–69**: 540
Customs, **1968–69**: 47 (p. 137), 678 (p. 1302)
  Conventions, **1968–69**: 261, 558
  Duties, **1967**: 13 (p. 44), 329
  Ports of entry inspection, **1968–69**: 388, 389
Customs, Bureau of, **1963–64**: 80, 752; **1965**:
  118, 125; **1967**: 13 (p. 57); **1968–69**:
  39 (p. 109), 59, 388, 389, 557 [8]
Customs Cooperation Council, convention estab-
  lishing, **1968–69**: 261
Customs Court, **1965**: 125
Customs Service, **1965**: 125
Cutler, Sir Arthur R. and Lady, **1966**: 544
Cutler, Lloyd N., **1968–69**: 298n.
Cyprus, **1963–64**: 211 [23], 597; **1968–69**: 14
  (p. 26), 242, 335, 504
  Archbishop Makarios, message to, **1963–64**: 70
  Assistance, **1963–64**: 210
  Conflict, **1967**: 100, 162, 518ftn. (p. 1093),
    519, 521, 545
  Greek-Turkish dispute, **1963–64**: 70, 170 [1],
    182, 192, 206, 210, 423, 429, 504 [5],
    511, 544, 560 [4], 746
  Kutchuk, Fazil, message to, **1963–64**: 70
  United Nations operations in, **1963–64**: 235,
    246 [4], 423; **1965**: 169
  U.S. Ambassador Fraser Wilkins, **1963–64**: 201
    [13]
  U.S. relations with, **1963–64**: 511
Czechoslovakia, **1967**: 34 [5], 347n.
  Invasion, **1968–69**: 455, 462, 467ftn. (p. 929),
    472, 474, 676 (pp. 1268, 1269)
  Refugees, **1968–69**: 467 [10]
Czestochowa, Shrine of Our Lady of, **1966**: 528

D-day, 20th anniversary, **1963–64**: 384
Daane, J. Dewey, **1967**: 371; **1968–69**: 317

Daddario, Repr. Emilio Q., **1963–64**: 603; **1967**: 391

Dade County, Fla.
  Mayor Charles Hall, **1968–69**: 547n.

Dairy imports, **1967**: 294

Dairy products, **1963–64**: 132 (p. 187), 256 [8]; **1965**: 377; **1966**: 62

Dakar, Senegal, **1965**: 141n., 144; **1966**: 488

Dale, Edwin L., Jr., **1966**: 373 [19]

D'Alesandro, Thomas, Jr., **1967**: 286

D'Alesandro, Thomas, III, **1963–64**: 703

Daley, John J., **1963–64**: 605; **1966**: 398

Daley, Richard J., **1963–64**: 287, 455 [10], 521 [5], 748; **1965**: 299, 415; **1966**: 183, 228; **1967**: 216, 223 [10], 515; **1968–69**: 171, 172, 183, 210

Daley, Mrs. Richard J., **1963–64**: 287; **1968–69**: 210

Dallas, George M., **1966**: 428

Dallas, Texas, **1968–69**: 96, 604
  Mayor Erik Jonsson, **1963–64**: 738
  Visit to, question of, **1963–64**: 780 [23]

Dallastown, Pa., **1966**: 428; **1968–69**: 94
  Mayor LaVerne Orwig, **1966**: 428

Dalton, John M., **1967**: 544; **1968–69**: 629

Dalton, Gov. John M., **1963–64**: 189, 217, 263, 695

Daly, Edward, **1968–69**: 470, 471

Danang, South Vietnam, **1966**: 346, 417 [12]; **1967**: 70 [8], 330 [1]

Dangerfield, George, "The Era of Good Tidings," **1963–64**: 303

Dangerous Drugs, Bureau of Narcotics and, **1968–69**: 59, 60, 217, 557 [8], 561, 678 (p. 1292)

Daniel, Bill, **1968–69**: 477

Daniel, Price (Director, Office of Emergency Preparedness), **1968–69**: 58, 100n., 102, 116, 296n., 325, 406, 477, 483n., 539, 570, 598

Daniel, Mrs. Price, **1968–69**: 102

Daniel, Maj. Walter F., **1965**: 219

Daniel Webster, U.S.S., **1963–64**: 560 [5]

Daniels, Repr. Dominick V., **1963–64**: 338; **1965**: 242; **1966**: 470, 504; **1967**: 413

Daniels, Jonathan M., **1965**: 442, 444n.

Daniels, Mrs. Philip, **1965**: 442

Dante Alighieri, **1967**: 389
  Commemorative stamp, **1965**: 367
  "Divine Comedy," **1965**: 367

Darien Gap, inter-American highway, **1967**: 173

Darrow, Clarence S., **1966**: 116, 431

Daughters of the American Revolution, **1963–64**: 275; **1966**: 478, 503

Davidson, Roy E., **1963–64**: 252, 284, 450

Davies, Don, **1967**: 396n.

Davies, Mrs. Dorothy, **1963–64**: 428n.

Davies, Harold, **1965**: 347 [10], 388 [6]

Da Vinci, Leonardo, **1966**: 216

Davis, Archie K., **1966**: 265

Davis, Repr. Clifford, **1963–64**: 645, 701

Davis, Mrs. Clifford, **1963–64**: 701

Davis, Rev. George R., **1967**: 87n.; **1968–69**: 705n.

Davis, Dr. I. P., **1965**: 642n.

Davis, Ilus W., **1967**: 382

Davis, Mrs. James, **1966**: 417 [3]

Davis, Sp4c. James T., **1966**: 246

Davis, Jefferson, **1967**: 538

Davis, John Edward, **1966**: 421

Davis, Repr. John W., **1963–64**: 330, 716

Davis, Lewis, **1967**: 4n.

Davis, Martin, **1963–64**: 751

Davis, Ross D., **1966**: 501 [1]

Davis, Sgt. Sammy L., **1968–69**: 594

Davis, Saville, R., **1966**: 599 [3]; **1968–69**: 1 [9, 11]

Davis, Sid, **1966**: 8 [11], 158 [11], 338 [8]

Davis, Spencer, **1966**: 338 [19]

Davis, Stella E., **1966**: 89

Davis, Watson, **1965**: 88

Davis, Will, **1968–69**: 497

Davis-Bacon Act, **1963–64**: 444; **1965**: 582

Davis Cup winners, **1963–64**: 106

Dawson, Repr. William L., **1963–64**: 287; **1965**: 299, 330, 503; **1966**: 523; **1968–69**: 57

Day, James V., **1965**: 371

Day care programs, **1967**: 15; **1968–69**: 3, 39 (p. 105), 47 (p. 142), 678 (p. 1294)

Dayton, Mrs. Mona M., **1966**: 165

Dayton, Ohio, **1966**: 434–435
  Campaign remarks, **1963–64**: 680
  Mayor Dave Hall, **1966**: 434–435

Deaf, International Games for the (1965), **1963–64**: 808

Deaf, National Technical Institute for the, establishment, **1965**: 401

Deaf-Blind Youth and Adults, National Center for, **1967**: 77, 413

Deaf persons, **1966**: 406; **1967**: 77, 413
  Employment, **1968–69**: 548
  Opportunities, **1963–64**: 808; **1965**: 305

Deakin, James, **1966**: 516 [17]; **1967**: 312 [16]

Dean, Alan L., **1965**: 263n.

Dean, Arthur, **1965**: 522n.

Dean, Arthur H., **1963–64**: 522, 563 [5], 688 [3, 8], 747; **1968–69**: 694

Dean, Noble E., **1966**: 331n.

Dean, Sir Patrick, **1965**: 335, 376; **1967**: 18n., 425; **1968–69**: 349n.

DeAngelis, Charles E., **1967**: 419n.

Deason, Bill, **1963–64**: 778

Death rate, **1968–69**: 262

DeBakey, Dr. Michael E., **1963–64**: 211 [6], 268n., 798; **1965**: 551, 594n.; **1966**: 166, 185, 189

Debates, presidential campaign, question of, **1963–64**: 54 [7], 201 [10], 455 [17], 475 [21], 486 [8], 516 [13], 560 [9]

Debré, Michel, **1968–69**: 169 [17], 533

Debt, consumer, **1963–64**: 173

Debt, national, **1963–64**: 132 (p. 181); **1965**: 32 (pp. 88, 96, 99), 146; **1966**: 26 (pp. 55, 65), 236 [11]; **1967**: 13 (pp. 44–46, 56), 264 [6], 329; **1968–69**: 39 (pp. 86, 91, 95, 96), 132, 678 (pp. 1280, 1282, 1285)

   Interest on, **1963–64**: 211 [28]

   Limit on, **1963–64**: 132 (p. 192), 379 [3]

   Reduction, **1963–64**: 199, 630

Debus, Kurt H., **1966**: 485, 625

Debye, Dr. Peter J. W., **1965**: 646n.; **1966**: 61n.

Deceptive sales bill of 1968, **1968–69**: 56

Dechant, Tony T., **1968–69**: 142

"Decision-Making in the White House," Theodore C. Sorensen, **1963–64**: 23n.

Decker, Gen. George H., **1966**: 495, 505

Declaration of Honolulu, **1968–69**: 452

Declaration of Human Rights, Universal, **1968–69**: 42, 611

Declaration of Independence, **1963–64**: 250, 441; **1965**: 80, 141, 397; **1966**: 120, 168, 243, 261, 305n., 323, 328n., 504, 551; **1968–69**: 157n., 214n., 246, 359, 479, 500, 511n., 676 (p. 1266)

Declaration of the Presidents of America, **1968–69**: 366

De Coubertin, Baron Pierre (founder of modern Olympics), **1963–64**: 782

Dedicatory occasions.
   See Addresses or remarks on commemorative or special occasions.

Deegan, Thomas J., Jr., **1963–64**: 282

Deer, Mr. and Mrs. A. F., **1968–69**: 453

Deere and Co., **1963–64**: 745

Defense
   Contractors, cost reduction program, **1963–64**: 18; **1965**: 211

   Contracts, **1963–64**: 285 [16], 409, 486 [2], 690n., 741; **1965**: 26, 211, 493; **1966**: 199, 313

      Economy measures, **1963–64**: 18, 170 [2]

      Increase, **1963–64**: 563 [6]

   Installations.
      See Military installations.

   National.
      See National security.

   Procurement, **1963–64**: 18, 216, 230, 486 [2]

   Production, **1968–69**: 112

   Spending, **1963–64**: 62, 227, 272, 276n., 307, 409, 482, 486 [2], 598, 733, 735, 775, 797; **1965**: 32 (pp. 84, 90), 176 [3], 179, 261n., 347 [11], 387; **1966**: 6 (p. 8), 26 (pp. 48, 55, 56–58), 34 (pp. 101,

Defense – *continued*
  Spending – *continued*
     103), 124 [15], 128, 141 [5], 334 [2, 8], 444, 464, 474 [2], 578 [2–3, 10], 631; **1967**: 13 (pp. 41, 43, 46), 16 (pp. 76–77), 193, 225 [3], 329, 330 [1], 417 [1], 524; **1968–69**: 2, 14 (p. 32), 38, 39 (pp. 83, 88, 97), 47 (pp. 131, 134), 76, 153 [12], 169 [8], 223 [11], 241, 425 [8], 483, 676 (p. 1267), 678 (pp. 1274, 1279, 1282, 1283, 1286)

   Economic impact, **1963–64**: 62; **1965**: 493; **1967**: 16 (p. 81); **1968–69**: 684 (p. 1312)

   Increase, **1963–64**: 266 [10], 493, 509, 516 [19], 533, 541, 588, 703, 749; **1965**: 26, 388 [1]

   News conference remarks, **1963–64**: 28 [5], 54 [6], 71 [3, 11], 170 [2], 211 [28], 218 [15], 266 [10], 285 [9], 336 [3], 516 [19], 619 [1, 2]; **1967**: 6 [12, 13]

   Overseas, **1965**: 60, 77; **1968–69**: 146, 449

   Reduction, **1963–64**: 18, 37, 71 [3, 11], 91 (pp. 113, 117), 96, 120, 129, 130, 131, 132 (pp. 176, 184, 185, 193, 194), 170 [2], 211 [28], 218 [15], 285 [9], 295, 327, 336 [3], 467, 531, 654, 657, 790; **1965**: 26, 362, 638; **1966**: 313, 327 [7], 444; **1968–69**: 1 [1, 15]

   Report, **1963–64**: 619 [2]

   Vietnam, **1966**: 277 [8, 18], 578 [2]

Defense, Canada–United States Permanent Joint Board on, **1965**: 432

Defense, Department of, **1963–64**: 26, 37, 132 (p. 181), 177, 218 [15], 227, 230, 272, 276, 298, 442, 482, 560ftn. (p. 1042), 612, 669, 735, 816; **1965**: 60, 81, 138n., 167, 176 [3], 211, 220n., 229n., 271, 280, 315, 319 [10], 395 [2], 396, 448 [1], 493n., 497, 503, 512, 514, 521, 528, 608; **1966**: 18, 41, 88 [24], 98, 108, 128, 139–140, 231n., 319, 324, 452, 464, 472, 521, 578 [6], 618, 654 [7]; **1967**: 159, 193, 375 [6], 408 [1], 412, 432n., 440; **1968–69**: 12, 18 [1,2], 99, 104, 223 [6], 248, 557 [8], 586, 669

   Antipoverty program participation, **1965**: 288

   Appropriations, **1966**: 444, 445 [1, 9, 16], 474 [2], 492 [9], 543; **1967**: 6 [20], 13 (p. 45), 44, 118, 329, 410, 518 [4], 556; **1968–69**: 39 (pp. 91, 97), 153 [12], 169 [8], 467 [3], 646 [3], 678 (pp. 1280, 1282, 1296)

   Budget, **1966**: 26 (p. 54), 578 [2, 6], 630 [2], 631, 642 [4–5, 12, 18]; **1968–69**: 12, 18 [1]

   Cost reduction program, **1965**: 26, 32 (pp. 90,

Defense, Department of – *continued*
  Cost reduction program – *continued*
      98), 77, 127, 274n., 387; **1966**: 6 (p. 8),
      26 (pp. 57, 67), 197, 313, 320 [7], 324,
      444, 603; **1967**: 13 (pp. 44, 48), 121,
      232, 324, 329, 410; **1968-69**: 39 (pp.
      98, 111), 516, 678 (p. 1304)
  Cost Reduction Week, **1963-64**: 467
  Meat purchases, **1963-64**: 246 [18], 316 [6],
      344, 732
  News conference remarks, **1963-64**: 54 [14],
      71 [2], 211 [28], 256 [2, 3], 266 [10],
      504 [11], 516 [3, 12], 560 [16], 563
      [6], 619 [3], 688 [8]
  Personnel reduction, **1963-64**: 28 [5], 91 (p.
      113), 132 (p. 194), 294 [4], 486 [5]
  Project 100,000, **1967**: 92
  Project Transition, veterans, **1967**: 345; **1968-
      69**: 40
  Report, **1965**: 360
  Research contracts, **1968-69**: 678 (p. 1293)
  Ship loan program, **1965**: 600
  Spending.
      See Spending *under* Defense.
  Training programs, **1968-69**: 678 (p. 1295)
Defense, Secretary of (Clark Clifford), **1968-69**:
      33, 40ftn. (p. 115), 105, 106, 109, 111,
      112, 153 [4, 12], 169 [18], 171, 185,
      187, 191 [4], 223 [1, 6, 10], 232, 248,
      292n., 353, 384, 398n., 400, 401, 425
      [5], 467 [3], 487, 516, 585, 590 [1, 2,
      4, 9], 598, 616, 646 [3], 669, 675
  Appointment, **1968-69**: 18 [1, 2]
  Memorandums, **1968-69**: 297, 361
  Swearing in, **1968-69**: 104
Defense, Secretary of (Robert S. McNamara),
      1963-64: 18, 19, 23, 26, 37, 54ftn. (p.
      66), 67, 83, 89, 105, 127, 132 (pp. 176,
      192), 175, 177, 218 [1, 23-26], 223,
      227, 233, 274, 276, 280 [8], 295, 298,
      314, 413, 425, 439, 442, 454, 467, 487,
      489, 509, 510, 513, 531, 533, 539, 600,
      665, 691, 696, 766, 771, 775, 793, 796,
      797, 809; **1965**: 26, 54, 60, 77, 81, 89,
      91, 112, 127, 136, 157, 158, 159n.,
      172n., 206n., 207, 212, 221, 222, 223,
      227, 229, 250, 257, 260, 261n., 268,
      274n., 277, 280, 288n., 339, 387, 420,
      421, 433, 438, 497, 528, 549, 561n.,
      599n., 607n., 608n., 617, 620, 632,
      633, 638, 660; **1966**: 39, 48, 100, 108,
      155, 202, 208, 214, 216, 231n., 235,
      261, 313, 324, 345, 407, 412, 414, 420,
      433, 464, 485-486, 496, 520, 570, 603,
      622, 626, 631, 636-637, 641, 645, 651;
      1967: 25, 80ftn. (p. 261), 92, 103, 116,
      121, 134, 159, 163, 167, 189, 195, 205,
      208, 232, 241, 248n., 254n., 255, 279,

Defense, Secretary of – *continued*
      286, 309, 310, 321, 322, 324, 326, 329,
      331, 345, 352, 360, 372, 379, 384, 410,
      420, 434, 485 [1-3, 5, 6], 492, 493,
      529; **1968-69**: 1 [1], 2, 15, 18 [1, 2],
      26, 40, 51 [1, 3, 9, 11], 79 [9, 12], 99,
      101, 102
  Campaign remarks on, **1963-64**: 605, 608,
      612, 622, 630, 654, 659, 667, 678, 680,
      702, 728, 733, 736, 745, 746, 747, 749,
      750
  Letter, **1963-64**: 816; **1965**: 161
  Memorandums, **1963-64**: 62, 440; **1965**: 396;
      1966: 476, 606; **1967**: 89, 412, 441,
      504
  News conference remarks on, **1963-64**: 28 [2,
      5], 54 [14], 71 [3, 11], 150 [1], 170
      [2, 12], 201 [5, 18], 211 [14, 33], 232
      [6], 242 [9, 20, 23], 246 [18], 266
      [5, 10, 18, 21], 271 [2, 8], 285 [9, 12],
      294 [17], 316 [2, 16], 336 [15], 379
      [1, 10, 11], 420 [3], 462 [2], 486 [5],
      504 [4, 11, 15], 516 [2, 3], 560 [5, 6],
      563 [1, 5, 6], 587 [5, 8], 619 [2, 3],
      688 [1, 8], 780 [5, 6, 22], 818 [4];
      1965: 117 [11], 208 [6], 295 [16],
      319 [12, 13, 19], 347 [1, 6, 11], 353
      [1, 6, 12], 388 [1, 13, 14], 395 [2],
      412 [2], 448 [1, 12, 20], 641 [2, 8];
      1966: 52 [2, 3], 65 [14], 88 [15-17,
      23-24], 124 [2, 9, 12, 15], 141 [10,
      12, 16], 158 [3-4], 188 [5], 236 [1],
      247 [5], 320 [2], 334 [1, 12], 373 [2,
      15, 19], 445 [1], 474 [2, 15], 501
      [20], 577 [14], 578 [1, 3-6, 10], 580
      [3], 607 [1, 8, 16], 628 [8], 630 [2],
      635 [2, 18], 642, 650 [1]; **1967**: 6 [16-
      18], 70 [1, 3, 7], 104 [2, 12, 14], 132
      [8], 204 [1, 2, 5], 225 [2], 312 [3],
      358 [10], 375 [1, 2, 5, 6, 12, 19], 408
      [1], 417 [14], 518 [4, 16]
  Report, **1965**: 321n.
  Report on cost reduction program, **1963-64**:
      619 [2]
  Resignation, **1967**: 518 [5, 13], 554 [15]
  Vietnam reports, **1966**: 320 [7], 521
  Visit to West Germany, **1963-64**: 316 [2]
  Visits to Vietnam, **1963-64**: 218 [23, 24, 26],
      316 [2, 16], 336 [15]
  World Bank, nomination as President, **1967**:
      511, 518 [5], 554 [15]
Defense, U.S.-Canada Joint Ministerial Commit-
      tee on, **1963-64**: 140
Defense Advisory Committee on Women in the
      Services, **1963-64**: 298
Defense appropriations bill, **1965**: 388 [1]
Defense Communications Agency, **1965**: 26
Defense Contract Audit Agency, **1965**: 26; **1967**:
      315n.

Defense and Disarmament, Committee on the
  Economic Impact of, **1963–64**: 62,
  486ftn. (p. 908); **1965**: 493
Defense Establishment, **1967**: 511; **1968–69**: 99,
  516, 537
Defense Highways, National System of Interstate
  and, **1963–64**: 565
Defense Intelligence Agency, **1965**: 26
Defense loans, student, **1966**: 3n.
Defense Mobilization, Office of, **1965**: 167
Defense Planning Committee of the North Atlantic Treaty Organization, **1967**: 204ftn.
  (p. 497)
Defense Satellite Communications System, **1963–
  64**: 504 [6]
Defense Supply Agency, **1965**: 26; **1967**: 315n.
Defense Transportation Day, National, **1966**:
  187
Deferments, selective service, **1967**: 92
Deficit spending, **1963–64**: 124 (pp. 158, 159),
  132 (pp. 176, 177), 295, 462 [2], 472,
  661, 679, 728, 753n., 787; **1965**: 22
  [11], 32 (pp. 84, 85), 35 (p. 105), 110,
  319 [6, 8], 321, 326, 347 [4], 541,
  638; **1966**: 6 (p. 4), 26 (pp. 49–50), 320
  [8], 477 [3], 654 [14]
De Gaulle, Charles (President of France), **1963–
  64**: 8, 136n., 218 [25], 693, 701; **1965**:
  46 [5], 641 [9]; **1966**: 141 [12], 158
  [13], 188 [1], 273, 277 [12], 445
  [25], 607 [5, 7]; **1967**: 554 [5, 10];
  1968–69: 605, 652
  Meeting with, question of, **1963–64**: 211 [19],
    780 [9]
  News conference remarks on, **1963–64**: 28 [4,
    6], 170 [10, 14, 18], 211 [19], 246
    [14], 285 [5], 475 [6], 688 [8], 780
    [9, 19]
Degrees, honorary.
  See Honorary degrees and memberships.
DeGrove, John, **1967**: 4n.
Deike, Levi, **1965**: 596
DeKeyser, Henry L., **1968–69**: 301
De Kooning, Willem, **1963–64**: 568
De la Garza, Eligio (Kika), **1963–64**: 767; **1966**:
  467; **1967**: 408 [1, 5, 8]
Delaney, Repr. James J., **1965**: 361
De la Rosa, Diógenes, **1965**: 532
Delaware, **1966**: 391
  Campaign remarks, **1963–64**: 749, 750
  Candidates for public office, **1963–64**: 749,
    750
  Gov. Elbert N. Carvel, **1963–64**: 338, 749, 750
  Gov. Charles L. Terry, Jr., **1965**: 417, 434;
    1966: 427–428, 515; **1967**: 121n.;
    1968–69: 46n.
Delaware River, **1965**: 418, 434
Delaware River Basin, **1966**: 391

Delaware River Basin Commission, **1965**: 358,
  434; **1966**: 391
Delaware Water Gap National Recreation Area,
  1965: 471; **1968–69**: 547
Delgado, Enrique, **1965**: 393
Delinquency, National Council on Crime and,
  1967: 276
Dellinger, David, **1967**: 554 [8]
DelliQuadri, Frederick, **1968–69**: 329
Del Rosso, Bernice, **1965**: 322
DeLuca, John A., **1965**: 334n.
Del Valle, José, **1963–64**: 438n.; **1968–69**: 375
DeMaster, Jean Ann, **1963–64**: 315
DeMeuleneester, Pierre, **1965**: 331n.
Demilitarized Zone, Vietnam, **1966**: 501 [5];
  1967: 225 [20]; **1968–69**: 51 [1], 81
  [1], 170, 472, 520
Deming, Frederick L., **1963–64**: 818 [1]; **1967**:
  371; **1968–69**: 317
Democracy, definition of, **1963–64**: 313
Democratic Committee dinner, Atlantic City,
  N.J., **1963–64**: 338
Democratic conference, Western States, **1966**:
  417 [11], 418
Democratic-Farmer-Labor Party Convention,
  1963–64: 433
Democratic Governors conference, **1967**: 296,
  297
Democratic National Committee, **1963–64**: 96,
  542; **1966**: 403, 650 [4, 10, 16, 25];
  1967: 34 [8], 150, 225 [19], 421;
  1968–69: 17, 405, 568, 631
Democratic National Committee, Chairman
  (John M. Bailey), **1963–64**: 199, 224,
  228n., 338, 363, 508, 542n., 603; **1965**:
  329, 330
Democratic National Convention, **1963–64**: 218
  [19], 256 [22], 539, 540; **1968–69**:
  171, 460 [1, 3], 461
  Nomination, acceptance remarks, **1963–64**:
    541
  President's attendance, question of, **1963–64**:
    521 [8, 12]
  Press coverage, **1963–64**: 150 [7]
Democratic Party, **1963–64**: 228, 342, 363, 372,
  373, 415, 536, 542, 603, 612, 622n.,
  654, 746, 747; **1965**: 329, 330, 340,
  349, 394; **1966**: 221, 228, 320 [14],
  353, 418, 459, 510, 515, 650 [23];
  1967: 216, 281, 296, 514; **1968–69**: 17,
  109, 171, 210, 405, 467 [7], 564, 696
  [5]
  Candidate for Vice President, question of,
    1963–64: 211 [12, 15], 242 [20], 294
    [17], 455 [10], 486 [9, 16], 516 [7],
    521 [12], 539
  Conferences, **1967**: 514

Democratic Party – *continued*
  Congressional candidates, **1968–69**: 529, 557
    [12], 565, 566
  Congressional dinner, **1963–64**: 228
  Convention.
    See Democratic National Convention.
  Dinners, **1963–64**: 199, 287, 338, 372, 373,
    413, 415, 431, 434; **1965**: 299, 329,
    330; **1966**: 312, 403; **1967**: 150, 251,
    270, 421; **1968–69**: 210
  Finances, **1967**: 281
  History of, **1963–64**: 542
  New Congressmen, reception for, **1963–64**:
    799
  News conference remarks, **1963–64**: 211 [12,
    15], 218 [19], 242 [20], 246 [17],
    280 [6], 294 [17, 25], 455 [10, 19],
    475 [17], 486 [9, 16], 516 [7, 19, 20],
    521 [12], 539, 560 [10, 15]
  Platform, **1965**: 2; **1966**: 221, 312, 512, 524,
    650 [20, 24]; **1967**: 34 [4], 281, 296,
    460 [14]
  President's Club, **1966**: 401 [3]
  Rally, Newark, N.J., **1966**: 504
  Record in office, **1963–64**: 199, 363, 411, 413,
    541, 637, 640, 642, 644, 645, 646, 648,
    652, 702, 703, 713, 734, 750, 764;
    1966: 403, 504, 509, 516 [19]; **1967**:
    150, 251, 296, 421, 514, 534; **1968–69**:
    212, 529, 566-569
  State strength, **1966**: 610 [13]
  Texas, **1968–69**: 486, 497
  Voter registrations, **1963–64**: 566
  Young Democrats, **1963–64**: 372, 729
Democratic Victory Committee, **1968–69**: 576
Democratic Women, Campaign Conference for,
    1963–64: 305
Demonstration cities.
  See Model cities program.
Demonstration Cities and Metropolitan Develop-
    ment Act of 1966, **1966**: 30, 207n.,
    297, 394–396, 401 [4], 403, 501 [9],
    574; **1967**: 121
De Montfort, Simon, **1963–64**: 796n.
Dempsey, Dr. Edward, **1963–64**: 211 [6]
Dempsey, Jack, **1967**: 315
Dempsey, Gov. John N., **1963–64**: 285 [7], 382,
    383, 603; **1967**: 222n., 223 [1, 2, 11]
DeNeutville, Richard L., **1965**: 334n.
Deniau, Jean François, **1968–69**: 62
Denmark, **1963–64**: 394; **1965**: 68n.; **1966**: 133
  Ambassador Kield Gustav Knuth-Winterfeldt,
    1963–64: 394
  Assistance, **1963–64**: 394n.
  King Frederik IX, **1963–64**: 394; **1966**: 195
  Prime Minister Jens Otto Krag, **1963–64**: 266
    [7], 394; **1966**: 195; **1967**: 278
  Queen Ingrid, **1963–64**: 394; **1966**: 195

Denmark – *continued*
  Support of the United Nations, **1963–64**: 394
  U.S. Ambassador Katharine E. White,
    1963–64: 394
  U.S. relations with, **1963–64**: 394
Dennis, Dr. James L., **1967**: 419n.
Dennis, Ronald A., **1966**: 220
Denny, Brewster, **1963–64**: 242 [5]
Dent, Dr. Albert W., **1963–64**: 266 [4];
    1966: 208n.; **1967**: 500
Dent, Repr. John H., **1963–64**: 728; **1965**: 242,
    578; **1966**: 151, 479
Dental care, **1967**: 13 (p. 53), 16 (p. 85), 114
Dental and medical education.
  See Medical and dental education.
Dental schools, **1968–69**: 39 (p. 103)
Dentists, **1966**: 111, 253, 580 [10]
  Shortage of, **1965**: 5
Denton, Repr. Winfield K. (Winnie),
    1963–64: 643, 644, 729; **1965**: 188;
    1966: 350
Denton, Texas, **1967**: 408 [1]
Denver, Colo., **1966**: 413, 417 [4, 15]
  Campaign remarks, **1963–64**: 658
  Mayor Thomas G. Currigan, **1966**: 413–414
  U.S. Mint, **1965**: 297
Denver, University of, **1966**: 410, 413–414
Department of Agriculture and Related Agencies
    Appropriation Act, 1967, **1966**: 441
Department of Defense Appropriation Act,
    1968, **1967**: 410
Department of the Interior and Related Agencies
    Appropriation Act
  1968, **1967**: 417 [1]
  1969, **1968–69**: 411
Departments of Labor, and Health, Education,
    and Welfare Appropriation Act
  1968, **1967**: 217n., 479
  1969, **1968–69**: 220n.
Department of State, Justice, and Commerce, the
    Judiciary, and Related Agencies
    Appropriation Act
  1967, **1966**: 592
  1968, **1967**: 482
  1969, **1968–69**: 347n.
Department of Transportation Act of 1966,
    1966: 523; **1967**: 149; **1968–69**: 122,
    130
Deposit Insurance Corporation, Federal,
    1966: 88 [3], 473, 530; **1967**: 16 (p.
    87)
Depreciation allowances, **1963–64**: 619 [4], 724;
    1965: 60, 76, 100, 226, 505;
    1966: 26 (p. 52), 444, 445 [4, 7, 14,
    22], 451, 596; **1967**: 6 [13, 17], 104
    [1], 329
  Message to Congress, **1967**: 103

Depressed areas
  Appalachian area.
    See Appalachian area.
  Development programs, **1965**: 2, 132, 492
  Federal aid, **1965**: 132, 139, 149, 452n., 492;
    1968-69: 39 (pp. 102, 109)
  Federal redevelopment program, **1963-64**: 91
    (p. 114), 126, 132 (p. 188), 213, 219
  Food stamp program, **1965**: 492
  Unemployment, **1963-64**: 294 [4]
Depressions, **1963-64**: 255, 757, 764;
        1965: 37, 46 [1], 235, 268; **1966**: 108,
        115, 155, 168, 386, 412, 479;
        1967: 156, 286; **1968-69**: 24, 37, 86,
        94, 459, 462, 472, 612
  1929-37 depression, **1963-64**: 124 (p. 159),
        667, 733, 736, 745, 749, 750, 799
Deressa, Yilma, **1965**: 541n.
Derrick, Leland E., **1968-69**: 459
Desalination of water.
  See Water desalination.
Deschutes National Forest, Oreg., **1967**: 418
Desegregation.
  See Integration.
De Seynes, Philippe, **1967**: 230
Desha, Joseph, **1963-64**: 644; **1966**: 351
Desha, Phoebe Ann, **1963-64**: 644
Desk set, gift to the President, **1968-69**: 631n.
Des Moines, Iowa, **1966**: 312; **1967**: 358 [9]
  Campaign remarks, **1963-64**: 634
  Mayor Charles S. Iles, **1963-64**: 634
Desmond, John, **1963-64**: 635
Desolation Wilderness, Calif., **1968-69**: 122, 168
Detachment ALFA, Mine Squadron Eleven, USN,
        1967: 424
Dethlefsen, Maj. and Mrs. Merlyn H., **1968-69**: 48
DeTocqueville, Alexis, **1965**: 200; **1967**: 349n.,
        415
Detroit, Mich., **1963-64**: 356, 462 [3], 463, 560
        [12, 15]; **1965**: 490; **1966**: 430;
        1967: 114, 535; **1968-69**: 328
  Campaign remarks, **1963-64**: 562, 745
  Civil disorders, **1967**: 328 [2], 466;
        1968-69: 51 [11], 86, 114
    Armed Forces use, **1967**: 321, 322, 328 [2],
        331
    Disaster relief, **1967**: 325, 328 [20]
    Remarks, **1967**: 322, 326, 331
  Democratic fundraising dinner, **1963-64**: 431
  Mayor Jerome P. Cavanagh, **1963-64**: 356, 431,
        562; **1966**: 155, 401 [4], 431, 536;
        1967: 321, 322, 325, 328 [5, 14];
        1968-69: 452
  Remarks, **1968-69**: 452
De Valera, Eamon, **1963-64**: 256 [4], 364, 366,
        376, 682
De Valera, Mrs. Eamon, **1963-64**: 366, 376
De Varona, Donna, **1966**: 385n.

Developing nations, **1966**: 6 (p. 8), 62, 94, 266,
        288, 308, 311, 420, 483, 497;
        1967: 495 [5]; **1968-69**: 2, 47 (p. 136),
        365
  See also Less developed countries and new
        nations.
  Agricultural imports, **1968-69**: 247, 679
  Agricultural programs, **1967**: 33
  Assistance, **1966**: 6 (pp. 3, 7-8), 11, 22, 26
        (pp. 58, 60), 34 (pp. 103, 105), 41, 45,
        52 [1], 62, 154, 243, 331, 343-344, 368,
        406, 420, 441, 608; **1967**: 13 (p. 49),
        16 (p. 80), 157, 175, 271, 346, 423,
        442, 491, 519, 545; **1968-69**: 39 (p.
        99), 47 (pp. 130, 138), 63, 176, 524,
        676 (p. 1268), 679, 684 (p. 1321)
  Coffee exports, **1968-69**: 207
  Communist aggression, **1966**: 420
  Economic and social development, **1966**: 34
        (p. 104), 200, 410, 542; **1967**: 13 (p.
        49), 16 (p. 80), 390, 442, 545
  Family planning, **1968-69**: 47 (p. 138)
  Food aid, **1968-69**: 29
  Food needs, **1967**: 13 (p. 49), 33, 272, 448,
        476; **1968-69**: 39 (p. 100), 47 (p. 138),
        94, 176, 679
  Health, **1967**: 13 (p. 49)
  Investments, **1967**: 469
  Malnutrition, prevention, **1968-69**: 692
  Population, **1967**: 272; **1968-69**: 14 (p. 27),
        679
  Tariff preferences, **1968-69**: 47 (p. 138)
  Television, educational, **1966**: 629
  Trade, **1968-69**: 559
  United Nations aid, **1966**: 41, 62, 427;
        1967: 488
  Water resources development, **1966**: 427
Development, International Bank for Reconstruc-
        tion and, **1967**: 13 (p. 49), 33, 44, 153,
        401; **1968-69**: 39 (p. 99), 63, 99, 102,
        290, 500
Development, National Advisory Council on
        Education Professions, **1967**: 396
Development, Organization for Economic Coop-
        eration and, **1967**: 33, 44
Development, United Nations Conference on
        Trade and, **1967**: 100
Development Assistance Committee, Organization
        for Economic Cooperation and Develop-
        ment, **1966**: 343
Development Association, International,
        1967: 13 (p. 49), 16 (p. 80);
        1968-69: 14 (p. 27), 39 (p. 99), 47
        (p. 138)
Development Bank, African, **1968-69**: 63, 365,
        500, 508
Development Bank, Asian, **1966**: 14, 41, 88 [1,
        16], 93, 128, 304, 325, 328-329, 348,

Development Bank, Asian — *continued*
    420, 458-459, 461, 516 [1], 517, 533,
    542, 565-566; **1968-69**: 14 (p. 27), 39
    (p. 99), 47 (p. 138), 63, 275 [6], 500,
    525, 678 (p. 1282), 684 (p. 1321)
Development Bank, Inter-American, **1966**: 26
    (p. 58), 41, 125, 177, 386n.;
    1968-69: 39 (p. 99), 63, 206, 239,
    290, 366, 500, 665
Development districts, multicounty, **1968-69**: 39
    (p. 101)
Development Loan Fund, **1963-64**: 71 [16]
Development of natural resources.
    See Conservation and development of natural
    resources.
Development and Resources Corporation,
    1967: 73
Development Standards, Commission on Codes,
    Zoning, Taxation and, **1966**: 394;
    1967: 4, 16 (p. 84)
Devine, J. Murray, **1963-64**: 607
Devine, Dr. Kenneth D., **1966**: 575
De Vries, Lucien (Governor of Surinam),
    1967: 178
De Weldon, Felix, **1963-64**: 773; **1966**: 174n.
Dewey, Adm. George, **1963-64**: 303
Dewey, Thomas E., **1963-64**: 637; **1968-69**: 540
DeWitt, J. Doyle, **1963-64**: 604n.
Diabetes prevention, **1963-64**: 755
Dial, A. Clayton, **1963-64**: 741
Diamond stones, industrial, **1966**: 572n.
Diarrheal disease, **1966**: 45
Diaz Ordaz, Gustavo, **1963-64**: 619 [10], 767,
    768; **1965**: 179, 558; **1966**: 174-175,
    177, 467-468, 507, 630 [2, 10], 635
    [14], 639-640, 642 [2], 644;
    1967: 47, 70 [4], 408 [1, 7], 453, 454n.;
    1968-69: 66, 73, 169 [14], 199, 354,
    623, 624
    Visit, **1967**: 447, 448, 449, 451, 452
Diaz Ordaz, Mrs. Gustavo, **1963-64**: 619 [10],
    767, 768; **1966**: 174, 468, 639;
    1967: 447, 449, 449n., 451, 452, 453;
    1968-69: 623, 624
Dickens, Charles, **1968-69**: 262
Dickerson, Nancy H., **1963-64**: 527; **1965**: 388
    [15]
Dickey hydroelectric project, Maine, **1966**: 399
Dickey-Lincoln School project, Maine,
    1965: 350
Dickinson, John, **1967**: 68
Dickson, Mrs. Bobbie, **1968**: 518
Didier, Dr. Edward Paul, **1966**: 575
Diem, Ngo Dinh, **1963-64**: 218 [24],
    379 [1], 607, 612, 643, 693;
    1965: 347 [6]; **1966**: 88 [23]
Dien Bien Phu, **1963-64**: 750
Diggs, Repr. Charles C., Jr., **1963-64**: 745;
    1966: 431

Digital Equipment Corp., **1966**: 144n.
Dillard, Mrs. James, **1966**: 156
Dillard, Julie Alice, **1966**: 156
Dillon, C. Douglas, **1965**: 155, 365; **1966**: 86,
    182, 388ftn. (p. 832); **1968-69**: 218,
    227, 241, 317
    See also Treasury, Secretary of the (C.
    Douglas Dillon).
Dillon, Mrs. C. Douglas (Phyllis), **1963-64**: 382;
    1965: 146, 155
DiLuzio, Frank C., **1966**: 320 [5]; **1967**: 227
Dilworth, Richardson, **1963-64**: 742; **1965**: 273
Dingell, Repr. John D., **1963-64**: 356, 745;
    1965: 348; **1966**: 431
Dingell, John D., Sr., **1965**: 394
Diop, Ousmane Socé, **1966**: 243
Diori Hamani (President of Niger), **1967**: 400,
    403
Diori Hamani, Madame, **1967**: 400, 403
Diphtheria, **1968-69**: 111
Diplomatic Corps, **1963-64**: 42
    Farewell remarks to, **1968-69**: 681
    Reception for, **1965**: 63
Diplomatic posts, U.S., **1965**: 32 (p. 90)
Diplomats, U.S.
    See Foreign Service.
Dirksen, Sen. Everett McK., **1963-64**: 333, 502;
    1965: 46 [2], 107, 113, 299, 546;
    1966: 174n., 237, 240, 504, 518, 520,
    531, 576; **1967**: 6 [17], 7, 236, 278,
    495 [14], 546; **1968-69**: 242, 257, 258,
    292n., 467 [1], 488, 658, 676 (p. 1270),
    690, 695, 696 [17]
    Campaign remarks on, **1963-64**: 652, 656, 658,
    669, 679, 680, 693, 694, 702, 703, 712,
    713, 729, 733, 734, 736, 745, 747, 750
    Civil rights bill opposition, **1966**: 474 [7]
    Dinner honoring, **1967**: 502
    Gift from President, **1966**: 628 [13]
    Illinois judicial nominations role, **1966**: 401
    [16]
    News conference remarks on, **1963-64**: 28 [9],
    563 [16]; **1966**: 88 [22], 247 [10, 12],
    334 [1], 401 [16], 417 [1, 4-5], 492
    [9], 577 [2, 13], 599 [2], 628 [1, 15],
    630 [16]
    Vietnam briefings, call for, **1966**: 247 [12]
Dirksen, Mrs. Everett McK., **1968-69**: 696 [17]
Disability insurance, **1965**: 49; **1968-69**: 684 (p.
    1323)
Disabled, Advisory Council on Health Insurance
    for the, **1968-69**: 346n.
Disabled persons.
    See also Handicapped persons.
    Federal aid, **1963-64**: 755; **1965**: 5, 416, 425,
    456
Disadvantaged Children, National Advisory
    Council on the Education of, **1966**: 210,
    238, 632; **1967**: 77, 183n.

Disadvantaged Children, National Planning Con-
   ference on the Education of, **1966**: 238
DiSalle, Michael V., **1963–64**: 642, 679
Disarmament.
   See Arms control and disarmament.
Disarmament, Committee on the Economic Impact of Defense and, **1963–64**: 62,
   486ftn. (p. 908); **1965**: 493
Disarmament Agency, United States Arms Control and.
   See Arms Control and Disarmament Agency,
   United States.
Disarmament Committee, Eighteen-Nation,
   1965: 20, 353 [5, 11], 386, 430;
   1966: 32, 70, 450; **1967**: 64, 80 [2],
   204 [4], 340, 365, 367; **1968–69**: 16,
   27, 69, 392
Disaster Fund, President's, **1963–64**: 567;
   1965: 174
Disaster relief, **1965**: 139, 149, 174, 215, 329,
   330, 592, 605; **1966**: 25 (p. 55), 145,
   584; **1967**: 133n., 138, 369, 408, 449,
   451; **1968–69**: 55, 98, 354, 483
   Appropriations, **1963–64**: 567
   Detroit civil disorders, **1967**: 325, 328 [20]
Disaster Relief Act of 1966, **1966**: 584;
   1967: 325n.; **1968–69**: 98
Disaster Warning System, National, **1967**: 31n.
Disasters, natural
   Blizzards, **1968–69**: 28
   Coal mines, **1968–69**: 607
   Drought, Northeastern States, **1966**: 391
   Earthquakes
      Alaska, **1963–64**: 241, 242 [1, 16], 286, 294
      [7], 308, 319, 368, 371, 615; **1965**: 435;
      1966: 74; **1967**: 369
      Chile, **1965**: 431
      Iran, **1968–69**: 614n.
      Japan, **1963–64**: 408
      Philippines, **1968–69**: 432
   Floods, **1967**: 300; **1968–69**: 98, 565, 593
      Alaska, **1967**: 369
      California, **1965**: 74, 477
      Chile, **1965**: 431
      Colorado, **1965**: 319 [20]
      Costa Rica, **1963–64**: 438, 443
      Mexico, **1967**: 408, 447, 449, 451
      Midwestern States, **1965**: 187, 188, 189,
         190, 191, 193, 215, 239, 477
      Minnesota, **1965**: 187, 189, 193, 239
      Mississippi Delta, **1965**: 592
      Montana, **1963–64**: 573
      Ohio River Basin, **1963–64**: 217
      Oregon, **1965**: 74
      Pacific Northwest, **1965**: 317, 477
      Texas, **1967**: 408
   Hurricanes, **1963–64**: 493; **1968–69**: 98
      Florida, **1963–64**: 563 [4], 567 ; **1965**: 605

Disasters, natural – *continued*
   Hurricanes – *continued*
      Georgia, **1963–64**: 563 [4], 567
      Louisiana, **1963–64**: 618, 647; **1965**: 605
      Mexico, **1966**: 507; **1967**: 408
      Mississippi, **1965**: 605
      South Carolina, **1963–64**: 563 [4]
      Texas, **1967**: 408
   In 1964, **1965**: 188
   Prediction, study and control, **1963–64**: 597,
      705; **1965**: 188, 193, 247, 271, 477;
      1966: 79; **1967**: 31n., 120, 303, 329,
      408 [5]; **1968–69**: 430
   Tornadoes, Midwest, **1965**: 187, 188, 189, 190,
      191, 193, 215, 239; **1967**: 187
   Typhoons, Philippines, **1963–64**: 627
   Volcano eruption, **1968–69**: 421, 430
      Costa Rica, **1963–64**: 438n., 443
Disciples of Christ, **1968–69**: 156
Disciples of Christ Historical Society, **1963–64**:
   279
Discount rates, **1965**: 639, 641 [2];
   1968–69: 141, 445
Discover America, Inc., **1968–69**: 648
Discrimination.
   See Civil rights; Integration; Nondiscrimination.
Disease prevention, **1963–64**: 391, 396, 598, 620,
   656, 755, 798; **1965**: 2, 5, 6, 32 (p. 94),
   70, 115, 154, 406, 410, 475, 495, 525,
   531; **1966**: 26 (p. 62), 95, 271, 293, 301,
   395, 406, 433, 436, 593; **1967**: 6 [15],
   13 (pp. 53, 59), 77, 110, 271, 286, 477,
   479, 520, 532, 554 [12]; **1968–69**: 14
   (p. 29), 21, 28, 39 (p. 103), 56, 63, 109,
   111, 145, 262, 286, 304, 363, 364, 396,
   406, 442, 446, 475, 536, 589, 622, 678
   (pp. 1295, 1296)
   See also specific diseases.
   Communicable diseases, **1966**: 6 (p. 8), 41, 45–
      46, 166, 189, 461
   District of Columbia, **1965**: 29
   Foreign assistance, **1966**: 6 (p. 3)
   Heart disease, cancer, and stroke, **1963–64**: 179,
      268, 650, 656, 667, 669, 733, 798;
      1965: 2, 5, 32 (p. 94), 52, 89, 154, 156
      [3], 329, 330, 343, 401, 406, 433, 551,
      594; **1966**: 26 (p. 62), 49, 95, 156, 189,
      271, 395, 403, 436, 515
   Hodgkins disease, **1966**: 156
   International cooperation, **1965**: 202, 262, 364
   Leukemia, **1966**: 156
   Malaria, **1963–64**: 716
   Mental illness, **1963–64**: 132 (p. 189)
   Multiple sclerosis, **1963–64**: 312
   Polio, **1963–64**: 598, 667, 669
   Research, **1968–69**: 40
   Smallpox, **1965**: 5, 262

Disease prevention – *continued*
U.S.-Japan, cooperative program, **1965**: 12, 15,
175, 214, 544; **1966**: 45; **1968-69**: 685
Disney, Walter, **1963-64**: 568
Disosway, Gen. Gabriel P., **1967**: 485 [7]
Displaced persons, unemployment, **1965**: 490
Disraeli, Benjamin, **1966**: 149
Dissent, right of, **1967**: 495 [13], 502, 554 [8]
Distinguished Civilian Service Awards Board,
1963-64: 27
Distinguished Federal Civilian Service, President's
Award for, **1963-64**: 417; **1965**: 269,
296; **1966**: 25, 266; **1967**: 317;
1968-69: 604
Distinguished Flying Cross, **1968-69**: 610
Distinguished Service Medal, **1963-64**: 127, 425,
454, 487, 783; **1965**: 37, 158, 228, 399;
1967: 235, 308, 567; **1968-69**: 34, 353,
384, 669
Distinguished Unit Citation, **1966**: 107, 282
District of Columbia, **1963-64**: 16, 700;
1965: 2, 315, 402, 452, 454 [5];
1966: 226; **1967**: 307, 377, 406
See also National Capital Region.
Alcoholics, treatment, **1966**: 27
AMVETS Headquarters, dedication,
1966: 345
Antipoverty program, **1965**: 70
Appropriations and expenditures,
1968-69: 39 (p. 107), 95, 133, 436
Art Center, **1968-69**: 660
Assistant Commissioner Thomas W. Fletcher,
1968-69: 698
Beautification programs, **1965**: 545;
1966: 500; **1968-69**: 648
Black United Front, **1968-69**: 425 [10]
Borrowing authority, **1963-64**: 133
Budget, **1963-64**: 133; **1965**: 29, 40, 151;
1966: 27, 586; **1967**: 15, 71, 247;
1968-69: 95, 689
Campaign addresses, remarks, etc.,
1963-64: 548, 555, 570, 588, 590,
611, 622, 633
Capital improvement program, **1965**: 29, 40,
61, 151
Chanceries, **1967**: 71
Civil disorders, **1968-69**: 180n.
Commissioner Walter N. Tobriner,
1963-64: 211 [2], 704; **1966**: 162;
1967: 372n.
Commissioner Walter E. Washington,
1967: 406, 411 [1], 466, 544, 575
See also Mayor Walter E. Washington *below.*
Commissioners, **1965**: 70, 151; **1966**: 267,
354, 611
Congressional representation, **1967**: 71;
1968-69: 39 (p. 107)
Correctional systems, **1968-69**: 95

District of Columbia – *continued*
Council, swearing in, **1967**: 406, 466
Courts, **1966**: 611; **1967**: 15, 71, 350;
1968-69: 95, 133, 542
Crime and law enforcement, **1963-64**: 704;
1965: 29, 70, 102, 366, 381;
1966: 27, 116, 219, 354, 611, 656;
1967: 15, 27, 71, 337, 466, 575;
1968-69: 95, 133, 355, 436, 689
Education, **1963-64**: 116, 133, 457;
1965: 29, 70, 111, 151; **1966**: 27,
406, 586; **1967**: 15, 350, 399;
1968-69: 39 (p. 106), 95, 133, 203,
436, 648, 689
Employment, **1968-69**: 19, 133, 272, 689
Federal City College, **1968-69**: 436, 689
Federal funds for, **1963-64**: 133;
1965: 29, 40, 151
Federal payment, **1968-69**: 39 (p. 107), 95,
133
Firearms, registration of, proposed,
1965: 70; **1966**: 27
Firemen, **1968-69**: 272
Food stamp program, **1965**: 492
Fort Lincoln development, **1968-69**: 689
Government, **1968-69**: 39 (pp. 107, 109),
133, 134, 135, 152, 203, 355, 425 [10],
458, 689, 698
Reorganization, **1967**: 71, 225 [22], 247,
307, 337, 339, 341
Safety award, **1967**: 265
Gun control legislation, **1968-69**: 133, 355
Health and welfare services, **1963-64**: 133;
1965: 29, 70; **1967**: 15, 71, 574;
1968-69: 19, 20, 95, 689
Higher education facilities, proposed,
1963-64: 116, 457n.
Highway program, **1963-64**: 133; **1965**: 19,
29, 61, 70; **1966**: 27, 162
Home rule, **1963-64**: 16, 133; **1965**: 39, 70,
402, 443, 448 [10], 481; **1966**: 6 (p.
6), 8 [4], 26 (p. 62), 27; **1967**: 13 (p.
56), 15, 71, 247; **1968-69**: 39 (p. 107),
133, 477, 689, 698
Housing, **1963-64**: 704n.; **1965**: 70; **1967**: 15n.,
180, 372; **1968-69**: 19, 20, 133, 135,
152
Infant mortality, **1968-69**: 111
Inter-American foreign ministers meeting in,
1963-64: 455 [18], 475 [3, 13], 561
International center, **1968-69**: 133, 523
Judges, **1968-69**: 542
Junior Village, **1963-64**: 133; **1965**: 29
Juvenile delinquency, **1963-64**: 133, 537;
1965: 29, 70, 151, 381
Lafayette Square renovation, **1965**: 328n.

District of Columbia – *continued*

Law enforcement.

  See Crime and law enforcement *above.*

Legislation, **1966**: 607 [13]

Library facilities, **1963–64**: 133; **1965**: 151

Licenses and Inspections, Department of, **1968–69**: 133

Mayor Walter E. Washington, **1968–69**: 19, 36, 39 (p. 107), 95, 133, 152, 169 [5], 272, 420, 424, 429, 436, 442, 458, 629, 698

  See also Commissioner Walter E. Washington *above.*

Medicaid participation, **1967**: 574

Mental health responsibilities, **1963–64**: 133

Messages to Congress, **1965**: 70; **1966**: 27; **1967**: 15, 71, 247; **1968–69**: 133, 689

Minimum wage, **1966**: 27, 527

Monuments and memorials, **1963–64**: 172; **1965**: 70

Municipal services, **1968–69**: 689

Museum of History and Technology, dedication, **1963–64**: 141

National Training School for Boys, **1965**: 29

National Visitor Center, **1966**: 90; **1968–69**: 128, 133

National Zoological Park functions, **1966**: 267

Neighborhood centers and services, **1968–69**: 19, 20, 195

Occupational training programs, **1963–64**: 133; **1965**: 70, 111; **1966**: 586

Pennsylvania Avenue, plans for redevelopment, **1963–64**: 379 [12], 700; **1965**: 70, 538

Police, **1963–64**: 133; **1965**: 29, 70, 366, 381; **1966**: 27, 116, 354, 611; **1967**: 15, 27, 71, 441, 466; **1968–69**: 95, 133, 272, 355, 425 [10], 436, 689

Pollution control, **1968–69**: 95, 420

Poor People's campaign, **1968–69**: 51 [14], 169 [5], 223 [9], 275 [5], 339 [7]

Public health, **1968–69**: 19, 20, 95, 689

Public works, **1968–69**: 689

Reception for President, **1968–69**: 698

Recreational programs and facilities, **1963–64**: 133; **1965**: 29, 70, 151; **1967**: 15; **1968–69**: 133, 134, 689

Revenues, **1968–69**: 39 (p. 107), 95, 133

St. Elizabeths Hospital, **1963–64**: 133

School board, **1968–69**: 133, 203, 436, 689

School construction, **1963–64**: 133

Schools, **1966**: 27, 457, 586

Shaw Junior High School, **1965**: 29, 151

  Site, **1966**: 27, 457

Social services, **1968–69**: 95

Summer enrichment program, **1968–69**: 95

Taxes, **1963–64**: 133; **1965**: 29, 40; **1968–69**: 95, 133, 689

Teachers, **1968–69**: 133, 272

District of Columbia – *continued*

Transportation, **1966**: 27, 68, 84, 262; **1967**: 15, 71, 154; **1968–69**: 95, 458, 689

Urban renewal, **1965**: 70; **1966**: 27, 452; **1968–69**: 135, 458

Vietnam peace demonstrations, **1967**: 441

Visitors' center, proposed, **1965**: 70

Voter participation, **1965**: 39; **1966**: 21

Voter registration, **1963–64**: 167

Voting rights, **1968–69**: 332, 341

Washington Technical Institute, **1968–69**: 436

Welfare services, **1963–64**: 133

World Weather Center, **1963–64**: 705

District of Columbia, President's Commission on Crime in the, **1965**: 70, 366, 381, 526n.; **1966**: 116, 219, 354, 611, 656; **1967**: 15, 27, 71

District of Columbia, President's Committee on Public Higher Education in the, **1963–64**: 116n., 457; **1965**: 111

District of Columbia Air Pollution Control Act, **1968–69**: 420

District of Columbia Alley Dwelling Act, **1968–69**: 133ftn. (p. 393), 152n.

District of Columbia Appropriation Act of 1966, **1965**: 366

District of Columbia Appropriation Act of 1969, **1968–69**: 355n., 436, 689n.

District of Columbia Bureau of Criminal Statistics, **1967**: 71

District of Columbia Charter Act, **1965**: 39, 486

District of Columbia Council on Human Relations, **1967**: 15

District of Columbia Department of Corrections, **1967**: 71

District of Columbia Department of Licenses and Inspections, **1968–69**: 133

District of Columbia Elected Board of Education Act, **1968–69**: 203

District of Columbia General Hospital, **1967**: 15

District of Columbia Judicial Council, **1967**: 71

District of Columbia Minimum Wage Amendments Act of 1966, **1966**: 527

District of Columbia Police and Firemen's Salary Act Amendments of 1966, **1966**: 611n.

District of Columbia Police and Firemen's Salary Act Amendments of 1968, **1968–69**: 272

District of Columbia Public Education Act, **1966**: 586

District of Columbia Public Library, **1967**: 15

District of Columbia Redevelopment Land Agency, **1966**: 457; **1968–69**: 133, 135

District of Columbia Teachers College, **1965**: 111

District of Columbia Teachers' Salary Act Amendments of 1968, **1968–69**: 272

District Youth Services Office, **1967**: 71

Dividends, **1963–64**: 285 [15]; **1966**: 34 (p. 99), 347
  Tax treatment, **1963–64**: 731
"Divine Comedy."
  See "Divine Comedy" *under* Dante Aligheri.
Dix, Dorothea L., **1965**: 401
Dix, S. Sgt. Drew D., **1968–69**: 688
Dixon, James, **1967**: 193
Dixon, Melvin T., **1968–69**: 599n.
Dixon, Paul Rand (Chairman, Federal Trade Commission), **1963–64**: 701; **1968–69**: 56
Djakarta, Indonesia, **1968–69**: 198
Doar, John M., **1963–64**: 417; **1965**: 106 [1], 117 [1]; **1967**: 328 [19]
Dobbin, Muriel, **1963–64**: 587 [3]
Dobie, J. Frank, **1963–64**: 294 [9], 568
  Death of, **1963–64**: 584
Dobrynin, Anatoly F., **1963–64**: 271 [14], 674, 676, 678, 680, 686, 688 [1], 737; **1965**: 388 [10]; **1967**: 18n., 279, 282, 425; **1968–69**: 309n.
Dobzhansky, Theodosius, **1965**: 56n.
Docking, Gov. Robert B., **1967**: 485 [6]; **1968–69**: 452
DOD.
  See Defense, Department of.
Dodd, Robert H., **1966**: 331n.
Dodd, Sen. Thomas J., **1963–64**: 382, 383, 603; **1965**: 142, 256, 361
Dogs of war, **1968–69**: 462, 474
Dohanos, Stevan, **1966**: 358n.
Dolby, Mr. and Mrs. Charles L., **1967**: 407n.
Dolby, Daniel, **1967**: 407n.
Dolby, Sgt. David C., **1967**: 407
Dole, Repr. Robert, **1967**: 33
Dollahite, John, **1963–64**: 374
Dollar stability, **1963–64**: 196, 233, 295, 296, 299, 455 [13], 462 [2], 472, 506, 563 [6], 617, 630, 722, 740, 753, 787; **1965**: 2, 18, 35 (pp. 105, 107, 108), 46 [12], 60, 76, 77, 139, 146, 149, 347 [7], 365n., 541, 638; **1966**: 140, 473; **1967**: 411 [11], 417 [5], 524; **1968–69**: 1 [4, 8, 10], 2, 10, 12, 14 (p. 31), 39 (p. 84), 47 (pp. 131, 133, 135–137), 63, 76, 112, 136, 170, 171, 176, 218, 241, 277, 283 [11], 326, 343, 427, 500, 517, 582, 624, 677, 678 (p. 1273), 683, 684 (pp. 1313, 1319), 690, 696 [12]
Dollars for Democrats Drive, **1966**: 403
Dominican Reconciliation, Act of, **1965**: 463 [4]
Dominican Republic, **1963–64**: 143ftn. (p. 219); **1965**: 208 [7], 221, 223, 286, 295 [1, 4, 16], 300, 319 [16], 347 [2, 3], 353 [2], 364, 392, 429, 448 [18], 459, 463 [4]; **1966**: 65 [4], 264, 273, 277 [25], 320 [6], 353, 607 [1]; **1967**: 44, 100, 261, 436; **1968–69**: 148n.

Dominican Republic – *continued*
  Assistance, **1965**: 217, 221, 223, 227, 253, 286, 293, 295 [16], 473, 484; **1968–69**: 679
  Cease-fire in, **1965**: 16, 295 [4, 16], 319 [4, 16]
  Communist aggression, **1965**: 216, 221, 227, 286, 295 [9, 16]
  Elections, **1966**: 251, 277 [25], 320 [12]
  OAS contributions, **1965**: 295 [1, 4, 6, 16], 319 [16], 473, 484
  OAS mission to, **1965**: 218, 221, 223, 227, 253, 347 [3]; **1966**: 277 [3, 25]
  Peace Corps projects in, **1965**: 83
  Peace mission (1965), **1968–69**: 291
  President Joaquin Balaguer, **1966**: 277 [3, 25], 320 [6]; **1967**: 436
  President Hector García-Godoy, **1965**: 484; **1966**: 251, 277 [3, 25]
  Protection of Americans and foreign nationals, **1965**: 208 [7], 212, 216, 221, 223, 227, 286, 295 [16], 319 [16]
  Provisional Government, **1965**: 472, 473
    Negotiations participants, **1965**: 482
    U.S. recognition, **1965**: 484
  U.S. Ambassador W. Tapley Bennett, Jr., **1965**: 212n., 221, 223n., 227, 295 [1, 16], 319 [16], 342, 364n., 482
  U.S. Ambassador John Hugh Crimmins, **1966**: 277 [2]
  U.S. Embassy, attacks on, **1965**: 227, 319 [16]
  U.S. forces in, **1965**: 212, 216, 217, 221, 223, 227, 286, 289, 295 [1, 15, 16], 299, 319 [4, 16], 342; **1966**: 577 [15]
  U.S. peace mission to, **1965**: 221
Dominican Republic-Puerto Rican Economic Commission, Joint, **1967**: 436
Dominick, Sen. Peter H., **1966**: 410, 413–414
Domino theory, **1967**: 519
Donaho, William T., **1965**: 89, 603
Donahue, Thomas R., **1967**: 97
Donahue, Dr. Wilma, **1965**: 642n.
Donald, David, **1963–64**: 303
Donaldson, Jesse M., **1968–69**: 498
Donatello, Dominic, **1965**: 270
Donelon, Thomas F., **1963–64**: 648
Donlon, Mrs. Marion H., **1963–64**: 793
Donlon, Capt. Roger H. C., **1966**: 421
Donnelley, Dixon, **1966**: 65 [1]
Donner, Frederic, **1963–64**: 587 [1], 733
Donohue, Repr. Harold D., **1963–64**: 396, 727
Donohue, Mary Lynne, **1968–69**: 236
Donora, Pa., **1965**: 54
Donovan, William J., **1967**: 502
Doolittle, Gen. James A., **1965**: 115n.
Doran, Adron, **1967**: 396n.
Dore, Very Rev. Vincent C., **1965**: 237n.
Dorn, Repr. W. J. Bryan, **1963–64**: 719; **1966**: 345; **1967**: 374; **1968–69**: 229

Doughboy Station, Fort Benning, Ga., **1967**: 485 [1]

Dougherty, Bishop John, **1966**: 504

Doughton, Robert Lee, **1968–69**: 238

Douglas, Donald W., Jr., **1968–69**: 616

Douglas, John W., **1966**: 335; **1967**: 411 [2]

Douglas, Kirk, **1963–64**: 751

Douglas, Lewis W., **1963–64**: 796

Douglas, Sen. Paul H., **1963–64**: 287, 619 [15], 635, 636, 637, 694, 747, 748; **1965**: 299, 354, 415; **1966**: 228, 349, 401 [16], 579, 599 [1–2]; **1967**: 4, 16 (p. 84); **1968–69**: 167, 280, 704

Douglas, Mrs. Paul H., **1963–64**: 748

Douglas, Justice William O., **1965**: 72; **1967**: 256; **1968–69**: 301

Douglas Aircraft Co., Inc., **1965**: 448 [1]; **1966**: 144n.

Dover, Del., campaign remarks, **1963–64**: 749

Dover Air Force Base, Delaware, **1963–64**: 749

Dow, Repr. John G., **1966**: 394–395

Dowdy, Repr. John, **1966**: 586

Dow-Jones Industrial Average, **1963–64**: 211 [3], 246 [12], 271 [15], 455 [2], 563 [6]

Dowling, Edward, **1963–64**: 639

Downing, Repr. Thomas N., **1963–64**: 358; **1967**: 485 [8]

Downs, Anthony, **1967**: 4n.

Doyle, Francis, **1966**: 359

Doyle, Jack, **1967**: 324n.

Doylestown, Pa., **1966**: 528

Draft rejectees.
    See Military rejectees, training and rehabilitation.

Draft system.
    See Selective Service System.

Draper, Charles S., **1965**: 56n.; **1968–69**: 107

Drawing Rights, Special, **1968–69**: 2, 47 (p. 137), 76, 218, 317, 500, 684 (p. 1319)

Drew, J. Patterson, **1966**: 373ftn. (p. 808)

Drewry, Elizabeth B., **1965**: 91n.

Drico Oil Tools, Inc., **1967**: 231n.

Driver, William J., (Administrator of Veterans Affairs), **1963–64**: 815; **1965**: 22 [16], 46 [8], 156 [10]; **1966**: 208, 490, 505; **1967**: 25, 161, 374, 493; **1968–69**: 40, 160, 229, 419, 452, 554, 599

Driver education, **1966**: 187

Driver registration, national, **1966**: 449

Driving, the President's, comments on, **1963–64**: 246 [2, 16]

Drought control, **1966**: 593

Drug Abuse, President's Advisory Commission on Narcotic and, **1963–64**: 179, 458; **1965**: 102; **1968–69**: 59, 60

Drug Abuse Control, Bureau of, **1968–69**: 59, 60

Drug Abuse Control Amendments of 1965, **1965**: 361, 509; **1966**: 116

Drug Administration, Food and, **1967**: 35, 57, 77

Drug control legislation.
    See Federal Food, Drug, and Cosmetic Act, amendments.

Drug Reaction Center, International Adverse, **1965**: 202, 262

Drug safety bill (Narcotic Addict Rehabilitation Act of 1966), **1966**: 140, 307, 598

Drugs, **1967**: 3 (p. 7), 12
    See also Narcotics and dangerous drugs; *specific drugs.*
    Addiction, **1965**: 102; **1966**: 116–117; **1967**: 35, 285, 382
    Compendium, **1968–69**: 111
    Consumer protection, **1963–64**: 159, 173, 179, 391, 458; **1965**: 5, 102, 202, 361, 567; **1966**: 6 (p. 6), 34 (p. 108), 140, 307; **1967**: 214; **1968–69**: 336
    Control, **1967**: 35, 71, 94
    Costs, **1968–69**: 111, 678 (p. 1295)
    Dangerous, **1968–69**: 14 (p. 30), 57, 59, 60, 109, 111, 217, 336, 390, 406, 536, 678 (p. 1295)
    Illegal traffic, **1963–64**: 179, 193, 458; **1965**: 5, 102, 361; **1966**: 307, 526
    Inventories, **1967**: 121
    Reaction monitoring, worldwide, **1967**: 214, 215

Drugs, Information and Education Center on Narcotic and Dangerous (HEW), **1967**: 35

Druid Hill Park, Baltimore, Md., **1968–69**: 184

Dryden, Dr. Hugh L., **1965**: 81, 120, 121, 310, 318, 463 [13], 584, 634, 646; **1966**: 61; **1968–69**: 507, 646 [9]

Dryden, Mrs. Hugh L., **1966**: 61n.

Dubinsky, David, **1963–64**: 334, 387, 388, 669, 796n.; **1965**: 223, 242, 273, 459; **1966**: 165, 417 [2, 6], 479; **1967**: 30, 484; **1968–69**: 270, 672

Dubinsky, Mrs. David, **1963–64**: 388

DuBoff, Leonard David, **1968–69**: 230

Dubord, Richard, **1963–64**: 606

Dubrow, Evelyn, **1968–69**: 270

"Duck stamps," **1967**: 547

Duesenberry, James, **1966**: 44; **1968–69**: 76

Duesenberry, Mrs. James, **1966**: 44

Dugan, Frank J., **1967**: 170ftn. (p. 439), 207, 310

Duggan, Ervin S., **1968–69**: 17, 453

Duke, Angier Biddle, **1963–64**: 340, 819; **1968–69**: 291n., 362n.

Duke, Mrs. Angier Biddle, **1963–64**: 819

Duke, Brig. Gen. Charles M., **1965**: 366

Dulles, Allen W., **1963–64**: 14, 15, 563 [5], 591, 688 [3], 696; **1965**: 209; **1966**: 310; **1967**: 502n.

Dulles, John Foster, **1966**: 86, 273; **1967**: 495 [14]
Dulles International Airport, **1966**: 531, 570
Dulski, Repr. Thaddeus J., **1963-64**: 667; **1965**: 413; **1966**: 392, 651; **1968-69**: 321
Duncan, John B., **1967**: 81, 466
Duncan, John J., **1963-64**: 324
Duncan, Mrs. Robert V. H., **1963-64**: 275n.
Duncan Lake Dam, **1963-64**: 135
Dungan, Ralph A., **1963-64**: 69, 224, 513; **1965**: 22 [1]
Dunlop, John T., **1966**: 373ftn. (p. 808), 535n.; **1967**: 174, 188, 204 [5], 207, 310
Dunne, Rev. George H., **1966**: 455
Du Pont, Henry, **1963-64**: 211 [7]
Dupuy, Pierre, **1966**: 644n.; **1967**: 237, 238
Durable goods shipments, **1966**: 141 [5]
Durfee, Judge James R., **1967**: 5
Durham, Lord, **1963-64**: 576
Dutton, Frederick G., **1963-64**: 414
Dwyer, Repr. Florence P., **1966**: 523
Dwyer, John J., **1963-64**: 695n.
Dwyer, Robert F., **1965**: 465
Dyal, Ken W., **1963-64**: 735
Dysentery, **1966**: 395

"E" Awards, **1963-64**: 350; **1966**: 144; **1967**: 231
Early Bird satellite, **1966**: 40; **1967**: 346
Earthquakes
  Alaska, **1963-64**: 241, 242 [1, 16], 286, 294 [7], 308, 319, 368, 371, 615; **1965**: 435; **1966**: 74; **1967**: 369
  Chile, **1965**: 43
  Iran, **1968-69**: 614n.
  Japan, **1963-64**: 408
  Philippines, **1968-69**: 432
Earthquake Information Center, National, **1967**: 31n.
East African Economic Community, **1968-69**: 365, 508
East Chicago, Ill., **1963-64**: 639
  Mayor John Nicosia, **1963-64**: 639
East St. Louis, Ill., Mayor Alvin G. Fields, **1963-64**: 694
East-West Center (Honolulu), **1965**: 248; **1966**: 532-533, 551
East-West Center, National Review Board for the, **1965**: 248
East-West relations, **1963-64**: 71 [13], 76, 91 (p. 117), 109, 232 [8], 246 [11], 359, 399, 400, 795n.; **1965**: 46 [7]; **1966**: 261, 272, 486; **1967**: 162
East-West trade, **1963-64**: 266 [11]
Easter vacation, the President's, **1963-64**: 242 [25]

Eastern Airlines, Inc., **1966**: 256n., 322
Eastern Europe, trade with U.S., **1968-69**: 47 (p. 138)
Eastern Kentucky Emergency Program, **1963-64**: 41
Eastland, Sen. James O., **1963-64**: 97; **1968-69**: 339 [2], 467 [2]
Eastman Kodak Co., **1963-64**: 350n.
Eaton, Bob, **1963-64**: 336 [21]
Eaton, Charles A., **1963-64**: 750
Eaton, Fredrick, **1963-64**: 296
Eaton, William, **1963-64**: 619 [18]
Eaton, William O., **1965**: 135
Ebert, Dr. Robert H., **1966**: 208n.; **1967**: 500
Eckert, J. Presper, **1968-69**: 695n.
Eckhardt, Repr. Bob, **1968-69**: 575
Eckler, A. Ross, **1967**: 498
Eckstein, Otto, **1963-64**: 336 [7], 550; **1966**: 33, 44; **1967**: 87n.
Eckstein, Mrs. Otto, **1963-64**: 550
Economic Advisers, Council of.
  See Council of Economic Advisers.
Economic Affairs, Joint United States-Japan Committee on Trade and, **1965**: 15, 355; **1967**: 381, 491
Economic Affairs, U.S.-Canada Committee on Trade and, **1963-64**: 140
Economic assistance, **1963-64**: 45, 69, 91 (p. 117), 132 (pp. 176, 185), 227, 233, 280; **1965**: 32 (p. 90), 450, 495; **1966**: 26 (pp. 58-59), 34 (p. 104), 41, 308, 343; **1967**: 44, 423, 442, 469, 489
See also Foreign assistance; Military, U.S.; Technical assistance to developing nations; *specific countries.*
  Africa, **1965**: 18
  Asia, South Asia, and Southeast Asia, **1965**: 18, 26, 130, 199, 295 [3], 357, 628; **1966**: 18, 26 (p. 58), 420
  China, Republic of, **1965**: 7; **1966**: 368; **1967**: 219
  Developing and new nations, **1965**: 15, 18, 139, 149, 176 [3]; **1966**: 6 (p. 7), 22, 34 (p. 103), 41, 344, 368; **1967**: 13 (p. 49), 491
  Dominican Republic, **1965**: 253, 295 [16], 484; **1966**: 320 [6]
  Europe, **1966**: 6 (p. 7)
  India, **1966**: 152
  Iran, **1967**: 509
  Japan, **1966**: 368
  Jordan, **1965**: 18
  Korea, **1965**: 18, 257
  Laos, **1965**: 18, 26, 294
  Latin America, **1963-64**: 71 [5], 340, 769; **1965**: 149; **1966**: 125, 175, 386
  Malagasy Republic, **1963-64**: 483
  Malaysia, **1963-64**: 471n.

Economic assistance – *continued*
  Message to Congress, **1966**: 41; **1967**: 44
  Middle East, **1967**: 264 [10]
  Philippines, **1963–64**: 627
  Ryukyu Islands, **1965**: 15
  Thailand, **1963–64**: 476; **1965**: 294
  Upper Volta, **1965**: 144
  Vietnam, **1963–64**: 348; **1965**: 18, 130, 194,
      246, 250, 294, 295 [3]; **1966**: 6 (pp. 7,
      11), 18, 41, 54–55, 65 [10], 114
Economic Commission, Joint Dominican Re-
      public-Puerto Rican, **1967**: 436
Economic Commission for Africa, **1966**: 243
Economic Commission for Asia and the Far East,
      1966: 461, 557
Economic Commission for Asia and the Far East,
      United Nations, **1965**: 353ftn. (p. 736);
      1968–69: 237
Economic Community of Eastern Africa, **1966**:
      243
Economic Conference, West African, **1968–69**:
      157, 181
Economic cooperation, international, **1963–64**:
      472, 780 [3]; **1965**: 15, 35 (p. 111),
      365, 451, 541, 637, 659n.
Economic Cooperation and Development,
      Organization for, **1963–64**: 472; **1965**:
      18, 495; **1966**: 343; **1967**: 33, 44;
      1968–69: 214
Economic Development, Committee for, **1963–
      64**: 271 [15], 775
Economic Development, Federal Advisory
      Council on Regional, **1968–69**: 173
Economic Development Act of 1965, **1966**: 351;
      1967: 223 [4]
Economic Development Administration, **1966**:
      28, 122 [2], 351–352; **1968–69**: 39
      (p. 109), 153 [16]
Economic development and public works bill.
  See Public works and economic development
      bill.
Economic and fiscal policy.
  See Fiscal and monetary policy.
Economic gains, **1963–64**: 477n.
Economic growth, U.S., **1963–64**: 23, 124 (pp.
      156, 161, 164), 132 (pp. 178, 179, 182,
      191, 193), 197, 198, 199, 213, 233,
      235, 244, 290, 311, 314, 338, 350, 411,
      413, 415, 431, 434, 459, 472, 477, 484,
      506, 509, 531, 536, 624, 638, 689, 697,
      707, 708, 722, 757, 771, 775, 787;
      1965: 2, 17, 23, 32 (pp. 83, 84, 85, 99),
      35, 45, 76, 77, 97n., 110, 132, 139, 146,
      153, 156 [1], 164, 179, 208 [4], 226,
      243, 246, 250, 251, 255, 258, 285, 298,
      299, 319 [3, 6], 321, 322, 326, 330,
      338, 351, 388 [7], 480, 489, 513, 567,
      589, 590, 632, 641 [2], 644; **1966**: 6

Economic growth – *continued*
      (p. 4), 17, 26 (pp. 48–49, 50, 52, 60),
      34, 44, 83, 108, 110–112, 140, 144,
      155, 201, 206, 333, 346–347, 403, 415,
      431–432, 444, 453, 464, 477 [3], 596,
      630 [2], 631, 635 [18], 637
  See also Economy, national.
  Campaign remarks, **1963–64**: 541, 548, 555,
      562, 597, 604, 630, 635, 636, 640, 642,
      643, 645, 650, 657, 658, 659, 669, 679,
      694, 695, 703, 712, 716, 719, 729, 733,
      734, 735, 741, 742, 745, 746, 750, 751,
      761, 762
  News conference remarks, **1963–64**: 266 [2],
      271 [3, 15], 285 [15], 316 [5], 336
      [1, 20], 379 [5], 455 [13], 486 [4],
      563 [6], 619 [4], 780 [3, 4]
  Relation to antipoverty program, **1963–64**:
      336 [20]
  Statements, **1963–64**: 404, 811
Economic Impact and Conversion, Office of,
      1963–64: 486 [2]
Economic Impact of Defense and Disarmament,
      Committee on the, **1963–64**: 62; **1965**:
      493
Economic Integration, Central American Bank
      for, **1965**: 393; **1968–69**: 363, 365,
      366, 375
Economic opportunity, **1963–64**: 386
Economic Opportunity, National Advisory
      Council on, **1967**: 87n., 114; **1968–69**:
      315
Economic Opportunity, Office of, **1963–64**:
      300, 677; **1965**: 35 (p. 114), 100, 132,
      288n., 567, 618; **1966**: 8 [3], 26 (p.
      55), 28, 95, 123, 140, 169n., 319, 394,
      630 [4]; **1967**: 13 (p. 54), 27, 77, 114,
      193, 199, 203, 412; **1968–69**: 39 (pp.
      104, 110), 57, 59, 155n., 153 [3, 10],
      259n., 315, 429, 555, 629n., 678 (pp.
      1295, 1301), 684 (p. 1324)
  Appropriations, **1967**: 55; **1968–69**: 39 (p. 92),
      678 (p. 1281)
  Director (R. Sargent Shriver, Jr.), **1963–64**: 677,
      678, 680, 711, 778, 801, 802; **1965**:
      75n., 102, 259, 264n., 322, 323, 467,
      545; **1966**: 12, 93, 95, 105, 140, 236
      [13], 394, 490, 594, 607 [1]; **1967**:
      12, 39, 77, 87n., 114, 199, 211, 258,
      259, 286, 291; **1968–69**: 94, 113
  Memorandums, **1966**: 425, 606; **1967**: 259,
      412
  Establishment, proposed, **1963–64**: 219
  Report to Congress, **1967**: 277
Economic Opportunity Act of 1964, **1963–64**:
      537, 580, 620, 642, 677, 704n., 802;
      1965: 9, 29, 32 (p. 93), 47, 75, 100,
      268, 340, 463,[15], 490; **1966**: 171n.,

Economic Opportunity Act of – *continued*
    172, 250, 594; **1967**: 15, 87, 91, 114,
    199, 353, 378; **1968–69**: 75, 87, 113,
    212, 315, 442, 567, 678 (pp. 1291,
    1301), 684 (p. 1324)
  See also Antipoverty bill.
  Approval, **1963–64**: 528
  Passage in Congress, **1963–64**: 505
  Proposed, **1963–64**: 219, 235
Economic Opportunity Amendments of 1965,
    1966: 221
Economic Opportunity Amendments of 1966,
    1966: 594
Economic Opportunity Amendments of 1967,
    1967: 114, 119n., 358 [3]
Economic Opportunity Council, **1963–64**: 802;
    1967: 114
Economic Progress, National Commission on
    Technology, Automation, and, **1963–
    64**: 214, 525; **1965**: 100, 258; **1966**:
    111, 258
Economic reform, **1963–64**: 776
Economic Report to Congress, **1963–64**: 124,
    173; **1965**: 35; **1966**: 34; **1967**: 16;
    1968–69: 46, 47, 683, 684
  Comments, **1966**: 33, 83, 110; **1967**: 6, 121
Economic and Social Act of Rio de Janeiro,
    1966: 125, 177, 386
Economic and Social Council, Inter-American,
    1963–64: 769; **1965**: 593; **1966**: 175
Economic Symposium, **1966**: 83
Economist, The, magazine, **1966**: 420
Economists, tax recommendations, **1966**: 141
    [3]
Economy, national, **1963–64**: 62, 132 (p. 178),
    139, 213, 219, 228, 255, 264, 284, 295,
    297, 299, 305, 386, 406, 435, 472, 484,
    598, 787; **1965**: 60, 100, 132, 168, 192,
    196, 207, 326, 371, 460, 638, 639;
    1966: 109, 115, 123, 132, 155, 201,
    235, 237, 240, 324, 333, 336, 371, 379,
    399, 412–413, 419, 429, 431, 444, 451,
    473, 588, 596, 612; **1967**: 3 (p. 2),
    48n., 55, 114, 199, 286, 420, 427, 495,
    498, 525, 556; **1968–69**: 1 [8], 2, 10,
    24, 39 (p. 84), 46, 100n., 141, 169 [21],
    170, 226, 281, 282, 283 [8], 332, 343,
    377, 403, 404, 406, 449, 463, 467 [3],
    469, 500, 517, 534, 568, 569, 612, 646
    [3], 654, 676 (pp. 1264, 1268), 696
    [12], 706
  See also Economic growth, U.S.; Fiscal and
    monetary policy.
  Effect on elections, **1963–64**: 246 [17]
  Growth, **1967**: 3 (p. 7), 13 (pp. 39, 43, 51), 16
    (pp. 72, 76, 77), 224, 244, 270, 329,
    376, 460 [1, 12], 465, 512, 524, 554
    [13]; **1968–69**: 14 (pp. 31, 33), 39
    (p. 86), 47 (pp. 128, 129, 133, 138),

Economy national – *continued*
  Growth – *continued*
    56, 76, 86, 87, 109, 111, 229, 241, 593,
    678 (pp. 1273–1276), 684 (pp. 1312,
    1314, 1317, 1325)
  Impact of
    Automobile prices, **1966**: 474 [3]
    Copper industry labor dispute, **1968–69**:
      106, 112, 169 [21]
    Credit restrictions, **1967**: 13 (p. 43)
    Crime, **1966**: 117
    Defense spending, **1963–64**: 62; **1965**: 493;
      1966: 277 [8]; **1967**: 16 (p. 81)
    Federal budget, **1968–69**: 241, 678 (pp.
      1274, 1276), 684 (pp. 1312, 1313)
    Federal construction, **1968–69**: 39 (p. 101)
    Federal loans, **1968–69**: 39 (p. 84)
    Floods, **1966**: 374
    Foreign assistance, **1967**: 16 (p. 81)
    Imports, **1967**: 99
    Marine resources development, **1968–69**:
      692
    Railroad labor dispute, **1967**: 170, 188, 194,
      207, 310
    Steel prices, **1965**: 62; **1968–69**: 425 [1],
      427
    Strikes, **1963–64**: 780 [3]
    Tariff reduction, **1968–69**: 274
    Tax cuts, **1963–64**: 150 [18], 246 [12],
      379 [5]; **1965**: 100, 153, 255; **1968–
      69**: 47 (p. 131)
    Transportation industry, **1966**: 98
    Transportation system, **1968–69**: 693
    TVA, **1966**: 382
    Vietnam conflict, **1966**: 34 (p. 97), 121 [5],
      431, 477 [3], 578 [6], 654 [9]; **1967**:
      6 [12], 13 (p. 40), 16 (pp. 74, 75, 77,
      87), 89, 430, 524; **1968–69**: 2, 39 (p.
      87), 47 (pp. 131, 145), 684 (p. 1318)
  Inflation.
    See main heading, Inflation.
  Message to Congress, **1963–64**: 124; **1966**: 34;
    1967: 16, 329; **1968–69**: 47, 654, 658,
    684
    Comments on, **1968–69**: 646 [3, 14], 683
  News conference remarks, **1963–64**: 150 [18],
    211 [3], 246 [12, 15, 17], 271 [3],
    316 [26], 379 [5], 455 [2, 3, 13], 462
    [1], 486 [4, 14], 619 [4], 780 [3];
    1965: 319 [7], 448 [11], 463 [12];
    1966: 121 [5], 141 [3, 5], 236 [7],
    247 [4], 320 [8], 334 [2–3, 5, 10],
    373 [6], 401 [2], 445 [13, 18], 474
    [13], 477 [2], 494 [1], 577 [10], 610
    [8], 628 [1, 3], 630 [2], 635 [9–10,
    12], 654 [5–6, 11]; **1967**: 6, 70 [6],
    312 [4], 375 [11], 417 [5], 554 [13]
  Productivity, **1968–69**: 684 (p. 1316)

Economy, national – *continued*
  Stability, **1963–64**: 482
  Stabilization, **1965**: 47; **1966**: 26 (pp. 48, 52),
      108, 373ftn. (p. 805), 399, 403, 431;
      1967: 430; **1968–69**: 684 (pp. 1312,
      1313)
  Statement, **1963–64**: 463, 619 [4], 707, 708,
      714, 722, 723, 724, 730, 731, 739, 740,
      743, 776, 811; **1965**: 590
  Statistics, **1967**: 13 (p. 57), 121; **1968–69**: 39
      (p. 102), 47 (p. 144)
Economy measures, Federal.
  See Cost reduction program, Federal.
Ecuador, **1968–69**: 205
Edelman, John, **1966**: 253
Edie, Lionel D., **1966**: 110
Edinger, Lois V., **1965**: 89, 340
Edison, Thomas, **1967**: 388
Editorial Cartoonists, Association of American,
      1965: 246; **1968–69**: 260
Editorial Writers, National Conference of, **1966**:
      501 [2], 503–504
Editors, foreign, **1968–69**: 177
Editors Association, Newspaper Farm, **1963–64**:
      344
Edmondson, Repr. Ed, **1963–64**: 597; **1966**:
      410, 413, 415–416
Edmondson, Sen. J. Howard, **1963–64**: 597
Edmunds Wilderness, Maine, **1968–69**: 168
Edner, Lt. Col. Seldon R., **1966**: 246
Education, **1963–64**: 132 (p. 176), 211 [28],
      213, 219, 227, 228, 238, 287, 289, 297,
      391, 414, 482, 488, 598, 630, 631, 639,
      658, 668, 678, 680, 718, 778; **1965**: 9,
      32 (pp. 83, 84, 94), 36, 72, 100, 156
      [2], 183, 196, 250, 257, 289, 291, 340,
      374, 378, 475, 519, 541, 609, 614;
      1966: 95, 111, 228, 235, 237, 258, 263,
      325, 346, 395, 399, 413, 418, 424, 580
      [7]; **1967**: 13 (p. 55), 81, 82, 117, 185,
      266, 267, 270, 286, 413, 421, 423, 448,
      490, 492, 493, 495 [5], 498, 532, 540,
      554 [12]; **1968–69**: 28, 47 (p. 141), 50,
      77, 84, 87, 102, 154, 156, 164, 262,
      270, 281, 315, 417, 442, 444, 459, 460
      [2], 462, 536, 538, 564–567, 622, 625,
      631, 644, 678 (pp. 1283, 1286, 1293),
      684 (p. 1324)
  See also Colleges; Occupational training;
      Schools; Students; Teachers.
  Adult, **1963–64**: 47, 213, 327; **1965**: 72,.75,
      208; **1966**: 111, 189; **1967**: 77, 277;
      1968–69: 6, 54, 154, 262, 484, 538,
      648
  Antipoverty program aid, **1963–64**: 124 (p.
      164)
  Appalachian area, **1963–64**: 321; **1965**: 103;
      1966: 122 [2]; **1968–69**: 701

Education – *continued*
  Appropriations and expenditures, **1967**: 13
      (pp. 46, 55), 82, 201, 211, 223 [6],
      258, 261, 266, 286, 291, 329, 423, 448,
      452, 490; **1968–69**: 54, 66, 75, 109,
      111, 114, 219, 262, 339 [9], 612, 644,
      646 [13]
  Bilingual, **1968–69**: 4, 54, 68, 91, 437
  Centers and services, evaluation, **1968–69**: 52
  Children, **1965**: 527n., 592; **1966**: 26 (p. 64),
      95, 108, 210, 223, 238, 270, 273, 319,
      353, 392, 394, 533, 589, 632, 654 [3];
      1967: 3 (pp. 2, 5), 13 (p. 55), 15, 16
      (p. 85), 53, 55, 77, 110, 114, 183, 222,
      277, 286, 292, 423, 452, 479, 532, 540;
      1968–69: 96, 142, 164
  Civil disorders, **1968–69**: 611
  College, **1968–69**: 406, 463, 678 (p. 1294)
  Community colleges, **1963–64**: 413
  Community programs, **1965**: 9; **1968–69**: 312
  Computers, use, **1968–69**: 54, 145
  Consumers, **1965**: 567
  Cooperation.
      See Government cooperation with business,
      education, and labor.
  Cost of, **1965**: 9, 156 [2], 183
  Cultural exchange, **1963–64**: 280, 369, 385
  Deaf persons, **1966**: 406
  Disadvantaged persons, **1968–69**: 26, 37, 39
      (p. 106), 47 (pp. 130, 143), 54, 133ftn.
      (p. 387), 164, 493, 678 (pp. 1293,
      1294)
  District of Columbia, **1963–64**: 116, 133, 457;
      1965: 29, 70, 111, 151; **1966**: 27, 406,
      586; **1967**: 15, 350, 399; **1968–69**: 95,
      133, 203, 436, 689
  Drama in, **1968–69**: 64
  Driver, **1966**: 187
  Electronic equipment, use in, **1968–69**: 687
  Equal opportunity, **1963–64**: 91 (p. 116), 124
      (p. 165), 233, 235, 250, 277, 292, 301,
      342, 357, 375, 406, 412, 413, 433, 457,
      477, 482, 513, 541, 544, 590, 599, 639,
      642, 643, 644, 648, 657, 666, 667, 676,
      703, 709, 719, 728, 729, 732, 733, 734,
      746, 750, 760, 761, 798; **1965**: 2, 9, 10,
      27, 32 (p. 94), 35 (p. 116), 48, 70, 88, 89,
      90, 111, 137, 156 [2], 178, 181, 183,
      291, 305, 340, 433, 452, 470, 522, 539,
      615; **1966**: 34 (p. 100), 196, 273; **1967**:
      16 (p. 76), 554 [6]
  Exchanges, international.
      See Exchange programs.
  Expenditures, **1965**: 23; **1966**: 26 (pp. 50, 55,
      63–64), 100, 112, 121 [4], 158 [10],
      185, 235, 236 [13], 237, 253, 395, 417
      [3], 630 [4]

Education – *continued*
  Facilities, **1966**: 95, 319, 650 [11]; **1968–69**:
    4, 26, 39 (p. 106), 54, 678 (p. 1293)
    Expansion, **1963–64**: 754; **1965**: 9, 70,
      100, 522, 527
  Family planning, **1966**: 45, 95, 433
  Federal aid, **1963–64**: 47, 53, 91 (p. 114), 124
    (p. 164), 132 (pp. 182, 189, 191), 213,
    219, 336 [16], 338, 413, 414, 601, 645,
    669, 676, 680, 683, 709, 728, 754, 775,
    780 [20]; **1965**: 2, 9, 29, 32 (p. 94),
    100, 178, 181, 225, 368, 369, 401, 479,
    485, 514, 519, 522, 527, 539, 592, 603,
    625; **1966**: 6 (pp. 3, 5), 26 (p. 63), 27,
    34 (p. 103), 38, 95, 111, 166, 168, 188
    [6, 8], 189, 273, 504, 508, 512, 524,
    586, 588; **1967**: 13 (p. 55), 16 (pp. 75,
    82), 35, 67, 77, 114, 164, 193, 223 [6],
    304, 378, 396n., 490, 495 [5], 532,
    534, 540; **1968–69**: 4, 6, 39 (pp. 106,
    110), 50, 54, 212, 406, 473, 538, 557
    [8], 564, 567–569, 601, 612, 622, 625,
    676 (pp. 1264, 1267), 678 (pp. 1292,
    1293), 684 (pp. 1313, 1314, 1322)
  Fellowships and scholarships, **1965**: 100, 340,
    368, 369, 374, 479, 514, 603
  Foreign aid, **1966**: 6 (p. 3), 26 (p. 58), 34 (p.
    105), 406; **1967**: 44
  Government employees, **1967**: 121, 184; **1968–
    69**: 39 (p. 110), 84, 312, 526, 539, 667,
    673
  Handicapped persons, **1963–64**: 47, 389, 808;
    1965: 9, 70, 305, 401, 592; **1966**: 406;
    1968–69: 39 (p. 106), 54, 503, 678
    (p. 1293)
  Health, **1967**: 217
  Health and medical personnel, **1968–69**: 39
    (pp. 103, 107), 40, 111, 447, 678 (p.
    1296)
  Impacted areas program, **1965**: 592
  Impacted school aid, **1968–69**: 425 [2]
  Indians, **1963–64**: 120; **1965**: 204; **1968–69**:
    113
  International, **1966**: 41, 45–46, 88 [1], 339,
    406; **1968–69**: 54
  Kindergartens, **1968–69**: 113
  Land-grant colleges, **1963–64**: 219
  Language training, **1968–69**: 4, 39 (p. 106), 54,
    68, 91, 437
  Leaders, conference, **1968–69**: 327, 644
  Legislation, **1963–64**: 78, 150 [5], 620, 642,
    650, 654, 657, 661, 667, 669, 680, 703,
    728, 750; **1965**: 9, 89, 94, 99, 100, 124,
    137, 154, 156 [2], 171, 173, 177, 178,
    179, 250, 319 [21], 329, 330, 340, 368,
    369, 455, 457, 463 [15], 479, 485, 514,
    522, 527, 539, 578; **1966**: 26 (pp. 63–
    64), 41, 77, 95, 265, 299, 319, 353, 392,

Education – *continued*
  Legislation – *continued*
    403, 431, 433, 501 [6], 504–505, 509–
    510, 512, 515, 520, 524, 533, 545, 573,
    589, 599 [6]; **1967**: 13 (p. 55), 77, 82,
    204 [15], 216, 270, 286, 291, 358 [3],
    413, 423, 452, 484, 490; **1968–69**: 4,
    39 (p. 106), 47 (p. 143), 50, 54, 109,
    111, 154, 164, 212, 238, 473, 538, 550,
    565, 567, 601, 644, 655, 672, 676
    (p. 1264), 678 (p. 1292)
    See also Higher Education Facilities Act of
      1963; National Defense Education Act
      Amendments, 1964; *specific acts.*
  Librarians, **1965**: 9
  Materials, importation, **1966**: 45
  Medical and dental, **1963–64**: 47, 132 (p. 189),
    179, 213, 520, 557, 620, 755; **1965**: 2,
    5, 6, 32 (p. 94), 100, 551, 579
  Medical personnel, **1966**: 95, 111, 208, 253,
    573, 580 [7, 10]; **1967**: 15; **1968–69**:
    39 (pp. 103, 107), 40, 111, 447, 678
    (p. 1296)
  Mentally retarded, **1963–64**: 403; **1968–69**:
    39 (p. 106), 493
  Message to Congress, **1966**: 95; **1967**: 77, 78;
    1968–69: 54
  Migrant workers, **1968–69**: 91
  Military personnel, **1963–64**: 382; **1965**: 26;
    1967: 25; **1968–69**: 40
  Minority groups, **1963–64**: 388; **1966**: 136;
    1968–69: 26, 227, 612
  Navajo Indians, **1968–69**: 28, 259
  Negro colleges fundraising campaign, **1963–64**:
    79
  Negroes, **1963–64**: 277, 287, 297, 301; **1965**:
    301, 353 [19], 615; **1966**: 196; **1967**:
    55; **1968–69**: 429
  Nondiscrimination, **1968–69**: 26, 54, 82, 91,
    611
  Philippine children, **1966**: 505
  Physical, **1967**: 160
  Physical fitness programs, **1968–69**: 111
  Preschool program.
    See Project Head Start.
  Presidential policy paper, **1963–64**: 754
  Presidential Scholars program, **1963–64**: 266
    [4]; **1965**: 306
  Public, **1963–64**: 219; **1965**: 9
  Quality, **1968–69**: 678 (pp. 1292, 1293)
  Research, **1965**: 9; **1966**: 45, 319; **1967**: 540;
    1968–69: 4, 39 (pp. 89, 106), 54
  Rural areas, **1965**: 47, 340; **1966**: 6 (p. 5),
    28–29; **1967**: 479; **1968–69**: 4, 96, 142
  Scholarships, **1963–64**: 457n., 601
  School dropouts, **1963–64**: 47, 53, 213, 218
    [15], 233, 246 [20], 398, 658, 680,
    733, 754; **1965**: 9, 10, 70, 90, 100, 156

Education – *continued*
  School dropouts – *continued*
      [2], 178, 183, 322, 340, 438, 453, 490;
      1966: 95, 111, 317, 385, 392, 580 [7],
      589; **1967**: 55, 193, 199, 413, 532, 540;
      1968–69: 4, 6, 39 (p. 106), 54, 113,
      329, 568, 569
    Back-to-school campaign, **1963–64**: 84
  Science, **1966**: 95, 111, 586; **1967**: 165, 217,
      230
  Scientific and engineering, **1963–64**: 132 (p.
      190), 391, 456, 709, 738; **1965**: 2, 32
      (p. 95), 88, 225, 271, 514, 522; **1968–
      69**: 41, 145, 687, 692
  Seminars in 1964, **1963–64**: 78
  Statistics, **1965**: 340
  Summer school programs, **1966**: 632
  Task forces, **1965**: 183, 374, 519, 541
  Teacher training, **1968–69**: 39 (p. 106), 54,
      145, 678 (p. 1293)
  Teachers, **1963–64**: 213, 357
  Television, educational, **1963–64**: 173; **1965**:
      468; **1967**: 3 (p. 6), 13 (p. 55), 77, 176,
      346, 474, 477, 492, 559; **1968–69**: 14
      (p. 27), 77, 370
  Unemployed, **1968–69**: 24
  Urban areas, **1965**: 90, 340; **1967**: 479
  U.S. system, **1963–64**: 601
  Veterans, **1963–64**: 419, 642, 709; **1966**: 26
      (p. 64), 100–101, 158 [10], 353, 571;
      1967: 25, 345, 374; **1968–69**: 39 (p.
      106), 40, 67, 160, 554, 599, 601, 678
      (p. 1293)
  War widows, **1968–69**: 678 (p. 1299)
  Work-study program, **1963–64**: 53, 132 (p.
      189), 219; **1965**: 9, 32 (p. 93), 75, 195,
      208 [13], 603; **1966**: 95, 111, 172, 189
  Work-training program, **1963–64**: 219
  Young people, **1963–64**: 267, 737; **1965**: 9,
      10, 35 (p. 114), 70, 100, 132, 137, 354,
      603; **1966**: 34 (p. 100), 429
Education, Commissioner of (Francis Keppel),
    1963–64: 78, 84, 397n., 414, 513, 622;
    1965: 70, 89, 181, 183, 264n., 305,
    340, 467, 485, 527, 539, 578
Education, Council on International, **1966**: 45
Education, Department of, proposed, **1965**: 388
    [17]
Education, Interagency Committee on, **1965**:
    100
Education, International Conference on the
    World Crisis in, **1966**: 627; **1967**: 423
Education, National Advisory Committee on
    Adult Basic, **1968–69**: 484
Education, National Advisory Council on
    Extension and Continuing, **1967**: 185;
    1968–69: 312

Education, Office of, **1965**: 9, 32 (p. 94), 183,
    340, 401, 470, 485, 514; **1966**: 77, 95,
    182, 196, 319, 584; **1967**: 77, 82, 164,
    193, 304n.; **1968–69**: 6, 133, 145, 238,
    419
  Appropriations, **1968–69**: 39 (p. 92), 678 (p.
      1284)
Education, White House Conference on, **1965**:
    183, 291, 340, 374, 385
Education Association, National, **1963–64**:
    676n.; **1965**: 250, 340
Education Award of 1966, National, **1966**: 77
Education of Disadvantaged Children, National
    Advisory Council on the, **1966**: 210,
    238, 632; **1967**: 77, 183n.
Education of Disadvantaged Children, National
    Planning Conference on the, **1966**: 238
Education in the District of Columbia, President's
    Committee on Public Higher, **1963–64**:
    116n.; **1965**: 111
Education of Henry Adams, The, Henry Adams,
    1967: 344
Education and Labor, House Committee on,
    1967: 338n.
Education opportunity bill, **1968–69**: 14 (p. 31),
    47 (p. 143), 54
Education Placement Service, American, **1966**:
    45
Education Professions Development, National
    Advisory Council on, **1967**: 396
Education Professions Development Act of 1967,
    1967: 77, 292; **1968–69**: 39 (p. 105),
    47 (p. 143), 54, 113
Education for public service bill, **1968–69**: 84
Education Week, American, **1965**: 609
Educational, Scientific, and Cultural Materials,
    Agreement on the Importation of
    (Florence Agreement), **1965**: 292, 604;
    1966: 45, 519, 601
Educational, Scientific, and Cultural Organiza-
    tion, United Nations, **1963–64**: 480;
    1967: 198n.
Educational Broadcasters, National Association
    of, **1967**: 474
Educational Cooperation, Center for (HEW),
    1966: 45, 406, 533, 627
Educational and Cultural Affairs, Bureau of,
    1966: 378n.
Educational Interchange, Joint United States-
    Japan Conference on Cultural and,
    1965: 15
Educational Legislation, National Conference on,
    1965: 89
Educational Opportunity Grants program, **1967**:
    304n.
Educational Program, Mid-Career, **1966**: 129n.
Educators, Foreign Policy Conference for, **1967**:
    272

Edwards, Corwin D., **1967**: 342n.
Edwards, Mrs. India, **1963-64**: 208, 257n.
Edwards, Dr. Lena F., **1963-64**: 568
Edwards, Leverett (Chairman, National Mediation Board), **1966**: 410, 413, 415-416
Edwards Air Force Base, California, **1963-64**: 201 [2], 409; **1965**: 219
EEC.
See European Economic Community.
Egal, Mohamed Ibrahim (Prime Minister of the Somali Republic), **1968-69**: 137, 140
Egal, Mrs. Mohamed Ibrahim, **1968-69**: 137, 140
Egan, Gov. William A., **1963-64**: 241, 242 [16], 615; **1966**: 244, 494 [1], 567-568; **1967**: 369
Egypt.
See United Arab Republic.
Egypt-Israeli conflict, **1966**: 630 [17]
Ehrenkrantz, Ezra, **1967**: 4n.
Eighteen-Nation Committee on Disarmament, **1965**: 20, 353 [5, 11], 386, 430; **1966**: 32, 70, 450; **1967**: 64, 80 [2], 204 [4], 367; **1968-69**: 16, 27, 69, 392
U.S. Representative, **1967**: 64n., 340, 365, 367
8th Armored Division Association, **1966**: 377
82nd Airborne Division, **1968-69**: 109
Eilberg, Repr. Joshua, **1967**: 291
Eilers, Col. A. J., **1967**: 210; **1968-69**: 625
Einstein, Albert, **1963-64**: 511; **1965**: 634; **1967**: 266
Eisele, Maj. Donn F., **1968-69**: 533n., 552, 574
Eisenhower, Dwight D., President, **1963-64**: 2, 12, 29, 45, 80, 96, 182, 207, 218 [1, 9, 24], 280 [8], 295, 303, 314, 340, 359, 499, 500, 506, 577, 591, 638, 641, 698, 775, 778, 784, 809; **1965**: 34, 76, 134, 160n., 255, 318, 357, 370, 397, 417, 418, 420, 430, 503, 549, 550, 554; **1966**: 6 (p. 8), 21, 62, 86, 125, 136, 168, 175, 182, 199, 221, 228, 240, 273, 312, 330, 415-416, 504, 509, 523, 573, 639; **1967**: 3 (p. 9), 16 (p. 88), 38, 44, 83, 99, 110, 143, 158n., 233, 236, 248n., 251, 281, 358 [10], 409, 425, 495 [14], 502, 510n., 515, 518 [3, 14]; **1968-69**: 27, 81 [3], 87, 102, 104, 109, 111, 153 [9], 185, 191 [6], 223 [14], 283 [6], 290, 301, 341, 378, 384, 399, 425 [11], 431, 452, 454, 472, 473, 488, 536n., 537n., 538, 550, 567, 576, 589, 646 [12], 665, 676 (p. 1270), 696 [20]
Asian visit, question of, **1966**: 401 [14]
Campaign remarks on, **1963-64**: 562, 601, 603, 604, 607, 612, 622, 634, 635, 637, 639, 640, 642, 643, 645, 646, 648, 652, 656, 658, 659, 669, 679, 680, 693, 694, 695, 702, 703, 712, 713, 718, 728, 729, 733, 734, 736, 745, 747, 748, 749, 750, 762

Eisenhower, Dwight D., President — *continued*
Golden wedding anniversary, **1966**: 300
Letter to Ngo Dinh Diem, **1963-64**: 218 [24], 379 [1], 607, 612, 643, 693
Letter to the President, **1965**: 227n.
Library, Abilene, Kans., **1965**: 412 [1]
News conference remarks on, **1963-64**: 54 [9], 71 [7, 10, 12], 201 [5], 211 [21, 29], 266 [10], 271 [10], 285 [17], 420 [1], 462 [2], 504 [11], 560 [10, 16]; **1965**: 46 [6], 106 [4], 117 [8], 156 [6], 176 [1], 208 [2], 319 [17], 347 [6], 353 [8], 388 [1], 412 [1, 4], 448 [12]; **1966**: 88 [17], 236 [6], 320 [1], 401 [4], 417 [1, 3, 6], 501 [12, 14], 516 [9], 577 [10, 15], 599 [2], 610 [1], 650 [13]
Telegrams to, **1965**: 414, 565, 607
Eisenhower, Mrs. Dwight D., **1963-64**: 96; **1965**: 607n.; **1966**: 300; **1968-69**: 488
Eisenhower, John S. D., **1968-69**: 399n., 488
Eisenhower, Milton S., **1963-64**: 266 [4], 397n., 587 [2], 612; **1965**: 172, 306n., 319 [17], 397, 400, 420; **1966**: 185n.; **1967**: 474; **1968-69**: 66, 77n., 293, 298
Eisenhower College, **1966**: 300; **1968-69**: 550
Eisenhower Lock, St. Lawrence Seaway, **1967**: 398
Eisenhower Week, Salute to, **1968-69**: 488
Eklund, Sigvard, **1965**: 537
El Paso, Tex., **1965**: 487, 641 [1]; **1966**: 597; **1967**: 451, 452, 460 [2]; **1968-69**: 91, 623, 624
El Paso Times, **1963-64**: 587 [6]
El Salvador, **1967**: 44; **1968-69**: 368
Ambassador Ramón de Clairmont Dueñas, **1965**: 472, 473
Peace Corps projects in, **1965**: 83
President Fidel Sanchez Hernandez, **1968-69**: 363, 365, 366, 369-371
Visit, **1968-69**: 363-372
El Toro Marine Base, Santa Ana, Calif., **1967**: 485 [2], 493
El Toro Marine Corps Air Station, Calif., **1968-69**: 81 [2], 109
Elco Corp., **1967**: 231n.
Eleanor Roosevelt Golden Candlestick award, presentation of, **1963-64**: 208
Eleanor Roosevelt Memorial Foundation, **1963-64**: 161; **1965**: 273
Election
1844, **1966**: 428
1855, **1967**: 538
1928, **1968-69**: 568
1936, **1963-64**: 640
1941, **1966**: 221
1948, **1963-64**: 637; **1966**: 516 [6]; **1968-69**: 109, 568, 569

Election — *continued*
  1954, **1966**: 221
  1960, **1963–64**: 171, 201 [5], 290, 508, 652,
    667; **1966**: 512
  1964, **1963–64**: 211 [31], 266 [19], 475
    [15], 508; **1966**: 228, 353, 403, 577
    [13], 403; **1967**: 281, 554 [1, 11]
  Candidacy, the President's.
    See Candidacy for reelection, the
      President's.
  Candidates for President.
    See Candidates for President.
  Candidates for Vice President.
    See Candidates for Vice President.
  Effect of civil rights on, **1963–64**: 266 [23],
    420 [10], 796n.
  Effect of economy on, **1963–64**: 246 [17]
  Predictions by press, **1963–64**: 266 [13]
  Primary.
    See Primary elections.
  Victory, remarks following, **1963–64**: 765
  Voter participation, **1963–64**: 57, 560 [1];
    1965: 39
    See also Voting rights.
  Voter registration, **1963–64**: 167, 750
  Women, **1963–64**: 289
  1966
  Addresses.
    See Election campaigns, addresses or
      remarks.
  Civil disorders impact, **1966**: 401 [6], 580
    [19]
  Democratic outlook, **1966**: 401 [11]
  Great Society, impact on program, **1966**:
    599 [1], 610 [6]
  Labor vote, **1966**: 141 [9]
  News conference remarks, **1966**: 188 [6],
    492 [10], 580 [19], 599 [1–3, 6], 650
    [7, 13–14]
  President's participation, **1966**: 141 [12],
    277 [23], 320 [20], 338 [15], 516
    [12], 577 [9]
  Southern Governors, **1966**: 501 [3]
  Vietnam conflict impact, **1966**: 141 [12],
    188 [7], 577 [2]
  White backlash impact, **1966**: 580 [15, 20],
    599 [3]
  1968, **1966**: 401 [1, 10, 17], 650 [17, 21,
    23]; **1967**: 225 [19], 297 [13], 375
    [15], 460 [10], 495 [8], 518 [11, 16],
    554 [9]; **1968–69**: 153 [13], 223 [6,
    10], 467 [7], 480, 557 [3, 4, 10], 604,
    676 (p. 1268), 696 [5]
  Candidacy, the President's, **1966**: 320 [20]
    See also Candidacy for reelection, the
      President's.
  Candidates.
    See also specific candidates.

Election — *continued*
  Candidates — *continued*
    Post election telegrams, **1968–69**: 578, 579
    Primaries, **1967**: 495 [10]
  Election campaign, **1963–64**: 713
  Ethics of, **1963–64**: 619 [13]
  1936, **1963–64**: 325
  1960, **1963–64**: 338, 563 [17], 645, 693, 728
  1964, **1963–64**: 170 [9], 218 [13, 19], 475
    [19], 486 [13], 504 [10], 516 [19, 21],
    560 [13], 587 [9], 680, 780 [23]
  Campaign issues, **1963–64**: 462 [10], 475
    [9, 17, 22], 560 [14, 16], 638, 654
  Conduct of candidates, **1963–64**: 462 [7],
    475 [11, 15], 718
  Debates.
    See Debates, presidential campaign,
      question of.
  Memorandum on, **1963–64**: 654
  Use of television and radio, **1963–64**: 201
    [15]
  Election campaigns, addresses or remarks, **1963–
    64**: 633
  August 27, Atlantic City, N.J., **1963–64**: 541
  August 28, Atlantic City, N.J., **1963–64**: 542
  August 29, Stonewall, Tex., **1963–64**: 544
  September 1, Washington, D.C., **1963–64**: 548,
    555
  September 5
    Battle Creek, Mich., **1966**: 432–433
    Dayton, Ohio, **1966**: 435
    Detroit, Mich., **1966**: 430
    Lancaster, Ohio, **1966**: 437
    Port Columbus, Ohio, **1966**: 436
    Vandalia, Ohio, **1966**: 434
  September 7, Detroit, Mich., **1963–64**: 562
  September 10, Harrisburg, Pa., **1963–64**: 566
  September 14, Washington, D.C., **1963–64**: 570
  September 15, Miami Beach, Fla., **1963–64**: 571
  September 17
    Portland, Oreg., **1963–64**: 578
    Sacramento, Calif., **1963–64**: 579
  September 21, Washington, D.C., **1963–64**: 588
  September 22, Atlantic City, N.J., **1963–64**: 589
  September 23, Washington, D.C., **1963–64**: 590
  September 25
    Eufaula, Okla., **1963–64**: 597
    Oklahoma City, Okla., **1963–64**: 598
    Texarkana, Tex.-Ark., **1963–64**: 599
  September 28
    Burlington, Vt., **1963–64**: 605
    Hartford, Conn., **1963–64**: 603, 604
    Manchester, N.H., **1963–64**: 607
    Portland, Maine, **1963–64**: 606
    Providence, R.I., **1963–64**: 601
  September 30, Washington, D.C., **1963–64**: 611
  October 1, Baltimore, Md., **1963–64**: 612

Election campaigns – *continued*
  October 3, Washington, D.C., **1963–64**: 622
  October 6
    Alexandria, Va., **1963–64**: 628
    Raleigh, N.C., **1963–64**: 631
    Washington, D.C., **1963–64**: 629, 630
  October 7
    Broadcast from the White House, **1963–64**: 638
    Des Moines, Iowa, **1963–64**: 634
    Newark, N.J., **1966**: 504
    Peoria, Ill., **1963–64**: 636, 637
    Springfield, Ill., **1963–64**: 635
    Washington, D.C., **1963–64**: 633
  October 8
    Cleveland, Ohio, **1963–64**: 642
    Indianapolis, Ind., **1963–64**: 640
    Lake County, Ind., **1963–64**: 639
  October 9
    Louisville, Ky., **1963–64**: 643, 644
    Nashville, Tenn., **1963–64**: 645
    New Orleans, La., **1963–64**: 646, 648
  October 11
    Las Vegas, Nev., **1963–64**: 652
    Long Beach, Calif., memorandum issued, **1963–64**: 654
    Phoenix, Ariz., **1963–64**: 649
    San Francisco, Calif., **1963–64**: 651
    South Gate, Calif., **1963–64**: 650
  October 12
    Baltimore, Md., **1966**: 509
    Boise, Idaho, **1963–64**: 659
    Brooklyn, N.Y., **1966**: 511
    Butte, Mont., **1963–64**: 656
    Casper, Wyo., **1963–64**: 657
    Denver, Colo., **1963–64**: 658
    Long Island, N.Y., **1966**: 512
    Reno, Nev., **1963–64**: 655
    Staten Island, N.Y., **1966**: 510
  October 13, Wilmington, Del., **1963–64**: 515
  October 14
    Bergen, N.J., **1963–64**: 660
    New York City, **1963–64**: 662
    Wilkes-Barre-Scranton, Pa., **1963–64**: 661
  October 15
    Brooklyn, N.Y., **1963–64**: 668
    Buffalo, N.Y., **1963–64**: 667
    New York City, **1963–64**: 669, 670
    Rochester, N.Y., **1963–64**: 666
  October 16
    Cincinnati, Ohio, **1963–64**: 678, 679
    Dayton, Ohio, **1963–64**: 680
  October 21
    Akron, Ohio, **1963–64**: 693
    Belleville, Ill., **1963–64**: 694
    St. Louis, Mo., **1963–64**: 695
  October 24
    Baltimore, Md., **1963–64**: 703

Election campaigns – *continued*
  October 24 – *continued*
    Chattanooga, Tenn., **1963–64**: 702
    Memphis, Tenn., **1963–64**: 701
  October 25, Boca Raton, Fla., **1963–64**: 709
  October 26
    Augusta, Ga., **1963–64**: 718
    Columbia, S.C., **1963–64**: 719
    Jacksonville, Fla., **1963–64**: 713
    Macon, Ga., **1963–64**: 716
    Orlando, Fla., **1963–64**: 712
  October 27
    Boston, Mass., **1963–64**: 727
    Evansville, Ind., **1963–64**: 729
    Pittsburgh, Pa., **1963–64**: 728
  October 28
    Albuquerque, N. Mex., **1963–64**: 732
    Los Angeles, Calif., **1963–64**: 733
    Riverside, Calif., **1963–64**: 734
    San Bernardino, Calif., **1963–64**: 735
    San Diego, Calif., **1963–64**: 736
  October 29
    Philadelphia, Pa., **1963–64**: 742
    Salt Lake City, Utah, **1963–64**: 737
    Wichita, Kans., **1963–64**: 741
  October 30
    Chicago, Ill., **1963–64**: 748
    Detroit, Mich., **1963–64**: 745
    Milwaukee, Wis., **1963–64**: 746
    Rockford, Ill., **1963–64**: 747
  October 31
    Dover, Del., **1963–64**: 749
    New York City, **1963–64**: 751
    Wilmington, Del., **1963–64**: 750
  November 2
    Austin, Tex., **1963–64**: 763
    Houston, Tex., **1963–64**: 760, 761
    Pasadena, Tex., **1963–64**: 762
  November 4
    Austin, Tex., **1963–64**: 765
    Taped address to the American people, **1963–64**: 764
  Casting of ballot, **1966**: 590
  Citizens for Humphrey-Muskie, **1968–69**: 569
  Democratic Party rally, Astrodome, Houston, **1968–69**: 575
  Democratic Victory Committee, **1968–69**: 576
  Election reform bill, **1966**: 241, 499, 612
  International Ladies' Garment Workers Union, **1968–69**: 529
Election Campaigns, Advisory Board on Funds for Presidential, **1967**: 236
Election polls.
  See Political polls.
Election reform bills, **1967**: 236
  See also Voting rights.
  Campaigning by Members of Congress, **1966**: 21

Election reform bills – *continued*
   Financing of campaigns, **1966**: 6 (p. 7), 241,
      403, 610 [5], 612; **1967**: 204 [8], 236
   Message to Congress, **1967**: 236
   Presidential, **1963-64**: 471n., 638; **1967**: 236
   Procedural reform, **1967**: 3 (p. 6)
   Ryukyu Islands, **1968-69**: 44
   Voting rights.
     See main heading, Voting rights.
Electoral college, **1965**: 2, 34; **1966**: 21
Electors, comments on, **1963-64**: 316 [21]
Electric Cooperative Association, National Rural,
   1963-64: 227; **1967**: 267; **1968-69**: 96,
   305
Electric power, **1966**: 140, 269, 411n.; **1967**:
   286, 342, 515; **1968-69**: 47 (p. 129),
   330, 345
   Consumer protection, **1968-69**: 56
   Powerplant site selection, **1968-69**: 653
   Project construction, **1968-69**: 39 (p. 91)
   Rural, **1967**: 13 (p. 50), 267, 270; **1968-69**:
     39 (p. 101), 94, 96, 305, 629n.
   See also Rural electrification.
Electric power failures
   Blackouts, **1967**: 57, 253; **1968-69**: 684 (p.
     1322)
   Northeastern States, **1965**: 608, 640, 641 [1]
   Texas, **1965**: 641 [1]
Electric power industry, increasing demands on,
   1963-64: 803; **1965**: 186
Electric power reactors, **1963-64**: 545
Electrical, Radio and Machine Workers, Interna-
   tional Union of, **1966**: 496
Electrical Workers, International Brotherhood of,
   1965: 298
Electrical Workers, International Union of, **1963-
   64**: 590
Electrification Administration, Rural, **1966**: 258,
   273; **1967**: 13 (pp. 46, 51); **1968-69**:
   39 (p. 101), 96, 629n.
Electron accelerator, **1968-69**: 145
Electron volt accelerator, **1967**: 515
Electronic computing equipment, **1968-69**: 687
Electronic eavesdropping, **1967**: 3 (p. 6), 35
Elementary and Secondary Education Act of
   1965, **1965**: 173, 183, 207, 340, 397,
   401, 463 [15], 539, 578, 592, 603;
   1966: 26 (pp. 63-64), 45, 77, 95, 121 [4],
   171n., 189, 238, 273, 319, 385n., 392,
   394-395, 403, 436, 504, 510, 632;
   1967: 13 (p. 55), 16 (p. 85), 39, 77,
   120, 193, 199, 353, 532; **1968-69**: 4,
   39 (p. 106), 47 (p. 143), 50, 52n., 54,
   87, 113, 154, 406, 484n., 567, 622,
   678 (p. 1293), 684 (p. 1324)
   See also Education.
   Approval, **1965**: 527
Elementary and Secondary Education Amendments of 1966, **1966**: 573

Elementary and Secondary Education Amend-
   ments of 1967, **1967**: 204ftn. (p. 502)
Elevator incident, Pentagon, **1968-69**: 101n.,
   102, 109, 110, 139
Eliot, George, **1967**: 306
Eliot, Thomas Stearns, **1963-64**: 568
Elisabeth, Queen of Belgium, death of, **1965**:
   627
Elizabeth II, Queen (United Kingdom), **1963-64**:
   187, 796; **1965**: 616; **1966**: 342, 359;
   1967: 540n.; **1968-69**: 65, 273, 479,
   525
Elkhart, Ind., **1965**: 188
Elkus, Abram I., **1963-64**: 208ftn. (p. 335)
Ellender, Sen. Allen J., **1963-64**: 150 [7], 546,
   646, 648; **1965**: 555; **1966**: 508; **1967**:
   405, 533; **1968-69**: 96, 417, 472
Ellenville, N.Y., **1966**: 395
   Community Hospital, **1966**: 395
   Mayor Eugene Glusker, **1966**: 395
Ellington, Buford, **1963-64**: 701; **1966**: 124
   [6], 145, 650 [15]; **1967**: 87n., 115-
   117; **1968-69**: 102, 345, 483n.
   See also Emergency Planning, Office of, Direc-
   tor.
Ellington, Mrs. Buford (Catherine), **1965**: 98;
   1967: 115
Elliott, Carl, **1966**: 424n.
Elliott, Tom, **1963-64**: 285 [7]
Ellis, Clyde T., **1965**: 308, 357; **1966**: 258; **1967**:
   267; **1968-69**: 96
Ellis, Mr. and Mrs. Robert, **1966**: 532
Ellis Island, **1965**: 242
Elmendorf Air Force Base, Alaska, **1966**: 567
Elson, Roy L., **1963-64**: 649
Elstad, Leonard M., **1963-64**: 389n.
Eltanin research ship, **1965**: 220
Emancipation Proclamation, **1963-64**: 111, 266
   [20], 277, 290, 301, 334, 342, 391, 511,
   522, 669, 728, 778, 800; **1965**: 48, 107,
   436; **1966**: 353; **1968-69**: 70, 158, 195,
   212
Embassies, U.S.
   Attacks on, **1965**: 59, 145, 156 [6], 208 [16],
     227, 276, 319 [16]
   Saigon, proposed construction of chancery in,
     1965: 152
Emergency Committee for Gun Control, **1968-
   69**: 339ftn. (p. 748)
Emergency Planning, Office of, **1963-64**: 368,
   567, 647; **1965**: 174, 418; **1966**: 124
   [6], 584, 636; **1967**: 508
   Director (Farris Bryant), **1966**: 121 [7], 124
     [6], 145, 187, 228, 252, 273, 408n.,
     416, 509, 584, 607 [1], 635 [2], 636n.,
     650 [15]; **1967**: 92, 121, 123, 187, 222,
     223 [2, 7], 296, 325n., 328 [20], 408
     [1], 558
   Memorandum, **1966**: 606; **1967**: 186

Emergency Planning – *continued*
  Director (Price Daniel), **1968–69**: 58, 100n.,
    102, 116, 296n., 325, 406, 483n., 539
  Director (Buford Ellington), **1965**: 187, 188,
    189, 319 [20], 418, 434, 554, 618
  Letter, **1965**: 167
  Memorandum, **1965**: 617
  Report, **1965**: 174
  Swearing in, **1965**: 98
  Director (Edward A. McDermott), **1963–64**:
    62, 217, 218 [1], 242 [1], 308, 567,
    615, 618
  Name change proposed, **1968–69**: 483
Emergency Preparedness, Office of, **1968–69**:
    586
  Director (Price Daniel), **1968–69**: 477, 570,
    598
Emerson, Ralph Waldo, **1963–64**: 533, 578;
    1965: 44, 53, 306, 340, 403, 653;
    1966: 101, 306, 435, 545, 557; **1967**:
    158, 323, 344, 347n., 364, 514; **1968–
    69**: 239, 345, 459, 536, 616
Emphysema, **1967**: 20
Employer of the Year award, **1967**: 388; **1968–
    69**: 548
Employment, **1963–64**: 124 (pp. 156, 158, 164,
    166), 233, 235, 289, 290, 379 [7], 388;
    1965: 32 (p. 84), 132, 148, 453, 475;
    1966: 26 (p. 63), 34 (p. 100), 111, 258,
    399, 412, 430, 434, 437, 444, 504, 512,
    654 [5]; **1967**: 16 (p. 79), 81, 97, 276;
    1968–69: 25, 47 (p. 141), 86, 102, 114,
    165, 220, 281, 315, 462, 566–569, 593,
    622, 631, 676 (pp. 1264, 1266)
  See also Labor force, growth of; Unemploy-
    ment.
  Armed Forces Reserves, members, **1968–69**:
    448
  Automation, effect on, **1963–64**: 99, 126, 213,
    233
  Community action programs, **1967**: 114
  Concentrated program, **1968–69**: 24, 39 (p.
    104), 40, 47 (p. 142), 94, 113, 220,
    678 (p. 1294)
  Construction industry, **1967**: 199; **1968–69**: 87
  Depressed areas, **1968–69**: 39 (p. 109)
  Disabled persons.
    See Handicapped persons *below*.
  District of Columbia, **1968–69**: 133
  Effect of tax reduction on, **1965**: 153
  Equal opportunity, **1966**: 136, 196, 248, 250,
    320 [17], 475; **1967**: 12, 16 (p. 76), 55,
    95, 354, 548; **1968–69**: 14 (p. 31), 24,
    26, 47 (p. 130), 84, 87, 91, 195, 209,
    347, 437, 458, 596, 611, 684 (pp. 1311,
    1324)
    See also Equal employment opportunity.
  Federal.
    See Government employees.

Employment – *continued*
  Fiscal policy impact, **1966**: 494 [14]
  Foreign workers, **1965**: 38
  Full employment, **1963–64**: 433, 566, 589,
    639, 693, 729, 743, 747; **1965**: 2, 35
    (pp. 103, 105, 106, 108, 109, 112, 117),
    255, 351, 490; **1966**: 34 (p. 98), 83, 111,
    158 [3], 235, 236 [8], 250, 373 [6],
    432, 444, 451, 501 [6], 545; **1967**: 16
    (p. 82)
  Government contract workers, **1965**: 582
  Handicapped persons, **1963–64**: 179, 302, 345,
    403, 808; **1966**: 111; **1967**: 199, 388,
    413; **1968–69**: 39 (p. 104), 548
  Increase, **1963–64**: 22, 23, 40, 91 (pp. 112,
    115), 160, 166, 199, 213, 297, 314,
    334, 338, 386, 404, 405, 413, 415, 431,
    463, 472, 477, 506, 525, 550, 647, 689,
    743, 791; **1965**: 23, 32 (p. 84), 35 (pp.
    104, 106), 100, 165, 207, 223, 226, 258,
    285, 298, 319 [7], 321, 322, 351, 408,
    438, 480, 489, 490, 590, 598, 632, 644;
    1966: 6 (p. 4), 26 (p. 49), 34 (p. 96),
    111, 155, 157, 347, 353, 415, 429, 479,
    492 [1], 515, 516 [19], 635 [8, 18];
    1967: 3 (p. 2), 13 (p. 39), 16 (pp. 72,
    73, 88), 63, 97, 121, 199, 270, 354,
    393, 534, 554 [13]; **1968–69**: 14 (p.
    28), 24, 39 (p. 86), 37, 46, 47 (pp. 128,
    129, 131, 138), 50, 86, 154, 229, 282,
    345, 350, 442, 462, 463, 564, 654, 672,
    678 (pp. 1291, 1294, 1299), 683, 684
    (pp. 1312, 1313)
  Campaign remarks, **1963–64**: 548, 604, 631,
    636, 639, 644, 645, 650, 652, 656, 666,
    669, 694, 695, 702, 703, 713, 719, 729,
    732, 733, 734, 735, 742, 746, 761, 762
  News conference remarks, **1963–64**: 211 [3],
    246 [15], 266 [2], 285, [15], 294 [4],
    316 [5, 26], 336 [1], 379 [5], 455 [2],
    504 [7], 521 [3], 619 [4], 780 [3]
  Increased opportunities, **1963–64**: 197, 271 [15],
    411, 558, 571, 599, 603, 605, 630, 635,
    640, 643, 648, 679, 690n., 704n., 708,
    728, 746; **1965**: 2, 32 (p. 96), 35 (pp.
    104, 106, 112), 38, 47, 79, 90, 132,
    153, 156 [1], 165, 255, 270, 326, 408,
    452, 480, 489, 490; **1966**: 189, 588
  Indians, **1968–69**: 113, 678 (p. 1295)
  Labor force, growth of, **1963–64**: 213
  Message to Congress, **1968–69**: 24
  Migrant farm workers, **1963–64**: 305
  Military personnel, **1967**: 199
  Minority groups, **1963–64**: 205, 213, 812n.;
    1968–69: 24, 26, 47 (p. 142), 596, 667
  Negroes, **1963–64**: 205, 277, 301; **1965**: 100,
    165, 412 [3], 480; **1966**: 34 (p. 98),
    248, 475; **1968–69**: 47 (p. 129), 429,
    596, 631

[References are to items except as otherwise indicated]

Employment — *continued*
  Neighborhood programs, **1968–69**: 471
  Nonwhite, **1963–64**: 213
  Older persons, **1963–64**: 178, 213, 431, 690n.;
      1966: 253, 270; **1967**: 12, 114, 199,
      548; **1968–69**: 24, 75
  Overtime, **1963–64**: 91 (p. 116), 124 (p. 163);
      1965: 258
  Prisoners, **1966**: 111, 116, 463, 588
  Public assistance recipients, **1967**: 16 (p. 83),
      114
  Puerto Ricans, **1968–69**: 596
  Rural areas, **1963–64**: 344, 434; **1966**: 26 (p.
      59), 428; **1967**: 114; **1968–69**: 94, 96,
      142, 450
  Safety, **1968–69**: 684 (p. 1321)
  Scientists and engineers, **1963–64**: 456n.
  Self-employed, taxes, **1966**: 34 (p. 102)
  Service work, **1965**: 38, 79, 99, 582
  Services, **1968–69**: 40, 86, 100, 406, 471
  Skilled workers, **1967**: 16 (p. 74)
  Social workers, **1966**: 95
  Spanish-speaking Americans, **1968–69**: 91, 437
  Special Impact program, **1968–69**: 678 (p.
      1291)
  State, **1966**: 34 (p. 98), 89, 111, 216, 499;
      1967: 199
  Statistics, **1965**: 223, 322, 351, 408, 438, 480;
      1967: 57; **1968–69**: 442, 462, 463, 654
  Steel industry, **1963–64**: 290, 780 [5]; **1965**:
      226
  Students, **1966**: 26 (p. 63), 105, 171; **1967**:
      378
  Tax reduction incentives, **1963–64**: 386
  Teachers, **1966**: 105; **1967**: 292, 396
  Textile industry, **1963–64**: 719
  Training.
      See Occupational training.
  Transportation industry, **1966**: 98
  Unskilled workers, **1963–64**: 213; **1965**: 165,
      480
  Urban areas, **1968–69**: 39 (p. 102), 87, 153 [16]
  Urban renewal, **1966**: 30
  Veterans, **1967**: 345, 374, 432, 493; **1968–69**:
      14 (p. 31), 39 (p. 106), 40, 67, 406, 411,
      667, 678 (p. 1295)
  Welfare recipients, **1968–69**: 39 (p. 105), 678
      (p. 1294)
  Women, **1963–64**: 213; **1965**: 91, 165; **1966**:
      89, 105; **1967**: 93, 95; **1968–69**: 133,
      138
  Work-experience program, **1966**: 26 (p. 63),
      111
  Work-study program, **1966**: 111, 172, 189;
      1967: 13 (p. 55), 39, 77, 378
  Work-training program, **1965**: 100, 208 [13],
      268; **1966**: 588; **1967**: 13 (p. 54), 55,
      114, 199

Employment — *continued*
  Workweek, **1966**: 34 (p. 99), 445 [5]
  Youth, **1965**: 35 (p. 114), 99, 132, 165, 193,
      207, 224, 268, 298, 436; **1966**: 34 (p.
      98), 105, 111, 171–172, 306, 385, 388,
      588; **1967**: 39, 114, 199, 203, 277;
      1968–69: 24, 87, 328, 526, 570, 678
      (pp. 1294, 1295), 689
      See also Youth, employment and training.
  Youth Employment Act, proposed, **1963–64**:
      132 (p. 184)
Employment Act of 1946, **1963–64**: 124 (p.
      155), 311, 375, 550, 648, 771; **1965**:
      35 (pp. 103, 104, 105, 107); **1966**: 34
      (p. 97), 83, 250; **1967**: 16 (p. 89); **1968–
      69**: 24, 684 (pp. 1312, 1325)
Employment of the Handicapped, Governors'
      Committees on, **1968–69**: 548n.
Employment of the Handicapped, President's
      Committee on, **1963–64**: 302; **1967**:
      388; **1968–69**: 548n.
  Distinguished Service Award, **1963–64**: 235,
      302n., 389
Employment Opportunity, President's Committee
      on Equal, **1963–64**: 111, 139, 213, 277
Employment Opportunity Commission, Equal,
      1967: 55; **1968–69**: 26
Employment program, concentrated, **1968–69**:
      24, 39 (p. 104), 40, 47 (p. 142), 94,
      113, 220, 678 (p. 1294)
Employment Service, State, **1968–69**: 86, 100
Employment Service, U.S., **1963–64**: 89, 178;
      1965: 35 (p. 112), 268, 340; **1967**: 13
      (p. 54)
Encyclopaedia Britannica, Inc., **1967**: 540
Endangered species preservation, **1966**: 522
Enders, Dr. John F., **1963–64**: 27
Endowment for the Arts, National, **1966**: 440;
      1967: 53; **1968–69**: 54, 64, 686
Endowment for the Humanities, National, **1966**:
      327; **1967**: 54, 77; **1968–69**: 45, 54, 61,
      703
Energy resources policy, **1967**: 20
Engel, Annette, **1967**: 396n.
Engelhard, Charles W., **1963–64**: 721; **1968–69**:
      672n.
Engelhard, Mrs. Charles W., **1968–69**: 672n.
Engineering
  Education, **1963–64**: 709
  Manpower utilization, **1963–64**: 271 [5]
  Research, **1963–64**: 308, 629
Engineering, National Academy of, **1968–69**: 361
Engineering, National Council on Marine Re-
      sources and, **1966**: 326
Engineering Development, National Council for
      Marine Resources and, **1967**: 20, 101,
      240; **1968–69**: 124

Engineering Manpower, Committee on Utilization of Scientific and, **1963-64**: 271ftn.
(p. 488), 456n.
Engineering research, **1965**: 225
Engineers, **1963-64**: 493; **1966**: 89, 111
Employment, **1963-64**: 456n.
Utilization, reports on, **1963-64**: 271ftn. (p.
488), 456
Engineers, Corps of, **1963-64**: 132 (p. 187), 198,
308, 567, 718; **1965**: 32 (p. 92), 174,
400, 418, 560; **1966**: 98, 374, 427, 630
[4]; **1967**: 6 [5, 10, 13], 120, 240, 408
[2, 4]; **1968-69**: 39 (pp. 92, 101), 223
[11], 252, 297, 467 [3]
Engineers, International Union of Operating,
1966: 141 [4]
Engineers, overseas service, **1968-69**: 63
Engineers and Scientists for Johnson, **1963-64**:
629
Engle, Sen. Clair, **1963-64**: 413, 486 [6], 650;
1965: 143
Engle, Dr. H. Martin, **1966**: 293n.
English, John F., **1966**: 512
English, Richard, **1963-64**: 650n.
Engstrom, Elmer W., **1965**: 11
Enrico Fermi Award, **1963-64**: 19; **1965**: 17;
1968-69: 608
Enterprise, U.S.S., **1963-64**: 560 [6], 619 [5];
1967: 484, 485 [5], 493, 494, 495 [3]
Enterprise system, **1963-64**: 8, 40, 91 (p. 115),
111, 124 (p. 166), 139, 158, 218 [36],
233, 248, 250, 264, 266 [3], 267, 270,
271 [15], 280 [11], 284, 290, 295,
297 [2], 299, 314, 350, 391, 402, 431,
506, 598, 599, 604, 617, 757, 760, 787;
1965: 18, 25, 38, 76, 223, 258, 590,
632
Environmental Health Sciences, National Center
for, proposed, **1965**: 54
Environmental Health Service, Consumer Protection and, **1968-69**: 336
Environmental Quality, Committee on, **1968-69**:
577n.
Environmental Research, Institutes for, **1967**:
31n.
Environmental Satellite Center, National, **1967**:
31n.
Environmental Science Services Administration,
1965: 247; **1966**: 143; **1967**: 31; **1968-
69**: 678 (p. 1302)
Epilepsy, **1968-69**: 111, 329
Episcopalians, **1968-69**: 156
Equal employment opportunity, **1963-64**: 91
(p. 116), 124 (p. 165), 213, 221, 233,
235, 250, 277, 379 [7], 398, 406, 412,
413, 448, 650, 680, 737, 743; **1965**:
153, 156 [1], 351, 384, 436; **1966**: 136,
196, 248, 250, 320 [17], 475; **1967**:

Equal employment opportunity – *continued*
12, 16 (p. 76), 55, 95, 354; **1968-69**:
14 (p. 31), 24, 26, 47 (p. 130), 84, 87,
91, 195, 209, 347, 437, 458, 596, 611,
684 (pp. 1311, 1324)
Business, responsibilities of, **1963-64**: 40, 111,
139, 250, 342, 448
Government service, **1963-64**: 111, 139, 168,
213, 277; **1965**: 91, 100, 150, 197
Labor, responsibilities of, **1963-64**: 139
Minority groups, **1963-64**: 40, 111, 205, 213,
342; **1965**: 76, 100, 384
Negroes, **1963-64**: 40, 111, 301; **1965**: 100,
480
Older persons, **1963-64**: 178n.
Women, **1963-64**: 170 [16], 213, 398; **1965**:
91
Equal Employment Opportunity, President's
Committee on, **1963-64**: 40, 111, 139,
205, 213, 221, 277, 342, 379 [7], 448,
812n.; **1965**: 448 [6], 530n.; **1966**:
196
Equal Employment Opportunity, White House
Conference on, **1965**: 384, 436
Equal Employment Opportunity Commission,
1965: 290, 384; **1966**: 196, 475; **1967**:
55, 258; **1968-69**: 26, 91, 347, 596
Chairman (Clifford L. Alexander, Jr.), **1967**:
291, 333, 460 [1]; **1968-69**: 17, 42,
429, 596, 631
Equal justice, message to Congress, **1967**: 55, 56
Equal opportunity, **1963-64**: 32, 34, 233, 235,
292, 293, 765; **1965**: 2, 27, 32 (p. 83),
35 (pp. 107, 108), 45, 48, 54, 85, 102,
107, 132, 179, 210, 301, 305, 340, 349,
377, 384, 388 [2], 392, 426, 433, 436,
452, 470, 530; **1966**: 168, 196, 273,
299, 335, 346, 394, 396, 408, 497;
1967: 261, 270, 297ftn. (p. 673), 450,
481; **1968-69**: 84, 111, 162, 487, 596,
612, 678 (p. 1286)
See also Equal Employment Opportunity; Nondiscrimination.
Education, **1966**: 34 (p. 100), 196, 273; **1967**:
16 (p. 76), 554 [6]
Mexican-Americans, **1966**: 158 [8], 236 [14];
1967: 452
Negroes, **1967**: 55, 463
Voting rights, **1967**: 55
Women, **1967**: 475
Equal Opportunity, President's Council on, **1965**:
50, 530n.
Equal opportunity agreements, **1963-64**: 40, 111,
139, 250, 342, 448; **1965**: 530n.; **1966**:
196
Equal opportunity awards, **1968-69**: 596
Equal Pay, National Committee for, **1963-64**:
398n.

Equal Pay Act of 1963, **1963–64**: 213, 398;
    1966: 299; **1967**: 548
Equal Pay Conference, **1963–64**: 398
"Era of Good Tidings, The," George Dangerfield,
    1963–64: 303
Erdmann, Marion S., **1963–64**: 573
Erhard, Ludwig, **1963–64**: 26, 87, 693, 701, 734;
    1965: 22 [7], 57, 333n., 463 [7], 659,
    660; **1966**: 88 [9], 484, 503, 506;
    1967: 306, 554 [5]
  Joint statements with, **1963–64**: 76, 400;
    1965: 300, 600
  Message, **1965**: 520
  News conference remarks on, **1963–64**: 28 [4],
    54 [8, 16], 71 [6, 8, 13], 266 [8], 316
    [25], 475 [3], 688 [8]
  Visit, **1963–64**: 72–76, 399, 400; **1966**: 474
    [9], 482, 485–486
Erhard, Mrs. Ludwig, **1966**: 482
Erhardt, Rev. Charles R., **1963–64**: 649n.
Erickson, Edward, **1963–64**: 693
Erickson, Mrs. Edward, **1963–64**: 693
Eriksson, Leif, **1967**: 313n.
Erosion, **1968–69**: 593
Ertola, John A., **1963–64**: 651n.
Ervin, Sen. Sam J., Jr., **1963–64**: 326, 327, 328,
    329, 631; **1966**: 286, 335
Erwin, Frank, **1968–69**: 97, 625
Eshkol, Levi (Prime Minister of Israel), **1963–64**:
    337, 378, 380, 672; **1966**: 365n.; **1968–
    69**: 7–9, 78
Eshkol, Mrs. Levi, **1963–64**: 377n., 378; **1968–
    69**: 7, 8
Espin, Mr. and Mrs. Carlos, **1965**: 336n.
ESSA satellites, **1966**: 222
Essex, Martin Walker, **1966**: 472
Essex, U.S.S., **1968–69**: 552n.
Estes, Billie Sol, **1963–64**: 728
Estes, Thomas S., **1965**: 142n.
Etherington, Edwin, **1968–69**: 470
Ethiopia, **1967**: 51, 52, 245; **1968–69**: 140n.
  Emperor Haile Selassie I, **1968–69**: 433, 639
  U.S. Ambassador Edward M. Korry, **1966**: 243
  U.S. assistance, **1968–69**: 21
Eufaula, Okla., campaign remarks, **1963–64**: 597
Eufaula Dam, Oklahoma, **1963–64**: 587 [2],
    597, 598
EURATOM (European Atomic Energy Com-
    munity), **1966**: 48n.; **1967**: 64
Eurich, Alvin, **1966**: 424n.
Europe, **1965**: 200n.; **1968–69**: 194, 204, 271n.
  See also specific countries.
  Assistance, **1963–64**: 617; **1965**: 235; **1968–
    69**: 143
  Economic and social development, **1968–69**:
    47 (pp. 134, 136), 151, 193n., 500
  Foreign investments, **1968–69**: 290
  Foreign trade, **1968–69**: 47 (p. 136)

Europe — *continued*
  Unification, **1963–64**: 76, 272, 662n., 788;
    1965: 112, 200n., 203, 235; **1966**: 6
    (p. 8), 142, 200, 486, 503
  U.S. relations with, **1963–64**: 272; **1965**: 2,
    235, 307, 347 [2, 7], 463 [8]
Europe, Cooperative for American Remittances
    to, **1967**: 153
Europe, Eastern, **1963–64**: 562, 638, 686, 719,
    785; **1965**: 299, 302; **1968–69**: 462,
    472, 474, 585
  See also specific countries.
  Communications, global satellite, **1968–69**:
    288
  Communist aggression, **1968–69**: 467 [15]
  INTELSAT participation, **1967**: 346
  Radio Free Europe broadcasts to, **1963–64**:
    785
  Relations with West, **1963–64**: 612; **1965**: 235,
    300, 660; **1967**: 272
  Trade exhibitions, **1967**: 245; **1968–69**: 204
  Trade with U.S., **1965**: 2, 4, 235, 266; **1966**:
    6 (pp. 3, 9), 200, 247 [9], 272, 503,
    528; **1967**: 3 (p. 10), 16 (p. 80), 80
    [2], 157, 225 [18], 231
  U.S. policy, **1968–69**: 474
  U.S. relations with, **1963–64**: 359, 785; **1965**:
    463 [8], 595; **1966**: 6 (p. 9), 261, 272;
    1967: 3 (p. 10), 34 [5], 225 [18], 346
  Vietnam conflict peace efforts, **1966**: 607 [6]
Europe, Western, **1963–64**: 400, 736, 780 [1];
    1967: 306n., 508
  See also specific countries.
  Assistance, **1966**: 6 (p. 7); **1968–69**: 63, 524
  Capital markets in, **1965**: 60
  Communist aggression, **1968–69**: 472
  Customs Union, **1968–69**: 348
  Defense, **1963–64**: 608, 780 [8]; **1965**: 172,
    200n., 235; **1966**: 200, 482, 506; **1967**:
    347, 351; **1968–69**: 472
  East-West relations, **1966**: 503
  Economic and political integration, **1963–64**:
    49, 76, 708; **1965**: 300; **1966**: 200,
    359n.; **1967**: 306n., 351
  Economic and social development, **1968–69**:
    62, 110, 274
  Immigration to U.S., **1966**: 30
  Investments, **1968–69**: 2
  Nuclear forces in, **1963–64**: 467; **1965**: 300
  Nuclear weapons in, **1963–64**: 413; **1965**: 300,
    387
  Postwar buildup, **1966**: 62, 142
  Postwar recovery, **1967**: 519
  Regional cooperation, **1968–69**: 676 (p. 1268)
  Relations with Western Hemisphere, **1963–64**:
    192
  U.S. Armed Forces in, **1963–64**: 49, 132 (p.
    184), 382; **1965**: 235, 300;

Europe — *continued*
  U.S. Armed Forces in — *continued*
    1966: 445 [24], 486, 506; **1967**:
      348; **1968-69**: 223 [14]
  U.S. policy, **1966**: 200, 482, 501 [2], 506,
      607 [3]
  U.S. relations with, **1963-64**: 49, 399n., 788;
      1966: 200, 607 [5]; **1967**: 390, 554
      [5]; **1968-69**: 62, 211, 472, 474, 676
      (p. 1268)
  U.S. trade with, **1963-64**: 76, 788
European Atomic Energy Community
  See EURATOM.
European Coal and Steel Community, **1963-64**:
    788; **1965**: 429
European Communities, Commission of the,
    1968-69: 62, 348
European Economic Community, **1963-64**: 71
    [8, 13], 788; **1965**: 112, 235, 347 [7],
    660; **1967**: 246n., 250, 442, 508, 545;
    1968-69: 517
  Housing, Building and Planning Commission,
    1968-69: 434
  U.S. trade with, **1963-64**: 757
European Space Research Organization, **1966**:
    485n.
Evans, C. E., **1963-64**: 778; **1965**: 603
Evans, David, **1966**: 472
Evans, Repr. Frank E., **1963-64**: 658; **1966**: 410,
    413-414
Evans, Rowland, Jr., **1968-69**: 459
Evansville, Ind., **1966**: 353
  Campaign remarks, **1963-64**: 729
  Mayor Frank McDonald, **1963-64**: 729
Everett, Repr. Robert A., **1963-64**: 358, 645,
    701
Evers, Medgar, **1968-69**: 298
Evins, Repr. Joe L., **1963-64**: 645, 701, 702;
    1965: 330, 554; **1968-69**: 345
Evins, Mary, **1968-69**: 345
EX-10 torpedo, **1963-64**: 382
Excavation technology, **1967**: 20
Exceptional Service Award, NASA, **1965**: 318
Exchange Commission, Securities and, **1967**: 57,
    103, 104 [1]
Exchange peace corps.
  See Exchange programs.
Exchange programs, **1963-64**: 280; **1965**: 248,
    292, 552, 553; **1966**: 200, 378, 503,
    545, 557
  American Field Service, **1963-64**: 465; **1965**:
    372
  Cultural, **1967**: 272, 344
  Educational, **1967**: 77, 344
  Message to Congress, **1965**: 36
  Peace Corps volunteers, **1966**: 45, 46, 332n.,
    406, 455
  Report, **1967**: 344

Exchange programs — *continued*
  Scientists, **1965**: 319 [5], 519; **1966**: 200,
    503
  Students, **1966**: 45, 177, 545, 557; **1967**:
    143n., 344
  Teachers, **1966**: 45, 406; **1967**: 344
  U.S.-Soviet scientific and cultural, **1966**: 483
Excise Tax Reduction Act of 1965, approval,
    1965: 326
Excise tax reduction bill, **1965**: 319 [3], 321
Excise taxes, **1963-64**: 132 (p. 180), 271 [3],
    379 [4, 5], 407, 724; **1965**: 2, 32 (pp.
    83, 84, 86), 76, 100, 326, 632; **1966**:
    6 (p. 5), 26 (pp. 49, 52), 34 (pp. 100,
    102), 155, 240, 444, 654 [6]; **1967**: 6
    [17], 16 (p. 76), 329, 420; **1968-69**: 39
    (pp. 87, 88), 47 (pp. 131, 133), 343,
    632, 678 (pp. 1274, 1277) 684 (p.
    1322)
  Automobile, **1965**: 255, 326; **1966**: 6 (p. 5), 8
    [14], 17, 26 (pp. 49, 52), 155
  Reduction, **1965**: 32 (p. 87), 251, 255, 319
    [3], 321, 326n., 505, 567; **1966**: 8 [14]
  Telephone, **1966**: 6 (p. 5), 8 [14], 17, 26 (pp.
    49, 52), 155
  User charges, **1965**: 32 (p. 87), 35 (pp. 108,
    116), 255; **1966**: 225
Executive, Legislative, and Judicial Salaries,
    Commission on, **1968-69**: 676 (pp.
    1266, 1267), 678 (p. 1305), 694
Executive Boards, Federal, **1968-69**: 464
Executive branch, **1963-64**: 201 [9]; **1965**: 2,
    42, 100, 117 [3], 209, 290, 296, 317,
    329, 330, 440; **1967**: 11, 99
  Antipoverty agency, question of, **1963-64**:
    218 [16]
  Appropriations, **1966**: 445 [16]; **1967**: 140,
    417, 518 [9], 556
  Automatic date processing, **1966**: 26 (p. 66),
    27, 296
  Budgetary decisions, **1968-69**: 678 (p. 1274),
    684 (p. 1317)
  Cabinet.
    See main heading, Cabinet.
  Civil rights compliance, **1965**: 50, 197n., 530;
    1966: 59, 60n., 501 [13]
  Communications with the public, **1965**: 249n.
  Congressional relations, **1966**: 206, 216, 270,
    292; **1967**: 417 [4]
  Economy measures in, **1963-64**: 37, 54 [6],
    71 [3, 10, 11], 100, 132 (p. 193), 211
    [9, 10], 218 [15], 240, 271 [7], 294
    [4], 295, 336 [3], 462 [2], 619 [1,
    14], 630, 689, 749, 775, 790; **1965**:
    127, 264, 267, 274, 311, 362, 497, 512
    See also Cost reduction program, Federal.
  Ethical standards in, **1965**: 241
  Inter-agency committees, councils, and boards,
    1965: 282, 631

Executive branch — *continued*
  Management improvement, **1963–64**: 17, 100,
    132 (pp. 176, 193), 168, 213, 240, 261,
    307; **1965**: 32 (pp. 97, 98), 125, 129,
    244, 249, 264, 274; **1966**: 6 (p. 4), 26
    (pp. 49, 55, 65–68), 129, 376
  Message to Congress: **1967**: 121
  Overseas programs, economic operation of,
    1965: 129
  Reduction of employees, **1963–64**: 240
  Regulatory agencies, **1966**: 34 (p. 108)
  Relations with Congress, **1963–64**: 11, 81, 527,
    777; **1965**: 440, 495, 502, 515
  Reorganization, **1965**: 32 (p. 97), 43, 94, 125;
    1966: 6 (p. 3), 26 (p. 65), 59, 98, 232,
    267, 292, 302
  Staffing of executive positions, **1965**: 213, 240
  Staffing of international organizations, assist-
    ance, **1963–64**: 519
  Transfer of power, **1968–69**: 480
Executive Branch of the Government, Commis-
    sion on Organization of the, **1963–64**:
    71 [12]; **1965**: 441; **1966**: 190, 438,
    523; **1967**: 99, 121; **1968–69**: 59, 60,
    227
Executive Institute, Federal, **1967**: 184n.
Executive Office of the President, **1968–69**: 297
Executive orders
  Arms import control, **1968–69**: 553n.
  Board of inquiry in labor dispute, **1968–69**:
    636n.
  Closing of Government agencies on November
    25, 1963, **1963–64**: 4
  Commission on Postal Organization, **1967**: 168
  Commission to Report Upon the Assassination
    of President John F. Kennedy, **1963–64**:
    15
  Department of Transportation Act, effective
    date, **1967**: 149
  Export Expansion Advisory Committee, estab-
    lishment, **1968–69**: 422
  Federal Council for Science and Technology,
    enlargement, **1967**: 478
  Federal Development Planning Commission for
    Appalachia, establishment, **1963–64**:
    711
  Federal law enforcement and crime prevention
    program, **1968–69**: 57
  Federal-State liaison and cooperation, **1968–
    69**: 483n.
  Foreign Service personnel system, **1968–69**:
    581
  John F. Kennedy Space Center, designation of
    name, **1963–64**: 13
  List, Appendix B, **1963–64**: p. 1702; **1965**: p.
    1197; **1966**: p. 1491; **1967**: p. 1221;
    1968–69: p. 1398
  National Advisory Commission on Civil Dis-
    orders, **1967**: 327

Executive orders — *continued*
  National Commission on the Causes and Pre-
    vention of Violence, establishment,
    1968–69: 298
  President's Advisory Council on Cost Reduc-
    tion, **1967**: 232
  President's Commission for the Observance of
    Human Rights Year, 1968, **1968–69**: 42
  Ryukyu Islands, administration, **1968–69**: 44
  Urban programs, coordination, **1966**: 380
  Vietnam veterans, civil service appointments,
    1968–69: 67
Executive privilege, **1965**: 160
Executive Seminar Center, **1965**: 379
Executive Service Corps, International, **1963–64**:
    227, 402; **1965**: 18; **1966**: 41; **1968–69**:
    63
Executives, retired, **1968–69**: 75
Executives, Service Corps of Retired, **1968–69**:
    75
Exemplary Rehabilitation Certificate, Armed
    Forces, **1966**: 529
Exhibitions, special international, **1965**: 553;
    1967: 245; **1968–69**: 204
Expenditure account budget, **1968–69**: 39 (p.
    84), 678 (p. 1274)
Expenditures.
  See Spending.
Explorations of Antarctica, **1965**: 220, 265
Explorations of man, **1963–64**: 117
Explorer I spacecraft, **1968–69**: 41
Explorer Scouts, uniform imports, **1966**: 178
EXPO '67 (Canadian Universal and International
    Exhibition), **1966**: 644; **1967**: 237, 238,
    239, 245; **1968–69**: 204
Export Control Act, **1966**: 592
Export Expansion, Cabinet Committee on, **1963–
    64**: 248, 592
Export Expansion, White House Conference on,
    1963–64: 248, 592
Export Expansion Advisory Committee, **1968–
    69**: 422
Export Expansion Council, National, **1965**: 465;
    1967: 231
Export-Import Bank of Washington, **1965**: 448
    [6]; **1966**: 182, 248, 503, 528; **1967**:
    13 (p. 49), 16 (p. 81), 176
Export-Import Bank of the United States, **1968–
    69**: 2, 39 (p. 96), 47 (p. 136), 136, 146,
    377, 422
  Chairman (Harold F. Linder), **1968–69**: 136
Exports, **1963–64**: 124 (pp. 157, 162), 739, 757,
    787; **1965**: 21, 35 (p. 111), 338, 465;
    1966: 34 (p. 104), 125, 144, 272, 445
    [6], 461, 503; **1967**: 13 (pp. 49, 51),
    228, 231, 329, 451, 476, 508, 524;
    1968–69: 2, 136, 434, 636
  See also specific commodities; specific exports.
  Administrative paperwork reduction, **1966**: 98

Exports – *continued*
  Agricultural products, **1963-64**: 71 [8, 13],
    475 [2], 484, 592, 634, 636, 757;
    1967: 63; **1968-69**: 39 (p. 100), 94,
    176, 247, 406, 417
  Associations, joint, **1968-69**: 146
  Decrease, **1968-69**: 39 (p. 87), 47 (pp. 13?
    135)
  Expansion program, **1963-64**: 248, 472, 722
  Government financing assistance, **1968-69**: 39
    (pp. 99, 102), 377, 442, 449
  Increase, **1963-64**: 246 [12], 350, 592, 695,
    753n., 757; **1965**: 35 (pp. 105, 106,
    111), 60, 77, 307, 465, 564, 638n.;
    1967: 231; **1968-69**: 2, 39 (pp. 99,
    102), 47 (p. 135), 146, 422, 684 (p.
    1319)
  Industrial goods, **1963-64**: 636, 722
  Insurance, **1968-69**: 377
  Marketing programs, **1963-64**: 566; **1965**: 47,
    77
  Military, **1963-64**: 132 (p. 191)
  Restrictions, limitation on, **1963-64**: 193
  Surplus, **1967**: 3 (p. 8), 16 (pp. 75, 81); **1968-
    69**: 47 (p. 133)
Extension Service, Cooperative, **1966**: 331n.
Extremist groups, **1963-64**: 462 [6], 475 [20,
    23], 656; **1965**: 22 [15], 135
Eye disease, **1968-69**: 111, 446
Eye Institute, National, **1968-69**: 446
Eyring, Henry, **1966**: 652n.; **1967**: 37n.

F-111 bomber, **1963-64**: 382; **1965**: 26, 339
FAA.
  See Federal Aviation Agency.
Fabric safety, **1967**: 57, 200, 342, 393, 465,
    499, 520, 534, 539; **1968-69**: 14 (p.
    29), 56, 545
Factory wages, **1966**: 34 (p. 96), 111, 228, 399,
    403, 426, 635 [8-9]; **1968-69**: 47 (p.
    128)
Factory workers, **1965**: 644
Fahy, Charles, **1967**: 174, 188, 204 [5], 207,
    301
FAIR (fair and impartial random) selective serv-
    ice, **1967**: 92, 205; **1968-69**: 43, 678
    (p. 1304)
Fair Deal, **1966**: 330; **1967**: 251, 281
Fair employment practices.
  See Equal employment opportunity.
Fair employment practices act.
  See Civil Rights Act of 1964.
Fair housing.
  See Housing; Civil Rights Act of 1968.
Fair Labor Standards Act of 1938, **1963-64**: 124
    (p. 163), 213, 334, 642; **1965**: 35 (p.

Fair Labor Standards Act of 1938 – *continued*
    114), 100, 258, 582; **1966**: 26 (p. 62),
    111, 168, 479; **1967**: 114
  Proposed amendments, **1963-64**: 166
Fair Labor Standards Amendments of 1961,
    1963-64: 22
Fair Labor Standards Amendments of 1966,
    1966: 111n., 479, 512
Fair Packaging and Labeling Act, **1966**: 576
Fairchild, Thomas E., **1966**: 320 [4]
Fairhall, Allen, **1967**: 562
Fairs and exhibitions, **1968-69**: 204
Faisal, King (Saudi Arabia), **1965**: 463 [6];
    1966: 284-285, 287
Falcon Dam, **1966**: 640; **1967**: 408 [5]
Falk, Adrien J., **1963-64**: 410
Fallon, Repr. George H., **1963-64**: 703; **1965**:
    317; **1967**: 286
Fallout, radioactive, **1963-64**: 434, 653n., 675n.,
    686; **1965**: 54, 284
Fallout shelters, **1963-64**: 132 (p. 185); **1965**:
    26
Families with dependent children, aid (AFDC),
    1967: 16 (p. 83), 39
Family Breadwinners: Their Special Training
    Needs, report, **1963-64**: 160
Family income and assets, **1968-69**: 47 (p. 129),
    684 (p. 1312)
Family planning, **1966**: 45, 95, 433; **1967**: 469;
    1968-69: 14 (p. 27), 39 (pp. 89, 104),
    47 (p. 138), 63, 111, 393, 408, 417,
    467 [9], 500, 659, 679, 684 (p. 1312)
  Developing nations, **1968-69**: 679
  Report, **1968-69**: 659
  Services, **1968-69**: 3
Family Planning, Committee on Population and,
    1968-69: 393, 659
Family relocation aid, **1967**: 353
Family unit, **1965**: 301, 392
Fanfani, Amintore, **1965**: 198, 200n., 203; **1967**:
    278, 389, 390, 391, 572
Fannie and John Hertz Foundation Award, **1966**:
    194
Fannin, Gov. Paul, **1963-64**: 649
Far East.
  See Asia, South Asia, and Southeast Asia.
Far East, Economic Commission for Asia and,
    1966: 461, 557
Far East, United Nations Economic Commission
    for Asia and the, **1965**: 353ftn. (p. 736);
    1968-69: 237
Farah, Empress (Iran), **1963-64**: 385; **1967**: 364
Farber, Dr. Sidney, **1963-64**: 211 [6]
Farbstein, Repr. Leonard, **1965**: 242; **1966**: 510
Farley, James A., **1963-64**: 224, 228, 751; **1965**:
    596; **1966**: 49; **1968-69**: 498
Farm bill, **1963-64**: 54 [9, 11], 71 [8], 242
    [12], 246 [12]

Farm cooperatives, **1965**: 47

Farm Credit Administration, **1967**: 315n.

  Governor (R. B. Tootell), **1967**: 156

Farm economy, **1963–64**: 124 (pp. 156, 158, 162), 132 (p. 187), 225, 249, 255, 267, 271 [3], 344, 433, 434, 475 [2], 484; **1965**: 32 (p. 91), 35 (pp. 106, 116), 46 [1], 100, 168, 192, 377, 452, 460, 590, 597

  See also Agriculture; Agricultural commodities.

  Campaign remarks, **1963–64**: 544, 570, 597, 631, 634, 643, 655, 657, 667, 712, 719, 746

  Message to Congress, **1965**: 47

Farm Editors Association, Newspaper, **1963–64**: 344

Farm Labor Contractor Registration Act of 1963, **1965**: 100

Farm prices and income.

  See Farm economy.

Farm programs, **1963–64**: 54 [9], 344, 570, 598; **1965**: 2, 32 (p. 91), 46 [1], 47, 85, 168, 597

  See also Agriculture and agricultural programs.

  Campaign remarks, **1963–64**: 620, 631, 634, 638, 643, 645, 649, 680, 701

  Presidential policy paper, **1963–64**: 757

Farmer, James L., **1965**: 412 [3], 436

Farmer-Labor Party Convention, Democratic, **1963–64**: 433

Farmers, **1965**: 5, 100, 490; **1967**: 228, 525; **1968–69**: 96, 142, 155, 174, 534

  Leaders, remarks, **1967**: 63

  Message to Congress, **1968–69**: 94

  Migrant, **1963–64**: 219, 305

  Social security, **1967**: 12

"Farmers Almanac, The," **1968–69**: 142

Farmers of America, Future, **1966**: 295n.; **1968–69**: 390

Farmers Home Administration, **1963–64**: 132 (p. 187); **1965**: 605; **1966**: 182, 584; **1967**: 120; **1968–69**: 94, 113, 467 [13], 678 (p. 1289)

Farmers Home Administration Act, Consolidated, **1968–69**: 450

Farmers' Home Administration Act of 1949, **1965**: 452

Farmers Organization, National, **1963–64**: 255

Farmers Union, Minnesota, **1963–64**: 255

Farmers Union, National, **1963–64**: 225, 242 [10]; **1968–69**: 75n., 142

Farmers Union Grain Terminal Association, **1963–64**: 255

Farms and farm programs.

  See Agriculture and agricultural programs.

Farnsley, Repr. Charles P., **1963–64**: 643, 644; **1966**: 351

Farnum, Repr. Billie S., **1963–64**: 745; **1966**: 431

Farr, Fred, **1965**: 277n.

Farr, George, **1963–64**: 433

Farrell, Raymond F., **1963–64**: 588n.; **1968–69**: 388n.

Farwell, Frank L., **1968–69**: 36

Fascell, Repr. Dante B., **1963–64**: 198, 199, 571, 709, 710; **1965**: 503; **1968–69**: 547

Faubus, Gov. Orval E., **1963–64**: 599

Faubus, Mrs. Orval E., **1963–64**: 599

Faulkner, William, **1963–64**: 141; **1967**: 442

Fauntroy, Rev. Walter E., **1967**: 406, 466

Fay, Dr. Marion, **1963–64**: 211 [6]

Fay, Paul B., Jr., **1963–64**: 354

Fay, William P., **1963–64**: 366

Fayette, Frederick J., **1963–64**: 605

FB–111 bomber, **1966**: 26 (p. 56); **1968–69**: 39 (p. 98), 169 [10, 18]

FBI.

  See Federal Bureau of Investigation.

FCC.

  See Federal Communications Commission.

Federal Advisory Council on Regional Economic Development, **1968–69**: 173

Federal aid, **1967**: 3 (p. 4), 121, 123, 124, 203, 222, 223 [6, 13]

  Agriculture, **1968–69**: 425 [2]

  Appalachia, **1967**: 11, 514, 576

  Arts and humanities support, **1968–69**: 686

  Business, **1968–69**: 39 (p. 102)

  Child welfare, **1967**: 39

  Colleges and universities, **1967**: 413, 423, 490; **1968–69**: 39 (p. 106), 54, 567, 678 (pp. 1292, 1293)

  Community development, **1968–69**: 684 (p. 1321)

  Crime prevention, **1968–69**: 59, 235, 355, 424

  Depressed areas, **1968–69**: 39 (p. 102)

  Disaster relief, **1967**: 408 [1]

  Education, **1967**: 13 (p. 55), 16 (pp. 75, 82), 35, 67, 70 [6], 71, 77, 114, 164, 193, 223 [6], 304, 378, 396n., 490, 495 [5], 532, 534, 540; **1968–69**: 4, 6, 39 (pp. 106, 110), 50, 54, 212, 406, 473, 538, 557 [8], 564, 567–569, 601, 612, 622, 625, 676 (pp. 1264, 1267), 678 (pp. 1292, 1293), 684 (pp. 1313, 1314, 1322)

  Electric power projects, **1968–69**: 39 (p. 91)

  Family relocation, **1967**: 353

  Health, **1967**: 223 [6], 477

  Health programs, **1968–69**: 24, 442, 468, 557 [8], 612, 676 (p. 1267), 678 (pp. 1295, 1303)

  Highways, **1967**: 6 [3, 10], 114, 120; **1968–69**: 39 (p. 91), 243, 458, 467 [3]

  Hospitals and medical care facilities, **1967**: 13 (p. 53), 419; **1968–69**: 678 (p. 1296)

  Housing, **1968–69**: 39 (p. 102), 426, 612, 676 (p. 1265), 678 (p. 1289)

Federal aid – *continued*
  Humanities, teachers' grants, **1968–69**: 703
  Law enforcement, local and State, **1968–69**:
      320, 557 [8], 678 (pp. 1281, 1291)
  Libraries, **1967**: 507
  Merchant marines, **1968–69**: 535
  Multi-county planning, **1967**: 114
  Nondiscrimination in, **1968–69**: 611
  Occupational training, **1967**: 91
  Police, **1967**: 482, 530
  Poultry inspection, **1968–69**: 451
  Processing time, **1967**: 458
  Research, **1968–69**: 678 (p. 1293)
  Rural development, **1967**: 114
  Science, **1968–69**: 687
  State and local governments.
    See Federal aid to States.
  Students, **1967**: 148, 378, 413, 423; **1968–69**:
      39 (p. 106), 54, 569
  Transportation, **1967**: 542
  Urban areas, **1967**: 16 (p. 85), 114, 179, 328
      [14, 17, 26], 353, 358 [8], 380, 458,
      467; **1968–69**: 39 (p. 110), 678 (p.
      1290)
  Vocational education, **1968–69**: 54, 684 (p.
      1316)
  Welfare programs, **1968–69**: 612
Federal Aid Highway Act of 1956, **1963–64**:
    453, 512
Federal Aid Highway Act of 1962, **1963–64**: 154
Federal Aid Highway Act of 1964, approval,
    1963–64: 512
Federal Aid Highway Act of 1968, **1968–69**:
    113, 458
Federal aid to States, **1963–64**: 132 (pp. 177,
    191), 598, 730, 746; **1965**: 32 (p. 85);
    1966: 26 (p. 60), 34 (p. 101), 121 [2,
    4], 392, 413, 492 [1, 2], 606; **1967**:
    458, 576; **1968–69**: 678 (pp. 1302,
    1303)
  Airports, **1963–64**: 215, 410, 453, 598
  Appalachian area, **1963–64**: 314, 711; **1965**:
      32 (p. 88), 35 (p. 115), 100, 103, 215,
      245; **1966**: 122 [2], 123
  Area redevelopment, **1963–64**: 124 (p. 165),
      152, 213; **1965**: 47, 90, 132, 148, 245
  Beautification programs, **1965**: 54, 545
  Commerce and transportation, **1963–64**: 132
      (p. 187)
  Depressed areas, **1963–64**: 132 (p. 188), 213,
      219; **1965**: 132, 139, 149, 452n., 492
  Disaster relief, **1965**: 174; **1966**: 74, 145
    Alaska earthquake, **1963–64**: 241, 286, 308,
        319, 368, 371, 615; **1965**: 435
    California floods, **1965**: 74
    Colorado flood, **1965**: 319 [20]
    Florida hurricane, **1963–64**: 563 [4], 567;
        1965: 605

Federal aid to States – *continued*
  Disaster relief – *continued*
    Georgia hurricane, **1963–64**: 563 [4], 567
    Louisiana hurricane, **1963–64**: 618, 647;
        1965: 605
    Midwestern floods and tornadoes, **1965**:
        187, 188, 189, 190, 191, 193, 215, 239,
        477
    Minnesota floods, **1965**: 187, 189, 193, 239
    Mississippi Delta flood, **1965**: 592
    Mississippi hurricane, **1965**: 605
    Montana flood, **1963–64**: 573
    Ohio River basin flood, **1963–64**: 217
    Oregon floods, **1965**: 74
    South Carolina hurricane, **1963–64**: 563 [4]
  Eastern Kentucky emergency program, **1963–
      64**: 41
  Education, **1963–64**: 47, 53, 91 (p. 114), 124
      (p. 164), 132 (pp. 189, 191), 213, 219,
      336 [16], 338, 413, 414, 676, 683, 709,
      754, 775, 780 [20]; **1965**: 2, 9, 29, 32
      (p. 94), 100, 178, 181, 225, 368, 369,
      401, 479, 485, 514, 519, 522, 527, 539,
      592, 603, 625; **1966**: 6 (pp. 3, 5), 26
      (p. 63), 27, 34 (p. 103), 38, 95, 111,
      166, 168, 188 [6, 8], 189, 273, 504,
      508, 512, 524, 586, 588
  Family planning, **1966**: 95
  Handicapped persons, **1966**: 127
  Health programs, **1963–64**: 179, 520, 755;
      1965: 5, 361; **1966**: 6 (p. 3), 95, 166,
      168, 188 [6, 8], 235, 237, 253, 524
  Highways, **1963–64**: 410, 453; **1965**: 30, 32
      (p. 85), 35 (p. 116), 54, 245, 277, 279,
      460, 487, 576n.; **1966**: 47, 98, 252,
      416, 492 [8]
  Historic landmarks preservation, **1966**: 82
  Hospitals and medical care facilities, **1963–64**:
      179; **1966**: 95, 189, 395
  Hydroelectric power projects, **1966**: 399
  Libraries, **1966**: 337
  Library services and construction, **1963–64**:
      181
  Police forces, **1966**: 487
  Public works, **1965**: 47, 148; **1966**: 416, 494
      [7]
  Recreational programs and facilities, **1963–64**:
      132 (p. 187); **1965**: 30, 54, 70, 168,
      222, 277, 279, 471, 477, 487, 521;
      1966: 26 (p. 60), 27, 352, 351–352,
      398, 518
  Rural areas, **1965**: 47, 75
  Technical services, **1966**: 26 (p. 60)
  Transportation, **1963–64**: 410, 453; **1966**:
      187, 442
  Unemployment insurance, **1963–64**: 132 (p.
      189)

Federal aid to States – *continued*
  Urban areas, **1966**: 6 (p. 3), 30, 207, 401 [6],
    428, 525
  Urban renewal, **1963–64**: 189; **1965**: 35 (p.
    114), 54, 90, 452, 511, 585
  Vocational rehabilitation services, **1965**: 5
  Waste disposal research, proposed, **1965**: 54
  Water pollution control, **1965**: 54
  Water resources development, **1965**: 32 (p. 92),
    54, 487
  Welfare services, **1963–64**: 213; **1965**: 501
  West Virginia, **1963–64**: 586
Federal Airport Act, amendment, **1963–64**: 215
Federal anti-riot bill of 1968, **1968–69**: 59
Federal Aviation Administration, **1967**: 392;
    1968–69: 93, 693
  Cost reduction program, **1968–69**: 39 (p. 111)
Federal Aviation Agency, **1963–64**: 294 [6],
    310, 336 [3], 351, 355n., 462 [2];
    1965: 138n., 255, 319 [19], 339, 512n.;
    1966: 26 (pp. 54, 67), 98, 244, 321,
    630 [4]; **1967**: 139n., 265
  Administrator (Najeeb E. Halaby), **1963–64**:
    215, 242 [9], 294 [6], 310, 355n., 409,
    586; **1965**: 319 [19]
  Administrator (William F. McKee), **1965**: 339;
    1966: 321, 322, 654 [12]; **1967**: 265,
    392
Federal Budget, Commission on the, **1967**: 85
Federal Building, San Francisco, Calif., dedica-
    tion, **1963–64**: 411
"Federal Buildings, Architectural Standards for,"
    report, **1965**: 249n.
Federal Bureau of Investigation, **1963–64**: 7, 14,
    28ftn. (p. 38), 90, 218 [4], 420 [12],
    455 [9], 475 [4], 504 [3], 563 [9, 11,
    13, 15], 619 [11], 700, 752; **1965**: 46
    [10], 102, 106 [1, 5], 117 [1, 5], 135,
    608; **1966**: 116, 196, 204, 491, 577
    [11]; **1967**: 105, 146, 326; **1968–69**:
    57, 133, 292n., 320, 324, 334, 498, 557
    [8], 604, 678 (p. 1292)
  Agents and staff increase, **1968–69**: 14 (p. 30),
    678 (p. 1292)
  Director (J. Edgar Hoover), **1963–64**: 199, 201
    [3], 315, 333, 455 [9], 468, 475 [20],
    504 [3], 600, 619 [11], 671, 688 [5,
    8], 780 [11, 14]; **1965**: 102, 135, 155,
    290, 336, 366, 443, 500; **1966**: 196,
    204, 289, 491; **1967**: 34 [1], 105, 146,
    204 [14], 275, 326, 385, 530; **1968–69**:
    57, 236, 292n., 320
  Draft evaders, prosecution, **1966**: 158 [11]
  National Academy, **1966**: 526; **1968–69**: 59,
    320, 678 (p. 1292)
  Report on urban riots, **1963–64**: 600
  Riot control, **1963–64**: 600, 603
Federal Bureau of Prisons, **1965**: 509

Federal Campaign, Combined, **1967**: 288
Federal Children's Bureau, **1967**: 39
Federal City College, D.C., **1966**: 586; **1968–69**:
    436, 689
Federal Civil Defense Act of 1950, **1968–69**:
    196n.
Federal Civilian Service, President's Award for
    Distinguished, **1963–64**: 417; **1965**:
    269, 296; **1966**: 266; **1967**: 317;
    1968–69: 604
Federal Claims Collection Act of 1966, **1966**: 335n.
Federal Coal Mine Safety Act, **1966**: 237
Federal Coal Mine Safety Act Amendments of
    1965, **1966**: 151
Federal Communications Commission, **1963–64**:
    256 [15], 266 [16]; **1965**: 126, 287n.,
    567; **1966**: 277 [5], 278; **1967**: 77,
    346; **1968–69**: 59, 298
  Chairman (Rosel H. Hyde), **1966**: 277 [5],
    278, 366, 410–413, 415; **1968–69**: 298
Federal Contract Compliance, Office of, **1968–
    69**: 26
Federal Corrupt Practices Act of 1925, **1966**:
    241; **1967**: 236
Federal Council on the Arts and the Humanities,
    1966: 327; **1967**: 274
Federal Council for Science and Technology,
    1963–64: 229, 231, 456n.; **1965**: 92,
    271, 275, 514; **1966**: 138, 222; **1967**:
    478; **1968–69**: 577
Federal Credit Programs, Committee on, **1966**:
    182
Federal credit programs, private investments,
    1965: 506
Federal Credit Union Act, amendment, **1967**:
    537
Federal Criminal Laws, National Commission on
    Reform of, **1968–69**: 59
Federal Deposit Insurance Corporation, **1963–64**:
    144, 642, 787; **1966**: 88 [3], 473, 530;
    1967: 16 (p. 87)
  Chairman (K. A. Randall), **1965**: 60; **1966**:
    473
Federal Development Planning Commission for
    Appalachia, establishment, **1963–64**:
    711; **1965**: 117 [3]
Federal Disaster Act of 1950, **1965**: 174
Federal employees.
    See Government employees.
Federal Employees Association, **1963–64**: 305
Federal Employees' Compensation Act Amend-
    ments of 1966, **1966**: 318
Federal Employees' Compensation Act of 1916,
    1966: 102, 318
Federal Employees' Incentive Awards, **1963–64**:
    467n., 790; **1965**: 540
Federal Employees' Salary Act of 1965, **1965**:
    589

Federal Executive Board Chairman, National
    Conference of, **1965**: 264
Federal Executive Boards, **1968-69**: 464
    Management and efficiency in Government
    operations, **1963-64**: 100
Federal Executive Institute, **1967**: 184n.
Federal Executive Salary Act of 1964, **1965**:
    240
Federal Expenditures, Committee on Reduction
    of Nonessential, **1963-64**: 316 [4]
Federal Extension Service, **1968-69**: 91
Federal Field Committee for Development
    Planning in Alaska, **1963-64**: 615
Federal Firearms Act, **1965**: 102
Federal Food and Drug Act of 1906, **1966**: 307
Federal Food, Drug, and Cosmetic Act, **1963-64**:
    173, 179; **1965**: 5; **1967**: 57; **1968-69**:
    14 (p. 30), 336, 561
Federal Hazardous Substances Labeling Act,
    1966: 140
Federal Highway Act, **1968-69**: 113
Federal Highway Administration, **1968-69**: 93,
    693
Federal Highway Administrator (Rex M. Whitton),
    1963-64: 217; **1965**: 30
Federal Home Loan Bank Board, **1963-64**: 814;
    1965: 127; **1966**: 473, 530, 642 [3, 19];
    1967: 3 (p. 8), 6 [11], 16 (p. 87), 88,
    315n., 420; **1968-69**: 72
    Chairman (John E. Horne), **1966**: 473; **1967**:
        420; **1968-69**: 72
Federal Home Loan Bank System, **1967**: 420
Federal Housing Administration, **1963-64**: 152,
    179, 690n.; **1965**: 47, 90, 415, 585;
    1966: 67, 373 [15]; **1967**: 88; **1968-
    69**: 19, 39 (p. 103), 47 (p. 141), 87,
    114, 229, 402, 435
Federal Insecticide, Fungicide, and Rodenticide
    Act, amendment, approval, **1963-64**:
    341
Federal Interstate Highway System, **1963-64**:
    512, 565, 598, 656, 661; **1965**: 29, 32
    (p. 88), 54, 255, 279, 460, 499
Federal Judicial Center, **1967**: 35, 560; **1968-69**:
    59
Federal Magistrates Act, **1968-69**: 542
Federal Maritime Commission, **1963-64**: 469;
    1965: 371; **1966**: 98
    Chairman (John Harllee), **1963-64**: 316 [3];
        1965: 371
Federal Mediation and Conciliation Service,
    1963-64: 614n.; **1966**: 496; **1967**: 104
    [15]; **1968-69**: 112
    Director (William E. Simkin), **1963-64**: 316
        [3]; **1965**: 448 [11]; **1966**: 496
Federal Metal and Nonmetallic Mine Safety Act
    of 1966, **1966**: 237, 462

Federal National Mortgage Association, **1963-64**:
    152, 688 [4]; **1965**: 90; **1966**: 182,
    199, 451; **1967**: 88, 114, 179; **1968-69**:
    39 (pp. 89, 96), 87, 402, 678 (pp. 1283,
    1285)
    Charter Act, **1968-69**: 402
Federal Personnel, Committee on Retirement
    Policy for, **1965**: 49
Federal Power Commission, **1963-64**: 173, 455
    [11], 780 [18], 803; **1965**: 117 [3],
    418, 567, 608n., 640, 641 [1]; **1966**:
    97, 140, 268; **1967**: 57, 253; **1968-69**:
    653n.
    Chairman (Joseph C. Swidler), **1963-64**:
        803; **1965**: 608, 641
    Chairman (Lee C. White), **1966**: 65 [1], 88
        [8], 97, 202; **1967**: 288
    Memorandum, **1967**: 186
Federal Prison Industries, **1967**: 71
Federal Property and Administrative Services Act
    of 1949, **1965**: 411n.
    Amendments, **1963-64**: 481
Federal Radiation Council, **1963-64**: 653n.,
    675n.
Federal Railroad Administration, **1968-69**: 93,
    693
Federal Reconstruction and Development
    Planning Commission for Alaska, **1963-
    64**: 241n., 294 [7], 308, 368, 615
    Report, **1963-64**: 319
Federal Records Centers, **1965**: 14; **1966**: 58n.
Federal Register, **1966**: 276n.
Federal Regulation of Lobbying Act, **1967**: 236
Federal Reports, President's Advisory Council on,
    1963-64: 583
Federal Reserve Act (Gold Cover Act), **1965**:
    173
Federal Reserve banks, **1965**: 297
Federal Reserve Board, **1963-64**: 211 [2]; **1965**:
    155, 319 [3]
Federal Reserve notes, **1968-69**: 47 (p. 136)
Federal Reserve System, **1963-64**: 294 [3], 295,
    563 [10], 714, 780 [3], 787; **1965**: 35
    (p. 110), 60, 638n.; **1966**: 34 (p. 102),
    401 [19], 419n., 445 [3], 530, 635
    [13]; **1967**: 3 (p. 8), 6 [18], 16 (pp. 75,
    81), 70 [6], 312 [4], 329, 420; **1968-
    69**: 47 (p. 135), 684 (pp. 1318, 1319)
    Board of Governors, **1965**: 319 [8], 639, 641
        [2]; **1966**: 88 [2], 115, 155, 248, 338
        [14], 444, 473; **1967**: 16 (p. 87), 88-
        89, 103, 104 [1, 9], 330 [1], 371, 411
        [11]; **1968-69**: 141, 418, 631, 684
        (p. 1318)
    Chairman (William McC. Martin, Jr.), **1963-
    64**: 295, 299, 486 [4], 530, 714, 780
        [3], 787; **1965**: 60, 77, 155, 638, 641;
        1966: 115, 155, 158 [4], 473; **1967**: 6

Federal Reserve System — *continued*
  Board of Governors — *continued*
    Chairman — *continued*
      [18], 104 [9], 329, 371, 420; **1968–69**:
        2, 169 [17], 170, 317, 418, 684 (p.
        1318)
    Discount rate, **1968–69**: 141, 445
    Loans, foreign, **1968–69**: 1 [1], 2
Federal Safety Council, **1966**: 75
Federal Salaries, Special Panel on, **1965**: 244, 612
Federal Salary Act of 1967, **1968–69**: 303
Federal Salary and Fringe Benefits Act of 1966,
    1966: 108n., 333
Federal Salary Reform Act of 1962, **1963–64**:
    132 (p. 194), 168, 222; **1965**: 244;
    1966: 108
Federal Savings and Loan Insurance Corporation,
    1966: 530
Federal Science Exhibit, **1965**: 170
Federal Service Entrance Examination, **1965**:
    591n.
Federal Staff Retirement Systems, Cabinet
    Committee on, **1965**: 49; **1966**: 108;
    1967: 25
Federal-State Appalachian Commission,
    proposed establishment, **1963–64**:
    294 [2]
Federal-State employment service, **1963–64**:
    99
Federal-State-local governmental responsibilities,
    1963–64: 8, 509, 513, 516 [21], 566,
    606, 656, 669, 702; **1965**: 98, 100, 406;
    1966: 418; **1967**: 121; **1968–69**: 24, 84,
    406
  Accident prevention, **1963–64**: 565
  Air pollution, **1968–69**: 409n.
  Antipoverty program, **1963–64**: 91 (p. 114),
    120, 124 (p. 166), 132 (pp. 176, 184),
    314, 316 [28]; **1965**: 32 (p. 93), 208
    [13]; **1967**: 297 [10]; **1968–69**: 173
  Appalachian area, economic development,
    1963–64: 711
  Arts and humanities, support of, **1965**: 534;
    1968–69: 686
  Beautification programs, **1965**: 2, 54, 277, 446,
    545
  Boat safety, **1968–69**: 56
  Civil defense, **1968–69**: 196
  Civil rights enforcement, **1963–64**: 330, 446,
    462 [5], 792; **1966**: 59; **1967**: 55
  College education, **1963–64**: 482; **1968–69**: 406
  Community development, **1963–64**: 152, 757;
    1965: 47, 103, 132, 493; **1967**: 372
  Consumer protection, **1966**: 140, 307
  Creative federalism, **1966**: 34 (p. 98), 416,
    606, 607 [1]; **1967**: 13 (p. 57), 296
  Crime control, **1967**: 3 (p. 6), 35, 222
  Crime eradication, **1963–64**: 523
  Cropland conversion, **1965**: 168

Federal-State-local government — *continued*
  Development planning coordination, **1966**: 425
  Disaster relief, **1965**: 174, 191, 605; **1966**: 145,
    584
  Domestic programs, **1968–69**: 678 (p. 1302)
  Draft rejectees, training and rehabilitation,
    1963–64: 336 [2]
  Drug control, **1963–64**: 179; **1968–69**: 60
  Economic, **1963–64**: 521 [2, 4]; **1966**: 34
    (p. 98), 477 [2]; **1967**: 576
  Economic growth, **1963–64**: 745
  Education, **1963–64**: 709, 754; **1965**: 340,
    527; **1966**: 95; **1967**: 77, 117
  Emergency preparedness, **1968–69**: 196
  Employee exchange and training, **1968–69**: 84,
    100, 678 (p. 1303)
  Employment, **1968–69**: 406, 444
  Family planning services, **1968–69**: 393
  Firearms control, **1965**: 102
  Fiscal policies, **1963–64**: 730
  Flood control, **1966**: 374
  Food stamp program, **1968–69**: 684 (p. 1324)
  Government employees, training, **1968–69**: 667
  Health programs, **1963–64**: 798; **1966**: 95, 157,
    169, 185; **1967**: 77; **1968–69**: 39 (p.
    103), 111, 678 (p. 1296)
  Highway safety, **1965**: 460; **1966**: 98, 449
  Housing, **1968–69**: 87
  Indian education, **1968–69**: 113
  Industrial waste disposal, **1963–64**: 578
  Interstate highway system, **1963–64**: 512
  Labor-management relations, **1963–64**: 729
  Law enforcement, **1963–64**: 462 [10], 468,
    475 [15], 563 [9], 600, 603, 655;
    1965: 102, 117 [1, 5], 526; **1966**: 26
    (p. 64), 116, 204, 491, 492 [1], 526,
    598, 611; **1967**: 297 [7], 382; **1968–
    69**: 14 (p. 30), 39 (p. 107), 50, 57, 59,
    100, 320, 325, 542, 553, 557 [8], 676
    (p. 1266), 678 (pp. 1281, 1291)
  Management improvement, **1966**: 26 (p. 66)
  Manpower development, **1966**: 536; **1967**: 16
    (p. 83), 199
  Model cities, **1968–69**: 406
  Natural resources development, **1965**: 32 (p.
    96)
  Occupational training and employment, **1963–
    64**: 99; **1965**: 32 (p. 96), 38, 207, 268,
    322, 416, 438, 490; **1968–69**: 6, 39 (p.
    108), 47 (p. 142)
  Older persons, **1965**: 354; **1967**: 296
  Pollution control, **1966**: 26 (p. 62), 34 (p.
    106), 82, 91, 392, 574; **1967**: 20;
    1968–69: 122
  Preschool education, **1968–69**: 678 (p. 1293)
  Public welfare, **1963–64**: 213; **1965**: 425, 492,
    501
  Recreation programs, **1966**: 352
  Recreational facilities, **1963–64**: 422; **1965**: 521

Federal-State-local government – *continued*
Rural development, **1966**: 6 (p. 5); **1967**: 114
School desegregation, **1965**: 470
School lunch program, **1966**: 340
Staffing of international organizations, assistance, **1963-64**: 519
Surface mining, regulation, **1968-69**: 39 (p. 102)
Transportation, **1963-64**: 453; **1966**: 98
Unemployment insurance, **1965**: 425; **1966**: 318
Urban development, **1966**: 26 (p. 62), 30, 302
Urban mass transportation, **1968-69**: 351
Urban renewal, **1963-64**: 693; **1965**: 32 (p. 93), 90, 510
Vaccination programs, **1965**: 406
Veterans' employment, **1967**: 345
Vocational rehabilitation, **1963-64**: 179
Voting rights, equal opportunity to exercise, **1965**: 108
Water resources, **1966**: 138, 481; **1968-69**: 593, 600
Water shortage and pollution control, **1965**: 54, 358, 375, 418, 434, 543
Youth Opportunity Campaign, **1965**: 298
Federal-State-local relations, **1966**: 121 [2, 6], 122 [2], 124 [3], 217, 273, 418, 428, 483; **1967**: 3 (p. 4), 11, 13 (pp. 57-58), 121, 123-125, 148, 223 [1, 7, 8, 12], 234, 297 [5], 458; **1968-69**: 39 (p. 110), 84, 102, 438n., 539
Federal-State Partnership for Health program, **1968-69**: 678 (p. 1296)
Federal-State Regional Commission, **1963-64**: 300
Federal surplus property, **1965**: 14, 54, 277
Transfer to States, **1963-64**: 422, 534
Federal system of government, **1967**: 13 (p. 58); **1968-69**: 539
Federal Task Force on Community Assistance, proposed, **1965**: 493n.
Federal Tort Claims Act, **1966**: 335n.
Federal Trade Commission, **1963-64**: 80, 173; **1966**: 140; **1967**: 518 [2]; **1968-69**: 14 (p. 29), 56, 684 (p. 1322)
Chairman (Paul Rand Dixon), **1963-64**: 701; **1968-69**: 56
Federal Voting Assistance Act of 1955, amendments, **1968-69**: 314
Federal Wage Board, **1966**: 630 [8]
Coordination of, **1965**: 612
Federal Water Pollution Control Administration, **1966**: 82, 88 [4], 91, 111, 215, 232, 428; **1967**: 13 (pp. 51, 57); **1968-69**: 39 (p. 109), 678 (p. 1301)
Federal Water Research Program (1966), **1965**: 275
Federal Woman's Award, **1965**: 91; **1966**: 89; **1967**: 93; **1968-69**: 138
Study Group, **1967**: 95

Federalism, creative, **1966**: 34 (p. 98), 416, 606, 607 [1]; **1967**: 13 (p. 57), 296
Federalist Papers, **1966**: 21
Federalists, **1968-69**: 109
Federation of Aeronautics, International, **1965**: 219
Federation of Commercial, Clerical, and Technical Employees, International, **1967**: 442
Federation of Independent Business, National, **1965**: 438
Federation of Teachers, American, **1965**: 539
Fee, George, **1963-64**: 679
Feed grains, **1963-64**: 132 (p. 187), 757; **1965**: 168; **1966**: 281, 608; **1967**: 13 (p. 50); **1968-69**: 94, 247
Feighan, Repr. Michael A., **1963-64**: 97, 405, 406, 642; **1965**: 190, 546
Feinberg, Abraham, **1963-64**: 175; **1965**: 44, 273
Feldman, Myer, **1963-64**: 246 [13]; **1965**: 22 [1], 273
Fellowship Advisory Board, Urban Studies, **1967**: 359
Fellowships and scholarships, **1963-64**: 601; **1965**: 2, 6, 9, 100, 340, 368, 369, 374, 479, 514, 603; **1966**: 26 (p. 63), 45, 486; **1967**: 1, 13 (p. 55), 148, 217, 359, 451, 490; **1968-69**: 66, 84, 113, 214n., 442, 447, 453, 459, 687
Felt, Adm. Harry D., **1963-64**: 454
Fenoaltea, Sergio, **1963-64**: 149n., 651n.; **1965**: 82; **1966**: 478, 513
Ferency, Zoltan A., **1966**: 431
Fergerstrom, Robert, **1963-64**: 60n.
Ferguson, Clarence C., **1965**: 366
Ferguson, James E., **1966**: 417 [4]
Ferguson, Mrs. Miriam A., **1963-64**: 374
Ferguson, Rev. Robert R., **1963-64**: 579
Ferguson, Thomas C., **1963-64**: 544n.
Fergusson, Sir Bernard (Governor-General of New Zealand), **1966**: 539, 540n.
Fergusson, Lady, **1966**: 539
Fermi, Enrico, **1965**: 449; **1967**: 391
Fermi, Mrs. Enrico, **1967**: 515
Fernandez, Sp4c. Daniel, **1967**: 166
Fernandez, Mr. and Mrs. Jose I., **1967**: 166
Fertilizer, foreign assistance, **1968-69**: 679
Fertilizer prices, **1963-64**: 352
FHA.
See Federal Housing Administration.
Fiber, Committee on Food and, **1965**: 597
Fiber, National Advisory Commission on Food and, **1965**: 597; **1966**: 26 (p. 59); **1967**: 525
Fiber Policy, Commission on U.S. Food and, proposed, **1965**: 47
Fiber production, **1967**: 305

Fiber Products Identification Act, **1966**: 576
Field, Mrs. Marshall, **1963–64**: 211 [7]; **1965**: 273
Field installations, reduction of, **1963–64**: 462 [2]
Fields, Alvin G., **1963–64**: 694
Fields, Kenneth E., **1965**: 400
Fields, Maj. Gen. Lewis J., **1967**: 485 [3]
Figueres, José, **1965**: 221
File cabinet purchases, Government, **1966**: 58n.
Film Institute, American, proposed, **1965**: 534
Finan, Thomas B., **1963–64**: 320, 321, 703
Finance, Senate Committee on, **1967**: 137n.; **1968–69**: 160, 651
Finance Corporation, International, **1966**: 94
Financial Institutions Supervisory Act of 1966, **1966**: 530, 582
Financial Problems, National Advisory Council on International Monetary and, **1965**: 110, 282
Finch, Robert H., **1968–69**: 657
Findley, Repr. Paul, **1963–64**: 201 [14]
Fine Arts, Commission on, **1963–64**: 700
Fine Arts, National Collection of, **1966**: 227; **1968–69**: 225
Finkelstein, Jerry, **1963–64**: 751
Finland, **1965**: 1, 491
　　Urho Kekkonen, **1963–64**: 564
Fire Island National Seashore, New York, **1965**: 521; **1966**: 518; **1968–69**: 122, 547, 601
　　Bill, **1963–64**: 554n.
Fire prevention, **1966**: 376n.
Fire Research and Safety Act of 1968, **1968–69**: 14 (p. 29), 56, 105
Fire safety, **1968–69**: 56, 105
　　Bill, **1967**: 57, 342
Firearms control, **1966**: 116, 364, 373 [14], 526; **1967**: 3 (p. 7), 35, 71, 326, 353, 382, 385, 468, 482, 560, 575; **1968–69**: 14 (p. 30), 59, 87, 235, 257, 263, 293, 296, 298, 302, 316, 320, 324, 325, 333, 339 [3], 355, 356, 358, 406, 530, 553, 557 [8], 678 (p. 1292), 696 [16]
　　District of Columbia, **1968–69**: 133
　　Legislation.
　　　　See Gun Control Act of 1968; Omnibus Crime Control and Safe Streets Act of 1968.
　　Message to Congress, **1968–69**: 334
　　Need for, **1965**: 70, 102
Firemen
　　District of Columbia, **1968–69**: 272
　　Pay, Washington, D.C., **1966**: 27
　　Veterans as, **1968–69**: 40, 419
Firmage, Edwin B., **1965**: 334n.
1st Air Cavalry, **1966**: 348
1st Cavalry Division (Airmobile), **1967**: 384, 407
1st Infantry Division, **1966**: 348

1st Squadron, 4th Cavalry, 1st Infantry Division, **1967**: 226
Fiscal and monetary policy, U.S., **1963–64**: 105, 120, 124 (pp. 157, 160, 161), 139, 182, 196, 197, 218 [17], 299, 307, 472, 506, 589, 617, 689, 775, 787; **1965**: 32, 35, 60, 255, 297, 638; **1966**: 17, 26 (pp. 49–54), 34 (pp. 97, 101, 104, 107), 83, 88 [20], 108, 141 [3], 333, 336, 379, 445 [18], 473, 486, 494 [4, 12]; **1967**: 63, 88, 121, 371, 420, 497, 524, 556; **1968–69**: 1 [8], 2, 38, 46, 90, 170, 229, 241, 283 [8], 326, 343, 350, 612, 632, 684 (pp. 1312, 1314–1316, 1318)
　　Cabinet meeting on, **1966**: 379
　　Campaign remarks, **1963–64**: 630, 640, 654, 679, 742
　　End of Vietnam conflict, planning for, **1968–69**: 684 (p. 1318)
　　International reserves, **1967**: 519, 545; **1968–69**: 136, 146, 170, 218, 684 (p. 1319)
　　Message to Congress, **1963–64**: 132; **1966**: 444; **1967**: 13, 16; **1968–69**: 39, 47, 646 [3, 14], 654, 658, 678, 684
　　News conference remarks, **1963–64**: 71 [2, 10, 11, 16], 256 [13], 455 [13], 780 [3]
　　Statements on, **1963–64**: 707, 708, 714, 722–724, 730, 731, 739, 740; **1966**: 477 [2]
Fischer, John H., **1966**: 210n.
Fish, Rabbi Judah, **1965**: 623n.
Fish
　　Protein concentrates, **1967**: 33, 101, 176; **1968–69**: 63, 124, 692
　　Safety, **1968–69**: 14 (p. 30), 56, 105, 390
Fish Protein Concentrate Act, **1966**: 568, 569; **1967**: 101ftn. (p. 298)
Fish and wildlife resources, **1965**: 54
Fisher, Adrian S., **1968–69**: 14 (p. 26), 73
Fisher, Maj. and Mrs. Bernard F., **1967**: 9
Fisher, Joseph Jefferson, **1968–69**: 109
Fisher, Sterling W., **1965**: 378
Fisheries of the North Pacific Ocean, International Convention for the High Seas, **1963–64**: 559; **1965**: 15
Fisheries resources, **1965**: 92; **1966**: 569
Fishing agreement, United States-Mexico, **1967**: 451
Fishing in territorial waters of United States, **1968–69**: 412
　　Prohibition, **1963–64**: 353
Fishtrap Dam, Ky., dedication, **1968–69**: 565
Fisk, Dr. James B., **1965**: 344n.; **1967**: 416n.
Fissionable materials, **1966**: 32
　　Private ownership of, **1963–64**: 538
　　Production decrease, **1963–64**: 91 (p. 117), 122, 129, 130, 131, 132 (p. 185), 272, 285 [3], 287, 294 [14], 295, 395, 434, 435, 486 [1, 2], 562, 642, 820; **1965**: 20, 196, 537

Fitch, William C., **1965**: 642n.
FitzGerald, Desmond, **1967**: 383
FitzGerald, Mrs. Desmond, **1967**: 383
Fitzgerald, F. Scott, **1963–64**: 208
Fitzhugh, Gilbert W., **1967**: 380; **1968–69**: 471n.
Flag, postage stamp of history, **1968–69**: 321
Flag, U.S., **1965**: 95
Flag of battle, presentation to the President, **1963–64**: 119
Flajnik, Bruno, **1966**: 272
Flaming Gorge National Recreation Area, Utah-Wyoming, **1965**: 54; **1966**: 82; **1968–69**: 505, 547
Flammable fabric safety, **1968–69**: 545
Flammable Fabrics Act amendments, **1967**: 57, 342, 393, 465, 534, 539; **1968–69**: 14 (p. 29)
Flanagan, Rev. E. J., **1965**: 242
Flanagan, Capt. William R., **1968–69**: 81 [3]
Flannagan, Bishop Bernard J., **1963–64**: 396
Flat Tops Wilderness, Colo., **1968–69**: 122, 168
Flathead Tunnel, Montana, opening, **1968–69**: 330
Fleming, Msgr. E. J., **1963–64**: 190n.
Fleming, Joe W., II, **1968–69**: 58
Fleming, Robert H., **1966**: 65 [2], 88 [13], 207n., 209n., 211n., 356n.; **1967**: 518 [7]
Fleming, Thomas F., **1963–64**: 709, 712, 713
Flemming, Arthur S., **1963–64**: 513; **1966**: 184n.
Fletcher, Thomas W., **1967**: 377, 406, 411 [1], 466; **1968–69**: 698
Fletcher, Mrs. Thomas W., **1967**: 406
Flint River Basin, Ga., **1963–64**: 716
Flood, Repr. Daniel J., **1963–64**: 661
Flood control, **1963–64**: 132 (p. 187), 134, 135, 193, 217, 391, 578, 597, 599, 645, 650, 729, 756; **1965**: 186, 193, 275, 477; **1966**: 427, 593; **1967**: 31n., 120, 303, 329, 408 [5]; **1968–69**: 330, 565
Floods, **1967**: 300; **1968–69**: 593
  Alaska, **1967**: 369; **1968–69**: 98
  California, **1965**: 74, 477
  Chile, **1965**: 431
  Colorado, **1965**: 319 [20]
  Costa Rica, **1963–64**: 438, 443
  Italy, **1966**: 591
  Mexico-United States Cooperation, **1967**: 303, 408, 447, 449, 451
  Midwestern States, **1965**: 187, 188, 189, 190, 191, 193, 215, 239, 477
  Minnesota, **1965**: 187, 189, 193, 239
  Mississippi Delta, **1965**: 592
  Montana, **1963–64**: 573
  Ohio River Basin, **1963–64**: 217
  Oregon, **1965**: 74
  Pacific Northwest, **1965**: 317, 477

Floods — *continued*
  Texas, **1966**: 401 [7]
  Victims, assistance, **1966**: 381
Florence Agreement (Agreement on the Importation of Educational, Scientific, and Cultural Materials), **1965**: 292, 604; **1966**: 45, 519, 601
Florida, **1963–64**: 710
  Campaign remarks, **1963–64**: 571, 709, 712, 713
  Candidates for public office, **1963–64**: 712
  Cross-state barge canal, ground breaking, **1963–64**: 198
  Gov. Farris Bryant, **1963–64**: 12, 198, 199, 567, 571, 709, 710n., 712, 713, 719
  Gov. Haydon Burns, **1965**: 248; **1966**: 494 [1]
  Hurricane relief, **1963–64**: 563 [4], 567; **1965**: 605
  Wilderness preservation, **1968–69**: 547
Florida Atlantic University, dedication, **1963–64**: 709
Flowers, J. G., **1963–64**: 778
Fluorspar stockpile, **1966**: 218
Flynt, Repr. John J., Jr., **1963–64**: 330, 716, 718
FNMA.
  See Federal National Mortgage Association.
Fogarty, John A., **1967**: 420n.
Fogarty, Repr. John E., **1963–64**: 174, 601; **1965**: 354, 401, 406, 410, 551; **1966**: 49, 334 [6]; **1967**: 3 (p. 2), 39; **1968–69**: 408
  Death, **1967**: 2
Fogarty International Center for Advanced Study in the Health Sciences, **1967**: 217; **1968–69**: 408
Folcarelli, John, **1966**: 396
Foley, Edward H., **1966**: 403; **1968–69**: 694
Foley, Eugene P. (Small Business Administrator), **1963–64**: 217, 362, 434, 531; **1965**: 270, 448 [5], 452, 454 [5]; **1966**: 410, 413, 415, 501 [1]
Foley, Capt. Robert F., **1968–69**: 221
Foley, Repr. Thomas S., **1966**: 269
Folliard, Edward T., **1963–64**: 246 [17]
Follow Through, **1967**: 13 (p. 54), 16 (p. 85), 39, 55, 77, 114; **1968–69**: 39 (p. 104), 54, 678 (p. 1293), 684 (p. 1324)
  See also Project Head Start.
Folsom, Marion B., **1963–64**: 211 [6], 666; **1965**: 32ftn. (p. 96), 410, 522n., 594n., **1966**: 185
Fong, Sen. Hiram L., **1965**: 413, 449, 568n.; **1967**: 555; **1968–69**: 197, 198
Fontanne, Lynn, **1963–64**: 568
Food, **1968–69**: 625, 631
  See also Agriculture and agricultural programs.
  Assistance programs, **1968–69**: 678 (p. 1297)

Food — *continued*
  Consumer protection, **1963–64**: 173, 179, 242
    [10]; **1965**: 5; **1966**: 140; **1968–69**: 14
    (p. 31), 336, 684 (p. 1322)
    See also specific food.
  Developing nations, **1967**: 13 (p. 49), 33, 272;
    1968–69: 47 (p. 138), 176, 679, 692
  India, **1967**: 44, 63; **1968–69**: 691
  Marine resources, **1967**: 20, 101, 491; **1968–
    69**: 63, 124, 692
  Marketing programs, **1963–64**: 455 [7]; **1965**:
    47; 1966: 26 (p. 59), 294
  National bank, **1968–69**: 94, 142, 155, 247,
    534
  Needy and unemployed persons, **1963–64**:
    67, 690n., 732, 757; **1965**: 47, 453;
    1966: 245, 515
    Stamp program, **1963–64**: 91 (p. 114), 219,
      225, 235, 242 [12], 249, 266 [21],
      267, 268, 297, 305, 314, 434, 546, 598,
      620, 634, 757; **1965**: 47, 492; **1966**:
      245, 520; **1967**: 63, 353, 405; **1968–69**:
      39 (p. 105), 94, 519, 678 (p. 1297),
      684 (p. 1324), 696 [14]
  New uses, proposed, **1963–64**: 344
  Ocean resources, **1965**: 92; **1966**: 326, 461
  Overseas distribution, **1963–64**: 91 (p. 117),
    344, 546, 641, 662n.; **1965**: 18, 47,
    139, 149, 172, 199, 223, 227, 246, 286,
    293, 295 [16]; **1966**: 6 (p. 3), 11, 22,
    26 (p. 59), 41, 52 [1], 62, 63, 153, 164,
    166, 180, 308, 343, 355, 441, 504, 509,
    569; **1967**: 3 (p. 11), 33, 44, 63, 153,
    156, 157, 228, 264 [19], 271, 287, 423,
    469, 476, 496, 525; **1968–69**: 14 (p.
    27), 29, 39 (p. 100), 94, 142, 176, 417,
    462, 691
  Prices, **1965**: 47, 168, 597; **1966**: 141 [3],
    155, 399, 403, 413, 635 [18]; **1967**:
    3 (p. 8), 63, 228; **1968–69**: 94
  Production, **1963–64**: 352; **1966**: 461, 509,
    520, 545, 608; **1967**: 13 (p. 49), 63,
    271, 305, 448, 476, 496, 554 [12];
    1968–69: 63, 622, 679, 696 [14]
  Protein fortification, **1966**: 569; **1967**: 33,
    101, 176
  Radioactivity in, **1963–64**: 653n., 675n.
  Research, **1966**: 461; **1967**: 449n.
  School programs, **1963–64**: 292; **1965**: 47;
    1966: 26 (p. 63), 95, 340, 508, 520;
    1967: 39, 63, 228, 353
  Surplus, **1963–64**: 292; **1965**: 47, 139, 149;
    1966: 52 [1], 62, 164, 550, 608; **1967**:
    469
  World needs, **1967**: 448, 449, 469, 476; **1968–
    69**: 21, 47 (p. 138), 63, 467 [9], 500,
    696 [12]

Food, Drug and Cosmetic Act, Federal, **1963–64**:
    173, 179; **1965**: 5
Food and Agriculture Act of 1965, **1965**: 597;
    1966: 26 (p. 59), 154, 203, 281, 355,
    403; **1967**: 156, 228; **1968–69**: 94, 142,
    155, 247, 390, 462, 534
Food and Agriculture Organization of the United
    Nations, **1966**: 94, 153; **1967**: 33
Food Aid Convention, **1968–69**: 29
Food and Drug Administration, **1963–64**: 132
    (p. 189), 173; **1965**: 5, 202, 361; **1966**:
    4, 140, 225, 307; **1967**: 35, 57, 77,
    214n., 215
Food and Fiber, Committee on, **1965**: 597
Food and Fiber, National Advisory Commission
    on, **1965**: 597; **1966**: 26 (p. 59); **1967**:
    525
Food and Fiber Policy, Commission on U.S.,
    proposed, **1965**: 47
Food for freedom bill.
    See Food for Peace Act of 1966.
Food for freedom program, **1966**: 26 (p. 58), 45,
    62, 63, 308, 417 [5, 6], 441, 461, 504,
    515, 528, 608, 630 [4]; **1967**: 33, 63,
    264 [19]; **1968–69**: 14 (p. 27), 29, 39
    (p. 99), 63, 94, 142, 176, 417, 462, 529
Food Fund, Agricultural, **1967**: 33
Food industry, message to Congress, **1963–64**:
    242 [10]
Food Marketing, National Commission on, **1963–
    64**: 455 [7]; **1965**: 567; **1966**: 294
Food Panel, World, report foreword, **1967**: 271
Food for Peace Act of 1966, **1966**: 62, 63, 433,
    608; **1967**: 157; **1968–69**: 47 (p. 138),
    142
Food for peace program, **1963–64**: 124 (p. 162),
    132 (p. 187), 546, 627, 634, 641, 757;
    1965: 18, 47, 139, 149, 257, 377, 569
Food program, world, **1965**: 149
Food Stamp Act of 1964, **1965**: 492; **1968–69**:
    94
  Amendments, **1967**: 405; **1968–69**: 390, 519
  Approval, **1963–64**: 546
Foot-and-mouth disease (rinderpest) prevention,
    1968–69: 364
Football, **1967**: 480
Football Coaches Association, American, **1966**: 7
Foote, Emerson, **1963–64**: 211 [6]
Forand, Aime J., **1965**: 348, 354, 394, 410
Ford, Frederick W., **1963–64**: 336 [7]; **1965**:
    126
Ford, Repr. Gerald R., Jr., **1963–64**: 14, 15;
    1965: 45n., 353 [18], 448 [12],
    463ftn. (p. 950); **1966**: 188 [5], 277
    [23], 334 [1], 628 [7, 14]; **1967**: 7,
    236, 495 [9], 502; **1968–69**: 655, 658,
    676 (p. 1270)
Ford, Henry, **1966**: 403

Ford, Henry, II, **1963-64**: 294 [23], 299, 356,
    431n., 455 [13], 745; **1968-69**: 24, 25,
    37, 86, 92, 100, 105, 114, 115, 141,
    227, 328n., 498, 549, 672n.
Ford, Mrs. Henry, II, **1968-69**: 672n.
Ford, Bishop Louis H., **1966**: 228
Ford, Wendell, **1968-69**: 565
Ford, Repr. William D., **1963-64**: 745; **1965**:
    592; **1966**: 431
Ford Foundation, **1963-64**: 451n., 537; **1965**:
    70; **1966**: 551; **1967**: 375 [17], 449n.;
    1968-69: 686
Ford Motor Company, **1963-64**: 587 [9], 745;
    1966: 474 [3]; **1968-69**: 549
Foreign affairs, **1963-64**: 42, 71 [7]; **1965**: 185
Foreign Affairs, House Committee on, **1967**:
    195, 358 [10], 375 [16]; **1968-69**:
    394, 395
Foreign Affairs, Panel of Consultants on, **1963-
    64**: 696
Foreign Agricultural Service, **1966**: 308n.
Foreign Aid, Advisory Committee on Private
    Enterprise in, **1963-64**: 227; **1965**: 18,
    450; **1966**: 41
Foreign aid bill, **1965**: 208 [17], 294n., 448
    [19], 495, 502
Foreign Aid and Related Agencies Appropriation
    Act, **1963-64**: 45n., 240
Foreign assistance, **1963-64**: 91 (p. 112), 124
    (p. 162), 189, 280, 344, 394n., 435,
    546, 607, 634, 641, 662, 695, 702, 722,
    737; **1965**: 22 [11], 26, 32 (p. 90), 35
    (pp. 107, 111, 112), 77, 142, 149, 319
    [8], 357, 406, 476, 495, 541, 570;
    1966: 42, 63, 246, 247 [1, 15], 368,
    469, 497, 504; **1967**: 44, 157, 401, 423,
    469, 489, 524; **1968-69**: 39 (p. 99), 47
    (p. 133), 143, 394, 395, 524, 678 (p.
    1280), 684 (pp. 1319, 1321)
    See also Economic assistance; Military, U.S.;
    Technical assistance to developing
    nations; *specific countries.*
Afghanistan, **1967**: 143n., 144n.
Africa, **1963-64**: 45, 227, 617; **1965**: 7, 18,
    136; **1966**: 45, 243; **1968-69**: 63, 524
Appropriations, **1963-64**: 45, 48, 218 [33],
    227; **1965**: 7, 18, 60, 638; **1966**: 26
    (p. 58), 88 [16], 445 [11], 492 [9];
    1967: 375 [16], 417 [1], 489, 495
    [12]; **1968-69**: 676 (p. 1268)
Argentina, **1963-64**: 269
Asia, South Asia, and Southeast Asia, **1963-64**:
    45, 186, 227, 379 [1], 420 [1], 597,
    617, 662n., 675, 686, 693, 797; **1965**:
    7, 18, 26, 106 [4], 130, 136, 172, 176
    [1, 3], 179, 199, 208 [17], 227, 229,
    294, 295 [3], 357, 628; **1966**: 11n.,
    18, 26 (p. 58), 133, 420; **1967**: 13 (pp.

Foreign assistance – *continued*
    Asia – *continued*
        46, 48), 44; **1968-69**: 39 (pp. 91, 99),
        63, 170, 524, 678 (pp. 1273, 1274)
    Bolivia, **1963-64**: 340; **1968-69**: 21
    Brazil, **1963-64**: 340; **1966**: 11n.; **1968-69**:
        63, 679
    Business participation in, **1963-64**: 227, 402,
        617; **1965**: 18, 154
    Central America, **1968-69**: 63, 363-366, 368
    Chile, **1963-64**: 227; **1966**: 11n.; **1968-69**: 63,
        679
    China, Republic of, **1965**: 7; **1966**: 41, 368;
        1967: 219; **1968-69**: 63, 176
    Colombia, **1963-64**: 227, 340; **1968-69**: 63,
        679
    Cyprus, **1963-64**: 210
    Denmark, **1963-64**: 394n.
    Developing and new nations, **1963-64**: 45, 51,
        76, 91 (p. 117), 124 (pp. 162, 166),
        132 (p. 185), 227, 280, 361, 400, 482n.,
        483, 617, 702; **1965**: 7, 15, 18, 32 (p.
        90), 35 (pp. 107, 112), 47, 117 [3],
        136, 139, 149, 169, 172, 176 [1, 3],
        194, 203, 294, 450, 495, 660; **1966**:
        6 (pp. 3, 7-8), 11, 22, 26 (pp. 58, 60),
        34 (pp. 103, 105), 41, 45, 52 [1], 62,
        154, 243, 331, 343-344, 368, 406, 420,
        441, 608; **1967**: 16 (p. 80), 271, 442,
        491, 519; **1968-69**: 39 (p. 99), 47 (pp.
        130, 138), 176, 524, 676 (p. 1268), 679
    Dominican Republic, **1965**: 217, 221, 223,
        227, 253, 286, 293, 295 [16], 484;
        1966: 320 [6]; **1968-69**: 679
    Economic impact in U.S., **1967**: 16 (p. 81)
    Embargo on countries trading with North
        Vietnam, **1966**: 441
    Ethiopia, **1968-69**: 21
    Europe, **1963-64**: 617; **1965**: 235; **1966**: 6
        (p. 7); **1968-69**: 63, 143, 524
    Foreign aid bill, **1963-64**: 11, 54 [17], 71
        [14], 379ftn. (p. 734), 455 [16]
    Greece, **1963-64**: 424n.; **1966**: 6 (p. 7), 41;
        1967: 44, 107, 108, 158; **1968-69**: 63
    Guyana, **1966**: 341
    India, **1963-64**: 227, 379 [17]; **1966**: 11n.,
        41, 52 [1], 152-54, 164, 166, 180, 247
        [7]; **1967**: 3 (p. 10), 44, 153; **1968-69**:
        39 (p. 99), 63, 417, 679
    Indonesia, **1966**: 501 [8]; **1968-69**: 63, 679
    Interdepartmental committee to review, **1963-
        64**: 69
    International cooperation, **1963-64**: 227;
        1965: 15, 18, 169, 172, 176 [1, 3],
        194, 203, 495
    Iran, **1966**: 41; **1967**: 509; **1968-69**: 63, 524,
        679

Foreign assistance – *continued*
  Israel, **1963-64**: 377, 378, 380; **1965**: 117 [6];
      1968-69: 63, 176, 524
  Italy, **1968-69**: 176
  Japan, **1966**: 368; **1968-69**: 176
  Jordan, **1963-64**: 227; **1965**: 18; **1966**: 11n.
  Korea, **1963-64**: 150 [6], 227; **1965**: 18, 254,
      257; **1966**: 11n., 41; **1967**: 44, 113,
      563; **1968-69**: 63, 176, 201, 524, 679
  Laos, **1963-64**: 227; **1965**: 18, 26, 294; **1966**:
      11n.; **1968-69**: 63
  Latin America, **1963-64**: 45, 71 [5, 9], 227,
      272, 340, 617, 662n., 769; **1965**: 7, 18,
      136, 139, 149; **1966**: 125, 175, 386;
      1967: 44, 152, 173, 175, 176, 357;
      1968-69: 39 (pp. 91, 99), 63, 365, 524
  Malagasy Republic, **1963-64**: 483
  Malaysia, **1963-64**: 471, 474, 797
  Messages to Congress, **1963-64**: 227, 348, 617;
      1965: 18; **1966**: 11, 41; **1967**: 44, 45;
      1968-69: 21, 63, 679
  Middle East and Near East, **1963-64**: 797;
      1967: 264 [10]; **1968-69**: 63
  Multilateral, **1968-69**: 63, 684 (p. 1321)
  Nicaragua, **1963-64**: 227; **1968-69**: 679
  Nigeria, **1963-64**: 227; **1966**: 11n., 41; **1968-
      69**: 21, 433, 482, 679
  Pakistan, **1963-64**: 227; **1965**: 649; **1966**:
      11n., 41; **1967**: 3 (p. 10), 44; **1968-69**:
      39 (p. 99), 63, 679
  Panama, **1963-64**: 285 [6]; **1968-69**: 679
  Peru, **1963-64**: 227, 340
  Philippines, **1963-64**: 627; **1966**: 461; **1968-
      69**: 63, 176, 679
  Poland, **1966**: 528
  Policy change, **1965**: 136
  Policy study, **1963-64**: 71 [9]
  Private organizations, participation, **1963-64**:
      617; **1965**: 7, 18, 450, 484; **1966**: 11
  Reduction, **1963-64**: 71 [16], 462 [2]; **1968-
      69**: 11, 684 (p. 1319)
  Reorganization of program, proposed, **1963-
      64**: 48, 69
  Ryukyu Islands, **1965**: 15
  Self-help, **1967**: 44; **1968-69**: 14 (p. 27), 63
  Ship loan program, **1965**: 600
  Spain, **1968-69**: 176
  Taiwan, **1968-69**: 524
  Thailand, **1963-64**: 476; **1965**: 294; **1966**: 41;
      1968-69: 63, 237, 679
  Tunisia, **1966**: 11n.
  Turkey, **1963-64**: 227; **1966**: 6 (p. 7), 11n.,
      41; **1967**: 44, 158, 162; **1968-69**: 63
  Upper Volta, Republic of, **1965**: 144, 250;
      1966: 45
  Venezuela, **1968-69**: 63
  Vietnam, **1963-64**: 83, 150 [6], 192, 201 [5],
      211 [33], 218 [24], 223, 227, 246 [4],

Foreign assistance – *continued*
  Vietnam – *continued*
      272, 280 [8], 285 [12], 379 [1, 19],
      400, 420 [1], 436n., 511, 591, 627,
      652, 662, 693, 780ftn. (p. 1616), 793,
      797; **1965**: 2, 18, 51, 106 [4], 117 [2,
      8], 130, 145, 152, 156 [11], 172, 194,
      206, 208 [2, 14, 16, 20], 227, 229, 230,
      234, 246, 250, 254, 257, 261, 276, 294,
      295 [3], 316, 388 [1, 2, 5, 11, 14],
      476, 551n., 588; **1967**: 13 (p. 49), 44
    See also main entry, Vietnam.
    Message to Congress, **1963-64**: 348
  Vietnam, South.
    See main entry, Vietnam, South.
Foreign Assistance Act of 1961, **1965**: 18; **1966**:
      18n.
Foreign Assistance Act of 1963, **1963-64**: 48,
      227
Foreign Assistance Act of 1965, **1965**: 294n.,
      502
    See also Foreign aid bill.
    Approval, **1965**: 495
Foreign Assistance Act of 1966, **1966**: 41n., 469
Foreign Assistance Act of 1967, **1967**: 44n., 489
Foreign Assistance Act of 1968, **1968-69**: 63,
      394, 395, 524n.
Foreign Assistance Programs, General Advisory
      Committee on, **1965**: 136
Foreign Assistance and Related Agencies
      Appropriation Act, 1966, approval,
      1965: 570
Foreign Claims Settlement Commission, **1963-
      64**: 684
Foreign currencies, **1965**: 110, 149
Foreign editors, **1968-69**: 177
Foreign Intelligence, President's Advisory Board
      on, **1966**: 320 [2]; **1968-69**: 18 [2]
Foreign investments, regulation, **1968-69**: 1 [1,
      15], 2
Foreign Investors Tax Act of 1966, **1966**: 612;
      1968-69: 2
Foreign language newspaper publishers, remarks
      to, **1963-64**: 496
Foreign language press, **1968-69**: 162
Foreign leaders.
    See Joint statements with foreign leaders;
      Messages to foreign leaders; Visitors,
      foreign leaders.
Foreign ministers meetings
    Inter-American meeting, Washington, D.C.,
      1963-64: 455 [18], 475 [3, 13], 561
    North Atlantic Council, **1963-64**: 28ftn.
      (p. 34)
    North Atlantic Treaty Organization, **1963-64**:
      316 [27]
Foreign Policy, National Conference on, **1963-
      64**: 280

Foreign policy, U.S., **1963–64**: 11, 37, 189, 192, 218 [2, 14, 28, 29], 227, 244, 272, 295, 346, 529, 533, 596, 616, 638, 641, 689, 788; **1965**: 2, 18, 26, 27, 136, 139, 142, 169, 179, 185, 198, 233, 285, 286, 289, 299, 302, 305, 329, 330, 346, 430, 436, 450, 495, 516, 519; **1966**: 14, 26 (p. 48), 86, 153, 158 [2], 216–217, 261, 273, 312, 320 [13], 346, 349, 353, 368, 379, 388, 392, 395, 406–407, 414, 417 [12], 431, 441, 446, 469, 480, 497–498, 503, 525, 528, 542; **1967**: 3 (p. 9), 46, 169, 261, 425, 442, 464, 484, 495 [14], 519; **1968–69**: 39 (p. 83), 50, 132, 143, 162, 176, 249, 250n., 394, 395, 439, 472, 479, 529, 581, 598, 599, 603, 611

Africa, **1966**: 414; **1967**: 3 (p. 9); **1968–69**: 249, 255

Asia, South Asia, and Southeast Asia, **1963–64**: 211 [27], 379 [1], 420 [1]; **1965**: 106 [4], 172, 199, 201, 203, 229, 257, 321n; **1966**: 26 (p. 48), 216, 325, 338 [9], 418, 437, 443, 450, 459, 482, 501 [17], 514, 533, 542, 577 [16]; **1967**: 357, 434, 446, 460 [9], 519; **1968–69**: 50, 81 [3], 109, 170, 178, 200, 221, 225, 232n., 233, 237, 255, 273, 400, 452, 462, 472, 522, 676 (p. 1269), 678 (pp. 1273, 1274), 682, 683

Australia, **1968–69**: 277

Bipartisanship, **1966**: 277 [23]

Cambodia, **1968–69**: 634

Campaign remarks, **1963–64**: 544, 606, 607, 608, 622, 630, 634, 635, 639, 640, 642, 643, 645, 646, 648, 650, 652, 655, 656, 657, 658, 662, 678, 680, 693, 694, 695, 701, 702, 703, 712, 713, 718, 719, 728, 729, 732, 733, 734, 735, 736, 741, 745, 746, 747, 748, 749, 750, 762

China, Communist, **1966**: 141 [7], 445 [23]; **1967**: 312 [15], 554 [14]; **1968–69**: 14 (p. 26)

Communist bloc, **1966**: 414; **1968–69**: 472

Conference for business executives, **1967**: 519

Congo, **1967**: 519

Criticism of, **1965**: 208 [9, 14], 223, 227n., 295 [7], 319 [14, 21]; **1966**: 65 [5], 236 [3, 9]

Cuba, **1963–64**: 316 [23]

Cyprus, **1968–69**: 14 (p. 26)

Dominican Republic, **1966**: 277 [25]

Economic, **1966**: 34 (p. 103)

Effect of immigration quota system on, **1965**: 13

Europe, **1965**: 235; **1966**: 200, 482, 501 [2], 506, 607 [3]; **1967**: 3 (p. 10); **1968–69**: 62, 211, 472, 474

Foreign policy – *continued*
France, **1968–69**: 652

Germany, **1966**: 486

Iran, **1968–69**: 307, 615

Israel, **1967**: 554 [3]

Japan, **1968–69**: 340

Korea, North, **1968–69**: 35, 51 [16]

Korea, South, **1968–69**: 51 [15], 79 [13], 200, 201

Kuwait, **1968–69**: 618–620

Laos, **1963–64**: 272; **1965**: 22 [4]

Latin America, **1966**: 414; **1968–69**: 148, 665 Report, **1965**: 429n.

Mexico, **1968–69**: 354, 623, 624

Middle East, **1967**: 3 (p. 9), 233, 251, 264 [1, 10, 12], 270, 272, 278, 279, 281, 488; **1968–69**: 14 (p. 26), 169 [20], 249, 250n., 255, 474, 557 [11]

New Zealand, **1968–69**: 528

News conference remarks, **1963–64**: 201 [5, 8], 211 [21, 27], 242 [11], 246 [4], 271 [1, 18], 280 [8], 285 [13, 17], 294 [19], 316 [23, 24], 379 [1], 420 [1, 8], 462 [12], 475 [3, 22], 688 [1, 8]; **1965**: 22 [18], 295 [15], 319 [21], 347 [2], 448 [19]

Nigeria, **1968–69**: 508, 639

Overseas programs, economic operation of, **1965**: 129

Philippine support of, **1963–64**: 626n.

Presidential responsibility, **1968–69**: 452, 590 [2]

President's advisory panel on, **1963–64**: 563 [5, 8]

Relation to antipoverty program, **1963–64**: 280

Remarks on, **1968–69**: 327

Review of, **1965**: 202n.

Social science research on, **1965**: 404

Southern Rhodesia, **1966**: 243

Soviet Union, **1966**: 483; **1967**: 282; **1968–69**: 14 (p. 26), 51 [13], 309, 339 [8], 472, 474, 585, 676 (p. 1268, 1269)

Teach-ins, **1965**: 295 [7], 353 [21], 397

Thailand, **1968–69**: 237

Tunisia, **1968–69**: 255

United Kingdom, **1966**: 359; **1968–69**: 65

Vietnam, **1963–64**: 186, 211 [21], 218 [25, 27], 246 [4], 280 [8], 420 [8], 626n.; **1965**: 26, 46 [7, 11], 51n., 76, 106 [4], 117 [2, 8], 130, 152, 156 [6, 11, 12], 162, 172, 194, 200, 208 [2, 9, 14, 19, 20], 227, 229, 230, 234, 246, 294, 319 [14], 388 [1, 5, 11, 14, 16], 390, 395 [5], 397, 412 [4], 421, 476

See also Vietnam, North; Vietnam, South.

Foreign Policy Conference for Educators, **1967**: 272

Foreign press, **1963–64**: 475 [23]
Foreign Relations.
    See Foreign policy.
Foreign Relations, Council on, **1967**: 306n.
Foreign Relations, Senate Committee on, **1967**:
        34 [7], 195, 204ftn. (p. 497), 358 [10],
        375 [16], 495 [14]; **1968–69**: 132, 153
        [1], 275 [6], 691
Foreign Relations Committee, Senate, **1966**: 52
        [3], 65 [6], 273
Foreign Service, **1963–64**: 227, 619 [8], 621;
        1965: 18, 129, 185, 233, 319 [8];
        1966: 45, 261; **1967**: 464, 495 [14];
        1968–69: 498
    Dependents overseas, **1963–64**: 266 [17]
    Officers, **1968–69**: 454, 581
Foreign Service Act of 1946, **1965**: 185, 233
Foreign Service Day, **1967**: 464
Foreign Service Institute, **1966**: 142, 261
    Vietnam Training Center, **1968–69**: 149
Foreign Service, Board of, **1965**: 282
Foreign Service Officers Corps, Department of
        State, **1968–69**: 454
Foreign visitor program, President's, **1968–69**:
        116
Foreign visitors.
    See Visitors, foreign leaders.
Foreign workers, employment in U.S., **1965**: 38
Foreman, Repr. Ed, **1963–64**: 316 [16], 504
        [11]
Forensic League, National, **1963–64**: 343, 455
        [17]
Forest Service, **1965**: 497; **1966**: 376; **1968–69**:
        91, 510
Forests, national, **1963–64**: 357, 554; **1965**: 53,
        54; **1966**: 26 (p. 60), 82, 376n., 518;
        1967: 418; **1968–69**: 39 (p. 101), 94,
        510, 700
Formosa (Taiwan), **1963–64**: 122; **1966**: 6 (p. 8),
        62, 368, 516 [16]
    See also China, Republic of.
Formosa Straits, **1963–64**: 607, 638, 694, 702,
        713, 728, 729, 733, 734, 736, 749, 750
Forrest, Iren, **1967**: 87n.
Forrest, Nathan Bedford, **1963–64**: 702
Forrestal, James, **1963–64**: 455 [5]; **1965**: 91,
        157, 315; **1967**: 241; **1968–69**: 18 [2]
Forrestal, James V., U.S.S., **1967**: 330 [1]
Forrestal, Michael V., **1963–64**: 455 [5]
Forrestal Building, **1965**: 315
Fort Benning, Georgia, **1965**: 117 [5]; **1967**: 485
        [1], 493
Fort Bragg, North Carolina, **1965**: 117 [5];
        1968–69: 81 [1], 109
Fort Campbell, Ky., **1966**: 348, 351–352
Fort DeRussy, Hawaii, **1967**: 440
Fort Des Moines, Iowa, **1967**: 475
Fort Gordon, Ga., **1963–64**: 718

Fort Lincoln model community, District of
        Columbia, **1968–69**: 152, 689
Fort Mitchell, Ky., **1968–69**: 499
Fort Peck Dam, **1963–64**: 656
Fort Worth, Texas, **1968–69**: 281, 282
Fortas, Justice Abe, **1965**: 388 [4]; **1966**: 226,
        368; **1967**: 264 [9], 335, 406, 512;
        1968–69: 115, 216
    Nomination as Chief Justice, **1968–69**: 339
        [2], 425 [11], 467 [2, 5], 509, 527,
        696 [6]
Fortune magazine, **1965**: 459
Fosburgh, James W., **1963–64**: 211 [7]
Fosdick, Harry Emerson, **1963–64**: 314
Fossil fuels, **1967**: 186
Foster, Spec. 4 John W., **1966**: 183
Foster, Mrs. Lincoln, **1966**: 645n.
Foster, William C., **1965**: 20, 353 [5], 430;
        1966: 32; **1967**: 64n., 340, 365, 367;
        1968–69: 27, 69
    See also United States Arms Control and Dis-
        armament Agency, Director.
Foster grandparents program, **1966**: 594; **1967**:
        12, 39, 114; **1968–69**: 75
Foundation for Science and Technology, Inter-
        American, **1967**: 176
Foundations, tax exemptions, **1966**: 34 (p. 107)
Foundations, taxes, **1967**: 16 (p. 86)
Founding Fathers, **1968–69**: 100
Fountain, Repr. L. H., **1963–64**: 327, 328
Four freedoms, **1967**: 105, 112n.
4–H Club, **1966**: 295n.
Fowler, Judge Conrad M., **1967**: 419n.
Fowler, Henry H., **1963–64**: 144, 296; **1965**:
        113, 117 [3]
    See also Treasury, Secretary of the.
Fowler, Mrs. Henry H. (Trudye), **1965**: 113, 155
Fox, George, **1966**: 295
Fox, Dr. Lay M., **1966**: 575
Foy, Fred C., **1963–64**: 169n.; **1965**: 465
France, **1963–64**: 617; **1965**: 68n., 220; **1966**:
        142n., 373 [6, 13], 437; **1968–69**: 169
        [17], 204
    Aircraft, Anglo-French supersonic transport,
        1965: 319 [19]
    Ambassador Hervé Alphand, **1963–64**: 188,
        189
    Couve de Murville, Maurice, **1965**: 78; **1966**:
        607 [2, 7]
    Disarmament conference proposal, **1965**: 208
        [11]
    Foreign Minister Michel Debré, **1968–69**: 533
    Foreign policy, **1963–64**: 266 [14]
    Foreign relations, **1968–69**: 313, 652
    Franc value, **1968–69**: 283 [11], 605
    NATO forces, withdrawal, **1966**: 158 [13],
        607 [3]

France – *continued*
  Paris Air Show, **1965**: 320
  President Charles de Gaulle, **1965**: 46 [5], 641
    [9]; **1966**: 141 [12], 188 [1], 273, 277
    [12], 445 [25], 607 [3, 7]; **1967**: 554
    [5, 10]; **1968–69**: 605, 652
    See also main entry, DeGaulle, Charles.
  Prices, **1967**: 430
  Recognition of Communist China, **1963–64**:
    150 [11, 15], 170 [1], 218 [31, 32]
  U.S. Ambassador Charles E. Bohlen, **1963–64**:
    211 [19], 218 [24]; **1966**: 134, 485n.
  U.S. Ambassador R. Sargent Shriver, **1968–69**:
    153 [1, 5, 10], 305
  U.S. relations, **1963–64**: 211 [19]; **1967**: 63,
    554 [10]; **1968–69**: 652
Francis, Connie, **1963–64**: 751
Franconia Notch, N.H., **1966**: 392
Frankel, Max, **1966**: 494 [16], 516 [12]; **1968–
  69**: 1 [8], 153 [8]
Frankfurter, Felix, **1963–64**: 27; **1965**: 102, 242;
  1968–69: 193
Franklin, Benjamin, **1963–64**: 350, 366n., 772;
  1965: 34, 45, 78, 463 [8, 9]; **1966**:
  258, 609; **1967**: 204 [13]; **1968–69**:
  499, 500, 648, 695
Franklin, John Hope, **1967**: 81
Franklin D. Roosevelt Birthday Memorial Award,
  1967: 21
Franklin D. Roosevelt Lake, **1965**: 186
Franklin Delano Roosevelt Memorial Park, Dis-
  trict of Columbia, **1968–69**: 707n.
Fraser, Repr. Donald M., **1963–64**: 434; **1965**:
  189
Fraternal organizations, remarks, **1967**: 397
Frear, Mr. and Mrs. J. Allen, Jr., **1966**: 515
Fredericksburg, Tex., **1963–64**: 74; **1965**: 623n.
  News conferences, **1966**: 580, 610
  Releases, **1966**: 581, 611–613
Frederickson, Dr. Donald S., **1966**: 580 [8]
Frederik IX (King of Denmark), **1963–64**: 394;
  1966: 195
Frederika, Queen, **1963–64**: 153, 209, 424
Fredman, Milton, **1966**: 644n.
Free, Brig. Gen. Richard H., **1965**: 236
Free enterprise system, **1966**: 6 (p. 6), 98, 187,
  396, 403, 444, 451, 473, 483; **1967**:
  57, 268
  See also Enterprise system.
Freedmen's Hospital, District of Columbia, **1967**:
  15
Freedom Award, National, **1966**: 86
Freedom House, **1966**: 86n.
Freedom Share savings note, **1967**: 66; **1968–69**:
  10, 12, 284, 537
Freeman, Mrs. Frankie M., **1963–64**: 201 [1],
  695; **1967**: 81
Freeman, Fulton, **1963–64**: 54ftn. (p. 70), 767;
  1966: 176, 620 [2], 639

Freeman, Mrs. Fulton, **1966**: 176
Freeman, Gaylord A., **1967**: 252n., 500
Freeman, Gordon M., **1963–64**: 302n.; **1968–69**:
  106n.
Freeman, Orville L.
  See Agriculture, Secretary of.
Freeman, Mrs. Orville L., **1963–64**: 358; **1966**:
  164n., 295
Freeport, Tex., salt water conversion demonstra-
  tion plant, **1965**: 417n.
Freer, Charles L., **1966**: 227, 587
Freer Gallery of Art, **1966**: 227
Frei Montalva, Eduardo (President of Chile),
  1963–64: 560 [2]; **1965**: 431; **1966**:
  649
Frelinghuysen, Repr. Peter, Jr., **1963–64**: 305
French, Daniel Chester, **1967**: 49
Friday, William, **1963–64**: 622
Fried, Edward, **1968–69**: 169 [17]
Friedel, Repr. Samuel N., **1963–64**: 703; **1967**:
  286
Friedkin, Joseph F., **1966**: 630 [2]; **1967**: 408
  [5]
Friedman, Eugene, **1963–64**: 338
Friedman, Herbert, **1963–64**: 417; **1968–69**:
  695n.
Friends, Society of, **1963–64**: 391
Friendship, United States-Mexico Commission
  for Border Development and, **1967**: 451;
  1968–69: 223 [2], 354, 623, 624n.
Friesen, Ernest C., Jr., **1966**: 88 [5]
Frost, Robert, **1963–64**: 313, 340, 788; **1966**:
  257, 522
Fucino, Italy, **1967**: 389
Fuel taxes, **1966**: 26 (p. 54)
Fuels
  Additives, air pollution control, **1967**: 20
  Fossil, **1967**: 186
  Nuclear, **1966**: 179; **1967**: 515
Fulbright, Sen. J. W., **1963–64**: 58, 153, 201
  [11], 242 [11], 246 [5], 316 [24],
  502, 575, 577, 599, 778; **1965**: 4, 46
  [6], 112, 156 [12], 412 [4], 418, 495;
  1966: 52 [3], 141 [7], 272, 417 [13],
  517; **1967**: 112, 278, 554 [1]; **1968–69**:
  139, 691
  Exchange act.
  See Mutual Educational and Cultural Ex-
    change Act of 1961.
Full Employment Act of 1946, **1963–64**: 642
Fuller, Edgar, **1968–69**: 219
Fuller, Ida, **1965**: 496
Fuller, R. Buckminster, **1966**: 644n.
Fulton, Maj. Fitzhugh L., Jr., **1963–64**: 569
Fulton, Repr. James G., **1963–64**: 290; **1966**:
  428; **1968–69**: 616
Fulton, Repr. Richard H., **1963–64**: 324, 325,
  358, 645, 701; **1967**: 115; **1968–69**:
  345

Fulton, Mrs. Richard H., **1967**: 115
Fulton, Mo., **1963-64**: 263
Fundraising campaigns
  Heart fund, **1965**: 52
  Multiple Sclerosis Society, **1963-64**: 312
  Negro colleges, **1963-64**: 79
  Red Cross, **1963-64**: 202; **1965**: 84
  Savings bond, **1963-64**: 306; **1965**: 11
  Winston Churchill Memorial Library, **1963-64**: 263
Fundy, Bay of, **1963-64**: 138
Funerals for officials, protocol, **1965**: 46 [6]
Funston, G. Keith, **1963-64**: 296
Fuqua, Repr. Don, **1963-64**: 198, 199
Fuqua, J. B., **1963-64**: 330, 716, 718
Fur bill, **1966**: 568
Furgurson, Ernest B. (Pat), **1965**: 319 [14], **1966**: 494 [15]
Furness, Betty, **1967**: 86, 200, 342, 393, 465, 499, 539, 541; **1968-69**: 105, 264, 280, 418, 545
Furniture, Government procurement, **1966**: 58n.
Furr, Roy, **1967**: 448n.
Fussler, Herman, **1966**: 424n.
Future Farmers of America, **1966**: 295n.; **1968-69**: 390
Future Homemakers of America, **1966**: 295n.

Gagarin, Yuri, **1965**: 318; **1968-69**: 161, 387
Gainesville, Ga., **1963-64**: 331, 332
  Mayor Henry Ward, **1963-64**: 331, 332
Galaxy, C-5A cargo plane, **1968-69**: 110, 125
Galbraith, William E., **1968-69**: 472
Galbreath, John W., **1963-64**: 323
Gallagher, Repr. Cornelius E., **1963-64**: 338; **1966**: 504
Gallagher, Jeffrey J., **1966**: 289
Gallatti, Stephen, Jr., **1963-64**: 465
Gallatti, Stephen, Sr., **1963-64**: 465
Gallaudet College, **1963-64**: 389, 808; **1965**: 305
Gallery of Art, National, **1967**: 470
Gallipolis, Ohio, **1967**: 558; **1968-69**: 58
Gallogly, Edward P., **1963-64**: 601
Gallup, George H., **1966**: 320 [14]; **1967**: 466, 495 [2]
Gallup Poll, **1963-64**: 542; **1966**: 65 [11], 320 [14], 654 [10]; **1967**: 297 [13], 328 [3, 11]; **1968-69**: 568, 569
Galveston, Tex., **1963-64**: 733
Gambling and wagering, **1968-69**: 59
Gammon, Samuel Rhea, III, **1963-64**: 26
Gandhi, Mrs. Indira (Prime Minister of India), **1966**: 52 [1], 65 [9], 141 [15], 153-154, 164, 180, 247 [7], 273, 329, 514
  Visit, **1966**: 148-149, 152
Gandhi, Mahatma, **1966**: 149, 153

Garcia, Dan, **1966**: 589
Garcia, Dr. Hector P., **1967**: 87n., 452; **1968-69**: 437
García-Godoy, Hector, **1965**: 484; **1966**: 251, 277 [3, 25]
Gardner, John W., **1963-64**: 568, 622; **1965**: 183, 291, 334, 374, 385, 388 [17], 406, 410, 418; **1968-69**: 227, 560, 570
  See also Health, Education, and Welfare, Secretary of.
  "Self Renewal; the Individual and the Innovative Society," **1965**: 385n.
Gardner, Mrs. John W., **1965**: 433
Garfield, James A., **1965**: 34; **1967**: 68; **1968-69**: 138, 298, 462
Garland, Charles S., **1965**: 172
Garmartz, Repr. Edward A., **1963-64**: 703; **1967**: 286
Garment Workers Union, International Ladies, **1963-64**: 387, 388; **1968-69**: 529
Garner, John Nance, **1963-64**: 599; **1965**: 622
  Birthday, **1966**: 624
  Death, **1967**: 471
Garrison, James, **1967**: 80 [6]
Gary, Ind., **1963-64**: 639; **1967**: 20
  Mayor A. Martin Katz, **1963-64**: 639
Gary Job Corps Center, San Marcos, Tex., **1965**: 179
Garza, Judge Reynaldo G., **1963-64**: 767
Gas pipeline safety, **1967**: 57, 200, 342, 393, 430, 465, 499, 520, 534, 539; **1968-69**: 105, 338, 390, 441
Gas rates, **1963-64**: 173, 352
Gases, non-lethal
  Use in civil disorders, **1965**: 156 [12]
  Use in Vietnam, **1965**: 156 [12]
Gasoline, **1966**: 27, 140
  Rates, **1965**: 567
  Taxes, **1965**: 29, 32 (p. 88), 255
Gaspari, Ramon, **1965**: 333n.
Gaston Marin, Gheorghe, **1963-64**: 336 [6]
Gates, Thomas S., Jr., **1966**: 315n., 320 [10]
Gathings, Repr. E. C. (Tuck), **1963-64**: 599, 701
GATT.
  See General Agreement on Tariffs and Trade.
Gaud, William S., **1966**: 52 [2], 141 [10]; **1967**: 352; **1968-69**: 11, 63, 361, 691
  Administrator, Agency for International Development, **1966**: 368, 407
Gaulle, Charles de.
  See De Gaulle, Charles.
Gavin, James M., **1963-64**: 401; **1966**: 65 [6, 7]
Gaylord, Edward L, **1963-64**: 598
Gaynor, Mitzi, **1963-64**: 373
Gaza Strip, **1967**: 233
Gearreald, Karen L., **1966**: 220
Gehlbach, Arthur L., **1966**: 331n.

Geilo, Norway, **1968–69**: 650n.
Gemini space flights, **1965**: 81, 120, 121; **1966**: 40, 371, 485
    No. 3, **1965**: 120, 121, 134
    No. 4, **1965**: 295 [12], 298, 302, 303, 304, 310, 318, 320
    No. 5, **1965**: 448 [2], 459, 462, 463 [2, 13]
    No. 6, **1965**: 448 [2], 636n., 647, 651, 652n., 656
    No. 7, **1965**: 636, 651, 652n., 656
    No. 8, **1966**: 135
    No. 12, **1966**: 618
Gemini space program, **1963–64**: 211 [32]; **1965**: 81, 120, 121, 310, 318, 320, 463 [2]; **1967**: 24, 431n.; **1968–69**: 39 (p. 100), 574, 616
    Conclusion of program, **1966**: 625
Geneen, Harold S., **1968–69**: 25
General Accounting Office, **1965**: 39, 508; **1967**: 236
    Reports, **1963–64**: 307
General Advisory Committee on Foreign Assistance Programs, **1965**: 136
General Agreement on Tariffs and Trade, **1967**: 142, 224, 508; **1968–69**: 2, 47 (p. 137), 274, 275 [2], 439
    Kennedy Round negotiations, **1963–64**: 109, 140, 186, 246 [19], 256 [21], 272, 336 [12], 394n., 400, 592, 739, 757, 787, 788; **1965**: 35 (p. 111), 47, 60, 76, 112, 564, 660; **1966**: 34 (p. 104), 471, 486, 503; **1968–69**: 2, 14 (p. 26), 29, 47 (pp. 129, 137), 62, 94, 146, 214n., 274, 275 [2], 517, 559, 684 (p. 1320)
    See also main heading, Kennedy Round trade negotiations.
General Aniline and Film Corp., **1965**: 309
General Assembly, U.N.
    See United Nations.
General Dynamics Corporation, **1963–64**: 170 [3], 383n., 515n.
General Electric Co., **1965**: 339, 448 [1]; **1966**: 496, 535; **1967**: 197
General Motors Corp., **1963–64**: 624, 713, 733, 745; **1968–69**: 492
    Labor dispute, **1963–64**: 687
General Services Administration, **1963–64**: 307, 792n.; **1965**: 14, 93, 138n., 222, 288n., 412 [1], 498n.; **1966**: 98, 296, 390, 464, 595, 630 [4]; **1967**: 315n., 412; **1968–69**: 99, 287, 427n., 470
    Administrator (Bernard L. Boutin), **1963–64**: 171n., 411, 481n.
    Administrator (Lawson B. Knott, Jr.), **1965**: 315, 328, 411; **1966**: 58n., 202, 206, 218, 390, 464, 635 [20]; **1967**: 16 (p. 87), 121, 232, 372, 412, 504; **1968–69**: 407

General Services Administration – *continued*
    Administrator – *continued*
        Acting, **1965**: 14, 54
        Letter, **1965**: 14
        Report, **1965**: 249n.
    Spending cutbacks, **1967**: 6 [7]
Genesis, Book of, **1967**: 515; **1968–69**: 589
Genetic research, **1968–69**: 145
Geneva, Switzerland, **1967**: 340
Geneva accords
    Laos (1962), **1967**: 439, 564; **1968–69**: 237, 240, 275 [1], 288, 400, 406, 452
    Vietnam and prisoners of war, **1966**: 6 (p. 11), 54, 65ftn. (p. 177), 338 [1], 549; **1967**: 34 [2], 80 [4], 83, 116, 118, 144, 145, 312ftn. (p. 702), 366, 462, 564; **1968–69**: 170, 400, 406, 452
Geneva Agreement of 1962, **1963–64**: 201 [7], 272, 294 [16], 420 [1], 500, 780ftn. (p. 1616); **1965**: 26, 106 [6]
Geneva agreements on Indochina (1954), **1965**: 26, 106 [6], 388 [1], 397, 448 [15]
Geneva conferences, **1965**: 331, 653
    Atomic energy, peaceful uses of, **1963–64**: 396; **1965**: 537
    Disarmament, **1963–64**: 91 (p. 116), 94, 109, 170 [15], 186, 382, 394n., 395, 529, 693, 736; **1965**: 20, 353 [5, 11], 386, 388 [10], 430, 463 [7]; **1966**: 32, 70, 401 [12]; **1968–69**: 378
        Resumption of meetings, **1963–64**: 122, 130, 131
        U.S. proposals, **1963–64**: 129
    Kennedy Round, GATT trade negotiations, **1963–64**: 109, 140, 186, 246 [19], 256 [21], 272, 336 [12], 394n., 400, 592, 739, 757, 787, 788; **1965**: 35 (p. 111), 47, 60, 76, 112, 564, 660
    Radio Conference on Space Communications, **1963–64**: 180n.
    Trade and Development, United Nations Conference on, **1963–64**: 201 [11], 237
    World Health Assembly, **1965**: 262
Gentry, Louise, **1967**: 342n.
Geodetic Survey, Coast and, **1963–64**: 308; **1967**: 31n.
Geodetic Survey, Inter-American, **1967**: 336
Geographic Society, National, **1963–64**: 117, 427
Geological Survey, **1963–64**: 308; **1968–69**: 430
Geophysical Year, International, **1963–64**: 551; **1965**: 318
George, Heard, **1963–64**: 716
George, Walter F., **1963–64**: 716
George III, King, **1965**: 376
George VI (King of the United Kingdom), **1968–69**: 65
George-Deen Vocational Act, **1968–69**: 238
George Rogers Clark National Historical Park, Ind., **1966**: 350

George Washington, U.S.S., **1963–64**: 383

Georgetown University, **1963–64**: 788; **1965**: 88; **1966**: 455

Georgia, **1963–64**: 171
  Antipoverty program, **1963–64**: 330, 331, 332
  Campaign remarks, **1963–64**: 716, 718
  Franchise for 18-year-olds, **1968–69**: 341
  Gov. Lester G. Maddox, **1967**: 297 [2], 485 [1]; **1968–69**: 46n., 110
  Gov. Carl E. Sanders, **1963–64**: 330, 332, 567, 716, 718, 719; **1965**: 245, 319 [7]; **1966**: 122 [1]
  Hurricane relief, **1963–64**: 563 [4], 567
  Medal of Honor winners from, **1968–69**: 688, 691
  Medical College of, **1963–64**: 718
  President's visit to, **1963–64**: 336 [9]
  Remarks, **1968–69**: 110
  School desegregation, **1965**: 470
  State motto, **1963–64**: 330, 716
  Voting registration, **1965**: 448 [9]

Geothermal steam, **1967**: 20
  Bill, **1966**: 614

Gerhart, Gen. John K., **1965**: 158

German Development Aid Service, **1963–64**: 76

German measles, **1967**: 319; **1968–69**: 19, 111

Germany, **1963–64**: 591; **1965**: 68n., 235, 660; **1966**: 437, 506
  See also Germany, East; Germany, West.
  Aid to less developed countries, **1963–64**: 400; **1965**: 660
  Ambassador Karl Heinrich Knappstein, **1965**: 57
  Arms supply to Israel, **1965**: 117 [6]
  Berlin.
    See main heading, Berlin.
  Change in leadership, **1963–64**: 694, 746
  Development Aid Service (peace corps), **1963–64**: 76, 347; **1965**: 660
  Erhard, Ludwig, **1963–64**: 26, 28 [4], 54 [8, 16], 71 [6, 8, 13], 72, 73, 74, 75, 76, 87, 266 [8], 316 [25], 399, 400, 475 [3], 688 [8], 693, 701, 734; **1965**: 22 [7], 57, 300, 333n., 463 [7], 520, 659, 660; **1966**: 88 [9], 474 [9], 482, 484–486, 503, 506
  Foreign Affairs Minister Gerhard Schroeder, **1966**: 486
  Foreign policy, **1963–64**: 788
  Immigration quota to U.S., **1963–64**: 97
  Income tax convention and protocol with U.S., **1965**: 535
  Lübke, Heinrich, **1963–64**: 73
  Nuclear weapons use, **1966**: 474 [9], 486
  Pollution control, **1966**: 88 [9]
  Relations with West, **1963–64**: 788

Germany — *continued*
  Reunification, question of, **1963–64**: 76, 122, 244, 359, 399, 400, 788; **1965**: 2, 57, 235, 300, 659, 660; **1966**: 200, 486, 503
  Schröder, Gerhard, **1963–64**: 28 [4], 72n., 75, 76, 400, 780 [8]; **1965**: 660
  Ships for, **1965**: 600
  Soviet relations with, **1963–64**: 316 [25]
  Space research with U.S., **1965**: 659, 660; **1966**: 485
  U.S. Ambassador George C. McGhee, **1963–64**: 818 [4]
  U.S. expenditures in, agreement on, **1963–64**: 76
  U.S. forces in, **1963–64**: 76
  U.S. relations with, **1963–64**: 72, 73, 76, 399; **1966**: 486, 610 [4]; **1968**: 57, 300, 659, 660
  Vietnam assistance, **1966**: 482, 486
  Visit of Secretary McNamara, **1963–64**: 316 [2]
  Von Hassel, Kai-Uwe, **1965**: 660

Germany, East, **1968–69**: 313n.
  See also Germany.
  RB–66 plane incident, **1963–64**: 170 [1], 182, 246 [4]
    Release of fliers, **1963–64**: 232 [2], 242 [18, 26]
  Treaty with the Soviet Union, **1963–64**: 400

Germany, West, **1967**: 545
  See also Germany.
  Ambassador Heinrich Knappstein, **1967**: 349
  Chancellor Kurt Georg Kiesinger, **1967**: 181, 191, 204 [2–4], 264 [18], 312 [2], 347–349, 351, 371, 373, 554 [5]; **1968–69**: 313
  Communist aggression, **1968–69**: 142, 154, 165
  Defense, **1967**: 272, 306n.
  Erhard, Ludwig (former Chancellor), **1967**: 306; **1968–69**: 151
  Foreign aid, **1968–69**: 63
  Foreign relations, **1967**: 347n.
  President Heinrich Luebke, **1967**: 181
  Prices, **1967**: 430
  Relations with U.S., **1967**: 191, 306n., 347–349, 351
  Reunification, **1967**: 351; **1968–69**: 474
  U.S. forces, **1967**: 204 [2, 3], 348, 519, 554 [5]
  Vice Chancellor Willy Brandt, **1967**: 347–349, 351
  Visit, **1967**: 191

Gestido, Oscar D. (President of Uruguay), **1967**: 171, 175n., 176
  Death, **1967**: 523

Gettys, Tom S., **1963–64**: 719

Gettysburg, Pa. (Eisenhower farm), **1968–69**: 411

Ghana, **1963–64**: 35; **1965**: 388 [6]; **1968–69**: 204, 433n.
    Ambassador Miguel Augustus Ribeiro, **1963–64**: 35n.
    Chairman, National Liberation Council, Lt. Gen. Joseph A. Ankrah, **1967**: 426
    Nkrumah, Kwame, **1963–64**: 88

GI bill of rights (Servicemen's Readjustment Act of 1944), **1963–64**: 419, 611, 642, 709; **1966**: 100, 158 [10], 188 [6], 353
    See also Veterans Readjustment Benefits Act of 1966.

G.I. Forum of the United States, American, **1966**: 236 [14]

Giap, General.
    See Vo Nguyen Giap.

Gibbon, Edward, **1967**: 256

Gibbons, Repr. Sam M., **1963–64**: 198, 199

Gibby, Mabel Kunce, **1968–69**: 138n.

Gibson, Phil S., **1966**: 294

Gifford, Selene, **1963–64**: 204n.

Gilford, Mrs. Dorothy Morrow, **1965**: 91n.

Gill, Jocelyn R., **1966**: 89

Gill, Lt. Gov. Thomas P., **1967**: 555

Gilligan, Repr. John J., **1963–64**: 679; **1965**: 190

Gillis, Simon, **1968–69**: 625

Gilpatric, Roswell L., **1963–64**: 37n., 54ftn. (p. 66), 563 [5], 688 [3]; **1965**: 28n.; **1966**: 220

Gilroy, Norman Cardinal, **1966**: 545

Gilruth, Robert E., **1965**: 310; **1966**: 625; **1968–69**: 107, 533n.

Gilstrap, Sam P., **1966**: 533

Ginsburg, David, **1966**: 256–257, 322, 360; **1967**: 168n., 170ftn. (p. 439), 204 [5], 207, 310, 328 [1]

Girl Scouts of the U.S.A., **1966**: 295n.

Girls Clubs of America, **1966**: 295n.

Girls Nation, **1967**: 332

Givens, Dr. Everett, **1963–64**: 763

Glacier Peak Wilderness, Wash., **1968–69**: 510n.

Gladstone, William E., **1966**: 149; **1968–69**: 227

Glass, Andrew, **1963–64**: 486 [9]

Glass, Marshall, **1963–64**: 315

Glass, sheet, tariffs, **1967**: 16 (p. 79), 428

Glassboro, N.J., **1967**: 279–283, 554 [2]
    1967 meetings with Premier Kosygin, **1968–69**: 14 (p. 26), 51 [13], 349, 425 [9], 467 [17]
    State College, commencement address, **1968–69**: 288

Glass-Steagall Act, 1933, **1963–64**: 144

Glaves, Jack, **1963–64**: 741

Gleason, John S., Jr., **1963–64**: 152, 178n., 611, 654; **1965**: 46 [8], 163

Glen Canyon Dam, Arizona, **1963–64**: 256 [16]

Glenn, Lt. Col. John H., Jr., **1963–64**: 374; **1965**: 120; **1968–69**: 339 [3], 616
    Promotion, **1963–64**: 725, 733

Glennan, Keith T., **1968–69**: 507

Glenview Naval Air Station, Ill., **1968–69**: 183

Glusker, Eugene, **1966**: 395

Glynn, William E., **1963–64**: 603

Glynn, William G., **1968–69**: 236

GNP (gross national product).
    See National product; Gross national product.

Goddard, James L., **1966**: 4, 307

Goddard, Mary, **1965**: 91

Goddard, Robert H., **1965**: 170

Goddard, Mrs. Robert H., **1966**: 134

Goddard, Gov. Sam, **1966**: 494 [1, 2]

Goddard Trophy, Robert H., **1966**: 134

Godwin, Gov. Mills E., Jr., **1966**: 122 [1], 650n.

Goethe, Johann Wolfgang von, **1967**: 349; **1968**: 659

Goheen, Robert F., **1966**: 216

Gold, **1967**: 371, 497, 524; **1968–69**: 47 (pp. 136, 137), 169, 582
    Outflow from U.S., **1963–64**: 722, 775; **1965**: 35 (p. 105), 60
    Prices, **1968–69**: 14 (p. 33), 47 (p. 128), 146, 500, 684 (p. 1320)
    Reserves, **1963–64**: 379 [6], 753; **1965**: 35 (p. 110), 60, 77, 110, 541; **1968–69**: 1 [4], 2, 14 (p. 33), 47 (p. 136), 141, 142, 146, 218
    Sales, **1968–69**: 2, 47 (p. 133), 146, 500
    Standard, **1965**: 46 [12], 60, 77

Gold Coast, **1967**: 426

Goldberg, Arthur J., **1963–64**: 139; **1965**: 155, 346, 370, 371, 374; **1968–69**: 335, 696 [6]
    See also United Nations, U.S. Representative (Arthur J. Goldberg).

Goldberg, Mrs. Arthur J. (Dorothy), **1965**: 370n., 383; **1967**: 461; **1968–69**: 335

Goldberg, Robert, **1965**: 370n.

Goldberger, Marvin L., **1965**: 166n.

Goldman, Eric F., **1963–64**: 303, 513; **1966**: 216

Goldner, Herman W., **1963–64**: 285 [7]

Goldsboro, N.C., **1963–64**: 326, 329

Goldstein, E. Ernest, **1968–69**: 1 [1], 388n.

Goldstein, Louis L., **1963–64**: 703

Goldwater, Sen. Barry, **1963–64**: 96, 218 [32], 287, 311, 352, 498; **1966**: 188 [5], 577 [13, 15]; **1968–69**: 228ftn. (p. 573), 690
    Campaign remarks on, **1963–64**: 542, 612, 631, 643, 655, 657, 659, 680, 693, 703, 713, 716, 718, 719, 728, 729, 733, 736, 748, 749, 762, 764
    News conference remarks on, **1963–64**: 71 [14],

Goldwater – *continued*
   News conference remarks on – *continued*
         150 [12], 211 [30], 242 [23], 271 [13],
         285 [1], 420 [7, 10, 11], 455 [13, 20],
         462 [6, 9, 10, 12], 475 [5, 7, 9, 12, 15,
         17, 21, 23], 504 [10], 516 [2, 6, 10, 13,
         17], 560 [9, 13, 14, 16], 563 [10, 12,
         14], 619 [15, 18]
Goldy, Daniel L., **1963–64**: 248
Gompers, Samuel, **1963–64**: 430; **1966**: 235
Gonard, Samuel A. (President, International Com-
      mittee of the Red Cross), **1965**: 546
Gondwe, Vincent H. B., **1965**: 354
Gonzalez, Repr. Henry B., **1963–64**: 767;
         1965: 621; **1966**: 160, 168; **1967**: 151,
         449; **1968–69**: 7
Good Neighborhood Bridge, **1967**: 454
Goodell, Sen. Charles E., **1968–69**: 540
Goodman, Philip, **1963–64**: 703
Good-neighbor policy, **1963–64**: 104, 220, 285
         [13], 340, 561; **1966**: 125, 175
Goodpaster, Lt. Gen. Andrew J., **1966**: 320 [1];
         1968–69: 191 [6]
Goodrich, Warren, **1963–64**: 199, 709, 712, 713
Goodwin, Richard N., **1963–64**: 727;
         1965: 22 [1]
Goodwin, S. Sgt. William, **1966**: 246
Gordon, Elinor L., **1968–69**: 42
Gordon, Jerald, **1963–64**: 808n.
Gordon, John, **1963–64**: 431
Gordon, Kermit, **1965**: 290, 365n., 611n.;
         1966: 208n., 493; **1967**: 500;
         1968–69: 38, 215, 350, 677
   See also Budget, Bureau of the, Director
         (Kermit Gordon).
Gordon, Lincoln, **1963–64**: 561n.; **1966**: 13,
         141 [12], 277 [2], 342, 366, 501 [1],
         630 [2], 635 [14], 642 [2]; **1967**: 1
Gordon, Comdr. Richard F., Jr., **1966**: 485
Gore, Sen. Albert, **1963–64**: 323, 324, 325, 619
         [16], 645, 701, 702; **1965**: 46 [7], 231;
         1966: 65 [5]; **1967**: 117; **1968–69**: 345,
         691
   Amendment to Interest Equalization Tax Act,
         1965: 60, 77
Gore, Mrs. Albert (Pauline), **1963–64**: 645, 702;
         1967: 115, 117
Gorham, William, **1965**: 620; **1968–69**: 215
Gorrell, Frank C., **1967**: 116
Gorton, John (Prime Minister of Australia),
         1967: 562; **1968–69**: 223 [7], 271, 273,
         275 [1, 2], 276, 277, 283 [1, 3–6], 290,
         513n.
Gorton, Mrs. John, **1968–69**: 271, 273, 283 [1]
Goshen, Ind., **1965**: 188
Gossett, William T., **1968–69**: 694
Goulart, João, **1963–64**: 66
Gould, Dr. Wilbur J., **1966**: 575

Govatos, Mr. and Mrs. John, **1963–64**: 153n.
Government, American, quality of, message,
         1967: 121
Government, Commission on Organization of the
         Executive Branch of the, **1967**: 121;
         1968–69: 59, 60, 227
Government, continuity in transition,
         1963–64: 6, 8, 28 [4]
Government communications with the public,
         report, **1965**: 249n.
Government contracts, **1968–69**: 26, 587, 678
         (p. 1280)
Government cooperation with business education,
         and labor, **1963–64**: 295, 456, 472;
         1965: 76; **1966**: 6 (p. 5), 26 (p. 49),
         44, 83, 115, 199, 206, 347, 410, 416,
         444; **1967**: 16 (pp. 81, 89), 114, 119,
         286
   Anti-inflation measures, **1968–69**: 14 (pp. 32,
         33)
   Area redevelopment, **1965**: 132
   Arts and humanities, support of, **1968–69**: 686
   Balance of payments, **1965**: 319 [8], 638;
         1968–69: 2, 136
   Dollar stability, **1965**: 60, 77
   Economic, **1965**: 321, 513, 632; **1966**: 155,
         201, 453, 473, 477 [2]; **1967**: 524;
         1968–69: 684 (pp. 1312, 1316, 1321)
   Education exchanges, international, **1966**: 45
   Equal employment opportunity, **1966**: 475;
         1967: 199; **1968–69**: 47 (p. 142), 50,
         91, 141, 678 (p. 1294)
   Federal career development, **1966**: 404
   Food distribution, **1966**: 62
   Housing, **1968–69**: 47 (p. 140), 278, 470, 471,
         506, 678 (p. 1289)
   Increase, **1963–64**: 805
   Insurance in riot-affected areas, **1968–69**: 36
   International scientific exchange, **1965**: 519
   Investment deferments, **1966**: 155
   Job training, **1968–69**: 14 (p. 28), 24, 25, 37,
         105, 164, 220, 227, 328, 498
   Manpower training, **1966**: 111
   Manpower utilization, **1963–64**: 456
   Marine and water resources development,
         1967: 101; **1968–69**: 593, 692
   Nuclear fuel reprocessing, **1966**: 179
   Personnel interchange, **1965**: 124; **1968–69**:
         490, 498
   Pollution control, **1966**: 82; **1967**: 20, 240
   Power projects, **1963–64**: 803
   Price stability, **1968–69**: 47 (pp. 127, 140), 76,
         89, 241, 350, 404, 427, 469, 492, 612
   Recreational programs, **1966**: 352
   Research, **1963–64**: 124 (p. 163)
   Scientific research, **1965**: 115, 196, 514, 522;
         1968–69: 687
   Strategic and critical materials, release from
         stockpiles, **1965**: 599; **1966**: 218

Government cooperation – *continued*
  Strike prevention, **1968-69**: 47 (p. 135)
  Student summer employment, **1966**: 172
  Supersonic civil transport, **1967**: 197
  Technological research, **1963-64**: 124 (p. 163)
  Trade, international, **1968-69**: 274
  Transportation, **1965**: 536; **1966**: 187;
    1968-69: 118
  Urban renewal, **1965**: 510; **1968-69**: 115
  Wage-price policy, **1967**: 16 (pp. 78, 79)
Government employees, **1963-64**: 462 [2], 780
    [4]; **1965**: 351, 403, 413, 631;
    1966: 6 (p. 3), 26 (p. 67), 216, 388,
    404, 650 [18]; **1968-69**: 84, 280, 498,
    526, 570, 630, 667
  Accident prevention, **1965**: 73, 287n.
  Associations of Federal officials, **1968-69**: 464
  Awards, **1965**: 263, 269, 296, 540; **1966**: 25,
    198
  Benefits, **1966**: 102, 108
  Blood donors, **1965**: 525
  Career development, **1965**: 379; **1966**: 216,
    266, 404; **1967**: 13 (p. 58), 121
  College students, summer intern program,
    1965: 403
  Combined Federal Campaign, **1967**: 288
  Comments, **1966**: 108, 216, 261, 310, 330;
    1967: 121, 317
  Constitution, upholding of, **1965**: 128
  Education, **1967**: 121, 184; **1968-69**: 39 (p.
    110), 84, 312, 526, 539, 667, 673
  Employee-management cooperation,
    1963-64: 151; **1967**: 379
  Equal employment opportunity, **1963-64**: 100,
    111, 139, 168, 213, 277; **1965**: 91, 100,
    150, 197; **1968-69**: 84
  Ethical standards, **1963-64**: 150 [9], 170 [7],
    226 [16]; **1965**: 241; **1966**: 276
  Executive assignment system, **1966**: 619;
    1967: 121; **1968-69**: 84, 667
  Foreign Service officers, **1968-69**: 454
  Handicapped persons, **1963-64**: 213, 302, 345,
    403; **1965**: 100, 140; **1966**: 318;
    1968-69: 548
  Hazardous duty benefits, **1967**: 568
  Health and medical care, **1965**: 324; **1966**:
    108-109; **1967**: 25
  Hiring restrictions, **1968-69**: 344, 678 (pp.
    1282, 1284, 1285)
  Holidays, **1968-69**: 342
  Incentive awards.
    See main heading, Government Employees
    Incentive Awards.
  Increase, **1965**: 298
  Insurance, **1965**: 49; **1966**: 318, 453;
    1967: 343
  Interchange with private sector, **1968-69**: 490,
    498
  Law enforcement officials, **1966**: 204-205

Government employees – *continued*
  Legislation, **1966**: 438, 453
  Manpower control and utilization,
    1963-64: 17, 38
  Minority groups, **1963-64**: 205, 213, 812;
    1966: 136; **1968-69**: 667
  Negroes, **1963-64**: 205; **1965**: 150, 197n.;
    1966: 96, 136, 248; **1968-69**: 631
  Occupational training, **1967**: 184
  Officials, **1965**: 209, 241, 530
    Ethical standards, **1963-64**: 266 [16]
    Pay, **1963-64**: 132 (p. 194), 295
  Older persons, **1963-64**: 213, 712
  Overseas, **1963-64**: 218 [15]; **1965**: 18, 129,
    185, 233, 319 [8]; **1968-69**: 2, 11, 15,
    47 (p. 135), 63, 146, 169 [1]
    Absentee voting, **1968-69**: 314
  Pay, **1963-64**: 17, 132 (p. 194), 222, 266 [21],
    267, 268, 270, 295-297, 402, 411, 456,
    514, 688 [6]; **1965**: 32 (p. 96), 244,
    448 [14, 15], 589, 612, 632; **1966**: 26
    (pp. 55, 56), 34 (p. 103), 108-109, 158
    [10], 299, 333, 453, 630 [6, 8];
    1967: 6 [13], 13 (pp. 43, 46, 47), 16
    (p. 78), 121, 140, 163, 329, 330, 343,
    417, 420, 546; **1968-69**: 14 (p. 32), 39
    (pp. 88, 91, 92, 97, 98), 303, 667, 678
    (pp. 1280, 1282, 1305)
  Peace Corpsmen, former, recruitment for
    Federal civilian service, **1963-64**: 347
  Personnel management, **1963-64**: 100, 132
    (pp. 176, 193), 168, 213
  Political activity, **1966**: 241, 499
  Production, **1963-64**: 132 (p. 193), 307, 462
    [2]; **1965**: 93, 324
  Recruiting, **1968-69**: 84
  Red Cross support, **1968-69**: 55
  Reduction, **1963-64**: 28 [5], 68, 71 [2, 11],
    91 (pp. 112, 113), 132 (pp. 176, 186,
    193, 194), 197, 211 [9], 240, 271 [3],
    294 [4], 295, 307, 316 [4], 462 [2],
    486 [5], 606, 619 [1, 2], 630, 650,
    652, 655, 659, 661, 669, 679, 688 [2,
    4, 6], 723, 749, 775; **1965**: 32 (p. 97),
    127, 138, 244, 319 [8, 9], 512;
    1966: 234, 321; **1968-69**: 63, 403
  Retirement, **1965**: 49; **1966**: 26 (p. 56), 108-
    109; **1967**: 12; **1968-69**: 678 (p. 1298)
  Safety, **1966**: 75-76, 102, 291, 449;
    1967: 265; **1968-69**: 489
  Savings bond purchases, **1966**: 72, 137, 164,
    358; **1967**: 315; **1968-69**: 174
  Scientific and technical, **1963-64**: 213
  Seasonal workers, **1963-64**: 294 [4]
  Spanish speaking, **1968-69**: 437
  State Department employees, **1963-64**: 26
  State and local, **1968-69**: 84, 100, 312, 539
  Travel allowances, **1965**: 512; **1966**: 234;
    1967: 25

[References are to items except as otherwise indicated]

Government employees – *continued*
  Unemployment insurance, **1966**: 318
  United Community Campaigns, **1966**: 476
  Veterans, **1968–69**: 40, 67, 667
    Vietnam service, **1967**: 25
  Voter registration, **1963–64**: 167
  Wage board, **1965**: 612
  Women, **1963–64**: 150 [16], 204, 208, 211
      [5], 213, 242 [2–7, 24], 257, 289, 298,
      305, 360, 398, 619 [7, 9]; **1965**: 91,
      100, 150, 263, 392; **1966**: 89, 96, 299;
      1967: 93, 95; **1968–69**: 138
  Youth, **1965**: 268, 298; **1966**: 172, 258, 306,
      388; **1967**: 41, 121, 148; **1968–69**: 305,
      570, 667, 673
Government Employees Incentive Awards,
    1963–64: 467n., 790; **1965**: 528
Government Employees Salary Reform Act of
    1964, **1963–64**: 514; **1966**: 108
Government Employees Trust Fund,
    1963–64: 688 [4]
Government management, **1967**: 13 (p. 57);
    1968–69: 39 (p. 109)
Government Operations Committee, House,
    1967: 337
Government Personnel, Commission on Political
    Activity of, **1966**: 499
Goverment Printing Office, **1965**: 287n.
Government publications, questionnaires, reports,
    etc., reduction, **1963–64**: 211 [10], 307,
    362, 462 [2], 583, 630, 749
Government securities, **1965**: 60; **1966**: 431, 444,
    445 [2], 451, 477 [2, 4], 492 [1], 494 [1],
    578 [3]
Government services, **1965**: 32 (p. 87), 255, 591;
    1966: 26 (p. 53), 88 [12], 225
Government Special Task Force on Travel, In-
    dustry, **1968–69**: 1ftn. (p. 1), 2n.
Government spending.
  See Spending.
Government-wide planning and budgeting system,
    1965: 447, 448 [3]
Governors, **1965**: 98; **1967**: 312 [5]
  Appalachia, **1965**: 103; **1966**: 121–123;
    1967: 11
  Colorado River Basin States, **1965**: 119
  Conferences, **1968–69**: 100, 102, 334, 406,
    483
    See also Governors' conferences.
  Crime, statement to, **1966**: 491
  Democratic, **1967**: 296, 297
  Law enforcement and gun control, letter to,
    1968–69: 325
  Meetings with the President, **1963–64**: 8, 521
    [2, 5, 7], 536
  Midwestern, **1967**: 375 [10]
  New England, **1967**: 222, 223, 542
  News conferences with, **1966**: 121–122, 124;
    1967: 223

Governors – *continued*
  Northeastern area, **1965**: 434
  Presidential relations, **1966**: 650 [12, 14];
    1967: 123
  Republican, **1967**: 297 [6]
  Southern candidates, **1966**: 501 [3]
  U.S. fiscal policy, response, **1966**: 494 [4, 12]
  Vietnam visits, **1966**: 124 [5, 14]
  Westmoreland, Gen. William C., luncheon
    honoring, **1967**: 189, 195
Governors' Association, Republican, **1967**: 297
    [6]
Governors' Commission on the Status of Women,
    1965: 392
Governors' Committees on Employment of the
    Handicapped, **1968–69**: 548n.
Governors' conferences, **1965**: 388 [14];
    1966: 252, 320 [1], 536
  Appalachian, **1963–64**: 285 [2], 293, 294 [2],
    300
  Executive committee, **1966**: 121 [1, 6], 124
    [1, 3, 5]
  Japanese, **1967**: 234
  National, **1967**: 234
  New England, **1967**: 222, 223, 225 [21]
  Remarks, **1967**: 123–125
  Vietnam resolution, **1966**: 124 [4, 7, 10]
Graberra, John, **1963–64**: 290
Grace, Judge Charles, **1966**: 168n.
Graduate Public Health Training Amendments of
    1964, **1968–69**: 111
Graduate Research Center of the Southwest,
    1963–64: 738
Grady, Henry, **1963–64**: 330, 716; **1968–69**: 575
Graf, David E., **1968–69**: 219
Graf, Leroy, **1967**: 538
Graham, Brig. Gen. Henry, **1965**: 117 [5]
Graham, Jerry R., **1963–64**: 680
Graham, Otto, **1968–69**: 109, 419
Graham, Philip L., **1965**: 353 [23]
Graham, Richard, **1965**: 290; **1967**: 292
Graham, Thomas, **1967**: 409
Graham, Rev. William F. (Billy), **1963–64**: 172,
    238, 631; **1965**: 157, 158, 223;
    1966: 77–78, 213, 273, 395;
    1967: 267
Grain, **1966**: 355; **1968–69**: 29, 94, 679
  Feed grains, **1963–64**: 132 (p. 187); **1965**: 47,
    168; **1966**: 281, 311; **1967**: 13 (p. 50),
    508
  India, shipments to, **1966**: 153
  Inspection, **1963–64**: 132 (p. 187)
  Storage, **1963–64**: 570
Grain Terminal Association, Farmers Union,
    1963–64: 255
Grainger, Joseph W., **1965**: 194
Grains Arrangement, International, **1967**: 476,
    508; **1968–69**: 29, 63, 94
Grand Canyon National Park, Ariz., **1968–69**: 547

Grand Coulee Dam, **1965**: 186; **1966**: 269
Grand Turk Island, **1963–64**: 725
Grandson, the President's.
 See Nugent, Patrick Lyndon.
Grant, Arnold M., **1965**: 273
Grant, Lt. Gen. H. W., **1965**: 339
Grant, Nellie (Mrs. Algernon Sartoris),
 1968–69: 648
Grant, Richard H., **1967**: 342n.
Grant, Ulysses S., **1967**: 57, 130, 256;
 1968–69: 648
Grantee Directory, United States (1965),
 1966: 378
Grant-in-aid processing time, task force,
 1967: 458
Grants, **1967**: 121, 123, 124
 Education, **1968–69**: 684 (pp. 1313, 1322)
 Humanities, **1968–69**: 686, 703
 Processing time, **1968–69**: 39 (p. 110)
 Research, **1967**: 6 [6]
 Scientific research, **1968–69**: 687
 Student, **1967**: 164
"Grapes of Wrath," John Steinbeck, **1967**: 114
Grasshopper, Ariz., **1965**: 419
Gray, Mrs. Georgia, **1963–64**: 741
Gray, Repr. Kenneth J., **1966**: 349;
 1968–69: 128
Gray, Susan W., **1967**: 396n.
Grazing land, **1968–69**: 91
Great Basin National Park, Nevada, **1965**: 54;
 1966: 82
Great Britain.
 See United Kingdom.
Great Falls, Mont., **1963–64**: 573, 574
 Mayor Marion S. Erdmann, **1963–64**: 573
Great Lakes area.
 See also Area redevelopment.
 Development, **1968–69**: 124
 Pollution control, **1966**: 392–393; **1967**: 101
  U.S.-Canada cooperation, **1965**: 54
 Shipping, U.S. and Canada, **1963–64**: 140
 Unemployment, **1963–64**: 213
Great Lakes Basin Commission, **1968–69**: 593,
 666
Great Northern Railroad, **1968–69**: 330
Great Salt Lake borderlands, **1966**: 255
Great Seal of the United States, **1963–64**: 411;
 1966: 609
Great Society, **1965**: 2, 27, 29, 32 (pp. 83, 94,
 99), 33, 35 (p. 107), 76, 80, 90, 100,
 105, 133, 223, 250, 277, 301, 354,
 362, 372, 374, 429, 439, 447, 489, 519,
 526, 632, 659, 660; **1966**: 33, 77, 111,
 119, 121 [4], 149n., 158 [1], 188 [8],
 221, 237, 330, 347, 351, 394, 399, 417
 [3], 418, 429, 444, 483, 484n., 493,
 497, 518, 545, 557, 599 [1, 6], 619;
 1967: 258, 291, 514, 532, 554 [15];
 1968–69: 4, 75, 96

Great Society – *continued*
 Election impact, **1966**: 610 [6]
 Republican support, **1966**: 628 [2]
 Statement, **1963–64**: 776
 Vietnam conflict impact, **1966**: 501 [10]
Great Swamp Wilderness, N.J., **1968–69**: 168,
 502
Greece, **1963–64**: 153, 424n., 607, 638, 694,
 702, 713, 728, 729, 733, 734, 736, 749;
 1965: 235, 325, 378; **1966**: 6 (p. 7), 41,
 62, 132, 478
 Ancient, **1963–64**: 106, 424
 Assistance, **1967**: 44, 107, 108, 158;
  1968–69: 63
 Communist aggression, **1967**: 397, 409;
  1968–69: 142, 154, 165
 Cyprus dispute, **1963–64**: 70, 170 [1], 182,
  192, 206, 210, 423, 429, 504 [5], 511,
  544, 560 [4], 607, 749; **1967**: 100, 162,
  518ftn. (p. 1093), 519, 521, 545;
  1968–69: 14 (p. 26), 504
 Immigration quota to U.S., **1963–64**: 97
 King Constantine II, **1963–64**: 209; **1967**: 108
 King Paul I, **1963–64**: 153, 209, 211 [1]
 Papandreou, George, **1963–64**: 424, 429
 Princess Irene, **1963–64**: 153
 Queen Frederika, **1963–64**: 153, 209, 424
 U.S. Ambassador Henry R. Labouisse,
  1965: 353 [4]
 U.S. relations with, **1963–64**: 424, 511
 Visit of Sen. Fulbright, **1963–64**: 316 [24]
Greeley, Horace, **1963–64**: 413; **1965**: 155;
 1967: 251
Green, Repr. Edith, **1963–64**: 36, 47, 398, 578,
 676
Green, Marshall, **1965**: 448ftn. (p. 926)
Green, Ray E., **1963–64**: 709, 712, 713
Green, Theodore Francis, **1963–64**: 587 [2], 601;
 1965: 410; **1966**: 230, 396;
 1968–69: 108
Green, William, **1967**: 484
Green, Repr. William J., **1963–64**: 63, 742;
 1967: 291
Green River, **1968–69**: 505
Green Thumb, Operation, **1967**: 114
Greene, Gen. Wallace M., Jr. (Marine Corps
 Commandant), **1966**: 516 [9], 641;
 1967: 361, 375 [6, 19], 446; **1968–69**:
 34
Greene, Mrs. Wallace M., Jr., **1968–69**: 34
Greenewalt, Crawford H., **1963–64**: 785
Greenfield, James L., **1966**: 65 [1, 3]
Gregory, Thomas W., **1965**: 66
Greig, Edvard, **1968–69**: 214
Greigg, Repr. Stanley L., **1966**: 312, 358
Gresham, Perry, **1963–64**: 279n.
Grider, George W., **1963–64**: 645, 701;
 1966: 472
Gridiron Club, **1963–64**: 298

Grieves, Howard C., **1965**: 269, 296n.
Griffin, Msgr. Christopher P., **1963–64**: 727
Griffin, Robert P., **1963–64**: 356; **1966**: 431
Griffiths, Repr. Martha W., **1963–64**: 356, 745;
    1966: 431
Grimes, Conrad, **1966**: 435
Grissom, Virgil I., **1965**: 120, 121, 134, 310;
    1968–69: 387
  Death, **1967**: 19, 38
Griswold, Erwin N., **1967**: 275n., 411 [2, 8], 443;
    1968–69: 236
Griswold, Mrs. Erwin N., **1967**: 443
Gromyko, Andrei A., **1963–64**: 365; **1965**: 388
    [10]; **1966**: 249n., 516 [8, 17], 577
    [6]; **1967**: 279–281, 283
Gronouski, John A., **1965**: 595, 596; **1966**: 141
    [12], 200, 228, 236 [15], 528;
    1967: 225 [18]
  See also Postmaster General (John A. Gronou-
    ski).
Gronouski, Mrs. John A., **1965**: 78, 463 [1], 595
Gross, Repr. H. R., **1968–69**: 696 [17]
Gross national product (GNP), **1966**: 11, 26
    (pp. 48–49, 60), 33, 34 (p. 96), 155,
    189, 228, 240, 247 [4], 324, 444, 494
    [1], 509, 635 [5, 8, 18], 642 [12], 654
    [9]; **1967**: 3 (p. 7), 13 (pp. 40, 41), 16
    (pp. 73, 76–78), 55, 63, 225 [9], 312
    [4], 328 [23], 329, 375 [16], 420, 484,
    493, 495 [9], 532; **1968–69**: 14 (p. 27),
    39 (p. 87), 46, 47 (pp. 129, 131, 133),
    50, 109, 229, 262, 467 [3], 524, 612,
    676 (p. 1268), 678 (p. 1287), 684 (pp.
    1312, 1313, 1315)
  See also National product.
Grosvenor, Melville B., **1963–64**: 117;
    1968–69: 501, 510, 525
Groton, Conn., **1963–64**: 383
Group of Ten (International Monetary Fund),
    1966: 486
Gruening, Sen. Ernest, **1966**: 567–569
Gruenther, Gen. Alfred M., **1963–64**: 211 [6],
    217, 241, 244; **1965**: 163
Guadalupe Mountains National Park, Texas,
    1965: 54; **1966**: 82, 518, 522;
    1967: 20; **1968–69**: 122, 411
Guam, **1966**: 128, 600; **1967**: 218;
    1968–69: 165, 402, 477
  Governor, election of, **1968–69**: 477
  Gov. Manuel F. L. Guerrero, **1967**: 126, 134;
    1968–69: 477
  Releases, **1967**: 129, 131
  Vietnam conference, **1967**: 126–128, 130–132
    [1], 134–135
Guam, College of, **1968–69**: 477
Guam Elective Governor Act, **1968–69**: 477
Guam International Airport, **1967**: 126

Guantanamo naval base, Cuba, **1965**: 325
  Cuban personnel, reduction, **1963–64**: 177
  U.S. guarantee of security, **1963–64**: 177
  Water supply, **1963–64**: 175, 182, 192, 218
    [29], 235, 295, 330, 544, 607, 612, 634,
    635, 639, 642, 643, 645, 648, 652, 726,
    736, 749, 750
Guaranteed loan program, **1968–69**: 54
  See also Students.
Guatemala, **1966**: 277 [6], 320 [12]; **1967**: 44;
    1968–69: 205n., 368
  President Mendez Montenegro, **1966**: 277 [6];
    1968–69: 366, 374–376
  Visit, **1968–69**: 376
Guerrero, Lorenzo (President of Nicaragua),
    1966: 369; **1967**: 173
Guerrero, Gov. Manuel F. L., **1967**: 126, 134;
    1968–69: 477
Guerrero, Mexico, **1967**: 447n.
Guerrilla warfare, **1963–64**: 223, 272, 382, 703;
    1965: 26, 223, 227, 229
Guevara, Ernesto, **1963–64**: 246 [5]
Guillermo Elio, Tomas, **1968–69**: 362n.
Gulf of Mexico, canal to Atlantic Ocean,
    1963–64: 198
Gulf of Mexico, U.S. coastline, **1965**: 521
Gulf of Tonkin resolution, **1966**: 88 [17]
Gun Control, Emergency Committee for,
    1968–69: 339ftn. (p. 748)
Gun Control Act of 1968, **1968–69**: 50, 59, 235,
    257, 296, 302, 316, 320n., 324, 325,
    333, 334, 530, 553, 678
Gun control legislation, **1968–69**: 14 (p. 30),
    235, 257, 263, 293, 296, 298, 302, 316,
    320, 324, 325, 333, 339 [3], 355, 356,
    358, 406, 530, 553, 557 [8], 561, 676
    (p. 1266), 678 (p. 1292), 696 [16]
  See also Gun Control Act of 1968; Omnibus
    Crime Control and Safe Streets Act of
    1968.
  District of Columbia, **1968–69**: 355
  Message to Congress, **1968–69**: 334
Gunn, Donald, **1963–64**: 694, 695
Guns, imports, **1968–69**: 553
Gursel, Cemal (President of Turkey), **1966**: 146,
    460
  Message to, **1963–64**: 70
Gursel, Mrs. Cemal, letter, **1966**: 460
Guy, Gov. William L., **1966**: 312, 491n., 492
    [1], 536; **1967**: 419n.; **1968–69**: 46n.
Guyana, **1966**: 341
  Ambassador Sir John Carter, **1966**: 342
  Prime Minister Linden F. Burnham,
    1966: 341–342
Gwinn, William P., **1968–69**: 10

Haar, Charles, **1966**: 12, 493; **1968–69**: 114
Haas, Walter A., Jr., **1968–69**: 25
Hackler, Loyd, **1968–69**: 7n.
Haddon, Dr. William J., Jr., **1966**: 449
Hagan, Repr. G. Elliott, **1963–64**: 330
Hagan, Richard C., **1967**: 230
Hagemeister, Sp5c. Charles C., **1968–69**: 246
Hagen, Repr. Harlan, **1963–64**: 409; **1965**: 405;
    1966: 508
Hagerty, William W., **1963–64**: 266 [4]
Haggerty, C. J., **1963–64**: 235, 444; **1965**: 223;
    1967: 261; **1968–69**: 154
Haggerty, James J., **1963–64**: 661
Hague, Capt. Dennis, **1967**: 9
Hague, The, **1963–64**: 316ftn. (p. 622)
Haile Selassie I, Emperor (Ethiopia), **1967**: 51,
    52; **1968–69**: 433, 639
Haines, Gen. Ralph E., Jr., **1967**: 384, 407;
    1968–69: 283 [2]
Haiphong, North Vietnam, **1966**: 124 [7], 312,
    338 [19]; **1967**: 70 [10], 308, 375 [1,
    3]
Halaby, Najeeb E. (Administrator, Federal Avia-
    tion Agency), **1963–64**: 215, 242 [9],
    294 [6], 310, 355n., 409, 586;
    1965: 339
Haley, Repr. James A., **1963–64**: 199
Hall, Charles, **1968–69**: 547n.
Hall, Dave, **1966**: 434–435
Hall, Hal David, **1963–64**: 339; **1965**: 260
Hall, Ralph, **1968–69**: 599n.
Hall, Comdr. Ralph E., **1966**: 345
Hall, Dr. Robert, **1968–69**: 589
Hall, William O., **1966**: 198n.
Hall of Heroes, Pentagon, **1968–69**: 246
Halleck, Repr. Charles A., **1963–64**: 96, 501
Hallenbeck, Dr. George, **1965**: 549n.;
    1966: 575
Hallstein, J. Walter, **1965**: 112
Halpern, Repr. Seymour, **1966**: 394, 395
Halsted, Mrs. Anna (Roosevelt), **1965**: 210n.;
    1967: 28; **1968–69**: 42, 611
Hamilton, Alexander, **1966**: 435; **1968–69**: 291n.
Hamilton, Deborah Lee, **1966**: 353n.
Hamilton, Douglas Nelson, **1966**: 353n.
Hamilton, Ed, **1968–69**: 17
Hamilton, Repr. Lee H., **1965**: 188; **1966**: 353
Hamilton, Mrs. Lee H., **1966**: 353
Hamilton, Mr. and Mrs. Thomas H., **1966**: 533
Hamilton, Tracy Lynn, **1966**: 353n.
Hamilton, W. C., **1965**: 161n.
Hamlett, Gen. Barksdale, **1963–64**: 349n.
Hammarskjold, Dag, **1963–64**: 435, 502;
    1965: 299
Hammer, Dr. Armand, **1963–64**: 137
Hammer, Harry, **1963–64**: 137
Hammer, Victor, **1963–64**: 137
Hammer v. *Dagenhart*, **1968–69**: 270ftn. (p. 636)

Hammerstein, Mrs. Oscar, **1967**: 248n.
Hammett, Louis P., **1968–69**: 71n.
Hammond, Ind., **1963–64**: 639
    Mayor Edward Dowling, **1963–64**: 639
Hanan, Rubin M., **1965**: 642n.
Hand, Learned, **1967**: 110; **1968–69**: 282
Hand, Lloyd N., **1963–64**: 819; **1966**: 85
Handel, George Frederick, **1966**: 482
Handicapped, National Commission on Archi-
    tectural Barriers to Rehabilitation
    of the, **1966**: 192; **1968–69**: 287
Handicapped, President's Committee on Em-
    ployment of the, **1963–64**: 302;
    1967: 388
    Distinguished Service Award, **1963–64**: 235,
        302n., 389
Handicapped American of the Year, President's
    Trophy for the, **1963–64**: 302n.
Handicapped Children's Early Education Assist-
    ance Act, **1968–69**: 503
Handicapped persons, **1963–64**: 297;
    1965: 478, 556; **1966**: 34 (p. 100);
    1967: 388
    Aid, **1963–64**: 415; **1965**: 5, 416;
        1966: 127, 189, 318, 509, 588; **1968–
        69**: 678 (pp. 1295, 1299)
    Architectural barriers, elimination, **1966**: 192;
        1968–69: 287, 440
    Blind, **1967**: 77, 413; **1968–69**: 230, 446, 503,
        548
    Children, **1965**: 401, 592; **1966**: 95, 317, 362;
        1967: 13 (pp. 55, 59), 39, 77, 260,
        517; **1968–69**: 4, 39 (p. 106), 111, 329,
        503, 678 (p. 1293)
    Crippled, **1968–69**: 111, 503
    Deaf, **1967**: 77, 413; **1968–69**: 548
    Education, **1963–64**: 47, 808; **1965**: 9, 70,
        305, 401, 592; **1966**: 406; **1968–69**:
        39 (p. 106), 54, 503, 678 (p. 1293)
    Employment, **1963–64**: 179, 302, 345, 403,
        808; **1965**: 100, 140, 425; **1966**: 111;
        1967: 199, 388, 413; **1968–69**: 24, 39
        (p. 104), 548
    Equal opportunity, **1963–64**: 389
    Government employment, **1963–64**: 213, 302,
        403; **1966**: 318
    Health care, **1968–69**: 111, 678 (p. 1296)
    Housing, **1965**: 415
    Income, **1968–69**: 39 (p. 105)
    Library services, **1966**: 362
    Medical care, **1967**: 3 (p. 6), 114
    Medicare benefits, **1966**: 516 [6]
    Mentally, **1967**: 199, 285, 517; **1968–69**: 54,
        493, 503, 678 (p. 1294)
    Military personnel, **1967**: 25
    Occupational training, **1963–64**: 179, 213, 302,
        305; **1966**: 26 (p. 63), 111, 127; **1967**:
        413

Handicapped persons — *continued*
  Rehabilitation, physical, **1966**: 588; **1967**: 413; **1968-69**: 678 (pp. 1294, 1299)
  Veterans, **1968-69**: 40, 452, 599, 678
  See also main heading, Veterans.
  Widows, **1967**: 12
Handler, Philip, **1963-64**: 211 [6]; **1968-69**: 513n.
"Handling of Toxicological Information" report, President's foreword, **1966**: 279
Hanford, Wash., **1963-64**: 486 [2]
Hanify, Edward B., **1966**: 210n.
Hanisch, Arthur, **1963-64**: 211 [6]
Hanley, Repr. James M., **1966**: 394-395, 510
Hanna, Mrs. Jane, **1963-64**: 208
Hanna, Repr. Richard T., **1963-64**: 414; **1967**: 227, 485 [2, 3]
Hannah, John A., **1963-64**: 513; **1965**: 85, 615
Hannan, Bishop Philip M., **1963-64**: 784
Hanoi, **1963-64**: 420 [1, 5]; **1965**: 152, 223; **1966**: 94, 246, 311-312, 325, 329, 346, 397; **1967**: 375 [1]
  See also Vietnam, North.
  News conference remarks, **1966**: 141 [14], 277 [11], 338 [19], 492 [6], 654 [1, 13]
  Radio, **1967**: 136n.
Hansberger, R. V., **1967**: 252n.
Hansen, Gov. Clifford P., **1966**: 121 [1]
Hansen, Repr. George V., **1966**: 410-411
Hansen, Repr. John R., **1966**: 312
Hansen, Repr. Julia Butler, **1968-69**: 386
Hanshus, Jon A., **1966**: 289
Hanson, Royce, **1963-64**: 703
Hanson Scale Co., **1963-64**: 350n.
Hard-core unemployment.
  See Unemployment.
Hardeman, Dorsey B., **1965**: 285
Hardin, Clifford M., **1968-69**: 664, 695, 696 [14]
Harding, Bertrand M., **1963-64**: 455 [4]; **1965**: 150; **1968-69**: 153 [3], 259n.
Harding, Ralph R., **1963-64**: 659; **1966**: 410-411
Harding, 1st Lt. Revier, **1966**: 246
Harding, Warren G., **1966**: 650 [13]; **1968-69**: 138
Hardy, Repr. Porter, Jr., **1965**: 205
Hardy, Thomas, **1963-64**: 347
Hare, Raymond A., **1965**: 353 [4]
Harkins, Gen. Paul D., **1963-64**: 170 [5], 294 [5], 425
Harkins, Mrs. Paul D., **1963-64**: 425
Harkness, Richard L., **1966**: 516 [6]
Harlan, Justice John M., **1966**: 475; **1967**: 268
Harlech, Lord (David Ormsby Gore), **1963-64**: 187n., 263n., 796

Harlech, Lady (Lady Ormsby Gore), **1963-64**: 187
Harlem, New York City, **1967**: 55
  Juvenile delinquency, **1963-64**: 334
Harley, William, **1967**: 474
Harlingen, Texas, **1967**: 408
Harllee, John (Chairman, Federal Maritime Commission), **1963-64**: 316 [3]; **1965**: 371
Harlow, Harry F., **1968-69**: 71n.
Harmel, Pierre, **1966**: 236 [5]
Harmon, Col. Clifford B., **1963-64**: 569; **1967**: 431; **1968-69**: 610n.
Harmon International Aviation Trophies, **1963-64**: 569; **1967**: 431; **1968-69**: 610
Harmon Trust, Clifford B., **1967**: 431n.
Harper, John D., **1968-69**: 25
Harriman, W. Averell, **1963-64**: 26, 336 [6], 358, 588n., 666, 667, 668, 780 [6], 796n.; **1965**: 221, 353 [7, 11], 388 [10], 412 [2], 491, 632; **1966**: 8 [2], 22, 56, 85, 88 [18], 236 [9], 320 [1], 397, 401 [15], 466, 474 [17], 577 [3, 6], 607 [2-8, 11], 610 [8]; **1967**: 21, 116, 251; **1968-69**: 42, 170, 188, 198, 223 [1], 242, 275 [1], 301, 339 [5], 400, 460 [3], 572, 611, 646 [14]
Harriman, Mrs. W. Averell, **1963-64**: 358
Harrington, Rev. Donald, **1963-64**: 669
Harrington Lake, **1967**: 239
Harris, Sen. Fred R., **1966**: 410, 413, 415-416; **1967**: 326; **1968-69**: 417
Harris, Rev. Frederick B., **1966**: 326
Harris, George S., **1968-69**: 36
Harris, Repr. Oren, **1963-64**: 50, 215, 520, 557, 599; **1965**: 319 [19], 361, 401, 406, 410, 536, 551, 568n.
  Letter, **1963-64**: 154
Harris, Mrs. Oren, **1963-64**: 599
Harris, Mrs. Patricia Roberts, **1963-64**: 242 [5], 257n., 750; **1965**: 301n.; **1966**: 136n.; **1967**: 81; **1968-69**: 293
Harris, Ralph, **1963-64**: 563 [17]
Harris (Louis) survey, **1963-64**: 542; **1966**: 52 [7], 320 [14], 654 [10]; **1967**: 297 [13], 502; **1968-69**: 568
Harrisburg, Pa., **1963-64**: 560 [13], 563 [17]
  Campaign remarks, **1963-64**: 566
Harrison, Gov. Albertis S., Jr., **1963-64**: 359, 471; **1965**: 205
Harrison, Repr. William Henry, **1968-69**: 505
Harry S. Truman Center for the Advancement of Peace (Jerusalem), **1966**: 22, 212
Harsha, Repr. William H., **1963-64**: 323
Hart, Parker T., **1967**: 158n.
Hart, Sen. Philip A., **1963-64**: 97, 356, 357, 431, 562, 745; **1966**: 294, 431, 433, 576; **1968-69**: 293
  Letter, **1968-69**: 82

Hart, Mrs. Philip A. (Jane), **1963–64**: 310
Hart-Celler packaging bill, **1963–64**: 173
Hartford, Conn.
  Campaign remarks, **1963–64**: 603, 604
  Chamber of Commerce, **1963–64**: 71 [3]
  Mayor William E. Glynn, **1963–64**: 603
Hartke, Sen. Vance, **1963–64**: 67, 288, 639, 640,
    729; **1965**: 188, 231; **1966**: 346–347,
    350, 353, 579; **1967**: 554 [1]
Hartke, Mrs. Vance, **1963–64**: 640, 729
Harvard University, **1963–64**: 399
Harvey, Repr. James, **1963–64**: 356
Harwick, J. William, **1965**: 163
Haskew, Dr. Lawrence D., **1967**: 396n.
Haskins, Caryl, **1966**: 424n.
Haskins, Ralph W., **1967**: 538n.
Hasluck, Paul M. C., **1967**: 562
Hassan II, King (Morocco), **1967**: 43, 46
Hassel, Kai-Uwe von, **1963–64**: 316 [2]
Hastie, Judge William, **1963–64**: 622; **1967**: 201;
    1968–69: 227
Hastings, George E., **1967**: 408 [1]
Hatch Act of 1887, **1965**: 9
Hatch Political Activity Act, **1966**: 499; **1967**:
    236; **1968–69**: 133, 305
Hatcher, Andrew T., **1963–64**: 104n., 150 [8]
Hatcher, Bishop E. C., **1966**: 484n.
Hatcher, Harlan H., **1963–64**: 357
Hatfield, Gov. Mark O., **1963–64**: 575, 578;
    1965: 388 [14]; **1966**: 124 [7]
Hathaway, William D., **1963–64**: 606; **1966**:
    396–399
Hathaway, Mrs. William D., **1966**: 398
Haughton, Daniel J., **1968–69**: 10, 110
Hawaii, **1965**: 448 [10]; **1966**: 157, 533; **1968–**
    69: 178, 179, 341, 525
  Civil rights in, **1963–64**: 534
  East-West Center, report, **1963–64**: 336 [6]
  Gov. John A. Burns, **1963–64**: 336 [6]; **1966**:
    121 [1], 326, 459n., 484, 532–533;
    1967: 555; **1968–69**: 197–199, 398n.
  Remarks, **1968–69**: 197–200, 398
  Statehood, fifth anniversary, **1963–64**: 534
  Transfer of land to, **1963–64**: 534
  Visit, **1966**: 532, 568; **1967**: 555; **1968–69**:
    197–201, 398, 400, 401
Hawaii, University of, **1966**: 601
Hawley, Samuel W., **1968–69**: 114
Haworth, Leland J. (Director, National Science
    Foundation), **1965**: 71, 265, 271; **1966**:
    424n., 637; **1967**: 20; **1968–69**: 361,
    695
Hayden, Sen. Carl, **1963–64**: 11, 98, 649, 793;
    1965: 329, 477, 543; **1966**: 395; **1967**:
    85n., 413, 536; **1968–69**: 228, 258, 501
Hayes, A. J., **1963–64**: 158, 571
Hayes, Col. Anna Mae, **1967**: 475
Hayes, Carleton J., **1968–69**: 78

Hayes, John S., **1966**: 401 [18]
Hayes, Rutherford B., **1968–69**: 147n.
Haygood, Atticus, **1963–64**: 330
Haynes, Eldridge, **1965**: 4
Hays, Brooks, **1963–64**: 113, 238; **1965**: 22 [1];
    1966: 51; **1968–69**: 156
Hays, Repr. Wayne L., **1963–64**: 323, 582; **1965**:
    233
  Exchange act.
  See Mutual Educational and Cultural Ex-
    change Act of 1961.
Haywood, Mrs. Margaret A., **1967**: 406, 466n.
Head Start.
  See Project Head Start.
Heads of state and government.
  Meetings, **1963–64**: 54 [8]
  Messages to.
  See Messages to foreign leaders.
Heald, Henry T., **1966**: 517
Healey, Denis, **1963–64**: 796, 797
Health, **1963–64**: 132, (pp. 176, 191), 268, 305,
    341, 387, 414, 552, 557; **1965**: 32 (pp.
    83, 84), 35 (p. 116), 115, 154, 222, 410,
    424
  See also Medical care.
  Campaign remarks, **1963–64**: 598
  Effect of smoking on, **1963–64**: 211 [25]
  Hazards to, **1965**: 5
  International, **1963–64**: 396; **1965**: 12, 15,
    175, 214, 262, 343, 531, 544, 649
  Legislation, **1963–64**: 620, 703; **1965**: 5, 179,
    183, 319 [21], 329, 330, 531
  See also specific acts.
  Message to Congress, **1963–64**: 179; **1965**: 5
  Older persons, **1965**: 176 [2]
  Presidential policy paper, **1963–64**: 755
  Research, **1965**: 54, 72
Health, Education, and Welfare, Department of,
    1963–64: 132 (p. 181), 173, 179, 218
    [16], 219, 271 [7], 516 [12], 792n.;
    1965: 9, 75, 94, 115n., 127, 138n., 140,
    184, 202n., 319 [21], 418, 433, 453,
    485, 503, 514, 527, 546, 620; **1966**: 26
    (p. 54), 28, 45, 82, 95, 98, 157, 185,
    215, 271n., 279–280, 307, 308n., 320
    [5], 344 [2, 8], 494ftn. (p. 1106), 580
    [7], 629, 630 [4]; **1967**: 6 [14], 13
    (pp. 57, 59), 27, 186, 199, 215, 217n.,
    223 [6], 265, 412, 432n.; **1968–69**: 30,
    39 (pp. 104, 108, 110), 57, 100, 145,
    153 [2], 155n., 287, 329, 336, 388,
    446, 586, 653n., 657, 678 (pp. 1280,
    1293, 1302)
  Alcoholism study, **1968–69**: 59
  Appropriations, **1967**: 13 (p. 46), 77, 411 [10],
    417 [1], 479; **1968–69**: 39 (p. 92), 408,
    678 (p. 1280)

HEW — *continued*
　Center for Educational Cooperation, **1966**: 406,
　　533, 627
　Disease prevention centers, **1967**: 6 [15]
　Drug Abuse Control, Bureau of, **1968–69**: 59,
　　60, 678, (p. 1292)
　Drug inventories, **1967**: 121
　Health services authority, **1966**: 190
　Reorganization, **1966**: 95, 580 [13]; **1968–69**:
　　678 (p. 1302)
　Spending cutbacks, **1967**: 6 [6]
　Water pollution control authority, **1966**: 91
　Health, Education, and Welfare, Secretary of
　　(Anthony J. Celebrezze), **1963–64**: 89,
　　99, 105, 178n., 288, 291, 292, 297, 320,
　　321, 322, 323, 325, 326, 327, 328, 405,
　　406, 488n., 537, 543, 581, 600, 711;
　　1965: 5, 54, 72, 94, 115, 181, 183, 200,
　　215, 231n., 282, 305, 324, 340, 354, 388
　　[17], 394, 401, 406, 410
　Campaign remarks on, **1963–64**: 588n., 642,
　　653n.
　News conference remarks on, **1963–64**: 170
　　[4], 211 [25], 256 [14], 266 [21],
　　285 [2]
　Report, **1963–64**: 675n.; **1965**: 184, 249n.,
　　394n., 416
　Resignation, **1965**: 389
　Health, Education, and Welfare, Secretary of
　　(Wilbur J. Cohen), **1968–69**: 111ftn.
　　(p. 331), 329, 346n., 388, 393n., 397,
　　409n., 419, 420, 459, 475, 481, 493,
　　503, 536, 538, 545, 565, 567, 589, 622,
　　640, 659
　Acting Secretary of, **1968–69**: 117
　Letter, **1968–69**: 396
　Memorandums, **1968–69**: 389, 538n.
　Swearing in, **1968–69**: 253
　Health, Education, and Welfare, Secretary of
　　(John W. Gardner), **1965**: 437, 443,
　　519, 527, 539, 551, 568n., 576, 611n.,
　　615, 620, 642; **1966**: 3n., 4, 31, 45, 54,
　　56, 86, 95, 105, 106n., 132, 140, 157,
　　161, 165, 168, 185, 190, 192n., 208,
　　214, 216, 223, 237, 253, 257, 270–271,
　　292–293, 298, 301, 306, 317, 327, 337,
　　388ftn. (p. 832), 395, 404n., 424n.,
　　462, 490, 493, 509, 523, 533, 573,
　　581, 627; **1967**: 12, 20, 35, 39, 71, 77,
　　82, 114, 115, 117, 121, 147, 148, 184,
　　199, 214n., 223 [2, 6], 225 [21], 258,
　　266, 298, 304n., 338, 373, 413, 423,
　　460 [1], 474, 490, 493, 503, 517, 520,
　　539; **1968–69**: 3, 6, 19, 24, 26, 42, 54,
　　74, 79 [5], 91, 94, 111, 113, 122, 153
　　[16]
　Letters, **1965**: 544, 618; **1966**: 127, 169, 280,
　　307, 319; **1967**: 215

HEW, Secretary — *continued*
　Memorandums, **1966**: 425, 606; **1967**: 186,
　　259, 412, 458
　News conference remarks on, **1966**: 52 [2],
　　88 [1], 188 [4], 247 [1], 494 [10],
　　501 [13], 516 [1], 578 [10], 580 [5,
　　8–9, 14, 19], 607 [1], 650 [11]
　Report to the President, **1968–69**: 473n.
　Reports, **1965**: 501, 545
　Resignation, **1968–69**: 30
　Swearing in, **1965**: 433
　Vietnam task force, **1966**: 141 [10]
　Health, International Career Service in, **1966**: 45
　Health, National Institutes of, **1963–64**: 132 (p.
　　189), 179; **1965**: 115, 410, 475, 514;
　　1966: 293, 301, 319, 433; **1967**: 12,
　　217, 319, 540
　Health, Partnership for, **1967**: 77; **1968–69**: 111
　Health, the President's, **1968–69**: 646 [4]
　Health, White House Conference on, **1965**: 183,
　　424, 594
　Health Agencies, National, **1967**: 288
　Health Assembly, World, **1965**: 202n., 262
　Health Association, American Public, **1966**:
　　185n.
　Health Association, International, **1966**: 45
　Health Benefits Act of 1959, **1966**: 108
　Health Center, International Ladies Garment
　　Workers Union, **1963–64**: 388
　50th anniversary, **1963–64**: 387
　Health Council, National, **1966**: 185n.
　Health Facilities, National Advisory Commission
　　on, **1967**: 77, 419; **1968–69**: 622
　Health and health programs, **1963–64**: 132 (pp.
　　188, 189), 305, 391, 661; **1965**: 32 (p.
　　95), 71, 72, 475, 525, 594; **1966**: 34
　　(p. 100), 95, 166, 208, 236 [13], 263,
　　273, 307, 394–395, 399, 573; **1967**: 13
　　(pp. 46, 58, 59), 267, 271, 286, 329,
　　412, 419, 500, 532, 540, 554 [6, 12];
　　1968–69: 39 (p. 92), 47 (pp. 141, 143),
　　84, 100, 102, 109, 164, 262, 282, 354,
　　396, 460 [2], 481, 566, 589, 622, 625,
　　631, 676 (p. 1265), 684
　See also Disease prevention; Health; Medical
　　care; Medicare; Safety.
　Administrative reforms, **1966**: 95, 190
　Antipoverty program aid, **1963–64**: 124 (p.
　　164)
　Appalachian region, **1968–69**: 701
　Centers, **1968–69**: 19, 20, 39 (p. 104), 111,
　　113, 536, 565, 622, 678 (pp. 1295,
　　1296), 689
　Children and youth, **1963–64**: 403, 490, 590,
　　755; **1965**: 2, 5, 6, 29, 32 (p. 94), 70,
　　149, 259, 401, 406, 453, 467, 501, 594;
　　1966: 26 (p. 62), 27, 45, 95, 157, 271,
　　317, 392, 395, 508, 569, 573, 576, 580

Health and health programs — *continued*
  Children and youth — *continued*
      [11], 589, 654 [3]; **1967**: 13 (p. 53),
      16 (pp. 75, 85), 39, 77, 86, 160, 176,
      222, 251, 353, 405; **1968-69**: 3, 4, 14
      (p. 29), 47 (p. 143), 111, 113, 270, 406,
      442, 446, 567, 568, 569, 622, 684 (p.
      1324)
      See also Infant, *below.*
  Coal mines, **1968-69**: 475
  Community services, **1967**: 353
  Costs, **1968-69**: 14 (pp. 28, 31), 47 (p. 143),
      100, 111, 397, 676 (p. 1265), 678 (p.
      1295)
  Disadvantaged persons, **1968-69**: 39 (p. 104),
      47 (pp. 130, 143), 111, 678 (pp. 1295,
      1296), 684 (p. 1324)
  District of Columbia, **1963-64**; 133; **1965**: 29,
      70; **1966**: 27; **1967**: 15; **1968-69**: 19,
      20, 95, 689
  Drugs, payment, **1968-69**: 678 (p. 1295)
  Education, **1967**: 217
  Expenditures, **1966**: 26 (pp. 50, 55, 58, 62),
      185, 189, 228, 395, 417 [3], 520;
      1967: 201, 211, 217, 258, 260, 261,
      286, 291, 329, 423; **1968-69**: 39 (p.
      103), 66, 75, 109, 111, 114, 262, 612,
      644
  Facilities, construction, **1968-69**: 39 (p. 92),
      468
  Federal aid, **1963-64**: 179, 520, 669; **1965**: 5,
      361; **1966**: 6 (p. 3), 95, 166, 168, 188
      [6, 8], 235, 237, 253, 524; **1967**: 477;
      1968-69: 24, 442, 468, 557 [8], 676
      (p. 1267), 678 (pp. 1280, 1295, 1303)
  Federal-State-local governmental responsi-
      bilities, **1967**: 77
  Federal-State partnership program, **1968-69**:
      678 (p. 1296)
  Foreign assistance, **1966**: 26 (p. 58), 34 (p.
      105); **1967**: 44
  Government employees, **1965**: 324; **1966**:
      108-109
  Handicapped persons, **1968-69**: 111, 678 (p.
      1296)
  Hazards, **1966**: 462
  Heart disease, cancer and stroke, **1968-69**: 111
  Indians, **1968-69**: 113, 259
  Industrial, **1965**: 324; **1966**: 237; **1968-69**: 24
  Infant, **1968-69**: 14 (p. 29), 26, 39 (pp. 89,
      103, 104), 47 (p. 143), 111, 113, 262,
      270, 406, 429, 442, 568, 569, 596, 622,
      676 (p. 1265), 678 (pp. 1295-1297),
      684 (p. 1324)
  Information exchange, **1968-69**: 408
  Insurance, **1966**: 26 (pp. 53, 55), 169; **1968-
      69**: 111
      Railroad, **1968-69**: 331

Health and health programs — *continued*
  International, **1966**: 6 (pp. 7-8), 22, 41, 45-
      46, 49, 157, 166, 339, 406
  International cooperation, **1965**: 202, 262, 343
  Legislation, **1966**: 6 (pp. 7-8), 22, 41, 45-46,
      49, 95, 166, 394-395, 403, 433, 490,
      501 [6], 509, 512, 515, 520, 524, 573,
      599 [6]; **1967**: 270, 413, 500, 520;
      1968-69: 39 (p. 104), 50, 154, 536,
      565, 567, 589, 601, 622, 655, 678
  Manpower development and training, **1967**: 16
      (p. 85), 77
  Maternal and prenatal, **1966**: 95, 189, 580
      [11]; **1967**: 353, 479; **1968-69**: 3,
      14 (p. 29), 39 (pp. 89, 104), 47 (p.
      143), 111, 113, 270, 442, 568, 569,
      662, 676 (p. 1265), 678 (p. 1296),
      684 (p. 1324)
  Mental health and retardation, **1966**: 26 (p.
      62), 27, 95, 189, 271, 293, 395, 515;
      1967: 285, 353, 373; **1968-69**: 39 (p.
      103), 111, 442, 678 (p. 1295)
      See also Mental health and mental health
      programs.
  Message to Congress, **1965**: 5; **1966**: 95; **1967**:
      77, 78; **1968-69**: 111
  Migrant workers, **1965**: 5, 406; **1967**: 114;
      1968-69: 91, 536
  Military personnel and veterans, **1968-69**: 39
      (p. 106), 40, 111, 678 (p. 1296)
  Minority groups, **1968-69**: 26, 91, 429, 442
  Neighborhood centers, **1967**: 13 (p. 53), 16 (p.
      76), 77, 114, 452
  Older persons, **1963-64**: 91 (p. 112), 105, 268,
      270; **1965**: 176 [2], 501; **1966**: 95,
      353; **1967**: 12, 13 (p. 53); **1968-69**: 19,
      20, 39 (p. 103), 47 (p. 143), 75, 87,
      108, 111, 114, 154, 346, 406, 567, 672,
      678 (pp. 1286, 1295, 1296)
  Organ transplants, **1968-69**: 611
  Partnership for Health program, **1967**: 77;
      1968-69: 111
  Personnel, **1968-69**: 39 (pp. 103, 107), 40, 47
      (p. 143), 111, 408, 419, 442, 447, 678
      (p. 1296)
  Personnel training, **1966**: 26 (p. 62), 573, 580
      [7, 10]; **1967**: 285
  Prenatal.
      See Maternal and prenatal *above.*
  Red Cross, **1963-64**: 202
  Regional programs, **1968-69**: 536, 678 (p. 1295)
  Research, **1966**: 95, 189, 293, 403; **1967**: 12,
      16 (p. 85), 77, 260, 319
  Rural areas, **1966**: 6 (p. 5)
  State, **1967**: 13 (p. 53), 223 [6]
  Statement, **1965**: 6; **1966**: 293
  Unemployed persons, **1968-69**: 24
  Urban, **1968-69**: 87

[References are to items except as otherwise indicated]

Health and health programs – *continued*
Veterans.
See also Military personnel; Veterans.
Civilian employment, **1967**: 432
Health Insurance for the Aged Act, **1966**: 314n.
See also Medicare.
Health Insurance Benefits Advisory Council,
approval of appointment of members,
1965: 611
Health Insurance for the Disabled, Advisory
Council on, **1968–69**: 346n.
Health insurance under social security.
See Social security.
Health Manpower, National Advisory Com-
mission on, **1966**: 169, 208, 301, 490,
536; **1967**: 77, 500; **1968–69**: 111
Health Manpower Act of 1968, **1968–69**: 111,
447
Health Organization, Pan American, **1965**: 262;
1966: 45, 386
Health Organization, World, **1963–64**: 179; **1965**:
202n., 262; **1966**: 45, 94; **1967**: 214n.,
215
Health personnel bill of 1968, **1968–69**: 111
Health of the President, **1965**: 46 [9], 641 [10],
648n., 649n.; **1966**: 8 [7], 417 [1],
575, 577 [1, 4], 580 [2, 18], 599 [5],
607 [9], 610 [7], 622, 628 [17], 630
[13], 642 [17]
Comments on, **1963–64**: 218 [20], 316 [22],
539n., 619 [11], 688 [7]
Surgery, **1965**: 549, 572n.
Health Professions Educational Assistance Act of
1963, **1963–64**: 179; **1965**: 5, 579;
1966: 111; **1968–69**: 111, 447
Amendments of 1965, **1965**: 579; **1966**: 95
Health Research Facilities Act of 1956, **1965**: 5;
1968–69: 111, 447
Amendments of 1965, **1965**: 329, 330
Approval, **1965**: 410
Health Sciences, John E. Fogarty International
Center for Advanced Study in the,
1967: 217; **1968–69**: 408
Health Sciences, National Center for Environ-
mental, proposed, **1965**: 54
Health Service.
See Public Health Service.
Health Services, National Commission on
Community, **1966**: 185
Health Services Research and Development,
National Center for, **1967**: 77
Healy, Patrick, **1966**: 155
Hearing problems, **1968–69**: 111, 577
Hearn, George H., **1963–64**: 469
Hearnes, Gov. Warren E., **1965**: 394; **1966**:
650n.; **1967**: 297 [1]
Hearst, William Randolph, **1965**: 48

Hearst, William Randolph, Jr., **1963–64**: 339;
1965: 260
Hearst Foundation, William Randolph, **1966**:
35; **1968–69**: 33n.
Journalism awards, **1963–64**: 339
Presentation, **1965**: 260
Heart Association, American, **1965**: 52
Heart disease, **1966**: 26 (p. 62), 49, 95, 156, 189,
271, 395, 403, 436, 515; **1967**: 6 [15],
77, 477; **1968–69**: 39 (p. 103), 111,
536, 589
Prevention, **1963–64**: 268, 391, 650, 656, 667,
669, 733, 755, 798; **1965**: 2, 5, 32 (p.
94), 52, 89, 154, 156 [3], 401, 406,
433, 551, 594
Heart Disease, Cancer, and Stroke, President's
Commission on, **1963–64**: 179, 211 [6],
268, 617, 798; **1965**: 5, 343
Heart Disease, Cancer and Stroke Amendments
of 1965, **1967**: 477
Approval, **1965**: 551
Heart disease, cancer, and stroke bill, **1965**: 329,
330, 448 [19]
Heart fund, **1965**: 52
Heart Institute, National, **1968–69**: 589
Heart transplants, **1968–69**: 111, 108
Heart-of-the-Year Award, **1966**: 49
Presentation, **1963–64**: 164
Heath, William Womack, **1963–64**: 375; **1965**:
411, 412; **1966**: 417 [3]
Heaton, Gen. Leonard D., **1968–69**: 488
Hébert, Repr. F. Edward, **1967**: 533
Hechinger, John W., **1967**: 406n., 466; **1968–69**:
272, 698
Hechler, Repr. Ken, **1963–64**: 360, 586; **1966**:
427–428; **1967**: 552n.; **1968–69**: 564,
567
Hecht, George J., **1965**: 614
Hedde, Charles, **1966**: 349
Heeney, A. D. P., **1965**: 352
Heffernan, John W. (Pat), **1968–69**: 696 [1]
Heidelberger, Michael, **1968–69**: 71n.
Heineman, Ben W., **1966**: 51, 88 [10], 248, 407,
408n.; **1968–69**: 3, 47 (p. 143), 100
Heinkel, Fred, **1963–64**: 54ftn. (p. 68)
Helicopters, **1967**: 13 (p. 48)
Heller, Jean, **1963–64**: 339
Heller, Walter W., **1963–64**: 771; **1965**: 347 [7];
1966: 121 [9], 635 [18]; **1968–69**:
151
See also Council of Economic Advisers,
Chairman (Walter W. Heller).
"Hello Dolly" Broadway musical, **1966**: 516 [8]
Tour in Vietnam, **1965**: 561
Hellwig, Fritz, **1968–69**: 62
Helms, Richard M., **1965**: 209, 263n.; **1966**: 277
[5, 14], 310; **1967**: 147, 255; **1968–69**:
585

Helsinki, Finland, **1965**: 491
Helstoski, Repr. Henry, **1963-64**: 338, 660; **1965**: 242; **1966**: 504
Helwig, Dr. Elson B., **1966**: 266
Hemingway, Ernest, "The Moveable Feast," **1963-64**: 526
HemisFair 1968, **1966**: 160; **1968-69**: 169 [14], 357, 362
  Remarks, **1968-69**: 359
Henderson, Douglas, **1968-69**: 362n.
Henderson, James Pinckney, **1963-64**: 576
Hendrick, James P., **1966**: 447n.
Hennington, Burnett, **1963-64**: 257n.
Henry, E. William, **1966**: 277 [5]
Henry, Joseph, **1968-69**: 695
Henry, O. (William Sydney Porter), **1968-69**: 625
Henry, Patrick, **1965**: 142n.; **1966**: 310
Hensley, Debs B., **1968-69**: 459n.
Hepatitis, **1968-69**: 56
Herbert Hoover Birthplace Foundation, **1965**: 420
Herbert Hoover National Historic Site, **1965**: 420, 498
Heritage Foundation, American, **1963-64**: 560 [1]
Herlong, Repr. A. Sydney, Jr., **1963-64**: 198, 199, 712
Hermitage, home of Andrew Jackson, **1967**: 115, 116
Hernandez, Mrs. Aileen, **1965**: 290
Herndon, Charles, **1966**: 411
Heroin, **1967**: 35; **1968-69**: 59
Herrera, Felipe, **1968-69**: 290
Herrick, Maj. Gen. Curtis J., **1966**: 246; **1967**: 49
Herring, Sir Edmund F. and Dame Mary, **1966**: 543
Herron, Mr. and Mrs. Leslie J., **1966**: 545
Hershey, Lt. Gen. Lewis B., **1963-64**: 89, 314; **1967**: 92, 104 [12], 205; **1968-69**: 696 [1]
Herter, Christian A., **1963-64**: 256 [21], 278, 336 [12], 605, 747; **1967**: 142, 508
  Death, **1966**: 655
Herter, Mrs. Christian A., **1967**: 545
Hertz Foundation Award, Fannie and John, **1966**: 194
Hesburgh, Rev. Theodore M., **1963-64**: 568
Hess, Arthur E., **1967**: 317n.
Hess, Audrey Stern, **1963-64**: 257n.
Heuss, Theodor, **1963-64**: 76
Hewgley, James M., Jr., **1966**: 415
Hewitt, William A., **1968-69**: 239, 471n.
Heyman, Jennifer, **1966**: 497n.
Heyman, Ken, **1966**: 497n.
Heyn, Robert N., **1968-69**: 604
Hibbs, 2d Lt. Robert J., **1968-69**: 148

Hibbs, Mr. and Mrs. Walter E., **1968-69**: 148
Hickel, Walter J., **1967**: 555; **1968-69**: 664
Hickenlooper, Sen. Bourke B., **1963-64**: 634, 635, 643, 693, 694, 712, 750, 796; **1965**: 46 [6], 420; **1967**: 204ftn. (p. 500)
Hickey, J. J., **1963-64**: 657
Hickey, Margaret, **1966**: 299
Hides, skins and leather exports, **1966**: 592
Higginbotham, Judge A. Leon, Jr., **1967**: 291, 333; **1968-69**: 293
Higgins, Msgr. George G., **1968-69**: 106, 112, 626n.
High-speed ground transportation study, approval, **1965**: 536
High Uintas Wilderness, Utah, **1968-69**: 700
Higher Education Act of 1965, **1966**: 3n., 26 (p. 63), 95, 100, 265, 273, 392, 436; **1967**: 13 (p. 55), 39, 77, 164, 185, 199, 338, 540; **1968-69**: 39 (p. 106), 50, 54, 113, 154, 312, 406, 538
  Approval, **1965**: 603
Higher Education Amendments of 1966, **1966**: 573
Higher Education Amendments of 1968, **1968-69**: 14 (p. 31), 154, 164, 390, 538, 539
Higher education bill, **1965**: 329, 330, 340, 457, 463 [15], 578
  House action on, **1965**: 455
  Senate passage, **1965**: 479
Higher Education in the District of Columbia, President's Committee on, report, **1965**: 111
Higher Education Facilities Act of 1963, **1963-64**: 36, 53n., 133, 338, 375, 620; **1965**: 32 (p. 94), 340, 514; **1966**: 95; **1967**: 77; **1968-69**: 54, 538
  Approval, **1963-64**: 47
Hightower, John M., **1963-64**: 246 [3]
Highway Act.
  See Federal-Aid Highway Act of 1956.
Highway Administration, Federal, **1968-69**: 93, 693
Highway Beautification Act of 1965, **1968-69**: 122
  Approval, **1965**: 576
Highway beautification bill, **1965**: 418, 448 [19]; **1968-69**: 14 (p. 31), 122
Highway Safety Act of 1966, **1966**: 47, 290, 449; **1967**: 57, 200, 342, 393, 465, 534; **1968-69**: 122, 243, 264
Highway Safety Advisory Committee, National, **1968-69**: 693
Highway Safety Board, Interdepartmental, **1966**: 98
Highways, **1963-64**: 579, 589, 643, 669; **1966**: 34 (p. 106), 98

Highways – *continued*
  Appalachian area, **1963–64**: 300; **1965**: 245;
    1966: 26 (p. 60), 122 [2], 123, 426;
    1968–69: 701
  Automobile junkyards along, **1965**: 54, 277,
    279
  Beautification programs, **1965**: 2, 30, 54, 279,
    545, 576; **1966**: 119, 398, 500; **1967**:
    20, 295; **1968–69**: 14 (p. 31), 122, 458,
    470, 567
  Chamizal area, **1966**: 597
  Construction, **1965**: 19, 32 (p. 85); **1966**: 630
    [2, 4], 631; **1967**: 261, 369; **1968–69**:
    173, 223 [11], 458, 567
  District of Columbia, **1966**: 27; **1968–69**: 458
  Federal aid, **1963–64**: 410, 453; **1965**: 30, 32
    (p. 85), 35 (p. 116), 54, 245, 277, 279,
    460, 487, 576n.; **1966**: 47, 98, 252,
    416, 492 [8]; **1967**: 6 [3, 10], 70 [6],
    114, 120; **1968–69**: 39 (p. 91), 458,
    467 [3]
  Indian areas, **1968–69**: 113
  Interstate system, **1963–64**: 133, 512, 565,
    578, 598, 656, 661; **1965**: 29, 32 (p.
    88), 54, 255, 279, 460, 499; **1966**: 27,
    98, 492 [8]; **1968–69**: 458, 693
  National Capital Region, **1965**: 29, 61, 70, 499
  Safety program, **1963–64**: 234; **1965**: 460,
    488; **1966**: 6 (p. 6), 26 (p. 61), 34 (p.
    106), 47, 98, 187, 228, 252, 273, 290–
    291, 423, 449, 630 [4]; **1967**: 13 (p.
    52), 20, 86, 200, 534; **1968–69**: 39 (p.
    102), 56, 57, 111, 122, 243, 244, 264,
    545, 693
  Traffic control devices, **1966**: 98
  Trust fund, **1963–64**: 132 (pp. 188, 191), 234;
    1965: 32 (p. 85), 255, 460
  Urban, **1968–69**: 93, 458, 693
  User charges, **1965**: 32 (p. 88), 35 (p. 116),
    255; **1966**: 26 (p. 53), 34 (p. 105);
    1967: 16 (p. 86)
Hill, Clinton J., **1968–69**: 549, 604
Hill, Sen. Lister, **1963–64**: 53, 174, 389, 557,
    693; **1965**: 183, 305, 361, 401, 406,
    410, 433, 534, 551; **1966**: 49, 395;
    1967: 338n., 413, 517; **1968–69**: 22,
    536, 589
  Hospital Act.
    See Hospital Survey and Construction
    Amendments of 1949.
Hill, Murray, **1967**: 416n.
Hill, Raymond A., **1965**: 400
Hill-Burton Act (Hospital Survey and Con-
    struction Act), **1966**: 416; **1967**: 12,
    77, 353, 419; **1968–69**: 406, 536, 622,
    678 (p. 1296)
  See also Hospital Survey and Construction
    Amendments of 1949.

Hillman, Sidney, **1963–64**: 334; **1967**: 484
Hilsman, Roger, **1963–64**: 201 [18]
Hilton, William Barron, **1968–69**: 525
Hilts, Wesley J., **1963–64**: 667
Hincks, Peter J., **1966**: 398
Hines, Brig. Gen. Frank T., **1967**: 161
Hines, Rt. Rev. John E., **1965**: 289
Hirohito, Emperor of Japan, **1965**: 12, 355n.;
    1967: 381, 487
Hirshhorn, Joseph H., **1966**: 226, 587; **1968–69**:
    660
Hirshhorn, Mrs. Joseph H., **1966**: 226; **1968–69**:
    660
Hirshhorn Foundation, Joseph H., **1966**: 227
Hirshhorn Museum and Sculpture Garden,
    Joseph H., **1966**: 226–227, 587; **1968–
    69**: 660
Historic Landmarks, Registry of National, **1965**:
    54
Historic landmarks preservation, **1963–64**: 275;
    1965: 70, 242, 498, 538; **1966**: 26 (p.
    60), 82, 518, 522; **1967**: 553; **1968–69**:
    39 (p. 101)
Historic Preservation in the United States,
    National Trust for, **1965**: 54; **1966**: 82
Historic Sites, Buildings and Monuments, Ad-
    visory Board on National Parks, **1965**:
    538n.
Historical Commission, Tennessee, **1967**: 538n.
Historical documents bill, approval, **1963–64**:
    481
Historical Publications Commission, National,
    1963–64: 481n.; **1967**: 538n.
History and Technology, Museum of, **1967**: 540n.
Hitler, Adolf, **1963–64**: 548, 648, 662, 703, 736,
    749; **1965**: 48, 88, 388 [1]; **1966**: 168,
    228, 273, 312, 515, 540, 563; **1967**:
    495 [14]; **1968–69**: 50, 109, 142, 165
Ho Chi Minh (President of North Vietnam),
    1965: 347ftn. (p. 730), 448ftn. (p.
    924); **1966**: 52 [5], 320 [18], 514–515,
    540; **1967**: 80 [4], 195, 225 [5], 281,
    312 [14, 16], 358 [5], 395, 409, 495
    [3, 6], 534; **1968–69**: 51 [1], 109, 170,
    250n.
  Letter, **1967**: 135, 136
Hobby, William, **1963–64**: 392
Hobby, Mrs. William (Oveta Culp), **1963–64**:
    392, 750; **1965**: 94; **1966**: 106n., 315n.,
    320 [10]; **1967**: 475, 532
Hodges, Luther H., **1965**: 25, 345, 465; **1967**:
    268
  See also Commerce, Secretary of (Luther H.
    Hodges).
Hodges, Mrs. Luther H., **1963–64**: 358
Hodges, Seaman Duane D., **1968–69**: 641
Hodgkins disease, **1966**: 156
Hoefly, Col. Ethel A., **1967**: 475

Hoff, Gov. Philip H., **1963–64**: 32n., 605; **1965**: 555; **1966**: 396–398, 494 [1–2], 650n.; **1967**: 223 [1, 2, 3, 4, 6, 7, 9, 10, 13], 544

Hoff, Mrs. Philip H., **1963–64**: 605; **1966**: 398

Hoffer, Eric, **1967**: 397, 490, 493; **1968–69**: 224, 293

Hoffman, Mrs. Anna Rosenberg, **1966**: 315n.; **1968–69**: 3

Hoffman, 1st Lt. George J., **1966**: 409

Hoffman, S. Sgt. Henry, **1966**: 409

Hoffman, Mr. and Mrs. Henry J., **1966**: 409

Hoffman, Paul G., **1963–64**: 563 [5], 591, 696; **1965**: 136

Hoffman, L/Cpl. Richard, **1966**: 409

Hoffman, Cpl. Robert T., **1966**: 409

Hoffman, Sgt. Walter, **1966**: 409

Holcomb, Rev. Luther J., **1965**: 290

Holden, Donald, **1967**: 241

Holderness, James S., **1966**: 331n.

Holding companies, **1966**: 34 (p. 108)

Holidays, national, uniform, **1968–69**: 342

Holifield, Repr. Chet, **1963–64**: 538, 650, 733; **1966**: 361, 410–411, 523; **1967**: 227; **1968–69**: 57

Holland, Capt. David I., release from East Germany, **1963–64**: 242 [18, 26]

Holland, Repr. Elmer J., **1963–64**: 728

Holland, Jerome H., **1966**: 404n.; **1967**: 184

Holland, Ransome G., **1967**: 324n.

Holland, Sen. Spessard L., **1963–64**: 55, 57, 145, 171, 198, 199, 709, 710, 712, 713, 719; **1967**: 541; **1968–69**: 547

Holland, food aid for India, **1967**: 33

Holland Society, **1968–69**: 661

Hollingsworth, Robert E., **1966**: 266

Hollybush meetings, **1967**: 279–283, 286

Holmes, Adm. Ephraim P., **1967**: 485 [7]

Holmes, Oliver Wendell, **1966**: 91, 223; **1968–69**: 270

Holt, Andrew D., **1967**: 538

Holt, Harold E. (Prime Minister of Australia), **1966**: 328–329, 492 [4], 514, 541–547, 549; **1967**: 246, 248, 267, 272, 329 [9], 409, 550, 551, 555, 561, 564, 565, 567, 573; **1968–69**: 273, 648

Death, **1967**: 550, 551, 555, 561

Election victory, message, **1966**: 630 [12]

Visit, **1966**: 304–305, 328; **1967**: 248

Holt, Mrs. Harold E., **1966**: 304, 541, 544–547; **1967**: 246, 248, 551, 561

Holt, James C., "Magna Carta," **1965**: 376

Holton, Karl, **1963–64**: 27

Holy Angels Church, Aurora, Ill., **1965**: 298

Holy Cross College, **1963–64**: 396; **1965**: 202n.

Holyoake, Keith J. (Prime Minister of New Zealand), **1963–64**: 464; **1966**: 514, 538–540, 549; **1967**: 409; **1968–69**: 522, 525, 528

Holyoake, Mrs. Keith J., **1966**: 538–539; **1968–69**: 522, 525

Homaira, Queen (Afghanistan), **1967**: 143–145

Home, Alec Douglas-, **1963–64**: 26, 272

News conference remarks on, **1963–64**: 28 [4], 285 [3, 21], 475 [3], 619 [15]

Visit, **1963–64**: 184–187

Home, Lady Douglas-, **1963–64**: 184

Home Administration, Farmers, **1967**: 120; **1968–69**: 94, 113, 467 [13], 678 (p. 1289)

Home Builders, National Association of, **1965**: 243; **1968–69**: 229

Home Health Aides (OEO), **1967**: 39

Home Loan Bank Board, Federal, **1966**: 473, 530, 642 [3, 19]; **1967**: 3 (p. 8), 6 [11], 16 (p. 87), 88, 315n., 420; **1968–69**: 72

Home rule.
See District of Columbia.

Homemakers of America, Future, **1966**: 295n.

Homestead Act, **1965**: 452; **1967**: 397

Honduras, **1967**: 44; **1968–69**: 368

President Oswaldo López Arellano, **1968–69**: 366, 374, 375

Visit, **1968–69**: 375

Honolulu, East-West Center, **1965**: 248

Honolulu, Hawaii, **1966**: 53–54, 55n., 320 [2], 532–533; **1968–69**: 178

Conference with President Thieu of South Vietnam, **1968–69**: 398, 400, 401

Mayor Neal S. Blaisdell, **1967**: 555

Releases, **1967**: 557; **1968–69**: 201, 399, 400

Remarks, **1968–69**: 197–200, 398

U.S. officials meeting in, **1963–64**: 379 [1, 9, 11]

Visit, **1967**: 555

Honolulu conference, **1966**: 52 [2, 4], 56, 65 [8], 86, 88, [16], 188 [2, 3], 320 [2], 383, 501 [2], 520, 532; **1967**: 130, 131, 132 [1]

Declaration, **1966**: 54–56, 85, 277 [7], 458n.

Honolulu International Airport, **1966**: 53

Honorary Chairmanship of Brotherhood Week for 1964, acceptance, **1963–64**: 113

Honorary degrees or memberships, acceptance, **1963–64**: 192n., 316 [12], 343, 357n., 375n., 382, 391n., 499n.; **1965**: 301n., 302n.; **1966**: 216n.; **1967**: 448

Hoover, Allan H., **1965**: 420

Hoover, Herbert, **1963–64**: 2, 12, 295, 303, 477n.; **1965**: 414, 420, 498; **1966**: 312, 395, 417 [3, 6]; **1967**: 70ftn. (p. 224), 258, 291, 490; **1968–69**: 540, 567, 576, 612, 648

Campaign remarks on, **1963–64**: 601, 643, 694, 695, 747

Death of, **1963–64**: 691, 692

News conference remarks on, **1963–64**: 71 [12], 619 [18]

Hoover, Mrs. Herbert, **1965**: 498n.; **1968–69**: 648

Hoover, Herbert, Birthplace Foundation, **1965**: 420

Hoover, Herbert, National Historic Site, **1965**: 420, 498

Hoover, J. Edgar (Director, Federal Bureau of Investigation), **1963–64**: 199, 201 [3], 315, 333, 455 [9], 468, 475 [20], 504 [3], 600, 619 [11], 671, 688 [5, 8], 780 [11, 14]; **1965**: 102, 135, 155, 290, 336, 366, 443, 500; **1966**: 196, 204, 289, 491; **1967**: 34 [1], 105, 146, 204 [14], 275, 326, 385, 530; **1968–69**: 57, 236, 292n., 320

Hoover Commission (Commission on Organization of the Executive Branch of the Government), **1963–64**: 71 [12]; **1966**: 190, 438, 523; **1967**: 99, 121; **1968–69**: 59, 60, 227

Hope, Bob, **1963–64**: 31

Hopkins, George, **1966**: 589

Hopkins, Harry, **1963–64**: 513

Hopkins, William J., **1966**: 330; **1968–69**: 588

Hopper, Walter E., **1968–69**: 661

Horn, Francis H., **1966**: 396

Horn, Rev. John F., **1967**: 115

Horne, John E. (Chairman, Federal Home Loan Bank Board), **1966**: 473; **1967**: 420; **1968–69**: 72

   Appointment, **1963–64**: 814

Horner, Garnett D., **1966**: 338 [3]; **1967**: 375 [4]; **1968–69**: 467 [8]

Hornig, Donald F. (Director, Office of Science and Technology), **1963–64**: 804; **1965**: 4, 12n., 54, 56n., 88, 92n., 257, 344n., 375, 404, 407, 417, 418, 446, 514, 547n., 649; **1966**: 61, 98ftn. (p. 261), 138, 143, 216, 326, 424n., 635 [3], 637; **1968–69**: 71, 122, 277, 297, 434, 453, 513n., 577, 608, 695

   See also Science and Technology, Office of, Director.

Hornig, Mrs. Donald F. (Lilli), **1965**: 344n., 407; **1968–69**: 513n.

Horning, Anson, **1963–64**: 255

Horsfall, Dr. Frank, **1963–64**: 211 [6]

Horsky, Charles A., **1963–64**: 16, 537; **1967**: 411 [1], 466

Horstman, Robert, **1963–64**: 680

Horton, Repr. Frank J., **1966**: 394

Horwitz, Dr. Abraham, **1966**: 386

Horwitz, Solis, **1963–64**: 442

Hosmer, Repr. Craig, **1967**: 227

Hospital Association, American, **1966**: 271, 314, 490

Hospital Survey and Construction Act (Hill-Burton Act), **1963–64**: 91 (p. 115), 132

Hospital Survey, Construction Act — *continued* (p. 189), 178, 179, 305, 434, 693; **1966**: 416; **1967**: 12, 77, 353, 419; **1968–69**: 536, 622, 678 (p. 1296)

   Extension, approval, **1963–64**: 520

Hospital Survey and Construction Amendments of 1949, **1965**: 5; **1966**: 95, 395, 509

Hospitals and medical care facilities, **1963–64**: 132 (pp. 189, 191), 305, 388, 598, 606, 669; **1965**: 6, 38, 70, 90, 122, 154, 531, 551; **1966**: 169, 185, 271, 395, 401 [2], 490; **1967**: 77, 298, 477; **1968–69**: 111, 447, 622, 684 (p. 1321)

   See also Health and health programs; Medicare; Medical care.

   Appalachian region, **1968–69**: 701

   Chronic disease hospitals, **1963–64**: 179

   Construction and modernization, **1963–64**: 91 (p. 112), 179, 415, 520, 620, 755; **1965**: 5; **1966**: 26 (p. 62), 95, 253, 394, 406, 515; **1967**: 261, 353, 419; **1968–69**: 111, 536, 678 (p. 1296)

   District of Columbia, **1967**: 15; **1968–69**: 19, 20

   Fallout shelters in, **1963–64**: 132 (p. 185)

   Federal aid, **1963–64**: 178, 179, 755; **1965**: 32 (p. 85); **1966**: 95, 189, 395; **1967**: 13 (p. 53), 77, 419; **1968–69**: 678 (p. 1296), 684 (p. 1321)

   Integration, **1967**: 55, 77

   Mentally ill, **1965**: 5; **1966**: 293; **1967**: 285

   Nondiscrimination, **1968–69**: 26

   Older persons, **1963–64**: 434, 755; **1967**: 12

   Philippine veterans, **1966**: 461, 495, 505

   Rural areas, **1966**: 28–29; **1968–69**: 96

   Safety, **1967**: 534

   Veterans, **1965**: 22 [16], 46 [8], 156 [10], 163; **1966**: 26 (pp. 64, 67), 505; **1967**: 13 (p. 55), 25; **1968–69**: 39 (106), 40

   Vietnam, **1966**: 433

Hostetler, C. A., **1966**: 567–568

Hot Springs, Va., **1963–64**: 336ftn. (p. 660); **1968–69**: 241

"Hotline" (U.S.-Soviet communications link), **1967**: 59, 264 [16], 297 [3]; **1968–69**: 14 (p. 26), 27, 69, 647

Houghton, Daniel J., **1966**: 625n.

Houghton, Brig. Gen. Kenneth J., **1968–69**: 541

Houphouet-Boigny, Felix (President of the Ivory Coast), **1967**: 356

Houphouet-Boigny, Madame Felix, **1967**: 356

House committees.

   See other parts of title.

House of President's birth, **1963–64**: 295

House Service for Aging, Inc., **1966**: 344n.

Household product safety, **1967**: 200, 534, 539

Housewives' strike, **1966**: 158 [7]

Housing, **1963–64**: 132 (pp. 176, 182), 150 [1,
    8], 219, 292, 541, 579, 642, 667, 668,
    669, 746, 780 [3]; **1965**: 2, 32 (pp. 84,
    88, 93), 35 (p. 114), 415, 454 [5], 463
    [15]; **1966**: 26 (pp. 50, 55, 61–62), 88
    [22], 155, 394, 445 [7], 630 [4]; **1967**:
    276, 330 [1], 420, 498, 512; **1968–69**:
    47 (p. 133), 50, 102, 153 [16], 156,
    283 [8], 406, 442, 460 [2], 462, 470,
    506, 567, 625, 631, 676 (p. 1265), 678
    (p. 1288)
Appalachian region, **1968–69**: 701
Blind persons, **1966**: 277 [1]
College, **1965**: 90, 415, 585; **1966**: 26 (p. 63),
    182; **1967**: 179; **1968–69**: 678 (p. 1281)
Construction, **1963–64**: 124 (pp. 156, 160),
    152, 189, 271 [3], 294 [23], 314, 463,
    669; **1965**: 35 (p. 108), 90, 243, 453,
    511, 585; **1966**: 141 [3], 445 [7], 451,
    596, 628 [1], 642 [3]; **1967**: 4, 16
    (pp. 75, 78, 85), 70 [6], 88, 103, 114,
    180, 353, 369, 411 [11], 417 [5, 6],
    420, 430, 531, 554 [6]; **1968–69**: 14
    (pp. 28, 29, 31), 26, 39 (p. 102), 47
    (pp. 128, 129, 132, 133, 141), 84, 87,
    91, 154, 164, 229, 319, 382, 406, 434,
    445, 506, 568, 569, 622, 625, 631,
    676 (p. 1265), 678 (p. 1289), 684 (pp.
    1313–1315, 1322), 699
Cooperatives, **1965**: 511; **1967**: 88
District of Columbia, **1963–64**: 704n.; **1965**:
    70; **1967**: 180; **1968–69**: 133, 135, 152
    Pilot project, **1968–69**: 19, 20
Equal opportunity, **1963–64**: 91 (p. 116), 152
Federal aid, **1968–69**: 39 (p. 102), 114, 426,
    612, 676 (p. 1265), 678 (p. 1289)
Handicapped persons, **1965**: 415
Home improvements, **1968–69**: 56
Home ownership, **1967**: 114
Housing bill, **1963–64**: 170 [13], 235, 434
Indians, **1963–64**: 120; **1966**: 193; **1968–69**:
    113
Industry, **1968–69**: 39 (p. 103), 229
Insurance for inner city, **1968–69**: 278
International exchange of information, **1968–
    69**: 434
Legislation, **1966**: 168; **1967**: 358 [3], 554
    [6]; **1968–69**: 278, 429, 565, 655, 696
    [12]
Low income, **1963–64**: 91 (p. 115), 132 (p.
    188), 152, 173, 728; **1965**: 90, 415,
    453, 585; **1966**: 26 (p. 61), 30, 67, 158
    [10], 223, 236 [13], 277 [1], 413,
    525; **1967**: 4, 13 (p. 60), 88, 114, 120,
    179, 355, 467; **1968–69**: 14 (p. 29), 19,
    26, 39 (p. 102), 50, 87, 91, 94, 133, 152,
    154, 164, 278, 319, 382, 402, 426, 435,
    470, 471, 506, 625, 676 (p. 1265), 678

Housing – *continued*
  Low income – *continued*
    (pp. 1289, 1290), 684 (pp. 1324, 1325),
    699
  Message to Congress, **1963–64**: 152
  Middle income, **1968–69**: 14 (p. 29), 19, 26,
    39 (p. 102), 87, 91, 94, 133, 278, 319,
    382, 402, 506, 625, 678 (pp. 1281,
    1289), 699
  Military personnel, **1963–64**: 152; **1965**: 26;
    1966: 141 [5], 159; **1967**: 70 [6]
  Minority groups, **1966**: 136
  Mortgages and credit, **1966**: 338 [14], 445
    [7], 451, 473, 642 [3, 19]; **1967**: 6
    [4, 10, 11], 88, 103, 114, 120, 179,
    329, 420; **1968–69**: 39 (pp. 87, 103),
    47 (p. 144), 72, 87, 94, 113, 229, 402,
    599
  National goals, **1968–69**: 699
  Negroes, **1966**: 196, 417 [4]; **1968–69**: 429
  Nondiscrimination (open housing), **1966**: 6
    (pp. 3, 5), 30, 196, 247 [10], 375, 474
    [14], 475; **1967**: 3 (p. 5), 55; **1968–
    69**: 14 (p. 31), 26, 47 (p. 130), 82, 87,
    91, 114, 126, 131, 158, 182, 191 [1],
    192, 195, 212, 380, 596, 611, 631, 676
    (p. 1266), 678 (p. 1289)
    See also Civil Rights Act of 1968.
    Military personnel, **1968–69**: 26, 158
  Nonprofit sponsors, **1968–69**: 87, 133
  Older persons, **1963–64**: 91 (p. 115), 124 (p.
    164), 132 (p. 188), 152, 178, 415, 431,
    590, 712; **1965**: 415; **1966**: 26 (p. 61),
    253, 509; **1967**: 12, 179; **1968–69**: 19,
    20, 678 (p. 1289)
  Private enterprise role, **1967**: 355, 380, 412
  Private organizations role, **1966**: 223, 277 [1]
  Public, **1963–64**: 124 (p. 163), 132 (p. 188),
    211 [28], 213; **1965**: 70, 90; **1966**:
    26 (p. 61), 223, 236 [13], 237, 428,
    439; **1967**: 114, 355n., 380, 412;
    1968–69: 87, 278, 382, 426, 435, 442,
    625, 678 (p. 1289), 684 (p. 1325)
  Rent supplements, **1965**: 90, 397; **1966**: 6 (p.
    6), 26 (p. 61), 30, 67, 158 [10], 168,
    223, 236 [13], 253, 277ftn. (p. 625),
    344, 373 [15], 394, 403, 417 [3], 436,
    439, 525; **1967**: 13 (p. 52), 15, 16 (pp.
    75, 85), 23, 88, 114, 179, 223 [13],
    225, [13], 261, 312 [6], 353, 358 [3,
    8], 359, 370, 380, 460 [3, 10], 467,
    534, 554 [6, 16]; **1968–69**: 47 (p. 141),
    87, 114, 234, 278, 380, 426, 470, 678
    (p. 1289)
  Rural, **1963–64**: 132 (p. 187), 152, 344; **1965**:
    32 (p. 91), 46 [1], 47, 415; **1966**: 28–
    29; **1968–69**: 94, 96, 142, 678 (p. 1289)
  Spanish-speaking persons, **1968–69**: 437

Housing – *continued*
    Standards, **1967**: 4
    Temporary commission on, **1965**: 90
    Tenants rights, **1966**: 394
    Turnkey project, **1967**: 355n., 372, 412, 460
        [10], 467; **1968–69**: 47 (p. 141), 87,
        133, 152
    Urban, **1963–64**: 91 (p. 115), 357; **1965**: 54,
        90, 337, 510, 511; **1966**: 13, 30, 320
        [17]; **1967**: 16 (p. 85), 23, 114, 252,
        355, 380, 412, 460 [10]; **1968–69**: 47
        (p. 140), 164, 697, 704
    Vacancy rates, **1963–64**: 314
    Veterans, **1963–64**: 419; **1965**: 415; **1968–69**:
        39 (p. 103), 40, 47 (p. 141), 229, 414,
        599
Housing, President's Committee on Urban, **1967**:
        252, 355, 358 [8], 412; **1968–69**: 87,
        471n., 704
Housing Act of 1949, **1963–64**: 152; **1965**: 415;
        1966: 196; **1968–69**: 47 (p. 140), 87,
        704
Housing Act of 1954, **1965**: 585; **1967**: 114;
        1968–69: 87
Housing Act of 1961, **1963–64**: 132 (p. 188),
        152, 422
Housing Act of 1964, **1963–64**: 549, 642, 654,
        728; **1965**: 54
Housing Administration, Federal, **1967**: 88;
        1968–69: 19, 39 (p. 103), 47 (p. 141),
        87, 114, 229, 402, 435
Housing Authority, National Capital, **1967**: 180;
        1968–69: 133, 152
Housing bill, **1965**: 319 [2], 329, 330, 337, 397,
        406, 415, 510
Housing code, **1965**: 70
Housing and Community Development, Depart-
        ment of, proposed, **1963–64**: 132 (p.
        194), 152
Housing and Home Finance Agency, **1963–64**:
        132 (p. 181), 152, 792n.; **1965**: 90, 174,
        453, 585; **1966**: 13, 30
    Administrator (Robert C. Weaver), **1963–64**:
        120, 170 [13], 178n., 288, 320, 321,
        322, 323, 325, 326, 327, 328, 537, 711;
        1965: 415, 511n., 545
    See also Housing and Urban Development,
        Secretary of.
Housing industry, **1965**: 90
Housing Partnership, National, **1968–69**: 278,
        382, 470, 471, 506, 678 (p. 1289), 704n.
Housing and Urban Development, Department of,
        1965: 2, 32 (p. 93), 35 (p. 114), 90,
        418, 503, 511, 512n., 605, 618; **1966**:
        8 [3, 13], 12, 30, 67, 98, 196, 207, 334
        [2], 380, 428, 511; **1967**: 4, 13 (pp. 57,
        59), 15, 16 (p. 84), 121, 139, 179, 193,
        223 [10], 315n., 358 [8], 359, 369,

HUD, Department of – *continued*
        412, 478, 542; **1968–69**: 39 (pp. 109,
        110), 57, 59, 87, 91, 93, 130n., 442,
        470, 678 (pp. 1289, 1301, 1302), 686
    Appropriations, **1967**: 13 (pp. 46, 53), 114,
        417 [1], 467; **1968–69**: 39 (pp. 91,
        102), 234, 380, 678 (p. 1281)
    Assistant Secretary for research, technology,
        engineering, **1967**: 114
    Building development, **1968–69**: 470
    First anniversary remarks, **1966**: 604
    Reports, **1968–69**: 697
    Urban mass transportation program, **1968–69**:
        351
Housing and Urban Development, Secretary of
        (Robert C. Weaver), **1966**: 98, 105, 216,
        223, 236 [13], 277 [1], 379–381, 394,
        442, 451–452, 524, 574, 604, 607 [1],
        628 [1], 628n.; **1967**: 4, 12, 39, 55,
        88, 114, 179, 186, 252, 258, 267n.,
        356, 358 [8], 359, 372, 380, 460 [1],
        467, 542; **1968–69**: 19, 26, 36, 42, 59,
        87, 91, 94, 113, 114, 122, 130, 153 [16],
        229, 306, 351, 426, 429, 435, 442, 470,
        471, 631
    Letters
        International exchange of housing informa-
            tion and technology, **1968–69**: 434
        Mortgage commitments, **1968–69**: 402
    Memorandums, **1966**: 344, 425, 606; **1967**:
        259, 355, 412, 458
    Swearing in, **1966**: 13
Housing and Urban Development Act of 1965,
        1965: 510; **1966**: 30, 277ftn. (p. 625),
        302, 504; **1967**: 179
    See also Housing bill.
    Approval, **1965**: 415
Housing and Urban Development Act of 1968,
        1968–69: 87, 278, 319, 382, 390, 426,
        470, 471, 506, 625, 676 (p. 1265), 678
        (pp. 1288, 1289), 684 (p. 1324), 699,
        704
Houssay, Bernardo, **1967**: 473
Houston, Col. Herbert, **1968–69**: 599n.
Houston, Sam, **1963–64**: 238, 325, 645, 702;
        1965: 89; **1967**: 115; **1968–69**: 575
Houston, William V., **1965**: 115n.
Houston, Texas, **1968–69**: 106n., 533n.
    Campaign remarks, **1963–64**: 760, 761
    Manned Spacecraft Center, **1965**: 310
    Mayor Louis Welch, **1963–64**: 760; **1967**: 87n.;
        1968–69: 442
    Port of, 50th anniversary, **1963–64**: 766
    Remarks, **1968–69**: 107, 442, 575
Houston, U.S.S., **1966**: 551
Houston Teachers Association, **1965**: 183
Hoveyda, Amir Abbas (Prime Minister of Iran),
        1968–69: 613–615

Hoveyda, Mrs. Amir Abbas, **1968–69**: 614, 615
Howard, Frank, **1967**: 388
Howard, James, **1963–64**: 338; **1966**: 504
Howard, Gunnery Sgt. Jimmie E., **1967**: 361
Howard, Mrs. Jimmie E., **1967**: 361n.
Howard Foundry Company, defense contract,
　　1963–64: 285 [16]
Howard University, **1963–64**: 116; **1965**: 301,
　　319 [17], 548; **1966**: 136; **1967**: 80
　　[1], 81
　Medical School, **1968–69**: 19
Howe, Arthur, Jr., **1965**: 372; **1966**: 339
Howe, Harold, II, **1966**: 3n., 223, 238, 265, 406,
　　501 [13]; **1967**: 82, 292, 338, 396n.,
　　493; **1968–69**: 219
Howlett, Michael J., **1963–64**: 635, 636, 637,
　　747
Hoyt, Palmer, **1963–64**: 521 [2]; **1966**: 417 [4]
Hrezo, John V., **1967**: 193
Hruska, Sen. Roman L., **1965**: 242; **1968–69**:
　　293, 542
Hubbard, Mrs. Charlotte M., **1963–64**: 316 [8]
Hubbard, William N., Jr., **1966**: 424n.
Huber, Conrad, **1965**: 449
Hudson River, **1965**: 54; **1966**: 393, 481
Hudson River Basin pollution control bill, **1966**:
　　481
Huerta, Alberto, **1966**: 223
Huffman, John, **1963–64**: 644; **1966**: 351
Hughes, Bernard, **1963–64**: 635
Hughes, Charles Evans, **1968–69**: 78
Hughes, Gov. Harold E., **1963–64**: 634; **1965**:
　　307, 420; **1966**: 312, 650; **1967**: 297
　　[1], 409
Hughes, Mrs. Harold E., **1963–64**: 634; **1966**:
　　312
Hughes, Harry R., **1963–64**: 703
Hughes, Howard, **1968–69**: 125
Hughes, Phillip S., **1966**: 88 [6]; **1968–69**: 677
Hughes, Gov. Richard J., **1963–64**: 338, 422,
　　660; **1965**: 291n., 417, 434, 471; **1966**:
　　77, 121 [1], 155, 216, 428, 504, 536;
　　1967: 70 [6], 112, 280–282; **1968–69**:
　　32, 36, 87, 171, 270, 288, 540
Hughes, Mrs. Richard J., **1967**: 282; **1968–69**:
　　32
Hughes, Judge Sarah T., **1963–64**: 1n., 218 [1];
　　1967: 475
Hughes Aircraft Co., **1963–64**: 201 [2]
Huitt, Ralph K., **1965**: 437
Hull, Cordell, **1966**: 185
Hull, Repr. W. R., Jr., **1963–64**: 189
Human Development, National Institute of Child
　　Health and, **1966**: 95; **1968–69**: 111
Human Relations, District of Columbia Council
　　on, **1967**: 15
Human Reproduction, Center for Population
　　Studies and, **1968–69**: 111

Human Rights, National Conference on Con-
　　tinuing Action for, **1968–69**: 611n.
Human rights, treaties on, **1968–69**: 611
Human Rights, Universal Declaration of (U.N.),
　　1967: 488; **1968–69**: 42, 611
Human Rights Award, Labor, **1967**: 484n.
Human Rights Year, 1968, **1968–69**: 42, 428,
　　611
Humanities, Federal Council on the Arts and the,
　　1966: 327; **1967**: 274
Humanities, National Council on the, **1966**: 101;
　　1968–69: 45, 61
Humanities, National Endowment for the, **1966**:
　　327; **1967**: 54, 77; **1968–69**: 45, 54, 61,
　　703
Humanities, National Foundation on the Arts
　　and the, **1965**: 2, 105, 314, 534; **1967**:
　　77; **1968–69**: 54
Humanities bill.
　See Arts and humanities bill.
Humann, Walter J., **1968–69**: 570
Humelsine, Carlisle H., **1963–64**: 365
Hummel, Don, **1966**: 207n.
Humphrey, Sen. Hubert H., **1963–64**: 387, 388,
　　433, 434, 435, 676, 782, 796, 800, 802,
　　810; **1965**: 20
　See also Vice President.
　Campaign remarks on, **1963–64**: 548n., 555,
　　606, 628, 631, 635, 637, 639, 643, 661,
　　666, 670, 678, 679, 680, 694, 728, 735,
　　741, 748, 750, 761, 762, 765
　Candidacy for Vice President, **1963–64**: 540,
　　541, 542, 544
　News conference remarks on, **1963–64**: 336
　　[14], 521 [9], 780 [15, 20, 22]
Humphrey, Mrs. Hubert H., **1963–64**: 544, 765;
　　1965: 45, 320; **1966**: 85, 570, 646;
　　1967: 169, 211, 216, 373, 421, 449,
　　480, 487, 517; **1968–69**: 32, 65, 140,
　　148, 159, 167, 193, 214, 575, 579, 615,
　　616, 619
Humphrey, Mrs. Hubert H., Sr., **1965**: 242
Humphrey, National Independent Committee for
　　Johnson and, **1963–64**: 555
Humphrey-Johnson, Rural Americans for, **1963–
　　64**: 570
Humphrey-Muskie, Citizens for, **1968–69**: 569
Humphreys, Maj. Gen. James W., Jr., **1967**: 132
　　[1], 235
Hundley, William G., **1966**: 204n.
Hungary, **1967**: 245; **1968–69**: 204
Hunger, **1968–69**: 21, 63, 94, 678 (pp. 1296,
　　1297)
Hungry Horse Dam, **1963–64**: 656
Hunt, Russell, **1966**: 415
Hunter, T. W., **1968–69**: 96
Huntington, W. Va., **1963–64**: 293; **1968–69**:
　　564

Huong, Tran Van, **1963–64**: 780ftn. (p. 1616)

Huot, J. Oliva, **1963–64**: 607; **1966**: 397

Hurd, Peter, **1965**: 395 [3], 405

    Portrait of President, **1968–69**: 696 [1]

Hurd, Mrs. Peter, **1965**: 395 [3]

Huron Islands Wilderness, Mich., **1968–69**: 168

Hurricanes, **1963–64**: 493; **1967**: 31n., 408

    Florida, **1963–64**: 563 [4], 567

    Florida, Louisiana, and Mississippi, **1965**: 605

    Georgia, **1963–64**: 563 [4], 567

    Louisiana, **1963–64**: 618, 647

    Mexico, **1966**: 507

    South Carolina, **1963–64**: 563 [4]

    Texas, **1968–69**: 98

Hurst, Dr. J. Willis, **1963–64**: 211 [6], 330;
    1966: 575; **1968–69**: 42, 589

Hussein I, King, visit of, **1963–64**: 258, 259, 265

Hussey, Dr. Hugh, **1963–64**: 211 [6]

Huston, Maj. Gen. Vincent G., **1966**: 625n.

Hutchinson, Repr. Edward, **1963–64**: 356

Hutchinson, Everett, **1967**: 485 [8]

Huxley, Thomas, **1966**: 420

HWOCR (heavy-water-moderated, organic-
    cooled reactor), **1967**: 98

Hyde, Rosel H. (Chairman, Federal Communica-
    tions Commission), **1966**: 277 [5], 278,
    366, 410–413, 415; **1968–69**: 298

Hyde Park, N.Y. (Franklin D. Roosevelt home),
    1968–69: 411

Hydroelectric power projects, **1963–64**: 193;
    1965: 186, 418, 471, 477; **1966**: 269,
    399, 411; **1968–69**: 330

Hydrological Decade, International, **1963–64**:
    231n.

Hye, Tex., **1963–64**: 71 [4]; **1965**: 596

Hyman, Sidney, **1963–64**: 303

Hypertension, **1967**: 319

Ia Drang Valley, South Vietnam, **1967**: 384

IAEA.

    See International Atomic Energy Agency.

Iakovos, Archbishop Demetrios A. C., **1963–64**:
    211 [1], 810n.

Ibn Saud, King (Saudi Arabia), **1966**: 285

Ibsen, Henrik, **1968–69**: 214

ICBM (intercontinental ballistic missile), **1963–
    64**: 150 [12], 382, 413, 607, 635, 703;
    1965: 26, 37n.; **1966**: 642 [15]

Ice patrol, **1968–69**: 124

Iceland, **1967**: 313

    Ambassador Petur Thorsteinsson, **1967**: 313

    Bjarni Benediktsson, **1963–64**: 521ftn. (p. 978)

    Foreign Minister Emil Jonsson, **1967**: 313

    President Asgeir Asgerisson, **1967**: 313

    U.S. Ambassador Karl F. Rolvaag, **1967**: 313

Ichord, Repr. Richard H., **1963–64**: 189

Ickes, Harold L., **1966**: 518

ICY.

    See International Cooperation Year.

Idaho, **1963–64**: 135

    Campaign remarks, **1963–64**: 659

    Candidates for public office, **1963–64**: 659

    Gov. Robert Smylie, **1963–64**: 285 [7]; **1966**:
       407, 410–411

Idaho Falls, Idaho, **1966**: 412

Idaho State University, **1966**: 410

Iglehart, Lewis, **1967**: 538

Ignatius, Paul R. (Secretary of the Navy), **1967**:
    446; **1968–69**: 34, 129, 267, 541, 556,
    675, 688

Ihnen, Edward, **1963–64**: 338, 660

Ikeda, Hayato, **1963–64**: 8, 236, 408, 747

Iles, Charles S., **1963–64**: 634

Iles, Mrs. Charles S., **1963–64**: 634

ILGWU.

    See International Ladies Garment Workers
       Union.

Illia, Arturo (President of Argentina), **1966**: 175

Illinois, **1963–64**: 590; **1965**: 132; **1966**: 157,
    401 [16]

    Campaign remarks, **1963–64**: 635, 636, 637,
       694, 747, 748

    Candidates for public office, **1963–64**: 635,
       636, 747, 748

    Gov. Otto Kerner, **1963–64**: 217, 287, 635,
       636, 637, 694, 747, 748; **1965**: 299;
       1966: 228, 349; **1967**: 187, 326, 327,
       328 [1]; **1968–69**: 210

    Lt. Gov. Samuel H. Shapiro, **1968–69**: 183

    Remarks, **1968–69**: 172, 210

Illinois Central Railroad, **1963–64**: 252; **1968–
    69**: 626

Illinois State Federation of Labor, **1963–64**: 637

Illiteracy, **1967**: 77, 423; **1968–69**: 109

    Indians, **1968–69**: 113

    U.S., **1965**: 154; **1966**: 95, 240; **1967**: 540,
       554 [12]

    World, **1967**: 442, 448, 554 [12]; **1968–69**:
       50, 63, 66, 227

Illueca, Jorge, **1963–64**: 285 [6], 316 [11]

Image, the President's public, **1966**: 654 [10]

IMF.

    See International Monetary Fund.

Immigration bill, **1963–64**: 280 [7]; **1965**: 13,
    398, 448 [13], 449

Immigration Board, proposed establishment,
    1965: 13

Immigration laws, **1963–64**: 91 (p. 116), 97, 115,
    268, 270, 581, 639, 746; **1965**: 2, 13,
    242, 398, 449, 546

Immigration and Nationality Act, **1966**: 403,
    436, 478, 510, 602

    Amendments, **1965**: 546; **1968–69**: 352

Immigration and Naturalization Service, **1963–64**: 90, 115; **1966**: 602; **1968–69**: 88, 388, 389

Immigration to U.S., **1963–64**: 387; **1965**: 100, 398, 546; **1966**: 30, 403, 478; **1967**: 397, 534; **1968–69**: 270, 499
  Cuban, **1965**: 546, 601, 618
  Equal opportunity, **1963–64**: 139
  Italian, **1963–64**: 581
  National origins system, termination, **1968–69**: 352
  Quotas, **1963–64**: 97; **1965**: 13, 242
  Report, **1963–64**: 115; **1965**: 547n.

Imperial Beach, Calif., **1967**: 303

Importation of Educational, Scientific, and Cultural Materials, Agreement on the (Florence Agreement), **1965**: 292, 604; **1966**: 45, 519, 601

Imports, **1963–64**: 739; **1965**: 577; **1966**: 34 (p. 100), 45, 125, 155, 451, 445 [6], 519, 601; **1967**: 16 (pp. 75, 79–80), 223 [3], 294, 329, 375 [20], 414, 428, 476, 508; **1968–69**: 2, 207, 241, 274, 439, 483, 562, 671
See also specific commodities.
  Duty-free
    Limitations on tourists, **1965**: 60, 338
    Scientific instruments, **1965**: 604
  Economic impact, **1963–64**: 246 [12, 18]; **1967**: 99; **1968–69**: 274
  Educational materials, **1965**: 292
  Increase, **1965**: 465; **1968–69**: 39 (p. 87), 47 (pp. 132, 135, 137)
  Marking requirements, lumber, **1963–64**: 80
  Quotas, **1968–69**: 47 (pp. 134, 137)
  Reduction, **1963–64**: 246 [18], 344

Inaugural address, **1965**: 27

Incentive Awards
  Armed Forces, **1965**: 528
  Government Employees', **1963–64**: 467n., 790; **1965**: 528

Income, **1967**: 13 (pp. 41–42), 16 (p. 74), 420
  Appalachian area, **1965**: 103
  Business, **1966**: 26 (p. 49), 34 (p. 99)
  College graduates, **1968–69**: 26
  Consumers, **1963–64**: 124 (p. 157); **1966**: 26 (p. 49), 34 (p. 99)
  Corporate, **1963–64**: 731; **1966**: 6 (p. 5); **1967**: 13 (p. 42)
  Depressed areas, **1965**: 132
  Family, **1968–69**: 47 (p. 129)
  Farm, **1963–64**: 434; **1966**: 6 (p. 5), 34 (p. 96), 189, 228, 334 [4], 346–347, 355, 403, 412, 415, 428, 436–437, 451, 479, 654 [3]; **1967**: 3 (p. 7), 13 (p. 50), 16 (p. 73), 63, 156, 228, 270, 305, 329, 358 [9], 496, 525; **1968–69**: 14 (pp. 28, 31), 39 (p. 100), 47 (p. 128), 91,

Income – *continued*
  Farm – *continued*
    94, 142, 155, 247, 462, 534, 683, 684 (p. 1312)
    See also Farm economy.
  Guaranteed, **1967**: 16 (p. 82)
  Handicapped persons, **1968–69**: 39 (p. 105)
  Increase, **1965**: 35 (p. 105), 90; **1966**: 492 [1], 515; **1967**: 3 (p. 7), 13 (p. 40), 16 (pp. 72–73, 88–89), 57, 199, 329, 376, 393; **1968–69**: 39 (p. 86), 47 (pp. 128, 129), 170, 678 (p. 1275)
  Indians, **1963–64**: 120; **1968–69**: 113
  Labor, **1963–64**: 22, 124 (p. 157), 299, 311, 314, 316 [5], 571
  Maintenance, **1968–69**: 47 (pp. 141, 143), 100
  Minority groups, **1968–69**: 26
  National, **1963–64**: 132 (p. 178), 305, 415; **1965**: 32 (p. 85), 35 (p. 107), 103, 164, 208 [4], 319 [6], 321, 362; **1966**: 6 (p. 4), 26 (pp. 51–52), 132, 141 [5], 420; **1967**: 13 (p. 41); **1968–69**: 87 (pp. 84, 87)
  Negroes, **1967**: 55; **1968–69**: 423, 429, 596
  Older persons, **1963–64**: 178, 338, 590, 667; **1965**: 176 [2], 215, 461; **1966**: 168, 253; **1968–69**: 39 (p. 105)
  Personal, **1967**: 354, 376; **1968–69**: 39 (p. 86), 47 (pp. 128, 131, 133), 229, 262, 282, 429, 442, 566, 569, 596, 612, 678 (p. 1276), 684 (pp. 1312, 1313)
  See also Personal income.
  Real, **1968–69**: 229
  Relation to schooling, **1965**: 178
  Rural areas, **1965**: 32 (p. 91); **1966**: 28–29; **1967**: 13 (p. 50)
  Security, **1968–69**: 678 (p. 1297)
  Support, **1968–69**: 678 (p. 1299), 684 (p. 1325)
  Survivors and dependents, **1968–69**: 39 (p. 105)
  Taxes.
    See main heading, Income Taxes
  World, **1963–64**: 323; **1966**: 420

Income accounts budget, national, **1967**: 13 (pp. 41, 43, 59), 16 (pp. 76–77), 330 [1]

Income budget, national, **1966**: 635 [6, 17]

Income Maintenance Programs, Commission on, **1968–69**: 3, 47 (p. 143), 678 (p. 1298), 684 (p. 1325)

Income taxes, **1963–64**: 730; **1965**: 35 (p. 109), 183, 505; **1966**: 8ftn. (p. 20), 17, 26 (pp. 50, 52), 34 (p. 102), 96; **1967**: 16 (p. 76), 328 [23]
  Corporate, **1966**: 17, 26 (pp. 49, 52), 34 (p. 102), 124 [13], 155, 444, 445 [9]
  Increase, **1966**: 124 [13], 492 [9]
  Military personnel, **1966**: 389, 571

[References are to items except as otherwise indicated]

Income taxes – *continued*
  Reduction and reform, **1963–64**: 43n., 91 (pp.
      112, 115), 92, 93, 124 (pp. 156, 157,
      159–161, 164), 132 (pp. 177, 179,
      190), 139, 150 [18], 176, 182, 197,
      199, 211 [3], 213, 218 [15], 219, 221,
      233, 235, 295, 299, 305, 311, 316 [5],
      338, 350, 379 [5], 388, 411, 413, 415,
      431, 434, 455 [13], 477, 563 [10],
      604, 635, 639, 640, 644, 678, 708, 724,
      731, 771, 787; **1965**: 2, 32 (pp. 83, 84,
      86), 60, 146, 255, 326, 330, 347 [11],
      505
  Surcharge, **1967**: 3 (p. 8), 6 [3, 17], 16 (p. 77),
      104 [3], 204 [6], 225 [9], 312 [4],
      328 [8, 21], 329, 330 [1, 5, 6–8], 362,
      375 [8], 411 [11], 417 [1, 5–8, 10, 12],
      420, 421, 427, 430, 460 [4, 12], 465,
      495 [9], 518 [4, 6, 9], 554 [13], 556
Tax bill.
  See main heading, Tax bill.
  U.S.-Germany convention and protocol, **1965**:
      535
  Withholding, **1963–64**: 91 (p. 115), 124 (pp.
      158, 159), 132 (p. 179), 271 [3], 336
      [18]
Independence, Mo., **1965**: 394n.; **1966**: 22;
      1968–69: 224, 532
Independence Day, **1967**: 301; **1968–69**: 358,
      359
Independence movements, national, **1966**: 6 (p.
      9)
Independent Business, National Federation of,
      1965: 438
Independent Offices Appropriation Act, 1964,
      approval, **1963–64**: 56
Independent Offices Appropriation Act, 1967,
      1966: 394n., 439
Independent Offices and Department of Housing
      and Urban Development Appropriation
      Act, 1968, **1967**: 114n., 370n., 467
Independent Offices and Department of Housing
      and Urban Development Appropriation
      Act of 1969, **1968–69**: 234, 380
Independent regulatory agency heads, remarks
      to, **1963–64**: 20
Independent Theater Owners Association, **1963–
      64**: 354
India, **1963–64**: 35; **1965**: 176 [3], 347 [2],
      388 [6]; **1966**: 14, 277 [7], 304, 311,
      338 [2]; **1967**: 16 (p. 80), 83, 449, 452
  Ambassador B. K. Nehru, **1963–64**: 35n.
  Assistance, **1963–64**: 227, 379 [17]; **1966**:
      11n., 41, 52 [1], 152–154, 164, 166,
      180, 247 [7]; **1967**: 3 (p. 10), 44, 153;
      1968–69: 39 (p. 99), 63, 417, 679
    Canadian, **1966**: 153–154
  Change in leadership, **1963–64**: 688 [8], 747

India – *continued*
  Chinese Communist relations, **1966**: 152–153
  Communist aggression, **1965**: 227
  Economic and social development, **1966**: 149,
      152–154; **1967**: 44, 153; **1968–69**: 63
  Food, **1968–69**: 63, 417, 679
    Aid, **1967**: 33, 44, 63, 153, 156, 228, 264
      [19], 375 [21–23]; **1968–69**: 691,
      696 [14]
    Resources, **1967**: 153, 157, 375 [21], 469
    Shortage, **1966**: 308, 311
  Grain shipments to, **1966**: 52 [1], 311–312
  Kashmir dispute, **1963–64**: 607; **1965**: 169,
      208 [10], 463 [5], 524, 529; **1967**:
      100
  Nehru, Jawaharlal, **1963–64**: 367
  Pakistan, relations with, **1965**: 176 [1], 649n.,
      650; **1966**: 41, 148, 153–154; **1968–69**:
      335
  Peace Corps projects in, **1965**: 83; **1966**: 149,
      154
  Press briefings on food aid, **1966**: 154
  Prime Minister Indira Gandhi, **1966**: 52 [1],
      65 [9], 141 [15], 148–149, 152–154,
      164, 180, 247 [7], 273, 329, 514
  Radhakrishnan, Sarvepalli, **1963–64**: 367
  Rainmaking projects, **1967**: 230
  Shastri, Lal Bahadur, **1963–64**: 379 [2, 17],
      381, 693, 701, 737, 747; **1965**: 208
      [17], 529
  U.S. Ambassador Chester Bowles, **1967**: 33
  U.S. relations with, **1965**: 208 [17]; **1966**:
      148, 152
  Wheat shipments to, **1967**: 375 [21, 22, 23]
India Food Consortium, **1967**: 375 [21]
Indian Affairs, Bureau of, **1963–64**: 120; **1968–
      69**: 629n.
Indian Affairs, Commissioner of (Philleo Nash),
      1963–64: 120
Indian Claims Commission, **1967**: 518 [3]
Indian Claims Commission Act, **1968–69**: 113
Indian Ocean, U.S. warships in, question of,
      1963–64: 54 [14]
Indian Opportunity, National Council on,
      1968–69: 113
Indian resources development bill of 1968,
      1968–69: 113
Indiana, **1966**: 346–347
  Automobile industry, **1963–64**: 288, 289, 295,
      297, 482 [6]
  Campaign remarks, **1963–64**: 639, 640, 729
  Candidates for public office, **1963–64**: 639,
      640, 729
  Gov. Roger D. Branigin, **1965**: 188; **1966**: 228,
      346–348, 350, 353, 491n., 492 [1]
  Gov. Matthew E. Welsh, **1963–64**: 217, 288,
      639, 640, 729

Indiana — *continued*
  Primary election, **1963–64**: 246 [7], 256 [19],
    316 [18]
  South Bend, closing of Studebaker facilities,
    1963–64: 67
  Unemployment, **1963–64**: 67, 288, 289, 295,
    297, 486 [2]
  Visit to, **1965**: 188
Indiana Dunes National Lakeshore, Indiana,
    1965: 54; **1966**: 82, 579; **1967**: 20;
    1968–69: 122
Indianapolis, Ind., **1963–64**: 641n.; **1966**: 346–
    347
  Campaign remarks, **1963–64**: 640
  Mayor John J. Barton, **1966**: 346–347
Indians, American, **1966**: 95, 193, 594; **1967**:
    3 (p. 5), 114
  Antipoverty program benefits, **1963–64**: 120;
    1965: 204
  Assistance, **1967**: 97, 138
  Education and health, **1968–69**: 113, 259
  Job training, **1968–69**: 678 (pp. 1294, 1295)
  Message to Congress, **1968–69**: 113
Indians, American, National Congress of, **1963–
    64**: 120
  Navajos, **1968–69**: 28, 259
Indochina, **1963–64**: 475 [6]
  See also Cambodia; Laos; Vietnam, North;
    Vietnam, South.
  Geneva agreements on (1954), **1965**: 26, 106
    [6], 388 [1], 397, 448 [15]; **1968–69**:
    170, 400, 406, 452
Indonesia, **1965**: 176 [3]; **1966**: 277 [7], 312,
    346, 542, 563; **1967**: 44, 246n., 401
  Assistance, **1966**: 501 [8]; **1968–69**: 63, 679
  Communist aggression, **1967**: 409
  Dispute with Malaysia, **1963–64**: 156n., 170
    [1], 471n., 474, 626n., 627; **1965**: 448
    [21]
  Dispute with Philippines, **1963–64**: 156n.
  Economic and social development, **1967**: 272;
    1968–69: 63, 170
  Foreign Minister Adam Malik, **1966**: 484
  U.S. Ambassador Marshall Green, **1965**:
    448ftn. (p. 926)
Indo-United States Foundation, **1966**: 149, 152–
    154
Indus Basin development, **1963–64**: 227
Industrial Association, National Security, **1965**:
    211
Industrial College of the Armed Forces, **1963–64**:
    533
Industrial Conference Board, National, **1963–64**:
    402; **1965**: 76; **1966**: 445 [5]; **1967**:
    57
Industrial Development Organization, U.N.,
    1967: 100, 488
Industrial Fair, Budapest, **1966**: 272

Industrial goods, **1965**: 35 (p. 111)
  Exports, **1963–64**: 722, 729
Industrial Payroll Savings Committee, U.S., **1965**:
    11; **1968–69**: 10
Industrial research, U.S.-Korea cooperation,
    1965: 257, 344, 407
Industrial Research and Technology, Central
    American Institute of, **1968–69**: 366
Industrial Technology and Applied Science,
    Korean Institute for, **1965**: 257, 344,
    407
Industry, U.S., **1963–64**: 271 [15], 379 [13],
    406, 462 [1], 455 [3], 606, 729; **1965**:
    60, 71, 322, 337, 483, 513; **1966**: 34
    (p. 96), 155, 418; **1967**: 121, 442;
    1968–69: 612
  See also specific industries.
  Accident prevention, **1963–64**: 421
  Capacity, **1963–64**: 91 (p. 115), 124 (p. 158),
    132 (p. 178); **1965**: 255
  Beautification programs, **1966**: 295
  Cooperation with colleges, Government, etc.
    See also Government cooperation with
      business, education, and labor.
    Cooperation with colleges, **1963–64**: 456
    Cooperation with Government, **1963–64**:
      456, 803, 805
  Durable goods shipments, **1966**: 141 [5]
  Effect of tax reduction on, **1963–64**: 379 [5];
    1965: 76
  Employment of handicapped, **1963–64**: 403
  Equal employment responsibilities, **1965**: 384
  Expansion of, **1963–64**: 233
  Export associations, **1968–69**: 146
  Exports, **1968–69**: 684 (p. 1319)
  Gains since 1961, **1963–64**: 697
  Government-regulated, **1963–64**: 266 [16]
  Hard-core unemployed, retraining, **1968–69**:
    14 (p. 28), 24, 25, 37, 86, 87, 92, 100,
    105, 114, 115, 133, 164, 220, 406, 555
  Health programs, **1965**: 324; **1966**: 237; **1968–
    69**: 24
  Housing, **1965**: 90
  Improvement of, **1965**: 148
  Labor costs, **1965**: 326
  Machinery orders, **1967**: 103
  Manufactured goods, **1963–64**: 463
  Nuclear fuel reprocessing, **1966**: 179
  Overtime employment in, **1963–64**: 91 (p.
    116), 124 (p. 163)
  Participation in foreign assistance, **1963–64**:
    617
  Plant closings, **1963–64**: 690
  Plant and equipment modernization, **1963–64**:
    211 [3], 233, 285 [9], 431, 459, 589,
    619 [4], 689, 708, 717, 724; **1965**: 23,
    35 (p. 106), 76, 226, 326, 590; **1966**:
    26 (p. 49), 34 (pp. 98–99), 158 [4],

Industry, U.S. – *continued*
  Plant, equipment modernization – *continued*
      444, 445 [4–5], 451, 470, 635 [10,
      18]; **1967**: 6 [9], 70 [6], 412; **1968–
      69**: 684 (pp. 1311, 1315)
  Plant equipment not utilized, **1963–64**: 91 (p.
      115), 132 (pp. 178, 191), 297; **1965**:
      32 (p. 84)
  Pollution control, **1963–64**: 578, 756; **1966**:
      392; **1967**: 16 (p. 85), 20, 186;
      1968–69: 122
  Prices, **1968–69**: 47 (p. 139)
  Production, **1963–64**: 23, 124 (p. 156), 132
      (p. 178), 199, 271 [3], 307, 404, 477,
      506, 555, 640, 780 [3]; **1965**: 35 (p.
      104), 76, 168, 319 [3], 326; **1966**: 34
      (p. 96), 155; **1967**: 13 (p. 40); **1968–
      69**: 47 (p. 128), 684 (pp. 1311, 1316)
  Reduction in reports to Government, **1963–64**:
      462 [2]
  Regulation, **1968–69**: 534
  Representatives in Peace Corps, **1963–64**: 745
  Research, **1963–64**: 589; **1965**: 257
  Research leaders, visit to Soviet Union, **1963–
      64**: 804; **1965**: 4
  Rural areas, **1965**: 47
  Rural credit, **1968–69**: 94
  Safety, **1968–69**: 24, 154, 164
  Slum renewal efforts, **1967**: 252
  Special Impact program, **1968–69**: 678 (p.
      1291)
  Stock owned by Government officials, **1963–
      64**: 266 [16]
  Textiles, **1963–64**: 602; **1965**: 168
  Unemployment, **1965**: 598
  Urban areas, **1968–69**: 87
  Veterans, employment, **1968–69**: 40
  Wages, **1966**: 34 (p. 96), 399, 403, 426, 635
      [8–9]
  Waste products, **1965**: 54; **1966**: 82
  Workweek, **1966**: 445 [5]
Industry committee, tripartite, proposed, **1963–
      64**: 91 (p. 116)
Industry-Government Special Task Force on
      Travel, **1967**: 16ftn. (p. 81); **1968–69**:
      1ftn. (p. 1), 2n., 83, 88, 116
Inez, Ky., **1963–64**: 295
Infant health, **1968–69**: 14 (p. 29), 26, 39 (pp.
      89, 103, 104), 47 (p. 143), 111, 113,
      262, 270, 406, 429, 442, 568, 569, 596,
      622, 676 (p. 1265), 678 (pp. 1295–
      1297), 684 (p. 1324)
Infant mortality, **1963–64**: 179; **1965**: 70, 301,
      401, 406; **1966**: 95, 395, 433, 580
      [11]; **1967**: 13 (p. 59), 39, 70, 114,
      286, 319, 532, 540, 554 [6, 12]
Inflation, **1963–64**: 299; **1965**: 326, 377, 641
      [2], 663; **1966**: 8 [15], 34 (p. 97),

Inflation – *continued*
      108–109, 111, 115, 141 [5], 155, 158
      [3], 234, 236 [7], 240, 275, 312, 333,
      334 [6], 336, 371, 373 [4, 17], 399,
      403, 413, 419, 428–429, 431, 444, 453,
      473, 504, 577 [10], 592, 596, 603,
      630 [2], 631; **1967**: 3 (p. 8), 13 (pp.
      40–41, 51), 16 (p. 88), 63, 70 [6], 329,
      343, 420, 430, 460 [6]; **1968–69**: 39
      (pp. 84, 87, 88), 47 (pp. 138, 139), 90,
      169 [21], 229, 241, 469, 612, 654
  Economy, national, **1967**: 465
  Increase, **1967**: 417 [5, 6]
  News conference remarks, **1963–64**: 246 [15],
      294 [23], 379 [13]
  Prevention and control, **1963–64**: 431, 787;
      1966: 6 (p. 5), 26 (p. 49), 34 (p. 109),
      83, 347, 441, 444, 464, 473–494 [4];
      1967: 103, 120, 312 [4], 329, 411
      [11], 430, 460 [4, 6], 490, 495, 556;
      1968–69: 1 [11], 2, 14 (pp. 32, 33), 39
      (p. 86), 46, 56, 146, 226, 274, 322, 326,
      343, 350, 404, 425 [1], 427, 469, 485,
      567, 612, 676 (p. 1268), 678 (pp. 1273,
      1275), 684 (pp. 1312, 1314, 1316,
      1319)
Influenza control, **1965**: 5
Information, **1966**: 26 (p. 59), 337, 338 [18]
  Availability to presidential candidates, **1963–
      64**: 272, 280 [6], 285 [1, 17], 294
      [15], 462 [9], 516 [11]
  Declassified, **1963–64**: 266 [22]
  Privileged, **1965**: 160; **1966**: 316
  Toxicological, **1966**: 279–280, 307
Information agency.
  See United States Information Agency.
Information Center, National Earthquake, **1967**:
      31n.
Information and Education Center on Narcotic
      and Dangerous Drugs (HEW), **1967**: 35
Information Interchange, Standard Code for,
      1968–69: 127
Information Service, United States, **1966**: 243
Informational Media Guarantee Program, **1966**:
      45
Ing, Mr. and Mrs. Andrew T. F., **1966**: 532
Ingram, Mr. and Mrs. W. B., Jr., **1963–64**: 701
Ingrid, Queen (Denmark), **1963–64**: 394; **1966**:
      195
Ink, Dwight A., **1966**: 198n.; **1967**: 458n.
Inland Steel Co., **1966**: 373ftn. (p. 805); **1968–
      69**: 427n.
Inland waterways, **1963–64**: 132 (pp. 180, 181)
  User charges, **1966**: 26 (p. 54), 34 (p. 105)
Inonu, Ismet, **1963–64**: 416, 418, 423
Inonu, Mrs. Ismet, **1963–64**: 416n.
Inouye, Sen. Daniel K., **1968–69**: 197, 198
Inouye, Mrs. Daniel K., **1967**: 555

Insecticides, **1963–64**: 758
  See also Pesticides.
  Consumer protection, **1963–64**: 341
  Regulation, **1963–64**: 173, 179
Institute of Architects, American, **1965**: 315
Institute for the Deaf, National Technical,
    establishment, **1965**: 401
Institute for Free Labor Development in Latin
    America, **1965**: 450
Institute of Industrial Research and Technology,
    Central American, **1968–69**: 366
Institute for Industrial Technology and Applied
    Science, Korean, **1965**: 257, 344, 407
Institute for Public Administration, Central
    American, **1968–69**: 366
Institute of Public Affairs, National, **1966**: 129n.
Institute of Public Affairs, University of Texas,
    1968–69: 690
Institute of Urban Development, **1967**: 114
Institutes for Environmental Research, **1967**:
    31n.
Institutes of Health, National, **1966**: 293, 301,
    319, 433; **1967**: 12, 217, 319, 500, 540;
    1968–69: 396, 408, 446, 536, 589
Insurance
  Automobile, study of, **1968–69**: 14 (p. 30),
    56, 264
  Bank deposits, **1966**: 34 (p. 108); **1967**: 57,
    200, 303
  Congressmen, **1967**: 343
  Coverage in riot-affected areas, **1968–69**: 36,
    87, 287
  Disability, **1965**: 49; **1966**: 318; **1968–69**:
    684 (p. 1323)
  Executives, urban programs role, **1967**: 380,
    460 [10], 467
  Export, **1968–69**: 377
  Financial institutions, **1966**: 530
  Flood victims, **1966**: 381
  Government employees, **1965**: 49; **1966**: 318,
    453; **1967**: 343
  Health, **1968–69**: 111
    Under social security.
    See Social security; Medicare.
  Medical, **1966**: 26 (pp. 53, 55)
  Military personnel, **1966**: 26 (p. 64); **1967**: 25;
    1968–69: 39 (p. 106), 40
  Mortgage, **1963–64**: 178n., 179; **1965**: 32 (p.
    93), 47, 90, 415, 585; **1966**: 95; **1967**:
    88
  Natural disasters, **1968–69**: 36
  Old-age and survivors, **1963–64**: 132 (p. 191),
    590, 648; **1965**: 49; **1966**: 453
  President's life insurance, **1963–64**: 143 [3]
  Railroad, **1968–69**: 331
  Retirement, **1967**: 244
  Role of companies in urban renewal, **1968–69**:
    87, 115

Insurance – *continued*
  Savings, **1967**: 86
  Savings and loan, **1966**: 34 (p. 108), 530
  Social, **1968–69**: 47 (p. 141), 684 (p. 1321)
  Student loans, **1966**: 3
  Unemployment, **1966**: 6 (p. 5), 26 (p. 62), 34
    (p. 106), 111, 235, 237, 318, 394;
    1967: 12, 16 (p. 84), 114, 199, 548;
    1968–69: 39 (p. 104), 47 (p. 142), 463,
    678 (pp. 1278, 1299), 684 (p. 1323)
  See also Unemployment insurance.
  Veterans, **1966**: 505
  Workmen's compensation, **1968–69**: 678 (p.
    1299), 684 (p. 1323)
Insurance Corporation, Federal Deposit, **1966**:
    473; **1967**: 16 (p. 87)
Insurance Development Corporation, National,
    proposed, **1968–69**: 36
Insurance in Riot-Affected Areas, President's
    National Advisory Panel on, **1968–69**:
    36, 87
Insured Loans to Students, Advisory Council on,
    1966: 3
Insured Savings Associations, National League of,
    1963–64: 617
Integration, **1963–64**: 220, 235; **1965**: 90
  See also Civil rights; Nondiscrimination.
  Hospitals, **1967**: 55, 77
  Housing, **1967**: 3 (p. 5), 55
  Public accommodations, **1963–64**: 91 (p. 116),
    111, 201 [16], 250, 301, 744; **1967**: 55
  Schools, **1963–64**: 413, 642, 744; **1965**: 340,
    443, 470, 615; **1966**: 95, 196, 235, 375,
    492 [3] 494 [5, 10], 501 [13]; **1967**:
    55, 77, 225 [12]
Integration Fund, Central American, **1967**: 44
Intelligence, President's Advisory Board on
    Foreign, **1966**: 320 [2]
INTELSAT (International Telecommunications
    Satellite Consortium), **1967**: 122, 346
Interagency Committee for Control of Pollution
    by Oil and Hazardous Materials,
    National, **1968–69**: 586
Interagency Committee on Education, **1965**: 100
Interagency Committee on International Meteor-
    ological Programs, **1966**: 143
Interagency Committee on Mexican American
    Affairs, **1967**: 258, 259; **1968–69**: 91,
    437
Interagency Committee on Oceanography, **1963–
    64**: 229
Interama Cultural and Trade Center, Miami, Fla.,
    1963–64: 710
Inter-American Bank, **1963–64**: 340
Inter-American Committee on the Alliance for
    Progress, **1963–64**: 211 [8], 220, 227,
    340, 475 [3], 726, 769; **1965**: 18, 136,
    393, 429; **1966**: 41, 125, 158 [2], 177,
    386n., 501 [1]; **1968–69**: 290

Inter-American conference, **1965**: 593, 624;
    1966: 41
Inter-American cooperation, **1963–64**: 220, 285
    [13]; **1965**: 200, 295 [4]; **1966**: 175,
    639
    Economic and social development, **1963–64**:
        340; **1965**: 18, 429
    U.S.-Colombia, sea-level canal survey, **1963–
        64**: 266 [5]
Inter-American Cooperation Program, Catholic,
    1963–64: 123
Inter-American Cultural Council, **1966**: 16;
    1968–69: 66, 77
Inter-American Development Bank, **1963–64**:
    132 (p. 186), 220; **1965**: 18, 32 (p. 90),
    131, 215, 393; **1966**: 26 (p. 58), 41,
    125, 177, 386n.; **1967**: 16 (p. 80), 44,
    110, 176, 177n., 394, 401; **1968–69**:
    39 (p. 99), 63, 206, 239, 290, 366, 500,
    665
    Fund for Special Operations, **1968–69**: 39 (p.
        99), 63, 290
Inter-American Development Bank Act, **1965**:
    173
    Amendment, **1968–69**: 290
Inter-American Economic and Social Council,
    1963–64: 769; **1965**: 593; **1966**: 175
Inter-American Force (OAS), **1965**: 286, 295 [1,
    4, 10], 319 [4, 16], 342, 463 [4]
Inter-American foreign ministers meeting,
    Washington, D.C., **1963–64**: 455 [18],
    475 [3, 13], 561
Inter-American Foundation for Science and
    Technology, **1967**: 176
Inter-American Geodetic Survey, **1967**: 336
Inter-American Peace Committee, **1963–64**: 104,
    143 [1], 150 [14]
Inter-American system, **1963–64**: 232 [1], 245,
    272, 340, 438, 486 [3]; **1965**: 216,
    218, 221, 286, 295 [15]
Intercontinental ballistic missile.
    See ICBM.
Interdepartmental Committee for Savings Bonds,
    1966: 137
Interdepartmental Highway Safety Board, **1966**:
    98
Interest equalization tax, **1963–64**: 91 (p. 117),
    124 (p. 162), 132 (p. 190); **1965**: 15,
    60, 77, 638n.; **1967**: 16 (p. 81)
Interest Equalization Tax Act, **1963–64**: 722;
    1965: 60, 77
Interest Equalization Tax Extension Act of 1967,
    1968–69: 684 (p. 1319)
Interest on national debt, **1963–64**: 211 [28]
Interest rates, **1963–64**: 132 (p. 190), 350, 654,
    722, 775, 787; **1965**: 35 (pp. 106, 111),
    60, 77, 639, 641 [2]; **1966**: 140, 182,
    201, 338 [14], 444, 445 [3], 501 [7],

Interest rates – *continued*
    596, 642 [3]; **1967**: 3 (p. 7), 13 (pp.
    39, 41), 16 (pp. 75, 88), 57, 103, 104
    [1, 9], 415, 460 [12]; **1968–69**: 678
    (pp. 1273, 1275, 1276)
    Bank deposits, **1966**: 338 [14]
    Ceiling, **1968–69**: 47 (p. 141)
    Consumer purchases, **1963–64**: 173
    Federal, **1968–69**: 39 (p. 88)
    Housing mortgages, **1967**: 103; **1968–69**: 39
        (p. 103), 87
    Increase, **1966**: 401 [19], 472; **1967**: 16 (p.
        75), 329, 411 [11], 417 [1, 5], 420,
        427, 556; **1968–69**: 14 (p. 31), 39 (pp.
        84, 86, 87), 47 (pp. 127, 132, 133), 56,
        141, 170, 229, 241, 283 [8], 343, 684
        (p. 1313)
    Legislation, **1966**: 473, 642 [3]
    Mortgages, **1963–64**: 714
    News conference remarks, **1963–64**: 211 [34]
    Reduction, **1963–64**: 714; **1968–69**: 445
    Savings bonds and Freedom Shares, **1966**: 15,
        72–73, 137, 150, 164; **1968–69**: 284
    Statement responding to remarks of President
        Truman, **1966**: 419
    Truth in lending, **1967**: 16 (p. 86), 57, 342,
        393, 430, 460 [5], 465, 499, 503, 520,
        534, 539; **1968–69**: 49, 154, 164, 270,
        280, 281, 545
    Water projects, **1968–69**: 39 (p. 101)
Intergovernmental Cooperation Act of 1968,
    1968–69: 539, 678 (p. 1303)
Intergovernmental manpower bill, **1967**: 121,
    148; **1968–69**: 39 (p. 110), 84, 100
Intergovernmental Marine Consultative Organi-
    zation, **1967**: 240
Intergovernmental personnel bill, **1968–69**: 539
Intergovernmental Relations, Advisory Commis-
    sion on, **1966**: 606, 607 [1]; **1968–69**:
    598
Interior, Department of the, **1963–64**: 179, 271
    [7], 420 [2], 462 [2], 480, 619 [1],
    792n.; **1965**: 54, 127, 138n., 143, 271,
    287n., 319 [5], 325, 420, 487, 498n.,
    503, 560; **1966**: 26 (p. 60), 69, 82, 215,
    232, 320 [5], 373 [15], 374, 428, 595,
    615, 630 [4]; **1967**: 6 [5, 10, 13], 13
    (pp. 51, 57), 20, 186, 369; **1968–69**:
    653n., 664, 678 (p. 1302), 700
    Job training for Indians, **1968–69**: 678 (p.
        1295)
    Oil spillage control, **1968–69**: 297, 586
    Water pollution control, **1966**: 91, 392–393
Interior, Secretary of the (Stewart L. Udall),
    1963–64: 34n., 65n., 120, 134, 422,
    427, 461, 554, 575, 577, 649, 711, 778,
    782, 810; **1965**: 12, 54, 119, 132, 143,
    186, 277, 350, 358, 375, 417, 418, 434,

Interior, Secretary of the — *continued*
  471, 477, 521, 538n., 545, 558, 560,
  576n., 583n., 586, 641 [5], 659; **1966:**
  69n., 82, 88 [9], 90, 151, 193, 202, 215,
  226, 227n., 232, 255, 269, 295, 486,
  518, 522, 607 [1, 8], 614, 630 [2], 639,
  646; **1967:** 15n., 20, 227, 230, 300,
  358 [11], 360, 387, 417 [1], 450, 460
  [1], 544, 547; **1968–69:** 63, 113, 122,
  128, 150, 167, 168, 259, 386, 411, 457,
  475, 477, 501, 510, 547, 600, 629, 644,
  664, 700, 707
  Memorandums, **1966:** 425, 606; **1967:** 186,
    240; **1968–69:** 297, 361
  News conference remarks on, **1963–64:** 170
    [4], 316 [4]
  Report, **1963–64:** 715
Internal Revenue Act of 1962, **1963–64:** 697,
  731
Internal Revenue Act of 1964.
  See Revenue Act of 1964.
Internal Revenue Code, **1968–69:** 651
Internal Revenue Code of 1954, **1963–64:** 148n.
Internal Revenue Service, **1963–64:** 90, 182, 336
  [3], 455 [4], 752; **1965:** 150, 505;
  1966: 88 [5], 96, 204, 422n., 630 [5];
  1967: 13 (p. 60)
  Commissioner (Mortimer M. Caplin), **1963–64:**
    182
  Commissioner (Sheldon S. Cohen), **1965:** 150,
    478
International Adverse Drug Reaction Center,
  1965: 202, 262
International Agency for Research on Cancer,
  1965: 343
International Agreements (1964).
  See also specific subjects.
  Communications satellite system, global com-
    mercial, **1963–64:** 532
  U.S.-Canada
    Columbia River agreement, **1963–64:** 134,
      135, 576
    Roosevelt Campobello International Park
      Agreement, **1963–64:** 137, 138
  U.S.-Israel joint water desalting study, **1963–
    64:** 672
  U.S.-Italy, space exploration, **1963–64:** 807
  U.S.-Mexico, Chamizal Zone agreement, **1963–
    64:** 58, 596
  U.S.-NATO, exchange of atomic information,
    1963–64: 439
  U.S.-Panama, sea-level canal study, **1963–64:**
    809
  U.S.-Philippines, tax convention, **1963–64:**
    627
  U.S.-Soviet
    Consular Convention, **1963–64:** 365
    Exchange of weather information, **1963–64:**
      705

International agreements (1965).
  See also specific subjects.
  Japan-Korea basic relations treaty, **1965:** 427,
    657
  U.S.-Canada, automotive products trade agree-
    ment, **1965:** 21, 147
  U.S.-Germany, income tax protocol, **1965:** 535
  U.S.-Mexico, water desalination in the Colo-
    rado River, **1965:** 119
  U.S.-Mexico-IAEA, saline water study, **1965:**
    558
International Air Transport Association, **1968–
  69:** 116
International Antidumping Code, **1968–69:** 559
International Association of Chiefs of Police,
  1966: 354; **1967:** 382, 385
International Association of Lions Clubs, **1965:**
  438, 529
International Association of Machinists and Aerospace Workers, **1966:** 256n., 322, 360,
  535
International Atomic Energy Agency, **1963–64:**
  29, 175, 545, 715; **1965:** 319 [5], 523,
  537, 558; **1966:** 32, 48n., 177, 516 [3];
  1967: 59, 64, 515; **1968–69:** 349, 378,
  392
International Award of the Kennedy Foundation,
  1963–64: 174
International Bank for Reconstruction and Development, **1963–64:** 220, 227; **1965:**
  18, 136, 541; **1966:** 41, 94, 125, 152–
  154, 565; **1967:** 13 (p. 49), 33, 44, 153,
  401, 511, 554 [15]; **1968–69:** 39 (p.
  99), 63, 99, 102, 290, 500
  President, nomination of Secretary McNamara,
    1967: 511, 554 [15]
International Boundary and Water Commission,
  U.S.-Mexico, **1963–64:** 193; **1965:** 119;
  1966: 177, 467–468; **1967:** 47, 303,
  408 [2, 8], 451, 454n.; **1968–69:** 623
International Brotherhood of Electrical Workers,
  1965: 298
International Career Service in Health, **1966:** 45
International center, District of Columbia, **1968–
  69:** 133, 523
International Center for Advanced Study in the
  Health Sciences, Fogarty, **1967:** 77, 217;
  1968–69: 408
International Cereals Arrangements, **1967:** 33
International Christian Leadership, Inc., **1967:**
  32n.; **1968–69:** 43n.
International Civil Aviation Organization, **1968–
  69:** 494
International Claims Settlement Act, amendment,
  approval, **1963–64:** 684
International Coffee Agreement, **1963–64:** 193,
  662, 728; **1965:** 272, 429; **1966:** 9, 125;
  1967: 10, 175–176; **1968–69:** 23, 207,
  366, 559

International Coffee Agreement — *continued*
  Act of 1965, **1966:** 9
International Committee of the Red Cross, **1966:**
  338 [1], 549; **1967:** 287, 312ftn. (p.
  702); **1968–69:** 381, 433, 580
International Conference on Education, **1966:**
  627
International Conference on the Peaceful Uses of
  Atomic Energy, **1963–64:** 545; **1965:**
  537
International Conference on Water for Peace,
  1966: 427, 593; **1967:** 230
International Conference on the World Crisis in
  Education, **1967:** 423
International Control Commission, **1963–64:**
  420 [1], 500; **1966:** 65ftn. (p. 177);
  1967: 83
International Convention for the High Seas
  Fisheries of the North Pacific Ocean,
  1963–64: 559; **1965:** 15
International cooperation, **1963–64:** 51, 66, 220,
  396, 438, 616; **1965:** 32 (p. 91), 179,
  203, 294, 295 [2], 319 [21], 393, 516,
  630; **1966:** 6 (p. 8), 417 [13], 448, 646;
  1967: 13 (p. 39), 157, 444, 488, 545
  Aid for less developed countries and new
    nations, **1963–64:** 51, 227, 361; **1965:**
    15, 18, 169, 172, 176 [1, 3], 194, 203,
    495; **1966:** 62, 200, 311
  Antarctic, exploration and research, **1965:** 220,
    265
  Antarctica, prohibition of nuclear activity in,
    1963–64: 551
  Arms control and disarmament, **1968–69:** 474
  Asia-U.S., economic development, **1966:** 88
    [1]
  Asian development, **1965:** 355n.; **1966:** 459,
    548
  Asian Development Bank, **1965:** 628
  Atomic energy, peaceful uses, **1963–64:** 29;
    1965: 319 [5], 523; **1966:** 48n., 361,
    480
  Australia-U.S., space research, **1966:** 546
  Automated Merchant Vessel Report, **1965:**
    312
  Central American countries, economic and
    social planning, **1965:** 393
  Communications satellite system, **1965:** 68,
    69, 81; **1967:** 346
  Conservation of natural resources, **1963–64:**
    756
  Cultural exchange, **1963–64:** 280, 369, 385;
    1965: 36, 292, 552, 553
  Customs reform, **1968–69:** 261
  Drug control, **1967:** 35
  Drug reactions, monitoring of, **1965:** 202, 262
  Economic, **1966:** 34 (pp. 98, 104); **1967:** 442
  Education, **1966:** 41, 45–46, 88 [1], 339, 406

International cooperation — *continued*
  Exchanges.
    See Exchange programs.
  Fairs and exhibitions, **1967:** 245; **1968–69:**
    204
  Fiscal and monetary policy, **1968–69:** 684 (p.
    1319)
  Flood control, **1967:** 303, 408, 447, 449, 451
  Food aid, **1967:** 33, 157
  Foot-and-mouth disease (rinderpest) preven-
    tion, **1968–69:** 364
  Foreign aid, **1963–64:** 227
  Germany-U.S.
    Pollution control, **1966:** 88 [9]
    Space research, **1965:** 659, 66; **1966:** 485
  Health programs, **1965:** 202, 262, 343; **1966:**
    6 (pp. 7–8), 22, 41, 45–46, 49, 157, 166,
    339, 406
  Housing information, exchange, **1968–69:** 434
  Indo-United States Foundation, **1966:** 149,
    152, 154
  Israel-U.S., water desalination, **1963–64:** 175,
    377, 378, 380, 480, 672; **1965:** 325;
    1966: 516 [3], 607 [1]
  Latin American development, **1966:** 125, 175,
    639
  Maritime, **1968–69:** 124
  Medical, **1968–69:** 408
  Mekong River projects, **1966:** 133
  Mexico-U.S.
    Amistad Dam, **1966:** 630 [2, 10], 638–640
    Water desalination, **1966:** 177, 467–468
  Monetary policy, **1963–64:** 472, 780 [3];
    1965: 15, 35 (p. 111), 110, 235, 365,
    451, 541, 637, 659n.; **1967:** 16 (p. 82),
    524; **1968–69:** 151, 218, 317, 500
  Moon exploration, **1963–64:** 518
  Nigerian aid, **1968–69:** 381, 580
  Nuclear energy, peaceful uses, **1968–69:** 349
  Oceanic research, **1966:** 326; **1968–69:** 14
    (p. 27), 692
  People-to-people program, **1966:** 339
  Philippines-U.S., **1963–64:** 627, 695
    Space research, **1966:** 461
    Veterans benefits, **1966:** 495
  Population control, **1966:** 45; **1968–69:** 393
  Proclamation on, **1963–64:** 616
  Report on, **1965:** 96
  Scientific research, **1963–64:** 529; **1965:** 523;
    1966: 503
  Space research and exploration, **1963–64:** 56,
    155, 493; **1965:** 81, 318, 333, 391, 463
    [2], 659, 660; **1966:** 209, 249, 260,
    272, 277 [13], 371, 461, 485–486,
    546, 626; **1967:** 38, 57, 425; **1968–69:**
    107, 662
  Trade.
    See Trade, international.

International cooperation — *continued*
  U.S.-Canada
    Columbia River development, **1965**: 186
    Defense production sharing program, **1963–64**: 140
    Electric energy resources development, **1965**: 350
    Great Lakes pollution control, **1965**: 54
    Shipping in Great Lakes area, **1963–64**: 140
  U.S.-Italy, space exploration, **1963–64**: 807
  U.S.-Japan, **1965**: 355n.
    Air pollution and insecticides control, **1965**: 15, 175
    Assistance to Ryukyu Islands, **1965**: 15
    Health and medical research, **1965**: 12, 15, 175, 214, 544; **1966**: 45; **1968–69**: 686
    Scientific, **1967**: 491
  U.S.-Korea, scientific and industrial research, **1965**: 257, 344, 407
  U.S.-NATO, exchange of atomic information, **1963–64**: 439, 440
  U.S.-OAS, aid to Dominican Republic, **1965**: 473, 484
  U.S.-Soviet Union, **1963–64**: 365, 420 [2], 435, 480n., 695, 705, 804
    Scientific exchanges, **1965**: 319 [5]
  Water desalination, **1963–64**: 175, 377, 378 380, 420 [2], 435, 480, 545, 672, 693, 695, 705, 715, 804; **1965**: 143, 319 [5], 325, 417, 494, 547, 588; **1966**: 177, 361, 427, 467–468, 516 [3], 607 [1]
  Water resources development, **1967**: 47, 230, 366
  Weather prediction and control, **1963–64**: 705; **1965**: 271; **1966**: 94, 143, 222; **1967**: 157; **1968–69**: 361
International Cooperation, White House Conference on, **1965**: 96, 630, 632; **1966**: 370; **1967**: 157
International Cooperation Year (1965), **1963–64**: 396; **1965**: 96, 202, 220, 262, 292, 331, 343, 346, 564, 630; **1966**: 94, 370; **1967**: 100, 157
  Proclamation, **1963–64**: 616
International Cotton Institute, **1966**: 177
International Cultural Exchange Program (1963), message to Congress, **1965**: 36
International Decade of Ocean Exploration, **1968–69**: 122, 692
International Development, Agency for, **1963–64**: 132 (pp. 185, 191), 227, 348, 480, 619 [1]; **1965**: 7, 18, 60, 127, 138n., 149, 233, 246, 294, 393n., 450, 511
See also Agency for International Development.
  Administrator (David E. Bell), **1963–64**: 48, 69, 227, 402; **1965**: 7, 18, 60, 77, 136, 407, 638, 649

International Development — *continued*
    Directors to Latin American nations, **1963–64**: 211 [8]
    Foreign assistance programs, **1963–64**: 617
International Development, National Committee for, **1965**: 7
International Development Association, **1963–64**: 227, 361; **1965**: 18; **1966**: 41, 94; **1967**: 13 (p. 49), 16 (p. 80); **1968–69**: 14 (p. 27), 39 (p. 99), 47 (p. 138), 63, 275 [6], 290, 500, 678 (p. 1282), 684 (p. 1321)
International Development Association Act, **1963–64**: 361, 462 [11], 617
International Development Association bill, **1963–64**: 346
International Education, Council on, **1966**: 45
International Education Act of 1966, **1966**: 6 (p. 8), 22, 41, 45–46, 77, 406, 533, 557, 627; **1967**: 77, 344; **1968–69**: 538
International education bill, **1968–69**: 54
International Executive Service Corps. **1963–64**: 227, 402; **1965**: 18; **1966**: 41; **1968–69**: 63
International exhibitions, **1965**: 553; **1967**: 245; **1968–69**: 204
International Federation of Aeronautics, **1965**: 219
International Federation of Commercial, Clerical, and Technical Employees, **1967**: 442
International Finance Corporation, **1966**: 94; **1968–69**: 500n.
International Games for the Deaf (1965), **1963–64**: 808
International Geophysical Year, **1963–64**: 551; **1965**: 318
International Grains Arrangement, **1967**: 476, 508; **1968–69**: 29, 63, 94
International groups.
  See Addresses or remarks to foreign or international groups.
International Harvester Co., **1963–64**: 745
International Health Association, **1966**: 45
International health bill, **1966**: 6 (pp. 7–8), 22, 41, 45–46, 49, 166
International Health Research Act of 1960, **1965**: 544; **1967**: 215; **1968–69**: 286n.
International Human Rights Year, **1968–69**: 428
International Hydrological Decade, **1963–64**: 231n.
International Labor Conference (1964), **1966**: 250
International Labor Organization, **1965**: 370
  Convention, **1966**: 122, 250
International Labor Press Association, **1963–64**: 297; **1966**: 237
International Ladies Garment Workers Union, **1963–64**: 387, 388; **1968–69**: 270, 529

International law, **1965**: 59, 346, 516; **1966**:
     498
International loans, **1968-69**: 1 [1, 15], 11, 47
     (p. 135), 146, 241 684 (p. 1319)
International Longshoremen's Association, **1963-
     64**: 195, 494, 614; **1965**: 58, 65; **1968-
     69**: 636
International Machinists Union, **1963-64**: 571
International Media Guarantee Program, U.S.-
     Poland, **1966**: 200
International Meteorological Programs, Inter-
     agency Committee on, **1966**: 143
International Monetary Arrangements, Advisory
     Committee on, **1965**: 365; **1968-69**:
     218
International Monetary and Financial Problems,
     National Advisory Council on, **1965**:
     110, 282
International Monetary Fund, **1963-64**: 472;
     1965: 32 (p. 91), 35 (p. 112), 60, 110,
     541; **1966**: 486; **1967**: 16 (p. 82), 351,
     371, 390, 497, 519, 524, 545; **1968-
     69**: 2, 47 (p. 129), 218, 317, 500, 684
     (p. 1319)
   Special Drawing Rights, **1968-69**: 2, 47 (p.
     137), 76, 218, 317, 500, 684 (p. 1319)
International Monetary Fund Agreement, **1968-
     69**: 317
International monetary system, **1965**: 15, 35 (p.
     111), 110, 235, 365, 451, 541, 659n.;
     1968-69: 2, 14 (p. 33), 47 (pp. 129,
     136, 137), 146, 151, 170, 194, 218,
     226, 317, 449, 500, 582, 676 (p. 1268),
     684 (p. 1319)
International Narcotics Control Board, **1967**: 35
International Narcotics Enforcement Officers
     Association, **1968-69**: 217
International Optical Co., Dallas, Tex., **1967**:
     388
International Organization of Masters, Mates and
     Pilots of America, **1965**: 428
International organizations
   Staffing of, memorandum, **1963-64**: 519
   U.S. contributions to, **1963-64**: 45; **1966**: 41,
     45, 130
International Peace Arch, **1963-64**: 563 [3],
     576
International Peace Garden, N. Dak., **1966**: 601
International Peace Park, Wash., **1966**: 448
International Platform Association, **1965**: 397
International Programs for Youth Leaders and
     Social Workers, Council of, **1967**: 365
International Red Cross, **1965**: 546
International Rice Research Institute, **1966**: 459,
     550
International Rice Year, **1966**: 62
International Rural Development, Conference on,
     1963-64: 482

International Service Agencies, **1967**: 288
International Settlements, Bank for, **1963-64**:
     472, 780 [3]
International Symposium on Water Desalination,
     1965: 325, 494, 547, 558
International Telecommunication Union, **1963-
     64**: 532
International Telecommunications Satellite Con-
     sortium (INTELSAT), **1967**: 122, 346
International trade.
   See Trade, international.
International Union of Electrical, Radio and
     Machine Workers, **1966**: 496
International Union of Electrical Workers, **1963-
     64**: 590
International Union of Operating Engineers,
     1966: 141 [4]
International Union of United Automobile, Aero-
     space and Agricultural Implement
     Workers of America, **1965**: 377;
     1966: 535; **1967**: 476
International Wheat Conference, **1968-69**: 29
Interoceanic Canal Study Commission, Atlantic-
     Pacific, **1965**: 400; **1967**: 336; **1968-69**:
     466
Interparliamentary Conference, Mexico-United
     States, **1968-69**: 199
Interstate Commerce Act, **1963-64**: 154
Interstate Commerce Commission, **1963-64**:
     154, 211 [2], 351, 360; **1965**: 281;
     1966: 98, 187, 322
   Chairman (John W. Bush), **1966**: 240, 322,
     434, 436-437
   Chairman (Laurence K. Walrath), **1963-64**:
     211 [2]
Interstate cooperation, water resources develop-
     ment, **1963-64**: 461
Interstate and Defense Highways, National Sys-
     tem of, **1963-64**: 565
Interstate Highway System, Federal, **1963-64**:
     512, 565, 598, 656, 661; **1965**: 29, 32
     (p. 88), 54, 255, 279, 460, 499; **1966**:
     27, 98, 492 [8]
Interstate land sales full disclosure bill, **1967**: 57
Interviews of the President, transcripts
   Lawrence, William H., Eric Sevareid, and David
     Brinkley, **1963-64**: 218
   U.S. officials held captive by Bolivian miners,
     1963-64: 60
Inventions, **1967**: 65
Inventories, business, **1967**: 16 (p. 78)
Inventory statistics, **1966**: 141 [3]
Investigations, criminal, **1968-69**: 59, 678 (p.
     1292)
Investment Company Act of 1940, **1967**: 57;
     1968-69: 418

Investments, **1963-64**: 211 [34], 233, 295, 771, 775, 787; **1965**: 32 (p. 93), 319 [8], 638n.; **1966**: 110, 155, 158 [4], 240, 444, 451, 494 [2]; **1967**: 16 (p. 74), 70 [6], 460 [12]; **1968-69**: 47 (p. 129)

Appalachia, **1963-64**: 711; **1968-69**: 173

Capital goods, **1963-64**: 124 (pp. 158, 160), 132 (p. 190), 139, 197, 211 [3], 246 [12], 271 [15], 285 [9], 544, 589, 598, 775; **1965**: 132; **1966**: 34 (pp. 99, 101)

Communications satellite program, **1963-64**: 517

Consumer protection, **1963-64**: 173

Control program, **1968-69**: 684 (p. 1319)

Depressed areas, **1965**: 132

Developing nations, **1966**: 41; **1967**: 469

Federal credit programs, **1965**: 506; **1966**: 26 (pp. 55, 66), 34 (p. 102), 182, 199, 451

Foreign in U.S., **1963-64**: 196, 296; **1965**: 35 (p. 111), 60, 77, 638n.; **1966**: 34 (p. 104), 607 [14], 612; **1967**: 16 (p. 81); **1968-69**: 47 (pp. 133, 135), 449

Increase, **1963-64**: 411, 531; **1965**: 255

Industrial plant and equipment, **1968-69**: 684 (p. 1313)

Latin America, **1963-64**: 169

Machine tool industry, **1966**: 451

Mutual funds investor protection, **1968-69**: 684 (p. 1322)

Small business, **1966**: 582

Tax credit plan, **1963-64**: 91 (p. 115), 124 (pp. 157, 159, 161), 132 (pp. 178, 179, 194), 227, 295, 350, 589, 724, 731, 787; **1965**: 18, 60, 76, 226, 326, 450, 505; **1966**: 26 (p. 52), 34 (p. 104), 444, 445 [4, 6, 22], 473, 492 [1], 494 [2], 596, 631, 642 [6], 654 [6]; **1967**: 204 [6], 329

Tax incentives, **1967**: 6 [2, 9, 13, 17], 16 (p. 76), 103, 104 [1]

Message to Congress, **1967**: 103

Transportation, **1966**: 98

U.S. abroad, **1963-64**: 91 (p. 117), 196, 296, 483, 617, 726; **1965**: 15, 18, 60, 77, 149, 450; **1966**: 125, 243; **1967**: 16 (p. 81), 524; **1968-69**: 1 [1, 15], 2, 47 (pp. 133, 134, 135), 142, 146, 241, 290, 449

Investor protection, **1967**: 57

Iowa, **1966**: 320 [14], 401 [11]

Campaign remarks, **1963-64**: 634

Gov. Harold E. Hughes, **1963-64**: 634; **1965**: 307, 420; **1966**: 312, 650; **1967**: 297 [1], 409

Iowa State University, **1963-64**: 634

Iowa Trade Mission, **1965**: 307

IPA.

See International Platform Association.

Iran, **1963-64**: 385; **1967**: 449, 452

AID programs, **1967**: 509

Art exhibit in U.S., **1963-64**: 369, 385

Assistance, **1966**: 41; **1967**: 44, 509; **1968-69**: 63, 524, 679

Cooperation with U.S., **1968-69**: 307, 615

Earthquake, **1968-69**: 614n.

Economic and social development, **1967**: 363, 364, 366, 509; **1968-69**: 304, 307, 613-615

Empress Farah, **1963-64**: 385; **1967**: 364

Khosrovani, Khosro, **1965**: 517n.

Prime Minister Amir Abbas Hoveyda, **1968-69**: 613, 614, 615

Shah Mohammad Reza Pahlavi, **1963-64**: 369, 385; **1965**: 517; **1967**: 363, 364, 366, 509; **1968-69**: 304, 307, 613-615

U.S. policy, **1968-69**: 307

U.S. relations with, **1965**: 517; **1967**: 366, 509

Water resources study, U.S. cooperation, **1967**: 366

Iran-America Society, **1963-64**: 369

Iraq, **1967**: 245

Ireland, **1965**: 68n.

Aiken, Frank, **1963-64**: 366

Ambassador William P. Fay, **1963-64**: 366

De Valera, Eamon, **1963-64**: 256 [4], 364, 366, 376, 682

Support of the United Nations, **1963-64**: 366, 376

U.S. relations with, **1963-64**: 366, 376

Irene, Princess of Greece, **1963-64**: 153

Irr, Henry P., **1968-69**: 114

Irrigation, foreign assistance, **1968-69**: 679

Irvine, Calif., University of California branch, dedication, **1963-64**: 414

Irwin, Repr. Donald J., **1968-69**: 221

Irwin, James E., **1963-64**: 701n.

Irwin, John N., **1965**: 532

Isaiah, **1966**: 78, 189, 312, 543; **1967**: 281; **1968-69**: 474, 501

Isgar, Mrs. Yeadis M., **1967**: 324n.

Island Bay Wilderness, Fla., **1968-69**: 168

Islands, conservation, **1968-69**: 167

Ismay, Lord, **1963-64**: 608n.

Isolationism, **1963-64**: 244

Isotopes, radioactive, **1965**: 196

Israel, **1965**: 68n.; **1966**: 405, 630 [17]; **1967**: 233, 257, 264 [1, 12, 13], 312 [18], 488, 554 [3]

Arab relations.

See Middle East.

Assistance, **1963-64**: 377, 378, 380; **1965**: 117 [6]; **1968-69**: 63, 176, 524

Food, **1968-69**: 176

Israel — *continued*
  Assistance — *continued*
    Military, **1968–69:** 524
  Conflict with Egypt.
    See Middle East conflict.
  Defense, **1968–69:** 9
  Foreign investments, **1968–69:** 290
  Germany, relations with, **1965:** 117 [6]
  President Schneor Zalman Shazar, **1966:** 365
  Prime Minister Levi Eshkol, **1963–64:** 377,
    378, 380, 672; **1966:** 365n.; **1968–69:**
    7, 8, 9, 78
  U.S. relations with, **1963–64:** 377, 378
  Water desalinization, cooperation with U.S.,
    1963–64: 175, 377, 378, 380, 480,
    672; **1965:** 325; **1966:** 516 [3], 607
    [1]
Isthmus of Panama, **1966:** 411
Italian-American Professional and Businessmen's
    Association, **1966:** 513
Italian Migration, American Committee on, **1968–
    69:** 352
Italian Space Commission, **1963–64:** 807
Italy, **1963–64:** 101, 149, 581, 607, 651; **1965:**
    68n., 198, 200, 235, 325; **1966:** 373
    [6, 13], 437, 478, 486
  Ambassador Sergio Fenoaltea, **1963–64:** 149n.,
    651n.; **1965:** 82; **1966:** 478, 513
  Artists from, **1965:** 82
  Change in leadership, **1963–64:** 693, 694, 746,
    747
  Earthquakes, Sicily, **1968–69:** 13
  Economic and social growth, **1963–64:** 102;
    1965: 82; **1967:** 389
  Fanfani, Amintore, **1965:** 198, 200n., 203;
    1967: 278, 389–391, 572
  Floods, **1966:** 591
  Food aid, **1968–69:** 176
  Immigrants from, **1963–64:** 581
  Immigration quota to U.S., **1963–64:** 97
  India food aid, **1967:** 33
  Journalists from, **1963–64:** 149
  Prices, **1967:** 430
  Prime Minister Aldo Moro, **1963–64:** 44;
    1965: 198, 200, 203; **1967:** 204 [4],
    278, 572
  San Marco satellite, launching, **1963–64:** 807
  Saragat, Giuseppe, **1963–64:** 101, 102n., 107,
    109, 118, 149, 817; **1965:** 200; **1966:**
    591; **1967:** 389–391, 515, 572; **1968–
    69:** 13
  Segni, Antonio, **1963–64:** 149
    Letter, **1963–64:** 794
    News conference remarks on, **1963–64:** 28
      [4], 54 [8], 475 [3]
    Visit of, **1963–64:** 101, 102, 107, 109, 118
  Ships for, **1965:** 600

Italy — *continued*
  Space exploration, cooperation with U.S.,
    1963–64: 807
  Trade with U.S., **1968–69:** 562
  U.S. Ambassador Gardner Ackley, **1968–69:**
    1 [17]
  U.S. Ambassador G. Frederick Reinhardt, **1968–
    69:** 13
  U.S. relations with, **1963–64:** 101, 102, 107,
    109, 118, 817; **1965:** 200n.; **1967:**
    389–391
  Visit, **1967:** 570–572
Ives, Mrs. Ernest, **1965:** 504n.
Ivory Coast
  Economic and social development, **1967:** 356
  President Felix Houphouet-Boigny, **1967:** 356
Iwo Jima, capture in World War II, **1968–69:** 267

J–58 aircraft engine, **1963–64:** 201 [2]
J. M. Kaplan Fund, Inc., **1968–69:** 686
J. Percy Priest Project, dedication, **1968–69:** 345
Jackson, Andrew, **1963–64:** 645; **1965:** 2, 299,
    409; **1966:** 216; **1967:** 115–117, 121,
    125, 216, 290, 495 [11]; **1968–69:** 109,
    238, 575, 648
Jackson, Beverly, **1965:** 322n.
Jackson, Elmer C., **1968–69:** 429
Jackson, Sen. Henry M., **1963–64:** 554, 575, 577;
    1965: 375, 417, 521; **1966:** 119, 193,
    202, 269, 448, 522–523; **1967:** 227;
    1968–69: 171, 386, 411, 457, 477, 501,
    505, 510
  Letter, bombing of North Vietnam, **1967:** 83
Jackson, Lt. Col. Joe M., **1968–69:** 688
Jackson, Lady (Barbara Ward), **1965:** 48, 410
Jackson, Robert H., **1967:** 443; **1968–69:** 31
Jackson, Samuel C., **1965:** 290
Jackson, Miss., civil rights march, **1966:** 277 [10]
Jackson Hole, Wyo., **1963–64:** 657; **1967:** 297
    [6]
Jacksonville, Fla., **1965:** 467, 508
  Campaign remarks, **1963–64:** 713
  Mayor Haydon Burns, **1963–64:** 571, 712, 713
Jacobs, Andrew, Jr., **1963–64:** 640; **1966:** 346–
    347
Jacobsen, Jake, **1966:** 188 [5]
Jacobsen, Melvin, **1968–69:** 599n.
Jacobson, Mrs. Dorothy H., **1963–64:** 257n.
Jacquinot, Louis, **1965:** 333n.
Jamaica
  Immigrants to U.S., **1965:** 13
  U.S. Ambassador Walter N. Tobriner, **1967:**
    466
James, Col. Daniel, Jr., **1967:** 536
James, Eldon, **1966:** 420–421; **1968–69:** 599n.
James, Frances M., **1968–69:** 138n.

James, Dr. George, **1965**: 115n., 594n.
James, George F., **1963–64**: 296
James, Hatcher M., Jr., **1967**: 352n.
James, Jack N., **1965**: 391n.
James, William, **1963–64**: 351, 397; **1966**: 45–46, 77, 497
James I, King (Great Britain), **1966**: 359
James V. Forrestal, U.S.S., **1967**: 330 [1]
Jamshid, Sultan Seyyid bin Abdulla, **1963–64**: 32
Japan, **1963–64**: 617; **1965**: 68n., 194, 220, 235, 451, 628; **1966**: 14, 133, 373 [6, 13], 420, 437, 542, 566; **1967**: 16 (p. 80), 272; **1968–69**: 44, 218, 340
  Air transport agreement, **1966**: 64
  Asian Bank aid, **1967**: 401
  Assistance, **1966**: 368
  Assistance to Asia, **1965**: 15
  Balance of payments, **1967**: 491, 492
  Bonin Islands, return of, **1968–69**: 340
  Cabinet ministers, remarks, **1967**: 381
  Change in leadership, **1963–64**: 737, 747
  Communications with U.S., **1963–64**: 408
  Earthquakes, **1963–64**: 408
  Economy, **1965**: 8, 12, 15
  Emperor Hirohito, **1965**: 12, 355n.; **1967**: 381, 487
  Fisheries in North Pacific, **1963–64**: 559
  Fishing in territorial waters of U.S., **1963–64**: 353
  Foreign aid and investments, **1968–69**: 63, 290
  Governors, remarks, **1967**: 234
  Health and medical research, **1966**: 45
  Ikeda, Hayato, **1963–64**: 8, 236, 408
  Interest equalization tax exemption, proposed, **1965**: 60
  Miki, Takeo, **1965**: 355n.
  Olympic games (1964), **1963–64**: 632, 699, 782
  Peace corps, establishment of, **1963–64**: 347
  Prices, **1967**: 430
  Prime Minister Eisaku Sato, **1965**: 8, 12, 15, 175, 214, 355n., 544; **1967**: 437, 486, 487, 491, 492, 493n.; **1968–69**: 44, 340, 685
  Rail rapid transit, **1967**: 234
  Relations with other countries
    Communist China, **1965**: 15
    Korea, **1965**: 256n., 257, 427, 657
    Republic of China, **1965**: 15
    U.S., **1965**: 8, 12, 15, 355n.; **1967**: 381, 437, 486, 491
  Shiina, Etsusaburo, **1965**: 12, 15, 355
  Support of United Nations, **1965**: 15
  Trade, **1967**: 508; **1968–69**: 517, 524
  U.S. aid, **1968–69**: 176
  U.S. Ambassador Edwin O. Reischauer, **1963–64**: 236; **1966**: 154

Japan — *continued*
  U.S. cooperation with, **1965**: 355n.
    Air pollution and insecticides control, **1965**: 15, 175
    Health and medical research, **1965**: 12, 15, 175, 214, 544; **1968–69**: 286, 685
    Scientific, **1967**: 491
  U.S. investments in, **1965**: 15
  U.S.-Japan, communication satellite television, **1963–64**: 632
  Visit of Cabinet ministers to U.S., **1965**: 355
Japan Committee on Trade and Economic Affairs, Joint United States, **1967**: 491
Japan Conference on Development and Utilization of Natural Resources, United States, **1967**: 491
Japan Cooperative Medical Science Program, United States, **1968–69**: 286, 685
Japan-United States Civil Air Transport Agreement, **1965**: 15
Japan-United States Committee on Scientific Cooperation, **1965**: 15
Japan-United States Committee on Trade and Economic Affairs, **1965**: 15, 355; **1967**: 381, 491
Japan-United States Conference on Cultural and Educational Interchange, Joint, **1965**: 15
Jarman, Repr. John, **1966**: 410, 413, 415–416
Jarring, Gunnar, **1967**: 554 [2]
  U.N. mission to Middle East, **1968–69**: 9, 14 (p. 26), 169 [20], 255, 288, 474, 615, 620, 652
Jaszi, George, **1965**: 263n.
Javan, Ali, **1966**: 194
Javits, Sen. Jacob K., **1965**: 242, 410, 546; **1966**: 392, 394–395, 417 [5]; **1967**: 484; **1968–69**: 540, 672
Jaworski, Leon, **1965**: 422n.; **1967**: 455
Jay, John, **1966**: 128
Jaycees, United States, **1967**: 23, 100, 286, 291
Jefferson, Thomas, **1963–64**: 19, 96, 172, 188, 218 [36], 233, 339, 388, 391, 397, 398, 414, 426n., 477, 510, 523, 754, 774; **1965**: 2, 5, 6, 54, 56, 91, 98, 108, 181, 198, 299, 302, 307, 314, 329, 336, 366, 370n., 410, 429, 503, 603; **1966**: 21, 120, 193, 248, 253, 323, 353, 395, 412, 435, 479, 489, 499–500, 528, 573, 576, 609; **1967**: 3 (p. 11), 17, 115, 193, 201, 216, 301, 423, 444, 485 [1]; **1968–69**: 94, 99, 104, 109, 210, 242, 282, 291n., 359, 538, 576, 648
  Campaign remarks on, **1963–64**: 542, 571, 598, 658, 659, 745, 746, 749, 750, 751
Jeffersonville, Ind., **1966**: 353
  Mayor Richard Vissing, **1966**: 353
Jenkins, Herbert, **1967**: 326

Jenkins, Howard, Jr., **1966**: 410, 413, 415
Jenkins, John A., **1965**: 308
Jenkins, Walter, **1963-64**: 170 [17], 516 [16], 671, 688 [5], 728
Jenner, Albert E., Jr., **1968-69**: 293
Jennings, S. Sgt. Delbert O., **1968-69**: 487
Jennings, Paul J., **1966**: 315n.; **1968-69**: 106n.
Jennings, Repr. W. Pat, **1963-64**: 358
Jensen, Maj. Gen. James C., **1963-64**: 242 [1]
Jensen, James H., **1967**: 490
Jersey City, N.J., Job Corps Conservation Center, **1965**: 242
Jerusalem, **1967**: 272, 297 [3], 312 [18]; **1968-69**: 474
Jessel, George, **1966**: 395
Jester, Beauford H., **1967**: 210
Jet Aircraft Noise Panel, **1966**: 98ftn. (p. 261)
Jewish High Holy Days, **1966**: 405
Jewish Labor Committee, **1967**: 484
Jewish people, **1968-69**: 474
Jewish Women, National Council of, **1965**: 438
Jews, National Conference of Christians and, **1963-64**: 113; **1968-69**: 78
Jidda, Saudi Arabia, **1965**: 325
Job, Book of, **1968-69**: 78
Job Corps, **1965**: 32 (p. 93), 75, 208 [13], 308; **1966**: 111, 189, 417 [2], 594; **1967**: 13 (p. 54), 16 (p. 75), 39, 81, 114, 199, 211, 277, 291; **1968-69**: 24, 47 (p. 142), 555, 678 (p. 1294)
  Proposed, **1963-64**: 323, 516 [4]
  Student participation, **1965**: 75
  Training centers, **1963-64**: 219; **1965**: 75, 106 [8], 179, 208 [5], 288n., 603
Job Corps Conservation Center, Jersey City, N.J., **1965**: 242
Job development program, statements, **1965**: 38, 79
Job Opportunities in Business Sector (JOBS), **1968-69**: 24, 25, 91, 92, 105, 678 (p. 1294), 684 (pp. 1314, 1324)
Job training.
  See Occupational training.
JOBS.
  See Job Opportunities in the Business Sector.
Joel, Sp6c. Lawrence, **1967**: 102
Joelson, Repr. Charles S., **1963-64**: 338; **1965**: 242; **1966**: 504
Johansen, Repr. August E., **1963-64**: 356
John, King, of England, **1965**: 376
John Birch Society, **1963-64**: 462 [6]
John E. Fogarty International Center for Advanced Study in the Health Sciences, **1967**: 217; **1968-69**: 408
John F. Kennedy, U.S.S., **1963-64**: 560 [6]; **1967**: 241
John F. Kennedy Center for the Performing Arts, **1963-64**: 142, 784; **1966**: 227

John F. Kennedy Educational, Civic and Cultural Center, Mitchel Field, N.Y., dedication, **1963-64**: 337
John F. Kennedy Memorial Library, Boston, Mass., **1963-64**: 773
John F. Kennedy Space Center (NASA), **1963-64**: 12; **1966**: 485
  Designation of name, Executive order, **1963-64**: 13
John F. Kennedy Square, Texarkana, dedication, **1963-64**: 599
John Fitzgerald Kennedy National Historic Site, Mass., **1967**: 242
John Foster Dulles International Airport, departure remarks, **1966**: 531
John XXIII, Pope, **1963-64**: 27, 123, 224, 396; **1965**: 302; **1966**: 396; **1968-69**: 78
John Wiley & Sons, Inc., **1963-64**: 350n.
Johns, Thomas L., **1965**: 22 [1]; **1968-69**: 549, 604
Johns Hopkins University, **1963-64**: 612; **1965**: 172, 294; **1968-69**: 170
Johnsen, Richard E., **1968-69**: 604
Johnson, Andrew, **1963-64**: 58, 137; **1967**: 81, 82, 376, 538; **1968-69**: 238
Johnson, Augustus C., **1963-64**: 628
Johnson, Catherine, **1967**: 332n.
Johnson, Charles Richard, **1966**: 455
Johnson, Clarence L., **1963-64**: 568, 593; **1965**: 646n.; **1966**: 61n.
Johnson, Daniel, **1967**: 237
Johnson, Donald E., **1965**: 388 [5]
Johnson, Sp. 5c. Dwight H., **1968-69**: 594
Johnson, Edwin C., **1963-64**: 658
Johnson, Emil, **1967**: 313
Johnson, G. Griffith, **1963-64**: 532n.
Johnson, Glen R., **1968-69**: 537
Johnson, Gen. Harold K., **1965**: 280; **1966**: 348, 516 [9]; **1967**: 166, 331, 358 [1, 6], 375 [7, 19], 485 [1], 494; **1968-69**: 79ftn. (p. 234), 81 [1], 153 [4], 221, 353, 384
Johnson, Mrs. Harold K., **1968-69**: 353
Johnson, Repr. Harold T., **1967**: 227
Johnson, Howard W., **1966**: 184n.
Johnson, Hugh S., **1966**: 493
Johnson, Iner, **1963-64**: 435
Johnson, Mr. and Mrs. J. Lee, III, **1968-69**: 281
Johnson, Repr. Jed, Jr., **1966**: 410, 413, 415-416
Johnson, Jeh, **1967**: 4n.
Johnson, Jesse, **1963-64**: 330
Johnson, John A., **1967**: 324n.
Johnson, John H., **1966**: 315n.
Johnson, Keen, **1963-64**: 643
Johnson, Kelly, **1965**: 219
Johnson, Lester D., **1968-69**: 388n.
Johnson, Louis A., **1968-69**: 18 [2]
  Death, **1966**: 191

Johnson, Mrs. Louis A., **1966**: 191
Johnson, Lucy (Luci) Baines, **1963–64**: 58, 208,
    270, 289, 318, 334, 465, 526, 680, 810;
    1965: 88, 205, 289, 306, 372, 405, 419,
    462, 467
    See also Nugent, Mrs. Patrick J.
    Campaign remarks on, **1963–64**: 644, 645, 646,
        648, 650, 680, 729, 732, 751, 760, 761,
        763, 765
    News conference remarks on, **1963–64**: 143
        [3], 516 [1], 587 [9]
Johnson, Lynda Bird, **1963–64**: 208, 270, 318,
    320n., 321, 322n., 323n., 326, 327, 328,
    330, 334, 372, 394, 397, 465, 526, 810;
    1965: 205, 260, 403, 419; **1966**: 72,
    119, 240, 339, 373 [18], 417 [8], 513,
    518, 528
    See also Robb, Mrs. Charles S.
    Campaign remarks on, **1963–64**: 622, 628,
        631n., 644, 648, 650, 732, 751, 760,
        761, 763, 765
    News conference remarks on, **1963–64**: 143
        [3], 294 [26], 336 [20], 516 [1], 587
        [9]
Johnson, Lyndon B.
    Bust, **1966**: 345
    Candidacy for reelection (1968), **1967**: 104
        [13], 225 [19], 411 [9], 495 [8], 518
        [17], 554 [9]
    Foreword to "Why Vietnam" booklet, **1965**:
        388ftn. (p. 795)
    Grandson.
        See Nugent, Patrick Lyndon.
    "Handling of Toxicological Information"
        report, foreword, **1966**: 279
    Health, **1966**: 8 [7], 417 [1], 575, 577 [1, 4],
        580 [2, 18], 599 [5], 607 [9], 610 [7],
        622, 628 [17], 630 [13], 642 [17]
    Image, public, **1966**: 654 [10]
    Institute of Public Service, Austin, Tex., **1965**:
        411n.
    "My Hope for America," **1963–64**: 560 [8]
    Personal reminiscences.
        See Reminiscences, the President's.
    Political philosophy, **1966**: 395, 410, 415, 432,
        437, 483, 504, 545
    Presidential library, Austin, Tex., **1965**: 411,
        412
    Protester, role as, **1967**: 264 [17]
    Public opinion polls, **1967**: 225 [7], 297 [4,
        13]
    Public support, **1967**: 358 [4], 495 [2], 554
        [11]
    Reminiscences.
        See Reminiscences, the President's.
    Retirement question, **1967**: 328 [6]
    Surgery, **1966**: 575, 577 [1, 4], 580 [2, 17],
        599 [4], 610 [1, 7]

Johnson, Lyndon B. – *continued*
    "This America," prologue and epilogue, **1966**:
        497
    USIA biographical film, **1966**: 401 [8]
    Work habits, **1966**: 516 [14]
    World Food Panel report, foreword, **1967**: 271
Johnson, Mrs. Lyndon B., **1963–64**: 1n., 27, 72,
    73n., 75, 77, 91 (p. 118), 96, 101, 107,
    118, 121, 153, 161, 172, 187n., 204,
    238, 244, 247, 257, 259, 267, 270, 273,
    275, 287, 288n., 289, 290, 291, 292,
    295, 297, 310, 313, 318, 320, 326, 328,
    330, 334, 337n., 338, 343, 352, 358,
    363, 364n., 373, 375n., 376, 377n.,
    378n., 382, 385n., 392, 394, 397, 399n.,
    416n., 424, 431, 434, 441n., 471n.,
    478n., 479n., 501n., 502n., 526, 527,
    584, 626n., 671, 673, 692, 728, 736,
    767n., 768, 782, 794, 796, 810, 817,
    819; **1965**: 11, 48, 54n., 87, 91, 101,
    141, 142, 146, 154n., 156 [11], 162,
    170, 200n., 222, 236, 238, 243, 254n.,
    256n., 259, 260, 277, 280, 285, 289,
    296, 305, 306, 314n., 323, 330, 334,
    341, 357, 366, 372, 392, 394, 397, 399,
    403, 412, 418, 419, 445, 454 [2], 459,
    491, 554, 559, 561, 565, 595, 616, 627,
    648, 649, 655, 659n.; **1966**: 1, 61, 72,
    118, 134, 148–149, 155, 160, 164–165,
    175–176, 189, 191, 226, 232, 240, 258,
    263n., 271, 299–300, 304n., 311, 339,
    345–346, 349, 353, 359, 363, 365n.,
    367, 398–399, 409–410, 412–413, 416,
    418, 426–428, 432, 434, 443, 458n.,
    459–460, 465, 468, 482, 505, 522, 528,
    532n., 533n., 538, 540–541, 543–547,
    554, 559, 561, 565–566a, 568, 570,
    590, 626, 638, 644–645, 647, 653;
    1967: 2, 7n., 8, 17n., 19n., 21, 28, 52,
    63, 109, 111, 112, 124, 155, 158n.,
    162, 206, 210–213, 246, 248n., 249n.,
    264 [17], 267, 289, 290n., 293, 313n.,
    347, 349, 356n., 363–365, 389, 400,
    403n., 409n., 426n., 447, 449n., 451,
    453, 461n., 462, 480, 486, 487n., 493,
    529, 540, 550, 551, 559; **1968–69**: 8n.,
    32, 65n., 72, 78, 80, 99, 102n., 104,
    105, 109, 132, 137n., 140n., 147n.,
    148, 154, 157, 159n., 167, 171, 177n.,
    179, 193n., 210–212, 214n., 224, 225,
    227, 232n., 233, 242, 260, 262, 271,
    273, 283 [5], 289, 291, 294, 300, 304,
    357, 368–371, 374, 385, 386, 405, 411,
    459, 460 [1, 3], 479, 488, 508, 510,
    511, 522, 525, 529, 547, 552, 567, 568,
    570, 576, 582, 585, 588, 589, 595, 598,
    599, 601, 602, 604, 613, 614n., 616,
    618n., 619, 622, 623n., 624n., 631,

Johnson, Mrs. Lyndon B. – *continued*
  644, 646 [2, 13–15], 655, 660, 662,
  672, 681, 695, 696 [1, 17–19], 698
"A View From the White House," **1968–69**:
  648
Beautification program support, **1966**: 202,
  295, 500, 501 [18], 518
Campaign remarks on, **1963–64**: 544, 598,
  599, 603n., 605n., 606, 607, 628, 631,
  644, 646n., 648, 650, 657, 659, 670,
  693, 695, 701, 719, 728, 729, 732, 733,
  735, 736n., 741n., 742, 745n., 748n.,
  749n., 751, 760, 761, 763, 764, 765
News conference remarks on, **1963–64**: 54
  [16], 143 [3, 4], 211 [1], 256 [15],
  266 [7, 16], 336 [20, 21], 516 [1, 15],
  560 [10, 13], 563 [17], 587 [2, 9];
  1966: 141 [15], 417 [1, 8, 14], 516
  [1], 580 [17], 599 [2], 610 [1], 630
  [2], 635 [14]
Stockholdings, **1963–64**: 256 [15], 266 [16]
Johnson, Nicholas (Maritime Administrator),
  1963–64: 203; **1966**: 277 [5], 278
Johnson, Gov. Paul B., Jr., **1963–64**: 563 [12,
  14]; **1966**: 121 [1], 494 [1–2]
Johnson, Rebekah Baines, **1965**: 286n.; **1966**:
  156, 158 [7], 427, 435, 542; **1968–69**:
  19, 165, 595, 648
Johnson, Sam Ealy, Jr., **1965**: 183n., 285n.,
  1966: 273, 427, 435, 542; **1967**: 529,
  532, 539; **1968–69**: 97, 648
Johnson, Samuel, **1963–64**: 352; **1967**: 475
Johnson, Tom, **1967**: 2n.
Johnson, U. Alexis, **1963–64**: 26, 420 [1, 4],
  780 [6]; **1965**: 46 [11], 145; **1966**:
  401 [18], 474 [17]
Johnson, Wilfrid E., **1966**: 320 [5], 361
Johnson, Mrs. Wilfrid E., **1966**: 361
Johnson, William, **1965**: 554
Johnson, Wyatt T., Jr., **1965**: 334n.; **1968–69**:
  17, 51 [1], 110, 171, 180n., 213 [5],
  332, 570, 604, 641n., 645n., 646 [1],
  663, 668n.
Johnson Australian Science Scholars, Lyndon B.,
  1966: 545–546; **1967**: 1
Johnson City, Tex., **1963–64**: 71, 73, 76, 87,
  242n., 462n., 504n., 547n., 761, 766n.,
  767n., 768n., 779n., 780n., 818n.;
  1965: 21n., 22n., 113n., 117n., 181n.,
  192n., 194n., 341n., 395n., 459, 462n.,
  463n., 595n., 632n., 641n., 643n.,
  644n.; **1967**: 267, 411; **1968–69**: 96,
  110, 537, 691
High School, **1963–64**: 374
News conferences, **1966**: 320, 417, 578, 599,
  607, 628, 650, 654
Releases, **1966**: 590, 625, 653; **1968–69**: 4
Remarks, **1968–69**: 1, 283, 574

"Johnson Doctrine," **1965**: 295 [15]
Johnson Hill, Suwon, Korea, **1966**: 564
Johnson and Humphrey, National Independent
  Committee for, **1963–64**: 555
Johnson-Humphrey, Rural Americans for,
  1963–64: 570
Johnson Library, Lyndon B., **1968–69**: 260, 646
  [15], 655
Johnsson, Hans-Ingvar, **1965**: 378
Johnston, Sen. Olin D., **1963–64**: 718, 719;
  1965: 154, 413
Johnston, Wayne A., **1963–64**: 252
Johnstown, Pa., **1965**: 490
Joint Board for Settlement of Jurisdictional
  Disputes, National, **1965**: 41
Joint Chiefs of Staff, **1963–64**: 37, 54 [6, 16],
  266 [18], 467, 510, 612, 619 [3], 645,
  702, 809; **1965**: 26, 223, 295 [16],
  387, 448 [12]; **1966**: 39, 88 [24], 158
  [14], 312, 320 [1, 11], 324, 412, 445
  [1], 630 [5], 641, 642 [5, 10]; **1967**:
  104 [2], 116, 189, 195, 204 [1], 309
  [1], 329, 375 [1, 6, 19], 495 [1, 14],
  518 [7]; **1968–69**: 51 [1, 3, 6, 11], 79
  [8, 9], 153 [4–6], 170, 191 [4, 6],
  267, 572, 585, 603, 669, 688
Chairman (Gen. Maxwell D. Taylor), **1963–64**:
  37, 211 [33], 223, 379ftn. (p. 735),
  420 [1, 4, 13]
Chairman (Gen. Earle G. Wheeler), **1963–64**:
  420 [1], 504 [11], 533, 563 [1], 587
  [5], 780ftn. (p. 1616); **1965**: 212, 221,
  223, 387; **1966**: 52 [3], 124 [2, 12],
  183, 214, 246, 320 [7], 324, 516 [9],
  628 [1], 642 [4]; **1967**: 134, 204 [1],
  255, 278, 309, 324, 358 [6], 493, 518
  [4]; **1968–69**: 100, 101, 153 [4, 5, 9],
  185n., 299, 398n., 401, 487, 516, 669
Joint Commission on the Coinage, proposed,
  1965: 297
Joint Cooperation Committee, U.S. and Panama,
  1963–64: 104
Joint Dominican Republic-Puerto Rican Economic Commission, **1967**: 436
Joint funding simplification bill, **1967**: 121n.;
  1968–69: 39 (p. 110), 100
Joint Mexican-U.S. Trade Committee, **1966**: 177
Joint Ministerial Committee on Defense, U.S.-
  Canada, **1963–64**: 140
Joint Philippine-U.S. Veterans Commission,
  1966: 495, 505
Joint Salary Commission, **1967**: 163
Joint Savings Bank-Savings and Loan Committee
  on Urban Problems, **1968–69**: 114
Joint statements with foreign leaders
  Afghanistan, Prime Minister Maiwandwal,
  1967: 145

Joint statements with foreign leaders – *continued*
  Australia
    Prime Minister Gorton, **1968–69**: 277
    Prime Minister Holt, **1966**: 329
    Prime Minister McEwen, **1967**: 562
  Austria, Chancellor Josef Klaus, **1968–69**: 194
  Burma, Chairman Ne Win, **1966**: 450
  Canada, Prime Minister Pearson, **1963–64**: 135, 138, 140
  Central American Presidents, **1968–69**: 366
  China, Republic of, Vice President Yen, **1967**: 219
  Commission of the European Communities, President Rey, **1968–69**: 62
  Costa Rica, President Orlich, **1963–64**: 443
  Dominican Republic, President Balaguer, **1967**: 436
  European Economic Community, President of the Commission, Walter Hallstein, **1965**: 112
  Germany
    Chancellor Erhard, **1963–64**: 76, 400; **1965**: 300, 660; **1966**: 486
    Chancellor Kiesinger, **1967**: 351
  Greece, Prime Minister Papandreou, **1963–64**: 429
  Guam conference.
    See Guam.
  India, Prime Minister Gandhi, **1966**: 152
  Iran, Shah Pahlavi, **1967**: 366; **1968–69**: 307
  Israel, Prime Minister Eshkol, **1963–64**: 380; **1968–69**: 9
  Italy
    President Saragat, **1967**: 390
    President Segni, **1963–64**: 109
    Prime Minister Moro, **1965**: 203
  Japan, Prime Minister Sato, **1965**: 15; **1967**: 491
  Jordan, King Hussein I, **1963–64**: 265
  Korea
    President Park, **1965**: 257; **1966**: 566; **1967**: 563; **1968–69**: 201
    Prime Minister Chung, **1967**: 113
  Kuwait, Amir Shaikh Sabah, **1968–69**: 620
  Liberia, President Tubman, **1968–69**: 181
  Malagasy Republic, President Tsiranana, **1963–64**: 483
  Malaysia, Prime Minister Rahman, **1963–64**: 474
  Manila Conference.
    See main heading, Manila Conference.
  Mexico
    President López Mateos, **1963–64**: 193
    President Diaz Ordaz, **1966**: 177, 640; **1967**: 451
  Nepal, King Mahendra, **1967**: 462
  New Zealand, Prime Minister Holyoake, **1968–69**: 528

Joint statements with foreign leaders – *continued*
  Pakistan, President Ayub, **1965**: 650; **1967**: 569
  Philippines
    President Macapagal, **1963–64**: 627
    President Marcos, **1966**: 461
  Saudi Arabia, King Faisal, **1966**: 287
  Singapore, Prime Minister Lee, **1967**: 435
  Thailand
    King Bhumibol Adulyadej, **1967**: 293
    Prime Minister Thanom Kittikachorn, **1968–69**: 237
  Tunisia, President Bourguiba, **1968–69**: 255
  Turkey
    President Sunay, **1967**: 162
    Prime Minister Inonu, **1963–64**: 423
  United Kingdom
    Prime Minister Douglas-Home, **1963–64**: 186
    Prime Minister Wilson, **1963–64**: 797
  Upper Volta, President Yameogo, **1965**: 144
  Vietnam
    Chief of State Thieu and Prime Minister Ky, **1966**: 54
    President Thieu, **1967**: 564; **1968–69**: 400
Joint United States-Japan Committee on Trade and Economic Affairs, **1965**: 15, 355; **1967**: 381, 491
Joint United States-Japan Conference on Cultural and Educational Interchange, **1965**: 15
Jonas, Franz (President of Austria), **1966**: 605; **1968–69**: 193
Jones, Billy, **1968–69**: 429
Jones, Boisfeuillet, **1963–64**: 330; **1965**: 424n., 594n.; **1966**: 185n.; **1967**: 419; **1968–69**: 622
Jones, Casey, **1963–64**: 644
Jones, Judge Herman, **1965**: 341
Jones, Mr. and Mrs. Howard P., **1966**: 533
Jones, James, **1967**: 291
Jones, James R., **1966**: 415–416; **1968–69**: 17, 142, 191 [3], 598, 604
Jones, Jesse, **1965**: 113
Jones, Marvin, **1963–64**: 455 [7]
Jones, Repr. Robert E., **1965**: 452; **1966**: 393–394; **1967**: 408 [1, 5]
Jong, Choi Si, **1966**: 564n.
Jonsson, Erik, **1963–64**: 738
Jordan, Sen. B. Everett, **1963–64**: 326, 327, 328, 329, 631; **1965**: 330; **1966**: 362; **1968–69**: 417
Jordan, Sen. Len B., **1966**: 410, 411, 417 [5]
Jordan, Vernon E., Jr., **1966**: 315n.
Jordan, **1967**: 257
  Assistance, **1963–64**: 227; **1965**: 18; **1966**: 11n.

Jordan — *continued*
  Conflict with Israel.
    See Middle East conflict.
  King Hussein I, visit of, **1963–64**: 258, 259, 265
  U.S. relations with, **1963–64**: 258, 259, 265
Jorden, William J., **1968–69**: 425ftn. (p. 861)
Joseph, Mrs. Burton, **1963–64**: 433
Joseph H. Hirshhorn Foundation, **1966**: 227
Joseph H. Hirshhorn Museum and Sculpture Garden, **1966**: 226–227, 587; **1968–69**: 660
Joseph P. Kennedy, Jr., Foundation, **1963–64**: 403
International awards, **1963–64**: 174
Jossem, E. Leonard, **1967**: 396n.
Juárez, Benito, **1963–64**: 193, 596; **1966**: 175, 177; **1967**: 395, 449n., 451, 453; **1968–69**: 623, 624n.
Juárez, Mexico, **1967**: 453; **1968–69**: 623
Judge Advocate General's Corps, **1967**: 527
Judicial appointments.
  See Appointments and nominations.
Judicial branch, **1965**: 42
Judicial Center, Federal, **1967**: 35, 560; **1968–69**: 59
Judicial Salaries, Commission on Executive, Legislative, and, **1968–69**: 676 (p. 1266), 678 (p. 1305), 694
Judicial system, **1968–69**: 14 (p. 30), 39 (p. 107), 57, 59, 95, 133, 209, 320, 355, 542
Judiciary, House Committee on, **1968–69**: 302, 324, 334
Judiciary, pay increase, **1963–64**: 132 (p. 194)
Judiciary, Senate Committee on the, **1968–69**: 26, 316, 334, 339 [2], 425 [11], 467 [2]
Judiciary Act of 1789, **1966**: 286
Judiciary Committee, House, **1967**: 276
Juliana, Queen (Netherlands), **1966**: 118
"Julius Caesar," William Shakespeare, **1967**: 248n.
June buying, **1966**: 224
"Jungle, The," Upton Sinclair, **1967**: 541
Jupiter Crocket, **1968–69**: 41
Jupiter probe, **1965**: 659
Jurisdictional Disputes, National Joint Board for Settlement of, **1965**: 41
Jury selection, nondiscrimination, **1966**: 6 (p. 3), 196; **1967**: 55; **1968–69**: 14 (p. 31), 26, 82, 158, 611
Jury Selection and Service Act of 1968, **1968–69**: 26, 158
Justice, Department of, **1963–64**: 7, 28 [12], 218 [16], 285 [11, 16], 315, 452n., 516 [12], 752, 780 [13]; **1965**: 102, 104, 106 [1], 117 [1], 127, 309, 319

Justice, Department of — *continued*
  [10], 366, 409, 486, 508, 530n., 546; **1966**: 51ftn. (p. 141), 59, 60n., 88 [5], 116, 204–205, 303, 577 [11]; **1967**: 13 (p. 57), 35, 55, 65, 71, 105, 264 [7], 269, 328 [19], 335, 411 [1], 443, 530; **1968–69**: 57, 59, 79 [6], 209, 236n., 425 [11], 514, 678 (pp. 1289, 1301)
  Appropriations, **1967**: 417 [1], 482; **1968–69**: 678 (p. 1281)
  Civil rights cases, **1968–69**: 26
  Civil rights enforcement, **1966**: 6 (p. 5), 196
  Consumer counsel, proposed, **1968–69**: 14 (p. 30), 56, 336
  Corrections service, proposed, **1968–69**: 59
  Narcotics and Dangerous Drugs, Bureau of, **1968–69**: 59, 60, 217, 561, 678 (p. 1292)
Justice, equal, message to Congress, **1967**: 55–56
Justice, President's Commission on Law Enforcement and Administration of, **1965**: 102, 381, 382, 422, 437, 500, 526; **1966**: 116, 491, 492 [1], 494 [1], 526, 611, 630 [9]; **1967**: 3 (p. 6), 13 (p. 56), 35, 39, 60, 146, 221, 276, 382, 385; **1968–69**: 59, 235, 257, 301, 320, 553, 678 (p. 1291)
Juvenile delinquency, **1963–64**: 133, 213, 266 [21], 280 [5], 590, 630, 658, 680; **1965**: 2, 90, 102, 183, 361, 382, 422; **1966**: 30, 117, 219, 317, 399, 491, 494 [1]; **1967**: 3 (p. 7), 15, 27, 35, 39, 71, 276, 353, 560; **1968–69**: 39 (p. 107), 57, 59, 329, 424, 553, 557 [8], 678 (p. 1291)
  District of Columbia, **1963–64**: 537, 704; **1965**: 29, 70, 151, 381
  Harlem, **1963–64**: 334
  Juvenile delinquency bill, **1965**: 329, 330
  Prevention bill, **1967**: 39, 276
  Senate Subcommittee on, **1968–69**: 316, 334
Juvenile Delinquency Prevention and Control Act of 1968, **1968–69**: 14 (p. 31), 59, 390, 424, 542, 553, 678 (p. 1291)
Juvenile Delinquency and Youth Crime, President's Committee on, **1963–64**: 133, 334, 537, 704n.; **1965**: 282, 381
Juvenile Delinquency and Youth Offenses Control Act of 1961, **1965**: 102, 282; **1967**: 39

Kachlein, George, **1963–64**: 317n.
Kaiser, Edgar F., **1966**: 184n., 217, 373 [8]; **1967**: 252, 355n., 358 [8], 412; **1968–69**: 50, 87, 241, 435, 470, 471, 506, 704

Kaiser, Henry J., death, **1967**: 368
Kaltenborn, H. V., **1966**: 516 [6]
Kampelman, Max, **1967**: 406
Kanawha River Basin, W. Va., **1966**: 427
Kane, R. Keith, **1965**: 522n.
Kansas, **1963–64**: 486 [7]; **1967**: 485 [6]
  Campaign remarks, **1963–64**: 741
  Candidates for public office, **1963–64**: 741
  Gov. William Avery, **1966**: 407n., 494 [1]
  Gov. Robert B. Docking, **1967**: 485 [6]; **1968–69**: 452
Kansas City, Mo., **1967**: 382
  Mayor Ilus W. Davis, **1967**: 382
Kaplan Fund, J. M., Inc., **1968–69**: 686
Kappel, Frederick R., **1963–64**: 23, 568; **1965**: 643; **1967**: 163, 168, 312 [1, 3]; **1968–69**: 391, 676 (p. 1266), 694
Kappel, Mr. and Mrs. William J., **1965**: 231
Kapranopoulos, 1st Lt. John, **1966**: 397
Karachi, Pakistan, release, **1967**: 569
Karelsen, Frank E., **1966**: 210n.
Karkheck, Jim, **1965**: 55
Karlen, Russel V., **1965**: 405
Karlsefni, Thorfinnur, **1967**: 313n.
Karsten, Repr. Frank M., **1963–64**: 188, 694, 695
Karth, Repr. Joseph E., **1963–64**: 433, 434; **1965**: 189
Kashmir dispute, **1963–64**: 607; **1965**: 169, 208 [10], 463 [5], 524, 529
  India-Pakistan, **1967**: 100
Katmai National Monument, Alaska, **1968–69**: 707n.
Katz, A. Martin, **1963–64**: 639
Katzenbach, Nicholas deB., **1966**: 474 [17], 477 [5], 491, 492 [1], 516 [11], 520, 526, 635 [2], 645; **1967**: 68, 94n., 104 [6], 113, 146, 147, 272, 290, 309 [1], 403, 426n., 444, 461; **1968–69**: 15, 190, 223 [12], 273, 508, 590 [1], 691
  See also Attorney General; Attorney General, acting.
  Swearing in as Under Secretary of State, **1966**: 498
  Vietnam visit, press briefing, **1966**: 521
Katzenbach, Mrs. Nicholas deB., **1965**: 66; **1966**: 498; **1968–69**: 273, 691
Kaunda, Kenneth D., **1963–64**: 721; **1966**: 243
Kazan, Repr. Abraham, Jr., **1967**: 408 [1], 409; **1968–69**: 7, 281
Kazan-Komarek, Vladimir, **1967**: 34ftn. (p. 133)
Keating, Sen. Kenneth B., **1963–64**: 97, 201 [14], 793
Kee, Repr. James, **1966**: 427
Keenan, Joseph D., **1965**: 223; **1966**: 431, 435, 437; **1967**: 30, 252n.
Keener, J. Ward, **1966**: 184n.
Keeney, Barnaby, **1963–64**: 587 [2], 601; **1966**: 327

Keeney, Mrs. Barnaby, **1966**: 327
Keeney, Elizabeth, **1966**: 327
Keeton, Page, **1966**: 184n.
Kefauver, Estes, **1963–64**: 702
Keith, Alexander M., **1965**: 189
Kekkonen, Urho, **1963–64**: 564
Kekumano, Msgr. Charles, **1966**: 533
Kellam, Jesse, **1963–64**: 778; **1965**: 603; **1967**: 87n.
Keller, Charles, Jr., **1967**: 252n.
Keller, Francis, **1963–64**: 703
Keller, Helen, **1963–64**: 568
  Death, **1968–69**: 285
Keller, Sgt. Leonard B., **1968–69**: 487
Kelley, Clarence M., **1967**: 382
Kelley, Ralph H., **1963–64**: 702
Kellogg, John, **1966**: 433
Kelly, Repr. Edna F., **1963–64**: 668; **1966**: 510; **1967**: 251, 503
Kemble, Fanny, **1968–69**: 648
Kennan, George F., **1966**: 65 [6, 7]
Kennedy, Caroline, **1963–64**: 12; **1967**: 241
Kennedy, David M., **1967**: 85; **1968–69**: 646 [3], 677n.
Kennedy, Sen. Edward M., **1963–64**: 142, 174n., 727; **1965**: 368, 369, 546, 551; **1967**: 241; **1968–69**: 599, 655
Kennedy, Mrs. Edward M., **1963–64**: 174, 727
Kennedy, John F., **1963–64**: 9, 12, 20, 26, 29, 37, 41, 42, 45, 65, 66, 72, 73, 76, 79n., 91 (pp. 113, 116, 117), 100, 101n., 102n., 108, 109, 112, 116, 117, 122, 126, 127, 132 (p. 178), 133, 135, 146, 152, 154, 161n., 173, 175, 179, 190, 193, 199, 205, 213, 218 [1, 2, 3, 8, 9, 11, 19, 20, 24, 29, 34], 220, 224, 228, 233, 250, 287, 296, 303, 340, 354, 363, 364, 373, 387, 391, 396, 397, 403, 411, 413, 424, 428n., 431, 433, 438, 447n., 448, 456n., 457n., 481n., 499, 502, 523, 526, 529, 577, 602, 625, 638, 641, 698, 705, 715, 740, 759, 775, 778, 784, 799; **1965**: 20, 25, 26, 29, 34, 44, 72, 93, 102, 134, 142n., 159, 160, 179, 183, 200n., 213, 221, 223, 254n., 299, 302, 318, 330, 339, 348, 355, 357, 370, 393, 394, 397, 399, 413, 429, 430, 433, 436, 439, 443, 445, 468, 538, 546, 549, 550, 557, 621, 649n.; **1966**: 6 (p. 8), 62, 86, 93, 125, 134, 140, 151, 175, 182, 185, 199, 228, 235, 246, 268, 365, 386, 392, 394, 399, 426, 428, 455, 483, 498, 504, 512, 515, 520; **1967**: 3 (p. 9), 12, 38, 44, 80 [4], 83, 99, 110, 121, 144, 150, 163, 207, 216, 233, 236, 241, 242, 248n., 251, 270, 281, 346, 357, 361, 384, 409, 421, 442, 443, 444n., 454n., 460 [14], 495 [14], 501, 514, 517, 554

Kennedy, John F. – *continued*
    [4]; **1968-69**: 18 [2], 27, 53, 75, 87,
    96, 99, 103, 104, 109, 111, 114, 148n.,
    164, 170, 207, 223 [6], 227, 282, 291,
    293, 296, 298, 301n., 378, 454, 472,
    479, 487, 493, 529, 540, 541, 567-569,
    574, 576, 598, 603, 623, 631, 646 [12],
    662, 665, 668, 669, 676 (p. 1270)
  Assassination, **1963-64**: 1, 8, 11, 21n., 51, 174,
    201 [9]
    First anniversary, **1963-64**: 773
    Investigations, **1963-64**: 7, 14, 28ftn (p. 38)
    Second anniversary, **1965**: 623
  Birthday tribute to, **1963-64**: 370
  Bust of, unveiling, **1963-64**: 773
  Campaign remarks on, **1963-64**: 541, 562, 599,
    605, 606, 607, 612, 622, 635, 637, 639,
    640, 642, 643, 644, 645, 646, 648, 650,
    651, 652, 656, 657, 658, 659, 662, 666,
    667, 669, 679, 680, 693, 694, 695, 702,
    703, 712, 713, 727, 728, 729, 732, 733,
    734, 736, 741, 742, 745, 746, 747, 748,
    749, 750, 751, 761, 762, 763
  Candlelight memorial service for, **1963-64**: 64
  Commission to report on assassination of.
    See Commission to Report Upon the Assassi-
    nation of President John F. Kennedy.
  50-cent pieces, **1965**: 297
    Message to Congress, **1963-64**: 33
  Funeral plans for, **1963-64**: 2, 5
  Medal of Freedom, posthumous award, **1963-
    64**: 27
  Message to Armed Forces on death of, **1963-
    64**: 6
  National Cultural Center, renaming as John F.
    Kennedy Center for the Performing
    Arts, **1963-64**: 39
  National day of mourning for
    Closing of Government agencies, **1963-64**: 4
    Proclamation, **1963-64**: 3
  News conference remarks on, **1963-64**: 54 [6],
    201 [9], 285 [13], 462 [2]; **1965**: 46
    [10], 106 [4, 9], 176 [3], 208 [2],
    295 [15], 353 [4, 8, 23], 388 [1], 412
    [4], 448 [14], 463 [2, 8, 9]; **1966**: 158
    [3], 334 [12], 401 [4], 417 [6], 577
    [11], 580 [5], 610 [1]
  Painting presented to White House in memory
    of, **1963-64**: 24
  Portrait on savings bonds, **1963-64**: 306
  Rededication, proclamation, **1963-64**: 774
  Thanksgiving Day Proclamation, statement on,
    1963-64: 10
Kennedy, Mrs. John F., **1963-64**: 1, 12, 24, 27,
    58, 137, 142, 161n., 172, 211 [7, 35],
    218 [1, 6], 267, 280, 285 [23], 309,
    773, 784; **1965**: 48; **1967**: 241
Kennedy, John F., Jr., **1963-64**: 12; **1967**: 241

Kennedy, Brig. Gen. John T., **1966**: 288
Kennedy, Joseph P., Jr., **1963-64**: 728
Kennedy, Mrs. Joseph P., Sr., **1963-64**: 174n.;
    1967: 241, 373, 517
Kennedy, Robert F., **1963-64**: 174n., 784, 793;
    1965: 66n., 183, 421, 546; **1966**: 86,
    392, 394-395, 510-512; **1967**: 104 [2],
    241, 251, 554 [9]; **1968-69**: 141,
    148n., 153 [14], 171, 298, 307
  See also Attorney General (Robert F.
    Kennedy).
  Campaign remarks on, **1963-64**: 666, 667, 668,
    669, 670, 751
  Death, **1968-69**: 294
  News conference remarks on, **1963-64**: 379
    [14, 18], 455 [10], 516 [8]; **1966**:
    188 [8], 320 [14], 401 [1, 10], 417
    [6], 474 [21], 577 [11]
  Proclamation, **1968-69**: 295
  Shooting, **1968-69**: 292, 293
Kennedy, Mrs. Robert F., **1963-64**: 174n., 452,
    523, 666, 667, 668, 670; **1968-69**: 294
Kennedy, Seth, **1965**: 230n.
Kennedy, Commission to Report Upon the
    Assassination of President John F.,
    1963-64: 14, 232 [5], 280 [10], 281,
    462 [8], 780 [11]; **1966**: 577 [11];
    1967: 80 [5]
  Appointment of executive order, **1963-64**:
    15
  Report, **1963-64**: 595, 619 [11, 17]
Kennedy, John F., Center for the Performing
    Arts, **1963-64**: 142, 784; **1966**: 227
Kennedy, John F., Educational, Civic and
    Cultural Center, Mitchel Field, N.Y.,
    dedication, **1963-64**: 337
Kennedy, John F., Memorial Library, Boston,
    Mass., **1963-64**: 773; **1965**: 412 [1]
Kennedy, John F., Space Center (NASA), **1963-
    64**: 12; **1966**: 485
  Designation of name, Executive order, **1963-
    64**: 13
Kennedy, John F., Square, Texarkana, dedication,
    1963-64: 599
Kennedy, John F., U.S.S., **1967**: 241
Kennedy, John Fitzgerald, National Historic Site,
    1967: 242
Kennedy, Joseph P., Jr., Foundation, **1963-64**:
    403
  International awards, **1963-64**: 174
Kennedy Round, GATT trade negotiations,
    1963-64: 109, 140, 186, 246 [19], 256
    [21], 272, 336 [12], 394n., 400, 592,
    739, 757, 787, 788; **1965**: 35 (p. 111),
    47, 60, 76, 112, 564, 660; **1966**: 34 (p.
    104), 471, 486, 503; **1967**: 16 (p. 79),
    33, 142, 169n., 175, 223 [3], 224, 225
    [17], 231, 250, 272, 371, 390, 442,

Kennedy Round, GATT – *continued*
445, 476, 491, 492, 495 [5], 508, 519, 554 [5]
See also General Agreement on Tariffs and Trade.
Proclamation, **1967**: 545
Kenney, Thomas S., **1963–64**: 712
Kenny, John, **1963–64**: 338
Kent, Sherman, **1967**: 317n.
Kentucky, **1966**: 351–352; **1968–69**: 341, 564
Antipoverty program, **1963–64**: 292, 334
Campaign remarks, **1963–64**: 643, 644
Candidates for public office, **1963–64**: 643, 644
Coal industry, **1963–64**: 297
Eastern, emergency program for, **1963–64**: 41
Eastern, Neighborhood Youth Corps in, **1965**: 195
Gov. Edward T. Breathitt, Jr., **1963–64**: 41, 217, 291, 292, 643, 644, 678, 729; **1965**: 80; **1966**: 122 [1], 228, 348
Remarks, **1968–69**: 499, 565
Unemployment, **1963–64**: 213, 297
Kenya, **1968–69**: 140n.
Independence, **1963–64**: 34
U.S. relations with, **1963–64**: 34
Kenyatta, Jomo, **1963–64**: 34
Keogh, Repr. Eugene J., **1963–64**: 668; **1966**: 510
Keppel, Francis (Commissioner of Education), **1963–64**: 78, 84, 397n., 414, 513, 622; **1965**: 70, 89, 181, 183, 264n., 305, 340, 467, 485, 527, 539, 578; **1966**: 106n.
Kern, Frank, **1963–64**: 736
Kerner, Gov. Otto, **1963–64**: 217, 287, 635, 636, 637, 694, 747, 748; **1965**: 299; **1966**: 228, 349; **1967**: 187, 326, 327, 328 [1]; **1968–69**: 210
Kerner, Mrs. Otto, **1963–64**: 287
Kerr, Clark, **1963–64**: 192n., 201 [1], 414, 587 [1]
Kerr, Mrs. Clark, **1963–64**: 750
Kerr, Robert S., **1963–64**: 598; **1966**: 415–416
Kerr-Mills legislation.
See Social Security Act of 1935, amendments.
"Land, Wood and Water," **1963–64**: 597
Kervick, John A., **1966**: 504
Kessler, Dr. Henry H., **1968–69**: 346n.
Kessler, Capt. Melvin J., release from East Germany, **1963–64**: 242 [18, 26]
Key, Francis Scott, "The Star-Spangled Banner," **1965**: 95
Key West, Fla., **1967**: 284
Keyserling, Mrs. Mary, **1963–64**: 208, 257n.
Khanh, Maj. Gen. Nguyen, **1963–64**: 218 [24], 223, 348

Khanh, Maj. Gen. Nguyen – *continued*
Message to, **1963–64**: 170 [5]
News conference remarks on, **1963–64**: 170 [1, 5], 256 [2], 420 [4], 475 [3]
Khe Sanh, Vietnam, **1968–69**: 185n., 186, 189, 267
Kheel, Theodore W., **1963–64**: 253, 256 [1], 271 [17], 284, 297 [2]; **1967**: 312 [1, 3]
Khoman, Thanat, **1967**: 290
Khorat, Thailand, **1967**: 565, 573
Khosrovani, Khosro, **1965**: 517n.
Khrushchev, Nikita S., **1963–64**: 26, 129, 130, 131, 182, 210, 272, 686, 775; **1966**: 411, 417 [12], 516 [8]; **1967**: 80 [2], 83, 554 [4]
Campaign remarks on, **1963–64**: 642, 643, 645, 646, 650, 652, 656, 657, 659, 667, 678, 680, 702, 703, 727, 733, 734, 735, 741, 745, 746, 747, 749, 750, 762
Meeting with, question of, **1963–64**: 54 [1], 211 [23], 218 [7]
Messages to, **1963–64**: 82, 122, 200
News conference remarks on, **1963–64**: 54 [1], 150 [10], 211 [23], 246 [11], 256 [10], 285 [3, 22], 294 [19], 316 [17], 379 [15], 504 [12], 688 [1]
Replacement of, **1963–64**: 669
Kieff, Elaine Marie, **1963–64**: 315
Kienzle, George J., **1963–64**: 339
Kiesinger, Kurt Georg (Chancellor of West Germany), **1967**: 181, 204 [2, 4], 264 [18], 371, 373, 554 [5]; **1968–69**: 313
Exchange of remarks, **1967**: 191
Visit, **1967**: 312 [2], 347–349, 351
Kiesinger, Mrs. Kurt Georg, **1967**: 191, 347–349
Kiewit, Peter, **1967**: 252n.
Kiker, Douglas, **1963–64**: 347
Kilduff, Malcolm M., **1963–64**: 560 [1], 780 [6]
Killeen, Tex., **1967**: 532
Killian, James R., **1968–69**: 18 [2]
Killian, James R., Jr., **1963–64**: 116n., 271 [5], 456; **1967**: 473
Kilpatrick, Carroll, **1966**: 154; **1967**: 460 [11]; **1968–69**: 242, 460 [3]
Kim, Eva Soonhe, **1967**: 352n.
Kim, Mr. and Mrs. Hyon-ok, **1966**: 561
Kim, Hyun Chul, **1965**: 256; **1967**: 113
Kim, Mrs. Hyun Chul, **1965**: 256
Kim, Se Won, **1968–69**: 200
Kim, Sung Eun, **1965**: 257; **1966**: 566; **1967**: 113; **1968–69**: 79 [13]
Kimberly, John R., **1967**: 231
Kimpo International Airport, Seoul, Korea, **1966**: 566a
Kincaid, Capt. James W., **1967**: 485 [8]
Kindergartens, **1968–69**: 113
Kindleberger, Charles, **1965**: 365n.

King, Repr. Cecil R., **1963–64**: 105, 733; **1965**: 122, 133, 394; **1966**: 271
Medical care bill.
  See King-Anderson medical care bill.
King, David S., **1963–64**: 737
King, Gov. John W., **1963–64**: 607; **1966**: 396–399; **1967**: 222n., 223 [3, 5, 8]
King, Rev. Martin Luther, Jr., **1963–64**: 780 [11]; **1965**: 126, 156 [4], 412 [3], 436; **1966**: 277ftn. (p. 631); **1967**: 204 [7]; **1968–69**: 51 [4], 169 [16], 195n., 214n., 293, 298, 648
  Assassination, **1968–69**: 179, 180
  Day of mourning for, **1968–69**: 180
King, Mrs. Martin Luther, Jr., **1968–69**: 179
King, W. L. MacKenzie, **1963–64**: 136, 574; **1965**: 432n.
King-Anderson medical care bill, **1963–64**: 516 [9]
  See also Social security.
King Crab fishery, Japan, **1963–64**: 353
Kinnard, Lt. Gen. Harry W. O., **1967**: 384
Kintner, Robert E., **1966**: 158 [1, 6, 10], 607 [1]
Kintner, Mrs. Robert E., **1965**: 273; **1966**: 158 [1]
Kinzel, Dr. Augustus B., **1966**: 194n.
Kiphuth, Robert J., **1963–64**: 27
Kipling, Rudyard, **1966**: 133, 398; **1968–69**: 65n.
Kirk, Norman, **1966**: 540
Kirkland, Lane, **1968–69**: 154
Kirkpatrick, Evron, **1966**: 404n.; **1967**: 184
Kirkpatrick, Lyman B., Jr., **1963–64**: 417
Kirwan, Repr. Michael J., **1963–64**: 198, 199, 228, 597; **1965**: 329, 330; **1967**: 216
Kistiakowsky, George B., **1963–64**: 563 [5], 591, 688 [3, 8]; **1968–69**: 71n.
Kittikachorn, Thanom (Prime Minister of Thailand), **1966**: 549, 554, 557n.
  See also under Thailand.
Kitty Hawk, N.C., **1967**: 431
Kitty Hawk, U.S.S., **1968–69**: 635
Kivett, Jerry D., **1968–69**: 604
Klaus, Josef (Chancellor of Austria), **1965**: 87; **1968–69**: 190, 193, 194
Klaus, Mrs. Josef, **1968–69**: 190, 193
Kleberg, Richard M., **1963–64**: 612n., 761n.
Kleberg, Richard M., Sr., **1968–69**: 595n., 696 [18]
Kleberg, Robert J., Jr., **1963–64**: 612
Kleeb, John M., **1967**: 420n.
Klein, Herbert G., **1968–69**: 646 [3]
Klieman, Paul, **1968–69**: 163
Klinck, Jeannine, **1965**: 171n.
Klinck, Richard E., **1965**: 171
Klinck, Mrs. Richard E., **1965**: 171n.
Kline, Hugo, **1965**: 183
Kluczynski, Repr. John C., **1965**: 299; **1966**: 228

Kluttz, Jerry, **1963–64**: 514
Klutznick, Philip M., **1963–64**: 161n.
Knap, Ted, **1966**: 338 [13]
Knappstein, Karl Heinrich, **1965**: 57; **1967**: 349
Knappstein, Mrs. Karl Heinrich, **1967**: 349
Knight, Douglas M., **1966**: 424
Knight, John S., **1965**: 298
Knight, Maj. William J., **1968–69**: 610
Knipling, Edward Fred, **1966**: 652n.; **1967**: 37n.
Knott, Lawson B., Jr. (Administrator of General Services), **1966**: 58n., 202, 206, 218, 390, 464, 635 [20]; **1967**: 16 (p. 87), 121, 232, 372, 412, 504
  See also General Services Administrator.
Knous, Robert L., **1966**: 413–414
Knowland, William F., **1963–64**: 733, 747
Knowles, Gov. Warren P., **1965**: 189
Knowlton, Winthrop, **1966**: 277 [5]
Know-Nothings, **1967**: 538
Knox, Frank, **1963–64**: 747
Knox, Repr. Victor A., **1963–64**: 356
Knoxville, Tenn., **1963–64**: 324, 325
  Mayor John J. Duncan, **1963–64**: 324
Knuth-Winterfeldt, Count and Countess Kield Gustav, **1963–64**: 394
Knutsen, Fred A., **1967**: 156
Kobach, Col. Ethel R., **1967**: 475
Kodiak, Alaska, **1963–64**: 242 [1]; **1967**: 369
Kohler, Foy D., **1963–64**: 365; **1965**: 319 [5]; **1966**: 474 [17]
Komarov, Col. Vladimir, **1968–69**: 387
  Death, **1967**: 190
Komer, Robert W., **1965**: 319 [21], 641 [2]; **1966**: 141 [8, 10, 16], 154, 158 [6], 214, 273, 277 [7, 21], 320 [1], 521, 578 [11], 580 [3]; **1967**: 104 [14], 116, 126, 131, 132 [5], 134, 225 [2], 309 [1], 503, 526, 567
  Press briefing on Vietnam, **1967**: 73
Kontum, South Vietnam, **1967**: 309 [3]
Koontz, Elizabeth D., **1966**: 210n.
Kootenai River, **1963–64**: 135
Korea, **1963–64**: 35, 272, 607; **1966**: 542, 564, 566
  See also Korea, North; Korea, South.
  Aid for Vietnam, **1965**: 257, 423
  Ambassador Hyun Chul Kim, **1965**: 256
  Assistance, **1963–64**: 150 [6], 227; **1965**: 18, 254, 257; **1966**: 11n., 41
  Communist aggression, **1966**: 6 (p. 7), 562, 565, 568
  Economic growth, **1965**: 254, 256, 257, 407
  Economic and social development, **1966**: 561–566a
  Japanese relations, **1965**: 256n., 257, 427, 657; **1966**: 566
  Moon, Duk Choo, **1965**: 257
  Mutual Defense Treaty, **1965**: 257; **1966**: 566

Korea — *continued*
President Chung Hee Park, **1965**: 254, 256,
257, 344n., 407, 423; **1966**: 492 [4],
514, 516 [1], 549, 561–562, 565–566a
Prime Minister Il Kwon Chung, **1966**: 561–564,
566
Unification, **1965**: 257
U.S. Ambassador Winthrop G. Brown, **1966**:
566
U.S. forces, **1965**: 257; **1966**: 563, 570, 577
[8]
U.S. relations with, **1965**: 254, 256, 257
U.S. scientific mission to, **1965**: 257, 344, 407
Vietnam assistance, **1966**: 53, 311, 516 [13],
520, 540, 561–562, 566
Visit, **1966**: 561–566a
Korea, North, **1967**: 113, 563
See also Korea.
Address to the Nation, **1968–69**: 35
Attack on U.S. patrol, **1966**: 577 [8]
Pueblo, U.S.S., seizure, **1968–69**: 35, 48, 51
[4, 7, 8, 15], 65n., 79 [13], 169 [7],
201, 223 [12], 467 [6], 557 [5]
Crew release, **1968–69**: 641, 643
U.S. relations, **1968–69**: 35, 51 [16]
Korea, South, **1967**: 272, 401
See also Korea.
Armed Forces, **1968–69**: 201, 323, 413
Assistance, **1967**: 44, 113, 563
Communist aggression, **1967**: 111; **1968–69**:
35, 63, 109, 142, 154, 165, 201, 472
Economic and social development, **1967**: 44,
111–113; **1968–69**: 63, 417
Japanese relations, **1967**: 112n.
Mutual defense treaty, **1967**: 113
President Chung Hee Park, **1967**: 111n., 112n.,
113, 409, 563; **1968–69**: 35, 51 [15],
79 [13], 197, 198, 200, 201, 223 [7],
224
Prime Minister Il Kwon Chung, **1967**: 111–113;
1968–69: 79 [13]
U.S. Ambassador Winthrop G. Brown, **1967**:
223 [8, 12]
U.S. Ambassador William J. Porter, **1967**: 317
U.S. assistance, **1968–69**: 63, 176, 201, 524,
679
U.S. forces, **1968–69**: 51 [15], 170
U.S. relations, **1968–69**: 51 [15], 79 [13],
200, 201
Vietnam assistance, **1967**: 83, 112n., 113, 195,
246; **1968–69**: 35, 149, 201, 273, 283
[4], 323, 413, 525
Korean conflict (1950–1953), **1963–64**: 703;
1965: 127, 254, 542; **1966**: 6 (p. 8),
311, 324, 345, 540, 561, 563–565;
1967: 13 (p. 40), 16 (p. 78), 100, 358
[10], 361, 397, 409, 430, 495 [2, 9];
1968–69: 50, 142, 165, 172, 200, 232,
452, 541, 572, 583

Korean Institute for Industrial Technology and
Applied Science, **1965**: 257, 344, 407
Korean National Assembly, address, **1966**: 565
Kornberg, Arthur, **1967**: 540, 544n.
Kornegay, Repr. Horace R., **1963–64**: 327, 328
Koror Island, **1967**: 133n.
Korry, Edward M., **1966**: 243
Korth, Fred (former Secretary of the Navy),
1963–64: 612
Kosciusko, Thaddeus, **1966**: 528
Kossuth, Louis, **1967**: 397
Kosygin, Aleksei N. (Premier of the Soviet
Union), **1963–64**: 737, 820; **1965**: 46
[4, 7], 412 [2]; **1966**: 8 [2], 516 [17],
577 [6]; **1967**: 80 [27], 104 [8], 157,
246 [16], 281, 286, 312 [13], 346,
554 [2]; **1968–69**: 14 (p. 26), 51 [13],
169 [13], 288, 339 [14], 349, 425ftn.
(p. 862)
Meeting with Vice President Humphrey, **1966**:
8ftn. (p. 15)
Visit, **1967**: 279, 280, 282, 283
Kowal, Chester, **1963–64**: 667
Krag, Jens Otto (Prime Minister of Denmark),
1963–64: 266 [7], 394; **1966**: 195;
1967: 278
Krag, Mme. Jens Otto, **1963–64**: 266 [7], 394
Krash, Abe, **1965**: 366
Krebs, Paul J., **1963–64**: 338; **1966**: 504
Krim, Arthur B., **1963–64**: 373; **1966**: 228, 403;
1967: 281, 421; **1968–69**: 213 [6],
672n.
Krim, Mrs. Arthur B., **1968–69**: 672n.
Kristula, Michael A., **1963–64**: 60
Krol, Archbishop John J., **1966**: 200, 528
Kroll, Cedric W., **1968–69**: 280
Kross, Judge Anna M., **1963–64**: 208
KTBC–TV, Austin, Tex., **1963–64**: 256 [15],
266 [16]
Ku Klux Klan, **1963–64**: 462 [6], 656; **1965**:
22 [15], 135, 436; **1968–69**: 78, 298
Kuala Lumpur, Malaysia, **1966**: 559–560
Conference, **1968–69**: 277
Kuchel, Sen. Thomas H., **1963–64**: 192, 444,
563 [16], 733; **1965**: 405, 417; **1967**:
227, 303; **1968–69**: 386, 510
Kunkel, Repr. John C., **1966**: 428
Kupferman, Repr. Theodore R., **1966**: 394–395
Kutchuk, Fazil, message to, **1963–64**: 70
Kuwait
Amir Shaikh Sabah al-Salim al-Sabah, **1968–69**:
618, 619
Shaikh Abdullah al-Salim al-Sabah, **1965**: 629
Shaikh Sabah al-Salim al-Sabah, **1965**: 629
U.S. relations, **1968–69**: 618–620
Kuykendall, Repr. Dan, **1968–69**: 661
Kuykendall, Jerome K., **1967**: 518 [3]
Ky, Premier.
See Nguyen Cao Ky.

Kyle, Maj. Gen. Wood, **1967**: 485 [3] ; **1968-69**: 81 [2]
Kynes, James, **1963-64**: 709, 712, 713

La Bahia Mission, Texas, **1968-69**: 648
Labeling and packaging, **1963-64**: 173; **1966**: 6 (p. 6), 34 (p. 108), 140, 576; **1967**: 57, 86, 200, 393, 465, 534; **1968-69**: 56, 545
Labor, **1963-64**: 124 (pp. 157, 158, 160-162), 132 (p. 191), 213, 233, 248, 388, 406, 415, 448; **1965**: 23, 35 (p. 111), 100, 207, 223, 338, 384, 391, 438, 511, 644; **1966**: 34 (p. 100), 111, 235, 429, 431, 444; **1967**: 13 (p. 57), 121, 354; **1968-69**: 87, 154
African-American labor center, **1965**: 450
Antipoverty program responsibilities, **1963-64**: 297, 336 [20]
Arbitration record, **1963-64**: 334
Child, **1967**: 39
Civil rights responsibilities, **1963-64**: 139, 221, 314, 342, 350
Cooperation with Government, business, etc.
   See Government cooperation with business, education, and labor.
Displaced persons, **1963-64**: 99, 126, 213, 233
Economic responsibilities, **1963-64**: 294 [23], 311; **1966**: 34 (pp. 102, 109), 347, 399, 431, 453
Imports, effect on, **1968-69**: 47 (p. 137)
Leaders, meetings with, **1966**: 158 [3]
Legislation, **1966**: 26 (pp. 62-63), 34 (pp. 103, 106)
Manpower.
   See Manpower resources.
Message to Congress, **1965**: 258
Movement, **1968-69**: 50, 270, 463
News conference remarks, **1963-64**: 271 [15], 294 [23], 379 [13], 462 [1]
Political independence, **1966**: 141 [9]
Productivity, **1968-69**: 684 (p. 1316)
Representatives in Peace Corps, **1963-64**: 745
Shortages, **1966**: 34 (pp. 96, 103), 155, 201, 445 [5]; **1967**: 345
State laws, **1966**: 6 (p. 5)
Tax increases, reaction, **1967**: 330 [7]
Urban programs role, **1968-69**: 114
Workweek, **1967**: 270
Labor, American Federation of, **1963-64**: 430n.
Labor, Department of, **1963-64**: 132 (p. 181), 160n., 213, 218 [16], 219, 271 [7, 8], 336 [2], 398n., 504 [7], 516 [12], 792n.; **1965**: 62, 153, 156 [1], 167, 193, 195, 268, 351, 408, 438, 480, 490, 503, 527, 530n., 618; **1966**: 28, 108,

Labor, Department of — *continued*
   111, 172, 385n., 422, 529, 577 [10], 630 [4]; **1967**: 97, 193, 199, 217n., 345, 412, 428, 432n., 460 [1], 484; **1968-69**: 26, 39 (pp. 104, 110), 59, 162, 220n., 629n., 706n.
Appropriations, **1967**: 417 [1], 479; **1968-69**: 678 (p. 1281)
Commerce Department, proposed merger, **1968-69**: 670
Cost reduction program, **1968-69**: 39 (p. 111)
Hard-core unemployment, program, **1968-69**: 37
Law enforcement, **1968-69**: 57, 59
Manpower Administration, **1968-69**: 24, 39 (p. 111), 86
President's Safety Award presented to, **1963-64**: 351
Reorganization, **1967**: 3 (p. 4), 11, 13 (p. 57), 16 (p. 86), 121, 148
Report on unemployment, **1963-64**: 211 [3]
Labor, Department of Business and, proposed, **1967**: 3 (p. 4), 11, 13 (p. 57), 16 (p. 86), 121, 148
Labor, HEW, and related agencies appropriations bill, **1965**: 475
Labor, Illinois State Federation of, **1963-64**: 637
Labor, Secretary of (W. Willard Wirtz), **1963-64**: 22, 23, 40, 58, 67, 85, 89, 99, 111, 178n., 199, 213, 214, 235, 251, 252, 253n., 264, 284, 289, 291, 292, 297, 302, 320, 321, 322, 323, 325, 351, 398, 421, 430n., 448, 456, 494, 537, 622, 711, 806; **1965**: 4, 38, 58, 65, 73, 79, 86, 100, 183, 193, 207, 224, 239, 264n., 268, 298, 322, 324, 374, 428, 433, 466, 483, 530n., 575, 582; **1966**: 59, 102, 105, 111, 116, 184n., 201, 208, 216, 228, 235, 236 [13], 237, 275, 291, 299, 322, 373 [7], 422, 431, 434, 436, 462, 479, 490, 496, 529, 580 [10], 607 [1, 8], 654 [11]; **1967**: 12, 13 (p. 57), 30, 39, 57, 77, 95, 97, 114, 170, 199, 258, 310, 311, 345, 345n., 379, 388, 415, 420, 484, 529, 548; **1968-69**: 1 [5], 2, 24, 25, 37, 40, 42, 47 (p. 135), 56, 75, 76, 79 [1], 86, 90, 91, 94, 106, 112, 113, 139, 274, 425 [5], 489, 587, 670
Airlines strike statement, **1966**: 338 [3]
Government safety report, **1966**: 75
Letter, **1965**: 153
Memorandum, **1963-64**: 62; **1966**: 606; **1967**: 89, 259, 412, 458; **1968-69**: 89
News conference remarks on, **1963-64**: 170 [4], 256 [14], 266 [21], 285 [2], 294 [2], 316 [3], 379 [7], 504 [7]; **1965**: 156 [1], 463 [3]; **1967**: 6 [17, 18], 104 [15], 204 [5], 264 [8], 312 [3]

Labor, Secretary of – *continued*
  Report on manpower resources, **1963-64**: 212
  Reports, **1965**: 67, 99, 490
Labor Advisory Council.
  See President's Committee on Equal Employ-
    ment Opportunity.
Labor Board, War, **1967**: 310
Labor contracts
  Automobile industry, **1963-64**: 624
  Railroads, **1963-64**: 284, 287, 290, 294 [11],
    295, 297 [2], 338, 678
Labor Day, **1966**: 423, 429, 430, 449; **1967**:
    354, 376; **1968-69**: 463
  Statement, **1963-64**: 558; **1965**: 488, 489
Labor Development in Latin America, Institute
    for Free, **1965**: 450
Labor disputes, **1968-69**: 2
  Airlines, **1966**: 256-257, 322, 338 [3], 360,
    373 [5, 7, 12], 399
  Automobile industry, **1963-64**: 687, 733, 780
    [3]; **1967**: 375 [11]
  Copper industry, **1967**: 375 [12]; **1968-69**:
    106, 112, 141, 169 [21]
  Decrease, **1963-64**: 85, 266 [3], 316 [7], 472,
    695, 713, 733
  Electrical workers, **1966**: 496
  Garbage collectors, Memphis, Tenn., **1968-69**:
    166n., 169 [5, 16]
  General Electric Co., **1966**: 535
  Legislation, **1966**: 6 (pp. 5-6), 338 [13]
  Maritime industry, **1963-64**: 195, 494n., 614;
    1965: 58, 65, 428; **1968-69**: 636
    Agreement, **1965**: 463 [3], 465
  New York City transit, **1966**: 8 [15], 34 (p.
    106)
  Railroad, **1963-64**: 250, 251, 252, 253, 256
    [1, 6], 262, 266 [12], 270, 271 [9, 17],
    280 [11], 587 [7], 659; **1968-69**: 132,
    626
    See also Labor disputes *under* Railroads
  Shipbuilding industry, **1967**: 104 [15]
  Steel industry, **1965**: 448 [11, 15], 454 [1, 3],
    463 [10, 12, 14], 466, 478
    Agreements, **1965**: 208 [3, 21], 483, 632
Labor force, growth of, **1965**: 35 (pp. 106, 112),
    165, 255, 408, 480, 578
"Labor Force, Monthly Report of the," **1963-
    64**: 211ftn. (p. 338)
Labor Human Rights Award, **1967**: 484n.
Labor Leaders, National Conference of, **1963-
    64**: 379 [7]
Labor leaders, remarks to, **1963-64**: 477
Labor-Management Policy, President's Advisory
    Committee on, **1963-64**: 126, 213;
    1965: 428; **1966**: 111, 184, 201, 474
    [20]; **1967**: 121; **1968-69**: 469
Labor-management relations, **1963-64**: 85, 218
    [36], 233, 311, 316 [7], 336 [17],

Labor-management relations – *continued*
    350, 406, 506, 587 [9], 589, 604, 607,
    657, 658, 667, 729, 740, 745, 780 [3,
    5]; **1965**: 2, 35 (p. 106), 38, 41, 156
    [1], 326, 338, 448 [11], 454 [1], 463
    [10, 12, 14], 483, 632; **1966**: 34 (p.
    106); **1967**: 13 (p. 57), 114, 121; **1968-
    69**: 684 (p. 1317)
Labor-Management Relations Act (Taft-Hartley
    Act), 1947, **1963-64**: 614; **1966**: 237,
    504, 535; **1967**: 170, 375 [12]; **1968-
    69**: 636
  Section 14(b), **1966**: 6 (p. 5), 26 (p. 62), 34
    (p. 106), 237, 431, 504
Labor movement, **1963-64**: 297, 558; **1967**:
    484
  International, **1965**: 370
Labor Organization, International, **1965**: 370;
    1966: 250
Labor organizations, **1963-64**: 350, 589, 703;
    1967: 121, 524; **1968-69**: 26, 471, 534
  AFL-CIO, **1963-64**: 22, 111, 195, 221, 235,
    255, 379 [7], 548, 745; **1965**: 223,
    438, 641 [7], 644; **1966**: 88 [20], 125,
    431, 535; **1967**: 30, 534; **1968-69**: 50,
    154, 164, 165, 241, 670, 686
  Automobile, Aerospace and Agricultural
    Implement Workers of America,
    International Union of the United,
    1966: 535
  Automobile Workers of America, United, **1963-
    64**: 67, 233, 336 [17], 563 [2], 624,
    687, 713, 733; **1966**: 235
  Brotherhood of Railroad Trainmen, **1968-69**:
    626
  Clothing Workers, Amalgamated, 50th anniver-
    sary, **1963-64**: 334
  Commercial, Clerical, and Technical Em-
    ployees, International Federation of,
    1967: 442
  Communications Workers of America, **1963-64**:
    406
  Electrical, Radio and Machine Workers,
    International Union of, **1966**: 496
  Electrical Workers, International Brotherhood
    of, **1965**: 298
  Electrical Workers, International Union of,
    1963-64: 590
  Labor, American Federation of, **1963-64**: 430n.
  Ladies Garment Workers Union, International,
    1963-64: 387, 388; **1968-69**: 270, 529
  Locomotive Engineers, Brotherhood of, **1963-
    64**: 252, 284
  Longshoremen's Association, International,
    1963-64: 195, 494, 614; **1965**: 58, 65
    1968-69: 636
  Machinists and Aerospace Workers, Interna-
    tional Association of, **1966**: 256n.,
    322, 360, 535

Labor organizations – *continued*
  Machinists Union, International, **1963–64**: 571
  Marine Engineers' Beneficial Association,
      National, **1965**: 428
  Maritime Union of America, National, **1963–
      64**: 195
  Masters, Mates and Pilots of America, Inter-
      national Organization of, **1965**: 428
  Operating Engineers, International Union of,
      1966: 141 [4]
  Radio Association, American, **1965**: 428
  Steelworkers of America, United, **1963–64**:
      289, 290, 587 [9], 589, 780 [5]; **1965**:
      208 [3, 21], 226, 454 [1], 466, 483
  Transport Workers Union of America, **1966**:
      8ftn. (p. 19), 373ftn. (p. 808)
Labor Party Convention, Democratic-Farmer,
    1963–64: 433
Labor Press Association, International, **1963–64**:
    297; **1966**: 237
Labor and Public Welfare, Senate Committee on,
    1967: 188, 207, 338n.; **1968–69**: 160
Labor Statistics, Bureau of, **1965**: 298, 319 [3];
    1966: 95, 111, 413, 445 [5], 635 [8];
    1967: 460 [2], 463; **1968–69**: 423, 429
Laboratories
  Licensing, **1967**: 57, 77
  Manned orbiting, **1967**: 24
  Standards, **1968–69**: 56
Labouisse, Henry R., **1965**: 353 [4]
Laclede, Pierre, **1963–64**: 189
"Lady Bird Special" campaign train, **1963–64**:
    646
LaFollette, Bronson, **1963–64**: 746; **1967**: 342n.
LaFollette, Robert M., **1965**: 397; **1966**: 193
Lafon, Dr. Robert P., **1963–64**: 174
LaGuardia, Fiorello, **1963–64**: 373; **1965**: 242
Lai Chia-chiu, **1967**: 219
Laird, Repr. Melvin R., **1963–64**: 379 [19];
    1967: 70 [3]; **1968–69**: 646ftn. (p.
    1215)
Laise, Carol (Mrs. Ellsworth Bunker), **1965**:
    91n.; **1967**: 460 [11], 461
Laitin, Joseph, **1965**: 395ftn. (p. 815) and [1, 2],
    427n., 515n., 520n., 607n., 633n., 634n.,
    635n., 641 [1], 661n., 662n.; **1966**: 65
    [2], 184n.
Lake Barkley State Park, Ky., **1966**: 351–352
Lake Champlain, **1966**: 398
Lake Chelan National Recreation Area, Wash.,
    1968–69: 510n.
Lake County, Ind., campaign remarks, **1963–64**:
    639
Lake Erie, pollution of, **1965**: 54; **1966**: 82, 392–
    393, 398
Lake Superior, **1966**: 82
Lake Tahoe, Nevada, **1963–64**: 655
Laking, George R., **1968–69**: 525n.

Lalla Aicha, Princess (Morocco), **1967**: 43n.
Lamar, Mirabeau Buonaparte, **1963–64**: 330,
    513, 601, 738; **1965**: 9, 48, 181, 340n.;
    1966: 189; **1967**: 193n.
Lamb, Charles, **1963–64**: 506, 513, 796n.; **1967**:
    279
Lamb, Frank, **1963–64**: 666
Lamb, Gerald A., **1967**: 342n.
Lampasas, Texas, **1968–69**: 109
Lancaster, Ohio, **1966**: 437
  Mayor William E. Burt, **1966**: 436–437
Lance missile, **1963–64**: 382
Land, Edwin H., **1963–64**: 27; **1968–69**: 71n.
Land
  Airport vicinity, use, **1967**: 139, 328 [15]
  Cost of Federal acquisition, **1966**: 82
  Federal, **1967**: 13 (p. 51), 114, 372, 380, 412,
      531; **1968–69**: 563
  Model communities, **1967**: 531
  Powerplant vicinity, **1968–69**: 653
  Rights, Alaska, **1968–69**: 113
  Sales, consumer protection, **1968–69**: 56
  Sales frauds, **1967**: 57, 342, 465, 499
  Surplus Federal, **1965**: 54, 277
    Transfer to States, **1963–64**: 422, 534
  Waterfowl refuges, **1967**: 547
Land Agency, District of Columbia Redevelop-
    ment, **1966**: 457
Land banks, Federal, **1967**: 156
Land Between the Lakes recreation area, Ky.,
    1968–69: 122
Land development
  Open-space program, **1965**: 54
  State agencies for, Federal aid, **1965**: 90
Land Grant Act, **1965**: 452
Land-Grant College Act of 1862, **1963–64**: 36,
    482
Land-grant colleges, **1963–64**: 219; **1965**: 9, 18
  Association of State Universities and, **1963–64**:
      482n.
  National Association of State Universities and,
      1967: 490n.
Land-locked states, convention of transit trade
    of, **1968–69**: 383
Land-use program, **1963–64**: 300
Land and Water Conservation Fund, **1963–64**:
    578, 756; **1965**: 47, 54; **1966**: 398;
    1968–69: 39 (p. 101), 122, 386
Land and Water Conservation Fund Act of 1965,
    1963–64: 554, 620, 654, 756; **1965**: 32
    (p. 92); **1967**: 13 (p. 51), 20, 553
  Amendment, **1968–69**: 386
"Land, Wood and Water," Robert S. Kerr, **1963–
    64**: 597
Landmarks, Registry of National Historic, **1965**:
    54

Landon, Alfred M., **1963–64**: 334
Landrum, Repr. Phil M., **1963–64**: 330, 332, 716
Lane, Dr. Walter, **1967**: 87n.
Langen, Repr. Odin, **1965**: 189
Langley Air Force Base, Va., **1967**: 485 [7]
Language courses for U.S. dependents overseas, **1963–64**: 266 [17]
Lanier, Maj. Glenard E., **1968–69**: 602
Lanier, William L., **1967**: 342n.
Lankford, Mrs. Richard E., **1963–64**: 172
Lansdale, Gen. Edward G., **1966**: 52 [2]
Laos, **1963–64**: 201 [7], 746, 780ftn. (p. 1616); **1966**: 514, 516 [11]; **1967**: 309 [9, 10], 480
　Assistance, **1963–64**: 227; **1965**: 18, 26, 294; **1966**: 11n., 41; **1968–69**: 63, 679
　Communism in, **1963–64**: 201 [7], 294 [16], 400, 420 [1, 5], 474, 500, 504 [4]; **1965**: 26
　Crown Prince Vong Savang, **1967**: 480
　Economic and social development, **1967**: 44
　Geneva accords, **1967**: 564; **1968–69**: 237, 240, 275 [1], 288, 400, 406, 452
　King Sri Savang Vatthana, **1963–64**: 336 [8]; **1967**: 438n.; **1968–69**: 240
　Minister of Foreign Affairs Sisouk Na Champassak, **1967**: 439
　National Day of the Kingdom of Laos, **1968–69**: 240
　Neutrality, **1963–64**: 499
　North Vietnamese infiltration, **1967**: 80 [4], 83, 132 [3, 4] 409, 480, 554 [1]
　Pathet Lao, **1963–64**: 201 [7]
　Philippine assistance to, **1963–64**: 626
　Prime Minister Souvanna Phouma, **1966**: 513–514, 516 [5, 11]; **1967**: 438, 439, 448, 480
　Prince Souvanna Phouma, **1963–64**: 285 [4], 294 [16], 336 [8]
　Princess Moune Souvanna Phouma, **1967**: 439
　U.S. Ambassador Leonard Unger, **1963–64**: 285 [4], 294 [16]
　U.S. policy in, **1963–64**: 272; **1965**: 22 [4]
　U.S. relations with, **1963–64**: 294 [16]
Lard, embargo on, proposed, **1963–64**: 201 [14]
Laredo, Texas, **1968–69**: 91
Larrick, George P., **1966**: 4n.
Larsen, Lt. Gen. Stanley R., **1967**: 358 [6]
Larson, Arthur, **1963–64**: 563 [5], 591, 747
Larson, J. Edwin, **1963–64**: 709, 712, 713
Larson, Jess, **1966**: 221
Larson, Roy E., **1963–64**: 336 [6]
Las Vegas, Nev., campaign remarks, **1963–64**: 652

Lasker, Albert, special award, **1966**: 166
Lasker, Mrs. Albert (Mary), **1965**: 551; **1966**: 166, 500; **1968–69**: 167, 589, 672n.
Lassen, Lt. Clyde E., **1968–69**: 688
Lassen Volcanic Wilderness, Calif., **1968–69**: 168
Latin America, **1963–64**: 54 [4], 285 [13]; **1965**: 272; **1966**: 6 (p. 9), 501 [1], 610 [8], 654 [3]
　See also American Republics; Organization of American States; *specific countries.*
　Alliance for Progress.
　　See main heading, Alliance for Progress.
　Ambassadors, remarks, **1967**: 151
　Assistance, **1963–64**: 45, 71 [5, 9], 227, 272, 340, 617, 662n., 769; **1965**: 7, 18, 136, 139, 149; **1966**: 125, 175, 386; **1967**: 44, 110, 152, 173, 175–176, 357; **1968–69**: 39 (pp. 91, 99), 63, 363, 365, 366, 368, 524
　Balance of payments, **1968–69**: 366
　Benito Juárez Scholars, **1968–69**: 66
　Common market, **1967**: 110, 173, 175–178, 357, 442, 451; **1968–69**: 39 (p. 99), 147n., 205, 467 [13]
　Communist aggression, **1963–64**: 220, 272, 443, 702; **1965**: 18, 295 [10]; **1967**: 395; **1968–69**: 110
　Conference, **1966**: 474 [11]
　Cuban subversion in, **1963–64**: 186
　Cultural exchanges, **1967**: 53
　Economic and social development, **1963–64**: 66, 71 [5], 123, 169, 186, 193, 220, 227, 316 [9], 340, 769; **1965**: 18, 139, 429, 450; **1966**: 125, 141 [12], 175, 177, 247 [1, 15], 254, 264, 320 [12], 386, 639, 642 [2]; **1967**: 3 (p. 9), 110, 152, 173, 176, 177, 272, 357, 394, 451, 473; **1968–69**: 39 (p. 99), 63, 110, 147, 148, 151n., 205, 206, 239, 290, 362, 363, 365–368, 370, 376, 394, 472, 665
　Education, **1968–69**: 239, 374
　Elections, **1966**: 320 [12]
　Foreign aid, **1968–69**: 63
　Free trade area, **1963–64**: 769
　Good-neighbor policy, **1963–64**: 104, 220, 285 [13], 340, 561
　Health problems, **1965**: 262
　Journalists from, **1963–64**: 475 [3]
　Military budgets, **1966**: 386
　Nuclear free zone, **1967**: 64
　　Treaty, **1968–69**: 13, 73, 349, 392
　Pan American Highway, **1968–69**: 696 [11]
　Peace Corps projects, **1965**: 83; **1966**: 125
　Regional cooperation, **1968–69**: 14 (p. 26), 147, 148n., 362, 363, 365–367, 374, 375, 665
　Science and technology, multinational program, **1967**: 473

Latin America – *continued*
Summit meeting.
See Punta del Este meeting of American chiefs of state.
Trade, **1967**: 110, 173, 175–178; **1968–69**: 204, 366, 559
U.S. investments in, **1963–64**: 169, 726
U.S. policy in, **1965**: 429n., **1966**: 414
U.S. private citizens, contact with, **1963–64**: 316 [9]
U.S. relations with, **1963–64**: 9, 220, 246 [1], 662, 726; **1965**: 558; **1968–69**: 148, 151n., 655; **1966**: 175, 273
Visit to, **1968–69**: 364–376
Proposed, **1968–69**: 339 [15]
Latin America, Business Group for, **1963–64**: 169, 688 [8]
Latin America, Council on, **1966**: 125
Latin America, Institute for Free Labor Development in, **1965**: 450
Latin American Citizens, League of United, **1966**: 236 [14]
Latin American Free Trade Association, **1966**: 177; **1968–69**: 239, 362, 665
Laughlin Air Force Base, Tex., **1966**: 638
Launch vehicles, **1966**: 26 (p. 59), 485, 625; **1967**: 13 (p. 48), 19n., 24, 76, 483, 533
Jupiter C, **1968–69**: 41
Saturn V, **1968–69**: 39 (p. 100), 41
Lausche, Sen. Frank J., **1963–64**: 310; **1966**: 434–437
Lava Beds Wilderness, Calif., **1968–69**: 168
Lavalle, Juan Bautista de, **1963–64**: 232 [1]
Law.
Administration of, **1967**: 121, 323
International, **1965**: 346
Law, Conference on World Peace Through, **1965**: 516
Law enforcement, **1963–64**: 462 [10], 468, 475 [15], 563 [9], 600, 603, 655, 752, 760; **1965**: 70, 102, 106 [1], 117 [1, 5, 10], 128, 135, 382, 426, 436, 448 [9]; **1966**: 117, 196, 204–205, 487, 498; **1967**: 13 (p. 44), 146, 297 [7], 382, 443, 455, 575; **1968–69**: 14 (p. 31), 26, 39 (p. 107), 59, 102, 164, 684 (p. 1314)
See also Crime; Police.
Assistance, **1967**: 35
Citations, **1967**: 71
Civil disorders, **1968–69**: 14 (p. 31)
Crime information center, **1968–69**: 678 (p. 1292)
District of Columbia, **1965**: 70, 102, 381; **1966**: 116, 611; **1967**: 27, 71, 466; **1968–69**: 95, 355, 436
Investigations, **1968–69**: 59, 678 (p. 1292)
Legislation, **1965**: 500; **1967**: 468

Law enforcement – *continued*
Memorandum, **1966**: 205
Message to Congress, **1966**: 116; **1968–69**: 59
Personnel and facilities, **1965**: 2, 29, 70, 102, 381, 509, 526; **1966**: 116, 204–205, 335, 598; **1967**: 71, 441, 482; **1968–69**: 14 (p. 30), 39 (p. 107), 57, 59, 202, 217, 320, 325, 355, 678 (p. 1292)
Pledge, Philadelphia Police Athletic League, **1968–69**: 163
Privacy, right of, **1967**: 105
Public cooperation, **1965**: 102; **1966**: 116, 396
Research, **1965**: 102; **1967**: 35
State and local, **1968–69**: 14 (p. 30), 39 (p. 107), 50, 57, 59, 100, 235, 320, 325, 542, 553, 557 [8], 678 (pp. 1281, 1291)
Statement to Governors, **1966**: 491
Warrants, arrest, **1967**: 71
Law Enforcement and Administration of Justice, President's Commission on, **1965**: 102, 381, 382, 422, 437, 500, 526; **1966**: 116, 491, 492 [1], 494 [1], 526, 611, 630 [9]; **1967**: 3 (p. 6), 13 (p. 56), 35, 39, 60, 146, 221, 276, 382, 385; **1968–69**: 59, 235, 257, 301, 320, 553, 678 (p. 1291)
Law Enforcement Assistance, Office of, **1966**: 116
Law Enforcement Assistance Act of 1965, **1965**: 102, 509, 526; **1966**: 26 (p. 64), 59, 116, 354, 487, 491, 526, 598, 611, 633n.; **1967**: 3 (p. 6), 13 (p. 56), 27, 35, 71, 146, 482; **1968–69**: 39 (p. 107), 553
Law Enforcement and Criminal Justice, National Institute of, **1968–69**: 59, 320
Law Enforcement and Criminal Justice Assistance, Office of, **1967**: 35
Law and order, issue of, **1968–69**: 154, 163, 298, 406, 553, 557 [8], 567
Postage stamp, **1968–69**: 257
Lawrence, David L., **1963–64**: 290, 338, 542, 566, 661, 728, 742; **1966**: 528, 623
Lawrence, Leonard G., **1967**: 382
Lawrence, William H., **1963–64**: 218
Lawrenceville, Ill., **1966**: 349
Mayor Charles Hedde, **1966**: 349
Laws, National Commission on Reform of Federal Criminal, **1966**: 598; **1968–69**: 59
Lawson, Earl C., **1966**: 350
Lawson, Marjorie M., **1965**: 366; **1968–69**: 631
Lawyers Association, American Trial, **1966**: 47
Lawyers Association, National Trial, **1967**: 114
Lawyers Conference on Crime Control, **1967**: 221
Lay, Donald P., **1966**: 320 [4]

Layton, John B., **1965**: 366; **1966**: 219; **1968-69**: 425 [10]
Lazarus, Ralph, **1967**: 168n.
Lazzari, Pietro, **1965**: 210n.; **1968-69**: 51n.
LBJ Ranch, Johnson City, Texas, **1963-64**: 242, 295, 462, 504, 547n., 766n., 767n., 768n., 779n., 780, 818n.; **1965**: 21n., 22, 113n., 117, 192, 194n., 341n., 395, 462n., 595, 632n., 641, 643n., 644n.; **1966**: 628 [12]
  News conferences, **1966**: 320, 578, 607, 654
  Releases, **1966**: 626
Lead, imports, **1965**: 577; **1966**: 125
Leader, George M., **1963-64**: 566; **1966**: 428
Lead-Zinc Small Producers Stabilization Act of Oct. 3, 1961, **1965**: 577
League of Cities, National, **1965**: 438; **1966**: 155
League of Nations, **1963-64**: 435, 662n., 695, 736; **1965**: 235; **1967**: 52; **1968-69**: 250n.
League of Red Cross Societies, **1966**: 549
League of United Latin American Citizens (LULACS), **1966**: 236 [14]
  Proclamation, **1968-69**: 68
League of Women Voters, **1963-64**: 289
Leather, hides, and skins exports, **1966**: 592
Leavitt, Dr. Milo D., Jr., **1968-69**: 408
Lebanon crisis (1957), **1968-69**: 472
Le Baron, Eddie, **1966**: 385n.
Lederman, Leon M., **1965**: 646n.; **1966**: 61n.
Ledesma, Oscar, **1963-64**: 626n.
Lee, H. Rex (Governor of American Samoa), **1966**: 266, 537; **1968-69**: 370
Lee, Mrs. H. Rex, **1966**: 537
Lee, Maj. Howard V., **1967**: 446
Lee, Mrs. Howard V., **1967**: 446n.
Lee, Hu Rak, **1966**: 566; **1967**: 113
Lee, Katharine, **1965**: 289
Lee, Capt. Kent L., **1967**: 485 [5]
Lee, Dr. Philip R., **1966**: 293n.
Lee, Ray, **1967**: 210
Lee, Robert E., **1963-64**: 599, 646, 648
Lee, Robert R., **1965**: 334n.
Lee, Maj. Ronald B., **1965**: 334n.
Lee, Tong Won, **1966**: 566
Lee Kuan Yew (Prime Minister of Singapore), **1967**: 409, 433-435
Lee Kuan Yew, Mrs., **1967**: 433, 434
Leeb, Bryant, **1965**: 522n.
Lefschetz, Solomon, **1965**: 56n.
Legal aid programs, **1967**: 114, 221, 277
Legal services, **1966**: 394, 594
Legion of Merit, **1967**: 475
Legislation, private, objections to tax exemption provisions, **1963-64**: 61
Legislation, remarks or statements upon approval
  Administrative Procedure Act amendment, **1966**: 316

Legislation – *continued*
  Adult Indian Vocational Training Act, amendment, **1965**: 204
  Age Discrimination in Employment Act of 1967: **1967**: 548
  Agricultural Act of 1964, **1963-64**: 255
  Agricultural Trade Development and Assistance Act of 1954, extension, **1963-64**: 641; **1968-69**: 417
  Air Quality Act of 1967, **1967**: 503
  Alaska Omnibus Act, amendment, **1963-64**: 371
  Alaska Purchase Centennial, 1967, **1966**: 147
  Allied Health Professions Personnel Training Act of 1966, **1966**: 573
  American Embassy in Saigon, appropriation authorization, **1965**: 276
  American Revolution Bicentennial Commission, **1966**: 323
  Animals, research, humane treatment, **1966**: 402
  Appalachian Regional Development Act of 1965, **1965**: 103
  Appropriations, continuing, **1967**: 417, 556
  Architectural barriers to the handicapped, elimination, **1968-69**: 440
  Armed Forces, appropriation authorization, **1963-64**: 230
  Armed Forces, equal opportunity for women, **1967**: 475
  Armed Forces Exemplary Rehabilitation Certificates, **1966**: 529
  Armed Forces incentive cash award program, **1965**: 528
  Arms Control and Disarmament Act, extension, **1965**: 284
  Asian Development Bank Act of 1966, **1966**: 133
  Assateague Island Seashore National Park, **1965**: 521
  Atlantic-Pacific interoceanic canal, study, **1963-64**: 594
  Atomic Energy Act of 1954, amendment, **1965**: 446
  Auburn-Folsom South project, Calif., **1965**: 477
  Bail Reform Act of 1966, **1966**: 286
  Bankhead-Jones Farm Tenant Act amendment, **1966**: 595
  Bartlett, Mrs. Margaret Patterson, relief bill, **1963-64**: 61
  Beirut Agreement implementation, **1966**: 519
  Bighorn Canyon National Recreation Area, Mont.-Wyo., **1966**: 522
  Biscayne National Monument, Fla., establishment, **1968-69**: 547
  Cape Lookout National Seashore, N.C., **1966**: 119

Legislation – *continued*

Central Intelligence Agency Retirement Act of 1964 for Certain Employees, **1963–64:** 664

Chamizal boundary area highway, **1966:** 597

Child Nutrition Act of 1966, **1966:** 508

Child Protection Act of 1966, **1966:** 576

Children, social security, **1966:** 581

Civil Rights Act of 1964, **1963–64:** 446

Civil Rights Act of 1968, **1968–69:** 195

Claims by or against U.S. Government, disposition, **1966:** 335

Clean Air Act, **1963–64:** 50
   Amendments, **1965:** 568

Clean Water Restoration Act of 1966, **1966:** 574

Coast Guard, procurement and construction appropriation approved, **1963–64:** 216

Coast Guard appropriations, **1966:** 159

Coinage Act of 1965, **1965:** 380

College work-study programs, **1967:** 378

Colorado River Basin Project Act, **1968–69:** 501

Commodity Exchange Act, amendments, **1968–69:** 85

Community Health Services Extension Amendments of 1965, **1965:** 406

Comprehensive Health Planning and Public Health Services Amendments of 1966, **1966:** 573

Consolidated Farmers Home Administration Act, amendments, **1968–69:** 450

Consumer Credit Protection Act, **1968–69:** 280

Criminal investigations, **1967:** 468

Customs conventions, implementing certain, **1968–69:** 558

Davis-Bacon Act, amended, **1963–64:** 444

Defense, Department of
   Appropriation Act of 1968, **1967:** 410
   Supplemental appropriations, **1967:** 118

Delaware Water Gap National Recreation Area, **1965:** 471

Demonstration Cities and Metropolitan Development Act of 1966, **1966:** 574

Department of Agriculture and Related Agencies Appropriation Act, 1967, **1966:** 441

Department of Housing and Urban Development, establishment, **1965:** 503

Department of the Interior and Related Agencies Appropriation Act, 1969, **1968–69:** 411

Department of Transportation, creation, **1966:** 523

Departments of State, Justice, and Commerce, the Judiciary, and Related Agencies Appropriation Act, 1968, **1967:** 482

Depreciation allowances suspension, **1966:** 596

Legislation – *continued*

Disabled veterans, bills providing additional benefits for, **1965:** 456

Disaster Relief Act of 1966, **1966:** 584

District of Columbia
   Crime bill, **1967:** 575
   Medicaid, **1967:** 574

District of Columbia Air Pollution Control Act, **1968–69:** 420

District of Columbia Appropriation Act, 1966, **1965:** 366

District of Columbia Appropriation Act, 1969, **1968–69:** 436

District of Columbia Elected Board of Education Act, **1968–69:** 203

District of Columbia Minimum Wage Amendments of 1966, **1966:** 527

District of Columbia Police and Firemen's Salary Act Amendments of 1968, **1968–69:** 272

District of Columbia Public Education Act, **1966:** 586

District of Columbia Teachers' Salary Act Amendments of 1968, **1968–69:** 272

Drug Abuse Control Amendments of 1965, **1965:** 361

Drug traffic or possession, **1968–69:** 561

Economic Opportunity Act of 1964, **1963–64:** 528

Economic Opportunity Amendments of 1966, **1966:** 594

Elementary and Secondary Education Act of 1965, **1965:** 181, 527

Elementary and Secondary Education Amendments of 1966, **1966:** 573

Elementary and Secondary Education Amendments of 1967, **1968–69:** 4

Eisenhower College, funds for, **1968–69:** 550

Endangered species preservation, **1966:** 522

Excise Tax Reduction Act of 1965, **1965:** 326

Explorer Scouts uniform import duties, relief, **1966:** 178

Export-Import Bank Act, amendments, **1968–69:** 136

Export-Import Bank of the United States, extension of authority, **1968–69:** 377

Fair Labor Standards Amendments of 1966, **1966:** 479

Fair Packaging and Labeling Act, **1966:** 576

Federal-Aid Highway Act of 1964, **1963–64:** 512

Federal-Aid Highway Act of 1968, **1968–69:** 458

Federal Airport Act, amendment, **1963–64:** 215

Federal Coal Mine Safety Act Amendments of 1965, **1966:** 151

Federal Credit Union Act, amendment, **1967:** 537

[References are to items except as otherwise indicated]

Legislation – *continued*
Federal Employees Compensation Act Amendments of 1966, **1966**: 318
Federal Employees Salary Act of 1965, **1965**: 589
Federal Food, Drug, and Cosmetic Act, amendments, **1968–69**: 561
Federal Insecticide, Fungicide, and Rodenticide Act, amendment, **1963–64**: 341
Federal Judicial Center, **1967**: 560
Federal Magistrates Act, **1968–69**: 542
Federal Metal and Nonmetallic Mine Safety Act, **1966**: 462
Federal Property and Administrative Services Act, amendments to, **1963–64**: 481
Federal Salary and Fringe Benefits Act of 1966, **1966**: 333
Federal Voting Assistance Act of 1955, amendments, **1968–69**: 314
Financial Institutions Supervisory Act of 1966, **1966**: 530
Fire Research and Safety Act of 1968, **1968–69**: 105
Fish Protein Concentrate Act, **1966**: 569
Fishing in territorial waters of the United States, **1968–69**: 412
　Prohibition, **1963–64**: 353
Five-day workweek for postmasters, **1965**: 413
Flaming Gorge National Recreational Area, establishment, **1968–69**: 505
Flammable Fabrics Act, amendment, **1967**: 539
Florence Agreement implementation, **1966**: 519
Food and Agriculture Act of 1965: **1965**: 597
　Extension, **1968–69**: 554
Food for Freedom program, extension, **1968–69**: 417
Food for Peace Act of 1966, **1966**: 608
Food Stamp Act of 1964, **1963–64**: 546
　Amendment, **1967**: 405; **1968–69**: 519
Foreign Assistance Act of 1963, **1963–64**: 48
Foreign Assistance Act of 1965, **1965**: 495
Foreign Assistance Act of 1966, **1966**: 469
Foreign Assistance Act of 1967, **1967**: 489
Foreign Assistance Act of 1968, **1968–69**: 524
Foreign Assistance and Related Agencies Appropriation Act, 1966, **1965**: 570
Foreign Investors Tax Act of 1966, **1966**: 612
Foreign Service information officer corps, establishment, **1968–69**: 454
Freight car shortage reductions, **1966**: 240
George Rogers Clark National Historical Park, Ind., **1966**: 350
Government employees
　Hazardous duty benefits, **1967**: 568
　Pay raises, **1967**: 546
Government Employees Salary Reform Act of 1964, **1963–64**: 514

Legislation – *continued*
Government personnel legislation codification, **1966**: 438
Grand Coulee Dam powerplant, **1966**: 269
Great Salt Lake borderlands conveyance to Utah, **1966**: 255
Great Seal of the United States, reproduction and use, **1966**: 609
Great Swamp National Wildlife Refuge Wilderness Area, designation, **1968–69**: 502
Guadalupe Mountains National Park, Texas, **1966**: 522
Guam Elective Governor Act, **1968–69**: 477
Gun Control Act of 1968, **1968–69**: 553
Handicapped Children's Early Education Assistance Act, **1968–69**: 503
Handicapped persons library services, **1966**: 362
Health Manpower Act of 1968, **1968–69**: 447
Health Professions Educational Assistance Amendments of 1965, **1965**: 579
Health Research Facilities Amendments of 1965, **1965**: 410
Heart Disease, Cancer, and Stroke Amendments of 1965, **1965**: 551
Herbert Hoover National Historic Site, establishment, **1965**: 420
Higher Education Act of 1965; **1965**: 603
Higher Education Amendments of 1966, **1966**: 573
Higher Education Amendments of 1968, **1968–69**: 538
Higher Education Facilities Act of 1963, **1963–64**: 47
High-speed ground transportation study, **1965**: 536
Highway Beautification Act of 1965, **1965**: 576
Highway Safety Act of 1966, **1966**: 449
Historic preservation, national, **1966**: 522
Historical documents bill, **1963–64**: 481
Home loan interest rate increase, **1968–69**: 229
Hospital Survey and Construction Act of 1949, extension, **1963–64**: 520
Housing Act of 1964, **1963–64**: 549
Housing mortgage credit, **1966**: 451
Housing and Urban Development Act of 1965, **1965**: 415
Housing and Urban Development Act of 1968, **1968–69**: 426
Hudson River Basin pollution control, **1966**: 481
Immigration and Nationality Act, amendments, **1965**: 546
Independent Offices Appropriation Act, 1964, **1963–64**: 56
Independent Offices Appropriation Act, 1967, **1966**: 439

Legislation – *continued*

Independent Offices and Department of
    Housing and Urban Development
    Appropriation Act, 1968, **1967**: 467
India food relief, **1966**: 180; **1967**: 153
Indiana Dunes National Lakeshore, Ind., **1966**:
    579
Inter-American Development Bank Act
    Amendment, **1968–69**: 290
    Contribution, **1967**: 394
    Resources increase, **1965**: 131
Interest rate control, **1966**: 473
Intergovernmental Cooperation Act of 1968,
    1968–69: 539
International center site in District of Columbia,
    1968–69: 523
International Claims Settlement Act, amend-
    ment, **1963–64**: 684
International Coffee Agreement, U.S. partici-
    pation, **1965**: 272
International Development Association bill,
    1963–64: 361
International Education Act, **1966**: 557
Interstate highway system, bill appropriating
    funds for, **1965**: 460
Investment tax credit suspension, **1966**: 596
John F. Kennedy Center for the Performing
    Arts, bill concerning, **1963–64**: 142
John Fitzgerald Kennedy National Historic
    Site, Mass., **1967**: 242
Joseph H. Hirshhorn Museum and Sculpture
    Garden, **1966**: 587
Judges in the District of Columbia, **1968–69**:
    542
Jury Selection and Service Act of 1968, **1968–
    69**: 158
Juvenile Delinquency Prevention and Control
    Act of 1968, **1968**: 424
Labor, HEW, and related agencies appropria-
    tions bill, **1965**: 475; **1967**: 479
Land and Water Conservation Fund Act of
    1964, **1963–64**: 554
Land and Water Conservation Fund Act of
    1965, amendments, **1968–69**: 386
Law Enforcement Assistance Act of 1965,
    1965: 526
Law Enforcement Assistance Act Amendment,
    1966: 598
Law enforcement officers, indemnity payments,
    1968–69: 202
Library Services Act, amendment, **1963–64**:
    181
Library Services and Construction Act,
    amendments, **1967**: 507
Library Services and Construction Act Amend-
    ments of 1966, **1966**: 337
Manpower Act of 1965, **1965**: 207
Manpower Development and Training Act of
    1962, amendments, **1963–64**: 55

Legislation – *continued*

Manpower Development and Training Amend-
    ments of 1966, **1966**: 588
Medical Library Assistance Act of 1965, **1965**:
    581
Medicare extension, **1966**: 168
Mental Health Amendments of 1967, **1967**:
    285
Mental Retardation Amendments of 1967,
    1967: 517
Mental Retardation Facilities and Community
    Mental Health Centers Construction Act
    Amendments of 1965, **1965**: 401
Merchant Marine Act of 1936, amendment,
    1968–69: 535
Migratory waterfowl refuges, **1967**: 547
Military appropriations, **1966**: 128
Military Construction Authorization Act,
    1965: 518
Military Construction Authorization Act,
    1967, **1966**: 452
Military Construction Authorization Act,
    1968, **1967**: 440
Military Justice Act of 1968, **1968–69**: 556
Military pay bill, **1963–64**: 510; **1965**: 439
Military pay raises, **1967**: 546
Military personnel, benefits, **1968–69**: 5
Motor vehicle insurance, joint resolution
    authorizing study, **1968–69**: 264
Narcotic Addict Rehabilitation Act of 1966,
    1966: 598
National Aeronautics and Space Administra-
    tion Authorization Act, 1967, **1966**:
    371
National Aeronautics and Space Administra-
    tion Authorization Act, 1968, **1967**:
    362
National Capital Transportation Act of 1965,
    1965: 499
National Commission on Product Safety, **1967**:
    499
National Commission on Reform of Federal
    Criminal Laws, **1966**: 598
National Commission on Technology, Automa-
    tion, and Economic Progress, establish-
    ment, **1963–64**: 525
National Defense Education Act Amendments,
    1964, **1963–64**: 676
National Eye Institute, establishment, **1968–
    69**: 446
National Foundation on the Arts and the
    Humanities Act of 1965, **1965**: 534
National Park Foundation, establishment,
    1967: 553
National parks bill, concession rights in, **1965**:
    560
National Teacher Corps appropriations, **1966**:
    223

Legislation – *continued*
  Extension, **1967**: 292
  National Technical Institute for the Deaf Act,
    1965: 305
  National Traffic and Motor Vehicle Safety Act
    of 1966, **1966**: 449
  National Trails System Act, **1968–69**: 510
  National Visitor Center Facilities Act of 1968,
    1968–69: 128
  National Vocational Student Loan Insurance
    Act of 1965, **1965**: 578
  Natural Gas Pipeline Safety Act of 1968,
    1968–69: 441
  Navajo Indians, **1968–69**: 259
  Navy Judge Advocate General's Corps, estab-
    lishment, **1967**: 527
  Nurse Training Act of 1964, **1963–64**: 557
  Older Americans Act of 1965, **1965**: 354
  Older Americans Act Amendments of 1967,
    1967: 299
  Omnibus Crime Control and Safe Streets Act
    of 1968, **1968–69**: 320
  Pacific Islands, Trust Territory of the, appro-
    priations, **1967**: 218
  Pacific Northwest Disaster Relief Act of 1965,
    1965: 317
  Parcel post, **1966**: 470
  Park areas in State of Washington, establish-
    ment, **1968–69**: 510
  Partnership for Health Amendments of 1967,
    1967: 520
  Patrick V. McNamara Federal Office Building.
    Detroit, **1967**: 535
  Peace Corps Act, extension, **1965**: 445
  Peace Corps Act amendment, **1966**: 455
  Philippines
    Veterans benefits, **1966**: 495, 505
    War orphans aid, **1966**: 495
  Pictured Rocks National Lakeshore, Mich.,
    1966: 522
  Point Reyes National Seashore, Calif.,
    1966: 522
  Political Activity of Government Personnel,
    Commission on, **1966**: 499
  Postage stamps, photographic reproductions,
    1968–69: 321
  Postal Revenue and Federal Salary Act of 1967,
    1967: 546
  Postal savings system abolition, **1966**: 150
  Presidential Election Campaign Fund Act of
    1966, **1966**: 612
  Private Ownership of Special Nuclear Materials
    Act, **1963–64**: 538
  Proclamations.
    See main heading, Proclamations.
  Protection of investors in securities, **1968–69**:
    418
  Public Broadcasting Act of 1967, **1967**: 474

Legislation – *continued*
  Public Health Service Act, amendments,
    1968–69: 536
  Public Works Appropriation Act, 1964,
    1963–64: 81
  Public Works and Economic Development Act
    of 1965, **1965**: 452
  Radiation Control for Health and Safety Act
    of 1968, **1968–69**: 545
  Railroad labor dispute settlement provisions,
    1967: 311
  Railroad "no strike" period extension,
    1967: 174
  Redwood National Park, Calif., establishment,
    1968–69: 510
  Rehabilitative techniques for adult offenders,
    1965: 509
  Renegotiation Act extension, **1966**: 313
  Renegotiation Amendments Act of 1968,
    1968–69: 559
  Rent supplements, **1966**: 223, 439
  Reserve and National Guard members, re-
    employment rights, **1968–69**: 448
  Reserve Officers' Training Corps Vitalization
    Act of 1964, **1963–64**: 665
  Revenue Act of 1964, **1963–64**: 197
  Revenue and Expenditure Control Act of 1968,
    1968–69: 343
  Rinderpest, cooperation with Central America
    for prevention, **1968–69**: 364
  Rio Grande salinity control, **1966**: 467
  River and Harbor Act of 1965, **1965**: 587
  St. Louis University, 150th anniversary,
    1968–69: 551
  Saline Water Conversion Act, **1965**: 417
  San Antonio commemorative medals, **1966**: 160
  San Juan Island Historical Park, Wash.,
    1966: 448
  San Rafael Wilderness, Calif., an act to designate,
    1968–69: 150
  Savings and Loan Holding Company Amend-
    ment of 1967, **1968–69**: 72
  School Disaster Aid Act, **1965**: 592
  Scientific instruments
    Bills for duty-free entry of, **1965**: 604
    Import tariffs, **1966**: 601
  Second Supplemental Appropriation Act, 1965,
    1965: 215
  Second Supplemental Appropriation Act, 1966,
    1966: 223
  Securities Acts Amendments of 1964,
    1963–64: 530
  Securities registration, bill increasing fees for,
    1965: 580
  Service Contract Act of 1965, **1965**: 582
  Shaw Junior High School site, Washington, D.C.,
    1966: 457
  Small Business Act Amendments, **1966**: 199

[References are to items except as otherwise indicated]

Legislation – *continued*
  Small Business Act Amendments of 1967,
      1967: 427
  Small Business Investment Act Amendments of
      1966, **1966**: 582
  Social Security Amendments of 1965,
      1965: 394
  Social Security Amendments of 1967,
      1968–69: 3
  Social security for children, **1966**: 581
  Solid Waste Disposal Act, **1965**: 568
  Southeast Asia, promotion of peace and security
      in, **1963–64**: 507
  Southeast Hurricane Disaster Relief Act of 1965,
      1965: 605
  Southern Nevada water project, approval of
      bill, **1965**: 586
  Special Drawing Rights Act, **1968–69**: 317
  State Technical Services Act of 1965, **1965**: 513
  Stockpile disposals, **1966**: 173, 206, 218, 283,
      572; **1967**: 506
  Supplemental Appropriation Act, 1969,
      1968–69: 550
  Supplemental Defense Appropriation Act, 1967,
      1967: 159
  Tariff Schedules of the United States, amend-
      ments, **1968–69**: 558, 562
  Tax Adjustment Act of 1966, **1966**: 132
  Tobacco marketing quotas, **1965**: 192
  Tourists, bill limiting duty-free imports,
      1965: 338
  TVA bonds, marketing authority, **1966**: 382
  25th amendment to the Constitution, Presi-
      dential inability, **1967**: 68
  Uniform holidays, **1968–69**: 342
  United Nations Participation Act of 1945,
      amendment, **1965**: 533
  Urban Mass Transportation Act of 1964,
      1963–64: 453
  Urban Mass Transportation Act amendment,
      1966: 442
  Urban study fellowships, **1967**: 359
  U.S.-Canadian agreement on automotive pro-
      ducts, bill implementing, **1965**: 574
  Vessel safety and financial responsibility,
      1966: 583
  Veterans benefits, **1968–69**: 414
      Educational, **1968–69**: 554
      Pensions, **1968–69**: 160
      Philippine, **1966**: 495, 505
  Veterans' life insurance and pension bill,
      1963–64: 663
  Veterans' Pension and Readjustment Assistance
      Act of 1967, **1967**: 374
  Veterans' Readjustment Benefits Act of 1966,
      1966: 100
  Veterans of Vietnam, American Legion member-
      ship, **1966**: 421

Legislation – *continued*
  Vice President, official residence, **1966**: 170
  Vietnam, appropriations for military require-
      ments in, **1965**: 234
  Vietnam servicemen welfare, **1966**: 571
  Virgin Islands Elective Governor Act,
      1968–69: 457
  Vocational Education Act of 1963, **1963–64**:
      53
  Vocational Education Amendments of 1968,
      1968–69: 538
  Vocational Rehabilitation Act Amendments of
      1967, **1967**: 413
  Voting Rights Act of 1965, **1965**: 409
  War orphans' educational assistance allowance
      bill, **1965**: 542
  Warships, sale or loan to friendly countries,
      1965: 600
  Watch and clock import tariffs, **1966**: 600
  Water desalination
      California, **1967**: 227
      Research, **1967**: 284
  Water for peace conference, **1966**: 593
  Water Quality Act of 1965, **1965**: 543
  Water Resources Planning Act, **1965**: 375
  Water Resources Research Act of 1964,
      1963–64: 461
  Water and sanitation systems in rural areas bill,
      1965: 555
  Wholesome Meat Act, **1967**: 541
  Wholesome Poultry Products Act, **1968–69**: 451
  Wild and Scenic Rivers Act, **1968–69**: 510
  Wilderness Act, **1963–64**: 554
  Wolf Trap Farm Park, Va., **1966**: 522
  Woodrow Wilson Memorial Act of 1968,
      1968–69: 560
  Wool fabrics, imports of certain, **1968–69**: 562
  Zinc and nickel, bills authorizing release from
      national stockpile, **1965**: 599
Legislative, and Judicial Salaries, Commission on
      Executive, **1968–69**: 676 (p. 1266), 678
      (p. 1305), 694
Legislative branch, **1965**: 42, 317, 440
  Relations with executive branch, **1963–64**: 527;
      1965: 440, 495, 502, 515
Legislative Branch Appropriation Act, 1967,
      1966: 417 [6]
Legislative Conference, National, **1967**: 409
Legislative Leaders Conference, National,
      1966: 273
Legislative program, the President's, **1963–64**: 11,
      22, 91, 158, 173, 199, 218 [14], 219,
      221, 228, 233, 235, 238, 267, 268, 270,
      280 [6], 287, 290, 292, 297, 311, 314,
      322, 323, 326, 334, 338, 373, 388, 391,
      398, 406, 415, 431, 434, 477, 482, 488,
      496, 755, 798; **1965**: 249, 277, 319 [1];
      1966: 6 (p. 3), 8 [5], 26 (pp. 48, 55–56,

Legislative program – *continued*
63–64), 34 (p. 101), 353, 436, 474 [21],
477 [1], 487, 545, 599 [1, 6], 607 [13],
610 [2]; **1967**: 204 [15], 225 [12–14],
253, 328 [7], 353, 358 [3, 8, 12], 393,
417 [1, 13], 420, 430, 460 [5, 14], 465,
467, 468, 482, 499, 500, 554 [6, 16],
575n.; **1968–69**: 4, 14 (p. 29), 153 [16],
154, 155, 171, 192, 195, 212, 275 [5],
332, 336, 338, 339 [7], 350, 380, 390,
406, 418, 467 [1], 481, 499, 529, 532,
564, 565, 566, 567, 601, 640n., 644,
646 [14], 655, 672, 676 (p. 1264), 690
Campaign remarks on, **1963–64**: 571, 630, 635,
745
News conference remarks, **1963–64**: 54 [6, 10],
170 [13], 242 [12, 22], 266 [21], 271
[7], 285 [15], 294 [2], 316 [13], 420
[9], 462 [11], 486 [14], 780 [20, 22,
24], 818 [1]
Lehman, Herbert H., **1963–64**: 25, 27, 157, 373;
1966: 510; **1967**: 540
Lehman, Mrs. Herbert H., **1963–64**: 157
Le'iato, Chief T., **1966**: 537
Leibman, Morris, **1963–64**: 563 [5], 591;
1967: 87
Leighton, Robert B., **1965**: 391
LeMay, Gen. Curtis E., **1963–64**: 266 [18], 610;
1965: 37; **1968–69**: 568, 569
LeMay, Mrs. Curtis E., **1965**: 37
Lemberger, Ernst, **1966**: 272
Lend-lease, **1967**: 313n.
Leness, George J., **1963–64**: 296
Lenin, Nikolai, **1963–64**: 686; **1967**: 395;
1968–69: 50
Lenz, Winthrop C., **1967**: 85n.
Leonard, Edward J., **1963–64**: 547
Leonard, Ernest, **1963–64**: 693
Leonard, Mrs. Kitty C., **1963–64**: 374
Leonard, W. W., **1967**: 1n.
Leonardo Da Vinci, **1966**: 216
Leoni, Raul (President of Venezuela), **1966**: 366
Leonov, Lt. Col. Aleksei, **1965**: 106;
1968–69: 387
Leopold, Aldo, **1968–69**: 700
Leprosy, prevention, **1968–69**: 685
Lerner, Marjorie, **1967**: 396n.
Lesinski, Repr. John, **1963–64**: 356
Less developed countries and new nations,
1963–64: 32, 34, 244, 272, 631, 643;
1965: 2, 200, 325, 378, 541
See also Developing nations; *specific countries.*
Africa, **1965**: 2, 141, 142n.
Asia, **1965**: 2
Assistance, **1963–64**: 45, 51, 76, 91 (p. 117),
124 (pp. 162, 166), 132 (p. 185), 227,
280, 361, 400, 482n., 483, 617, 702;
1965: 7, 15, 18, 32 (p. 90), 35 (pp. 107,

Less developed countries – *continued*
Assistance – *continued*
112), 47, 117 [3], 136, 139, 149, 169,
172, 176 [1, 3], 194, 203, 294, 450,
495, 660
Communist aggression, **1965**: 18
Economic and social development, **1965**: 18,
139, 149
Economy of, **1963–64**: 396, 634, 641, 702, 757
Exports, **1963–64**: 193
Peace Corps projects in, **1965**: 83
Private investment in, **1963–64**: 617; **1965**: 18,
450
Standards of living, **1963–64**: 77
Trade, **1963–64**: 248
Leto, Carlo J., **1967**: 324n.
Leukemia, **1966**: 156; **1968–69**: 111
Levin, Sam, **1968–69**: 548
Levinson, Lawrence E., **1968–69**: 17, 332
Leviticus, Book of, **1966**: 365
Levitt, Arthur, **1966**: 510–512
Lewis, Lt. Fred M., **1967**: 324n.
Lewis, John L., **1963-64**: 568; **1967**: 484
Lewis, John P., **1963–64**: 336 [7]
Lewis, Meriwether, **1963–64**: 573
Lewis, Roger, **1966**: 625n.
Lewis, Warren K., **1965**: 646n.
Lewis, Dr. Warren Kendall, **1966**: 61n.
Lewiston, Maine, **1966**: 399
Lexington, Va., **1963–64**: 359
Li Kwoh-ting, **1967**: 219
Libby Dam, Mont., **1963–64**: 135, 563 [3], 573,
656; **1968–69**: 330
Liberation Front, National, **1967**: 80 [4], 132
[7], 312ftn. (p. 702), 554 [1], 564
Liberia, **1968–69**: 181, 433n.
President William V. S. Tubman, **1968–69**: 157,
159, 181
Liberty, U.S.S., **1967**: 264 [4]
Liberty Bell, **1966**: 323, 365
Miniature, gift, **1966**: 472
"Liberty Bell," Mercury II nickname, **1965**: 120
Liberty bonds, **1966**: 472
Liberty Island National Monument, **1965**: 242
Liberty State Park, New Jersey, **1965**: 242
Libonati, Repr. Roland V., **1963–64**: 356
Librarian of Congress (L. Quincy Mumford),
1966: 424n.
Librarians, need for, **1965**: 9
Libraries, **1966**: 337, 424; **1967**: 507
Appalachian region, **1968–69**: 701
Construction, **1963–64**: 91 (p. 112)
District of Columbia, **1965**: 151; **1966**: 27
Dwight D. Eisenhower Library, Abilene, Kans.,
1965: 412 [1]
Franklin D. Roosevelt Library, Hyde Park, N.Y.,
1965: 210, 412 [1]

Libraries — *continued*
  George C. Marshall Research Library, dedica-
      tion, **1963–64**: 359
  Handicapped persons, services, **1966**: 362
  Harry S. Truman Library, Independence, Mo.,
      1965: 412 [1], 420
  John F. Kennedy Library, Cambridge, Mass.,
      1965: 412 [1]
    Proposed, **1963–64**: 773
  Legislation, **1963–64**: 650, 669
  Library of Congress, **1965**: 412 [1]; **1966**: 362;
      1967: 423
  Lyndon Baines Johnson Presidential Library,
      Austin, Tex., **1965**: 411, 412; **1968–
      69**: 260, 646 [15], 655
  Medical, **1965**: 581
  National Library Week, 1964, **1963–64**: 254
  Public, **1966**: 95, 337
  Rural areas, **1968–69**: 142
  School and college, **1965**: 9, 455, 479, 527;
      1968–69: 4, 54
  Winston Churchill Memorial Library,
      1963–64: 263
Libraries, National Advisory Commission on,
    1966: 424
Libraries, President's Committee on, **1966**: 424
Library Commission, National, **1966**: 337
Library of Congress, **1965**: 412 [1]; **1966**: 362;
    1967: 423
Library Services Act, **1967**: 507
  Amendment, **1963–64**: 181
Library Services and Construction Act, **1965**: 32
    (p. 94), 340
  Amendments, **1967**: 507
  Amendments of 1966, **1966**: 95, 337
Lichtenstein, Zalmen, **1965**: 642n.
Lie, Trygve, **1968–69**: 214, 650
Life expectancy, **1963–64**: 178, 179, 642, 650,
    755; **1965**: 72, 154, 354, 378, 401, 406;
    1966: 228, 271, 273, 395; **1967**: 55,
    77, 114, 286; **1968–69**: 108, 113, 442
Life insurance bill for Federal employees, veto,
    1966: 453
Life magazine, **1965**: 459
  Kosygin interview, **1968–69**: 51 [13]
Lifesaving awards, AAA, **1963–64**: 317; **1965**:
    232
Lilienthal, David E., **1966**: 154, 549ftn. (p.
    1261); **1967**: 73, 104 [14], 116, 117,
    131, 364, 364n.; **1968–69**: 304
Lillie, Mildred L., **1966**: 210n.
Limousine, presidential, **1968–69**: 549
Lin, Dato Ong Yoke, **1963–64**: 471n.
Lin Piao, **1966**: 420
Lincoln, Abraham, **1963–64**: 111, 139, 185, 198,
    204, 228, 250, 277, 290, 301, 334, 342,
    533, 596, 693, 770, 773, 778, 796n.,
    800, 808; **1965**: 47, 48, 78, 94, 107,

Lincoln, Abraham — *continued*
    117 [1], 141, 154, 179, 213, 299, 305,
    356, 436, 503, 551, 644; **1966**: 2, 19,
    44, 51, 60, 66, 78, 175, 177, 248, 349–
    350, 353, 394–395, 414, 504, 509,
    558; **1967**: 3 (pp. 2, 7), 32, 35, 49, 55,
    81, 144, 161, 229, 251, 323, 346, 382,
    387, 407, 449n., 451, 453, 481, 487,
    495 [11]; **1968–69**: 40, 65n., 70, 138,
    143, 148, 158, 163, 195, 210, 212, 225,
    227, 230n., 238, 298, 305, 452, 540,
    576, 612, 624n., 648
  Birthday commemoration, **1965**: 64
  Campaign remarks on, **1963–64**: 588, 590, 603,
      635, 649, 667, 669, 677, 678, 680, 727,
      728, 732, 746, 747, 748, 751, 765
  News conference remarks on, **1963–64**: 150
      [4], 170 [13], 266 [20]
  Statue presented to Mexico, **1966**: 174–175,
      177
  White House dinner service collection,
      1965: 101
Lincoln, Franklin B., Jr., **1968–69**: 646 [3]
Lincoln, Gould, **1968–69**: 212
Lincoln Memorial, **1963–64**: 185; **1965**: 64, 70;
    1967: 49, 387, 441
Lindbergh, Charles A., **1968–69**: 616
Lindbergh, Charles A., Sr., **1965**: 242
Linder, Harold F. (Chairman, Export-Import Bank
    of the United States), **1968–69**: 136
Lindsay, John V., **1966**: 401 [4]; **1967**: 251, 326,
    327, 460 [10]; **1968–69**: 191 [9], 260n.,
    339 [3], 540, 672
Lindsay, Mrs. John V., **1968–69**: 540
Lindsay, Robert G., **1966**: 510
Lindsay, Vachel, **1968–69**: 87
Linen, James A., **1965**: 459; **1967**: 510n.;
    1968–69: 596
Ling, James, **1968–69**: 470, 471
Linnehan, John, **1967**: 223 [4]
Linowitz, Sol M., **1963–64**: 402; **1965**: 7;
    1966: 501 [1], 635 [14], 642 [2]
Lions Clubs, International Association of,
    1965: 438, 529
Lipchitz, Jacques, **1963–64**: 397n.
Lipmann, Fritz Albert, **1966**: 652n.; **1967**: 37n.
Lippman, Walter, **1963–64**: 26, 568, 608;
    1968–69: 242, 260, 459, 696 [1]
Lisagor, Peter, **1965**: 353 [20]; **1966**: 338 [9];
    1967: 330 [1]; **1968–69**: 275 [3]
Liskany, Michael, **1966**: 435
Liteky, Chaplain (Capt.) Angelo J., **1968–69**: 594
Literacy Corps, Iran, **1967**: 363
Litter control, **1968–69**: 122
Little, Malcolm (Malcolm X), **1968–69**: 298
"Little Congress," **1968–69**: 212
Liu Chieh, **1967**: 219

Liuzzo, Mrs. Viola, **1968–69**: 298
  Death of, **1965**: 135
Liverpool, Earl of, **1966**: 359
Livestock, **1968–69**: 85, 94
  Emergency feed, **1967**: 138
  Exports, **1965**: 47
  Foot-and-mouth disease (rinderpest) preven-
    tion, **1968–69**: 364
  Industry, **1963–64**: 732; **1965**: 168
  Prices, **1966**: 357, 592, 630 [14]
  Screwworm eradication, **1966**: 357; **1967**: 319,
    448; **1968–69**: 624
Living standard, **1968–69**: 612
Llano, Texas, **1966**: 417 [15]
Lleras Camargo, Alberto, **1963–64**: 9n.
Loan Bank Board, Federal Home, **1966**: 473,
    530, 642 [3, 19]; **1967**: 3 (p. 8), 6 [11],
    16 (p. 87), 88, 315n., 420
Loan Committee on Urban Problems, Joint Sav-
    ings Bank-Savings and, **1968–69**: 114
Loane, Archbishop Marcus, **1966**: 545
Loans, **1966**: 444; **1967**: 13 (p. 41, 59), 420
  Agricultural, **1967**: 6 [8], 305
  Bank policies, **1966**: 444, 473
  Business, **1966**: 26 (pp. 55, 63, 66), 141 [3, 5],
    155, 199, 445 [5]
  Construction, **1968–69**: 587
  Consumer credit, **1966**: 6 (p. 6), 34 (p. 108),
    140, 394, 445 [8]; **1967**: 200
  Effect on economy, **1968–69**: 39 (p. 84)
  Export, **1968–69**: 39 (p. 99, 102), 377, 422,
    449
  Farmers, **1968–69**: 247
  Federal, **1968–69**: 39 (p. 90), 467 [3]
  Federal programs, private investment in,
    1965: 506; **1966**: 182, 199
  Foreign, voluntary restraint, **1968–69**: 684 (p.
    1319)
  Fraud, **1968–69**: 678 (p. 1292)
  Housing, **1968–69**: 39 (p. 87, 103), 40, 47 (p.
    141), 72, 87, 94, 113, 229, 402, 599,
    678 (p. 1281)
  Housing mortgage, **1966**: 338 [14], 445 [7],
    451, 473, 642 [3, 19]
  Indian development, **1968–69**: 113
  Interest rates.
    See main heading, Interest rates.
  International, **1963–64**: 617; **1965**: 18, 60,
    149, 257, 319 [8], 393, 495, 638n.;
    1966: 41, 243; **1968–69**: 1 [1, 15],
    2, 11, 47 (p. 135), 146, 241, 684 (p.
    1319)
  Mortgage, **1965**: 90; **1967**: 88, 420
  Private, **1966**: 401 [19]
  Rural areas, **1965**: 75; **1966**: 584; **1967**: 114;
    1968–69: 39 (p. 101)
  Savings and loan associations, **1967**: 3 (p. 8);
    1968–69: 42 (p. 141), 72, 87, 114, 115

Loans — *continued*
  Small business, **1965**: 38, 75, 270; **1966**: 30,
    199, 231; **1967**: 427, 504
  Student, **1963–64**: 47, 53, 132 (p. 189), 413,
    676, 755; **1965**: 2, 5, 9, 100, 455, 479,
    539, 578, 603; **1966**: 3, 26 (p. 63), 95,
    189, 265, 392, 584; **1967**: 77, 304, 338,
    490; **1968–69**: 39 (p. 106), 54, 320,
    473, 678 (p. 1293), 684 (p. 1322)
    Advisory Council on Insured, **1966**: 3
  Truth in lending, **1967**: 16 (p. 86), 57, 342,
    393, 430, 460 [5], 465, 499, 503, 520,
    534, 539; **1968–69**: 49, 154, 164, 270,
    280, 281, 545
  Urban development, **1968–69**: 676 (p. 1265)
  Waste disposal systems, **1966**: 584; **1967**: 114
  Water programs, **1968–69**: 39 (p. 101), 678
    (p. 1301)
Lobbying, **1967**: 236
Loc, Prime Minister.
  See Nguyen Van Loc.
Local government, **1966**: 34 (p. 98); **1967**: 121,
    123; **1968–69**: 416
  See also Federal-State-local governmental
    responsibilities; Federal-State-local re-
    lations.
  Credit, **1968–69**: 39 (p. 87)
  Employees, **1968–69**: 84, 100, 312, 678 (p.
    1303)
  Federal aid, **1968–69**: 678 (p. 1303)
  Law enforcement, **1968–69**: 14 (p. 30), 39 (p.
    107), 50, 57, 59, 100, 235, 325, 542,
    553, 557 [8], 678 (pp. 1281, 1291,
    1292)
  Police, **1968–69**: 202
Locher, Ralph S., **1963–64**: 405, 406, 543, 642
Lockbourne Air Force Base, Ohio, **1963–64**: 322
Locke, Eugene M., **1966**: 247ftn. (p. 567);
    1967: 116, 126–128, 131, 134, 225 [2],
    309 [1], 567
Lockheed Aircraft Corporation, **1963–64**: 201
    [2]; **1965**: 339
Lockheed aircraft plant, Georgia, **1963–64**: 330
Locomotive Engineers, Brotherhood of,
    1963–64: 252, 284
Locomotives, inspection, **1965**: 281
Lodge, Henry Cabot, **1963–64**: 83, 218 [23, 25,
    26], 223, 274, 290, 348, 379ftn. (p.
    735), 436, 502, 605, 612; **1965**: 347
    [1, 5, 6], 353 [1, 12], 370, 388 [1],
    412 [3], 421; **1966**: 52 [2], 65 [8, 12],
    86, 141 [10], 188 [3], 214, 228, 236
    [1], 273, 334 [4], 338 [19], 383, 492
    [1], 578 [11], 628 [1], 642n., 645;
    1967: 3 (p. 12), 104 [5, 14, 17], 70 [1],
    116, 126–128, 130n., 131, 132, [1, 4,
    11, 13], 134, 201, 225 [2, 11], 309 [1],
    352, 375ftn. (p. 820)

Lodge, Henry Cabot — *continued*
  News conference remarks on, **1963–64**: 170
      [5], 201 [5, 18], 211 [22], 246 [4], 256
      [2, 5, 9], 285 [1, 17], 336 [15], 420 [1,
      4, 6, 13], 504 [4, 9, 11], 516 [11], 560
      [3], 780 [6]
Lodge, Mrs. Henry Cabot, **1965**: 347 [5], 421
Loeb, John, **1968–69**: 470, 471, 672n.
Loeb, Mrs. John, **1968–69**: 672n.
Loeser, Charles, **1963–64**: 24
Loevinger, Lee, **1963–64**: 434
London, Commonwealth Prime Ministers' Con-
      ference, **1965**: 319 [14], 331
London, visit of Robert F. Kennedy to,
      1963–64: 156
London Times, **1967**: 371
Loney, Mrs. Kate Deadrich, **1965**: 181, 183n.
Long, Repr. Clarence D., **1963–64**: 703;
      1966: 509; **1967**: 286
Long, Sen. Edward V., **1963–64**: 188, 189, 263,
      694, 695; **1965**: 394; **1966**: 22, 442
Long, Repr. Gillis W., **1963–64**: 648
Long, Huey, **1963–64**: 648; **1965**: 72, 223, 319
      [17], **1966**: 509
Long, Sen. Russell B., **1963–64**: 197, 646, 648;
      1965: 163, 183, 251, 319 [17], 321,
      329, 330, 394; **1966**: 88 [22], 132,
      157, 158 [10], 221, 237, 509; **1967**: 6
      [17], 204 [8], 216, 533; **1968–69**: 2,
      554, 599
  Letter, tariffs on reprocessed wool fabrics,
      1968–69: 671n.
Long, Mrs. Russell B., **1963–64**: 648
Long, Stuart, **1966**: 630 [14]
Long Beach, Calif., **1963–64**: 654n.
Long Beach, U.S.S., **1963–64**: 619 [5]
Long Island, N.Y., **1966**: 512
Long Island Sound bridge, **1967**: 223 [11]
Longfellow, Henry Wadsworth, **1963–64**: 606,
      764; **1966**: 326; **1968–69**: 122
Longshoremen's Association, International,
      1963–64: 195, 494, 614; **1965**: 58, 65
  Strike, **1968–69**: 636
  See also Maritime labor disputes.
Longworth, Mrs. Nicholas (Alice Roosevelt),
      1965: 3, 201; **1967**: 450
Lonstein, Benjamin, **1966**: 395
Look Magazine, **1963–64**: 593; **1965**: 171;
      1966: 165; **1967**: 182n.; **1968–69**: 219n.
Lop Nor, China, **1963–64**: 686
López, Arellano, Oswaldo (President of Hon-
      duras), **1968–69**: 366, 374, 375
López, Arellano, Mrs. Oswaldo, **1968–69**: 374
López Mateos, Adolfo, **1963–64**: 58, 598, 599;
      1965: 119; **1966**: 174, 630 [3], 639;
      1967: 408 [7], 454; **1968–69**: 623, 624
  News conference remarks on, **1963–64**: 28
      [14], 54 [8], 71 [1], 587 [2, 6]

López Mateos, Adolfo — *continued*
  Visit, **1963–64**: 192, 193, 194, 596
López Mateos, Señora, **1963–64**: 192, 194, 596
Lord, Bishop John Wesley, **1966**: 189
Los Alamos Scientific Laboratory, **1967**: 76
Los Angeles, Calif., **1963–64**: 192, 194; **1965**: 54;
      1967: 281, 418; **1968–69**: 114, 292n.
  Campaign remarks, **1963–64**: 733
  Civil disorder, **1965**: 426, 436, 448 [17], 452,
      453, 454 [5], 463 [15]
  Democratic fundraising dinner, **1963–64**: 415
  Federal assistance, **1965**: 453
  Mayor Samuel W. Yorty, **1963–64**: 194;
      1965: 453; **1966**: 56, 236ftn. (p. 537);
      1967: 227
  Public powerplant, **1963–64**: 486 [7]
  Report on, **1965**: 453n.
  Small business development center, proposed,
      1965: 453
  Watts area, **1966**: 236 [13]; **1967**: 55
Los Angeles International Airport, **1966**: 56
Los Angeles Times, **1967**: 281
Los Banos, the Philippines, **1966**: 550
Los Chorros picnic site, El Salvador, **1968–69**: 371
Los Padres National Forest, Calif., **1967**: 20, 29,
      96
Louchheim, Mrs. Katie S., **1963–64**: 204n.;
      1965: 91, 392; **1966**: 509; **1967**: 93;
      1968–69: 138
Louise Lykes, S.S., keel-laying ceremony,
      1963–64: 110
Louisiana, **1967**: 270
  Campaign remarks, **1963–64**: 646, 648
  Gov. John J. McKeithen, **1963–64**: 618, 646,
      647, 648; **1967**: 297 [2], 533
  Hurricane relief, **1963–64**: 618, 647; **1965**: 605
  Remarks, **1967**: 533; **1968–69**: 472
  School desegregation, **1965**: 470
  Voting registration, **1965**: 448 [9]
Louisville, Ky., **1966**: 351
  Campaign remarks, **1963–64**: 643, 644
  Mayor Kenneth Schmied, **1966**: 351
Louisville & Nashville Railroad, **1968–69**: 626
Love, Gov. John A., **1965**: 319 [20]; **1966**: 413–
      414, 436, 491n., 492 [1]
Love, Rodney M., **1963–64**: 680; **1965**: 190;
      1966: 431, 434–435
Lovelace, Terry, **1968–69**: 238n.
Lovelace, Dr. W. Randolph, II, **1963–64**: 273;
      1965: 652
Lovell, James A., Jr., **1965**: 636, 656; **1966**: 618,
      625; **1967**: 431; **1968–69**: 616, 637n.,
      647, 652, 662
Lovell, Mrs. James A., Jr., **1968–69**: 645n.
Lovett, Robert A., **1963–64**: 27, 359, 563 [5],
      591, 605, 688 [3, 8], 696, 747
Low income housing, **1966**: 26 (p. 61), 30, 67,
      158 [10], 223, 236 [13], 277 [1], 413,

Low income housing – *continued*
    525; **1967**: 4, 13 (p. 60), 88, 114, 120,
    179, 355, 467; **1968–69**: 14 (p. 29), 19,
    26, 39 (p. 102), 50, 87, 91, 94, 133,
    152, 154, 164, 278, 319, 382, 402,
    426, 435, 470, 471, 506, 625, 676 (p.
    1265), 678 (pp. 1289, 1290), 684 (pp.
    1324, 1325), 699
  Experimental project, **1968–69**: 435
Lowe, E. C., **1966**: 413
Lowe, Linda, **1966**: 289
Lowell, Robert, Jr., **1965**: 403
Lower Mekong Basin Coordinating Committee,
    1965: 199, 294
Lownds, Col. David E., **1968–69**: 267
Loyal Legion of the United States, Military
    Order of the, **1967**: 49n.; **1968–69**: 70n.
LSD (Lysergic Acid Diethylamide), **1968–69**: 14
    (p. 30), 59, 60, 109, 217, 390, 561, 678
    (p. 1292)
Lubbock, Texas, **1967**: 448
Lübke, Heinrich (President of West Germany),
    1963–64: 73; **1967**: 181
Lucas, C. Payne, **1967**: 317n.
Lucas, Capt. Jon, **1967**: 9
Lucas, Scott, **1963–64**: 635
Luce, Henry, death, **1967**: 75
Lucey, Patrick J., **1963–64**: 746
Lucey, Archbishop Robert E., **1966**: 167–168;
    1968–69: 499n.
Luevano, Daniel M., **1963–64**: 201 [1], 442;
    1966: 315n.
LULAC (League of United Latin American Citi-
    zens), **1966**: 236 [14]; **1968–69**: 68
Lumber imports, **1963–64**: 80
Lumley, Kathryn, **1967**: 396n.
Luna 9, Soviet spacecraft, **1966**: 50
Lunar Science Institute, **1968–69**: 107
Lunch programs in schools, **1963–64**: 292;
    1965: 47, 139, 149; **1966**: 26 (p. 63),
    95, 340, 508, 520; **1967**: 15, 39, 63,
    228, 353, 405; **1968–69**: 94, 678 (p.
    1297)
Lung cancer, **1968–69**: 39 (p. 104)
Lunt, Alfred, **1963–64**: 568
Lush, Jay L., **1968–69**: 695n.
Lusitania, U.S.S., **1963–64**: 493, 648, 703;
    1965: 88; **1966**: 563; **1968–69**: 142
Luther, Martin, **1967**: 18
Luxembourg, U.S. Ambassador Patricia Roberts
    Harris, **1965**: 301n.; **1966**: 136n.
Luxon, Norval Neil, **1963–64**: 339
Lykes Bros. Steamship Co., **1963–64**: 110n.
Lynch, Barbara Ann, **1965**: 336n.
Lynch, Thomas, **1965**: 422n.
Lyndon B. Johnson Australian Science Scholars,
    1966: 545–546; **1967**: 1; **1968–69**: 453
Lyndon B. Johnson Library, **1968–69**: 260, 646
    [15], 655

Lyndon B. Johnson School, San Salvador, El
    Salvador, **1968–69**: 369, 370
Lynn, Lt. Col. Frank, **1966**: 246
Lyons, John, **1967**: 4n.
Lysergic Acid Diethylamide.
  See LSD.

Maas, Maj. Gen. Melvin J., **1963–64**: 260, 271
    [6], 302
Macapagal, Diosdado, **1963–64**: 587 [2], 623,
    626, 627; **1965**: 655
Macapagal, Mrs. Diosdado, **1963–64**: 626;
    1965: 655
MacArthur, Arthur, **1963–64**: 247
MacArthur, Gen. Douglas A., **1963–64**: 247,
    266 [22]; **1966**: 52 [3], 410, 546;
    1968–69: 384
MacArthur, Mrs. Douglas, **1963–64**: 247
Macaulay, Thomas Babington, **1963–64**: 187;
    1965: 308; **1966**: 86, 216
MacDonald, Maj. Gen. A. L., **1968–69**: 283 [4]
MacDonald, Gordon, **1965**: 166n.
MacDonald, J. Clifford, **1963–64**: 27
MacDonald, Mrs. J. Clifford, **1963–64**: 27
Macdonald, Repr. Torbert H., **1963–64**: 727;
    1967: 474
Macedonia, **1965**: 280, 378
MacFarlane, W. D., **1963–64**: 297
MacGregor, Repr. Clark, **1965**: 189
Mach 2.3 aircraft, proposed, **1963–64**: 310
Machen, Hervey G., **1963–64**: 703; **1967**: 193,
    286
Machine Workers, International Union of Elec-
    trical, Radio and, **1966**: 496
Machinery, **1966**: 34 (p. 100), 141 [5], 445 [5,
    7], 451; **1967**: 16 (p. 79), 103, 104 [1]
Machinist Non-Partisan Political League, National
    Planning Committee of the, **1963–64**:
    158
Machinists and Aerospace Workers, International
    Association of, **1966**: 256n., 322, 360,
    535
Machinists Union, International, **1963–64**: 571
Mack Trucks Inc., **1963–64**: 745
Mackay, Repr. James A., **1965**: 242
Mackensen, Judith, **1963–64**: 606
Mackin, Catherine, **1966**: 338 [16]
MacLeish, Archibald, **1966**: 216; **1967**: 387
MacLeod, Dr. Colin M., **1965**: 175, 214
Macnaughton, Alan Aylesworth, **1966**: 400
Macomber, William B., **1966**: 154
Macon, Ga., **1963–64**: 717
  Campaign remarks, **1963–64**: 716
  Mayor B. F. Merritt, Jr., **1963–64**: 716
Macy, John W., Jr. (Chairman, Civil Service
    Commission), **1966**: 8 [1], 88 [12],
    105, 108, 116, 129, 136–137, 158 [1],

Macy, John W., Jr. – *continued*
    198, 208, 216, 239, 241, 247 [2], 266,
        276, 388, 404, 438, 580 [5]; **1967**: 95,
        121, 163, 184, 232, 343, 379, 388, 546;
        1968–69: 40, 67, 227, 303, 464, 480n.,
        516, 526, 539, 570, 581, 604
    See also Civil Service Commission, Chairman.
Madden, Repr. Ray J., **1963–64**: 639;
        1966: 579
Maddox, Gov. Lester G., **1967**: 297 [2];
        1968–69: 46n., 110
Maddox, U.S.S., **1963–64**: 498, 499
Madison, Dolley, **1966**: 359; **1968–69**: 648
Madison, James, **1963–64**: 513; **1965**: 39, 440,
        481; **1966**: 21, 77, 359, 435;
        1967: 115, 495 [11]; **1968–69**: 138
Magazines, **1968–69**: 64, 111
Magistrates, U.S., **1968–69**: 542
Magna Carta, **1963–64**: 413, 796n.;
        1968–69: 26
"Magna Carta," James C. Holt, **1965**: 376
Magnesium, **1968–69**: 47 (p. 144)
Magnuson, Sen. Warren G., **1963–64**: 136n.,
        198, 199, 215, 228, 382, 383, 575, 577;
        1965: 329, 330, 339; **1966**: 221, 240,
        269, 290, 326, 449, 520, 567, 568;
        1967: 231, 370, 474, 539; **1968–69**: 264
    Letter, **1963–64**: 154
Maguire, Charles, **1965**: 334n.; **1968–69**: 17
Maguire, John E., Sr., **1963–64**: 523n.
Maguire, Richard, **1963–64**: 224, 363, 396
Mahendra, King (Nepal), **1967**: 459, 461, 462
Mahon, Repr. George H., **1963–64**: 455 [1],
        763, 780 [4]; **1965**: 227n., 339;
        1966: 470, 494 [8], 628n.; **1967**: 85n.,
        105n., 156, 358 [12], 420, 448;
        1968–69: 169 [4], 677
Mahon, Lacy, Jr., **1963–64**: 713
Mahoney, Mrs. Florence, **1963–64**: 211 [6]
Mahoney, George P., **1966**: 494 [11]
Maier, Henry W., **1963–64**: 746; **1966**: 394n.
Mail, the President's, **1963–64**: 211 [3]
Mail order sale of guns, **1968–69**: 235, 296, 302,
        316, 320, 325, 333, 334, 355, 530, 553
Mail service, **1967**: 13 (pp. 43, 46, 52), 163, 168,
        546
    See also Postal service.
    Military personnel in Vietnam, **1966**: 37, 322,
        389, 571, 651
    Servicemen's, **1965**: 573
    Transportation, **1965**: 78
Maiman, Theodore H., **1966**: 194
Maine, **1963–64**: 602n., 788; **1965**: 350; **1966**:
        320 [14]; **1967**: 223 [3, 5]
    Campaign remarks, **1963–64**: 606
    Candidates for public office, **1963–64**: 606
    Gov. Kenneth M. Curtis, **1967**: 222n., 223 [3,
        6], 225 [21]

Maine – *continued*
    Gov. John H. Reed, **1963–64**: 455 [14], 606;
        1965: 291n.; **1966**: 121 [1, 5, 6], 124,
        [1–3, 7–8, 10], 320 [1], 397–399, 491n.,
        492 [1, 10]
    Passamaquoddy tidal power project,
        1963–64: 606
Maisel, Sherman, J., **1965**: 155, 319 [8]
Maiwandwal, Mohammed Hashim (Prime Minis-
        ter of Afghanistan), **1967**: 143–145
Maize shipments to India, **1966**: 52 [1]
Makarios, Archbishop, message to, **1963–64**: 70
"Making of the President, The, " Theodore H.
        White, **1965**: 353ftn. (p. 743)
Malagasy and African States, Union of,
        1965: 144
Malagasy Republic
    Assistance, **1963–64**: 483
    Tsiranana, Philibert, **1963–64**: 478, 479, 483
    U.S. relations with, **1963–64**: 478, 479, 483
Malaria, **1966**: 6 (p. 8), 45, 166, 461; **1967**: 110;
        1968–69: 304, 363
    Control, **1965**: 5
    Eradication, **1963–64**: 179, 716
Malawi, **1968–69**: 103
    Ambassador Vincent H. B. Gondwe, **1965**: 354
    President H. Kamuzu Banda, **1967**: 256
Malaysia, **1963–64**: 186, 475 [3]; **1966**: 559–
        560, 563, 568; **1967**: 401
    Ambassador Dato Ong Yoke Lin, **1963–64**:
        471n.
    Assistance, **1963–64**: 471, 474, 797
    Assistance to Vietnam, **1963–64**: 474
    British troop withdrawals, **1967**: 312 [17]
    Communist aggression, **1963–64**: 471
    Dispute with Indonesia, **1963–64**: 156n., 170
        [1], 471n., 474, 626n., 627;
        1965: 448 [21]
    Dispute with Philippines, **1963–64**: 156n.
    Economic and social development, **1963–64**:
        471, 474
    King Nasiruddin, **1966**: 559n., 560n.
    Prime Minister Abdul Rahman, **1966**: 559n.,
        560n.; **1967**: 409
    Queen Zaharah, **1966**: 559n., 560n.
    Rahman, Tunku Abdul, **1963–64**: 470, 471,
        474
    U.S. relations with, **1963–64**: 470, 471
    Visit, **1966**: 559–560
    Visit of Robert F. Kennedy, **1963–64**: 150 [17]
Malcolm, W. C., **1965**: 124
Malcolm X (Malcolm Little), **1968–69**: 298
Malik, Adam, **1966**: 484
Malnutrition, **1968–69**: 63, 113, 408, 463, 519,
        622, 678 (p. 1296), 685
    Research, **1966**: 45
Malone, Ross L., Jr., **1965**: 422n.
Malta, Giorgio Borg Olivier, **1963–64**: 585

Management.
See Labor-management relations.
Management, Government, **1967**: 13 (p. 57)
Management Policy, President's Advisory Committee on Labor, **1968-69**: 469
Managua, Nicaragua, remarks, **1968-69**: 373
Manatos, Mike N., **1963-64**: 211 [1], 657; **1966**: 478, 520
Manchester, N. H., **1966**: 397
Campaign remarks, **1963-64**: 607
Mayor Roland S. Vallee, **1966**: 397
Manes, Mrs. Jane, **1968-69**: 419
Manescu, Corneliu, **1968-69**: 308n.
Manganese dioxide, **1966**: 572n.
Manganese stockpiles, **1966**: 390
Manger, Julius, **1963-64**: 522
Mangla Dam, Pakistan, **1967**: 569
Manhattan Insurance Company, **1963-64**: 143 [3]
Manila, **1963-64**: 623
Releases, **1966**: 550-551
Manila Conference, **1966**: 401 [12], 461, 492 [1, 4], 501 [15], 514, 516 [13], 521, 531-532, 550-551, 554, 561, 563-566a, 568, 570, 577 [15-16], 578 [1], 607 [2-3]; **1967**: 112n., 127n., 130-131, 132 [1], 246; **1968-69**: 201, 232, 237, 400, 452
Agreement, **1966**: 580 [16]
Communique, **1966**: 577 [15]
Declaration of Goals of Freedom, **1966**: 549
Declaration on Peace and Progress in Asia and the Pacific, **1966**: 549
Joint statement, **1966**: 549
Message to the American people, **1966**: 553
Remarks, **1966**: 548
Statement, **1966**: 516 [1]
Manila conference on Asian Development Bank, **1965**: 628
Manila Pact (Southeast Asia Collective Defense Treaty), **1963-64**: 499; **1965**: 117 [8], 130, 156 [6], 227, 229, 230, 319 [17], 353 [8]; **1966**: 88 [17]
Mann, Fredric R., **1968-69**: 476
Mann, Horace, **1963-64**: 601
Mann, Thomas C., **1963-64**: 69, 95, 104, 220, 227, 269, 596, 726, 767, 809; **1965**: 295 [4], 319 [16], 347 [2]; **1966**: 247 [2], 266, 397, 401 [18], 474 [17]
Letter, **1963-64**: 46
News conference remarks on, **1963-64**: 54 [2, 4, 15], 71 [5, 9], 150 [2, 7, 14], 201 [6], 232 [1], 285ftn. (p. 522), 316 [9], 455 [16], 486 [3], 688 [8]
Manned orbiting laboratory, **1965**: 353 [10], 448 [1]

Manned space flights, **1965**: 117 [9], 310, 318, 448 [1]; **1966**: 40, 135, 371, 485, 618, 625
See also Astronauts; Space research and exploration.
Gemini.
See Gemini space flights.
Mercury, **1965**: 120, 121
Moon exploration, **1963-64**: 56, 132 (p. 186)
Soviet, **1965**: 116
Manned Spacecraft Center, **1965**: 310; **1968-69**: 107, 533n., 645n.
Manning, Bayless, **1966**: 373ftn. (p. 808)
Manning, Rt. Rev. Joseph L., **1965**: 623n.
Mannington, West Va., mine disaster, **1968-69**: 607
Manpower, National Advisory Commission on Health, **1966**: 169, 208, 301, 490, 536
Manpower, President's Committee on, **1963-64**: 212, 213; **1965**: 100; **1966**: 111, 536
Establishment, **1963-64**: 264
Manpower Act of 1965, **1965**: 173, 207, 490
Manpower Administration, **1967**: 412; **1968-69**: 24, 39 (p. 111), 86
Manpower Conservation, Task Force on, report, **1963-64**: 89
Manpower Conservation Program, **1963-64**: 213
Manpower Conservation Units, **1963-64**: 89
Manpower Development and Training Act of 1962, **1963-64**: 22, 53, 67, 99, 132 (p. 189), 133, 213, 219, 221, 235, 264, 290, 297, 305, 451n., 636, 642, 690n.; **1965**: 5, 29, 32 (p. 94), 38, 99, 100, 207, 340; **1966**: 26 (pp. 62-63), 111, 172, 250; **1967**: 13 (p. 54), 16 (p. 75), 39, 55, 199, 353; **1968-69**: 24, 26, 113, 220n., 587, 678 (p. 1295), 706n.
Amendments, approval, **1963-64**: 55
Amendments of 1966, **1966**: 111n., 588
Manpower Planning System, Cooperative Area, **1968-69**: 24, 444
Manpower resources, **1963-64**: 132 (p. 178), 287, 295; **1966**: 34 (p. 103), 112, 275, 301
Construction industry, **1968-69**: 699
Consultative committee, Federal-State-local, **1966**: 536
Development, **1963-64**: 47, 89, 124 (pp. 158, 162), 132 (pp. 176, 181, 182, 189), 160, 213, 227, 235, 264, 271 [5], 314, 406, 743, 787; **1965**: 5, 9, 32 (p. 94), 35 (pp. 106, 108, 112, 113), 38, 79, 92, 100, 102, 129, 132, 156 [2], 207, 215, 351, 480, 632; **1966**: 26 (p. 55), 111, 235, 275, 536, 588; **1967**: 12, 13 (p. 57), 16 (p. 83), 77, 121, 199, 412, 458; **1968-69**: 24-26, 39 (pp. 89, 104), 47

Manpower resources — *continued*
  Development — *continued*
      (p. 142), 75, 86, 91, 94, 109, 113, 114,
      444, 655, 678 (pp. 1281, 1294), 684
      (pp. 1313, 1314, 1316, 1319)
    Health, **1968-69**: 39 (p. 104), 408, 447
    Machinists, **1967**: 104 [1]
    Message to Congress, **1968-69**: 220
    Military, **1967**: 3 (p. 6)
    Peace Corps veterans, **1965**: 33
    Report, **1963-64**: 211 [3], 212, 213
    Report of the President, **1965**: 99, 100;
      1966: 111, 250, 275; **1967**: 199;
      1968-69: 706
    Scientific, **1963-64**: 456; **1968-69**: 687
    Shortages, **1967**: 16 (p. 79), 103, 104 [1]
    Utilization program, Federal, **1963-64**: 17, 38
Mansera, Frank (Pancho), **1967**: 452
Mansfield, Sen. Mike, **1963-64**: 28 [9], 58, 99,
      218 [25], 224, 267, 316 [24], 336 [14],
      527, 563 [15], 573, 575, 577;
      1965: 22 [16], 107, 113, 133, 156 [2],
      183, 223, 242, 329, 330, 394, 395 [5],
      412 [2], 413n., 415, 534, 546, 551, 555,
      559, 568n., 592; **1966**: 164n., 174n.,
      187, 188 [10], 221, 223, 237, 277 [12,
      17], 334 [1], 396-397, 399, 401 [15],
      445 [24], 470, 492 [9], 505, 518, 520,
      522-524, 531, 628 [1, 15]; **1967**: 6
      [17], 7, 34 [4], 169, 204 [2], 216, 236,
      264 [1], 278, 358 [3], 375 [18], 460 [5,
      9], 467, 502; **1968-69**: 191 [1], 212,
      258, 259, 292n., 330, 467 [1], 479, 510,
      536, 623, 624, 654, 655, 658, 672, 676
      (p. 1270), 690, 691
  Campaign remarks on, **1963-64**: 605, 656, 658,
      679
  Letters
    Crime control legislation, **1968-69**: 235
    Middle East conflict, **1967**: 257
    Railroad dispute, **1967**: 310
    Steel price increase, **1968-69**: 427
    Urban legislation, **1967**: 353
  Meat imports bill, **1963-64**: 344
  Vietnam conflict proposals, **1966**: 8 [12], 607
      [10]
Mansfield, Mrs. Mike, **1963-64**: 267, 656;
      1966: 397; **1967**: 216
Manufacturers, National Association of,
      1963-64: 402; **1965**: 438; **1968-69**: 25,
      548n.
Manufacturers taxes, **1965**: 255
Ma'o, Chief Tima, **1966**: 537
Maplethorpe, Wade L., **1963-64**: 211 [3]
Maracay, Venezuela, **1968-69**: 77
Marble Canyon National Monument, Ariz.,
      1968-69: 707n.
Marburger, Carl, **1967**: 396n.

March on Washington, Poor People's,
      1968-69: 51 [14], 169 [5], 275 [5],
      339 [7]
Marciano, Rocky, **1966**: 385n.
Marconi, William, **1965**: 449
Marcos, Ferdinand E. (President of the Philip-
      pines), **1965**: 655; **1966**: 417 [9],
      492 [4], 495, 501 [2], 505, 514, 516
      [1], 548-551, 577 [16]; **1967**: 328
      [12], 409; **1968-69**: 432
  Visit, **1966**: 458-459, 461
Marcos, Mrs. Ferdinand E., **1966**: 458-459, 550-
      551
Marden, Orison, **1967**: 221
Mare Island Naval Shipyard, California,
      1963-64: 449n.
Mares, Leonard V., **1967**: 324n.
Margain, Hugo B., **1965**: 558n.; **1966**: 174, 639;
      1967: 408 [7]
Margaret, Princess, **1965**: 616
Margolies, Daniel F., **1967**: 416n.; **1968-69**: 513n.
Mariana Islands, **1967**: 360
Marietta, Ga., **1968-69**: 109, 110
Marijuana, **1968-69**: 59, 60, 109, 390
Marine Band, **1965**: 519n.
Marine Consultative Organization, Intergovern-
      mental, **1967**: 240
Marine Corps, **1963-64**: 516 [3], 611, 703, 716,
      736; **1965**: 26, 212, 217, 223, 227, 229,
      319 [16]; **1967**: 485 [2, 3], 493, 518
      [1, 7], 527; **1968-69**: 34, 39 (p. 98),
      81 [2, 3], 109, 129, 267, 516, 521,
      537n., 541, 603, 688
  Commandant (Gen. Leonard F. Chapman),
      1968-69: 34, 129, 232, 267, 541
  Commandant (Gen. Wallace M. Greene, Jr.),
      1966: 516 [9], 641; **1967**: 361, 375
      [6, 19], 446
  Hoffman brothers in, letter, **1966**: 409
Marine Engineers' Beneficial Association, Na-
      tional, **1965**: 428
Marine resources, **1967**: 20, 101, 176;
      1968-69: 122, 124, 145, 692
  Food, **1967**: 20, 101, 491
  Pollution, **1967**: 240
  Report to Congress, **1967**: 101
  Sea grant colleges and programs, **1967**: 101
Marine Resources and Engineering Development,
      National Council on, **1966**: 326;
      1967: 20, 101, 240; **1968-69**: 124,
      692
Marine Resources and Engineering Development
      Act of 1966, **1966**: 326n.; **1967**: 101;
      1968-69: 692
Marine Science, Engineering, and Resources,
      Commission on, **1967**: 101
Mariner IV, **1965**: 27, 81, 305, 345, 391;
      1966: 40, 249; **1968-69**: 616

Mariner space project, **1965**: 27, 81
Marines, Women, **1966**: 8 [16]
Maritime Administration, **1966**: 98, 523;
  1968–69: 535, 678 (p. 1302)
Maritime Administrator (Nicholas Johnson),
  1963–64: 203; **1966**: 277 [5], 278
Maritime Advisory Committee, establishment of,
  1963–64: 316 [3]
Maritime Commission, Federal, **1966**: 98
Maritime fleet, **1965**: 17
Maritime labor disputes, **1963–64**: 195, 494n.,
  614; **1965**: 58, 65, 428; **1968–69**: 636
  Agreement, **1965**: 463 [3], 465
Maritime policy, U.S., **1965**: 459, 463 [3];
  1966: 474 [19]
Maritime Union of America, National,
  1963–64: 195
Maritime workers, **1965**: 459
Markel, Hazel, **1963–64**: 150 [16]
Marketing programs, **1963–64**: 248; **1965**: 2, 77
  Agricultural, **1963–64**: 255, 455 [7], 566,
    631, 757; **1965**: 46 [1], 47, 139, 149,
    168, 192, 307, 377, 597; **1966**: 62, 294
Marketing Service, Consumer and, **1966**: 140,
  245n.
Markman, Sherwin J., **1968–69**: 17
Marks, Leonard H. (Director, United States Infor-
  mation Agency), **1965**: 353 [4, 17], 468;
  1966: 141 [16], 537, 629, 644n.;
  1967: 238, 352; **1968–69**: 581
Marks, Mrs. Leonard, **1965**: 468
Marland, Sidney P., Jr., **1966**: 210n.; **1967**: 87n.
Mars, planet probes, **1965**: 27, 81, 305, 391;
  1966: 40
Mars exploration, **1967**: 13 (p. 50); **1968–69**: 39
  (p. 100), 107, 507, 616
Marsh, Jane, **1966**: 440
Marsh, Repr. John O., Jr., **1963–64**: 358
Marsh, William, **1965**: 115n.
Marshal Day, proclamation, **1963–64**: 523n.
Marshall, Burke, **1965**: 117 [1]; **1966**: 315n.,
  320 [10], 388; **1967**: 92, 104 [12],
  205
Marshall, Fred, **1963–64**: 455 [7]
Marshall, Gen. George C., **1963–64**: 294 [11],
  297 [2], 358, 612; **1965**: 156 [6],
  302; **1966**: 345; **1968–69**: 42, 109,
  283 [6], 384, 594, 696 [19]
Marshall, Mrs. George C., **1963–64**: 359
Marshall, George C., Research Library, dedica-
  tion, **1963–64**: 359
Marshall, Thurgood, **1965**: 353 [3], 443;
  1966: 136n., 248, 289n.; **1967**: 81,
  221, 264 [21], 266; **1968–69**: 631
  Question of successor, **1967**: 264 [7]
  Supreme Court appointment, **1967**: 263, 264
    [9, 21], 266, 267n.
Marshall, Mrs. Thurgood, **1965**: 443

Marshall Islands, **1967**: 360
Marshall plan, **1963–64**: 189, 244, 359, 562,
  607, 617, 648; **1965**: 18, 235, 450,
  570; **1966**: 11, 62, 200, 212, 272, 497,
  557; **1967**: 169n., 306n., 313n., 347n.;
  1968–69: 63, 143, 211, 214n.
Marshals, U.S., **1965**: 106 [5], 117 [1, 5]
  Conference, **1966**: 487
Marston, Dr. Robert Q., **1968–69**: 396, 589n.
Martha's Vineyard, Mass., **1967**: 290
Martin, Clarence D., Jr., **1965**: 290
Martin, Eddie, **1967**: 281
Martin, J. M., **1967**: 420n.
Martin, Repr. Joseph W., Jr., **1963–64**: 297
  [2]; **1965**: 420; **1966**: 361, 417 [15]
  Death, **1968–69**: 120
Martin, Louis, **1968–69**: 631
Martin, Mary, **1965**: 561
Martin, Paul, **1963–64**: 134, 135, 140; **1965**: 21,
  22 [1]; **1967**: 237, 238
Martin, Mrs. Ruby Grant, **1968–69**: 138n.
Martin, Thomas M., **1963–64**: 60
Martin, Mrs. Thomas M., **1963–64**: 60
Martin, Tony, **1963–64**: 199
Martin, William McC., Jr. (Chairman, Board of
  Governors, Federal Reserve System),
  1963–64: 295, 299, 486 [4], 530, 714,
  780 [3], 787; **1965**: 60, 77, 155, 638,
  641; **1966**: 115, 155, 158 [4], 473;
  1967: 6 [18], 104 [9], 329, 371, 420;
  1968–69: 2, 169 [17], 170, 317, 418
Martinez, Robert, **1965**: 322
Martínez Francisco, Antonio, **1965**: 221
Martini, Steve, **1966**: 478
Marx, Karl, **1966**: 386
Marxist system.
  See Communism.
Maryland, **1963–64**: 321; **1965**: 61, 70; **1966**:
  494 [11]; **1967**: 15
  Antipoverty program, **1963–64**: 321
  Assateague Island, **1965**: 54, 521
  Bloomington Dam, **1963–64**: 320
  Campaign remarks, **1963–64**: 612, 703
  Candidates for public office, **1963–64**: 703
  Gov. Spiro T. Agnew, **1967**: 286; **1968–69**: 184,
    529, 540, 567, 598, 599, 604, 696 [20]
  Gov. J. Millard Tawes, **1963–64**: 703;
    1965: 499, 521; **1966**: 122 [1, 2], 494
    [1, 2, 11]
  Primary election, **1963–64**: 246 [7], 256 [19],
    266 [24], 316 [15]
  Rail rapid transit system, **1965**: 499; **1967**: 154
  Remarks, **1967**: 135, 193, 319
Maryland, University of, **1968–69**: 38
Masferrer, Alberto, **1968–69**: 370, 372
Mason, Jerry, **1966**: 497n.
Mason, Jimilu, **1966**: 345n.
Mason, Walter, **1963–64**: 235

Mass spectrometer import tariffs, **1966**: 601
Mass Transportation Administration, Urban, proposed, **1968-69**: 93
Massachusetts, **1967**: 223 [2]
  Campaign remarks, **1963-64**: 727
  Gov. Endicott Peabody, **1963-64**: 338, 396, 727
  Gov. John A. Volpe, **1966**: 121 [1], 396-399, 407; **1967**: 222n., 223 [3, 4]; **1968-69**: 46n., 102, 406, 539, 646 [3]
Massey, Vincent, death, **1967**: 577
Masters, Mates and Pilots of America, International Organization of, **1965**: 428
Mateos, Lopez
  See López Mateos, Adolfo.
Material witnesses to crimes, interrogation, **1966**: 611
Maternal health services, **1963-64**: 755; **1965**: 5; **1966**: 95, 189, 580 [11]; **1967**: 39, 353, 479; **1968-69**: 3, 14 (p. 29), 39 (pp. 89, 104), 47 (p. 143), 111, 113, 270, 442, 568, 569, 662, 676 (p. 1265), 678 (pp. 1296, 1297), 684 (p. 1324)
Mathe, Brig. Gen. Robert E., **1967**: 466
Mather, Lt. Gen. G. R., **1967**: 532
Mathews, Charles W., **1965**: 310, 318, 320; **1966**: 625n.
Mathias, Repr. Charles McC., Jr., **1963-64**: 320, 321
Mathiasen, Mrs. Geneva, **1968-69**: 117
"Matinée sur la Seine; Beautemps," Claude Monet, **1963-64**: 24
Matson, Ollie, **1966**: 385n.
Matsunaga, Repr. Spark M., **1966**: 532-533
Matthews, Judge Burnita Shelton, **1963-64**: 257n.
Matthews, Repr. D. R. (Billy), **1963-64**: 198, 199, 713
Mattingly, Rev. T. J., **1963-64**: 325
Mattson, Everett, **1968-69**: 470, 471
Mauldin, William H. (Bill), **1965**: 554
Maurer, Ion Gheorghe (Prime Minister of Romania), **1967**: 312 [15]
Maverick, Maury, **1963-64**: 297; **1965**: 459; **1966**: 168, 417 [2]
Maxwell Air Force Base, Alabama, **1965**: 117 [5]
May, Mrs. Elizabeth Stoffregen, **1963-64**: 242 [4]
Maynard, Alex, **1965**: 179
Mayo, Dr. Charles C., **1968-69**: 415n.
Mayo, Dr. Charles W., **1963-64**: 211 [6]
  Death, **1968-69**: 415
Mayo, Robert P., **1968-69**: 677n.
Mayo, Dr. William H., **1968-69**: 415n.
Mayo Clinic, **1968-69**: 536
Mayo State Vocational School, Paintsville, Ky., **1963-64**: 291
Mayors, meetings with, **1966**: 155, 158 [3], 525
Mayors, United States Conference of, **1965**: 438; **1966**: 536; **1967**: 337

Mays Manufacturing Co., Inc., **1967**: 231n.
Mazzilli, Ranieri, **1963-64**: 243, 256ftn. (p. 458)
McAllister, W. W., **1966**: 168n.; **1967**: 151n.; **1968-69**: 357, 359
McBride, James W., **1967**: 420n.
McCain, Adm. John S., Jr., **1968-69**: 191 [4, 6, 7], 197, 198
McCall, Abner V., **1965**: 286n.
McCandless, Susan, **1966**: 25
McCandless, William F., **1966**: 25
McCarter, Walter J. (Administrator, National Capital Transportation Agency), **1966**: 84
McCarthy, Sen. Eugene J., **1963-64**: 433, 434, 435; **1965**: 181, 189; **1967**: 182, 495 [10], 518 [11]; **1968-69**: 142, 339 [10], 540
  Presidential candidacy (1968), **1967**: 554 [9]
McCarthy, Msgr. John F., **1963-64**: 97
McCarthy, Joseph R., **1963-64**: 462 [6]; **1966**: 155
McCarthy, Richard D., **1963-64**: 667; **1966**: 392, 510
McClanahan, Sidney B., **1963-64**: 695
McClellan, Sen. John L., **1963-64**: 597, 599; **1965**: 478; **1966**: 523; **1968-69**: 57
McClendon, Sarah, **1966**: 338 [14], 516 [16]; **1967**: 358 [9, 10], 375 [20]; **1968-69**: 51 [3], 171, 696 [1]
McCloy, John J., **1963-64**: 14, 15, 27, 349n., 563 [5], 591, 605, 688 [3, 8], 696, 747; **1966**: 482n., 506, 610 [8], 622, 626; **1967**: 502n., 545; **1968-69**: 1 [16]
McConaughy, Walter P., **1967**: 219
McCone, John A., **1965**: 209, 319 [19]; **1966**: 277 [14], 310, 315n.; **1967**: 252n.
  See also Central Intelligence Agency, Director.
McConnell, Gen. John P., **1968-69**: 48, 110; **1966**: 20, 516 [9]; **1967**: 9, 106, 485 [6]
McConnell, John W., **1967**: 170ftn. (p. 439), 207, 310
McConnell, Thomas R., **1963-64**: 116n.
McConnell Air Force Base, Kans. **1967**: 485 [6]
McCord, James N., **1963-64**: 645
McCormack, Repr. John W.
  See Speaker of the House of Representatives.
McCormack, Mrs. John W., **1963-64**: 228, 366; **1965**: 302; **1967**: 7n., 206, 216; **1968-69**: 32
McCracken, Paul W., **1967**: 85n.; **1968-69**: 677n.
McCrocklin, James H., **1963-64**: 778; **1965**: 603; **1966**: 315n., 404n.; **1967**: 184, 490n.; **1968-69**: 459
McCulloch, Repr. William M., **1965**: 107, 353 [18]; **1967**: 326; **1968-69**: 57, 293, 542
McCurdy, Robert, **1968-69**: 599
McDermott, Edward A.
  See Emergency Planning, Office of, Director.

McDivitt, Lt. Col. (Maj.) James A., **1965**: 304, 306, 310, 318, 320
McDonald, David, **1963-64**: 289, 290, 589, 728
McDonald, Adm. David L., **1963-64**: 619ftn. (p. 1194); **1966**: 516 [9], 645; **1967**: 308
McDonald, Frank, **1963-64**: 729
McDonald, Bishop William J., **1963-64**: 810n.; **1965**: 302
McDonnell, J. S., **1968-69**: 616
McDonnell, James C., Jr., **1968-69**: 25
McDonnell, James Smith, Jr., **1966**: 625n.
McDowell, Repr. Harris B., Jr., **1963-64**: 749, 750; **1966**: 515
McDowell County, W. Va., **1966**: 245
McElroy, Dr. William D., **1965**: 115n.
McEwen, John, **1966**: 541-542; **1967**: 561, 562
McEwen, Mrs. John, **1966**: 541
McEwen, Repr. Robert C., **1966**: 394
McEwen, Robert J., **1967**: 342n.
McFarland, Ernest W., **1963-64**: 649; **1968-69**: 501
McFarland, Mrs. Ernest W. (Edna), **1963-64**: 649
McFarland, Helen Hayes, **1968-69**: 108
McFarlane, William D., **1966**: 168, 417 [2]
McFarley, Curtis, **1965**: 566
McFeatters, Dale, **1965**: 88
McGannon, Donald, **1967**: 87n.
McGee, Sen. Gale W., **1963-64**: 242 [10], 657; **1966**: 188 [4], 500; **1967**: 33; **1968-69**: 505
McGhee, George C., **1963-64**: 818 [4]
McGiffert, David E., **1965**: 319 [10]
McGill, Ralph, **1963-64**: 568
McGinnis, Edward F., **1967**: 502
McGinty, 2d Lt. and Mrs. John J., III, **1968-69**: 129
McGovern, Frances, **1963-64**: 693
McGovern, Sen. George, **1968-69**: 691
McGowan, Richard, **1968-69**: 213 [9]
McGrath, Repr. Thomas C., Jr., **1963-64**: 338; **1966**: 504
McGraw-Hill, Inc., Media Information Bureau, **1963-64**: 285 [9]
McGrory, Mary, **1968-69**: 242
McHugh, Brig. Gen. Godfrey T., **1963-64**: 773
McIntyre, Sen. Thomas J., **1963-64**: 607; **1966**: 396-399
McIntyre, Mrs. Thomas J., **1966**: 396, 398
McKay, David O., **1963-64**: 736, 737n., **1965**: 101
McKay, Robert E., **1965**: 89
McKee, Rose, **1963-64**: 208, 362
McKee, Gen. William F., **1963-64**: 487; **1965**: 208 [6], 319 [19]; **1966**: 321-322, 654 [12]; **1967**: 265, 392
   See also Federal Aviation Agency, Administrator.

McKeldin, Theodore R., **1963-64**: 516 [16], 703; **1965**: 521; **1966**: 155, 189, 394n.; **1967**: 87n., 286
McKenna, Joseph, **1968-69**: 270
McKeon, William H., **1963-64**: 666, 667, 668, 669
McKinley, William, **1968-69**: 298
"McKinley, In the Days of," Margaret Leech Pulitzer, **1963-64**: 303
McKinney, Jerry E., **1968-69**: 604
McKinney, Robert, **1963-64**: 296; **1968-69**: 1 [1], 2, 83n., 116
McLain, George, **1963-64**: 733
McLean, Hunter, **1963-64**: 763
McLeay, Sir John and Lady, **1966**: 541-542
McLeod, Daniel R., **1963-64**: 719
McLeod, Yancey A., **1963-64**: 719
McMahon, William, **1967**: 562
McMahon Atomic Energy Act, **1968-69**: 378
McMichael, James F., **1965**: 642n.
McMillan, Repr. John L., **1963-64**: 719; **1965**: 486; **1966**: 586
McMillan, William M., **1963-64**: 207
McMullin, Sir Alister M. and Lady, **1966**: 541
McMurdo Station, Antarctica, **1965**: 220
McKeithen, Gov. John J., **1963-64**: 618, 646, 647, 648; **1967**: 297 [2], 533
McNair, Robert E., **1963-64**: 719; **1966**: 122 [1, 2], 650n.
McNally, Dave, **1966**: 509
McNally, John J., Jr., **1963-64**: 396
McNamara, Sen. Pat (Patrick V.), **1963-64**: 50, 356, 357, 431, 444; **1965**: 317, 354, 568n., 582; **1966**: 430-431; **1967**: 535
   Campaign remarks on, **1963-64**: 562, 745
   Letter, **1963-64**: 39n.
   McNamara-O'Hara Act.
      See Service Contract Act of 1965.
McNamara, Mrs. Patrick V., **1966**: 431
McNamara, Robert S., **1968-69**: 104, 110, 139n., 153 [4], 171, 174, 215, 500, 516, 669
   See also Defense, Secretary of.
McNamara, Mrs. Robert S., **1963-64**: 298; **1965**: 387; **1966**: 345; **1967**: 87n.; **1968-69**: 99
McNaughton, John T., **1963-64**: 201 [1], 316 [2], 442
   Death, **1967**: 316
McNaughton, Mrs. John T., **1967**: 316
McNerney, 1st Sgt. David H., **1968-69**: 487
McNichols, Stephen L. R., **1963-64**: 658
McPherson, Harry C., Jr., **1965**: 347 [8]; **1966**: 65 [1], 408n.; **1967**: 460 [1]; **1968-69**: 498
McVicker, Roy H., **1963-64**: 658; **1966**: 410, 413-414
Meader, Repr. George, **1963-64**: 357
Means, Marianne, **1966**: 338 [7]; **1967**: 104 [13]

Meany, George, **1963-64**: 22, 27, 221, 255, 379
       [7], 444, 513, 587 [1], 806; **1965**:
       223, 428, 539, 644; **1965**: 223, 428,
       539, 644; **1966**: 88 [20], 158 [3], 373 [8
       [8], 408n., 474 [20], 479, 573; **1967**:
       30, 168n., 252n., 261, 312 [1, 3], 534;
       1968-69: 42, 50, 141, 154, 164, 165,
       471, 670, 694
    Campaign remarks on, **1963-64**: 669, 745
    Dinner honoring, **1967**: 484
    Letter, **1963-64**: 195
Measles, **1966**: 45; **1967**: 286, 319; **1968-69**:
       19, 111, 442, 678 (p. 1295)
    Immunization in Africa, **1963-64**: 396
Meat
    Imports, **1963-64**: 211 [31], 344, 516 [14],
       732
    Inspection, **1963-64**: 132 (p. 187), 173;
       1967: 57, 465, 499, 503, 520, 522, 534,
       539, 541; **1968-69**: 39 (p. 101), 56,
       270, 451, 545
       Fees, **1965**: 32 (p. 88)
    Prices, **1963-64**: 242 [10], 246 [18]
    Production and sale of, **1963-64**: 246 [18]
Meat Inspection Act, **1967**: 7, 522, 541
Meatpacking industry, **1963-64**: 316 [6]
Medal of Honor.
    See under Awards and Citations.
Medal of Science, National.
    See Science, National Medal of.
Medals, presentation or acceptance.
    See Awards and citations.
Medendorp, Lt. Col. Alfred, **1966**: 246
Mediation Board, National, **1963-64**: 297 [2];
       1967: 207, 310
Mediation and Conciliation Service, Federal,
       1963-64: 614n.; **1966**: 496; **1967**:
       104 [15]; **1968-69**: 112
Medicaid, **1966**: 650 [11, 18]; **1967**: 13 (pp.
       46, 53), 16 (pp. 76, 85), 39, 77, 419,
       554 [6], 574; **1968-69**: 14 (pp. 29,
       32), 38, 39 (p. 103), 47 (p. 143), 50,
       87, 100, 111, 397, 467 [3], 678 (pp.
       1280, 1295, 1296), 684 (p. 1324)
Medical Association, American, **1965**: 295 [3],
       394; **1966**: 271, 395, 490
Medical Association, National, **1968-69**: 19, 20
Medical care, **1963-64**: 297, 444, 588, 746,
       750; **1965**: 5, 6, 89, 115, 525; **1966**:
       141 [3], 156, 208, 270, 346, 392, 395,
       490, 494 [6]; **1967**: 13 (p. 53), 39, 77,
       276, 291, 532
    See also Hospitals and medical care facilities;
       Health and health programs; Medicare.
    Children, **1967**: 13 (p. 60), 39, 114
    Consumer protection, **1963-64**: 173
    Costs, **1963-64**: 179; **1966**: 271, 401 [2],
       403; **1967**: 77

Medical care — *continued*
    District of Columbia, **1965**: 70
    Families with dependent children, **1966**: 26
       (p. 63)
    Federal-State program, **1966**: 157; **1967**:
       13 (p. 53)
    Government employees, **1967**: 25
    Group practice, **1963-64**: 179
    Handicapped persons, **1967**: 3 (p. 6), 114
    Highway accident casualties, **1966**: 98
    Maternal care, **1967**: 39, 353, 479
    Medicare bill.
       See main heading, Medicare bill.
    Military personnel, **1966**: 6 (p. 6), 334 [2],
       389, 433, 571; **1967**: 25, 92
    Older persons, **1963-64**: 219, 267, 292, 297,
       406, 541, 548, 640, 648, 667, 680;
       1965: 5, 32 (p. 94), 348, 394, 632;
       1966: 26 (p. 55), 95, 122 [2], 189,
       253, 271, 273, 309, 353, 429, 433, 509,
       545, 580 [7]; **1967**: 3 (p. 2), 12, 15, 81,
       114, 286, 298, 574
    Under social security.
       See Social security.
    Regional programs, report, **1967**: 477
    Rural areas, **1965**: 47
    Urban areas, **1965**: 9
    U.S. aid to foreign countries, **1965**: 223, 227,
       229, 246, 250, 293, 295 [3, 16], 406,
       649; **1966**: 22, 41, 45, 54, 77
    Veterans, **1965**: 163; **1967**: 13 (p. 55), 25
Medical Center, American Samoan Tropical,
       1966: 537
Medical College of Georgia, **1963-64**: 718
Medical complexes, **1965**: 5
Medical Costs, National Conference on, **1967**: 77
Medical and dental education, **1963-64**: 47,
       132 (p. 189), 179, 213, 520, 557, 620,
       755; **1965**: 2, 5, 6, 32 (p. 94), 100, 551,
       579
Medical device safety bill, **1967**: 57
Medical devices, consumer protection, **1966**: 140
Medical libraries, **1965**: 581
Medical Library Assistance Act of 1965, **1965**:
       581
Medical personnel, **1966**: 45, 169, 185, 495;
       1968-69: 47 (p. 143), 442, 678 (p.
       1296)
    Education, **1966**: 95, 111, 208, 253, 573, 580
       [7, 10]; **1967**: 15, 77; **1968-69**: 39
       (pp. 103, 107), 40, 111, 447, 678 (p.
       1296)
    Leaders, meeting with, **1966**: 271
    Military service, **1967**: 92
    Negroes, **1968-69**: 442
    Scholarships, **1968-69**: 447
    Shortage of, **1963-64**: 179, 520, 755; **1965**:
       5, 531, 551, 579, 594; **1966**: 89, 95,
       208, 253, 301, 347, 394, 490, 580 [10]

Medical personnel – *continued*
  U.S. mission to Pakistan, **1965**: 649
  Veterans, **1968–69**: 111
Medical research, **1963–64**: 179, 403, 733, 755,
      775, 808; **1965**: 2, 5, 12, 115, 154, 175,
      196, 214, 343, 410, 531, 544, 551, 581;
      1966: 45, 95, 156, 185, 271, 273, 293,
      353, 395, 403, 483, 495; **1967**: 13 (p. 53),
      77, 161, 319, 477, 500; **1968–69**: 39
      (p. 107), 40, 41, 47 (p. 143), 108, 111,
      286, 396, 408, 442, 446, 468, 589,
      695
  U.S.-Japan cooperation, **1965**: 12, 15, 175,
      214, 544
Medical Science Program, United States-Japan,
      1965: 544; **1968–69**: 286, 685
Medicare, **1966**: 95, 122 [2], 141 [3], 156, 164,
      168–169, 189, 208, 228, 240, 271, 301,
      314, 392, 394–395, 403, 433, 436, 494
      [2], 504, 509–510, 512, 515, 650 [24];
      1967: 3 (pp. 2, 6), 12, 13 (pp. 43–44,
      53), 16 (pp. 76, 85), 77, 216, 251, 296,
      299, 329, 419, 484, 532, 534, 539, 540,
      554 [6]; **1968–69**: 3, 4, 14 (pp. 29, 32),
      38, 39 (pp. 88, 91, 103), 47 (p. 143),
      50, 75, 87, 91, 96, 108, 109, 154, 164,
      262, 270, 281, 397, 406, 442, 459, 499,
      529, 555, 564–569, 601, 622, 625, 676
      (p. 1264), 678 (pp. 1279, 1295, 1296)
  Anniversary, **1967**: 298
    Second, **1968–69**: 346
  Appalachian area, **1966**: 123
  Benefits extension, **1967**: 12, 16 (p. 78);
      1968–69: 108
  Enrollment extension, **1966**: 161, 168
  Handicapped persons, **1966**: 516 [6]
  Inauguration, **1966**: 26 (p. 62), 271, 298, 309,
      353
  Legislation, **1968–69**: 253, 506, 569
    See also Social Security Amendments of
      1965.
  Nondiscrimination, **1966**: 253, 271, 395;
      1967: 298
  Taxes, **1966**: 155, 444
Medicare Alert, Operation, **1966**: 169n., 253;
      1967: 12
Medicare bill, **1963–64**: 22, 91 (p. 115), 158,
      219, 228, 233, 235, 267, 268, 270, 287,
      292, 295, 297, 305, 314, 334, 338, 406,
      413, 728; **1965**: 72, 133, 173, 176 [2],
      329, 330, 348, 354
  See also Social Security Amendments of 1965.
  News conference remarks, **1963–64**: 150 [5],
      170 [13], 211 [28], 266 [21], 379 [16],
      516 [9], 619 [16]
  Senate passage of, **1963–64**: 552
  Statement, **1965**: 122
Meech, J. V., **1966**: 538

Meeds, Repr. Lloyd, **1966**: 448
Meeker, Leonard C., **1965**: 208 [6]
Meiklejohn, Alexander, **1963–64**: 27
Meir, Golda, **1967**: 484
Mejía, Rev. Jorge, **1963–64**: 123n.
Mekong Coordinating Committee, **1965**: 199,
      294; **1967**: 401
Mekong Delta Valley, **1965**: 177, 199
Mekong River, **1965**: 172, 294, 295 [3]; **1966**:
      514; **1967**: 16 (p. 80), 73, 401, 480
  Development, **1966**: 133, 328–329, 348, 458n.,
      542, 557; **1968–69**: 233, 327, 365
Melbourne, Australia, **1966**: 543
Melchior Station, Argentina, **1965**: 220
Mellody, Patrick J., **1963–64**: 661
Mellon, Andrew W., **1965**: 155; **1966**: 227, 587;
      1967: 470; **1968–69**: 612
Mellon, Paul, **1966**: 227n.
Mellon, Mrs. Paul, **1963–64**: 267, 280, 285 [23],
      309
Melson, Dr. William G., **1968–69**: 430
Memorandums of Disapproval.
  See Veto Messages and Memorandums of
      Disapproval.
Memorandums to Federal agencies or officials
  Agricultural surpluses, sales to United Arab
      Republic, **1965**: 661
  Air pollution, **1967**: 186
  Air routes, transoceanic, **1966**: 64
  Aircraft noise and land use in vicinity of
      airports, **1967**: 139
  Atomic information, exchange with NATO and
      member nations, **1963–64**: 440
  Balance of payments, **1966**: 114
    Reduction, **1968–69**: 11
  Blood donations, voluntary, **1965**: 525
  Brotherhood Week, **1963–64**: 113; **1966**: 81
  Budget expenditures in 1966, **1966**: 131
  Budget preview and program planning for fiscal
      1967, **1965**: 249
  Campaign issues, **1963–64**: 654
  Career training programs, **1968–69**: 526, 673
  Combined Federal Campaign, **1967**: 288
  Committee on the Economic Impact of
      Defense and Disarmament, **1963–64**: 62
  Computer use and management, **1966**: 296
  Construction activity, reduction of seasonal
      variation, **1968–69**: 587
  Copper Stockpile releases, **1965**: 617; **1966**:
      139, 636
  Cost reduction program, **1965**: 360; **1966**:
      181, 197, 239, 464, 620; **1968–69**:
      403
  Creative federalism, **1966**: 606
  Crime prevention, **1966**: 205
  Development planning coordination, **1966**: 425
  Drug reaction monitoring, worldwide, **1967**:
      215

Memorandums — *continued*
Employment control, **1963–64:** 68
Employment record, **1965:** 35.1
Executive Seminar Center, **1965:** 379
Federal loan programs, financing through private capital, **1965:** 506
Federal staff retirement systems, **1965:** 49
Financial management improvement program, joint, **1963–64:** 261
Food for peace program, **1965:** 569
Government employees
Benefits, **1966:** 102
Employee management cooperation, **1967:** 379
Employment control, **1966:** 234
Ethical standards, **1966:** 276
Safety, **1966:** 76
Travel allowances, **1966:** 234
Government's services to the public, **1965:** 591
Grant-in-aid processing time, **1967:** 458
Handicapped persons, employment of, **1963–64:** 345
Housing, private enterprise role, **1967:** 355
Information Interchange, Standard Code for, **1968–69:** 127
International Cooperation, White House Conference on, **1966:** 370
International organizations, support, **1966:** 130
June buying, **1965:** 267; **1966:** 224
Management of executive branch, **1963–64:** 17
Management improvement, **1966:** 129
Medicare inauguration, **1966:** 169
Mexican American Affairs, Inter-Agency Committee on, **1967:** 259
Military personnel, use of, **1965:** 396
Mission SAFETY-70, **1968–69:** 489
National Capital Transportation Agency, **1966:** 84
Oil pollution of coastal waters, **1967:** 240
Oil spill emergencies, contingency plans, **1968–69:** 297
Overseas expenditures, **1966:** 114
Overseas personnel and travel, reduction, **1968–69:** 15
Ports of entry, one-stop inspection, **1968–69:** 389
Postal practices, Federal agencies, **1968–69:** 407
Power failure in Northeastern States, **1965:** 608
President's Award for Distinguished Federal Civilian Service, **1965:** 269, 296n.
Price Stability, Cabinet Committee on, **1968–69:** 89, 90
Procurement guidelines, **1966:** 104
Public services, user charges, **1966:** 225
Red Cross, American National, **1967:** 22
Support, **1968–69:** 55

Memorandums — *continued*
Rent supplement program, **1966:** 344
Savings bonds interest rates, **1966:** 73
Science, strengthening academic capability for, **1965:** 514
Small business aid, **1967:** 504
Staffing of international organizations, **1963–64:** 519
Summer domestic programs, **1966:** 105
Summer Youth Opportunity Campaign, **1966:** 385
Supersonic air transport, **1963–64:** 294 [6]
Television in developing nations, **1966:** 629
Toxicological information, **1966:** 280
Unemployment, **1967:** 412
United Community Campaigns of America, **1966:** 476
Vietnam conflict
Economic planning for end, **1967:** 89
Peace demonstrations, **1967:** 441
Wage board activities, coordination, **1965:** 612
World Weather Watch, **1968–69:** 361
ZIP Code system, use of, **1965:** 332
Memorial Day, **1966:** 246; **1968–69:** 245, 279, 342
Messages, exchange with Chairman Thieu of South Vietnam, **1967:** 243
Prayer for Peace proclamation, **1966:** 242; **1967:** 229
Memphis, Tenn., **1968–69:** 179n.
Campaign remarks, **1963–64:** 701
Civil disorders, **1968–69:** 166
Civil rights march, **1966:** 277 [10]
Garbage collectors' strike, **1968–69:** 166, 169 [5, 16]
Mayor W. B. Ingram, Jr., **1963–64:** 701
Mende, Eric, **1966:** 466
Mendez Montenegro, Julio Cesar (President of Guatemala), **1966:** 277 [6]; **1968–69:** 366, 374–376
Mendez Montenegro, Mrs. Julio Cesar, **1968–69:** 374
Mental Health Amendments of 1967, **1967:** 114n., 285
Mental health centers, **1968–69:** 39 (p. 103), 111, 442, 678 (p. 1295)
Mental health and mental health programs, **1963–64:** 132 (p. 182), 133, 179, 305, 755; **1965:** 2, 5, 6, 32 (p. 94), 70, 329, 330, 401; **1966:** 26 (p. 62), 27, 95, 189, 271, 293, 395, 515; **1967:** 39, 71, 77, 199, 285, 353, 373, 382, 517, 534
Mental illness and mental retardation, **1963–64:** 132 (p. 189), 403, 620, 755; **1965:** 5, 70, 94, 100, 140, 401, 592; **1968–69:** 39 (p. 106), 54, 113, 481, 493, 503, 678 (pp. 1293, 1294)
Clinics, **1968–69:** 39 (p. 103), 111, 678 (p. 1295)

Mental Retardation, President's Committee on,
 1966: 95; **1967**: 373, 517; **1968–69**:
 481, 493
Mental Retardation Amendments of 1967,
 1967: 517
Mental Retardation Facilities and Community
 Mental Health Centers Construction
 Act of 1963, **1965**: 401; **1967**: 77,
 517n.
Mental Retardation Facilities and Community
 Mental Health Centers Construction
 Act Amendments of 1965.
 See also Community mental health centers bill.
 Approval, **1965**: 401
Menzies, Robert G., **1963–64**: 426; **1965**: 303;
 1966: 24, 305, 542–543; **1967**: 551
Merchant, Livingston T., **1965**: 352; **1967**: 511
Merchant marine, U.S., **1963–64**: 110; **1965**:
 2, 463 [3]; **1966**: 98
 Absentee voting by seamen, **1968–69**: 314
 Federal aid, **1968–69**: 535
 Legislation, **1968–69**: 535
Merchant Marine Act of 1936, amendment,
 1968–69: 535
Merchant Marine Council, **1967**: 240
Merchant Marine Institute, American, **1965**: 428
Merchant Vessel Report, Automated, **1965**: 312
Mercury space program, **1965**: 120, 121; **1966**:
 625; **1968–69**: 39 (p. 100), 616
Mercury II spacecraft, **1965**: 120
Meridian, Miss., **1967**: 443
Merriam, Ida C., **1966**: 89
Merrill, Allen H., **1966**: 220
Merrill, Robert, **1963–64**: 751; **1967**: 388;
 1968–69: 65
Merritt, B.F., Jr., **1963–64**: 716
Merry del Val, Marquis de, **1966**: 478
Meson Physics Laboratory, **1967**: 76
Messages to the American people
 Armed Forces
 Christmas message, **1963–64**: 313; **1965**:
 654; **1966**: 647; **1967**: 549
 Thanksgiving Day, **1965**: 626
 Campaign issues, **1963–64**: 638
 Civil Rights Act of 1964, **1963–64**: 446
 District of Columbia home rule petition,
 signing by House Members, **1965**: 481
 Dominican Republic, **1965**: 221
 Heart Month, proclamation, **1965**: 52
 Manila Conference, **1966**: 553
 North Vietnam attacks on U.S. vessels, **1963–
 64**: 498
 Railroad labor dispute, **1963–64**: 252
 Railroad labor settlement, **1963–64**: 284
 Red Cross campaign, **1965**: 84
 Russia, China, and U.K., recent events in,
 1963–64: 686
 Southeast Asia, signing of resolution to promote
 peace and security in, **1963–64**: 507

Messages to the American people — *continued*
 Steel industry
 Postponement of shutdown, **1965**: 466
 Settlement of dispute, **1965**: 483
 Thanksgiving Day, **1963–64**: 12
 U.S. policy in Vietnam, **1965**: 172
 Vietnam conflict, **1966**: 553
 Voting rights, duty to exercise, **1963–64**: 764
Messages to Congress.
 See Congress, messages to.
Messages to foreign leaders
 African Unity, Organization of, **1965**: 571
 Australia, Prime Minister Menzies, **1966**: 24
 Austria
 Chancellor Klaus, **1965**: 87
 President Jonas, **1966**: 605
 Brazil
 President Castelo Branco, **1963–64**: 561
 President Goulart, **1963–64**: 66
 President Mazzilli, **1963–64**: 243
 Canada
 Governor-General Michener, **1967**: 577
 Prime Minister Pearson, **1965**: 432
 Chile, President Frei Montalva, **1965**: 431
 Commission of the European Communities,
 President Rey, **1968–69**: 348
 Costa Rica, President Trejos Fernandez, **1968–
 69**: 421, 430
 Cyprus
 Archbishop Makarios, **1963–64**: 70
 Vice President Kutchuk, **1963–64**: 70
 Ethiopia, Emperor Haile Selassie I., **1968–69**:
 433
 Finland, President Kekkonen, **1963–64**: 564
 France, President de Gaulle, **1968–69**: 605, 652
 Germany
 Chancellor Erhard, **1965**: 520
 Chancellor Kiesinger, **1968–69**: 313
 Ghana, President Nkrumah, **1963–64**: 88
 Greece, King Constantine, **1967**: 108
 India
 President Radhakrishnan, **1963–64**: 367
 Prime Minister Shastri, **1963–64**: 381
 Iran, Shah Mohammad Reza Pahlavi, **1965**: 517
 Ireland, President de Valera, **1963–64**: 376, 682
 Italy
 President Saragat, **1963–64**: 817; **1966**: 591;
 1968–69: 13
 President Segni, **1963–64**: 118, 794
 Prime Minister Moro, **1963–64**: 44
 Japan, Prime Minister Ikeda, **1963–64**: 236
 Kenya, Prime Minister Kenyatta, **1963–64**: 34
 Korea, President Park, **1965**: 423
 Kuwait, Shaikh Sabah Al-Salim Al-Sabah,
 1965: 629
 Laos, King Sri Savang Vatthana, **1963–64**:
 336 [8]; **1968–69**: 240
 Malta, Prime Minister Olivier, **1963–64**: 585

Messages to foreign leaders – *continued*
  Mexico, President Diaz Ordaz, **1966**: 468, 507
  Netherlands, Queen Juliana, **1966**: 118
  Nicaragua, President Guerrero, **1966**: 369
  Philippines
    President Macapagal, **1965**: 655
    President Marcos, **1968–69**: 432
  Soviet Union
    Chairman Brezhnev, **1963–64**: 82
    Chairman Kosygin, **1963–64**: 820
    Chairman of the Presidium Anastas I.
      Mikoyan, **1963–64**: 820; **1965**: 116
    Chairman of the Presidium Podgorny, **1966**:
      50; **1967**: 472
    Premier Khrushchev, **1963–64**: 82, 122, 210
  Thailand, King Phumiphon Adundet, **1963–64**:
    30
  Turkey
    President Gursel, **1963–64**: 70
    President Sunay, **1967**: 109
  United Arab Republic, President Nasser,
    1963–64: 460
  United Kingdom, Prime Minister Wilson,
    1963–64: 681
  Vatican City, Pope Paul VI, **1967**: 42
  Vietnam, North, President Ho Chi Minh,
    1967: 136
  Vietnam, South
    Chairman Thieu, **1967**: 243
    General Minh, **1963–64**: 83
    Major General Khanh, **1963–64**: 170 [5]
  Zambia, President Kaunda, **1963–64**: 721
  Zanzibar, Sultan Jamshid, **1963–64**: 32
Messel, Harry, **1966**: 545ftn., (p. 1251); **1967**:
  1; **1968–69**: 453
Messer, Elizabeth F., **1963–64**: 204n.
Metals, **1967**: 16 (p. 79)
  Prices, **1966**: 155, 635 [7]
  Stockpikes, **1965**: 599, 617, 632
Metcalf, Sen. Lee, **1963–64**: 267, 573, 575, 656;
  1965: 592
Meteorological Day, World, **1966**: 143
Meteorological Organization, World, **1963–64**:
  705; **1966**: 94, 143, 461; **1967**: 157;
  1968–69: 361
Meteorological Programs, Interagency Committee
  on International, **1966**: 143
Methodism, American, bicentennial, **1966**: 189
Methodist Church, Social Creed of the, **1966**: 189
Methodist Episcopal Church, African, **1966**: 484
Methodists, **1968–69**: 156
Metropolitan Area Transit Authority, Washington,
  1967: 154
Metropolitan Life Insurance Co., **1967**: 160n.
Metropolitan Motion Picture Theater Association,
  1963–64: 354
Metropolitan Museum of Art, **1967**: 198
Metropolitan Opera Association (New York),
  1966: 466, 482

Metropolitan Washington Council of Govern-
  ment, **1966**: 302; **1968–69**: 355
Metropolitan Water District of Southern Cali-
  fornia, **1967**: 13 (p. 51), 284
Metzger, Stanley R. (Chairman, United States
  Tariff Commission), **1968–69**: 562n.
Mexican-American Affairs, Inter-Agency
  Committee on, **1967**: 258, 259;
  1968–69: 91, 437
Mexican-American Conference, **1967**: 452
Mexican-Americans, **1966**: 158 [8], 236 [14],
  589; **1967**: 199, 258, 259, 397, 452,
  460 [2]; **1968–69**: 26, 54, 87, 91, 437,
  631
Mexican-U.S. Trade Committee, Joint, **1966**: 177
Mexican War, **1967**: 495 [11]
Mexico, **1965**: 325
  Amistad Dam, **1966**: 630 [2, 10], 638–640
  Border development, **1968–69**: 199, 354
  Carrillo Flores, Antonio, **1963–64**: 58, 596,
    767; **1966**: 175, 247 [15]; **1967**: 447,
    449, 452, 454n.
  Chamizal boundary, **1967**: 447, 451–454;
    1966: 177, 597; **1968–69**: 199, 623, 624
  Chamizal Zone agreement with U.S., **1963–64**:
    58, 193, 194, 316 [10], 587 [6], 596,
    598, 599; **1965**: 487
  Diaz Ordaz, Gustavo, President, **1965**: 179,
    558; **1966**: 174–175, 177, 467–468,
    507, 630 [2, 10], 635 [14], 639–640,
    642 [2], 644; **1967**: 47, 70 [4], 408
    [1, 7], 447–449, 451–453, 454n.;
    1968–69: 66, 73, 169 [14], 199, 354,
    623, 624
  Economic and social development, **1963–64**:
    193, 194
  Exports, **1963–64**: 193
  Fishing agreement with U.S., **1967**: 451
  Floods, **1967**: 408, 447, 449, 451
  Hurricanes, **1967**: 408
    Damage, **1966**: 507
  International Boundary and Water Commission,
    1963–64: 193
  López Mateos, Adolfo, **1963–64**: 28 [14],
    54 [8], 58, 71 [1], 192, 193, 194, 587
    [2, 6], 596, 598, 599; **1965**: 119
  Margain, Hugo B., Ambassador, **1965**: 558n.;
    1966: 174, 639; **1967**: 408 [7]
  Relations with U.S., **1963–64**: 192, 193, 194,
    767, 768; **1965**: 558; **1966**: 174, 247
    [15], 597; **1967**: 447, 449, 451, 453,
    454; **1968–69**: 354, 623, 624
  Rio Grande salinity control, **1966**: 467–468;
    1967: 47
  Screwworm eradication, **1966**: 357
  Space satellite for Latin America, proposed,
    1968–69: 205
  Tijuana River flood control with U.S., **1967**:
    303

Mexico — *continued*
  U.S. Ambassador Fulton Freeman, **1963–64**:
      767; **1966**: 176, 630 [2], 639
  U.S. Ambassador Thomas C. Mann, **1963–64**:
      46
  U.S. trade with, **1963–64**: 193; **1966**: 177
  Visit, **1966**: 174, 176–177, 639; **1967**: 453;
      1968–69: 623n., 696 [10]
  Water desalination, U.S. cooperation, **1965**:
      119, 558; **1966**: 177, 467–468;
      1967: 448
  Wheat research, **1967**: 448, 449, 452, 453
Mexico, International Boundary and Water
      Commission, United States and, **1965**:
      119; **1966**: 177, 467–468; **1967**:
      303, 408 [2, 8], 451; **1968–69**: 623
Mexico City, Mexico, **1966**: 174, 176, 177n.;
      1968–69: 73n., 392n., 571
Mexico-United States Commission for Border
      Development and Friendship, **1967**:
      451; **1968–69**: 223 [2], 354, 623,
      624n.
Mexico-United States Interparliamentary
      Conference, **1968–69**: 199
Mexico-United States Joint Trade Committee,
      1967: 451
Meyer, Mrs. Agnes E., **1963–64**: 116n.
Meyer, Albert Cardinal, **1965**: 180
Meyer, André, **1963–64**: 296; **1965**: 365n.;
      1968–69: 471n., 672n.
Meyer, Mrs. André, **1968–69**: 672n.
Meyer, Mrs. Eugene, **1968–69**: 601
Meyer, Eugene and Agnes E., Foundation,
      1965: 70
Meyer, Garson, **1965**: 642n.; **1968–69**: 117
Meyer, Dr. John, **1963–64**: 211 [6]
Meyner, Robert B., **1963–64**: 338; **1968–69**: 42
Miami, Fla., **1963–64**: 710; **1965**: 618
Miami Beach, Fla., campaign remarks, **1963–64**:
      199, 571
Mica Creek dam, **1963–64**: 135
Mica stockpiles, **1966**: 218
Micah, **1967**: 261
Micah, Book of, **1966**: 365
Michel, Repr. Robert H., **1966**: 164
Michelangelo, **1965**: 200; **1966**: 216
Michener, Roland (Governor-General of Canada),
      1967: 577
Michigan, **1966**: 320 [14]
  Area redevelopment programs, **1965**: 132
  Automobile industry, **1963–64**: 462 [3], 463
  Campaign remarks, **1963–64**: 562, 745
  Candidates for public office, **1963–64**: 745
  Disaster relief, **1965**: 239
  Gov. George W. Romney, **1963–64**: 271 [11],
      356, 357, 562; **1966**: 431, 491n.,
      492 [1, 7, 10], 599 [3]; **1967**: 70 [11],
      321, 322, 325, 328 [2], 331; **1968–69**:
      79 [7]

Michigan — *continued*
  National Guard, **1967**: 321, 322
  Unemployment, **1963–64**: 462 [3], 463
Michigan, University of, **1966**: 93: **1967**: 306
Michigan Islands Wilderness, Mich., **1968–69**:
      168
Michigan State University, **1965**: 223
Michoud Assembly Facility (NASA), **1967**: 533
Micronesia, **1967**: 360; **1968–69**: 103
Mid-America Industrial Site, Pryor, Okla.,
      groundbreaking, **1966**: 416
Mid-Career Educational Program, **1966**: 129n.
Middle East, **1966**: 610 [8], 630 [17], 654 [3];
      1967: 44, 239, 246n., 249n., 270, 272,
      286, 363, 442; **1968–69**: 9, 194, 242,
      250, 255, 288, 307, 335, 445n., 504,
      613n., 615, 620, 652, 676 (p. 1269)
      See also Middle East Conflict; Middle East and
      Near East.
  Arms control, **1967**: 272, 281, 312 [12]
  Assistance, **1963–64**: 797; **1967**: 264 [10]
  Discussions with Soviet Union, **1968–69**:
      557 [11]
  Economic and social development, **1963–69**:
      380
  "Hot line" use in crisis, **1968–69**: 14 (p. 26)
  Maritime rights, **1967**: 272, 281
  Refugee problem, **1967**: 264 [15], 272, 281;
      1968–69: 619, 620
  Regional cooperation, **1967**: 264 [11], 272;
      1968–69: 365
  Relations with U.S., **1967**: 233, 264 [20], 272,
      375 [20]
  Territorial rights, **1967**: 272, 281
  Trade missions to, **1968–69**: 204
  United Nations operations, **1965**: 169
  U.N. role, **1968–69**: 9, 249, 250n., 255, 307,
      504, 676 (p. 1269)
    Jarring (Gunnar) mission, **1968–69**: 9, 14 (p. 26),
      169 [20], 255, 288, 474, 615, 620, 652
  U.S. policy, **1967**: 3 (p. 9), 233, 264 [1, 12],
      270, 272; **1968–69**: 8, 63, 169 [20],
      249, 250n., 255, 474, 585
Middle East conflict, **1967**: 239, 261, 270, 272,
      280, 283, 297 [2, 3, 9], 347, 364, 366,
      375 [17], 390, 404, 438n., 462, 484,
      488, 519, 554 [2]
      See also Middle East.
  "Hotline" role, **1967**: 264 [16], 297 [3]
  Jerusalem, **1967**: 272, 297 [3]
  Liberty, U.S.S., attack by Israel, **1967**: 264 [4]
  Mansfield, Sen. Mike, letter, **1967**: 257
  National Security Council committee, **1967**:
      255, 375ftn. (p. 821)
  Oil supply impact, **1967**: 358 [11]
  Statements, **1967**: 233, 254, 272, 287
  Soviet policy, **1967**: 264 [3], 279
  United Nations resolution, **1967**: 297 [3]

Middle East conflict — *continued*
  United Nations role, **1967:** 233, 239, 254, 255,
      257, 272, 287, 488, 519, 554 [2]
  U.S. participation, Arab charges, **1967:** 264
      [13]
  U.S. policy, **1967:** 251, 264 [1], 270, 278,
      279, 281, 297 [3], 488, 554 [3]
  Victims, relief, **1967:** 287, 510
Middle East and Near East, **1963–64:** 265;
      1965: 117 [6], 378
  See also specific countries.
  Water desalinization, **1963–64:** 378
  Yemen cease-fire agreement, **1965:** 463 [6]
Middle income housing, **1968–69:** 14 (p. 29), 19,
      26, 39 (p. 102), 87, 91, 94, 133, 278,
      319, 382, 402, 506, 625, 678 (pp.
      1281, 1289), 699
Midwestern Governors conference, **1967:** 375
      [10]
Mies van der Rohe, Ludwig, **1963–64:** 27
Migrant workers, **1963–64:** 213, 219, 305;
      1965: 5, 100, 406; **1966:** 95, 594;
      1967: 3 (p. 5), 97, 114, 199, 201;
      1968–69: 91, 536
Migratory waterfowl refuges, **1967:** 547
Mihlbaugh, Robert, **1963–64:** 680; **1966:** 434
Miki, Takeo, **1965:** 15, 355n.
Mikoyan, Anastas, **1963–64:** 26, 218 [7], 820;
      1965: 116
Milam, Ben, **1968–69:** 631
Milburn, Gen. C. L., Jr., **1965:** 229
Military, U.S.
  See also Selective Service System; Armed
      Forces, U.S.
  Aides to the President, **1968–69:** 603
  Aircraft, **1968–69:** 39 (p. 98)
  Appropriations, **1967:** 518 [4]; **1968–69:**
      223 [11]
  Construction, **1966:** 155, 452; **1967:** 417 [14],
      440, 460 [5]
    Authorization bill, **1965:** 440, 448 [22]
  Equipment, **1968–69:** 39 (p. 98)
  Policy, **1966:** 407
  Veterans Day tour, **1967:** 485
Military Academy, United States, **1967:** 19n.,
      495 [14]
Military affairs authorization bill, **1966:** 88 [16]
Military Assistance Command, Vietnam,
      Commander.
  See Westmoreland, Gen. William C.
Military assistance and defense support, **1963–64:**
      69, 71 [9, 16], 132 (p. 176), 150 [6],
      218 [24], 227, 435, 607, 638, 693, 695,
      703, 722, 797; **1965:** 26, 60, 319 [17],
      476, 495, 600; **1966:** 26 (p. 54), 41,
      114, 420, 445 [25], 461; **1967:** 13 (pp.
      45, 46, 48), 44; **1968–69:** 39 (p. 91),

Military assistance, defense support — *continued*
      47 (p. 133), 51 [6], 63, 678 (p. 1280),
      684 (p. 1319)
  See also Foreign assistance.
  Asia, **1963–64:** 186, 189, 379 [1], 500, 597,
      627, 662n., 675, 686, 693; **1965:** 26,
      106 [4], 130, 176 [3], 179; **1966:**
      11n.
  China, Republic of, **1966:** 41
  Dominican Republic, **1965:** 217, 227
  Europe, **1965:** 235
  Greece, **1966:** 6 (p. 7), 41
  India, **1963–64:** 379 [17]
  Iran, **1966:** 41
  Israel, **1965:** 117 [6]
  Korea, **1965:** 254, 257; **1966:** 41
  Laos, **1965:** 26
  Legislation, **1966:** 41
  Less developed countries and new nations,
      1963–64: 132 (p. 185), 280; **1965:**
      18, 176 [3]
  Malaysia, **1963–64:** 474
  Message to Congress, **1963–64:** 348
  Statement, **1963–64:** 498
  Turkey, **1966:** 6 (p. 7), 41
  Vietnam, **1963–64:** 192, 201 [5], 211 [33],
      223, 246 [4], 272, 280 [8], 285 [12],
      379 [1, 19], 400, 420 [1], 436n., 498,
      511, 591, 627, 652, 662, 693, 780ftn.
      (p. 1616), 793; **1965:** 2, 51, 106 [4],
      117 [2, 8], 130, 145, 152, 172, 194,
      206, 208 [2, 14, 16, 20], 227, 229,
      234, 246, 254, 257, 261, 316, 388 [1,
      2, 5, 11, 14], 476, 588
  See also main heading, Vietnam; Vietnam
      conflict.
Military Command System, National, **1965:** 26
Military Construction Authorization Act,
      approval, **1965:** 518
Military Construction Authorization Act, 1967,
      1966: 452
Military Construction Authorization Act, 1968,
      1967: 440
Military coups, Vietnam, **1963–64:** 271 [12]
Military exports, **1963–64:** 132 (p. 191)
Military installations, U.S., **1965:** 261n., 277;
      1966: 202, 444, 452, 461; **1967:** 440,
      485
  Closing of, **1963–64:** 54 [6], 71 [3, 11], 91
      (pp. 113, 117), 132 (p. 194), 218 [15],
      285 [9], 295, 669, 690n., 790; **1965:**
      26, 222, 440, 518
  Panama Canal Zone area, **1965:** 532
  Review and study of, **1963–64:** 54 [6], 71
      [3, 11]; **1965:** 360
  Ryukyu and Bonin Islands, **1965:** 15
  Surplus, use by Job Corps, **1965:** 288n.
  Tour, **1968–69:** 81

Military Justice Act of 1968, **1968–69**: 556
Military Order of the Loyal Legion of the United
      States, **1967**: 49n.; **1968–69**: 70n.
Military pay raise bill, **1965**: 439
Military personnel, **1965**: 395 [2], 396; **1968–
      69**: 498, 630, 669
  See also Armed Forces, U.S.
  Absentee voting, **1968–69**: 314
  Benefits, **1968–69**: 5
  Christmas message, **1963–64**: 313; **1965**: 654;
      1966: 647; **1967**: 549
  Commemorative stamp, **1966**: 358
  Dependents, **1968–69**: 223 [14]
  Dependents overseas, **1963–64**: 211 [14],
      266 [17], 475 [10]; **1965**: 51
  Draft and enlistment.
    See Selective Service System.
  Draft policy, **1963–64**: 271 [2, 8]
  Education, **1963–64**: 382; **1965**: 26; **1967**: 25;
      1968–69: 40
  Employment, **1967**: 199
  Handicapped, **1967**: 25
  Health care, **1968–69**: 111, 678 (p. 1296)
  Housing, **1963–64**: 152; **1965**: 26; **1966**:
      141 [5], 159; **1967**: 70 [6]; **1968–69**:
      26, 158
  Incentive awards, **1967**: 208; **1968–69**: 248
  Income taxes, **1966**: 571
  Insurance, **1966**: 26 (p. 64); **1967**: 25; **1968–
      69**: 39 (p. 106), 40
  Job training, **1968–69**: 39 (p. 106), 678
      (p. 1295)
  Leave, **1966**: 571; **1968–69**: 5
  Legal services, **1968–69**: 556
  Mail, **1966**: 37, 322, 389, 571, 651
  Medical care, **1966**: 6 (p. 6), 334 [2], 389,
      433, 571; **1967**: 25, 92
  Memorial Day message, **1968–69**: 279
  Message to Congress, **1967**: 25, 26; **1968–69**:
      40
  Military justice, **1968–69**: 556
  Negroes, **1967**: 55, 104 [12]
  Overseas, **1965**: 60; **1968–69**: 15
  Pay, **1963–64**: 132 (pp. 182, 194), 295, 467,
      510, 688 [6]; **1965**: 26, 32 (p. 96),
      244, 439, 633; **1966**: 26 (p. 55), 158
      [10], 333, 389; **1967**: 13 (pp. 43,
      46–47), 16 (p. 78), 25, 92, 140, 163,
      329, 330 [1], 343, 546; **1968–69**:
      5, 14 (p. 32), 39 (pp. 88, 91, 92, 97,
      98), 556, 678 (pp. 1280, 1282, 1305)
  Political and diplomatic functions, **1963–64**:
      816
  Reception for, **1965**: 280
  Red Cross services, **1966**: 476
  Rehabilitation, **1966**: 529
  Retirement, **1965**: 49; **1967**: 92; **1968–69**:
      678 (pp. 1298, 1305)

Military personnel – *continued*
  Savings bond purchases, **1967**: 66, 315;
      1968–69: 12
  Spending abroad, **1968–69**: 2
  Taxes, **1966**: 389, 571
  Tours of duty, **1967**: 309 [4]
  USO services, **1966**: 476
  Widows of, **1968–69**: 678 (p. 1299)
  Women, **1967**: 92, 475, 527
  Wounded, **1968–69**: 301, 305
Military rejectees, training and rehabilitation,
      1963–64: 89, 126, 179, 218 [17],
      266 [21], 270, 297, 314, 327, 328,
      336 [2], 755; **1965**: 5, 9, 26, 100,
      156 [2]
Military research, **1963–64**: 132 (p. 185); **1965**:
      26, 32 (p. 90); **1966**: 26 (p. 57); **1967**:
      13 (p. 48); **1968–69**: 678 (p. 1279)
Military scholarships, **1963–64**: 665
Military Selective Service Act of 1967, **1967**:
      92n., 297ftn. (p. 676); **1968–69**:
      678 (p. 1305)
Military strength, U.S., **1963–64**: 37, 91 (p. 116),
      96, 132 (p. 184), 227, 228, 233, 272,
      295, 382, 383, 413, 415, 435, 493, 509,
      577, 638, 654, 689, 775, 788; **1965**:
      2, 20, 26, 32 (p. 90), 37, 185, 347 [9],
      353 [6], 387, 388 [1], 396; **1966**:
      6 (p. 8), 346, 353, 521; **1967**: 3 (p. 6);
      1968–69: 39 (pp. 83, 98)
  Campaign remarks, **1963–64**: 541, 562, 599,
      603, 607, 611, 635, 639, 640, 648, 652,
      657, 662n., 679, 686, 693, 694, 695,
      701, 702, 729, 733, 734, 735, 736, 737,
      741, 745, 747, 748, 760
  Draft requirements to maintain, **1965**: 388 [1],
      395 [2]; **1963–64**: 271 [2]
  Growth, **1963–64**: 533
  News conference remarks, **1963–64**: 266 [10],
      619 [3]
Military Training and Service Act of 1951,
      Universal, **1963–64**: 89
Milk
  Prices, **1967**: 294
  Programs, **1966**: 26 (p. 63), 62, 95, 153
    School, **1967**: 228; **1968–69**: 94, 678
      (p. 1297)
Milk Producers, Inc., **1968–69**: 462
Miller, Arjay, **1968–69**: 215
Miller, Mrs. Betty, **1963–64**: 569
Miller, Repr. Clarence E., **1967**: 552n.
Miller, Mrs. Emma Guffey, **1963–64**: 566, 728
Miller, Repr. George P., **1963–64**: 409, 413, 414;
      1965: 134; **1966**: 134; **1968–69**: 616
Miller, George William, **1963–64**: 250n.; **1968–
      69**: 37
Miller, Mrs. Henry, **1963–64**: 332
Miller, Herbert J., Jr., **1965**: 366

Miller, J. Irwin, **1965**: 266; **1966**: 208, 490;
        1967: 168n., 252n., 500; **1968–69**: 215
Miller, Sen. Jack, **1965**: 420; **1967**: 33
Miller, Mitch, **1963–64**: 751
Miller, Neal E., **1965**: 56n.
Miller, Paul, **1963–64**: 272; **1966**: 320 [5]
Miller, Roger, **1963–64**: 709
Miller, Tom, **1963–64**: 763; **1967**: 210
Miller, Rabbi Uri, **1963–64**: 301
Miller, Wilbur C., **1966**: 414
Miller, William E., **1963–64**: 642, 667; **1966**:
        504; **1967**: 421
Milliken, Frank R., **1965**: 11; **1968–69**: 106n.
Milliken, William H., **1965**: 189
Mills, Mrs. Frances J., **1963–64**: 643, 644
Mills, Repr., Wilbur D., **1963–64**: 196, 197, 599,
        642; **1965**: 113, 122, 133, 251, 321,
        329, 394, 478; **1966**: 17, 124 [13],
        132, 157, 221, 445 [10], 509; **1967**:
        6 [1, 9, 14, 17, 19], 264 [6], 330 [1,
        4], 411 [10], 414, 420, 495 [9], 518
        [5]; **1968–69**: 2, 223 [11], 462, 658,
        671n.
    Kerr-Mills legislation.
    See Social Security Act amendments.
    Letter, **1963–64**: 196
    News conference remarks on, **1963–64**: 379
        [4, 5, 15], 563 [10], 619 [16]
Milnor, John Willard, **1966**: 652n.; **1967**: 37n.
Milton, John, **1965**: 556; **1966**: 220
Milwaukee, Wis.
    Campaign remarks, **1963–64**: 746
    Mayor Henry W. Maier, **1963–64**: 746; **1966**:
        394n.
Miner, Thomas H., **1967**: 231
Mineral County, West Va., **1968–69**: 567
Minerals and mining, **1968–69**: 345
    Development, **1968–69**: 39 (p. 101)
    Disaster, West Va., **1968–69**: 607
    Industry, **1965**: 54
    Offshore deposits, **1967**: 101; **1968–69**: 122
    Resources, **1963–64**: 300, 396; **1965**: 92
    Safety, **1966**: 462; **1968–69**: 475
        Bill, **1965**: 329, 330
    Strip and surface, **1967**: 300; **1968–69**: 39
        (p. 102), 122
    Uranium, **1968–69**: 39 (p. 104)
Mines, Bureau of, **1965**: 54
Minh, Gen. Duong Van, **1963–64**: 83
Minimum wage, **1963–64**: 22, 213, 219, 235,
        290, 297, 305, 334, 388; **1965**: 70, 99,
        258; **1966**: 111, 216, 237, 394–395,
        417 [2, 6], 431, 433, 504; **1967**:
        3 (p. 2), 16 (p. 76), 30, 97, 216, 251,
        267, 534; **1968–69**: 50, 91, 154, 164,
        212, 227, 406, 437, 442, 499, 672
    Campaign remarks, **1963–64**: 548, 562, 566,
        589, 590, 597, 599, 605, 637, 642, 643,
        644, 678, 680, 703, 733, 745, 762

Minimum wage — *continued*
    District of Columbia, **1966**: 27, 527
    Expansion of coverage, **1963–64**: 91 (p. 114),
        297 [1], 338, 406; **1965**: 2, 100; **1966**:
        6 (p. 5), 470, 512
    Increase, **1966**: 26 (p. 62), 34 (p. 106)
Minish, Repr. Joseph G., **1963–64**: 338; **1965**:
        242; **1966**: 504
Mink, Repr. Patsy T., **1965**: 368, 369, 449;
        1966: 157; **1968–69**: 197, 198
Minneapolis, Minn., **1965**: 189
    Democratic fundraising dinner, **1963–64**: 434
    Governors' Conference, **1965**: 388 [14]
    Remarks, **1968–69**: 142
    Swedish Day picnic, **1963–64**: 435
Minneapolis-St. Paul International Airport,
        1963–64: 432
Minneapolis Tribune, **1967**: 358 [7]
Minnesota, **1965**: 454 [5]; **1966**: 157
    Candidates for public office, **1963–64**: 435
    Flood relief, **1965**: 187, 189, 193, 239
    Gov. Karl F. Rolvaag, **1963–64**: 432, 433, 434,
        435; **1965**: 189; **1966**: 491n., 492
        [1, 10], 650n.
    Visit to, **1965**: 189
Minnesota Farmers Union, **1963–64**: 255
Minority groups, **1965**: 100, 301; **1966**: 95, 111,
        136, 396, 431, 433, 479, 545; **1968–
        69**: 26, 87, 91, 131, 565, 678 (p. 1291)
    See also specific groups.
    Education, **1963–64**: 388; **1966**: 136; **1968–
        69**: 26, 227, 612
    Employment, **1968–69**: 24, 26, 47 (p. 142),
        596
        Equal opportunity, **1963–64**: 40, 111, 205,
        213, 342, 812n., **1965**: 76, 100, 384
        Government, **1963–64**: 100, 213, 812;
        1968–69: 667
    Government service, **1966**: 136
    Housing, **1966**: 136
    Jury service, **1966**: 196
    Unemployment, **1965**: 100, 408, 598, 632;
        1966: 111
Minow, Newton N., **1967**: 216
Mint, Bureau of the, **1963–64**: 33; **1965**: 252,
        380
    Director (Eva Adams), **1965**: 297
Mint Act of 1792, **1965**: 297
Mints, United States, **1965**: 297
Minuteman award, **1968–69**: 12
Minuteman missiles, **1963–64**: 132 (p. 185), 199,
        382, 656; **1965**: 26
Mirnyy Station, Antarctica, **1965**: 220
Missile Sites Commission, **1963–64**: 235
Missiles, **1963–64**: 211 [30], 579; **1965**: 26,
        37n., 209, 375; **1966**: 26 (p. 56), 310,
        387, 607 [16], 642 [8, 14–16, 20];
        1968–69: 39 (pp. 92, 98)

Missiles — *continued*
  See also main headings for specific missiles.
  Antiballistic, **1967**: 3 (p. 11), 13 (p. 48), 157,
      167, 225 [17], 328 [25]; **1968-69**:
      39 (p. 92), 557 [6], 676 (p. 1268)
  Antitank missile system, **1963-64**: 170 [3],
      382
  Defense systems, **1963-64**: 783
  Disarmament, **1968-69**: 425 [9], 467 [8],
      557 [6]
  ICBM, **1963-64**: 150 [12], 382, 413, 607,
      635, 703
  Lance, **1963-64**: 382
  Minuteman, **1963-64**: 132 (p. 185), 199, 382,
      656; **1965**: 26
  Minuteman III, **1966**: 642 [15, 20]
  Nike X, **1963-64**: 382
  Polaris, **1963-64**: 382, 413, 560 [5], 635, 703
  Redeye, **1963-64**: 170 [3]
  Reliability, question of, **1963-64**: 211 [30]
  Shillelagh, **1963-64**: 170 [3]
Mission SAFETY-70, **1966**: 75-76, 291; **1967**:
    70, 265; **1968-69**: 489
Mississippi
  Civil rights workers, death, **1968-69**: 26
  Disappearance of civil rights workers, investiga-
      tion, **1963-64**: 420 [12], 455 [9], 504
      [3, 8], 563 [9, 12, 14]
  Food stamp program, **1965**: 492
  Gov. Paul B. Johnson, Jr., **1963-64**: 563 [12,
      14]; **1966**: 121 [1], 494 [1, 2]
  Gov. John Bell Williams, **1968-69**: 46n.
  Hurricane relief, **1965**: 605
  Poll tax, **1965**: 409
  School integration, **1963-64**: 642; **1965**: 470
  Voting registration, **1965**: 448 [9]
Mississippi Delta flood, **1965**: 592
Mississippi River, **1967**: 480
Mississippi River Basin, **1966**: 427
Missouri
  Campaign remarks, **1963-64**: 695
  Candidates for public office, **1963-64**: 695
  Disaster relief, **1965**: 239
  Gov. John M. Dalton, **1963-64**: 189, 217,
      263, 695
  Gov. Warren E. Hearnes, **1965**: 394;
      1966: 650n.; **1967**: 297 [1]
  Remarks, **1967**: 296, 297, 382; **1968-69**: 224,
      532
Missouri Compromise, **1968-69**: 575
Missouri River, **1967**: 401
Mitchell, Albert K., **1963-64**: 455 [7], 732
Mitchell, Clarence, **1968-69**: 631, 696 [12]
Mobilization for Youth program, **1963-64**: 451
Mock, Gary, **1963-64**: 310n.
Mock, Roger, **1963-64**: 310n.
Mock, Russell, **1963-64**: 310
Mock, Mrs. Russell (Jerrie), **1963-64**: 310
Mock, Valerie, **1963-64**: 310

Model cities program, **1966**: 30, 207, 237, 297,
    373 [15], 392, 394, 414, 417 [3, 5, 6],
    491, 524-525, 574; **1967**: 3 (p. 5), 12,
    13 (pp. 46, 52, 58), 16 (p. 84), 23, 114,
    124, 179, 216, 223 [13], 225 [13], 252,
    261, 276, 286, 312 [6], 353, 358 [8],
    359, 370, 458, 460 [3, 10], 467, 484,
    534, 554 [6, 16]; **1968-69**: 4, 14 (p.
    28), 19, 26, 39 (pp. 89, 92, 103, 109),
    47 (p. 140), 59, 87, 91, 114, 133, 135,
    212, 234, 278, 380, 406, 426, 437, 470,
    565, 568, 569, 676 (p. 1265), 678 (p.
    1290), 684 (pp. 1314, 1325), 697
  Statement, **1966**: 356
Modrzejewski, Maj. and Mrs. Robert J.,
    1968-69: 129
Moe, Henry Allen, **1966**: 101, 327
Moeller, Raymond, **1963-64**: 317n.
Moeller, Repr. Walter H., **1966**: 436-437
Mohammed Ben Abdallah, Sultan Sidi, **1967**: 43n.
Mohole oceanographic project, **1966**: 229, 401
    [3]
Mohr, Charles, **1965**: 641 [8]
Molina Urena, José, **1965**: 212n.
"Molly Brown," Gemini 3 nickname, **1965**: 120
MOLNIYA Soviet telecommunications satellite
    system, **1967**: 346
Molybdenum stockpiles, **1966**: 206; **1967**: 506
Momyer, Lt. Gen. William W., **1967**: 567
Mondale, Sen. Walter F., **1965**: 189; **1967**: 541;
    1968-69: 142
Monet, Claude, "Matinée sur la Seine; Beautemps,"
    1963-64: 24
Monetary Arrangements, Advisory Committee on
    International, **1965**: 365; **1968-69**: 218
Monetary conference, Stockholm, **1968-69**: 169
    [17], 170
Monetary cooperation, international, **1963-64**:
    472, 780 [3]
Monetary Council, Central American, **1968-69**:
    365, 366
Monetary and Financial Problems, National Ad-
    visory Council on International,
    1965: 110, 282
Monetary Fund, International, **1963-64**: 472;
    1965: 32 (p. 91), 35 (p. 112), 60, 110,
    541; **1966**: 486; **1967**: 16 (p. 82), 351,
    371, 390, 497, 519, 524, 545;
    1968-69: 2, 47 (p. 129), 218, 317, 500,
    684 (p. 1319)
Monetary policy.
  See Fiscal and monetary policy.
Monetary reserve asset creation, **1967**: 371
Monetary system, international, **1965**: 15, 35 (p.
    111), 110, 235, 365, 451, 541, 659n.;
    1968-69: 2, 14 (p. 33), 47 (pp. 129,
    136, 137), 146, 151, 170, 194, 218,
    226, 317, 449, 500, 582, 676 (p. 1268),
    684 (p. 1319)

Monetary systems, **1963–64**: 244
Money and Credit, Commission on, **1966**: 182, 199
Mongkut, King (Thailand), **1966**: 558
Monnet, Jean, **1963–64**: 27; **1967**: 545
Monomoy Island Wilderness, Mass., **1968–69**: 168
Monroe, James, **1965**: 66; **1968–69**: 157
Monroney, Sen. A. S. Mike, **1963–64**: 215, 309, 358, 587 [2], 597, 598, 789; **1965**: 330, 413; **1966**: 410, 413, 415–416, 470; **1967**: 546; **1968–69**: 110, 125, 292n., 616
Monroney, Mrs. A. S. Mike, **1963–64**: 358; **1966**: 416; **1968–69**: 616
Montana, **1963–64**: 135
  Campaign remarks, **1963–64**: 656
  Candidates for public office, **1963–64**: 656
  Flood relief, **1963–64**: 573
  Gov. Tim M. Babcock, **1963–64**: 267, 575; **1966**: 491n., 492 [1]
  Territorial centennial, **1963–64**: 267
Montana centennial medallion and coin, acceptance, **1963–64**: 267
Montenegro, Mendez (President of Guatemala), **1966**: 277 [6]; **1968–69**: 366, 374–76
Montfort, Simon de, **1963–64**: 796n.
Montgomery, John, **1963–64**: 741
Montgomery, Ala., civil rights march to, **1965**: 104, 114, 117 [1, 5, 10], 126n., 135
Montoya, Joseph M., **1963–64**: 732, 767; **1967**: 258, 541; **1968–69**: 417, 624
Montreal, Canada, **1967**: 237
  Mayor Jean Drapeau, **1967**: 237
Monuments, Advisory Board on National Parks, Historic Sites, Buildings and, **1965**: 538n.
Monuments, national, **1963–64**: 172; **1965**: 70, 242; **1968–69**: 707
Moon, Duk Choo, **1965**: 257
Moon exploration, **1963–64**: 56, 91 (p. 117), 132 (pp. 176, 186), 493, 709; **1965**: 32 (p. 91), 81n., 123, 134, 463 [13]; **1966**: 26 (p. 59), 40, 50, 134, 209, 249, 272, 277 [13], 371, 643; **1967**: 13 (pp. 49–50), 24, 38, 48n., 104 [18], 533; **1968–69**: 39 (pp. 99, 100), 107, 507, 533, 574, 610, 611, 616, 637, 645, 646 [9, 12], 647, 660, 662, 676 (p. 1264), 678 (p. 1273), 695
  See also Apollo space program.
  Funds for, **1963–64**: 455 [15]
  International cooperation, **1963–64**: 56
  U.S. photographs of moon, **1963–64**: 492, 501n., 504 [2], 518
Moore, Repr. Arch A., Jr., **1966**: 427
Moore, Dr. Carl V., **1965**: 115n.

Moore, Dan K., **1963–64**: 631; **1966**: 122 [1, 2], 491n., 492 [1], 650n.
Moore, T. Sgt. Francis D., **1967**: 324n.
Moore, Matthew, **1963–64**: 290
Moore, Maurice P., **1965**: 522n.
Moore, Rt. Rev. Paul, Jr., **1965**: 519
Moorer, Adm. Thomas H., **1967**: 485 [2, 3, 5]; **1968–69**: 675
Moorhead, Repr. William S., **1963–64**: 728
Moose, Richard M., **1968–69**: 17
Moot, Robert C., **1966**: 613; **1968–69**: 94, 122
Mora, José A., **1965**: 227, 286, 295 [1, 4, 6], 473, 482; **1966**: 386, 478; **1967**: 357, 395; **1968–69**: 205, 239
Morals in U.S., **1963–64**: 280 [5]; **1965**: 302
  Young people, **1963–64**: 246 [20], 280 [5], 622, 750
Moran, Eugene F., Jr., **1963–64**: 224
Moreell, Rear Adm. Ben, **1965**: 157
Morelos Dam, **1965**: 119
Moreno, Edward, **1967**: 396n.
Moreno Reyes, Mario (Cantinflas), **1967**: 449
Morgan, Edward P., **1966**: 338 [6]
Morgan, Graham J., **1967**: 252n.
Morgan, J. P., **1968–69**: 227, 498
Morgan, Mr. and Mrs. James, **1965**: 101
Morgan, Nicholas G., Sr., **1965**: 101
Morgan, Repr. Thomas E., **1963–64**: 290, 566, 728; **1965**: 330, 495; **1966**: 455; **1967**: 278
Morgan Guaranty Trust Co., **1963–64**: 455 [13]
Morgantown, W. Va.
  Airport, dedication, **1963–64**: 586
  Mayor Arthur W. Buehler, **1963–64**: 586
  Remarks, **1968–69**: 566, 567
Morison, Samuel Eliot, **1963–64**: 568
Moro, Aldo, **1963–64**: 44; **1965**: 198, 200, 203; **1967**: 204 [4], 572
  Visit, **1967**: 278
Morocco, **1967**: 46
  King Hassan II, **1967**: 43, 46
  Prince Moulay Abdallah, **1967**: 43n.
  Princess Lalla Aicha, **1967**: 43n.
Morrill Act, **1965**: 9; **1967**: 397, 474
Morris, Staff Sgt. and Mrs. Charles B., **1967**: 494
Morris, Douglas, **1967**: 494
Morris, Thomas D., **1963–64**: 71 [3]
Morris, Repr. Thomas G., **1963–64**: 732
Morris, William H., **1967**: 382
Morrisett, Lloyd, **1967**: 396n.
Morrison, Gov. Frank B., **1963–64**: 609; **1966**: 311, 312
Morrison, Mrs. Frank B., **1966**: 311
Morrison, Repr. James H., **1963–64**: 648; **1966**: 470
Morrison, Mrs. Thomas J., **1968–69**: 540
Morrisroe, Rev. Richard F., **1965**: 442n., 444
Morse, Marston, **1965**: 56n.

Morse, Otis B., IV, **1963-63**: 566
Morse, Robert W., **1963-64**: 442, 601; **1965**: 92n.
Morse, Samuel, **1967**: 474
Morse, Sen. Wayne, **1963-64**: 36, 47, 53, 136n.,
        150 [7], 340, 444, 575, 577, 578, 676;
        1965: 58, 156 [2], 183, 250, 305, 317,
        340, 354, 368, 369, 457, 483, 578;
        1966: 88 [17], 151, 256-257, 322, 360,
        527, 586, 642 [21]; **1967**: 204 [5], 312
        [1], 358 [10], 386, 466
Mortality rate, **1967**: 540
Mortgage Association, Federal National,
        1966: 451; **1967**: 88, 114, 179;
        1968-69: 39 (pp. 89, 96), 87, 402, 678,
        (pp. 1283, 1285)
Mortgages, **1966**: 95, 199, 338 [14], 445 [7],
        451, 473, 642 [3, 19]; **1967**: 13 (p.
        44), 120, 179, 329, 420, 528
  Government held, **1963-64**: 132 (pp. 188, 190),
        690n.
  Housing, **1967**: 6 [4, 10-11], 103; **1968-69**: 39
        (pp. 87, 103), 40, 47 (p. 141), 72, 87,
        229, 402
  Insurance, **1963-64**: 178n., 179; **1965**: 32 (p.
        93), 47, 90, 415, 585; **1967**: 88
  Interest rates, **1963-64**: 714
  Ship, **1967**: 72
Mortimer, Charles G., **1963-64**: 79
Morton, Dr. Luis M., Jr., **1967**: 532
Morton, Sen. Thruston, **1963-64**: 96; **1966**: 348,
        351; **1967**: 328 [17]
Morvant, Ray, **1963-64**: 648
Moscoso, Teodoro, **1963-64**: 71 [5], 227, 340,
        563 [5], 591; **1965**: 221
Moscow, **1963-64**: 705; **1965**: 223
  Telecommunications, direct link with Washing-
        ton, **1965**: 20
  U.S. Embassy, attack on, **1965**: 59
Moseman, Dr. Albert H., **1967**: 416n.
Moseman, Albert I., **1965**: 344n.
Moses, Robert, **1963-64**: 282
Mosher, Repr. Charles A., **1965**: 190
Mosk, Stanley, **1963-64**: 415
Moss, Sen. Frank E., **1963-64**: 737; **1966**: 255;
        1967: 33; **1968-69**: 125, 505, 629
Moss, Repr. John E., **1963-64**: 579;
        1968-69: 264
  Letter, **1965**: 160
Motion Picture Association of America, **1968-
    69**: 686
Motion Picture Exhibitors, Allied States As-
    sociation of, **1963-64**: 354
Motion Picture Organizations, Inc., Council of,
    1963-64: 354
Motion Picture Theater Association, Metro-
    politan, **1963-64**: 354
Motion Picture Theater Owners of Maryland,
    Inc., Allied, **1963-64**: 354

Motley, Mrs. Constance Baker, **1966**: 136n.
Motor Vehicle Safety Advisory Council, Na-
    tional, **1968-69**: 693
Motor vehicles
  Insurance study, **1968-69**: 264
  Safety standards, **1968-69**: 244
Moudy, James M., **1968-69**: 282
Moulay Abdallah, Prince, **1967**: 43n.
Moulton, Dr. Barbara, **1967**: 93n.
Mount Baldy Wilderness, Ariz., **1968-69**: 122,
    168
Mount Hood National Forest, Oreg., **1967**: 418
Mount Irazu, **1963-64**: 438n., 443
Mount Jefferson Wilderness, Oreg., **1967**: 418;
    1968-69: 122
Mount McKinley, **1965**: 583
Mount McKinley National Park, Alaska,
    1968-69: 707
Mount Vernon, replica on coin, **1965**: 380
Mountbatten, Earl Louis, **1963-64**: 796;
    1967: 502n.
Moursund, Mr. and Mrs. Albert Wadel III,
    1966: 417 [3]
"Moveable Feast, The," Ernest Hemingway,
    1963-64: 526
Moyers, Bill D., **1963-64**: 238, 818 [4];
    1965: 382n., 388ftn. (p. 795), 412,
    422n., 423n., 424n., 441n., 442n., 444n.,
    445, 449n., 456n., 457n., 474n., 485n.,
    507n., 522n., 524n., 528n., 549, 554n.,
    565n., 571n., 598n., 601n., 608n., 619n.,
    622n., 627n., 629n., 652n., 657n.;
    1966: 5n., 12, 50n., 93, 135n., 139n.,
    154, 203n., 230n., 244n., 259n., 274n.,
    314n., 315n., 363n., 364n., 369n., 548,
    575, 618n.
  News conference remarks on, **1965**: 22 [1],
    106 [9], 295 [16], 319 [9], 347 [2, 8],
    448 [17], 641 [1, 2]; **1966**: 8 [10, 16],
    65 [1, 2], 88 [13], 121 [1, 2], 122 [2],
    124 [1, 6, 12], 141 [3, 8, 10, 13], 158
    [6], 236 [5], 247 [1, 8], 320 [14], 401
    [8], 417 [9], 445 [24], 477 [2], 492
    [4], 494 [2, 10], 501 [5], 516 [1], 628
    [1]
Moyers, James H., death, **1966**: 465
Moyers, Mrs. James H., **1966**: 465
Moyers, Karen, **1966**: 465
Moyers, Melinda, **1966**: 465
Mueller, George E., **1966**: 625; **1968-69**: 662
Muirhead, Peter P., **1966**: 265
Mulford, David C., **1965**: 334n.
Mulford, Stewart, **1963-64**: 480
Mullaney, Paul, **1963-64**: 396
Mullet, David, **1965**: 179
Mulroy, John, **1966**: 394
Multer, Repr. Abraham J., **1963-64**: 668;
    1965: 242; **1966**: 394-395, 510, 527

Multilateral nuclear force, NATO, proposed,
    1963-64: 76, 109, 150 [10], 186, 272,
    400, 780 [1, 8]; **1965**: 22 [7, 17]
Multiple Sclerosis Society, **1963-64**: 312
Mumford, L. Quincy (Librarian of Congress),
    1966: 424n.
Mumford, Lewis, **1963-64**: 568
Mundt, Sen. Karl E., **1963-64**: 343
Munich, **1965**: 235
Municipal bonds, **1966**: 141 [3, 5]
Municipal budgets, **1966**: 30
Municipal Center, Washington, D.C., **1966**: 27
Muñoz Marín, Gov. Luis, **1963-64**: 27, 387, 388
Munro, Ed., **1966**: 536
Murphy, Charles S., **1965**: 208 [6], 290;
    1966: 64, 322; **1968-69**: 79 [2, 4],
    125, 480, 646 [3]
Murphy, Mrs. Charles S., **1968-69**: 125
Murphy, Frank, **1963-64**: 333
Murphy, Franklin D., **1963-64**: 192n.
Murphy, Sen. George, **1967**: 335
Murphy, Msgr. John F., **1968-69**: 499
Murphy, Repr. John M., **1963-64**: 668;
    1966: 394-395, 510; **1968-69**: 221
Murphy, Michael J., **1963-64**: 468
Murphy, Robert, **1966**: 516 [4]
Murphy, Robert D., **1968-69**: 590 [1, 2, 4], 598
Murphy, W. Beverly, **1965**: 632; **1966**: 158 [3],
    184n., 373 [8], 408n.; **1967**: 168n.
Murphy, Repr. William T., **1965**: 299; **1966**: 228
Murray, Dr. Grover, **1967**: 448n.
Murray, Very Rev. Msgr. Harrold A., **1967**: 419n.
Murray, James E., **1965**: 348, 394
Murray, Rev. John Courtney, **1966**: 315n.
Murray, Philip, **1963-64**: 290, 431, 589, 639,
    656; **1965**: 242; **1967**: 484
Murray, Repr. Tom, **1963-64**: 701; **1965**: 154;
    1966: 470
Murrow, Edward R., **1963-64**: 200n., 568;
    1965: 208 [8], 468; **1966**: 248
    See also United States Information Agency,
        Director.
Museum of Art, Metropolitan, **1967**: 198
Museum of History and Technology, Smith-
    sonian Institution, **1965**: 95;
    1967: 540n.
    Dedication, **1963-64**: 141
Museum and Sculpture Garden, Joseph H.
        Hirshhorn, **1968-69**: 660
Museums, **1968-69**: 64
Museums in America, **1967**: 274
Musial, Stanley (Stan), **1963-64**: 188, 490, 695,
    782; **1965**: 625n.
Muskie, Sen. Edmund S., **1963-64**: 50, 602, 606;
    1965: 242, 415, 452, 503, 568n.;
    1966: 200, 398-400, 459, 607 [1];
    1967: 216, 503; **1968-69**: 486, 497, 539,
    576, 598, 672

Muskie, Sen. Edmund S. – *continued*
    Vice Presidential candidacy, **1968-69**: 529, 565,
        567-569, 575
Muskie, Mrs. Edmund S., **1963-64**: 606;
    1966: 398, 400
Musmanno, Judge Michael A., **1963-64**: 289,
    728, 742
Musser, Virgil, **1966**: 435, 437
Mussolini, Benito, **1968-69**: 50
Mutual defense treaties, **1966**: 461, 566;
    1967: 113, 219
Mutual Defense Treaty, U.S.-Korea, **1965**: 257
Mutual Educational and Cultural Exchange Act
        of 1961, **1965**: 36, 552, 553; **1966**:
        378; **1967**: 245, 344; **1968-69**: 204
Mutual funds
    Investor protection, **1967**: 57, 342
    Proposed reforms, **1968-69**: 56, 390, 418
Mutual savings institutions, **1968-69**: 47 (p. 141)
"My Hope for America," Lyndon B. Johnson,
    1963-64: 560 [8]
Myers, Lt. Col. Dafford W., **1967**: 9
Myers, Francis J., **1963-64**: 742
Myers, William I., **1967**: 156

Na Champassak, Sisouk, **1967**: 439
Nabrit, James M., Jr., **1965**: 301, 448 [4], 533;
    1967: 81
Nabrit, Samuel M., **1963-64**: 116n.; **1966**: 277
    [5], 361
Nabrit, Mrs. Samuel M., **1966**: 361
Naden, Kenneth D., **1963-64**: 54ftn. (p. 68)
Nakai, Raymond, **1968-69**: 28
Nam Dong, Vietnam, **1963-64**: 793
Nam Ngum Dam (Laos), **1965**: 294; **1966**: 133;
    1967: 401
Napoleon I, **1963-64**: 334, 578
Narasimhan, Chakravarthi, **1965**: 331n.
Narcotic Addict Rehabilitation Act of 1966,
    1966: 140, 307, 598; **1968-69**: 39 (p.
    107), 678 (p. 1291)
Narcotic addict rehabilitation bill, **1967**: 35
Narcotic Drugs, Single Convention on, **1967**: 35, 94
Narcotics, Bureau of, **1963-64**: 90, 752;
    1965: 102; **1966**: 116, 204; **1967**: 35;
    1968-69: 59, 60, 217, 557 [8], 561,
    678 (p. 1292)
Narcotics Control Board, International, **1967**: 35
Narcotics and dangerous drugs, **1968-69**: 109,
    336, 406
    See also specific narcotic or drug.
    Addiction, **1968-69**: 57, 59, 111, 536
    Control, **1965**: 5, 102, **1968-69**: 14 (p. 30),
        59, 60
    Federal agents, **1968-69**: 14 (p. 30), 59, 217
    Illegal traffic, **1963-64**: 179; **1968-69**: 59, 390,
        561, 678 (p. 1292)

Narcotics and Dangerous Drugs, Information and
    Education Center on (HEW), **1967**: 35
Narcotics and Drug Abuse, President's Advisory
    Commission on, **1963-64**: 159, 179,
    458; **1965**: 102; **1968-69**: 59, 60
Narcotics Enforcement Officers Association,
    International, **1968-69**: 217
NASA.
    See National Aeronautics and Space Adminis-
    tration.
Nash, Ogden, **1963-64**: 282
Nash, Philleo (Commissioner of Indian Affairs),
    1963-64: 120
Nasher, Raymond D., **1966**: 370n.; **1967**: 157,
    252n.
Nashville, Tenn., **1967**: 116
    Campaign remarks, **1963-64**: 645
    Mayor Beverly Briley, **1967**: 115n.; **1968-69**:
    345
    Remarks, **1968-69**: 345
Nasiruddin, King (Malaysia), **1966**: 559n., 560n.
Nason, Howard, **1966**: 637n.
Nassau County (N.Y.), **1966**: 512
Nasser, Gamal Abdel, **1963-64**: 460; **1965**: 463
    [6]
Nast, Thomas, **1968-69**: 260
Natcher, Repr. William H., **1963-64**: 643, 644
Natchitoches, La., **1968-69**: 441
National Academy of Engineering, **1968-69**: 361
National Academy of Sciences, **1963-64**: 271
    [5], 308, 355n., 456n.; **1966**: 79, 200,
    461; **1967**: 101; **1968-69**: 107, 361
National Advisory Commission on Civil Dis-
    orders, **1967**: 326, 327, 328 [1, 10, 23];
    1968-69: 59, 114, 142, 153 [16], 191
    [9], 301
National Advisory Commission on Food and
    Fiber, **1965**: 597; **1966**: 26 (p. 59);
    1967: 525
National Advisory Commission on Health Facili-
    ties, **1967**: 77, 419; **1968-69**: 622
National Advisory Commission on Health Man-
    power, **1967**: 77, 500; **1968-69**: 111
National Advisory Commission on Libraries,
    1966: 424
National Advisory Commission on Rural
    Poverty, **1966**: 28; **1967**: 114
National Advisory Commission on Selective Ser-
    vice, **1966**: 315n., 388, 536; **1967**: 3
    (p. 6), 92, 104 [12], 205n.
National Advisory Committee on Adult Basic
    Education, **1968-69**: 484
National Advisory Committee on Self-Help,
    1967: 44
National Advisory Council, Peace Corps,
    1965: 33; **1966**: 93
National Advisory Council on Economic Oppor-
    tunity, **1967**: 87n., 114; **1968-69**: 315

National Advisory Council on the Education of
    Disadvantaged Children, **1966**: 210,
    238, 632; **1967**: 77, 183n.
National Advisory Council on Education Pro-
    fessions Development, **1967**: 396
National Advisory Council on Extension and
    Continuing Education, **1967**: 185;
    1968-69: 312
National Advisory Council on International Mone-
    tary and Financial Problems, **1965**: 110,
    282
National Advisory Council for Small Business,
    1963-64: 362
National Advisory Council of the Small Business
    Administration, **1965**: 270n.
National Advisory Council on Supplementary
    Centers and Services, **1968-69**: 52
National Advisory Panel on Insurance in Riot-
    Affected Areas, President's, **1968-69**: 36,
    87
National Aeronautics Association, **1963-64**: 593
National Aeronautics and Space Act of 1958,
    1963-64: 155; **1965**: 81, 117 [9];
    1967: 533; **1968-69**: 107, 507, 696
    [9]
National Aeronautics and Space Acting Ad-
    ministrator (Dr. Thomas O. Paine),
    1968-69: 574, 616, 646 [1, 5, 9], 647,
    662
National Aeronautics and Space Administration,
    1963-64: 56, 132 (p. 186), 351, 632n.,
    654; **1965**: 68n., 81, 127, 134, 271,
    287n., 319 [19], 514, 647; **1966**: 26
    (pp. 54, 59), 58, 98, 111, 134, 141
    [5], 249, 630 [4, 7]; **1967**: 13 (p. 50),
    76, 104 [18], 139n., 220; **1968-69**:
    507, 533, 610, 616, 646 [12]
    Appropriations, **1967**: 362, 417 [1];
    1968-69: 39 (pp. 92, 100), 467 [3],
    678 (p. 1281)
    Awards, **1965**: 134, 318, 391n.; **1968-69**: 574,
    616, 662
    Cost reduction program, **1967**: 121; **1968-69**:
    39 (p. 111), 678 (p. 1304)
    Distinguished Service Medal, **1968-69**: 662
    Launch Operations Center, Florida, redesigna-
    tion, **1963-64**: 13
    Manned Spacecraft Center, **1965**: 310;
    1968-69: 107
    Michoud Assembly Facility, **1967**: 533
    News conference remarks, **1963-64**: 455 [15],
    462 [2], 619 [1], 780 [22]
    Report, **1965**: 584
National Aeronautics and Space Administration
    Authorization Act, **1963-64**: 780 [22]
National Aeronautics and Space Administration
    Authorization Act, 1967, **1966**: 371

National Aeronautics and Space Administration
  Authorization Act, 1968, **1967**: 362
National Aeronautics and Space Administrator
  (James E. Webb), **1963–64**: 273, 493,
  572, 598, 654; **1965**: 81, 91, 120, 121,
  134, 207, 268, 298, 304, 310, 318, 320,
  339, 391, 462, 584, 636n., 659;
  1966: 134–135, 249, 410, 413–416,
  427, 485–486, 618, 625; **1967**: 77, 425,
  533; **1968–69**: 107, 174, 507, 552
  Memorandum, **1963–64**: 62; **1967**: 504;
    1968–69: 361
  News conference remarks on, **1963–64**: 242
    [9], 780 [22]; **1965**: 117 [9], 319
    [19], 448 [2], 463 [2, 9, 13]
  Telegram, **1965**: 651
National Aeronautics and Space Council,
  1965: 353 [10], 448 [1]; **1967**: 315;
  1968–69: 41n.
National Agricultural Advisory Commission,
  1963–64: 255, 484; **1965**: 47
National Air Museum, **1966**: 630 [4]
National Airlines, Inc., **1966**: 256n., 322
National Airspace System, **1968–69**: 39 (p. 111)
National Alliance of Businessmen, **1968–69**: 24,
  25, 37, 74, 92, 100, 105, 115, 141, 220,
  227, 328, 506, 678 (p. 1294), 684 (p.
  1324)
National Anthem trailer film, **1963–64**: 354
National Archives and Records Service,
  1965: 412 [1]; **1966**: 78, 577 [11]
National Arts and Cultural Development Act of
  1964, **1963–64**: 784n.; **1965**: 177
National Association for the Advancement of
  Colored People, **1965**: 443; **1968–69**:
  696 [12]
National Association of Attorneys General,
  1968–69: 334
National Association of Broadcasters,
  1968–69: 172
National Association of Counties, **1963–64**: 509;
  1966: 536; **1968–69**: 416
National Association of Educational Broadcasters,
  1967: 474
National Association of Home Builders,
  1965: 243; **1968–69**: 229
National Association of Manufacturers,
  1963–64: 402; **1965**: 438;
  1968–69: 25, 548n.
National Association of Postmasters,
  1968–69: 498
National Association of Purchasing Agents,
  1963–64: 211 [3]
National Association of Real Estate Boards,
  1966: 158 [10]
National Association of State Aviation Offi-
  cials, **1963–64**: 215
National Association of State Universities and
  Land-Grant Colleges, **1967**: 490n.

National Association of Wheat Growers,
  1963–64: 255
National Ballet Company, proposed, **1965**: 534
National Bar Association, **1967**: 114;
  1968–69: 429
National Better Business Bureau, **1968–69**: 56
National Broadcasting Company, **1967**: 518
  [14]; **1968–69**: 529n., 576n.
National Bureau of Standards, **1965**: 247;
  1967: 31n.; **1968–69**: 127, 133, 523
National Cancer Institute, **1966**: 156
National Capital Affairs, President's Advisor for
  (Charles A. Horsky), **1963–64**: 16, 537
National Capital Housing Authority, **1967**: 180;
  1968–69: 133
  Report, **1968–69**: 152
National Capital Planning Commission, **1963–64**:
  700; **1966**: 27, 452; **1967**: 15, 71;
  1968–69: 133
National Capital Region, **1963–64**: 133
  See also District of Columbia.
  Transportation, **1966**: 27, 68, 84, 262;
    1965: 19, 32 (p. 93), 61, 70, 499
National Capital Regional Planning Council,
  1966: 302
National Capital Transportation Act of 1960,
  1965: 61; **1966**: 262
National Capital Transportation Act of 1965,
  1965: 61, 499; **1966**: 27
National Capital Transportation Agency,
  1963–64: 133; **1965**: 19, 61;
  1966: 68; **1967**: 15, 154
  Administrator (Walter J. McCarter), **1966**: 84
National Cathedral School for Girls, **1965**: 289
National Center for Deaf-Blind Youth and
  Adults, **1967**: 77, 413
National Center for Environmental Health Sci-
  ences, proposed, **1965**: 54
National Center for Health Services Research
  and Development, **1967**: 77
National Christmas Tree, **1963–64**: 65, 810;
  1965: 653; **1966**: 646; **1967**: 544;
  1968–69: 629
National Citizens' Commission, **1966**: 370
National Citizens Committee for Community Re-
  lations, **1963–64**: 522
National City Christian Church, Washington,
  1968–69: 705n.
National City Managers Association, **1965**: 438
National Civil Defense Advisory Council,
  1968–69: 196
National Civil Service League awards, **1965**:
  263; **1966**: 198
National Collection of Fine Arts, **1966**: 227;
  1968–69: 225
National Commission on Architectural Barriers to
  Rehabilitation of the Handicapped,
  1966: 192; **1968–69**: 287

National Commission on the Causes and Prevention of Violence, **1968–69**: 293, 298, 301

National Commission on Codes, Zoning, Taxation and Development Standards, Temporary, **1965**: 90

National Commission on Community Health Services, **1966**: 185

National Commission on Consumer Finance, **1968–69**: 280

National Commission on Food Marketing, **1963–64**: 455 [7]; **1965**: 567; **1966**: 294

National Commission on Product Safety, **1967**: 57, 342, 499; **1968–69**: 14 (p. 29)

National Commission on Reform of Federal Criminal Laws, **1966**: 598; **1968–69**: 59

National Commission on Technology, Automation, and Economic Progress, **1963–64**: 214, 525; **1965**: 110, 258; **1966**: 111, 258

National Committee for Equal Pay, **1963–64**: 398n.

National Committee for International Development, **1965**: 7

National Committee for a More Beautiful Capital, **1966**: 501 [18]

National Communications System, **1968–69**: 127

National Conference of Christians and Jews, **1963–64**: 113; **1968–69**: 78
Brotherhood Award, **1968–69**: 78n.

National Conference on Continuing Action for Human Rights, **1968–69**: 611n.

National Conference on Crime Control, **1967**: 146

National Conference of Editorial Writers, **1966**: 501 [2], 503–504

National Conference on Educational Legislation, **1965**: 89

National Conference of Federal Executive Board Chairmen, **1965**: 264

National Conference on Foreign Policy, **1963–64**: 280

National Conference of Labor Leaders, **1963–64**: 379 [7]

National Conference on Medical Costs, **1967**: 77

National Congress of American Indians, **1963–64**: 120

National Co-op Month, 1967, **1967**: 415

National Council on Aging, **1968–69**: 75n., 117

National Council on the Arts, **1963–64**: 524, 784; **1965**: 177, 534; **1966**: 440; **1967**: 53n.; **1968–69**: 64, 601, 686

National Council of Churches of Christ in the U.S.A., **1965**: 438

National Council on Crime and Delinquency, **1967**: 276

National Council on the Humanities, **1966**: 101; **1968–69**: 45, 61

National Council on Indian Opportunity, **1968–69**: 113

National Council of Jewish Women, **1965**: 438

National Council on Marine Resources and Engineering, **1966**: 326; **1967**: 20, 101, 240; **1968–69**: 124, 692

National Council of Senior Citizens, **1966**: 253; **1968–69**: 75n.

National Council for Small Business Management Development, **1965**: 270n.

National Council of State Governments, **1968–69**: 334

National Crime Commission.
See President's Commission on Law Enforcement and Administration of Justice.

National Crime Information Center, **1968–69**: 334

National Cultural Center, renaming, **1963–64**: 39. 142

National Cultural Center Act, **1963–64**: 784n.

National Day of Prayer, **1965**: 557

National debt.
See Debt, national.

National defense.
See National security.

National Defense Act of 1916, **1963–64**: 665

National Defense Education Act of 1958, **1963–64**: 47, 53, 488; **1966**: 95, 111, 116; **1967**: 77; **1968–69**: 54, 538, 550
10th anniversary, **1968–69**: 473

National Defense Education Act Amendments of 1964, **1963–64**: 620, 676, 678

National Defense Education Act Amendments of 1965, **1966**: 28

National defense education legislation, **1965**: 9, 32 (p. 94), 514

National defense student loan program, **1967**: 304n.

National Defense Transportation Day, **1966**: 187

National Defense Transportation Day and National Transportation Week, **1968–69**: 118

National Disaster Warning System, **1967**: 31n.

National Earthquake Information Center, **1967**: 31n.

National economy.
See Economy, national.

National Education Association, **1963–64**: 676n.; **1965**: 250, 340

National Education Award of 1966, **1966**: 77

National Education Improvement Act, proposed, **1963-64**: 47

National Endowment for the Arts, **1966**: 440; **1967**: 53; **1968–69**: 54, 64, 686

National Endowment for the Humanities, **1966**: 327; **1967**: 54, 77; **1968–69**: 45, 54, 61, 703
Chairman (Barnaby C. Keeney), **1966**: 327

National Environmental Satellite Center,
    1967: 31n.
National Export Expansion Coordinator (Daniel
    L. Goldy), **1963–64**: 248
National Export Expansion Council, **1965**: 465;
    1967: 231
National Eye Institute, establishment,
    1968–69: 446
National Farmers Organization, **1963–64**: 255
National Farmers Union, **1963–64**: 225, 242 [10];
    1968–69: 75n., 142
National Federation of Independent Business,
    1965: 438
National First Voters Week, **1963–64**: 706
National Food Bank, proposed, **1968–69**: 94,
    142, 155, 247, 534
National Forensic League, **1963–64**: 343, 455
    [17]
National Forest System, **1966**: 376n.
National Foundation on the Arts and the Human-
    ities, **1965**: 2, 105, 314, 534; **1967**: 77;
    1968–69: 54
National Foundation on the Arts and the Human-
    ities Act of 1965, **1966**: 101n.;
    1968–69: 39 (p. 106), 45, 61n., 686
    See also Arts and humanities bill.
    Approval, **1965**: 534
National Freedom Award, **1966**: 86
National Gallery of Art, **1966**: 227; **1967**: 470;
    1968–69: 133
    Iranian Art exhibit in, **1963–64**: 369, 385
National Geographic Society, **1963–64**: 117, 427
    Building, dedication, **1963–64**: 117
National Grange, **1967**: 496
National Guard, **1963–64**: 600, 816; **1965**: 26,
    114, 117 [1, 5, 11], 191, 353 [9];
    1966: 124 [9]; **1967**: 92, 321, 322,
    327n.
    Members, reemployment rights, **1968–69**: 448
    Riot control training, **1967**: 326
National Health Agencies, **1967**: 288
National Health Council, **1966**: 185n.
National Heart Institute, 20th anniversary,
    1968–69: 589
National Highway Safety Advisory Committee,
    1968–69: 693
National Highway Safety Bureau, **1968–69**: 243
National Historic Landmarks, Registry of,
    1965: 54
National historic preservation, **1966**: 522
National Historical Publications Commission,
    1963–64: 481n.; **1967**: 538n.
National Housing Act, **1967**: 88; **1968–69**: 26,
    402, 589n.
National Housing Partnership, **1968–69**: 278,
    382, 470, 506, 704n.
    Incorporators, nomination, **1968–69**: 471

National income accounts budget, **1967**: 13 (pp.
    41, 43, 59), 16 (pp. 76–77), 330 [1];
    1968–69: 47 (p. 131)
National income budget, **1966**: 635 [6, 17]
National Independent Committee for Johnson
    and Humphrey, **1963–64**: 555
National Industrial Conference Board,
    1963–64: 402; **1965**: 76; **1966**: 445
    [5]; **1967**: 57
National Institute of Child Health and Human
    Development, **1963–64**: 403; **1966**: 95;
    1968–69: 111
National Institute of Law Enforcement and
    Criminal Justice, **1968–69**: 59, 320
National Institute of Mental Health, **1963–64**:
    179; **1966**: 395
National Institute of Neurological Diseases,
    1963–64: 312
National Institute of Neurological Diseases and
    Blindness, **1968–69**: 446
National Institute of Public Affairs, **1966**: 129n.
National Institutes of Health, **1963–64**: 132 (p.
    189), 179; **1965**: 115, 410, 475, 514;
    1966: 293, 301, 319, 433; **1967**: 12,
    217, 319, 500, 540; **1968–69**: 396, 408,
    446, 536, 589
National Insurance Development Corporation,
    proposed, **1968–69**: 36, 87
National Inter-Agency Committee for Control of
    Pollution by Oil and Hazardous Materials,
    1968–69: 586
National Joint Board for Settlement of Juris-
    dictional Disputes, **1965**: 41
National Labor Relations Act, 1947 (Taft-Hartley
    Act), **1965**: 2, 258, 448 [16], 644
National Labor Relations Act (Wagner-Connery
    Labor Relations Act), **1968–69**: 463
National Labor Relations Board, **1965**: 117 [3],
    127
National League of Cities, **1965**: 438; **1966**: 155,
    536
National League of Insured Savings Associations,
    1963–64: 617
National Legislative Conference, **1967**: 409
National Legislative Leaders Conference,
    1966: 273
National Liberation Front (Vietnam), **1967**: 80
    [4], 132 [7], 312ftn. (p. 702), 554 [1],
    564; **1968–69**: 51 [12], 250n., 425 [6],
    572
    See also Vietcong.
National Library Commission, **1966**: 337
National Library Week, 1964, **1963–64**: 254
National Marine Engineers' Beneficial Association,
    1965: 428
National Maritime Union of America,
    1963–64: 195

National Medal of Science, **1965**: 56, 646;
    1966: 61, 652; **1967**: 37; **1968–69**: 71,
    695
  Presentation, **1963–64**: 98
National Medal of Science, President's Committee
    on the, **1963–64**: 98n.; **1965**: 646n.;
    1966: 61n.; **1967**: 37n.; **1968–69**:
    695n.
National Mediation Board, **1963–64**: 297 [2];
    1967: 207, 310
  Chairman (Leverett Edwards), **1966**: 410,
    413, 415–416
  Chairman (Francis A. O'Neill, Jr.), **1963–64**:
    251, 284, 297 [2]; **1967**: 170, 310
National Medical Association, **1968–69**: 19, 20,
    442
National Merit Scholarship Corporation,
    1966: 545ftn. (p. 1251)
National Military Command System, **1965**: 26
National monuments, **1968–69**: 707
National Mortgage Association, Federal,
    1966: 451; **1967**: 179; **1968–69**: 39
    (pp. 89, 96), 87, 402, 678 (pp. 1283,
    1285)
National Motor Vehicle Safety Advisory Coun-
    cil, **1968–69**: 693
National Multiple Sclerosis Society, **1963–64**:
    312
National Newspaper Publishers Association,
    1967: 297 [14]
National Oceanographic program, **1965**: 92
National Opera Company, proposed, **1965**: 534
National Paint-Up, Clean-Up, Fix-Up Week,
    1968–69: 122
National Park Foundation, **1967**: 553
National Park Service, **1963–64**: 427; **1965**: 53,
    222, 277, 521, 583n.; **1966**: 27, 411n.,
    579; **1967**: 553
National Park System, **1968–69**: 510
National parks.
  See Parks, national.
National Parks, Historic Sites, Buildings and
    Monuments, Advisory Board on,
    1965: 538n.
National parks bill, concession rights in,
    1965: 560
National Planning Committee of the Machinist
    Non-Partisan Political League,
    1963–64: 158
National Planning Conference on the Education
    of Disadvantaged Children, **1966**: 238
National Portrait Gallery, **1966**: 227;
    1968–69: 225n.
National Power Survey, **1965**: 567
  Report, **1963–64**: 803
National Press Club, **1963–64**: 298; **1968–69**:
    696

National product, **1963–64**: 22, 23, 40, 91 (p.
    115), 124 (pp. 156, 157–160), 132 (pp.
    178, 179, 191, 192), 173, 199, 213, 219,
    250, 270, 280, 289, 290, 295, 297
    [2], 305, 404, 411, 459, 463, 477, 506,
    531, 555, 589, 603, 640, 689, 724, 728,
    775, 787; **1965**: 23, 26, 32 (p. 84), 35
    (pp. 104, 108, 109), 76, 77, 97, 285,
    433, 438, 632, 641 [2]
  See also Gross national product.
  News conference remarks, **1963–64**: 54 [9],
    266 [2], 316 [5], 379 [5], 619 [4], 780
    [4]
National Railway Labor Conference, **1963–64**:
    284
National Reactor Testing Station, Arco, Idaho,
    1966: 411
National Recreation and Park Association,
    1966: 518
National Research Bureau, **1963–64**: 455 [13]
National Review Board for the East-West Center,
    1965: 248
National Rural Electric Cooperative Association,
    1963–64: 227, 617; **1965**: 308, 357;
    1966: 258; **1967**: 267; **1968–69**: 96,
    305
National Safety Council, **1968–69**: 475
National School Lunch Act, **1966**: 508
National School Lunch Week, 1966, **1966**: 508
National Science Board, **1965**: 283
National Science Foundation, **1963–64**: 132
    (p. 190), 308, 792n.; **1965**: 9, 32, (p.
    95), 71, 220n., 225, 271, 283, 514;
    1966: 38, 111, 229, 319, 545ftn. (p.
    1251); **1967**: 1, 77, 165, 193, 314,
    540; **1968–69**: 54, 453, 495, 678 (p.
    1293), 687
  See also Science Foundation, National
  Director (Leland J. Haworth), **1965**: 71, 265,
    271; **1966**: 424n., 637; **1967**: 20;
    1968–69: 695
  Memorandum, **1968–69**: 361
  Report, **1968–69**: 145
  Weather modification, **1966**: 79
National Science Foundation Act of 1950,
    1965: 71, 283
National Sea Grant College and Program Act of
    1966, **1968–69**: 122
National security, **1963–64**: 37, 48, 49, 117, 120,
    124 (p. 166), 132 (p. 176), 272, 276,
    382, 409, 413, 493, 662n., 689;
    1965: 2, 17, 20, 32 (pp. 83, 90), 35 (p.
    108), 47, 92, 167, 185, 196, 211, 221,
    244, 277, 284, 362, 387, 432, 440, 460,
    468, 490, 493, 518; **1966**: 70, 99, 145,
    316, 324, 494 [15], 535, 599 [2];
    1967: 3 (p. 6), 13 (pp. 39, 46, 48), 16
    (p. 88), 48n., 92, 107, 108, 205, 329,

National security – *continued*
      343, 384, 409, 417 [1, 12], 420, 460
      [9], 485 [7], 495 [14], 515, 518 [4, 6],
      519, 533; **1968-69**: 39 (pp. 88, 97, 98),
      41, 47 (pp. 135, 136), 106, 112, 169
      [8], 394, 395, 403, 449, 483, 632, 678
      (pp. 1279, 1286, 1288), 692
   Campaign remarks, **1963-64**: 598, 608, 622,
      667, 669, 680, 686, 694, 695, 703,
      735, 746
   Congressional investigation, **1965**: 106 [3]
   Message to Congress, **1965**: 26
   News conference remarks, **1963-64**: 486 [1],
      516 [13], 619 [3], 780 [1]; **1965**: 106
      [3], 208 [18], 319 [21], 388 [5], 448
      [1]
National Security, Panel of Consultants on Peace
      and, **1963-64**: 591
National Security Act, **1967**: 375 [1, 6];
      1968-69: 104
National Security Council, **1963-64**: 223, 245,
      266 [22], 370, 645, 648, 652, 656, 657,
      666, 680, 693, 702, 736, 749, 750;
      1965: 51, 98, 319 [12, 14, 21];
      1966: 124 [6], 145, 214; **1967**: 83,
      255, 375ftn. (p. 821); **1968-69**: 86,
      213 [8], 483, 669
National Security Industrial Association,
      1965: 211
National Security Medal, **1965**: 209n.; **1966**: 99,
      387; **1967**: 383
National Service Corps, proposed, **1963-64**: 89,
      91 (p. 114), 132 (pp. 184, 189)
   See also Service Corps.
National Service Life Insurance, **1963-64**: 663
National System of Interstate and Defense
      Highways, **1963-64**: 565
National Teacher Corps, **1965**: 340, 368, 369,
      479, 603; **1966**: 6 (pp. 5-6), 26 (p. 63),
      28, 67, 77, 111, 158 [10], 223, 257,
      373 [15], 388, 394, 417 [3], 477 [1],
      580 [7, 12]; **1967**: 6 [13], 13 (p. 55),
      15, 16 (pp. 75, 85), 77, 182-183, 223
      [13], 225 [13], 266, 275, 276, 291,
      292, 479, 534; **1968-69**: 678 (p.
      1293)
National Technical Institute for the Deaf,
      establishment, **1965**: 401
National Technical Institute for the Deaf Act,
      1965: 305, 401
National Theater, proposed, **1965**: 534
National Trade Union Council for Human
      Rights, **1967**: 484n.
National Traffic and Motor Vehicle Safety Act
      of 1966, **1966**: 98, 187n., 290, 423,
      433, 449, 576; **1967**: 86, 342, 393,
      465, 534; **1968-69**: 122, 244, 264
National Traffic Safety Bureau, **1966**: 449

National Trails System, **1968-69**: 39 (p. 101),
      122, 406, 510
National Trails System Act, **1968-69**: 411,
      547, 570
National Training School for Boys, **1967**: 15, 372
   Site, **1968-69**: 133
National Transportation Safety Board, **1966**: 98
National Transportation Week, **1966**: 187
National Trial Lawyers Association, **1967**: 114
National Trust for Historic Preservation,
      1965: 54; **1966**: 82
National Turkey Federation, **1963-64**: 772n.
National Urban League, **1965**: 438; **1968-69**:
      596, 604, 631
National Urban League's Community Action
      Assembly, **1963-64**: 800
National Visitor Center, **1966**: 90; **1968-69**: 128,
      133
National Visitor Center Facilities Act of 1968,
      1968-69: 128
National Vocational Student Loan Insurance Act
      of 1965, **1965**: 578; **1967**: 77
National War College, **1963-64**: 533
National Water Commission, **1966**: 82;
      1968-69: 39 (p. 101), 122, 345, 501n.,
      600
   Proposed, **1967**: 13 (p. 51)
National Water Commission Act, **1968-69**: 122ftn.
      (p. 360)
National Wild Rivers System, **1966**: 82
   Proposed, **1965**: 54
National Wild and Scenic Rivers System,
      1968-69: 14 (p. 31), 39 (p. 101), 122,
      345, 510
National Wilderness Preservation System,
      1965: 53, 54; **1967**: 20, 29;
      1968-69: 122, 168, 311, 502, 700
National Women Voters Week, **1963-64**: 289
National Wool Act of 1954, **1965**: 47, 168
National Youth Administration, **1963-64**: 53,
      289, 622; **1965**: 268; **1966**: 49, 228,
      417 [2], 500; **1967**: 211, 258;
      1968-69: 97, 305
National Youth Conference on Natural Beauty
      and Conservation, **1966**: 295, 653
National ZIP Code Week, **1966**: 470
National Zoological Park, **1966**: 267; **1967**: 265
Nationalism, **1967**: 442, 444
NATO.
   See North Atlantic Treaty Organization.
Natural Beauty, Citizens' Advisory Committee on
      Recreation and, **1966**: 202, 653; **1967**:
      295; **1968-69**: 122, 167
Natural Beauty, President's Council on Recrea-
      tion and, **1966**: 202, 653; **1967**: 295;
      1968-69: 122, 167
Natural Beauty, White House Conference on,
      1965: 2, 30, 54, 183, 277, 446

Natural beauty in America, joint report on,
    1965: 545
Natural Beauty and Conservation, National
    Youth Conference on, **1966**: 295, 653
Natural Beauty and Conservation Year Proc-
    lamation, Youth for, **1966**: 653
Natural Gas Pipeline Safety Act of 1968,
    1968–69: 14 (p. 29), 56, 105, 338, 390,
    441
Natural gas pipeline safety bill, **1967**: 57
Natural Resources, United States-Japan Con-
    ference on Development and Utiliza-
    tion of, **1967**: 491
Natural resources conservation.
    See Conservation and development of natural
        resources.
Naturalization Service, Immigration and,
    1966: 602
Nautilus, U.S.S., **1965**: 17
Navajo Economic Opportunity, Office of,
    1968–69: 28
Navajo Indians
    Centennial of peace treaty with U.S.,
        1968–69: 259
    Education and health, **1968–69**: 28, 259
    Message, **1968–69**: 28
Naval Academy, U.S., **1967**: 440
Naval Hospital, Bethesda, Md.
    See Bethesda (Md.) Naval Hospital.
Naval Observatory, **1966**: 170
Naval Operations, Chief of (Adm. D. L. Mc-
    Donald), **1963–64**: 619ftn. (p. 1194)
Naval Ordnance Test Station, China Lake, Calif.,
    1963–64: 170 [3]
Navigation, **1963–64**: 132 (p. 187), 410, 597
    Air, **1967**: 13 (p. 44)
    Safety, **1966**: 98
Navorr, JoAnn, **1966**: 223
Navy, **1963–64**: 665; **1965**: 223; **1967**: 308,
    410, 424, 440, 485 [5], 527;
    1968–69: 39 (p. 98), 81 [3], 124, 129,
    153 [5], 169 [18], 265, 516, 584, 603,
    635, 675, 688
    Assistance to foreign navies, **1965**: 600
    Man-in-sea project, **1966**: 229
    Modernization, **1963–64**: 467
    Nuclear-powered carriers, **1966**: 26 (p. 56)
    Patrols off North Vietnam, **1963–64**: 497
    Seabees, **1963–64**: 438n., 443; **1966**: 456
    Shipbuilding program, **1963–64**: 382;
        1965: 26, 600
    Strength, increase in, **1963–64**: 611; **1965**: 26
    Submarine operations, **1968–69**: 692
Navy, Department of the, **1963–64**: 294 [21],
    351, 516 [3]; **1967**: 265, 440;
    1968–69: 18 [2]
Navy, Secretary of the (Ignatius, Paul R.),
    1967: 446; **1968–69**: 34, 129, 267,
    541, 556, 675, 688

Navy, Secretary of the (Nitze, Paul H.),
    1963–64: 37, 316 [3], 351, 510, 619
    ftn. (p. 1194), 725; **1965**: 228, 319
    [11]; **1966**: 456, 641; **1967**: 202, 241,
    265, 308
Navy League luncheon remarks, **1966**: 397
NBC television, **1968–69**: 529n., 576n.
Ne Win, General (Chairman of the Revolutionary
    Council of the Union of Burma),
    1966: 443, 446, 450, 514
Ne Win, Mrs., **1966**: 443, 446, 450
NEA.
    See National Education Association.
Near East.
    See also Middle East and Near East; Middle
        East.
    Emergency Donations (NEED), **1967**: 510
Nebraska
    Gov. Frank B. Morrison, **1963–64**: 609;
        1966: 311–312
    University of, **1966**: 601; **1968–69**: 696 [14]
Neches River Basin, **1965**: 236
Nedzi, Repr. Lucien N., **1963–64**: 356, 745;
    1966: 431
Negro College Development Campaign, United,
    1963–64: 79
Negro College Fund, United, **1963–64**: 79
Negroes, **1965**: 353 [19], 426, 429, 436, 443;
    1966: 183, 196, 646; **1967**: 326, 397,
    460 [2], 554 [6]; **1968–69**: 47 (p. 141),
    87, 158, 195, 406, 442, 487, 499
    See also Civil rights; Voting rights.
    Antipoverty program benefits, question of,
        1963–64: 256 [14]
    Armed Forces, **1967**: 55, 104 [12]
    Civil rights, **1967**: 55, 81, 463
    Colleges, fundraising campaign, **1963–64**: 79
    Education, **1963–64**: 277, 287, 297, 301;
        1965: 301, 615; **1966**: 196; **1968–69**:
        429
    Employment, **1963–64**: 205, 277, 301, 787;
        1965: 100, 165, 412 [3], 480;
        1966: 34 (p. 98), 248, 475; **1967**: 16
        (p. 73), 55, 199; **1968–69**: 47 (p. 129),
        429, 596, 631
        Opportunities, **1963–64**: 40, 111
    Equal rights, **1963–64**: 218 [35], 800, 816;
        1965: 64, 201, 301, 409, 448 [9], 548,
        613; **1966**: 30, 235, 248, 320 [17], 396,
        408, 436, 484
    Family unit, **1965**: 301, 392
    Government employment, **1963–64**: 205;
        1965: 150, 197n.; **1966**: 96, 136, 248
    Health, **1968–69**: 429, 442
    Housing, **1966**: 196, 417 [4]
    Infant mortality, **1965**: 301; **1966**: 395, 433
    Lincoln, Abraham, role in liberation, **1967**: 49
    National Guard membership, **1967**: 327n.

Negroes – *continued*
  Office holding, **1968–69**: 26
  Personal income, **1965**: 301
  Physicians, **1968–69**: 442
  Presidential appointees, **1968–69**: 631
  Rural areas, **1965**: 85
  Social and economic conditions, **1967**: 55, 463;
      1968–69: 423, 429, 596
  Teachers, **1965**: 340
  Unemployment, **1965**: 76, 301, 322, 351, 480,
      632; **1966**: 34 (p. 100), 111–112, 196,
      475
  Urban areas, concentration in, **1965**: 301
  Veterans, **1968–69**: 131
  Voting rights and participation, **1966**: 66, 96,
      196, 277ftn. (p. 631), 403, 436;
      1968–69: 26, 672
  See also Voting rights.
Nehru, B. K., **1963–64**: 35n.
Nehru, Jawaharlal, **1963–64**: 625, 693, 737, 747,
      790; **1966**: 5, 148n., 149
  Death of, **1963–64**: 367
Neighborhood centers, **1968–69**: 19, 39 (pp.
      104, 110), 95, 315, 678 (p. 1296)
  Antipoverty, **1967**: 15, 114, 458, 467
  Health, **1966**: 594; **1967**: 13 (p. 53), 16 (p.
      76), 77, 114, 452; **1968–69**: 19, 20, 39
      (p. 104), 111, 622, 678 (p. 1296), 689
  Older Persons, **1968–69**: 19, 20
Neighborhood development program, proposed,
      1968–69: 87
Neighborhood facilities program, **1967**: 12
Neighborhood legal services, **1966**: 394, 594
Neighborhood Youth Corps, **1965**: 32 (p. 93),
      67, 75, 86, 193, 195, 224, 239, 268,
      298, 308, 322, 438; **1966**: 111, 172,
      189, 236 [13], 385n., 594; **1967**: 3
      (p. 3), 13 (p. 54), 16 (p. 75), 39, 55, 77,
      81, 97, 114, 199, 211, 277, 291, 408
      [4]; **1968–69**: 24, 26, 47 (p. 142), 87,
      678 (p. 1294)
Neihuss, Marvin L., **1963–64**: 356
Neilan, Edwin P., **1963–64**: 295
Nelsen, Repr. Ancher, **1966**: 586
Nelson, Sen. Gaylord, **1963–64**: 746; **1965**: 368,
      369
Nelson, Herman, **1968–69**: 462
Nelson, Lord, **1965**: 616
Nelson, Richard H., **1963–64**: 619 [11]
Nelson, Dr. Russell, **1965**: 163; **1966**: 208n.;
      1967: 500
Nelson, Thomas W., **1963–64**: 71 [3]
Nemerovski, Howard N., **1965**: 334n.;
      1967: 419n.
Nepal
  Crown Prince Birendra, **1967**: 459n., 461n.,
      462
  Economic and social development, **1967**: 459,
      461, 462

Nepal – *continued*
  Foreign Minister Kirti Nidhi Bista, **1967**: 462
  Government, **1967**: 461n.
  King Mahendra, **1967**: 459, 461, 462
  Queen Ratna, **1967**: 461n., 462
  U.S. Ambassador Carol Laise, **1967**: 460 [11],
      461
Netherlands, **1965**: 68n; **1966**: 133
  Food aid for India, **1967**: 33
  Princess Beatrix, **1966**: 118
  Queen Juliana, **1966**: 118
Nettinga, Rev. James Z., **1966**: 19
Networks for knowledge bill, **1968–69**: 54
Neuberger, Sen. Maurine B., **1963–64**: 136, 575,
      577, 578; **1966**: 299, 599 [1]; **1967**:
      342n.
Neurological Diseases, National Institute of,
      1963–64: 312
Neurological Diseases and Blindness, National
      Institute of, **1968–69**: 446
Neurological diseases control, **1965**: 5
Neustadt, Richard E., **1963–64**: 303; **1966**:
      256–257, 322, 360, 612; **1968–69**: 215
Nevada
  Campaign remarks, **1963–64**: 652, 655
  Candidates for public office, **1963–64**: 652,
      655
  Gov. Grant Sawyer, **1963–64**: 575, 652, 655;
      1966: 407
  Southern, water project, **1965**: 586
Nevins, Allan, **1968–69**: 96, 655
Nevins, Jim, **1966**: 332n.
Nevius, John A., **1967**: 406, 466n.
New Brunswick, N.J., **1963–64**: 338
New careers program, **1968–69**: 678 (p. 1295)
New communities bill of 1968, **1968–69**: 87
New Deal, **1966**: 235, 330, 351, 386, 429;
      1967: 156, 176, 251, 281, 460 [14],
      514
New Delhi, India, **1968–69**: 198
New England
  Governors, **1967**: 542
  Oceanography, **1967**: 223 [5]
  Textile industry, **1963–64**: 602
  Transportation, **1967**: 223 [2]
New England Governors' conference, **1967**: 222,
      223, 225 [21]
New England Regional Commission, **1967**:
      223 [4]
New England River Basins Commission, **1968–
      69**: 593, 666
New Frontier, **1966**: 330; **1968–69**: 75
New Guinea, **1966**: 345
New Hampshire, **1966**: 320 [14]; **1967**: 233 [5]
  Campaign remarks, **1963–64**: 607
  Candidates for public office, **1963–64**: 607
  Gov. John W. King, **1963–64**: 607; **1966**:
      396–399; **1967**: 223 [3, 5, 8]

New Hampshire – *continued*
  Presidential primary, **1968–69**: 132
  Primary campaign, **1963–64**: 199
  Primary election, **1963–64**: 211 [12], 218
    [23]
New Haven Railroad, **1965**: 536; **1967**: 223 [2],
    542; **1968–69**: 102
New Jersey, **1966**: 320 [14], 391
  Campaign remarks, **1963–64**: 541, 542, 589,
    660
  Candidates for public office, **1963–64**: 338,
    660
  Civil disorders, **1967**: 312 [6]
  Democratic Committee State dinner, **1963–64**:
    338
  Firearms control, **1967**: 385
  Gov. Richard J. Hughes, **1963–64**: 338, 422,
    660; **1965**: 291n., 417, 434, 471; **1966**:
    77, 121 [1], 155, 216, 428, 504, 536;
    1967: 70 [6], 112, 280–282; **1968–69**:
    32, 36, 87, 171, 270, 288, 540
  Liberty State Park, **1965**: 242
  Remarks, **1967**: 279, 280, 282, 283; **1968–69**:
    270, 288
  Transfer of land to, **1963–64**: 422
  Water problems, **1965**: 434
New Jersey State Democratic Committee,
    remarks to, **1963–64**: 338
New London, Conn., **1963–64**: 382
New Mexico, **1967**: 258, 270; **1968–69**: 259
  Campaign remarks, **1963–64**: 732
  Candidates for public office, **1963–64**: 732
  Gov. Jack M. Campbell, **1963–64**: 732; **1966**:
    413, 416, 491n., 492 [1]
New Orleans, La., **1965**: 54; **1967**: 533; **1968–**
    69: 107, 473n.
  Campaign remarks, **1963–64**: 646, 648
  Mayor Victor H. Schiro, **1963–64**: 648; **1967**:
    533
  Remarks, **1968–69**: 472
New York, **1965**: 434; **1966**: 391; **1967**: 223
    [2, 11], 542
  Antipoverty program, **1963–64**: 334
  Campaign remarks, **1963–64**: 662, 666–670,
    751
  Candidates for public office, **1963–64**:
    666–670, 751
  Fire Island National Seashore, **1965**: 521
  Gov. Nelson A. Rockefeller, **1963–64**: 96,
    211 [19], 218 [25], 282, 285 [1], 287,
    311, 462 [6], 468, 499, 662n., 746;
    1965: 417, 418, 434; **1966**: 122 [1,
    2], 392, 394, 417 [5], 494 [1–2, 6];
    1967: 70 [6], 223 [11]; **1968–69**:
    153 [13], 260n., 299, 540, 567, 672
  Remarks, **1968–69**: 262, 568, 672
  Water pollution control, **1966**: 481
New York Central Railroad, **1967**: 223 [2], 542

New York City, **1963–64**: 174n., 175, 224, 272,
    334, 336, 387, 388, 511; **1965**: 54,
    312, 340, 434, 467; **1966**: 86
  Campaign remarks, **1963–64**: 662, 669, 670,
    751
  Democratic fundraising dinner, **1963–64**: 372
  Democratic Gala, **1963–64**: 373
  Mayor John V. Lindsay, **1966**: 401 [4];
    1967: 251, 326, 327, 460 [10];
    1968–69: 191 [9], 260n., 339 [3],
    540, 672
  Mayor Robert F. Wagner, **1963–64**: 282, 294
    [9], 334, 387n., 388, 521 [5], 666,
    667, 669, 751; **1965**: 295 [5], 403,
    415, 418, 422n., 434, 566
  Mobilization for Youth program, **1963–64**: 451
  News conference, **1966**: 514
  Remarks, **1968–69**: 262, 568, 672
  Riots, **1963–64**: 468, 475 [4, 20]
  Sniper attack in Central Park, **1968–69**: 356
  Transit Authority, **1966**: 8ftn. (p. 19), 373
    [3]
  Transit strike, **1966**: 8 [15], 34 (p. 106)
  Urban problems, **1967**: 20, 55, 71, 542
  Urban renewal project, **1965**: 566
  Verrazano-Narrows Bridge, **1963–64**: 581
  Von Steuben Day parade, **1966**: 466
  World's Fair (1939), **1963–64**: 282
  World's Fair (1964–65), **1963–64**: 282
    Civil rights demonstrations, **1963–64**:
      285ftn. (p. 521), 290
    Singer Bowl, **1963–64**: 334n.
    Time capsule, **1963–64**: 282
    United States Pavilion, **1963–64**: 283
    Venezuelan Pavilion, **1963–64**: 335
New York Herald Tribune, **1963–64**: 486 [9];
    1966: 88 [23]
New York Shipping Association, **1963–64**: 494
New York Stock Exchange, **1963–64**: 750
New York Times, **1963–64**: 455 [13]; **1966**:
    236 [3], 277 [20], 312, 373 [19],
    417 [7, 9], 477 [5], 492 [9], 516
    [18], 654 [2, 7]; **1967**: 312 [10];
    1968–69: 260
New Zealand, **1963–64**: 475 [3]; **1965**: 220,
    628; **1966**: 133, 516 [1], 540;
    1968–69: 522, 525, 528
  Ambassador Frank H. Corner, **1968–69**: 525
  Foreign relations, **1968–69**: 522n., 525
  Governor General Sir Bernard Fergusson,
    1966: 539–540
  Holyoake, Keith, **1963–64**: 464; **1966**: 514,
    538–540, 549; **1967**: 409; **1968–69**:
    522, 525, 528
  Meat exports from, **1963–64**: 267
  Minister of Agriculture (Brian E. Talboys),
    1963–64: 267
  U.S. relations with, **1963–64**: 464

New Zealand – *continued*
  Vietnam assistance, **1966**: 53, 516 [13], 520;
      1967: 83, 246; **1968-69**: 283 [4], 522,
      525, 528
  Visit, **1966**: 538–540
Newark, N.J., **1965**: 67; **1967**: 312 [6]
  Civil disorders, **1968-69**: 86, 114
  Mayor Hugh J. Addonizio, **1965**: 434; **1966**:
      504
Newell, Homer E., **1963-64**: 492n., 493n.;
      1965: 263n., 269, 296n.; **1968-69**: 574
Newhouse, Samuel I., **1963-64**: 499
  Communications Center, dedication, **1963-64**:
      499
Newhouse, Mrs. Samuel I., **1963-64**: 499n.
Newman, Sidney, **1966**: 637n.
Newmark, Nathan M., **1968-69**: 695n.
Newport News, Va., **1963-64**: 59; **1967**: 241n.
News conferences, comments on, **1963-64**: 28
      [7], 54 [13], 150 [20], 170 [8], 316
      [20]; **1965**: 106 [7], 117 [4]
News conferences, the President's
  1964
      January 23, **1963-64**: 143
      January 25, **1963-64**: 150
      February 1, **1963-64**: 170
      February 29, **1963-64**: 201
      March 7, **1963-64**: 211
      March 21, **1963-64**: 232
      March 28, Johnson City, Tex., **1963-64**: 242
      April 4, **1963-64**: 246
      April 11, **1963-64**: 256
      April 16, **1963-64**: 266
      April 18, **1963-64**: 271
      April 23, **1963-64**: 285
      April 25, **1963-64**: 294
      May 6, **1963-64**: 316
      May 9, **1963-64**: 336
      June 2, **1963-64**: 379
      June 23, **1963-64**: 420
      July 10, **1963-64**: 455
      July 18, Johnson City, Tex., **1963-64**: 462
      July 24, **1963-64**: 475
      July 30, **1963-64**: 486
      August 8, Johnson City, Tex., **1963-64**: 504
      August 15, **1963-64**: 516
      August 18, **1963-64**: 521
      August 26, **1963-64**: 539
      September 5, **1963-64**: 560
      September 9, **1963-64**: 563
      September 21, **1963-64**: 587
      October 3, **1963-64**: 619
      October 19, **1963-64**: 688
      November 28, Johnson City, Tex., **1963-64**:
          780
      December 7, 1963, **1963-64**: 28
      December 18, 1963, **1963-64**: 54
      December 27, 1963, Johnson City, Tex.,
          1963-64: 71

News conferences, the President's – *continued*
  1964 – *continued*
      December 28, Johnson City, Tex., **1963-64**:
          818
  1965
      January 16, Johnson City, Tex., **1965**: 22
      February 4, **1965**: 46
      March 13, **1965**: 106
      March 20, Johnson City, Tex., **1965**: 117
      April 1, **1965**: 156
      April 8, **1965**: 176
      April 27, **1965**: 208
      June 1, **1965**: 295
      June 17, **1965**: 319
      July 9, **1965**: 347
      July 13, **1965**: 353
      July 28, **1965**: 388
      August 25, **1965**: 448
      August 26, **1965**: 454
      August 29, Johnson City, Tex., **1965**: 463
      December 6, Johnson City, Tex., **1965**: 641
  1966
      January 13, **1966**: 8
      February 4, **1966**: 52
      February 11, **1966**: 65
      February 26, **1966**: 88
      March 12, **1966**: 121, 122, 124
      March 22, **1966**: 141
      March 31, **1966**: 158
      April 22, **1966**: 188
      May 21, **1966**: 236
      June 1, **1966**: 247
      June 18, **1966**: 277
      July 5, **1966**: 320
      July 19, **1966**: 334
      July 20, **1966**: 338
      August 9, **1966**: 373
      August 24, **1966**: 401
      August 27, **1966**: 417
      September 8, **1966**: 445
      September 12, **1966**: 454
      September 21, **1966**: 474
      September 22, **1966**: 477
      September 29, **1966**: 492
      September 30, **1966**: 494
      October 6, **1966**: 501
      October 13, **1966**: 514, 516
      November 3, **1966**: 575
      November 4, **1966**: 577
      November 5, **1966**: 578
      November 6, **1966**: 580
      November 10, **1966**: 599
      November 11, **1966**: 607
      November 13, **1966**: 610
      November 25, **1966**: 628
      November 29, **1966**: 630
      December 2, **1966**: 635
      December 6, **1966**: 642

News conferences, the President's — *continued*
  1966 — *continued*
    December 21, **1966**: 650
    December 31, **1966**: 654
  1967
    January 17, **1967**: 6
    February 2, **1967**: 34
    February 27, **1967**: 70
    March 2, **1967**: 80
    March 9, **1967**: 104
    March 21, **1967**: 132
    May 3, **1967**: 204
    May 18, **1967**: 225
    June 13, **1967**: 264
    July 1, **1967**: 297
    July 13, **1967**: 309
    July 18, **1967**: 312
    July 31, **1967**: 328
    August 3, **1967**: 330
    August 18, **1967**: 358
    September 1, **1967**: 375
    September 28, **1967**: 408
    September 30, **1967**: 411
    October 5, **1967**: 417
    November 1, **1967**: 460
    November 17, **1967**: 495
    December 4, **1967**: 518
  1968
    January 1, **1968-69**: 1
    January 19, **1968-69**: 18
    February 2, **1968-69**: 51
    February 16, **1968-69**: 79
    March 22, **1968-69**: 153
    March 30, **1968-69**: 169
    March 31, **1968-69**: 171
    April 10, **1968-69**: 191
    April 25, **1968-69**: 213
    May 3, **1968-69**: 223
    May 28, **1968-69**: 275
    May 30, **1968-69**: 283
    June 26, **1968-69**: 339
    July 31, **1968-69**: 425
    August 27, **1968-69**: 460
    September 6, **1968-69**: 467
    October 24, **1968-69**: 557
    November 15, **1968-69**: 590
    December 27, **1968-69**: 646
  1969
    January 17, **1968-69**: 696
News media, **1968-69**: 298
Newsom, Herschel D., **1963-64**: 54ftn. (p. 68),
  225; **1967**: 496
Newspaper Editors, American Society of, **1963-
  64**: 266 [1], 270, 285ftn. (p. 524)
Newspaper Farm Editors Association, **1963-64**:
  344
Newspaper Publishers Association, National,
  1967: 297 [14]

Newspaper publishers (foreign language), remarks
  to, **1963-64**: 496
Newspapers, **1968-69**: 111, 242
Newsweek, **1968-69**: 1 [10]
Newton, Isaac, **1967**: 37
Newton, Quigg, **1965**: 115n.; **1966**: 208n.;
  1967: 500
Neyman, Jerzy, **1968-69**: 695n.
Ngo Dinh Diem, **1966**: 88 [23]
Nguyen Cao Ky, **1966**: 53-54, 56n., 520, 549,
    552; **1967**: 73, 132 [1, 3, 4, 7, 10, 13],
    134, 135, 297 [15], 352, 358 [5], 567
  Guam conference, **1967**: 127, 129, 131
  News conference remarks on, **1966**: 52 [2],
    65 [7], 88 [19, 21], 188 [2, 4],
    236 [4], 277 [21]
Nguyen Dang Thuc, **1966**: 549ftn. (p. 1261)
Nguyen Duy Trinh, **1965**: 388 [6]; **1967**:
    34 [6]; **1968-69**: 1 [6], 65n.
Nguyen Van Loc (Prime Minister of South
    Vietnam), **1967**: 564
Nguyen Van Thieu (President of South Vietnam),
    1966: 52 [2], 53-54, 56n., 549, 552;
    1967: 297 [15], 352, 358 [5], 460
    [11], 554 [1]; **1968-69**: 51 [12], 170,
    172, 189, 223 [7], 339 [13], 398, 400,
    401, 406, 425 [4], 452, 472, 572,
    590 [5]
  Guam conference, **1967**: 127, 130-131
  Joint statement, **1967**: 564
  Memorial Day messages exchange, **1967**: 243
Niagara-Mohawk power system, **1965**: 608n.
Nicaragua, **1963-64**: 809; **1967**: 44, 336;
    1968-69: 368, 373
  Ambassador Guillermo Seville-Sacasa,
    1963-64: 42n.; **1966**: 263, 478;
    1968-69: 371, 373, 681
  Assistance, **1963-64**: 227; **1966**: 11n., 41;
    1968-69: 679
  Canal route mapping, **1966**: 384
  Economic development, **1963-64**: 352
  Guerrero, Lorenzo (President), **1967**: 173
  Shick Gutiérrez, René (President), **1966**: 263,
    264, 367, 369
  Somoza Debayle, Anastasio (President), **1968-
    69**: 366, 373
  Visit, **1968-69**: 373
Nichols, Frances, **1966**: 223
Nichols, Judge Philip, Jr., **1963-64**: 613
Nichols, Mrs. Philip, Jr., **1963-64**: 613
Nichols, Roy, **1963-64**: 303
Nichols, Tom, **1963-64**: 778; **1965**: 603
Nicholson, James M., **1967**: 518 [2]
Nickel, **1966**: 572n.; **1968-69**: 47 (p. 144)
  Release from national stockpile, **1965**: 599
  Use in coinage system, **1965**: 297
Nickerson, Albert L., **1968-69**: 25, 241
Nickerson, Eugene H., **1963-64**: 337; **1966**: 512

Nicklin, George F. R., **1966**: 546
Nicks, Oran, **1965**: 391n.
Nicosia, John, **1963-64**: 639
Niebuhr, Reinhold, **1963-64**: 568
Neiderlehner, Leonard, **1965**: 263n.
Niger, **1967**: 400, 403; **1968-69**: 433n.
    Hamani, Diori (President), **1967**: 400, 403
    Peace Corps projects, **1967**: 400n.
Nigeria
    Civil war, **1968-69**: 242, 482, 508, 511n.,
        639
        Aid to victims, **1968-69**: 381, 433, 580
    U.S. assistance, **1963-64**: 227; **1968-69**: 21,
        433, 482, 580, 679
    U.S. policy, **1968-69**: 508, 639
Nigeria, Consultative Committee on (Organization
    of African Unity), **1968-69**: 433
Nightingale, Florence, **1963-64**: 557
NIH.
    See National Institutes of Health.
Nike X missile, **1963-64**: 382; **1965**: 26; **1966**:
    642 [16]; **1967**: 13 (p. 48)
Nikezic, Marko, **1967**: 375 [17]
Nimetz, Matthew, **1968-69**: 17
Nimitz, Fleet Adm. Chester W., **1966**: 1, 80
1964 Amendments to the Alaska Omnibus Act,
    1965: 435
Nirenberg, Marshall W., **1965**: 56n.
Nitze, Paul H. (Secretary of the Navy), **1966**:
    456, 641; **1967**: 202, 241, 265, 308;
    1968-69: 101, 384, 516, 556, 604,
    669
    See also Navy, Secretary of the.
Nix, Repr. Robert N. C., **1963-64**: 742; **1967**:
    291
Nixon, Richard M., **1963-64**: 218 [9], 287,
    295, 297, 542, 728; **1965**: 549, 550;
    1966: 401 [1, 12, 17], 577 [2, 13,
    15], 580 [16], 610 [1]
    Congratulatory telegram, **1968-69**: 578
    News conference remarks on, **1963-64**: 201
        [12], 285 [1, 17], 560 [10], 619 [18]
    President-elect, **1968-69**: 578, 585, 590 [1,
        2, 4, 8], 598, 604, 646 [12], 657n.,
        664, 676 (pp. 1267, 1270), 677, 691,
        695, 696 [2, 4, 20]
    Presidential candidacy, **1968-69**: 467 [14,
        16], 480n., 529, 540, 557 [8],
        567-569
    Visit to Vietnam, **1963-64**: 285 [17]
Nixon, Mrs. Richard M., **1968-69**: 540, 578,
    585
Nkrumah, Kwame, **1963-64**: 88
NLF.
    See National Liberation Front.
NMEBA.
    See National Marine Engineers Beneficial
        Association.

Nobel Prize, **1965**: 56
Noble, Bob, **1966**: 358n.
Noble, Jeanne, **1963-64**: 309; **1966**: 315n.
Noise abatement, **1968-69**: 122, 577
Nominations.
    See Appointments and nominations.
Nonaligned nations conference, Cairo, **1963-64**:
    625
Nondiscrimination, **1968-69**: 50, 156, 162, 180,
    406, 423, 442, 460 [2]
    Education, **1968-69**: 26, 54, 82, 91
    Employment, **1968-69**: 14 (p. 31), 24, 26, 47
        (p. 130), 87, 91, 195, 209, 347, 437,
        458, 596, 611
    Government, **1968-69**: 84
    Federal projects, **1968-69**: 26
    Hospitals and medical care facilities, **1968-69**:
        26
    Housing, **1968-69**: 14 (p. 31), 26, 47 (p. 30),
        82, 87, 91, 114, 126, 131, 158, 182,
        191 [1], 192, 195, 212, 380, 596, 611,
        631, 676 (p. 1266), 678 (p. 1289)
        Military personnel, **1968-69**: 26
    Jury selection, **1968-69**: 14 (p. 31), 26, 82,
        158, 611
    Public accommodations, **1968-69**: 26, 82, 87,
        195, 212, 459, 596, 611
    School district boundaries, **1968-69**: 91
    Unions, **1968-69**: 26
    Voting, **1968-69**: 26, 82, 87, 195, 209, 212,
        459, 596, 672, 696 (p. 1264)
Non-immigrant visa bill of 1968, **1968-69**: 88
Nonprofit organizations, housing projects,
    1968-69: 87
Nordberg Manufacturing Co., Inc., **1967**: 231n.
Norfolk, Va., **1965**: 205
Normandy, France, **1963-64**: 384; **1965**: 303;
    1967: 361
Norris, George, **1963-64**: 644, 645; **1966**: 49,
    382, 518
Norris, James J., **1965**: 302
Norstad, Gen. Lauris, **1963-64**: 244, 608
North American Air Defense Command, **1965**:
    158
North Atlantic Alliance, **1965**: 507
North Atlantic Council, **1963-64**: 28ftn. (p. 34),
    49; **1965**: 507
North Atlantic Treaty Organization, **1963-64**:
    44, 54 [14, 15], 76, 177, 182, 384,
    394, 399, 416, 424, 495, 511, 582, 607,
    608, 685, 702, 788; **1965**: 26, 106 [6],
    319 [21], 347 [2], 463 [7], 507, 659,
    660; **1966**: 124 [11], 141 [6, 12], 142,
    200, 228, 236 [5-6], 247 [8], 261,
    395, 482, 486, 503, 506, 577 [6],
    610 [8]; **1967**: 109, 155n., 158n., 162,
    169n., 204 [2], 264 [20], 272, 306n.,
    313n., 347n., 351, 390, 485 [5], 495

North Atlantic Treaty Organization — *continued*
[14], 545, 554 [5]; **1968–69**: 2, 214,
224, 472, 585, 590 [2]
Atomic information, exchange with U.S.,
agreement, **1963–64**: 439, 440
Brussels conference, **1966**: 273
Expansion or revision, question of, **1963–64**:
246 [8]
15th Anniversary, **1963–64**: 244
French withdrawal, **1966**: 158 [13], 607 [5]
Germany, integration of, **1963–64**: 788
Joint Declaration, **1966**: 142n.
Military strength, **1963–64**: 49, 244, 703
Multilateral nuclear force, proposed, **1963–64**:
76, 109, 150 [10], 186, 272, 400,
780 [1, 8]; **1965**: 22 [7, 17]
Nuclear Planning Working Group, **1967**: 167
Parliamentarians, remarks to, **1963–64**: 582
Secretary General (Manlio Brosio), **1963–64**:
587 [2], 608, 609, 610, 612; **1966**:
506; **1967**: 521
Letters, **1963–64**: 495, 685
17th Anniversary, **1966**: 163
U.S. participation, **1965**: 507; **1966**: 445 [24],
607 [3], 654 [3]; **1967**: 3 (p. 10), 44,
348
U.S.-U.K.-German discussions, **1966**: 506
North Atlantic Treaty Organization, Defense
Planning Committee of the, **1967**:
204ftn. (p. 497)
North Carolina, **1966**: 95; **1968–69**: 81 [1]
Antipoverty program, **1963–64**: 103, 326,
327, 328, 329
Campaign remarks, **1963–64**: 631
Candidates for public office, **1963–64**: 631
Gov. Dan K. Moore, **1966**: 122 [1, 2], 491n.,
492 [1], 650n.
Gov. Terry Sanford, **1963–64**: 103, 326, 327,
328, 329, 631, 643, 644
School desegregation, **1965**: 470
North Carolina Fund, **1963–64**: 103, 327
North Cascades National Park, Wash., **1966**: 82;
1967: 13 (p. 51), 20; **1968–69**: 39
(p. 101), 122, 345, 510n., 547, 700
North Dakota, **1966**: 157
Gov. William L. Guy, **1966**: 312, 491n., 492
[1], 536; **1967**: 419n.; **1968–69**: 46n.
North Pacific Ocean, Convention for the High
Seas Fisheries of the, **1965**: 15
Northwest Airlines, Inc., **1966**: 256n., 322
Northwest Ordinance of 1787, **1963–64**: 482;
1965: 9
Northwest-Southwest power transmission
intertie, **1963–64**: 578; **1965**: 186
Northwest Territory, **1966**: 350
Norway, **1965**: 68n.; **1968–69**: 211, 214
King Olav V, **1968–69**: 211, 214
Norwich, Conn., **1967**: 223 [10]

Norwood, William R. (High Commissioner,
Trust Territory of the Pacific Islands),
1967: 133
Novak, Robert D., **1968–69**: 459
Novy, James, **1963–64**: 77
Novy, Louie, **1963–64**: 77
Nuclear attack on U.S., defense measures,
1963–64: 199, 577, 579, 607, 688
[1], 719, 786; **1965**: 26, 32 (p. 90)
Nuclear energy
Peaceful uses, **1966**: 48; **1967**: 336, 367;
1968–69: 27, 308, 349, 378
Research, **1967**: 515; **1968–69**: 145, 308, 608
Nuclear forces in Western Europe, **1963–64**: 467
Nuclear Fuel Services, Inc., **1966**: 179
Nuclear materials, **1965**: 20, 196, 537; **1966**: 32
Private ownership of, **1963–64**: 538
Production decrease, **1963–64**: 91 (p. 117),
122, 129, 130, 131, 132 (p. 185), 272,
285 [3], 287, 294 [14], 295, 395, 434,
435, 486 [1, 2], 562, 642, 820
Nuclear Materials Act, Private Ownership of
Special, approval, **1963–64**: 538
Nuclear Planning Working Group, **1966**: 486;
1967: 167
Nuclear power, **1963–64**: 545; **1965**: 196, 558
Nuclear power projects, **1963–64**: 480; **1965**:
17, 319 [5]; **1966**: 26 (p. 60), 411;
1967: 515
Nuclear-powered ships.
See Ships, nuclear-powered.
Nuclear Proliferation, Committee on, **1965**: 28
Nuclear reactors, **1963–64**: 396; **1965**: 196,
537; **1966**: 48n.; **1967**: 98, 515
Nuclear Research Foundation (University of
Sydney), **1966**: 545
Nuclear rocket propulsion, **1967**: 13 (p. 50), 76
Nuclear test ban treaty, **1963–64**: 91 (p. 116),
122, 132 (p. 185), 186, 199, 382, 395,
413, 434, 435, 529, 625, 638, 686;
1965: 2, 15, 20, 26, 196, 284, 386,
430; **1966**: 32, 411, 450, 483, 503,
560, 643; **1967**: 18n., 59; **1968–69**:
27, 69, 345, 349, 378, 387, 529, 531,
568, 569, 676
Campaign remarks, **1963–64**: 541, 562, 590,
599, 605, 607, 635, 642, 650, 651, 656,
658, 662n., 667, 680, 693, 694, 702,
713, 727, 728, 729, 732, 736, 747, 749,
764
First anniversary, **1963–64**: 486 [1], 653
Safeguards, **1963–64**: 276, 486 [1]
Nuclear war, **1963–64**: 91 (p. 116), 122, 129,
130, 235, 431, 433, 786; **1965**: 26,
284, 430
Campaign remarks, **1963–64**: 562, 607, 695,
701, 728, 733, 760
Nuclear wastes, disposal, **1963–64**: 551

Nuclear weapons, **1963–64**: 132 (p. 184), 382, 413, 467, 736; **1965**: 26, 196, 284, 387; **1966**: 400, 411, 486, 642 [15]; **1967**: 167, 192, 515; **1968–69**: 39 (p. 98), 143, 557 [6]
  See also Missiles; Nuclear weapons tests.
  Antarctica, **1967**: 59
  Civilian-military relationship on, **1963–64**: 475 [7]
  Communist Chinese, **1963–64**: 673, 676, 678, 679, 686, 688 [1], 693, 735, 736, 737, 745, 780 [23], 797; **1966**: 654 [4]
  Control, **1967**: 38, 59, 80 [2]
    See also Arms control and disarmament.
  Decrease, proposed, **1963–64**: 130, 131, 199, 295
  Defense systems, **1963–64**: 780 [1], 788; **1965**: 235
  Europe, **1963–64**: 413; **1965**: 300, 387
  First U.S. nuclear task force, **1963–64**: 619 [5]
  Germany, **1966**: 474 [9]
  Latin America free zone, **1967**: 64; **1968–69**: 13, 73, 349, 392
  Materials for.
    See Nuclear materials.
  Nonproliferation treaty, **1967**: 64, 80 [2], 157, 162, 169n., 192, 204 [4], 225 [17], 272, 280, 328 [24], 340n., 348, 365, 367, 371, 373, 390, 492, 495 [5], 515, 519, 545; **1968–69**: 14 (p. 26), 16, 27, 51 [13], 69, 73, 194, 214n., 288, 308, 310, 335, 345, 350, 371, 378, 387, 390, 392, 425 [8], 467 [5], 531, 567–569, 590 [6], 654, 663, 676 (p. 1268)
    Signing, **1968–69**: 349
  North Atlantic Treaty Organization, multilateral force, proposed, **1963–64**: 76, 109, 150 [10], 186, 272, 400, 780 [1, 8]; **1965**: 22 [7, 17]
  Peaceful uses, **1967**: 64
  Presidential control of, **1963–64**: 760, 762; **1965**: 26, 208 [18]
  Proliferation, **1963–64**: 51, 122, 129, 130, 131, 619 [15], 686, 696, 820; **1965**: 20, 22 [7], 28, 284, 386, 430, 463 [7], 523, 660; **1966**: 32, 70, 411, 450, 480, 486, 560, 654 [4]
    Danger of, **1963–64**: 797; **1965**: 284, 319 [5], 347 [2]
  Research and development, **1963–64**: 170 [3]; **1965**: 196
  Soviet, **1963–64**: 382, 395, 413, 653
  Space, **1963–64**: 395, 486 [1], 579, 686; **1966**: 209, 272, 411; **1967**: 18, 38, 59, 64, 80 [2], 425, 488; **1968–69**: 14 (p. 26)
  United Kingdom, **1963–64**: 653

Nuclear weapons — *continued*
  Use in Southeast Asia, question of, **1965**: 208 [18]
  Vietnam conflict, **1966**: 501 [14]
  Vietnam use, question, **1963–64**: 516 [2, 6], 638; **1968–69**: 79 [9]
  War, **1966**: 480, 483, 642 [15, 20]
Nuclear weapons tests
  Ban or suspension, **1963–64**: 109, 140, 170 [15], 186, 272, 394n., 529, 651, 702, 719, 736, 764, 797, 820; **1965**: 15, 20
  Treaty.
    See Nuclear test ban treaty.
  U.S. proposals, **1963–64**: 91 (pp. 116, 117), 122, 129, 130, 131, 693
  Fallout.
    See Radioactive fallout.
  Geneva conferences.
    See Geneva conferences.
  Inspection and control, **1963–64**: 91 (p. 116), 132 (p. 185), 276
  Prohibition
    In Antarctica, **1963–64**: 551
    In space, **1965**: 284
  Scientific and technical data, dissemination, **1963–64**: 462 [5]
  Soviet, **1963–64**: 653
  Underground, **1963–64**: 132 (p. 185), 462 [4]
  United Kingdom, **1963–64**: 653
Nuevo Laredo, Mexico, **1968–69**: 91
Nugent, Patrick J., **1966**: 338ftn. (p. 750), 417 [1], 513; **1967**: 225 [16], 529; **1968–69**: 233, 460 [2], 576, 588, 603n., 630, 646 [14], 648, 688n., 690, 691, 696 [17]
Nugent, Mrs. Patrick J. (Luci Baines Johnson), **1966**: 65 [10], 72, 168, 240, 257, 338ftn. (p. 750), 413, 417 [1, 8], 484, 513; **1967**: 210, 225 [16], 273, 278n., 332, 420, 493, 517, 529, 538, 540; **1968–69**: 50, 96n., 171, 299n., 305, 368, 369, 374, 567, 576, 588, 602, 604, 623, 630, 646 [2], 655, 696 [17]
  See also Johnson, Luci Baines.
Nugent, Patrick Lyndon, **1967**: 225 [16], 270, 273, 278, 281, 498n., 529; **1968–69**: 8n., 142, 165, 225, 233, 260, 368, 460ftn. (p. 916), 499, 510, 537, 549, 568–570, 576, 588, 595, 602, 603n., 623, 631, 646 [14], 648, 655, 661, 690, 695, 696 [17]
Nulato, Alaska, Christmas tree, **1968–69**: 629n.
Nurse Training Act of 1964, **1965**: 340; **1966**: 95; **1968–69**: 111, 447
  Approval, **1963–64**: 557

Nurses, **1966**: 89, 95, 253, 580 [10]; **1967**: 15, 77
  Education and training, **1963–64**: 91 (p. 115), 132 (p. 189), 179, 557, 620, 755; **1965**: 100
  Shortage of, **1963–64**: 520; **1965**: 531
Nurses Association, American, **1966**: 490
Nursing homes, **1963–64**: 178, 179, 415, 755; **1965**: 5; **1966**: 27, 509, 515, 580 [7]; **1967**: 12, 13 (p. 53), 298, 419; **1968–69**: 19
Nutritional program, Project Head Start, **1966**: 45
NYA.
  See National Youth Administration.

Oak Ridge, Tenn., **1963–64**: 297 [2], 648, 650, 657, 659, 701
Oakes, E. M., **1967**: 420n.
Oakes, John, **1963–64**: 622; **1968–69**: 227
OAS.
  See Organization of American States.
Oates, James F., Jr., **1963–64**: 211 [6]
Oath of office, first official remarks following, **1963–64**: 1
O'Boyle, Patrick A., **1963–64**: 301, 788; **1968–69**: 78, 470, 629
O'Brien, Daniel J., **1963–64**: 605
O'Brien, Davy, **1968–69**: 282
O'Brien, Dorothy, **1963–64**: 635, 636, 747
O'Brien, James C., **1965**: 642n.
O'Brien, Lawrence F., **1963–64**: 224, 396, 727; **1965**: 22 [1], 394, 448 [19], 463 [1, 9], 559; **1968–69**: 216
  See also Postmaster General (Lawrence F. O'Brien).
O'Brien, Mrs. Lawrence F., **1965**: 463 [1]; **1966**: 470
O'Brien, Repr. Leo W., **1965**: 568n.; **1966**: 522
O'Brien, Robert, **1963–64**: 666
O'Brien, Repr. Thomas J., **1963–64**: 287, 763
Obscene literature, **1966**: 611
Occupational safety, **1967**: 77
Occupational Safety, Conference on, **1963–64**: 421
Occupational safety and health bill of 1968, **1968–69**: 24, 111, 154, 390, 475, 607, 678 (p. 1293), 684 (p. 1323)
Occupational training, **1963–64**: 47, 53, 124 (p. 165), 132 (pp. 176, 181, 182), 213, 219, 228, 235, 288, 289, 290, 291, 292, 295, 297, 327, 338, 386, 406, 413, 431, 486 [2], 589, 598, 603, 606, 775; **1965**: 35 (p. 113), 452, 453, 475, 632; **1966**: 26 (pp. 55, 63–64), 34 (pp. 99, 103), 111, 127, 258, 422, 429, 588; **1967**: 3 (p. 2), 13 (p. 54), 16 (pp. 79, 83), 55, 114, 193, 199, 261, 286, 291,

Occupational training – *continued*
    412, 479, 512; **1968–69**: 6, 14 (p. 28), 39 (pp. 105, 110), 24, 47 (p. 142), 54, 75, 91, 105, 162, 219, 238, 262, 390, 442, 484, 538, 565–569, 676 (pp. 1264, 1266), 678 (p. 1294), 684 (pp. 1311, 1313, 1316), 701
  Construction workers, **1968–69**: 684 (p. 1322)
  District of Columbia programs, **1963–64**: 133, 457n.; **1965**: 70, 111; **1966**: 586
  Federal aid, **1963–64**: 55, 132 (pp. 189, 191); **1965**: 204, 207, 215, 509; **1966**: 95, 100, 586; **1967**: 13 (p. 54), 16 (p. 82), 67, 91
  Federal-State-local responsibility, **1968–69**: 39 (p. 108)
  Foreign assistance, **1966**: 34 (p. 105)
  Government employees, **1966**: 404; **1967**: 184
  Handicapped persons, **1963–64**: 179, 213, 302, 305; **1966**: 26 (p. 63), 111, 127; **1967**: 413
  Hard-core unemployed program, **1968–69**: 24–26, 37, 39 (p. 104), 50, 87, 91, 92, 105, 133, 141, 227, 555, 678 (p. 1294), 684 (pp. 1314, 1324)
  Health personnel, **1966**: 26 (p. 62); **1967**: 16 (p. 85), 77, 285
  Indians, **1965**: 204; **1968–69**: 113
  Law enforcement personnel, **1965**: 2, 70, 102, 381, 526; **1966**: 116; **1967**: 3 (p. 6); **1968–69**: 14 (p. 30), 59, 133, 320, 355, 557 [8]
  Migrant workers, **1967**: 114
  Military personnel, **1968–69**: 39 (p. 106)
  Military rejectees, **1963–64**: 266 [21], 336 [2]
  Minority groups, **1966**: 136
  Older persons, **1963–64**: 213; **1965**: 72; **1966**: 253, 270
  Prisoners, **1965**: 509; **1966**: 111, 116, 588; **1967**: 71
  Report, **1963–64**: 160; **1968–69**: 6
  Schools, **1967**: 193
  Scientists, **1965**: 514; **1966**: 95
  Task force, **1967**: 199
  Teachers, **1965**: 9, 70, 111, 368, 369, 401, 479; **1967**: 13 (p. 55), 77
  Unemployed workers, **1963–64**: 99, 160, 213, 321, 504 [7], 669, 690n.; **1965**: 38, 70, 79, 100, 165; **1966**: 588
  Veterans, **1965**: 456; **1966**: 26 (p. 64), 100
  Women, **1967**: 93
  Work-experience program, **1966**: 26 (p. 63), 111; **1967**: 55, 199
  Work-study program, **1966**: 95, 111, 172, 189; **1967**: 13 (p. 55), 39
  Work-training program, **1965**: 100, 208 [13], 268; **1966**: 588; **1967**: 13 (p. 54), 114; **1968–69**: 24, 86, 87, 94, 684 (p. 1311)

Occupational training – *continued*
  Young people, **1963–64**: 55, 89, 199, 213, 218 [15], 267, 451n., 504 [7], 658, 704n., 742, 787, 791; **1965**: 35 (p. 114), 100, 208 [5], 268, 322, 340, 578; **1966**: 105, 172, 588; **1967**: 114, 193, 484
Ocean Eagle, **1968–69**: 122, 586
Ocean Exploration, International Decade of, proposed, **1968–69**: 122, 692
Oceanic research, **1963–64**: 229; **1965**: 71, 92, 247; **1966**: 229, 326, 461
Oceanic resources.
  See also Marine resources.
  Fish resources, **1966**: 569
Oceanographer research ship, **1966**: 326; **1967**: 20
Oceanographic program, national, **1965**: 92
Oceanography, **1967**: 20, 101, 223 [5]; **1968–69**: 14 (p. 27), 122, 124, 227, 288, 504
Oceanography, Interagency Committee on, **1963–64**: 229
Ochel, Ernest A., **1967**: 388
O'Connell, Gen. John P., **1967**: 433
O'Connor, Basil, **1967**: 21
O'Connor, Frank D., **1966**: 510–513
O'Connor, Herbert R., Jr., **1963–64**: 703
O'Connor, Lawrence J., Jr., **1966**: 268
Odegaard, Charles, **1966**: 208n.; **1967**: 500
Odell, Arthur Gould, Jr., **1965**: 315n.
Odell, Charles E., **1965**: 642n.
Odlin, Reno, **1968–69**: 537
Odlum, Floyd B., dinner honoring, **1968–69**: 262
Odlum, Mrs. Floyd B. (Jacqueline Cochran), **1968–69**: 262, 616
O'Donnell, P. Kenneth, **1963–64**: 224, 396, 727; **1965**: 22 [1]
OECD.
  See Organization for Economic Cooperation and Development.
Officer, Charles B., **1963–64**: 607
Official funerals, protocol of, **1965**: 46 [6]
Offshore mineral deposits, **1967**: 101
Offutt Air Force Base, Nebraska, **1963–64**: 609, 610
Ohakea, New Zealand, **1966**: 538
O'Hara, Repr. Barratt, **1965**: 142; **1966**: 228
O'Hara, Repr. James G., **1963–64**: 356; **1965**: 582; **1966**: 431
O'Hare, John, **1963–64**: 590
O'Hare International Airport, Chicago, **1968–69**: 183
Ohio
  Antipoverty program, **1963–64**: 322, 323
  Area redevelopment programs, **1965**: 132
  Campaign remarks, **1963–64**: 642, 678, 679, 680, 693

Ohio – *continued*
  Candidates for public office, **1963–64**: 642, 678, 679, 680, 693
  Democratic State convention, **1966**: 417 [10]
  Gov. James A. Rhodes, **1963–64**: 217, 322, 323; **1965**: 190, 191; **1966**: 122 [1, 2], 124 [2, 4, 8, 10], 434, 599 [3]; **1967**: 552n., 558; **1968–69**: 58, 406
  Remarks, **1968–69**: 406
  Visit to, **1965**: 190
Ohio River Basin, **1963–64**: 597, 644, 729; **1966**: 427
  Flood, **1963–64**: 217
Ohio River Bridge, **1967**: 558
Ohio State University, **1963–64**: 339
Ohio University, **1963–64**: 323; **1965**: 132
Ohmart, Goehler E., **1967**: 420n.
Oil
  Coastal waters pollution, **1967**: 240; **1968–69**: 122, 124, 390, 684 (p. 1321)
  Continental Shelf, **1968–69**: 411, 547, 567, 646 [13]
  Depots in North Vietnam, bombing, **1966**: 338 [19]
  Imports, **1965**: 641 [5]
  Industry, **1968–69**: 644
  Middle East conflict, supply impact, **1967**: 358 [11]
  Shale processing, **1967**: 358 [11]
  Spill emergencies, **1968–69**: 297, 586
Oil, United States National Committee for the Prevention of Pollution of the Seas by, **1967**: 240
Oil and Hazardous Materials, National Inter-Agency Committee for Control of Pollution by, **1968–69**: 586
Oil Pollution Act, 1924, **1968–69**: 297
Oil pollution and hazardous substance control bill of 1968, **1968–69**: 122
Oil Pollution Industry Advisory Board, **1967**: 240
Okefenokee Wilderness, Ga., **1968–69**: 168
O'Kelly, Sean T., **1963–64**: 364n.
Okinawa, administration of, **1968–69**: 44
Oklahoma, **1963–64**: 486 [7]; **1965**: 132; **1966**: 157, 416, 417 [1]; **1967**: 270
  Campaign remarks, **1963–64**: 597, 598
  Eufaula Dam, dedication, **1963–64**: 597
  Gov. Dewey Bartlett, **1968–69**: 46n.
  Gov. Henry Bellmon, **1963–64**: 597, 598; **1966**: 401 [7], 415–416, 417 [1], 491n., 492 [1, 10]
Oklahoma City, Okla., campaign remarks, **1963–64**: 598
Okun, Arthur M., **1963–64**: 771; **1966**: 33
  See also Council of Economic Advisers, Chairman.
Okun, Mrs. Arthur M., **1968–69**: 76

Olav V (King of Norway), **1968-69**: 211, 214
Old, Dr. Bruce S., **1967**: 416n.
Old-age assistance bill.
  See Social Security Amendments of 1965.
Old Man of the Mountain, N.H., **1966**: 392
Older Americans, Advisory Committee on,
    1965: 642
Older Americans Act of 1965, **1965**: 354;
    1966: 95; **1967**: 12, 299; **1968-69**: 75
Older Americans Act Amendments of 1967,
    1967: 12n., 296, 297 [9], 299
Older persons, **1963-64**: 297, 630; **1965**: 354,
    642; **1966**: 34 (p. 100), 235, 509;
    1967: 261, 296, 297 [9], 299, 534;
    1968-69: 39 (p. 105, 110), 117, 164,
    331, 397
  See also Medicare.
  "A Republican Approach to the Needs of the
    Aging," **1966**: 509
  Community service projects, **1968-69**: 75
  District of Columbia, **1967**: 574
  Employment, **1963-64**: 178, 213, 431, 690n.;
    1965: 72; **1966**: 253, 270; **1967**: 12,
    114, 199; **1968-69**: 24, 75
  Equal opportunity, **1963-64**: 415
  Federal aid, **1965**: 461
  Federal programs, **1967**: 12
  Government service, **1963-64**: 213, 712
  Health, **1963-64**: 91 (p. 112); **1965**: 90, 176
    [2], 501; **1966**: 95, 353; **1967**: 12, 13
    (p. 53), 179; **1968-69**: 19, 20, 39
    (p. 103), 47 (p. 143), 75, 87, 108, 111,
    114, 154, 346, 406, 567, 672, 678 (pp.
    1286, 1295, 1296)
  Housing, **1963-64**: 91 (p. 115), 124 (p. 164),
    132 (p. 188), 152, 178, 415, 431, 590,
    712; **1965**: 415; **1966**: 26 (p. 61), 253,
    509; **1968-69**: 19, 20, 678 (p. 1289)
  Income, **1963-64**: 178, 338, 590, 667;
    1965: 176 [2], 215, 461; **1966**: 168,
    253
  Legislation, **1968-69**: 655
  Library services for, **1966**: 362
  Medical care, **1963-64**: 219, 267, 292, 297,
    406, 541, 548, 640, 648, 667, 680;
    1965: 5, 32 (p. 94), 348, 394, 632;
    1966: 26 (p. 55), 95, 122 [2], 189,
    271, 273, 309, 353, 429, 433, 509,
    545, 580 [7]; **1967**: 3 (p. 2), 12, 15,
    81, 114, 286, 298, 574
  Message to Congress, **1967**: 12
  Neighborhood center, **1968-69**: 19, 20
  Public service volunteers, **1963-64**: 712
  Retirement, **1963-64**: 431
  Senior Citizens Month, **1965**: 72
  Social security.
    See main heading, Social Security.

Older persons – *continued*
  Welfare of, **1968-69**: 47 (p. 141), 108, 678
    (p. 1298)
  Welfare measures, District of Columbia,
    1963-64: 133
Olds, Col. Robin, **1967**: 536
Olive, Mr. and Mrs. Milton B., Jr., **1966**: 183
Olive, Pfc. Milton L., III, **1966**: 183
Oliver, Bernard, **1966**: 637n.
Oliver, Covey T., **1968-69**: 66, 362n., 368
Olivier, Giorgio Borg, **1963-64**: 585
Ollendorff, Henry B., **1967**: 365
Olsen, Repr. Arnold, **1963-64**: 267, 656;
    1968-69: 330
Olson, Repr. Alec G., **1963-64**: 434; **1965**: 189
Olson, R. A., **1963-64**: 590
Olympic Committee, United States, **1963-64**: 699
Olympic games, ancient, **1963-64**: 106
Olympic Games (1964), **1963-64**: 632, 699, 782
  Medal winners, U.S., **1963-64**: 782
Olympic Games for the Deaf (1965),
    1963-64: 808
Olympic team, U.S., **1963-64**: 699; **1968-69**: 571
Omaha, Nebr., **1963-64**: 609, 610, 685;
    1966: 277 [1], 311
  Mayor A. V. Sorensen, **1966**: 311
O'Malley, Brian, **1966**: 641
O'Malley, Gen. C. S., Jr., **1968-69**: 70
O'Malley, Daniel, **1966**: 641
O'Malley, John, **1966**: 641
O'Malley, Mrs. John, **1966**: 641
O'Malley, Sgt. Robert E., **1966**: 641
Omar, Haji Farah Ali, **1968-69**: 137
O'Meara, Gen. Andrew P., **1963-64**: 95
Omnibus Crime Control and Safe Streets Act of
    1968, **1968-69**: 14 (p. 30), 39 (p.
    107), 50, 57, 59, 87, 133, 235, 257,
    263, 296, 302n., 325, 333-355, 542,
    553, 561, 567, 655, 676 (p. 1266), 678
    (p. 1291)
  See also Safe Streets and Crime Control bill.
  Signing, **1968-69**: 320
101st Airborne Division, Army, **1966**: 348, 353
121st Aviation Company (Air Mobile Light),
    USA, **1966**: 107
173rd Airborne Brigade, **1966**: 348
O'Neil, Joseph R., Jr., **1967**: 352n.
O'Neill, Francis A., Jr. (Chairman, National
    Mediation Board), **1963-64**: 251, 284,
    297 [2]; **1967**: 170, 310
O'Neill, Richard W., **1967**: 4n.
O'Neill, Repr. Thomas P., Jr., **1963-64**: 727
Onsager, Lars, **1968-69**: 695n.
Open arms program, **1966**: 501 [2]
Open housing (nondiscrimination), **1966**: 6 (pp.
    3, 5), 30, 196, 247 [10], 375, 474 [14],
    475; **1967**: 3 (p. 51), 55
  See also Housing; Civil Rights Act of 1968.

[References are to items except as otherwise indicated]

Opera Association, Metropolitan (New York), **1966**: 466, 482

Opera Company, National, proposed, **1965**: 534

Operation Green Thumb, **1967**: 114

Operation Medicare Alert, **1966**: 169n., 253

Operation Outreach, **1968-69**: 94

Operation TAP (Talent for America's Progress), **1966**: 619

Opium stockpiles, **1966**: 283n.

Oppenheimer, Dr. J. Robert, **1963-64**: 19; **1968-69**: 608
  Death, **1967**: 62

Oppenheimer, Mrs. J. Robert, **1963-64**: 19

Opportunities Industrialization Center, Philadelphia, Pa., **1967**: 291

Opportunity, equal.
  See Equal opportunity.

Optometric Association, American, **1965**: 467

Orbiter spacecraft, **1967**: 13 (p. 50); **1968-69**: 107

Orchestras, symphony, **1968-69**: 64

Order of the Loyal Legion of the United States, Military, **1967**: 49n.

Oregon, **1963-64**: 135, 590; **1967**: 418
  Campaign remarks, **1963-64**: 578
  Flood relief, **1965**: 74
  Gov. Mark O. Hatfield, **1963-64**: 575, 578; **1965**: 388 [14]; **1966**: 124 [7]
  Primary election, **1963-64**: 211 [22]

Oregon, U.S.S., **1963-64**: 578

Oregon Dunes National Seashore, Oreg., **1966**: 82
  Proposed, **1965**: 54

Organic Act of Guam, **1968-69**: 477

Organization of African Unity, **1963-64**: 191, 460; **1965**: 571; **1966**: 243; **1967**: 51n., 52; **1968-69**: 140n., 157, 181, 508, 511n.
  Consultative Committee on Nigeria, **1968-69**: 433
  Fifth annual assembly, message, **1968-69**: 482

Organization of American States, **1963-64**: 91 (p. 117), 177, 193, 695; **1965**: 212, 216, 217, 221, 227, 286, 293, 342, 393, 429, 463 [4], 632; **1966**: 16, 125, 273, 341, 386n.; **1967**: 100, 152, 395; **1968-69**: 239, 479
  See also American Republics.
  Ad Hoc Committee, **1965**: 364, 463 [4]
  Ambassadors meeting, **1963-64**: 218 [34]
  Charter, Protocol of Amendments to, **1968-69**: 205, 206
  Communist aggression, defense measures, **1963-64**: 443
  Dominican Republic
    Aid to, **1965**: 295 [1, 4, 6, 16], 319 [16], 473, 484
    Mission to, **1965**: 218, 221, 223, 227, 253, 347 [3]; **1966**: 277 [3, 25]

Organization of American States — *continued*
  Inter-American conference, Rio de Janiero, **1965**: 593, 624
  Inter-American Force, **1965**: 286, 295 [1, 4, 10], 319 [4, 16], 342, 463 [4]
  Inter-American Peace Committee, **1963-64**: 104, 143 [1], 150 [14]
  Joint committee on U.S.-Panama dispute, **1963-64**: 104, 232 [1], 245
  News conference remarks, **1963-64**: 54 [15], 143 [1], 150 [14], 211 [8], 232 [1], 455 [18], 486 [3], 688 [8]
  Secretary General (José A. Mora), **1965**: 227, 286, 295 [1, 4, 6], 473, 482; **1966**: 386, 478; **1967**: 357, 395; **1968-69**: 205
  U.S. Representative (Ellsworth Bunker), **1965**: 221, 227, 347 [3], 353 [2], 364, 448 [18], 472, 473, 482, 632; **1966**: 501 [1]
  U.S. Representative (Sol M. Linowitz), **1966**: 635 [14]

Organization of Central American States, **1968-69**: 365-367

Organization for Economic Cooperation and Development, **1963-64**: 472; **1965**: 18, 495; **1966**: 343; **1967**: 33, 44, 306n.; **1968-69**: 47 (p. 138), 214

Organization of the Executive Branch of the Government, Commission on, **1966**: 190, 438, 523; **1967**: 99, 121; **1968-69**: 59, 60, 227

Organized crime, **1966**: 116, 204-205, 487; **1967**: 35, 382, 468; **1968-69**: 39 (p. 107), 59, 553, 561

Orioles (Baltimore Baseball Club, Inc.), **1966**: 509

Orlando, Fla.
  Campaign remarks, **1963-64**: 712
  Mayor Robert S. Carr, **1963-64**: 712

Orlich, Francisco J., **1963-64**: 438, 441, 443, 455 [16]

Orlich, Mrs. Francisco J., **1963-64**: 438

Orly Airport, Paris, **1963-64**: 54ftn. (p. 70)

Ormsby Gore, David (Lord Harlech), **1963-64**: 187n., 263n., 796

Ormsby Gore, Lady (Lady Harlech), **1963-64**: 187

O'Rourke, Paul, **1963-64**: 580n.

Orphans
  Benefits for, **1967**: 114
  Philippine, **1966**: 495
  Social security benefits, **1968-69**: 3

Orthopedic handicaps, **1968-69**: 111

Orwig, LaVerne, **1966**: 428

Osborne, Stanley de J., **1963-64**: 201 [2]

O'Shea, Bernard, **1963-64**: 605

Osler, Sir William, **1967**: 201

Oswald, John W., **1965**: 80
Oswald, Lee Harvey, **1965**: 102
Otenasek, Mildred, **1963–64**: 703
Otepka, Otto F., **1965**: 106 [3]
Ottawa, Canada, **1967**: 239n.
Outdoor advertising, control, **1965**: 54, 277, 279, 576n.
Outdoor Recreation, Bureau of, **1963–64**: 578, 756
Outer Continental Shelf, **1968–69**: 39 (p. 101)
Outer Space, United Nations Committee on Peaceful Uses of, **1963–64**: 705; **1966**: 277ftn. (p. 631); **1967**: 18n., 557
Outer space treaty.
  See Space research and exploration; Space treaty.
Overby, Charles, **1963–64**: 331
Over-exposure of the President, question of, **1963–64**: 316 [20], 336 [10]
Overhage, Carl, **1966**: 424n.
Owen, Henry D., **1966**: 277 [5]
Owen, Mr. and Mrs. William F., **1968–69**: 397
Owens, Hugh, **1963–64**: 211 [2]; **1966**: 416
Owings, Nathaniel, **1968–69**: 167
Oxford teach-in on Vietnam, **1965**: 347 [5]
Ozark National Scenic Riverways bill, **1963–64**: 554n.

Pace, Frank, Jr., **1967**: 510n.; **1968–69**: 370
Pachios, Hal, **1966**: 399
Pacific area, U.S. troops in, **1966**: 37
Pacific-Atlantic Interoceanic Canal Study Commission, **1965**: 400
Pacific-Atlantic sea-level canal, proposed, **1963–64**: 266 [5], 594; **1965**: 400
Pacific community, **1965**: 256
Pacific Council, Asian and, **1966**: 542, 564–565; **1967**: 44, 111, 219; **1968–69**: 525
Pacific Crest Trail, **1968–69**: 510
Pacific Islands, Trust Territory of the, **1967**: 133, 218, 360
Pacific Northwest Disaster Relief Act of 1965, **1965**: 317
Pacific Northwest fisheries, **1963–64**: 559; **1965**: 15
Pacific Northwest power projects, **1966**: 269
Pacific Northwest River Basins Commission, **1968–69**: 593, 666
Pacific Ocean, Convention for the High Seas Fisheries of the North, **1965**: 15
Pacific Ocean, trans-oceanic telephone cable, **1963–64**: 408
Pacific partnership, **1963–64**: 91 (p. 117); **1965**: 8, 12, 15
Pacific Pumps, Inc., **1967**: 231n.

Packaging and labeling, **1963–64**: 173; **1965**: 35 (p. 115); **1966**: 6 (p. 6), 34 (p. 108), 140, 576; **1967**: 57, 86, 200, 393, 465, 534; **1968–69**: 56, 545
Packard, David, **1965**: 522n.
Packard, George R., **1968–69**: 101n.
Packers and Stockyards Act, amendment, **1968–69**: 94
Padre Island National Seashore, Texas, **1968–69**: 648
Page, Robert, **1968–69**: 106n.
Page School, Capitol, **1966**: 270
Pages, Capitol Page School, **1965**: 316
Pago Pago, American Samoa, **1966**: 537; **1967**: 559
Pahlavi, Shah Mohammad Reza, **1963–64**: 369, 385; **1965**: 517; **1967**: 363, 364, 366, 509; **1968–69**: 304, 307, 613, 614
Paiewonsky, Gov. Ralph M., **1968–69**: 457, 477
Paine, Thomas, **1963–64**: 579; **1966**: 542, 634; **1967**: 549; **1968–69**: 291n.
Paine, Dr. Thomas O. (National Aeronautics and Space Acting Administrator), **1968–69**: 574, 616, 646 [1, 5, 9], 647, 662
Painter, Capt. W. B., **1965**: 114
Paintings in the President's collection, **1965**: 82
Paintsville, Ky., **1963–64**: 291, 292
Pak, Chung Hee.
  See Park, Chung Hee.
Pake, George, **1965**: 166n.
Pakistan, **1965**: 347 [2]; **1966**: 148, 153, 277 [17]; **1967**: 297 [3], 449, 452, 569
  Ambassador Ghulam Ahmed, **1965**: 649
  Assistance, **1963–64**: 227; **1965**: 649; **1966**: 11n., 41; **1967**: 3 (p. 10), 44; **1968–69**: 39 (p. 99), 63, 679
  Bhutto, Zulfikar Ali (Foreign Secretary), **1965**: 649
  Economic and social progress, **1965**: 649n.
  Food needs, **1967**: 469
  Indian relations, **1965**: 176 [1], 649n., 650; **1966**: 41, 148, 153–154; **1968–69**: 335
  Kashmir dispute, **1963–64**: 607; **1965**: 169, 208 [10], 463 [5], 524, 529; **1967**: 100
  President Mohammed Ayub Khan, **1965**: 208, 529, 641 [3], 648, 649, 650; **1966**: 247 [7], 273, 514; **1967**: 569
  U.S. Ambassador Eugene Locke, **1967**: 116
  U.S. medical mission to, **1965**: 649
  U.S. relations with, **1965**: 208 [17], 649n., 650
  Visit, **1967**: 569
Palatka, Fla., **1963–64**: 198
Palm Springs, Calif., **1963–64**: 193
Palmer, Lt. Gen. Bruce, Jr., **1965**: 286, 295 [1], 299, 319 [4], 342; **1967**: 567; **1968–69**: 283 [1]

Palmer, H. Bruce, **1965**: 76
Palmer, Lester, **1963–64**: 72n., 763; **1967**: 210
Palmer, Mrs. Lester, **1967**: 210
Palmer, Joseph, 2d, **1966**: 141 [12]
Palmerston, Lord, **1966**: 359
Pan American Airways, **1966**: 64
Pan American Congress of Architects, Eleventh, **1965**: 315
Pan American Day and Week proclamation, **1967**: 152
Pan American Development Foundation, **1967**: 357n.
Pan American Health Organization, **1965**: 262; **1966**: 45, 386
Pan American Highway, **1966**: 175; **1968–69**: 696 [11]
Pan American Society Gold Medal Award, **1968–69**: 665
Pan American Union, **1965**: 482
Panama, **1963–64**: 594, 688 [6]; **1967**: 44, 336; **1968–69**: 66, 205, 364
  Ambassador Ricardo Arias Espinosa, **1965**: 532
  Assistance, **1963–64**: 285 [6]; **1968–69**: 679
  Canal study, **1968–69**: 466
  Canal Zone, **1965**: 400
  Canal Zone dispute.
    See main heading, Canal Zone dispute, U.S.-Panama.
  Chiari, Roberto F., **1963–64**: 95, 201 [6], 232 [1], 245, 316 [11], 607
  Diplomatic relations with, renewal, **1963–64**: 245
  President Marco A. Robles, **1965**: 532
  Sea-level canal, **1966**: 384
    Proposed, **1965**: 532
  U.S. Ambassador Jack Hood Vaughn, **1963–64**: 245n., 246 [4], 285 [6], 316 [11], 809
  U.S. economic team to, report, **1963–64**: 316 [11]
  U.S. relations with, **1963–64**: 143 [1], 150 [2], 170 [1], 201 [6], 218 [30], 242 [11], 246 [1, 10], 272, 285 [13], 316 [11], 809
  U.S. Special Ambassador Robert B. Anderson, **1963–64**: 245
  U.S. troops in, **1965**: 532
Panama, Isthmus of, **1966**: 411
Panama Canal
  See Panama.
Panama Canal Company, **1963–64**: 81
Panama Canal Treaty, proposed revision, **1963–64**: 220, 232 [1], 246 [10], 809
Panel of Consultants on Foreign Affairs, **1963–64**: 696
Panel of Consultants on Peace and National Security, **1963–64**: 591

Panel on Federal Salaries, Special, **1965**: 244, 612
Papandreou, George, **1963–64**: 424, 429
Pappas, Judge John, **1963–64**: 211 [1]
Papper, Dr. E. M., **1963–64**: 211 [6]
Parachute jumping, incentive pay for hazardous duty involving, **1965**: 633
Paraguay, **1968–69**: 205
  Economic and social development, **1968–69**: 147, 148n.
  President Alfredo Stroessner, **1968–69**: 147, 148
Paramaribo, Surinam, **1967**: 178
Parasitic diseases, prevention, **1968–69**: 685
Parcel post bill, **1966**: 470
Parents' Magazine award, **1965**: 614
Pargo submarine, keel laying, **1963–64**: 383
Paris, France, report on Ho Chi Minh statement, **1966**: 320 [18]
Paris, North Atlantic Council, foreign ministers meeting, **1963–64**: 28ftn. (p. 34)
Paris Air Show, **1965**: 320
Paris peace talks on Vietnam, **1968–69**: 223 [1, 6], 224, 225, 233, 237, 241, 242, 246, 267, 271n., 273, 275 [1, 3], 277, 280, 283 [3, 4, 9], 307, 339 [5, 10], 398, 400, 401, 425 [8], 452, 467 [12, 14], 472, 511n., 529, 564, 572, 590 [5, 9], 606, 611, 646 [3, 6, 11], 676 (pp. 1267, 1269), 678 (pp. 1274, 1276), 682, 683
Park, Chung Hee (President of South Korea), **1965**: 344n., 407; **1966**: 492 [4], 514, 516 [1], 549, 561–562, 565–566a; **1967**: 111n., 112n., 113, 409, 563; **1968–69**: 35, 51 [15], 79 [13], 197, 198, 200, 201, 223 [7], 224
  Letter, **1965**: 423
  Visit, **1965**: 254, 256, 257
Park, Mrs. Chung Hee, **1965**: 256; **1966**: 561–562, 566a; **1967**: 111n.
Park, Chung Hun, **1967**: 113
Park, Tai Wan, **1966**: 564
Park Association, National Recreation and, **1966**: 518
Park Foundation, National, **1967**: 553
Park Police, United States, **1966**: 27
Park Service, National, **1966**: 27, 411n., 579; **1967**: 553
Parking facilities, **1967**: 114
Parkinson, C. Jay, **1968–69**: 106n.
Parks, Rev. A. Gene, **1963–64**: 571
Parks, **1968–69**: 458, 470, 672, 676 (p. 1264), 684 (p. 1321)
  See also specific parks.
  National, **1963–64**: 357, 427, 578, 620, 642, 669, 756; **1965**: 53, 222, 277, 471, 521, 560; **1966**: 26 (p. 60), 82, 119, 202,

Parks — *continued*
National — *continued*
    398, 448, 518, 522, 524, 579; **1967**:
    13 (pp. 44, 51), 20, 90, 96, 418, 534;
    1968-69: 122, 123, 167, 345, 386, 406,
    510, 547, 567, 601, 655, 707
Public, **1963-64**: 287
Roadside, **1968-69**: 122
State and local, **1963-64**: 422; **1965**: 54, 242,
    277; **1966**: 26 (p. 60), 398
Trails, proposed projects, **1965**: 54
Parks, Historic Sites, Buildings and Monuments,
    Advisory Board on National, **1965**:
    538n.
Parole and probation, **1968-69**: 59
Parr, David L., **1968-69**: 462
Parsons, Irene, **1966**: 89
Parsons, Judge James B., **1965**: 422n.
Participation certificates, **1967**: 13 (p. 44), 329,
    330, 420; **1968-69**: 39 (pp. 96, 108)
Federal, **1966**: 596
Participation Sales Act of 1966, **1966**: 182,
    199n., 231
Partners of the Alliance program, **1968-69**: 63
Partnership for Health Amendments of 1967,
    1967: 12, 57, 77, 318n., 520, 539;
    1968-69: 111
Partridge, Robert D., **1968-69**: 305n.
Pasadena, Tex., campaign remarks, **1963-64**: 762
Pasayten Wilderness, Washington, **1968-69**:
    510n.
Paso del Norte Bridge, El Paso, Texas, **1967**:
    454; **1968-69**: 623n.
Passage Key Wilderness, Fla., **1968-69**: 168
Passamaquoddy-St. John River Basin develop-
    ment, **1965**: 350
Passamaquoddy title power project, **1963-64**:
    606
Passman, Repr. Otto E., **1963-64**: 150 [7];
    1968-69: 691
Passow, A. Harry, **1968-69**: 133ftn. (p. 387)
Pasteur, Louis, **1966**: 166
Pastore, Sen. John O., **1963-64**: 149, 538, 540,
    560 [10], 581, 601, 602; **1965**: 200, 242,
    449; **1966**: 396, 417 [15], 478, 513;
    1967: 225 [1], 391, 474; **1968-69**:
    378
Patent fees, **1965**: 32 (p. 88)
Proposed revision, **1963-64**: 132 (p. 181)
Patent Office, **1965**: 249n., 497
User charges, **1966**: 225
Patent reform bill, **1967**: 65
Patent system, **1967**: 16 (p. 87), 65
Patent System, President's Commission on the,
    1966: 635 [3], 637
Pathet Lao, **1963-64**: 201 [7]; **1966**: 514

Patman, Repr. Wright, **1963-64**: 120, 150 [19],
    410, 599, 763; **1965**: 155, 230, 415;
    1966: 110, 231, 442, 451, 473; **1967**:
    465, 537; **1968-69**: 72, 280, 317, 426,
    625
Patman, Mrs. Wright, **1963-64**: 599
Patricelli, Robert E., **1965**: 334n.
Patrick V. McNamara Office Building, **1967**: 535
Patriotism, President's views, **1966**: 420
Patronage, **1966**: 650 [11]
Patten, Repr. Edward J., **1963-64**: 338; **1966**:
    504
Patterson, Eugene C., **1963-64**: 271 [4]
Patterson, Mrs. Eugene C., **1963-64**: 271 [4]
Patton, Gen. George S., Jr., **1967**: 512
Patton, James G., **1963-64**: 54ftn. (p. 68), 225;
    1968-69: 142
Paul, Alice, **1963-64**: 366n.
Paul, Norman S., **1963-64**: 298
Paul I, King, **1963-64**: 153, 424
Death of, **1963-64**: 209, 211 [1]
Paul VI, Pope.
    See Pope Paul VI.
Paxton, Frank, **1963-64**: 643n., 678
Pay.
    See also Personal income; Wages.
Cabinet members, **1963-64**: 297
Congress, Members of, **1963-64**: 132 (p. 194),
    222, 267, 270, 271 [10]
Equal, conference on, **1963-64**: 398
Factory workers, **1966**: 34 (p. 96), 111, 228,
    399, 403, 426, 635 [8-9]
Firemen, **1966**: 27
Government employees, **1963-64**: 17, 132 (p.
    194), 222, 266 [21], 267, 268, 270,
    295, 296, 297, 402, 411, 456, 514, 688
    [6]; **1965**: 32 (p. 96), 244, 448 [14,
    15], 589, 612, 632; **1966**: 26 (pp. 55,
    56), 34 (p. 103), 108-109, 158 [10],
    299, 333, 453, 630 [6, 8]
    Pay bill, **1963-64**: 222, 267, 268, 270, 296,
    297, 402, 411
Government officials, **1963-64**: 132 (p. 194),
    295
Judiciary, **1963-64**: 132 (p. 194)
Military personnel, **1963-64**: 132 (pp. 182,
    194), 295, 467, 510, 688 [6]; **1965**:
    26, 32 (p. 96), 244, 439, 633; **1966**:
    26 (p. 55), 158 [10], 333, 389
Pay bill, **1965**: 244
Police, **1966**: 27, 526
Teachers, **1963-64**: 132 (p. 189); **1965**: 527,
    539
Pay, National Committee for Equal, **1963-64**:
    398n.
Payne, John W., **1967**: 388
Payroll Savings Committee, U.S. Industrial,
    1965: 11; **1968-69**: 10

Payroll taxes, **1966**: 26 (p. 53); **1968–69**: 39 (p. 88), 678 (p. 1278)

Paz Esténssoro, Victor, **1963–64**: 52

Pazhwak, Abdul Rahman, **1967**: 143

Peabody, Gov. Endicott, **1963–64**: 338, 396, 727

Peace, Harry S. Truman Center for the Advancement of, **1966**: 22, 212

Peace corps, German, **1963–64**: 76, 347; **1965**: 660

Peace Corps, U.S., **1963–64**: 76, 132 (p. 186), 147, 280, 357, 413, 471n., 474, 562; **1965**: 22 [13], 102, 308, 445, 450, 519; **1966**: 6 (p. 7), 12, 26 (p. 59), 93, 125–126, 149, 154, 257, 339, 388, 406, 417 [6], 455, 489, 497, 629; **1967**: 90, 133n., 218, 266, 275, 292, 400n.; **1968–69**: 75, 153 [10], 181, 314, 332, 341, 529, 568, 569

  Anniversary, **1966**: 93

  Appropriations, **1963–64**: 112, 347; **1965**: 83

  Campaign remarks, **1963–64**: 607, 702, 736, 745

  Congressional support, **1966**: 93

  Director (R. Sargent Shriver, Jr.), **1963–64**: 76, 147, 347, 428n., 489, 745; **1965**: 33, 208 [12], 445

  Director (Jack Hood Vaughn), **1966**: 12–13, 332n., 455

    Swearing in, **1966**: 93

  Exchange program, **1966**: 45, 46, 332n., 406, 455

  Expansion, **1963–64**: 759; **1965**: 32 (p. 91), 83

  Fourth anniversary, **1965**: 33, 83

    Statement, **1963–64**: 759

  India projects, **1966**: 149, 154

  Industry participation, **1963–64**: 745

  Labor participation, **1963–64**: 745

  Movement, spread to other countries, **1963–64**: 347, 759; **1965**: 83

  Older persons serving, **1963–64**: 712

  Reports, **1968–69**: 103, 656

  School-to-school program, **1966**: 332, 455

  Veterans

    Federal employment, **1963–64**: 347, 759

    Recruitment for public service, proposed, **1965**: 33

    Training in human rights fields, **1963–64**: 161n.

  Vietnam projects, **1966**: 93

  Volunteers, **1963–64**: 289, 347, 759; **1965**: 33, 80, 83, 286; **1966**: 93, 126, 332n., 455

  Women in, **1963–64**: 289

Peace Corps Act, **1965**: 83n., 445

  Amendment, **1966**: 455

Peace Corps National Advisory Council, **1963–64**: 802; **1965**: 33; **1966**: 93

Peace Corps Volunteers, Conference of Returned, **1965**: 33

Peace Garden, International, N. Dak., import tariffs on gifts, **1966**: 601

Peace and National Security, Panel of Consultants on, **1963–64**: 591

Pearl Harbor, **1965**: 88; **1966**: 128, 563; **1968–69**: 142

  25th anniversary, **1963–64**: 796

Pearl Harbor Day proclamation, **1966**: 634

Pearson, Drew, **1965**: 113, 397, 401; **1966**: 52 [5], 155, 158 [10]; **1968–69**: 167, 459, 681

Pearson, Lester B. (Prime Minister of Canada), **1963–64**: 174n., 575; **1965**: 21, 22 [1], 147, 186, 352, 574; **1966**: 269, 400, 417 [5]; **1967**: 237, 239, 272, 543

  Campaign remarks on, **1963–64**: 598, 599, 656, 695, 709

  Message, **1965**: 432

  News conference remarks on, **1963–64**: 28 [14], 54 [8], 170 [15], 563 [3]

  Visit, **1963–64**: 128, 134–138, 140; **1965**: 162

Pearson, Mrs. Lester B., **1963–64**: 128; **1966**: 400

Pearson, Paul, **1965**: 397

Peay, Oscar, **1967**: 324n.

Peck, Gregory, **1963–64**: 373, 751; **1966**: 156

Peck, Mrs. Gregory, **1966**: 156

Peck, Merton J., **1968–69**: 76, 350, 683

Peck, Mrs. Merton J., **1968–69**: 76

Peden, Katherine, **1967**: 326; **1968–69**: 565

Pedernales Electric Cooperative, **1963–64**: 352; **1965**: 230; **1968–69**: 96

Pedernales River, **1963–64**: 597, 728, 736, 747; **1965**: 2; **1966**: 232; **1968–69**: 510, 630, 647, 672

Peeler, Jimmy, **1963–64**: 645

Pei, I. M., **1965**: 449

Peking, **1965**: 223; **1966**: 94, 246

Pelican Island Wilderness, Fla., **1968–69**: 168

Pell, Sen. Claiborne, **1963–64**: 382, 383, 601; **1965**: 177, 534, 536; **1966**: 19, 396–399

Pelley, James, **1966**: 434

Penal institutions, **1965**: 9, 70, 102, 509

Penal systems, **1965**: 381

Pengel, Johan (Minister President of Surinam), **1967**: 178

Penn, Lt. Col. Lemuel A., **1963–64**: 462ftn. (p. 866); **1968–69**: 298

Penn, William, **1963–64**: 390, 742

Penna Marinho, Illmar, **1965**: 472, 473

Pennsylvania, **1966**: 157, 391, 428

  Area redevelopment programs, **1965**: 132

  Bureau of Rehabilitation, **1967**: 413

  Campaign remarks, **1963–64**: 566, 661, 728, 742

Pennsylvania – *continued*
  Candidates for public office, **1963–64**: 566, 661, 728, 742
  Delaware Water Gap National Recreation Area, **1965**: 471
  Food stamp program, **1965**: 492
  Gov. William W. Scranton, **1963–64**: 217, 285 [1], 287, 516 [11], 566, 728; **1965**: 417, 418, 434, 471; **1966**: 121 [1], 122 [1, 2], 407, 428, 501 [20]
  Gov. Raymond P. Shafer, **1967**: 426
  Remarks, **1967**: 291
  Unemployment, steel industry, **1963–64**: 297
  Veterans' employment programs, **1967**: 345
Pennsylvania Avenue, President's Council on, **1965**: 538
  Report, **1963–64**: 379 [12] and ftn., 700
Pennsylvania Avenue, Temporary Commission on, **1965**: 538; **1967**: 71; **1968–69**: 133, 560
Pennsylvania Avenue National Historic Site, **1965**: 538
Pennsylvania Railroad, **1965**: 536; **1967**: 223 [2], 542
Penrose, Dr. Lionel S., **1963–64**: 174
Pension funds, **1963–64**: 132 (p. 191); **1968–69**: 47 (p. 129)
Pension Funds and Other Private Retirement and Welfare Programs, Presidential Committee on Corporate, **1965**: 35 (p. 113)
Pension plans, consumer protection, **1967**: 57, 200
Pension programs, **1965**: 72
  Veterans, **1965**: 215
Pentagon, **1963–64**: 266 [22]; **1965**: 387
  Elevator incident, **1968–69**: 101n., 102, 109, 110, 139
  Hall of Heroes, **1968–69**: 246
  Peace demonstrations, **1967**: 441
People-to-people program, **1963–64**: 45, 316 [9]; **1965**: 18; **1966**: 339
"People's Business, The," **1963–64**: 352n.
Peoria, Ill., campaign remarks, **1963–64**: 636, 637
Pepper, Repr. Claude, **1963–64**: 198, 199, 571, 709, 710; **1967**: 28; **1968–69**: 589
Perakis, Katherine M., **1966**: 581
Percy, Sen. Charles H., **1968–69**: 219
Pericles, **1963–64**: 337, 576, 784
Perkins, Repr. Carl D., **1963–64**: 41, 53, 291, 292, 643, 644, 676; **1965**: 183, 368, 369; **1967**: 30n., 193, 338n., 413; **1968–69**: 565
Perkins, Frances, **1963–64**: 208, 388
Perkins, James, **1963–64**: 563 [5], 688 [3]; **1966**: 533, 627; **1967**: 423
Permanent Joint Board on Defense, Canada-United States, **1965**: 432

Perrin, Robert, **1966**: 431; **1968–69**: 555
Perry, Edgar H., **1963–64**: 763; **1967**: 210; **1968–69**: 625
Perry, Dr. Richard E., **1968–69**: 438
Pershing, Gen. John J., **1968–69**: 153 [9], 283 [6], 384, 556, 594
Personal income, **1963–64**: 22, 91 (p. 115), 124 (pp. 156, 157, 164), 132 (p. 178), 160n., 218 [36], 219, 244, 280, 404, 431, 434, 455 [2], 544, 555, 562, 571, 589, 689, 724, 731, 735; **1965**: 23, 32 (pp. 84, 91), 35 (p. 104), 38, 76, 100, 132, 425; **1966**: 6 (p. 4), 17, 34 (pp. 96, 99), 166, 312, 398, 413, 434, 444, 472
  See also Income; Pay; Wages.
  After taxes, **1963–64**: 124 (p. 156), 463, 477
  Appalachian area, **1963–64**: 321
  Increase, **1963–64**: 23, 197, 266 [2], 280, 299, 311, 314, 316 [5], 459, 603, 605, 631, 635, 636, 642, 650, 659, 669, 694, 702, 713, 716, 718, 746; **1965**: 164, 243, 285, 298, 299, 489, 590, 632, 644; **1966**: 155, 189, 235, 237, 240, 373 [17], 403, 415, 420, 428, 431–432, 444, 477 [3], 479, 494 [1], 504, 512, 516 [19]
  Indians, American, **1966**: 193
  Negroes, **1965**: 301; **1966**: 196
  Older persons, **1966**: 168
  Statement, **1963–64**: 811
  Tennessee Valley area, **1966**: 382
Personal reminiscences.
  See Reminiscences, the President's.
Personnel Interchange, Advisory Panel on, **1968–69**: 490, 498
Peru, **1967**: 44; **1968–69**: 103, 205
  Assistance, **1963–64**: 227, 340
  Peace Corps projects in, **1965**: 83
Pesticides, **1963–64**: 758
  Consumer protection, **1963–64**: 341
  Control, **1965**: 15, 29, 54, 94, 175
  Foreign assistance, **1968–69**: 679
  Regulations, **1963–64**: 173, 179
Peterson, Mrs. Esther, **1963–64**: 86, 233, 398; **1965**: 91, 392, 567; **1966**: 299; **1967**: 86
Peterson, Rudolph A., **1967**: 168n.
Peterson, Sherrill Rae, **1968–69**: 230
Petrified Forest Wilderness, Ariz., **1968–69**: 168
Petroleum, **1967**: 358 [11]
  Prices, **1966**: 34 (p. 100)
Petrosyants, Andronik M., **1965**: 319 [5]
Pham Van Dong, **1965**: 208 [12]
Philadelphia, Pa., **1963–64**: 390; **1965**: 434; **1967**: 291; **1968–69**: 419, 499
  Campaign remarks, **1963–64**: 742

Philadelphia, Pa. – *continued*
  Mayor James H. J. Tate, **1963-64**: 390n., 742; **1965**: 434; **1967**: 291
  Police Athletic League, **1968-69**: 163
  U.S. Mint, **1965**: 297
Philadelphia Inquirer, **1963-64**: 516 [2]
Philadelphia-Torresdale water intake, **1966**: 391
Philbin, Repr. Philip J., **1963-64**: 727; **1966**: 218, 283, 572
Philippine National Science Development Board, **1966**: 461
Philippines, **1965**: 448 [10]; **1966**: 288, 458, 461
  AID program, **1968-69**: 63
  Aid for Southeast Asia, **1963-64**: 626, 627
  Ambassador Oscar Ledesma, **1963-64**: 626n.
  Communist aggression, **1966**: 568
  Dispute with Indonesia and Malaysia, **1963-64**: 156n.
  Earthquake, **1968-69**: 432
  Economic and social development, **1963-64**: 626, 627; **1968-69**: 63, 417, 679
  Education, **1966**: 505
  Food aid, **1968-69**: 176
  Immigration to U.S., **1966**: 478
  Macapagal, Diosdado, President, **1963-64**: 587 [2], 623, 626, 627; **1965**: 655
  Marcos, Ferdinand, President, **1965**: 655; **1966**: 417 [9], 458-459, 461, 492 [4], 495, 501 [2], 505, 514, 516 [1], 548-551, 577 [16]; **1967**: 328 [12], 409; **1968-69**: 432
  Orphans, assistance, **1966**: 495
  Rice research, **1967**: 448
  Ships for, **1965**: 600
  Tax convention with U.S., **1963-64**: 627
  Typhoon damage control, **1966**: 461
  Typhoon relief, **1963-64**: 627
  U.S. Ambassador William McC. Blair, Jr., **1963-64**: 394, 626; **1966**: 550
  U.S. relations with, **1963-64**: 623, 626, 627; **1966**: 458, 459, 495, 505
  Veterans, **1966**: 461, 495, 505
    World War II, **1963-64**: 627
  Vietnam assistance, **1966**: 458, 461, 516 [13], 520, 551; **1967**: 83, 246; **1968-69**: 283 [4], 525
  Visit, **1966**: 550-551
  War damage legislation, **1963-64**: 627
Philippines, University of the, College of Agriculture, **1966**: 550
Philippine-U.S. Veterans Commission, Joint, **1966**: 495, 505
Phillips, Mrs. Robert J., **1963-64**: 289
Phillips, Wendell, **1963-64**: 339
Phillips, William W., Jr., **1968-69**: 108
Philosophical Society, American, **1968-69**: 695
Phoenix, Ariz., campaign remarks, **1963-64**: 649
Photography program of the White House, **1965**: 16

Phumiphon Adundet, King, **1963-64**: 30
Physical education, **1967**: 160
Physical fitness, **1963-64**: 89, 106, 126, 401, 490
Physical Fitness, President's Council on, **1963-64**: 188, 490; **1965**: 625, 645n.; **1967**: 160
Physical Fitness Awards program, establishment, **1965**: 645
Physical Fitness Leadership Awards, **1965**: 222; **1967**: 160
Physical Fitness and Sports, President's Council on, **1968-69**: 111
Physical rehabilitation, **1967**: 413
Physical Society, American, **1967**: 192
Physicians, **1966**: 95, 111, 208, 253, 347, 401 [2], 403, 580 [10]; **1967**: 39, 77
  Shortage of, **1963-64**: 47, 179, 755; **1965**: 5, 531
Physicians for Vietnam, Volunteer, **1968-69**: 438
Piccione, Attilio, **1963-64**: 807n.
Pickering, William H., **1963-64**: 492, 493n.; **1965**: 391; **1966**: 134
Pickle, Repr. J. J., **1963-64**: 72, 544, 763, 778; **1965**: 142, 179; **1966**: 520, 635 [14]; **1967**: 485 [1-3, 5-7]; **1968-69**: 12, 97, 108, 109, 625
Pickle, Mrs. J. J. (Beryl), **1963-64**: 763; **1968-69**: 109
Pictured Rocks National Lake Shore, Mich., **1966**: 518, 522; **1967**: 20
Pierce, Alfred R., **1965**: 434
Pierce, Gregory, **1966**: 87
Pierce, John R., **1963-64**: 98
Pierce, Kelley, **1966**: 87
Pierce, S. Sgt. Larry S., **1966**: 87
Pierce, Mrs. Larry S., **1966**: 87
Pierce, Mrs. Lillie, **1966**: 87n.
Pierce, Theresa, **1966**: 87
Pierce, William J., **1967**: 342n.
Pieri, Msgr. Paul, **1963-64**: 761n.
Pierpoint, Robert C., **1966**: 338 [12]; **1968-69**: 1 [7], 425 [4, 11], 481
Pierson, W. DeVier, **1968-69**: 411
Pifer, Alan, **1967**: 474
Pig War (1859), **1966**: 448
Pikesville, Ky., remarks, **1968-69**: 565
Pilago Magallanes, Kenneth, **1965**: 336n.
Pilcher, Repr. J. L., **1963-64**: 330, 716
Pilcher, Palmer C., **1963-64**: 709
Pinchot, Gifford, **1965**: 521; **1966**: 398; **1968-69**: 122, 212, 345, 386
Pine, Judge David A., **1965**: 366
Pine Mountain Wilderness, Ariz., **1968-69**: 122, 168
Pinnacles Wilderness, Calif., **1968-69**: 168
Pioneer Memorial, Fredericksburg, Tex., **1963-64**: 74

Pipeline safety, gas, **1967**: 57, 200, 342, 393, 430, 465, 499, 520, 534, 539; **1968–69**: 105, 338, 390, 441
Piper, Norman, **1963–64**: 607
Pistol registration bill, **1966**: 27
Pittman, Sgt. Richard A., **1968–69**: 246
Pitts, Mark, **1968–69**: 617n.
Pitts, Capt. and Mrs. Riley L., **1968–69**: 617
Pitts, Stacie, **1968–69**: 617n.
Pittsburgh, Pa., **1963–64**: 289, 290; **1965**: 448 [11], 490
  Campaign remarks, **1963–64**: 728
  Mayor Joseph M. Barr, **1963–64**: 290, 728; **1966**: 536; **1967**: 252n.
  Occupational training projects, **1968–69**: 162
  Unemployment, steel industry, **1963–64**: 289, 295
Pittsburgh Symphony Orchestra, **1963–64**: 728
Pitzer, Kenneth, **1965**: 166n.
Pizzello, Ralph J., **1967**: 324
PKU test for detection of mental retardation, **1963–64**: 403
Plainfield, N.J., **1967**: 312 [6]
Planetary probes, **1963–64**: 132 (p. 187)
Planning System, Cooperative Area Manpower, **1968–69**: 24
Planning-Programming-Budgeting System, **1965**: 447, 448 [3]; **1966**: 129, 620; **1967**: 13 (pp. 59, 60), 121; **1968–69**: 39 (p. 108), 678 (pp. 1303, 1304)
Plans for Progress.
  See Equal opportunity agreements.
Plasterers' and Cement Masons' International Association of the United States and Canada, Operative, **1963–64**: 547
Platform Association, International, **1965**: 397
Platinum, **1968–69**: 47 (p. 144)
  Stockpiles, **1966**: 173
Plato, **1963–64**: 452; **1966**: 257
Platt, Mrs. Frank C., **1963–64**: 735
Platt, Frank K., **1966**: 77
Platt, Joseph B., **1965**: 115n.
Plaza, Galo, **1968–69**: 290
"Plea for Realism, A," **1967**: 225ftn. (p. 543)
Pleiku, South Vietnam, **1967**: 309 [3]
Pless, Maj. Stephen W., **1968–69**: 688
Plowshare program (peaceful uses for nuclear explosives), **1967**: 336
Plumides, John, **1963–64**: 211 [1]
Plutonium, **1967**: 491, 515; **1968–69**: 378
  Decrease in production, **1963–64**: 91 (p. 117), 132 (p. 185), 272
Plymouth Rock, **1963–64**: 611
Pneumonia, **1966**: 395; **1968–69**: 113
Poage, Repr. W. R., **1963–64**: 763; **1965**: 555; **1966**: 398, 403, 428; **1967**: 33, 405, 541; **1968–69**: 96, 142
Pocatello, Idaho, **1966**: 410

Podgorny, Nikolai V. (Chairman of the Presidium of the Supreme Soviet, U.S.S.R.), **1966**: 50; **1967**: 104 [8], 190, 472
Poiner, Arthur B., **1968–69**: 260
Point 4 program, **1966**: 22, 62, 175
Point Loma Desalting Plant, **1965**: 325
Point Pleasant, W. Va., **1967**: 558; **1968–69**: 58
Point Reyes National Seashore, Calif., **1966**: 522
Poland, Dr. Eleanor, **1963–64**: 208
Poland, **1966**: 273, 528; **1967**: 83, 245, 347n.; **1968–69**: 204
  Constitution of 1791, **1966**: 200
  International Media Guarantee Program, **1966**: 200
  National and Christian millenium, **1966**: 200
  U.S. Ambassador John M. Cabot, **1963–64**: 420 [5], 548
  U.S. Ambassador John A. Gronouski, **1965**: 595, 596; **1966**: 141 [12], 200, 228, 236 [15], 528; **1967**: 225 [18]
  U.S. relations with, **1965**: 463 [8], 562, 595; **1966**: 200, 503, 528
  U.S. trade with, **1963–64**: 272
  Warsaw Uprising, 20th anniversary, **1963–64**: 491
Polaris missiles, **1963–64**: 382, 383, 413, 560 [5], 635, 703, 786; **1965**: 26, 209; **1966**: 26 (p. 56), 310, 387
Police, **1966**: 6 (p. 6), 116, 491; **1967**: 146, 382, 455; **1968–69**: 26, 59, 100, 202, 235, 320
  See also Law enforcement.
  Action in civil disorders, **1968–69**: 213 [9]
  Community relations, **1968–69**: 59
  District of Columbia, **1965**: 29, 70, 366, 381; **1966**: 27, 116, 611; **1967**: 15, 27, 71, 441, 466; **1968–69**: 95, 133, 272, 355, 425 [10], 436, 689
  Equipment and facilities, **1967**: 482; **1968–69**: 59, 133, 320
  Federal aid, **1966**: 487, 598; **1967**: 3 (p. 6), 71, 146, 482, 530; **1968–69**: 164
  Interrogation of suspects, **1966**: 611
  Pay, **1966**: 27, 526; **1967**: 27, 382, 482, 575; **1968–69**: 14 (p. 30), 59, 133, 202, 272, 320, 325, 355, 436, 557 [8]
  Standards, **1967**: 35
  Training, **1965**: 2, 70, 102, 381, 526; **1967**: 3 (p. 6); **1968–69**: 14 (p. 30), 59, 133, 320, 355, 557 [8]
  Veterans of Armed Forces as, **1968–69**: 40, 419
  Warrants, arrest, **1967**: 71
  White House, **1968–69**: 602, 630
Police Athletic League, Philadelphia, Pa., **1968–69**: 163
Policy Advisory Committee, District of Columbia, **1966**: 27

Poliomyelitis, **1966**: 271, 293, 395, 433; **1967**: 286; **1968-69**: 111, 442
  Control, **1965**: 5
  Prevention, **1963-64**: 598, 667, 669
Polish Academy of Science, **1966**: 200
Political Activity of Government Personnel, Commission on, **1966**: 499
Political contributions, **1967**: 204 [8], 236
  Voluntary deductions for, **1966**: 6 (p. 7), 241
Political Education, Committee on (AFL-CIO), **1968-69**: 50, 164, 165
Political experience of the President, **1963-64**: 486 [11]
Political nicknames for the President, **1963-64**: 256 [12], 732
Political philosophy, the President's, **1963-64**: 124 (p. 156), 218 [18], 560 [10], 612, 617, 648, 693, 718, 736, 741, 747; **1966**: 395, 410, 415, 432, 437, 483, 504, 545; **1968-69**: 17, 170, 212, 406
Political polls, **1963-64**: 542, 642, 680, 693, 734
Political slogans, **1963-64**: 218 [18], 256 [12], 536; **1965**: 76
Political support of the President, **1963-64**: 548n., 622n., 629, 765
  News conference remarks, **1963-64**: 232 [4], 336 [9], 521 [11], 542, 563 [14], 587 [9]
Political system, U.S., **1965**: 555; **1966**: 6 (p. 7), 98, 396, 403, 483, 491, 599 [2]; **1967**: 123-124, 236, 502
Polk, James K., **1966**: 428; **1967**: 117
Poll tax, **1963-64**: 57; **1965**: 208 [15], 353 [16], 409; **1966**: 96
  Federal elections, **1968-69**: 332, 341
    Abolishment, **1963-64**: 145
  Ratification of constitutional amendment, **1963-64**: 171
Pollak, Stephen J., **1967**: 225 [22], 411 [1], 466
Polls, public opinion, **1965**: 353 [15]; **1966**: 52 [7], 65 [11], 141 [12], 188 [6], 236 [8], 237, 277 [16], 320 [14], 401 [10], 417 [1], 428, 607 [5], 654 [10]; **1967**: 41, 225 [7, 15], 251, 297 [4, 13], 328 [3, 11], 375 [15], 466, 495 [2, 7], 502
Pollution bill, **1965**: 452
Pollution control, **1966**: 34 (p. 106), 215, 229, 232, 394-395, 406, 427, 436, 593, 653; **1967**: 23, 421, 484; **1968-69**: 14 (p. 31), 102
  Air, **1966**: 6 (p. 6), 26 (p. 62), 82, 353, 398, 403, 485-486, 515, 545; **1967**: 3 (p. 5), 13 (p. 53), 20, 149, 186, 216, 222, 295, 329, 503, 534; **1968-69**: 14 (p. 28), 39 (pp. 89, 103), 84, 87, 95, 122, 123, 167, 345, 409, 420, 447, 470, 648, 653, 678 (p. 1296), 684 (pp. 1311, 1321)

Pollution control − *continued*
  Chemical compounds, environmental, **1966**: 280n.
  Federal installations, **1966**: 82
  Government cooperation with business, education, and labor, **1967**: 20
  Great Lakes, **1966**: 392-393; **1967**: 101
  Industrial, **1966**: 392; **1967**: 16 (p. 85), 186; **1968-69**: 122
  Marine resources, **1967**: 240
  Memorandum, **1967**: 186
  Oil, **1968-69**: 122, 124, 297, 390, 586, 684 (p. 1321)
  Research, **1966**: 82; **1967**: 20, 186
  U.S.-German cooperation, **1966**: 88 [9]
  Water, **1966**: 6 (p. 3), 26 (p. 62), 34 (p. 106), 82, 91, 215, 229, 232, 334 [2], 353, 392-393, 398, 403, 427, 481, 485-486, 518, 545, 574, 630 [4]; **1967**: 3 (p. 2), 13 (p. 51), 16 (p. 85), 20, 101, 222, 223 [6], 295, 300, 329, 503, 534; **1968-69**: 14 (p. 28), 39 (pp. 89, 101), 84, 87, 95, 113, 122, 123, 167, 297, 345, 447, 470, 501, 593, 648, 653, 678 (p. 1301), 684 (pp. 1311, 1321), 692
Pollution Control Administration, Federal Water, **1966**: 232; **1967**: 13 (pp. 51, 57)
Pollution by Oil and Hazardous Materials, National Inter-Agency Committee for Control of, **1968-69**: 586
Pollution of the Seas by Oil, United States National Committee for the Prevention of, **1967**: 240
Pool, Repr. Joe R., **1963-64**: 760
  Death, **1968-69**: 385
Pool, Mrs. Joe R., **1968-69**: 385
Poole, Cecil, **1963-64**: 411
Poor People's March on Washington, **1968-69**: 51 [14], 169 [5], 223 [9], 275 [5], 339 [7]
Pope John XXIII, **1963-64**: 27, 123, 224, 396; **1965**: 302; **1966**: 396; **1968-69**: 78
Pope Paul VI, **1963-64**: 123, 147, 188; **1965**: 142n.; **1966**: 39, 153; **1967**: 346, 570, 573; **1968-69**: 53, 78, 696 [10]
  Birth control encyclical, **1968-69**: 467 [9]
  Message, **1967**: 42
  Vietnam peace efforts, **1966**: 474 [5], 513, 549, 577 [7], 607 [4, 15]; **1967**: 42, 116, 135, 411 [5], 571, 573; **1968-69**: 1 [6], 14 (p. 26)
  Visit with, **1967**: 571, 572; **1968-69**: 1 [10]
Population, **1965**: 464
  Average age in U.S., **1965**: 80; **1966**: 257, 435
  Developing nations, **1967**: 272; **1968-69**: 14 (p. 27), 679
  Family planning, **1967**: 469; **1968-69**: 14 (p. 27), 39 (pp. 89, 104), 47 (p. 138),

Population – *continued*
  Family planning – *continued*
        63, 111, 393, 408, 417, 467 [9], 500,
        659, 679, 684 (p. 1321)
  Growth, **1963-64**: 54 [6], 132 (pp. 182, 193),
        152, 179, 211 [28], 213, 244, 323, 363,
        372, 374, 388, 391, 413, 578, 579, 604,
        607, 619 [3, 12], 630, 650, 701, 756,
        775, 780 [4]; **1965**: 2, 47, 54, 76, 132,
        258, 275, 331, 511; **1966**: 30, 34 (p.
        105), 41, 45, 62, 207, 240, 258, 308,
        312, 347, 386, 394, 399, 413, 428, 433,
        478, 550, 608; **1967**: 92, 270, 498;
        1968-69: 47 (p. 138), 63, 111, 118,
        227, 406, 593
  Migration, **1963-64**: 669, 680; **1965**: 47, 90;
        1966: 235
  National Capital Region, **1966**: 262
  Report, **1968-69**: 659
  Research, **1968-69**: 393
  Rural areas, **1965**: 47
  200 millionth American, **1967**: 498, 499
  Urban, **1965**: 9, 54, 76, 90, 102, 330;
        1967: 234, 503
  Western Hemisphere, **1966**: 386; **1967**: 110
  World, **1966**: 22, 420, 428; **1967**: 63, 286,
        469, 476, 491, 519; **1968-69**: 696
        [14]
Population Conference, United Nations World,
        1965: 464
Population and Family Planning, Committee on,
        1968-69: 393, 659
Population Studies and Human Reproduction,
        Center for, proposed, **1968-69**: 111
Pornographic literature, **1966**: 611
Port Columbus, Ohio, **1966**: 436
Porter, Albert, **1963-64**: 406, 642
Porter, Katherine Anne, **1963-64**: 266 [4]
Porter, Sylvia, **1963-64**: 455 [13]
Porter, William J., **1966**: 141 [10], 188 [3],
        214, 273-274, 277 [7, 21]; **1967**: 104
        [14], 131, 317n.
Porter, William Sydney (O. Henry),
        1968-69: 625
Portillo, Señorita Valentina, **1968-69**: 369
Portland, Maine, **1963-64**: 602n.
  Campaign remarks, **1963-64**: 606
Portland, Oreg., campaign remarks, **1963-64**: 578
Portrait Gallery, National, **1966**: 227;
        1968-69: 225n.
Portrait of the President, unveiling, **1965**: 285
Ports of entry, one-stop inspection, **1968-69**: 388,
        389
Portugal, **1965**: 68n.; **1966**: 478
  U.S. Ambassador W. Tapley Bennett, Jr.,
        1966: 277 [2]
Poseidon missiles, **1966**: 26 (p. 56), 642 [8, 20];
        1967: 13 (p. 48); **1968-69**: 39 (p. 78)
  Proposed, **1965**: 26

Post, Mrs. Merriweather, **1963-64**: 784
Post, Wiley, **1963-64**: 598
Post, Saturday Evening, **1963-64**: 238
Post Office Department, **1963-64**: 71 [2], 207,
        211 [28], 271 [7], 336 [3], 462 [2],
        619 [1], 654; **1965**: 32 (pp. 93, 98), 78,
        127, 138n., 140, 274n., 329, 330, 332,
        573, 596; **1966**: 26 (p. 67), 470;
        1967: 13 (p. 46), 121, 163, 168, 312 [1];
        1968-69: 216, 437, 678 (p. 1301)
  Appropriations, **1968-69**: 39 (p. 92), 39 (p.
        111), 678 (p. 1281)
  Beautification awards, **1966**: 353
  Improvement and modernization, **1968-69**:
        407
  Postage stamps, **1966**: 358, 500
  History of the flag, **1968-69**: 321
  Law and order issue, **1968-69**: 257
  Photographic reproductions, **1968-69**: 321
Postal Field Service, **1963-64**: 205; **1965**: 413
Postal Organization, Commission on,
        1967: 168; **1968-69**: 216, 391, 676 (p.
        1266), 678 (p. 1301)
Postal Policy Act of 1958, **1967**: 163
Postal rates, **1968-69**: 39 (p. 92)
Postal Revenue and Federal Salary Act of 1967,
        1967: 330ftn. (p. 741), 417 [1], 546
Postal service, **1963-64**: 132 (pp. 176, 188),
        207; **1965**: 332; **1966**: 10, 150, 336;
        1968-69: 216, 630, 676 (p. 1266), 678
        (pp. 1281, 1301)
  See also Mail service.
  Federal agencies, **1968-69**: 407
Postal Service's Honor Award, **1968-69**: 630
Postmaster General (John A. Gronouski),
        1963-64: 139, 207, 588n., 642, 654,
        747; **1965**: 78, 154, 332, 413, 463 [1,
        8, 9], 504
  Letter, **1965**: 373
Postmaster General (Lawrence F. O'Brien),
        1965: 596; **1966**: 137, 240, 247 [1, 3,
        14], 322, 336, 353, 358, 470, 500, 504,
        524n., 580 [19], 651; **1967**: 30, 216,
        237n., 315, 379, 546
  Letters, **1966**: 10, 37
  Resignation, **1968-69**: 191 [2, 10]
Postmaster General (W. Marvin Watson),
        1968-69: 191 [1, 2], 257, 260, 267,
        391, 588, 630
  Swearing in, **1968-69**: 216
Postmasters, 5-day work week for, **1965**: 413
Potofsky, Jacob S., **1963-64**: 334; **1965**: 242;
        1966: 479
Potomac River, **1963-64**: 578, 756, 784n.;
        1965: 2, 54, 70, 418, 543; **1966**: 34 (p.
        106), 82, 391
Potomac Valley, **1967**: 13 (p. 51), 20;
        1968-69: 122
Potts, Frederic A., **1967**: 291

Poultry
  Inspection, **1963-64**: 132 (p. 187), 173;
        1968-69: 14 (p. 30), 56, 105, 390, 451,
        545
  Producers, **1968-69**: 94
Poultry and Egg National Board, **1963-64**: 772n.
Pound devaluation, British, **1967**: 497, 499, 519,
        524
Poverty, **1967**: 291, 354, 376, 442, 444, 448,
        514, 517, 538; **1968-69**: 3, 24, 28, 39
        (pp. 86, 89, 104, 105), 46, 47 (pp. 129,
        141, 143), 75, 109, 154, 156, 162, 164,
        173, 223 [11], 227, 241, 262, 281,
        282, 315, 331, 339 [7], 350, 423, 429,
        442, 444, 459, 463, 493, 555, 565, 567–
        569, 631, 676 (p. 1266), 678 (pp.
        1276, 1300), 684 (pp. 1312, 1313)
  See also Antipoverty programs.
  Citizens Crusade Against, **1965**: 75
  Conference on Women in the War on,
        1967: 211
  Indians, **1968-69**: 113
  Legislation, **1968-69**: 223 [9]
  Message to Congress, **1967**: 114
  Minority groups, **1968-69**: 26
  National Advisory Commission on Rural,
        1967: 114
  Presidential Report to the Nation on,
        1965: 75n.
  Rural areas, **1968-69**: 39 (p. 100), 94
  Urban, **1968-69**: 47 (p. 140), 86, 87
  World, **1968-69**: 39 (p. 99), 282
Powell, Repr. Adam C., **1963-64**: 47, 53, 676;
        1965: 183, 305, 329, 330, 534;
        1966: 479; **1967**: 80 [3]
Powell, John Wesley, **1968-69**: 505
Powell, Lewis F., Jr., **1965**: 422n.
Powell, Paul, **1963-64**: 636, 637, 694, 747
Power, Dennis J., **1965**: 336n.
Power, Gen. Thomas S., **1963-64**: 596, 609, 610,
        783
Power failures
  Northeastern States, **1965**: 608, 640, 641 [1]
  Texas, **1965**: 641 [1]
Power lines, underground installation proposed,
        1965: 54
Power projects, **1963-64**: 598, 756; **1965**: 54;
        1966: 398; **1968-69**: 39 (p. 91)
  Columbia River project, **1963-64**: 134, 135;
        1965: 186; **1966**: 269
  Hydroelectric, **1963-64**: 193; **1965**: 186, 418,
        471, 477; **1966**: 269, 399, 411;
        1968-69: 330
  Northwest-Southwest intertie, **1965**: 186
  Nuclear, **1963-64**: 480; **1965**: 17, 319 [5];
        1966: 26 (p. 60), 411; **1967**: 515
  Pacific Northwest, **1966**: 269
  Passamaquoddy-St. John River Basin,
        1965: 350

Power projects — *continued*
  Public, **1963-64**: 713
  Public-private cooperation, **1963-64**: 486 [7],
        578, 803; **1965**: 186
  Site selection, **1968-69**: 653
  U.S.-Canada cooperation, **1965**: 350
Power Survey, National, **1965**: 567
  Report, **1963-64**: 803
Powers, Charles, **1965**: 260
Powers, David F., **1963-64**: 224, 727; **1965**: 22
        [1]
Powers, Dr. Grover Francis, **1963-64**: 174
Pratt Arnold School, Philadelphia, Pa.,
        1968-69: 419
Pratt and Whitney Aircraft Division, **1963-64**: 201
        [2]; **1965**: 339
Prayer, National Day of, **1965**: 557
Prayer, the President's, **1968-69**: 705
Prayer breakfast, presidential, **1963-64**: 172;
        1965: 45; **1966**: 78; **1967**: 32;
        1968-69: 43
Prayer day for those in Vietnam, **1965**: 606
Prayer for Peace, Memorial Day, proclamation,
        1966: 242; **1967**: 229
Preacher, Brooks C., **1966**: 58
Prenatal and maternal health, **1967**: 39, 114;
        1968-69: 3, 14 (p. 29), 39 (pp. 89,
        104), 47 (p. 143), 111, 113, 270, 442,
        568, 569, 662, 676 (p. 1265), 678
        (pp. 1296, 1297), 684 (p. 1324)
Prentice-Hall International, Inc., **1966**: 144n.
Prentiss, Miss., **1965**: 448 [9]
Presbyterians, **1968-69**: 156
Presentation ceremonies.
  See Addresses or remarks at presentation cere-
        monies.
Presidency, **1967**: 115
  Administration, assessment of, **1968-69**: 696
        [12]
  Candidacy, the President's.
        See Candidacy for reelection, the
        President's.
  Candidates for.
        See Candidates for President.
  Comments on, **1963-64**: 172, 199, 218 [36],
        266 [15], 270, 303, 506, 531, 633, 661,
        679, 747, 764; **1965**: 117 [3], 289, 314,
        388 [15], 555, 587; **1966**: 158 [3],
        168, 483, 520; **1967**: 34 [3], 495 [5];
        1968-69: 32, 170, 171, 172, 223 [13],
        242, 576, 588, 672, 690, 691, 696 [1]
  First 100 days, comments on, **1963-64**: 201
        [9], 211 [4], 218
  Function in collective bargaining, **1963-64**: 266
        [12]
  Government reorganization authority,
        1965: 43
  Institutional study, proposed, **1968-69**: 227

Presidency — *continued*
Letters on transfer of power, **1968-69**: 480
175th anniversary year, **1963-64**: 303, 304
Powers, **1965**: 39, 317, 388 [13], 412 [4],
440, 448 [22]; **1966**: 88 [17];
1967: 358 [10], 375 [18]
Responsibilities of office, **1963-64**: 218 [5],
280, 472, 604, 612, 655; **1965**: 117
[4], 213, 440, 454 [1]; **1966**: 236
[3], 273, 277 [15], 312, 399, 417 [2],
483; **1967**: 159, 358 [10]
Salary increase, **1968-69**: 655, 690, 691
Security measures, **1963-64**: 201 [3], 218
[4], 294 [1, 8], 619 [11]
Succession or disability, **1963-64**: 54 [3], 211
[13, 29], 218 [1, 9], 780 [15];
1965: 2, 34, 549, 550; **1967**: 68
Support for successor, plea for, **1968-69**: 696
[20]
President pro tempore of the Senate.
See Congress, letters to Members of; *specific*
entries.
President of the United States, Seal of the,
1966: 609
Presidential advisers, **1965**: 22 [1]
Presidential appointments, **1963-64**: 777;
1965: 213
Presidential Board on the Arts, proposed,
1963-64: 266 [6]
Presidential Citation, Stephen Gallatti, Sr., post-
humous presentation, **1963-64**: 465
Presidential Committee on Corporate Pension
Funds and Other Private Retirement and
Welfare Programs, **1965**: 35 (p. 113)
Presidential Committee on Manpower, proposed,
1963-64: 212
Presidential disability and succession bill,
1965: 329, 330
Presidential documents published in Federal
Register, **1967**: Appendix B (p. 1219);
1968-69: Appendix B (p. 1396)
Presidential Election Campaign Fund, Advisory
Board on the, **1967**: 236
Presidential Election Campaign Fund Act of 1966,
1966: 612; **1967**: 236
Presidential libraries, **1965**: 411, 412, 420
Presidential limousine, **1968-69**: 549
Presidential Medal of Freedom, **1963-64**: 27,
157, 447, 568; **1967**: 567; **1968-69**:
99, 592, 616, 691
Presidential policy papers
Conservation of natural resources, **1963-64**:
756
Education, **1963-64**: 754
Farm programs, **1963-64**: 757
Health, **1963-64**: 755
Presidential primaries
New Hampshire, **1968-69**: 132, 169 [2]
Wisconsin, **1968-69**: 169 [2]

Presidential Report to the Nation on Poverty,
1965: 75n.
Presidential reports to Congress.
See also Congress, reports to, messages transmitting.
List, Appendix C, **1963-64**: p. 1706;
1967: p. 1225; **1968-69**: p. 1401
Presidential Scholars, **1967**: 201, 266;
1968-69: 282, 300, 570
Commission on, **1963-64**: 266 [4], 309;
1965: 171; **1966**: 257
Remarks to, **1966**: 257
Presidential Scholars Award, presentation,
1963-64: 397; **1965**: 306
Presidential Transition Act of 1963,
1963-64: 336 [4]; **1968-69**: 480
Presidential Unit Citations, **1965**: 206, 588;
1966: 20, 616-617, 621; **1967**: 61,
106, 226, 302, 334, 384, 407, 424,
456, 457
Attack Carrier Air Wing Eleven, **1968-69**: 635
Battery B, 7th Battalion, 9th Artillery, USA,
1968-69: 609
Company A, 1st Battalion, 5th Cavalry Regi-
ment, 1st Cavalry Division (Airmobile),
USA, **1968-69**: 546
Company A, 1st Battalion, 8th Infantry,
1968-69: 487
Company A, 1st Battalion, 35th Infantry,
United States Army, **1968-69**: 456
Company A, 3d Battalion, 60th Infantry, 9th
Infantry Division, **1968-69**: 487
Company B, 2d Battalion, 35th Infantry U.S.
Army, **1968-69**: 456
Company C, 1st Battalion (Airborne), 12th
Cavalry, 1st Air Cavalry Division,
1968-69: 487
Company D, 6th Battalion, Royal Australian
Regiment, **1968-69**: 283 [4, 5]
Delta River Patrol Group (Task Group 116.1),
U.S. Naval Forces, Vietnam,
1968-69: 265
1st Battalion (Less Company A), 8th Cavalry,
1st Cavalry Division (Airmobile), USA,
1968-69: 544
1st Battalion (Airborne), 12th Cavalry and
Attached Units, 1st Cavalry Division
(Airmobile), USA, **1968-69**: 410
1st Brigade, 101st Airborne Division (Airmobile), USA, specified elements assigned
and attached, **1968-69**: 512
1st Marine Aircraft Wing, **1968-69**: 521
1st Marine Division (Reinforced) Fleet Marine
Force, Pacific, **1968-69**: 520
1st Platoon, Company B, 1st Battalion, 69th
Armor, USA, **1968-69**: 323
2d Battalion, 31st Regiment, 21st Infantry
Division, Army of the Republic of
Vietnam, **1968-69**: 222

Presidential Unit Citations — *continued*
  2d Battalion, 327th Infantry, 1st Brigade,
    101st Airborne Division, USA,
    1968–69: 544
  3d Brigade, 4th Infantry Division, USA,
    1968–69: 491
  3d Platoon, Company C, 1st Battalion, 35th
    Infantry, **1968–69**: 487
  3d Squadron, 5th Cavalry, 9th Infantry Divi-
    sion, USA, **1968–69**: 609
  3d Tactical Fighter Wing, Pacific Air Forces,
    1968–69: 379
  3d Troop, 8th Reconnaissance Squadron,
    ARVN, **1968–69**: 674
  5th Marine Regiment (Reinforced), 1st Marine
    Division (Reinforced), **1968–69**: 541
  8th Tactical Fighter Wing, Pacific Air Forces,
    1968–69: 337
  9th Company, 1st Cavalry Regiment, Republic
    of Korea Army, **1968–69**: 413
  11th Tactical Reconnaissance Squadron,
    Pacific Air Forces, **1968–69**: 318
  12th Air Commando Squadron, Pacific Air
    Forces, **1968–69**: 543
  14th Air Commando Wing, USAF,
    1968–69: 268
  20th Tactical Reconnaissance Squadron,
    Pacific Air Forces, **1968–69**: 231
  21st Tactical Air Support Squadron, Pacific
    Air Forces, **1968–69**: 627
  23d Tactical Air Support Squadron, Pacific
    Air Forces, **1968–69**: 254
  26th Marines (Reinforced), 3d Marine Divi-
    sion (Reinforced), **1968–69**: 267
  36th Tactical Fighter Squadron, Pacific Air
    Forces, **1968–69**: 269
  41st Regimental Headquarters, 1st and 3d
    Battalions, 41st Regiment, Army of
    the Republic of Vietnam, **1968–69**:
    674
  42d Ranger Battalion, 21st Infantry Division,
    Army of the Republic of Vietnam,
    1968–69: 119
  74th Tactical Wing, Vietnamese Air Force,
    1968–69: 518
  336th Tactical Fighter Wing, Pacific Air
    Forces, **1968–69**: 478
  355th Tactical Fighter Wing, Pacific Air
    Forces, **1968–69**: 251
  460th Tactical Reconnaissance Wing, Pacific
    Air Forces, **1968–69**: 628
  602d Fighter Squadron, Pacific Air Forces,
    1968–69: 266, 597
  6234th Tactical Fighter Wing, 7th/13th Air
    Force (Southeast Asia), Pacific Air
    Forces, **1968–69**: 144
  Headquarters and Headquarters Company; 3d
    Platoon, 5th Company; and 6th Com-

Presidential Unit Citations — *continued*
  Headquarters — *continued*
    pany, 2d Battalion, 9th Regiment, 5th
    Infantry Division, Army of the Re-
    public of Vietnam, **1968–69**: 443
  Seal Team One, USN, **1968–69**: 584, 675
  Troops A, B, C, and D and Headquarters and
    Headquarters Troops, 1st Squadron,
    9th Cavalry, 1st Cavalry Division (Air-
    mobile), U.S. Army, **1968–69**: 649
  U.S.S. *Kitty Hawk* and Attack Carrier Air
    Wing 11, USN, **1968–69**: 635
President's Advisory Board on Foreign Intelli-
    gence, **1966**: 320 [2]
President's Advisory Commission on Narcotic
    and Drug Abuse, **1963–64**: 159, 179,
    458; **1965**: 102; **1968–69**: 59, 60
President's Advisory Committee on Labor-
    Management Policy, **1963–64**: 126,
    213; **1965**: 428; **1966**: 111, 184, 201,
    474 [20]; **1967**: 121; **1968–69**: 469
President's Advisory Committee on Supersonic
    Transport, **1963–64**: 242 [9, 17], 294
    [6]; **1965**: 339
President's Advisory Council on Cost Reduction,
    1967: 121, 232; **1968–69**: 678 (p.
    1304)
President's Advisory Council on Federal Re-
    ports, **1963–64**: 583
President's advisory panel on foreign affairs,
    establishment, **1963–64**: 563 [5, 8]
President's Appalachian Regional Commission,
    1963–64: 293n., 294 [2], 300
President's Award for Distinguished Federal
    Civilian Service, **1963–64**: 417; **1965**:
    269, 296; **1966**: 25, 266; **1967**: 317;
    1968–69: 604
"President's Choice" photography program,
    1965: 16
President's Club, Democratic Party, **1966**: 401
    [3]; **1967**: 421n.
  Dinner remarks, **1967**: 281
President's Commission on Budget Concepts,
    1968–69: 39 (pp. 84, 96, 107, 108),
    678 (p. 1274)
President's Commission on Campaign Costs,
    1967: 236
President's Commission on Crime in the District
    of Columbia, **1965**: 70, 366, 381,
    526n.; **1966**: 116, 219, 354, 611, 656;
    1967: 15, 27, 71
President's Commission on Heart Disease, Can-
    cer, and Stroke, **1963–64**: 179, 211
    [6], 268, 617, 798; **1965**: 5, 343
President's Commission on Law Enforcement
    and Administration of Justice,
    1965: 102, 381, 382, 422, 437, 500,
    526; **1966**: 116, 491, 492 [1], 494
    [1], 526, 611, 630 [9]; **1967**: 3 (p. 6),

President's Commission — *continued*
13 (p. 56), 35, 39, 60, 146, 221, 276, 382, 385; **1968–69**: 59, 235, 257, 301, 320, 553, 678 (p. 1291)

President's Commission for the Observance of Human Rights Year 1968, **1968–69**: 42, 611

President's Commission on the Patent System, **1966**: 635 [3], 637

President's Commission on Postal Organization, **1968–69**: 216, 391, 676 (p. 1266), 678 (p. 1301)

President's Commission on Registration and Voting Participation, **1963–64**: 57, 167

President's Commission on the Status of Women, **1963–64**: 294 [21]; **1965**: 392

President's Commission on White House Fellows, **1965**: 334; **1968–69**: 227

President's Committee on Consumer Interests, **1963–64**: 86, 173; **1965**: 567; **1966**: 140; **1967**: 86, 200, 393, 430, 465; **1968–69**: 56, 336

President's Committee on the Distinguished Service Award, **1963–64**: 235, 302n., 389

President's Committee on Employment of the Handicapped, **1963–64**: 302; **1967**: 388; **1968–69**: 548n.

President's Committee on Equal Employment Opportunity, **1963–64**: 40, 111, 139, 205, 213, 221, 277, 342, 379 [7], 448, 812n.; **1965**: 448 [6], 530n.; **1966**: 196

President's Committee on Juvenile Delinquency and Youth Crime, **1963–64**: 133, 334, 537, 704n.; **1965**: 282, 381

President's Committee on Libraries, **1966**: 424

President's Committee on Manpower, **1963–64**: 212, 213, 264; **1965**: 100; **1966**: 111, 536

President's Committee on Mental Retardation, **1967**: 373, 517; **1968–69**: 481, 493

President's Committee on the National Medal of Science, **1963–64**: 98n.; **1965**: 646n.; **1966**: 61n.; **1967**: 37n.; **1968–69**: 471n., 695n.

President's Committee on Population and Family Planning, **1968–69**: 393, 659

President's Committee on Public Higher Education in the District of Columbia, **1963–64**: 116n., 457
Report, **1965**: 111

President's Committee on Traffic Safety, **1963–64**: 565; **1966**: 98

President's Committee on Urban Housing, **1967**: 252, 355, 358 [8], 412; **1968–69**: 87, 704

President's Council on Aging, **1963–64**: 178, 415; **1965**: 72

President's Council on Equal Opportunity, **1965**: 50, 530n.

President's Council on Pennsylvania Avenue, report, **1963–64**: 379 [12], 700

President's Council on Physical Fitness, **1963–64**: 188, 490; **1965**: 625, 645n.; **1967**: 160; **1968–69**: 111

President's Council on Recreation and Natural Beauty, **1966**: 202, 653; **1967**: 295; **1968–69**: 122, 167

President's Council on Youth Opportunity, **1968–69**: 24, 686

"President's Country" television program, **1966**: 270

President's Disaster Fund, **1963–64**: 567; **1965**: 174

President's Foreign Intelligence Advisory Board, **1968–69**: 18 [2]

President's foreign visitor program, **1968–69**: 116

President's foreword to "Why Vietnam" booklet, **1965**: 388ftn. (p. 795)

President's health.
See Health of the President.

President's National Advisory Panel on Insurance in Riot-Affected Areas, **1968–69**: 36, 87

President's portrait, unveiling, **1965**: 285

"Presidents and Recessions Since 1837," **1963–64**: 477n.

President's Review Committee for Development Planning in Alaska, **1963–64**: 615

President's Safety Awards, **1963–64**: 351; **1965**: 73, 287

President's salute to Congress, **1965**: 559

President's Science Advisory Committee, **1963–64**: 179, 271 [5], 456n., 758; **1965**: 166, 602; **1966**: 62, 82, 279–280, 326; **1967**: 33, 48, 101, 271; **1968–69**: 63

President's Task Force on Career Advancement, **1966**: 404

President's Trophy for the Handicapped American of the Year, **1963–64**: 302n.

Presley, Sp. 6 Robert M., **1965**: 161n.

Press.
See also News conferences.
Civil rights responsibilities, **1963–64**: 496
Comments on, **1963–64**: 149, 150 [8], 170 [8], 218 [11], 280 [4], 336 [13], 339, 496, 504 [1]; **1965**: 117 [4], 353 [15], 459, 463 [1]; **1966**: 477 [2, 3, 5], 502
Conferences.
See main heading, News conferences.
Coverage of Alaska earthquake, **1963–64**: 242 [1]

Press – *continued*
  Coverage of Democratic convention, **1963–64**:
      150 [7]
  Criticism of the President, **1963–64**: 218 [11]
  Election predictions for 1964, **1963–64**: 266
      [13]
  Families of reporters at news conference,
      1963–64: 316 [1]
  Foreign, **1963–64**: 475 [23]; **1968–69**: 162
  Freedom of, **1966**: 338 [18]; **1967**: 286, 495
      [13], 502
  President's relations with, **1965**: 353 [15];
      1967: 34 [3]; **1968–69**: 242, 696 [1]
  Printing of declassified material, **1963–64**: 266
      [22]
  Remarks to, **1965**: 133, 162, 395; **1966**: 154,
      214, 298, 383, 407, 517, 626; **1967**:
      536; **1968–69**: 19, 25, 185, 187–189,
      242, 299, 388, 431, 481, 585, 598, 654,
      657, 658
  White House Press Corps, **1963–64**: 339;
      1965: 117 [4], 222, 412
Press Association, International Labor, **1966**:
    237
Press Club, National, **1963–64**: 298
Press Club, Women's National, **1963–64**: 208
Press Institute, World, **1965**: 378
Prettyman, E. Barrett, **1963–64**: 159, 458n.;
    1965: 163; **1966**: 13, 97n., 113n.;
    1968–69: 31
Price, Gwilym A., **1965**: 115n.
Price, Leontyne, **1963–64**: 568
Price, Margaret, **1963–64**: 305, 338; **1966**: 403,
    431; **1967**: 216, 421
  Death, **1968–69**: 405, 631
Price, Repr. Melvin, **1963–64**: 189, 694
Price Administration, Office of, **1963–64**: 297
Price Index, Consumer, **1963–64**: 124 (p. 160),
    211 [3], 463, 619 [4]; **1965**: 35 (p.
    104); **1966**: 88 [22], 185, 336, 373
    [6], 401 [2], 403; **1967**: 430
Price Index, Wholesale, **1963–64**: 23, 124 (p.
    160), 294 [3], 336 [1], 463; **1965**: 35
    (p. 104)
Price Stability, Cabinet Committee on, **1968–69**:
    46, 47 (p. 140), 76, 89, 90, 404, 425
    [1, 3], 469, 485, 492, 612n., 684 (p.
    1317)
Price supports, **1963–64**: 634, 757; **1965**: 35 (p.
    116), 46 [1], 47, 168, 192
  See also specific commodities.
Prices, **1963–64**: 80, 211 [3]; **1965**: 168, 567,
    632; **1966**: 312, 346, 444, 445 [5],
    474 [3], 596; **1967**: 228, 294, 460
    [12], 476, 496, 497, 518 [18], 545
  American selling price system, **1968–69**: 274,
      275 [2]
  Consumer, **1963–64**: 619 [4]; **1968–69**: 39
      (p. 86)

Prices – *continued*
  Controls, **1967**: 13 (p. 40), 16 (p. 78), 518
      [9]; **1968–69**: 1 [5], 2, 241, 612, 684
      (pp. 1315, 1316)
  Effect of tax reduction on, **1965**: 319 [3],
      326n.
  Farm, **1968–69**: 94, 534, 679
  Food, **1967**: 228
  Gold, **1968–69**: 14 (p. 33), 47 (p. 129), 146,
      500, 684 (p. 1320)
  Guidelines, **1968–69**: 1 [13], 404
  Increase, **1963–64**: 124 (p. 161); **1965**: 663;
      1966: 155, 158 [7], 201, 236 [8], 240,
      347, 371, 373 [3–4, 13, 17], 399, 401
      [2], 403, 412–413, 415, 428, 437, 444,
      492 [5], 504, 512, 515, 557 [10]; **1967**:
      3 (p. 7), 13 (p. 40), 16 (pp. 72, 74–76,
      78, 89), 57, 63, 329, 417 [1, 6], 420,
      430, 460 [12], 495 [9], 524, 534;
      1968–69: 1 [11], 14 (p. 31), 39 (p. 86),
      46, 47 (pp. 127–131, 133, 135, 138,
      139), 56, 169 [21], 142, 170, 229, 241,
      274, 425 [1, 5], 427, 431, 469, 485,
      567, 612, 654, 677, 678 (p. 1276), 684
      (p. 1313)
  Industrial, **1968–69**: 47 (p. 139)
  International trade, **1968–69**: 29, 274
  Reduction, proposed, **1963–64**: 271 [15], 295
  Retail, **1965**: 255; **1966**: 155
  Stability, **1963–64**: 23, 43, 124 (p. 157), 132
      (pp. 178, 190), 173, 233, 266 [2], 272,
      294 [3, 23], 297 [1], 299, 311, 316
      [5], 336 [17], 350, 379 [5], 455 [2, 3,
      13], 463, 477, 504 [16], 506, 589,
      624, 640, 662n., 708, 722, 738, 740,
      745, 771, 775, 787, 788; **1965**: 2, 32
      (p. 84), 35 (pp. 104, 105, 110, 111,
      112, 117), 60, 76, 77, 226, 251, 255,
      272, 285, 319 [3], 326, 448 [11, 14],
      632, 644; **1966**: 34 (pp. 100, 103, 109),
      108, 111, 140, 201, 312, 333, 336, 373
      [3, 13], 399, 444, 577 [10], 635 [18];
      1967: 3 (p. 7), 16 (pp. 75, 78), 430,
      524, 534; **1968–69**: 39 (p. 86), 47 (pp.
      127, 130, 138–140), 76, 89, 90, 207,
      229, 404, 427, 449, 469, 492, 678 (pp.
      1273, 1276), 684 (pp. 1311, 1315,
      1316, 1319)
  United Kingdom, **1966**: 359n.
  Wage-price policy, **1963–64**: 124 (p. 160), 232
      [10], 242 [8], 294 [23], 311, 316 [5],
      350, 624, 740; **1965**: 35 (pp. 106, 110,
      111), 60, 77, 208 [4], 226, 258, 326,
      338, 413, 448 [11, 14]; **1966**: 8 [15],
      34 (pp. 96, 109), 44, 88 [20], 108–
      109, 140, 141 [3–4], 155, 201, 333,
      334 [2, 7], 336, 347, 373 [3, 8, 11,
      13, 17], 403, 473, 474 [20]; **1967**: 16

Prices — *continued*
  Wage-price policy — *continued*
    (p. 78), 518 [9], 524; **1968-69**: 350,
      684 (pp. 1313, 1315, 1316)
    Wholesale, **1963-64**: 124 (p. 157), 271 [3],
      472, 619 [4], 630, 657, 689, 740, 775;
      1965: 632; **1966**: 34 (p. 101), 155,
      201, 347, 494 [1], 577 [10]; **1967**: 16
      (pp. 75, 78, 88); **1968-69**: 39 (p. 86),
      47 (p. 131)
Priest, Harriet Frances, **1968-69**: 345
Priest, J. Percy, **1968-69**: 345
Priest, Mrs. J. Percy, **1968-69**: 345
Primary elections, **1963-64**: 266 [24]
  Alabama, **1963-64**: 316 [14, 21]
  Effect on Vice Presidential nominations, **1963-
    64**: 211 [12, 17]
  Indiana, **1963-64**: 246 [7], 256 [19], 316 [18]
  Maryland, **1963-64**: 246 [7], 256 [19], 266
    [24], 316 [15]
  New Hampshire, **1963-64**: 199, 211 [12],
    218 [23]
  Oregon, **1963-64**: 211 [22]
  Wisconsin, **1963-64**: 246 [7], 256 [7], 316
    [18]
Prince, Don, **1966**: 228
Princess telephones, acceptance of gift, **1963-64**:
  406
Princeton University, **1966**: 216
Pringle, Sandy MacGregor, **1968-69**: 430
Prison Industries, Inc., Federal, **1967**: 71
Prisoners, **1965**: 183; **1967**: 13 (p. 56), 71, 146,
  382
  Occupational training, **1965**: 509; **1966**: 111,
    116, 588
  Probation and parole, **1968-69**: 59
  Rehabilitation, **1966**: 116, 491, 526; **1968-69**:
    39, 678 (p. 1291)
  Treatment of, **1965**: 381
  Work release program, **1966**: 463
Prisoners of war
  Geneva accords, **1966**: 6 (p. 11), 54, 65ftn. (p.
    177), 338 [1], 549; **1967**: 34 [2], 80
    [4], 83, 116, 118, 144, 145, 366, 462,
    564
  Vietnam conflict, **1966**: 54, 338 [1, 4-5, 17],
    549; **1967**: 312 [7], 572, 573; **1968-
    69**: 169 [7]
Prisons.
  See Correctional institutions.
Prisons, Bureau of, **1966**: 463, 633; **1968-69**: 59
Pritel, Dr. Philip A., **1968-69**: 438
Privacy, right of, **1967**: 35, 105; **1968-69**: 320
Private Enterprise in Foreign Aid, Advisory
  Committee on, **1963-64**: 227; **1965**:
  18, 450; **1966**: 41
Private organizations
  Antipoverty program participation, **1965**: 529

Private organizations — *continued*
  Community development, **1965**: 529
  Cultural exchange participation, **1965**: 553
  Economic responsibilities, **1963-64**: 589
  Employment responsibilities, **1965**: 268
  Federal and State charters, **1965**: 508
  Foreign aid participation, **1963-64**: 617; **1965**:
    7, 18, 450, 484
  International cooperation participation, **1963-
    64**: 616
  Participation in Federal programs, **1966**: 11,
    223, 277 [1]; **1967**: 412
  Tax-exemption provisions, **1965**: 32 (p. 88)
Private Ownership of Special Nuclear Materials
  Act, approval, **1963-64**: 538
Private Resources, Office of (AID), **1967**: 44
Privileged information, **1966**: 316
Procaccino, Mario, **1968-69**: 568n.
Prochacci, William, **1963-64**: 338
Proclamations
  Additions to national park system, statement,
    1968-69: 707
  Columbus Day, **1966**: 478
  Commemoration of the Beginnings of the
    Office of the Presidency of the United
    States, **1963-64**: 304
  Dairy import reductions, **1967**: 294
  Day of dedication and prayer for those in
    Vietnam, **1965**: 606
  Hoover, Herbert, death of, **1963-64**: 691
  International Cooperation Year, **1963-64**: 616
  Kennedy, John F., a Rededication, **1963-64**:
    774
  Kennedy, Sen. Robert F., death of, **1968-69**:
    295
  King, Rev. Martin Luther, Jr., death, **1968-69**:
    180
  League of United Latin American Citizens,
    anniversary, **1968-69**: 68
  List, Appendix B, **1963-64**: p. 1700; **1965**:
    p. 1197; **1966**: p. 1489; **1967**: p. 1219;
    1968-69: p. 1396
  Marshal Day, **1963-64**: 523n.
  Memorial Day, Prayer for Peace, **1966**: 242;
    1967: 229; **1968-69**: 245
  National Day of Mourning for President
    Kennedy, **1963-64**: 3
  National Day of Prayer, **1965**: 557
  National Defense Transportation Day and
    National Transportation Week, **1968-
    69**: 118
  National ZIP Code Week, **1966**: 470
  Navajo Indian Tribe-United States Peace
    Treaty Centennial, **1968-69**: 259
  Pan American Day and Week, **1967**: 152
  Pearl Harbor Day, **1966**: 634
  President Truman's role in creation of United
    Nations, **1968-69**: 532

Proclamations – *continued*
 Salute to Eisenhower Week, **1968–69**: 399, 488
 Senior Citizens Month, **1968–69**: 108
 Tariff reductions, **1967**: 545
 Thanksgiving Day, **1963–64**: 770; **1965**: 610; **1966**: 534; **1967**: 481; **1968–69**: 591
 Truman, Harry S., birthday, **1966**: 212
 United Nations Day, **1968–69**: 532
 Warsaw Uprising Day, **1963–64**: 491
 Youth for Natural Beauty and Conservation Year, **1966**: 653
Procurement, Federal, **1963–64**: 18, 132 (p. 191), 216, 703, 716, 486 [2]; **1965**: 149, 261n.; **1966**: 104, 159, 396, 464
Product Safety, National Commission on, **1967**: 57, 342, 499; **1968–69**: 14 (p. 29)
Production, **1963–64**: 43, 233, 235, 244, 290; **1965**: 35 (p. 107); **1967**: 13 (p. 41); **1968–69**: 112
 Agricultural, **1963–64**: 124 (p. 162), 132 (p. 187), 352, 570; **1965**: 47, 168, 377, 597; **1966**: 26 (p. 59), 62, 281, 355, 461, 550; **1967**: 156, 496, 525; **1968–69**: 63, 94, 406, 534, 679, 696 [14]
 Consumer goods, **1966**: 34 (p. 101)
 Costs, **1968–69**: 684 (p. 1313)
 Cotton, **1963–64**: 758; **1965**: 168
 Defense, **1966**: 320 [7]; **1968–69**: 112
  Cooperation with Canada, **1963–64**: 140
 Food, **1967**: 13 (p. 49), 271, 476, 496, 554 [12]
 Government employee, **1963–64**: 307, 462 [2]; **1965**: 93, 324
 Increase, **1963–64**: 124 (pp. 157, 158, 161, 166), 197, 316 [5], 350, 459, 639, 708, 713, 734; **1965**: 32 (p. 84), 35 (pp. 106, 108, 109), 60, 235, 326; **1966**: 347, 444; **1967**: 16 (pp. 72, 73, 78, 89), 199, 270, 554 [13]; **1968–69**: 39 (p. 86), 678 (pp. 1273, 1276)
 Industrial, **1963–64**: 23, 124 (p. 156), 132 (p. 178), 199, 271 [3], 307, 404, 477, 506, 555, 640, 780 [3]; **1965**: 35 (p. 104), 76, 168, 319 [3], 326; **1966**: 34 (p. 96), 155; **1967**: 13 (p. 40), 498; **1968–69**: 47 (p. 128), 684 (pp. 1311, 1316)
 Meat, **1963–64**: 246 [18]
 Nuclear materials, decrease, **1963–64**: 91 (p. 117), 122, 129, 130, 131, 132 (p. 185), 272, 285 [3], 287, 294 [14], 295, 395, 434, 435, 486 [1, 2], 562, 642, 820; **1965**: 20, 196, 537
 Steel, **1963–64**: 504 [16], 563 [6], 780 [5]; **1965**: 208 [21], 226; **1966**: 206
 Weapons, **1963–64**: 797
 Wheat, **1966**: 62, 311, 608
Professional Training and Cooperation Amendments, proposed, **1966**: 307

Profits, **1963–64**: 91 (p. 115), 124 (pp. 158–160), 199, 350, 455 [2], 599, 604, 619 [4], 639, 708, 728, 771, 775; **1966**: 401 [2], 431, 444, 654 [5]; **1967**: 3 (p. 7), 270, 420, 524, 534, 554 [13]; **1968–69**: 50, 241, 676 (p. 1268)
 Agricultural, **1963–64**: 484
 Corporate, **1965**: 23, 35 (p. 104), 60, 76, 223, 250, 285, 298, 326, 406, 590, 632, 644; **1966**: 17, 34 (p. 96), 155, 199, 347, 444; **1967**: 3 (p. 40), 16 (p. 73), 329; **1968–69**: 76, 109, 229, 612, 678 (p. 1276), 684 (p. 1312)
 Increase, **1965**: 32 (p. 84), 35 (p. 108); **1966**: 237, 401 [2], 403, 412, 415, 428, 432, 437
 Steel industry, **1963–64**: 504 [16], 780 [5]; **1965**: 226
Programing-Budgeting System, Planning, **1967**: 121; **1968–69**: 39 (p. 108)
Project Head Start, **1965**: 2, 9, 75, 80, 259, 308, 323, 436, 467; **1966**: 26 (p. 63), 45, 77, 95, 111, 171n., 189, 299, 385n., 509, 524, 533, 594; **1967**: 3 (pp. 3, 5), 13 (p. 54), 16 (pp. 75, 85), 39, 55, 77, 81, 114, 211, 277, 286, 291, 397, 452, 495 [5], 532, 540; **1968–69**: 39 (p. 104), 47 (p. 143), 50, 54, 87, 111, 113, 154, 262, 270, 459, 493, 555, 567, 568, 648, 676 (p. 1264), 678 (p. 1293), 684 (p. 1324)
 Insignia, **1965**: 323
Project Mohole, **1966**: 229, 401 [3]
Project 100,000 (Department of Defense), **1967**: 92; **1968–69**: 40
"Project Remed," **1967**: 432n.
Project Transition, veterans' program, **1967**: 345; **1968–69**: 40
Property disposal, Federal, **1963–64**: 81, 617; **1966**: 464
Property rights, **1968–69**: 596
Protectionism, **1967**: 465
Protein fortification in food, **1967**: 33, 101, 176; **1968–69**: 124
Protestor, President as, **1967**: 264 [17]
Prouty, Sen. Winston L., **1965**: 551; **1966**: 396–399
Prouty, Mrs. Winston L., **1966**: 397–398
Proverbs, Book of, **1966**: 189
Providence, R.I., **1963–64**: 601, 602n.
 Housing projects, **1966**: 277 [1]
Providence College Veritas Medal, presentation, **1965**: 237
Province, Harry, **1967**: 532
Proxmire, Sen. William, **1963–64**: 746; **1965**: 437; **1968–69**: 280
Pryor, William C., **1968–69**: 631

Psalms, Book of, **1966**: 392; **1967**: 238
Psychiatric research, **1966**: 293
Psychiatrists, shortage of, **1965**: 5
Public accommodations, **1967**: 55
   Equal access to, **1963–64**: 91 (p. 116), 111,
      201 [16], 250, 301, 744, 800
   Nondiscrimination, **1968–69**: 26, 82, 87, 195,
      212, 459, 596, 611
Public Administration, Central American Insti-
      tute for, **1968–69**: 366
Public Advisory Committee on Trade Negotia-
      tions, **1963–64**: 278
Public Advisory Committee on Trade Policy,
      1968–69: 517
Public Affairs, National Institute of, **1966**: 129n.
Public assistance, **1963–64**: 219, 590; **1965**: 32
      (p. 94), 35 (p. 113), 132, 215; **1967**: 13
      (pp. 44, 46), 114
   See also Welfare programs.
   District of Columbia, **1967**: 15
   Expenditures, **1967**: 329
   Migrant workers, **1967**: 114
   State, **1967**: 13 (p. 54), 16 (p. 83)
   Taxes, **1967**: 16 (p. 83)
   Unemployed, **1967**: 13 (p. 54), 16 (p. 83), 114
Public Broadcasting, Corporation for, **1967**: 77,
      474; **1968–69**: 39 (p. 106), 54, 370
Public Broadcasting Act of 1967, **1967**: 77, 346,
      474, 490
Public buildings, architectural barriers to the
      handicapped, **1968–69**: 440
Public debt.
   See Debt, national.
Public education, **1963–64**: 219; **1965**: 9
Public Health Association, American, **1966**:
      185n.
Public Health Service, **1963–64**: 179, 211 [25],
      312, 567, 675n.; **1965**: 115, 174, 514,
      531; **1966**: 22, 45, 95, 292, 462, 524;
      1967: 13 (p. 57), 193, 520; **1968–69**:
      39 (p. 109), 113, 122, 389, 447, 536
   Alcoholism research center, **1966**: 95
   Reorganization, **1966**: 190, 292
Public Health Service Act, **1968–69**: 113, 447,
      536
Public Health Services Amendments of 1966,
      1967: 16 (p. 85), 121
Public health training programs, **1963–64**: 179
Public Higher Education in the District of
      Columbia, Committee on, **1963–64**:
      116n., 457
   Report, **1965**: 111
Public housing, **1963–64**: 124 (p. 163), 132 (p.
      188), 211 [28], 213; **1965**: 70, 90;
      1966: 26 (p. 61), 223, 236 [13], 237,
      428, 439; **1967**: 114, 355n., 380, 412;
      1968–69: 87, 278, 382, 426, 625, 678
      (p. 1289), 684 (p. 1325)

Public opinion, comments on, **1963–64**: 211
      [12], 232 [1]
Public opinion polls.
   See Polls, public opinion.
Public order, **1968–69**: 100
Public Roads, Bureau of, **1963–64**: 234, 567;
      1965: 30, 174, 255, 274n., 460; **1966**:
      98; **1967**: 369
Public service, **1968–69**: 676 (p. 1264)
   Careers for veterans, **1968–69**: 14 (p. 31), 40,
      160, 419
   Community service projects for older Ameri-
      cans, **1968–69**: 75
   Education bill, **1967**: 121, 148; **1968–69**: 100
   Urban areas, **1968–69**: 87
Public television, **1967**: 77, 346, 474, 490, 559
Public Utility Holding Company Act of 1935,
      1963–64: 295
Public welfare, **1963–64**: 132 (p. 188), 775;
      1965: 425
Public works, **1963–64**: 120, 132 (p. 188), 271
      [3], 300, 590; **1965**: 32 (p. 85), 90,
      415, 454 [5]; **1966**: 26 (p. 60), 122
      [2], 182, 416, 494 [7]; **1967**: 6 [5,
      10], 114, 329, 330 [1]; **1968–69**: 223
      [11], 567, 678 (p. 1303), 689
   Depressed areas, **1965**: 132
   District of Columbia, **1968–69**: 689
   Federal aid, **1965**: 47, 148
Public Works Acceleration Act, **1963–64**: 22,
      290, 297, 667
Public Works Appropriation Act, 1964, ap-
      proval, **1963–64**: 81
Public Works and Economic Development Act of
      1965, **1965**: 452, 454 [5]; **1966**: 111,
      250, 352
Public works and economic development bill,
      1965: 148, 418, 448 [5]
Publications
   Consumer, **1963–64**: 173
   Government, reduction, **1963–64**: 211 [10],
      307, 362, 462 [2], 630, 749
Publications Commission, National Historical,
      1963–64: 481n.; **1967**: 538n.
Publishers Association, National Newspaper,
      1967: 297 [14]
Publishers of obscene literature, **1966**: 611
Pucinski, Repr. Roman C., **1965**: 242, 299, 449;
      1966: 228
Pueblo, U.S.S., **1968–69**: 35, 48, 51 [4, 7, 8,
      15], 65n., 79 [13], 169 [7], 201, 223
      [12], 467 [6], 557 [5], 641, 643
Puerto Rican-Dominican Republic, Joint Eco-
      nomic Commission, **1967**: 436
Puerto Rico, **1965**: 448 [10]; **1966**: 157, 372;
      1967: 199, 397; **1968–69**: 54, 87, 91,
      437, 457, 596
   Economic growth, **1963–64**: 393

Puerto Rico — *continued*
  Gov. Luis Muñoz Marín, **1963–64**: 27, 387, 388
  Gov. Roberto Sánchez-Vilella, **1967**: 436
  U.S. citizenship, 50th anniversary, **1967**: 84
  U.S. relations with, **1963–64**: 393
Puerto Rico, Study Commission on Statehood for, **1963–64**: 242 [5]
Puerto Rico, United States-Puerto Rico Commission on the Status of, **1963–64**: 393; **1966**: 372
Puget Sound Naval Shipyards, Bremerton, Wash., **1963–64**: 430n.
Pulaski, Casimir, **1965**: 562, 595; **1966**: 120, 528
Pulitzer, Margaret Leech, "In the Days of McKinley," **1963–64**: 303
Puller, 1st Lt. Lewis B., Jr., **1968–69**: 537n., 541n.
Puller, Lt. Gen. Lewis B., **1968–69**: 537n., 541
Pulliam, Eugene C., **1966**: 347
Punta del Este Charter, **1963–64**: 9, 45, 46, 340, 443, 561, 769; **1965**: 286, 624; **1966**: 125, 177, 254, 386; **1967**: 152, 451
Punta del Este conference (1967), **1968–69**: 14 (p. 26), 39 (p. 99), 63, 66, 77, 147, 148, 199, 205, 207, 289, 362n., 366, 524
Punta del Este meeting of American Chiefs of State, **1967**: 70 [4], 272, 357, 394, 448, 451, 473, 495 [5], 519, 523
  Message to Congress, **1967**: 110
  Releases, **1967**: 171–175, 177
  Remarks, **1967**: 171, 173, 175–178
Purcell, Repr. Graham, **1967**: 405; **1968–69**: 281
Purchasing Agents, National Association of, **1963–64**: 211 [3]
Pure Food and Drug Act, **1966**: 576
Pure Food and Drug Act of 1906, **1967**: 57
Pure Food and Drug Act of 1907, **1968–69**: 601
Pyle, Ernie, **1967**: 494

Qantas Airways, **1966**: 64
Quaison-Sackey, Alex, **1965**: 331n.
Quakers, **1963–64**: 391
Quang Tri Province, South Vietnam, **1967**: 309 [5]
Quayle (Oliver) poll, **1963–64**: 542; **1966**: 320 [14]
Quebec, Canada, Premier Daniel Johnson, **1967**: 237
Queen Ann Democratic Club, Los Angeles, Calif., **1963–64**: 71 [3]
Quesada, Lt. Gen. Elwood R., **1965**: 319 [19]
"Quick," Munich publication, **1963–64**: 316ftn. (p. 621)

Quie, Repr. Albert H., **1965**: 189; **1967**: 182
Quigley, James M., **1966**: 88 [4], 428
Quill, Dan, **1965**: 621
Quilter, Gen. Charles J., **1967**: 485 [2]; **1968–69**: 81 [2]
Quinn, Lt. Gen. William W., **1967**: 502n.

Raab, Julius, **1968–69**: 193n.
Rabinowitz, Rabbi Stanley, **1963–64**: 77
Raboff, Stanley B., **1968–69**: 310
Raborn, Vice Adm. William F., Jr., **1965**: 209; **1966**: 310, 387, 410–411
  See also Central Intelligence Agency, Director.
Raborn, Mrs. William F., Jr., **1966**: 387
Racial Discrimination, Convention on the Elimination of all Forms of (U.N.), **1967**: 488
Racial and religious discrimination, **1966**: 320 [17]
Racism, **1968–69**: 26, 262
Radcliffe, George L., **1963–64**: 703
Radhakrishnan, Sarvepalli, **1963–64**: 367
Radiation belts probe, **1965**: 659
Radiation Control for Health and Safety Act of 1968, **1968–69**: 56, 390, 545
Radiation Council, Federal, **1963–64**: 653n., 675n.
Radiation research, **1967**: 31n.
Radiation safety, **1968–69**: 14 (p. 30), 56, 390, 545
Radiation Surveillance Center, **1963–64**: 675n.
Radio, **1967**: 286, 474, 477
  Health programs, **1968–69**: 111
  Noncommercial, **1968–69**: 54
  Police aid, **1968–69**: 59
  Use in 1964 Presidential campaign, **1963–64**: 201 [15]
Radio Association, American, **1965**: 428
Radio Conference on Space Communications, Geneva, **1963–64**: 180n.
Radio Free Europe, **1963–64**: 785
Radio Hanoi, **1967**: 136n.
Radio and Machine Workers, International Union of Electrical, **1966**: 496
Radio Propagation Laboratory, Central, **1967**: 31n.
Radio and television addresses.
  See Messages to the American people; Addresses to the Nation.
Radio and Television Service, Armed Forces, **1966**: 648
Radioactive fallout, **1963–64**: 434, 605, 653n., 675n., 686, 732; **1965**: 54, 284; **1967**: 59
Radioactive isotopes, **1965**: 196

Rahman, Abdul (Prime Minister of Malaysia), **1963–64**: 470, 471, 474; **1966**: 559n., 560n.; **1967**: 409

Railroad Administration, Federal, **1968–69**: 93, 693

Railroad Retirement Board, **1967**: 244, 315n.; **1968–69**: 331

Railroads, **1966**: 98; **1967**: 223 [2], 286; **1968–69**: 330

Freight car shortage, **1966**: 240

Labor contracts, **1963–64**: 284, 287, 290, 294 [11], 295, 297 [2], 338, 659, 678

Labor disputes, **1963–64**: 250, 251–253, 256 [1, 6], 262, 266 [12], 270, 271 [9, 17], 280 [11], 587 [7]; **1967**: 204 [5, 9], 310, 312 [1, 3]; **1968–69**: 132, 626

Economic impact, **1967**: 170, 188, 194, 207, 310

Emergency board, **1967**: 207, 310, 386

Joint resolution to provide for settlement, **1967**: 311

Messages to Congress, **1967**: 170, 207

"No strike" period, **1967**: 172, 174, 194, 310

Special panel, **1967**: 174, 188, 207, 310

Statements, **1967**: 172, 174, 188

Rapid transit systems, **1966**: 27, 68, 84, 240, 262, 353, 442; **1967**: 154, 234, 353, 358 [3]; **1968–69**: 693

Proposed, **1965**: 2, 32 (p. 93), 61, 97, 536

Retirement system, **1967**: 12, 244; **1968–69**: 331, 678 (pp. 1296, 1298)

Safety operations, **1965**: 281

Wages, **1967**: 188

Railway Labor Act, **1966**: 322; **1967**: 170, 172, 188, 204 [5, 9], 207, 310; **1968–69**: 626

Rainmaking projects in India, **1967**: 230

Rains, Albert, **1963–64**: 453, 549; **1967**: 87n.

Raleigh, N.C., campaign remarks, **1963–64**: 631

Rama III, King (Thailand), **1967**: 290n.

Ramey, James T., **1963–64**: 285 [10]

Rampton, Calvin, **1963–64**: 737; **1966**: 255, 410–411, 413, 491n. 492 [1]; **1968–69**: 125

Ramsey, Judge William F., **1967**: 79

Ranchers, **1968–69**: 94

Rand Development Corp., **1966**: 392

Randall, Clarence B., **1963–64**: 27

Randall, K. A. (Chairman, Federal Deposit Insurance Corporation), **1965**: 60; **1966**: 473

Randall, Repr. Wm. J., **1963–64**: 189

Randolph, A. Philip, **1963–64**: 568; **1965**: 436, 548, 613; **1966**: 248, 407, 408n.; **1967**: 484; **1968–69**: 42

Randolph, Edmund, **1965**: 66

Randolph, Sen. Jennings, **1963–64**: 360, 586; **1966**: 151, 426–427, 505; **1967**: 503; **1968–69**: 128, 160, 229, 566, 567

Randolph, Phillip, **1963–64**: 669

Randolph Air Force Base, Texas, **1967**: 151n.; **1968–69**: 7n.

Random House publishing company, **1963–64**: 560 [8]

Ranger space project, **1965**: 134

Ranger spacecraft, **1963–64**: 492, 501n., 504 [2], 518; **1965**: 81, 123; **1966**: 40, 249; **1968–69**: 107

Rangoon, Burma, **1968–69**: 198

Rankin, Lee, **1963–64**: 595; **1967**: 68

Rankin, Jeannette, **1965**: 319 [17]

Ransom, Harry, **1963–64**: 375, 482, 513, 622; **1965**: 412; **1966**: 363, 424n., 635 [3], 637; **1968–69**: 625

Rare earths, **1967**: 506

Rat control, **1968–69**: 95

Bill, **1967**: 114, 318, 326, 328 [7], 358 [3], 534, 539, 554 [16]

Rather, Dan, **1967**: 529, 554; **1968–69**: 1 [9]

Rather, Mary Alice, **1968–69**: 595

Ratna, Queen (Nepal), **1967**: 461n., 462

Ravitch, Richard, **1967**: 4n.

Raw materials, **1966**: 34 (p. 100); **1967**: 16 (p. 79)

Ray, C. B., **1963–64**: 255

Rayburn, Sam, **1963–64**: 23, 59, 96, 199, 290, 295, 305, 324, 325, 330, 338, 434, 506, 786, 799; **1965**: 81, 223, 236, 353 [23], 554; **1966**: 271, 273, 306, 353, 395, 416, 433, 509, 512, 516 [9]; **1967**: 63, 150, 156, 206, 228, 262, 296, 496; **1968–69**: 14 (p. 25), 109, 114, 301, 536, 575, 592, 595, 648, 676 (p. 1270)

Campaign remarks on, **1963–64**: 599, 604, 631, 642, 643, 645, 648, 659, 693, 732, 736, 763

News conference remarks on, **1963–64**: 294 [11], 297 [2], 516 [8]

Rayburn House Office Building, dedication of Carl Vinson Hearing Room in, **1965**: 157

Raye, Martha, **1967**: 196

RB–66 aircraft incident over East Germany, **1963–64**: 170 [1], 182, 232 [2], 242 [18, 26], 246 [4]

Re, Edward D., **1965**: 367

REA.

See Rural Electrification Administration.

Reactor Testing Station, National, Arco, Idaho, **1966**: 411

Reactors, nuclear, **1966**: 48n.; **1967**: 98, 515

Reader's Digest Foundation, **1965**: 335n.; **1966**: 306n.; **1968–69**: 332n.

Reading, the President's, **1963–64**: 218 [12]

Reagan, Ronald, **1966**: 577 [13], 599 [3]
Real Estate Boards, National Association of,
    1966: 158 [10]
Real estate taxes, **1966**: 30
Reams, Frazier, Jr., **1966**: 434–437
Recessions, **1965**: 46 [1]; **1966**: 34 (p. 97), 108,
    115, 155, 635 [18]; **1967**: 16 (p. 88);
    1968–69: 47 (p. 127), 612, 684 (p.
    1312)
  1957–58 recession, **1963–64**: 639
  1960 recession, **1963–64**: 411
  1960–61 recession, **1965**: 76, 490
  Preventive measures, **1963–64**: 124 (p. 159),
    295, 316 [26], 415, 431, 472, 477,
    550, 589, 708, 749, 775, 787; **1965**:
    2, 35 (p. 109)
Reciprocal Tariff Act, **1968–69**: 274
Reclamation, Bureau of, **1963–64**: 132 (p. 187);
    1965: 32 (p. 92); **1968–69**: 39 (p. 101),
    467 [3]
Reclamation Project Act of 1939, **1963–64**: 554
Reclamation projects, **1965**: 193, 471
Reconstruction and Development, International
    Bank for, **1965**: 18, 136, 541; **1966**:
    41, 94, 125, 152–154, 565; **1968–69**:
    39 (p. 99), 63, 99, 102, 290, 500
Reconstruction and Development Planning
    Commission for Alaska, Federal, **1963–
    64**: 241n.
Recording for the Blind, Inc., **1966**: 220n.;
    1968–69: 230n.
Records Centers, Federal, **1965**: 14; **1966**: 58n.
Recreation Advisory Council, **1965**: 54; **1966**:
    202
Recreation Department, District of Columbia,
    1966: 27
Recreation and Natural Beauty, Citizens' Ad-
    visory Committee on, **1966**: 202, 653;
    1967: 295; **1968–69**: 122, 167
Recreation and Natural Beauty, President's
    Council on, **1966**: 202, 653; **1967**: 295;
    1968–69: 122, 167
Recreation and Park Association, National,
    1966: 518
Recreation programs and facilities, **1963–64**:
    132 (p. 187), 133, 213, 287, 357, 422,
    427, 490, 516 [1], 554, 578, 597, 620,
    642, 667, 669, 704n., 756; **1965**: 35
    (p. 115), 47, 53, 90, 415; **1966**: 82,
    105, 398, 427, 545, 595; **1967**: 13 (p.
    51), 15, 29, 240; **1968–69**: 39 (p. 101),
    94, 122, 123, 270, 311, 330, 345, 386,
    406, 411, 470, 505, 547, 565, 593, 601,
    612, 653, 672, 676 (p. 1264)
  Beautification, **1965**: 2
  Children, **1966**: 105, 394; **1967**: 160, 203, 209
  Construction, **1965**: 2, 90; **1966**: 398, 515,
    520; **1967**: 20

Recreation programs and facilities – *continued*
  District of Columbia, **1965**: 29, 70, 151; **1968–
    69**: 133, 134, 689
  Federal aid, **1965**: 30, 54, 70, 168, 222, 277,
    279, 471, 477, 487, 521; **1966**: 26 (p.
    60), 27, 351–352, 398, 518
  Legislation, **1968–69**: 510
  Rural, **1967**: 114; **1968–69**: 94
  Seashore, **1966**: 26 (p. 60); **1967**: 553
  State, **1967**: 203
  Trails, **1967**: 20
  Urban, **1966**: 26 (p. 61), 373 [15], 398;
    1967: 114, 553; **1968–69**: 87
Recreational boat safety bill of 1968, **1968–69**:
    56
Red Cross, **1963–64**: 202, 217, 241, 567, 647;
    1965: 74, 84, 174, 191, 436, 525, 605;
    1966: 92, 476; **1967**: 22, 287; **1968–
    69**: 55, 121
Red Cross, International, **1965**: 546
Red Cross, International Committee of the,
    1966: 338 [1], 549; **1967**: 287, 312ftn.
    (p. 702); **1968–69**: 381, 433, 580
Red Cross Societies, League of, **1966**: 549
Redevelopment Land Agency, District of
    Columbia, **1966**: 457; **1968–69**: 135
Redeye heat-seeking missile, **1963–64**: 170 [3]
Redskins Pro Football, Inc., Washington, **1968–
    69**: 109
Redwood forests, **1963–64**: 427; **1966**: 8 [9]
Redwood National Park, Calif., **1966**: 26 (p. 60),
    82; **1967**: 20; **1968–69**: 39 (p. 101),
    345, 510, 547
  Proposed, **1963–64**: 427; **1965**: 54
Redwood preservation, **1968–69**: 14 (p. 31),
    122, 167, 411
Redwoods League, Save the, **1963–64**: 427
Reeb, Rev. James, murder of, **1965**: 107
Reed, Frank J., **1963–64**: 728
Reed, Gov. John H., **1963–64**: 455 [14], 606;
    1965: 291n.; **1966**: 121 [1, 5, 6], 124
    [1–3, 7–8, 10], 320 [1], 397–399,
    491n., 492 [1, 10]
Reedy, George E., **1963–64**: 224, 232ftns. (pp.
    404, 408), 236n., 270, 296, 415, 450n.,
    451n., 485n., 503n., 539, 794n., 806;
    1965: 22 [1], 46 [3], 106 [9], 113, 126,
    162; **1966**: 315n.; **1968–69**: 3, 106, 112
  Campaign remarks on, **1963–64**: 579, 639
  News conference remarks on, **1963–64**: 150
    [8, 20], 242 [25], 271 [5, 15], 294
    [7], 336 [7], 504 [1, 6], 521 [1],
    560 [13, 15], 563 [3, 5], 619 [1, 8],
    780 [13, 14], 818 [1, 2]
Reeves, Lt. Gen. Raymond J., **1963–64**: 241
Reform of Federal Criminal Laws, National
    Commission on, **1968–69**: 59
Reforms in Government, statement, **1963–64**:
    776

Refugees
  Czechoslovakian, **1968-69**: 467 [10]
  Middle East, **1967**: 264 [15], 272, 281
  Protocol for status of, **1968-69**: 428
Regional Action Planning Commissions, **1965**:
      132
Regional Economic Development, Federal Ad-
      visory Council on, **1968-69**: 173
Regional recovery program, proposed, **1965**: 2
Register, Lynn, **1968-69**: 238n.
Registration.
  See Voting participation and registration.
Registration and Voting Participation, President's
      Commission on, **1963-64**: 57, 167
Registry of National Historic Landmarks, **1965**:
      54
Regulatory agencies
  Management activities, **1963-64**: 20
  Powers, **1966**: 34 (p. 108)
Rehabilitation.
  See also Vocational rehabilitation.
  Criminals, **1967**: 13 (p. 56), 71, 382
  Handicapped persons, **1968-69**: 678 (p. 1299)
  Physical, **1966**: 588
Rehabilitation of the Handicapped, National
      Commission on Architectural Barriers
      to, **1966**: 192
Rehabilitation, Bureau of, Pennsylvania, **1967**:
      413
Rehabilitation Service, Social and, **1968-69**: 39
      (p. 109)
Reid Cabral, Donald, **1965**: 212n.
Reid, Repr. Charlotte T., **1968-69**: 219
Reilly, Col. John, **1968-69**: 210
Reilly, John R., Jr., **1967**: 518 [2]
Reinecke, Repr. Ed, **1967**: 227
Reinert, Msgr. Paul C., **1963-64**: 188
Reinhardt, G. Frederick, **1968-69**: 13
Reininger, Robert M., **1968-69**: 665n.
Reischauer, Edwin O., **1963-64**: 236; **1966**: 154
Reitz, J. Wayne, **1965**: 115n., 260
Relay communication satellite, **1963-64**: 779n.
Rembrandt van Rijn, **1966**: 328n.
Reminiscences, the President's, **1965**: 179, 357,
      481, 521, 621
  Awards and citations, **1968-69**: 212
  Baptist heritage, **1963-64**: 238
  Birthplace, **1965**: 2
  Boyhood impressions and experiences, **1963-
      64**: 9, 172, 293, 484, 493, 562, 597,
      650, 652, 695, 728, 749, 763; **1965**:
      89, 191, 223, 277, 388 [2], 459, 576,
      596; **1966**: 232, 273, 417 [2], 543,
      564; **1968-69**: 429, 567, 644
  Candidacy for Congress, **1963-64**: 232 [11]
  Coaching high school debate, **1963-64**: 343;
      1965: 89

Reminiscences, the President's – *continued*
  College days, **1965**: 603; **1966**: 417 [2], 589;
      1968-69: 219, 459
    Newspaper activity, **1963-64**: 339
    Record, **1965**: 397
  Congressional career, **1966**: 353; **1968-69**: 50,
      143, 212, 228, 258, 672, 676 (p. 1269),
      690, 698
  Depressions, **1966**: 410; **1967**: 286; **1968-69**:
      86
  Early employment, **1963-64**: 292, 321, 658,
      673, 735; **1965**: 4, 329, 405, 519;
      1966: 509; **1967**: 211, 267
  Election campaigns, **1966**: 221, 399, 410, 504,
      512, 520
    Congress, **1963-64**: 732
  Experience with press, **1963-64**: 149
  Food aid to India, support, **1968-69**: 691
  Forebears, **1963-64**: 292; **1965**: 89; **1966**:
      351, 417 [2]
  Former Presidents, **1963-64**: 9, 165, 303, 650;
      1965: 48; **1966**: 400, 417 [2]; **1967**:
      21, 28
  Government service, **1966**: 193
  Graduation from high school, **1963-64**: 374,
      658, 761n.
  Heart attack in 1955, **1963-64**: 143 [3], 157,
      606; **1965**: 154; **1968-69**: 672
  Job-hunting experiences, **1963-64**: 413, 650,
      658, 733, 734, 735
  Kennedy, John F., events surrounding assassi-
      nation, **1968-69**: 604
  Marriage, **1968-69**: 357
  Mexican immigrant families, associations,
      1963-64: 194; **1965**: 107; **1966**: 176
  National Youth Administration, **1966**: 500
  Parents, **1965**: 183, 286, 406, 529; **1966**: 168,
      176, 417 [2, 4]
    Memories of father, **1963-64**: 327, 496,
      658, 733, 763
    Memories of mother, **1963-64**: 172, 658,
      673; **1968-69**: 165
  Public life, early, **1963-64**: 75, 372, 496, 578,
      607, 612, 648, 650, 733, 761n., 763;
      1965: 142, 157, 179, 233, 236; **1966**:
      155, 168, 232, 361, 388, 415-416,
      417 [2], 433, 439, 479
  Public service, **1968-69**: 33, 97, 174, 227, 305,
      460 [1, 2], 499, 603, 698
  Rural electrification support, **1967**: 267;
      1968-69: 96, 305
  Savings bonds purchases, **1965**: 11
  Schooling, **1963-64**: 327, 658, 778; **1965**: 89,
      181, 183, 374; **1966**: 455
  Space program support, **1967**: 38
  Teaching experiences, **1965**: 89, 107, 183,
      250, 301, 539, 541, 603; **1966**: 223,
      417 [2], 455, 508, 589; **1967**: 258;

Reminiscences, the President's — *continued*
  Teaching experiences — *continued*
        1968–69: 68, 125, 158, 459, 595, 596,
        624, 631, 644
  Term of office, highlights of, **1968–69**: 696
        [9]
  United Nations, 1958 appearance before,
        1965: 318
  Visits abroad, **1963–64**: 182; **1965**: 378; **1968–
        69**: 199
    See also Visits to foreign countries.
    Africa, **1963–64**: 280, 297 [1]
    American Samoa, **1967**: 559
    Asia, **1967**: 272
    Australia, **1966**: 516 [1]; **1968–69**: 604
    Berlin, **1963–64**: 87, 349
    Canada, **1967**: 237
    Denmark, **1963–64**: 394
    Finland, **1965**: 491
    Germany, **1966**: 482
    Greece, **1963–64**: 153
    Iceland, **1967**: 313
    India, **1966**: 149
    Iran, **1963–64**: 385; **1967**: 363, 364, 509
    Italy, **1963–64**: 101, 149, 581, 607, 651;
        1965: 82
    Korea, **1967**: 112; **1968–69**: 696 [1]
    Mexico, **1967**: 447; **1968–69**: 199
    New Zealand, **1966**: 516 [1], 540; **1968–
        69**: 522, 525
    Pakistan, **1965**: 648
    Senegal, **1966**: 488
    Southeast Asia, **1965**: 248
    Thailand, **1963–64**: 476; **1965**: 177; **1966**:
        554, 557; **1967**: 289, 290; **1968–69**: 48
    Turkey, **1963–64**: 416
    Uruguay, **1968–69**: 147
    Vatican, **1968–69**: 603
    Vietnam, **1965**: 159; **1967**: 446; **1968–69**:
        79 [8]
  Wedding and wedding trip, **1966**: 160, 174–
        176
  World War II service, **1963–64**: 426, 493;
        1965: 228; **1966**: 345, 538–540, 546–
        547, 568; **1968–69**: 603
Remittances to Europe, Cooperative for Ameri-
        can, **1967**: 33, 153
Renegotiation Act extension, **1966**: 313; **1968–
        69**: 559
Renne, Roland, **1963–64**: 656
Reno, Nev., campaign remarks, **1963–64**: 655
Rent supplements, **1965**: 90, 397; **1966**: 6 (p. 6),
        26 (p. 61), 30, 67, 158 [10], 168, 223,
        236 [13], 253, 277ftn. (p. 625), 344,
        373 [15], 394, 403, 417 [3], 436, 439,
        525; **1967**: 13 (p. 52), 15, 16 (pp. 75,
        85), 23, 88, 114, 179, 223 [13], 225
        [13], 261, 312 [6], 353, 358 [3, 8],

Rent supplements — *continued*
        359, 370, 380, 460 [3, 10], 467, 534,
        554 [6, 16]; **1968–69**: 47 (p. 141), 87,
        114, 234, 279, 380, 426, 470, 678 (p.
        1289)
Renwick, James, **1965**: 328n.
Reorganization Act of 1949, **1965**: 43, 125;
        1966: 267, 302
Reorganization plans, **1965**: 43
  Abolition of certain committees, councils, and
        boards, **1965**: 282
  Authority, **1968–69**: 678 (p. 1302)
  Bureau of Customs, **1965**: 125
  Community Relations Service, **1966**: 59–60
  District of Columbia, **1967**: 247, 307, 337,
        339
    Recreation functions, **1968–69**: 134
    Redevelopment Land Agency, **1968–69**:
        135
  Emergency Planning, Office of, **1968–69**: 483
  Environmental Science Service Administration,
        1965: 247
  Locomotive inspection, **1965**: 281
  Narcotics and drug abuse control, **1968–69**: 60
  National Capital Regional Planning Council
        1966: 302
  National Science Foundation, **1965**: 283
  National Zoological Park, **1966**: 267
  President's authority to submit to Congress,
        1968–69: 39, 678
  Public Health Service, **1966**: 190
  Ships' mortgages, **1967**: 72
  Tariff Commission, United States, **1967**: 99
  Urban mass transportation, **1968–69**: 93, 130,
        351
  Water pollution control, **1966**: 91
Repair work, consumer protection, **1968–69**: 56
"Report to the President—The President's Com-
        mittee on Equal Employment Oppor-
        tunity," **1963–64**: 111n.
Reports to Congress.
    See also Congress, reports to, messages trans-
        mitting; Presidential reports to
        Congress.
  List, Appendix C, **1965**: p. 1203; **1966**: p.
        1494; **1967**: p. 1225; **1968–69**: p. 1401
Reports to the President.
  Ackley, Gardner, effect of excise tax reduction
        on consumer prices, **1965**: 326n.
  Acting Attorney General Katzenbach, crime
        and law enforcement, **1963–64**: 752
  Advisory Committee on Private Enterprise in
        Foreign Aid, **1965**: 450
  Anderson, Sen. Clinton P., Alaska reconstruc-
        tion, **1963–64**: 319
  Antarctic Policy Group, **1965**: 220, 265

Reports to the President – *continued*
  Appalachian Governors, Conference of, **1963–64**: 293n.
  Atomic Energy Commission
    Activities in 1964, **1965**: 196
    Water desalinization, **1963–64**: 715n.
  Attorney General Katzenbach
    Immigration and naturalization, **1965**: 547n.
    President's Commission on Law Enforcement and the Administration of Justice, **1965**: 437n.
    Voting rights implementation, **1965**: 409n.
  Attorney General Kennedy
    Immigration, **1963–64**: 115
    Organized crime and racketeering, **1963–64**: 90
  Beautification programs, **1965**: 277n.
  Budget, Bureau of the, cost reduction program, **1965**: 497
  Career training for young Federal employees, **1968–69**: 673
  Citizens' Advisory Committee on Recreation and Natural Beauty, **1967**: 295
  Civil Service Commission
    Executive Seminar Center, **1965**: 379
    Federal personnel management, **1963–64**: 168
  Commission on Civil Rights, equal opportunity in Federal farm programs, **1965**: 85
  Commission to Report on the Assassination of President John F. Kennedy, **1963–64**: 595
  Committee on the Economic Impact of Defense and Disarmament, **1965**: 493
  Committee on Equal Opportunity in the Armed Forces, **1963–64**: 816
  Committee on Urban Housing, **1968–69**: 704
  Committee on Utilization of Scientific and Engineering Manpower, **1963–64**: 271ftn. (p. 488)
  Cost reduction program, Federal, **1965**: 184, 249n., 360, 497
  Council of Economic Advisers, **1963–64**: 124 (pp. 161, 162); **1965**: 62, 226, 590n.; **1966**: 34 (p. 103)
  Defense Department, cost reduction, **1965**: 360
  Education, **1965**: 111, 527n.
  Education Task Force, **1965**: 519n.
  Employment record for August, **1965**: 480
  Family Breadwinners: Their Special Training Needs, **1963–64**: 160
  Federal Power Commission
    National power survey, **1963–64**: 803
    Power failure in Northeastern States, **1965**: 640
  Federal Radiation Council, radioactive fallout, **1963–64**: 653n.

Reports to the President – *continued*
  Federal taxes, collection during fiscal year 1965, **1965**: 505
  Federal Water Resources Research Program, **1963–64**: 231
  Foreign trade policy, **1968–69**: 680
  Government employment of minority groups, **1963–64**: 812
  Government publications, reduction, **1963–64**: 211 [10]
  Health, Education, and Welfare, Secretary of
    Federal aid to college students, **1968–69**: 473n.
    Programs and goals, **1968–69**: 640
    Vocational education, **1968–69**: 6
  Hoover, J. Edgar, **1963–64**: 688 [5]
  Housing and Urban Development, Secretary of, rent supplements, **1966**: 344
  Inter-Agency Committee on Mexican American Affairs, **1968–69**: 437
  International cooperation, **1965**: 96
  June buying, **1965**: 31
  Keppel, Francis, education for children of low-income families, **1965**: 527n.
  Knott, Lawson B., Jr., architectural standards for Federal buildings, **1965**: 249n.
  Labor, Department of, unemployment, **1963–64**: 211 [3]
  Layton, John B., crime in the District of Columbia, **1966**: 219
  Limited test ban treaty safeguards, **1963–64**: 276
  Los Angeles, Calif., **1965**: 453n.
  Macy, John W., Jr.
    Federal incentive awards program, **1965**: 540
    Government communications with and services to the public, **1965**: 249n., 591n.
    Voting rights implementation, **1965**: 409n.
  Manpower Conservation, Task Force on, **1963–64**: 89
  Mansfield, Sen. Mike, Vietnam conflict, **1966**: 8 [12]
  Maritime industry labor dispute, **1963–64**: 614n.
  National Advisory Commission on Food and Fiber, **1967**: 525
  National Advisory Commission on Health Facilities, **1968–69**: 622
  National Commission on Community Health Services, **1966**: 185
  National Conference of Federal Executive Board Chairmen, **1965**: 264
  National Institutes of Health study committee, **1965**: 115
  National Oceanographic Program, **1963–64**: 229

Reports to the President — *continued*
Natural beauty in America, **1965**: 545
Noise in the environment, **1968-69**: 577
Northeastern States
Drought, **1965**: 358n.
Power failure, **1965**: 640, 641ftn. (p. 1140)
Panama, economy of, **1963-64**: 316 [11]
Panama Canal Zone dispute, **1963-64**: 104
Powerplant site selection, **1968-69**: 653
President's Advisory Commission on Narcotic
and Drug Abuse, **1963-64**: 458
President's Advisory Committee on Labor-
Management Policy, automation, **1965**:
428
President's Advisory Committee on Supersonic
Transport, **1965**: 339
President's Appalachian Regional Commission,
1963-64: 293n.
President's Commission on Crime in the
District of Columbia, **1966**: 354
President's Commission on Heart Disease,
Cancer, and Stroke, **1963-64**: 798
President's Commission on Law Enforcement
and Administration of Justice, **1967**: 60
President's Commission on Postal Organization,
1968-69: 391
President's Commission on Registration and
Voting Participation, **1963-64**: 57
President's Committee on Equal Employment
Opportunity, **1963-64**: 448
President's Committee on Mental Retardation,
1968-69: 493
President's Committee on Population and
Family Planning, **1968-69**: 659
President's Committee on Public Higher Educa-
tion in the District of Columbia, **1963-
64**: 457; **1965**: 111
President's Committee for Traffic Safety,
1963-64: 565
President's Council on Aging, **1963-64**: 178
President's Council on Pennsylvania Avenue,
1963-64: 379 (ftn.) (p. 738), 700
President's Council on Physical Fitness, **1963-
64**: 490
President's National Advisory Panel on Insur-
ance in Riot-Affected Areas, **1968-69**:
36
President's Science Advisory Committee, **1966**:
326
Pollution, **1965**: 602
Space program, **1967**: 48
Railroad labor dispute panel, **1967**: 188
Railway labor dispute, emergency board in-
vestigating, **1968-69**: 626
Red Cross disaster operations in Oregon and
California, **1965**: 74
School dropouts, 1963 back-to-school cam-
paign, **1963-64**: 84

Reports to the President — *continued*
SEATO meeting, **1963-64**: 274
Secretary Celebrezze
Civil Rights Act implementation, **1965**:
249n.
Cost reduction, **1965**: 184
Radioactive fallout, **1963-64**: 675n.
Social Security Administration, **1965**: 394n.
Secretary Connor, Patent Office operations,
1965: 249n.
Secretary Dillon, balance of payments, **1963-
64**: 753
Secretary Fowler
Balance of payments, **1965**: 249n.; **1968-69**:
449
International monetary system, **1965**: 451n.
Secretary Freeman
Drought in Northeastern States, **1965**:
358n.
Economy program in the Department of
Agriculture, **1965**: 249n.
Forest Service, **1966**: 376
Secretary Gardner, social security benefits to
young people, **1965**: 501
Secretary McNamara
Defense cost reduction, **1963-64**: 467
Defense spending, **1963-64**: 619 [2]
International situation, **1965**: 321n.
Selective Service System study, **1963-64**:
619 [3]
Vietnam, **1963-64**: 218 [24]
Secretary Rusk
East-West Center in Hawaii, **1963-64**: 336
[6]
International situation, **1965**: 321n.
Secretary Udall
Outdoor advertising restrictions, **1965**:
576n.
Salt water conversion demonstration plant,
Freeport, Tex., **1965**: 417n.
Water desalinization, **1963-64**: 715
Secretary Wirtz
Employment, **1965**: 490
First Neighborhood Youth Corps project,
1965: 67
Government safety program, **1966**: 75
Manpower, **1963-64**: 212
Social and economic conditions of the Ameri-
can Negro, **1968-69**: 423
Space Program in the Post Apollo Period,
1967: 48
Special Panel on Federal Salaries, **1965**: 244,
612
Soviet science and technology, **1963-64**: 804
Summer domestic programs, **1966**: 171
Supersonic transport program, **1963-64**: 355
Swidler, Joseph C., Jr., power failure in North-
eastern States, **1965**: 641ftn. (p. 1140)

Reports to the President – *continued*
Task force on foreign investments, **1963-64**: 296
Taylor, Gen. Maxwell D., Vietnam, **1965**: 412 [2, 3]
Toward Better Utilization of Scientific and Engineering Talent, **1963-64**: 456
Treasury, Secretary of the, balance of payments, **1966**: 6 (p. 5)
U.S. trade with Eastern Europe and the Soviet Union, **1965**: 266
Valenti, Jack J., salt water conversion demonstration plant, Freeport, Tex., **1965**: 417n.
Vaughn, Jack H., Latin American policy of U.S., **1965**: 429n.
Vice President, Dominican Republic, **1966**: 320 [6]
Vice President Humphrey, civil rights activities in Government, **1965**: 50
Vietnam mission, **1963-64**: 223
Vocational rehabilitation, Federal-State program, **1965**: 416
Water Resources Council, **1965**: 358n., 375
Westmoreland, Gen. William C., Vietnam conflict, **1966**: 383
White House Conference on Natural Beauty, **1965**: 277
White House Conference "To Fulfill These Rights," **1965**: 548n.; **1966**: 408
White House Fellows Association, Federal Government and the student community, **1968-69**: 570
Youth Opportunity Campaign, **1965**: 438n.
Reports required by Government, reduction, **1963-64**: 307, 362, 583
Republic Powdered Metals, Inc., **1963-64**: 350n.
Republic Steel Co., **1968-69**: 427
"Republican Approach to the Needs of the Aging, A," **1966**: 509
Republican Coordinating Committee, **1966**: 501 [12]; **1967**: 330 [9]
Republican Governors Association, **1967**: 297 [6]
Republican National Committee
Chairman (Dean Burch), **1963-64**: 508
Republican National Convention (1964), **1963-64**: 170
Republican Party, **1963-64**: 280 [6], 342, 617; **1965**: 330, 340, 349, 353 [18, 19], 388 [17], 555; **1966**: 459, 504, 510, 516 [6], 599 [2, 3], 610 [13]; **1967**: 225 [13], 251, 375 [15]; **1968-69**: 210, 233, 460 [2], 467 [7, 14]
Campaign remarks, **1963-64**: 542, 555n., 603, 605, 660, 680, 693, 695, 713, 747, 764; **1968-69**: 529, 565-569, 575
Great Society programs, support, **1966**: 628 [2]

Republican Party – *continued*
News conference remarks, **1963-64**: 150 [9, 18], 201 [16], 246 [4], 256 [12], 285 [15], 455 [19, 20], 475 [7], 486 [16], 560 [10], 619 [18]
Nickname for the President, **1963-64**: 256 [12]
Platform, **1963-64**: 475 [7], 680
Record in Congress, **1966**: 504, 510, 610 [6]; **1967**: 150, 479, 534
Record in office, **1963-64**: 764
Vietnam conflict criticism, **1966**: 474 [4]; **1967**: 204 [10, 16]
Rescue of accident victims, **1968-69**: 111
Research, **1963-64**: 389, 601
Accident prevention, **1963-64**: 565
Administrative systems, **1966**: 98
Agricultural, **1963-64**: 124 (p. 162); **1965**: 47, 54, 168; **1966**: 62, 441, 550; **1967**: 13 (p. 60), 449n.; **1968-69**: 176
Alcoholism, **1966**: 95
Animals, humane treatment, **1966**: 395, 402
Automobile and highway, **1968-69**: 243, 244
Biomedical, **1965**: 115; **1966**: 293; **1967**: 76, 77, 540
Child health, **1967**: 39
Construction technology, **1968-69**: 684 (p. 1322)
Crime, **1965**: 2, 102, 381, 422, 437, 500, 509, 526; **1966**: 526; **1967**: 35, 382
Prevention, **1968-69**: 320
Defense, **1963-64**: 797
Education, **1965**: 9; **1966**: 45, 319; **1967**: 540; **1968-69**: 4, 39 (pp. 89, 106), 54
Electronic computing equipment, use in, **1968-69**: 687
Engineering, **1963-64**: 308, 629; **1965**: 225
Federal aid, **1968-69**: 678 (p. 1293)
Federal cooperation with colleges, **1963-64**: 482
Fire safety, **1967**: 57
Food production, **1966**: 461
Government sponsored, **1968-69**: 54
Grants, **1967**: 6 [6]
Health, **1965**: 54, 72; **1966**: 95, 189, 293, 403; **1967**: 16 (p. 85), 77, 260, 319
Highway safety, **1966**: 98, 187, 449
Industrial, **1963-64**: 589; **1965**: 257
Law enforcement, **1965**: 102; **1967**: 35
Malnutrition, **1966**: 45
Medical, **1963-64**: 179, 403, 733, 755, 775, 808; **1965**: 2, 5, 12, 15, 115, 154, 175, 196, 214, 343, 410, 531, 544, 551, 581; **1966**: 45, 95, 156, 185, 271, 273, 293, 353, 395, 403, 483, 495; **1967**: 13 (p. 53), 77, 161, 319, 477, 500; **1968-69**: 39 (p. 107), 40, 41, 47 (p. 143), 108, 111, 286, 396, 408, 442, 446, 468, 589, 685, 695

Research — *continued*
  Mental health, **1966**: 95, 293, 395
  Military, **1963-64**: 132 (p. 185); **1965**: 26, 32
      (p. 90); **1966**: 26 (p. 57); **1967**: 13
      (p. 48); **1968-69**: 39 (p. 98), 678 (p.
      1279)
  Natural resources conservation, **1963-64**: 132
      (p. 187); **1965**: 35 (p. 115)
  Nuclear, **1963-64**: 462 [4]; **1965**: 196;
      1967: 76, 515; **1968-69**: 145, 308, 608
  Oceanic, **1963-64**: 229, 650; **1965**: 71, 92,
      247; **1966**: 229, 326, 461; **1967**: 20,
      101, 176; **1968-69**: 124, 692
  Pesticides, **1965**: 54
  Pollution control, **1965**: 54; **1966**: 82; **1967**:
      20, 186
  Population control, **1968-69**: 393
  Rice, **1967**: 448
  Scientific, **1963-64**: 117, 124 (p. 163), 132
      (p. 191), 231, 308, 396, 529, 629, 715,
      738, 756, 758; **1965**: 9, 32 (p. 95), 56,
      71, 88, 92, 115, 166, 170, 196, 220,
      225, 247, 257, 265, 271, 319 [5], 514,
      522, 523, 558; **1966**: 38, 79, 111, 222,
      326, 402; **1967**: 37, 165, 491, 540;
      1968-69: 145, 227, 288, 687, 692
  Ship design, **1966**: 98
  Social science, **1965**: 404; **1968-69**: 145
  Space.
      See Space research and exploration.
  Technological, **1963-64**: 804; **1965**: 143, 513
  Transportation, **1965**: 32 (p. 93), 97, 536;
      1966: 26 (p. 61), 98; **1967**: 16 (p. 87);
      1968-69: 39 (p. 102), 306
  Urban, **1967**: 114, 353, 359, 370; **1968-69**: 39
      (p. 103), 87, 215
  Waste disposal, **1965**: 54
  Water resources, **1963-64**: 231, 461, 756;
      1965: 54, 143, 275, 325, 547;
      1966: 138; **1967**: 284
  Weather, **1963-64**: 597; **1965**: 247, 271;
      1968-69: 495
      See also Weather prediction and control.
  Wheat, **1967**: 448, 449, 452, 453
Research, Institutes for Environmental,
      1967: 31n.
Research on Cancer, International Agency for,
      1965: 343
Research Center of the Southwest, Graduate,
      1963-64: 738
Reserve Board.
  See Federal Reserve System.
Reserve forces, **1965**: 26, 353 [6, 9], 388 [1],
      395 [5], 396; **1966**: 65 [14], 124 [9],
      324, 521; **1967**: 92, 309 [1], 410, 475,
      485 [6]; **1968-69**: 170, 448
  Mobilization, **1963-64**: 382
Reserve Officers' Training Corps, **1963-64**: 665

Reserve Officers' Training Corps Vitalization Act
      of 1964, approval, **1963-64**: 665
Reserve System.
  See Federal Reserve System.
Reservoirs, **1965**: 54, 418, 434
Residency voting bill, **1967**: 236; **1968-69**: 314
Resignations and retirements
  Ambassador to the Soviet Union, **1966**: 474
      [17]
  Atomic Energy Commission, member,
      1966: 277 [5]
  Central Intelligence Agency, Director,
      1966: 277 [5, 14]
  Chief Justice of the United States, **1968-69**:
      339 [1], 425 [11], 527
  Civil Aeronautics Board, Chairman,
      1968-69: 79 [2]
  Commerce, Department of, Assistant Secre-
      tary and Director of Economic Devel-
      opment, **1966**: 501 [1]
  Commerce, Secretary of, **1967**: 8; **1968-69**: 79
      [1, 3], 80
  Federal Communications Commission, member,
      1966: 277 [5]
  Health, Education, and Welfare, Secretary of,
      1968-69: 30
  Justice, Department of, Attorney General,
      1966: 474 [17]
  Postmaster General, **1968-69**: 191 [2, 10]
  Physician to the President, **1968-69**: 668
  State, Department of, Under Secretary,
      1966: 474 [17]
  Treasury, Department of the, Assistant
      Secretary (International Affairs),
      1966: 277 [5]
  Treasury, Secretary of the, **1968-69**: 582
  White House staff, member, **1966**: 186
  United Nations, U.S. Representatives,
      1968-69: 213 [1, 3, 8], 496
Resignations or retirements, letters or remarks
  Celebrezze, Anthony J., **1965**: 389
  Dillon, C. Douglas, **1965**: 146
  Hodges, Luther H., **1963-64**: 805
  Kennedy, Robert F., **1963-64**: 556
  LeMay, Gen. Curtis E., **1965**: 37
  Lodge, Henry Cabot, **1963-64**: 420 [1]
  Murrow, Edward R., **1963-64**: 125
  Sorensen, Theodore C., **1963-64**: 108
Resnick, Harry, **1966**: 395n.
Resnick, Repr. Joseph Y., **1966**: 394-395
Resor, Stanley R., **1965**: 117 [3], 319 [10, 13],
      399; **1966**: 183, 288; **1967**: 102, 166,
      331, 384, 407, 494, 558; **1968-69**: 58,
      221, 353, 384, 487, 594, 669, 688
Resources Corporation, Development and,
      1967: 73
Respiratory ailments, **1967**: 20

Reston, James B., **1968–69**: 242
Resurrection City, U.S.A., **1968–69**: 223ftn. (p. 558)
Retail prices, **1965**: 255; **1966**: 155
Retail sales, **1963–64**: 463, 619 [4], 689; **1966**: 141 [3]
Retardation, President's Committee on Mental, **1967**: 373, 517
Retired Executives, Service Corps of, **1968–69**: 75
Retirement
  Federal programs, **1968–69**: 678 (pp. 1298, 1305)
  Government employees and military personnel, **1965**: 49; **1966**: 26 (p. 56), 108–109; **1967**: 12
  Insurance, **1967**: 245
  Military, **1967**: 92
  Older persons, **1963–64**: 431
  President's plans, **1968–69**: 213 [5], 281, 301, 459, 646 [15], 696 [1, 4, 7, 10]
  Railroad employees, **1967**: 12, 244; **1968–69**: 331, 678 (pp. 1296, 1298)
Retirement Board, Railroad, **1968–69**: 331
Retirement Policy for Federal Personnel, Committee on, **1965**: 49
Retirement Systems, Cabinet Committee on Federal Staff, **1966**: 108; **1967**: 25
  Proposed, **1965**: 49
Retirement and Welfare Programs, Presidential Committee on Corporate Pension Funds and Other Private, **1965**: 35 (p. 113)
Reuss, Repr. Henry S., **1963–64**: 746; **1965**: 503; **1966**: 442
Reuter, Richard W., **1963–64**: 585; **1965**: 139, 569
Reuters News Agency, **1966**: 188 [1]; **1968–69**: 169 [17]
Reuther, Victor G., **1966**: 210n.
Reuther, Walter P., **1963–64**: 233n., 294 [9, 23], 336 [17], 431, 513, 562, 733, 745, 780 [3]; **1966**: 158 [3], 235, 373 [8], 431, 435, 437; **1967**: 252n.; **1968–69**: 106n.
Revenue Act of 1962, **1965**: 326, 505; **1966**: 26 (p. 52)
Revenue Act of 1964, **1963–64**: 197, 228, 233, 235, 338, 531, 604, 620, 697, 723, 724, 731; **1965**: 32 (p. 85), 100, 155, 255, 326; **1966**: 26 (p. 50), 34 (p. 99)
  Campaign remarks, **1963–64**: 562, 589, 605, 636, 642, 643, 644, 667, 669, 693, 713, 718, 728, 729, 732, 741, 745, 746, 750
  News conference remarks, **1963–64**: 246 [12, 15], 271 [15], 336 [18], 379 [5], 462 [11]
Revenue and Expenditure Control Act of 1968, **1967**: 329n., 375ftn. (p. 819), 411ftn. (p. 886), 420ftn. (p. 905), 427n., 430n., 495ftn. (p. 1050), 518ftn. (p. 1089),

Revenue and Expenditure – *continued*
  554ftn. (p. 1171); **1968–69**: 1ftn. (p. 3), 46, 76n., 169ftn. (p. 468), 213ftn. (p. 538), 218n., 226, 241n., 229n., 274n., 275ftn. (p. 654), 283ftn. (p. 675), 322, 326, 339 [12], 344, 350, 403, 404, 427, 445, 449, 517, 678 (pp. 1277, 1278, 1282, 1283), 684 (pp. 1312, 1313)
  Signing, **1968–69**: 343
Revenues, District of Columbia, **1968–69**: 95
Revenues, Federal, **1966**: 6 (p. 4), 26 (pp. 49, 52–54), 34 (p. 98), 121 [9], 628 [5]; **1967**: 13 (p. 39), 16 (p. 77), 329, 330 [1, 8], 358 [12], 411 [11], 417 [1], 430, 495 [9]; **1968–69**: 14 (p. 32), 39 (pp. 84, 85, 88, 95), 47 (pp. 131, 132), 59, 547, 646 [3], 654, 676 (p. 1267), 677, 678 (pp. 1277, 1288), 683, 684 (pp. 1312, 1314, 1315)
Revolutionary War, **1967**: 485 [3], 495 [11]
Rey, Jean (President of the Commission of the European Communities), **1968–69**: 62, 348
Reynolds, Don B., **1963–64**: 143 [3]
Reynolds, Frank, **1966**: 622; **1967**: 529, 554
Reynolds, James, **1963–64**: 195n., 252, 253n., 284, 297 [2]; **1966**: 322; **1967**: 97, 170, 204 [5], 312 [3]
Reynolds, Gov. John, **1963–64**: 746
Rhee, Hyo Sang, **1966**: 562, 564n.
Rhee, Mrs. Hyo Sang, **1966**: 562
Rheumatic fever
  Control, **1965**: 5
  Prophylaxis program, District of Columbia, **1966**: 27
Rheumatism, **1963–64**: 755
Rhode Island, **1963–64**: 602n.; **1967**: 223 [2]
  Campaign remarks, **1963–64**: 601
  Gov. John H. Chafee, **1963–64**: 601; **1966**: 396–397, 494 [1, 2]; **1967**: 222n., 223 [2, 3]
Rhode Island, University of, **1966**: 396
Rhodes, Repr. George M., **1966**: 428
Rhodes, Gov. James A., **1963–64**: 217, 322, 323; **1965**: 190, 191; **1966**: 122 [1, 2], 124 [2, 4, 8, 10], 434, 599 [3]; **1967**: 552n., 558; **1968–69**: 58, 406
Rhodes, Mrs. James A., **1963–64**: 323; **1968–69**: 406
Rhodes, Robert, **1966**: 397
Rhodesia, Southern, **1966**: 243; **1967**: 74, 488
Rhodium stockpiles, **1966**: 218
Rhyne, Charles S., **1965**: 516
Ribeiro, Miguel Augustus, **1963–64**: 35n.
Ribicoff, Sen. Abraham, **1963–64**: 50, 341, 382, 383, 603; **1965**: 242, 394, 433, 503; **1966**: 290
  Unveiling of portrait of, **1965**: 94

Ribicoff, Mrs. Abraham, **1965**: 94
Rice, William M., **1968–69**: 599n.
Rice, **1965**: 47, 168; **1966**: 62, 355; **1967**: 448
Rice Research Institute, International, **1966**: 459, 550
Rice University, **1968–69**: 107, 644
Rice Year, International, **1966**: 62
Rich, Robert F., **1966**: 65 [1], 113
Richardson, Dorsey, **1963–64**: 296
Richardson, Mr. and Mrs. William S., **1966**: 532
Richardson, Tex., Mayor Herbert Ryan, **1963–64**: 738
Richman, Harold A., **1965**: 334n.
Richmond, Julius B., **1965**: 467
Rickover, Vice Adm. Hyman G., **1963–64**: 164, 560 [6]; **1965**: 17, 242
Riddleberger, James W., **1966**: 272
Ridgway, Gen. Matthew B., **1963–64**: 244; **1968–69**: 51 [3]
Rieke, Mary, **1967**: 396n.
Rielly, John E., **1966**: 85
Rifkin, Bernard, **1963–64**: 60
Rifkind, Simon H., **1966**: 635 [3], 637
Rifle sales to Singapore, **1967**: 104 [19]
Right of privacy bill, **1967**: 35; **1968–69**: 59, 320
Riis, Jacob, **1963–64**: 394; **1967**: 114, 146
Riley, James Whitcomb, **1965**: 397
Riley, Paul H., **1966**: 198n.
Rinderpest, prevention, **1968–69**: 364
Rine, Phyllis, **1963–64**: 780ftn. (p. 1612)
Rio de Janeiro, **1967**: 351, 390
    Inter-American conference, **1965**: 593, 624; **1966**: 41
Rio de Janeiro, Economic and Social Act of, **1966**: 125, 177, 386
Rio Grande River, **1963–64**: 193; **1965**: 487; **1966**: 467–468, 597, 630 [2], 640; **1967**: 47, 408 [5], 447, 454; **1968–69**: 623, 624
Riot-Affected Areas, President's National Advisory Panel on Insurance in, **1968–69**: 36, 87
Riots, **1966**: 373 [15], 484, 501 [12]
    See also Civil disorders.
    New York City, **1963–64**: 468, 475 [4, 20]
    Urban areas, **1963–64**: 600
Ripley, S. Dillon (Secretary, Smithsonian Institution), **1965**: 328, 519; **1966**: 90, 193, 226n.; **1967**: 265, 274, 540; **1968–69**: 225, 660
Ritchie, A. Edgar, **1966**: 644n.; **1967**: 237
Ritter, Joseph Cardinal, **1963–64**: 189
River Basins Commission
    New England, **1968–69**: 593, 666
    Pacific Northwest, **1968–69**: 593, 666
    Souris-Red-Rainy, **1968–69**: 593, 666
River and Harbor Act of 1965, **1965**: 587

River and water development, **1963–64**: 410, 486 [7], 563 [3], 597, 598, 756
Rivers, Repr. L. Mendel, **1963–64**: 487; **1965**: 157n., 227n.; **1966**: 218, 283, 572; **1968–69**: 110, 153 [4, 12]
Rivers, Repr. Ralph J., **1966**: 567–569
Rivers and harbors development, **1966**: 6 (p. 3), 82, 98, 393
    See also specific rivers.
Rivers System, National Wild, **1966**: 82; **1968–69**: 14 (p. 31), 39 (p. 101), 122, 345, 510
    Proposed, **1965**: 54
Rivers system, scenic, **1967**: 20
Rivers and waterways.
    See Water resources; *specific rivers.*
Riverside, Calif., campaign remarks, **1963–64**: 734
Roads, Bureau of Public, **1967**: 369
Roadside parks, **1968–69**: 122
Roanoke, Va., **1963–64**: 358
Robb, Maj. Charles S., **1967**: 529; **1968–69**: 34, 233, 460 [2], 576, 588, 603n., 630, 646 [14], 648, 655, 688n., 696 [19]
    Message on birth of daughter, **1968–69**: 573
Robb, Mrs. Charles S., (Lynda Bird Johnson), **1967**: 420, 493, 517, 529, 533; **1968–69**: 34, 50, 171, 229n., 460 [2], 567, 573n., 576, 588, 602, 604, 630, 646 [2], 655, 660, 696ftn. (p. 1361)
    See also Johnson, Lynda Bird.
Robb, Lucinda Desha, **1968–69**: 537n., 566–570, 573, 576, 588, 602, 646 [2, 14], 655
Roberts, A. Addison, **1968–69**: 36
Roberts, Mrs. Anne Mason, **1967**: 93n.
Roberts, Charles W., **1963–64**: 285 [20, 23]; **1967**: 132 [4]
Roberts, Edmund, **1967**: 290n.
Roberts, Emory P., **1965**: 22 [1]; **1968–69**: 604
Roberts, Mrs. Juanita D., **1965**: 412 [1]; **1968–69**: 595
Roberts, Repr. Kenneth A., **1963–64**: 50, 557
Roberts, Roy, death, **1967**: 69
Robertson, Sen. A. Willis, **1965**: 205; **1966**: 231, 442, 451, 473
Robertson, J. L., **1963–64**: 211 [2]; **1965**: 319 [8], 638
Robertson, James, **1965**: 64n.
Robins Air Force Base, Ga., **1963–64**: 716
Robinson, Aubrey E., Jr., **1965**: 366
Robinson, Dr. Henry S., Jr., **1968–69**: 442
Robinson, Lt. Col. Hugh G., **1967**: 536
Robinson, Joseph T., **1965**: 223; **1968–69**: 568
Robinson, Spottswood W., III, **1967**: 81
Robinson, Thomas E., **1967**: 279n., 281, 282; **1968–69**: 288
Robinson, Mrs. Thomas E., **1967**: 282
Robinson, Warren A., **1968–69**: 599n.
Robles, Marco A., **1965**: 532

Robson, John, **1968-69**: 276
Rochester, N.Y.
  Campaign remarks, **1963-64**: 666
  Mayor Frank Lamb, **1963-64**: 666
Rockefeller, David, **1963-64**: 169n., 402, 622,
    688 [8]; **1965**: 334, 365n.;
    1968-69: 470, 471
Rockefeller, John D., Jr., **1963-64**: 601
Rockefeller, John D., 3d, **1968-69**: 393n., 467
    [9], 659
Rockefeller, Laurence S., **1965**: 54, 277, 446;
    1966: 202, 500, 518; **1967**: 295;
    1968-69: 122, 150, 167, 411, 672
  "Beauty for America—Proceedings of the
    White House Conference on Natural
    Beauty," **1965**: 418ftn. (p. 870)
Rockefeller, Mrs. Laurance S., **1966**: 518;
    1968-69: 167, 672n.
Rockefeller, Gov. Nelson A., **1963-64**: 96, 211
    [19], 218 [25], 282, 285 [1], 287, 311,
    462 [6], 468, 499, 662n., 746;
    1965: 417, 418, 434; **1966**: 122 [1, 2],
    392, 394, 417 [5], 494 [1, 2, 6];
    1967: 70 [6], 223 [11]; **1968-69**: 153
    [13], 260n., 299, 540, 567, 672
Rockefeller, Mrs. Nelson A., **1963-64**: 499
Rockefeller Foundation, **1966**: 550-551;
    1967: 448, 449
Rocket propulsion, nuclear, **1967**: 13 (p. 50),
    76
Rockets, **1965**: 196
  See also Launch vehicles.
  Mariner IV, **1965**: 27, 81, 305, 345, 391
  Saturn I, **1963-64**: 162, 170 [1]
  Titan III-C, **1965**: 448 [1]
Rockford, Ill.
  Campaign remarks, **1963-64**: 747
  Mayor Benjamin T. Schleicher, **1963-64**: 747
Rockne, Knute, **1965**: 242; **1967**: 480
Rockwell, George Lincoln, **1968-69**: 298
Rocky Mount, N.C., **1963-64**: 327, 328
Rocky Mountain Dental Products Co.,
    1966: 144n.
Rocky Mountains, oil shale processing,
    1967: 358 [11]
Rodgers, Maj. Marie L., **1967**: 475
Rodino, Repr. Peter W., Jr., **1963-64**: 149, 338,
    651; **1965**: 200, 242; **1966**: 504;
    1967: 391
Roe, Robert A., **1963-64**: 422
Roeder, Vice Adm. Bernard F., **1968-69**: 81 [3]
Rogers, Alfred C., **1968-69**: 332
Rogers, Repr. Byron G., **1963-64**: 658;
    1966: 410, 413-414
Rogers, Repr. Paul G., **1963-64**: 198, 199, 709
Rogers, Stephen, **1966**: 394
Rogers, Repr. Walter, **1965**: 417

Rogers, Will, **1963-64**: 598, 799; **1965**: 81;
    1966: 221; **1967**: 449; **1968-69**: 291
Rogers, William P., **1965**: 366, 422n.;
    1968-69: 646ftn. (p. 8), [14]
Rogg, Nathaniel H., **1968-69**: 229
Rogovin, Mitchell, **1963-64**: 818 [2]; **1966**: 88
    [5]
Roland, Bill, **1965**: 298
Roland, Adm. Edward J., **1963-64**: 382
Rolland, Shirley, **1965**: 322
Rollings, John I., **1963-64**: 590
Rolvaag, Gov. Karl F., **1963-64**: 432, 433, 434,
    435; **1965**: 189; **1966**: 491n., 492 [1,
    10], 650n.; **1967**: 313
Rolz-Bennett, José, **1967**: 521
Roman, Repr. Daniel J., **1966**: 228
Roman y Vega, Albino, **1968-69**: 367n.
Romania, **1967**: 347n.
  Prime Minister Ion Gheorghe Maurer,
    1967: 312 [15]
Rome, Italy
  Releases, **1967**: 570, 571, 572
  Visit, **1967**: 570
Rome, Treaty of, **1967**: 391n.
Romero Losa, José, **1968-69**: 362n.
Romney, Carl F., **1967**: 317n.
Romney, Gov. George W., **1963-64**: 271 [11],
    356, 357, 562; **1966**: 431, 491n., 492
    [1, 7, 10], 599 [3]; **1967**: 70 [11], 322,
    328 [2], 331, 375 [10]; **1968-69**: 79
    [7]
  Telegrams, **1967**: 321, 325
Romney, Mrs. George W., **1963-64**: 562
Romualdez, Benjamin, **1966**: 550
Ronan, Daniel J. (Jim), **1963-64**: 747
Ronan, James A., **1963-64**: 635, 636, 694
Roncalio, Teno, **1963-64**: 657
Roney, Jay, **1965**: 642n.
Rooney, Repr. John J., **1963-64**: 668;
    1965: 82, 248; **1966**: 511; **1968-69**: 568
Roosa, Robert V., **1963-64**: 299, 780 [13], 818
    [1]; **1965**: 365n.
Roosevelt, Mr. and Mrs. Curtis, **1963-64**: 208n.
Roosevelt, Eleanor, **1963-64**: 208; **1965**: 392;
    1966: 299; **1968-69**: 260, 611, 648
  Bust of, President's acceptance of, **1965**: 210
  Commemorative stamps, **1963-64**: 35;
    1965: 504
Roosevelt, Eleanor, Memorial Foundation,
    1963-64: 161; **1965**: 273
Roosevelt, Franklin D., **1963-64**: 12, 51, 65, 136,
    137, 138, 144, 182, 184, 199, 208, 218
    [15], 220, 224, 228, 233, 267, 289, 290,
    297, 303, 306, 321, 324, 325, 327, 330,
    332, 334, 340, 342, 373, 388, 406, 413,
    414, 431, 434, 554, 574, 576, 586, 677,
    698, 778, 799; **1965**: 47, 48, 72, 142,
    156 [9], 218, 223, 231, 299, 302, 319

Roosevelt, Franklin D. – *continued*
  [18], 357, 394, 415, 425, 432n., 436,
  448 [4], 527, 576, 585; **1966**: 35, 62,
  86, 100, 119, 125, 158, 168, 216, 223,
  228, 273, 284, 285, 351, 392, 395, 399–
  400, 414, 417 [2, 7], 433, 439, 478, 503,
  509–515, 516 [1], 518, 520, 542, 568,
  599 [3], 634, 650 [13]; **1967**: 7n., 12,
  21, 25, 28, 39, 40, 43n., 57, 92, 105,
  112n., 114, 121, 176, 211, 216, 241,
  249, 251, 267, 270, 281, 299, 409, 470,
  485 [5], 495 [11], 505, 512, 514, 537,
  554 [6]; **1968–69**: 3, 33, 42, 43, 53, 54,
  65, 86, 87, 94, 96, 108–110, 117, 122,
  125, 129, 143, 157, 159n., 164, 165,
  218, 227, 238, 270, 274, 298, 305n.,
  336, 373, 386, 397, 411, 418, 426, 442,
  460 [3], 472, 500, 536, 547, 554, 555,
  567, 568, 575, 576, 601, 611, 625, 630,
  648, 661, 665n.
  Campaign remarks on, **1963–64**: 541, 605, 606,
    622, 637, 639, 642, 644, 645, 650, 667,
    678, 728, 732, 733, 736, 746, 747, 751,
    764
  82d anniversary of birth, **1963–64**: 165
  Library, Hyde Park, N.Y., **1965**: 210, 412 [1]
  20th anniversary of death, **1965**: 182
Roosevelt, Franklin D., Jr., **1963–64**: 41, 208n.,
    285 [2], 291, 293, 320, 321, 322, 323,
    324, 325, 326, 327, 328, 332, 711n.;
    1965: 210n., 290, 319 [18], 384, 436;
    1967: 28
Roosevelt, Mrs. Franklin D., Jr., **1963–64**: 208n.
Roosevelt, Repr. James, **1963–64**: 208n., 444,
    650, 733; **1965**: 210n., 394, 448 [4],
    533
Roosevelt, Mrs. James, **1963–64**: 208n.
Roosevelt, John, **1963–64**: 208n.; **1967**: 28
Roosevelt, Mrs. John, **1963–64**: 208n.
Roosevelt, Theodore, **1963–64**: 58, 137, 303,
    527, 554, 590, 607, 622, 655, 695, 790;
    1965: 48, 101, 103, 237, 521, 543, 551,
    559; **1966**: 325, 353, 392, 398, 417 [7,
    9], 612; **1967**: 39, 57, 114, 121, 125,
    201, 262, 281, 450, 465, 541;
    1968–69: 109, 122, 212, 270, 298, 345,
    386, 451, 547, 576, 601
  46th anniversary of death, **1965**: 3
Roosevelt, Theodore, Memorial, **1967**: 450
Roosevelt Association, Theodore, **1967**: 450
Roosevelt Birthday Memorial Award, Franklin
    D., **1967**: 21
Roosevelt Campobello International Park,
    1963–64: 136n., 137, 138, 140;
    1965: 350; **1966**: 448
Roosevelt Campobello International Park Com-
    mission, **1963–64**: 455 [14]; **1965**: 350
Roosevelt (Franklin D.) Lake, **1965**: 186

Roper, Daniel C., **1968–69**: 241n.
Roper (Elmo) and Associates, Presidential election
    polls, **1963–64**: 542
Rose, Alex, **1963–64**: 334, 388, 669; **1967**: 484
Rose, Dr. Arnold M., **1965**: 642n.
Rose, William Cumming, **1966**: 652n.; **1967**: 37n.
Rosellini, Gov. Albert D., **1963–64**: 575, 576,
    577
Rosen, Abe S., **1967**: 291
Rosen, Joseph, **1966**: 210n.
Rosenblatt, Peter, **1968–69**: 17
Rosenblith, Walter A., **1967**: 252n.
Rosenbush, Mervin, **1966**: 472
Rosendahl, Vice Adm. Charles E., **1968–69**: 610
Rosengard, Dr. David E., **1967**: 419n.
Rosenthal, Repr. Benjamin S., **1963–64**: 341;
    1966: 510
Rosenthal, Jacob, **1965**: 336n.; **1966**: 289n.
Rosh Hashanah, **1966**: 405
Ross, Charles R., **1963–64**: 455 [11]; **1965**: 117
    [3]
Ross, Stanford, **1968–69**: 17, 276
Ross, William, **1966**: 12
Ross Lake National Recreation Area, Washington,
    1968–69: 510n.
Rossiter, Clinton, **1963–64**: 303
Rostenkowski, Repr. Dan, **1965**: 299; **1966**: 228
Rostow, Eugene V., **1966**: 474 [17]; **1967**: 33,
    230; **1968–69**: 289
Rostow, Walt W., **1963–64**: 340, 455 [16];
    1965: 256; **1966**: 158 [2, 6], 214, 236
    [1], 247 [1, 8], 277 [5], 320 [1], 370,
    501 [1], 521, 566, 622, 626, 642 [4, 6]
    1967: 113, 157, 254n., 255, 264 [11,
    19], 519, 562; **1968–69**: 1 [1], 18 [2],
    292n., 362n., 398n., 496, 590 [1, 2],
    696 [19]
ROTC.
  See Reserve Officers Training Corps.
Roth, William (Special Representative for Trade
    Negotiations), **1965**: 112ftn. (p. 295);
    1967: 142, 428, 545; **1968–69**: 274,
    517, 680
Rous, F. Peyton, **1965**: 646n.; **1966**: 61n.
Roush, Repr. J. Edward, **1966**: 579
Rousseau, Jean Jacques, **1966**: 35
Rover rocket, **1967**: 76
Rover space project, **1963–64**: 54 [12]
Roving Leader program, **1967**: 15, 71
Rowan, Carl T., **1963–64**: 200, 280 [5], 619
    [8], 621; **1965**: 468; **1966**: 248
  See also United States Information Agency,
    Director (Carl T. Rowan).
Rowan, Mrs. Carl T., **1963–64**: 200; **1965**: 468
Rowe, Gary T., Jr., **1965**: 135
Rowe, James H., Jr., **1963–64**: 242 [5], 393
Rowen, Henry S., **1968–69**: 3
Rowlett, Frank B., **1965**: 269, 296n.; **1966**: 99

Rowley, James J., **1963–64**: 21, 619 [11];
  1968–69: 292n., 549, 602, 604
Royal, Darrell, **1966**: 7; **1968–69**: 109
Royal Thai Air Force Base, Khorat, Thailand,
  1967: 565
Roybal, Repr. Edward R., **1963–64**: 733
Rozmarek, Charles, **1963–64**: 491
Rubber stockpiles, **1966**: 390
Rubella, **1967**: 319
Rubey, William W., **1965**: 646n.; **1966**: 61n.
Rubin, Bishop Ladislaus, **1966**: 528
Ruby, Cecil B., **1965**: 179
Rudder, Gen. James E., **1966**: 141 [10, 11]
Rudolph, Wilma, **1966**: 385n.
Rules governing this publication, Appendix D,
  1967: p. 1227; **1968–69**: p. 1403
Rumania, U.S. relations with, **1963–64**: 336
  [6]
Rural Americans for Johnson-Humphrey,
  1963–64: 570
Rural areas, **1963–64**: 357, 570, 754, 757;
  1965: 32 (p. 83), 100, 168, 313, 357,
  545, 555, 597; **1966**: 26 (p. 59), 34 (p.
  100), 428, 441, 584; **1967**: 13 (p. 60),
  512
  Antipoverty program, **1963–64**: 54 [9], 132
    (p. 184), 219, 225, 344, 434, 528;
    1967: 3 (p. 5); **1968–69**: 39 (p. 100)
  Beautification programs, **1965**: 54; **1966**: 500
  Community action program, **1963–64**: 219
  Conference, **1968–69**: 155
  Credit, **1968–69**: 94, 142, 450
  Development, **1963–64**: 132 (p. 187), 344,
    571; **1965**: 47, 90, 132; **1966**: 6 (p. 5),
    28–29, 594–595; **1967**: 13 (p. 57), 114;
    1968–69: 39 (p. 101), 94, 96, 305, 450
  Education, **1963–64**: 658; **1965**: 47, 340;
    1966: 6 (p. 5), 28–29; **1967**: 479;
    1968–69: 4, 96, 142
  Electrification.
    See main heading, Rural electrification.
  Employment, **1963–64**: 344, 434; **1966**: 26
    (p. 59), 428; **1967**: 114, 199;
    1968–69: 39 (p. 104), 94, 96, 142, 450
  Extension service, **1963–64**: 482
  Federal aid, **1965**: 47, 75
  Food stamp program, **1965**: 492
  Health programs, **1966**: 6 (p. 5)
  Hospitals, **1968–69**: 96
    Construction, **1963–64**: 179
  Housing, **1963–64**: 132 (p. 187), 152, 344;
    1965: 32 (p. 91), 46 [1], 47, 415;
    1966: 28–29; **1968–69**: 94, 96, 142,
    678 (p. 1289)
  Income, **1965**: 32 (p. 91); **1966**: 28–29;
    1967: 13 (p. 50)
  Legislation, **1968–69**: 155
  Libraries, **1968–69**: 142
  Loans, **1966**: 584; **1967**: 114

Rural areas – *continued*
  Medical care, **1965**: 47; **1966**: 28–29
  Message to Congress, **1966**: 28; **1967**: 114;
    1968–69: 94
  Negroes, **1965**: 85
  Operation outreach, **1968–69**: 94
  Recreation areas, **1968–69**: 94
  Telephones, **1968–69**: 39 (p. 101), 94
  Transportation, **1965**: 38; **1968–69**: 142
  Unemployment, **1965**: 47
  Urban migration, **1968–69**: 39 (p. 100), 87,
    94, 416, 568, 569, 696 [9]
  Water resources, **1966**: 398, 403, 428
  Water and sewer systems, **1968–69**: 94
Rural Community Development Service,
  1966: 28, 111
Rural Development, Conference on Inter-
  national, **1963–64**: 482
Rural Electric Cooperative Association, Na-
  tional, **1963–64**: 227, 617;
  1965: 308, 357; **1966**: 258; **1967**: 267;
  1968–69: 96, 305
Rural electric cooperatives, **1963–64**: 352;
  1965: 308, 313, 357
Rural electrification, **1963–64**: 132 (p. 191),
  336 [3], 344, 391, 590, 631, 646, 648,
  701, 716, 733; **1965**: 47, 230, 308, 313,
  357; **1966**: 228, 258, 382, 398, 417,
  564; **1967**: 13 (p. 50), 267, 270; **1968–
  69**: 39 (p. 101), 94, 96, 305
Rural Electrification Act of 1936, **1966**: 398,
  403
Rural Electrification Administration, **1965**: 230,
  274n., 295 [3], 308, 313, 357;
  1966: 258, 273; **1967**: 13 (pp. 46, 51);
  1968–69: 39 (p. 101), 96, 305, 629n.,
  653n.
Rural electrification bank bill, **1968–69**: 96
Rural Poverty, National Advisory Commission on,
  1966: 28; **1967**: 114
Rush-Bagot Agreement, **1967**: 237n.
Rusk, Dean.
  See State, Secretary of.
Rusk, Mrs. Dean, **1963–64**: 194; **1965**: 63n.,
  463 [1]; **1966**: 176; **1967**: 447, 449,
  480, 519; **1968–69**: 137, 140, 157, 159,
  232, 271, 476, 522n., 613, 619, 681,
  691
Rusk, Dr. Howard, **1963–64**: 211 [6];
  1965: 469, 551; **1966**: 166, 433
Russell, Mrs. A. M. G., **1965**: 642n.
Russell, Charles, **1963–64**: 267
Russell, Sen. Donald, **1965**: 207n., 413
Russell, Gov. Donald S., **1963–64**: 718, 719
Russell, Mrs. Donald S., **1963–64**: 719
Russell, George, **1963–64**: 271 [3]
Russell, Harold, **1963–64**: 271 [6], 302;
  1967: 388; **1968–69**: 548

Russell, Norman, **1963–64**: 599
Russell, Sen. Richard B., **1963–64**: 14, 15, 150
    [1, 12], 153, 230, 330, 716, 718, 719;
    1966: 52 [3], 88 [17], 218, 283, 445
    [16], 470, 572; **1967**: 493; **1968–69**:
    110, 132, 153 [4, 12], 301, 676 (p.
    1270), 690
Russell, Robert L., Jr., **1963–64**: 330
Russell, Mrs. Ruth, **1963–64**: 645
Russellville, Ky., **1966**: 351
Russia.
    See Soviet Union.
Ruthenium stockpiles, **1966**: 218
Rutland, Vt., Mayor John J. Daley, **1963–64**: 605
Ruttenberg, Mr. and Mrs. Stanley H., **1966**: 275
Ryan, Repr. Harold M., **1963–64**: 356
Ryan, Herbert, **1963–64**: 738
Ryan, Gen. John D., **1967**: 555
Ryan, Repr. William F., **1967**: 554 [1]
Ryan, William J., **1963–64**: 605
Ryukyu Islands, **1967**: 491
    Administration of, **1965**: 15
    Chief executive, election of, **1965**: 658;
        1968–69: 44
    High Commissioner Ferdinand T. Unger,
        1968–69: 44
    U.S. military installations on, **1965**: 15

Sabin, Dr. Albert B., **1963–64**: 679
Sabine, Tex., **1965**: 641 [1]
SAC.
    See Strategic Air Command.
Sacramento, Calif., **1963–64**: 580n.; **1965**: 477
    Campaign remarks, **1963–64**: 579
Safe drinking water bill of 1968, **1968–69**: 122
Safe streets and crime control bill, **1967**: 3 (p. 6),
        35–36, 146, 221, 276, 297 [7], 326,
        382, 455, 468, 482, 530, 560, 575
    See also Omnibus Crime Control and Safe
        Streets Act of 1968.
Safety, **1966**: 98, 102, 290–291, 423, 449, 462
    Accident prevention, **1967**: 499
    Appliances, **1968–69**: 56
    Automobile, **1966**: 98, 187, 252, 290–291,
        449, 474 [3]; **1967**: 77; **1968–69**: 56,
        212, 244, 264, 270, 545, 693
    Aviation, **1966**: 98, 321; **1967**: 392;
        1968–69: 14 (p. 31), 39 (p. 102), 41,
        47 (p. 144), 693
    Boating and water, **1968–69**: 56
    Bridge, **1967**: 558
    Coal mine, **1966**: 151, 237; **1968–69**: 475,
        607, 684 (p. 1323)
    Consumer protection, message, **1968–69**: 56
    Drug, **1967**: 214

Safety – *continued*
    Fabric, **1967**: 57, 200, 393, 465, 499, 520,
        534, 539; **1968–69**: 14 (p. 29), 56, 545
    Fire, **1968–69**: 56, 105
        Prevention, **1967**: 57
    Fish, **1968–69**: 14 (p. 30), 56, 105, 390
    Gas pipeline, **1967**: 57, 200, 342, 393, 430,
        465, 499, 520, 534, 539; **1968–69**: 105,
        338, 390, 441
    Government employees, **1966**: 75–76, 102,
        291, 449; **1967**: 265; **1968–69**: 489
    Highway, **1966**: 6 (p. 6), 26 (p. 61), 34 (p.
        106), 47, 98, 187, 228, 252, 273, 290–
        291, 423, 449, 630 [4]; **1967**: 13 (p.
        52), 20, 86, 200, 534; **1968–69**: 39
        (p. 102), 56, 57, 111, 122, 243, 244,
        264, 545, 693
    Hospitals, **1967**: 534
    Household, **1967**: 200, 499, 534, 539
    Interstate Commerce Commission programs,
        1966: 98
    Meat, **1967**: 57, 465, 499, 503, 520, 522, 534,
        539, 541; **1968–69**: 39 (p. 101), 56,
        270, 451, 545
    Mine, **1966**: 462
    Motor vehicle standards, **1968–69**: 244
    Occupational, **1963–64**: 421; **1967**: 77;
        1968–69: 24, 39 (p. 104), 111, 154,
        164, 390, 406, 475, 607, 684 (pp.
        1321, 1323)
    Poultry, **1968–69**: 14 (p. 30), 56, 105, 390,
        451, 545
    Radiation, **1968–69**: 14 (p. 30), 56, 390, 545
    Ship, **1966**: 98, 583
    Tire, **1967**: 342
    Toys, **1966**: 140, 576; **1967**: 86, 393, 465, 534;
        1968–69: 56, 545
    Transportation, **1967**: 149
    Water supply, **1968–69**: 14 (p. 30)
Safety Awards, President's, **1965**: 73, 287
    Presentation, **1963–64**: 351
Safety Board, National Transportation,
        1966: 98
Safety of the President, comments on,
        1963–64: 201 [3], 218 [4], 246 [2],
        294 [1, 8], 619 [11]
Safety programs
    Government, **1965**: 73, 287n.
    Highways, **1965**: 460, 488
    Railroads, **1965**: 281
SAFETY-70, Mission, **1966**: 75, 76, 291;
        1967: 265; **1968–69**: 489
Saigon, **1963–64**: 54ftn. (p. 70), 274; **1967**: 73,
        309 [5]
    See also Vietnam.
    News conference remarks, **1963–64**: 28 [2],
        211 [14], 475 [10]

Saigon — *continued*
  U.S. chancery, proposed construction,
      1965: 152
  U.S. Embassy bombing, **1965**: 145, 208 [16],
      276
  U.S. military dependents in, **1963–64**: 211 [14],
      475 [10]
Saigon, University of, **1966**: 549ftn. (p. 1261)
Saint Elizabeth's Hospital, District of Columbia,
      1967: 15
Salaries.
  See Pay; Wages.
Salaries, Commission on Executive, Legislative
      and Judicial, **1968–69**: 676 (pp. 1266,
      1267), 678 (p. 1305), 694
Salaries, Special Panel on Federal, **1965**: 244
Salary Commission, Joint, **1967**: 163
Sales, fraud, **1968–69**: 56
Saline Water, Office of, **1965**: 143, 325
Saline water conversion act of 1961, **1965**: 143
Saline water conversion act of 1965, **1965**: 417,
      418
Saline water study agreement, U.S.-Mexico-IAEA,
      1965: 558
Salinger, Pierre, E. G., **1963–64**: 409, 411, 413,
      415
  News conference remarks on, **1963–64**: 28 [1,
      4, 14], 71 [4], 150 [8], 201 [2, 15], 211
      [9], 232 [4, 11]
  Press Secretary to the President, **1963–64**: 30n.,
      31n., 36n., 41n., 52n., 63n., 88n., 95n.,
      144n., 176n., 177n., 209n.
  Senator, **1963–64**: 577, 579, 650, 651, 733,
      734, 735, 736
Salisbury, Harrison E., **1966**: 654 [7]
Salk, Dr. Jonas E., **1966**: 271
Salomon, Sidney, Jr., **1963–64**: 363
Salt Lake, Great, conveyance of borderlands to
      Utah, **1966**: 255
Salt Lake City, Utah, campaign remarks,
      1963–64: 737
Saltonstall, Leverett, **1967**: 312 [1, 3], 386
  Telegram, **1965**: 662
Salute to Eisenhower Week, proclamation,
      1968–69: 399, 488
Salvation Army Association of New York,
      1965: 643
Salvation Army award, **1965**: 643
Salzberg, Milton J., **1963–64**: 808n.
SAM (surface-to-air missiles), **1966**: 642 [14]
Sam Rayburn, U.S.S., **1963–64**: 59, 786
Sam Rayburn Dam, dedication of, **1965**: 236
Samoa.
  See American Samoa.
Samora, Julian, **1968–69**: 3, 91
Sampson, George, **1963–64**: 143 [3]
Samuel Gompers, U.S.S., proposed building of,
      1963–64: 430

Samuel I. Newhouse Communications Center,
      dedication, **1963–64**: 499
Samuels, Howard J., **1966**: 510, 512; **1967**: 512;
      1968–69: 139
San Andres, El Salvador, **1968–69**: 370
San Antonio, Tex., **1965**: 621
  Commemorative medals, **1966**: 160
  Hemisfair 1968, **1966**: 160
  Housing, **1967**: 531; **1968–69**: 19
  Mayor W. W. McAllister, **1966**: 168n.;
      1967: 151n.; **1968–69**: 7n., 357, 359
  Releases, **1966**: 105, 167–173, 178, 206–212,
      255, 316–319, 321–323, 419, 480, 579,
      582–590, 592–598, 600–604, 606, 608–
      609; **1967**: 85–92, 151, 179–180, 209,
      243, 293–295, 298–304, 378, 379, 410n.,
      455, 504, 506, 507, 530, 531, 574–577;
      1968–69: 2–5, 6, 9–11, 360, 361, 377,
      379, 396, 402, 489–492, 535, 577–579,
      606, 607, 653
  Remarks, **1968–69**: 7, 357, 359, 462
  Vietnam policy address, **1967**: 409, 411 [6],
      460 [13], 554 [1]
San Antonio formula.
  See Vietnam conflict.
San Bernardino, Calif., campaign remarks,
      1963–64: 735
San Diego, Calif., **1965**: 325; **1967**: 303
  Campaign remarks, **1963–64**: 736
  Mayor Frank Kern, **1963–64**: 736
San Francisco, Calif., **1965**: 295 [2], 297, 312,
      331; **1966**: 94
  Campaign remarks, **1963–64**: 651
  Cow Palace, **1963–64**: 415
  Democratic fundraising dinner, **1963–64**: 413
  Federal Building, dedication, **1963–64**: 411
  Mayor Joseph Alioto, **1968–69**: 333, 339 [3],
      568
  Mayor John F. Shelley, **1963–64**: 411, 413, 651,
      660n.
  Republican National Convention, **1963–64**: 462
      [6]
San Francisco Bay Area Rapid Transit Test Track,
      1963–64: 410
San Gabriel Wilderness, Calif., **1967**: 418;
      1968–69: 122
San José, Costa Rica, **1968–69**: 374
San Juan Island Historical Park, Wash., **1966**: 448
San Luis, Colo., **1967**: 452
San Marco satellite, Italy, **1963–64**: 807
San Marcos, Tex., **1963–64**: 778; **1965**: 179, 603n.;
      1968–69: 459n.
  Mayor Ellis Serur, **1965**: 179n.
San Marcos State Teachers College, Texas,
      1966: 589; **1968–69**: 644
San Mateo County, Calif., **1965**: 446
San Pedro Sula, Honduras, **1968–69**: 375

San Rafael Wilderness, Calif., **1967**: 20, 29, 96, 418; **1968–69**: 122, 150, 168
San Saba, Tex., **1965**: 467
San Salvador, El Salvador
  Charter of, **1968–69**: 366
  Releases, **1968–69**: 364, 366, 372
  Remarks, **1968–69**: 363, 365, 367–369
Sánchez Gavito, Vicente, **1963–64**: 596
Sanchez Hernandez, Fidel (President of El Salvador), **1968–69**: 363, 365, 366, 369–371
Sanchez Hernandez, Mrs. Fidel, **1968–69**: 369, 371
Sánchez-Vilella, Gov. Roberto, **1967**: 436
Sand, H. A., **1963–64**: 679
Sandburg, Carl, **1963–64**: 313, 568; **1966**: 2, 327, 579; **1967**: 320, 387; **1968–69**: 70, 230n.
"Abraham Lincoln: The Prairie Years and the War Years," **1963–64**: 796n.
Sandburg, Mrs. Carl, **1967**: 387
Sanders, Gov. Carl E., **1963–64**: 330, 332, 567, 716, 718, 719; **1965**: 245, 319 [7]; **1966**: 122 [1]; **1967**: 87n.
Sanders, Mrs. Carl E., **1963–64**: 330, 332
Sanders, Harold Barefoot, **1967**: 411 [2]
Sanders, Dr. William, **1968–69**: 239
Sandy Hook State Park, **1963–64**: 422
Sanford, Gov. Terry, **1963–64**: 103, 326, 327, 328, 329, 631, 643, 644; **1966**: 210n.
Sanford, Mrs. Terry, **1963–64**: 326
Sanger, Dr. Paul, **1963–64**: 211 [6]
Sanjines, Julio, **1968–69**: 362n.
Sanjines-Goytia, Julio, **1965**: 473n.
Santa Ana, Calif., **1967**: 485 [2]
Santa Cruz, Calif., University of California branch, **1963–64**: 414
Santiago, Dominican Republic, **1965**: 286
Santo Domingo, Dominican Republic, **1965**: 208 [7], 212n., 217, 223, 286, 482
  U.S. Embassy, attacks on, **1965**: 227, 319 [16]
Sanz de Santamaría, Carlos, **1963–64**: 211 [8], 220, 340, 726, 769; **1968–69**: 205, 290
Saragat, Giuseppe, **1963–64**: 101, 102n., 107, 109, 118; **1965**: 200; **1967**: 515, 572
  Election as President, **1963–64**: 817
  Flood message, **1966**: 591
  Message, **1968–69**: 13
  Visit, **1967**: 389–391
Sarnoff, David, **1963–64**: 211 [6]; **1965**: 242, 449
Sarnoff, Robert W., **1965**: 74
Sartoris, Mrs. Algernon (Nellie Grant), **1968–69**: 648
Satellite Center, National Environmental, **1967**: 31n.
Satellite Communications System, Defense, **1963–64**: 504 [6]
Satellite Consortium, International Telecommunications (INTELSAT), **1967**: 122, 346

Satellite Corporation, Communications (ComSat), **1967**: 122, 346; **1968–69**: 175
Satellites, earth, **1963–64**: 132 (p. 187), 579; **1967**: 346; **1968–69**: 616
  See also Space Research and exploration; Space vehicles.
  Anti-satellite systems, **1965**: 26
  Communications, **1966**: 40, 103, 243; **1967**: 122, 176, 346, 389, 423, 425, 474, 533; **1968–69**: 14 (p. 27), 77, 175, 233, 288
    See also Communications satellites.
  Defense, **1967**: 346
  Global system, **1967**: 346
  Italian San Marco, **1963–64**: 807
  Radiation probe, **1965**: 659
  Sputnik, **1967**: 533; **1968–69**: 39 (p. 99), 616, 646 [5, 9], 647
  Weather, **1963–64**: 132 (p. 187), 396, 597, 705, 733; **1966**: 222; **1967**: 121
Sato, Eisaku, **1965**: 8, 12, 15, 175, 214, 355n., 544; **1967**: 437; **1968–69**: 44, 340, 685
  Visit, **1967**: 486, 487, 491, 492, 493n.
Sato, Mrs. Eisaku, **1967**: 486, 487
Saturday Evening Post, **1963–64**: 238
Saturn space project, **1963–64**: 162, 170 [1]
Saturn V launch vehicle, **1966**: 26 (p. 59), 485, 625; **1967**: 19n., 24, 76, 483, 533
Saturn V rocket, **1968–69**: 39 (p. 100), 41
Saudi Arabia, **1965**: 325; **1966**: 284–285, 287
  King Faisal, **1965**: 463 [6]; **1966**: 284–285, 287
  Water desalination, U.S. cooperation, **1966**: 285
  Yemen cease-fire agreement, **1965**: 463 [6]
Saunders, Stewart T., **1963–64**: 299; **1968–69**: 471n.
Savage, Francis S., **1967**: 352
Savang Vatthana (King of Laos), **1967**: 438n.
Savannah, U.S.S., **1963–64**: 719
Savannah River nuclear production plant, **1963–64**: 716, 718, 719
Save the Redwoods League, **1963–64**: 427
Savings, personal, **1963–64**: 563 [6]; **1965**: 164, 285; **1966**: 432; **1967**: 16 (p. 76), 86, 420; **1968–69**: 47 (p. 129)
Savings Associations, National League of Insured, **1963–64**: 617
Savings bond campaign, **1963–64**: 306
Savings bonds, **1965**: 11; **1966**: 15, 164, 240, 247 [3]; **1967**: 66, 315; **1968–69**: 10, 174, 284, 537
  See also Bonds.
  Anniversary stamp, **1966**: 358
  Interest rates, **1966**: 15, 72–73, 137, 150, 164
  Minuteman Award, **1968–69**: 12
Savings Bonds, Interdepartmental Committee for, **1966**: 137
Savings and loan associations, **1963–64**: 814; **1966**: 34 (p. 108), 582; **1967**: 3 (p. 8),

Savings and loan associations – *continued*
  16 (p. 86), 88, 103, 104 [1], 420;
  1968–69: 47 (p. 141), 72, 87, 114, 115
  Urban areas role, **1968–69**: 114, 115
Savings and Loan Committee on Urban Problems,
  Joint Savings Bank, **1968–69**: 114
Savings and Loan Holding Company Amend-
  ments of 1967, **1968–69**: 72
Savings and loan insurance, **1963–64**: 598;
  1965: 32 (p. 93); **1966**: 34 (p. 108),
  530
Savings note, Freedom Share, **1967**: 66
Savings stamp programs, **1966**: 472
Sawyer, Gov. Grant, **1963–64**: 575, 652, 655;
  1966: 407
Sawyer, Mrs. Grant, **1963–64**: 655
Sawyer, Brig. Gen. Webb D., **1968–69**: 81 [2]
Saylor, Repr. John P., **1965**: 417; **1968–69**: 457,
  477, 510
Sayre, Very Rev. Francis B., Jr., **1965**: 289;
  1967: 387
Saxon, James J., **1966**: 228
Scales, James R., **1963–64**: 238
Scali, John, **1966**: 338 [17], 455
Scenic rivers system, **1967**: 20
Scenic Rivers System, National Wild and,
  1968–69: 14 (p. 31), 39 (p. 101), 122,
  345, 510
Scenic sites, preservation, **1966**: 26 (p. 60);
  1967: 13 (p. 51), 295; **1968–69**: 39 (p.
  101)
Scerra, Joseph A., **1968–69**: 132, 452
Schaert, Adolf, death of, **1965**: 87
Schary, Dore, **1965**: 44
Schechter, Mrs. Harvey B., **1963–64**: 257n.
Scheible, Goldie V., **1966**: 435
Scherer, Raymond L., **1966**: 223, 338 [11], 492
  [10], 494 [3], 516 [10]; **1967**: 225
  [19], 529, 554; **1968–69**: 101n., 171,
  481
Schick, Señora Carmen Renasco de, telegram,
  1966: 367
Schick Gutiérrez, René (President of Nicaragua),
  1966: 263, 264
  Death of, **1966**: 367, 369
Schiro, Victor H., **1963–64**: 648; **1967**: 533
Schirra, Capt. Walter M., Jr., **1965**: 647, 656;
  1967: 533; **1968–69**: 533n., 552, 574,
  616
Schleicher, Benjamin T., **1963–64**: 747
Schlesinger, A. W., **1968–69**: 108
Schlesinger, Arthur, Jr., **1963–64**: 218 [8];
  1965: 22 [1], 353 [23]; **1967**: 104 [4]
  "A Thousand Days—John F. Kennedy in the
  White House," **1965**: 353ftn. (p. 743)
Schlesinger Old Folks Home, Beaumont, Texas,
  1968–69: 108
Schmidhauser, Repr. John R., **1965**: 420;
  1966: 312

Schmied, Kenneth, **1966**: 351
Schneider, Mrs. Edythe, **1967**: 361n.
Schneiderman, Dan, **1965**: 81
Schnittker, John A., **1965**: 206 [6], 290;
  1967: 33, 476
Schnitzler, William F., **1963–64**: 221, 388
Schoendienst, Red, telegram, **1967**: 429
Scholars, Commission on Presidential,
  1963–64: 266 [4], 309; **1965**: 171;
  1966: 257
Scholars, Presidential, **1963–64**: 266 [4]
  Remarks to, **1966**: 257
Scholars, role in American culture, **1966**: 101,
  216, 327
Scholars, Woodrow Wilson Center for,
  1967: 71
Scholarship Corporation, National Merit,
  1966: 545ftn. (p. 1251)
Scholarships, **1963–64**: 457n., 588, 601;
  1965: 2, 6, 9, 100, 340, 368, 369, 374,
  479, 514, 603; **1966**: 26 (p. 63), 45,
  486; **1967**: 1, 13 (p. 55), 148, 217, 359,
  451, 490; **1968–69**: 66, 84, 113, 214n.,
  442, 447, 453, 459, 687
  Military, **1963–64**: 665
  Nursing, **1963–64**: 179
Scholastic achievement awards, **1966**: 220
Scholle, August, **1963–64**: 356; **1966**: 431
School Administrators, American Association of,
  1965: 250; **1966**: 77
School Disaster Aid Act, **1965**: 592
School Lunch Week, 1966, National, **1966**: 508
School Officers, Council of Chief State,
  1966: 165; **1967**: 182n.
School Safety Patrol awards, presentation,
  1963–64: 317; **1965**: 232
School-to-school partnerships, **1966**: 45
School-to-school program, Peace Corps,
  1966: 332, 445; **1967**: 90
Schools, **1963–64**: 213, 579, 709; **1965**: 181,
  609; **1966**: 45, 77, 111, 319, 394;
  1967: 276, 484
  See also Colleges; Education; Students.
  Appalachian area, **1963–64**: 325
  Campaign remarks, **1963–64**: 658
  Civil rights boycotts, **1963–64**: 242 [13]
  Community financing, **1968–69**: 684 (p. 1321)
  Computer uses, **1967**: 77
  Construction, **1963–64**: 91 (p. 112), 132 (p.
  189), 133, 571, 589, 603, 606, 650, 667,
  669, 754; **1965**: 2, 5, 6, 100, 592;
  1967: 532, 540; **1968–69**: 39 (p. 106)
  Dental, **1968–69**: 39 (p. 103)
  District boundaries, nondiscrimination,
  1968–69: 91
  Dropouts, **1963–64**: 47, 53, 84, 213, 218 [15],
  233, 246 [20], 398, 658, 680, 733, 754;
  1965: 9, 10, 70, 90, 100, 156 [2], 178,
  183, 322, 340, 438, 453, 490; **1966**: 95,

Schools — *continued*
  Dropouts — *continued*
      111, 317, 385, 392, 580 [7], 589;
      1967: 55, 193, 199, 413, 532, 540
  Facilities expansion, **1965**: 340; **1966**: 27, 95,
      105, 319, 406, 508, 654 [3]
  Fallout shelters in, **1963–64**: 132 (p. 185)
  Federal aid, **1963–64**: 47, 53, 91 (p. 112), 132
      (p. 191), 338, 754; **1965**: 2, 100, 479,
      539, 592, 625; **1966**: 95, 508
  Foreign, construction, **1966**: 332
  Integration, **1963–64**: 413, 642, 744;
      1965: 340, 443, 470, 615; **1966**: 95,
      196, 235, 375, 492 [3], 494 [5, 10],
      501 [13]; **1967**: 55, 77, 225 [12]
  Libraries, **1965**: 9, 527; **1968–69**: 4, 54
  Low-income districts, **1965**: 9
  Lunch and milk programs, **1963–64**: 292, 391,
      546, 713, 732; **1965**: 47, 139, 149;
      1966: 26 (p. 63), 95, 340, 508, 520;
      1967: 15, 39, 63, 228, 353, 405;
      1968–69: 94, 678 (p. 1297)
  Medical, **1968–69**: 39 (p. 103), 111
  Nursing, **1963–64**: 179
  Occupational training, **1963–64**: 53, 213;
      1967: 193
  Officials, **1965**: 183
  Overcrowding, **1963–64**: 357; **1965**: 9, 89
  Physical fitness programs, **1963–64**: 490;
      1965: 625
  Rural areas, **1963–64**: 658; **1965**: 47
  Savings stamp program, **1966**: 472
  Summer programs for children, **1966**: 632
  Superintendents, remarks to, **1963–64**: 488
  Urban, **1966**: 30; **1967**: 493
  U.S. abroad, **1966**: 45
  Washington, D.C., area, **1963–64**: 133; **1965**:
      29, 70, 151; **1966**: 27, 457, 586; **1967**:
      15
Schramm, Wilbur, **1966**: 424n.
Schreiber, Walter R., **1965**: 353 [4]
Schröder, Gerhard, **1963–64**: 28 [4], 72n., 75,
      76, 400, 780 [8]; **1965**: 660; **1966**:
      486
Schultze, Charles L. (Director, Bureau of the
      Budget), **1965**: 249, 290, 297, 319 [6,
      8], 324, 332, 347 [8], 362, 404, 418,
      447, 506, 512, 560; **1968–69**: 1 [16],
      2n., 15, 36, 38, 677
  See also Budget, Bureau of the, Director.
Schulz, Gen. Robert L., **1968–69**: 550
Schumacher, William E., **1966**: 331n.
Schuman, Robert, **1963–64**: 244; **1966**: 142
Schurman, Mrs. Beatrice, **1963–64**: 605
Schurmann, Carl W. A., **1968–69**: 661
Schurmeier, Harris M., **1965**: 134
Schwartz, Carl H., Jr., **1965**: 263n.
Schwartz, Margaret Wolman, **1963–64**: 204n.

Schweinhaut, Mrs. Margaret, **1965**: 642n.
Schweitzer, Dr. Albert, **1965**: 474; **1966**: 82,
      402
Schweitzer, Louis, **1966**: 286
Schweitzer, Pierre-Paul, **1965**: 541; **1968–69**: 500
Schwengel, Repr. Fred, **1968–69**: 655
Schwinger, Julian, **1965**: 56n.
Science, **1963–64**: 175, 408n., 650; **1966**: 101,
      418; **1967**: 192, 448; **1968–69**: 41, 71,
      687, 695
  Atmospheric programs, **1966**: 222
  Crime prevention role, **1966**: 491
  Education, **1963–64**: 132 (p. 190), 391, 456,
      709, 738; **1965**: 2, 32 (p. 95), 88, 225,
      271, 514, 522; **1966**: 95, 111, 586;
      1967: 165, 217, 230; **1968–69**: 145,
      687
  Exchange programs, **1963–64**: 434; **1965**: 292,
      519; **1966**: 200, 503
  Federal aid, **1968–69**: 687
  Instrument import tariffs, **1966**: 601
  Manpower utilization, **1963–64**: 271 [5]
  Research, **1963–64**: 117, 124 (p. 163), 132
      (p. 191), 231, 308, 396, 529, 629, 715,
      738, 756, 758; **1965**: 9, 32 (p. 95), 56,
      71, 88, 92, 115, 166, 170, 196, 220,
      225, 247, 257, 265, 271, 319 [5], 514,
      522, 523, 558; **1966**: 38, 79, 111, 222,
      326, 402; **1967**: 37, 165, 491, 540;
      1968–69: 145, 227, 288, 687, 692
  Teachers, Washington, D.C., **1966**: 27
  U.S.-Korean cooperation, **1965**: 257, 344, 407
  Waste products, **1965**: 54
Science, Korean Institute for Industrial Tech-
      nology and Applied, **1965**: 257, 344,
      407
Science, National Medal of, **1965**: 56, 646;
      1966: 61, 652; **1967**: 37; **1968–69**: 71,
      695
  Presentation, **1963–64**: 98
Science, Polish Academy of, **1966**: 200
Science, President's Committee on the National
      Medal of, **1963–64**: 98n.; **1965**: 646n.;
      1966: 61n.; **1967**: 37n.
Science, Weizmann Institute of, **1963–64**: 175
Science Adviser to the President.
  See Science and Technology, Office of.
Science Advisory Committee, President's,
      1963–64: 179, 271 [5], 456n., 758;
      1965: 166, 602; **1966**: 62, 82, 279–280,
      326; **1967**: 33, 48, 101, 271;
      1968–69: 63
Science Board, National, **1965**: 283
Science Foundation, National, **1963–64**: 308;
      1965: 9, 32 (p. 95), 71, 220n., 225,
      271, 283, 514; **1966**: 38, 79, 111, 229,
      319; **1967**: 1, 77, 165, 193, 314;
      1968–69: 54, 145, 453, 495, 678 (p.
      1293), 687

Science Foundation, National — *continued*
See also National Science Foundation.
Science Institute, Lunar, **1968-69**: 107
Science Scholars, Lyndon B. Johnson Australian,
  1966: 545-546; **1967**: 1; **1968-69**: 453
Science Services Administration, Environmental,
  1967: 31
Science Talent Search, remarks to winners of,
  1965: 88
Science and Technology, Federal Council for,
  1963-64: 229, 456n., **1965**: 92, 271,
  275, 514; **1966**: 138, 222; **1967**: 478;
  1968-69: 577
Science and Technology, Inter-American
  Foundation for, **1967**: 176
Science and Technology, Office of, **1963-64**: 179,
  229, 231, 480; **1967**: 20, 315n.;
  1968-69: 59, 297, 653
  Director (Donald F. Hornig), **1963-64**: 229n.,
    231n., 420 [2], 456, 480n., 493n., 513,
    601, 629, 804; **1965**: 4, 12n., 54, 56n.,
    88, 92n., 257, 344n., 375, 404, 407, 417,
    418, 446, 514, 547n., 649; **1966**: 61,
    98ftn. (p. 261), 138, 143, 216, 326,
    424n., 635 [3], 637; **1967**: 1, 20, 37, 65,
    82, 139n., 186, 192, 219, 388, 478n.;
    1968-69: 71, 122, 277, 434, 453, 513n.,
    577, 608, 695
  China, Republic of, mission, **1967**: 416
  Letter, **1963-64**: 308
  Memorandum, **1967**: 186; **1968-69**: 297
  Swearing in, **1963-64**: 146
Sciences, National Academy of, **1963-64**: 271
  [5], 308, 355n., 456n.; **1966**: 79,
  200, 461; **1967**: 101; **1968-69**: 107,
  361
Scientific, and Cultural Materials, Agreement on
  the Importation of Educational,
  1965: 292, 604; **1966**: 45, 529, 601
Scientific, and Cultural Organization, United
  Nations, Educational, **1963-64**: 480;
  1967: 198n.
Scientific, Professional and Cultural Employees,
  AFL-CIO Council for, **1968-69**: 686
Scientific Cooperation, United States-Japan
  Committee on, **1965**: 15
Scientific and Engineering Manpower, Commit-
  tee on Utilization of, **1963-64**: 271ftn.
  (p. 488), 456n.
Scientific instruments, approval of bills for duty-
  free entry of, **1965**: 604
Scientists, **1963-64**: 493; **1966**: 89, 95, 200;
  1967: 192
  American, comments on, **1965**: 56
  Employment, **1963-64**: 456n.
  Exchange programs, **1965**: 319 [5], 519
  Overseas service, **1968-69**: 63
  Training, **1965**: 514

Scientists — *continued*
  Utilization, reports on, **1963-64**: 271ftn. (p.
    488), 456
Scientists and Engineers for Johnson,
  1963-64: 629
SCORE (Service Corps of Retired Executives),
  1968-69: 75
Scorpion, U.S.S., **1968-69**: 275 [7]
Scott, Lt. Col. David, **1966**: 134-135
Scott, David W., **1968-69**: 225
Scott, Sen. Hugh, **1963-64**: 289, 290, 390;
  1967: 291
Scott, Sir Walter, **1966**: 368
Scott Aviation Corp., **1967**: 231n.
Scotton, Frank W., **1967**: 352n.
Scranton, Gov. William W., **1963-64**: 217, 285
  [1], 287, 516 [11], 566, 728;
  1965: 417, 418, 434, 471; **1966**: 121
  [1], 122 [1, 2], 407, 428, 501 [20];
  1968-69: 36, 590 [2]
Scranton, Mrs. William W., **1966**: 428
Scranton, Pa., campaign remarks, **1963-64**: 661
Screwworm eradication, **1966**: 357; **1967**: 319,
  448; **1968-69**: 624
Sculpture in cities, **1968-69**: 64
Sculpture Garden, Joseph H. Hirshhorn
  Museum and, **1968-69**: 660
Sea grant colleges and programs, **1967**: 101;
  1968-69: 122, 124, 145, 692
Seabeds, arms control, **1968-69**: 392
Seabees, **1963-64**: 438n., 443; **1966**: 456
Seaborg, Glenn T. (Chairman, Atomic Energy
  Commission), **1965**: 17, 88, 196, 319
  [1, 5], 417, 418, 523; **1966**: 48, 179,
  361, 410-411; **1967**: 227, 504, 515;
  1968-69: 310, 361, 608, 695
  See also Atomic Energy Commission, Chair-
    man.
Seal of the President of the United States,
  1966: 609
Seal of the United States, **1963-64**: 411;
  1966: 609
Seamans, Robert C., **1963-64**: 162n.
Seamans, Robert C., Jr., **1965**: 120, 121, 134,
  310, 462, 463 [2, 13]; **1966**: 625;
  1968-69: 507
Seashores
  Conservation, **1968-69**: 167
  National, **1963-64**: 357, 578, 620, 642;
    1965: 222, 521; **1966**: 119; **1967**: 553
SEATO.
  See Southeast Asia Treaty Organization.
Seattle, Wash., **1963-64**: 577
  Mayor J. D. Braman, **1963-64**: 577
Second Supplemental Appropriation Act, 1965,
  1965: 215
Second Supplemental Appropriation Act, 1966,
  1966: 67n., 223

Second Supplemental Appropriation Act, 1967,
		1967: 140n., 203n., 225ftn. (p. 541)
Secret Service, **1963–64**: 21, 90, 201 [3], 218
		[4], 268, 516 [17], 619 [11], 688 [5,
		8], 752; **1968–69**: 59, 549, 557 [8], 604
	Protection of presidential candidates,
		1968–69: 292n.
Secretaries, White House, **1968–69**: 595
Securities
	Consumer protection, **1963–64**: 173
	Corporate, **1965**: 60
	Foreign, **1965**: 60, 638n.
		Proposed tax on, **1963–64**: 196
	Government, **1965**: 60; **1966**: 431, 444, 445
		[2], 451, 477 [2, 4], 492 [1], 494 [1],
		578 [3]; **1968–69**: 418
	Investor protection, **1967**: 57; **1968–69**: 39
		(p. 96)
	Registration fees, **1965**: 580
Securities Act of 1933, amendments, **1965**: 580
Securities Acts Amendments of 1964, approval,
		1963–64: 530
Securities Exchange Act of 1934, **1963–64**: 604
Securities and Exchange Commission,
		1963–64: 211 [2], 530, 563 [6], 598,
		604, 642; **1965**: 164, 580, 641 [2];
		1966: 110, 445 [5], 470, 635 [18];
		1967: 57, 103, 104 [1]; **1968–69**: 418
	Chairman (William L. Cary), **1963–64**: 455
		[8]
	Chairman (Manuel F. Cohen), **1963–64**: 530;
		1968–69: 418
Security, national.
	See National security
Security Council.
	See United Nations Security Council.
Security Council, National, **1966**: 124 [6], 145,
		214; **1968–69**: 86, 213 [8], 483, 669
	See also National Security Council.
Security Industrial Association, National,
		1965: 211
Security Medal, National, **1965**: 209n.;
		1966: 99, 387; **1967**: 383
Sedita, Frank A., **1966**: 392, 511–512
"See the U.S.A." Committee, **1965**: 418, 419
"See the U.S.A." program, **1965**: 60, 419
Segal, Rabbi Henry, **1968–69**: 78
Segni, Antonio (President of Italy), **1963–64**:
		149
	Letter, **1963–64**: 794
	News conference remarks on, **1963–64**: 28 [4],
		54 [8], 475 [3]
	Visit, **1963–64**: 101, 102, 107, 109, 118
Segni, Signora Antonio, **1963–64**: 101, 102,
		107, 118
Segregation, **1968–69**: 611
Seidenberg, Jacob, **1966**: 535n.
Seismic sea waves, **1967**: 31n.

Seitz, Collins J., **1966**: 88 [11]
Seitz, Frederick, **1965**: 56n.; **1968–69**: 107
Seitz, Maj. Gen. Richard J., **1968–69**: 81 [1]
Selassie, Haile (Emperor of Ethiopia), **1967**: 51,
		52; **1968–69**: 433, 639
Seldovia, Alaska, **1967**: 369
Selective Service, National Advisory Commission
		on, **1966**: 315n., 388, 536; **1967**: 3 (p.
		6), 92, 104 [12], 205n.
Selective Service Act of 1948, **1967**: 92
Selective Service System, **1963–64**: 89, 560 [16];
		1965: 100; **1966**: 67, 315, 320 [10],
		388; **1967**: 3 (p. 5), 104 [12], 315n.;
		1968–69: 132, 676 (p. 1267)
	Director (Lt. Gen. Lewis B. Hershey),
		1967: 92, 104 [12], 205
	Draft
		Evaders, prosecution, **1966**: 158 [11]
		Increase, **1965**: 388 [1], 395 [2]
		Requirements, **1966**: 208, 521, 578 [2, 10];
			1967: 297 [9], 309 [4]
	FAIR (fair and impartial random) selection,
		1967: 92, 205; **1968–69**: 43, 678 (p.
		1304)
	Message to Congress, **1967**: 92
	Negroes, **1967**: 104 [12]
	Rejectees, **1967**: 92, 199
		See also Military rejectees, training and
			rehabilitation.
	State directors, remarks, **1967**: 205
	Study of, **1963–64**: 271 [2, 8], 619 [3]
	Voluntary enlistments, **1967**: 286
Self-Help, National Advisory Committee on,
		1967: 44
"Self Renewal; the Individual and the Innovative
		Society," John W. Gardner, **1965**: 385n.
Selfridge Air Force Base, Mich., **1967**: 321, 322
Sellers, Dennis K., **1966**: 331n.
Selma, Ala., **1965**: 201, 409
	Civil rights demonstrations in, **1965**: 106 [1,
		7], 107; **1968–69**: 596, 631, 696 [9]
	Civil rights march to Montgomery, **1965**: 104,
		114, 117 [1, 5, 10], 126n., 135
	Voting registration, **1965**: 46 [3, 13]
Sells, Leonard L., **1963–64**: 285 [8]
Semer, Milton P., **1966**: 88 [7], 399
Senate committees.
	See other parts of title.
Senate luncheon remarks, **1966**: 520
Senate Youth Program, **1966**: 35; **1968–69**: 33
	Participants, remarks to, **1965**: 48
Senators, Inc., baseball club, **1966**: 509
Senegal, **1966**: 489
	Ambassador Ousmane Socé Diop, **1966**: 243
	President Leopold S. Senghor, **1966**: 488–489
Seney Wilderness, Mich., **1968–69**: 168
Senior citizens.
	See Older persons.

Senior Citizens, National Council of, **1966**: 253;
   1968–69: 75n.
Senior Citizens Month, **1965**: 72
   Proclamation, **1968–69**: 108
Senior Interdepartmental Group, State Department, **1968–69**: 15
Senior Seminar in Foreign Policy, Foreign Service Institute, **1966**: 261
Senner, Repr. George F., Jr., **1963–64**: 649
Sensenbrenner, M. E., **1966**: 436
Sentinel missile defense system, **1968–69**: 39
   (p. 98)
Seoane, Edgardo, **1965**: 593
Seoul, Korea
   Mayor Hyon-ok Kim, **1966**: 561
   Release, **1966**: 564
   Visit, **1966**: 561–562, 565, 566a
Separation of church and state, **1965**: 302
Separation of powers of Government,
   1965: 440, 515, 587
Serkin, Rudolf, **1963–64**: 27
Serur, Ellis, **1965**: 179n.
Service Agencies, International, **1967**: 288
Service Contract Act of 1965, **1965**: 582
Service Corps, **1965**: 270
   Proposed, **1963–64**: 89, 91 (p. 114), 132 (pp. 184, 189)
Service Corps of Retired Executives (SCORE),
   1968–69: 75
Service work, **1965**: 38, 79, 99, 582
Servicemen.
   See Armed Forces, U.S.; Military, U.S.
Servicemen's Readjustment Act of 1944 (GI bill of rights), **1966**: 100, 158 [10], 188 [6], 353; **1968–69**: 554
Seryagin, Col. Eng. Vladmir, death, **1968–69**: 161
Sessions, Clinton F., **1967**: 275n.; **1968–69**: 236n.
Seton Hall University, **1963–64**: 190
Sevareid, Eric, **1963–64**: 218; **1966**: 52 [5]
"7,000 Years of Iranian Art," exhibit,
   1963–64: 369, 385
17-Nation Declaration on Vietnam, **1965**: 319 [14]
7th Airborne Battalion, Airborne Division, Army of the Republic of Vietnam, **1967**: 457
Sevilla-Sacasa, Guillermo, **1963–64**: 42n., 340; **1966**: 263, 478; **1968–69**: 371, 373, 681
Sewage facilities, **1965**: 555, 585
Seward, Alaska, **1963–64**: 242 [1]; **1967**: 369
Sewell, J. Richard, **1968–69**: 212n.
Sewell, James L., **1965**: 330
Sewer systems, **1968–69**: 94
Shackleton, Mrs. Polly, **1967**: 406, 466n.
Shafer, Eric E., **1967**: 41n.
Shafer, Kenneth, **1963–64**: 317n.
Shafer, Gov. Raymond P., **1967**: 426

Shaikh Sabah al-Salim al-Sabah (Amir of Kuwait), **1968–69**: 618–620
Shakespeare, William, **1966**: 289
   400th anniversary, **1963–64**: 784
   "Julius Caesar," **1967**: 248n.
Shamansky, Robert, **1966**: 436
Shanklin, John A., **1966**: 426
Shannon, Claude Elwood, **1966**: 652n.;
   1967: 37n.
Shannon, James A., **1965**: 410; **1966**: 266, 271;
   1967: 319; **1968–69**: 513n.
Shapiro, Samuel, **1963–64**: 636, 637, 694, 747;
   1968–69: 183, 210
"Share Your Summer" children's program,
   1967: 39, 209
Sharon, John H., **1968–69**: 53
Sharp, Jacqueline, **1966**: 295
Sharp, Thelma Parkinson, **1963–64**: 338
Sharp, Adm. U.S. Grant, Jr., **1966**: 52 [2], 320
   [2], 383, 474 [2, 10], 494 [1], 501
   [20], 532; **1967**: 134, 204 [1], 246n.;
   1968–69: 153 [5], 188, 189, 191 [4, 6], 197, 198
Sharp, Mrs. U.S. Grant, Jr., **1966**: 532
Sharpe Army Depot, Calif., safety record,
   1966: 75
Shastri, Lal Bahadur, **1963–64**: 379 [2, 17], 381, 693, 701, 737, 747; **1965**: 208 [17], 529; **1966**: 5, 8ftn. (p. 15), 141 [15], 148–149
Shaw, George Bernard, **1965**: 335; **1966**: 271, 526
Shaw Junior High School, Washington, D.C.,
   1966: 27, 457; **1967**: 15
Shazar, Schneor Zalman (President of Israel),
   1966: 365
Shea, Joseph, **1963–64**: 656n.
Sheet glass tariffs, **1967**: 428
Sheffer, 1st Lt. Eric S., **1965**: 161n.
Shell, Gen. George R. E., **1963–64**: 359
Shelley, Edwin F., **1968–69**: 117
Shelley, John F., **1963–64**: 411, 413, 651, 660n.
Shellfish, **1967**: 101
Shellworth, Eugene, **1963–64**: 660n.
Shen, Samson C., **1967**: 219
Shenker, Morris, **1963–64**: 695
Shepard, Comdr. Alan B., Jr., **1968–69**: 387
Shepard, Capt. Tazewell T., Jr., **1963–64**: 773
Shepherd, Repr. Harry R., **1963–64**: 735
Shepley, Steven C., **1967**: 352n.
Sheppard, Dr. Harold, **1965**: 642n.
Sheridan, Ann, **1963–64**: 713
Sherman, Allan, **1963–64**: 373
Sherman, Roger, **1967**: 376
Sherrill, William W., **1966**: 88 [3]
Sherwood, Don, **1965**: 554n.
Shevchenko, Taras, **1963–64**: 720
Shields, Barbara Diane, **1966**: 456

Shields, PO Marvin G., **1966**: 456
Shields, Mrs. Marvin G., **1966**: 456
Shiina, Etsusaburo, **1963–64**: 632n.; **1965**: 12,
	15, 355
Shillelagh antitank missile, **1963–64**: 170 [3]
Ship Mortgage Act, 1920, **1967**: 528
Shipbuilding industry labor disputes, **1967**: 104
	[15]
Shipley, Repr. George E., **1966**: 349
Shipp, Dr. Kathryn Grove, **1967**: 93n.
Ships, **1966**: 98, 159, 583
	AID-financed cargo, **1963–64**: 617
	Augusta, U.S.S., **1967**: 485 [5]
	Automated, **1965**: 428
	Cargo, gas turbine propulsion proposed,
		1965: 26
	Carriers, atomic propulsion proposed,
		1963–64: 170 [12]; **1965**: 26
	Constellation, U.S.S., **1968–69**: 81 [3], 102,
		109
	Construction, **1965**: 26, 387, 600; **1967**: 13
		(p. 48), 410, 528; **1968–69**: 39 (p. 98),
		535
	Contracts, **1967**: 410
	Design research, **1966**: 98
	Eltanin research ship, **1965**: 220
	Enterprise, U.S.S., **1963–64**: 560 [6];
		1967: 484, 485 [5], 493, 495 [3]
	Essex, U.S.S., **1968–69**: 552n.
	Forrestal, James V., U.S.S., **1967**: 330 [1]
	Houston, U.S.S., **1966**: 551
	Hydrofoils, **1966**: 98
	John F. Kennedy, U.S.S., **1963–64**: 560 [6];
		1967: 241
	Kitty Hawk, U.S.S., **1968–69**: 635
	Liberty, U.S.S., **1967**: 264 [4]
	Louise Lykes, S.S., keel-laying ceremony,
		1963–64: 110
	Lusitania, U.S.S., **1963–64**: 493, 648, 703;
		1965: 88; **1968–69**: 142
	Maddox, U.S.S., **1963–64**: 498, 499
	Maritime labor disputes, **1963–64**: 195, 494n.,
		614
		See also Maritime labor disputes.
	Masters, liens on wages, **1967**: 528
	Missiles based on, **1968–69**: 39 (p. 98)
	Mortgages, **1967**: 72, 528
	Nautilus, U.S.S., **1965**: 17
	Navy shipbuilding program, **1963–64**: 382
	Nuclear-powered
		Bainbridge, U.S.S., **1963–64**: 619 [5]
		Carriers, **1965**: 17; **1966**: 26 (p. 56)
		Enterprise, U.S.S., **1963–64**: 619 [5]
		Long Beach, U.S.S., **1963–64**: 619 [5]
		Savannah, U.S.S., **1963–64**: 719
	Ocean Eagle, **1968–69**: 122
	Oceanic research ships, construction, **1965**: 92

Ships — *continued*
	Oceanographer, **1966**: 326; **1967**: 20
	Oceanographic research, **1967**: 101
	Oregon, U.S.S., **1963–64**: 578
	Procurement, **1963–64**: 216
	Pueblo, U.S.S., seizure, **1968–69**: 35, 48, 51 [4,
		7, 8, 15], 65n., 79 [13], 169 [7], 201,
		223 [12], 467 [6], 557 [5], 641, 643
	Safety standards, **1966**: 98, 583
	Samuel Gompers, proposed building of,
		1963–64: 430
	Scorpion, U.S.S., **1968–69**: 275 [7]
	Submarines
		See main heading, Submarines.
	Torrey Canyon, **1967**: 240; **1968–69**: 122
	U.S. loan program, **1965**: 600
	Wasp, U.S.S., **1965**: 304n.
	Yarmouth Castle, **1966**: 98, 583
	Yorktown, U.S.S., **1968–69**: 647n.
Shivers, Alan, **1963–64**: 767
Shoe imports, **1963–64**: 285 [19]; **1967**: 223 [3]
Shoe industry, news conference remarks,
		1963–64: 246 [19]
Short, Dewey, **1965**: 157
Short, Robert E., **1965**: 419
Shoshone National Forest, Wyo., **1967**: 418
Shoumatoff, Madame Elizabeth, **1967**: 28
Shoup, Carl, **1967**: 85n.
Shoup, Gen. David M., **1963–64**: 127
Shoup, Mrs. David M., **1963–64**: 127
Shoup, David Monroe, **1966**: 315n.
Shriver, R. Sargent, Jr., **1963–64**: 174, 218 [16],
		219, 233, 267, 314, 323, 324, 403, 513,
		528, 606; **1965**: 179; **1966**: 12, 93, 95,
		105, 140, 236 [13], 394, 425, 490, 594,
		606, 607 [1]; **1968–69**: 153 [1, 3, 5, 10],
		305
	See also Economic Opportunity, Office of,
		Director; Peace Corps, Director.
	Director, Office of Economic Opportunity,
		1968–69: 94, 113
	Letter, **1963–64**: 183
	News conference remarks on, **1963–64**: 71
		[9], 150 [7], 170 [4], 256 [14], 294
		[2], 316 [26], 336 [20], 516 [4, 12]
Shriver, Mrs. R. Sargent, Jr., **1963–64**: 174n.,
		403, 773; **1967**: 373, 517
Shulman, Stephen N., **1966**: 475
Shuman, Charles, **1963–64**: 54ftn. (p. 68)
Shuster, George N., **1963–64**: 116n.
Siam, **1967**: 290
Sibelius, Jean, **1965**: 1
Sicily, earthquakes, **1968–69**: 13
Sickles, Repr. Carlton R., **1963–64**: 320, 321,
		703
Sidney, Hugh, **1963–64**: 294 [26]; **1968–69**: 696
		[10]

Siegel, Seymour N., **1967**: 474
Siemiller, P. L., **1966**: 360, 373 [12];
  1968–69: 106n., 110
Sierawski, Frank J., **1963–64**: 745
Sierra Club, **1963–64**: 427
Sihanouk, Prince Norodom (Chief of State of
  Cambodia), **1968–69**: 1 [9], 634
Sikes, Repr. Robert L. F., **1963–64**: 198, 199;
  1966: 145
Sikorsky, Igor, **1965**: 242; **1968–69**: 71n.
"Silent Spring," Rachel Carson, **1965**: 568ftn.
  (p. 1067)
Silk, Leonard S., **1967**: 85n.
Silver, Charles H., **1968–69**: 540
Silver, use in coinage system, **1965**: 297, 380
Silver Bridge, W. Va.-Ohio
  Collapse, **1967**: 552, 558
  Rebuilding, **1968–69**: 58
Silver and Coinage Study, Treasury Staff,
  1965: 297
Silver dollars, minting of, **1965**: 252, 297
Silver Star, **1966**: 350
  Presentation, **1963–64**: 535
Simeone, Fiorinda R., **1966**: 315n.
Simkin, Dr. Thomas E., **1968–69**: 430
Simkin, William E. (Director, Federal Mediation
  and Conciliation Service),
  1963–64: 316 [3]; **1965**: 448 [11];
  1966: 496
Simons, Milton, **1963–64**: 77
Simpson, Charles R. (Jim), **1965**: 478, 556n.
Simpson, Mrs. Charles R., **1965**: 478
Simpson, Donald F., **1967**: 458n.
Simpson, George G., **1965**: 646n.; **1966**: 61n.
Sinclair, Upton, "The Jungle," **1967**: 541
Singapore, **1967**: 433–435
  British troop withdrawals, **1967**: 312 [17]
  Economic and social development, **1967**: 433,
    434
  Prime Minister Lee Kuan Yew, **1967**: 409, 433–
    435
  Rifle purchases from U.S., **1967**: 104 [19]
Singer Bowl, World's Fair (1964–65),
  1963–64: 334n.
Single Convention on Narcotic Drugs, **1967**: 35,
  94
Singletary, Otis A., **1963–64**: 622ftn. (p. 1206);
  1965: 179
Sinkiang, China, **1963–64**: 686
Sinkin, William, **1968–69**: 357, 430
Sino-Soviet bloc.
  See Communist bloc.
Sioux City, Iowa, commemorative stamp,
  1966: 358
Siragusa, Ross David, **1966**: 228
Sirikit, Queen (Thailand), **1966**: 554n., 558n.;
  1967: 289, 290, 293; **1968–69**: 232n.,
  233

Sisco, Joseph J., **1966**: 198
Sisk, Repr. B. F., **1967**: 227
Sitterly, Mrs. Charlotte Moore, **1966**: 198n.
Sitton, Paul L., **1967**: 485 [8]
Six, Robert F., **1963–64**: 415
Sizer, Theodore, **1967**: 396n.
Skeen, Clyde, **1968–69**: 25
Skelton, Byron G., **1968–69**: 125
Skiff, Robert W., **1963–64**: 26
Skinner, B. Frederic, **1968–69**: 695n.
Skins, leather, and hides exports, **1966**: 592
Skouras, Spyros, **1965**: 242; **1968–69**: 540
Slack, Repr. John M., Jr., **1966**: 426–428
Slavery, **1967**: 49, 81
Sleeping Bear Dunes National Lakeshore, Mich.,
  1966: 82
  Proposed, **1965**: 54
Slums, **1967**: 286, 512, 517, 554 [6];
  1968–69: 26, 47 (p. 140), 50, 82, 86,
    87, 91, 227, 625, 678 (p. 1289)
  Clearance, **1963–64**: 590, 668, 669, 733;
    1965: 89, 90; **1966**: 6 (pp. 3, 6);
    1967: 23
  Rat control, **1967**: 114
  Renewal committee, **1967**: 252
  Unemployment, **1967**: 114; **1968–69**: 24, 26
  Youth, **1968–69**: 24
Small business, **1963–64**: 598, 606, 713;
  1965: 35 (p. 106), 590; **1966**: 231,
    582; **1967**: 427; **1968–69**: 39 (p. 87),
    227
  Federal aid, **1963–64**: 362; **1965**: 38, 75, 215,
    270
  Loans, **1965**: 38; **1966**: 26 (p. 63), 30, 231;
    1967: 427, 504
  Role in domestic economy, **1963–64**: 531
  Tax benefits, **1963–64**: 132 (pp. 180, 191),
    197
Small Business, National Advisory Council for,
  1963–64: 362
Small Business Act Amendments of 1966,
  1966: 199, 231n.
Small Business Act Amendments of 1967,
  1967: 427
Small Business Administration, **1963–64**: 336
  [3], 368, 567, 598, 615, 814;
  1965: 174, 215, 270, 453, 605, 618;
  1966: 172, 182, 199, 231, 582, 584,
    613, 630 [4]; **1967**: 315n., 369, 412,
    427, 428, 504; **1968–69**: 678 (p. 1291)
Small Business Administration, National Ad-
  visory Council of the, **1965**: 270n.
Small Business Administrator
  Bernard L. Boutin, **1966**: 231, 397, 613, 637;
    1967: 325n., 412; **1968–69**: 36
  Eugene P. Foley, **1963–64**: 217, 362, 434,
    531; **1965**: 270, 448 [5], 452, 454 [5]
  Robert C. Moot, **1968–69**: 94, 122

Small Business Investment Act Amendments of 1966, **1966**: 582

Small Business Investment Act of 1958, **1966**: 582

Small Business Management Development, National Council for, **1965**: 270n.

Small Business Week, **1965**: 270

Small Businessman of the Year award, presentation, **1963–64**: 362; **1965**: 270

Smallpox, **1966**: 6 (p. 8), 45, 166; **1967**: 110; **1968–69**: 304

  Control, **1965**: 5, 262

Smathers, Sen. George A., **1963–64**: 198, 199, 709, 710, 712, 713, 719; **1965**: 133, 183, 330, 345, 394; **1966**: 221; **1968–69**: 547

Smeder, Rear Adm. O.R., **1967**: 485 [8]

Smith, A. J., **1966**: 547

Smith, Adam, **1966**: 231; **1967**: 228

Smith, Sgt. Maj. Agrippa Warren, **1968–69**: 267

Smith, Alfred E., **1963–64**: 272, 338, 373, 387, 405, 434, 662, 678, 716, 736, 751; **1966**: 504, 510; **1968–69**: 78, 540, 568

Smith, Mrs. Alfred E., **1968–69**: 78

Smith, Bishop B. Julian, **1963–64**: 301

Smith, Benjamin A., II, **1963–64**: 559

Smith, Bromley K. (Executive Secretary of the National Security Council), **1963–64**: 417, 678

Smith, C.R.

  See Commerce, Secretary of.

Smith, Mrs. C.R., **1968–69**: 139

Smith, Chloethiel W., **1967**: 4n.

Smith, Courtney C., **1963–64**: 391n.

Smith, E. B. (Babe), Jr., **1965**: 230

Smith, Francis R., **1963–64**: 742

Smith, 1st Lt. George B., **1966**: 246

Smith, Adm. Harold P., **1963–64**: 244; **1965**: 228

Smith, Lt. Col. Haywood, **1968–69**: 345, 603

Smith, Repr. Henry P., III, **1966**: 392

Smith, Howard K., **1963–64**: 527; **1968–69**: 646 [14], 648

Smith, Repr. Howard W., **1965**: 133, 353 [18]; **1966**: 417 [2], 599 [6]

Smith, Gov. Hulett C., **1963–64**: 586; **1966**: 122 [1, 2], 348, 426–427, 650n.; **1967**: 514, 552n., 558; **1968–69**: 46n., 58

Smith, Mrs. Hulett C., **1968–69**: 564

Smith, Kate, **1963–64**: 199

Smith, Luther Napoleon, **1968–69**: 108

Smith, Sen. Margaret Chase, **1963–64**: 136, 199, 285 [1], 289, 606, 622; **1966**: 396–399; **1967**: 475

Smith, Merriman, **1963–64**: 170 [19], 232 [11], 246 [20], 256 [22], 316 [28], 455 [22], 475 [23], 516 [21]; **1965**: 106

Smith, Merriman – *continued*

  [9], 319 [14, 17], 347 [11], 353 [23]; **1966**: 65 [2, 4], 158 [2, 14], 236 [15], 320 [20], 334 [12], 338 [2], 373 [3, 16, 19], 401 [19], 445 [26], 501 [20], 516 [9]; **1967**: 80 [7], 104 [2, 19], 204 [16], 225 [22], 375 [1, 23], 460 [6, 14], 495 [14], 518 [19]; **1968–69**: 1 [14], 18 [2], 51 [16], 153 [6, 16], 171, 223 [14], 224, 683, 696 [1]

Smith, Repr. Neal, **1963–64**: 634; **1966**: 312

Smith, Preston, **1963–64**: 763; **1965**: 285; **1967**: 409

Smith, Roy J., **1967**: 532

Smith, Sam, **1967**: 538

Smith, Mrs. Stephen E., **1963–64**: 174n.

Smith, Warren, **1968–69**: 350

Smith, Adm. Willard J., **1963–64**: 382

Smith, Alfred E., Memorial Foundation, **1963–64**: 662

Smith-Hughes Act, **1967**: 67, 193; **1968–69**: 238

Smithson, James, **1966**: 227, 587

  Bicentennial celebration, **1965**: 519

Smithsonian Institution, **1965**: 519; **1966**: 90, 227, 267, 406, 519, 587; **1967**: 265, 540; **1968–69**: 133, 307, 430, 560, 695

  Art gallery, acquisition, **1965**: 328

  Museum of History and Technology, **1965**: 95

    Dedication, **1963–64**: 141

  National Collection of Fine Arts, **1968–69**: 225

  Secretary (S. Dillon Ripley), **1966**: 90, 193, 226n.; **1967**: 265, 274, 540; **1968–69**: 225, 660

Smoking, cigarette

  Discontinuance by President, **1963–64**: 218 [21]

  Effect on health, **1963–64**: 211 [25]

Smuts, Jan Christiaan, **1966**: 328n.

Smylie, Gov. Robert, **1963–64**: 285 [7]; **1966**: 407, 410–411

Snowdon, Lord (Antony Armstrong-Jones), **1965**: 616

Social Council, Inter-American Economic and, **1963–64**: 769; **1965**: 593; **1966**: 175

Social insurance, **1968–69**: 47 (p. 141), 678 (pp. 1277, 1279, 1282, 1287)

  Payments, **1968–69**: 678 (p. 1280)

  Trust funds, **1968–69**: 39 (pp. 86, 87, 91, 92)

Social and Rehabilitation Service, **1968–69**: 39 (p. 109)

Social science research, **1965**: 404; **1968–69**: 145

Social security, **1963–64**: 132 (p. 191), 325, 391, 477, 638; **1965**: 32 (pp. 83, 85, 94, 95), 49, 72, 176 [2], 231, 425, 632; **1966**: 164, 169, 216, 225, 240, 271,

Social security — *continued*
    395, 444, 509; **1967**: 6 [13], 12, 13 (p.
    42), 16 (pp. 76, 89), 23, 25, 216, 296,
    330 [1], 358 [3], 479; **1968–69**: 3, 38,
    39 (p. 88), 91, 108
  Adopted children, **1966**: 581
  Benefits extension, **1963–64**: 22, 388, 415;
    1965: 2, 32 (pp. 83, 87), 35 (pp. 108,
    113), 100, 394, 496, 501; **1966**: 26
    (p. 53), 34 (p. 100), 132, 168, 253,
    509, 515, 516 [6], 580 [6, 9, 11];
    1967: 3 (p. 5), 12, 13 (pp. 41, 54), 16
    (pp. 77–78, 83), 39, 81, 114, 244,
    499, 500, 505; **1968–69**: 3, 14 (p.
    32), 39 (p. 105), 75, 96, 108, 109,
    117, 397, 442, 481, 555, 565, 567, 568,
    676 (p. 1265), 678 (pp. 1274, 1279,
    1287, 1296, 1298), 684 (p. 1323)
  Campaign remarks, **1963–64**: 590, 597, 598,
    599, 605, 607, 635, 636, 637, 639,
    642, 643, 644, 648, 652, 655, 669,
    670, 680, 695, 701, 703, 712, 713,
    719, 728, 729, 733, 734, 742, 745, 748
  Expenditures, **1968–69**: 66
  Farmers, **1967**: 12
  First beneficiary, letter to, **1965**: 496
  Health insurance under, **1965**: 496, 501, 611
    Approval, **1965**: 394
    Proposed, **1963–64**: 22, 91 (p. 115), 105,
      124 (p. 165), 132 (p. 189), 150 [5],
      158, 170 [13], 178, 179, 211 [28],
      219, 228, 233, 235, 266 [21], 267,
      268, 270, 287, 292, 295, 297, 305,
      314, 334, 338, 379 [16], 413, 415,
      431, 434, 516 [9], 552, 562, 566, 571,
      589, 590, 604, 606, 619 [16], 637,
      642, 648, 712, 732, 733, 735, 746,
      748, 750, 755, 761; **1965**: 2, 5, 6, 32
      (pp. 83, 87, 94), 35 (p. 113), 72, 94,
      122, 133, 173, 176 [2], 231
  Legislation, **1967**: 312 [4]; **1968–69**: 253
  Taxes on, **1965**: 32 (p. 87); **1966**: 26 (p. 53),
    34 (p. 102), 155, 444; **1968–69**: 39
    (p. 88), 632, 678 (p. 1278)
  Trust fund, **1968–69**: 678 (pp. 1274, 1282)
  Twenty-millionth beneficiary, presentation of
    check to, **1965**: 231
  24 millionth beneficiary, **1968–69**: 397
Social Security Act of 1935, **1965**: 176 [2], 231,
    329, 330, 394, 425; **1966**: 168, 253,
    516 [6], 581; **1967**: 12, 15, 114, 299;
    1968–69: 212, 397, 506, 567, 678 (p.
    1298)
  Amendments, **1963–64**: 22, 133, 178, 179,
    745
  1965 amendments, **1965**: 5, 70, 173, 176 [2],
    397, 401, 406, 425, 496, 501; **1966**:
    494ftn. (p. 1105); **1967**: 12; **1968–69**:
    3n., 50, 108

Social Security Act of 1935 — *continued*
  1965 amendments — *continued*
    See also Medicare bill.
    Approval, **1965**: 394
  1966 amendments, **1968–69**: 3n.
  1967 amendments, **1967**: 244n., 505n.; **1968–
    69**: 3, 14 (p. 32), 39 (pp. 88, 105), 75,
    108, 109
Social Security Administration, **1966**: 26 (p. 67),
    161, 509; **1967**: 298
  Report, **1965**: 394n.
Social Security Headquarters, Baltimore, Md.,
    remarks, **1966**: 509
Social workers, **1966**: 95; **1967**: 15
Social Workers, Council of International Pro-
    grams for Youth Leaders and,
    1967: 365
Socialist Party, **1968–69**: 633n.
Society of Friends, **1963–64**: 391
Society of Jesus, **1968–69**: 551
Socrates, **1963–64**: 289; **1967**: 376
Soderstrom, Reuben, **1963–64**: 636, 637
Soil Bank Act, **1965**: 168
Soil erosion, **1967**: 300
Soil pollution, **1965**: 35 (p. 115), 602
Solicitor General (Erwin N. Griswold),
    1967: 275n., 443; **1968–69**: 236
Solicitor General (Thurgood Marshall).
    See Marshall, Thurgood.
Solid Waste Disposal Act, **1965**: 568;
    1968–69: 122, 536
Solomon, Anthony M., **1965**: 293, 295 [16]
Solomon, quote from, **1965**: 27
Solow, Robert M., **1968–69**: 3
Somali Republic, Foreign Minister Haji Farah Ali
    Omar, **1968–69**: 137, 140
Somoza, Luis, **1967**: 173
Somoza Debayle, Anastasio (President of
    Nicaragua), **1968–69**: 366, 373
Sonnabend, Roger P., **1968–69**: 25, 37
Sonorian Desert, Ariz., **1968–69**: 707
Sorensen, A. V., **1966**: 311
Sorensen, Philip C., **1966**: 311
Sorensen, Theodore C., **1963–64**: 108, 218 [8];
    1965: 22 [1]; **1967**: 104 [13];
    1968–69: 646 [12]
  "Decision-Making in the White House,"
    1963–64: 23
Sosa Rodriguez, Carlos, **1963–64**: 51n.
Sotoa, Chief Rapi, **1966**: 537
Souris-Red Rainy Basins Commission,
    1968–69: 593, 666
Sousa, John Philip, **1965**: 449
South Africa, **1965**: 220
South America, **1968–69**: 467 [13]
South Bend, Ind., **1963–64**: 288; **1965**: 188,
    490
  Occupational training, **1963–64**: 288

South Bend, Ind. — *continued*
  Studebaker facilities, closing of, **1963–64**: 67,
    288
  Unemployment, **1963–64**: 288, 289, 295, 297,
    486 [2]
South Carolina, **1967**: 115
  Campaign remarks, **1963–64**: 719
  Gov. Robert E. McNair, **1966**: 122 [1, 2],
    650n.
  Gov. Donald S. Russell, **1963–64**: 718, 719
  Hurricane relief, **1963–64**: 563 [4]
  School desegregation, **1965**: 470
South Dakota, **1963–64**: 171
  Gov. Nils A. Boe, **1966**: 494 [1, 2]
South Gate, Calif., campaign remarks,
    1963–64: 650
Southeast Asia, Association of, **1966**: 560
Southeast Asia, Joint Resolution on,
    1963–64: 503, 507
Southeast Asia Collective Defense Treaty,
    (Manila Pact), **1963–64**: 499, 500, 627;
    1965: 117 [8], 130, 156 [6], 227, 229,
    230, 319 [17], 353 [8]; **1966**: 88 [17],
    555
Southeast Asia Treaty Organization,
    1963–64: 272, 274, 285 [12], 499, 623,
    626; **1965**: 106 [6], 319 [16, 21], 347
    [5]; **1966**: 86, 228, 304; **1967**: 3 (p. 11),
    83, 116, 293, 409, 460 [9], 495 [14],
    519, 534, 554 [1]; **1968–69**: 232, 233,
    277, 452, 472, 525, 696 [13]
  Cholera Research Center in East Pakistan,
    1966: 45
  Support of South Vietnam, **1963–64**: 266
    [14]
Southeast Hurricane Disaster Relief Act of 1965,
    1965: 605; **1966**: 381
Southern Baptists Christian Leadership Seminar,
    1963–64: 238; **1968–69**: 156
Southern California, Metropolitan Water District
    of, **1967**: 13 (p. 51), 284
Southern Methodist University, **1966**: 189
Southern Rhodesia, **1966**: 243; **1967**: 74, 488
Southwest, Graduate Research Center of the,
    1963–64: 738
Southwest Texas State College, **1965**: 603;
    1967: 490n.; **1968–69**: 459
  Remarks, **1963–64**: 778
Souvanna Phouma, **1963–64**: 285 [4], 294
    [16], 336 [8]; **1966**: 513–514, 516
    [5, 11]; **1967**: 448, 480
  Visit, **1967**: 438, 439
Souvanna Phouma, Princess Moune, **1967**: 439
Soviet Life magazine, **1966**: 483
Soviet Union, **1963–64**: 8, 250, 619 [15], 737;
    1965: 208 [11], 220, 299, 302, 303,
    448 [2], 463 [11], 507; **1966**: 326,
    411, 414; **1967**: 80 [2, 7], 83, 245,
    328 [25], 401; **1968–69**: 50

Soviet Union — *continued*
  Academy of Sciences, **1965**: 448 [2]
  Aid to developing nations, **1965**: 18
  Aircraft
    Speed record, **1963–64**: 256 [3]; **1965**: 219
    Supersonic transport, **1965**: 319 [19]
  Ambassador Anatoly F. Dobrynin,
    1963–64: 271 [14], 674, 676, 678, 680,
    686, 688 [1]; 737; **1965**: 388 [10];
    1967: 18n., 279, 282, 425;
    1968–69: 309n.
  America Illustrated magazine, interview with
    the President, **1966**: 483
  Anniversary, **1967**: 472
  Antimissile defense system, **1967**: 3 (p. 11)
  Astronauts
    Gagarin, Maj. Yuri, **1965**: 318
    Leonov, Lt. Col. Aleksei, **1965**: 116
  Berlin blockade, **1965**: 37
  Brezhnev, Leonid, **1963–64**: 82; **1965**: 46
    [4]; **1966**: 516 [7], 577 [6]
  Burmese relations, **1966**: 450
  Business International roundtable, **1965**: 4
  Chairman of the Presidium, Supreme Soviet,
    Nikolai V. Podgorny, **1966**: 50;
    1967: 104 [8], 190, 472
  Change in leadership, **1963–64**: 669, 673, 676,
    678, 679, 680, 686, 688 [1, 8], 693,
    694, 734, 735, 736, 737, 745, 746,
    747, 750, 780 [23]
  Communication with U.S., **1963–64**: 395,
    413, 435, 504 [12], 607, 662n., 667,
    686
  Cooperation with U.S., **1967**: 495 [5];
    1968–69: 676 (p. 1268)
    Arms control, **1968–69**: 14 (p. 26), 39
    (p. 98), 51 [13], 69, 288, 345, 349, 378,
    387, 392, 394, 425 [9], 467 [17], 474,
    531, 557 [6]
    Astronaut rescue, **1968–69**: 14 (p. 27), 288,
    387
    Civil air agreement, **1967**: 80 [2];
    1968–69: 14 (p. 26), 288, 387
    Communications
      Global satellite system, **1968–69**: 288
      "Hotline," **1965**: 20; **1967**: 59, 264
      [16], 297 [3]; **1968–69**: 14 (p. 26), 27,
      69, 647
    Consular convention, **1963–64**: 365; **1967**:
      3 (p. 10), 34 [1], 80 [2], 104 [11],
      119, 157, 225 [17], 519; **1968–69**:
      14 (p. 26), 288, 309, 387
    Cultural, **1966**: 483, 503; **1967**: 80 [2];
      1968–69: 288
    Middle East crisis, **1968–69**: 557 [11]
    Missile talks, **1968–69**: 69, 647 [8], 676 (p.
      1268)
    Nuclear weapons control, **1966**: 320 [19];
      1967: 373

Soviet Union — *continued*
  Cooperation with U.S. — *continued*
    Scientific exchanges, **1965**: 319 [5];
      1966: 483
    Space exploration, **1966**: 277 [13], 411, 483,
      485; **1967**: 425, 519; **1968-69**: 14
      (p. 26), 69, 288
    Water desalinization, **1963-64**: 420 [2], 435,
      480n., 695, 804; **1965**: 325
  Cuban activities.
    See Cuba.
  Czechoslovakian invasion, **1968-69**: 455, 462,
    467ftn. (p. 929), 472, 474, 676 (pp.
    1268, 1269)
  Disarmament, question of, **1963-64**: 170 [15],
    382; **1965**: 353 [5, 11]
  Economy, **1963-64**: 23, 218 [36], 531, 604,
    804; **1965**: 4n.
  Foreign policy, **1963-64**: 680, 686; **1966**: 483
  Foreign relations, **1967**: 347n.
  Gromyko, Andrei A., **1963-64**: 365; **1965**: 388
    [10]; **1966**: 249n., 516 [8, 17], 577 [6];
    1967: 279, 280, 282, 283
  India food aid, **1967**: 33
  INTELSAT participation, **1967**: 346
  Khrushchev, Nikita S.
    See main heading, Khrushchev, Nikita S.
  Kosygin, Aleksei N., **1963-64**: 737, 820;
    1965: 46 [4, 7], 412 [2]; **1966**: 8 [2],
    516 [17], 577 [6]; **1967**: 80 [2, 7], 104
    [8], 157, 264 [16], 279-283, 286, 312
    [13], 346, 554 [2]; **1968-69**: 14 (p.
    26), 51 [13], 169 [13], 288, 339 [14],
    349, 425ftn. (p. 862)
  Meeting with new leaders, **1963-64**: 780 [7];
    1965: 2, 22 [8, 10], 44, 46 [4], 156 [7]
  Middle East conflict policy, **1967**: 264 [3], 279
  Mikoyan, Anastas, **1963-64**: 26, 218 [7], 820;
    1965: 116
  Military strength, **1963-64**: 266 [10];
    1967: 59
  Missile strength, **1966**: 607 [16], 642 [15, 20];
    1967: 13 (p. 48), 157
  MOLNIYA telecommunications satellite system,
    1967: 346
  Nuclear activity, **1963-64**: 276n.
  Nuclear materials, production decrease,
    1963-64: 294 [19], 642; **1965**: 20
  Nuclear weapons.
    See main heading, Nuclear weapons tests.
  Reduction in military spending, **1963-64**: 129,
    130, 131
  Relations with Communist China, **1963-64**: 182,
    246 [11], 643, 686
  Relations with Germany, **1963-64**: 316 [25]
  Relations with West, **1963-64**: 109
  Release of U.S. flier, **1963-64**: 232 [2], 242
    [18, 26]

Soviet Union — *continued*
  Sale of gold, **1963-64**: 379 [6]
  Science and technology, **1963-64**: 804
  Space exploration, **1963-64**: 579, 709, 733;
    1965: 116, 117 [9]; **1966**: 50;
    1967: 157; **1968-69**: 14 (p. 26), 39 (p.
    99), 69, 288, 574
  Supplies for North Vietnam, transportation in
    Communist China, **1966**: 642 [13]
  Tchaikovsky International Music Competition,
    1966: 440
  Threat to Vietnam, question of, **1963-64**: 201
    [5]
  Trade, **1968-69**: 47 (p. 138), 204
    U.S., **1963-64**: 211 [11, 18, 24], 266 [11],
    294 [20, 22]; **1965**: 2, 4, 266; **1967**:
    16 (p. 80)
    West, **1966**: 6 (p. 3), 272
  Treaty with East Germany, **1963-64**: 400
  U.S. Ambassador Foy D. Kohler, **1963-64**: 365;
    1965: 319 [5]; **1966**: 474 [17]
  U.S. Ambassador Llewellyn E. Thompson,
    1967: 80 [2], 104 [11], 282;
    1968-69: 170
  U.S. Embassy in Moscow, attack on, **1965**: 59
  U.S. industrial research leaders, visit to,
    1963-64: 804; **1965**: 4
  U.S. relations with, **1963-64**: 26, 54 [18], 82,
    199, 211 [23], 242 [26], 271 [14], 272,
    285 [13], 294 [14], 529, 638, 662,
    674, 678, 680, 686, 693, 733, 737,
    788, 820; **1965**: 2, 44, 59, 235, 299,
    353 [11], 388 [10]; **1966**: 417 [13],
    483, 503, 516 [8, 17]; **1967**: 3 (p. 10),
    80 [2, 5, 7], 104 [11], 264 [16], 272,
    279, 280, 282, 286, 346, 554 [2, 4];
    1968-69: 14 (p. 26), 51 [13], 288,
    309, 339 [8], 472, 474, 585, 676
    (p. 1268)
  Vietnam policy, **1965**: 353 [7, 20], 388 [8, 10];
    1966: 474 [16], 577 [6], 607 [3, 6];
    1967: 104 [8], 204 [12], 264 [5], 554
    [2]; **1968-69**: 170
  Weather prediction and control, cooperation
    with U.S., **1963-64**: 705
  Wheat sales to, **1963-64**: 139, 211 [11]
    Longshoremen's boycott of shipment,
    1963-64: 195
  Wilson, Harold, visit, **1966**: 88 [25]
Soybeans, **1965**: 47, 168; **1966**: 62, 355; **1968-69**: 94
Spaak, Paul-Henri, **1963-64**: 608n.
Spaatz, Gen. Carl, **1963-64**: 487
Space Administration.
  See National Aeronautics and Space Adminis-
    tration.
Space Commission, Italian, **1963-64**: 807

Space Council.
See National Aeronautics and Space Council.
Space objects, U.N. agreement for rescue and
  return, **1967**: 557
Space research and exploration, **1963–64**: 91 (p.
  117), 132 (pp. 176, 182, 186, 191),
  162, 374, 399, 409, 572; **1965**: 2, 27,
  32 (p. 83), 81, 117 [9], 121, 196, 271,
  298, 302n., 303, 304, 310, 320, 391,
  448 [1, 3], 462, 463 [2], 636, 651,
  656; **1966**: 26 (p. 59), 134, 442, 485;
  1967: 13 (p. 50), 18, 76, 425, 533, 557;
  1968–69: 107, 145, 233, 507, 552, 574,
  616, 624, 646 [5], 660, 695
See also Rockets; Manned space flights;
  Satellites, earth; Space vehicles.
Appropriations, **1967**: 13 (p. 50), 328 [14],
  362, 533; **1968–69**: 646 [12]
Astronaut assistance and return agreement,
  1968–69: 14 (p. 27), 41, 288, 309, 387,
  662
Campaign remarks, **1963–64**: 650, 654, 695,
  703, 709, 713, 733, 734, 735
Dinner honoring program members, **1968–69**:
  616
International cooperation, **1963–64**: 493;
  1965: 81, 318, 333, 391, 463 [2], 659,
  660; **1966**: 209, 249, 260, 272, 277
  [13], 371, 461, 485–486, 546, 626;
  1967: 38, 157, 425; **1968–69**: 107, 662
Jupiter probe, **1965**: 659
Laboratories, manned orbiting, **1967**: 24
  Proposed, **1965**: 353 [10]
Man-in-space.
  See Astronauts; Manned space flights.
Mars, **1965**: 27, 81, 305, 391; **1967**: 13 (p.
  50); **1968–69**: 39 (p. 100), 107, 507,
  616
Message to Congress, **1963–64**: 155
Moon, **1966**: 26 (p. 59), 40, 50, 134, 209, 249,
  272, 277 [13], 371, 643; **1967**: 13 (pp.
  49–50), 24, 48n., 104 [18], 533;
  1968–69: 39 (pp. 99, 100), 107, 507,
  533, 574, 610, 611, 616, 637, 645, 646
  [9, 12], 647, 660, 662, 676 (p. 1264),
  678 (p. 1273), 695
See also main heading, Moon exploration.
News conference remarks, **1963–64**: 54 [12],
  211 [28], 504 [2]
Nuclear weapons, **1968–69**: 14 (p. 26)
Peaceful uses, **1963–64**: 493; **1965**: 333, 448
  [2], 463 [2]; **1966**: 249, 260, 371,
  411, 626
President's support, **1966**: 417 [15]
Report, **1966**: 40; **1967**: 24, 48, 220; **1968–
  69**: 41
Soviet, **1968–69**: 14 (p. 26), 39 (p. 99), 66,
  288, 574
See also main heading, Soviet Union.

Space research and exploration — *continued*
  Sun probe, **1965**: 659
  Technological value, **1968–69**: 41
  Treaty governing, **1966**: 209, 249, 272, 277
    [13], 411, 474 [18], 643; **1968–69**: 14
    (pp. 26, 27), 27, 41, 69, 288, 309, 335,
    349, 387, 504, 662, 676 (p. 1268)
  See also main heading, Space treaty.
  U.S.-Germany cooperation, **1965**: 659, 660
  U.S.-Italy cooperation, **1963–64**: 807
  U.S.-Soviet cooperation, **1966**: 277 [13], 411,
    483, 485; **1967**: 157
  Venus, **1968–69**: 107, 507
  X–15 program, **1968–69**: 610
Space Research Organization, European, **1966**:
  485n.
Space treaty, **1967**: 24, 38, 59, 80 [2], 220, 225
  [17], 425, 488, 491, 519, 557
  Signing, **1967**: 18
Space vehicles.
  See also Rockets; Satellites, earth; Space
    research and exploration.
  Apollo, **1963–64**: 211 [32]; **1966**: 26 (p. 59),
    485, 625; **1967**: 19n., 24, 48, 104 [18],
    533; **1968–69**: 39 (p. 100), 41, 574,
    616
  Explorer I, **1968–69**: 41
  Gemini, **1963–64**: 211 [32]; **1965**: 120, 121,
    134, 298, 310, 318, 448 [2], 459, 462,
    463 [2, 13], 636, 647, 651, 656; **1967**:
    24; **1968–69**: 574, 616
  Manned orbiting laboratory, **1965**: 353 [10],
    448 [1]
  Mariner, **1965**: 27, 81, 305, 345, 391
  Mariner IV, **1966**: 40, 249; **1968–69**: 616
  Mercury, **1968–69**: 616
  Mercury II, **1965**: 120
  Orbiter, **1967**: 13 (p. 50); **1968–69**: 107
  Ranger, **1965**: 81, 123; **1966**: 40, 249; **1968–
    69**: 107
  Ranger VI, **1963–64**: 518
  Ranger VII, **1963–64**: 492, 501n., 504 [2],
    518
  Soviet, **1965**: 116
  Surveyor, **1967**: 13 (p. 50), 24; **1968–69**: 107
  Surveyor I, **1966**: 249, 260, 371
  Voyager, **1965**: 81n.; **1967**: 13 (p. 50); **1968–
    69**: 39 (p. 100)
Spacecraft Center, Manned (NASA), **1968–69**:
  107
Spain, **1965**: 68n., 325, 600
  Ambassador the Marquis de Merry del Val,
    1966: 478
  Food aid, **1968–69**: 176
Spanish-Americans, **1966**: 577 [12]
Spanish Peaks Wilderness, **1968–69**: 122, 168
Spanish-speaking Americans, **1968–69**: 68, 91,
  437

Sparkman, Sen. John, **1963–64**: 453, 549;
  1965: 415; **1966**: 231; **1967**: 537;
  1968–69: 72, 199n., 278, 426
Spaulding, Asa T., **1968–69**: 3
Speaker of the House of Representatives (John
  W. McCormack), **1963–64**: 2, 11, 26,
  55, 172, 197, 218 [9], 224, 228, 333,
  341, 366, 527, 528n., 540, 799; **1965**:
  2, 45, 81, 107, 133, 157n., 183, 223,
  297, 302, 330, 394, 409, 413, 415, 534,
  546, 559, 568n.; **1966**: 23, 164n., 221,
  237, 334 [1], 345, 499, 523–524, 531,
  576, 599 [6], 628 [11]; **1967**: 3 (p. 2),
  32, 105, 169, 216, 217n., 236, 338,
  420, 460 [5]; **1968–69**: 14 (p. 25), 71,
  180, 212, 259, 390, 567, 654, 655, 658,
  676 (pp. 1263, 1270), 694
  Campaign remarks on, **1963–64**: 541, 542, 727
  Dinner honoring, **1965**: 42; **1967**: 7, 206;
    1968–69: 32
  Letters.
    See main heading, Congress, letters to
    Members of.
  News conference remarks on, **1963–64**: 54 [3];
    1965: 22 [14], 106 [9], 448 [10, 13]
  Veritas Medal of Providence College, **1965**:
    237
Spears, Judge Adrian, **1965**: 319 [22], 341
Special Committee on Veterans Facilities, **1965**:
  163
Special Drawing Rights, **1968–69**: 2, 47 (p. 137),
  76, 218, 317, 500, 684 (p. 1319)
Special Drawing Rights Act, **1968–69**: 218
  Signing, **1968–69**: 317
Special Panel on Federal Salaries, **1965**: 244, 612
Speech, freedom of, **1967**: 286, 495 [13]; **1968–
  69**: 360
Speech defects, **1968–69**: 111
Spellman, Francis Cardinal, **1963–64**: 174n.,
  224n., 662; **1965**: 223; **1967**: 270, 516;
  1968–69: 540
Spellman, Dr. Mitchell W., **1968–69**: 442
Spence, Brent, **1963–64**: 678
Spending, **1963–64**: 11, 91 (pp. 112, 113), 124
  (p. 157), 179, 295, 300, 606, 650, 669,
  775, 776; **1965**: 176 [3], 179, 183,
  194, 439, 487; **1966**: 30, 236 [8], 237,
  239–240, 296, 324, 333, 334 [2, 8],
  353, 371, 444, 453, 464, 472–473, 477
  [2], 501 [7, 20], 603; **1967**: 13 (pp.
  39–40, 43), 16 (p. 77), 329, 330 [1],
  362, 417 [1, 10], 518 [6], 556; **1968–
  69**: 14 (p. 32), 38, 39 (pp. 83, 89), 47
  (pp. 131, 133), 54, 223 [11], 229, 343,
  467 [3], 654, 676 (p. 1267), 677, 678
  (p. 1286), 684 (pp. 1313–1315)
  See also Budget; Defense spending.
  Congressional ceilings, **1968–69**: 678 (p. 1278)

Spending – *continued*
  Control, **1963–64**: 100, 216, 261, 295, 467,
    688 [6], 787, 790
  Defense funds statement, **1967**: 120
  District of Columbia, **1968–69**: 689
  Economic Report, **1965**: 35
  Increase, **1965**: 362; **1966**: 392, 417 [3], 444;
    1967: 6 [2], 13 (p. 42), 16 (pp. 76, 79)
  Job creation, **1965**: 2, 132
  June buying, **1965**: 267, 311; **1966**: 224
  Letter to the Speaker of the House, **1963–64**:
    240
  Message to Congress, **1963–64**: 132; **1965**: 32
  News conference remarks, **1963–64**: 54 [6, 10],
    71 [3, 10, 11, 16], 150 [3], 211 [9, 10,
    28], 256 [13], 271 [3, 7], 294 [4, 6],
    316 [4], 336 [3], 379 [3], 462 [2],
    619 [1, 2], 688 [2, 4, 6], 780 [4], 818
    [3]
  Overseas, **1963–64**: 753n.; **1965**: 60, 129, 319
    [8], 362, 638; **1968–69**: 1 [1, 15], 2,
    11, 47 (p. 135), 449
  Priorities, **1967**: 328 [23], 358 [12], 556
    Low priority, **1966**: 444, 445 [1, 12, 17],
      473, 492 [1], 494 [3]
  Reduction, **1963–64**: 18, 37, 54 [6, 10], 71
    [3, 10, 11, 16], 80, 121, 150 [3], 168,
    197, 211 [9, 10, 28], 218 [17], 222,
    228, 256 [13], 271 [3, 7], 294 [4],
    307, 316 [4], 336 [3], 362, 462 [2],
    477, 531, 603, 619 [1, 2], 630, 640,
    650, 652, 654, 655, 657, 659, 661, 679,
    688 [2, 4], 689, 723, 728, 749, 753n.,
    760, 818 [3]
    See also main heading, Cost reduction pro-
    gram, Federal.
  State and local, **1968–69**: 684 (p. 1315)
  Supersonic civil transport, **1963–64**: 294 [6]
Spiewak, Irving, **1963–64**: 480
Spivack, Robert G., **1966**: 338 [15]
Spivak, Alvin A., **1963–64**: 54 [18], 242 [26],
  266 [24], 271 [18], 379 [20], 486
  [16], 504 [16], 521 [13], 560 [16];
  1965: 46 [14], 117 [11], 295 [16];
  1966: 277 [25], 654 [14]; **1967**: 70
  [12], 309 [8]
Spoelhof, William, **1968–69**: 694
Sports, President's Council on Physical Fitness
  and, **1968–69**: 111
Sports, proficiency in, **1963–64**: 106, 401
Springer, Repr. William L., **1965**: 410, 551,
  568n.; **1967**: 474
Springfield, Ill., campaign remarks, **1963–64**:
  635
Sprouse, James M., **1968–69**: 566, 567
Sprout, Waldron, and Co., Inc., **1966**: 144n.
Spruce Knob, Seneca Rocks National Recreation
  Area, West Virginia, proposed, **1965**: 54

Sputnik, **1967**: 425, 533; **1968–69**: 39 (p. 99), 616, 646 [5, 9], 647
  Earth satellites, **1965**: 117 [9]
SRAM (short range attack missile), proposed, **1965**: 26
Sri Savang Vatthana, King, **1963–64**: 336 [8]; **1968–69**: 240
Srisdi Dhanarajata, death of, **1963–64**: 30
SR–71 reconnaissance aircraft, **1963–64**: 475 [1]; **1965**: 26, 339
SST.
  See Supersonic civil transport.
St. Germain, Repr. Fernand J., **1963–64**: 601; **1966**: 396
St. Francis Xavier Roman Catholic Church, **1968–69**: 499n.
St. John, Jill, **1963–64**: 751
St. John, Gospel of, **1967**: 319
St. John River Basin project, **1965**: 350
St. Lawrence Seaway, shipping, **1963–64**: 140
St. Lawrence Seaway, tonnage transit record, **1968–69**: 693
St. Lawrence Seaway Development Corporation, **1967**: 398; **1968–69**: 252
St. Louis, Mo., **1963–64**: 188, 189; **1965**: 510
  Campaign remarks, **1963–64**: 695
  Democratic Governors conference, **1967**: 296, 297
  Mayor Raymond Tucker, **1963–64**: 188, 189
  News conference, **1967**: 297
St. Louis Cardinals, **1967**: 429
St. Louis University, 150th anniversary, **1968–69**: 551
St. Luke, **1965**: 45
St. Mary the Virgin Church, London, **1963–64**: 263n.
St. Onge, Repr. William L., **1963–64**: 383
St. Patrick's Day, **1963–64**: 224
St. Paul, **1967**: 376, 570; **1968–69**: 612
St. Paul, Minn., **1965**: 189
  Democratic-Farmer-Labor Party Convention, **1963–64**: 433
St. Peter, **1968–69**: 540, 612
Staats, Elmer B.
  See main heading, Comptroller General (Staats, Elmer B.).
Staats, Mrs. Elmer B., **1966**: 113
Staebler, Neil, **1963–64**: 356, 357, 431, 562, 745; **1967**: 34 [8]
Stafford, Repr. Robert T., **1966**: 396–398
Stafford, Maj. Thomas P., **1965**: 647, 656
Staggers, Repr. Harley O., **1963–64**: 586; **1966**: 240, 427, 449, 576; **1967**: 474, 517, 520, 539; **1968–69**: 118, 125, 264, 418, 566
  Dinner honoring, **1968–69**: 567
Stainless steel flatware tariffs, **1967**: 428
Stalbaum, Lynn E., **1963–64**: 746

Staley, Oren, **1963–64**: 54ftn. (p. 68), 255
Stalin, Joseph V., **1963–64**: 686; **1968–69**: 50, 474
Stamp album, gift to President, **1968–69**: 630n.
Stamp program, food, **1967**: 63, 353, 405
Stamps
  Commemorative
    Adlai E. Stevenson, **1965**: 373, 504
    Dante, **1965**: 367
    Eleanor Roosevelt, **1963–64**: 35; **1965**: 504
    Verrazano-Narrows Bridge, **1963–64**: 581
  Crusade Against Cancer, issuance, **1965**: 154
  Documentary, taxes on, **1965**: 255
  Food stamp program, **1963–64**: 91 (p. 114), 219, 225, 235, 242 [12], 249, 266 [21], 267, 268, 297, 305, 314, 434, 546, 598, 620, 634, 757; **1965**: 47, 492; **1966**: 245, 520
    See also under Food.
  Postage, **1966**: 358, 500
  "Register and Vote," issuance, **1963–64**: 508
  Savings, **1966**: 472
Standard Code for Information Interchange, **1968–69**: 127
Standard of Living, U.S., **1963–64**: 51, 120, 124 (p. 164), 166, 212, 214, 280, 287, 289, 297, 313, 396, 434, 589, 745, 803, 811; **1965**: 35 (p. 106), 47, 164, 258, 511; **1966**: 26 (p. 49), 140, 240, 347, 388, 395, 398–399, 412–413, 418, 428, 430–432, 434, 437, 444, 451, 473, 479, 504, 520, 545, 610 [8], 637; **1967**: 57, 393, 420, 498, 505; **1968–69**: 14 (p. 27), 39 (p. 86), 678 (p. 1273)
  Campaign remarks, **1963–64**: 597, 598, 631, 694, 747
Standard Packaging Corp., **1965**: 222n.
Standards, National Bureau of, **1967**: 31n.; **1968–69**: 127, 133, 523
Stanford, Lt. James B., **1966**: 183
Stanford University, **1965**: 124, 446; **1967**: 540; **1968–69**: 108
Stanforth, James K., **1966**: 353
Stanleyville, Republic of the Congo, **1963–64**: 780 [2, 16]
Stanton, Frank, **1963–64**: 23, 211 [2]
Star route postal contracts, **1966**: 336
"Star-Spangled Banner, The," Francis Scott Key, **1965**: 95
Stark, Abe, **1963–64**: 668; **1966**: 511
Stassen, Harold E., **1963–64**: 285 [1], 287, 516 [11]; **1967**: 421
State, Department of, **1963–64**: 37, 150 [16], 175, 272, 480, 612, 621; **1965**: 106 [3], 209, 220n., 233, 268, 319 [14], 454 [2], 463 [8], 482, 487, 503, 511, 535, 546, 569, 618; **1966**: 26 (p. 60), 41, 45, 62, 124 [5], 320 [3], 474 [17], 478, 502, 629; **1967**: 10n., 157, 198,

State, Department of – *continued*
    344n., 346, 365n., 460 [1], 461, 478,
    518 [12], 568; **1968-69**: 15, 79 [6],
    149n., 155, 223 [6], 291, 648, 671, 691
  Appropriations, **1967**: 417 [1]
  Budget, **1963-64**: 818 [4]
  Employees, remarks to, **1963-64**: 26
  Foreign Policy Conference for Educators,
    1967: 272
  Foreign Service, **1968-69**: 454, 581
  News conference remarks, **1963-64**: 150 [16],
    462 [2], 818 [4]
  Personnel changes, question of, **1963-64**: 818
    [4]
State, Secretary of (Rusk, Dean), **1963-64**: 19,
    26n., 37, 49n., 58, 72, 75, 76, 102n.,
    107, 109, 134, 135, 140, 186, 194, 218
    [25], 227, 272, 280 [8], 313, 340, 358,
    400, 425, 426n., 428n., 429, 439, 445,
    471n., 479n., 489, 498, 513, 531, 608,
    616, 621, 632n., 675, 684, 686, 696,
    726, 766, 778, 795, 796, 797, 809, 816;
    1965: 7, 8, 12, 13, 15, 21, 26, 63n., 89,
    112, 119, 129, 136, 144, 159n., 169,
    185, 203, 221, 227, 250, 257, 260, 296,
    318, 320, 352, 355n., 370, 397, 418,
    421, 429, 433, 436, 438, 519, 535, 544,
    549, 569, 617, 624n., 632, 644, 660;
    1966: 22, 39, 45, 48, 85–86, 93, 100,
    126, 130, 133–134, 139, 142n., 174–
    176, 200, 214, 235, 243, 261, 270, 273,
    325, 341n., 343n., 370, 397, 407, 414,
    459, 486, 498, 503, 515, 519, 521, 531,
    550–551, 561–562, 565, 567–568, 570,
    609, 622, 626, 638–639, 644–645;
    1967: 18, 71, 74, 80ftn. (p. 261), 116,
    134, 144, 147, 162, 189, 195, 219, 230,
    248n., 249n., 254n., 255, 256, 272,
    279, 280, 282, 283, 286, 287, 294, 348,
    356, 360, 390, 395, 409, 425, 426, 433,
    434, 446, 447, 449, 451, 454n., 461,
    480, 486, 488–490, 492, 519, 529, 545;
    1968-69: 1 [1], 2, 7, 18 [2], 29, 42,
    51 [5], 53, 62, 79 [9, 10, 12], 88,
    100n., 109, 115, 122, 124, 132, 133,
    137, 140, 143, 151, 153 [1, 10], 155,
    157, 159, 169 [20], 171, 181, 185, 187,
    205, 207, 211, 213 [8], 223 [1, 6, 10],
    232, 233, 271, 290, 291, 299, 301, 309,
    327, 349, 368, 371, 378, 383, 398n.,
    401, 422, 425 [4], 428, 434, 455n.,
    467 [1, 5], 476, 479, 494, 496, 522n.,
    524, 557 [1], 581, 585, 590 [1, 2],
    598, 603, 613, 618, 619, 669, 683, 688,
    690, 696 [19]
  Campaign remarks on, **1963-64**: 612, 622,
    656, 678, 680, 702, 709, 728, 733, 734,
    736, 741, 745, 746, 747, 749, 750

State, Secretary of – *continued*
  Communist China, proposed meeting with
    leaders, **1966**: 277 [17]
  Farewell reception for, **1968-69**: 681
  Letters to, **1965**: 233, 404
  Medal of Freedom, **1968-69**: 691
  Meeting with SEATO, report on, **1963-64**: 274
  Memorandum, **1965**: 661; **1967**: 186; **1968-
    69**: 15, 361
  News conference remarks on, **1963-64**: 54 [2,
    14], 71 [7, 9], 150 [13], 201 [5, 18],
    232 [6], 256 [2, 10], 266 [14], 271
    [12], 285 [1, 12, 13], 294 [15], 316
    [3, 16], 336 [6, 15], 379 [1, 11], 455
    [5, 16], 486 [3], 504 [4], 516 [14,
    19], 539, 563 [1, 5], 587 [5], 619 [8],
    688 [1, 8], 780 [5, 6, 8, 22], 818 [4];
    1965: 46 [6], 106 [3, 6], 117 [11],
    156 [6], 208 [10], 295 [16], 319 [12,
    14], 347 [2, 6], 353 [22], 388 [1, 13,
    14], 412 [2, 4], 448 [2, 15, 20, 21],
    463 [1, 2, 4, 5, 8, 9], 641 [2]; **1966**:
    8 [2, 17], 52 [1–3], 65 [3, 6], 88 [15–
    17, 21, 24], 124 [2, 5, 11], 141 [1, 7,
    12, 16], 158 [3, 4], 236 [1, 5], 247
    [8], 277 [2], 320 [6], 334 [1], 373
    [2], 445 [25], 477 [6], 501 [1], 516
    [11], 577 [6], 580 [3], 607 [2, 8, 10],
    610 [8], 635 [14]; **1967**: 34 [1], 70
    [1, 3, 4, 7], 104 [2, 10], 132 [8, 11],
    204 [2], 223 [8, 12], 225 [2], 264
    [20], 328 [25], 358 [10], 375 [1, 2],
    460 [7], 495 [13, 14], 554 [1, 5, 8]
  Report, **1965**: 321n.
  Report on East-West Center in Hawaii, **1963-
    64**: 336 [6]
  Resignation, question of, **1966**: 88 [23]
  Responsibilities, **1963-64**: 519
  Visit to Vietnam, **1963-64**: 316 [16]
State Aviation Officials, National Association,
    1963-64: 215
State Colleges and Universities, Association of,
    1967: 490n.
State Commissions on the Status of Women,
    Conference of, **1966**: 299
State Committees on Criminal Administration,
    Conference of, **1966**: 491, 492 [1], 526
State Employment Service, **1968-69**: 86
State Regional Commission, Federal-, **1963-64**:
    300
State School Officers, Council of Chief, **1966**:
    165; **1967**: 182n.; **1968-69**: 219n.
State Technical Services Act of 1965, **1965**: 513;
    1967: 148
State Technical Services Program, **1965**: 35 (p.
    116)
State of the Union Message, **1963-64**: 91; **1965**:
    2; **1966**: 6; **1967**: 3; **1968-69**: 14. 676

State of the Union Message – *continued*
  Comments on, **1965**: 18, 30, 105, 118, 125;
    1966: 8 [10], 121 [2, 8], 241, 474
    [14], 607 [1, 13]; **1967**: 11, 70 [3],
    77, 104 [3], 121, 124, 138, 148; **1968–
    69**: 19, 26, 32, 37, 51 [2], 63, 85, 264,
    441, 622, 646 [3, 7, 14], 654, 658
  News conference remarks, **1963–64**: 818 [1]
State Universities and Land-Grant Colleges,
    Association of, **1963–64**: 482n.; **1967**:
    490n.
Statehood, Hawaii, fifth anniversary, **1963–64**:
    534
Statements by the President.
  See also Joint statements with foreign leaders;
    Legislation, remarks or statements upon
    approval.
  Abu Simbel Egyptian temples, preservation,
    1967: 198
  Adenauer, Konrad, death, **1967**: 181
  Administrative Conference of the United
    States, **1968–69**: 208
  Agriculture message to Congress, **1965**: 46 [1]
  Aircraft, world speed record, **1965**: 219
  Airlines labor dispute, **1966**: 322
  Alabama
    Telegram to Governor, **1965**: 117 [1]
    Voter registration in, **1965**: 46 [3], 106 [1]
  Alliance for Progress, **1966**: 125
  Alliance for Progress, Inter-American Com-
    mittee on the, **1963–64**: 769
  American National Red Cross, support, **1968–
    69**: 121
  Antarctic Policy Group, report of, **1965**: 220
  Antipoverty program, **1965**: 24, 224, 288
  Appalachian programs, **1966**: 123
    Highway construction, **1965**: 245
  Appointments, **1965**: 117 [3], 208 [6], 319
    [10], 353 [3, 4], 388 [3, 4], 395 [1],
    448 [4–7], 463 [8, 9], 476, 485, 620
    Driver, William J., **1963–64**: 815
    Hand, Lloyd Nelson, **1963–64**: 819
    Horne, John E., **1963–64**: 814
  Appropriation bills, House action on, **1963–64**:
    455 [1]
  Arms Control and Disarmament Act, **1966**:
    480
  Arts and the Humanities, National Foundation
    on the, proposed, **1965**: 105
  Asia
    Development, **1966**: 88 [1]
    Visit, **1966**: 516 [1]
  Asian Development Bank
    Charter signing, **1965**: 637
    U.S. participation, **1965**: 628
  Astronaut rescue, U.N. agreement, **1967**: 557
  Athletic achievements, U.S., **1963–64**: 401
  Atomic Energy Commission budget, **1967**: 98

Statements by the President – *continued*
  Atomic energy program, **1965**: 319 [5]
  Attlee, Clement, death, **1967**: 422
  Austin, Texas, housing project, **1968–69**: 435
  Australia, science mission to, **1968–69**: 513
  Automobile industry dispute
    Negotiations, **1963–64**: 455 [3]
    New labor contracts, **1963–64**: 624
  Automobile prices, **1968–69**: 485, 492
  Automobile products, U.S.-Canada agreement
    on, **1965**: 575
  Balance of payments, **1968–69**: 1 [1], 2, 449
    Deficit, **1965**: 319 [8]
    Report, **1963–64**: 753
  Bartlett, Sen. E. L., death, **1968–69**: 621
  Baruch, Bernard M., death of, **1965**: 327
  Bethlehem Steel Co., price increase, **1965**: 663
  Big Thicket, Texas, preservation, **1968–69**: 702
  Bridge safety task force, **1967**: 558
  British pound devaluation, **1967**: 497
  Brown, Repr. Clarence J., death of, **1965**: 441
  Budget
    Deficit reduction, **1965**: 319 [6]
    Fiscal 1967, **1966**: 334 [1], 630 [2]
    Surplus, forecast, **1968–69**: 632
  Burkley, Vice Adm. George G., retirement,
    1968–69: 668
  California's plans under Equal Opportunity
    Act, **1963–64**: 580
  Cambodia, release of Americans, **1968–69**: 634
  Campaign tour, beginning, **1963–64**: 633
  Canal Zone dispute, U.S.-Panama, **1963–64**:
    232 [1]
  Career advancement task force, **1966**: 404
  Central American Common Market, **1966**: 254
  Central Intelligence Agency, relations with
    private voluntary organizations, **1967**:
    147
  Chaffee, Lt. Comdr. Roger B., death, **1967**: 19
  Chamizal Zone adjustment in El Paso, Tex.,
    1965: 487
  Chief Justice of the United States, nomination,
    1968–69: 509, 527
  Children, summer schools, **1966**: 632
  China, Communist, first nuclear device, **1963–
    64**: 675
  Churchill, Sir Winston S., death of, **1965**: 31
  Churchill Peaks, designation, **1965**: 583
  Civil defense, Federal, State, and local coopera-
    tion, **1968–69**: 196
  Civil disturbances, **1963–64**: 600
  Civil Rights Act of 1968, **1968–69**: 191 [1],
    192
    Senate passage of bill, **1968–69**: 126
  Civil rights bill, **1963–64**: 412
    Compliance, **1963–64**: 744, 792
    House approval, **1966**: 375
  Civil Service Commission, report, **1963–64**:
    168

Statements by the President — *continued*
 Coast Guard, procurement and construction
  appropriation approved, **1963–64**: 216
 College students, Federal aid, **1967**: 304
 Colorado River, desalination agreement, U.S.-
  Mexico, **1965**: 119
 Communications satellites, report to Congress,
  1963–64: 180; **1965**: 68
 Community development on site of National
  Training School, **1967**: 372
 Congress (89th), legislative record, **1965**: 173
 Congress, messages to.
  See main heading, Congress, messages to.
 Connally, Gov. John B., visit with, **1963–64**:
  281
 Conservation message, **1968–69**: 123
 Consular convention with Soviet Union, **1967**:
  34 [1], 119
 Cost reduction program, Federal, **1965**: 127,
  211, 274, 497, 512; **1966**: 464, 603,
  631
 Cotton insect pests control, **1963–64**: 758
 Crime and law enforcement, **1966**: 117, 491
 Cross, Maj. Carl S., death, **1966**: 259
 Cuban refugees
  Agreement covering movement to U.S.,
   1965: 601
  Resident applications, **1966**: 602
 Customs Bureau of, reorganization proposed,
  1965: 118
 Cyprus, Greece-Turkey dispute, **1967**: 521
 Cyprus crisis, U.N. Security Council resolution,
  1963–64: 206
 Czechoslovakia, Soviet invasion, **1968–69**: 455
 Davidson, Roy E., death of, **1963–64**: 450
 Defense cost reduction program, report, **1963–
  64**: 619 [2]
 Defense Department support of antipoverty
  program, **1965**: 288
 Defense expenditures, **1966**: 642 [4]
 Disadvantaged, National Conference on Educa-
  tion of the, **1966**: 238
 Disaster assistance
  In 1964, **1965**: 174
  Midwestern States, **1965**: 187, 193, 239
 Discount rates
  Raising of, **1965**: 639
  Reduction, **1968–69**: 445
 District of Columbia, **1963–64**: 16
  Crime, **1966**: 219, 354, 656
  Home rule, **1965**: 448 [10], 481
  Housing project, **1968–69**: 20
  Reorganization, **1967**: 307, 339, 341
 Dobie, J. Frank, death of, **1963–64**: 584
 Dominican Republic, **1965**: 216, 353 [2], 364
  Cease-fire, **1965**: 319 [4]
  Food and medical supplies for, **1965**: 293
  OAS contributions, **1965**: 218, 253, 463
   [4], 473

Statements by the President — *continued*
 Dominican Republic — *continued*
  Provisional Government, **1965**: 472, 484
  Renewed fighting, **1965**: 208 [7]
  U.S. forces in, **1965**: 212, 217, 295 [1], 342
 Drought in the Northeast, **1966**: 391
 Drug monitoring, international system, **1965**:
  202
 Drug reaction monitoring, worldwide, **1967**:
  214
 Dryden, Hugh L., death of, **1965**: 634
 Earthquake in Alaska, **1963–64**: 241
 Eastern Kentucky Emergency Program, **1963–
  64**: 41
 Economic development, regional, **1967**: 576
 Economic gains of 1964, **1965**: 23
 Economic issues, **1963–64**: 707, 708, 714, 722,
  723, 724, 730, 731, 739, 740, 743
 Economic Opportunity Act of 1964, passage in
  Congress, **1963–64**: 505
 Economic stability, **1968–69**: 404
 Economy
  Midyear review of the, **1963–64**: 455 [2]
  National, **1963–64**: 404, 463, 477, 619 [4],
   811; **1965**: 590; **1966**: 236 [8]
 Education
  Bills, **1965**: 137, 156 [2], 455, 457, 479
  Legislation, **1963–64**: 78
 Education, White House Conference on, **1965**:
  291
 Education Week, American, **1965**: 609
 Educational, Scientific and Cultural Materials,
  Agreement on the Importation of,
  1965: 292
 Educational opportunity for youth, **1965**: 10
 Educational programs, **1968–69**: 52, 640
 Eighteen-Nation Disarmament Committee,
  meeting with U.S. Representative,
  1967: 340
 88th Congress, legislative record, **1963–64**:
  620
 Electric power blackouts, **1967**: 253
 Elisabeth, Queen of Belgium, death of, **1965**:
  627
 Employment, **1963–64**: 791
  Statistics, **1965**: 408, 480, 490
 Engle, Sen. Clair, death of, **1963–64**: 486 [6]
 Equal Employment Opportunity, White House
  Conference on, **1965**: 384
 Equal Employment Opportunity Commission,
  anniversary, **1968–69**: 347
 European defense, **1966**: 506
 Excise tax bill, passage in Congress, **1965**: 319
  [3], 321
 Excise taxes, House action on, **1963–64**: 407
 Executive branch
  Policy-making position in, **1965**: 240
  Reduction of personnel levels, **1965**: 138

Statements by the President – *continued*
  Export Expansion Advisory Committee, establishment, **1968–69**: 422
  Export Expansion Council, National, **1965**: 465
  Exports of hides, skins, leather, **1966**: 592
  Family Breadwinners: Their Special Training Needs, report, **1963–64**: 160
  Federal cost reduction program, **1965**: 127, 211, 274, 497, 512
  Federal Council for Science and Technology, enlargement, **1967**: 478
  Federal education programs, signing of Executive order, **1963–64**: 683
  Federal programs, deferred funds, **1967**: 120
  Federal research grants to universities, **1965**: 225, 522
  Federal taxes, report, **1965**: 505
  Firearms control, **1966**: 364
  Fiscal policy, **1966**: 445 [1], 477 [2]
  Fogarty, Repr. John E., death, **1967**: 2
  Food, Drug, and Cosmetic Act, 30th anniversary, **1968–69**: 336
  Food marketing report, **1966**: 294
  Food for peace program, **1965**: 139
  Food stamp program, **1966**: 245
    Extension, **1965**: 492
  Foreign affairs consultants, meeting with, **1963–64**: 696
  Foreign aid bill, **1968–69**: 394
  Foreign assistance, proposed reduction in funds for, **1963–64**: 45
  Foreign Assistance Appropriation Act, House passage, **1965**: 502
  Foreign assistance programs, interdepartmental committee to review, **1963–64**: 69
  Foreign Service
    Change in, **1963–64**: 621
    Personnel system, **1968–69**: 581
  Foreign trade policy, **1968–69**: 680
  Freedom Share savings note, **1967**: 66
  Frei, President Eduardo, visit, **1966**: 649
  Gagarin, Col. Yuri, death, **1968–69**: 161
  Garner, John Nance, death, **1967**: 471
  Gemini space flights, **1965**: 121, 448 [2], 463 [2], 636, 647
    Final flight, **1966**: 618
    No. 8, safe return, **1966**: 135
  General Electric Co., labor dispute, **1966**: 496
  General Motors Corp., strike, **1963–64**: 687, 733, 780 [3]
  Geneva disarmament conference, **1963–64**: 395
    Resumption of meetings, **1963–64**: 130; **1965**: 353 [5], 463 [7]
  German Ambassador, meeting with, **1965**: 57
  Germany, pollution control, **1966**: 88 [9]
  Gestido, Oscar, death, **1967**: 523

Statements by the President – *continued*
  GI bill of rights, 20th anniversary, **1963–64**: 419
  Government, cost of, **1963–64**: 619 [1]
  Government employees
    Constitutional rights, upholding of, **1965**: 128
    Education, **1967**: 184
    Ethical standards, **1965**: 241
    Executive assignments, **1966**: 619
    Health service programs, **1965**: 324
    Incentive awards program, report, **1965**: 540
    Mentally retarded persons, **1965**: 140
    Mission SAFETY–70, **1966**: 75, 291
    Pay, **1967**: 140
    Reduction, **1965**: 319 [9]
    Safety policy, **1965**: 73; **1967**: 265
  Government employment of minority groups, **1963–64**: 812
  Government services, **1966**: 88 [12]
  Government-wide planning and budgeting system, **1965**: 447, 448 [3]
  Grains Arrangement, International, **1967**: 476
  Great Society, **1963–64**: 776
  Green, Theodore Francis, death, **1966**: 230
  Green, Repr. William J., death of, **1963–64**: 63
  Grissom, Lt. Col. Virgil I., death, **1967**: 19
  Gross national product and income, **1963–64**: 459
  Guatemala, presidential inauguration, **1966**: 277 [6]
  Gulf of Tonkin patrols, **1963–64**: 497
  Gun control bill, **1968–69**: 302, 316, 324, 333, 530
  Gursel, President Cemal, return to Turkey, **1966**: 146
  Handicapped children, task force, **1966**: 317
  Hawaii statehood, fifth anniversary, **1963–64**: 534
  Head Start project, **1965**: 323
  Health, Education, and Welfare, Department of, report, **1965**: 184
  Health, education, and welfare programs, **1968–69**: 640
    District of Columbia, **1968–69**: 20
  Health, National Institutes of, report on, **1965**: 115
  Health, White House Conference on, **1965**: 424
  Health Insurance Benefits Advisory Council, approval of appointment of members, **1965**: 611
  Health Manpower, National Advisory Commission on, **1966**: 208, 301
  Health manpower shortage, **1966**: 490
  Health programs, **1965**: 6

Statements by the President – *continued*
Health Sciences, International Center for Advanced Study in the, **1967**: 217
Herbert Hoover National Historic Site, **1965**: 498
Herter, Christian A., death, **1966**: 655
Higher education bill, **1965**: 455, 457, 479
Higher Education Facilities Act of 1963
Senate passage of Conference report on, **1963–64**: 36
Highway safety, Labor Day weekend, **1966**: 423
Hill, Sen. Lister, retirement, **1968–69**: 22
Holt, Harold E., death, **1967**: 550
Hoover, Herbert, death of, **1963–64**: 692
Honolulu Conference, **1968–69**: 401
Housing
Austin, Texas, **1968–69**: 435
Committee on Urban Housing, report, **1968–69**: 704
Congressional approval of bill, **1968–69**: 319, 380, 382
Construction, **1967**: 88
District of Columbia, **1968–69**: 20
Low income, **1966**: 277 [1]
Mortgages, **1966**: 642 [3]
Housing bills, House action on, **1965**: 319 [2], 337
Human Rights Year, establishment of Commission, **1968–69**: 42
Hurricane Hilda, **1963–64**: 647
Hurricane inspection trip to Florida and Georgia, **1963–64**: 567
Immigration bill, **1965**: 398
Immigration report, Attorney General Kennedy, **1963–64**: 115
Independence Day, **1967**: 301; **1968–69**: 358
India
Food shortage, **1966**: 52 [1]
Livestock feed relief, **1967**: 138
Wheat shipments, **1967**: 375 [21]
Industry gains, 1961–64, **1963–64**: 697
Insurance in Riot-Affected Areas, President's National Advisory Panel on, report, **1968–69**: 36
Interest rates, **1966**: 419
International Agency for Research on Cancer, U.S. participation, **1965**: 343
International Atomic Energy Agency, U.S. support of, **1963–64**: 29
International Cooperation, White House Conference on, **1967**: 157
International Cooperation Year (1965), observance of, **1965**: 96
International Development Association bill, House action on, **1963–64**: 346
International Labor Organization, Convention 122, employment policy, **1966**: 250

Statements by the President – continued
International monetary cooperation, **1963–64**: 780 [3]
International situation, Cabinet review, **1965**: 319 [12]
Iran, AID program, **1967**: 509
Italian San Marco satellite, launching of, **1963–64**: 807
Japan-Korea basic relations treaty, **1965**: 657
Jenkins, Walter, resignation of, **1963–64**: 671
Job Corps conservation camps, **1965**: 208 [5]
Job development program, **1965**: 38, 79
John E. Fogarty International Center for Advanced Study in the Health Services, establishment, **1968–69**: 408
June buying, **1965**: 311
Kashmir dispute between India and Pakistan, **1965**: 463 [5]
Cease-fire agreements, **1965**: 524
Keller, Helen, death, **1968–69**: 285
Kennedy, John F., 4th anniversary of assassination, **1967**: 501
Kennedy, Sen. Robert F., assassination, **1968–69**: 292, 294
Kennedy Round trade negotiations, **1967**: 224
King, Rev. Martin Luther, Jr., assassination, **1968–69**: 179
King Paul I, death of, **1963–64**: 209
Komarov, Vladimir, death, **1967**: 190
Korea
Basic relations treaty with Japan, **1965**: 427
Institute for Industrial Technology and Applied Science, **1965**: 407
U.S. scientific mission to, **1965**: 344
Labor Day, **1963–64**: 558; **1965**: 488, 489; **1966**: 429; **1967**: 354, 376; **1968–69**: 463
Labor-management relations, **1963–64**: 85
Lake Barkley State Park, Ky., **1966**: 352
Lands for model communities, **1967**: 531
Latin America, multinational science and technology program, **1967**: 473
Latin American conference.
See Punta del Este meeting of American Chiefs of State.
Law Enforcement and Administration of Justice, President's Commission on, **1965**: 382
Law enforcement and crime, **1966**: 117, 491
Lawrence, David L., death, **1966**: 623
Lead and zinc imports, proclamation on, **1965**: 577
League of United Latin American Citizens, anniversary, **1968–69**: 68
Lehman, Herbert H., death of, **1963–64**: 25
Libraries, President's Committee on, **1966**: 424
Lie, Trygve, death, **1968–69**: 650

Statements by the President — *continued*
  Lincoln, Abraham, anniversary of birth,
    1966: 66
  Longshoreman's strike, **1968–69**: 636
  Los Angeles
    Federal aid, **1965**: 453
    Restoration of order, **1965**: 426
  Louisiana, declaration as major disaster area,
    1963–64: 618
  Lovelace, Dr. W. Randolph, II, death of,
    1965: 652
  Luce, Henry, death, **1967**: 75
  Maas, Maj. Gen. Melvin J., death of,
    1963–64: 260
  MacArthur, Gen. Douglas, death of,
    1963–64: 247
  Manila Conference, **1966**: 516 [1]
  Manned orbiting laboratory, **1965**: 448 [1]
  Manpower Conservation, Task Force on,
    1963–64: 89
  Manpower control and utilization program,
    Federal, **1963–64**: 38
  Manpower programs, **1968–69**: 444
  Manpower resources, report, **1965**: 99
  Maritime labor dispute, **1965**: 58, 65
    Settlement, **1965**: 463 [3]
  Martin, Joseph W., Jr., death, **1968–69**: 120
  Mayo, Dr. Charles W., death, **1968–69**: 415
  McNaughton, John T., death, **1967**: 316
  Meat inspection bill, **1967**: 522
  Medical cooperation, U.S.-Japan, **1965**: 175,
    214
  Medical research, **1966**: 293
  Medicare
    First anniversary, **1967**: 298
    Second anniversary, **1968–69**: 346
    Program, inauguration, **1966**: 309
  Medicare bill
    Committee action, **1965**: 122
    Passage by Senate, **1963–64**: 552; **1965**: 348
  Memphis, Tenn., disorders, **1968–69**: 166
  Mentally retarded, Federal employment,
    1965: 140
  Mexican American Affairs, Inter-Agency Com-
    mittee on, recommendations,
    1968–69: 91
  Meyer, Albert Cardinal, death of, **1965**: 180
  Middle East conflict
    National Security Council committee,
      1967: 255
    Rising tensions, **1967**: 233
    United Nations cease-fire vote, **1967**: 254
    Victims, relief, **1967**: 287, 510
  Military personnel
    Christmas mail for servicemen in Asia,
      1965: 573
    Effective use of, **1965**: 395 [2]
    Parachute jumping, incentive pay for hazard-
      ous duty involving, **1965**: 633

Statements by the President — *continued*
  Mine disaster, Mannington, West Va.,
    1968–69: 607
  Mobilization for Youth program, New York
    City, **1963–64**: 451
  Model cities
    Program, **1966**: 207, 297, 356
    Senate committee action, **1967**: 370
  Monetary Arrangements, International Advisory
    Committee on, meeting with, **1965**: 365
  Monetary System, International, **1965**: 451
  Moon photographs sent to other nations,
    1963–64: 518
  Moyers, James H., death, **1966**: 465
  Murrow, Edward R., death of, **1965**: 208 [8]
  Narcotic and drug abuse, **1963–64**: 458
  National Aeronautics and Space Administration,
    10th anniversary, **1968–69**: 507
  National Alliance of Businessmen, **1968–69**: 92
  National Council on the Humanities, members,
    1968–69: 61
  National Defense Education Act, 10th anni-
    versary, **1968–69**: 473
  National First Voters Week, **1963–64**: 706
  National Gallery of Art construction gift,
    1967: 470
  National Library Week, 1964, **1963–64**: 254
  National park system, additions to, **1968–69**:
    707
  Natural beauty in America, joint report on,
    1965: 545
  Natural gas pipeline safety bill, **1968–69**: 338
  Negroes
    Social and economic conditions, **1968–69**:
      423
      Report, **1967**: 463
  Neighborhood Youth Corps, **1965**: 86, 195
    Disaster work, **1965**: 193, 239
    Report on first project, **1965**: 67
  New Haven Railroad, aid, **1967**: 542
  Nigeria
    Assistance, **1968–69**: 381, 580
    Truce, support of, **1968–69**: 639
  Nimitz, Fleet Adm. Chester W., death,
    1966: 80
  Noise in the environment, **1968–69**: 577
  North Atlantic Alliance, **1965**: 507
  North Atlantic Treaty Organization, **1966**: 163
  North Pacific fisheries, U.S.-Canada-Japan
    negotiations, **1963–64**: 559
  North Vietnam attacks on U.S. vessels,
    1963–64: 497
  Northeast drought, **1966**: 391
  Nuclear fuel reprocessing, **1966**: 179
  Nuclear nonproliferation treaty, **1967**: 367;
    1968–69: 16, 531
  Nuclear rocket and research facilities,
    1967: 76

Statements by the President — *continued*
Nuclear task force, U.S., first round-the-world cruise, **1963–64**: 619 [5]
Nuclear test ban treaty, first anniversary, **1963–64**: 486 [1], 653
Nuclear weapons
Latin America, treaty for prohibition, **1968–69**: 73
Spread of, **1965**: 28, 430
Ohio River Basin flood, **1963–64**: 217
Oil spills, national contingency plan, **1968–69**: 586
Older Americans, Advisory Committee on, **1965**: 642
Older citizens of low income, aid for, **1965**: 461
Olympic team, U.S. congratulations, **1968–69**: 571
On-the-job training, **1966**: 422
Oppenheimer, Dr. J. Robert, death, **1967**: 62
Organization of American States, meeting, **1963–64**: 486 [3]
Organized crime and racketeering, report by Attorney General Kennedy, **1963–64**: 90
Overseas program, economic operation of, **1965**: 129
Pacific Islands, meeting with High Commissioner of the Trust Territory, **1967**: 133
Pan American Society's Gold Medal Award, **1968–69**: 665
Panama treaty negotiations with U.S., **1965**: 532
Parachute jumping, incentive pay for hazardous duty involving, **1965**: 633
Paris peace talks, **1968–69**: 178, 223 [1], 275 [1], 606, 682
Patent system report, **1966**: 637
Peace Corps
4th anniversary, **1963–64**: 759
School-to-school program, **1966**: 332
Pearson, Prime Minister Lester B., retirement, **1967**: 543
Photography program of the White House, **1965**: 16
Plant closings, task forces to assist communities with, **1963–64**: 690
Pool, Repr. Joe R., death, **1968–69**: 385
Pope Paul VI, visit with, **1967**: 571
Postal organization, **1968–69**: 391
Postal Organization, Commission on, **1967**: 168
Power failure in Northeastern States, report, **1965**: 640
Powerplant site selection, report, **1968–69**: 653
Presidential appointments, **1963–64**: 777
Presidential Unit Citation to the Vietnamese 42d Ranger Battalion, **1965**: 588
President's Commission on Law Enforcement and Administration of Justice, report, **1967**: 60

Statements by the President — *continued*
President's Committee on Consumer Interest, establishment, **1963–64**: 86
President's Committee for Traffic Safety, report, **1963–64**: 565
President's Council on Aging, report, **1963–64**: 178
President's Council on Physical Fitness, report, **1963–64**: 490; **1965**: 625
Price, Mrs. Margaret, death, **1968–69**: 405
Public higher education in the District of Columbia, **1963–64**: 457
Pueblo, U.S.S., release of crew, **1968–69**: 641
Puerto Rico, report on status of, **1966**: 372
Railroad labor dispute, **1963–64**: 251, 252; **1967**: 172, 188
Settlement, **1963–64**: 284
Report, **1968–69**: 626
Ranger VII, flight of, **1963–64**: 492
Ranger IX flight to the moon, **1965**: 123
Rat extermination bill, **1967**: 318
Rent supplements, Senate committee action, **1967**: 370
Reorganization plans
Bureau of Prisons, **1966**: 633
Community Relations Service, **1966**: 60
Public Health Service, **1966**: 292
Rio Grande salinity control, U.S.-Mexico, **1967**: 47
Riots in New York City, **1963–64**: 468
Roberts, Roy, death, **1967**: 69
Rosh Hashanah, **1966**: 405
Roosevelt, Franklin D., 20th anniversary of death, **1965**: 182
Rural electric cooperatives, rate reduction by, **1965**: 313
Ryukyu Islands
Election of chief executive, **1965**: 658; **1968–69**: 44
Safe streets and crime control bill, **1967**: 530
San Salvador, departure, **1968–69**: 372
Sandburg, Carl, death, **1967**: 320
Saturn I, launching of, **1963–64**: 162
Saturn V rocket launch, **1967**: 483
Savings, personal, **1965**: 164
Savings bond program, **1968–69**: 10, 284
Savings bonds, interest rates, **1966**: 72
School desegregation, **1965**: 470
School dropouts, 1963 back-to-school campaign, **1963–64**: 84
Schools, aid for impacted, **1968–69**: 425 [2]
Science, strengthening academic capability for, **1965**: 514
Science Advisory Committee, President's
Appointment of new members, **1965**: 166
Report on pollution, **1965**: 602

[References are to items except as otherwise indicated]

Statements by the President – *continued*
 Science mission to Australia, **1968–69**: 513
 Screwworm eradication, Mexico, **1966**: 357
 Selective Service, National Advisory Commission on, **1966**: 315
 Selective Service System, study of, **1963–64**: 619 [3]
 Selma-to-Montgomery civil rights march, demonstrators in, **1965**: 104, 114
 "Share Your Summer" children's program, **1967**: 209
 Shastri, Lal Bahadur, death, **1966**: 5
 Shipping industry negotiations, **1963–64**: 494
 Ships, automated
  Manning disputes on, **1965**: 428
  Merchant vessel report, **1965**: 312
 Silver dollars, minting of, **1965**: 252
 Smallpox eradication, international program, **1965**: 262
 Smith-Hughes Act, anniversary, **1967**: 67
 Sniper attack in Central Park, New York City, **1968–69**: 356
 Social Security Act, 30th anniversary, **1965**: 425
 Social Security Amendments of 1965
  Benefits to young people, **1965**: 501
  House approval, **1965**: 176 [2]
 Social security beneficiary, 24 millionth, **1968–69**: 397
 Social security bill, Senate approval, **1967**: 505
 South Bend, Ind., closing of Studebaker facilities, **1963–64**: 67
 Southeast Asia
  Economic progress, **1965**: 199
  U.S. assistance to, **1965**: 176 [1], 295 [3]
 Southeast Asia, Joint Resolution on, passage by Congress, **1963–64**: 503
 Soviet Ambassador, meeting with, **1963–64**: 674
 Space exploration treaty, **1966**: 209, 643
 Space objects, U.N. agreement on return, **1967**: 557
 Space program report, **1967**: 48
 Space research, international cooperation, **1963–64**: 532
 Spellman, Francis Cardinal, death, **1967**: 516
 Staffing of international organizations, **1963–64**: 519
 State university presidents, meeting of, **1963–64**: 485
 Steel dispute, agreements, **1965**: 208 [3], 466, 483
 Steel prices, **1965**: 62, 226, 663
  Increases, **1968–69**: 425 [1]
 Steinbeck, John, death, **1968–69**: 638
 Stevenson, Adlai E., death of, **1965**: 356
 Stockpile disposal program, **1966**: 390
 Student grants, **1967**: 164

Statements by the President – *continued*
 Summer domestic programs, report, **1966**: 171
 Summer schools for children, **1966**: 632
 Supersonic civil transport, **1967**: 197
  Development, **1963–64**: 355, 789
 Surgery, plan to undergo, **1965**: 549; **1966**: 575
 Surveyor I
  Lunar photographs, **1966**: 260
  Moon landing, **1966**: 249
 Taras Shevchenko statue, sealing of documents in, **1963–64**: 720
 Tariff "escape clause" actions, **1967**: 428
 Tax bill
  House approval, **1968–69**: 326
  Senate approval of, **1963–64**: 176
  Senate committee action on, **1963–64**: 148
 Teacher Corps, **1967**: 183
 Television by communication satellite between U.S. and Japan, **1963–64**: 632
 Textile industry, **1963–64**: 717
  Economy, **1967**: 414
  New England States, **1963–64**: 602
 Thanksgiving Day, **1963–64**: 10
 Thomas, Repr. Albert, death, **1966**: 71
 Thomas, Norman, death, **1968–69**: 633
 Tijuana River flood control, **1967**: 303
 Tornado relief in Midwest, **1967**: 187
 Traffic safety bill, Senate approval, **1966**: 290
 Truman, Harry S., interest rate remarks, response, **1966**: 419
 Truth-in-lending bill, **1968–69**: 49
 24th amendment to the Constitution, adoption, **1963–64**: 145
 Unemployment
  Anaconda, Mont., **1963–64**: 99
  Decline in, **1963–64**: 386
  Statistics, **1965**: 156 [1], 165, 319 [7], 598
 United Arab Republic, U.S. relations with, **1965**: 46 [2]
 United Nations
  Meetings with U.S. Representative, **1965**: 395 [3]
  Twentieth anniversary, **1965**: 295 [2]
 U.S. Embassy in Saigon, bombing of, **1965**: 145
 U.S.-Israeli joint water desalting study, **1963–64**: 672
 U.S.-Mexico Commission for Border Development and Friendship, **1968–69**: 223 [2]
 U.S. officials held captive by Bolivian miners, **1963–64**: 52
 U.S.-Soviet agreement on exchange of weather information, **1963–64**: 705
 U.S.-Soviet Consular Convention, **1963–64**: 365
 U.S.S. *Samuel Gompers,* proposed destroyer tender, **1963–64**: 430
 Uranium, peaceful uses, **1966**: 48
 Urban Coalition, **1968–69**: 74

Statements by the President – *continued*
Urban programs, **1968–69**: 234
Coordination, **1966**: 380
Housing, **1968–69**: 704
Transportation, **1968–69**: 351
Veterans
Civilian health occupations, **1967**: 432
Employment, **1967**: 345
Hospitals, committee to review closing of,
1965: 163
Veterans Day, **1968–69**: 583
Vice presidential candidate, selection of,
1963–64: 489
Vietnam, **1965**: 130, 194
Agricultural Advisory Corps, **1966**: 331
Appropriations for military requirements in,
1965: 261
Bombing of the North, **1966**: 39
Conflict, **1968–69**: 51 [1]
Paris peace talks, **1968–69**: 178, 223 [1],
275 [1], 606, 682
U.S. veterans, civil service appointments,
1968–69: 67
Volunteer physician program of American
Medical Association, **1968–69**: 438
Development, **1966**: 274, 320 [1]
Health and education task force, **1966**: 106
Health and welfare needs in, **1965**: 469
Honolulu conference, **1966**: 52 [2]
Military situation, **1966**: 277 [7]
Negotiations proposal, **1965**: 208 [2]
Pacification programs, **1966**: 274
Political situation, **1966**: 236 [1]
U.S. dependents, withdrawal from, **1965**: 51
U.S. policy in, **1965**: 117 [2], 388 [1, 2]
Visit of Secretary McNamara and Ambassa-
dor Lodge, **1965**: 353 [1]
Vietnam, North, bombing by U.S., **1967**: 50
Vietnam, South, Constitution, **1967**: 129
Vocational rehabilitation, Federal-State pro-
gram, **1965**: 416
Voter participation in election, **1966**: 585
Voter registration in District of Columbia,
1963–64: 167
Voting Rights Act of 1965, compliance,
1965: 448 [9]
Voting rights bill, **1965**: 201
House action on, **1965**: 349
Senate passage, **1965**: 278
Wage-price stability in 1965, **1965**: 208 [4]
Walker, Joseph A., death, **1966**: 259
Wallace, George, disruption of speech,
1968–69: 360
Wallace, Henry A., death of, **1965**: 619
Water desalination, **1963–64**: 715
Water Desalination, International Symposium
on, **1965**: 325, 494, 547
Water Pollution Control Administration,
1966: 215

Statements by the President – *continued*
Water resource conservation, **1966**: 393
Water Resources Council, Ad Hoc, **1965**: 358
Waterman, Alan T., death, **1967**: 513
Wheat
Acreage allotments, **1966**: 203
Surplus reduction, **1966**: 281
Wheat-cotton and food stamp bills,
1963–64: 249
White, Lt. Col. Edward H., 2d, death,
1967: 19
White backlash, **1966**: 580 [20]
White House conferences
Education, **1965**: 291
Equal employment opportunity, **1965**: 384
Health, **1965**: 424
"To Fulfill These Rights," **1965**: 548;
1966: 88 [10], 408
White House seminars for college students,
1963–64: 428
White House staff, **1965**: 22 [1]
World Meteorological Day, **1966**: 143
Yemen agreement, **1965**: 463 [6]
YF-12A aircraft, world speed record, **1965**: 219
York, Sgt. Alvin, death of, **1963–64**: 553
Yoshida, Shigeru, death, **1967**: 437
Youth Opportunity Campaign, **1965**: 268;
1966: 172
Staten Island, N.Y., **1965**: 467
States.
See also Federal-State-local governmental re-
sponsibilities; Federal-State-local rela-
tions; *specific States.*
Appalachian area.
See main heading, Appalachian area; *specific
States.*
Charters for private organizations, **1965**: 508
Civil rights enforcement, **1966**: 6 (p. 3)
Commerce directors, remarks, **1967**: 148
Council of State Governments, **1963–64**: 178n.
Creative federalism, **1966**: 34 (p. 98), 416, 606,
607 [1]; **1967**: 13 (p. 57), 296
Credit, **1968–69**: 39 (p. 87)
Crime control, **1967**: 146
Cultural resources, **1967**: 53
Democratic Party strength, **1966**: 610 [13]
Depressed areas.
See main heading, Depressed areas.
Eastern Kentucky, **1965**: 195
Education, **1963–64**: 482; **1967**: 490
Education legislation seminars, **1963–64**: 78
Educational agencies, **1965**: 9
Educational facilities, **1966**: 650 [11]
Election laws, review of, **1963–64**: 57
Employees, **1966**: 34 (p. 98), 89, 111, 216, 499;
1967: 13 (pp. 53, 58), 121, 148
Employment, **1967**: 199; **1968–69**: 84, 100,
312, 406, 678 (p. 1303)

States — *continued*
  Federal aid.
    See main heading, Federal aid to States.
  Federal tax revenue sharing, **1966**: 121 [9], 635
      [19]; **1967**: 225 [21]
  Fiscal policies, **1963–64**: 730
  Governors, **1965**: 98, 119, 388 [14]
    See also main heading, Governors.
    Appalachian area, **1963–64**: 285 [2], 293,
      294 [2], 300, 711; **1965**: 103
    Meetings with the President, **1963–64**: 8,
      521 [2, 5, 7], 536
    Northeastern area, **1965**: 434
  Health programs, **1967**: 13 (p. 53), 223 [6]
  Health services, **1966**: 95
  Interstate business, taxes, **1966**: 121 [3]
  Jury selection, nondiscrimination, **1967**: 55
  Labor laws, **1966**: 6 (p. 5)
  Land development, Federal aid, **1965**: 90
  Law enforcement, **1968–69**: 14 (p. 30), 39 (p.
      107), 57, 59, 100, 202, 320, 678 (pp.
      1281, 1291, 1292)
    Assistance, **1967**: 35
  Legislative leaders conference, **1966**: 273
  Meat inspection, **1967**: 57, 541
  Middle Atlantic, **1965**: 358
  Midwestern, floods and tornadoes in, **1965**: 187,
      188, 189, 190, 191, 193, 215, 239, 477;
      1967: 187
  National Guard, **1965**: 26
    Integration in, **1963–64**: 816
  New England
    Resources development, **1965**: 350, 358
    Textile industry, **1963–64**: 602
    Transportation, **1967**: 223 [2]
  Northeastern
    Drought, **1966**: 391, 427
    Power failure, **1965**: 608, 640, 641 [1]
    Water problems, **1965**: 358, 375, 417, 418,
      434, 477
    Water resources, **1966**: 393
  Northwest-Southwest power transmission inter-
      tie, **1965**: 186
  Northwestern, **1963–64**: 134, 135
    Floods in, **1963–64**: 573; **1965**: 317, 477
  Public assistance, **1967**: 13 (p. 54), 16 (p. 83)
  Recreational facilities, **1967**: 203
  Revenue, **1966**: 34 (p. 99)
  Southern
    Electors from, **1963–64**: 266 [23]
    School desegregation, **1965**: 470
    Voter registration, **1965**: 448 [9]; **1966**: 66
  Southwest, water problem, **1963–64**: 294 [12]
  Spending control, **1966**: 124 [16], 492 [10],
      494 [9]
  Student aid, **1967**: 338
  Taxes, **1968–69**: 406
    State and local, **1966**: 121 [3]

States — *continued*
  University presidents, meeting of, **1963–64**: 485,
      513
  Utilities commissions, **1968–69**: 653n.
  Voting discrimination, **1965**: 104, 107, 108
  Western, Democratic conference, **1966**: 417
      [11], 418
  Withholding tax payments, **1963–64**: 197n.
Statistics.
  See specific entry.
Stats, Mrs. Herbert, **1963–64**: 208
Statue of Liberty, **1963–64**: 267
Stay-in-School Campaign, **1966**: 385;
      1968–69: 54
Steadman, Martin, **1966**: 512
Steam, geothermal, **1967**: 20
  Bill, **1966**: 614
Steed, Repr. Tom, **1966**: 410, 413, 415–416;
      1968–69: 292n.
Steel, **1966**: 141 [5], 206, 373 [4]; **1967**: 286
  Imports, **1968–69**: 427
  Prices, **1963–64**: 504 [16], 780 [5]; **1965**: 22
      [2], 35 (p. 111), 46 [14], 62, 226, 448
      [11], 663; **1967**: 375 [4], 518 [18];
      1968–69: 241, 425 [1, 3, 5], 427, 431
  Production, **1963–64**: 504 [16], 563 [6], 780
      [5]; **1965**: 208 [21], 226
  Profits, **1963–64**: 504 [16], 780 [5]; **1965**:
      226
Steel industry, **1965**: 62, 448 [11, 15], 459;
      1966: 373 [8]
  Employment, **1963–64**: 290, 780 [5];
      1965: 226
  Labor dispute, **1965**: 448 [11, 15], 454 [1, 3],
      463 [10, 12, 14], 466, 478
    Agreements, **1965**: 208 [3, 21], 483, 632
  News conference remarks, **1963–64**: 246 [19],
      780 [5]
  Unemployment, **1963–64**: 289, 295, 297
Steele, John, **1966**: 338 [5]
Steelworkers of America, United, **1963–64**: 289,
      290, 587 [9], 589, 780 [5]; **1965**: 208
      [3, 21], 226, 454 [1], 466, 483
Steffens, Lincoln, **1968–69**: 87
Stehling, Arthur, **1963–64**: 544
Stehling, Mrs. Arthur, **1963–64**: 544
Steichen, Edward, **1963–64**: 27
Steinbeck, John, **1963–64**: 568; **1966**: 350, 445
      [25]; **1968–69**: 638
  "Grapes of Wrath," **1967**: 114
Steingut, Stanley, **1966**: 511
Stellar, Raymond, **1965**: 288n.
Stennis, Sen. John, **1963–64**: 150 [12], 487;
      1965: 353 [13]; **1966**: 188 [11], 516
      [9]; **1968–69**: 169 [8]
  Vietnam conflict criticism, **1967**: 375 [3, 18]
Stephens, Repr. Robert G., Jr., **1963–64**: 330,
      716, 718

Stephens, Col. Robert L., **1965**: 219
Stephens, Roger F., **1963-64**: 784
Sterling, J. E. Wallace, **1966**: 257n.
Sternberg, Maj. Gen. and Mrs. Ben, **1966**: 348
Stevens, Col. Francis, **1966**: 328, 345, 547
Stevens, Capt. Francis R., Jr., **1966**: 328, 345, 547
Stevens, Roger I., **1963-64**: 266 [6], 524n.;
    1965: 177n.; **1966**: 226n.; **1968-69**: 601, 603
Stevenson, Adlai E., **1963-64**: 560 [16];
    1965: 176 [1, 3], 210; **1966**: 504;
    1967: 100, 532; **1968-69**: 53, 164, 210, 335, 460 [1]
    See also United Nations, U.S. Representative (Stevenson, Adlai E.).
    Commemorative stamps, **1965**: 373, 504
    Death of, **1965**: 355, 356, 359, 370, 371, 373, 376, 383
    Letter, **1963-64**: 161; **1965**: 273
    Memorial fellowships, proposed, **1965**: 374
Stevenson, Adlai E., 3d, **1965**: 504n.; **1966**: 228
Stevenson, Borden, **1965**: 504n.
Stever, Dr. Horton Guyford, **1966**: 637n.
Stewart, J. Harold, **1965**: 420
Stewart, Justice Potter, **1968-69**: 511
Stewart, Mrs. Robert J., **1963-64**: 289
Stewart, Dr. Sarah E., **1965**: 91n.
Stewart, Dr. William H., **1965**: 531; **1966**: 95, 190, 271, 292-293, 298, 301;
    1967: 57, 260, 477; **1968-69**: 468
Stickel, Lucille Farrier, **1968-69**: 138n.
Stigall, Lt. Col. and Mrs. Arthur D., **1967**: 485 [1]
Stigall, Susan, **1967**: 485 [1]
Stikker, Dirk, **1963-64**: 494n., 608n.
Stillman, Charles B., award for outstanding service to education, **1965**: 539
Stimson, George, **1968-69**: 696 [1]
Stimson, Henry L., **1963-64**: 294 [21], 747;
    1967: 70 [9]; **1968-69**: 227
Stipp, John E., **1967**: 420n.
Stock market, **1963-64**: 506, 530, 635, 636, 640, 695, 745, 750; **1966**: 445 [15], 501 [7];
    1967: 460 [12]
    Campaign remarks, **1963-64**: 604, 735, 750
    News conference remarks, **1963-64**: 211 [3], 246 [12]
    Rise, **1963-64**: 246 [12]
    Stockholdings, **1963-64**: 455 [2], 477n., 531, 555
Stock prices, **1966**: 141 [5]
Stockholm, Sweden, monetary conference, **1968-69**: 169 [17], 170
Stockpiles of strategic and critical materials, **1963-64**: 132 (p. 185); **1965**: 599, 617, 632; **1966**: 26 (p. 64), 34 (p. 103), 48, 139, 145, 173, 206, 218, 283, 390, 572,

Stockpiles — *continued*
    635 [2, 7, 15, 20], 636; **1967**: 16 (p. 87), 506; **1968-69**: 47 (p. 144), 483
    See also specific materials.
Stocks, **1968-69**: 47 (p. 129), 418
Stokes, Carl, **1968-69**: 141
Stone, Dewey, **1963-64**: 175
Stonewall, Tex., **1963-64**: 75; **1968-69**: 499n.
    Campaign remarks, **1963-64**: 544
Stoltenberg, Gerhard, **1966**: 486
Stolzenbach, C. Darwin, **1965**: 19n.
Storey, Robert, **1963-64**: 271 [4]; **1965**: 346, 400, 422n.
Story, Joseph, **1963-64**: 314
Straits of Tiran, **1968-69**: 474
Strassburg, Bernard, **1966**: 198n.
Straus, Roger W., **1968-69**: 78
Strauss, Nathan, **1968-69**: 426
Strauss, T. H., **1968-69**: 97
Strategic Air Command, **1963-64**: 475 [1], 610, 612, 685, 716, 783; **1965**: 26, 37
Strategic and critical materials.
    See also Stockpiles of strategic and critical materials.
    Procurement, **1963-64**: 703, 716; **1965**: 261n.
Strategic and Critical Materials Stock Piling Act, **1965**: 617; **1966**: 635 [2], 636
Strategic Service, Office of, **1967**: 502
Stratton, Julius A., **1965**: 115n.
Stratton, Repr. Samuel S., **1966**: 394-395
Straus, Michael W., **1966**: 232
Strauss, Mrs. Anna Lord, **1967**: 526
Strauss, Lewis L., **1965**: 420
Strecker, R. J., **1967**: 420n.
Strikes.
    See Labor disputes.
Stroessner, Alfredo (President of Paraguay), **1968-69**: 147, 148
Stroke, **1966**: 95, 156, 189, 395, 403, 436, 515; **1967**: 6 [15], 477
    Prevention, **1963-64**: 179, 268, 650, 656, 669, 733, 798; **1965**: 2, 5, 32 (p. 94), 52, 89, 154, 156 [3], 329, 330, 401, 406, 433, 551; **1968-69**: 39 (p. 103), 111, 536
Stroke, President's Commission on Heart Disease, Cancer and, **1963-64**: 179, 211 [6], 268, 617, 798; **1965**: 5, 343
Strong, Robert C., **1965**: 263n.
Stuart, Mrs. Robert J., **1965**: 422n.
Stubblefield, Repr. Frank A., **1963-64**: 643, 644; **1966**: 348
Studebaker Co., **1963-64**: 67, 288
Student Body Presidents National Advisory Committee, **1963-64**: 622n.
Student loan program, national defense, **1967**: 304n.
Students, **1963-64**: 622
    See also Colleges; Education; Schools.

Students – *continued*
  American Field Service, **1963–64**: 465;
      1965: 372; **1966**: 339
  Art, **1968–69**: 64
  Bilingual, **1968–69**: 4, 54, 68, 91, 437
  Campaign remarks on, **1963–64**: 622, 658
  Civic responsibilities, **1966**: 388
  College, **1968–69**: 14 (p. 31), 39 (pp. 104, 106,
      110); 47, (pp. 129, 143), 50, 113, 230,
      282, 459, 672, 676 (p. 1264), 678 (p.
      1293)
    Summer intern program, **1963–64**: 428;
        1965: 403
  College Students Registration Week,
      1963–64: 560 [1]
  Disadvantaged and handicapped, **1968–69**: 4,
      6, 26, 37, 39 (pp. 104, 106), 54, 133ftn.
      (p. 387), 164, 230, 493, 503, 678 (pp.
      1293, 1294)
  Dropouts, **1966**: 95, 111, 317, 385, 392, 580
      [7], 589; **1967**: 413; **1968–69**: 4, 6, 39
      (p. 106), 54, 113, 329, 568, 569
  Employment, **1966**: 26 (p. 68), 105, 171;
      1967: 378
  Exchange programs, **1963–64**: 280; **1965**: 36,
      519, 552; **1966**: 45, 177, 545, 557;
      1967: 143n., 344
  Federal aid, **1967**: 77, 148, 164, 338, 378, 413,
      423; **1968–69**: 14 (p. 31), 39 (pp. 106,
      110), 54, 320, 459, 473, 569, 678 (p.
      1293), 684 (p. 1322)
  Federal Government, relations to,
      1968–69: 570
  Foreign, **1963–64**: 313, 465; **1965**: 33, 36, 372;
      1966: 243, 312
  Grants, **1965**: 455
  High school, **1968–69**: 678 (p. 1294)
  Increase, **1965**: 340
  Job Corps participation, **1965**: 75
  Loan program, **1963–64**: 47, 53, 132 (p. 189),
      413, 676, 755; **1965**: 2, 5, 9, 100, 455,
      479, 539, 578, 603; **1966**: 3, 26 (p. 63),
      95, 111, 189, 265, 392; **1967**: 304, 338,
      490
  Lyndon B. Johnson Australian Science Scholars,
      1966: 545–546
  Military service, **1967**: 92
  Overseas travel, **1968–69**: 14 (p. 33)
  Political support of the President,
      1963–64: 622n.
  Protest movements, **1968–69**: 499, 696 [8]
  Selective service, **1967**: 205
  Senate Youth Program, **1966**: 35
    Participants, remarks to, **1965**: 48
  Sioux City, Iowa, sponsorship of commemora-
      tive stamp, **1966**: 358
  Suicides, **1967**: 285
  Summer trainee program, **1966**: 111, 172;
      1967: 201

Students – *continued*
  White House seminar, **1963–64**: 526
  Work-study programs, **1966**: 95, 111, 172, 189;
      1967: 13 (p. 55), 77, 304n., 378;
      1968–69: 39 (p. 106), 54, 678 (p.
      1294)
Students, Advisory Council on Insured Loans to,
    1966: 3
Study Commission on Statehood for Puerto
    Rico, **1963–64**: 242 [5]
Stulberg, Louis, **1967**: 342n., 484;
    1968–69: 270, 529
Stull, Lee T., **1963–64**: 26
Stumpf, S. Sgt. Kenneth E., **1968–69**: 487
Sturtevant, Alfred H., **1968–69**: 71n.
Submarines
  Missile equipped, **1966**: 387
  Names for, **1963–64**: 294 [21]
  Nuclear-powered, **1963–64**: 635; **1965**: 26;
      1967: 515
    Casimir Pulaski, **1963–64**: 515
    Daniel Webster, **1963–64**: 560 [5]
    George Washington, **1963–64**: 383
    Nautilus, **1965**: 17
    Pargo, **1963–64**: 383
    Polaris missile-equipped, **1963–64**: 383,
        449, 786; **1965**: 17, 26
    Poseidon missile-equipped, proposed,
        1965: 26
    Sam Rayburn, **1963–64**: 59, 786
    Vallejo, U.S.S., **1963–64**: 449
  U.S.S. *Scorpion*, **1968–69**: 275 [7]
Subsidies, Federal, **1963–64**: 211 [25];
    1966: 98, 193
Subway construction, **1967**: 20
Suez Canal, **1963–64**: 702, 728, 734, 736, 749,
    750; **1967**: 264 [14], 375 [22];
    1968–69: 474
Suffrage.
  See also Voting rights.
  Women, **1963–64**: 257
Suffridge, James A., **1966**: 315n., 431, 435,
    437; **1967**: 87n., 442
Sugar imports, **1965**: 429; **1966**: 125
Suicide, **1967**: 285
Sullivan, David, **1967**: 87n., 419n.; **1968–69**: 3
Sullivan, Ed, **1963–64**: 199
Sullivan, John L., **1966**: 397
Sullivan, Rev. Leon H., **1967**: 291
Sullivan, Repr. Leonor K., **1963–64**: 188, 189,
    546, 694, 695; **1965**: 361; **1967**: 393,
    405, 465; **1968–69**: 280
Sullivan, William H., **1963–64**: 455 [5]
Sullivan Law (New York), **1967**: 35
Sully, Thomas, **1968–69**: 648
Summer domestic programs, task force,
    1966: 105, 171–172
Summer schools for children, **1966**: 632

Summer Youth Opportunities, **1967**: 39
Summer Youth Opportunity Campaign,
    1966: 172, 385
Summersville, W. Va., **1966**: 427
  Mayor William S. Bryant, **1966**: 427
Summersville Dam, W. Va., dedication,
    1966: 427
Summitt, Robert M., **1963–64**: 645, 701, 702
Sun probe, **1965**: 659
Sunay, Cevdet (President of Turkey),
    1967: 109, 155, 158, 162
Sunay, Mrs. Cevdet, **1967**: 109, 155, 158, 162
Supersonic civil transport, **1963–64**: 132 (p.
    188), 201 [2], 242 [9], 294 [6], 355,
    789; **1965**: 32 (p. 89), 319 [19], 339;
    1966: 6 (pp. 6, 7), 26 (pp. 56, 61), 98,
    654 [12]; **1967**: 13 (pp. 48, 52), 31n.,
    197; **1968–69**: 39 (p. 102)
  Sale of planes to Israel, **1968–69**: 524n.
Supersonic Transport, President's Advisory Com-
    mittee on, **1963–64**: 242 [9, 17], 294
    [6]; **1965**: 339
Supplemental Appropriation Act
  1965, **1963–64**: 528n.
  1966, **1965**: 339n., 546n.
  1969, **1968–69**: 483n., 550, 689n.
Supplemental Defense Appropriation Act
  1966, **1966**: 18n.
  1967, **1967**: 14n., 159
Supreme Court of the United States,
    1963–64: 342, 780 [11]; **1965**: 301,
    317, 353 [3], 370, 371, 388 [4], 443;
    1966: 216, 235, 501 [13]; **1967**: 55,
    105, 263, 411 [8]; **1968–69**: 283 [12],
    339 [1], 467 [2], 631
  Chief Justice nomination, **1968–69**: 339 [2],
    425 [11], 467 [2, 5], 509, 527, 696
    [6]
  Decisions
    Church-state separation, **1963–64**: 271 [11]
    Reapportionment, **1965**: 295 [11]
    School desegregation, **1965**: 443
Supremes, The (singing group), **1967**: 281
Surcharge proposal.
  See Income taxes.
Surface mining reclamation bill of 1968,
    1968–69: 122
Surface-to-air missiles (SAM), **1966**: 642 [14]
Surgeon General (William H. Stewart),
    1967: 57, 260, 477; **1968–69**: 468
Surgery, the President's, **1965**: 549, 572n.;
    1966: 575, 577 [1, 4], 580 [2, 17],
    599 [4], 610 [1, 7]; **1968–69**: 696
    [1]
  Vice President's responsibilities, **1966**: 610
    [1]
Surinam
  Governor Lucien de Vries, **1967**: 178
  Minister President Johan Pengel, **1967**: 178

Surplus agricultural commodities.
  See Agricultural surpluses.
Surplus Federal lands, transfer to States,
    1963–64: 422, 534
Surplus property, disposal, **1963–64**: 81, 617;
    1965: 14
Surpluses.
  See specific commodity.
Surtax.
  See Taxes.
Surveyor spacecraft, **1966**: 249, 260, 371;
    1967: 13 (p. 50), 24; **1968–69**: 107
Survivors insurance, **1966**: 453; **1968–69**: 39
    (p. 105)
Suspects, interrogation of criminal, **1966**: 611
Sutherland, George, **1965**: 443
Sutphin, Robert F., **1966**: 246
Suttle, William W., **1967**: 23, 160, 286
Suwon, Korea, **1966**: 564
Swainson, John B., **1963–64**: 562
Swan, Dr. Lionel F., **1968–69**: 19, 442
Swanstrom, Bishop Edward E., **1965**: 302
Swarthmore, Pa., **1963–64**: 391
Swarthmore College, **1963–64**: 391
Swearing-in ceremonies
  Administrative Conference of the United
    States, Chairman, **1968–69**: 31
  Agency for International Development, Ad-
    ministrator, **1966**: 368
  Atomic Energy Commission, members,
    1966: 361
  Bureau of the Budget, Director, **1968–69**: 38
  Central Intelligence Agency, Director,
    1966: 310
  Civil Aeronautics Board, Chairman,
    1968–69: 125
  Commerce, Department of
    Secretary, **1967**: 268; **1968–69**: 115
    Under Secretary, **1967**: 512
  Community Relations Service, Director,
    1966: 51
  Comptroller General, **1966**: 113
  Consumer Affairs, Special Assistant for,
    1967: 200
  Council of Economic Advisers, members,
    1966: 44; **1968–69**: 76, 350
  Defense, Secretary of, **1968–69**: 104
  District of Columbia
    Commissioner and Assistant Commissioner,
      1967: 406
    Council, **1967**: 466
  Emergency Planning, Office of, Director,
    1966: 145
  Equal Employment Opportunity Commission
    Chairman, **1966**: 475; **1967**: 333
    Member, **1967**: 258
  Federal Power Commission, Chairman,
    1966: 97

Swearing-in ceremonies – *continued*
  Federal Reserve System, Board of Governors, member, **1966**: 115
  Health, Education, and Welfare, Department of
    Children's Bureau, Chief, **1968-69**: 329
    Secretary, **1968-69**: 253
  Housing and Urban Development, Department of, Secretary and Under Secretary, **1966**: 13
  Humanities, National Council on the, Chairman and members, **1966**: 101
  Humanities, National Endowment for the, Chairman, **1966**: 327
  Indian Affairs, Commissioner, **1966**: 193
  Justice, Department of
    Attorney General, **1967**: 105
    Deputy Attorney General, **1967**: 335
    Solicitor General, **1967**: 443
  Labor, Department of
    Assistant Secretary for Labor-Management Relations, **1967**: 97
    Assistant Secretary for Manpower and Manpower Administrator, **1966**: 275
    Under Secretary, **1967**: 97
  Peace Corps, Director, **1966**: 93
  Postmaster General, **1968-69**: 216
  Small Business Administrator, **1966**: 231
  State, Department of, Under Secretary, **1966**: 498
  Trade Negotiations, Special Representative for, **1967**: 142
  Transportation, Department of
    General Counsel, **1968-69**: 276
    Secretary, **1967**: 5
    Under Secretary, **1968-69**: 276
  United Nations, U.S. Representative, **1968-69**: 335, 515
Sweatt, Herman, **1968-69**: 631
Sweatt v. *Painter,* **1968-69**: 631
Sweden, **1965**: 68n.
Swedish Day picnic, Minneapolis, Minn., **1963-64**: 435
Sweeney, John, **1963-64**: 711n.; **1965**: 117 [3], 245; **1966**: 122 [2], 425
Sweeney, Robert E., **1963-64**: 679, 693; **1965**: 190
Swidler, Joseph C., Jr., **1965**: 608, 641; **1966**: 97
  Letter, **1963-64**: 803
Swift, Jonathan, **1966**: 482
Swing, Philip D., **1963-64**: 735
Switzer, Mary E., **1965**: 305, 416; **1966**: 192n., 198n.; **1967**: 413
Switzerland, **1965**: 68n.
  President Hans-Peter Tschudi, **1965**: 333n.
Swoboda, Frank, **1968-69**: 467 [17]
Swords, Very Rev. Raymond J., **1963-64**: 396

Swords Into Plowshares Award, **1968-69**: 310
Sycamore Canyon, **1968-69**: 122, 168
Sydney, Australia, **1966**: 544-545
Sydney (Australia), University of, **1966**: 545; **1967**: 1; **1968-69**: 453
Sydney (Australia) Morning World, **1966**: 545
Sylvester, Arthur, **1963-64**: 316 [2]; **1968-69**: 696 [1]
Symington, Sen. Stuart, **1963-64**: 188, 189, 263, 273, 487, 694, 695; **1965**: 394; **1966**: 22, 218, 283, 572; **1967**: 375 [1]
Symphony orchestras, aid to, **1968-69**: 64
Syncom communications satellites, **1963-64**: 180n., 632, 779n.
Syracuse, N.Y., **1966**: 393-394
  Mayor William Walsh, **1966**: 394
Syracuse University, **1963-64**: 499; **1966**: 394.
Syria, conflict with Israel, **1968-69**: 504
Szymanski, Frank Stanley, **1966**: 315n.

Tacoma, Wash., Mayor Harold M. Tollefson, **1966**: 536
Taconic Foundation, **1967**: 484
Tactical Air Command, 12th Air Force, **1968-69**: 12
Tae-an Myun agriculture demonstration center, Suwon, Korea, **1966**: 564
Taft, Robert A., **1963-64**: 612, 733, 747, 754; **1965**: 9, 183, 415; **1966**: 88 [17], 628 [13]; **1967**: 358 [10]; **1968-69**: 212
Taft, William Howard, **1963-64**: 560 [10], 590, 642, 734; **1965**: 101, 397; **1967**: 70ftn. (p. 224), 121, 281; **1968-69**: 138
Taft-Hartley Act, **1963-64**: 494n.; **1965**: 2, 258, 448 [16], 644
  See also Labor Management Relations Act.
Tafuna International Airport, Pago Pago, American Samoa, **1966**: 537
Taiwan.
  See China, Republic of; Formosa.
Talbot, Phillips, **1965**: 353 [4]
Talboys, Brian E., (New Zealand Minister of Agriculture), **1963-64**: 267
Talent for America's Progress (Operation TAP), **1966**: 619
Talent Search program, **1967**: 304n.
Talmadge, Sen. Herman E., **1963-64**: 330, 332, 336 [9], 716, 718, 719; **1968-69**: 110
Talmadge, Mrs. Herman E., **1963-64**: 330
Tamm, Quinn, **1967**: 382
Tanana River, Alaska, **1967**: 369
Tanner, N. Eldon, **1963-64**: 737
Taos County, N. Mex., **1967**: 452

Tape, Gerald F., **1966**: 277 [5]
Tariff Commission, United States, **1963–64**: 80;
    1965: 353 [4], 577; **1966**: 43;
    1967: 99, 414, 428, 508; **1968–69**: 562,
    671
  Chairman (Stanley R. Metzger), **1968–69**:
    562n.
Tariff Schedules of the United States, **1966**: 43,
    600
  Amendments, **1968–69**: 558, 562
Tariffs, **1967**: 175, 294; **1968–69**: 562
  See also Trade, international; *specific*
    commodities.
  American selling price system, **1968–69**: 274,
    275 [2]
  Automotive products, **1965**: 21, 22 [9], 147,
    574, 575
  Customs conventions, **1968–69**: 261, 558
  Developing nations, preference for,
    1968–69: 47 (p. 138)
  Educational materials, **1965**: 292; **1966**: 45
  "Escape clause" actions, **1967**: 428
  Geneva conference, **1963–64**: 400
  Increase, **1968–69**: 47 (p. 134)
  Reduction, **1967**: 142, 428, 442, 508, 545;
    1968–69: 2, 14 (p. 26), 47 (p. 137),
    274, 275 [2], 517, 562, 671
  Scientific instruments, **1966**: 601
  Watches and clocks, **1966**: 600
  Yarns, textured, **1966**: 43
Tariffs and Trade, General Agreement on,
    1965: 35 (p. 111), 47, 60, 76, 112,
    564, 660; **1966**: 34 (p. 104), 471, 486,
    503; **1967**: 142, 224, 508
  See also General Agreement on Tariffs and
    Trade; Kennedy Round negotiations.
Tashkent conference, India-Pakistan, **1966**:
    247ftn. (p. 567)
Tashkent Declaration, **1966**: 41, 152
Task Force on Community Assistance, Federal,
    proposed, **1965**: 493n.
Task forces, governmental, **1965**: 347 [2, 8],
    385, 395 [2]
  Bridge safety, **1967**: 558
  Budgetary savings, **1965**: 512
  Career advancement, Federal, **1966**: 404;
    1967: 184
  Civil rights, **1965**: 353 [19]
  Community assistance, **1965**: 100, 493n.
  Communications policy, **1967**: 346
  Cost reduction, **1965**: 362
  Crime prevention, **1965**: 381
  Cuban refugee program, **1965**: 618
  Defense spending, **1965**: 347 [11]
  Education, **1965**: 183, 374, 519, 541;
    1966: 95
  Flood control policy, Federal, **1966**: 374
  Grant-in-aid processing time, **1967**: 458

Task forces, governmental – *continued*
  Handicapped children and child development,
    1966: 317
  Income tax reduction, **1965**: 347 [11]
  Los Angeles riots, **1965**: 448 [17]
  Medical research, **1965**: 410
  Occupational training, **1967**: 199; **1968–69**: 37
  Silver Bridge tragedy, **1968–69**: 58
  Social workers, manpower, **1966**: 95
  Summer domestic programs, **1966**: 105, 171
  Tariffs on sheet glass and carpets, **1967**: 428
  Travel in U.S., **1965**: 419
  Travel to U.S., **1967**: 16ftn. (p. 81);
    1968–69: 1 [1], 2, 83, 116
  Vietnam health and education, **1966**: 106,
    141ftn. (p. 347)
  Youth opportunity, **1966**: 385
  Youth Opportunity Campaign, **1965**: 268,
    298, 436, 438
Tasman, Abel Janszoon, **1966**: 538
Tate, James H. J., **1963–64**: 390n., 742;
    1965: 434; **1967**: 291
Taussig, Dr. Helen, **1963–64**: 211 [6], 568;
    1966: 49
Tawes, Gov. J. Millard, **1963–64**: 703; **1965**: 499,
    521; **1966**: 122 [1, 2], 494 [1–2, 11]
Tax Adjustment Act of 1966, **1966**: 17n., 132,
    654 [6]
Tax bill, **1963–64**: 11, 22, 23, 91 (p. 115), 92,
    93, 105, 124 (pp. 158–160), 132 (pp.
    178, 179, 190), 148, 158, 176
  See also Revenue Act of 1964.
  Approval, **1963–64**: 197
  News conference remarks, **1963–64**: 28 [4, 9],
    54 [9], 143 [2], 150 [3, 4], 170 [13]
Tax convention, U.S.-Philippines, **1963–64**: 627
Tax Incentives, Central American Agreement on,
    1968–69: 366
Tax Reduction, Business Committee for,
    1963–64: 93, 299
Tax Reduction and Revision, Citizens Committee
    for, **1963–64**: 93
Taxation and Development Standards, Commis-
    sion on Codes, Zoning, **1966**: 394;
    1967: 4, 16 (p. 84)
  Temporary, **1965**: 90
Taxes, **1963–64**: 28 [4, 9], 211 [3], 787;
    1965: 32 (pp. 83, 87, 99), 35 (p. 106),
    90; **1966**: 8 [14, 18], 17, 26 (pp. 48,
    52), 96, 100, 110, 155, 444, 494 [2],
    501 [7]; **1968–69**: 467 [3], 677, 684
    (p. 1318)
  Automobile, **1966**: 6 (p. 5), 8 [14], 17, 26
    (pp. 49, 52), 155
  Aviation, **1966**: 26 (p. 54)
  Beautification allowances, **1965**: 54
  Business, **1966**: 121 [3], 444, 445 [21], 596,
    631, 642 [6], 654 [6]

Taxes – *continued*
  Capital gains, **1963–64**: 132 (p. 179)
  Collection, **1966**: 6 (p. 5), 26 (p. 52); **1967**: 13
      (pp. 44, 59), 16 (p. 76); **1968–69**: 59,
      498
  Continental Oil Shelf, **1968–69**: 411
  Corporate, **1963–64**: 124 (p. 159), 132 (pp.
      179, 180), 139, 197, 218 [15], 724;
      1965: 23, 35 (p. 109), 226, 406,
      505n.; **1966**: 6 (p. 5), 17, 26 (pp. 49,
      52), 34 (p. 102), 124 [13], 155, 444,
      445 [9]; **1967**: 6 [13], 13 (p. 41), 16
      (p. 77), 329, 330 [1, 6, 7], 417 [7];
      1968–69: 39 (pp. 85, 87), 47 (p. 132),
      229, 678 (p. 1277)
  Deductions, **1963–64**: 731
  Depreciation allowances, **1963–64**: 619 [4],
      724; **1965**: 60, 76, 100, 226, 505;
      1966: 26 (p. 52), 444, 445 [4, 7,
      14, 22], 451, 596
  District of Columbia, **1963–64**: 133; **1965**: 29,
      40; **1966**: 27; **1967**: 15; **1968–69**: 95,
      133, 689
  Effect on economy, **1963–64**: 723; **1965**: 100,
      153, 255
  Excise, **1963–64**: 132 (p. 180), 271 [3], 379
      [4, 5], 407, 724; **1967**: 6 [17], 16 (p.
      76), 329, 420; **1968–69**: 39 (pp. 87,
      88), 47 (pp. 131–133), 343, 632, 678
      (pp. 1274, 1277), 684 (p. 1322)
    See also main heading, Excise taxes.
  Exemption provisions
    Private foundations, **1965**: 32 (p. 88)
    Private legislation, **1963–64**: 61
  Federal-State revenue sharing, **1966**: 121 [9],
      635 [19]; **1967**: 225 [21]
  Foreign investment tax credit, **1963–64**: 227
  Foreign investments in U.S., **1966**: 607 [14],
      612
  Gasoline, **1965**: 29, 32 (p. 88), 255
  Income, **1968–69**: 2, 14 (p. 32), 38, 39 (pp.
      84, 85, 87), 46, 47 (pp. 131–133, 135,
      139, 145), 56, 76, 87, 132, 142, 169
      [4, 21], 226, 229, 241, 322, 326, 339
      [12], 343, 582, 632, 676 (p. 1267),
      678 (p. 1274), 684 (pp. 1313–1315),
      696 [12]
    See also main heading, Income taxes.
  Increase, **1966**: 27, 88 [22], 121 [10], 155,
      158 [4, 9], 201, 236 [12], 247 [16],
      277 [8], 334 [8], 415, 445 [9, 20–
      21], 474 [1], 494 [16], 501 [20],
      516 [9], 577 [14], 578 [3], 610 [11],
      628 [5], 630 [5], 635 [12], 642 [6],
      654 [6, 11]; **1967**: 3 (p. 8), 6 [3, 13,
      17, 19], 13 (p. 42), 16 (pp. 76, 77),
      104 [3], 204 [6], 225 [9], 312 [4], 328
      [8, 21], 329, 330 [1, 2, 5, 6–9], 358

Taxes – *continued*
  Increase – *continued*
      [12], 362, 375 [8], 411 [11], 417 [1,
      5–8, 10, 12], 420, 421, 427, 430, 460
      [4, 12], 465, 490, 495 [9], 518 [4, 6,
      9], 554 [13], 556; **1968–69**: 1 [5, 11],
      2, 14 (pp. 31, 32), 38, 39 (pp. 83–87,
      103), 46, 47 (pp. 127, 131–133, 135,
      139, 145), 56, 76, 87, 114, 132, 136,
      141, 142, 146, 169 [4, 21], 170, 213
      [4], 223 [11], 226, 229, 241, 274, 275
      [4], 283 [8, 10], 322, 326, 339 [12],
      343, 427, 500, 567, 582, 612, 676 (p.
      1267), 677, 684 (pp. 1312, 1313), 690
  Interest equalization tax, **1963–64**: 91 (p.
      117), 124 (p. 162), 132 (p. 190);
      1965: 15, 60, 77, 638n.; **1968–69**: 684
      (p. 1319)
  Investment incentive plan, **1963–64**: 91 (p.
      115), 124 (pp. 157, 159, 161), 132 (pp.
      178, 179, 194), 295, 350, 589, 724,
      731, 787; **1965**: 18, 60, 76, 226, 326,
      450, 505; **1966**: 26 (p. 52), 34 (p. 104),
      444, 445 [4, 6, 22], 473, 492 [1], 494
      [2], 596, 631, 642 [6], 654 [6];
      1967: 6 [2, 9, 13, 17], 16 (p. 76), 103,
      104 [1], 204 [6], 329
  Legislation, **1965**: 321; **1966**: 26 (p. 49), 141
      [3], 473
  Letter to Representative Mills, **1963–64**: 196
  Medicare, **1966**: 155, 444
  Military personnel, **1966**: 389, 571
  Payroll, **1966**: 26 (p. 53)
  Policy and reform, **1967**: 12, 13 (p. 40), 16
      (pp. 76, 81, 83, 86), 465, 533
  Political contributions, voluntary deductions,
      1966: 6 (p. 7), 241; **1967**: 204 [8],
      236
  Poll.
    See main heading, Poll tax.
  Presidential, **1965**: 154, 156 [3]
  Private foundations, **1966**: 34 (p. 107)
  Real estate, **1966**: 30
  Reduction and reform, **1965**: 35 (pp. 103,
      105, 106, 108, 109), 60, 76, 153,
      156 [1], 164, 319 [3], 326, 452, 505;
      1966: 6 (p. 5), 8 [14], 26 (p. 52),
      34 (pp. 100, 107), 324; **1968–69**: 14
      (p. 32), 39 (p. 86), 47 (p. 131), 343,
      651, 677, 678 (pp. 1276, 1288), 684
      (pp. 1312, 1315)
  Refunds, **1963–64**: 92
  Report, **1965**: 505
  Revenues, **1966**: 26 (p. 50), 520, 577 [14],
      635 [5–6]; **1967**: 13 (pp. 39, 43), 16
      (p. 77), 329, 330 [1, 8], 358 [12],
      411 [11], 417 [1], 430, 495 [9]
  Securities, foreign, **1963–64**: 196

Taxes – *continued*
  Social security, **1965**: 32 (p. 87); **1966**: 26
       (p. 53), 34 (p. 102), 155, 444;
       1968-69: 39 (p. 88), 678 (p. 1277)
  State, **1968-69**: 406
  State and local, **1965**: 90; **1966**: 121 [3]
  States, withholding payments, **1963-64**: 197n.
  Surcharge.
       See main heading, Income taxes.
  Surtax, **1966**: 635 [18]; **1968-69**: 2, 14 (p.
       32), 38, 39 (pp. 84, 85, 87), 46, 47
       (pp. 131-133, 135, 139, 145), 56, 76,
       87, 132, 142, 146, 169 [4, 21], 170,
       226, 241, 322, 326, 339 [12], 343,
       582, 676 (p. 1267), 677, 678 (pp. 1274,
       1277), 684 (pp. 1313-1315), 696 [12]
  Tax bill.
       See main heading, Tax bill.
  Tax incentives, **1968-69**: 36, 366
  Tobacco products, **1965**: 192, 255
  Transportation, **1968-69**: 39 (pp. 88, 102),
       678 (p. 1278)
  Trust fund, **1966**: 26 (50)
  Urban, **1967**: 4; **1968-69**: 87
  Withholding, **1966**: 34 (p. 102); **1967**: 16 (p.
       76)
Taylor, Bishop Prince Albert, Jr., **1966**: 504
Taylor, George W., **1963-64**: 27, 253, 256 [1],
       271 [17], 284, 297 [2]; **1967**: 174,
       188, 204 [5], 207, 310, 312 [1];
       1968-69: 106, 112
Taylor, H. Ralph, **1966**: 207n.
Taylor, Hobart, Jr., **1963-64**: 111, 246 [13],
       250n., 356, 448; **1965**: 448 [6];
       1966: 248n., 431; **1967**: 81
Taylor, Hobart, III, **1966**: 477 [2]
Taylor, Capt. James A., **1968-69**: 594
Taylor, Gen. Maxwell D., **1963-64**: 349n.;
       1965: 46 [7, 11], 117 [2], 156 [11],
       295 [8], 319 [19], 347 [5], 353 [1],
       403, 412 [2, 3], 421, 476; **1966**: 65
       [6], 124 [2], 482n.; **1967**: 80 [4],
       83, 134, 195, 225 [11], 328 [9, 12,
       16], 352, 384; **1968-69**: 51 [3], 79
       [8]
  See also Joint Chiefs of Staff, Chairman (Gen.
       Maxwell D. Taylor).
  Ambassador to Vietnam, **1963-64**: 445, 455
       [5], 475 [3], 533, 560 [3], 563 [1, 7],
       688 [8], 780 [6, 12], 793
  Visits to Vietnam, **1963-64**: 336 [15]
Taylor, Mrs. Otrie, **1967**: 342n.
Taylor, Robert H., **1968-69**: 549, 604
Taylor, Repr. Roy A., **1963-64**: 327, 328;
       1968-69: 510
Taylor, Thomas Jefferson, **1968-69**: 648
Taylor, William L., **1968-69**: 42
Taylor, Mrs. Willie Day, **1968-69**: 260

Taylor, Zachariah, **1963-64**: 645
Tchaikovsky International Music Competition
       winners, **1966**: 440
Teacher Corps.
  See National Teacher Corps.
Teacher of the Year Award.
  See under Awards and citations.
Teachers, **1963-64**: 357, 589, 606, 650, 667,
       669, 754; **1965**: 70, 183, 401;
       1966: 26 (p. 64); **1967**: 423;
       1968-69: 26, 39 (p. 89), 47 (p. 143)
  Comments on, **1965**: 170
  District of Columbia, **1967**: 15; **1968-69**: 133,
       272, 689
  Education and humanities, **1968-69**: 145, 678
       (p. 1293), 703
  Employment, **1966**: 105; **1967**: 292, 396
  Exchange program, **1965**: 36; **1966**: 45, 406;
       1967: 344
  Fellowships, **1965**: 340, 368, 369
  Indian schools, **1968-69**: 113
  Mexican-American children, work with,
       1968-69: 91
  Negro, **1965**: 340
  Overseas travel, **1968-69**: 14 (p. 33)
  Pay, **1963-64**: 132 (p. 189); **1965**: 527, 539;
       1967: 493; **1968-69**: 133, 272
  Shortage of, **1963-64**: 47; **1966**: 27, 89, 216,
       347; **1967**: 493
  Summer Teaching Corps, **1966**: 45
  Training, **1963-64**: 213, 357; **1965**: 9, 70, 111,
       368, 369, 401, 479; **1967**: 13 (p. 55),
       77; **1968-69**: 39 (p. 106), 54, 687
  Urban slums, **1968-69**: 419
  Veterans, **1968-69**: 40, 160, 419
Teachers, American Federation of, **1965**: 539
Teachers Association, Houston, **1965**: 183
Teaching aids, import tariffs, **1966**: 601
Teaching Professions, World Confederation of
       Organizations of, **1968-69**: 644n.
Teaching Professions Act of 1965, proposed,
       1965: 368, 369
Teach-ins on U.S. foreign policy, **1965**: 295
       [7], 353 [21], 397
Teague, Repr. Charles M., **1968-69**: 132
Teague, Repr. Olin E., **1963-64**: 763;
       1965: 46 [8], 163; **1966**: 100, 495,
       .505; **1967**: 374; **1968-69**: 132, 160,
       281, 282, 452, 472, 554, 599, 616
Teague, Mrs. Olin E., **1968-69**: 452
Tear gas and non-lethal gas
  Use in controlling civil disorders, **1965**:
       156 [12]
  Use in Vietnam, **1965**: 156 [12]
Technical assistance to less developed countries
       and new nations, **1963-64**: 45, 132
       (p. 185), 471n., 617; **1965**: 7, 18, 117
       [3], 149, 230, 246, 257, 294, 295 [3],

Technical assistance – *continued*
    357, 450; **1966**: 6 (pp. 3, 8), 11, 22,
    26 (pp. 58, 60), 34 (p. 105), 41, 45,
    54, 62, 77, 243, 331, 420; **1967**: 44,
    157, 175, 346, 423, 469, 545; **1968–69**:
    679
  See also Economic assistance; Foreign
    assistance.
Technical Employees, International Federation
    of Commercial, Clerical, and, **1967**: 442
Technical Institute for the Deaf, National,
    establishment, **1965**: 401
Technical Services Program, State, **1965**: 35
    (p. 116)
Technological progress, **1963–64**: 124 (p. 163),
    126, 132 (pp. 191, 194), 213, 214, 396,
    578, 589, 598, 629, 735, 756, 804, 805;
    1965: 35 (pp. 112, 113, 116), 54, 71,
    76, 97, 100, 143, 170, 219, 305, 334,
    378, 428, 446, 448 [1], 513, 523, 536;
    1966: 258, 306, 337, 462, 486; **1967**:
    37, 57, 65, 192, 193, 431, 448, 465,
    496; **1968–69**: 282
Technological Progress, National Commission
    on Automation and, proposed, **1963–
    64**: 214
Technology, Automation and Economic
    Progress, National Commission on,
    1963–64: 214, 525; **1965**: 100, 258;
    1966: 111, 258
Technology, Case Institute of, **1965**: 225
Technology, Federal Council for Science and,
    1963–64: 456n.; **1965**: 92, 271, 275,
    514; **1966**: 222; **1967**: 478; **1968–69**:
    577
Technology, Inter-American Foundation for
    Science and, **1967**: 176
Technology, Museum of History and, **1967**: 540n.
Technology, Office of Science and.
  See Science and Technology, Office of.
Tehran, Iran, **1967**: 363
Tejera-Paris, Enrique, **1963–64**: 335n.; **1966**: 366
Telecommunication Union, International,
    1963–64: 532
Telecommunications, **1968–69**: 175, 233, 366,
    483
Telecommunications Satellite Consortium,
    International (INTELSAT), **1967**:
    122, 346
Telephone, Trans-Pacific cable, **1963–64**: 408
Telephones, **1967**: 346
  Costs, reduction of rates, **1965**: 567
  Overhead utility lines, **1967**: 295
  Police aid, **1968–69**: 59
  Rural areas, **1968–69**: 39 (p. 101), 94
  Taxes, **1966**: 6 (p. 5), 8 [14], 17, 26 (pp. 49,
    52), 155; **1967**: 329; **1968–69**: 39 (p.
    88), 47 (p. 132), 678 (p. 1277)

Telephones – *continued*
  U.S.-Venezuela submarine cable, **1966**: 366
  White House operators, **1968–69**: 588, 595,
    630
Television, **1966**: 27, 403, 629; **1967**: 474;
    1968–69: 172
  "A Conversation With the President," **1967**:
    554
  Addresses.
    See main heading, Messages to the American
      people.
  Community antenna systems, **1963–64**:
    256 [15]
  Debates.
    See main heading, Debates, Presidential
      campaign, question of.
  Educational, **1963–64**: 173; **1965**: 468;
    1967: 3 (p. 6), 13 (p. 55), 77, 176,
    346, 474, 477, 492, 559; **1968–69**:
    14 (p. 27), 77, 111, 370, 701
  Intercontinental, **1968–69**: 507
  Interviews.
    See main heading, Interviews of the
      President.
  Noncommercial, **1968–69**: 54
  Operation on UHF channels, **1963–64**: 173
  President's use, **1966**: 52 [4]
  Public, **1967**: 77, 346, 474, 490, 559
  Safety, **1968–69**: 14 (p. 30), 56
  "The President's Country" program, **1966**: 270
  "Today" program, **1966**: 295
  Use in 1964 Presidential campaign, **1963–64**:
    201 [15]
Television and radio addresses.
  See Messages to the American people.
Telles, Raymond, **1963–64**: 54 [5]; **1968–69**:
    223 [2]
Temple, Larry E., **1968–69**: 17, 191 [3]
Temple University, **1968–69**: 419
Temporary Commission on Pennsylvania
    Avenue, **1965**: 538; **1967**: 71; **1968–
    69**: 133, 560
Temporary Extended Unemployment Compen-
    sation Act of 1961, **1963–64**: 22, 305
Temporary National Commission on Codes,
    Zoning, Taxation and Development
    Standards, **1965**: 90
Tennessee, **1966**: 320 [14], 391; **1967**: 115–117
  Antipoverty program, **1963–64**: 324, 325
  Campaign remarks, **1963–64**: 645, 701, 702
  Candidates for public office, **1963–64**: 645,
    701, 702
  Clement, Gov. Frank G., **1963–64**: 324, 325,
    645, 701, 702; **1966**: 122 [1, 2], 494
    [1, 2], 599ftn. (p. 1358)
  Ellington, Gov. Buford, **1967**: 87n., 115–17,
    1968–69: 102, 345, 483n.
  Remarks, **1965**: 554; **1968–69**: 345

Tennessee, University of, **1967**: 538n.
Tennessee Historical Commission, **1967**: 538n.
Tennessee Valley Authority, **1963–64**: 324, 325, 462 [2], 642, 643, 644, 645, 669, 680, 701, 702, 711, 713; **1965**: 32 (p. 92), 127, 172, 274n.; **1966**: 49, 233, 351–352, 374, 382, 509, 518, 520; **1967**: 13 (p. 46), 117, 315n.; **1968–69**: 39 (p. 91), 345, 653n.
   Chairman (Aubrey J. Wagner), **1963–64**: 320, 321, 322, 323, 324, 325, 326, 327, 328
Tennessee Valley Authority Act of 1933; **1966**: 233
Tenney, Mr. and Mrs. Roger, **1967**: 182
Tenzer, Repr. Herbert, **1966**: 510, 512
Ter Horst, J. F., **1966**: 338 [4]
Teran, José Fernandez, **1966**: 639
Terris, Bruce, **1968–69**: 425ftn. (p. 862)
Territo, Mrs. Dorothy, **1965**: 412 [1]
Territorial waters of U.S., fishing prohibition, **1963–64**: 353
Territory of the Pacific Islands, Trust, **1967**: 133, 218
Terry, Charles L., Jr., **1963–64**: 749; **1965**: 417, 434; **1966**: 427–428, 515; **1967**: 121n.; **1968–69**: 46n.
Terry, Luther L., **1963–64**: 211 [25]; **1965**: 202n., 410, 531n.; **1966**: 315n.
Test ban treaty.
   See Nuclear test ban treaty.
Tetanus, **1968–69**: 111
Texarkana, John F. Kennedy Square, dedication, **1963–64**: 599
Texas, **1963–64**: 72, 576, 788; **1965**: 48, 230, 285, 454 [4], 603; **1966**: 320 [14], 401 [7], 427–428; **1967**: 115, 397; **1968–69**: 12n., 574n., 648
   Big Thicket Wilderness Area, proposed, **1968–69**: 702
   Campaign addresses and remarks, **1963–64**: 544, 599, 680, 760, 761, 762, 763, 765
   Candidates for public office, **1963–64**: 544, 760, 761, 762
   Chamizal boundary and highway, **1966**: 177, 597
   Floods, **1967**: 408
   Gov. John B. Connally, **1963–64**: 72n., 280 [10], 281, 375, 596, 597, 598, 599, 738, 760, 761, 763, 765, 767, 778; **1965**: 179, 285, 291n.; **1966**: 121 [1], 277 [6], 415–416, 417 [3], 520, 630 [2], 635 [14], 638–639, 641, 650n.; **1967**: 408 [1, 4, 8], 452; **1968–69**: 97, 171, 191 [3], 260, 357, 359
   Hurricanes, **1967**: 408; **1968–69**: 98
   Poll tax, **1965**: 409
   Power failure, **1965**: 641 [1]

Texas — *continued*
   Remarks, **1967**: 210, 270, 409, 452, 532; **1968–69**: 7, 96, 97, 107–109, 281, 282, 357, 359, 442, 459, 460, 462, 575, 623–625
   Rio Grande salinity control with Mexico, **1967**: 47
   San Jacinto Day, **1963–64**: 281
   Visits to, comments on, **1963–64**: 780 [23]
   Water resources, **1965**: 236
Texas, University of, **1967**: 210, 385; **1968–69**: 109, 212, 213 [5], 260, 631, 690
   Mass shooting at, **1966**: 363–364
Texas Christian University, **1968–69**: 282
Texas Democratic Party, telegrams, **1968–69**: 486, 497
Texas Educational Foundation, Inc., **1965**: 179n.
Texas Electric Cooperatives, Inc., remarks at dinner for, **1965**: 230
Texas Instruments, Inc., **1966**: 144n.
Texas Municipal League, **1967**: 123
Texas Quarterly, **1968–69**: 212
Texas Technological College, Lubbock, Tex., **1967**: 448
Textile industry, **1965**: 168; **1966**: 516 [15]
   Employment, **1963–64**: 719
   Statements, **1963–64**: 602, 717
Textiles, **1967**: 223 [3], 414
Thackeray, William Makepeace, **1965**: 616
Thailand, **1963–64**: 476; **1965**: 177; **1966**: 41, 133, 516 [1], 554–555, 557–558; **1967**: 44, 272, 290, 401, 409, 480; **1968–69**: 204, 223 [7]
   Assistance, **1963–64**: 476; **1965**: 294; **1968–69**: 63, 237, 679
   Bases, U.S., **1966**: 401 [13]
   Charusathiara, Gen. Prapass, **1963–64**: 476
   Communist aggression, **1967**: 293, 409; **1968–69**: 237
   Economic and social development, **1968–69**: 232, 237
   Foreign Minister Thanat Khoman, **1967**: 290, 409
   King Bhumibol Adulyadej, **1966**: 554n., 555n., 557n., 558n.; **1967**: 289, 290, 293; **1968–69**: 232n., 233, 237
   King Phumiphon Adundet, **1963–64**: 30
   Peace corps movement in, **1965**: 83
   Prime Minister Thanom Kittikachorn, **1966**: 549, 554, 557n.; **1968–69**: 232, 233, 237
   Queen Sirikit, **1966**: 554n., 558n.; **1967**: 289, 290, 293; **1968–69**: 232n.
   Relations with U.S., **1967**: 289, 290, 293
   Srisdi Dhanarajata, death of, **1963–64**: 30
   U.S. forces, **1963–64**: 379 [9]; **1967**: 565, 573
   U.S.-Thai Treaty of Friendship, **1967**: 290n.

Thailand — *continued*
Vietnam assistance, **1966:** 555, 557; **1967:**
83, 246, 293; **1968–69:** 232, 237, 273,
283 [4], 525
Visit, **1966:** 554, 555, 557–558; **1967:** 565
Thalidomide tragedy, **1967:** 214n., 215
Thanat Khoman, **1967:** 409
Thanksgiving Day
Address to the American people, **1963–64:** 12
Message to the Armed Forces, **1963–64:** 779;
1965: 626
Proclamation, **1963–64:** 770; **1965:** 610;
1966: 534; **1967:** 481; **1968–69:** 591
Statement, **1963–64:** 10
Turkey, acceptance, **1963–64:** 772
Thanom Kittikachorn.
See under Thailand.
Thant (U).
See United Nations Secretary General.
Thatcher, William, **1963–64:** 255
"The President's Country" television program,
1966: 270
Theater Owners of America, Inc., **1963–64:** 354
Theater Owners Association, Independent,
1963–64: 354
Theis, Frank, **1963–64:** 741
Theodore Roosevelt Memorial, **1967:** 450
Thieu, President.
See Nguyen Van Thieu.
"This America," prologue and epilogue, **1966:**
497
3d Aerospace Rescue and Recovery Group,
Military Airlift Command, **1967:** 106
3d Marine Division, Reinforced, Fleet Marine
Force Pacific, **1967:** 456
Thomas, Repr. Albert, **1963–64:** 760, 761, 762;
1966: 71, 134
Thomas, Mrs. Albert, **1963–64:** 762
Thomas, B. D., **1965:** 344n.
Thomas, David D., **1965:** 339
Thomas, Eugene, **1965:** 135
Thomas, Helen, **1963–64:** 28 [15], 211 [18,
35], 420 [13], 486 [10]; **1966:** 455;
1967: 6 [20], 225 [19]; **1968–69:**
169 [6, 14, 21], 171, 191 [13], 229,
275 [7], 283 [15], 646 [5, 11, 13, 14]
Thomas, Lowell, **1968–69:** 172
Thomas, Norman, death, **1968–69:** 633
Thomas More College, **1968–69:** 499
Thomason, Robert Ewing, **1963–64:** 596
Thompson, Charles C., **1967:** 156
Thompson, Repr. Clark W., **1963–64:** 760
Thompson, Repr. Frank, Jr., **1963–64:** 338;
1965: 177, 534; **1966:** 504
Thompson, Llewellyn E., **1963–64:** 688 [1, 8];
1966: 501 [1]; **1967:** 80 [2], 104
[11], 282; **1968–69:** 170

Thompson, Rogene L., **1968–69:** 138n.
Thompson, Repr. T. A., **1963–64:** 648
Thompson, William S., **1965:** 516; **1967:** 406,
466n.; **1968–69:** 429, 442
Thomson, George, **1966:** 506
Thoreau, Henry David, **1963–64:** 578, 788;
1965: 521; **1966:** 116, 202; **1967:** 474
Thorium stockpiles, **1966:** 218
Thornberry, Judge Homer, **1963–64:** 207, 389n.;
1965: 305, 319 [22], 341; **1967:** 210;
1968–69: 339 [2], 425 [11], 527
Thornberry, Mrs. Homer (Eloise Engle), **1965:**
341; **1967:** 210
Thornberry, Mrs. Mary, **1963–64:** 389; **1965:**
305
Thornton, Charles, **1966:** 637n.; **1967:** 326
Thornton, J. R., **1965:** 179
Thorsteinsson, Petur, **1967:** 313
"Thousand Days—John F. Kennedy in the White
House," Arthur M. Schlesinger, Jr.,
1965: 353ftn. (p. 743)
Thrash, William G., **1967:** 485 [2]; **1968–69:**
81 [2]
388th Tactical Fighter Wing, **1967:** 565n.
Throckmorton, Lt. Gen. J. L., **1967:** 322, 331
Thua Thien province, South Vietnam, **1967:**
309 [5]
Thuc (Vu Quoc Thuc), **1967:** 131
Thucydides, **1967:** 301
Thunberg, Mrs. Penelope, **1965:** 91n., 353 [4];
1967: 95
Thurmond, Sen. Strom, **1963–64:** 382, 383;
1966: 516 [9]; **1968–69:** 467 [2],
567–569
Thurmont, Md., **1968–69:** 188n., 189n.
Tibbetts, Margaret Joy, **1963–64:** 242 [2, 24]
Tice, Frank, **1963–64:** 741n.
Tidal waves, **1967:** 31n.
Tijuana River, **1967:** 303
Time magazine, **1965:** 459; **1968–69:** 631
Timmerman, George Bell, **1963–64:** 719
Timmons, Bascom, **1968–69:** 696 [1]
Tiran, Straits of, **1967:** 272
Tire safety, **1966:** 98, 449, 576; **1967:** 342;
1968–69: 56
Tires, excise taxes, **1965:** 255
Tiros weather satellite, **1963–64:** 647; **1967:** 121
Titan launch vehicle, **1966:** 625
Titan missiles, **1965:** 26
Titan III–C boosters, **1965:** 448 [1]
Titanium metal development, **1963–64:** 201 [2]
Tito, Marshal Josip Broz, **1965:** 412 [2]; **1967:**
328 [13], 375ftn. (p. 821)
Tittle, Y. A., **1963–64:** 136n.
Tlatelolco (Mexico) treaty on nuclear weapons
in Latin America, **1968–69:** 13, 73,
349, 392

Tobacco
  Growers, Government subsidy to, **1963-64**:
    211 [25]; **1965**: 192
  Marketing quotas, approval, **1965**: 192
  Program, **1963-64**: 631, 644; **1965**: 47, 192
  Shipments to India, **1966**: 153-154
  Tariffs, **1968-69**: 274
  Taxes, **1965**: 192, 255
Tobago, immigrants to U.S., **1965**: 13
Tobin, Austin J., **1966**: 517
Tobriner, Walter N., **1963-64**: 211 [2]; **1966**:
    162, 646; **1967**: 372n., 466
  Letter, **1963-64**: 704
Tocks Island National Recreation Area, New
    Jersey-Pennsylvania, proposed, **1965**:
    54
Tocks Island Reservoir project, **1965**: 471
Tocqueville, Alexis de, **1965**: 519; **1967**: 349n.,
    415
"Today" television program, **1966**: 295
Todd, Repr. Paul H., Jr., **1966**: 431-433
Todd, Mrs. Paul H., Jr., **1966**: 432
Toiletries, taxes, **1965**: 255
Tokyo, Japan, **1963-64**: 632, 699; **1965**: 523;
    1968-69: 494
Toledo, Ohio, **1965**: 190, 191
Toll, Repr. Herman, **1963-64**: 742
Tollefson, Harold M., **1966**: 536
Tolley, William P., **1963-64**: 499
Tolson, Clyde A., **1965**: 269, 296n.
Toly, Caroline, **1966**: 257
Toly, Lucille, **1966**: 257
Toly, Michael T., **1966**: 257
Tombalbaye, Francois (President of Republic of
    Chad), **1968-69**: 508, 511
Tompkins, Pauline, **1963-64**: 208
Tonkin, Gulf of, **1963-64**: 497, 498, 499, 626,
    627; **1965**: 208 [2], 276; **1966**: 94
  Campaign remarks, **1963-64**: 607, 612, 634,
    635, 646, 648, 703, 733, 736
  News conference remarks, **1963-64**: 504 [2],
    516 [2], 560 [7], 587 [5, 8]
  Resolution, **1966**: 88 [17]; **1967**: 358 [10],
    460 [9], 495 [14], 534, 554 [1]
Toohey, Edward F., **1967**: 291
Tootell, R. B. (Governor, Farm Credit Adminis-
    tration), **1967**: 156
Tornadoes, **1967**: 31n., 187
  Midwestern States, **1965**: 187, 188, 189, 190,
    191, 193, 215, 239
Torpedo, EX-10, **1963-64**: 382
Torrey Canyon, **1967**: 240; **1968-69**: 122, 586
Torrez, Romaldo Perry, **1968-69**: 108
Tourism.
  See Travel.
Tourists.
  See Travel.

Tower, Sen. John G., **1966**: 635 [14]; **1967**:
    408 [1, 5, 8]; **1968-69**: 460 [1]
Townes, Charles H., **1967**: 192
Townsend, Lynn Alfred, **1966**: 240
Townsville, Australia, **1966**: 547, 570
  Mayor A. J. Smith, **1966**: 547
Toxicological information, **1966**: 279-280, 307
"Toxicological Information, Handling of,"
    President's foreword to report on,
    1966: 279
Toy safety, **1966**: 140, 576; **1967**: 86, 200, 393,
    465, 534; **1968-69**: 56, 545
Trade, General Agreement on Tariffs and.
  See General Agreement on Tariffs and Trade;
    Kennedy Round negotiations.
Trade, international, **1963-64**: 80, 91 (p. 117),
    124 (pp. 162, 166), 244, 248, 278, 295,
    311, 344, 529, 592, 717, 722, 734, 769,
    805, 809; **1965**: 2, 25, 35 (pp. 111,
    112), 47, 110, 112, 118, 149, 167, 168,
    255, 307, 465, 597; **1966**: 6 (p. 9), 34
    (p. 103), 94, 444, 471; **1967**: 16 (p.
    79), 121, 231, 250, 294, 442, 445, 465,
    476, 491, 497, 508, 519, 524, 525, 545,
    554 [5]; **1968-69**: 1 [1], 2, 10, 29,
    47 (p. 134), 62, 94, 146, 176, 194, 207,
    218, 241, 343, 366, 377, 422, 439, 500,
    517, 559, 636, 671, 676 (p. 1268)
  Automotive products, **1967**: 137; **1968-69**:
    256, 274, 275 [2], 465
  Barriers reduction, **1963-64**: 140; **1965**: 21,
    147, 292, 465, 574; **1967**: 16 (p. 79),
    424, 508, 545; **1968-69**: 47 (pp. 129,
    136, 137), 146, 214n., 274, 275 [2],
    517, 684 (pp. 1319, 1320)
  Canada-Communist China, **1965**: 21n.
  Coffee, **1968-69**: 23
  Cuba, U.S. opposition, **1966**: 608
  Customs, **1968-69**: 261, 558
  Developing nations, **1966**: 34 (p. 104)
  Expansion, **1963-64**: 695, 736, 739; **1965**:
    15, 235, 371
  Fairs and exhibitions, **1967**: 245; **1968-69**:
    146, 204
  GATT negotiations, Kennedy Round.
    See General Agreement on Tariffs and
    Trade.
  Land-locked states, **1968-69**: 383
  Latin America, **1963-64**: 66; **1965**: 429;
    1966: 125, 254
  Message to Congress, **1967**: 508; **1968-69**: 274
  North Vietnam, U.S. opposition, **1966**: 441,
    608
  Nuclear materials, **1966**: 32; **1968-69**: 378
  Protectionism, **1967**: 465, 492, 508, 545
  Quotas, **1967**: 492
  Trade agreements program, **1966**: 471; **1967**:
    445

Trade, international – *continued*
United Nations Conference on Trade and
        Development, **1963–64:** 201 [11], 237
U.S.-Asia, **1967:** 231
U.S. balance of trade, **1963–64:** 246 [12, 18],
        753n., 757; **1965:** 35 (pp. 107, 111),
        47, 60, 77, 192, 365n.
U.S.-Canada, **1963–64:** 80, 140; **1965:** 21, 22
        [9], 147, 574, 575, 638n.; **1967:** 137,
        508; **1968–69:** 256, 274, 275 [2], 465
U.S.-Communist bloc, **1963–64:** 294 [20, 22],
        641
U.S.-Communist China, **1966:** 338 [12]
U.S.-Eastern Europe, **1965:** 2, 4, 235, 266;
        1966: 6 (pp. 3, 9), 200, 247 [9], 272,
        503, 528; **1967:** 3 (p. 10), 16 (p. 80),
        80 [2], 157, 225 [18], 231; **1968–69:**
        47 (p. 138)
U.S.-Europe, **1963–64:** 76, 788; **1965:** 235
U.S.-Italy, **1968–69:** 562
U.S.-Japan, **1968–69:** 524
U.S.-Korea, **1965:** 257; **1966:** 566; **1967:** 113
U.S.-Latin America, **1967:** 110, 173, 175–178
U.S.-Malagasy Republic, **1963–64:** 483
U.S.-Mexico, **1963–64:** 193, 767; **1966:** 177;
        1967: 451; **1968–69:** 624
U.S.-New Zealand, **1968–69:** 528
U.S.-Philippines, **1963–64:** 627; **1966:** 461
U.S.-Poland, **1963–64:** 272
U.S. policy, **1968–69:** 47 (p. 133), 241, 274,
        275 [2], 283 [8]
    Report, **1968–69:** 680
U.S.-Republic of China, **1965:** 18
U.S.-Southern Rhodesia, **1967:** 74
U.S.-Soviet Union, **1963–64:** 211 [11, 18,
        24], 294 [20, 22], 266 [11]; **1965:**
        2, 4, 266; **1966:** 6 (p. 3), 272; **1967:**
        16 (p. 80); **1968–69:** 47 (p. 138)
U.S.-United Arab Republic, **1965:** 46 [2], 661
U.S.-Yugoslavia, **1963–64:** 272
Trade Agreements Act, **1965:** 564
Trade Agreements Act of 1962, **1963–64:** 592
Trade agreements program, **1965:** 564; **1968–
        69:** 517
Trade Association, Latin American Free, **1968–
        69:** 239, 362, 695
Trade Center, Inter-American, Miami, Fla.,
        1963–64: 710
Trade Centers, American, **1963–64:** 722
Trade Commission, Federal, **1967:** 518 [2];
        1968–69: 14 (p. 29), 56, 684 (p. 1322)
Trade Committee, Joint Mexican-U.S., **1966:**
        177; **1967:** 451
Trade Convention, Wheat, **1968–69:** 29
Trade and Development, United Nations Con-
        ference on, **1963–64:** 201 [11], 237;
        1966: 94; **1967:** 100

Trade and Economic Affairs, Joint United
        States-Japan Committee on, **1965:**
        15, 355; **1967:** 381, 491
Trade and Economic Affairs, U.S.-Canada
        Committee on, **1963–64:** 140
Trade Expansion Act of 1962, **1963–64:** 71 [13],
        91 (p. 117), 124 (p. 162), 278, 295,
        297, 642, 728, 739; **1965:** 147, 167,
        564, 575, 577; **1966:** 471; **1967:** 16
        (p. 80), 224, 428, 445, 508, 545;
        1968–69: 274, 275 [2], 517
Trade expansion bill of 1968, **1968–69:** 274,
        275 [2, 4], 390
Trade Mission, Iowa, **1965:** 307
Trade Negotiations, Public Advisory Committee
        on, **1963–64:** 278
Trade Negotiations, Special Representative for
        (William M. Roth), **1967:** 142, 428,
        545; **1968–69:** 274, 517, 680
Trade Policy, Public Advisory Committee on,
        1968–69: 517
Trade practices, **1963–64:** 173
Trade Union Council for Human Rights, National,
        1967: 484n.
Trade union movement, **1963–64:** 388; **1965:**
        370, 489; **1966:** 429
Trade Week, World, **1963–64:** 336 [5], 350;
        1967: 231
Trading with the Enemy Act, **1966:** 303
Trading with the Enemy Act of 1917, **1965:** 309
Traffic accidents, **1963–64:** 234, 565; **1965:**
        460, 488
Traffic accident prevention.
    See Safety.
Traffic Safety, President's Committee for,
        1963–64: 565; **1966:** 98
Traffic safety bill.
    See National Traffic and Motor Vehicle Safety
        Act of 1966.
Traffic Safety Bureau, National, **1966:** 449
Trails, nationwide system, **1967:** 20
Trails in national forests and parks, **1965:** 54;
        1966: 82
Trails System, National, **1968–69:** 39 (p. 101),
        122, 406, 510
Training.
    See Occupational training.
Training Act, Manpower Development and,
        1963–64: 690n.
Tran Van Huong (Prime Minister of South
        Vietnam), **1968–69:** 400
Trans World Airlines, **1966:** 256n., 322
Transit Authority
    New York, **1966:** 8ftn. (p. 19)
    Washington Metropolitan Area, **1966:** 262;
        1967: 15, 154
Transport Workers Union of America, **1966:**
        8ftn. (p. 19), 373ftn. (p. 808)

Transportation, **1963-64**: 91 (p. 112), 124
    (p. 163), 132 (p. 188), 213, 414, 579,
    603, 650, 669, 728, 733; **1965**: 32
    (p. 92), 35 (pp. 106, 115), 97, 251,
    290, 371, 460, 499; **1966**: 26 (pp. 60–
    61), 34 (p. 105), 187, 237, 240, 394,
    580 [5], 583; **1967**: 13 (p. 52), 149;
    1968-69: 47 (p. 144), 93, 102, 125,
    276, 282, 655, 684 (pp. 1311, 1321),
    695
  Air, **1963-64**: 215, 789; **1965**: 97; **1966**: 64,
    225
  Atlantic-Pacific sea-level canal, **1966**: 384
  Defense, proclamation, **1968-69**: 118
  District of Columbia, **1963-64**: 133; **1965**:
    32 (p. 93), 61, 70, 499; **1966**: 27, 68,
    84, 262; **1967**: 15, 154; **1968-69**: 95,
    458, 689
  Federal aid, **1963-64**: 132 (p. 187), 410;
    1966: 187, 442; **1967**: 542
  Highway.
    See main heading, Highways.
  Intercity, **1965**: 2, 32 (p. 93), 97, 536
  Letter, **1963-64**: 154
  Message to Congress, **1966**: 98
  New England, **1967**: 223 [2]
  Oceanic, **1966**: 229
  Rail, **1965**: 2, 32 (p. 93), 61, 97, 536
  Rapid rail transit systems, **1963-64**: 410;
    1965: 2, 29, 32 (p. 93), 61, 70, 90, 97,
    499, 536; **1966**: 27, 68, 84, 240, 262,
    353, 442; **1967**: 154, 234, 353, 358
    [3]; **1968-69**: 693
  Research, **1965**: 32 (p. 93), 97, 536; **1966**:
    26 (p. 61). 98; **1967**: 16 (p. 87); **1968-
    69**: 39 (p. 102), 306
  Rural, **1965**: 38; **1968-69**: 142
  Safety.
    See main heading, Safety.
  Saint Lawrence Seaway, **1967**: 398; **1968-69**:
    693
  Supersonic, **1963-64**: 132 (p. 188), 201 [2],
    242 [9], 294 [6], 355, 789
  Urban, **1963-64**: 91 (pp. 112, 115), 124 (p.
    163), 132 (p. 188), 152, 357, 410, 453,
    620, 630, 654; **1965**: 2, 9, 29, 32
    (p. 93), 35 (p. 114), 38, 61, 90, 97,
    499; **1966**: 26 (p. 61), 30, 98, 353, 394,
    428, 442; **1967**: 16 (p. 85), 20, 114,
    179, 234, 353, 358 [3], 412, 467, 542;
    1968-69: 39 (p. 102), 87, 93, 130, 306,
    351, 678 (p. 1302), 684 (p. 1321), 693,
    697
  User charges, **1965**: 32 (p. 87), 35 (p. 116),
    255; **1966**: 26 (p. 53), 34 (p. 105), 225,
    401 [2], 403; **1967**: 16 (p. 86); **1968-
    69**: 39 (pp. 88, 102), 678 (p. 1278)

Transportation, Department of, **1966**: 6 (pp. 3,
    6–7), 26 (p. 61), 34 (p. 105), 98, 187,
    240, 449, 474 [19], 523, 580 [5, 14];
    1967: 5, 13 (pp. 52, 57), 57, 121, 139,
    149, 223 [2], 478, 542; **1968-69**: 39
    (p. 109), 47 (p. 144), 58, 87, 93, 118,
    125, 130n., 243n., 244n., 276, 297,
    535, 586, 678 (pp. 1301, 1302), 693
  Appropriations, **1967**: 417 [1]
  Urban mass transportation program,
    1968-69: 351
  Transportation, Secretary of (Alan S. Boyd),
    1967: 6 [3], 20, 57, 70 [6], 72, 114,
    139n., 149, 170, 186, 197, 204 [5],
    208, 223 [2], 310, 542, 558;
    1968-69: 39 (p. 102), 47 (p. 144), 56,
    58, 59, 93, 111, 118, 122, 125, 130,
    248, 264, 276, 351, 441, 458, 498, 570
  Annual report, **1968-69**: 693
  Letter, **1967**: 392; **1968-69**: 490
  Memorandum, **1967**: 240; **1968-69**: 297, 361
  Swearing in, **1967**: 5
Transportation Agency, National Capital,
    1963-64: 133; **1965**: 19, 61;
    1967: 15, 154
Transportation Day, National Defense,
    1966: 187
Transportation Safety Board, National,
    1966: 98
Transportation Week, National, **1966**: 187
Travel
  Americans abroad, **1965**: 118, 307;
    1966: 503, 528; **1967**: 34 [1], 119,
    389; **1968-69**: 1 [1, 3, 15], 2, 14 (p.
    33), 15, 47 (pp. 134, 135), 142, 146
  Americans within U.S., **1963-64**: 516 [1];
    1965: 60, 77, 97, 279, 419, 488, 638n.;
    1966: 240
  Duty-free exemptions, **1965**: 60, 338
  Foreigners in U.S., **1963-64**: 516 [1];
    1965: 60, 77, 638n.; **1966**: 34 (p. 104),
    503, 528; **1967**: 13 (p. 51), 16 (p. 81),
    389; **1968-69**: 1 [1], 2, 47 (pp. 134,
    135), 83, 88, 116, 146, 449, 648, 684
    (p. 1319)
  Government employees, **1965**: 512;
    1967: 25
  Allowances, **1966**: 234
  National Capital visitors, **1966**: 90
  Ports of entry, inspection, **1968-69**: 388, 389
  President's, **1963-64**: 218 [4], 242 [19, 21],
    246 [6], 256 [14, 18], 316 [15], 336
    [9]; **1965**: 22 [5]; **1967**: 70 [5], 328
    [22]; **1968-69**: 169 [12, 14], 178, 179,
    223 [8], 339 [13–15], 431, 467 [8,
    13], 557 [2], 590 [7], 646 [2, 14], 696
    [9]

[References are to items except as otherwise indicated]

Travel — *continued*
  President's — *continued*
    See also Visits to foreign countries; *specific
      cities and countries.*
    Asia, **1966**: 373 [16], 492 [4], 501 [11, 15,
      17, 19], 505, 516 [1, 19]
    Europe, **1966**: 8 [11], 141 [13], 610 [9]
    Germany, **1966**: 610 [9]
    Laos, **1966**: 514
    Manila Conference, **1966**: 492 [4], 501 [11,
      15, 17, 19], 516 [1, 19]
    Mexico, **1966**: 630 [2, 10], 635 [14]
    Philippines, **1966**: 505
    South America, **1966**: 373 [16]
    United States, **1966**: 320 [20], 338 [15],
      401 [7], 474 [6]
    Vietnam, **1966**: 501 [4]
  See the U.S.A. program, **1965**: 60, 419
  Visas, **1968–69**: 88, 116, 146
  Virgin Islands, **1968–69**: 457
Travel, Industry-Government Special Task Force
    on, **1967**: 16ftn. (p. 81); **1968–69**: 1ftn.
    (p. 1), 2n., 83, 88, 116
Travel Service, United States, **1967**: 16 (p. 81);
    1968–69: 146
Travell, Dr. Janet G., **1965**: 22 [1]
Traynor, Richard, **1963–64**: 338
Treasury, Department of the, **1963–64**: 33, 271
    [7], 277, 462 [2], 512, 688 [8], 724;
    1965: 32 (pp. 87, 97), 40, 46 [12], 60,
    76, 102, 113, 127, 140, 146, 155, 267,
    297, 311, 319 [3], 321, 329, 330, 380,
    503, 512n., 535, 599, 641 [2];
    1966: 75, 204, 390, 445 [14], 630 [4,
    5], 654 [11]; **1967**: 13 (p. 56), 66, 88,
    264 [6], 312 [4], 315n., 330 [1], 420,
    524n.; **1968–69**: 39 (p. 96), 57, 651,
    654, 684
  Customs activities, **1968–69**: 678 (p. 1302)
  Exceptional Service Award, presentation,
    1963–64: 21
  Narcotics, Bureau of, **1968–69**: 59, 60, 678
    (p. 1292)
  Reduction in expenditures, **1963–64**: 294 [4]
Treasury, Post Office, and Executive Office Ap-
    propriation Act, 1968, **1967**: 417 [1]
Treasury, Secretary of the
  Barr, Joseph W., **1968–69**: 676 (p.1268), 677
  Dillon, C. Douglas, **1963–64**: 21n., 23, 105,
    132 (p. 192), 178n., 182, 196, 197,
    277, 296, 299, 306, 370n., 382, 531,
    714, 771, 796; **1965**: 11, 60, 77, 102,
    113, 117 [3], 125
    Campaign remarks on, **1963–64**: 588n., 605,
      659, 667, 747
    Letter, bank regulations, **1963–64**: 226
    Memorandum to, **1963–64**: 261

Treasury, Secretary of the — *continued*
  Dillon, C. Douglas — *continued*
    News conference remarks on,
      1963–64: 242 [9], 379 [3, 6], 486 [4],
      563 [10], 688 [5], 780 [5], 818 [1]
    Report on balance of payments position,
      1963–64: 753
    Resignation, **1965**: 146
  Fowler, Henry H., **1965**: 250, 251, 297, 319
    [6, 8, 12, 19], 326, 335, 339, 347 [2, 4,
    11], 365, 380, 433, 451, 506, 541, 575,
    599n., 617, 639, 641, 660; **1966**: 8
    [18], 83, 116, 121 [3], 133, 137n., 139,
    182, 236 [8], 239, 277 [8], 379, 401
    [19], 444, 445 [2], 451, 472–473, 486,
    523, 612, 630 [2], 631, 635 [2], 636,
    645; **1967**: 6 [17, 18], 35, 63, 74, 77,
    85, 89, 103, 236, 255, 330 [1, 4, 8],
    371, 373, 394n., 417 [1, 10], 511, 529,
    554 [13]; **1968–69**: 2, 10n., 36, 47 (p.
    135), 54, 90, 100n., 112, 136, 169 [17],
    170, 218, 223 [11], 226, 241, 274, 290,
    317, 388, 422, 425 [3, 5], 500, 537,
    553, 604, 612, 651, 691, 696 [15]
    Asian Development Bank report, **1966**: 14
    Balance of payments report, **1966**: 6 (p. 5);
      1968–69: 449
    Letter, **1965**: 638; **1966**: 15, 73, 447
    Memorandums, **1968–69**: 89, 389
    Reports, **1965**: 249n., 451n.
    Resignation, **1968–69**: 582
    Swearing-in ceremony, **1965**: 155
Treasury Staff Silver and Coinage Study,
    1965: 297
Treaties and other international agreements,
    proposed.
  See also specific subject.
  Aircraft based offenses, convention,
    1968–69: 494
  Astronaut rescue, **1968–69**: 14 (p. 27), 41,
    288, 309, 387, 662
  Coffee agreement, **1968–69**: 207
  Customs Cooperation Council, convention
    establishing, **1968–69**: 261
  Human rights treaties, **1968–69**: 611
  Land-locked states, convention on trade,
    1968–69: 383
  Latin America, nuclear weapons in,
    1968–69: 13, 73, 349, 392
  Nuclear nonproliferation treaty, **1967**: 64, 80
    [2], 157, 162, 169n., 192, 204 [4], 225
    [17], 272, 280, 328 [24], 340n., 348,
    365, 367, 371, 373, 390, 492, 495 [5],
    515, 519, 545; **1968–69**: 14 (p. 26), 16,
    27, 51 [13], 69, 73, 194, 214n., 288,
    308, 310, 335, 345, 349, 350, 371,
    378, 387, 390, 392, 425 [8], 467 [5],
    531, 567–569, 590 [6], 654, 663, 676
    (p. 1268)

Treaties – *continued*
　Nuclear weapons control, **1966**: 411, 483
　Outer space exploration, **1966**: 411, 474 [18]
　Refugees, protocol relating to status,
　　1968-69: 428
　Space exploration, **1967**: 18, 24, 38, 59, 80
　　[2], 220, 225 [17], 519, 557
Treaty of Rome, **1967**: 391n.
Treaty of Washington (1871), **1966**: 448
Tree-planting program, proposed, **1965**: 54
Trejos Fernandez, José Joaquín (President of
　　Costa Rica), **1968-69**: 289-291, 366,
　　374, 421, 430
Trejos Fernandez, Mrs. José Joaquín,
　　1968-69: 289, 291
Trezise, Philip H., **1965**: 269, 296n.
Tri Quang (Thich), **1966**: 236 [4]
Trial Lawyers Association, National, **1967**: 114
Tribbitt, Sherman W., **1966**: 515
Trimble, Repr. James W., **1963-64**: 599;
　　1965: 478
Trimble, Vice Adm. Paul E., **1967**: 485 [8]
Trinidad, immigrants to U.S., **1965**: 13
Trinidad and Tobago, **1967**: 152
Trippe, Juan, **1965**: 522n.
Tropical Medical Center, American Samoan,
　　1966: 537
Tropics, exploration, **1968-69**: 288
Troubadors Drum and Bugle Corps, Bridge-
　　port, Conn., **1966**: 178
Trout, Mrs. Lawana, **1963-64**: 309
Trowbridge, Alexander B.
　See Commerce, Secretary of.
Trowbridge, Mrs. Alexander B., **1967**: 268;
　　1968-69: 80, 139
Trowbridge, Kimberly, **1967**: 268n.
Trowbridge, Scott, **1967**: 268n.
Trowbridge, Stephen, **1967**: 268n.
Trucks, excise taxes, **1965**: 255
Trudeau, Pierre Elliott (Prime Minister of Canada),
　　1968-69: 339 [11]
Trueblood, Robert, **1967**: 85n.
Trued, Merlyn N., **1965**: 155n.; **1966**: 277 [5]
Truesdale, Rev. Norman, **1968-69**: 499n.
Trujillo Molina, Rafael L., **1965**: 221
Truman, Harry S., President, **1963-64**: 2, 12, 69,
　　161n., 189, 192, 199, 218 [1, 36], 244,
　　261, 303, 314, 318, 359, 391, 506, 511,
　　577, 582, 698, 778, 809; **1965**: 34, 66,
　　223, 255, 324, 329, 330, 331, 348, 370,
　　394, 397, 401, 420, 425, 559;
　　1966: 22, 62, 86, 88 [17], 168, 175,
　　183, 228, 273, 311-312, 433, 437, 504,
　　508-509, 516 [6], 561, 565; **1967**: 3 (p.
　　3), 12, 44, 55, 70 [10] and ftn. (p. 224),
　　99, 107, 108, 111-112, 121, 150, 158,
　　216, 233, 236, 251, 267, 270, 281, 358
　　[10], 375 [18], 421, 495 [2, 9], 539;

Truman, Harry S., President – *continued*
　　1968-69: 24, 26ftn. (p. 57), 32, 56, 75,
　　79 [4], 87, 99, 104, 109, 154, 164, 171,
　　211, 212, 223 [8], 227, 270, 298, 346,
　　394, 460 [3], 472, 529, 556, 569, 576,
　　604, 611, 622, 646 [15], 648, 655, 665n.,
　　676 (p. 1270)
　Birthday, telephone greeting, **1966**: 211
　Birthday anniversary, **1965**: 238
　Birthday proclamation, **1966**: 212
　Campaign remarks on, **1963-64**: 541, 562,
　　601, 605, 607, 612, 631, 634, 635, 637,
　　638, 639, 640, 642, 643, 645, 646, 648,
　　652, 656, 658, 659, 669, 679, 680, 693,
　　694, 702, 703, 712, 713, 728, 729, 733,
　　734, 736, 745, 747, 748, 749, 762
　Interest rate statement, **1966**: 419
　Korean policy, **1966**: 6 (p. 8)
　Library, Independence, Mo., **1965**: 412 [1],
　　420
　News conference remarks of, **1963-64**: 294
　　[11, 24]
　News conference remarks on, **1963-64**: 54 [9],
　　71 [12], 211 [1], 242 [14], 294 [1, 8];
　　1965: 46 [6], 117 [4], 176 [1], 208
　　[2], 319 [17]
　Proclamation on role in creation of United Na-
　　tions, **1968-69**: 532
　Visit with, **1968-69**: 224
Truman, Mrs. Harry S., **1963-64**: 161n., 211
　　[6]; **1965**: 238, 394; **1966**: 22, 168;
　　1968-69: 224, 532n., 604
Truman, Lt. Gen. Louis W., **1966**: 348
Truman, Harry S., Center for the Advancement
　　of Peace (Jerusalem), **1966**: 22, 212
Truman Doctrine, **1963-64**: 189, 424n., 648,
　　736; **1966**: 212; **1967**: 107-109, 155n.,
　　158, 162; **1968-69**: 154, 211
Trust Fund, Government Employees',
　　1963-64: 688 [4]
Trust funds, **1963-64**: 132 (pp. 177, 178, 181,
　　188, 191); **1965**: 32 (pp. 85, 87, 88),
　　255, 460; **1966**: 26 (pp. 50, 52, 54);
　　1967: 13 (pp. 41, 43, 45, 59);
　　1968-69: 14 (p. 32), 39 (pp. 84, 86-
　　88, 91, 92, 95, 108), 678 (pp. 1274,
　　1279, 1280), 684 (p. 1322)
Trust Territory of the Pacific Islands, **1967**: 133,
　　218, 360
　High Commissioner (William R. Norwood),
　　1967: 133
Truth in lending, **1966**: 394; **1967**: 16 (p. 86),
　　57, 342, 393, 430, 460 [5], 465, 499,
　　503, 520, 534, 539; **1968-69**: 49, 154,
　　164, 270, 280, 281, 545
　See also Consumer Credit Protection Act.
Truth in packaging, **1966**: 394, 576; **1967**: 57,
　　86, 200, 393, 465, 534; **1968-69**: 56,
　　545

Tschudi, Hans-Peter, **1965**: 333n.
Tshombe, Moise, **1963–64**: 455 [12], 475 [8]
Tsiranana, Philibert, **1963–64**: 478, 479, 483
Tsiranana, Mrs. Philibert, **1963–64**: 478n., 479n.
Tuberculosis, **1966**: 271, 293, 433; **1967**: 161
   Control, **1965**: 5
   Prevention, **1968–69**: 113, 685
Tubman, William V. S. (President of Liberia),
     1968–69: 157, 159, 181
Tubman, Mrs. William V. S., **1968–69**: 157,
     159, 181
Tuck, Repr. William M., **1965**: 353 [18]
Tucker, Joseph, **1963–64**: 780ftn. (p. 1612)
Tucker, Paul, **1963–64**: 317n.
Tucker, Raymond, **1963–64**: 188, 189
Tugwell, Rexford G., **1966**: 270; **1968–69**: 227
Tukey, John W., **1965**: 602n.
Tulsa, Okla., **1966**: 415
   Mayor James M. Hewgley, Jr., **1966**: 415
Tunisia, **1965**: 325; **1967**: 245
   Assistance, **1966**: 11n.
   Visit of President Habib Bourguiba,
     1968–69: 249, 250, 255
Tunnell, James M., Jr., **1966**: 515
Tunney, John V., **1963–64**: 734
Tuomioja, Sakari, death of, **1963–64**: 564
Tupper, Stanley R., **1966**: 396–398, 644n.;
     1967: 238
Turkey, **1963–64**: 416, 607, 638, 694, 702, 713,
     728, 729, 733, 734, 736, 749; **1965**:
     235; **1966**: 6 (p. 7), 11n., 41;
     1967: 449
   Assistance, **1963–64**: 227; **1967**: 44, 158, 162;
     1968–69: 63, 679
   Communist aggression, **1967**: 397, 409
   Cyprus dispute, **1963–64**: 70, 170 [1], 182, 192,
     206, 210, 423, 429, 504 [5], 511, 544,
     560 [4], 607, 746; **1967**: 100, 162,
     518ftn. (p. 1093), 519, 521, 545;
     1968–69: 14 (p. 26), 504
   Economic and social development, **1967**: 44,
     109, 155, 158, 162
   Economy, **1963–64**: 418
   Foreign Minister Ihsan Sabri Caglayangil,
     1967: 162
   Gursel, Cemal (President), **1966**: 146, 460
     Message to, **1963–64**: 70
   Inonu, Ismet, **1963–64**: 416, 418, 423
   Nuclear weapons, **1967**: 167
   Ships for, **1965**: 600
   Sunay, Cevdet (President), **1967**: 109, 155,
     158, 162
   U.S. Ambassador
     Hare, Raymond A., **1965**: 353 [4]
     Hart, Parker T., **1967**: 158n.
   U.S. relations with, **1963–64**: 416, 418, 511;
     1967: 109, 155, 158, 162
   Visit of Sen. Fulbright, **1963–64**: 316 [24]

Turkey Federation, National, **1963–64**: 772n.
Turku, Finland, "America Days" celebration,
     1965: 491
Turman, Solon B., **1963–64**: 110n.
Turner, Donald F., **1965**: 208 [6]
Turner, Frederick Jackson, **1967**: 236
Turner, J. C., **1967**: 406, 466n.
Turner, J. Douglas, **1963–64**: 577
Turner, Robert C., **1967**: 85n.
Turnkey housing project, **1967**: 355n., 372,
     412, 460 [10], 467; **1968–69**: 47 (p.
     141), 87, 133, 152
Turville, Edward A., **1963–64**: 106
Tuscaloosa, Ala., **1965**: 117 [5]
Tuss McLaughry Award, **1966**: 7
Tuten, Repr. J. Russell, **1963–64**: 716
TVA.
   See main heading, Tennessee Valley Authority.
Twain, Mark, **1963–64**: 796; **1965**: 200, 500,
     555, 616; **1966**: 164; **1967**: 275, 538;
     1968–69: 148, 467 [8]
Tweed, William M., **1968–69**: 260
21st Tactical Air Support Squadron, USAF,
     1967: 61
25th Infantry Division, **1966**: 348
Tydings, Joseph D., **1963–64**: 703; **1965**: 172;
     1966: 189; **1967**: 193, 286
Tydings, Millard E., **1963–64**: 703
Tyler, Ralph W., **1966**: 210n.
Tyler, Veronica, **1968–69**: 65
Typewriter ribbon cloth tariffs, **1967**: 428
Typhoons, Philippines, **1963–64**: 627; **1966**: 461
Typhus, **1966**: 395
   Control, **1965**: 5
Tyros IV weather satellite, **1963–64**: 733

U.A.R.
   See United Arab Republic.
UAW Social Justice Award, **1966**: 235n.
U Nyun, **1966**: 557
U Thant.
   See United Nations Secretary General.
U-235, **1966**: 48n.
   Nuclear fuel, **1967**: 491
Udall, Repr. Morris K., **1963–64**: 649; **1966**:
     579; **1968–69**: 501
Udall, Stewart L.
   See Interior, Secretary of the.
Udall, Mrs. Stewart L., **1963–64**: 649
Uinta National Forest, Utah, **1968–69**: 629n.
Ulysses, **1967**: 37
UNCTAD.
   See United Nations Conference on Trade and
     Development.
Underdeveloped countries.
   See Developing nations.

Unemployed workers.
See also Unemployment.
Aid to children of, **1963–64**: 133, 160;
   1965: 29
Antipoverty program aid, **1963–64**: 124 (p.
   165), 219, 267, 288, 289; **1965**: 132
Food for, **1963–64**: 67, 690n., 732, 757;
   1965: 47, 453, 492
   Stamp program, **1963–64**: 91 (p. 114), 219,
      225, 235, 242 [12], 249, 266 [21], 267,
      268, 297, 305, 314, 434, 546, 598, 620,
      634, 757
   See also under Food.
Increased benefits for, **1963–64**: 219;
   1965: 258
Occupational training, **1963–64**: 99, 160, 213,
   321, 504 [7], 598, 669, 690n.;
   1965: 38, 70, 79, 100, 165
Unemployment, **1963–64**: 22, 28 [9], 124 (pp.
   156, 158, 160), 132 (p. 178), 211 [3],
   213, 221, 287, 290, 293, 295, 297, 305,
   311, 388, 690, 775, 787; **1965**: 35
   (p. 113), 38, 76, 99, 100, 165, 351,
   436; **1966**: 34 (p. 97), 110n., 121 [5],
   141 [3], 155, 158 [3], 275, 395, 401
   [2], 426; **1967**: 13 (p. 40), 16 (p. 73),
   199, 286, 329; **1968–69**: 14 (p. 28),
   24, 46, 47 (pp. 139–142), 86, 112, 156,
   165, 241, 343, 406, 565, 567, 587, 612
See also Unemployed workers.
Appalachian area, **1963–64**: 213, 246 [6], 321,
   325
Automobile industry, **1963–64**: 67, 288, 289,
   295, 297, 462 [3], 463, 486 [2]
Blue-collar workers, **1965**: 598
Children of unemployed, aid, **1966**: 26 (p. 63),
   27
Coal industry, **1963–64**: 292, 295, 297
Crime, relationship to, **1966**: 116
Decrease, **1965**: 23, 32 (p. 84), 35 (pp. 104,
   106, 109), 45, 76, 153, 156 [1], 165,
   207, 255, 258, 298, 319 [7], 480, 489,
   490, 590, 598, 632, 644; **1966**: 17, 26
   (p. 49), 33, 34 (p. 96), 111, 132, 140,
   155, 189, 235, 237, 347, 394, 415,
   429, 431, 437, 444, 477 [2], 588, 635
   [8]; **1967**: 3 (p. 7), 13 (p. 39), 16 (pp.
   73, 82), 114, 199, 286, 354, 412;
   1968–69: 24, 25, 37, 39 (p. 86), 47
   (pp. 128, 131, 133), 76, 282, 564,
   678 (pp. 1273, 1276), 683, 684 (pp.
   1312, 1313, 1315)
See also main heading, Employment.
Defense programs, **1963–64**: 486 [2]
Depressed areas, **1963–64**: 294 [4]; **1965**: 132;
   1966: 111
Displaced persons, **1963–64**: 67, 99, 126;
   1965: 490
Great Lakes area, **1963–64**: 213

Unemployment – *continued*
Hard-core, **1967**: 13 (p. 54), 412, 427, 512,
   554 [6]; **1968–69**: 14 (p. 28), 19, 24–
   26, 37, 39 (pp. 104, 109), 50, 75n., 86,
   87, 91, 92, 100, 105, 114, 115, 133,
   141, 154, 164, 220, 227, 241, 328, 406,
   498, 555, 678 (p. 1294), 684 (pp. 1314,
   1324)
Indians, **1963–64**: 120; **1965**: 204
Insurance, **1963–64**: 91 (p. 114), 124 (pp. 163,
   165), 132 (pp. 189, 191), 213, 235, 246
   [12], 305, 388, 406, 444, 562, 589, 598,
   643, 703, 713; **1965**: 2, 32 (p. 94), 35
   (p. 114), 99, 100, 132, 258, 425, 644;
   1966: 6 (p. 5), 26 (p. 62), 34 (p. 106),
   111, 235, 237, 318, 394; **1967**: 12, 16
   (p. 84), 97, 114, 199, 548; **1968–69**: 39
   (p. 104), 47 (p. 142), 463, 678 (pp.
   1278, 1299), 684 (p. 1323)
Machinery industry, **1966**: 445 [5]
Minority groups, **1965**: 100, 408, 598, 632;
   1966: 111; **1967**: 16 (p. 73), 55, 199;
   1968–69: 24, 26, 47 (p. 142), 113,
   429, 596, 612
Negroes, **1965**: 76, 165, 301, 322, 351, 480,
   632; **1966**: 34 (p. 100), 111–112, 196,
   475
Older persons, **1967**: 12, 199; **1968–69**: 24
Programs, **1968–69**: 19, 39 (p. 104), 40, 354,
   678 (pp. 1286, 1294)
Rate, **1968–69**: 47 (p. 142), 133, 567–569,
   575, 596, 612, 622, 646 [3], 654, 676
   (p. 1264)
Report, **1963–64**: 160, 211 [3]
Rural, **1965**: 47; **1967**: 199; **1968–69**: 39 (p.
   104), 94
Statement, **1963–64**: 99
Statistics, **1965**: 153, 165, 298, 408, 632;
   1967: 55
Steel industry, **1963–64**: 289, 295, 297
Unskilled workers, **1965**: 490; **1966**: 111–112;
   1967: 16 (p. 73)
Urban, **1967**: 144, 199; **1968–69**: 14 (p. 28),
   24, 26, 47 (p. 140), 50, 82, 87, 115,
   678 (p. 1290)
Veterans, **1967**: 345
Youth, **1963–64**: 91 (p. 115), 246 [20], 386,
   451, 754, 771, 787, 791; **1965**: 9, 76,
   100, 165, 268, 298, 301, 322, 351, 408,
   436, 438, 463 [15], 480, 490, 590, 598.
   632; **1966**: 34 (p. 100), 111–112, 235;
   1967: 55, 199, 328 [19]; **1968–69**: 24
UNESCO.
See United Nations Educational, Scientific and
   Cultural Organization.
Unger, Gen. Ferdinand T. (High Commissioner
   of the Ryukyu Islands), **1968–69**: 44
Unger, Leonard, **1963–64**: 285 [4], 294 [16]

UNICEF.
See United Nations International Children's
  Emergency Fund.
Uniform Code of Military Justice, **1968–69**: 556
Uniformed Services Pay Act of 1963,
  1963–64: 132 (p. 194)
Union of African and Malagasy States, **1965**: 144
Union Bag-Camp Paper Corp., **1963–64**: 350n.
Union Programs for Fair Practices,   .
  1963–64: 221n.
Union Station, Washington, D. C., **1968–69**: 128
Unions.
  See Labor organizations.
United Air Lines, Inc., **1966**: 256n., 322
United Aircraft Corporation, **1963–64**: 201 [2]
United Arab Republic, **1965**: 325; **1967**: 198,
    233, 254n., 257, 264 [12, 13];
    1968–69: 504
  Conflict with Israel.
    See main heading, Middle East conflict.
  Cotton exports to U.S., **1967**: 375 [20]
  Nasser, Gamal Abdel, **1963–64**: 460;
    1965: 463 [6]
  Nonaligned nations conference, **1963–64**: 625
  U.S. relations with, **1965**: 46 [2]
  U.S. trade with, **1965**: 46 [2], 661
  Yemen cease-fire agreement, **1965**: 463 [6]
United Automobile Workers of America,
    1963–64: 67, 233, 336 [17], 563 [2],
    624, 687, 713, 733; **1966**: 235
United Community Campaigns of America,
    1966: 476; **1967**: 402
United Fund, **1966**: 476
United Givers Fund, **1965**: 436, 438; **1967**: 288
United Kingdom, **1963–64**: 617, 733, 764;
    1965: 68n., 194, 220; **1966**: 34 (p.
    100), 359n., 373 [6, 13], 478, 486;
    1967: 83, 204ftn. (p. 497);
    1968–69: 378, 479
  Aid to developing nations, **1965**: 18
  Aircraft, Anglo-French supersonic transport,
    1965: 319 [19]
  Ambassador Patrick Dean, **1965**: 335, 376;
    1967: 18n., 425; **1968–69**: 349n.
  Ambassador Lord Harlech (David Ormsby
    Gore), **1963–64**: 187n., 263n., 796
  Balance of payments, **1963–64**: 780 [3];
    1966: 359n.
  Butler, Richard A., **1963–64**: 184, 186, 187n.
  Change in leadership, **1963–64**: 680, 686, 688
    [8], 694, 701, 734, 735, 737, 746, 747
  Commonwealth Prime Ministers' Conference,
    1965: 319 [14], 331
  Control, **1966**: 359n.
  Cyprus dispute, **1963–64**: 70
  Defense, **1966**: 506
  Economy, **1963–64**: 780 [3]
  Foreign aid to other countries, **1968–69**: 63

United Kingdom – *continued*
  Foreign policy, **1968–69**: 65, 170, 250n., 277,
    313, 528, 620
  Foreign Secretary George Brown, **1966**: 520,
    607 [3], 654ftn. (p. 1458); **1967**: 278,
    404
  Home, Alec Douglas, **1963–64**: 26, 272
    News conference remarks on, **1963–64**: 28
    [4], 285 [3, 21], 475 [3], 619 [15]
    Visit, **1963–64**: 184–187
  Immigration quota to U.S., **1963–64**: 97
  Interest rates, increase, **1963–64**: 211 [34]
  Malaysia troop withdrawals, **1967**: 312 [17]
  Nuclear materials, production decrease,
    1965: 20
  Nuclear weapons, **1963–64**: 653
    Tests, **1963–64**: 462 [4], 653
  Pound devaluation, **1967**: 497, 499, 519, 524;
    1968–69: 2, 47 (pp. 128, 134), 500
  Price and wage controls, **1966**: 347, 359n.
  Prices, **1967**: 430
  Princess Margaret, **1965**: 616
  Queen Elizabeth II, **1963–64**: 187, 796;
    1965: 616; **1966**: 342, 359; **1967**: 540;
    1968–69: 65, 479
  Ship construction contracts with U.S.,
    1967: 410
  Singapore troop withdrawals, **1967**: 312 [17]
  Southern Rhodesia dispute, **1966**: 243
  Special Drawing Rights, **1968–69**: 218
  Support of United Nations, **1963–64**: 795n.,
    797
  Tariff reductions, **1968–69**: 517
  Trade, **1967**: 497, 508
    With Cuba, **1963–64**: 150 [13]
  U.S. Ambassador David K. E. Bruce,
    1963–64: 796; **1965**: 46 [6]; **1966**: 236
    [5]
  U.S. relations with, **1963–64**: 184, 187, 686,
    795, 796n., 797; **1966**: 448, 359
  Vietnam peace efforts, **1966**: 654 [1]
  Walker, Patrick Gordon, **1963–64**: 688 [1],
    796, 797
  Weapons purchases from U.S., **1967**: 410
  Wilson, Harold (Prime Minister), **1963–64**: 676,
    678, 679, 680, 681, 693, 800;
    1965: 22 [7], 319 [14], 333n., 347 [10],
    376, 388 [6], 641 [3], 653; **1966**: 88
    [25], 328n., 359; **1967**: 249, 250, 518
    [8, 10], 554 [5]; **1968–69**: 65, 79 [11,
    15], 588
    News conference remarks on, **1963–64**: 688
    [1], 780 [8]
    Visit, **1963–64**: 795–797
United Nations, **1963–64**: 28 [3], 193, 244, 396,
    426, 435, 566, 579, 590, 616, 651, 667,
    680, 693, 728, 734, 736, 764;
    1965: 68, 169, 194, 199, 254, 257, 262,

United Nations — *continued*
284, 318, 320, 330, 331, 359, 370, 378,
383, 390, 397, 464, 558; **1966**: 125,
246, 483–485, 492 [1]; **1967**: 100,
109, 111, 143n., 312 [12], 313n., 390,
404, 423, 435, 438, 459, 480, 488, 491;
1968–69: 53, 143, 159n., 194, 214,
271n., 511n., 522n., 525
Africa, action on, **1967**: 100, 488
Arms control policy, **1968–69**: 392
Astronaut assistance and return agreement,
1968–69: 14 (p. 27), 41, 288, 309,
387, 662
Astronauts and space objects, rescue and return, **1967**: 557
Brazilian support, **1963–64**: 561
British support, **1963–64**: 186, 795n., 797
Charter, **1963–64**: 122, 483, 502n., 507,
561n.; **1965**: 169, 331; **1966**: 94,
212, 338 [9, 12], 483, 540, 549;
1967: 46, 74, 100, 144n., 162, 233, 257,
272, 366, 488; **1968–69**: 349, 455, 462,
620
Children's Fund, **1963–64**: 227; **1966**: 41
Communist China, question of membership,
1963–64: 170 [6], 218 [32]; **1965**: 46
[5]; **1966**: 141 [7], 338 [9]; **1967**: 219
Congo operations, **1965**: 169
Convention on the Elimination of All Forms of
Racial Discrimination, **1967**: 488
Convention on transit trade of land-locked
states, **1968–69**: 383
Cyprus, **1963–64**: 235, 246 [4], 423;
1965: 169; **1967**: 100, 162, 518ftn. (p.
1093), 519, 521, 545; **1968–69**: 504
Czechoslovakia, Soviet invasion, **1968–69**: 455
Danish support of, **1963–64**: 394
Developing nations aid, **1965**: 136, 169;
1966: 41, 62, 427; **1967**: 100, 488;
1968–69: 233
Dominican Republic, **1967**: 100
Economic and Social Council.
See main heading, United Nations Economic
and Social Council.
Fellowships, proposed, **1965**: 374
Financial support, **1965**: 169, 319 [15];
1967: 100, 488
General Assembly, **1963–64**: 51, 529;
1965: 169, 355n., 395 [4], 516, 630;
1966: 32, 94, 566, 643; **1967**: 38, 100,
219, 233, 425, 488; **1968–69**: 16, 42,
53, 288, 308, 310, 349, 392, 428, 515,
611
Commemorative session, **1965**: 295 [2]
Geneva five-power conference on, proposed,
1965: 46 [5]
Human Rights Year, **1968–69**: 42
India, support, **1966**: 152

United Nations — *continued*
Indus Basin development, **1963–64**: 227
Irish support, **1963–64**: 366, 376
Japanese support, **1965**: 15
Kashmir, **1965**: 169; **1967**: 100
Korean conflict, **1966**: 565–566; **1967**: 100;
1968–69: 232
Members, meeting with, **1963–64**: 54ftn. (p.
67)
Message to Congress, **1966**: 94
Middle East conflict, **1965**: 169; **1967**: 233,
239, 254, 255, 257, 272, 287, 297 [3],
488, 519, 554 [2]; **1968–69**: 9, 14 (p.
26), 169 [20], 249, 250n., 255, 288,
307, 474, 504, 615, 620, 652, 676 (p.
1269)
Narcotic drug control, **1967**: 94
News conference remarks, **1965**: 46 [5], 106
[6], 319 [14, 15, 17, 21], 388 [1, 6, 12],
395 [3, 4], 448 [2, 4], 463 [5]
19th anniversary, **1963–64**: 698
Nuclear nonproliferation treaty, endorse-
ment, **1968–69**: 308, 378, 531
Nuclear weapons in space, **1963–64**: 395, 486
[1]; **1966**: 411
Pueblo incident, **1968–69**: 35
Record for 1963, **1963–64**: 529
Refugees, protocol for status of, **1968–69**: 428
Secretariat, **1968–69**: 650
Secretary General (U Thant), **1963–64**: 28 [3],
51, 429, 501, 502, 545n.; **1965**: 169,
172, 194, 199, 294, 331, 516, 524, 529;
1966: 39n., 153, 236 [9], 249n., 443,
474 [5], 504; **1967**: 18n., 70 [12], 144,
225 [8], 233, 328 [4], 411 [5], 488, 521;
1968–69: 9, 79 [11], 308, 428, 504
Letters, **1965**: 390, 464
Message, **1965**: 359
News conference remarks on, **1965**: 176 [1,
3], 295 [14], 388 [1, 12], 412 [2], 463
[5]
Vietnam peace efforts, **1966**: 654 [1, 13]
Security Council, **1963–64**: 122, 206, 218 [24],
429, 498, 499, 504 [5], 529, 561n.;
1965: 169, 331, 448 [4], 524, 533, 650;
1966: 39, 52 [5], 65 [13], 88 [15], 607
[10]; **1967**: 74, 100, 204 [13], 233,
239, 251, 254, 257, 312 [9], 488, 521;
1968–69: 9, 35, 148, 170, 249, 288,
307, 349, 455, 474, 504, 615, 620, 676
(p. 1269)
Southeast Asia operations, **1963–64**: 170 [1];
1965: 169, 172, 176 [1, 3], 246
Southern Rhodesia, **1967**: 488
Dispute, role, **1966**: 243
Space treaty, **1967**: 18, 24, 38, 59, 80 [2],
220, 225 [17], 519, 557; **1968–69**: 504

United Nations – *continued*
Trusteeship Council.
  See main heading, United Nations Trusteeship Council.
Twentieth anniversary, **1965**: 96, 295 [2], 331
Universal Declaration of Human Rights,
    1967: 488
U.S. participation and support, **1963–64**: 45,
    51, 91 (p. 117), 186, 191, 193, 206,
    227, 394n., 501, 502, 529, 638, 642,
    662n., 669, 702, 795n., 797; **1965**: 2,
    15, 32 (p. 90), 169, 464, 533;
    1966: 6 (p. 8), 26 (p. 59), 32, 94, 130,
    152, 498; **1967**: 100, 272, 488;
    1968–69: 53, 504
U.S. Representative (Ball, George W.),
    1968–69: 455, 496
  Swearing in, **1968–69**: 335
U.S. Representative (Goldberg, Arthur J.),
    1965: 388 [1, 12], 390, 395 [3], 397,
    412 [2, 3], 448 [2, 4, 15, 20], 463 [1,
    8, 9], 516, 524, 529, 533, 546, 595,
    632; **1966**: 8 [2], 39, 52, [5], 65 [13],
    86, 88 [23], 130, 209, 217, 236 [9],
    272, 338 [5], 397, 411, 443, 475, 477
    [6], 503, 580 [4], 607 [2, 10], 643,
    645; **1967**: 18n., 38, 70 [12], 100, 116,
    144, 204 [13], 233, 255, 257, 264 [1],
    272, 297 [3], 425, 461, 488, 518 [12],
    554 [2]; **1968–69**: 31, 53, 79 [11], 86,
    169 [20], 223 [1, 6]
  Resignation, **1968–69**: 213 [1, 3, 8]
  Swearing-in, **1965**: 383
U.S. Representative (Stevenson, Adlai E.),
    1963–64: 35n., 208, 228, 489, 498,
    502, 511, 529, 616, 669; **1965**: 176
    [1, 3], 355, 356, 359, 370, 371, 373,
    376, 383
  See also main heading, Stevenson, Adlai E.
U.S. Representative (Wiggins, J. Russell),
    1968–69: 515, 525, 696 [1]
Vietnam conflict, **1966**: 6 (p. 10), 52 [5], 65
    [13], 94, 607 [10], 654 [1]; **1967**: 100,
    132 [9], 144, 204 [13], 225 [6], 312
    [9], 409, 411 [5], 488, 495 [14], 518
    [12]; **1968–69**: 504
Water resources development, **1966**: 427;
    1967: 230
United Nations Committee on Peaceful Uses of
    Outer Space, **1963–64**: 705; **1967**: 18n.
United Nations Conference on Trade and Development (UNCTAD), **1963–64**: 201 [11],
    237; **1966**: 94; **1967**: 100; **1968–69**: 47
    (p. 138)
United Nations Day, **1966**: 217
  Proclamation, **1968–69**: 532
United Nations Development Program,
    1967: 100; **1968–69**: 504

United Nations Economic Commission for
    Africa, **1963–64**: 191
United Nations Economic Commission for Asia
    and the Far East, **1965**: 353ftn. (p.
    736); **1968–69**: 237
United Nations Economic and Social Council,
    1965: 169, 448 [4]
United Nations Educational, Scientific, and
    Cultural Organization (UNESCO),
    1963–64: 480; **1966**: 519, 556;
    1967: 198n.
United Nations Food and Agriculture Organization, **1966**: 153; **1967**: 33, 415n.;
    1968–69: 504
United Nations Industrial Development Organization, **1967**: 100, 488
United Nations International Children's Emergency Fund (UNICEF), **1963–64**: 227;
    1965: 149, 353 [4] ; **1966**: 41
United Nations Outer Space Committee,
    1966: 277ftn. (p. 631); **1967**: 557;
    1968–69: 387
United Nations Participation Act of 1945,
    1966: 94; **1967**: 74
  Amendment, **1965**: 533
United Nations Relief and Rehabilitation Administration, **1966**: 528
United Nations Relief and Works Agency
    (UNRWA), **1967**: 510
United Nations Relief and Works Agency for
    Palestine Refugees in the Near East,
    1965: 149
United Nations Trusteeship Council,
    1965: 448 [4]
United Nations World Population Conference,
    1965: 464
United Negro College Development Campaign,
    1963–64: 79
United Negro College Fund, **1963–64**: 79
United Planning Organization, **1963–64**: 537;
    1965: 70
United Press International, **1967**: 460 [5]
United Service Organizations (USO), **1966**: 476
United States Advisory Commission on Information, **1963–64**: 211 [2]
United States Armed Forces Institute, **1967**: 199
United States Arms Control and Disarmament
    Agency, **1963–64**: 382, 413; **1965**: 20,
    26, 284; **1966**: 70; **1967**: 59
  Director (William C. Foster), **1963–64**: 26, 62,
    94, 129n., 131n., 150 [10], 395;
    1965: 20, 353 [5], 430; **1967**: 64n.,
    340, 365, 367
United States attorneys, **1968–69**: 14 (p. 30),
    59, 209
United States-Canada
  Automotive products, trade agreement,
    1965: 21, 22 [9], 147, 574, 575

United States-Canada – *continued*
  Committee on Trade and Economic Affairs,
    1963–64: 140
  Joint Ministerial Committee on Defense,
    1963–64: 140
  Permanent Joint Board on Defense, **1965**: 432
United States Chamber of Commerce.
  See Chamber of Commerce of the United States.
United States Conference of Mayors, **1965**: 438;
    1966: 536; **1967**: 337
United States Courts of Appeals, **1965**: 353 [3],
    385
United States Employment Service, **1963–64**: 89,
    178; **1965**: 35 (p. 112), 340; **1966**: 111;
    1967: 13 (p. 54)
United States Food and Fiber Policy, Commis-
    sion on, proposed, **1965**: 47
United States Grantee Directory (1965),
    1966: 378
United States Housing Authority, **1963–64**: 642
United States image abroad, **1963–64**: 218 [28]
United States Industrial Payroll Savings Com-
    mittee, **1965**: 11; **1968–69**: 10
United States Information Agency, **1963–64**:
    200, 621, 688 [8]; **1965**: 117 [3],
    185, 223, 233, 319 [21], 353 [17],
    395 [1], 412 [2], 468; **1966**: 52 [7],
    445 [26], 519, 629; **1967**: 245n.,
    357n., 568; **1968–69**: 149n., 454, 581
  Director (Marks, Leonard), **1965**: 353 [4, 17],
    468; **1966**: 141 [16], 537, 629, 644n.;
    1967: 238, 352; **1968–69**: 581
  Director (Murrow, Edward R.), resignation,
    1963–64: 125
  Director (Rowan, Carl T.), **1963–64**: 200, 280
    [5], 619 [8], 621; **1965**: 117 [3], 353
    [4, 17]
  Johnson, Lyndon B., biographical film,
    1966: 401 [8]
United States Information and Educational Ex-
    change Act of 1948, **1966**: 45
United States Information Service, **1966**: 243
United States Interparliamentary Conference,
    Mexico, **1968–69**: 199
United States-Japan
  Civil Air Transport Agreement, **1965**: 15
  Committee on Scientific Cooperation,
    1965: 15
  Committee on Trade and Economic Affairs,
    Joint, **1965**: 15, 355; **1967**: 381, 491
  Conference on Cultural and Educational Inter-
    change, Joint, **1965**: 15
  Conference on Development and Utilization of
    Natural Resources, **1967**: 491
  Cooperative Medical Science Program,
    1965: 544; **1968–69**: 286, 685
United States Jaycees, **1967**: 23, 160, 286, 291

United States Junior Chamber of Commerce,
    1963–64: 403; **1965**: 222
United States marshals, **1963–64**: 523
United States-Mexico
  Commission for Border Development and
    Friendship, **1967**: 451; **1968–69**: 223
    [2], 354, 623, 624n.
  International Boundary and Water Commission,
    1965: 119; **1966**: 177, 467–468;
    1967: 408 [2, 8]
  Joint Trade Committee, **1967**: 451
United States Military Academy, **1967**: 19n.,
    495 [14]
United States National Committee for the Pre-
    vention of Pollution of the Seas by Oil,
    1967: 240
United States Naval Academy, **1967**: 440
United States Park Police, **1966**: 27
United States Pavilion, World's Fair, **1963–64**:
    283
United States Prisoners Rehabilitation Act,
    1968–69: 39 (p. 107)
United States-Puerto Rico, Commission on the
    Status of Puerto Rico, **1963–64**: 393;
    1966: 372
United States Steel Corp., **1963–64**: 246 [19],
    290; **1965**: 454 [1], 466; **1968–69**: 425
    [5], 427
United States Supreme Court.
  See Supreme Court of the United States.
United States Tariff Commission, **1963–64**: 80;
    1965: 353 [4], 577; **1966**: 43;
    1967: 99, 414, 428, 508
United States Tax Court, **1965**: 478; **1966**: 220
United States Travel Service, **1967**: 16 (p. 81)
United States Veterans Advisory Commission,
    1968–69: 40, 599
United Steelworkers of America, **1963–64**: 289,
    290, 587 [9], 589, 780 [5]; **1965**: 208
    [3, 21], 226, 454 [1], 466, 483
Universal Declaration of Human Rights,
    1968–69: 42, 611
Universal Military Training and Service Act,
    1963–64: 89; **1966**: 128
Universities.
  See Colleges; *specific universities.*
Universities, Association of State Colleges and,
    1967: 490n.
Universities and Land-Grant Colleges, National
    Association of, **1967**: 490n.
University Council, Central American,
    1968–69: 366
University of Akron, **1963–64**: 693
University of California, **1963–64**: 71 [1], 192
  Irvine Campus, dedication, **1963–64**: 414
  Santa Cruz campus, **1963–64**: 414
University of Florida, **1965**: 260
University of Kentucky, **1965**: 80

University of Maryland, **1963–64**: 808n.
University of Michigan, **1963–64**: 357; **1965**: 318
University of Nebraska, **1965**: 445
University of North Carolina, **1963–64**: 339
University of Oregon, **1965**: 225
University of Tennessee, **1963–64**: 339
University of Texas, **1963–64**: 375, 482;
    1965: 142, 181, 411, 412
  Lyndon Baines Johnson Institute of Public
    Service, **1965**: 411n.
University of Virginia, **1967**: 184n.
Unruh, Jesse M., **1963–64**: 415, 579
UNRWA.
  See United Nations Relief and Works Agency
Uplands R.C.A.F. Base, Ottawa, Canada,
    1967: 239n.
Upper Volta, Republic of, **1966**: 45
  Assistance, **1965**: 144, 250
  President Maurice Yameogo, **1965**: 141, 142,
    144, 154, 250; **1966**: 168n., 189n.
  U.S. Ambassador Thomas S. Estes, **1965**: 142n.
  U.S. relations with, **1965**: 141, 144
Upward Bound program, **1966**: 594; **1967**: 39,
    114, 211, 532; **1968–69**: 39 (p. 104),
    54, 87, 113
Uranium, **1968–69**: 28, 39 (p. 104), 678 (p.
    1281)
  Decrease in production, **1963–64**: 91 (p. 117),
    132 (p. 185), 272, 294 [10, 19]
  Peaceful uses, **1966**: 48
Urban areas, **1963–64**: 754; **1965**: 32 (p. 83),
    100, 315, 319 [2], 353 [19], 415, 460,
    545; **1966**: 6 (p. 6), 237, 388, 394, 414,
    491; **1967**: 4, 13 (p. 52), 23, 55, 222,
    326, 329, 421, 460 [10], 463, 498, 517;
    1968–69: 153 [16], 164, 167, 241, 462,
    655
  See also Federal-State-local governmental re-
    sponsibilities; Federal-State-local rela-
    tions.
  Antipoverty program, **1963–64**: 132 (p. 184),
    528; **1965**: 90; **1967**: 312 [6], 328 [19]
  Beautification programs, **1965**: 54, 90;
    1966: 26 (p. 61), 394, 500; **1967**: 295;
    1968–69: 697
  Civil disorders.
    See main heading, Civil disorders.
  College extension service, **1963–64**: 414
  Community development, **1965**: 90
  Crime, **1966**: 30; **1967**: 353, 455; **1968–69**: 59,
    82, 87, 320
  Development, **1963–64**: 213, 669, 680, 756:
    1965: 9, 24, 76, 90, 102, 277, 330,
    503, 511, 596; **1966**: 8 [1], 13, 26
    (pp. 61–62), 27, 30–31, 34 (p. 105),
    155, 302, 346, 401 [4], 428, 452, 486,
    497, 524, 630 [4]; **1967**: 3 (p. 2), 13

Urban areas — *continued*
  Development — *continued*
    (pp. 52, 60), 114, 179, 223 [10], 252,
    261, 353, 358 [3], 460 [10]; **1968–69**:
    39 (p. 103), 47 (p. 141), 50, 84, 87, 91,
    114, 135, 164, 165, 167, 227, 234,
    278, 380, 382, 406, 426, 458, 463,
    470, 506, 676 (p. 1265), 678 (pp. 1286,
    1289, 1290), 684 (p. 1313), 689, 697
  Disadvantaged children, **1966**: 30
  Education, **1963–64**: 725; **1965**: 90, 340;
    1966: 30; **1967**: 479, 493
  Employment, **1968–69**: 14 (p. 28), 24, 26, 39
    (p. 102), 47 (p. 140), 50, 82, 87, 115,
    153 [16], 678 (p. 1290)
  Federal aid, **1966**: 6 (p. 3), 30, 207, 401 [6],
    428, 525; **1967**: 13 (p. 52), 16 (p. 84),
    114, 179, 225 [1], 328 [14, 17, 26],
    353, 358 [8], 380, 458, 467, 576;
    1968–69: 39 (p. 110), 678 (p. 1290)
  Federal programs, coordination, **1966**: 30,
    380, 425
  Hospital modernization, **1963–64**: 179
  Housing, **1963–64**: 91 (p. 115), 357;
    1965: 54, 90, 337, 510, 511; **1966**: 13,
    30, 320 [17]; **1967**: 16 (p. 85), 23, 114,
    252, 355, 380, 412, 460 [10];
    1968–69: 47 (p. 140), 164, 697, 704
  Housing and urban development bill, **1965**: 319
    [2], 329, 330, 337, 397, 406, 415, 510
  Indian migration, **1968–69**: 113
  Industry, **1968–69**: 87
  Insurance coverage, **1968–69**: 36, 87, 114, 115,
    278
  Insurance firms, aid, **1967**: 380, 460 [10], 467
  Legal services, **1966**: 394, 594
  Legislation, **1966**: 401 [4], 524; **1967**: 353,
    358 [8], 460, [2, 10]
  Medical care, **1965**: 9
  Message to Congress, **1965**: 90; **1966**: 30;
    1967: 114; **1968–69**: 87
  Model cities program, **1966**: 30, 207, 237, 297,
    373 [15], 392, 394, 414, 417 [3, 5, 6],
    491, 524–525, 574; **1967**: 3 (p. 5), 12,
    13 (pp. 46, 52, 58), 16 (p. 84), 23, 114,
    124, 179, 216, 223 [13], 225 [13],
    252, 261, 276, 286, 312 [6], 326, 353,
    358 [8], 359, 370, 458, 460 [3, 10],
    467, 484, 534, 554, [6, 16];
    1968–69: 4, 14 (p. 28), 19, 26, 39 (pp.
    89, 92, 103, 109), 47 (p. 140), 59, 87,
    91, 114, 133, 135, 212, 234, 278, 380,
    406, 426, 437, 470, 565, 568, 569, 676
    (p. 1265), 678 (p. 1290), 684 (pp.
    1314, 1325), 697
  Municipal budgets, **1966**: 30
  Negro concentration in, **1965**: 301
  Open-space land program, **1965**: 54

Urban areas — *continued*
  Pollution control, **1968–69**: 14 (p. 28), 87, 122
  Population.
    See main heading, Population.
  Problems, **1968–69**: 14 (p. 28), 47 (pp. 130, 140), 74, 87, 95, 223 [11], 242, 354, 464, 470, 678 (p. 1289)
  Public services, **1968–69**: 87
  Recreational facilities, **1966**: 26 (p. 61), 373 [15], 398; **1967**: 114, 553
  Research, **1967**: 114, 353, 359, 370; **1968–69**: 39 (p. 103), 87, 215
  Riots, **1963–64**: 600; **1966**: 373 [15], 484, 501 [12]
  Rural migration to, **1968–69**: 39 (p. 100), 87, 94, 416, 568, 569, 696 [9]
  Sculpture in, **1968–69**: 64
  Slums, **1967**: 14, 23, 252, 286, 512, 517, 554 [6]; **1968–69**: 26, 47 (p. 140), 50, 82, 86, 87, 91, 227, 419, 625, 678 (p. 1289)
  Study fellowships, **1967**: 359
  Suburban migration, **1968–69**: 416
  Taxes, **1967**: 4
  Transportation, **1963–64**: 91 (pp. 112, 115), 124 (p. 163), 132 (p. 188), 152, 357, 410, 453, 620, 630, 654; **1965**: 2, 9, 29, 32 (p. 93), 35 (p. 114), 38, 61, 90, 97, 499; **1966**: 26 (p. 61), 30, 98, 353, 394, 428, 442; **1967**: 16 (p. 85), 20, 114, 179, 234, 353, 358 [3], 412, 467, 542; **1968–69**: 39 (p. 102), 87, 93, 130, 306, 351, 458, 678 (p. 1302), 684, (p. 1321), 693, 697
  Unemployment, **1967**: 199
  Water resources, **1966**: 30, 393; **1967**: 16 (p. 84), 230; **1968–69**: 697
  Welfare programs, **1966**: 26 (p. 61), 30
  Youth, **1968–69**: 87, 328
Urban Coalition, **1968–69**: 74, 220, 227
Urban Development, Department of Housing and, proposed, **1965**: 418
Urban Development, Institute of, **1967**: 114
  Proposed, **1965**: 90
Urban Development Bank, proposed, **1968–69**: 684
Urban Development Seminar, **1965**: 511
Urban Housing, President's Committee on, **1967**: 252, 355, 358 [8], 412; **1968–69**: 87, 471n., 704
Urban Institute, **1968–69**: 74, 87, 215
Urban League, National, **1965**: 438; **1968–69**: 596, 604, 631
Urban Mass Transportation Act of 1964, **1963–64**: 453; **1965**: 32 (p. 93); **1966**: 442; **1968–69**: 87
Urban Mass Transportation Act of 1966, amendments, **1968–69**: 306

Urban Mass Transportation Administration, proposed, **1968–69**: 93
Urban planning, **1963–64**: 756
Urban Problems, Commission on, **1968–69**: 704
Urban Problems, Joint Savings Bank-Savings and Loan Committee on, **1968–69**: 114
Urban renewal, **1963–64**: 91 (p. 115), 124 (p. 163), 132 (pp. 188, 194), 152, 211 [28], 324, 541, 578, 589, 603, 630, 650, 693, 728, 733; **1965**: 2, 32 (p. 93), 35 (p. 106), 90, 454 [5], 511
  District of Columbia, **1965**: 70
  Federal aid, **1963–64**: 189; **1965**: 35 (p. 114), 54, 90, 452, 511, 585
  Home improvement grants, **1965**: 510
  Legislation, approval, **1963–64**: 549
  New York City, **1965**: 566
Urban Renewal Administration, **1966**: 452
Urban Studies Fellowship Advisory Board, **1967**: 359
Uretz, Lester R., **1966**: 88 [5]
Urey, Harold C., **1965**: 56n.
Uribe, Eduardo, **1965**: 473n.
Uruguay, **1968–69**: 147
  President Oscar D. Gestido, **1967**: 171, 175n., 176, 523
  Visit, **1967**: 171, 173, 175, 176, 177
User Charges, transportation, **1968–69**: 39 (pp. 88, 102), 678 (p. 1278)
USIA.
  See United States Information Agency.
USO (United Service Organizations), **1966**: 476
U.S.S.R.
  See Soviet Union.
Utah, **1963–64**: 590; **1968–69**: 259
  Campaign remarks, **1963–64**: 737
  Gov. Calvin L. Rampton, **1966**: 255, 410–411, 413, 491n., 492 [1]; **1968–69**: 125
  Great Salt Lake borderlands, **1966**: 255
  Uinta National Forest, **1968–69**: 629n.
Utah State University, **1966**: 601
Utility lines, overhead, **1967**: 295
Utt, Repr., James B., **1963–64**: 414
Uttar Pradesh, India, **1967**: 33

Vaccination programs, **1963–64**: 305; **1965**: 262, 406, 410; **1966**: 45
Vagnozzi, Egidio, **1963–64**: 788n.; **1966**: 478
Vail, Thomas, **1966**: 208n.; **1967**: 500
Valdez, Alaska, **1963–64**: 242 [1]; **1967**: 369
Valenti, Jack, **1963–64**: 28 [10], 121, 149, 294 [26], 521 [8], 539, 560 [11], 581, 760, 778; **1965**: 22 [1], 82, 200, 270, 387, 417n.; **1966**: 85, 158 [1, 6], 202, 459, 478, 513; **1967**: 281, 391; **1968–69**: 260, 631

Valentine, Foy, **1963–64**: 238; **1968–69**: 156
Vallee, Roland S., **1966**: 397
Vallejo, Gen. Mariano Guadalupe, **1963–64**: 449
Vallejo, Calif., **1963–64**: 449
Vallejo, U.S.S., **1963–64**: 449
Valley Forge, Pa., **1963–64**: 473; **1967**: 361
Van Cleve, Ruth G., **1966**: 89
Van Deerlin, Repr. Lionel, **1963–64**: 736;
      1967: 303
Van Delden, Patricia G., **1963–64**: 204n.
Van Doren, Mark, **1967**: 387
Van Dyke, Dick, **1963–64**: 239n.
Van Heyde, Robert, **1966**: 436
Van Niel, Cornelis B., **1963–64**: 98
Van Petten, Harry O., **1963–64**: 650
Van Slyke, Donald D., **1965**: 646n.;
      1966: 61n.
Van Vleck, John Hasbrouck, **1966**: 652n.;
      1967: 37n.
Vanadium stockpiles, **1966**: 218
Vance, Cyrus R., **1963–64**: 467, 531, 533, 535;
      1965: 37n., 295 [4, 16], 319 [10, 16],
      387; **1966**: 141 [8, 10], 322, 324, 642
      [4, 6, 10], 645; **1967**: 166, 204 [1],
      208n., 321, 322, 325, 328 [2, 20], 331,
      518 [15], 519, 521; **1968–69**: 14 (p.
      26), 79 [13], 198, 215, 223 [1], 242,
      273, 275 [1, 3], 277, 280, 283 [3, 9],
      301, 400, 401, 467 [14], 504, 572, 646
      [3, 6, 11, 14]
   See also Army, Secretary of the (Cyrus R.
      Vance).
Vance, Mrs. Cyrus R., **1968–69**: 275 [1]
Vance, John T., **1967**: 518 [3]
Vancouver, B. C., Canada, **1963–64**: 575
Vandalia, Ohio, **1966**: 434
Vandenberg, Arthur H., **1963–64**: 144, 612, 622,
      634, 635, 643, 645, 648, 652, 656, 658,
      669, 679, 680, 693, 694, 702, 703, 712,
      713, 728, 729, 733, 734, 736, 745, 747,
      749, 750, 762; **1966**: 88 [17], 417 [15];
      1967: 495 [14]; **1968–69**: 341
Vanderburgh Humane Society, Evansville, Ind.,
      1963–64: 316 [12]
Vandergriff, Thomas, **1967**: 4n.
Vanik, Repr. Charles A., **1963–64**: 405, 406,
      642; **1965**: 190, 242
Varner, Rev. Robert M., **1968–69**: 452
Vasquez, Capt. Francisco, **1967**: 9
Vassallo, Elfrain D., **1966**: 231n.
Vatican City, **1965**: 68n.; **1967**: 571;
      1968–69: 603, 696 [10]
Vatican Council II, **1968–69**: 78
Vaughn, Jack H., **1963–64**: 245n., 246 [4], 285
      [6], 316 [11], 809; **1965**: 227, 295 [4,
      16], 319 [16], 429n., 593; **1966**: 12–
      13, 93, 332n., 455; **1968–69**: 314
VE Day, 20th anniversary, **1965**: 235

Veatch, Ellis H., **1966**: 198n.
Veblen, Thomas C., **1965**: 334n.
Vegetable oil shipments to India, **1966**: 153
Venereal disease control, **1965**: 29
Venezuela, **1963–64**: 143ftn. (p. 219);
      1968–69: 63, 205
   Ambassador Enrique Tejera-Paris, **1963–64**:
      335n.; **1966**: 366
   Communist aggression, **1967**: 453
      Defense against, **1963–64**: 220, 486 [3]
   President Raul Leoni, **1966**: 366
   U.S.-Venezuela communications cable,
      1966: 366
Venezuelan Pavilion, World's Fair (1964–65),
      1963–64: 335
Ventana Wilderness, Calif., **1968–69**: 122, 168
Venus exploration, **1968–69**: 107, 507
Veritas Medal of Providence College, presentation,
      1965: 237
Vermeil bowl, gift to President and First Lady,
      1968–69: 570n.
Vermont
   Campaign remarks, **1963–64**: 605
   Candidates for public office, **1963–64**: 605
   Gov. Philip H. Hoff, **1963–64**: 32n., 605;
      1965: 555; **1966**: 396–398, 494 [1, 2],
      650n.; **1967**: 223 [1–4, 6, 7, 9, 10, 13],
      544
Verne, Jules, **1968–69**: 610
Verrazano-Narrows Bridge, New York,
      1963–64: 581; **1966**: 510
Vessel Report, Automated Merchant, **1965**: 312
Vessels.
   See Ships.
Veterans, **1963–64**: 761; **1967**: 485 [1], 493,
      534
   AMVETS National Headquarters, **1966**: 345
   Beneficiaries, **1968–69**: 39 (p. 108), 678 (p.
      1299)
   Benefits, **1963–64**: 132 (pp. 176, 190), 642,
      663; **1965**: 32 (p. 95), 215, 438, 456;
      1966: 26 (pp. 55, 64), 100–101, 158
      [10], 420, 505; **1967**: 13 (pp. 44, 46,
      55), 25, 374; **1968–69**: 39 (pp. 88,
      106–108), 40, 452, 554, 599, 678 (pp.
      1281, 1282, 1287, 1299)
      To children of, **1965**: 542
   Burial, **1968–69**: 40
   Dependents, **1966**: 26 (p. 64)
   Disabled, **1968–69**: 40, 452, 599, 678 (p.
      1299)
   Education, **1963–64**: 419, 709; **1966**: 26 (p.
      64), 100–101, 158 [10], 353, 571;
      1967: 25, 345, 374; **1968–69**: 39 (p.
      106), 40, 67, 160, 554, 599, 601, 678
      (p. 1293)
   Employment, **1967**: 345, 374, 432, 493;
      1968–69: 14 (p. 31), 39 (p. 106), 406,
      414

Veterans – *continued*
  Employment – *continued*
    Assistance centers, **1968–69**: 40, 678 (p.
      1295)
    Government employment, **1968–69**: 67,
      667
    Health care, **1968–69**: 39 (p. 106), 40, 111,
      678 (pp. 1281, 1296)
    Hospitals, **1965**: 22 [16], 46 [8], 156 [10],
      163; **1966**: 26 (pp. 64, 67), 505;
      1967: 13 (p. 55), 25
    Housing, **1963–64**: 419; **1965**: 415;
      1968–69: 39 (p. 103), 40, 47 (p. 141),
      229, 414, 599
    Insurance, **1966**: 505
    Legislation, **1968–69**: 160, 414, 554, 599, 601
    Life insurance and pension bill, approval,
      1963–64: 663
    Medical care, **1966**: 26 (p. 64)
    Message to Congress, **1967**: 25–26;
      1968–69: 40
    Negro, **1968–69**: 131
    Occupational training, **1965**: 456; **1966**: 26
      (p. 64), 100
    Pensions, **1968–69**: 39 (p. 107), 40, 160, 554,
      678
    Philippine, **1966**: 505
    Project Remed, **1967**: 432n.
    Project Transition, **1967**: 345
    Public service, **1968–69**: 14 (p. 31), 40, 111,
      160, 419
    Rehabilitation, **1968–69**: 39 (p. 106), 414
    Unemployment, **1967**: 345
    Vietnam conflict, **1966**: 421, 645; **1967**: 13
      (p. 55), 25, 92, 161, 374; **1968–69**:
      40ftn. (p. 115), 67, 114, 131, 132, 229,
      419, 667
  Veterans Administration, **1963–64**: 71 [2], 132
    (p. 190), 152, 307, 462 [2], 611, 619
    [1], 654, 690n., 815; **1965**: 46 [8],
    138n., 140, 163, 512n.; **1966**: 26 (pp.
    21, 67), 182, 630 [4]; **1967**: 88, 161,
    193, 345, 432n.; **1968–69**: 40, 87, 114,
    678 (pp. 1293, 1296)
    Appropriations, **1968–69**: 678 (p. 1281)
    Mortgages, **1968–69**: 39 (p. 103), 40, 47 (p.
      141)
  Veterans Advisory Commission, U.S.,
    1968–69: 40, 599
  Veterans Affairs, Adminstrator of (Driver, W. J.),
    1965: 22 [16], 46 [8], 156 [10];
    1966: 208, 490, 505; **1967**: 25, 161,
    374, 493; **1968–69**: 40, 160, 229, 419,
    452, 554, 599
  Veterans Affairs, Administrator of (Gleason, John
    S., Jr.), **1963–64**: 152, 178n., 611, 654
  Veterans Affairs, House Committee on,
    1968–69: 160

Veterans Commission, Joint Philippine-U.S.,
    1966: 495, 505
Veterans Day, **1968–69**: 342, 583
  Tour of military installations, **1967**: 485
Veterans Facilities, Special Committee on,
    1965: 163
Veterans of Foreign Wars, **1968–69**: 132, 452
Veterans Memorial Hospital, Manila, the Philip-
    pines, **1966**: 495
Veterans Pension and Readjustment Assistance
    Act of 1967, **1967**: 25, 92, 374
Veterans in public service bill of 1968,
    1968–69: 40, 111, 160, 419
Veterans Readjustment Benefits Act of 1966,
    1966: 100, 188 [6], 353, 389;
    1967: 13 (p. 55), 25, 374; **1968–69**: 39
    (p. 106), 40, 67, 554, 678 (p. 1293)
Veth, Rear Adm. Kenneth L., **1967**: 567
Veto Messages and Memorandums of Disapproval
  See also **1963–64**: Appendix A.
  Colorado River, certain lands along,
    1968–69: 563
  Colorado River lands, ownership, **1966**: 615
  District of Columbia crime bill, **1966**: 611
  Geothermal steam bill, **1966**: 614
  Government employees life insurance,
    1966: 453; **1967**: 343
  Imported articles, marking of, disapproval,
    1963–64: 80
  Importing extra-long staple cotton,
    1968–69: 439
  Military construction authorization bill,
    1965: 440
  Nominations, effect of primary elections on,
    1963–64: 211 [12, 17]
  Responsibilities, **1963–64**: 486 [12], 780 [22]
  Ship masters, liens on wages, **1967**: 528
  Star route postal contracts price increase,
    1966: 336
  Succession to, **1963–64**: 218 [9]
  Youth Councils on Civic Affairs, incorporation
    of, disapproval, **1965**: 508
Veto power, comments on, **1965**: 317
Vice Presidency, **1965**: 34
  Candidates for.
    See main heading, Candidates for Vice Presi-
    dent.
  Comments on, **1968–69**: 529
  Constitutional amendment, Proposed, **1963–
    64**: 211 [13, 29], 218 [9]
Vice President (Humphrey, Hubert H.),
    1965: 2, 44, 45, 64, 72, 81, 98, 107,
    112, 133, 134, 183, 189, 207, 242, 268,
    277, 296, 297, 298, 318, 320, 322, 334,
    356, 383, 394, 409, 415, 419, 421, 429,
    433, 436, 438, 445, 448 [1], 452, 468,
    503, 504, 513, 534, 536, 546, 549, 550,
    567, 568n., 613, 630n., 653n., 659n.;

Vice President – *continued*
    1966: 13, 56, 60n., 72, 93, 100–101,
     115, 133–134, 136–137, 149, 170–172,
     216, 221, 223, 226, 235, 240, 243, 261,
     269–271, 305, 326, 361, 366, 370, 386,
     408n., 459, 499, 513, 541, 570, 573–
     574, 576, 646; **1967**: 3 (p. 2), 18, 20,
     32, 39, 52, 68, 101, 102, 105, 112, 121,
     167, 182, 216, 227, 228, 251, 255, 256,
     258, 261, 268, 278, 294, 313, 315, 338,
     356, 357, 373, 374, 403, 421, 439, 444,
     449, 475, 487, 514, 519, 520;
    1968–69: 14 (pp. 25, 26), 24, 53, 62,
     65, 71, 73n., 91, 102n., 109, 111, 113,
     124, 137, 140, 142, 148, 151, 159, 167,
     171, 180, 193, 211, 214, 233, 242, 250,
     253, 259, 280, 327, 335, 392n., 426 (pp.
     1263, 1270), 598, 614–616, 619, 622,
     662, 672, 676 (pp. 1263, 1270), 692,
     694, 695, 696 [20]
  See also Humphrey, Hubert H.
  Asian visit, **1966**: 85–86
  Candidacy for reelection (1968), **1966**: 401
    [17], 474 [12]; **1967**: 104 [13]
  Dinner honoring, **1965**: 42; **1967**: 7;
    1968–69: 32
  Dominican Republic mission, **1966**: 277 [3],
    320 [6]
  Kosygin, Premier Aleksei N., meeting with,
    1966: 8ftn. (p. 15)
  Letters, **1965**: 33, 50
  Letters to President of the Senate.
    See Congress, letters to Members of.
  Memorandum, **1965**: 530; **1966**: 385
  News conference remarks on, **1965**: 46 [6],
    117 [11], 319 [1, 12, 19]; **1966**: 8
    [2], 88 [15–16], 124 [2], 158 [3, 4],
    188 [4], 236 [13], 247 [1], 277 [3],
    401 [17], 607 [1], 628 [1]; **1967**: 104
    [6, 13], 225 [19], 264 [8], 297 [5],
    460 [4], 554 [8]
  Post election telegram, **1968–69**: 579
  Presidential candidacy, **1968–69**: 191 [12],
    461n., 467 [7, 16], 480n., 486, 497,
    529, 540, 557 [4, 10], 565–569, 575,
    576, 579
  President's surgery, agreement on responsi-
    bilities, **1966**: 610 [1]
  Residence, authorization, **1966**: 170
Vickers, Mrs. Marie, **1963–64**: 741
Victor, Eugene, **1963–64**: 60n.
Victor, Wilma Louise, **1967**: 93n.
Victor Comptometer Co., **1966**: 144n.
Victoria, Queen (Great Britain), **1966**: 149
Victory Committee, Democratic, **1968–69**: 576
Vienna, Austria, **1968–69**: 387
Vientiane, Laos, **1968–69**: 198

Vietcong, **1963–64**: 170 [1, 5, 10], 223, 793,
    780ftn. (p. 1616); **1965**: 117 [8], 152,
    172, 194, 206, 227, 276, 295 [8], 319
    [14], 347 [1], 388 [16], 412 [3], 469,
    588; **1966**: 35, 55, 77, 277 [7, 20],
    311, 348, 373 [9], 434, 501 [2], 516
    [1], 520, 532, 549, 577 [15], 578 [2,
    4], 642 [13]; **1967**: 73, 195, 226,
    309 [3], 352, 384, 409; **1968–69**: 34,
    51 [3, 11], 119, 221, 222, 265, 266,
    487, 491, 520, 521, 584, 594, 609,
    646 [10], 649, 675
  See also National Liberation Front.
  Casualties, **1967**: 116
  Infiltration in Cambodia and Laos, **1967**: 80
    [4], 83, 132 [3, 4], 409, 480, 554 [1]
  Negotiations with, question of, **1966**: 501 [16],
    654 [13]
  Peace negotiation efforts, **1967**: 132 [7], 460,
    495 [4]
  Terrorism, **1967**: 128–129, 131, 309 [5], 352,
    375 [13], 409
  U.S. Naval Hospital, Danang, attack, **1966**: 346
Vietnam, **1963–64**: 182, 201 [17], 207, 235,
    336 [15], 399n., 544, 562, 607, 642,
    703, 746, 749; **1965**: 15, 46 [7, 11],
    159, 176 [3], 183, 185, 191, 194, 203,
    223, 289, 295 [8], 296, 298, 308, 319
    [16], 347 [1, 2, 5], 353 [1, 6, 12], 362,
    387, 392, 395 [3], 397, 421, 448 [12,
    15, 20, 21], 459, 483, 641 [8], 644,
    653, 659, 660; **1966**: 88 [14, 25], 93,
    124 [2], 264, 346, 395, 492 [1, 6],
    515, 563, 610 [8]
  See also Vietnam, North; Vietnam , South;
    Vietnam conflict.
  Americans in, **1965**: 51, 106 [2], 145, 276
    Christmas message to, **1963–64**: 313
  Appropriations and expenditures, **1966**: 6 (p.
    8), 26 (pp. 48, 50, 54–58), 34 (p. 102),
    121 [5, 10], 128, 155, 277 [8, 18], 334
    [1, 8, 10, 11], 444, 445 [1], 474 [2, 8,
    15], 477 [3], 492 [9], 494 [1, 8], 501
    [10], 630 [5], 642 [4–5, 9, 18, 22]
  Appropriations for military requirements in,
    1965: 227, 229, 234, 261, 276
  Armed forces, Vietnamese, **1966**: 53–54, 188
    [4], 277 [7], 346, 348, 397
  Assistance.
    Asian nations, **1966**: 312, 516 [13], 553
    Australia, **1963–64**: 426; **1966**: 53, 304,
     516 [13], 520, 543, 546
    Germany, **1966**: 482, 486
    Korea, **1965**: 257, 423; **1966**: 53, 311, 516
     [13], 520, 540, 561–562, 566
    Malaysia, **1963–64**: 474
    Message to Congress, **1963–64**: 348
    New Zealand, **1966**: 53, 516 [13], 520

Vietnam – *continued*
 Assistance – *continued*
  Philippines, **1963–64**: 626; **1966**: 458, 461,
   516 [13], 520, 551
  Thailand, **1966**: 555, 557
  United States, **1963–64**: 83, 150 [6], 192,
   201 [5], 211 [33], 218 [24], 223, 227,
   246 [4], 272, 280 [8], 285 [12], 379
   [1, 19], 400, 420 [1], 436n., 511, 591,
   627, 652, 662, 693, 780ftn. (p. 1616),
   793, 797; **1965**: 2, 18, 51, 106 [4],
   117 [2, 8], 130, 145, 152, 156 [11],
   172, 194, 206, 208 [2, 14, 16, 20],
   227, 229, 230, 234, 246, 250, 254,
   257, 261, 276, 294, 295 [3], 316, 388
   [1, 2, 5, 11, 14], 476, 551n., 588;
   1966: 6 (pp. 7–8, 11), 8 [14], 11n.,
   17–18, 26 (p. 68), 41, 53–55, 65 [10],
   77, 114, 141 [3], 273–274, 288, 320
   [1], 331, 346, 577 [5]
 Bases, U.S., **1966**: 401 [13]
 Changes in Government, **1965**: 76
 Chief of State Nguyen Van Thieu, **1966**: 52
  [2], 53–54, 56n., 549, 552
 Communist aggression, **1963–64**: 37, 83, 170
  [1, 5, 10, 18], 201 [5, 17], 211 [33],
  218 [24], 223, 272, 280 [8], 313, 316
  [27], 348, 379 [1], 400, 474, 475 [3],
  497, 498, 499, 500, 504 [4], 507, 509,
  511, 560 [3], 561, 563 [1], 591, 627,
  662, 693, 793; **1965**: 2, 26, 46 [11], 51,
  117 [2], 130, 145, 152, 156 [11], 172,
  194, 206, 208 [2, 14, 16], 227, 229,
  234, 246, 254, 276, 295 [3], 300, 319
  [17], 331, 353 [1, 12], 388 [1, 5, 16],
  397, 412 [4], 421; **1966**: 6 (p. 7), 53,
  55, 77, 86, 93–94, 128, 188 [10], 236
  [1, 9], 246, 273–274, 277 [7], 304,
  311, 329, 346, 377, 383, 411, 415–416,
  420, 431, 437, 445 [25], 474 [10],
  540, 549, 553, 565–566, 568, 570, 577
  [15], 607 [3]
 Communist Chinese threat to, **1965**: 208 [12]
 Construction contracts, **1966**: 642 [21]
 Cultural presentations program, **1965**: 159
 Defense of, **1963–64**: 211 [33], 272, 313,
  626n., 662n., 688 [8], 793
 Dignitaries, U.S., visits by, **1966**: 56, 124 [5,
  14], 394, 521
  Bundy, McGeorge, **1965**: 46 [7]
  McNamara, Robert, **1963–64**: 28ftn. (p. 34),
   201 [5], 218 [23, 24, 26], 316 [2,
   16], 336 [15]; **1965**: 347 [1], 353
   [1, 6, 12], 633
  Nixon, Richard M., **1963–64**: 285 [17]
  Rusk, Dean, **1963–64**: 316 [16]
 Economic and social development, **1966**: 54–
  55, 77, 106, 141ftn. (p. 347), 214, 271,

Vietnam – *continued*
 Economic and social development – *continued*
  273–274, 277 [7], 311, 320 [1], 338
  [19], 348, 417 [12], 501 [2, 17], 516
  [1, 13], 520, 532, 548–549, 553, 607
  [3]
 Economy, **1965**: 246, 295 [3]
 Elections, **1966**: 247 [13, 14], 277 [7], 311,
  338 [19], 397, 414, 456, 501 [17],
  516 [1], 520, 532, 549, 553, 607 [3]
 Expansion of war, question of, **1963–64**: 597,
  607, 643, 693, 719, 780 [6, 12];
  1965: 208 [20], 295 [13], 388 [1, 5,
  10, 14]
 Health programs, **1966**: 106, 141ftn. (p. 347),
  271, 273, 331, 433
 Health and welfare needs, **1965**: 469
 "Hello Dolly" tour in, **1965**: 561
 Huong, Tran Van, **1963–64**: 780ftn. (p. 1616)
 Khanh, Maj. Gen. Nguyen.
  See main heading, Khanh, Maj. Gen.
  Nguyen.
 Mail service to, **1966**: 37, 322, 389, 571, 651
 Military Assistance Commander, U.S.
  See main headings, Abrams, Gen. Creighton
  W.; Westmoreland, Gen. William C.
 Military coups, **1963–64**: 271 [12]
 Minh, Gen. Duong Van, **1963–64**: 83
 Negotiated settlement, question of, **1965**: 46
  [7], 106 [6], 117 [11], 156 [8], 194,
  208 [2, 12], 246, 319 [14], 331, 353
  [14], 388 [1, 5, 6, 16], 390, 397, 412
  [2], 436, 448 [15, 20], 463 [11], 653,
  659
 Neutralization, question of, **1963–64**: 83, 170
  [10, 18], 218 [25], 544
 1954 agreements.
  See main heading, Geneva agreements on Indochina (1954).
 Oxford teach-in, **1965**: 347 [5]
 Political situation, **1966**: 141 [2], 158 [5], 188
  [2–3], 236 [1, 4], 246, 247 [5], 277 [7],
  311, 501 [2], 549, 607 [3]
 Prime Minister Nguyen Cao Ky, **1966**: 52 [2],
  53–54, 56n., 65 [7], 88 [19, 21], 188
  [2, 4], 236 [4], 277 [21], 520, 549,
  552
 Proclamation, **1965**: 606
 Relation to 1964 election campaign,
  1963–64: 504 [10]
 Report, **1965**: 412 [2, 3, 4]
 SEATO support, **1963–64**: 266 [14]
 Sino-Soviet threat to, question of,
  1963–64: 201 [5]
 Soviet policy in, **1965**: 353 [7, 20], 388 [8,
  10]
 Statements, **1966**: 39, 52 [2], 106, 236 [1],
  274, 277 [7], 320 [1], 331

Vietnam — *continued*
  U.S. Ambassador, Lodge, Henry Cabot,
    1963–64: 83, 170 [5], 201 [5, 18], 211
    [22], 218 [23, 25, 26], 223, 246 [4],
    256 [2, 5, 9], 285 [1, 17], 290, 336
    [15], 348, 379ftn. (p. 735), 420 [1, 4,
    6, 13], 436, 504 [4, 9, 11]; **1965**: 421;
    1966: 52 [2], 65 [8, 12], 86, 141 [10],
    188 [3], 214, 228, 236 [1], 273, 334
    [4], 338 [19], 383, 492 [1], 578 [11],
    628 [1], 642n., 645
  U.S. Ambassador, Taylor, Maxwell D.,
    1963–64: 445, 455 [5], 475 [3], 560
    [3], 563 [1, 7], 688 [8], 780 [6, 12],
    793; **1965**: 46 [7, 11], 117 [2], 156
    [11], 295 [8], 319 [19], 347 [5], 353
    [1, 12], 403, 412 [2, 3]
  U.S. chancery in Saigon, proposed construction,
    1965: 152
  U.S. dependents in, **1963–64**: 211 [14]
  U.S. Embassy bombing, **1965**: 145, 208 [16],
    276
  U.S. forces in, **1963–64**: 26, 83, 211 [33],
    223, 294 [5], 314, 379 [10], 793;
    1965: 46 [7, 11], 51, 206, 208 [20],
    227, 229, 234, 261, 289, 295 [13], 319
    [17], 347 [1, 9], 353 [1, 12, 14, 21],
    388 [1, 5, 11, 14], 395 [2], 396, 412
    [4], 421, 439, 445, 448 [11, 12, 20],
    561n., 573, 588, 632, 633; **1966**:
    6 (p. 9), 15, 18, 20, 37, 47, 53–54,
    85–87, 88 [24], 96, 107, 124 [15],
    128, 136–137, 141 [11], 158 [14],
    166, 188 [4, 5, 11], 228, 242, 273,
    277 [7], 311–312, 320 [7], 338 [19],
    345, 348, 350, 353, 373 [2, 19], 377,
    383, 389, 397, 412, 415–416, 420, 431,
    433–434, 445 [25], 449, 456, 485–
    486, 496, 515, 516 [10], 521, 533,
    543, 547, 552–553, 563, 568, 570–571,
    577 [5], 578 [2, 5], 607 [3], 638, 641,
    642 [10], 645, 651, 654 [3]
  U.S. health and economic missions to
    1965: 246, 551
  U.S. missions to, **1963–64**: 211 [33], 223, 256
    [2, 5]; **1966**: 56, 65 [10], 106, 141
    [8, 10], 227 [22], 331
  U.S. policy in, **1963–64**: 186, 201 [5], 211
    [21], 218 [25, 27], 246 [4], 280 [8],
    420 [8], 626n.; **1965**: 26, 46 [7, 11],
    51n., 76, 106 [4], 117 [2, 8], 130, 152,
    156 [6, 11, 12], 162, 172, 194, 200,
    208 [2, 9, 14, 19, 20], 227, 229, 230,
    234, 246, 294, 319 [14], 388 [1, 5, 11,
    14, 16], 390, 395 [5], 397, 412 [4],
    421, 476; **1966**: 6 (pp. 7, 10), 45, 65
    [6, 7], 86, 88 [16–17, 19, 21], 93, 120,
    124 [4, 7, 10, 12], 128, 152, 188 [5],

Vietnam — *continued*
  U.S. policy in — *continued*
    221, 228, 236 [3, 9], 246, 277 [7],
    311, 325, 338 [6], 377, 397, 411, 414–
    416, 437, 445 [18, 25], 450, 456, 474
    [10], 498, 501 [14, 17], 532, 540,
    547, 551–553, 554, 568, 570, 577 [2,
    15], 578 [7], 607 [3], 654 [3]
  Use of non-lethal gases in, **1965**: 156 [12]
  Vietcong.
    See main heading, Vietcong.
  Vietnamese Armed Forces, **1965**: 206, 347
    [1], 388 [11], 588
  Visit, **1966**: 552
  Vietnam, North, **1963–64**: 475 [16]; **1965**: 106
    [6], 156 [11], 208 [2], 246, 295 [13],
    319 [14], 388 [1, 5], 448 [12];
    1966: 128, 228, 312, 325, 501 [14],
    578 [2]; **1967**: 134–135, 352, 407, 460
    [7], 495 [7], 565; **1968–69**: 250n.
  See also Vietcong; Vietnam, South; Vietnam
    conflict; Vietnam.
  Aggression, **1965**: 353 [1, 11, 13, 20, 21];
    1966: 6 (p. 9), 158 [12], 246, 277 [7],
    311–312, 325, 329, 338 [19], 346, 348,
    397, 411, 515, 516 [1], 549, 577 [15],
    578 [2]; **1967**: 34 [2], 70 [8], 83, 104
    [10], 116, 131, 136, 272, 309 [5], 409,
    460 [8], 480; **1968–69**: 267, 283 [6],
    339 [4], 400, 401, 425 [4], 452, 512,
    522, 676 (p. 1269)
  American prisoners, **1966**: 338 [1, 4–5, 17];
    1968–69: 646 [16]
  Armed forces, **1967**: 309 [3, 5, 7, 9], 384;
    1968–69: 48, 51 [1], 81 [2], 129, 283
    [6], 323, 425 [4], 478, 487, 512, 520,
    521, 541, 544, 594, 649, 674
  Attacks on U.S. vessels, **1963–64**: 497, 498,
    499, 500, 504 [2, 4, 11], 560 [7],
    561n.; **1965**: 276; **1966**: 94
  U.S retaliatory action, **1963–64**: 499, 504
    [11], 507, 509, 516 [2, 6], 544, 561n.,
    607, 612, 626n., 627, 634, 635, 638,
    646, 648, 733, 736; **1965**: 208 [2]
  Bombing by U.S., **1965**: 22 [4], 117 [8], 156
    [6], 194, 208 [16], 227, 229, 319
    [14], 331, 448 [12], 463 [11]; **1966**:
    6 (pp. 9, 10), 39, 52 [5], 124 [7], 246,
    277 [7, 9, 20], 311, 320 [9, 16], 338
    [2], 346, 350, 397, 434, 474 [5], 477
    [6], 514, 516 [10], 547, 577 [7],
    578 [2, 7–8], 607 [4], 642 [7], 654
    [2, 7, 13]; **1967**: 34 [2, 6], 50, 70
    [7–8], 80 [4], 83, 100, 116, 136, 195,
    312 [14, 16], 358 [1, 5, 7], 375 [1–3,
    5, 6, 13, 19], 409, 411 [6], 460 [13],
    491, 495 [3, 4], 518 [8], 554 [1];
    1968–69: 170, 178, 201, 237, 251,

Vietnam, North — *continued*
  Bombing by U.S. — *continued*
      275 [1], 280, 283 [4], 288, 425 [4,
      8], 452, 472, 572
    Halt to, **1968-69**: 223 [3], 557 [9]
  Cambodia, infiltration into, **1968-69**: 1 [9]
  Casualties, **1966**: 578 [2]
  Chinese Communist aid to, **1965**: 26
  Defections, **1966**: 516 [1]
  Election in U.S., interpretation, **1966**: 610
      [12]
  Foreign Minister Nguyen Duy Tinh,
      1965: 388 [6]; **1967**: 34 [6];
      1968-69: 1 [6], 65n.
  Foreign policy, **1967**: 309 [7]
  Government, **1968-69**: 572
  Laos, infiltration, **1967**: 80 [4], 83, 132 [3,
      4], 409, 480, 554 [1]
  Missile sites in, **1965**: 388 [8]
  Morale, **1966**: 578 [2]
  Peace negotiation efforts, response to,
      1966: 338 [10], 474 [5], 607 [3, 4];
      1967: 50, 80 [4], 104 [10], 116, 118,
      131, 132 [9-10, 12], 136, 144, 195,
      204 [16], 358 [5], 409, 411 [7], 460
      [13], 495 [3], 518 [8], 554 [1], 564;
      1968-69: 14 (p. 25), 50, 51 [2, 8], 79
      [10], 169 [9], 170, 171, 177, 178,
      187, 188, 191 [8], 198, 213 [2], 223
      [1, 3, 5], 225, 241, 283 [4, 9], 288,
      400, 425ftn. (p. 861), 452, 472, 528,
      529, 557 [1, 9], 572, 590 [9]
  Pham Van Dong, **1965**: 208 [12]
  President Ho Chi Minh, **1965**: 347ftn. (p.
      730), 448ftn. (p. 924); **1966**: 52 [5],
      320 [18], 514-515, 540; **1967**: 80 [4],
      135, 136, 195, 225 [5], 281, 312 [14,
      16], 358 [5], 395, 409, 495 [3, 6],
      534; **1968-69**: 51 [1], 109, 170, 250n.
  Soviet aid, **1965**: 353 [20], 388 [8, 10]
  Trade, U.S. opposition, **1966**: 441, 608
  U.S. reconnaissance defense measures,
      1963-64: 587 [5]
  Use of chemical warfare in, question of,
      1965: 208 [19]
  Use of nuclear weapons in, question of,
      1963-64: 516 [2, 6], 638
  Vice Premier Vo Nguyen Giap, **1967**: 195
  Vietcong support, **1963-64**: 780ftn. (p.
      1616); **1965**: 117 [8], 172; **1966**: 325
  Visit of Kosygin, Aleksei N., **1965**: 46 [7]
Vietnam, 17-Nation Declaration on, **1965**: 319
      [14]
Vietnam, South, **1967**: 286, 480; **1968-69**: 189,
      250n.
  See also Vietcong; Vietnam, North; Vietnam
      conflict; Vietnam.
  AID programs, **1967**: 73, 116, 235

Vietnam, South — *continued*
  Appropriations and expenditures, **1967**: 13 (pp.
      40-41), 16 (p. 80), 43, 46, 48, 56, 328
      [14, 23], 329; **1968-69**: 47 (p. 145), 63,
      241, 678 (pp. 1274, 1279, 1282, 1286)
  Armed Forces (ARVN), **1967**: 55, 61, 73, 116,
      136, 195, 302, 309 [3, 5, 6], 457, 554
      [1]; **1968-69**: 51 [1], 96, 119, 170,
      185n., 186, 189, 201, 222, 223 [4], 283
      [6], 400, 401, 443, 472, 518, 572, 674
  Assistance, **1968-69**: 21, 63, 438
    Australia, **1967**: 83, 246, 555, 562, 567;
        1968-69: 271n., 273, 277, 283 [3, 4],
        525
    China, Republic of, **1967**: 219
    Korea, **1967**: 83, 112n., 113, 195, 246;
        1968-69: 35, 149, 201, 273, 283 [4],
        323, 413, 525
    Military, **1967**: 83, 195, 309 [1, 2, 10], 312
        [11]
    New Zealand, **1967**: 83, 246; **1968-69**: 283
        [4], 522, 525, 528
    Philippines, **1967**: 83, 246; **1968-69**: 283
        [4], 525
    Thailand, **1967**: 83, 246, 293; **1968-69**:
        232, 237, 273, 283 [4], 525
  Communist aggression, **1967**: 3 (p. 11), 13 (p.
      48), 83, 195, 219, 352, 384, 395, 397,
      401, 409, 438n., 442, 446, 460 [13],
      495 [6, 14], 565; **1968-69**: 14 (p. 25),
      50, 51 [1], 81 [1-3], 142, 154, 170,
      186, 267, 273, 283 [6], 339 [4], 398n.,
      425 [4], 452, 472, 491, 512, 522, 564,
      676 (p. 1269)
  Constituent Assembly, **1967**: 129, 131, 132 [1,
      2], 134, 135
  Constitution, **1967**: 127-129, 131, 132 [1, 2,
      4, 13], 134, 135
  Construction, **1967**: 460 [11]
  Directorate, **1967**: 131, 134, 135
  Economic, political, and social development,
      1967: 13 (p. 49), 44, 73, 116, 131, 134,
      135, 195, 219, 352, 409, 526, 564;
      1968-69: 34, 63, 149, 170, 400
  Elections, **1967**: 129, 132 [1], 297 [12, 15],
      352, 358 [1, 2, 5], 374, 375 [13], 409,
      460 [11], 495 [6], 502, 554 [1], 564;
      1968-69: 14 (p. 25), 110, 452
  Government, **1968-69**: 14 (p. 25), 51 [1], 81
      [1], 170, 189, 223 [4], 400, 452, 521,
      572, 590 [9], 606
  Government employees, U.S., **1967**: 25
  Health programs, **1967**: 235, 352, 409
  Komer, Robert, visit, **1967**: 73
  Lilienthal, David, visit, **1967**: 73
  Military Assistance Commander, U.S.
    See main headings, Abrams, Gen.
        Creighton W.; Westmoreland, Gen.
        William C.

Vietnam, South — *continued*
  Missions from U.S., **1967**: 526
  National Liberation Front, **1968–69**: 51 [12],
    250n., 425 [6], 572
  Peace negotiation efforts.
    See Vietnam conflict.
  Political situation, **1967**: 129, 132 [13], 352,
    358 [1], 409, 460 [11], 491, 564
  Population, **1967**: 73
  President Nguyen Van Thieu, **1967**: 127, 130,
    131, 243, 297 [15], 352, 358 [5], 460
    [11], 554 [1], 564; **1968–69**: 51 [12],
    170, 172, 189, 223 [7], 339 [13], 398,
    400, 401, 406, 425 [4], 452, 472, 572,
    590 [5]
    See also main heading, Nguyen Van Thieu.
  Prime Minister Nguyen Van Loc, **1967**: 564
  Prime Minister Tran Van Huong, **1968–69**: 400
  Prisoners, **1967**: 312ftn. (p. 702)
  Refugees, **1968–69**: 63
  Relations with United States, **1968–69**: 189
  U.S. Ambassador, Bunker, Ellsworth,
    1967: 309 [1], 352, 358 [2], 460 [11],
    461, 490, 493, 495 [6, 13, 14], 503,
    526, 567; **1968–69**: 51 [1], 109, 185,
    187–189, 197, 398n., 401
  U.S. Ambassador, Lodge, Henry Cabot,
    1967: 3 (p. 12), 70 [1], 104 [5, 14, 17],
    116, 126–128, 130n., 131, 132 [1, 4,
    11, 13], 134, 225 [2]
  U.S. forces, **1967**: 3 (p. 12), 9, 13 (p. 48), 14,
    25, 55, 61, 83, 104 [4], 132 [8, 12],
    134–136, 166, 195, 202, 204 [1, 3, 13],
    226, 229, 275, 308, 309 [1–4, 6, 8, 10],
    312 [10], 329, 330 [1, 3], 334, 358 [1],
    361, 374, 375 [7], 384, 409, 424, 434,
    446, 456, 460 [9], 475, 481, 485 [1, 3–
    5, 6, 8], 493, 494, 495 [1, 13], 518
    [14], 544, 554 [1], 566, 567, 573;
    1968–69: 5, 12, 34, 48, 51 [1, 6], 79
    [7, 14], 81 [1–3], 96, 109, 112, 129,
    144, 153 [11], 169 [3], 170, 171, 226,
    245, 265, 267, 271n., 283 [15], 384,
    410, 456, 487, 491, 512, 525, 528, 541,
    543, 544, 546, 564, 572, 583, 584, 594,
    609, 646 [3, 14], 649, 676 (p. 1269)
  Message to, **1968–69**: 186
  U.S. policy, **1967**: 13 (pp. 39, 48), 34 [2], 70
    [11], 80 [4], 83, 104 [2, 14, 16], 116,
    118, 126, 150, 162, 204 [7, 13], 219,
    225 [4, 5, 11, 15, 20], 229, 270, 272,
    286, 329, 352, 358 [1, 7], 361, 375
    [13], 395, 407, 409, 411 [6], 421, 446,
    460 [9, 13], 480, 491, 495 [14], 519,
    534, 554 [1], 564; **1968–69**: 50, 51
    [9], 79 [7], 81 [1–3], 96, 100n., 109,
    153 [9], 141–143, 169 [3, 6], 170, 172,
    178, 221, 232, 233, 237, 250n., 277,

Vietnam, South — *continued*
  U.S. policy — *continued*
    291, 398, 400, 401, 452, 472, 487, 504,
    522, 525, 528, 557 [1], 572, 585
  Vice President Nguyen Cao Ky, **1967**: 73, 127,
    129, 131, 132 [1, 3–4, 7, 10, 13], 134,
    135, 297 [15], 352, 358 [5], 567
  Visit, **1967**: 566, 567
Vietnam Civilian Service Awards, **1967**: 352
Vietnam conflict, **1966**: 32, 35–36, 77, 86, 93,
    107–109, 214, 234–235, 246, 312, 323,
    325, 328n., 329, 345, 388, 414–415,
    421, 486, 542, 548–549, 553, 567, 603,
    638, 646; **1967**: 166, 195, 239, 243,
    246n., 248n., 261, 280, 281, 283, 302,
    310, 311, 329, 334, 352, 361, 384,
    433n., 434, 435, 456, 457, 462, 481,
    484, 485 [3, 8], 492, 494, 514, 534,
    536, 563, 568, 569; **1968–69**: 43, 51
    [2, 3, 5–12], 144, 165, 200, 271n.,
    455n., 575
  See also Vietnam; Vietnam, North; Vietnam,
    South.
  Address to the Nation, **1968–69**: 170
  Appropriations and expenditures, **1968–69**: 14
    (p. 32), 39 (pp. 84, 87, 97, 98), 677
  Assistance
    Australia, **1968–69**: 283 [3, 4]
    Korea, **1968–69**: 283 [4], 323
    New Zealand, **1968–69**: 283 [4], 522
    Philippines, **1968–69**: 283 [4]
    Thailand, **1968–69**: 283 [4]
  Bombing policy, **1967**: 34 [2, 6], 50, 70 [7, 8],
    83, 104 [7, 10], 116, 136, 195, 358
    [1, 5, 7], 375 [1–3, 5, 6, 13, 19], 409,
    411 [6], 460 [13], 491, 495 [3, 4],
    518 [8], 554 [1]; **1968–69**: 14 (p. 25),
    48, 50, 65n., 169 [3], 170, 172, 198,
    201, 223 [3], 237, 275 [1], 280, 283
    [4, 7, 13], 288, 400, 425 [4, 8], 452,
    472, 572, 583
  Casualties, **1966**: 338 [19], 346, 395, 412,
    433, 449, 578 [2], 642 [14], 654 [2,
    7]; **1967**: 83, 116, 132 [1], 134–136,
    309 [5], 312 [10], 358 [1, 4], 409,
    460 [11], 485 [4], 495 [6];
    1968–69: 51 [11], 96, 105, 109, 170,
    262, 275 [1], 400, 557 [7], 646 [3]
  Chinese Communist policy, **1967**: 358 [7]
  Christmas truce, **1966**: 630 [11]
  Coast Guard and FAA, contributions to war
    effort, **1968–69**: 693
  Conferences.
    See main headings, Guam conference;
      Honolulu conference; Manila con-
      ference.
  Congressional views, **1966**: 52 [3], 65 [6], 88
    [16–17], 474 [4]; **1967**: 132 [10], 358
    [2, 10], 518 [12]

Vietnam conflict – *continued*
  Demilitarized zone, **1966**: 501 [5]; **1967**: 225
    [20], 309 [3], 554 [1]; **1968–69**: 51
    [1], 81 [1], 170, 472, 520
  Demonstrations against, **1967**: 225 [10], 441,
    460 [7], 495 [13], 554 [8];
    1968–69: 51 [11]
  Economic impact in U.S., **1966**: 34 (p. 97),
    121 [5], 431, 477 [3], 578 [6], 654
    [9]; **1967**: 6 [12], 13 (p. 40), 16 (pp.
    74, 75, 77, 87), 89, 430, 524;
    1968–69: 2, 39 (p. 87), 47 (pp. 131,
    145), 684
  Election impact in U.S., **1966**: 141 [12], 188
    [7], 577 [2]
  Geneva accords, **1966**: 6 (p. 11), 54, 65ftn.
    (p. 177), 338 [1], 549; **1967**: 34 [2],
    80 [4], 83, 116, 118, 144, 145, 312ftn.
    (p. 702), 366, 462, 564; **1968–69**: 170,
    400, 406, 452
  Mansfield, Sen. Mike, proposals, **1966**: 8 [12],
    607 [10]
  Message to the American people, **1966**: 553
  Military equipment, **1968–69**: 400
  Military situation, **1966**: 8 [6], 88 [19], 277
    [7, 20, 22], 320 [15], 338 [19], 373
    [2, 19], 474 [10], 494 [1], 520, 532,
    549, 599 [7], 628 [9]; **1967**: 70 [1, 3,
    8, 10], 116, 132 [1–2, 4], 134, 195,
    204 [3, 16], 225 [20], 261, 264 [5],
    309 [1, 3, 5], 329, 358 [1, 6], 409,
    460 [8], 495 [6], 564; **1968–69**: 14
    (p. 25), 51 [1, 3, 9–11], 81 [1, 2], 112,
    185, 189, 197, 198, 213 [7], 283 [6],
    339 [4], 400, 401, 452
    F-111 disappearance, **1968–69**: 169 [10]
    Khe Sanh seige, lifting of, **1968–69**: 186
    Nuclear weapons use, question, **1966**: 501
      [14]; **1968–69**: 79 [9]
    Tet offensive, **1968–69**: 79 [10], 142, 149,
      170, 185n., 188, 189
  News conference remarks, **1966**: 236 [9], 334
    [1], 401 [5], 417 [12], 494 [1], 501
    [2], 516 [9], 607 [3], 642 [11], 650
    [24]; **1967**: 70 [1, 3], 80 [4], 104
    [2, 4, 7, 10], 225 [11], 297 [9], 309
    [1, 7], 328 [4, 9], 330 [1, 2], 358 [1],
    375 [1–3, 19], 460 [7, 8], 495 [10],
    518 [14], 554 [4]
  Ordnance requirements, **1966**: 520, 578 [2, 6, 9]
  Pacification programs, **1966**: 274, 520–521, 578
    [2]; **1967**: 73, 132 [6, 8, 12], 135, 225
    [2], 375 [13], 564
  Peace negotiation efforts, **1966**: 6 (pp. 10–11),
    8 [2, 17], 18, 22–23, 39, 52 [5], 54,
    65 [7], 93–94, 141 [12, 14], 188 [10],
    236 [1, 15], 246, 277 [11], 329, 338

Vietnam conflict – *continued*
  Peace negotiation efforts – *continued*
    [19], 348, 350, 353, 373 [9], 397, 474
    [5], 477 [6], 516 [1], 531, 549, 654
    [1, 7–8, 13]; **1967**: 34 [2, 6], 42, 50,
    70 [9], 80 [4], 100, 104 [4, 7, 10],
    116, 118, 131, 132 [7, 9, 10, 12], 135–
    136, 144–145, 195, 204 [16], 229, 272,
    279ftn. (p. 673), 312 [16], 358 [5],
    374, 407, 409, 411 [5–7], 442, 460
    [11, 13], 495 [3, 11, 14], 518 [8], 534,
    554 [1], 564, 571–573; **1968–69**: 1 [2,
    6], 14 (pp. 25, 26), 50, 51 [2, 12], 65n.,
    79 [10], 141, 153 [8], 169 [9], 170,
    171, 177, 178, 186, 187, 188, 189, 191
    [8], 193n., 198, 201, 214n., 223 [1, 3,
    6], 224, 225, 233, 237, 241, 242, 246,
    255, 267, 271n., 273, 275 [1, 3], 277,
    280, 283 [3, 4, 9], 288, 307, 339 [5,
    10], 398, 400, 401, 406, 425 [8], 452,
    460 [2], 462, 467 [12, 14], 472, 511n.,
    522, 528, 529, 557 [1, 9], 564, 572,
    590 [5, 9], 606, 611, 646 [3, 6, 10,
    11, 14, 16], 652n., 676 (p. 1269), 678
    (pp. 1274, 1276), 682, 683, 690, 691,
    696 [19]
    Pope Paul VI peace efforts, **1966**: 474 [5],
      513, 549, 577 [7], 607 [4, 15]; **1967**: 42,
      135, 411 [5], 571, 573; **1968–69**: 1 [6],
      14 (p. 26)
    San Antonio formula, **1968–69**: 14 (p. 25),
      50, 51 [5], 65n., 79 [10], 169 [9], 170,
      280, 425 [4]
    U Thant's peace efforts, **1967**: 411 [5], 488
  Prisoner exchange, **1968–69**: 169 [7]
  Prisoners, **1966**: 54, 338 [1, 4–5, 17], 549;
    1967: 312 [7], 572, 573
  Public opinion, **1966**: 88 [16, 18], 445 [26];
    1967: 132 [10], 204 [10, 11, 13, 14,
    16], 211, 225 [15], 328 [3, 11], 407,
    409, 495 [7]; **1968–69**: 151n., 172
  San Antonio address, **1967**: 409, 411 [6],
    460 [13], 554 [1]
  SEATO signatories, role in, **1968–69**: 696
    [13]
  Soviet policy, **1966**: 474 [16], 577 [6], 607
    [3, 6]; **1967**: 104 [8], 204 [12], 264 [5],
    554 [2]
  Statement, **1968–69**: 51 [1]
  Television, role of, **1968–69**: 172
  Tonkin resolution, Gulf of, **1966**: 88 [17]
  United Kingdom, policy, **1968–69**: 65n.
  United Nations role, **1966**: 6 (p. 10), 52 [5],
    65 [13], 94, 607 [10], 654 [1];
    1967: 100, 132 [9], 144, 204 [13],
    225 [6], 312 [9], 409, 488, 495 [14],
    518 [12]

Vietnam conflict – *continued*
  Veterans, **1966**: 421, 645; **1967**: 13 (p. 55),
    25, 92, 161, 374; **1968–69**: 40ftn. (p.
    115), 67, 114, 131, 132, 229, 419,
    667
  Vietcong.
    See main heading, Vietcong.
  War, question of declaration, **1966**: 88 [17,
    21]
  Westmoreland, Gen. William C.
    See main heading, Westmoreland, Gen.
    William C.
Vietnam Training Center, Foreign Service Insti-
  tute, **1968–69**: 149
"View From the White House, A," **1968–69**:
  648
Vigorito, Repr. Joseph P., **1967**: 391
Villa Madonna College, **1968–69**: 499n.
Vincennes, Ind., **1966**: 350
  Mayor Earl C. Lawson, **1966**: 350
Vinson, Carl, **1963–64**: 230, 242 [26], 330, 332,
    487, 568, 716, 717, 718, 719;
    1965: 157, 158; **1968–69**: 110, 592
Vinson, Fred M., **1963–64**: 292, 643, 644
Vinson, Fred M., Jr., **1966**: 204
Violence, National Commission on the Causes
  and Prevention of, **1968–69**: 293,
  298, 301
Violence in the streets.
  See main heading, Civil disorders.
Virgil, **1966**: 93
Virgin Islands, **1968–69**: 457
  Gov. Ralph Paiewonsky, **1968–69**: 457, 477
  Watch imports, **1966**: 600
Virgin Islands Elective Governor Act,
  1968–69: 457
Virginia, **1965**: 61, 70; **1966**: 320 [14], 338
  [11], 391; **1967**: 15; **1968–69**: 241
  Campaign remarks, **1963–64**: 628
  Candidates for public office, **1963–64**: 628
  Goodwin, Gov. Mills E., Jr., **1966**: 122 [1],
    650n.
  Harrison, Gov. Albertis S., Jr., **1963–64**: 359,
    471; **1965**: 205
  Poll tax, **1965**: 409
  Rapid transit system, **1965**: 499; **1967**: 154
  Remarks, **1967**: 423, 485 [7, 8]
  School desegregation, **1965**: 470
Virginia, University of, **1966**: 395; **1967**: 184n.
Virginia Military Institute, **1963–64**: 359;
  1965: 463 [8]
Virus diseases, prevention, **1968–69**: 113, 685
Viruses, synthetic, **1967**: 540, 544
Visas, travel, **1968–69**: 88, 116, 146
Vision, Volunteers for, **1965**: 467; **1966**: 257
Visitor Center, National, **1968–69**: 128, 133
Visitor program, President's foreign, **1968–69**:
  116

Visitors, foreign leaders
  Afghanistan, Prime Minister Maiwandwal,
    1967: 143–144
  Australia
    Prime Minister Gorton, **1968–69**: 271, 273,
      277
    Prime Minister Holt, **1966**: 304–305, 328;
      1967: 246, 248
    Prime Minister Menzies, Robert G., **1963–
      64**: 426; **1965**: 303
  Austria, Chancellor Klaus, **1968–69**: 190, 193
  Barbados, Prime Minister Barrow, **1968–69**:
    476, 479
  Bolivia, Barrientos Ortuño, **1966**: 338 [16];
    1968–69: 362
  Brazil, President-elect Costa e Silva, **1967**: 17
  Burma, General Ne Win, **1966**: 443, 440, 450
  Cameroon, President Ahidjo, **1967**: 444
  Canada, Prime Minister Pearson, Lester B.,
    1963–64: 128, 134–138, 140, 574,
    576; **1965**: 21, 162
  Chad, Republic of, President Tombalbaye,
    1968–69: 508, 511
  China, Republic of, Vice President Yen, **1967**:
    212, 213, 219
  Costa Rica
    President Fernandez, Trejos, **1968–69**:
      289–291
    President Orlich, Francisco J., **1963–64**:
      438, 441, 443
  Denmark, Prime Minister Krag, **1963–64**: 394;
    1966: 195; **1967**: 278
  Ethiopia, Emperor Haile Selassie, **1967**: 51–52
  Germany
    Brandt, Willy, **1963–64**: 349; **1967**: 347–
      349, 351
    Chancellor Kiesinger, **1967**: 312 [2], 347–
      349, 351
    Erhard, Ludwig, **1963–64**: 72–76, 87, 399,
      400; **1965**: 659, 660; **1966**: 474 [9],
      482, 485–486; **1967**: 306; **1968–69**:
      151
  Ghana, Lt. Gen. Ankrah, **1967**: 426
  Greece, Prime Minister Papandreou, George,
    1963–64: 424, 429
  Guyana, Prime Minister Burnham, **1966**:
    341–342
  Iceland
    President Asgeirsson, **1967**: 313
    Prime Minister Bjarni, **1963–64**: 521ftn.
      (p. 978)
  India, Prime Minister Gandhi, **1966**: 148–149,
    152
  Iran
    Prime Minister Hoveyda, **1968–69**: 613–615
    Shah Mohammad Reza Pahlavi, **1963–64**:
      385, **1967**: 363, 364, 366; **1968–69**:
      304, 307

Visitors, foreign leaders – *continued*
  Ireland, De Valera, Eamon, **1963-64**: 364, 366, 376
  Israel
    Eshkol, Levi, **1963-64**: 377, 378, 380; **1968-69**: 7-9
    President Shazar, **1966**: 365
  Italy
    Foreign Minister Fanfani, **1967**: 278
    Moro, Aldo, **1965**: 198, 200, 203; **1967**: 278
    President Saragat, **1967**: 389-391
    Segni, Antonio, **1963-64**: 101, 102, 107, 109, 118
  Ivory Coast, President Houphouet-Boigny, **1967**: 356
  Japan, Prime Minister Sato, **1965**: 8, 12, 15; **1967**: 486, 487, 492
  Jordan, King Hussein I, **1963-64**: 258, 259, 265
  Korea
    Park, Chung Hee, **1965**: 254, 256; **1968-69**: 201
    Prime Minister Chung, **1967**: 111-113
  Kuwait, Amir Shaikh Sabah, **1968-69**: 618-620
  Laos
    Crown Prince Vong Savang, **1967**: 480
    Prime Minister Souvanna Phouma, **1967**: 438, 439
  Liberia, President Tubman, **1968-69**: 157, 159, 181
  Malagasy Republic, Tsiranana, Philibert, **1963-64**: 478, 479
  Malawi, President Banda, **1967**: 256
  Malaysia, Rahman, Tunku Abdul, **1963-64**: 470, 471
  Mexico
    López Mateos, Adolfo, **1963-64**: 192, 193, 194, 590
    President Diaz Ordaz, **1967**: 447-449, 451, 452; **1968-69**: 623, 624
  Morocco, King Hassan II, **1967**: 43, 46
  Nepal, King Mahendra, **1967**: 459, 461, 462
  New Zealand, Holyoake, Keith, **1963-64**: 464; **1968-69**: 522, 525, 528
  Nicaragua, President Schick, **1966**: 263-264
  Niger, President Diori, **1967**: 400, 403
  Norway, King Olav V, **1968-69**: 211, 214
  Pakistan, Ayub Khan, Mohammed, **1965**: 648, 649, 650
  Paraguay, President Stroessner, **1968-69**: 147, 148
  Philippines
    Macapagal, Diosdado P., **1963-64**: 623, 626
    President Marcos, **1966**: 458-459, 461
  Saudi Arabia, King Faisal, **1966**: 284-285, 287
  Senegal, President Senghor, **1966**: 488-489
  Singapore, Prime Minister Lee, **1967**: 433-435

Visitors, foreign leaders – *continued*
  Somali Republic, Prime Minister Egal, **1968-69**: 137, 140
  Soviet Union, Premier Kosygin, **1967**: 279, 280, 282, 283
  Thailand
    King Bhumibol Adulyadej and Queen Sirikit, **1967**: 289, 290, 293
    Prime Minister Kittikachorn, **1968-69**: 232, 233
  Tunisia, President Bourguiba, **1968-69**: 249, 250, 255
  Turkey
    Inonu, Ismet, **1963-64**: 416, 418, 423
    President Sunay, **1967**: 155, 158, 162
  United Kingdom
    Foreign Secretary Brown, **1967**: 278, 404
    Home, Alec Douglas-, **1963-64**: 184-187
    Wilson, Harold, **1963-64**: 795-797; **1966**: 359; **1967**: 249, 250; **1968-69**: 65
  Upper Volta, Yameogo, Maurice, **1965**: 141, 142, 144
  Vietnam
    President Thieu, **1966**: 53; **1967**: 127, 129-131; **1968-69**: 398, 400, 401
    Prime Minister Ky, **1966**: 53; **1967**: 127, 129-131
Visits to foreign countries.
  See also Reminiscences, the President's.
  Australia, **1966**: 541-547; **1967**: 561
  Canada, **1963-64**: 575, 576; **1967**: 237-239
  Costa Rica, **1968-69**: 374
  El Salvador, **1968-69**: 363, 365, 367-372
  Germany, **1967**: 191
  Guatemala, **1968-69**: 376
  Honduras, **1968-69**: 375
  Italy, **1967**: 570-572
  Korea, **1966**: 561-566a
  Malaysia, **1966**: 559-560
  Mexico, **1966**: 174, 176-177, 639; **1967**: 453; **1968-69**: 623n.
  New Zealand, **1966**: 538-540
  Nicaragua, **1968-69**: 373
  Pakistan, **1967**: 569
  Philippines, **1966**: 550-551
  Thailand, **1966**: 554, 555, 557-558; **1967**: 565
  Uruguay, **1967**: 171, 173, 175-177
  Vietnam, **1966**: 552; **1967**: 566, 567
Vissing, Richard, **1966**: 353
VISTA.
  See Volunteers in Service to America.
Visual Arts, Center for Advanced Study in the, **1967**: 470
Visual and Auditory Materials of an Educational, Scientific, and Cultural Character, Agreement for Facilitating the International Circulation of (Beirut Agreement), **1966**: 45, 519

VITA Corporation, **1968–69**: 63
Vivanco, José, **1968–69**: 223 [2]
Vivian, Weston E., **1963–64**: 745; **1966**: 431
VMI.
    See Virginia Military Institute.
Vo Nguyen Giap (Vice Premier of North
    Vietnam), **1967**: 195
Vocational education.
    See Occupational training.
Vocational Education Act of 1917 (Smith-
    Hughes Act), **1967**: 67, 193
Vocational Education Act of 1963, **1965**: 32
    (p. 94), 340; **1967**: 67, 77, 193; **1968–
    69**: 113, 538
Vocational Education Acts, **1963–64**: 53, 133,
    219; **1965**: 5; **1966**: 95, 172, 273
Vocational Education Amendments of 1968,
    1968–69: 54, 390, 538, 678 (p. 1283)
Vocational education and training.
    See Occupational training.
Vocational guidance, **1967**: 77
Vocational Industrial Clubs of America, **1968–
    69**: 238
Vocational rehabilitation, **1963–64**: 179, 213;
    1965: 5, 102, 140, 416, 425, 526;
    1968–69: 40
    See also Occupational training.
    Handicapped persons, **1968–69**: 39 (pp. 104,
      106), 678 (p. 1294)
    Veterans, **1968–69**: 39 (p. 106), 414
Vocational Rehabilitation Act Amendments of
    1965, **1966**: 192n.
Vocational Rehabilitation Act Amendments of
    1967, **1967**: 413
Vocational Rehabilitation Acts, **1963–64**: 488
Vocational Training Act of 1963, **1965**: 70
Voice of America, **1965**: 353 [17], 388 [3]
Volcanic eruption, Costa Rica, **1963–64**: 438n.,
    443; **1968–69**: 421, 430
Volker, Dr. Joseph, **1966**: 208n.; **1967**: 500
Vollmer, Clarence E., **1967**: 485 [6]
Volpe, Gov. John A., **1966**: 121 [1], 396–399,
    407; **1967**: 222n., 223 [3, 4]; **1968–
    69**: 46n., 102, 406, 539, 646 [3]
Volpe, Mrs. John A., **1968–69**: 406
Voltaire, François, **1968–69**: 360
Volunteer Physicians for Vietnam, **1968–69**: 438
Volunteers to America, **1967**: 365
Volunteers in Service to America (VISTA),
    1963–64: 801; **1965**: 32 (p. 94), 75,
    80, 102, 208 [13], 288n., 308; **1966**:
    111, 189, 257, 594; **1967**: 114, 266,
    275, 277; **1968–69**: 40, 75, 282, 332,
    341, 555
Volunteers for Vision, **1965**: 467; **1966**: 257
Von Braun, Wernher, **1963–64**: 75; **1966**: 485;
    1967: 533; **1968–69**: 616
Von Hase, Karl Guenther, **1967**: 264 [18]

Von Hassel, Kai-Uwe, **1965**: 660; **1966**: 486
Von Neumann, Dr. John, **1968–69**: 608
Von Steuben, Friedrich Wilhelm, **1966**: 466
Vong Savang, Crown Prince (Laos), **1967**: 480
Voorhis, Jerry, **1963–64**: 54ftn. (p. 68), 352
Vorenberg, James, **1965**: 437; **1966**: 526;
    1967: 146
Voskhod II space flight, **1965**: 116
Voting participation and registration, **1963–64**:
    508
    Alabama, **1965**: 46 [3, 13]
    Bill to eliminate barriers.
      See main heading, Voting rights bill.
    Discriminatory tests, **1965**: 107, 108
    District of Columbia, **1963–64**: 167; **1965**: 39
    Guam, election of governor, **1968–69**: 477
    Negroes, **1965**: 104, 106 [1], 107, 108; **1966**:
      66, 96, 196, 277ftn. (p. 631), 403, 436
    Southern States, **1965**: 448 [9]
    Virgin Islands, election of governor, **1968–69**:
      457
    Women, **1963–64**: 289
Voting Participation and Registration, President's
    Commission on, **1963–64**: 57, 167
Voting rights, **1963–64**: 91 (p. 116), 406, 413,
    433, 541, 800; **1965**: 39, 46 [3, 13],
    179, 201, 208 [15], 353 [18], 402,
    436, 448 [9], 452, 463 [15]; **1966**:
    21, 273, 320 [17], 353, 403, 585;
    1967: 55, 81, 201, 332; **1968–69**: 26,
    82, 87, 164, 195, 209, 212, 282, 332,
    459, 565, 596, 611, 631, 672, 676
    (p. 1264)
    Absentee, **1968–69**: 314
    Duty to exercise, **1963–64**: 57, 167, 171, 508,
      680, 702, 712, 719, 761, 764
    Equal opportunity, **1965**: 2, 104, 106 [1, 7,
      9], 107, 108, 109
    Franchise for 18-year-olds, **1968–69**: 282, 283
      [14], 305, 332, 341
    Message to Congress, **1965**: 108
    Negroes, **1965**: 2, 104, 106 [1], 107, 108, 349,
      409
    Ratification of constitutional amendment,
      1963–64: 171
    Young people, **1963–64**: 706
Voting Rights Act of 1965, **1965**: 117ftn. (p.
    305), 353ftn. (p. 741), 436, 448 [9],
    613; **1966**: 59, 196, 216, 403, 504;
    1967: 55, 216; **1968–69**: 26, 87, 111,
    195, 212, 332, 341, 596, 611, 631, 676
    (p. 1266), 696 [9]
    See also main heading, Voting rights bill.
    Approval, **1965**: 409
    Reports on, **1965**: 409n.
Voting rights bill.
    See also Voting Rights Act of 1965.
    House action on, **1965**: 349

Voting rights bill – *continued*
  Proposed, **1965**: 104, 106 [1, 9], 107, 108,
      109, 117 [7], 201, 208 [15], 301, 353
      [16, 18], 397
  Senate passage, **1965**: 278
Vournas, George, **1963–64**: 211 [1]
Voyager space program, **1968–69**: 39 (p. 100)
Voyager spacecraft, **1965**: 81n.; **1967**: 13 (p. 50)
Vu Quoc Thuc, **1967**: 131

WAAC (Women's Army Auxiliary Corps), **1967**:
      475
WAC (Women's Army Corps), **1966**: 8 [16]
Waco, Tex., **1965**: 286n.
Waddy, Joseph C., **1967**: 81
Wade, Hugh J., **1966**: 567–568
Wadsworth, James, **1963–64**: 563 [5], 591, 688
      [3], 750
Wadsworth, James J., Jr., **1965**: 126
Wage Policy Board, **1965**: 483
Wage-hour bill.
  See Fair Labor Standards Act, 1938.
Wages, **1963–64**: 213, 233, 235, 267, 297, 299,
      413, 415, 558, 566, 747, 761, 775, 787;
      1965: 38, 99; **1966**: 401 [2], 414, 430,
      432, 434, 444, 451, 512, 654 [5];
      1967: 329, 420, 554 [13]; **1968–69**:
      2, 50, 114, 280, 442, 631, 678 (p. 1276)
  See also Pay; Personal income.
  Agricultural.
    See main heading, Agriculture and agricul-
        tural programs.
  Airlines workers, **1966**: 338 [3]
  Congressmen, **1968–69**: 676 (p. 1267), 677,
      694
  Construction industry, **1963–64**: 444; **1966**:
      445 [7]
  Controls, **1967**: 13 (p. 40), 518 [9]; **1968–69**:
      1 [5], 241, 404, 684 (p. 1316)
  District of Columbia employees, **1968–69**: 133,
      689
  Factory and industrial, **1965**: 644; **1966**: 34
      (p. 96), 399, 403, 426, 635 [8–9];
      1968–69: 47 (p. 128)
  Farm workers, **1968–69**: 91
  Federal wage boards, **1965**: 612
  Firemen, **1968–69**: 272
  Garnishment, **1967**: 114
  Government employees, **1967**: 6 [13], 13
      (pp. 43, 46–47), 16 (p. 78), 121, 140,
      163, 329, 330 [1], 343, 417 [1], 420,
      546; **1968–69**: 14 (p. 32), 39 (pp. 88,
      91, 92, 97, 98), 303, 667, 678 (pp.
      1280, 1282, 1305), 694
  Guidelines, **1968–69**: 1 [13]

Wages – *continued*
  Increase, **1963–64**: 91 (p. 115), 124 (pp. 156,
      161), 166, 285 [15], 314, 327, 350,
      404, 405, 431, 434, 455 [2], 477, 506,
      548, 562, 599, 604, 640, 652, 655, 657,
      658, 695, 703, 708, 712, 713, 719, 728,
      733, 734, 745, 749, 750, 762, 771, 811;
      1965: 23, 35 (pp. 104, 106), 60, 208
      [4], 223, 326, 489, 567, 590, 632;
      1966: 34 (p. 96), 155, 189, 201, 228,
      236 [8], 237, 333, 336, 347, 373 [3,
      13], 399, 401 [2], 403, 412–413, 415,
      428, 431, 437, 479, 504, 515, 520, 577
      [10], 654 [3]; **1967**: 3 (p. 7), 16
      (p. 74), 270, 524, 534; **1968–69**: 46,
      47 (pp. 130, 131, 138, 139), 154, 169
      [17], 241, 469, 612, 654, 676 (p. 1268),
      683, 684 (pp. 1312, 1313)
  Medical personnel, **1966**: 185
  Military, **1967**: 13 (pp. 42, 46–47), 16 (p. 78),
      25, 92, 140, 163, 329, 330 [1], 343,
      546; **1968–69**: 5, 14 (p. 32), 39 (pp. 88,
      91, 92, 97, 98), 556, 678 (pp. 1280,
      1282, 1305)
  Minimum.
    See main heading, Minimum wage.
  Negroes, **1968–69**: 423, 429
  Police, **1967**: 27, 382, 482, 575; **1968–69**:
      14 (p. 30), 59, 133, 202, 272, 320, 325,
      355, 436, 557 [8]
  President's, **1968–69**: 655, 690, 691
  Railroads, **1967**: 188
  Ship masters, **1967**: 528
  Stabilization, **1963–64**: 124 (p. 157), 642;
      1965: 2, 644; **1966**: 155, 444
  Teachers, **1967**: 493; **1968–69**: 133, 272
  Wage-price policy, **1963–64**: 124 (p. 160),
      232 [10], 242 [8], 294 [23], 311, 350,
      624, 740; **1965**: 35 (pp. 106, 110, 111),
      60, 77, 208 [4], 226, 258, 326, 338,
      413, 448 [11, 14]; **1966**: 8 [15], 34
      (pp. 96, 109), 44, 88 [20], 108–109,
      140, 141 [3–4], 155, 201, 333, 334
      [2, 7], 336, 347, 373 [3, 8, 11, 13,
      17], 403, 473, 474 [20]; **1967**: 16
      (pp. 78, 79), 518 [9], 524; **1968–69**:
      1 [5], 47 (pp. 127, 130), 76, 89, 350,
      427, 684 (pp. 1313, 1315, 1316)
  Withholding rate, **1963–64**: 92, 132 (p. 179)
  Women, **1963–64**: 398; **1965**: 91; **1966**: 299
Wagner, Aubrey J.
  See Tennessee Valley Authority, Chairman.
Wagner, Robert F., **1963–64**: 282, 294 [9], 334,
      387n., 388, 521 [5], 666, 667, 669, 751;
      1965: 295 [5], 403, 415, 418, 422n.,
      434, 566
Wagner, Robert F., Sr., **1963–64**: 334, 373, 667;
      1965: 348, 394, 415

Wagner Act, **1963–64**: 642

Wagner-Connery Labor Relations Act (National Labor Relations Act), **1968–69**: 463

Wagner Housing Act, **1968–69**: 426

Wailes, Charles, **1966**: 472

Wakelin, James H., Jr., **1963–64**: 229n.

Wald, Patricia M., **1965**: 366

Waldheim, Kurt, **1966**: 272

Waldie, Repr. Jerome R., **1966**: 401ftn. (p. 881)

Waldron, Dr. Howard H., **1968–69**: 430

Walker, Charles E., **1966**: 265

Walker, E. S. (Johnny), **1963–64**: 732

Walker, Elmer E., **1963–64**: 571

Walker, Joseph A., death, **1966**: 259

Walker, Lloyd, **1963–64**: 660n.

Walker, Mort, **1965**: 554n.

Walker, Patrick Gordon, **1963–64**: 688 [1], 796, 797; **1965**: 227

Walker, Walton, **1966**: 564

Walker Hill, Seoul, Korea, **1966**: 564

Wallace, Gov. George C., **1963–64**: 246 [7], 256 [7, 19], 285 [1], 316 [14, 18, 21], 455 [19], 475 [18]; **1965**: 106 [1], 114, 117 [1, 5], 126n.; **1966**: 122 [1, 2]; **1968–69**: 360, 480n., 529, 568n., 569n.

Wallace, Henry A., death of, **1965**: 619

Wallace, J. E., **1968–69**: 300n.

Waller, John Keith, **1967**: 1, 246

Waller, Mrs. John Keith, **1967**: 246

Waller, Keith, **1968–69**: 273

Waller, Mrs. Keith, **1968–69**: 273

Waller, Theodore, **1966**: 424n.

Walleye guide bomb, **1963–64**: 170 [3]

Walling, Sgt. Harry A., **1963–64**: 535

Walling, Mrs. Harry A., **1963–64**: 535

Walrath, Laurence K. (Chairman, Interstate Commerce Commission), **1963–64**: 211 [2]

Walsh, Adam, **1963–64**: 606

Walsh, Jerry J., **1963–64**: 302

Walsh, Mrs. Lee, **1963–64**: 242 [6, 24]

Walsh, Michael H., **1965**: 334n.

Walsh, Rev. Michael P., **1963–64**: 266 [4]

Walsh, Thomas J., **1963–64**: 656

Walsh, William, **1966**: 394

Walsh-Healey Act, **1965**: 582; **1968–69**: 24

Walt, Lewis W., **1966**: 88 [14], 100; **1967**: 225 [11], 264ftn. (p. 613); **1968–69**: 34, 81 [1, 2]

Walter Reed Army Medical Center, **1963–64**: 476n.; **1966**: 146; **1968–69**: 431, 536, 537

Walters, Mrs. Adelaide, **1963–64**: 285 [7]

Walters, Herbert S., **1963–64**: 323, 324, 325, 645, 701, 702; **1968–69**: 345

Walworth, Arthur, **1963–64**: 303

Wanninayake, U. B., **1968–69**: 500

War, Department of, **1965**: 503; **1968–69**: 113

War, prevention of, **1965**: 88; **1966**: 480

War Claims Act of 1948, **1966**: 303

War Claims Fund, **1965**: 309; **1966**: 303

War College, National, **1963–64**: 533

War of 1812, **1965**: 95; **1966**: 359; **1967**: 495 [11]

War on Hunger, Office of (AID), **1967**: 44

War Labor Board, **1967**: 310

War orphans, **1966**: 26 (p. 64), 495

War Orphans' Education Assistance Act of 1956, **1965**: 542

War orphans' educational assistance allowance bill, approval, **1965**: 542

War on Poverty, **1968–69**: 4, 29, 124

See also Antipoverty program.

War on Poverty, Conference on Women in the, **1967**: 211

War on waste.

See Cost reduction program, Federal.

"War on Waste," cost reduction booklet, **1965**: 127

Ward, Barbara, **1963–64**: 289; **1965**: 48, 410

Ward, Henry, **1963–64**: 331, 332

Ward, Mrs. Henry, **1963–64**: 332

Wardwell, Capt. Arthur L., **1965**: 326

Warfare, subversive, **1963–64**: 382

Warheads, nuclear, **1963–64**: 382, 413

Warner, Mrs. John A., **1968–69**: 540

Warner Robins Air Force Base, Georgia, **1963–64**: 716

Warning System, National Disaster, **1967**: 31n.

Warrants, arrest, **1967**: 71

Warren, Earl (Chief Justice of the United States), **1963–64**: 2, 14, 15, 27, 117, 141, 153, 172, 426, 427, 733, 796; **1965**: 25, 42, 46 [6], 516, 519; **1966**: 22, 86, 570

See also Chief Justice of the United States.

Letter, **1963–64**: 595

Warren, Mrs. Earl, **1967**: 7n., 387; **1968–69**: 32, 78, 104, 140

Warren Commission (Commission to Report Upon the Assassination of President John F. Kennedy), **1966**: 577 [11]; **1967**: 80 [5]

See also Commission to Report Upon the Assassination of President John F. Kennedy.

Warsaw Pact nations, invasion of Czechoslovakia, **1968–69**: 455, 462, 467ftn. (p. 929), 472, 474, 676 (pp. 1268, 1269)

Warsaw (Poland) Uprising, 20th anniversary, **1963–64**: 491

Wartburg College, Waverly, Iowa, **1967**: 306

Washakie Wilderness, Wyo., **1967**: 418; **1968–69**: 122

Washington, George, **1963–64**: 101n., 141, 272, 295, 303, 402, 415, 473, 533, 566, 597,

Washington, George – *continued*
    623n., 774; **1965**: 25, 26, 80, 213, 299,
    543, 559; **1966**: 81, 189, 261, 353;
    1967: 43n., 200, 465, 502, 549;
    1968–69: 138, 147n., 148n., 156, 225,
    246, 476n., 479, 499, 644, 655
    Birthday, **1968–69**: 342
Washington, Martha, **1965**: 380
Washington, Walter E., **1965**: 263n.; **1967**: 377,
    411 [1], 466, 544, 575; **1968–69**: 19,
    36, 39 (p. 107), 95, 133, 152, 169 [5],
    272, 420, 424, 429, 436, 442, 458, 629,
    698
    Swearing in as Commissioner, District of
      Columbia, **1967**: 406
Washington, Mrs. Walter E., **1967**: 406
Washington, **1963–64**: 135
    Gov. Albert D. Rosellini, **1963–64**: 575, 576,
    577
Washington, D.C.
    See District of Columbia.
Washington Action for Youth, **1963–64**: 537
Washington Clearing House Association, **1967**:
    27
Washington Council of Governments, Metropoli-
    tan, **1966**: 302; **1968–69**: 355
Washington Metropolitan Area Transit Authority,
    1966: 262; **1967**: 15, 154
Washington Monument, **1963–64**: 623n.; **1965**:
    70
Washington Post, **1963–64**: 256 [12]; **1966**:
    8 [3], 52 [7], 88 [23], 277 [22];
    1967: 466; **1968–69**: 655
Washington Redskins Pro Football, Inc.,
    1968–69: 109
Washington Star, **1968–69**: 212, 655
Washington State, national park and wilderness
    areas, **1968–69**: 510n.
Washington State International Trade Fair,
    1967: 231n.
Washington Technical Institute, **1966**: 586;
    1968–69: 436, 689
Washington University, **1965**: 225
Wasilewski, Vincent Thomas, **1968–69**: 172
Wasp, U.S.S., **1965**: 304n.
Wasserman, Lew, **1967**: 281
Waste, program to combat.
    See Cost reduction program, Federal.
Waste disposal facilities, **1966**: 26 (p. 61), 30,
    584; **1967**: 16 (p. 85), 114, 458;
    1968–69: 94, 113, 122, 450, 536, 678
Waste products
    Disposal, **1965**: 54
    Industrial, **1966**: 82
Watch import tariffs, **1966**: 600; **1967**: 16
    (p. 79)
Watch movements, imported, **1965**: 167

Water Commission, National, **1966**: 82; **1968–**
    69: 39 (p. 101), 122, 345, 501, 600
    Proposed, **1967**: 13 (p. 51)
Water Commission, United States and Mexico,
    International Boundary and, **1966**:
    177, 467–468; **1967**: 47, 303, 408
    [2, 8], 451, 454n.; **1968–69**: 623
Water Conservation Fund, Land and, **1963–64**:
    756; **1965**: 47, 54; **1966**: 398; **1967**:
    13 (p. 51), 20, 553; **1968–69**: 39 (p.
    101), 122, 386
Water desalination, **1963–64**: 177, 396, 597,
    693, 732, 733, 756; **1965**: 17, 32 (p.
    92), 35 (p. 115), 143, 375, 417, 418,
    558; **1966**: 26 (p. 60); **1967**: 230
    Appropriations, **1967**: 284
    Atomic energy use, **1965**: 196; **1966**: 361,
    427; **1967**: 13 (p. 51), 227
    California, **1967**: 227
    Colorado River, **1963–64**: 193
    Conversion demonstration plant, Freeport,
      Tex., **1965**: 417n.
    International cooperation, **1963–64**: 545;
      1965: 143, 319 [5], 325, 417, 494,
      547, 558; **1966**: 177, 361, 427, 467–
      468, 516 [3], 607 [1]
    Reports, **1963–64**: 715
    Research, **1965**: 143, 325, 547; **1967**: 284
    Rio Grande, **1967**: 47
    U.S.-Israel cooperation, **1963–64**: 175, 377,
      378, 380, 480, 672; **1965**: 325; **1966**:
      516 [3], 607 [1]
    U.S.-Mexico, **1965**: 119; **1966**: 177, 467–468;
      1967: 448
    U.S.-Mexico-IAEA study agreement, **1965**: 558
    U.S.-Saudi Arabia, **1966**: 285
    U.S.-Soviet cooperation, **1963–64**: 420 [2],
      435, 480, 695, 804; **1965**: 325
Water Desalination, International Symposium on,
    1965: 325, 494, 547, 558
Water District of Southern California, Metro-
    politan, **1967**: 13 (p. 51), 284
Water Energy Conference, **1965**: 418
Water for Peace, International Conference on,
    1966: 427, 593; **1967**: 230
Water for Peace Office, **1967**: 230
Water for peace program, **1965**: 558
Water pollution, **1963–64**: 132 (p. 187), 179,
    357, 391, 422, 578, 669, 755
    See also under Water resources.
    Control, **1965**: 2, 9, 32 (p. 94), 35 (p. 115),
      54, 90, 92, 94, 275, 277, 418, 433, 452,
      543, 545, 602, 659
Water Pollution Control Act of 1965, **1966**: 82
Water Pollution Control Administration,
    Federal, **1966**: 82, 88 [4], 91, 111, 215,
    232, 428; **1967**: 13 (pp. 51, 57), 240;
    1968–69: 39 (p. 109), 678 (p. 1301)

Water Pollution Control Advisory Board, **1966:**
  91
Water Quality Act of 1965, **1965:** 543; **1966:**
  82, 392–393; **1967:** 13 (p. 51), 20;
  1968–69: 122, 593
Water quality bill, **1965:** 418
Water resources, **1967:** 13 (p. 51), 230; **1968–69:**
  39 (p. 101), 94, 330, 600, 624, 678
  (p. 1301)
  Appalachian region, **1968–69:** 701
  Coastal, oil pollution, **1967:** 240
  Community, **1968–69:** 14 (p. 30), 666
  Desalination.
    See main heading, Water desalination.
  Developing nations, **1966:** 427
  Development, **1963–64:** 132 (p. 187), 134,
    135, 175, 193, 198. 231, 396, 461,
    578, 620, 756; **1965:** 2, 17, 32 (p. 92),
    35 (p. 115), 54, 186, 236, 275, 277,
    358, 375, 417, 418, 452, 454 [5], 477,
    487, 543, 545, 555, 558, 587; **1966:**
    26 (p. 60), 49, 394; **1967:** 13 (p. 51),
    20, 227, 230, 458
    Campaign remarks, **1963–64:** 597, 598,
      606, 645, 650, 656, 760
  International conference, **1966:** 593
  Management, **1967:** 230
  Northeastern States, **1965:** 358, 375, 417,
    418, 434, 477; **1966:** 391, 393, 427
  Northwestern States, **1965:** 186
  Pollution, **1966:** 6 (p. 3), 26 (p. 62), 34 (p.
    106), 82, 91, 215, 229, 232, 334 [2],
    353, 392–393, 398, 403, 427, 481,
    485–486, 518, 545, 574, 630 [4];
    1967: 3 (p. 2), 13 (p. 51), 16 (p. 85),
    20, 101, 222, 233 [6], 240, 295, 300,
    329, 503, 534; **1968–69:** 14 (p. 28),
    39 (pp. 89, 101), 84, 87, 95, 113, 122,
    123, 167, 297, 345, 447, 470, 501, 593,
    648, 653, 678 (p. 1301), 684 (pp. 1311,
    1321), 692
    See also main heading, Water pollution.
  Research, **1965:** 54, 143, 275; **1966:** 138;
    1967: 284
  Rural, **1966:** 398, 403, 428
  Shortage, **1966:** 481; **1967:** 227
  Southwestern States, **1965:** 186
  Urban, **1966:** 393; **1967:** 16 (p. 84), 230;
    1968–69: 697
  User charges, **1967:** 16 (p. 86)
  Waste disposal facilities, **1966:** 26 (p. 61), 30,
    584; **1967:** 16 (p. 85), 114, 458
    See also main heading, Waste disposal
    facilities.
Water Resources Council, **1965:** 358, 375; **1966:**
  82, 91, 391; **1967:** 20; **1968–69:** 39
  (p. 101), 593
Water Resources Planning Act, **1963–64:** 597;
  1965: 173, 375; **1968–69:** 593, 666

Water Resources Research, Committee on, **1965:**
  275, 418; **1966:** 138
Water Resources Research Act of 1964, **1963–
  64:** 461, 756; **1965:** 32 (p. 92)
Water Resources Research Program, Federal
  (1966), **1965:** 275
Water and sanitation systems bill (1965), **1966:**
  398, 403, 428
Water and sanitation systems in rural areas bill,
  1965: 555
Water and sewer facilities, **1965:** 555, 585, 586
Water shortage, **1965:** 358
Water System, Tri-County, **1966:** 398
Waterfowl refuges, **1967:** 547
Waterloo, N.Y., **1966:** 242
Waterman, Alan T., **1963–64:** 27; **1965:** 71
  Death, **1967:** 513
Waterton-Glacier International Peace Park
  (Montana–British Columbia), **1966:**
  448
Waterways, inland, **1963–64:** 132 (p. 181)
  User charges, **1965:** 32 (p. 88), 35 (p. 116),
    255
Waterways, safety, **1968–69:** 56
Watson, Arthur, **1963–64:** 296; **1965:** 450
Watson, Barbara M., **1968–69:** 442
Watson, Bernard, **1967:** 396n.
Watson, Mark S., **1963–64:** 27
Watson, Thomas J., Jr., **1963–64:** 473, 568,
  601; **1965:** 55, 115n.; **1966:** 57;
  1968–69: 3
Watson, W. Marvin, **1963–64:** 780 [17]
  See also Postmaster General.
Wattenberg, Ben J., **1968–69:** 17
Watts, Repr. John C., **1963–64:** 643, 644
Watts area, Los Angeles, **1966:** 236 [13];
  1967: 55
  Civil disorders, (1965), **1968–69:** 114
Waukegan, Ill., **1968–69:** 690
Wauneka, Mrs. Annie D., **1963–64:** 27
WAVES (Women's Reserve, USNR), **1966:**
  8 [16]; **1967:** 475
Ways and Means, House Committee on, **1967:**
  6 [19], 330 [1, 4], 358 [3], 371, 411
  [10], 417 [1, 8, 10], 460 [4], 518
  [6], 554 [13]; **1968–69:** 223 [11],
  229, 425 [2], 651, 654
Weapons, **1966:** 246, 320 [7], 434; **1967:** 442
  See also Arms control and disarmament; Fire-
    arms control; Missiles; Nuclear weapons;
    Nuclear weapons tests.
  Arms control and disarmament, **1966:** 6 (p.
    8), 70, 320 [9], 411, 480, 483, 486,
    497, 503; **1967:** 3 (p. 11), 38, 59, 80
    [2, 5, 7], 162, 167, 281, 283, 328
    [24], 491
  Arms race, **1966:** 32

Weapons – *continued*
  Firearms control, **1966**: 116, 364, 373 [14],
    526; **1967**: 3 (p. 7), 35, 71, 326, 353,
    382, 385, 468, 482, 560, 575
  Importation control, **1965**: 102
  Laboratories, **1963–64**: 132 (p. 185)
  Missiles, **1965**: 26 (p. 56), 310, 387, 607
    [16], 642 [8, 14–16, 20]; **1967**:
    13 (p. 48), 328 [25]
  New and improved, **1963–64**: 382; **1965**: 26,
    284, 387
  Nuclear.
    See main heading, Nuclear weapons.
  Production, **1963–64**: 797
Weather Bureau, **1963–64**: 336 [3], 647; **1965**:
    247, 271; **1967**: 31n.
Weather Center, World, Washington, D.C.,
    1963–64: 705
Weather prediction and control, **1963–64**: 518,
    597, 647, 705, 756; **1965**: 81, 92,
    247; **1966**: 222, 229, 326; **1967**: 13
    (p. 52), 31n., 101; **1968–69**: 41, 122,
    124, 145, 227, 501, 507
  International cooperation, **1965**: 271; **1966**:
    94, 143, 222; **1967**: 157; **1968–69**:
    361
  Message to Congress, **1965**: 271
  Report, **1966**: 79; **1967**: 314; **1968–69**: 495
  Satellites, **1963–64**: 132 (p. 187), 396, 597,
    647, 705, 733, 756; **1966**: 222; **1967**:
    121, 533
Weather System, World, **1963–64**: 396, 705
Weather Watch, World, **1966**: 94, 222; **1967**:
    13 (p. 52), 157; **1968–69**: 361, 479
Weatherbee, Artemus E., **1965**: 263n.
Weatherford, Tex., **1965**: 561
Weaver, George L-P., **1968–69**: 631
Weaver, Robert C., **1965**: 415, 511n., 545;
    1966: 8 [1, 13], 12
  See also Housing and Home Finance Agency,
    Administrator; Housing and Urban
    Development, Secretary of.
Weaver, Mrs. Robert C., **1966**: 8 [1], 13, 295
Webb, James E., **1966**: 134–135, 249, 410,
    413–416, 485–486, 618, 625; **1967**:
    77, 425, 504, 533; **1968–69**: 107, 174,
    361, 507, 552, 616, 646 [9, 12], 647,
    662
  See also National Aeronautics and Space
    Administrator.
Webb, Mrs. James E., **1968–69**: 616
Webb, Walter Prescott, **1963–64**: 642; **1966**:
    427
Webster, Daniel, **1963–64**: 413, 606; **1966**: 21,
    335, 392; **1968–69**: 155, 592
Wechsler, Herbert, **1965**: 422n.
Weed, W. F., **1965**: 236
Weeds, Lt. Gen. Richard G., **1967**: 485 [7]

Wehle, Maj. Gen. Philip C., **1963–64**: 5
Weimer, Rae O., **1965**: 260
Weinberg, Sidney J., **1968–69**: 694
Weiner, Charles R., **1963–64**: 285 [7]
Weiner, Leon N., **1967**: 252n.; **1968–69**: 471n.
Weinheimer, Mrs. Tom, **1963–64**: 544
Weinman, Judge Carl A., **1966**: 535n.
Weirton, W. Va., **1967**: 20
Weisl, Edwin L., Jr., **1963–64**: 372, 751; **1967**:
    411 [2]
Weisl, Edwin L., Sr., **1967**: 251, 411 [2]; **1968–
    69**: 153 [14], 262, 672n.
Weizmann, Chaim, **1963–64**: 175
Weizmann Institute of Science, **1963–64**: 175
Welch, Lt. Harold W., release from East
    Germany, **1963–64**: 232 [2], 242
    [18, 26]
Welch, Louis, **1963–64**: 760; **1967**: 87n.; **1968–
    69**: 442
Welfare.
  See Public assistance; Welfare programs.
Welfare and pension plan protection bill, **1967**:
    57
Welfare programs, **1963–64**: 132 (p. 188), 669;
    1965: 94, 132, 475; **1966**: 22 (pp.
    61–62, 68), 27, 30, 34 (pp. 100–101,
    108), 127, 347, 444; **1968–69**: 3, 24,
    425 [2], 678 (pp. 1283, 1294, 1299)
  See also Antipoverty programs; Public
    assistance.
  Antipoverty.
    See main heading, Antipoverty program.
  Child care, **1968–69**: 39 (p. 105), 322, 678
    (p. 1294)
  Children and youth, **1965**: 501
  Cost of, **1965**: 9, 183
  District of Columbia, **1963–64**: 133; **1965**:
    29, 70
  Expenditures, **1968–69**: 39 (pp. 88, 91, 92),
    66, 109, 612, 678 (pp. 1280, 1282)
  Indians, **1963–64**: 120
  Job training, **1968–69**: 39 (p. 105)
  Older people, **1965**: 90
  Red Cross, **1963–64**: 202
  Reform, **1968–69**: 39 (p. 105), 47 (p. 143),
    100
  Work incentive program, **1968–69**: 86, 678
    (p. 1294)
Welfare Programs, Presidential Committee on
    Corporate Pension Funds and Other
    Private Retirement and, **1965**: 35
    (p. 113)
Welhausen, Judge, **1966**: 589
Welhausen Elementary School, Cotulla, Texas,
    1966: 589
Welles, Orson, **1965**: 391
Wellington, Duke of, **1967**: 216
Wellington, New Zealand, **1966**: 539–540

Wells, H. G., **1963-64**: 338; **1965**: 89; **1967**: 236

Welsh, Edward C., **1968-69**: 616, 662

Welsh, Gov. Matthew E., **1963-64**: 217, 288, 639, 640, 729

Weltner, Repr. Charles L., **1963-64**: 330, 716

Wentzel, Mrs. Volkmar, **1967**: 349

Werts, Leo R., **1967**: 458n.

Wesley, John, **1966**: 189

West African Economic Conference, **1968-69**: 157, 181

West Berlin.
See Berlin.

West Branch, Iowa, **1965**: 414, 420, 498

West Point, **1967**: 495 [14]

West Virginia, **1963-64**: 586; **1966**: 391
  Antipoverty program, **1963-64**: 293
  Barron, William W., Gov., **1963-64**: 217, 293, 360, 586
  Coal industry, **1963-64**: 295, 297
  Remarks, **1968-69**: 564, 566, 567
  Smith, Gov. Hulett C., **1966**: 122 [1, 2], 348, 426-427, 650n.; **1967**: 514, 552n., 558; **1968-69**: 46n., 58
  Unemployment, **1963-64**: 213, 295, 297

West Virginia University, **1968-69**: 567

Western Alliance, split in, question of, **1963-64**: 246 [14]

Western Hemisphere, **1963-64**: 177, 607, 695, 710, 726, 809; **1965**: 286, 393, 558; **1966**: 175, 386, 338 [16]; **1967**: 357, 395, 448, 451; **1968-69**: 239
  Communism in, **1963-64**: 26, 316 [23], 635; **1965**: 18, 223, 286, 295 [4, 15]
  Economic and social development, **1963-64**: 340, 443; **1965**: 295 [15]
  News conference remarks, **1963-64**: 54 [2, 15], 232 [1], 246 [1], 256 [17], 285 [13], 316 [23]
  Relations with Western Europe, **1963-64**: 192

Western Reserve University, **1965**: 225

Western States Democratic Conference, **1966**: 417 [11], 418

Westminster College, Missouri, **1963-64**: 263

Westmoreland, Mrs. James R., **1967**: 309 [1]

Westmoreland, Margaret, **1967**: 494

Westmoreland, William C., **1963-64**: 294 [5], 780 [6]; **1965**: 206n., 347 [1], 353 [1], 388 [1], 421, 561n.; **1966**: 86, 100, 214, 311-312, 388-389, 412, 520-521, 532, 548, 552-553, 563, 568, 570, 638, 641; **1967**: 3 (p. 12), 14, 25, 73, 116, 134, 135, 196, 308, 309, 329, 490, 494, 503, 526, 566, 567; **1968-69**: 51 [1, 6, 9, 11], 79 [8, 12, 14], 96, 109, 153 [4, 6-8], 169 [19], 171, 178n., 185, 189, 191 [5], 197, 232, 267, 276, 283 [1, 3, 5, 6, 13, 15],

Westmoreland, William C. – *continued*
    353, 384, 452, 487, 557 [7], 572, 594, 661, 688
  Birthday greetings, **1967**: 141
  Distinguished Service Medal, **1967**: 567
  Luncheon honoring, **1967**: 189, 195
  News conference remarks on, **1966**: 52 [2], 65 [8, 12, 14], 88 [19, 24], 141 [10], 158 [14], 188 [4-5, 9], 236 [1], 320 [7, 15], 334 [4], 338 [19], 445 [1], 474 [10], 492 [1], 494 [1], 501 [14, 20], 577 [5, 7], 578 [2, 6, 11], 628 [1], 642 [10], 654 [8]; **1967**: 104 [5, 14, 17, 19], 132 [1, 2, 4, 8], 204 [1, 3, 11], 225 [2], 312 [11], 358 [6], 485 [1, 6], 495 [1, 6, 13, 14], 518 [14], 554 [1]
  Vietnam conflict report, **1966**: 383

Westmoreland, Mrs. William C., **1966**: 52 [2], 383; **1967**: 309 [1], 494; **1968-69**: 384

Westrick, Ludger, **1966**: 486

Wetherby, Lawrence W., **1963-64**: 643, 644

Wetzel, Sp4c. Garry G., **1968-69**: 594

Wetzel, Walter, **1963-64**: 120

Wexler, Dr. William A., **1968-69**: 474

Wheat, Francis M., **1963-64**: 455 [8]

Wheat, **1963-64**: 132 (p. 187), 225, 249, 757; **1965**: 47; **1967**: 13 (p. 50), 63; **1968-69**: 247, 425 [2]
  Acreage allotments, **1966**: 203, 355
  Exports, **1966**: 355; **1967**: 476; **1968-69**: 29, 39 (p. 100), 696 [14]
  India, shipments to, **1966**: 52 [1], 311-312; **1967**: 375 [21, 22, 23]
  Marketing certificate program, **1963-64**: 255; **1965**: 168; **1963-64**: 255; **1965**: 168; **1967**: 476
  Prices, **1968-69**: 29, 94
  Production, **1966**: 62, 311, 608; **1967**: 448, 449, 452, 453
  Research, **1967**: 449n.
  Sale to Soviet Union, **1963-64**: 139, 211 [11], 266 [11]
    Longshoremen's boycott of shipment, **1963-64**: 195
  Storage, **1963-64**: 570
  Surpluses, **1966**: 281

Wheat Agreement, International, **1965**: 377; **1967**: 476

Wheat Conference, International, **1968-69**: 29

Wheat-cotton bill.
  See Agricultural Act of 1964.

Wheat Growers, National Association of, **1963-64**: 255

Wheat Trade Convention, **1968-69**: 29

Wheeler, Burton K., **1963-64**: 656

Wheeler, Gen. Earle G., **1963–64**: 119, 256
    [2], 316 [2]; **1965**: 212, 221, 223,
    387; **1966**: 52 [3], 124 [2, 12], 183,
    214, 246, 320 [7], 324, 516 [9], 628
    [1], 642 [4]; **1967**: 134, 204 [1],
    255, 278, 309, 324, 358 [6], 493, 518
    [4]; **1968–69**: 100n., 101, 153 [4, 5,
    9], 185n., 191 [6], 299, 384, 398n.,
    401, 487, 516, 585, 669
  See also Joint Chiefs of Staff, Chairman
    (Earle G. Wheeler).
Wheeler, Mrs. Earle G., **1968–69**: 669
Wheeler, John, **1963–64**: 522; **1968–69**: 470,
    471
Wheeler, Dr. and Mrs. John A., **1968–69**: 608
Wheeler, Pete, **1968–69**: 599n.
Whelan, Mrs. Annie Laurie, **1965**: 510
Whelan, Quintin, **1963–64**: 736
Wheller, John H., **1967**: 252n.
Whiskeytown-Shasta-Trinity National Recrea-
    tion area, Calif., proposed, **1965**: 54
White, Alvin S., **1967**: 431
White, Justice Byron R., **1963–64**: 782, 784;
    1965: 66; **1966**: 498; **1968–69**: 329
White, Repr. Compton I., **1963–64**: 659; **1966**:
    410–411
White, E. B., **1963–64**: 27
White, Lt. Col. Edward H., 2d, **1965**: 302n., 304,
    306, 310, 318, 320; **1968–69**: 387
  Death, **1967**: 19, 38
White, Mrs. Edward H., 2d, **1965**: 304
White, G. D. L., **1966**: 538
White, John, **1967**: 130n.
White, John C., **1963–64**: 767
White, John R., **1963–64**: 169n.
White, Mrs. Katharine Elkus, **1963–64**: 208,
    257n., 394
White, Lee C., **1963–64**: 246 [13], 458; **1965**:
    22 [1]; **1966**: 65 [1], 88 [8], 97, 202;
    1967: 186, 288
White, Dr. Paul Dudley, **1963–64**: 568; **1965**:
    154, 163
White, Robert M., **1968–69**: 513n.
White, Theodore H., "The Making of the
    President," **1965**: 353ftn. (p. 743)
White, William Allen, **1963–64**: 339; **1967**: 193
White, William S., **1965**: 454 [5]; **1966**: 492
    [9]
White backlash, **1966**: 401 [6], 580 [15, 20],
    599 [3]
White Cane Safety Day, **1965**: 556
White House
  Cabinet Room, new portraits in, **1963–64**: 344
  First night residence in, **1963–64**: 28 [1]
  Lawn, **1963–64**: 521 [1]
  Lighting, **1963–64**: 121, 139, 182, 208, 218
    [17], 238, 299, 352, 358, 657; **1965**:
    230

White House – *continued*
  Lincoln dinner service collection, **1965**: 101
  Photography program, **1965**: 16
  Police, **1968–69**: 602, 630
    Badge, gift to President, **1968–69**: 602n.
  President's life in, **1965**: 277
  Releases, list, Appendix A, **1966**: p. 1467;
    1967: p. 1197; **1968–69**: p. 1371
  Rose Garden, beautification, **1963–64**: 267,
    280, 285 [23], 309
  Savings bond award, **1967**: 315n.
  Savings bonds purchases by employees, **1966**:
    358
  Secretaries, **1968–69**: 595
  Seminar program, **1966**: 388
  Seminars for college students, **1963–64**: 428,
    526
  Staff, **1965**: 22 [1]
  See also Appointments and nominations.
  Telephone operators, **1968–69**: 588, 595, 630
  Tree planting, **1963–64**: 673, 678, 680
  Visitors to, **1963–64**: 280 [2]
"White House, A View From the," **1968–69**: 648
White House, Committee for the Preservation of
    the, **1963–64**: 211 [7, 35]
White House announcements or statements
  Certificate of Commendation, citation to
    Eddie Cantor, **1963–64**: 163
  Desalinization of sea water, **1963–64**: 480
  Employment of minority groups in Govern-
    ment, **1963–64**: 205
  Geneva Disarmament Conference, resumption,
    1963–64: 94
  Guantanamo naval base, Cuba, U.S. guarantee
    of security, **1963–64**: 177
  Kennedy, John F.
    Assassination investigation, **1963–64**: 7, 14
    Funeral plans for, **1963–64**: 2, 5
  Painting presented to White House by family
    of President Kennedy, **1963–64**: 24
  Panama Canal Zone dispute, **1963–64**: 95, 104,
    114
  Presidential inability, procedures for, **1965**: 550
  Test ban treaty safeguards, **1963–64**: 276
  U.S.-Canadian relations, **1965**: 352
  U.S. Embassy in Moscow, attack on, **1965**: 59
  Vietnam mission, **1963–64**: 223
White House Conference on Education, **1965**:
    183, 291, 340, 374, 385
White House Conference on Equal Employment
    Opportunity, **1965**: 384, 436
White House Conference on Export Expansion,
    1963–64: 248, 592
White House Conference on Health, **1965**: 183,
    424, 594
White House Conference on International
    Cooperation, **1965**: 96, 630, 632;
    1966: 370; **1967**: 157

White House Conference on Natural Beauty, **1965**: 2, 30, 54, 183, 277, 446
White House Conference "To Fulfill These Rights."
See under Civil rights.
White House Correspondents Association, **1968–69**: 242
White House Fellows, **1966**: 388; **1967**: 201, 266; **1968–69**: 227, 282, 498, 570
  Program, **1965**: 334
    Establishment, **1963–64**: 622
White House Fellows, President's Commission on, **1963–64**: 622; **1965**: 344; **1968–69**: 227
White House Festival of the Arts, **1965**: 314
White House Press Corps, **1963–64**: 339; **1965**: 117 [4], 222, 412
White Sulphur Springs, W. Va., **1966**: 650 [1]
Whitehead, Alfred North, **1965**: 651; **1967**: 268
Whitener, Repr. Basil L., **1966**: 586
Whitlam, Edward G., **1967**: 267
Whitman, Walt, **1965**: 13, 398; **1966**: 337, 489; **1967**: 387, 426; **1968–69**: 24, 46
Whitner, Charles, **1968–69**: 453
Whitney, John Hay (Jock), **1963–64**: 796
Whittemore, Mrs. Arthur, **1965**: 277n.
Whitten, Repr. Jamie L., **1968–69**: 96
Whitticoe, Dr. James M., Jr., **1968–69**: 442
Whitton, Rex M. (Federal Highway Administrator), **1963–64**: 217; **1965**: 30; **1967**: 6 [3]
Wholesale Price Index, **1963–64**: 23, 124 (p. 160), 294 [3], 336 [1], 463; **1965**: 35 (p. 104)
Wholesale prices, **1963–64**: 124 (p. 157), 271 [3], 472, 619 [4], 630, 657, 689, 740, 775; **1965**: 632; **1966**: 34 (p. 101), 155, 201, 347, 494 [1], 577 [10]; **1967**: 16 (pp. 75, 78, 88); **1968–69**: 39 (p. 86), 47 (p. 131)
Wholesome fish and fishery products bill of 1968, **1968–69**: 56
Wholesome Meat Act of 1967, **1967**: 342, 393, 520, 534, 539, 541; **1968–69**: 14 (p. 29), 39 (p. 101), 56, 451
Wholesome meat bill, **1967**: 57
Wholesome Poultry Products Act, **1968–69**: 56, 105, 390, 451
Whooping cough, **1968–69**: 111
"Why Vietnam" booklet, President's foreword, **1965**: 388ftn. (p. 795)
Whyte, William H., **1965**: 277n.
Wichita, Kans.
  Campaign remarks, **1963–64**: 741
  Mayor Clarence E. Vollmer, **1967**: 485 [6]
Wichita Mountains Wilderness, Okla., **1968–69**: 168
Wickersham, Repr. Victor, **1963–64**: 309

Widnall, Repr. William B., **1963–64**: 453; **1965**: 415; **1968–69**: 317
Widows, benefits, **1967**: 12; **1968–69**: 3, 678 (p. 1299)
Wiener, Norbert, **1963–64**: 98
Wiesner, Jerome B., **1963–64**: 98, 116, 146n., 175, 420 [2]; **1965**: 115n.
Wiggins, Chase, **1966**: 277 [1]
Wiggins, J. Russell, **1968–69**: 496, 498, 515
  See also United Nations, U.S. Representative.
Wiggins, Mrs. J. Russell, **1968–69**: 515, 525
Wiggins, M. E., **1965**: 161n.
Wiggins, Warren W., **1965**: 208 [6]
Wightman, Richard, **1966**: 338 [18]
Wigner, Eugene P., **1968–69**: 608, 695n.
Wilbur, Dr. Dwight, **1965**: 594n.; **1966**: 208n.; **1967**: 500
Wild and Scenic Rivers Act, **1968–69**: 345, 411, 510, 547
Wild and Scenic Rivers System, National, **1968–69**: 14 (p. 31), 39 (p. 101), 122, 345, 510
Wilde, Frazar B., **1963–64**: 775; **1966**: 182
Wilde, Oscar, **1963–64**: 224, 303
Wilder, Thornton, **1963–64**: 27
Wilderness Act, **1963–64**: 554, 578, 620, 657, 669, 728, 756; **1965**: 32 (p. 92); **1966**: 69, 398, 518; **1967**: 29, 96, 418; **1968–69**: 150, 311
Wilderness area, preservation, **1965**: 277, 471; **1967**: 295, 418; **1968–69**: 122, 150, 167, 168, 311, 406, 502, 547 684 (p. 1321), 700, 702
Wilderness Preservation System, National, **1965**: 53, 54; **1966**: 69; **1967**: 20, 29, 96; **1968–69**: 122, 168, 311, 502, 700
Wildlife conservation, **1965**: 53, 54; **1966**: 518; **1968–69**: 39 (p. 101), 707n.
Wilentz, David, **1963–64**: 338
Wilentz, Warren W., **1966**: 504
Wiles, Harry, **1963–64**: 741
Wiley, Dr. Harvey W., **1966**: 307
Wilhelm, Kaiser, **1963–64**: 648, 703; **1965**: 88
Wilkerson Corp., **1963–64**: 350n.
Wilkes-Barre, Pa., campaign remarks, **1963–64**: 661
Wilkes College, **1965**: 132
Wilkie, Wendell, **1963–64**: 622; **1966**: 86
Wilkins, Collie Leroy, Jr., **1965**: 135
Wilkins, Fraser (U.S. Ambassador to Cyprus), **1963–64**: 201 [13]
Wilkins, Roger C., **1963–64**: 604n.
Wilkins, Roger W., **1966**: 51; **1967**: 328 [19]; **1968–69**: 153 [16]
Wilkins, Roy, **1965**: 436; **1966**: 51, 431; **1967**: 326; **1968–69**: 153 [16]
Wilkinson, Charles B. (Bud), **1966**: 7
Wilklow, Harry, **1966**: 433

Willamette National Forest, Oreg., **1967**: 418

William I, Emperor (Germany), **1966**: 448

William II, Emperor (Germany), **1966**: 312

William Randolph Hearst Foundation, **1966**: 35; **1968-69**: 33n.

  Journalism awards, **1963-64**: 339; **1965**: 260

Williams, Lt. Charles Q., **1966**: 288, 456

Williams, Mrs. Charles Q., **1966**: 288

Williams, Dick, **1967**: 429

Williams, G. Mennen, **1963-64**: 356, 431, 478n., 562, 588n., 745; **1965**: 142; **1966**: 8 [2], 141 [12]

Williams, Mrs. G. Mennen, **1966**: 430-431

Williams, Sen. Harrison A., Jr., **1963-64**: 233, 338, 422, 453, 660; **1965**: 113; **1966**: 442, 504

Williams, Boatswain's Mate 1c. James E., **1968-69**: 246

Williams, Jerre S. (Chairman, Administrative Conference of the United States), **1968-69**: 31

Williams, Mrs. Jerre S., **1968-69**: 31

Williams, Gov. John Bell, **1968-69**: 46n.

Williams, John C., **1963-64**: 666

Williams, Sen. John J., **1963-64**: 256 [13], 775; **1966**: 88 [22], 132; **1967**: 6 [17]

Williams, Kenneth R., **1963-64**: 709

Williams, 1st Lt. Leland, **1966**: 246

Williams, Dr. Marjorie, **1967**: 93n.

Williams, Ransome J., **1963-64**: 719

Williams, Roger, **1963-64**: 601; **1966**: 396; **1967**: 365

Williams College, Mass., **1967**: 290

Williamsburg, Va., **1967**: 423

Williamson, Brig. Gen. Ellis W., **1966**: 124 [2, 12]

Willis, Repr. Edwin E., **1963-64**: 648; **1966**: 121 [3]

Willis, Sid, **1963-64**: 267

Willits, Perry, **1965**: 243

Wilmington, Del., **1966**: 515

  Campaign remarks, **1963-64**: 750

  Mayor John E. Babiarz, **1966**: 515

Wilson, Mr. and Mrs. Bassel, **1968-69**: 109

Wilson, David Phillip, **1965**: 285n.

Wilson, Donald M., **1965**: 395 [1]

Wilson, Edmund, **1963-64**: 27

Wilson, Mrs. Fay O., **1967**: 419n.

Wilson, Gen. George B., **1968-69**: 163

Wilson, Harold (Prime Minister of United Kingdom), **1963-64**: 676, 678, 679, 680, 681, 693, 800; **1965**: 22 [7], 319 [14], 333n., 347 [10], 376, 388 [6], 641 [3], 653; **1966**: 88 [25], 328n., 359; **1967**: 518 [8, 10], 554 [5]; **1968-69**: 65, 79 [11, 15], 588

Wilson, Harold — *continued*

  News conference remarks on, **1963-64**: 688 [1], 780 [8]

  Visit, **1963-64**: 795-797; **1967**: 249, 250

Wilson, Mrs. Harold, **1967**: 249, 250; **1968-69**: 65

Wilson, Joseph, **1966**: 208n.

Wilson, Kenneth L., **1963-64**: 782

Wilson, O. Meredith, **1963-64**: 622; **1966**: 210n., 632; **1967**: 183n.

Wilson, Owen M., **1966**: 184n.

Wilson, Robert E., **1963-64**: 242 [3]

Wilson, Lt. Gen. Walter K., Jr., **1963-64**: 217

Wilson, Woodrow, **1963-64**: 272, 287, 305, 314, 338, 357, 391, 433, 473, 566, 576, 588, 636, 695, 718, 719, 728, 736, 748, 799; **1965**: 12, 34, 66, 108, 124, 232, 286, 299, 316, 330, 440, 448 [8], 463 [2], 541, 559; **1966**: 216, 221, 392, 413-414, 470, 472, 504, 509, 650 [13]; **1967**: 67-68, 117, 121, 193, 413, 415, 495 [11, 14]; **1968-69**: 133, 207, 250n., 459, 560, 648, 670

Wilson, Woodrow, School for Public and International Affairs (Princeton University), **1966**: 216, 404

Windsor Locks, Conn., **1967**: 222

Winneke, Sir Henry and Lady, **1966**: 543

Winston, Ellen, **1965**: 72; **1966**: 157

Winston Churchill Memorial Library, **1963-64**: 263

Winter Olympic Games, **1968-69**: 214

Winters, Bud, **1965**: 459

Winters, Mr. and Mrs. Melvin, **1966**: 417 [3]

Winters, Robert, **1966**: 644n.

Winthrop, John, **1963-64**: 282

Wiretapping, **1966**: 630 [9]; **1967**: 3 (p. 6), 35; **1968-69**: 283 [12], 320

Wirth, Conrad L., **1966**: 518

Wirtz, Alvin J., **1965**: 459

Wirtz, W. Willard.

  See Labor, Secretary of.

Wisconsin

  Campaign remarks, **1963-64**: 746

  Candidates for public office, **1963-64**: 746

  Democratic primary, **1968-69**: 169 [2]

  Disaster relief for, **1965**: 239

  Gov. Knowles, Warren P., **1965**: 189

  Gov. Reynolds, John, **1963-64**: 746

  Primary election, **1963-64**: 246 [7], 256 [7], 316 [18]

Wisconsin Islands Wilderness, **1968-69**: 168

Wissenbach, Charles E., **1966**: 331n.

Withholding taxes.

  See Taxes.

Witnesses, crime, **1967**: 71

Wolf Trap Farm Park, Va., **1966**: 518, 522

Wolfe, J. E., **1963-64**: 284

Wolfe, Thomas, **1963–64:** 526; **1965:** 179;
    1966: 30, 435; **1967:** 251, 270
Wolff, Repr. Lester L., **1966:** 510, 512
Woman's Award, Federal, **1965:** 91; **1967:** 93
Woman's Award Study Group, Federal, **1967:** 95
Women, **1963–64:** 297, 388; **1965:** 210
  Antipoverty program, role in, **1963–64:** 289
  Armed Forces service, **1963–64:** 298; **1966:**
    8 [16]; **1967:** 92, 475, 527
  Community service, **1967:** 332
  Employment and training, **1963–64:** 213;
    1965: 91, 165; **1966:** 89, 105; **1967:**
    93, 95; **1968–69:** 133, 138
  Equal opportunity, **1963–64:** 170 [16], 213,
    398; **1965:** 91, 392; **1967:** 475
  Government service, **1963–64:** 150 [16], 204,
    208, 211 [5], 213, 242 [2–7, 24], 257,
    289, 298, 305, 306, 398, 619 [7, 9];
    1965: 91, 100, 150, 263, 392; **1966:**
    89, 96, 299; **1967:** 93, 95
  Housewives' strike, **1966:** 158 [7]
  Occupational training, **1967:** 93
  Peace Corps volunteers, **1963–64:** 289
  Politics, **1963–64:** 298
  State conference, remarks, **1966:** 299
  Submarines named for, question of, **1963–64:**
    294 [21]
  U.S. dependents overseas, **1963–64:** 266 [17]
  Voting and registration campaign, **1963–64:**
    289
  Voting rights, **1963–64:** 257; **1967:** 332;
    1968–69: 332, 341
  Wages, **1963–64:** 398; **1965:** 91; **1966:** 299
  Widows, **1965:** 496
  Working mothers, **1963–64:** 160n.
Women, Citizens' Advisory Council on the Status
  of, **1965:** 392n.; **1966:** 299
Women, Conference of State Commissions on the
  Status of, **1966:** 299
Women, Governors' Commission on the Status
  of, **1965:** 392
Women, President's Commission on the Status
  of, **1963–64:** 294 [21]; **1965:** 392
Women Accepted for Volunteer Emergency
  Service (WAVES), **1966:** 8 [16]
Women in the Services, Defense Advisory
  Committee on, **1963–64:** 298
Women in the War on Poverty, Conference on,
  1967: 211
Women Voters, League of, **1963–64:** 289
Women's Army Auxiliary Corps (WAAC),
  1967: 475
Women's Army Corps (WAC), **1966:** 8 [16]
Women's Aviation Committee, **1963–64:** 310
Women's National Press Club, **1963–64:** 208
Women's Reserve, USNR (WAVES), **1966:** 8
  [16]; **1967:** 475
Women's Wear Daily, **1966:** 338 [18]
Wood, C. Tyler, **1965:** 263n.

Wood, Robert C., **1966:** 8 [1, 3, 13], 12–13,
    493, 524, 574, 604; **1967:** 358 [8];
    1968–69: 114
Wood, Mrs. Robert C., **1966:** 8 [1], 13
Woodbury, Coleman, **1967:** 4n.
Woodford, L. E., **1967:** 420n.
Woodrich, Rev. C. B., **1966:** 508
Woodrow Wilson Center for Scholars, **1967:** 71;
    1968–69: 133, 560
Woodrow Wilson Memorial Act of 1968, **1968–
  69:** 560
Woodrow Wilson Memorial Commission, **1967:**
    71; **1968–69:** 133, 560
Woodrow Wilson School for Public and Interna-
    tional Affairs (Princeton University),
    1966: 216, 404
Woods, George D., **1965:** 347 [2], 541; **1967:**
    511, 517
Woods, Howard, **1965:** 117 [3]
Woodside, Dr. Nina Bencich, **1968–69:** 138n.
Woodside, Calif., **1965:** 446
Woodward, Maj. Gen. Gilbert H., **1968–69:** 641
Woodward, Robert B., **1965:** 56n.
Woodward, Warren G., **1966:** 315n.
Wool, **1965:** 47, 168; **1967:** 223 [3]
  Imports, **1963–64:** 717
Wool fabrics, imports, **1968–69:** 562, 671
Wool industry, **1963–64:** 246 [19], 602; **1965:**
    168
Wooldridge, Dr. Dean E., **1965:** 115n.
Woolnough, Gen. J. K., **1967:** 485 [7]
Worcester, Mass., **1963–64:** 396n.
  Mayor Paul Mullaney, **1963–64:** 396
Wordsworth, William, **1966:** 202, 213
Work-experience program, **1965:** 208 [13];
    1966: 26 (p. 63), 111; **1967:** 55, 199
Work habits, the President's, **1966:** 516 [14]
Work incentive programs, **1968–69:** 3, 24, 54,
    86, 87, 94, 678 (p. 1294)
  See also Incentive awards.
Work release program
  Bureau of Prisons, **1966:** 463
  Prisoners, **1967:** 146
Work-study program, **1963–64:** 132 (p. 189),
    219; **1965:** 9, 32 (p. 93), 75, 195, 208
    [13], 603; **1966:** 95, 111, 172, 189;
    1967: 13 (p. 55), 39, 77, 378
Work-training program, **1963–64:** 219; **1965:**
    100, 208 [13], 268; **1966:** 588; **1967:**
    13 (p. 54), 55, 114, 119
Workers, health and safety, **1968–69:** 39 (p.
    104), 406
Workers Defense League, **1967:** 484
Workmen's compensation, **1963–64:** 444; **1968–
  69:** 678 (p. 1299), 684 (p. 1323)
Workweek, **1963–64:** 91 (p. 116), 124 (p. 163),
    233, 404, 571, 590, 642, 669, 761;
    1965: 258, 413; **1966:** 34 (p. 99), 445
    [5]; **1967:** 270

World Affairs Council, **1967**: 246n.
World Bank.
  See International Bank for Reconstruction and
    Development.
World Confederation of Organizations of Teach-
    ing Professions, **1968–69**: 644n.
World Crisis in Education, International
    Conference on the, **1967**: 423
World Food Panel report, foreword, **1967**: 271
World food program, **1965**: 149
World Health Assembly, **1965**: 202n., 262
World Health Organization, **1963–64**: 179;
    1965: 202n., 262; **1966**: 45, 94; **1967**:
    214n., 215; **1968–69**: 408
World law.
  See International law.
World Law Day proclamation, remarks upon
    signing, **1965**: 346
World Leadership Award, **1968–69**: 459n.
World Meteorological Day, **1966**: 143
World Meteorological Organization, **1963–64**:
    705; **1966**: 94, 143, 461; **1967**: 157;
    1968–69: 361
World Peace Through Law, Conference on,
    1965: 516
World Population Conference, United Nations,
    1965: 464
World poverty, **1968–69**: 39 (p. 99)
World Press Institute, **1965**: 378
World Series, telegrams, **1967**: 429
World Trade Week, **1963–64**: 336 [5], 350;
    1967: 231
World War I, **1963–64**: 703; **1965**: 88, 235, 309,
    403; **1966**: 228, 273, 395, 515, 563;
    1967: 315, 438n., 495 [11], 554 [6];
    1968–69: 50, 142, 154, 165, 250n.,
    462, 472, 541, 583
World War II, **1963–64**: 37, 628, 648, 703, 764;
    1965: 37, 48, 88, 172, 309, 397, 448
    [12]; **1966**: 228, 273, 288, 359, 395,
    415, 433, 505, 563, 568; **1967**: 51–52, 13
    (p. 40), 111, 315, 361, 397, 409, 423,
    430, 437, 438n., 460 [6], 475, 485
    [8], 554 [6, 7]; **1968–69**: 2, 50, 94, 99,
    110, 129, 142, 154, 165, 172, 211n.,
    214, 249n., 250n., 271n., 291, 452,
    462, 472, 479, 541, 583, 603, 695
  Great Britain in, **1963–64**: 796
  Philippine veterans of, **1963–64**: 627
  President's service in, **1963–64**: 426
World War III, **1967**: 225 [8], 534, 567; **1968–
    69**: 110
  Question of, **1965**: 388 [14]
World Weather Center, Washington, D.C., **1963–
    64**: 705
World Weather System, proposed, **1963–64**: 396,
    705
World Weather Watch, **1966**: 94, 222; **1967**:
    13 (p. 52), 157; **1968–69**: 361, 479

World's Fair (1939), **1963–64**: 282
World's Fair (1964–65)
  Civil rights demonstrations, **1963–64**: 285ftn.
    (p. 521), 290
  Singer Bowl, **1963–64**: 334n.
  Time capsule, **1963–64**: 282
  United States Pavilion, **1963–64**: 283
  Venezuelan Pavilion, **1963–64**: 335
Worthington, Leslie B., **1963–64**: 290
Wotton, Sir Henry, **1967**: 359
Wozencraft, Frank M., **1966**: 88 [5]; **1968–69**:
    36
Wren, Sir Christopher, **1963–64**: 263n.
Wright, Dr. Irving S., **1963–64**: 211 [6]
Wright, Repr. James C., Jr., **1968–69**: 281, 497
Wright, Mrs. James C., Jr., **1968–69**: 281
Wright, Brig. Gen. James M., **1965**: 117 [5]
Wright, Dr. Jane, **1963–64**: 211 [6]
Wright, Maj. Gen. John MacNair, Jr., **1967**:
    485 [1]
Wright, Bishop Milton, **1967**: 533
Wright, Bishop R. R., Jr., **1966**: 484n.
Wright, Sp4c Raymond R., **1968–69**: 487
Wright, Sewall, **1966**: 652n.; **1967**: 37n.
Wright, Stephen, **1966**: 424n.
Wright brothers (Wilbur and Orville), **1963–64**:
    310, 680, 783; **1966**: 434; **1967**:
    431, 533; **1968–69**: 110
Wright-Patterson Air Force Base, Dayton, Ohio,
    1966: 434
Wriston, Walter, **1963–64**: 296
Writers, **1968–69**: 64
Writers, National Conference of Editorial,
    1966: 501 [2], 503–504
Wunder, George, **1965**: 554n.
Wyeth, Andrew, **1963–64**: 27
Wynn, Douglas C., **1963–64**: 701
Wyoming, **1967**: 418
  Campaign remarks, **1963–64**: 657
  Candidates for public office, **1963–64**: 657
  Gov. Clifford P. Hansen, **1966**: 121 [1]
Wyszynski, Stefan Cardinal, **1966**: 200n., 528

X–15 aircraft, **1968–69**: 610
XB–70 supersonic aircraft, **1967**: 431n.
XB–70A research aircraft, **1965**: 339
Ximenes, Dr. Edward T., **1965**: 642n.
Ximenes, Vicente T., **1967**: 258, 259, 452;
    1968–69: 437

Yameogo, Maurice (President of Upper Volta),
    1965: 141, 142, 144, 154, 250; **1966**:
    168n., 189n.
Yameogo, Mrs. Maurice, **1965**: 141, 142
Yankee Station, Vietnam, **1967**: 493; **1968–69**:
    81 [3]

Yarborough, Sen. Ralph, **1963–64**: 72, 375, 544, 596, 599, 676, 760, 761, 762, 763, 778; **1965**: 183, 230, 236, 319 [22], 361, 406, 413, 621; **1966**: 100, 160, 168, 345, 353, 467, 479, 522, 635 [14], 641; **1967**: 30, 374, 408 [1, 5, 8], 452, 493; **1968–69**: 281, 282, 359, 554, 575, 599, 624, 631, 677

Yarborough, Mrs. Ralph, **1963–64**: 544, 762, 763; **1968–69**: 281, 359, 575

Yarborough, Richard W., **1967**: 518 [3]

Yarborough, Maj. Gen. William P., **1963–64**: 535n.

Yarbrough, Willard V., **1963–64**: 645, 701

Yarmolinsky, Adam, **1963–64**: 504 [14], 516 [12]

Yarmouth Castle, **1966**: 98, 583

Yarns, textured, tariffs, **1966**: 43

Yates, Repr. Sidney R., **1965**: 299; **1966**: 228

Yeats, William Butler, **1963–64**: 220

Yeldell, Joseph, **1967**: 406, 466n.

Yellow fever, **1966**: 6 (p. 8)
  Control, **1965**: 5
  Eradication program, **1963–64**: 179

"Yellow peril," **1967**: 446

Yellowstone National Park, Wyo., **1966**: 82; **1968–69**: 411, 547

Yellowtail Dam, **1963–64**: 656

Yemen, cease-fire agreement, **1965**: 463 [6]

Yen, C. K. (Vice President of the Republic of China), visit, **1967**: 212, 213, 219, 416n.

Yen, Mrs. C. K., **1967**: 212, 213

Yerby, Dr. Alonzo, **1966**: 208n.; **1967**: 500

Yeshiva University, Urban League, **1965**: 340

YF–12A aircraft, speed record, **1965**: 219

York, Sgt. Alvin, **1966**: 221
  Death of, **1963–64**: 553

York, Mrs. Alvin, **1963–64**: 553

Yorkshire, England, **1963–64**: 796n.

Yorktown, U.S.S., **1968–69**: 647n.

Yorktown Coast Guard Station, Va., **1967**: 485 [8], 493

Yorty, Samuel W., **1963–64**: 194; **1965**: 453; **1966**: 56, 236ftn. (p. 537); **1967**: 227

Yorty, Mrs. Samuel W., **1963–64**: 194

Yoshida, Shigeru, death, **1967**: 437

Yost, Charles W., **1965**: 448 [4]

Young, Capt. Gerald O., **1968–69**: 246

Young, Repr. John, **1963–64**: 763; **1967**: 408 [1]

Young, John A., **1963–64**: 728

Young, John M., **1963–64**: 296

Young, Lt. Comdr. John W., **1965**: 120, 121, 134; **1968–69**: 387

Young, Joseph, **1963–64**: 514

Young, Sen. Milton R., **1967**: 85n.; **1968–69**: 677

Young, Ralph, **1963–64**: 296

Young, Robert C., **1967**: 132 [8]; **1968–69**: 275 [3]

Young, Sen. Stephen M., **1963–64**: 405, 406, 642, 678, 679, 680, 693; **1967**: 256

Young, Whitney M., Jr., **1963–64**: 800; **1965**: 422n.; **1967**: 87n., 252n.; **1968–69**: 141, 153 [16], 596, 631

Young American Medals, **1963–64**: 315; **1965**: 336; **1966**: 289; **1967**: 275; **1968–69**: 236

Young Democrats, **1968–69**: 165

Young Men's Christian Association, **1966**: 295n., 306
  Youth Governors Conference, **1965**: 335; **1966**: 306; **1968–69**: 332

Young Presidents' Organization, **1965**: 438

Young Women's Christian Association, **1966**: 295n.

Youngblood, Rufus W., **1963–64**: 21, 330, 619 [11]; **1968–69**: 549, 602, 604

Youngblood, Mrs. Rufus W., **1963–64**: 21

Youngdahl, Judge Luther W., **1965**: 422n.

Youth, **1963–64**: 622; **1965**: 179, 232, 403, 508, 614
  See also Children.
  Athletic achievements, **1963–64**: 106, 401
  Centers, **1968–69**: 40
  Comments on, **1965**: 159, 289; **1966**: 213, 257, 306, 435; **1967**: 286, 323, 446, 529, 554 [7]; **1968–69**: 17, 33, 165, 227, 236, 238, 282, 305, 332, 341, 526, 557 [8], 570
  Conservation activities, **1966**: 653; **1967**: 114
  Crime, **1963–64**: 537, 658; **1965**: 90, 102, 509; **1967**: 382
  Delinquency, **1963–64**: 133, 213, 266 [21], 280 [5], 334, 537, 590, 630, 658, 680, 704; **1965**: 2, 29, 70, 90, 102, 151, 183, 361, 381, 382, 422; **1966**: 30, 117, 219, 317, 399, 491, 494 [1]; **1967**: 3 (p. 7), 15, 27, 35, 39, 71, 276, 353, 560; **1968–69**: 39 (p. 107), 57, 59, 329, 424, 553, 557 [8], 678 (p. 1291)
  Disadvantaged, **1968–69**: 24, 39 (p. 104), 87, 328, 678 (pp. 1291, 1294)
  Drug addiction, **1968–69**: 57, 59, 217, 561
  Education, **1963–64**: 267, 737; **1965**: 9, 10, 35 (p. 114), 70, 100, 132, 137, 354, 603; **1966**: 34 (p. 100), 429; **1967**: 114, 277; **1968–69**: 672 (p. 1264), 678 (p. 1286)
  Employment and training, **1963–64**: 55, 89, 91 (p. 114), 132 (pp. 176, 181), 199, 213, 218 [15], 246 [20], 267, 451n., 504 [7], 658, 704n., 742, 787, 791; **1965**: 35 (p. 114), 99, 100, 132, 165, 193, 207, 208 [5], 224, 268, 298, 322, 340, 408, 436, 438, 453, 578; **1966**:

Youth — *continued*
  Employment and training — *continued*
      34 (p. 98), 105, 111, 171–172, 385, 588;
      1967: 39, 114, 199, 203, 277; **1968–69**:
      24, 87, 328, 526, 678 (p. 1294), 689
  Government employment, **1965**: 268, 298;
      1966: 172, 258, 306, 388; **1967**: 41,
      121, 148; **1968–69**: 305, 526, 570,
      667, 673
  Health and welfare, **1963–64**: 403, 490, 590,
      755; **1965**: 5, 32 (p. 94), 501; **1966**:
      26 (p. 62), 27, 45, 95, 157, 271, 317,
      392, 395, 508, 569, 573, 576, 580
      [11], 589, 654 [3]; **1967**: 39, 160
  Job Corps.
      See main heading, Job Corps.
  Job Corps recruitment, **1963–64**: 219
  Junior Chamber of Commerce, **1963–64**: 403
  Mental fitness, **1963–64**: 89, 126
  Message to Congress, **1967**: 39–40
  Mobilization for Youth program, **1963–64**: 451
  Morals of, comments on, **1963–64**: 246 [20],
      280 [5], 622, 750
  Neighborhood Youth Corps, **1965**: 32 (p. 93),
      67, 75, 86, 193, 195, 224, 239, 268,
      298, 308, 322, 438
      See also main heading, Neighborhood Youth
      Corps.
  Occupational training, **1967**: 193, 484
  Physical fitness, **1963–64**: 89, 106, 126, 401,
      490; **1965**: 625, 645
  Presidential Scholars program, **1963–64**:
      266 [4]; **1965**: 306; **1966**: 257
  Role in antipoverty program, **1963–64**: 323
  School dropouts, **1963–64**: 47, 53, 84, 213,
      218 [15], 233, 246 [20], 398, 658,
      680, 733, 754; **1965**: 9, 10, 70, 90, 100,
      156 [2], 178, 183, 322, 340, 438, 453,
      490; **1966**: 95, 111, 317, 385, 392,
      580 [7], 589
  Senate youth program participants, remarks
      to, **1965**: 48
  Social security benefits, **1965**: 501
  Unemployment, **1963–64**: 91 (p. 115), 246
      [20], 386, 451, 754, 771, 787, 791;
      1965: 9, 76, 100, 165, 268, 298, 301,
      322, 351, 408, 436, 438, 463 [15], 480,
      490, 590, 598, 632; **1966**: 34 (p. 100),
      111–112, 235; **1967**: 55, 199, 328
      [19]
  Volunteer services, **1965**: 308, 329, 334, 335,
      336; **1966**: 257–258, 339
  Voting rights, **1963–64**: 706
  White House conference, **1966**: 306
  "White House Fellows" program, establish-
      ment, **1963–64**: 622
  Work-study program, **1963–64**: 219; **1965**:
      9, 32 (p. 93), 75, 195, 208 [13], 603
  Work-training program, **1963–64**: 219

Young Democrats, **1963–64**: 372, 729
Youth, Washington Action for, **1963–64**: 537
Youth Activities, Advisory Committee on,
      Democratic National Committee,
      1968–69: 17
Youth Administration, National, **1963–64**: 622;
      1965: 268; **1966**: 49, 228, 417 [2],
      500; **1967**: 211, 258
Youth Authority, California, **1967**: 35
Youth Conference on Natural Beauty and
      Conservation, National, **1966**:
      295, 653
Youth Corps, Neighborhood.
      See Neighborhood Youth Corps.
Youth Councils on Civic Affairs, **1965**: 508
Youth Crime, President's Committee on Juvenile
      Delinquency and, **1963–64**: 334, 537,
      704n.; **1965**: 282, 381
Youth Employment Act, proposed, **1963–64**:
      89, 132 (pp. 184, 189)
Youth Governors Conference, YMCA, **1965**:
      335; **1966**: 306
Youth Leaders and Social Workers, Council of
      International Programs for, **1967**: 365
Youth for Natural Beauty and Conservation
      Year proclamation, **1966**: 653
Youth Opportunity, President's Council on,
      1968–69: 24, 686
Youth Opportunity Advisory Committee,
      1966: 385
Youth Opportunity Campaign, **1965**: 322, 480;
      1967: 39
  Business participation, **1965**: 298
  Report on, **1965**: 438n.
  Summer, **1966**: 172, 385
  Task forces, **1965**: 268, 298, 436, 438
Youth Opportunity Centers, **1965**: 100
Youth Opportunity Task Force, **1966**: 385
Youth Program, Senate, **1966**: 35; **1968–69**: 33
Youth Services Office, District, **1967**: 71
Yuen, Rev. Thomas, **1966**: 528
Yugoslavia, **1963–64**: 617; **1967**: 245; **1968–69**:
      204
  Foreign Secretary Marko Nikezic, **1967**: 375
      [17]
  President Josip Broz Tito, **1965**: 412 [2];
      1967: 328 [13], 375ftn. (p. 821)
  Relations with U.S., **1966**: 272
  U.S. trade with, **1963–64**: 272
Yuki, **1968–69**: 260
Yun, Suk Heun, **1963–64**: 35n.
Yuvabul, Cham Nan, **1966**: 554n.

Zablocki, Repr. Clement J., **1963–64**: 746; **1966**:
      141 [7], 236 [6]
Zachos, Kimon S., **1965**: 334n.
Zachry, H. B., **1968–69**: 357

[References are to items except as otherwise indicated]

Zagoria, Sam, **1965**: 117 [3]
Zahir, King Mohammed (Afghanistan), **1967**: 143–145
Zambia, **1966**: 243
  Independence, **1963–64**: 721
  Kaunda, Kenneth D., **1963–64**: 721; **1966**: 243
Zammit, Themistocles, **1963–64**: 585
Zanzibar, **1963–64**: 597, 607
  Independence celebration, **1963–64**: 32
  Sultan Jamshid, **1963–64**: 32
Zararah, Queen (Malaysia), **1966**: 559n., 560n.
Zariski, Oscar, **1965**: 646n.; **1966**: 61n.
Zembrzuski, Rev. Michael M., **1966**: 528
Zenith Radio Corp., **1967**: 231n.
Zimmerman, Charles, **1967**: 484
Zinc
  Imports, **1965**: 577; **1966**: 125
  Release from national stockpile, **1965**: 599

Zinc — *continued*
  Stockpiles, **1966**: 390
ZIP Code, **1965**: 332; **1967**: 163
ZIP Code Week, National, **1966**: 470
Zoning, Taxation and Development Standards, Temporary National Commission on Codes, **1965**: 90; **1966**: 394; **1967**: 4, 16 (p. 84)
Zoological Park, National, **1966**: 267; **1967**: 265
Zorthian, Barry, **1965**: 412 [3]
Zweig, Stefan, **1968–69**: 193
Zwick, Charles J. (Director, Bureau of the Budget), **1968–69**: 38, 54, 75, 89, 90, 153 [16], 169 [1], 283 [10], 303, 344, 391, 467 [3], 480n., 581, 587, 590 [4], 677
Zworykin, Vladimir Kosma, **1966**: 652n.; **1967**: 37n.

DATE DUE